Daniel

EDITORIAL BOARD
Dean O. Wenthe
General Editor

Christopher W. Mitchell
Old Testament and CPH Editor

Curtis P. Giese
New Testament Editor

CONCORDIA COMMENTARY VOLUMES
Leviticus, John W. Kleinig
Joshua, Adolph L. Harstad
Ruth, John R. Wilch
Ezra and Nehemiah, Andrew E. Steinmann
Proverbs, Andrew E. Steinmann
Ecclesiastes, James Bollhagen
The Song of Songs, Christopher W. Mitchell
Isaiah 40–55, R. Reed Lessing
Ezekiel 1–20, Horace D. Hummel
Ezekiel 21–48, Horace D. Hummel
Daniel, Andrew E. Steinmann
Amos, R. Reed Lessing
Jonah, R. Reed Lessing
Matthew 1:1–11:1, Jeffrey A. Gibbs
Matthew 11:2–20:34, Jeffrey A. Gibbs
**Mark 1:1–8:26*, James W. Voelz
Luke 1:1–9:50, Arthur A. Just Jr.
Luke 9:51–24:53, Arthur A. Just Jr.
**Romans 1–8*, Michael P. Middendorf
1 Corinthians, Gregory J. Lockwood
Colossians, Paul E. Deterding
Philemon, John G. Nordling
2 Peter and Jude, Curtis P. Giese
1–3 John, Bruce G. Schuchard
Revelation, Louis A. Brighton

For a current list of available Concordia Commentary volumes, visit our Web site at http://www.cph.org/commentaries.

*In preparation

CONCORDIA COMMENTARY

A Theological Exposition of Sacred Scripture

DANIEL

Andrew E. Steinmann

Concordia Publishing House
Saint Louis

Copyright © 2008 Concordia Publishing House
3558 S. Jefferson Avenue, St. Louis, MO 63118-3968
1-800-325-3040 • www.cph.org

All rights reserved. No part of this publication may be reproduced, stored in a retrieval system, or transmitted, in any form or by any means, electronic, mechanical, photocopying, recording, or otherwise, without the prior written permission of Concordia Publishing House.

Unless otherwise indicated, Scripture quotations are the author's translation.

Scripture quotations marked NKJV™ are taken from the New King James Version®. Copyright © 1982 by Thomas Nelson, Inc. Used by permission. All rights reserved.

Scripture quotations marked RSV are from the Revised Standard Version of the Bible, copyright 1952, © 1971 by the Division of Christian Education of the National Council of the Churches of Christ in the United States of America. Used by permission. All rights reserved. Revised Standard Version of the Bible, Apocrypha, copyright 1957; The Third and Fourth Books of the Maccabees and Psalm 151, copyright 1977 by the Division of Christian Education of the National Council of the Churches of Christ in the United States of America. Used by permission. All rights reserved.

Scripture quotations marked ESV are from The Holy Bible, English Standard Version®. Copyright © 2001 by Crossway Bibles, a publishing ministry of Good News Publishers, Wheaton, Illinois. Used by permission. All rights reserved.

Scripture quotations or quotations from the Apocrypha marked NRSV are from the New Revised Standard Version of the Bible with the Apocrypha, copyright 1989, Division of Christian Education of the National Council of the Churches of Christ in the United States of America. Used by permission. All rights reserved.

Scripture quotations marked NIV are taken from the Holy Bible, New International Version®. NIV®. Copyright © 1973, 1978, 1984 by International Bible Society. Used by permission of Zondervan Publishing House. All rights reserved.

Scripture quotations marked NASB are taken from the New American Standard Bible®. Copyright © 1960, 1962, 1963, 1968, 1971, 1972, 1973, 1975, 1977, 1995 by The Lockman Foundation. Used by permission.

Unless otherwise indicated, the quotations from the Lutheran Confessions in this publication are from THE BOOK OF CONCORD: THE CONFESSIONS OF THE EVANGELICAL LUTHERAN CHURCH, edited by Theodore G. Tappert, copyright © 1959 Fortress Press. Used by permission of Augsburg Fortress.

The SymbolGreek II, NewJerusalem, JacobiteLS, and TranslitLS fonts used to print this work are available from Linguist's Software, Inc., PO Box 580, Edmonds, WA 98020-0580, USA; telephone (425) 775-1130; www.linguistsoftware.com.

Manufactured in the United States of America

Library of Congress Cataloging-in-Publication Data

Steinmann, Andrew E.
    Daniel / Andrew E. Steinmann.
        p.   cm. — (Concordia commentary)
    Includes bibliographical references (p.) and indexes (p.).
    ISBN 978-0-7586-0695-2
    1. Bible. O.T. Joshua—Commentaries. I. Title. II. Series.

    BS1555.53.S75   2008
    224'.5077—dc22

                                                          2007050019

To Rebecca, my wife
May her name always be
"found written in the book" (Dan 12:1)

Contents

EDITORS' PREFACE	xii
AUTHOR'S PREFACE	xvi
PRINCIPAL ABBREVIATIONS	xviii
HEBREW AND ARAMAIC VERBAL SYSTEMS	xxi
ICONS	xxii
BIBLIOGRAPHY	xxiv
INTRODUCTION	

Date, Authorship, and Unity — 1

Date and Authorship according to the Book	1
Critical Theories about Date, Authorship, and Unity	3
Evidence—An Argument for the Traditional Date of Daniel	6
Hebrew Language Characteristics in Daniel	6
Aramaic Language Characteristics in Daniel	8
Persian and Greek Loanwords	9
Historical Data in the Book Itself	11
Evidence from Ben Sira	13
Ben Sira 3:30 (from Daniel 4:24 [ET 4:27])	13
Ben Sira 36:10 (from Daniel 8:19; 11:27, 35)	14
Ben Sira 36:22 (from Daniel 9:17)	15
Conclusion about Ben Sira 3:30; 36:10; and 36:22	16
Evidence from Qumran	17
Theological Threats Posed by the Critical Dating of Daniel	18

Overview of Daniel — 20

Organization of the Book: The Clearly Defined Sections	20
Daniel 1–6: Six Narratives	20
Daniel 7–12: Four Visions	21
Interlocked Chiasms and the Dual Language of the Book	21
Daniel 1–7: An Aramaic Chiasm with a Hebrew Introduction	24
Daniel 7–12: A Hebrew Chiasm with an Aramaic Introduction	25

Major Themes — 26

The Messiah in Daniel: An Overview	26
God as the Protector of His People	28
The Uselessness of False Gods and the Power of the True God	29
Maintaining the Integrity of One's Faith	30

Law and Gospel in Daniel — 31
God's Law in Daniel — 31
God's Gospel in Daniel — 36

Connections with Other Old Testament Books — 37
Daniel and Joseph — 37
Daniel and Esther — 39
Daniel and the Prophets — 40
Daniel and Wisdom Books — 42

Daniel in the New Testament — 43

Eschatology and Dispensational Premillennial Interpretations of Daniel — 51
Basic Dispensational Presuppositions — 52
    A Radical Distinction between Israel and the Church — 52
    The "Literal" Fulfillment of Prophecy — 53
    The Glorification of God as the Purpose of History — 54
Dispensational Interpretations of Daniel — 55
    Daniel 2 — 56
    Daniel 7 — 57
        A Literalistic Interpretation of Numbers Is Disproved by Daniel 1:20 and 3:19 — 57
    Daniel 8 — 58
    Daniel 9 — 60
    Daniel 12 — 60
    Summary — 60

The Text and Other Daniel Traditions — 63
The Hebrew and Aramaic Text — 63
    The Masoretic Text — 63
    Qumran Manuscripts — 63
Daniel in the Greek Traditions — 63
    The Old Greek and Theodotion — 63
    The Greek Additions to Daniel — 67
        Susanna — 67
        Bel and the Serpent — 68
        The Prayer of Azariah and the Song of the Three Young Men — 69
Qumran Daniel Traditions — 70
    The Prayer of Nabonidus (4QPrNab ar/4Q242) — 70
    Pseudo-Daniel (4QpsDan^{a-c} ar/4Q243–4Q245) — 71
    The Son of God Text (4QApocalypse ar/4Q246) — 73
    Summary — 73

COMMENTARY

1:1–21   The Judeans Are Steadfast in Practicing Their Faith

Introduction to Daniel 1		77
1:1–2	The Beginning of the Babylonian Captivity	79
1:3–7	Young Judeans from the Nobility Are Pressed into Service in the Babylonian Court	86
1:8–21	The Judeans Are Steadfast in Practicing Their Faith	95
Excursus	*Daniel's View of the Exile*	104

2:1–49   Nebuchadnezzar's Dream of the Statue: Four Kingdoms before the Kingdom of God

Introduction to Daniel 2		109
2:1–13	Nebuchadnezzar Challenges Babylon's Wise Men to Recount and Explain His Dream	113
2:14–23	God Reveals Nebuchadnezzar's Dream to Daniel	121
2:24–49	Daniel Recounts and Explains Nebuchadnezzar's Dream of the Statue	127
Excursus	*The Four-Kingdom Schema in Daniel*	144

3:1–30   God's Faithful Servants Are Saved from Death

Introduction to Daniel 3		161
3:1–7	Nebuchadnezzar's Officials Obey His Command to Worship His Idol	170
3:8–18	Despite the Death Threat, the Judeans Remain Faithful and Entrust Themselves to God	179
3:19–30	The Judeans Are Thrown into the Furnace but Are Miraculously Saved by God	188

3:31–4:34   Nebuchadnezzar Is Judged for His Arrogance against God (ET 4:1–37)

Introduction to Daniel 4 (MT 3:31–4:34; ET 4:1–37)		203
3:31–33	The Greeting of Nebuchadnezzar's Letter (ET 4:1–3)	212
Excursus	*Daniel 4 and the Prayer of Nabonidus*	215
4:1–15	Nebuchadnezzar Seeks the Meaning of His Dream of the Tree (ET 4:4–18)	229
4:16–24	Daniel Explains Nebuchadnezzar's Dream of the Tree (ET 4:19–27)	240
4:25–34	Nebuchadnezzar's Dream of the Tree Is Fulfilled (ET 4:28–37)	248

5:1–6:1   Belshazzar Is Judged for His Arrogance against God (ET 5:1–31)

Introduction to Daniel 5		257
5:1–12	Writing on the Wall at Belshazzar's Banquet	266
5:13–6:1	Daniel Interprets the Writing and Darius Receives the Kingdom (ET 5:13–31)	278
Excursus	*The Identity of Darius the Mede*	290

6:2–29   God's Faithful Servant Daniel Is Rescued from Death (ET 6:1–28)

Introduction to Daniel 6		299
6:2–29	God's Faithful Servant Daniel Is Rescued from Death (ET 6:1–28)	305

7:1–28   Daniel's Vision of Four Kingdoms and the Establishment of the Kingdom of God

Introduction to Daniel 7		327
7:1–14	Daniel's Vision of Four Beasts and the Coming of the Son of Man	336
7:15–28	An Angel Explains the Four Beasts and the Establishment of the Kingdom of God	361

8:1–27   Daniel's First Vision of Post-Babylonian Kingdoms

Introduction to Daniel 8		389
8:1–14	Daniel's Vision of the Ram and the Goat	392
8:15–27	Gabriel Explains the Vision of the Ram and the Goat	408
Excursus	*Dispensational Interpretations of Daniel 8*	418

9:1–27   Daniel's Prayer and Vision concerning Jerusalem during the Post-Babylonian Kingdoms

Introduction to Daniel 9		425
9:1–19	Daniel's Prayer	430
9:20–27	Gabriel Explains Jerusalem's Future	443

10:1–12:13   The Divine Man Explains Daniel's Second Vision of Post-Babylonian Kingdoms Plus the Antichrist, the Resurrection, and the End

Introduction to Daniel 10–12		479
10:1–11:1	Daniel's Vision of a Divine Man	487
11:2–35	The Divine Man Explains the First Two Post-Babylonian Kingdoms	508

11:36–45	The Divine Man Explains the Antichrist and the Time of the End	533
Excursus	*The Lutheran Confessions on the Antichrist in Daniel*	547
12:1–4	After the End, the Resurrection to Eternal Life or to Everlasting Abhorrence	556
12:5–13	The Divine Man Concludes His Revelation to Daniel about the Time of the End	564

INDEX OF SUBJECTS — 578
INDEX OF PASSAGES — 599

LIST OF FIGURES

Figure 1	Timeline of Daniel and Related Events	2
Figure 2	The Interlocked Chiastic Structure of Daniel	22
Figure 3	Timeline of Biblical Eschatology	48
Figure 4	Timelines of Millennial Eschatologies	50
Figure 5	Qumran Manuscripts of Daniel	62
Figure 6	Chronological Notices in Daniel	80
Figure 7	Nebuchadnezzar's Campaign of 605–604 BC	82
Figure 8	Events during Jehoiakim's Reign (Fall 609–December 598 BC)	85
Figure 9	Views on the Identity of the Kingdoms in Daniel	146
Figure 10	Comparison between the Little Horn in Daniel 7 and the Little Horn in Daniel 8	154
Figure 11	The Messiah's Enthronement in Daniel 7 and Psalms 2 and 110	360
Figure 12	The Seventy Weeks (Daniel 9:24–27)	454
Figure 13	Catchwords and Catch-Concepts in Daniel 11:2–12:4	485
Figure 14	Comparison of the Divine Figures in Daniel 10; Ezekiel 1; and Revelation 1	499
Figure 15	The Ptolemies and the Seleucids	521
Figure 16	The Symbolic Periods of Time in Daniel 12:7, 11–12	576

Editors' Preface

What may a reader expect from the Concordia Commentary: A Theological Exposition of Sacred Scripture?

The purpose of this series, simply put, is to assist pastors, missionaries, and teachers of the Scriptures to convey God's Word with greater clarity, understanding, and faithfulness to the divine intent of the text.

Since every interpreter approaches the exegetical task from a certain perspective, honesty calls for an outline of the presuppositions held by those who have shaped this commentary series. This also serves, then, as a description of the characteristics of the commentaries.

First in importance is the conviction that the content of the scriptural testimony is Jesus Christ. The Lord himself enunciated this when he said, "The Scriptures … testify to me" (Jn 5:39), words that have been incorporated into the logo of this series. The message of the Scriptures is the Good News of God's work to reconcile the world to himself through the life, death, resurrection, ascension, and everlasting session of Jesus Christ at the right hand of God the Father. Under the guidance of the same Spirit who inspired the writing of the Scriptures, these commentaries seek to find in every passage of every canonical book "that which promotes Christ" (as Luther's hermeneutic is often described). They are Christ-centered, *Christological* commentaries.

As they unfold the scriptural testimony to Jesus Christ, these commentaries expound Law and Gospel. This approach arises from a second conviction—that Law and Gospel are the overarching doctrines of the Bible itself and that to understand them in their proper distinction and relationship to one another is a key for understanding the self-revelation of God and his plan of salvation in Jesus Christ.

Now, Law and Gospel do not always appear in Scripture labeled as such. The palette of language in Scripture is multicolored, with many and rich hues. The dialectic of a pericope may be fallen creation and new creation, darkness and light, death and life, wandering and promised land, exile and return, ignorance and wisdom, demon possession and the kingdom of God, sickness and healing, being lost and found, guilt and righteousness, flesh and Spirit, fear and joy, hunger and feast, or Babylon and the new Jerusalem. But the common element is God's gracious work of restoring fallen humanity through the Gospel of his Son. Since the predominant characteristic of these commentaries is the proclamation of that Gospel, they are, in the proper sense of the term, *evangelical.*

A third, related conviction is that the Scriptures are God's vehicle for communicating the Gospel. The editors and authors accept without reservation that the canonical books of the Old and New Testaments are, in their entirety, the inspired, infallible, and inerrant Word of God. The triune God is the ultimate author of the Bible, and every word in the original Hebrew, Aramaic, and Greek is inspired by the Holy Spirit. Yet rather than mechanical dictation, in the mysterious process by which the Scriptures were divinely inspired (e.g., 2 Tim 3:16; 2 Pet 1:21), God made use of the human faculties, knowledge, interests, and styles of the biblical writers, whose individual books surely are marked by distinctive features. At the same time, the canon of Scripture has its own inner unity, and each passage must be understood in harmony with the larger context of the whole. This commentary series pays heed to the smallest of textual details because of its acceptance of *plenary and verbal inspiration* and interprets the text in light of the whole of Scripture, in accord with the analogy of faith, following the principle that *Scripture interprets Scripture.* The entirety of the Bible is God's Word, *sacred* Scripture, calling for *theological* exposition.

A fourth conviction is that, even as the God of the Gospel came into this world in Jesus Christ (the Word incarnate), the scriptural Gospel has been given to and through the people of God, for the benefit of all humanity. God did not intend his Scriptures to have a life separated from the church. He gave them through servants of his choosing: prophets, sages, evangelists, and apostles. He gave them to the church and through the church, to be cherished in the church for admonition and comfort and to be used by the church for proclamation and catechesis. The living context of Scripture is ever the church, where the Lord's ministry of preaching, baptizing, forgiving sins, teaching, and celebrating the Lord's Supper continues. Aware of the way in which the incarnation of the Son of God has as a consequence the close union of Scripture and church, of Word and Sacraments, this commentary series features expositions that are *incarnational* and *sacramental.*

This Gospel Word of God, moreover, creates a unity among all those in whom it works the obedience of faith and who confess the truth of God revealed in it. This is the unity of the one holy Christian and apostolic church, which extends through world history. The church is to be found wherever the marks of the church are present: the Gospel in the Word and the Sacraments. These have been proclaimed, confessed, and celebrated in many different cultures and are in no way limited nor especially attached to any single culture or people. As this commentary series seeks to articulate the universal truth of the Gospel, it acknowledges and affirms the confession of the scriptural truth in all the many times and places where the one true church has been found. Aiming to promote *concord* in the confession of the one scriptural Gospel, these commentaries seek to be, in the best sense of the terms, *confessional, ecumenical,* and *catholic.*

All of those convictions and characteristics describe the theological heritage of Martin Luther and of the confessors who subscribe to the *Book of Concord* (1580)—those who have come to be known as Lutherans. The editors and authors forthrightly confess their subscription to the doctrinal exposition of Scripture in the *Book of Concord.* As the publishing arm of The Lutheran Church—Missouri Synod, Concordia Publishing House is bound to doctrinal agreement with the Scriptures and the Lutheran Confessions and seeks to herald the true Christian doctrine to the ends of the earth. To that end, the series has enlisted confessional Lutheran authors from other church bodies around the world who share the evangelical mission of promoting theological concord.

The authors and editors stand in the exegetical tradition of Martin Luther and the other Lutheran reformers, who in turn (as their writings took pains to demonstrate) stood in continuity with faithful exegesis by theologians of the early and medieval church, rooted in the hermeneutics of the Scriptures themselves (evident, for example, by how the New Testament interprets the Old). This hermeneutical method, practiced also by many non-Lutherans, includes (1) interpreting Scripture with Scripture according to the analogy of faith, that is, in harmony with the whole of Christian doctrine revealed in the Word; (2) giving utmost attention to the grammar (lexicography, phonetics, morphology, syntax, pragmatics) of the original language of the text; (3) seeking to discern the intended meaning of the text, the "plain" or "literal" sense, aware that the language of Scripture ranges from narrative to discourse, from formal prose to evocative poetry, from archaic to acrostic to apocalyptic, and it uses metaphor, type, parable, and other figures; (4) drawing on philology, linguistics, archaeology, literature, philosophy, history, and other fields in the quest for a better understanding of the text; (5) considering the history of the church's interpretation; (6) applying the text as authoritative also in the present milieu of the interpreter; and (7) above all, seeing the present application and fulfillment of the text in terms of Jesus Christ and his corporate church; upholding the Word, Baptism, and the Supper as the means through which Christ imparts salvation today; and affirming the inauguration, already now, of the eternal benefits of that salvation that is yet to come.

To be sure, the authors and editors do not feel bound to agree with every detail of the exegesis of our Lutheran forefathers. Nor do we imagine that the interpretations presented here are the final word about every crux and enigmatic passage. But the work has been done in harmony with the exegetical tradition that reaches back through the Lutheran confessors all the way to the biblical writers themselves, and in harmony with the confession of the church: grace alone, faith alone, Scripture alone, Christ alone.

The editors wish to acknowledge their debt of gratitude for all who have helped make possible this series. It was conceived at CPH in 1990, and a couple of years of planning and prayer to the Lord of the church preceded its formal launch on July 2, 1992. During that time, Dr. J. A. O. Preus II volunteered his enthusiasm for the project because, in his view, it would nurture and advance the faithful proclamation of the Christian faith as understood by the Lutheran church. The financial support that has underwritten the series was provided by a gracious donor who wished to remain anonymous. Those two faithful servants of God were called to heavenly rest not long after the series was inaugurated.

During the early years, former CPH presidents Dr. John W. Gerber and Dr. Stephen J. Carter had the foresight to recognize the potential benefit of such a landmark work for the church at large. CPH allowed Dr. Christopher W. Mitchell to devote his time and energy to the conception and initial development of the project. Dr. Mitchell has remained the CPH editor and is also the Old Testament editor. Dr. Dean O. Wenthe has served on the project since its official start in 1992 and is the general editor, as well as a commentary author. Mrs. Julene Gernant Dumit (M.A.R.) has been the CPH production editor for the entire series. Dr. Jeffrey A. Gibbs, author of the Matthew commentary volumes, served on the editorial board as the New Testament editor from 1999 into 2012. Dr. Curtis P. Giese, author of the commentary on 2 Peter and Jude, joined the board as interim assistant New Testament editor in 2011 and now serves as the New Testament editor.

CPH thanks all of the institutions that have enabled their faculty to serve as authors and editors. A particular debt of gratitude is owed to Concordia Theological Seminary, Fort Wayne, Indiana, for kindly allowing Dr. Dean O. Wenthe to serve as the general editor of the series and to dedicate a substantial portion of his time to it for many years. CPH also thanks Concordia Seminary, St. Louis, Missouri, for the dedication of Dr. Jeffrey A. Gibbs during his tenure as the New Testament editor. Moreover, Concordia University Texas is granting Dr. Curtis P. Giese a reduced load to enable him to carry on as the New Testament editor of the series. These institutions have thereby extended their ministries in selfless service for the benefit of the greater church.

The editors pray that the beneficence of their institutions may be reflected in this series by an evangelical orientation, a steadfast Christological perspective, an eschatological view toward the ultimate good of Christ's bride, and a concern that the wedding feast of the King's Son may be filled with all manner of guests (Mt 22:1–14).

> Now to him who is able to establish you by my Gospel and the preaching of Jesus Christ, by the revelation of the mystery kept secret for ages past but now revealed also through the prophetic Scriptures, made known to all the nations by order of the eternal God unto the obedience of faith—to the only wise God, through Jesus Christ, be the glory forever. Amen! (Rom 16:25–27)

Author's Preface

The Gospel of the kingdom of God is not simply a proclamation of John the Baptist, Jesus, and the apostles in the New Testament. It finds its most consistent Old Testament treatment in Daniel. This book, often viewed as a combination of miraculous stories and fantastic visions, is much more than that. It is a picture of the Gospel of the promised Messiah and his eternal kingdom. However, interpreting Daniel is no easy task. While the stories about Daniel and his fellow Judeans appear simple (belying a rich theological complexity), the visions at the end of the book seem extraordinarily complicated. Thus the challenge for any commentator is to understand the book as a whole and to explain its rich and variegated presentation of the Gospel and its power.

Certainly every commentator on Daniel has struggled with the unique set of issues it presents, from the dual languages[1] of the book to its marriage of straightforward narrative and enigmatic vision. Certainly no commentary on this book will have the last word on its meaning. There will always be more insights into the book's message of hope that sustains God's people in faith despite living in a world hostile to our God.

Nevertheless, a commentary on this book is a necessity for the church to fully understand and properly apply its message. Since at least the first century before Christ, Daniel has been the subject of intense scrutiny by religious zealots seeking to view it as an eschatological road map for determining all sorts of misleading and harmful theologies of triumphalism and glory. Such an approach avoids the cross of Christ and distorts the divine plan of salvation revealed throughout Scripture. In our day, it is often manifested in millennial speculation. I have endeavored to show that Daniel is more than simply an adjunct to such theories, an oracle to be bent in service of eschatological speculations about an earthly messianic kingdom that provides escape from bearing the cross during this earthly life. Instead it is a book about Christ, who preserved his people throughout the Babylonian captivity and pointed them forward to the coming of his kingdom at his first as well as his second advent. For us who live between those two advents, Daniel sustains our faith that the God who accomplished our redemption through the suffering, death, and resurrection of Christ will preserve us until Christ's return, whereupon we shall be raised (Dan 12:1–3) and inherit eternal life the new heavens and new earth (Revelation 21–22).

Many people are responsible for this commentary. I am grateful to Concordia Publishing House for a grant that enabled a full year's writing leave to

---

[1] Dan 1:1–2:4a is in Hebrew, while 2:4b–7:28 is in Aramaic, and then 8:1–12:13 is in Hebrew again.

complete this work. My thanks are due to Dr. Christopher Mitchell and Mrs. Julene Dumit for their many fine suggestions that have greatly improved this commentary. Also, I owe a debt to my teacher Dr. Peter Machinist (currently Hancock Professor of Hebrew and Other Oriental Languages at Harvard University), whose guidance and patience with me during the writing of my dissertation on apocalyptic literature at the University of Michigan has borne fruit several places in this commentary. The encouragement and prayers of my colleagues at Concordia University Chicago have been greatly appreciated.

I pray that by God's grace this commentary may prove useful to the church and may lead many to Christ, the messianic King, whose gracious reign over his people is eternal.

December 17, 2007
Commemoration of Daniel the Prophet and the Three Young Men

Principal Abbreviations

Books of the Bible

Gen	2 Ki	Is	Nah	Rom	Titus
Ex	1 Chr	Jer	Hab	1 Cor	Philemon
Lev	2 Chr	Lam	Zeph	2 Cor	Heb
Num	Ezra	Ezek	Hag	Gal	James
Deut	Neh	Dan	Zech	Eph	1 Pet
Josh	Esth	Hos	Mal	Phil	2 Pet
Judg	Job	Joel	Mt	Col	1 Jn
Ruth	Ps (pl. Pss)	Amos	Mk	1 Thess	2 Jn
1 Sam	Prov	Obad	Lk	2 Thess	3 Jn
2 Sam	Eccl	Jonah	Jn	1 Tim	Jude
1 Ki	Song	Micah	Acts	2 Tim	Rev

Books of the Apocrypha and Other Noncanonical Books of the Septuagint

1–2 Esdras	1–2 Esdras
Tobit	Tobit
Judith	Judith
Add Esth	Additions to Esther
Wisdom	Wisdom of Solomon
Ben Sira	Sirach/Ecclesiasticus
Baruch	Baruch
Ep Jer	Epistle of Jeremiah
Azariah	Prayer of Azariah
Song of the Three	Song of the Three Young Men
Susanna	Susanna
Bel	Bel and the Serpent
Manasseh	Prayer of Manasseh
1–2 Macc	1–2 Maccabees
3–4 Macc	3–4 Maccabees
Ps 151	Psalm 151
Odes	Odes
Ps(s) Sol	Psalm(s) of Solomon

Reference Works and Scripture Versions

ABD	*Anchor Bible Dictionary.* Edited by D. N. Freedman. 6 vols. New York: Doubleday, 1992
AC	Augsburg Confession
AE	*Luther's Works.* St. Louis: Concordia, and Philadelphia: Fortress, 1955– [American Edition]
ANET	*Ancient Near Eastern Texts Relating to the Old Testament.* Edited by J. B. Pritchard. 3d ed. Princeton: Princeton University Press, 1969
ANF	*The Ante-Nicene Fathers.* Edited by A. Roberts and J. Donaldson. 10 vols. Repr. Peabody, Mass.: Hendrickson, 1994
Ap	Apology of the Augsburg Confession
BDB	Brown, F., S. R. Driver, and C. A. Briggs. *A Hebrew and English Lexicon of the Old Testament.* Oxford: Clarendon, 1979
BHS	*Biblia Hebraica Stuttgartensia*
BM	British Museum (Tablet)
CAD	*The Assyrian Dictionary of the Oriental Institute of the University of Chicago.* Chicago: Oriental Institute, 1956–
CAL	*The Comprehensive Aramaic Lexicon.* Cincinnati: Hebrew Union College—Jewish Institute of Religion; http://cal1.cn.huc.edu
DJD	Discoveries in the Judaean Desert
Ep	Epitome of the Formula of Concord
ESV	English Standard Version of the Bible
ET	English translation
FC	Formula of Concord
GKC	*Gesenius' Hebrew Grammar.* Edited by E. Kautzsch. Translated by A. E. Cowley. 2d ed. Oxford: Clarendon, 1910
HALOT	Koehler, L., W. Baumgartner, and J. J. Stamm. *The Hebrew and Aramaic Lexicon of the Old Testament.* Translated and edited under the supervision of M. E. J. Richardson. 5 vols. Leiden: Brill, 1994–2000
Jastrow	Jastrow, M., comp. *A Dictionary of the Targumim, the Talmud Babli and Yerushalmi, and the Midrashic Literature.* 2 vols. Brooklyn: P. Shalom, 1967

Joüon	Joüon, P. *A Grammar of Biblical Hebrew*. Translated and revised by T. Muraoka. 2 vols. Subsidia biblica 14/1–2. Rome: Editrice Pontificio Istituto Biblico, 1991
KJV	King James Version of the Bible
LC	Large Catechism by M. Luther
LEH	Lust, J., E. Eynikel, and K. Hauspie. *A Greek-English Lexicon of the Septuagint*. 2 vols. Stuttgart: Deutsche Bibelgesellschaft, 1992–1996
LSB	*Lutheran Service Book.* St. Louis: Concordia, 2006
LW	*Lutheran Worship.* St. Louis: Concordia, 1982
LXX	Septuagint
MT	Masoretic Text of the Hebrew Old Testament
NASB	New American Standard Bible
NIV	New International Version of the Bible
NKJV	New King James Version of the Bible
NPNF[2]	*The Nicene and Post-Nicene Fathers.* Series 2. Edited by P. Schaff and H. Wace. 14 vols. Repr., Peabody, Mass.: Hendrickson, 1994
NRSV	New Revised Standard Version of the Bible
NT	New Testament
OT	Old Testament
PG	Patrologia graeca. Edited by J.-P. Migne. 161 vols. Paris, 1857–1866
RSV	Revised Standard Version of the Bible
SA	Smalcald Articles
SC	Small Catechism by M. Luther
SD	Solid Declaration of the Formula of Concord
Treatise	Treatise on the Power and Primacy of the Pope
TWOT	*Theological Wordbook of the Old Testament.* Edited by R. L. Harris, G. L. Archer Jr., and B. K. Waltke. 2 vols. Chicago: Moody, 1980
WA	*D. Martin Luthers Werke: Kritische Gesamtausgabe.* 73 vols. in 85. Weimar: Böhlau, 1883– [Weimarer Ausgabe]
WA DB	*D. Martin Luthers Werke: Kritische Gesamtausgabe. Die Deutsche Bibel.* 12 vols. in 15. Weimar: Böhlau, 1906–1961 [Weimarer Ausgabe Deutsche Bibel]
Waltke-O'Connor	Waltke, B. K., and M. O'Connor. *An Introduction to Biblical Hebrew Syntax.* Winona Lake, Ind.: Eisenbrauns, 1990

Hebrew and Aramaic Verbal Systems

Hebrew Verbal System

	G-Stem System[1] *Basic*	D-Stem System *Doubling*[2]	H-Stem System *H-Prefix*
Active	G (Qal)	D (Piel)	H (Hiphil)
Passive	Gp (Qal passive)	Dp (Pual)	Hp (Hophal)
Reflexive/Passive	N (Niphal)	HtD (Hithpael)	

Aramaic Verbal System

	G-Stem System *Basic*	D-Stem System *Doubling*	H-Stem System *H-Prefix*[3]
Active	G (Peal)	D (Pael)	H (Haphel)
Passive	Gp (Peil)	Dp (Pual)	Hp (Hophal)
Reflexive/Passive[4]	HtG (Hithpeel)	HtD (Hithpaal)	HtH (Hishtaphal)

---

[1] "G" is from the German *Grundstamm*, "basic stem."

[2] This also includes other doubling patterns such as Polel (D), Pilpel (D), Polal (Dp), Polpal (Dp), Hithpolel (HtD), and Hithpalpel (HtD).

[3] This also includes Aphel (H), where the ה is written as א, and the Shaphel (H), with the prefix שׁ.

[4] This also includes patterns where the ה is written as א: Ithpeel (HtG) and Ithpaal (HtD).

Icons

These icons are used in the margins of this commentary to highlight the following themes:

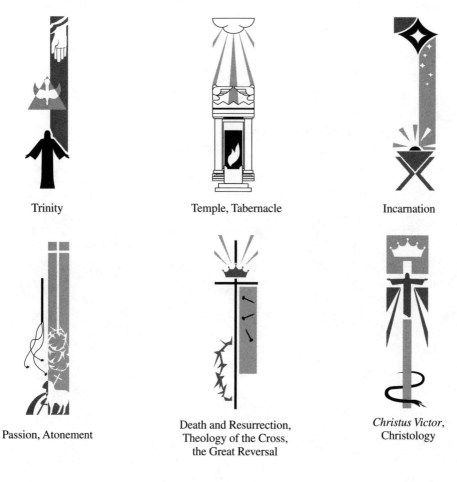

Trinity

Temple, Tabernacle

Incarnation

Passion, Atonement

Death and Resurrection,
Theology of the Cross,
the Great Reversal

Christus Victor,
Christology

Baptism

Catechesis,
Instruction, Revelation

Lord's Supper

Icons

Ministry of Word and Sacrament,
Office of the Keys

The Church,
Christian Marriage

Worship

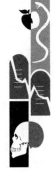

Sin, Law Breaking,
Death

Hope of Heaven,
Eschatology

Justification

Bibliography

Note: The secondary literature on Daniel is extensive. This bibliography is confined to secondary literature in English during the last fifty years. Exceptions were made for important older works and important works in French or German.

Adler, William. "The Apocalyptic Survey of History Adapted by Christians: Daniel's Prophecy of 70 Weeks." Pages 201–38 in *The Jewish Apocalyptic Heritage in Early Christianity*. Edited by James C. VanderKam and William Adler. Assen: Van Gorcum, 1996.

Albertz, Rainer. *Der Gott des Daniel: Untersuchungen zu Daniel 4–6 in der Septuagintafassung sowie zu Komposition und Theologie des aramäischen Danielbuches*. Stuttgarter Bibelstudien 131. Stuttgart: Katholisches Bibelwerk, 1988.

―――. *Israel in Exile: The History and Literature of the Sixth Century B.C.E.* Studies in Biblical Literature 3. Atlanta: Society of Biblical Literature, 2003.

Alexander, John B. "New Light on the Fiery Furnace." *Journal of Biblical Literature* 69 (1950): 375–76.

Alfrink, Bernardus J. "L'idée de résurrection d'après Dan 12,1–2." *Biblica* 40 (1959): 355–71.

Allegro, John M. *Qumrân Cave 4.I (4Q158–4Q186)*. Discoveries in the Judaean Desert 5. Oxford: Clarendon, 1968.

Anderson, Robert. *The Coming Prince, or, the Seventy Weeks of Daniel with an Answer to the Higher Criticism*. 7th ed. London: Hodder and Stoughton, 1903. First published in 1881. Repr., Grand Rapids: Kregel, 1957.

Applegate, John. "Jeremiah and the Seventy Years in the Hebrew Bible: Inner-Biblical Reflections on the Prophet and His Prophecy." Pages 91–110 in *The Book of Jeremiah and Its Reception*. Edited by A. H. W. Curtis and T. Römer. Louvain, Belgium: Leuven University Press, 1997.

Archer, Gleason L., Jr. "The Aramaic of the 'Genesis Apocryphon' Compared with the Aramaic of Daniel." Pages 160–69 in *New Perspectives on the Old Testament*. Edited by J. Barton Payne. Waco: Word, 1970.

―――. "The Hebrew of Daniel Compared with the Qumran Sectarian Documents." Pages 470–81 in *The Law and the Prophets: Old Testament Studies Prepared in Honor of Oswald Thompson Allis*. Edited by John H. Skilton, Milton C. Fisher, and Leslie W. Sloat. Nutley, N.J.: Presbyterian & Reformed, 1974.

―――. "Daniel." Pages 1–157 in vol. 7 of *The Expositor's Bible Commentary*. Grand Rapids: Zondervan, 1985.

Archer, Gleason L., Jr., trans. *Jerome's Commentary on Daniel*. Grand Rapids: Baker, 1958. Paperback ed., 1977.

Armerding, Carl E. "Asleep in the Dust." *Bibliotheca sacra* 121 (1964): 153–58.

Armistead, David B. "The Images of Daniel 2 and 7: A Literary Approach." *Stulos Theological Journal* 6 (1998): 63–66.

Arnold, Bill T. "Wordplay and Narrative Techniques in Daniel 5 and 6." *Journal of Biblical Literature* 112 (1993): 479–85.

———. "Word Play and Characterization in Daniel 1." Pages 231–48 in *Puns and Pundits: Word Play in the Hebrew Bible and Ancient Near Eastern Literature*. Edited by Scott B. Noegel. Bethesda: CDL, 2000.

Avalos, Hector I. "The Comedic Function of the Enumerations of Officials and Instruments in Daniel 3." *Catholic Biblical Quarterly* 53 (1991): 580–88.

———. "Daniel 9:24–25 and Mesopotamian Temple Rededications." *Journal of Biblical Literature* 117 (1998): 507–11.

Bailey, Daniel P. "The Intertextual Relationship of Daniel 12:2 and Isaiah 26:19: Evidence from Qumran and the Greek Versions." *Tyndale Bulletin* 51 (2000): 305–8.

Baillet, M., J. T. Milik, and R. de Vaux. *Les "Petites Grottes" de Qumrân*. Discoveries in the Judaean Desert 3. Oxford: Clarendon, 1962.

Baldwin, Joyce G. *Daniel: An Introduction and Commentary*. Tyndale Old Testament Commentaries. Downers Grove, Ill.: InterVarsity, 1978.

———. "Some Literary Affinities of the Book of Daniel." *Tyndale Bulletin* 30 (1979): 77–99.

Bampfylde, Gillian. "The Prince of the Host in the Book of Daniel and the Dead Sea Scrolls." *Journal for the Study of Judaism in the Persian, Hellenistic and Roman Period* 14 (1983): 129–34.

Barker, Kenneth L. "Premillennialism in the Book of Daniel." *Master's Seminary Journal* 4 (1993): 25–43.

Barthélemy, D., and J. T. Milik. *Qumran Cave 1*. Discoveries in the Judaean Desert 1. Oxford: Clarendon, 1955.

Bauckham, Richard J. "The Son of Man: 'A Man in My Position' or 'Someone.' " *Journal for the Study of the New Testament* 23 (1985): 23–33.

Bauer, Johannes B. "Wann heißt ʾappayim 'Zorn'? Ex 15,8; Prov 30,33; Dan 11,20." *Zeitschrift für die alttestamentliche Wissenschaft* 111 (1999): 92–94.

Beale, Gregory K. "The Danielic Background for Revelation 13:18 and 17:9." *Tyndale Bulletin* 31 (1980): 163–70.

———. "The Problem of the Man from the Sea in IV Ezra 13 and Its Relation to the Messianic Concept in John's Apocalypse." *Novum Testamentum* 25 (1983): 182–88.

———. "The Influence of Daniel upon the Structure and Theology of John's Apocalypse." *Journal of the Evangelical Theological Society* 27 (1984): 413–23.

———. "The Use of Daniel in the Synoptic Eschatological Discourse and in the Book of Revelation." Pages 129–53 in *The Jesus Tradition outside the Gospels.* Vol. 5 of *Gospel Perspectives*. Edited by David Wenham. Sheffield: JSOT Press, 1984.

———. "The Origin of the Title 'King of Kings and Lord of Lords' in Revelation 17:4." *New Testament Studies* 31 (1985): 618–20.

———. "A Reconsideration of the Text of Daniel in the Apocalypse." *Biblica* 67 (1986): 539–43.

———. "The Interpretative Problem of Rev 1:19." *Novum Testamentum* 34 (1992): 360–87.

Bealieu, Paul-Alain. *The Reign of Nabonidus, King of Babylon (556–539 B.C.).* Yale Near Eastern Researches 10. New Haven: Yale University Press, 1989.

Beasley-Murray, George R. "The Interpretation of Daniel 7." *Catholic Biblical Quarterly* 45 (1983): 44–58.

Becking, Bob. " 'A Divine Spirit Is in You': Notes on the Translation of the Phrase *rûaḥ ˀlāhîn* in Daniel 5,14 and Related Texts." Pages 515–19 in *The Book of Daniel in the Light of New Findings.* Edited by A. S. van der Woude. Louvain, Belgium: Leuven University Press, 1993.

Beckwith, Roger T. "Early Traces of the Book of Daniel." *Tyndale Bulletin* 53 (2002): 75–82.

Begg, Christopher T. "Daniel and Josephus: Tracing Connections." Pages 539–45 in *The Book of Daniel in the Light of New Findings*. Edited by A. S. van der Woude. Louvain, Belgium: Leuven University Press, 1993.

Bentzen, Aage. *King and Messiah*. London: Lutterworth, 1955.

Benveniste, E. "Eléments perses en araméen d'Egypte." *Journal asiatique* 242 (1954): 297–310.

Berger, Paul Richard. "Der Kyros-Zylinder mit dem Zusatzfragment BIN II Nr. 32 und die akkadischen Personennamen im Danielbuch." *Zeitschrift für Assyriologie* 64 (1975): 192–34.

Bergman, Ben Zion. "*Hanᶜel* in Daniel 2:25 and 6:19." *Journal of Near Eastern Studies* 27 (1968): 69–70.

Black, Matthew. "The Theological Appropriation of the Old Testament by the New Testament." *Scottish Journal of Theology* 39 (1986): 1–17.

Bloch, Ariel A. "Questioning God's Omnipotence in the Bible: A Linguistic Case Study." Pages 174–88 in *Semitic Studies in Honor of Wolf Leslau on the Occasion of His Eighty-fifth Birthday*. Wiesbaden: Harrassowitz, 1991.

Bonwetsch, Georg Nathanael, trans. *Kommentar zu Daniel*. Vol. 1, part 1 of *Hippolyt Werke*. 2d ed. Berlin: Akademie, 2000.

Boogaart, Thomas A. "Daniel 6: A Tale of Two Empires." *Reformed Review* 39 (1986): 106–12.

Boutflower, Charles. *In and around the Book of Daniel.* 1923. Repr., Grand Rapids: Eerdmans, 1963.

Braverman, Jay. *Jerome's Commentary on Daniel: A Study of Comparative Jewish and Christian Interpretations of the Hebrew Bible.* Catholic Biblical Quarterly Monograph Series 7. Washington, D.C.: Catholic Biblical Association of America, 1978.

Brensinger, Terry L. "Compliance, Dissonance and Amazement in Daniel 3." *Evangelical Journal* 20 (2002): 7–19.

Briant, Pierre. *From Cyrus to Alexander: A History of the Persian Empire.* Translated by Peter T. Daniels. Winona Lake, Ind.: Eisenbrauns, 2002.

Brighton, Louis A. *Revelation.* Concordia Commentary. St. Louis: Concordia, 1999.

Brueggemann, Walter. "2 Kings 18–19: The Legitimacy of a Sectarian Hermeneutic." *Horizons in Biblical Theology* 7 (1985): 1–42.

———. "At the Mercy of Babylon: A Subversive Rereading of the Empire." *Journal of Biblical Literature* 110 (1991): 3–22.

———. "The Old One Takes Notice." *Christian Century* 109 (1992): 867.

Bulman, James M. "The Identification of Darius the Mede." *Westminster Theological Journal* 35 (1973): 247–67.

Calvin, John. *Commentaries the Book of the Prophet on Daniel.* Translated by Thomas Myers. 2 vols. Grand Rapids: Eerdmans, 1948.

Caragounis, Chrys C. "History and Supra-History: Daniel and the Four Empires." Pages 387–97 in *The Book of Daniel in the Light of New Findings.* Edited by A. S. van der Woude. Louvain, Belgium: Leuven University Press, 1993.

Casey, P. Maurice. *Son of Man: The Interpretation and Influence of Daniel 7.* London: SPCK, 1979.

———. "General, Generic and Indefinite: The Use of the Term 'Son of Man' in Aramaic Sources and in the Teaching of Jesus." *Journal for the Study of the New Testament* 29 (1987): 21–56.

Chazan, Robert. "Daniel 9:24–27: Exegesis and Polemics." Pages 143–59 in *Contra Iudaeos: Ancient and Medieval Polemics between Christians and Jews.* Edited by Ora Limor and Guy G. Stroumsa. Tübingen: Mohr, 1996.

Chemnitz, Martin. *The Two Natures in Christ.* Translated by J. A. O. Preus. St. Louis: Concordia, 1971.

Christie-Miller, Ian. "Matfre Ermengaud's Breviari d'amor and Daniel 9.26." *Journal for the Study of the Old Testament* 66 (1995): 113–17.

Clanton, Dan W., Jr. "(Re)dating the Story of Susanna: A Proposal." *Journal for the Study of Judaism in the Persian, Hellenistic and Roman Period* 34 (2003): 121–40.

Clements, Ronald E. "The Interpretation of Prophecy and the Origin of Apocalyptic." *Baptist Quarterly* 33 (1989): 28–34.

Clermont-Ganneau, Claude. "Mané, thécel, pharès et le festin de Balthasar." *Journal asiatique* 8th series, 8 (1886): 36–67. ET: "Mene, Tekel, Peres, and the Feast of Belshazzar." *Hebraica* 3 (1887): 87–102.

Clouse, Robert G. *The Meaning of the Millennium: Four Views*. Downers Grove, Ill.: InterVarsity, 1977.

Colless, Brian E. "Cyrus the Persian as Darius the Mede in the Book of Daniel." *Journal for the Study of the Old Testament* 56 (1992): 113–26.

Collins, Adela Yarbro. "Numerical Symbolism in Jewish and Early Christian Apocalyptic Literature." Pages 1221–87 in *Principat 21, 2: Hellenistische Judentum in römischer Zeit: Philon und Josephus*. Edited by Wolfgang Haase. Berlin: Walter de Gruyter, 1984.

———. "The Origin of the Designation of Jesus as 'Son of Man.' " *Harvard Theological Review* 80 (1987): 391–407.

———. "Daniel 7 and Jesus." *Journal of Theology* 93 (1989): 5–19.

———. "The Apocalyptic Son of Man Sayings." Pages 220–28 in *The Future of Early Christianity: Essays in Honor of Helmut Koester*. Edited by Birger A. Pearson et al. Minneapolis: Fortress, 1991.

Collins, John J. "The Son of Man and the Saints of the Most High in the Book of Daniel." *Journal of Biblical Literature* 93 (1974): 50–66.

———. *The Apocalyptic Vision of the Book of Daniel*. Harvard Semitic Monographs 16. Missoula, Mont.: Scholars, 1977.

———. *Daniel with an Introduction to Apocalyptic Literature*. Forms of the Old Testament Literature 20. Grand Rapids: Eerdmans, 1984.

———. "The Son of Man in First-Century Judaism." *New Testament Studies* 38 (1992): 448–66.

———. *Daniel: A Commentary on the Book of Daniel*. Hermeneia. Minneapolis: Fortress, 1993.

———. "Stirring Up the Great Sea: The Religio-Historical Background of Daniel 7." Pages 121–36 in *The Book of Daniel in the Light of New Findings*. Edited by A. S. van der Woude. Louvain, Belgium: Leuven University Press, 1993.

———. "4QPrayer of Nabonidus ar." Pages 83–93 in *Qumran Cave 4.XVII: Parabiblical Texts, Part 3*. Discoveries in the Judaean Desert 22. Oxford: Clarendon, 1996.

Collins, John J., and Peter W. Flint. "4Qpseudo-Daniel[a-c] ar." Pages 95–164 in *Qumran Cave 4.XVII: Parabiblical Texts, Part 3*. Discoveries in the Judaean Desert 22. Oxford: Clarendon, 1996.

Collins, John J., and Peter W. Flint, eds. *The Book of Daniel: Composition and Reception*. 2 vols. Supplements to Vetus Testamentum 83. Leiden: Brill, 2001.

Cook, Edward M. " 'In the Plain of the Wall' (Dan 3:1)." *Journal of Biblical Literature* 108 (1989): 115–16.

Coxon, Peter W. "Greek Loan-Words and Alleged Greek Loan Translations in the Book of Daniel." *Glasgow University Oriental Society Transactions* 25 (1973–1974): 24–40.

———. "Daniel III 17: A Linguistic and Theological Problem." *Vetus Testamentum* 26 (1976): 400–409.

———. "A Philological Note on אשתיו Dan 5:3f." *Zeitschrift für die alttestamentliche Wissenschaft* 89 (1977): 275–76.

———. "The Syntax of the Aramaic of *Daniel*: A Dialectal Study." *Hebrew Union College Annual* 48 (1977): 107–22.

———. "The Distribution of Synonyms in Biblical Aramaic in the Light of Official Aramaic and the Aramaic of Qumran." *Revue de Qumran* 9 (1978): 497–512.

———. "The 'List' Genre and Narrative Style in the Court Tales of Daniel." *Journal for the Study of the Old Testament* 35 (1986): 95–121.

———. "Another Look at Nebuchadnezzar's Madness." Pages 211–22 in *The Book of Daniel in the Light of New Findings*. Edited by A. S. van der Woude. Louvain, Belgium: Leuven University Press, 1993.

———. "Nebuchadnezzar's Hermeneutical Dilemma." *Journal for the Study of the Old Testament* 66 (1995): 87–97.

Cross, Frank Moore. "Fragments of the Prayer of Nabonidus." *Israel Exploration Journal* 34 (1984): 260–64.

———. *The Ancient Library of Qumran*. 3d ed. Sheffield, England: Sheffield Academic Press, 1995.

Dahood, Mitchell J. "Egyptian *ʾiw*, 'Island,' in Jeremiah 10,9 and Daniel 10,5." Pages 101–3 in *Atti del Secondo Congresso Internazionale di Linguistica Camito-Semitica*. Florence: Ist di Linguistica e Lingue Orientali, U de Firenze, 1978.

David, Pablo. "Daniel 11,1: A Late Gloss?" Pages 505–14 in *The Book of Daniel in the Light of New Findings*. Edited by A. S. van der Woude. Louvain, Belgium: Leuven University Press, 1993.

Davies, Philip R. "Reading Daniel Sociologically." Pages 345–61 in *The Book of Daniel in the Light of New Findings*. Edited by A. S. van der Woude. Louvain, Belgium: Leuven University Press, 1993.

Day, John. "*Daʿat* 'Humiliation' in Isaiah LIII 11 in the Light of Isaiah LIII 3 and Daniel XII 4, and the Oldest Known Interpretation of the Suffering Servant." *Vetus Testamentum* 30 (1980): 97–103.

———. "The Daniel of Ugarit and Ezekiel and the Hero of the Book of Daniel." *Vetus Testamentum* 30 (1980): 174–84.

De Guglielmo, Antonine. "Daniel 5:25: An Example of a Double Literal Sense." *Catholic Biblical Quarterly* 11 (1949): 202–6.

Delcor, Mathias. "Les sources du chapitre 7 de Daniel." *Vetus Testamentum* 18 (1968): 290–312.

Dequeker, Luc. "The 'Saints of the Most High' in Qumran and Daniel." Pages 108–87 in *Syntax and Meaning: Studies in Hebrew Syntax and Biblical Exegesis.* By C. J. Labuschagne et al. Oudtestamentische Studiën 18. Leiden: Brill, 1973.

———. "King Darius and the Prophecy of Seventy Weeks: Daniel 9." Pages 187–210 in *The Book of Daniel in the Light of New Findings.* Edited by A. S. van der Woude. Louvain, Belgium: Leuven University Press, 1993.

DeSilva, David A. *Introducing the Apocrypha: Message, Context, and Significance.* Grand Rapids: Baker, 2002.

Deventer, Hans J. M., van. "The End of the End, or, What Is the Deuteronomist (Still) Doing in Daniel?" Pages 62–75 in *Past, Present, Future: The Deuteronomistic History and the Prophets.* Edited by Johannes C. de Moor and Harry F. van Rooy Leiden: Brill, 2000.

Di Lella, Alexander A. "Daniel 4:7–14: Poetic Analysis and Biblical Background." Pages 247–58 in *Melanges bibliques et orientaux en l'honneur de M Henri Cazelles.* Kevelaer: Butzon and Bercker, 1981.

Dimant, Devorah. "The Seventy Weeks Chronology (Dan 9,24–27) in the Light of New Qumranic Texts." Pages 57–76 in *The Book of Daniel in the Light of New Findings.* Edited by A. S. van der Woude. Louvain, Belgium: Leuven University Press, 1993.

Dommershausen, Werner. *Nabonid im Buche Daniel.* Mainz: Grünewald, 1964.

Dougherty, Raymond Philip. *Nabonidus and Belshazzar: A Study of the Closing Events of the Neo-Babylonian Empire.* Yale Oriental Series 15. New Haven: Yale University Press, 1929.

Doukhan, Jacques. "The Seventy Weeks of Dan 9: An Exegetical Study." *Andrews University Seminary Studies* 17 (1979): 1–22.

Dressler, Harold H. P. "The Identification of the Ugaritic Dnil with the Daniel of Ezekiel." *Vetus Testamentum* 29 (1979): 152–61.

Driver, Samuel Rolles. *An Introduction to the Literature of the Old Testament.* 14th ed. New York: Scribner, 1909.

Dunn, James D. G. " 'Son of God' as 'Son of Man' in the Dead Sea Scrolls? A Response to John Collins on 4Q246." Pages 198–210 in *The Scrolls and the Scriptures: Qumran Fifty Years After.* Edited by Stanley E. Porter and Craig A. Evans. Sheffield: Sheffield Academic Press, 1997.

Dyer, Charles H. "The Musical Instruments in Daniel 3." *Bibliotheca sacra* 147 (1990): 426–36.

Emerton, John A. "The Origin of the Son of Man Imagery." *Journal of Theological Studies,* n.s., 9 (1958): 225–42.

———. "Participles in Daniel 5:12." *Zeitschrift für die alttestamentliche Wissenschaft* 72 (1960): 262–63.

Eshel, Esther. "Possible Sources of the Book of Daniel." Pages 387–94 in vol. 2 of *The Book of Daniel: Composition and Reception.* Edited by John J. Collins and Peter W. Flint. Supplements to Vetus Testamentum 83. Leiden: Brill, 2001.

Fauna and Flora of the Bible. 2d ed. Helps for Translators 11. London: United Bible Societies, 1980.

Ferch, Arthur J. *The Son of Man in Daniel 7*. Andrews University Seminary Doctoral Dissertation Series 6. Berrien Springs, Mich.: Andrews University Press, 1979.

———. "Daniel 7 and Ugarit: A Reconsideration." *Journal of Biblical Literature* 99 (1980): 75–86.

———. "The Book of Daniel and the 'Maccabean Thesis.'" *Andrews University Seminary Studies* 21 (1983): 129–41.

Ferguson, Paul. "Nebuchadnezzar, Gilgamesh, and the 'Babylonian Job.'" *Journal of the Evangelical Theological Society* 37 (1994): 321–31.

Finegan, Jack. *Handbook of Biblical Chronology*. Revised ed. Peabody, Mass.: Hendrickson, 1998.

Fitzmyer, Joseph A, and Daniel J. Harrington. *A Manual of Palestinian Aramaic Texts (Second Century B.C.—Second Century A.D.)* Biblica et orientalia 34. Rome: Biblical Institute Press, 1978.

Flint, Peter W. "The Daniel Tradition at Qumran." Pages 329–67 in vol. 2 of *The Book of Daniel: Composition and Reception*. Edited by John J. Collins and Peter W. Flint. Supplements to Vetus Testamentum 83. Leiden: Brill, 2001.

Flusser, David. "The Four Empires in the Fourth Sibyl and in the Book of Daniel." *Israel Oriental Studies* 2 (1972): 148–75.

———. "Psalms, Hymns and Prayers." Pages 551–77 in *Jewish Writings of the Second Temple Period*. Edited by Michael E. Stone. Philadelphia: Fortress, 1984.

Ford, Desmond. *Daniel*. Anvil Biblical Studies. Nashville: Southern, 1978.

Fox, Douglas E. "Ben Sira on OT Canon Again: The Date of Daniel." *Westminster Theological Journal* 49 (1987): 335–50.

Francisco, Clyde T. "Seventy Weeks of Daniel." *Review and Expositor* 57 (1960): 126–37.

Frank, Richard M. "The Description of the 'Bear' in Dn 7,5." *Catholic Biblical Quarterly* 21 (1959): 505–7.

Freedman, David Noel. "The Prayer of Nabonidus." *Bulletin of the American Schools of Oriental Research* 145 (1957): 31–32.

Fröhlich, Ida. "Pesher, Apocalyptical Literature and Qumran." Pages 295–305 in *Madrid Qumran Congress*. Leiden: Brill, 1992.

———. "Daniel 2 and Deutero-Isaiah." Pages 266–70 in *The Book of Daniel in the Light of New Findings*. Edited by A. S. van der Woude. Louvain, Belgium: Leuven University Press, 1993.

Gadd, C. J. "The Harran Inscriptions of Nabonidus." *Anatolian Studies* 8 (1958): 35–92.

Gammie, John G. "On the Intention and Sources of Daniel 1–6." *Vetus Testamentum* 31 (1981): 282–92.

Gangel, Kenneth O. "Daniel 7: A Vision of Future World History." *Grace Theological Journal* 6 (1985): 247–56.

García Martínez, Florentino. "The *Prayer of Nabonidus*: A New Synthesis." Chapter 4 in *Qumran and Apocalyptic: Studies on the Aramaic Texts from Qumran*. Leiden: Brill, 1992.

Gardner, Anne E. "The Way to Eternal Life in Dan 12:1e–2 or How to Reverse the Death Curse of Genesis 3." *Australian Biblical Review* 40 (1992): 1–19.

———. "The Great Sea of Dan VII 2." *Vetus Testamentum* 49 (1999): 412–15.

———. "Daniel 7,2–14: Another Look at Its Mythic Pattern." *Biblica* 82 (2001): 244–52.

Gelston, Anthony. "Sidelight on the Son of Man." *Scottish Journal of Theology* 22 (1969): 189–96.

Gerhard, Johann. "[Notes on] Daniel." Pages 1029–58 in the Old Testament portion of *Biblia, das ist die ganze heilige Schrift Alten und Neuen Testaments verdeutscht von Doctor Martin Luther, und auf Herzog Ernst's Verordnung von etlichen reinen Theologen dem eigentlichen Wortoerstand nach erklärt*. Das Weimarische Bibelwerk. 3d ed. St. Louis: Fr. Dette, 1902. The first edition was published in 1640.

Gibbs, Jeffrey A. *Matthew 1:1–11:1*. Concordia Commentary. St. Louis: Concordia, 2006.

Gieschen, Charles A. *Angelomorphic Christology: Antecedents and Early Evidence*. Leiden: Brill, 1998.

Ginzberg, Louis. *The Legends of the Jews*. 7 vols. Philadelphia: Jewish Publication Society of America, 1909–1938.

Glasson, T. Francis. " 'Visions of Thy Head' (Daniel 2^{28}): The Heart and the Head in Bible Psychology." *Expository Times* 81 (1969–1970): 247–48.

Gnuse, Robert. "The Jewish Dream Interpreter in a Foreign Court: The Recurring Use of a Theme in Jewish Literature." *Journal for the Study of the Pseudepigrapha* 7 (1990): 29–53.

Goldingay, John E. "The Stories in Daniel: A Narrative Politics." *Journal for the Study of the Old Testament* 37 (1987): 99–116.

———. " 'Holy Ones on High' in Daniel 7:18." *Journal of Biblical Literature* 107 (1988): 495–97.

———. *Daniel*. Word Biblical Commentary 30. Dallas: Word, 1989.

———. "Story, Vision, Interpretation: Literary Approaches to Daniel." Pages 295–313 in *The Book of Daniel in the Light of New Findings*. Edited by A. S. van der Woude. Louvain, Belgium: Leuven University Press, 1993.

Gooding, David W. "The Literary Structure of the Book of Daniel and Its Implications." *Tyndale Bulletin* 32 (1981): 43–79.

Goudoever, J. van. "Time Indications in Daniel That Reflect the Usage of the Ancient Theoretical So-Called Zadokite Calendar." Pages 533–38 in *The Book of Daniel in the Light of New Findings*. Edited by A. S. van der Woude. Louvain, Belgium: Leuven University Press, 1993.

Gowan, Donald E. *Daniel*. Abingdon Old Testament Commentaries. Nashville: Abingdon, 2001.

Grabbe, Lester L. " 'The End of the Desolations of Jerusalem': From Jeremiah's 70 Years to Daniel's 70 Weeks of Years." Pages 67–72 in *Early Jewish and Christian Exegesis: Studies in Memory of William Hugh Brownlee*. Edited by Craig A. Evans and William F. Stinespring. Atlanta: Scholars, 1987.

———. "Fundamentalism and Scholarship: The Case of Daniel." Pages 133–52 in *Scripture: Meaning and Method*. Edited by Barry P. Thompson. Hull, England: Hull University Press, 1987.

———. "Another Look at the *Gestalt* of 'Darius the Mede.' " *Catholic Biblical Quarterly* 50 (1988): 198–213.

———. "The Belshazzar of Daniel and the Belshazzar of History." *Andrews University Seminary Studies* 26 (1988): 59–66.

———. "The Seventy-Weeks Prophecy (Daniel 9:24–27) in Early Jewish Interpretation." Pages 595–611 in *The Quest for Context and Meaning: Studies in Biblical Intertextuality in Honor of James A. Sanders*. Edited by Craig A. Evans and Shemaryahu Talmon. Leiden: Brill, 1997.

Greenfield, Jonas C. "Early Aramaic Poetry." *Journal of the Ancient Near Eastern Society of Columbia University* 11 (1979): 45–51.

Grelot, Pierre. "La prière de Nabonide (4 Q Or Nab)." *Revue de Qumran* 9 (1978): 483–95.

Gruenthaner, Michael J. "The Seventy Weeks." *Catholic Biblical Quarterly* 1 (1939): 44–54.

———. "The Last King of Babylon." *Catholic Biblical Quarterly* 11 (1949): 406–27.

Gunkel, Hermann. *Schöpfung und Chaos in Urzeit und Endzeit: Eine religionsgeschichtliche Untersuchung über Gen 1 und Ap Joh 12*. Göttingen: Vandenhoeck & Ruprecht, 1895.

Gurney, Robert J. M. "The Four Kingdoms of Daniel 2 and 7." *Themelios* 2 (1977): 39–45.

Haag, Ernst. *Die Errettung Daniels aus der Löwengrube: Untersuchungen zum Ursprung der biblischen Danieltradition*. Stuttgarter Bibelstudien 110. Stuttgart: Katholisches Bibelwerk, 1983.

———. "Daniel 12 und die Auferstehung der Toten." Pages 132–48 in vol. 1 of *The Book of Daniel: Composition and Reception*. Edited by John J. Collins and Peter W. Flint. Supplements to Vetus Testamentum 83. Leiden: Brill, 2001.

Habel, Norman C. "Introducing the Apocalyptic Visions of Daniel 7." *Concordia Theological Monthly* 41 (1970): 10–26.

Hanhart, Robert. "The Translation of the Septuagint in Light of Earlier Tradition and Subsequent Influences." Pages 339–79 in *Septuagint, Scrolls and Cognate Writings*. Edited by George J. Brooke and Barnabus Lindars. Atlanta: Scholars, 1992.

Hanson, Paul D. "Apocalyptic Literature." Pages 465–88 in *The Hebrew Bible and Its Modern Interpreters*. Edited by Douglas A. Knight and Gene M. Tucker. Chico, Calif.: Society of Biblical Literature, 1985.

Hardy, Frank W. "The Hebrew Singular for 'Week' in the Expression 'One Week' in Daniel 9:27." *Andrews University Seminary Studies* 32 (1994): 197–202.

Harrington, Daniel J. "The Ideology of Rule in Daniel 7–12." Pages 540–51 in *Society of Biblical Literature 1999 Seminar Papers*. Atlanta: Society of Biblical Literature, 1999.

Harstad, Adolph L. *Joshua*. Concordia Commentary. St. Louis: Concordia, 2004.

Hartman, Louis F., and Alexander A. Di Lella. *The Book of Daniel*. Anchor Bible 23. New York: Doubleday, 1978.

Harton, George M. "An Interpretation of Daniel 11:36–45." *Grace Theological Journal* 4 (1983): 205–31.

Hasel, Gerhard F. "The Identity of 'The Saints of the Most High' in Daniel 7." *Biblica* 56 (1975): 173–92.

———. "The First and Third Years of Belshazzar (Dan 7:1; 8:1)." *Andrews University Seminary Studies* 15 (1977): 153–68.

———. "The Four World Empires of Daniel 2 against Its Near Eastern Environment." *Journal for the Study of the Old Testament* 12 (1979): 17–30.

———. "The Book of Daniel: Evidences Relating to Persons and Chronology." *Andrews University Seminary Studies* 19 (1981): 37–49.

———. "The Book of Daniel and Matters of Language: Evidences Relating to Names, Words, and the Aramaic Language." *Andrews University Seminary Studies* 19 (1981): 211–25.

———. "The Hebrew Masculine Plural for 'Weeks' in the Expression 'Seventy Weeks' in Daniel 9:24." *Andrews University Seminary Studies* 31 (1993): 105–18.

Hengstenberg, E. W. *Christology of the Old Testament and a Commentary on the Messianic Predictions*. Translated by James Martin. 2d ed. Vol. 3. Edinburgh: T&T Clark, 1864.

Henten, Jan Willem van. "Antiochus IV as a Typhonic Figure in Daniel 7." Pages 223–43 in *The Book of Daniel in the Light of New Findings*. Edited by A. S. van der Woude. Louvain, Belgium: Leuven University Press, 1993.

———. "Daniel 3 and 6 in Early Christian Literature." Pages 149–69 in vol. 1 of *The Book of Daniel: Composition and Reception*. Edited by John J. Collins and Peter W. Flint. Supplements to Vetus Testamentum 83. Leiden: Brill, 2001.

Henze, Matthias. "The Ideology of Rule in the Narrative Frame of Daniel (Dan 1–6)." Pages 527–39 in *Society of Biblical Literature 1999 Seminar Papers*. Atlanta: Society of Biblical Literature, 1999.

Hilton, Michael. "Babel Reversed—Daniel Chapter 5." *Journal for the Study of the Old Testament* 66 (1995): 99–112.

Hindley, J. Clifford. "The Son of Man: A Recent Analysis." *Indian Journal of Theology* 15 (1966): 172–78.

Hoekema, Anthony A. *The Bible and the Future.* Grand Rapids: Eerdmans, 1979.

Holladay, William L. "Indications of Segmented Sleep in the Bible." *Catholic Biblical Quarterly* 69 (2007): 215–21.

Holm, Tawny L. "Daniel 1–6: A Biblical Story-Collection." Pages 149–66 in *Ancient Fiction: The Matrix of Early Christian and Jewish Narrative*. Edited by Jo-Ann A. Brant et al. Atlanta: Society of Biblical Literature, 2005.

Horbury, W. "The Messianic Associations of 'The Son of Man.' " *Journal of Theological Studies*, n.s., 36 (1985): 34–55.

Horsley, Richard A. "The Politics of Cultural Production in Second Temple Judea: Historical Context and Political-Religious Relations of the Scribes Who Produced 1 Enoch, Sirach, and Daniel." Pages 123–45 in *Conflicted Boundaries in Wisdom and Apocalypticism*. Edited by Benjamin G. Wright III and Lawrence M. Wills. Atlanta: Society of Biblical Literature, 2005.

Hummel, Horace D. *Ezekiel 1–20*. Concordia Commentary. St. Louis: Concordia, 2005.

———. *Ezekiel 21–48*. Concordia Commentary. St. Louis: Concordia, 2007.

Instone Brewer, David. "*Mene Mene Teqel Uparsin*: Daniel 5:25 in Cuneiform." *Tyndale Bulletin* 42 (1991): 310–16.

Jeansonne, Sharon Pace. *The Old Greek Translation of Daniel 7–12*. Catholic Biblical Quarterly Monograph Series 19. Washington, D.C.: Catholic Biblical Association of America, 1988.

Jones, Bruce William. "The Prayer in Daniel IX." *Vetus Testamentum* 18 (1968): 488–93.

Jones, Ivor H. "Musical Instruments in the Bible, Pt 1." *Bible Translator* 37 (1986): 101–16.

Jongeling, B., C. J. Labuschagne, and A. S. van der Woude. *Aramaic Texts from Qumran with Translations and Annotations*. Vol. 1. Semitic Study Series, n.s., 4. Leiden: Brill, 1976.

Judisch, Douglas. *An Evaluation of Claims to the Charismatic Gifts*. Baker Biblical Monograph. Grand Rapids: Baker, 1978.

———. "The Saints of the Most High." *Concordia Theological Quarterly* 53 (1989): 96–103.

Kee, Howard C. "Messiah and the People of God." Pages 341–58 in *Understanding the Word: Essays in Honour of Bernhard W. Anderson*. Journal for the Study of the Old Testament Supplement Series 37. Sheffield: JSOT Press, 1985.

Keil, C. F. *Biblical Commentary on the Book of Daniel*. Translated by M. G. Easton. Cambridge: T&T Clark, 1877. Repr., Grand Rapids: Eerdmans, 1978.

Keil, Volkmar. "Onias III—Märtyrer oder Tempelgründer." *Zeitschrift für die alttestamentliche Wissenschaft* 97 (1985): 221–33.

Kitchen, K. A. "The Aramaic of Daniel." Pages 31–79 in *Notes on Some Problems in the Book of Daniel*. Edited by D. J. Wiseman. London: Tyndale, 1965.

Kleinig, John W. *Leviticus*. Concordia Commentary. St. Louis: Concordia, 2003.

Kliefoth, Theodor. *Übersetzung des Buches Daniel*. Schwerin: Sandmeyer, 1866.

Knibb, Michael A. " 'You Are Indeed Wiser Than Daniel': Reflections on the Character of the Book of Daniel." Pages 399–411 in *The Book of Daniel in the Light of New Findings*. Edited by A. S. van der Woude. Louvain, Belgium: Leuven University Press, 1993.

Kooij, Arie van der. "A Case of Reinterpretation in the Old Greek of Daniel 11." Pages 72–80 in *Tradition and Re-interpretation in Jewish and Early Christian Literature: Essays in Honour of Jürgen C. H. Lebram*. Edited by J. W. van Henten. Leiden: Brill, 1986.

———. "The Concept of Covenant ($B^er\hat{\imath}t$) in the Book of Daniel." Pages 495–501 in *The Book of Daniel in the Light of New Findings*. Edited by A. S. van der Woude. Louvain, Belgium: Leuven University Press, 1993.

Kratz, Reinhard G. "The Visions of Daniel." Pages 91–113 in vol. 1 of *The Book of Daniel: Composition and Reception*. Edited by John J. Collins and Peter W. Flint. Supplements to Vetus Testamentum 83. Leiden: Brill, 2001.

Krauss, Samuel. "Some Remarks on Daniel 8.5 ff." *Hebrew Union College Annual* 15 (1940): 305–11.

Kvanvig, Helge S. "An Akkadian Vision as Background for Dan 7?" *Studia theologica* 35 (1981): 85–89.

———. *Roots of Apocalyptic: The Mesopotamian Background of the Enoch Figure and of the Son of Man*. Wissenschaftliche Monographien zum Alten und Neuen Testament 61. Neukirchen-Vluyn: Neukirchener, 1988.

———. "The Relevance of the Biblical Visions of the End Time: Hermeneutical Guidelines to the Apocalyptic Literature." *Horizons in Biblical Theology* 11 (1989): 35–58.

Laato, Antti. "The Seventy Yearweeks in the Book of Daniel." *Zeitschrift für die alttestamentliche Wissenschaft* 102 (1990): 212–25.

Lacocque, André. "The Vision of the Eagle in 4 Esdras, a Rereading of Daniel 7 in the First Century C.E." Pages 237–58 in *Society of Biblical Literature 1981 Seminar Papers*. Edited by Kent Harold Richards. Chico, Calif.: Scholars, 1981.

———. *Daniel in His Time*. Studies on Personalities in the Old Testament. Columbia: University of South Carolina Press, 1988.

———. "The Socio-Spiritual Formative Milieu of the Daniel Apocalypse." Pages 315–43 in *The Book of Daniel in the Light of New Findings*. Edited by A. S. van der Woude. Louvain, Belgium: Leuven University Press, 1993.

———. "Allusions to Creation in Daniel 7." Pages 114–31 in vol. 1 of *The Book of Daniel: Composition and Reception*. Edited by John J. Collins and Peter W. Flint. Supplements to Vetus Testamentum 83. Leiden: Brill, 2001.

Lancaster, Jerry R., and R. Larry Overstreet. "Jesus' Celebration of Hanukkah in John 10." *Bibliotheca sacra* 152 (1995): 318–33.

Lawson, Jack N. " 'The God Who Reveals Secrets': The Mesopotamian Background to Daniel 2.47." *Journal for the Study of the Old Testament* 74 (1997): 61–76.

Lenglet, Ad. "La structure littéraire de Daniel 2–7." *Biblica* 53 (1972): 169–90.

Lessing, R. Reed. *Jonah*. Concordia Commentary. St. Louis: Concordia, 2007.

Leupold, H. C. *Exposition of Daniel*. 1949. Repr., Grand Rapids: Baker, 1969.

Lindenberger, James M. "Daniel 12:1–4." *Interpretation* 39 (1985): 181–86.

Longenecker, Richard N. " 'Son of Man' as a Self-Designation of Jesus." *Journal of the Evangelical Theological Society* 12 (1969): 151–58.

Lucas, Ernest C. "The Origin of Daniel's Four Empires Scheme Re-examined." *Tyndale Bulletin* 40 (1989): 185–202.

———. "The Source of Daniel's Animal Imagery." *Tyndale Bulletin* 41 (1990): 161–85.

———. *Daniel*. Apollos Old Testament Commentary 20. Downers Grove, Ill.: InterVarsity, 2002.

Lurie, David H. "A New Interpretation of Daniel's 'Sevens' and the Chronology of the Seventy 'Sevens.' " *Journal of the Evangelical Theological Society* 33 (1990): 303–9.

Lust, Johan. "The Septuagint Version of Daniel 4–5." Pages 39–53 in *The Book of Daniel in the Light of New Findings*. Edited by A. S. van der Woude. Louvain, Belgium: Leuven University Press, 1993.

Martin, W. J. "The Hebrew of Daniel." Pages 28–30 in *Notes on Some Problems in the Book of Daniel*. Edited by D. J. Wiseman. London: Tyndale, 1965.

Mastin, Brian Arthur. "Daniel 2^{46} and the Hellenistic World." *Zeitschrift für die alttestamentliche Wissenschaft* 85 (1973): 80–93.

———. "The Reading of 1QDan[a] at Daniel II 4." *Vetus Testamentum* 38 (1988): 341–46.

———. "The Meaning of $H^a l \bar{a}^{\jmath}$ at Daniel IV 27." *Vetus Testamentum* 42 (1992): 234–47.

McComiskey, Thomas Edward. "The Seventy 'Weeks' of Daniel against the Background of Ancient Near Eastern Literature." *Westminster Theological Journal* 47 (1985): 18–45.

McGarry, Eugene P. "The Ambidextrous Angel (Daniel 12:7 and Deuteronomy 32:40): Inner-Biblical Exegesis and Textual Criticism in Counterpoint." *Journal of Biblical Literature* 124 (2005): 211–28.

McGinn, Bernard. *Antichrist: Two Thousand Years of the Human Fascination with Evil*. San Francisco: HarperSanFrancisco, 1994.

McKay, Gretchen Kreahling. "The Eastern Christian Exegetical Tradition of Daniel's Vision of the Ancient of Days." *Journal of Early Christian Studies* 7 (1999): 139–61.

McLay, R. Timothy. *The OG and Th Versions of Daniel*. Septuagint and Cognate Studies 43. Atlanta: Scholars, 1996.

———. "The Old Greek Translation of Daniel IV–VI and the Formation of the Book of Daniel." *Vetus Testamentum* 55 (2005): 304–23.

Meadowcroft, Tim. "Point of View in Storytelling: An Experiment in Narrative Criticism in Daniel 4." *Didaskalia* 8 (1997): 30–42.

———. "Exploring the Dismal Swamp: The Identity of the Anointed One in Daniel 9:24–27." *Journal of Biblical Literature* 120 (2001): 429–49.

———. "Who Are the Princes of Persia and Greece (Daniel 10)? Pointers towards the Danielic Vision of Earth and Heaven." *Journal for the Study of the Old Testament* 29 (2004): 99–113.

Mercer, Mark K. "Daniel 1:1 and Jehoiakim's Three Years of Servitude." *Andrews University Seminary Studies* 27 (1989): 179–92.

Meyer, Rudolf. *Das Gebet des Nabonid. Eine in den Qumran-Handschriften wiederentddeckte Weisheitserzählung*. Sitzungsberichte der Sächsischen Akademie der Wissenschaften zu Leipzig 107.3. Berlin: Akademie, 1962.

Milik, J. T. " 'Prière de Nabonide' et autres écrits d'un cycle de Daniel." *Revue biblique* 63 (1956): 407–15.

Millard, Alan R. "Daniel 1–6 and History." *Evangelical Quarterly* 49 (1977): 67–73.

———. "Daniel and Belshazzar in History." *Biblical Archaeology Review* 11 (1985): 73–78.

———. "The Etymology of *Nebraštāʾ*, Daniel 5:5." *Maarav* 4 (1987): 87–92.

Miller, James E. "Dreams and Prophetic Visions." *Biblica* 71 (1990): 401–4.

Miller, Stephen R. *Daniel*. New American Commentary 18. Nashville: Broadman & Holman, 1994.

Mitchell, Christopher W. *Our Suffering Savior: Exegetical Studies and Sermons for Ash Wednesday through Easter Based on Isaiah 52:13–53:12*. St. Louis: Concordia, 2003.

———. *The Song of Songs*. Concordia Commentary. Saint Louis: Concordia, 2003.

Mitchell, Terence C. "The Music of the Old Testament Reconsidered." *Palestine Exploration Quarterly* 124 (1992): 124–43.

———. "And the Band Played On ... But What Did They Play On? Identifying the Instruments in Nebuchadnezzar's Orchestra." *Bible Review* 15 (December 1999): 32–39.

Mitchell, T. C., and R. Joyce. "The Musical Instruments in Nebuchadrezzar's Orchestra." Pages 19–27 in *Notes on Some Problems in the Book of Daniel*. Edited by D. J. Wiseman. London: Tyndale, 1965.

Montgomery, James A. *A Critical and Exegetical Commentary on the Book of Daniel*. International Critical Commentary. Edinburgh: T&T Clark, 1927.

Moore, Carey A. *Daniel, Esther, and Jeremiah: The Additions*. Anchor Bible 44. Garden City, N.Y.: Doubleday, 1977.

Moore, Michael S. "Resurrection and Immortality: Two Motifs Navigating Confluent Theological Streams in the Old Testament (Dan 12:1–4)." *Theologische Zeitschrift* 39 (1983): 17–34.

Morgenstern, Julian. " 'Son of Man' of Daniel 7:13 f.: A New Interpretation." *Journal of Biblical Literature* 80 (1961): 65–77.

Mosca, Paul G. "Ugarit and Daniel 7: A Missing Link." *Biblica* 67 (1986): 496–517.

Muilenburg, James. "Son of Man in Daniel and the Ethiopic Apocalypse of Enoch." *Journal of Biblical Literature* 79 (1960): 197–209.

Newman, Robert C. "Daniel's Seventy Weeks and the Old Testament Sabbath-Year Cycle." *Journal of the Evangelical Theological Society* 16 (1973): 229–34.

Niditch, Susan. *The Symbolic Vision in Biblical Tradition*. Harvard Semitic Monographs 30. Chico, Calif.: Scholars, 1983.

———. "Legends of Wise Heroes and Heroines." Pages 445–63 in *The Hebrew Bible and Its Modern Interpreters*. Edited by Douglas A. Knight and Gene M. Tucker. Philadelphia: Fortress, 1985.

Niskanen, Paul. "Daniel's Portrait of Antiochus IV: Echoes of a Persian King." *Catholic Biblical Quarterly* 66 (2004): 378–86.

Nordling, John G. *Philemon*. Concordia Commentary. Saint Louis: Concordia, 2004.

Noth, Martin. "Die Heiligen des Höchsten." *Norsk Theologisk Tidsskrift* 56 (1955): 146–57. Reprinted as pages 274–90 in *Gesammelte Studien zum Alten Testament* by Martin Noth. Munich: C. Kaiser, 1957.

Nuñez, Samuel. "The Vision of Daniel 8: Interpretations from 1700 to 1900." *Andrews University Seminary Studies* 25 (1987): 305.

Otzen, Benedikt. "Heavenly Visions in Early Judaism: Origin and Function." Pages 199–215 in *In the Shelter of Elyon: Essays on Ancient Palestinian Life and Literature in Honour of G. W. Ahlström*. Edited by W. Boyd Barrick and John R. Spencer. Sheffield: JSOT Press, 1984.

Ozanne, C. G. "Three Textual Problems in Daniel." *Journal of Theological Studies*, n.s., 16 (1965): 445–48.

Parker, Richard A., and Waldo H. Dubberstein. *Babylonian Chronology 626 B.C.–A.D. 75*. Brown University Studies 19. Providence, R.I.: Brown University Press, 1956.

Patterson, Richard D. "The Key Role of Daniel 7." *Grace Theological Journal* 12 (1991): 245–61.

———. "Holding On to Daniel's Court Tales." *Journal of the Evangelical Theological Society* 36 (1993): 445–54.

Paul, Shalom M. "Daniel 3:29—A Case Study of 'Neglected' Blasphemy." *Journal of Near Eastern Studies* 42 (1983): 291–94.

———. "Dan 6,8: An Aramaic Reflex of Assyrian Legal Terminology." *Biblica* 65 (1984): 106–10.

———. "Decoding a 'Joint' Expression in Daniel 5:6, 16." *Journal of the Ancient Near Eastern Society* 22 (1993): 121–27.

———. "Gleanings From the Biblical and Talmudic Lexica in Light of Akkadian." Pages 242–56 in *Minḥah le-Naḥum: Biblical and Other Studies Presented to Nahum M. Sarna in Honour of His 70th Birthday*. Edited by Marc Brettler and Michael Fishbane. Journal for the Study of the Old Testament Supplement Series 154. Sheffield: JSOT Press, 1993.

———. "The Mesopotamian Background of Daniel 1–6." Pages 55–68 in vol. 1 of *The Book of Daniel: Composition and Reception*. Edited by John J. Collins and Peter W. Flint. Supplements to Vetus Testamentum 83. Leiden: Brill, 2001.

———. "Daniel 12:9: A Technical Mesopotamian Scribal Term." Pages 115–18 in *Sefer Moshe: The Moshe Weinfeld Jubilee Volume: Studies in the Bible and the Ancient Near East, Qumran, and Post-Biblical Judaism*. Edited by Chaim Cohen, Avi Hurvitz, and Shalom M. Paul. Winona Lake, Ind.: Eisenbrauns, 2004.

Payne, J. Barton. "The Goal of Daniel's Seventy Weeks." *Journal of the Evangelical Theological Society* 21 (1978): 97–115.

Péter-Contesse, René, and John Ellington. *A Handbook on the Book of Daniel*. UBS Handbook Series. New York: United Bible Societies, 1993.

Pfandl, Gerhard. "Interpretations of the Kingdom of God in Daniel 2:44." *Andrews University Seminary Studies* 34 (1996): 249–68.

Pieper, Francis. *Christian Dogmatics*. 3 vols. St. Louis: Concordia, 1950–1953.

Pierce, Ronald W. "Spiritual Failure, Postponement, and Daniel 9." *Trinity Journal*, n.s., 10 (1989): 211–22.

Pinches, T. G. "On a Cuneiform Inscription Relating to the Capture of Babylon by Cyrus and the Events Which Preceded and Led to It." *Transactions of the Society of Biblical Archaeology* 7 (1882): 139–76.

Pinker, Aron. "A Dream of a Dream in Daniel 2." *Jewish Biblical Quarterly* 33 (2005): 231–40.

Polak, Frank H. "The Daniel Tales in Their Aramaic Literary Milieu." Pages 249–65 in *The Book of Daniel in the Light of New Findings*. Edited by A. S. van der Woude. Louvain, Belgium: Leuven University Press, 1993.

Polaski, Donald C. "*Mene, Mene, Tekel, Parsin*: Writing and Resistance in Daniel 5 and 6." *Journal of Biblical Literature* 123 (2004): 649–69.

Porteous, Norman W. *Daniel: A Commentary*. 2d rev. ed. Old Testament Library. London: SCM, 1979.

Poythress, Vern Sheridan. "The Holy Ones of the Most High in Daniel VII." *Vetus Testamentum* 26 (1976): 208–13.

———. "Hermeneutical Factors in Determining the Beginning of the Seventy Weeks (Daniel 9:25)." *Trinity Journal*, n.s., 6 (1985): 131–49.

Prinsloo, G. T. M. "Two Poems in a Sea of Prose: The Content and Context of Daniel 2.20–23 and 6.27–28." *Journal for the Study of the Old Testament* 59 (1993): 93–108.

Qimron, Elisha. *The Hebrew of the Dead Sea Scrolls*. Harvard Semitic Studies 29. Atlanta: Scholars, 1986.

Quaegebeur, Jan. "On the Egyptian Equivalent of Biblical *Ḥarṭummîm*." Pages 162–72 in *Pharaonic Egypt: The Bible and Christianity*. Edited by Sarah Israelit-Groll. Jerusalem: Magnes, 1985.

Raabe, Paul R. "Daniel 7: Its Structure and Role in the Book." *Hebrew Annual Review* 9 (1985): 267–75.

Rabinowitz, Isaac. "*Pēsher/Pittārōn*: Its Biblical Meaning and Its Significance in the Qumran Literature." *Revue de Qumran* 8 (1973): 219–32.

Rappaport, Uriel. "Apocalyptic Vision and Preservation of Historical Memory." *Journal for the Study of Judaism in the Persian, Hellenistic and Roman Period* 23 (1992): 217–26.

Raurell, Frederic. "The *Doxa* of the Seer in Dan-LXX 12,13." Pages 520–32 in *The Book of Daniel in the Light of New Findings*. Edited by A. S. van der Woude. Louvain, Belgium: Leuven University Press, 1993.

Redditt, Paul L. "Calculating the 'Times': Daniel 12:5–13." *Perspectives in Religious Studies* 25 (1998): 373–79.

———. "Daniel 11 and the Sociohistorical Setting of the Book of Daniel." *Catholic Biblical Quarterly* 60 (1998): 463–74.

———. "Daniel 9: Its Structure and Meaning." *Catholic Biblical Quarterly* 62 (2000): 236–49.

Reeves, Eileen. "Daniel 5 and the Assayer: Galileo Reads the Handwriting on the Wall." *Journal of Medieval and Renaissance Studies* 21 (1991): 1–27.

Robertson, David. "Tragedy, Comedy, and the Bible: A Response." *Semeia* 32 (1984): 99–106.

Rosenberg, Roy A. "The Slain Messiah in the Old Testament." *Zeitschrift für die alttestamentliche Wissenschaft* 99 (1987): 259–61.

Rosenthal, Franz. *A Grammar of Biblical Aramaic*. 7th, expanded ed. Porta linguarum orientalium, n.s., 5. Wiesbaden: Harrassowitz, 2006.

Rosscup, James E. "Prayer Relating to Prophecy in Daniel 9." *Master's Seminary Journal* 3 (1992): 47–71.

Roth, Norman. "Seeing the Bible through a Poet's Eyes: Some Difficult Biblical Words Interpreted by Moses Ibn Ezra." *Hebrew Studies* 23 (1982): 111–14.

Rowland, Christopher. "A Man Clothed in Linen: Daniel 10.6ff. and Jewish Angelology." *Journal for the Study of the New Testament* 24 (1985): 99–110.

Rowley, H. H. *Darius the Mede and the Four World Empires in the Book of Daniel: A Historical Study of Contemporary Theories*. Cardiff: University of Wales, 1935.

———. "The Unity of the Book of Daniel." Pages 235–68 in *The Servant of the Lord and Other Essays on the Old Testament*. London: Lutterworth, 1952.

Royer, Wilfred Sophrony. "The Ancient of Days: Patristic and Modern Views of Daniel 7:9–14." *Saint Vladimir's Theological Quarterly* 45 (2001): 137–62.

Russell, D. S. *Daniel*. The Daily Study Bible. Edinburgh: Saint Andrew Press, 1981.

Ryrie, Charles C. *Dispensationalism Today*. Chicago: Moody, 1965.

Schaberg, Jane. "Daniel 7, 12 and the New Testament Passion-Resurrection Predictions." *New Testament Studies* 31 (1985): 208–22.

Schechter, Solomon, and Charles Taylor. *The Wisdom of Ben Sira: Portions of the Book of Ecclesiasticus from Hebrew Manuscripts in the Cairo Genizah Collection Presented to the University of Cambridge by the Editors*. Cambridge: Cambridge University Press, 1899.

Scofield, C. I., E. Schuyler English, et. al., eds. *Oxford NIV Scofield Study Bible*. Oxford: Oxford University Press, 1967, 1978, 1984.

Shea, William H. "An Unrecognized Vassal King of Babylon in the Early Achaemenid Period (Part 1)." *Andrews University Seminary Studies* 9 (1971): 51–67.

———. "An Unrecognized Vassal King of Babylon in the Early Achaemenid Period (Part 2)." *Andrews University Seminary Studies* 9 (1971): 99–128.

———. "An Unrecognized Vassal King of Babylon in the Early Achaemenid Period (Part 3)." *Andrews University Seminary Studies* 10 (1972): 88–117.

———. "An Unrecognized Vassal King of Babylon in the Early Achaemenid Period (Part 4)." *Andrews University Seminary Studies* 10 (1972): 147–78.

———. "Poetic Relations of the Time Periods in Dan 9:25." *Andrews University Seminary Studies* 18 (1980): 59–63.

———. "Daniel 3: Extra-Biblical Texts and the Convocation on the Plain of Dura." *Andrews University Seminary Studies* 20 (1982): 29–52.

———. "Darius the Mede: An Update." *Andrews University Seminary Studies* 20 (1982): 229–47.

———. "Nabonidus, Belshazzar, and the Book of Daniel: An Update." *Andrews University Seminary Studies* 20 (1982): 133–49.

———. "A Further Note on Daniel 6: Daniel as 'Governor.' " *Andrews University Seminary Studies* 21 (1983): 169–71.

———. "Wrestling with the Prince of Persia: A Study on Daniel 10." *Andrews University Seminary Studies* 21 (1983): 225–50.

———. "Further Literary Structures in Daniel 2–7: An Analysis of Daniel 4." *Andrews University Seminary Studies* 23 (1985): 193–202.

———. "Further Literary Structures in Daniel 2–7: An Analysis of Daniel 5, and the Broader Relationships within Chapters 2–7." *Andrews University Seminary Studies* 23 (1985): 277–95.

———. "Mutilation of Foreign Names by Bible Writers: A Possible Example from Tell el-ʿUmeiri." *Andrews University Seminary Studies* 23 (1985): 111–15.

———. "The Neo-Babylonian Historical Setting for Daniel 7." *Andrews University Seminary Studies* 24 (1986): 31–36.

———. "Bel(te)shazzar Meets Belshazzar." *Andrews University Seminary Studies* 26 (1988): 67–81.

———. "Darius the Mede in His Persian-Babylonian Setting." *Andrews University Seminary Studies* 29 (1991): 235–57.

———. "The Search for Darius the Mede (Concluded), or, The Time of the Answer to Daniel's Prayer and the Date of the Death of Darius the Mede." *Journal of the Adventist Theological Society* 12 (2001): 97–105.

———. "Supplementary Evidence in Support of 457 B.C. as the Starting Date for the 2300 Day-Years of Daniel 8:14." *Journal of the Adventist Theological Society* 12 (2001): 89–96.

Shuckburgh, Evelyn S., trans. *The Histories of Polybius*. 2 vols. London: Macmillan, 1889. Repr., Bloomington: Indiana University Press, 1962. Available on http://www.perseus.tufts.edu.

Siegman, Edward F. "The Stone Hewn from the Mountain (Daniel 2)." *Catholic Biblical Quarterly* 18 (1956): 364–79.

Smith, Charles R. "The Book of Life." *Grace Theological Journal* 6 (1985): 219–30.

Soesilo, Daud H. "Belshazzar's Scales: Towards Achieving a Balanced Translation of Daniel 5." *Bible Translator* 40 (1989): 426–32.

———. "Translating the Poetic Sections of Daniel 1–6." *Bible Translator* 41 (1990): 432–35.

———. "Why Did Daniel Reject the King's Delicacies? (Daniel 1.8)." *Bible Translator* 45 (1994): 441–44.

Sparks, H. F. D. "On the Origin of 'Darius the Mede' at Daniel V. 31." *Journal of Theological Studies* 47 (1946): 41–46.

Stefanovic, Zdravko. "Thematic Links between the Historical and Prophetic Sections of Daniel." *Andrews University Seminary Studies* 27 (1989): 121–27.

———. *The Aramaic of Daniel in the Light of Old Aramaic*. Journal for the Study of the Old Testament Supplement Series 129. Sheffield: JSOT Press, 1992.

———. "Daniel: A Book of Significant Reversals." *Andrews University Seminary Studies* 30 (1992): 139–50.

Steiner, Richard C. "Meaninglessness, Meaningfulness, and Super-Meaningfulness in Scripture: An Analysis of the Controversy Surrounding Dan 2:12." *Jewish Quarterly Review*, n.s., 82 (1992): 431–39.

Steinmann, Andrew E. "The Shape of Things to Come: The Genre of the Historical Apocalypse in Ancient Jewish and Christian Literature." Ph.D. diss., University of Michigan, 1990.

———. "The Tripartite Structure of the Sixth Seal, the Sixth Trumpet, and the Sixth Bowl of John's Apocalypse (Rev 6:12–7:17; 9:13–11:14; 16:12–16)." *Journal of the Evangelical Theological Society* 35 (1992): 69–79.

———. "The Graded Numerical Saying in Job." Pages 288–97 in *Fortunate the Eyes That See: Essays in Honor of David Noel Freedman in Celebration of His Seventieth Birthday*. Edited by Astrid B. Beck, Andrew H. Bartelt, Paul R. Raabe, and Chris A. Franke. Grand Rapids: Eerdmans, 1995.

———. *The Oracles of God: The Old Testament Canon*. St. Louis: Concordia, 1999.

———. "The Chicken and the Egg: A New Proposal for the Relationship between the *Prayer of Nabonidus* and the *Book of Daniel*." *Revue de Qumran* 20 (2002): 557–70.

———. *Fundamental Biblical Aramaic* (with *Fundamental Biblical Hebrew* by Andrew Bartelt). St. Louis: Concordia, 2004.

———. *Is God Listening? Making Prayer a Part of Your Life*. St. Louis: Concordia, 2004.

———. "Is the Antichrist in Daniel 11?" *Bibliotheca sacra* 162 (2005): 195–209.

Stevens, David E. "Daniel 10 and the Notion of Territorial Spirits." *Bibliotheca sacra* 157 (2000): 410–31.

Stone, Michael E. "A Note on Daniel 1:3." *Australian Biblical Review* 7 (1959): 69–71.

———. "Apocalyptic Literature." Pages 383–441 in *Jewish Writings of the Second Temple Period: Apocrypha, Pseudepigrapha, Qumran Sectarian Writings, Philo, Josephus*. Edited by Michael E. Stone. Assen: Van Gorcum, 1984.

Stuckenbruck, Loren T. " 'One Like a Son of Man as the Ancient of Days' in the Old Greek Recension of Daniel 7,13: Scribal Error or Theological Translation?" *Zeitschrift für die neutestamentliche Wissenschaft und die Kunde der älteren Kirche* 86 (1995): 268–76.

———. "The Throne-Theophany of the Book of Giants: Some New Light on the Background of Daniel 7." Pages 211–20 in *The Scrolls and the Scriptures: Qumran Fifty Years After*. Edited by Stanley E. Porter and Craig A. Evans. Sheffield: Sheffield Academic Press, 1997.

Surburg, Raymond F. "Justification as a Doctrine of the Old Testament: A Comparative Study in Confessional and Biblical Theology." *Concordia Theological Quarterly* 46 (1982): 129–46.

Süring, Margit L. "The Horn-Motifs of the Bible and the Ancient Near East." *Andrews University Seminary Studies* 22 (1984): 327–40.

Tanner, J. Paul. "Daniel's 'King of the North': Do We Owe Russia an Apology?" *Journal of the Evangelical Theological Society* 35 (1992): 315–28.

———. "The Literary Structure of the Book of Daniel." *Bibliotheca sacra* 160 (2003): 269–82.

Tawil, Hayim. "Hebrew נַפֵּץ יָד = Akkadian *qāta napāṣu*: A Term of Non-Allegiance." *Journal of the American Oriental Society* 122 (2002): 79–82.

Taylor, Richard A. "The Peshitta of Daniel: Questions of Origin and Date." Pages 31–42 in *VI Symposium Syriacum, 1992*. Rome: Pontificio Istituto Orientale, 1994.

Theodoret of Cyrus. *Commentary on Daniel*. Translated by Robert C. Hill. Writings from the Greco-Roman World 7. Atlanta: Society of Biblical Literature, 2006.

Thiele, Edwin R. *The Mysterious Numbers of the Hebrew Kings*. 3d ed. Grand Rapids: Zondervan, 1983. Repr., Grand Rapids: Kregel, 1994.

Thomas, D. Winton. "Note on הַדָּעַת in Daniel XII. 4." *Journal of Theological Studies*, n.s., 6 (1955): 226.

Thomas, Robert L. "The Mission of Israel and of the Messiah in the Plan of God." *Master's Seminary Journal* 8 (1997): 191–210.

Toorn, Karel van der. "In the Lions' Den: The Babylonian Background of a Biblical Motif." *Catholic Biblical Quarterly* 60 (1998): 626–40.

Tov, Emanuel. *Textual Criticism of the Hebrew Bible*. 2d ed. Minneapolis: Fortress, 2001.

Towner, W. Sibley. "Poetic Passages of Daniel 1–6." *Catholic Biblical Quarterly* 31 (1969): 317–26.

———. "Tribulation and Peace: The Fate of Shalom in Jewish Apocalyptic." *Horizons in Biblical Theology* 6/2 (1984): 1–26.

———. "Daniel 1 in the Context of the Canon." Pages 285–98 in *Canon, Theology, and Old Testament Interpretation: Essays in Honor of Brevard S. Childs*. Edited by Gene M. Tucker, David L. Petersen, and Robert R. Wilson. Philadelphia: Fortress, 1988.

Trever, John C. "The Book of Daniel and the Origin of the Qumran Community." *Biblical Archaeologist* 48 (1985): 89–102.

Ulrich, Eugene. "Daniel Manuscripts from Qumran, Part 1: A Preliminary Edition of 4QDan[a]." *Bulletin of the American Schools of Oriental Research* 268 (1987): 17–37.

———. "Daniel Manuscripts from Qumran, Part 2: Preliminary Editions of 4QDan^b and 4QDan^c." *Bulletin of the American Schools of Oriental Research* 274 (1989): 3–26.

Ulrich, Eugene, et al. *Qumran Cave 4.XI: Psalms to Chronicles*. Discoveries in the Judaean Desert 16. Oxford: Clarendon, 2000.

Valeta, David M. "Court or Jester Tales? Resistance and Social Reality in Daniel 1–6." *Perspectives in Religious Studies* 32 (2005): 309–24.

Vasholz, Robert I. "Qumran and the Dating of Daniel." *Journal of the Evangelical Theological Society* 21 (1978): 315–21.

Vaucher, Alfred-Félix. "Daniel 8:14 en occident jusqu'au Cardinal Nicolas de Cusa." *Andrews University Seminary Studies* 1 (1963): 139–51.

Walker, William O., Jr. "Daniel 7:13–14." *Interpretation* 39 (1985): 176–81.

Waltke, Bruce K. "The Date of the Book of Daniel." *Bibliotheca sacra* 133 (1976): 319–29.

Walton, John H. "The Four Kingdoms of Daniel." *Journal of the Evangelical Theological Society* 29 (1986): 25–36.

———. "The Decree of Darius the Mede in Daniel 6." *Journal of the Evangelical Theological Society* 31 (1988): 279–86.

———. "The *Anzu* Myth as Relevant Background for Daniel 7?" Pages 69–89 in vol. 1 of *The Book of Daniel: Composition and Reception*. Edited by John J. Collins and Peter W. Flint. Supplements to Vetus Testamentum 83. Leiden: Brill, 2001.

Walvoord, John F. "The Prophecy of the Ten-Nation Confederacy." *Bibliotheca sacra* 124 (1967): 99–105.

———. *Daniel: The Key to Prophetic Revelation*. Chicago: Moody, 1971.

Wambacq, B. N. "Les prières de Baruch 1:15–2:19, et de Daniel 9:5–19." *Biblica* 40 (1959): 463–75.

Watts, John D. W. "Babylonian Idolatry in the Prophets as a False Socio-Economic System." Pages 115–22 in *Israel's Apostasy and Restoration: Essays in Honor of Roland K. Harrison*. Edited by Avraham Gileadi. Grand Rapids: Baker, 1988.

Weisberg, David B. *Texts from the Time of Nebuchadnezzar*. New Haven: Yale University Press, 1980.

Weitzman, Steven. "Plotting Antiochus's Persecution." *Journal of Biblical Literature* 123 (2004): 219–34.

Wenham, David. "The Kingdom of God and Daniel." *Expository Times* 98 (1986–1987): 132–34.

Wesselius, J. W. "Language and Style in Biblical Aramaic: Observations on the Unity of Daniel 2–6." *Vetus Testamentum* 38 (1988): 194–209.

Whitcomb, John C. *Darius the Mede: A Study in Historical Identification*. Grand Rapids: Eerdmans, 1959.

Wilch, John R. *Ruth*. Concordia Commentary. Saint Louis: Concordia, 2006.

Wilson, Gerald H. "The Prayer of Daniel 9: Reflection on Jeremiah 29." *Journal for the Study of the Old Testament* 48 (1990): 91–99.

Wilson, Robert R. "Creation and New Creation: The Role of Creation Imagery in the Book of Daniel." Pages 190–203 in *God Who Creates: Essays in Honor of W. Sibley Towner*. Edited by William P. Brown and S. Dean McBride, Jr. Grand Rapids: Eerdmans, 2000.

Winkle, Ross E. "Jeremiah's Seventy Years for Babylon: A Re-assessment, Part 1: The Scriptural Data." *Andrews University Seminary Studies* 25 (1987): 201–14.

Wiseman, D. J. *Chronicles of Chaldean Kings (626–556 B.C.) in the British Museum*. London: Trustees of the British Museum, 1956. Repr., 1961.

———. "The Last Days of Babylon." *Christianity Today* 2/4 (November 25, 1957): 7–10.

———. "Some Historical Problems in the Book of Daniel." Pages 9–18 in *Notes on Some Problems in the Book of Daniel*. Edited by D. J. Wiseman. London: Tyndale, 1965.

———. *Nebuchadrezzar and Babylon*. Oxford: Oxford University Press, 1985.

Wolter, Michael. " 'Revelation' and 'Story' in Jewish and Christian Apocalyptic." Translated by Mary Deasey Collins and Robert Morgan. Pages 127–44 in *Revelation and Story: Narrative Theology and the Centrality of Story*. Edited by Gerhard Sauter and John Barton. Aldershot, England: Ashgate, 2000.

Wolters, Albert M. "The Riddle of the Scales in Daniel 5." *Hebrew Union College Annual* 62 (1991): 155–77.

———. "Untying the King's Knots: Physiology and Wordplay in Daniel 5." *Journal of Biblical Literature* 110 (1991): 117–22.

———. "*Zōhar hārāqîaʿ* (Daniel 12.3) and Halley's Comet." *Journal for the Study of the Old Testament* 61 (1994): 111–20.

Wong, G. C. I. "Faithful to the End: A Pastoral Reading of Daniel 10–12." *Expository Times* 110 (1999): 109–13.

Woodard, Branson L., Jr. "Literary Strategies and Authorship in the Book of Daniel." *Journal of the Evangelical Theological Society* 37 (1994): 39–53.

Wooden, R. Glenn. "The Recontextualization of Old Greek Daniel 1." Pages 47–68 in *Ancient Versions and Traditions*. Vol. 1 of *Of Scribes and Sages: Early Jewish Interpretation and Transmission of Scripture*. Edited by Craig Evans. 2 vols. London: T&T Clark, 2004.

Woude, Adam S. van der. "Prophetic Prediction, Political Prognostication, and Firm Belief: Reflections on Daniel 11:40–12:3." Pages 63–73 in *The Quest for Context and Meaning: Studies in Biblical Intertextuality in Honor of James A. Sanders*. Edited by Craig A. Evans and Shemaryahu Talmon. Leiden: Brill, 1997.

Yamauchi, Edwin M. "The Greek Words in Daniel in the Light of Greek Influence in the Near East." Pages 170–200 in *New Perspectives on the Old Testament*. Edited by J. Barton Payne. Waco: Word, 1970.

———. "Archaeological Backgrounds of the Exilic and Postexilic Era, Part 1: The Archaeological Background of Daniel." *Bibliotheca sacra* 137 (1980): 3–16.

———. "Hermeneutical Issues in the Book of Daniel." *Journal of the Evangelical Theological Society* 23 (1980): 13–21.

———. "Daniel and Contacts between the Aegean and the Near East before Alexander." *Evangelical Quarterly* 53 (1981): 37–47.

———. *Persia and the Bible*. Grand Rapids: Baker, 1990.

Young, Edward J. *The Prophecy of Daniel: A Commentary*. Grand Rapids: Eerdmans, 1949. Repr., Eugene, Oreg.: Wipf and Stock, 1998.

Young, Ian. *Diversity in Pre-Exilic Hebrew.* Forschungen zum Alten Testament 5. Tübingen: Mohr (Siebeck): 1993.

———. "Concluding Reflections." Pages 312–17 in *Biblical Hebrew: Studies in Chronology and Typology*. Edited by Ian Young. Journal for the Study of the Old Testament: Supplement Series 369. London: T&T Clark, 2003.

Young, Ian, ed. *Biblical Hebrew: Studies in Chronology and Typology*. Journal for the Study of the Old Testament: Supplement Series 369. London: T&T Clark, 2003.

Young, Rodger C. "When Did Solomon Die?" *Journal of the Evangelical Theological Society* 46 (2003): 589–603.

———. "When Did Jerusalem Fall?" *Journal of the Evangelical Theological Society* 47 (2004): 21–38.

Zerbe, Gordon. " 'Pacifism' and 'Passive Resistance' in Apocalyptic Writings: A Critical Evaluation." Pages 65–95 in *The Pseudepigrapha and Early Biblical Interpretation*. Edited by James H. Charlesworth and Craig A. Evans. Sheffield: JSOT Press, 1993.

Zevit, Ziony. "Structure and Individual Elements of Daniel 7." *Zeitschrift für die alttestamentliche Wissenschaft* 80 (1968): 385–96.

Ziegler, Joseph, and Olivier Munnich, eds. *Susanna, Daniel, Bel et Draco*. Second ed. Septuaginta: Vetus Testamentum Graecum 16.2. Göttingen: Vandenhoeck & Ruprecht, 1999.

Zimmermann, Frank. "The Writing on the Wall: Dan. 5:25 f." *Jewish Quarterly Review*, n.s., 55 (1965): 201–7.

Introduction

Date, Authorship, and Unity

Perhaps no other OT prophetic book has been dissected and denied as the work of its putative author as Daniel has been. Critical scholars date its various sections much later than the dates given in the book itself and view none of the events in the book as historical. This critical view has even influenced some authors who claim to be more conservative and evangelical, but who adopt some form of the critical theories and attempt to modify them to make them compatible with an evangelical view of inspiration.[1] However, the majority of Christian evangelicals defend the traditional view, which was also held by Luther and the reformers. This view accepts the book as coming from the pen of Daniel and understands the events related in the book as historically accurate.

Date and Authorship according to the Book

Daniel divides neatly into ten major sections. Each of the first nine chapters (in English Bibles)[2] is a distinct story from the Babylonian captivity (Daniel 1–6) or a vision received by Daniel (Daniel 7–9). The tenth section is a vision that spans the final three chapters, Daniel 10–12. The visions all claim to be from the pen of Daniel as testified by the frequent notice "I, Daniel" (אֲנָה דָנִיֵּאל, 7:15, 28, or אֲנִי דָנִיֵּאל, 8:1, 15, 27; 9:2; 10:2, 7; 12:5) and by the statement that Daniel "wrote the dream" he relates in chapter 7 (see the commentary on 7:1). Traditionally, both Christians and Jews have understood the entire book, including the third person narratives of Daniel 1–6, as coming from the pen of Daniel.

The various accounts in Daniel 1–6 contain historical references that enable a reconstruction of the time of the events narrated. Depending on the type of notice given in each account, the time frame may span several years or may be pinpointed to a particular month or day. (For details, see the commentary on 1:1–2 and the introductions to the subsequent chapters.) The narratives of Daniel 1–6 are in chronological order from earliest to latest:

Chapter	Date of Events in the Chapter
1	Summer 605 BC to sometime between March 22, 603, and fall 603
2	Fall 603 or Winter 603–602
3	Late December 594 or January 593
4	Probably sometime between 573 and 569
5	October 11, 539
6	Between late October 539 and late March 538

---

[1] E.g., Lucas, *Daniel*, 306–15. Lucas equivocates on the date and authorship of Daniel.

[2] The English chapter divisions are the same as the Hebrew except that MT 3:31–33 is part of chapter 4 in English (4:1–3), and MT Dan 6:1 is included at the end of chapter 5 in English (5:31). See "Introduction to Daniel 4" and "Introduction to Daniel 6."

Introduction

Daniel is the first of the prophets to date all of his visions to the years of the reigning king.[3] The visions, like the narratives, are in chronological order. However, the visions overlap the last narratives: Daniel received the visions of Daniel 7 and 8 after the events of Daniel 4 but before the events of Daniel 5. The visions of Daniel 9 and 10–12 were received after the events of Daniel 6.

Chapter(s)	Date of the Vision
7	Sometime between April 7, 553, and April 25, 552 or between April 5, 550, and April 22, 549
8	Sometime between April 16, 551, and April 4, 550 or between April 13, 548, and April 1, 547
9	Sometime between March 24, 538, and Cyrus' 538 decree allowing the exiles to return home
10–12	April 23, 536

Therefore, the visions are chronologically interlocked with the narratives, pointing to a unity of the book despite its two different genres of historical narrative and visionary description, as shown in figure 1.

Figure 1

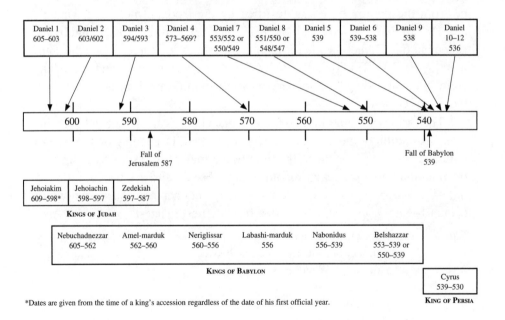

Timeline of Daniel and Related Events

---

[3] Ezekiel was a contemporary of Daniel, but dates his prophecies according to the exile of King Jehoiachin, and not all of his prophecies are dated. For a list of Ezekiel's dates, one may see Hummel, *Ezekiel 21–48*, 740–41.

The book itself cannot have existed in its present form before 536 BC, since that is the date of the final vision. Moreover, there are some indications that the entire book in its present form was written after that final vision. Dan 1:21 indicates that Daniel served in the Babylonian court until the first official year of Cyrus (spring 538–spring 537 BC), so the final form of the account of the earliest incidents in Daniel (chapter 1) was composed after the Persian conquest of Babylon. Also indicative of the date of composition is the presence of Old Persian loanwords throughout Daniel.[4] (See the discussion of Persian loanwords below.) These words are mainly administrative terms or words connected with the palace, which would have quickly been added to any Babylonian courtier's Aramaic vocabulary, though they may have penetrated the Aramaic of common people more slowly.

Therefore, the earliest date for the writing of Daniel is 536 BC. Given the fact that Daniel was probably in his early eighties at this time,[5] it is unlikely that Daniel wrote the book later than about 530 BC. Daniel probably committed his experiences in Babylon to writing during the same time that the construction of the second temple was beginning in Jerusalem (Ezra 3:8; cf. Ezra 4:24).

Critical Theories about Date, Authorship, and Unity

Higher critical scholarship has long challenged the traditional date and authorship of Daniel as well as its unity. The objections that have led to this rejection of the traditional view fall into two broad categories: historical concerns that question the book's authenticity and literary-critical concerns.

Historical concerns about the book date back to Porphyry, a virulent anti-Christian Neo-Platonist philosopher of the late third century, whose writings are no longer extant, but are known only through a number of refutations of his position contained in Jerome's commentary on Daniel. Porphyry challenged especially the visions in Daniel 7–12, believing them to have been written after the events they supposedly predict. While conceding that the visions were largely historically accurate, Porphyry presupposed that there was no such thing as genuine divine revelation of the future. Instead, he argued that Daniel was written as if it were predictive prophecy, but was actually written during the first half of second century BC after the supposed events that it prophesied concerning Antiochus IV Epiphanes (175–164 BC). The prophecies that attempted to prophesy events later in the reign of Antiochus (11:40–45) were inaccurate, demonstrating that there is no divinely revealed predictive prophecy, and also betraying the author's real identity: a Jew in Palestine about the year 165 BC. While Porphyry's views found little support at the time, this same approach to understanding and dating Daniel's visions as *ex eventu* ("after the event")

---

[4] Kitchen, "The Aramaic of Daniel," 35–44.

[5] If Daniel was ten years old when he was first taken to Babylon (605 BC), he would have been seventy-nine in 536 BC. He may have been older than ten in 605 BC, but he probably was less than twenty years old.

prophecies was revived with the rise of higher critical approaches to the Bible. Modern critics assume that the visions are compositions from the Hellenistic era (late fourth to early second centuries BC).

Modern critics also raise objections about other historical references in the book. For instance, the first historical notice in Daniel, that Nebuchadnezzar besieged and captured Jerusalem in the third year of Jehoiakim (Dan 1:1–2), is challenged both as to whether such an event actually happened and because it seemingly conflicts with Jer 25:1, which dates the siege to Jehoiakim's fourth year. Both objections are answerable (see the commentary on 1:1–2), but critical scholars often dismiss any explanations. Often they are much more inclined to search for apparent historical anomalies to bolster their theories concerning the late composition of Daniel than to accept valid explanations of these apparent inaccuracies.

A good example of this critical inclination is the issue of the person of Belshazzar, who is mentioned in Daniel 5, 7, and 8. Until the 1860s, no source outside the book of Daniel or those dependent upon Daniel (e.g., Baruch 1:11) could provide independent confirmation of the existence of Belshazzar. Since he is not mentioned in any of the Greek historians, many nineteenth-century critical scholars viewed Daniel 5 as a purely fictional account about a fictional king. Following the lead of Josephus, defenders of the historicity of Daniel often countered that "Belshazzar" might have been another name for Nabonidus.[6]

However, beginning in the 1860s, Babylonian sources came to light naming Belshazzar the son of Nabonidus and demonstrating that he was made regent over Babylon in the third year of his father's reign. It would seem that the historical nature of Daniel's account had been vindicated. Since all memory of Belshazzar had been lost to history outside of the Bible and works dependent on it, this seemed to furnish proof positive that the writer of Daniel 5 had to have been a contemporary of the events, since later writers, especially Maccabean era writers, would have had no knowledge of Belshazzar.

Despite the clear refutation of their skepticism concerning Belshazzar's existence, critical scholars continue to dismiss the story of Belshazzar as largely fictionalized. They challenge two statements about Belshazzar in Daniel 5: that he was a son of Nebuchadnezzar (5:2, 11, 13, 18, 22) and that he was king (e.g., 5:1).[7] Since critical scholars often dismiss both of these claims, they also dismiss the rest of the account as legendary. Their challenges can be met with

---

[6] Josephus, *Antiquities*, 10.231; Keil, *Daniel*, 169.

[7] Collins, *Daniel*, 32–33; Grabbe, "The Belshazzar of Daniel and the Belshazzar of History," 62–64; Hartman and Di Lella, *Daniel*, 186. However, it should be noted that Hartman and Di Lella concede:

> Belshazzar was, for all practical purposes, ruler of the Neo-Babylonian empire. It is also historically true that he had this position when the city of Babylon was captured by a foreign ruler in 539 B.C. ... At best, he may have been a descendant of Nebuchadnezzar on his mother's side ... , although this is based on legendary, rather than historical evidence.

equally strong reasons defending the accuracy of Daniel's portrayal of this ruler (see the commentary on 5:1–4), but these reasons are often unjustifiably dismissed by critical scholars.

Ironically, contemporary critical scholars often take a similar approach to the person of Darius the Mede.[a] Since no such person is known from ancient sources, critics assume that this person is a fictional figure invented to explain a Median presence in the conquest of Babylon (cf. Jer 51:11, 28). However, given the experience with the identity of Belshazzar, some caution is in order concerning the identity of Darius, and several reasonable explanations for his identity are available (see the excursus "The Identity of Darius the Mede").

(a) Daniel 6:1, 2, 7, 10, 26, 29 (ET 5:31; 6:1, 6, 9, 25, 28); 9:1; 11:1

Critical scholars often supplement these historical objections by other observations that are said to be indicative of a date of composition later than the sixth century BC. Among these are the presence of Persian and Greek loanwords as well as the type of Aramaic and Hebrew found in the book. S. R. Driver's oft-quoted statement summarizes the classical critical position concerning this evidence:

> The *Persian* words presuppose a period after the Persian empire had been well established: the Greek words *demand*, the Hebrew *supports*, and the Aramaic *permits*, a date *after the conquest of Palestine by Alexander the Great* (B.C. 332).[8]

Thus Daniel is viewed by critical scholars as a composition from the Hellenistic era.

The other line of objections—those arising from literary-critical concerns—has led not only to a denial of the book's authorship by Daniel, but also to challenges to its unity. Until the late nineteenth century, both conservative and critical scholars accepted the unity of the book. Critical scholars since that time have tended to view literary features of the book as testifying to it being the work of several authors, although among critical scholars, its unity of authorship was defended as late as 1952 by Rowley.[9] However, the trend among critics has been to view Daniel as a compilation or accretion of several Daniel sources. Most radical of these is the theory that there are ten distinct authors for the book, one for each major section.[10] Less radical are various developmental theories that posit a different setting for the composition of larger sections of the book based on several literary features; the most prominent features are the presence of both Hebrew (1:1–2:4a; 8:1–12:13) and Aramaic (2:4b–7:28) and the use of both narrative accounts (Daniel 1–6) and visions (Daniel 7–12). These developmental theories often suppose that the earliest materials in the book are the several stories about Daniel and his friends, which allegedly were independent compositions eventually collected into one book, possibly in Maccabean times.

---

[8] Driver, *An Introduction to the Literature of the Old Testament*, 508.

[9] Rowley, "The Unity of the Book of Daniel." Rowley dated the book to the Maccabean period, but maintained that it came from the pen of a single author.

[10] Hartman and Di Lella, *Daniel*, 13–14.

The visions are said to be products of the Maccabean era and supposedly were combined with the earlier stories by a Maccabean editor, who also added some redactional touches to the earlier material.[11]

This does not mean that there is widespread critical agreement as to the composition of the stories in Daniel 1–6. According to some critics, they may have originally been oral tales. Some view them as originating in the eastern Jewish Diaspora, while others argue that they are Palestinian in origin. Any number of studies seek to find a social or political setting that gave rise to the tales, looking for clues within the tales themselves.[12] While older critics often viewed the stories as Maccabean in origin, later scholars have tended to view the stories as originating earlier, most often in the third century BC.[13] While there is little consensus, therefore, among critical scholars on the origin of the stories in Daniel 1–6, there is widespread agreement that the composition of the visions in Daniel 7–12 as well as the final redaction of the book took place in Maccabean times (ca. 165 BC).

Evidence—An Argument for the Traditional Date of Daniel

While critical theories concerning the unity and composition of Daniel dominate modern scholarship on the book, conservative and evangelical scholars have continued to defend the traditional date of the book. Several lines of reasoning converge to suggest that the matter is not as settled as critical commentaries and essays on Daniel would lead one to believe. Some of these lines of reasoning undermine assertions made by critical scholars, while others bring unnoticed evidence to bear on the question.

Hebrew Language Characteristics in Daniel

When Driver wrote his much-quoted dictum about the language characteristics of Daniel (quoted above), he could not have possibly foreseen the effect of later research and discoveries on the study of ancient Hebrew. His assertion that "the Hebrew *supports* ... a date *after the conquest of Palestine* by Alexander the Great" has been called into question on several grounds. Driver supported his assertion with a list of expressions that he claimed never or very rarely occurred in earlier Hebrew literature. After examining these, Martin concludes:

> To make out a plausible case for the lateness of Daniel on lexical grounds, one would have to show not only that the words or idioms did not occur earlier, but that there was *prima facie* evidence against the possibility of their appearing. There is no intrinsic probability that any of the terms listed could

---

[11] An example of this type of treatment can be found in Collins, *Daniel*, 38.

[12] Some of these proposals are Collins, *Apocalyptic Vision*; Gammie, "On the Intention and Sources of Daniel 1–6"; Gnuse, "The Jewish Dream Interpreter in a Foreign Court"; Goldingay, "The Stories in Daniel"; Henze, "The Ideology of Rule in the Narrative Frame of Daniel (Dan 1–6)"; Millard, "Daniel 1–6 and History"; Niditch, "Legends of Wise Heroes and Heroines"; Patterson, "Holding On to Daniel's Court Tales"; Paul, "The Mesopotamian Background of Daniel 1–6"; Robertson, "Tragedy, Comedy, and the Bible: A Response."

[13] The last major critical study to defend a Maccabean date for Daniel 1–6 was Rowley, "The Unity of the Book of Daniel" (1952).

not have been used much earlier. In fact, one must proceed with the utmost caution in making pronouncements on the extent of a given vocabulary. It is well known that words that are not recorded in the literary language are to be found in the dialects. All that one is justified in saying is that a certain word occurs in the extant documents for the first time. *There is nothing about the Hebrew of Daniel that could be considered extraordinary for a bilingual or, perhaps in this case, a trilingual speaker of the language in the sixth century BC.*[14]

Moreover, Daniel's Hebrew can now be compared to the Hebrew of the sectarian scrolls discovered at Qumran. These sectarian documents from the second century BC onward show a number of characteristics of the Hebrew language as it was written in the Hasmonean (165–37 BC) and Herodian (after 36 BC) periods. The differences between the Hebrew portions of Daniel and the Hebrew of these documents is striking. Already as early as 1974, before all of the Qumran scrolls (or Dead Sea Scrolls) were published, Archer came to the following conclusion when comparing Daniel to these sectarian writings:

> It seems abundantly clear that a second-century date for the Hebrew chapters of Daniel is no longer tenable on linguistic grounds. In view of the markedly later development exhibited by these second-century documents in the areas of syntax, word order, morphology, vocabulary, spelling, and word-usage, there is absolutely no possibility of regarding Daniel as contemporary. ... Otherwise we must surrender linguistic evidence altogether and assert that it is completely devoid of value in the face of subjective theories derived from antisupernaturalistic bias. ... This verdict carries with it some far-reaching consequences. The possibility of explaining the predictive portions of this work as mere prophecy after the event is completely excluded.[15]

Subsequent research into the Hebrew of the Dead Sea Scrolls has not added any information to challenge Archer's conclusion.[16] Thus with the discovery of the Qumran sectarian documents it is possible to contradict Driver's statement: the Hebrew of Daniel *does not* support a date of composition after 332 BC.

Moreover, recent studies of the history of Hebrew during the OT period demonstrate that it is difficult, if not impossible, to date any Hebrew text solely on the basis of linguistic evidence.[17] Young notes a number of unresolved questions in regard to attempts to date Hebrew texts linguistically:

---

[14] Martin, "The Hebrew of Daniel," 30; emphasis added.

[15] Archer, "The Hebrew of Daniel Compared with the Qumran Sectarian Documents," 480–81.

[16] The survey of Qimron, *The Hebrew of the Dead Sea Scrolls*, demonstrates this. There are no significant grammatical or lexical features found both in Daniel and in the Dead Sea Scrolls that are not also found in other Persian-era biblical books (e.g., Ezra, Nehemiah, Esther, Haggai, Zechariah, Malachi). If the Hebrew portions of Daniel were written in the Maccabean period, one would expect to find that Daniel shared features with the Qumran documents that were not found in other biblical books.

[17] A good discussion of the problems associated with linguistic arguments for dating OT texts is found in the various articles in Young, *Biblical Hebrew: Studies in Chronology and Typology*.

> Given the attestation of LBH [Late Biblical Hebrew] features in pre-exilic inscriptions, my article also raised another question, less important for the current debate: Why couldn't a work with a concentration of LBH elements be written before the exile? ...
>
> If SBH [Standard Biblical Hebrew] could be used after the exile, and LBH before the exile, is it at all possible, given the current state of our knowledge of ancient Hebrew, to date the language of any part of biblical literature? ...
>
> Without chronological presuppositions, does LBH really exist as a distinct entity within BH [Biblical Hebrew]? The LBH books were grouped together first of all on the basis that they were the ones known to be post-exilic (as opposed to other clearly earlier books). However, purely on linguistic grounds, are the links between Esther, Ezra, Nehemiah, Chronicles and Daniel strong enough to single this group of books out from BH in general? Or does every book of the Hebrew Bible simply have its own linguistic profile?
>
> If LBH really is a distinct entity, do the linguistic variations reflect social realities? If the differences between SBH and LBH are not to be explained chronologically, what sociolinguistic factors lead to the co-existence of these varieties of Hebrew? If LBH is not in fact "late" BH, is there a need to invent a new term to describe it?[18]

Given our fragmentary state of knowledge about the history of linguistic developments in Biblical Hebrew, use of linguistic evidence to argue for a late date of Daniel's Hebrew is unwarranted since the linguistic evidence is, at best, mixed. The most that can be said is that Daniel's Hebrew is much more like the Hebrew of other acknowledged exilic books of the OT than like the Hebrew of the Qumran documents, making Daniel unlikely to be a composition from the Hellenistic era as higher critics contend.

Aramaic Language Characteristics in Daniel

Driver was less certain about the Aramaic evidence and so stated only that he thought it *permitted* a date after 332 BC. Subsequent studies have confirmed that the Aramaic of Daniel is Imperial Aramaic, which was current from about the seventh century BC to about 300 BC. Already in 1965 Kitchen concluded:

> The word-order of the Aramaic of Daniel (and Ezra) places it squarely in full-blooded Imperial Aramaic—and in striking contrast with *real* Palestinian post-Imperial Aramaic of the second and first centuries BC as illustrated by the Dead Sea Scrolls. ...
>
> There is nothing to decide the date of composition of the Aramaic of Daniel *on the grounds of Aramaic* anywhere between the late sixth and the second century BC. Some points hint at an early (especially pre-300), not late, date. ... The date of the book of Daniel, in short, cannot be decided upon linguistic grounds alone. It is equally obscurantist to exclude dogmatically a sixth–fifth (or fourth) century date on the one hand, or to hold such a date as mechanically proved on the other, *as far as the Aramaic is concerned*.[19]

---

[18] Young, "Concluding Reflections," 313–14.

[19] Kitchen, "The Aramaic of Daniel," 78–79.

Later studies have supported Kitchen's conclusion. Coxon, who accepts a second-century date for the final editing of Daniel, nevertheless concludes:

> While it would be unwise to conclude that as far as syntax is concerned the Aramaic of Daniel has great antiquity it would be equally amiss to insist that it is a late regional dialect. The language shares a high proportion of features which bear the stamp of Official Aramaic but this may reflect nothing more than the literary facility of a later writer. The treatment of the accusative preposition ל and the verb יכל ["be able to," e.g., 2:10, 27, 47] supports this view. On the other hand an intriguing feature is the apparent "eastern" word order which distinguished the Aramaic of Daniel from Official Aramaic and the later dialects. A fundamental change of this kind in sentence structure may be highly significant and would certainly point to a date [for Daniel] before the second century B.C.[20]

Coxon's further study of synonyms in Aramaic from both Official Aramaic and the Aramaic Qumran documents found only one connection between Daniel's Aramaic and the Qumran documents, and that one connection he considers to be indeterminate of date.[21] Otherwise, he concludes:

> Accepting the validity of the method [used by Coxon in his study] can only conclude that Biblical Aramaic is a brand of Official Aramaic and bears the marks of the antiquity of that language.[22]

Studies by Archer and Vasholz have confirmed that the second-century Aramaic documents from Qumran demonstrate that Daniel's Aramaic is older.[23] Therefore, the Aramaic of Daniel may permit a date as late as 300 BC, but the evidence favors an earlier date and does not rule out the date indicated in the book itself—sometime shortly after 536 BC.

Persian and Greek Loanwords

Daniel's Hebrew and Aramaic use a relatively high proportion of loanwords from two languages: Akkadian and Old Persian. In addition, three Greek loanwords are used in Daniel 3. The Akkadian loanwords are of little significance in dating the composition of the book.[24] However, the Old Persian and Greek loanwords have been used in arguments concerning the date of Daniel.

That Daniel contains loanwords from Old Persian is acknowledged by nearly all scholars, though some caution should be exercised in identifying them since little actual evidence of Old Persian survives, and a number of words are

---

[20] Coxon, "The Syntax of the Aramaic of *Daniel*," 122.
[21] Coxon, "The Distribution of Synonyms in Biblical Aramaic," 510.
[22] Coxon, "The Distribution of Synonyms in Biblical Aramaic," 511.
[23] Archer, "The Aramaic of the 'Genesis Apocryphon' Compared with the Aramaic of Daniel"; Vasholz, "Qumran and the Dating of Daniel."
[24] This is conceded by all. See, for example, Collins, *Daniel*, 18.

said to be derived from reconstructed theoretical Old Persian forms.²⁵ Kitchen recognizes the significance of these Old Persian words in Daniel:

> The Persian words in Daniel are specifically *Old Persian* words. The recognized divisions of Persian language-history within Iranian are: Old down to *c.* 300 BC, Middle observable during *c.* 300 BC to *c.* AD 900, and New from *c.* AD 900 to the present. Now, the fact that the Iranian element in Daniel is from *Old* Persian and not Middle indicates that the Aramaic of Daniel is in this respect pre-Hellenistic, drew on no Persian from after the fall of that empire—and not on any Middle Persian words and forms that might have penetrated Aramaic in Arsacid times (*c.* 250 BC, ff.).²⁶

A contention of critical scholars is that Daniel could not have used any Persian loanwords in his Aramaic since it would have taken a considerable time for such words to be adopted into Aramaic. However, that contention is false. As Kitchen notes:

> If a putative Daniel in Babylon under the Persians (and who had briefly served them) were to write a book some time after the third year of Cyrus (Dn. 10:1), then a series of Persian words is no surprise. Such a person in the position of close contact with Persian administration that is accorded to him in the book would have to acquire—and use in his Aramaic—many terms and words from his new Persian colleagues (just like the Elamite scribes of Persepolis), from the conquest by Cyrus onwards.²⁷

We could add that Daniel's initial audience may well have been fellow Judeans living in Babylon, and probably more than a few of them served the new Persian administration. They would have readily understood such Persian words, which had recently become current in their environment. Therefore, the presence of Persian words in Daniel does not present an argument for a date of composition later than about 560 BC.

The Greek words in Daniel are often considered the strongest indication that Daniel was written, or at least received its final editing, in the second century BC. Coxon observes:

> Of all the linguistic arguments which have been used in the debate concerning the age of the Aramaic sections of *Daniel* and the date of the composition of the book, the Greek loans seem to provide the strongest evidence in favor of the second century B.C.²⁸

Yet Coxon also presents evidence that this is not the case. For instance, he points out that the form of the word קִיתָרוֹס, "lyre" (Dan 3:5, 7, 10, 15), indicates

---

²⁵ See the discussion in Young, *Diversity in Pre-Exilic Hebrew*, 69–71. Also see Kitchen, "The Aramaic of Daniel," 43, n. 65.
²⁶ Kitchen, "The Aramaic of Daniel," 43–44.
²⁷ Kitchen, "The Aramaic of Daniel," 41–42.
²⁸ Coxon, "Greek Loan-Words and Alleged Greek Loan Translations in the Book of Daniel," 24.

that it was borrowed from Ionic κίθαρις rather than Attic κιθάρα, indicating that it was an early (pre-332 BC) loanword.[29]

In fact, there are only three Greek loanwords in Daniel, all of them musical instruments mentioned in Daniel 3.[30] Yamauchi has amassed much evidence of contacts between the ancient Near East and the Aegean long before Alexander, even providing instances of early Semitic influence on the Greek language and Greek culture.[31] This led him to conclude: "We may safely say that the presence of Greek words in an Old Testament book is not a proof of Hellenistic date, in view of the abundant opportunities for contacts between the Aegean and the Near East before Alexander."[32]

Such evidence has even led critical scholars to admit that "the evidence for Greek influence on Daniel is too slight to prove anything."[33]

Therefore, neither the Persian nor the Greek loanwords offer any proof that Daniel is a late composition. Of themselves, they also do not provide any conclusive evidence that the book is an early Persian composition. The same is true of the other linguistic evidence, both Hebrew and Aramaic. The best that can be said about the linguistic evidence is that it suggests that Daniel was not written before about 560 BC and not later than 300 BC.

Historical Data in the Book Itself

As discussed earlier, critical scholars label much of the historical data found in the text of Daniel as inaccurate or erroneous. There are three primary reasons for such claims.

Lack of Extrabiblical Evidence: This is clearly the case for the person called "Darius the Mede" (e.g., 6:1 [ET 5:31]), for whom no confirming ancient Near Eastern evidence has yet been uncovered. This was also once true for Belshazzar, but confirming extrabiblical evidence has now been found for him.[34] Several other cases in Daniel could be added here. However, "absence of evidence is not evidence of absence."[35] When we simply do not have any extrabiblical evidence that confirms that an event or person in Daniel is historical, this does not mean that these events and persons are fictional. It only means that we have no surviving evidence from outside the Scriptures to confirm them.

---

[29] Coxon, "Greek Loan-Words and Alleged Greek Loan Translations in the Book of Daniel," 31.

[30] The three are קַתְרוֹס, "lyre," פְּסַנְתֵּרִין, "triangular harp," and סוּמְפֹּנְיָה, "drum." See the textual notes on them in 3:5. A fourth word, כָּרוֹז, is now recognized to be a Persian loanword into both Aramaic and Greek; see the textual note on it in 3:4.

[31] Yamauchi, "The Greek Words in Daniel in the Light of Greek Influence in the Near East"; "Daniel and Contacts between the Aegean and the Near East before Alexander," especially pages 44–47.

[32] Yamauchi, "The Greek Words in Daniel in the Light of Greek Influence in the Near East," 192.

[33] Collins, *Daniel*, 20.

[34] See above under "Critical Theories about Date, Authorship, and Unity."

[35] To quote Carl Sagan.

Nevertheless, we do have the historical evidence provided by the book of Daniel itself, which is at least as reliable as other historical sources.[36] Moreover, as the discussion of various historical notices in Daniel in the commentary below demonstrates, the events related in Daniel fit well into what is known about ancient Near Eastern chronology of this period. That they fit well does not prove that the events happened, but provides a compelling reason not to assume that they did not happen. For example, Nebuchadnezzar's convocation at the dedication of the gold statue (Daniel 3) is not recorded in the extant Babylonian annals. However, the information given by Daniel fits well with what we know about the chronology of Nebuchadnezzar's reign and can be convincingly given a probable date (see "Introduction to Daniel 3").

Apparent Contradictions: If there is an apparent contradiction between Daniel and some other data, critics automatically understand Daniel to be in error. This assumption of Daniel's lack of trustworthiness means that critics do not bother to consider possible solutions that may show that what at first blush appears to be a contradiction is not actually contradictory. In this category belongs the contention that Dan 1:1–2 is contradicted by Jer 25:1 (see the commentary on Dan 1:1–2). We could also add the contention that the portrayal of Belshazzar in Daniel 5 is inaccurate because he is called "king" while Nebuchadnezzar is called his "father" and he is called Nebuchadnezzar's "son." (See the discussion of the person and office of Belshazzar in "Introduction to Daniel 5.") These apparent contradictions are resolved if one pays attention to the ways that information was reported in ancient sources and understands them according to their own conventions, rather than imposing modern conventions upon them.

Antisupernaturalistic Bias: An often unstated bias held by critics is the bias against accepting reports of miraculous, divine intervention among human affairs, such as God revealing to Daniel the content of Nebuchadnezzar's dream (Daniel 2), the survival of the men in the fiery furnace (Daniel 3), or the rescue of Daniel from the lions' den (Daniel 6). Critics consider these events unhistorical on their face since they involve God's direct involvement in history. The assumption that the visions of Daniel are *ex eventu* ("after the event") prophecies involves the same antisupernaturalistic bias since critics reject out of hand the possibility of predictive prophecy.

None of these reasons for the "unhistorical" nature of Daniel is sufficient to prove that Daniel contains historical errors or even to demonstrate that it may be in error. As the commentary demonstrates, a close examination of the historical references in Daniel reveals no reason to label the events as erroneous.

---

[36] This commentary considers Daniel to be inspired and so inerrant, as are the rest of the Scriptures. But even if one considers Daniel simply to be an ancient document and argues on the basis of human reason alone, there are compelling reasons to regard it as historically accurate.

Evidence from Ben Sira[37]

While scholars often date the book of Jesus son of Sirach (Yeshua ben Sira) to about 180 BC, some fifteen years before Antiochus Epiphanes' persecution of the Jews, it often goes unnoticed that Ben Sira (Sirach or Ecclesiasticus) may have known the book of Daniel. However, Solomon Schechter, the first editor of the Hebrew fragments of Ben Sira discovered in the *genizah* of the Cairo synagogue in the late nineteenth century, thinks differently. Schechter proposes three possible adaptations of Daniel: in Ben Sira 3:30 (from Dan 4:24 [ET 4:27]); in Ben Sira 36:10 (from Dan 8:19, 11:27, 35); and in Ben Sira 36:22 (from Dan 9:17).[38]

Ben Sira 3:30 (from Daniel 4:24 [ET 4:27])

Schechter proposes that the words חטאת תכפר צדקה in Ben Sira 3:30 were adapted from Dan 4:24 (ET 4:27). The problem of comparing Ben Sira to Daniel is that Dan 4:24 (ET 4:27) is Aramaic, while Ben Sira is Hebrew. Therefore, we must also determine whether the words in Ben Sira appear to be a Hebrew representation of this Aramaic text.

Dan 4:24 (ET 4:27) reads (following the Qere):

לָהֵן מַלְכָּא מִלְכִּי יִשְׁפַּר עֲלָךְ וַחֲטָאָךְ בְּצִדְקָה
פְרֻק וַעֲוָיָתָךְ בְּמִחַן עֲנָיִן הֵן תֶּהֱוֵא אַרְכָה לִשְׁלֵוְתָךְ׃

Therefore, Your Majesty, let my advice be pleasing to you: *break away from your sins with righteousness* and from your iniquities by showing mercy to the poor. Perhaps your prosperity will be prolonged.

Ben Sira 3:30 reads:

חטאת תכפר צדקה כן מים יכבו לוהטת אש

Righteousness [NRSV: almsgiving] *atones for sin* just as water extinguishes a blazing fire.

The question of whether the language of this passage in Ben Sira is drawn from Daniel revolves around the equivalence of Daniel's Aramaic verb, פְּרַק, "break/tear away," and Ben Sira's Hebrew verb, כִּפֵּר, "atone." Admittedly, פְּרַק is difficult to understand in this context. However, we should note that both the Old Greek and Theodotion translate this verb in Dan 4:24 (ET 4:27) in a way that is similar to the Hebrew verb in Ben Sira. Both Greek versions use λυτρόω, which normally means "redeem," but in the context of this verse can only mean "atone by your actions," that is, "your actions will pay the price to redeem you and therefore atone for your sins."

The Old Greek of Dan 4:24 (ET 4:27) is as follows:

πάσας τὰς ἀδικίας σου ἐν ἐλεημοσύναις λύτρωσαι.

---

[37] This discussion is drawn from Steinmann, *Oracles of God*, 44–49.

[38] Schechter and Taylor, *The Wisdom of Ben Sira*, 13, 17, 18. The versification of Ben Sira followed here will be that of the NRSV. Schechter follows a slightly different versification so that Ben Sira 36:10 is 36:8 in his list and 36:22 is 36:17 in his list.

Atone for all your unrighteousness with donations to the poor.

Theodotion reads:

τὰς ἁμαρτίας σου ἐν ἐλεημοσύναις λύτρωσαι.

Atone for your sins with donations to the poor.

Interestingly, both of these translations understand the "righteousness" (צְדָקָה) of the Aramaic text as charitable giving, probably from the mention of showing mercy to the oppressed later in the verse. This same connection is made by Ben Sira's grandson in his translation of Ben Sira 3:30, confirming the identification of Ben Sira's language with Dan 4:24 (ET 4:27):

πῦρ φλογιζόμενον ἀποσβέσει ὕδωρ καὶ ἐλεημοσύνη ἐξιλάσεται ἁμαρτίας.

As water extinguishes a blazing fire, so a donation to the poor atones for sin.

All of this evidence points in the direction of Ben Sira being dependent on Daniel, not the reverse. We can easily explain the extant texts based on the assumption that Ben Sira, the Greek translation of Ben Sira, and the two Greek translations of Daniel are dependent on the older, original Aramaic text of Daniel. The other scenario is highly improbable: that only fifteen years after Ben Sira was written, Daniel borrowed this thought and transformed its vocabulary into Aramaic, then thirty years later, Ben Sira's grandson interpreted the older Ben Sira 3:30 in light of a younger book of Daniel, and that at about the same time Daniel was translated in the Old Greek with the same understanding.[39] Therefore, we have ancient confirmation that Ben Sira 3:30 does reflect the language of Dan 4:24 (ET 4:27).

Ben Sira 36:10 (from Daniel 8:19; 11:27, 35)

The parallel between Dan 8:19; 11:27, 35 and Ben Sira 36:10 has been recognized not only by Schechter but also by Torrey[40] and Fox.[41] All have noted the same thing. The collocation of the Hebrew words קֵץ, "end," and מוֹעֵד, "appointed time," occurs in the OT only in Dan 8:19; 11:27, 35 (cf. Deut 31:10; Hab 2:3).

The three OT passages are as follows:

... כִּי לְמוֹעֵד קֵץ׃

... because it concerns the appointed time of the end. (Dan 8:19)

... כִּי־עוֹד קֵץ לַמּוֹעֵד׃

... because an end is yet for an appointed time. (11:27)

---

[39] Old Greek Daniel most probably dates to the late second century BC. See Collins, *Daniel*, 8; Hartman and Di Lella, *Daniel*, 78; Montgomery, *Daniel*, 38.

[40] C. C. Torrey, "The Hebrew of the Geniza Sirah," in *The Alexander Marx Jubilee Volume* (ed. Saul Lieberman; New York: Jewish Theological Seminary of America, 1950), 597.

[41] Fox, "Ben Sira on OT Canon Again."

... וְלַלְבֵּן עַד־עֵת קֵץ כִּי־עוֹד לַמּוֹעֵד׃

... and make them white until the time of the end for it is still for an appointed time. (11:35)

This same collocation of קֵץ, "end," and מוֹעֵד, "appointed time," is found in Ben Sira 36:10:

החיש קץ ופקוד מועד ...

Hasten the end, and remember the appointed time ...

God's judgment at this eschatological appointed time of the end is the theme in Ben Sira 36:1–11:

> ¹Have mercy upon us, O God of all,
>   ²and put all the nations in fear of you.
> ³Lift up your hand against foreign nations
>   and let them see your might.
> ⁴As you have used us to show your holiness to them,
>   so use them to show your glory to us.
> ⁵Then they will know, as we have known,
>   that there is no God but you, O Lord.
> ⁶Give new signs, and work other wonders;
>   ⁷make your hand and right arm glorious.
> ⁸Rouse your anger and pour out your wrath;
>   ⁹destroy the adversary and wipe out the enemy.
> ¹⁰Hasten the day [Hebrew: the end],[42] and remember the appointed time,
>   and let people recount your mighty deeds.
> ¹¹Let survivors be consumed in the fiery wrath,
>   and may those who harm your people meet destruction. (NRSV)

If we keep in mind Schechter's observation that "when the same phrase occurs in one of the canonical writers and in B. S. [Ben Sira], the balance of probability is strongly in favour of the supposition that B. S. was the imitator of the canonical writer and not *vice versa*,"[43] we are led to the conclusion that Ben Sira was borrowing from Daniel at this point.

Ben Sira 36:22 (from Daniel 9:17)

Ben Sira 36:22 says:

תשמע תפלת עבדיך ...

Listen to the prayers of your servants ...

The collocation of the Hebrew words שָׁמַע, "hear," תְּפִלָּה, "prayer," and עֶבֶד, "servant," occurs in the OT only in Dan 9:17 and Neh 1:6 (cf. 1 Ki 8:28–29 ‖ 2 Chr 6:19–20). However, Nehemiah uses the infinitive construct לִשְׁמֹעַ, "to

---

[42] NRSV is following the Greek text, which apparently misunderstood the Hebrew. The NRSV's decision to follow the Greek is probably an ideological one. It assumes that Ben Sira could not be borrowing from Daniel since critical opinion dates Daniel after Ben Sira.

[43] Schechter and Taylor, *The Wisdom of Ben Sira*, 35.

hear," whereas Daniel uses the imperative שְׁמַע, "hear, listen to." Since the imperfect תשמע, "may you hear, listen to," in Ben Sira 36:22 is probably to be understood as an injunction, that is, a request[44] (the Greek translates it with the imperative εἰσάκουσον, "hear, listen"), Dan 9:17 has a much stronger claim as the source used by Ben Sira. Its syntax more easily aligns with the syntax in Ben Sira, whereas the syntax of Neh 1:6 is much more distant.

Conclusion about Ben Sira 3:30; 36:10; and 36:22

These three verses in Ben Sira have clear parallels in Daniel. One could argue that the parallels are coincidental. However, these parallels are of the same type as those in Ben Sira that allude to other OT books. To deny that these are parallels to Daniel, one would have to deny practically every reference to other OT books as well. Since scholars generally view those other parallels as Ben Sira's deliberate use of the OT, that approach is precluded.

On the other hand, one could argue that Daniel borrowed from Ben Sira. However, besides being contrary to the fact that Ben Sira is known to be an adapter of earlier biblical material, this would also raise the question as to why Daniel borrowed at only these three places. The parallel in Ben Sira 36:10 to Daniel 8 and 11 could possibly be seen as Daniel adapting an eschatological passage for his own use since his book is eschatologically oriented, and the author of Daniel might have been interested in using another well-respected book to boost his own. However, little reason could be found for adopting the two other passages. Indeed, given the interest in wisdom in the first part of Daniel, one would expect much more borrowing there, especially in the contexts where wisdom is explicitly mentioned. However, we find in Daniel only two other parallels to Ben Sira, and neither in the immediate proximity of references to wisdom. Indeed, Daniel 4 is a different kind of wisdom than found in Ben Sira—wisdom and insight that allow Daniel to interpret dreams, not the proverbial wisdom characteristic of Ben Sira. It seems that Ben Sira is adopting Daniel for his purposes, as he does other biblical books.

Therefore, Ben Sira appears to have drawn upon Daniel 4, 8, and 11, and also most probably drew on chapter 9. This means that Ben Sira used even those chapters (8–12) that critical scholars date as late compositions. Since he also used chapter 4, which some scholars date as earlier, Ben Sira appears to have been using the book of Daniel as we have it in the Hebrew OT or something very similar to it. Whether these parallels to Daniel are real or only apparent is an issue that has seldom been addressed. For our immediate purposes we can only state that there is no obvious reason (other than the critical scholarly consensus on the late date of Daniel) for maintaining that Ben Sira did not know and use Daniel.

If this is the case, then Daniel was an older and respected book when Ben Sira wrote (ca. 180 BC). This implies that Daniel was indeed predictive

---

[44] See Waltke-O'Connor, § 31.5b.

prophecy. Even if we were to date Daniel as late as about 300 BC (about as late as possible if it were to become a revered book by Ben Sira's day), the detailed descriptions in Daniel 11 of the reigns of the Ptolemaic kings Ptolemy III through Ptolemy VI and the details of the reigns of the Seleucid kings Antiochus I through Antiochus IV would not have been *ex eventu* ("after the event") prophecy, since those events had not yet taken place. Yet the book does accurately describe details from the reigns of these kings (see the commentary on Daniel 11). The most logical explanation is that Daniel 11 (and the rest of Daniel) contains actual predictive prophecy revealed to Daniel by God, as the book itself claims.

Evidence from Qumran

One of the eight manuscripts of Daniel from Qumran, 4QDan^c, is among the oldest biblical manuscripts discovered there, and is commonly dated to 120–115 BC. Cross, who assumes the standard critical dating for Daniel, states that this copy of Daniel is "no more than about a half century younger than the autograph."[45] This would mean that this manuscript is a copy of Daniel produced no later than about 115 BC.

There can be no doubt that Daniel was considered a genuine prophetic book by the Qumran sectarians. In the work known as 4QFlorilegium, Daniel is grouped among the prophets. In column 2, line 3, we read:[46]

כתוב בספר דניאל הנביא ...

As is written in the book of the prophet Daniel ... (Quotations from Dan 12:10 and 11:32 follow.)

This is identical to the earlier references to Isaiah and Ezekiel in column 1, lines 15 and 16:

כתוב בספר ישעיה הנביא ...

As is written in the book of the prophet Isaiah ... (A quotation from Is 8:11 follows.)

כתוב עליהמה בספר יחזקאל הנביא ...

As is written about them in the book of the prophet Ezekiel ... (Quotations from Ezek 37:23 and possibly 44:15 follow.)

This treatment of Daniel as on par with Isaiah and Ezekiel agrees with what we know about Jewish attitudes in general about Daniel, since both Josephus[47] and the NT[48] accept Daniel as a genuine prophet.

To account for the widespread evidence for the acceptance of Daniel as canonical, the supposition that Daniel was only composed in about 165 BC would require it to have gained very rapid acceptance as a genuine prophecy

---

[45] Cross, *The Ancient Library of Qumran*, 43.
[46] The Hebrew text is from Allegro, *Qumrân Cave 4.I*, 53–54.
[47] See "Daniel and the Prophets" in "Connections with Other Old Testament Books" below.
[48] See "Daniel in the New Testament" below.

by virtually all known Jewish sects in the late Hellenistic and early Herodian periods.[49] The probability of this rapid and widespread acceptance of a recent composition is extremely remote. It is made even more remote by the fact that critical scholars often claim that the end of Daniel 11 and the end of Daniel 12 were attempts at genuine prophecy by the author of Daniel, but they proved to be inaccurate. If they were recent and inaccurate (false) prophecies, it is almost impossible to image that there has survived no record of controversy among Jewish sects about the prophetic status of Daniel. Surely some would have objected that Daniel was a false prophet (cf. Deut 18:20–22) and that the book was only a recent work and a forgery attributed to a much earlier figure from the Babylonian and Persian periods.

However, just the opposite happened. Daniel was received as a genuine prophetic book and was so popular that other Daniel works were produced under his name (see "The Text and Other Daniel Traditions" below), though none of these later works was universally received as a genuine prophetic book. The widespread acceptance of Daniel as canonical only makes sense if Daniel and his book were generally accepted as genuine *before* the rise of Jewish sects following Antiochus' persecution (167–164 BC). Like the evidence from Ben Sira, this implies that Daniel was already revered some length of time before 165 BC.

Thus the Qumran evidence, like the evidence from Ben Sira, strongly implies that Daniel is older than the early second century, which would of necessity make it genuine predictive prophecy. This evidence is in harmony with the view of its authorship by Daniel around the year 536 BC.

Theological Threats Posed by the Critical Dating of Daniel

While it may seem at first blush that the main threat posed by critical theories about the date and composition of Daniel concerns the inspiration of the Scriptures, the problem runs much deeper than that. The theology presented in Daniel is intimately tied to the historicity of the events it describes and the reliability of its predictive prophecy. These, in turn, are dependent on a theme that runs throughout the book, both in its early chapters relating events in Babylon and in its later chapters that relay Daniel's visions: God is in complete control of human events, both in the near term and in the more distant future.

The book makes clear that God governs all that happens (1:2; 2:21–22; 4:32 [ET 4:35]) for the sake of his kingdom: the fall of Jerusalem to Nebuchadnezzar, the Babylonian king's dreams, the events in the fiery furnace, the fall of Babylon to the Persians, and the future events seen by Daniel. If the book is not historically accurate, then this assertion about God's governance for his kingdom is false. Daniel would be nothing more than a series of documents manufactured by human minds in an attempt to grant hope and confidence (albeit falsely

---

[49] On the acceptance of the OT canon in general by the Pharisees, Sadducees, and Essenes in the first century AD, see Steinmann, *Oracles of God*, 118–21.

founded) to its readers. If Daniel is not reliable, then neither is its message that God governs human events and administers his kingdom in order to bring about redemption according to his good pleasure.

The reason that Daniel emphasizes God's control over all things is that it serves the four major theological themes of the book: the messianic kingdom of God, God as the protector of his people, God's superiority over false gods, and encouragement for God's people to maintain their faith in him with integrity (see "Major Themes" below). If the critics were correct, then Daniel would not speak of the Messiah and the coming of the kingdom of God in Jesus. Then the NT appropriation of Daniel in this respect would be later Christian ideology based on an understanding of the book not intended by the original author(s) or the final editor. Therefore, those Christian messianic understandings that are based on Daniel would be built on a false foundation.

If God were not in control of history as Daniel portrays him, he therefore would not necessarily (or not absolutely) act as the protector of his people (3:17–18). They would have no certainty that he is able to provide them with eternal security in his everlasting kingdom (e.g., 3:33 [ET 4:3]; 4:31 [ET 4:34]; 7:14).

If God were not in complete control of history, Daniel's portrayal of him as powerful, in contrast the impotence of the false gods of Babylon, would be mistaken. He would be no more reliable than the pagan gods, if the critics were correct. He could not or would not necessarily thwart the plans of kings, direct the history of nations, or intervene to rescue his people in history. How could they be certain that he will do similar things at the end of history in the resurrection, or even that there will be an end to human history and a resurrection (12:1–3)? If the critics were correct, then worshiping a false god would perhaps be an offense to God, but not one that would lead to any more grave consequences than having a false, misplaced hope in the true God, since he would be unable or unwilling to intervene in human history.

Finally, if God were not in complete control over history, then Daniel's example of maintaining one's faith in the face of persecution and cultural pressure would perhaps be quaint and would be nothing more than the result of the strength of the human will against great odds. Maintaining one's religious integrity through resisting temptations to compromise one's piety and faith would be simply a triumph of the human spirit, if the critics were correct. However, Daniel portrays it as something else: perseverance in faith is the gracious work of God in the lives of his people. The critical view relegates God to the sidelines and exalts human capacities and effort, despite the fact that Daniel places human achievement far below God's wonderful work of granting his people faith and the integrity to maintain that faith (2:30).

Overview of Daniel
Organization of the Book: The Clearly Defined Sections

Unlike many books of Scripture, Daniel is organized into ten distinct sections. With the exception of the transition from 6:1 (ET 5:31) to 6:2 (ET 6:1), these sections are clearly delineated from one another by obvious beginnings and endings.

Daniel 1–6: Six Narratives

Daniel contains six narratives that relate incidents from the lives of Daniel and his three Judean companions in the Babylonian captivity. These narratives are arranged in chronological order.[50] Each is its own chapter in the English versions of Daniel, demonstrating that later readers understood these major breaks between the narratives.[51] The first two narratives start with chronological notices (1:1; 2:1), clearly marking their beginnings. The third narrative does not start with a chronological notice, but with a new action by Nebuchadnezzar: the erecting of a statue (3:1). To further delineate this as the beginning of a new narrative, 3:1 does not begin with a conjunctive *waw* (neither did 1:1 and 2:1). The fourth narrative begins with a letter by Nebuchadnezzar to all of his subjects (3:31 [ET 4:1]). Like the third narrative (3:1), it starts with the king's name without a conjunctive *waw*. The fifth narrative starts with the name "Belshazzar" (5:1) in the same fashion as did the third and fourth narratives with "Nebuchadnezzar" (3:1 and 3:31 [ET 4:1]). Thus each of the first five narratives is clearly set off from the preceding one.

However, the sixth narrative flows more smoothly from the fifth. The fifth narrative ends with the notice that "Darius the Mede received the kingdom, being about sixty-two years old" (6:1 [ET 5:31]). Immediately afterward, the sixth narrative opens with "it seemed good to Darius ... " creating a smooth transition (6:2 [ET 6:1]). However, here too the Aramaic text marks a new beginning as it opens with a verb without a conjunctive *waw* (שְׁפַר, 6:2 [ET 6:1]), thereby syntactically disconnecting this narrative from the previous one.

Thus all six narratives in Daniel are clearly delineated accounts of events during the exile in Babylon. They are designed so that they may be read as self-contained units. Their connection to one another is not through a continuing narrative, but is signaled by other means, both thematic and structural.[52]

---

[50] See figure 1, "Timeline of Daniel and Related Events."

[51] The English chapter divisions are the same as the Hebrew except that MT 3:31–33 is part of chapter 4 (4:1–3) in English and MT Dan 6:1 is included in chapter 5 (5:31) in English. See "Introduction to Daniel 4" and "Introduction to Daniel 6" on the history of chapter division and verse numbering in those chapters.

[52] For thematic connections, see "Major Themes." For structural connections, see "Interlocked Chiasms and the Dual Language of the Book" in "Overview of Daniel."

Daniel 7–12: Four Visions

The four visions in Daniel, like the six narratives, are clearly delineated and separated from one another. This was generally recognized by readers, since each of the first three visions (chapters 7, 8, and 9) constitute their own chapter in Daniel, while the fourth and longest vision (chapters 10–12) is divided into three chapters.[53] Each of the four visions opens with a chronological notice (7:1; 8:1; 9:1; 10:1) that signals its beginning and places the vision in chronological order. However, it should be noted that the visions overlap the narratives in time sequence.[54] Therefore, like the narratives, the visions are designed so that they can be read as self-contained units, and their connection to one another is not through a continuing narrative, but is signaled by other means, both thematic and structural. These thematic connections will be discussed later in this introduction.[55] We now turn to the structural features that bind these ten separate sections to one another.

Interlocked Chiasms and the Dual Language of the Book

The book of Daniel is unique in form among the books of the OT. It is extant as a work in two languages: 1:1–2:4a and 8:1–12:13 are in Hebrew, and 2:4b–7:28 is in Aramaic. It contains two parts: (1) stories of Daniel and his companions in Babylon (1:1–6:29 [ET 1:1–6:28]) and (2) visions seen by Daniel (7:1–12:13). In the first part of the book, Daniel is referred to in the third person, while in the second part, he narrates the visions in the first person. The stories are arranged in chronological order, taking place during the reigns of Nebuchadnezzar (1:1; 2:1; 3:1; 3:31 [ET 4:1]), Belshazzar (5:1), and Darius (6:2 [ET 6:1]). The visions too are in chronological order, but their order begins before the events of Daniel 5. Thus the book divides into two parts—the stories and the visions—but each part contains both Hebrew and Aramaic.

While scholars have often debated the reason for Daniel as a bilingual text,[56] the key to understanding the author's reason for the dual languages is recognizing the interlocked chiastic structure of the book. Chiasm is the concentric arrangement of parts, such as ABC : C'B'A', or some longer or shorter variation. Chiasm was often employed as a literary technique in both the Old and New Testaments. A classic instance is Gen 9:6:

שֹׁפֵךְ֙ דַּ֣ם הָֽאָדָ֔ם בָּֽאָדָ֖ם דָּמ֣וֹ יִשָּׁפֵ֑ךְ
  A   B   C   C'   B'   A'

Whoever *sheds* the *blood* of *man*, by *man* his *blood* will be *shed*.

---

[53] In Daniel 7–12 the chapter divisions are the same in the MT as in later versions, including the LXX, Vulgate, Peshitta, and English translations.

[54] See figure 1, "Timeline of Daniel and Related Events."

[55] See "Major Themes."

[56] Critical scholars (e.g., Collins, *Daniel*, 24) have proposed redactional schemes or even that some chapters may have been written in Aramaic originally and later were translated into Hebrew.

In Daniel, large divisions of material are arranged chiastically.

The chiastic arrangement of the Aramaic portion of Daniel was first demonstrated by Lenglet and has since been followed by a number of scholars, including Collins, Baldwin, and Lacocque.[57] However, scholars have been slower to recognize the chiastic structure of the second part of the book and the unique way in which the two chiasms are joined.[58] See figure 2, "The Interlocked Chiastic Structure of Daniel."

Figure 2

The Interlocked Chiastic Structure of Daniel

Introduction 1: Prologue (1:1–21)		NARRATIVE	*Hebrew*
A	Nebuchadnezzar dreams of four kingdoms and the kingdom of God (2:1–49)	NARRATIVE	*Aramaic*
B	Nebuchadnezzar sees God's servants rescued (3:1–30)	NARRATIVE	*Aramaic*
C	Nebuchadnezzar is judged (3:31–4:34 [ET 4:1–37])	NARRATIVE	*Aramaic*
C'	Belshazzar is judged (5:1–6:1 [ET 5:1–31])	NARRATIVE	*Aramaic*
B'	Darius sees Daniel rescued (6:2–29 [ET 6:1–28])	NARRATIVE	*Aramaic*
A'	Introduction 2: Daniel has a vision of four kingdoms and the kingdom of God (7:1–28)	VISION	*Aramaic*
D	Details on the post-Babylonian kingdoms (8:1–27)	VISION	*Hebrew*
E	Jerusalem restored (9:1–27)	VISION	*Hebrew*
D'	More details on the post-Babylonian kingdoms (10:1–12:13)	VISION	*Hebrew*

---

[57] Lenglet, "La structure littéraire de Daniel 2–7"; Collins, *Apocalyptic Vision*, 11; *Daniel*, 33–34; Baldwin, *Daniel*, 59–60; Lacocque, *Daniel in His Time*, 11. Lacocque also proposes a chiastic structure for chapters 8–12, though different in form from the one proposed here.

[58] The first work to recognize the interlocked construction of the two chiasms in Daniel was Steinmann, "The Shape of Things to Come," 38–42. Pierce, "Spiritual Failure, Postponement, and Daniel 9," 221, and van Deventer, "The End of the End, or, What Is the Deuteronomist (Still) Doing in Daniel?" 73, recognize the two chiasms, but do not recognize that they are interlocked.

Both chiasms are bilingual. The first (1:1–7:28) begins with a Hebrew introduction (1:1–21) followed by the chiasm proper in Aramaic (2:1–7:28). The second chiasm (7:1–12:13) has an Aramaic introduction (7:1–28) followed by the chiasm proper in Hebrew (8:1–12:13). The two chiasms, moreover, are interlocked, since the first vision (7:1–28) serves both as the end of the first chiasm by virtue of its four-kingdom parallel to Nebuchadnezzar's dream and its Aramaic language, and also as the introduction to the visions by virtue of its visionary style and its chronological placement in the first year of Belshazzar.

Both introductions contain themes developed later in the book. The first introduction (1:1–21) presents three themes: first, the captured vessels of the Jerusalem temple (1:2), which play a pivotal role in chapter 5; second, the wisdom of Daniel (1:4), which plays a role in chapters 2, 4, and 5; and third, Daniel's companions Hananiah (Shadrach), Mishael (Meshach), and Azariah (Abednego), who are the heroes of chapter 3. The second introduction (7:1–28) also involves three features: first, it presents the vision style, which dominates the second half of the book; second, it introduces animal imagery, which is used also in chapter 8; and third, it is the first section of the book to present an angelic interpreter who explains the revelations to Daniel, as is done in all three of the subsequent visions.

This produces two interlocked chiasms: a Hebrew introduction followed by an Aramaic chiasm interlocked with an Aramaic introduction and a Hebrew chiasm. Instead of indicating some long process of accumulation and redaction of narrative tales and visions, the Hebrew and Aramaic languages of the sections of Daniel were carefully chosen to serve as a way to unite two different genres (narrative and vision) in one book. Therefore, the dual languages and two genres of the book are not a problem stemming from the book's redactional history, but a deliberate result of its careful composition. Moreover, the interlocking of the two parts of Daniel (narrative and vision) is achieved both through the dual languages and also by the overlapping chronology of the two parts, since the sequence of narratives and the sequence of visions are each arranged in chronological order. However, in time, the sequence of the visions overlaps the sequence of the narratives, since chronologically the first vision takes place before the fifth narrative. See figure 1, "Timeline of Daniel and Related Events."

The last part of the first chiasm (7:1–28) also serves as the first part of the second chiasm. This section of Daniel shares the Aramaic language of the first chiasm, but is a vision instead of a narrative, thereby matching the genre of the second chiasm. Thus it rounds out the first chiasm by repeating the four kingdom theme of 2:1–49 while simultaneously serving as an introduction to the second chiasm by giving readers their first view of Daniel the seer and his visions.

Moreover, since chapter 7 serves as the hinge connecting the two parts of the book,[59] the author has highlighted it as the pivotal chapter of the entire book.

---

[59] For further details on how Daniel 7 serves to unite the two parts of Daniel, see "The Importance of Daniel 7 in the Book of Daniel" in "Introduction to Daniel 7."

It is this chapter that introduces the Son of Man (7:13–14), an important messianic concept that is taken up by Jesus himself in the Gospels. It is this chapter that first discusses the role of the saints in God's eternal kingdom. Therefore, Daniel 7 is the key to understanding the major themes that run throughout the book: God's control over history, the eschatological kingdom of God, the messianic promise, and the protection God affords his people even during the darkest hours of persecution. Thus Daniel, like Scripture as a whole, revolves around Christ, his kingdom, and his work for the benefit of his people.

Daniel 1–7: An Aramaic Chiasm with a Hebrew Introduction

While the thematic parallels in the individual elements of the first chiasm can easily be observed by readers, the author has also left linguistic clues that point to the chiastic parallels. The parallels in the first chiasm are easily seen merely by their content, as the outline above shows.[60] Moreover, there are a few similarities in language that also highlight the parallels. The similarity in the descriptions of God's eternal kingdom in both A and A' is striking:

יְקִים֩ אֱלָ֨הּ שְׁמַיָּ֜א מַלְכוּ֙ דִּ֣י לְעָלְמִין֙ לָ֣א תִתְחַבַּ֔ל

The God of heaven will establish a kingdom that will never be destroyed. (Or, more literally: "the God of heaven will establish a kingdom that forever/eternally will not be destroyed," 2:44)

וּמַלְכוּתֵ֖הּ דִּי־לָ֥א תִתְחַבַּֽל׃

And his kingdom is one that will not be destroyed. (7:14)

מַלְכוּתֵהּ֙ מַלְכ֣וּת עָלַ֔ם

His kingdom is an eternal kingdom. (7:27)

The malicious accusation of the three young men in B and of Daniel in B' is described by the same idiom, which occurs only in these two chapters:

קְרִ֣בוּ גֻּבְרִ֣ין כַּשְׂדָּאִ֑ין וַאֲכַ֥לוּ קַרְצֵיה֖וֹן דִּ֥י יְהוּדָיֵֽא׃

Chaldean men approached and ate pieces of [maliciously accused] the Judeans. (3:8)

גֻּבְרַיָּ֣א אִלֵּ֗ךְ דִּֽי־אֲכַ֤לוּ קַרְצ֙וֹהִי֙ דִּ֣י דָנִיֵּ֔אל ...

These men who ate pieces of [maliciously accused] Daniel ... (6:25 [ET 6:24])

The clearest parallel is the direct reference in C' to the events of C using the same terminology. In 5:18–21 Daniel reminds Belshazzar of Nebuchadnezzar's arrogance against God, which should have been a lesson to Belshazzar. The description in 5:18–21 of the events of chapter 4 imitates the expressions used in chapter 4. See further the textual notes on 5:18–21.

These examples show that Daniel carefully used linguistic markers to reinforce the structural and thematic parallels that comprise his first chiasm. The chiasm, therefore, is not simply happenstance, nor something perceived

---

[60] See figure 2, "The Interlocked Chiastic Structure of Daniel."

by scholars without any intent on the part of the author. Instead, Daniel left unambiguous clues as to his method of choosing and organizing the Aramaic chiasm.

Daniel 7–12: A Hebrew Chiasm with an Aramaic Introduction

In a similar way, Daniel used clues to highlight the chiastic parallels in the Hebrew chiasm. The parallels in the second chiasm are, again, easily seen in their content. Both D and D' relate the history of the kingdoms that followed the Babylonian Empire, in contrast with A and A', which included the Babylonian Empire. The vision in E stands alone (since there are an odd number of Hebrew visions) in relating the history of Jerusalem without reference to the dominant world empires. The unique position of E is also highlighted by the unique prayer that begins this vision. This is the only prayer of confession in the entire book of Daniel and the only prayer in the visions.[61]

There are similarities in language that serve to draw the reader's attention to the parallel nature of D and D'. In both visions, Daniel relates the beginning of his visionary experience with "I lifted up my eyes and I saw: and behold, …" (… וְהִנֵּה וְאֶרְאֶה עֵינַי וָאֶשָּׂא, 8:3; … וְהִנֵּה וָאֵרֶא עֵינַי־אֶת וָאֶשָּׂא, 10:5). Both refer to "the appointed time of the end" (קֵץ לְמוֹעֵד כִּי, 8:19; קֵץ לְמוֹעֵד כִּי־עוֹד, 11:27; לְמוֹעֵד כִּי־עוֹד קֵץ עַד־עֵת, 11:35). Both use similar clauses with identical syntax to describe the actions of the wicked king who will arise. Note the exact syntactic parallel in the Hebrew: conjunction plus preposition, noun (in construct), noun (genitive), verb (imperfect third person masculine singular):

וְעַל־שַׂר־שָׂרִים יַעֲמֹד

And he will arise against the Prince of princes. (8:25)

וְעַל אֵל אֵלִים יְדַבֵּר

And against the God of gods he will speak. (11:36)

In addition, it should be noted that at the beginning of both the visions in D and D', Daniel is standing at the bank of a body of water: in 8:2 he is on the bank of the Ulai Canal and in 10:4 he is on the bank of the Tigris River. In the other visions, Daniel's geographic location is not given.

Therefore, Daniel is clearly an intricately arranged book, whose inspired author carefully chose the languages and genres he used to produce his work. Although each of its major units can be read as an independent account of an event or vision, these independent accounts are bound together into a larger whole that has its own literary integrity (despite the first impression to the contrary given by the book's two distinct genres and two languages). This intricate structure, in turn, serves to point the reader to the central importance of Daniel 7 and its messianic portrait of the Son of Man.

---

[61] Prayers in the narratives are prayers of praise: 2:20–23 and 4:31–32 (ET 4:34–35).

Major Themes
The Messiah in Daniel: An Overview

Since the structure of Daniel is intended to highlight the central, messianic figure called the "Son of Man" (Dan 7:13), it should not be surprising that the book contains many other messianic passages. Most of these messianic passages are part of a section of the book that contains eschatologically oriented revelation: Daniel 2, 7, 9, and 10–12. This is consistent with the OT perspective that the end times will begin with the Messiah's arrival (first advent). In fact, the Scriptures as a whole depict a divine division of human history into two great periods by the use of phrases such as "in the *latter/last days*," which implies an earlier period, "in the *former/first days*" (e.g., Rom 15:4). The latter or last days commence with the coming of the Messiah and his kingdom (Num 24:14; Is 2:2 ‖ Micah 4:1; also see Jer 48:47; 49:39; Ezek 38:16; Hos 3:5). The reference to the messianic era as the latter days is also found in Daniel (2:28; 10:14).[62] The NT clarifies this. Both Peter and the writer to the Hebrews understood that the last days began with the first advent of Christ and confirm that they and their hearers or readers were already in the last days (Acts 2:17; Heb 1:2). The apostles' use of the phrase "in the last days" to describe conditions that were already present as they wrote is further confirmation of this (2 Tim 3:1; James 5:3; 2 Pet 3:3; see also ἐσχάτη ὥρα, "last hour," in 1 Jn 2:18, and ἐπ' ἐσχάτου τοῦ χρόνου, "in the last time," in Jude 18). Therefore, from Daniel's viewpoint, even the first advent of Christ is eschatological.

This eschatological view first surfaces in Nebuchadnezzar's dream of a large statue (Daniel 2). In this dream the statue, representing four kingdoms, is shattered and crushed by a rock from heaven. This stone was hewn "not by [human] hands," a reference to Christ's divine origins (2:34, 45; cf. Micah 5:1 [ET 5:2]; Jn 1:1). The rock not only crushes the kingdoms, but itself grows into a greater kingdom. The picture of the Messiah as bringing an end to earthly kingdoms and establishing God's kingdom is always part of Daniel's portrayal of the coming of the Messiah. Therefore, the NT connection between the coming of Christ and the nearness of God's kingdom[b] is a continuation of this theme from the OT, including especially Daniel.

(b) Mt 3:2; 4:17; 10:7; 12:28; Mk 1:15; 9:1; Lk 9:27; 10:9, 11; 11:20; 17:21; 21:31

The Messiah appears as "a son of gods" in 3:25 and possibly as the "angel" in 6:23 (ET 6:22). However, it is left to the vision of the Son of Man who appears before the Ancient of Days to make this connection explicit (see the commentary on 7:13–14). This messianic passage not only depicts the Son of Man as divine, thereby showing forth the two natures, divine and human, in Christ, but it also states that he receives "dominion, honor, and a kingdom" (7:14).

---

[62] For the prophetic phrases "the latter years" (Ezek 38:8) and "the latter days" (Ezek 38:16), one may see Hummel, *Ezekiel 21–48*, 1103, 1109, 1113, 1119–20, who says in part: "In Dan 2:28 and 10:14, 'in the latter days' is a full-fledged eschatological phrase that looks to the coming of God's eternal kingdom at the first advent of Jesus Christ" (p. 1119).

This picture of the Messiah as king is assumed in Daniel 9, when Gabriel reveals Jerusalem's future to Daniel. Here "Messiah" (9:25–26) is also called "a Most Holy One" (9:24) and "a Leader" (9:25–26) who confirms a covenant. In an explicit reference to Christ's crucifixion and vicarious atonement, "Messiah will be cut off and have nothing" (9:26) in order "to end transgression, to finish sin, and to atone for iniquity" (9:24).

The Son of God is called "the Prince of the army" in 8:11, and 10:4–21 develops his military role as Israel's champion, the one who battles and conquers the demonic forces arrayed against God's people.

Finally, there is an oblique reference to the coming of the Messiah in Daniel's final vision. In 11:30 it is prophesied that ships will come from Kittim. The combination of "ships" and "Kittim" occurs elsewhere in Scripture only in Num 24:24, part of Balaam's messianic prophecy of a star that will arise from Jacob (Num 24:17). The implication is that during the time to which the prophecy in Dan 11:30 refers (168 BC, during the reign of Antiochus Epiphanes), the Messiah's coming was near. In comparison with Balaam's day (1407 BC), that time was indeed near (less than two centuries before) the advent of the Messiah. Daniel, therefore, adds detail to Balaam's prediction and thereby renews the hope of the people of Judah in his exilic era and beyond.

Daniel in 12:2–3 has perhaps the clearest depiction of resurrection in the OT. The promise that "many of those sleeping in the dusty earth will awake, some to everlasting life" is part of the revelation given Daniel by the radiant Son of God who fights the battle on behalf of his people (10:4–21). His promise that believers shall be raised to shine like the stars (12:3) suggests that they shall be conformed to the likeness of his glorified body (Phil 3:21). This connection would be made explicit by the revelation of God through Christ himself, who would not only speak of his own resurrection (e.g., Mt 20:19; 26:32), but become "the firstfruits of those who sleep" (1 Cor 15:20; see also 1 Cor 15:40–57).

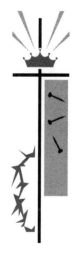

In summary, the depiction of the Messiah in Daniel is that of a King who is both divine and human and who brings his people into the kingdom of God. His death and atonement are described in Daniel 9 as the basis of the new "covenant" (9:27) that God will make with his people. Thus Jesus is the focus of Daniel. He is both King and suffering Savior, and his work is for the benefit of God's people, "to bring everlasting righteousness" for them (9:25) so that they may be raised "to everlasting life" (12:2).

The three remaining major themes in Daniel find their greatest fulfillment in the Messiah but are often developed in sections of Daniel where the Messiah is not in direct view. Thus God is depicted as the great protector of his people, a role ultimately fulfilled in the Messiah. God's superiority to all other gods is emphasized several times in Daniel. This is demonstrated most clearly in Christ and his cross. The emphasis on maintaining the integrity of one's faith is found throughout Daniel. This faith is sustained first and foremost through the messianic promise that Daniel's prophecy renews and reinvigorates.

God as the Protector of His People

Throughout Daniel, God is the protector of his people. This has an ironic touch to it, since the beginning of Daniel depicts God as handing his people over to Nebuchadnezzar (1:1–2). However, this is only an apparent abandonment of the people of Judah. By the end of Daniel 1, it is clear to the reader that God is still with his people. He grants them favor in the sight of their Babylonian overlords (1:9) and gives them intelligence and wisdom (1:17) so that they can survive and even prosper in a foreign land. Thus Daniel 1 introduces the two primary means through which God protects his people throughout Daniel: he controls events, present and future, among humans, and he grants his people useful gifts and abilities.

God's control over human events is found in every major section in Daniel. In Daniel 2 he controls the events surrounding Nebuchadnezzar's dream so that Daniel alone is able to interpret the dream. The dream itself demonstrates how God governs the future as it prophesies four world kingdoms and then God's kingdom.[63] God not only remains in control in Daniel 3, but by rescuing the three young men from the fiery furnace, he demonstrates to Nebuchadnezzar that he, not the Babylonian king, has control over life and death. Daniel 4 reemphasizes God's lordship to Nebuchadnezzar as the king is humbled because of his arrogance. God revealed to the king in a dream that he would be humbled, and then God brought it about, leading even Nebuchadnezzar to acknowledge God's power and greatness. The continued arrogance of Babylonian rulers in Daniel 5 affords another occasion to demonstrate God's control over all events as he first pronounces judgment on Belshazzar through the mysterious handwriting on the wall and then sees that this judgment is carried out through the conquest of Babylon by the Persians. The Persians too are not exempt from being under the Almighty's dominion, and his control over life and death is made plain by the rescue of Daniel from the lions' den (Daniel 6).

Of course, Daniel's visions (Daniel 7–12), all of which prophesy about future events, clearly demonstrate that God will never lose control over human history, but that he will always govern world kingdoms for the sake of his own kingdom and ultimate purposes. These prophecies are so detailed in their description of future events that critical scholars have often regarded them as *ex eventu* prophecies written "after the events" they depict. This supposedly explains why they are so accurate, even in many details. However, this explanation for the accuracy of Daniel's prophecies not only denies the very power of God to inspire his prophets, it also misses the point of this major theme of the book: God is in control over all things, and through his foreknowledge as well as his active guidance of events, he brings about judgment and salvation.

---

[63] For a further discussion of God's foreknowledge in relation to his eternal election of believers to salvation, see the commentary on 2:27–30, which cites FC Ep and SD XI, "Eternal Foreknowledge and Divine Election."

These accurate prophecies demonstrating God's control are not intended merely to demonstrate God's omnipotence. They are primarily designed to comfort God's people. He is in control of all human history *for their benefit*. While this benefit may be seen in the short term (as when Daniel is rescued from the lions' den or the young men from the fiery furnace), often it is not immediately evident (as in the capture of Jerusalem by Nebuchadnezzar or the persecution of God's people under Antiochus IV Epiphanes). Yet Daniel emphasizes that God always has his people's welfare in mind, so that by his mighty hand, often unseen in the course of human events, "all things work together for good for those who are called according to his purpose" (Rom 8:28).

God also protects his people by granting them gifts and abilities. Daniel can interpret dreams (Daniel 2 and 4) and mysteries (Daniel 5). Shadrach, Meshach, and Abednego are given the gift of steadfast loyalty to God in the face of seemingly certain death (Daniel 3), while Daniel is moved to worship God even when forbidden by royal decree (Daniel 6). Moreover, Daniel is given visions. Once again, all of these gifts given to Daniel and the young Judeans are for the benefit of God's people—both themselves and others.

At times the benefit may be immediate and personal (rescue from death in Daniel 2, 3, and 6). However, the wider benefit of these gifts may be less obvious and immediate. Certainly, Daniel's ability to receive visions could be at first a frightening experience (7:28; 8:27). The prophecy of the future persecution of God's people (Daniel 8 and 11) could seem to be no blessing. However, both of these prophecies yield benefits for God's people as they are encouraged by knowing that their God knew their circumstances before they ever faced them and that through these trials he will "refine them, purify [them], and make [them] white" (11:35). Of course, God's governance of world history is best demonstrated in his Son, whom Daniel prophesies as the "Son of Man" (7:13) and "Messiah" (9:25–26), God's greatest gift to his people (Jn 4:10; Rom 6:23; Eph 2:8). Daniel's detailed depiction of the coming of the Messiah into human history confirms that God accomplishes his redemptive work for his people in "the fullness of time" (Gal 4:4; Eph 1:10).

The Uselessness of False Gods and the Power of the True God

Most every reader of Daniel will see Daniel 3, the account of Shadrach, Meshach, and Abednego, as a confrontation between worship of idols and trust in the true God. This narrative, more than any other, confirms that gods like those set up by Nebuchadnezzar are powerless, whereas Israel's God is omnipotent and can save his people from death. Yet this theme is not confined to this chapter. Already in Daniel 1 the confrontation between God and the pagan gods serves as a subtext for the narrative. Nebuchadnezzar believes that his gods, especially Marduk, have shown their superiority to Israel's God by enabling him to conquer Jerusalem. Therefore, the king put the vessels from Jerusalem's temple in the temple of his god (1:2). However, it is the servants of Israel's God that are shown to be wiser and better than the wise men who claim allegiance to the

pagan gods (1:20). This continues in Daniel 2, where Daniel, the servant of the "God of gods, Lord of kings, and Revealer of mysteries" (2:47), can do what no servant of the gods can do: tell Nebuchadnezzar his dream and its interpretation. The God of Israel is superior since he does indeed dwell with humans, unlike the pagan gods (2:11).

This same superiority of the true God is demonstrated in Daniel 4 and 5 as Daniel once again is the only wise man in the Babylonian court who can interpret God's revelations. Even in Daniel 6, God is superior to all gods since he can rescue from the lions, something the pagan courtiers never suspected that a god could or would do. This is reinforced by Daniel's visions, which reveal the power of the true God to accurately predict even the details of future history several centuries in advance, something no diviner dedicated to the gods of the nations could ever do.

Yet the point of emphasizing God's superiority to the gods of the nations is not simply to motivate readers to worship and trust in the true God because of his omnipotence and omniscience. Instead, it is designed to reveal the graciousness of God. The Lord who created the universe is also the Savior who has pity on humans, who understands their sins and weaknesses. He is patient with them, as he was with Nebuchadnezzar, granting him the time and opportunity to repent (4:24 [ET 4:27]; although Nebuchadnezzar did not avail himself of this opportunity). He is the God who, unlike the pagan gods, is not capricious or fickle. Instead, he keeps his promises (as in the fulfilling of Daniel's prophecies), shows mercy through his Messiah, and never abandons his people. He is reliable, and his people rely on him. Daniel portrays the God of Israel as a true God. He is never a false god, either in terms of nonexistence (like the idols) or in any failure to keep his promises, which are sacred and inviolable (cf. 1 Cor 1:9; 1 Thess 5:24; 2 Tim 2:11–13; Heb 10:23; Rev 22:6).

Maintaining the Integrity of One's Faith

The fourth major theme in Daniel is the ability of God's people to maintain their faith with integrity. Throughout Daniel, this ability is implied to be from God himself. Thus Daniel and his friends are able to resist defiling themselves with the king's food because of God's strength that is in them, and that strength becomes evident even in their appearance (1:8–15). Shadrach, Meshach, and Abednego are able to resist Nebuchadnezzar's order to worship the idol he had erected because God is with them, as becomes evident in the fiery furnace (3:25). Daniel worships God daily without ceasing even under the threat of death (6:7–11 [ET 6:6–10]), a testimony to the work of God's Spirit in his life.

(c) Dan 11:33, 35; 12:3, 10; cf. 1:4, 17; 5:11–12, 14; 9:22

The visions also are intended to offer the strength of God to his people who read and believe his promises. He will "refine them, purify [them], and make [them] white" (11:35) so that they can maintain their faith with integrity, even in the face of persecution. He will make them insightful enough to avoid compromising their faith,[c] and he will also awaken them from death, raise them bodily, and make them shine like the brightness of the sky forever (12:2–3).

This integrity of faith in the face of persecution is not simply the product of belief in a omnipotent God. Instead, it is the product of faith in a merciful God who will keep his promise to send his Messiah and establish his kingdom. Daniel and his friends can defy errant and arrogant human kings because they are servants of the eternal King, the Son of Man (7:13–14), who establishes his eternal covenant (9:27) with his people.

Law and Gospel in Daniel

Throughout the Scriptures God speaks both Law and Gospel. In his Law, exemplified in the Decalogue, he commands that his will be done, and his Law curbs sinful behavior, convicts people of their guilt as sinners, and guides the believer's new life of faith.[64] In his Gospel, he forgives sin and declares both OT and NT believers righteous on account of Christ.[65] Through his Gospel, he also grants faith and strength by his Spirit to do good works and live according to his will.[66]

Daniel's particular contribution to the proclamation of God's Word in both Law and Gospel revolves around the experience of the Babylonian captivity and the abiding confidence of faithful Judeans in God's promise to establish his eternal kingdom. Both of these factors shape God's revelation of his gracious will in the Messiah.

God's Law in Daniel

Daniel's message is obviously related to the First Commandment (Ex 20:3–6; Deut 5:7–10) because of his life of faith in the true God in contrast to his pagan environment and because he emphasizes the power of the one true and triune God.[67] The First Commandment comes to the fore in two narratives in Daniel. The first of these narratives is Daniel 3, the refusal of Shadrach, Meshach, and Abednego to worship the idol set up by Nebuchadnezzar. These Judeans' faithful adherence to the commandment is vindicated when God rescues them from the fiery furnace, as they had affirmed he could do. Yet they had also declared that even if God might not rescue them from the furnace, they still would not worship any other god (3:17–18).

---

[64] These are traditionally called the three uses of the Law. See SA III II 1–5, and FC Ep and SD VI; FC Ep VI 1 is quoted below.

[65] See AC and Ap IV. That OT believers too were justified through faith alone is St. Paul's theme in Romans 4, where he cites Gen 15:6 and the example of Abraham.

[66] See AC VI and XX.

[67] While the OT book of Daniel naturally does not contain a full revelation of the three persons of the one true and triune God, it does contain adumbrations of the Trinitarian theology revealed in the NT. For example, the "Son of Man" in 7:13–14 is portrayed as having both a human and a divine nature, as the NT affirms about God the Son. While Nebuchadnezzar speaks from his polytheistic perspective, his affirmation that in Daniel is "the spirit of the holy gods" (4:5–6, 15 [ET 4:8–9, 18]) seems to reflect that Daniel was filled with God the Holy Spirit (cf. 1 Pet 1:11; 2 Pet 1:21).

The other narrative that highlights the First Commandment is Daniel 5, the account of the handwriting on the wall. When Belshazzar and the revelers at his feast praise the pagan gods while drinking from the vessels from the Jerusalem temple, the judgment of God falls upon them. Clearly, God will tolerate no rivals! The use of his vessels to praise other gods was a direct challenge to the God of Israel, and even the Babylonians become subject to his wrath under the First Commandment because of their arrogance.

The First Commandment is also in the background of the other narratives in Daniel. In Daniel 1, Nebuchadnezzar captures the vessels from the temple in Jerusalem and places them in the temple of Marduk, which sets up a confrontation between God and the gods of Babylon. The Judean exiles remain faithful to God, and their refusal to eat the king's provisions—probably related directly to the dietary laws of the OT—is ultimately motivated by their desire to worship the only true God. In Daniel 2 and 4, God's superiority over the gods of Babylon is demonstrated by Daniel. Only the servant of Israel's God can interpret the king's dreams, and the wise men who revere Babylon's gods are powerless to do so. These chapters, while not directly stating that there is only one God,[68] give a reason for keeping the First Commandment: because God alone among all the gods is the living God who can accomplish great works.

The First Commandment is also in the background in Daniel's visions (chapters 7–12). The vision of Daniel 7 is about the establishment of God's kingdom, which belongs to the "Son of Man" (Dan 7:13). This establishment comes at the end of a series of four world kingdoms, all of whom stem from polytheistic peoples. One subtextual theme in this chapter is that the eternal God and his eternal kingdom will outlast the kingdoms of humans who worship the gods of the nations, which are mere human inventions.

The two visions of Daniel 8 and 10–12 both depict the religious persecution of God's people. These visions reveal that God's people will remain faithful to him and will refuse to worship other gods. They demonstrate the First Commandment in action in the lives of believers.

Daniel's use of themes related to the other commandments flows from his emphasis on the First Commandment. For instance, the Second Commandment (Ex 20:7; Deut 5:11) and its corollary, the proper use of God's name,[69] lie behind the titles for God that are found in Daniel. Daniel frequently refers to God in terms that are understandable, but not offensive to Babylonian kings. He uses phrases such as "the God of heaven" (2:18–19, 37, 44) or "the Most High (God)" (3:26; 3:32 [ET 4:2]; 4:14, 21–22, 29, 31 [ET 4:17, 24–25, 32, 34]; 5:18, 21). These terms enable Daniel to communicate truths about the one true God with-

---

[68] God is said to be greater than the other gods (e.g., 2:47), but there is no direct monotheistic statement in these accounts.

[69] The Second Commandment prohibits the false use of God's name. In its larger context, this commandment also supports the biblical examples and commands to use and call upon God's name rightly in faith (e.g., Gen 12:8; Deut 6:13; 10:20; Is 12:4; Joel 3:5 [ET 2:32]).

out associating his name with polytheistic beliefs. Yet he is able to speak without confusing language to Nebuchadnezzar, who assumes that there are many gods. The use of "the Most High (God)" also affects Daniel's use of titles for God in the visionary accounts when there is no need to communicate to polytheistic kings. For instance, God is called "the Most High" in 7:18, 22, 25, 27.

Faithful worship of God on any day fulfills the intent of the Third Commandment, which reserves the Sabbath for worship (Ex 20:8–11; Deut 5:12–15).[70] Daniel's depiction of faithfulness to the Third Commandment also flows from the First Commandment and is evident in both the narratives and the visions. In Daniel 6, the account of the lions' den, Daniel continues to pray to God even when Darius' decree forbids it. Daniel was not required by Darius' decree in Daniel 6 to worship any particular god. Instead, he was forbidden from praying to his God. Therefore, the emphasis in this account is on the Third Commandment and that a believer should not avoid persecution by neglecting to worship God, but should affirm belief in him. The distinction between chapters 3 and 6 is that Daniel 3 pertains most directly to the negatively worded First Commandment, "You shall have no other gods" (in other words, "*Do not* worship other gods"), whereas chapter 6 relates most directly to the positively worded Third Commandment, "Remember the Sabbath day by keeping it holy," or in other words, "*Do* worship the true God."

Daniel could have avoided any accusation against himself simply by not worshiping God for a month. However, Daniel felt an obligation to worship God. Moreover, his trust in God as the only source of life, forgiveness, comfort, and aid drew him to prayer three times each day. He could not give this up, even to conform to a decree of the king. Therefore, the account in Daniel 6 supplements the message of Daniel 3 by reminding readers that not only is it important to avoid idolatry in the face of persecution, we also must not compromise our faith by neglecting the worship of God, even when that worship might expose us to persecution. Such neglect is as much a denial of the true God as bowing down to idols. As Jesus declared, "Every person who confesses me before people, I also will confess him before my Father, who is in heaven. But every person who denies me before people, I also will deny him before my Father, who is in heaven" (Mt 10:32–33; cf. Lk 12:8–9). Therefore, in Daniel's view, obedience to the Third Commandment flows from faithfulness to the First Commandment.

Daniel's devotion to the Third Commandment also motivates his prayer in Daniel 9, as he fervently confesses his sin and asks God to restore Jerusalem and its temple. Daniel desires that God once again establish this place of worship so that his people can resume the practice dictated by the OT laws of worship

---

[70] Thus Luther explained the Third Commandment as mandating worship in faith especially on the day set aside for worship, but also on every day: "Indeed, we Christians should make every day a holy day and give ourselves only to holy activities—that is, occupy ourselves daily with God's Word and carry it in our hearts and on our lips" (LC I 89).

and sacrifice that flow from the Third Commandment. God not only heard Daniel's prayer, but his answer in the form of Gabriel's depiction of the future of Jerusalem (9:25–27) focuses this worship toward the Messiah (9:25–26), which prepares for the NT emphasis on Christian worship in every place (Jn 4:20–26; 1 Cor 1:2; 1 Tim 2:8).

The same can be said about the Fourth Commandment in Daniel: it also flows from the First Commandment. The mandate to honor one's parents (Ex 20:12; Deut 5:16) also applies more generally to all human authorities under God (see Rom 13:1–10). Daniel and his Judean companions are willing to submit to the authority of the Babylonians and Persians because of their faith commitment to God and acknowledgement that all legitimate human authority derives from God (Dan 2:21). This is emphasized most clearly Daniel 1 as Daniel and his companions submit to Babylonian authority—except in those ways that would require a denial of their faith in God (cf. Acts 5:29). They receive Babylonian education, tolerate the imposition of Babylonian personal names, and acknowledge the authority of the king and those he has appointed over them.

The Fourth Commandment is also acknowledged elsewhere in Daniel. Daniel states his commitment to it in 6:22 (ET 6:21). Moreover, Nebuchadnezzar's dream in Daniel 2, as well as the visions of chapter 7, chapter 8, and chapters 10–12, all view a succession of human kingdoms raised up to rule the earth, and all assume that the Fourth Commandment remains valid until the eschaton.[71]

At times Daniel also depicts faithful obedience to some of the other commandments (e.g., the Ninth and Tenth Commandments in 5:17), but the emphasis is always on the First Commandment as the command from which all others flow. Luther states the same in the Large Catechism: "Where the heart is right with God and this commandment [the First Commandment] is kept, fulfillment of all the others will follow of its own accord" (LC I 48). This is also the message of Daniel with respect to the commandments.

Since Daniel is primarily depicting the voluntary and joyful commitment of God's people to his Law, most of the examples of the Law in Daniel are in the category of the third use of the Law.[72] However, Daniel also at times depicts the first use of the Law, especially when dealing with Nebuchadnezzar and Belshazzar: God's Law is used to restrain Nebuchadnezzar's sinful desires

---

[71] Thus passages such as Mt 22:15–21; Acts 25:10–12; and Rom 13:1–10 teach that throughout the church age, Christians are to submit to lawful authorities (although we must obey God rather than men if those authorities demand a compromise or denial of faith in Christ [Acts 5:29]). However, in the eschaton or eternal state, God himself will graciously reign over his people directly (Revelation 21–22) without using human authorities as his intermediaries.

[72] The Law's three uses are "(1) to maintain external discipline against unruly and disobedient men, (2) to lead men to a knowledge of their sin, (3) after they are reborn, and although the flesh still inheres in them, to give them on that account a definite rule according to which they should pattern and regulate their entire life" (FC Ep VI 1).

and Belshazzar's arrogance, especially in the judgment on Nebuchadnezzar in Daniel 4 and the fall of Babylon in Daniel 5. For these polytheistic kings (and the ones spoken of in the later visions in Daniel), the first use of the Law curbs their sinful inclinations.

The Law in its second use is seldom explicitly found in Daniel, but is always present implicitly, since *lex semper accusat*, "the Law always accuses."[73] The goal of the second use is to drive a person to repent and recognize his need for salvation through faith. This chief and proper use of the Law[74] is found at two important places in Daniel. Daniel uses the Law to appeal to Nebuchadnezzar to repent so that he might avoid God's judgment (4:24 [ET 4:27]). In this case, the Law does not move Nebuchadnezzar toward true repentance and faith in Israel's God, even after God's judgment falls on the king. His actions following the restoration of his sanity (4:31 [ET 4:34]) demonstrate that Nebuchadnezzar had grown in his knowledge about the God of Israel, but these actions fall short of indicating true faith. They exhibit a type of expanding civil righteousness (a result of the first use of the Law)[75] in recognizing God's knowledge, sovereignty, and power, but they do not demonstrate a reliance on God as a forgiving, gracious God (the need for which is made plain by the second use of the Law). Moreover, Nebuchadnezzar never makes a clear monotheistic confession of

---

[73] Ap IV 38 states that the Law cannot justify us sinners:

> Paul says (Rom. 4:15), "The law brings wrath." He does not say that by the law men merit the forgiveness of sins. For the law always accuses and terrifies consciences. It does not justify, because a conscience terrified by the law flees before God's judgment. It is an error, therefore, for men to trust that by the law and by their works they merit the forgiveness of sins.

[74] The Confessions call the second use of the Law its main or chief use. FC SD V 17 cites Luther: " 'Everything that rebukes sin is and belongs to the law, the proper function of which is to condemn sin and to lead to a knowledge of sin' (Rom. 3:20; 7:7)" (see WA 39/1:342–58).

[75] "Civil righteousness" refers to outward obedience to the Second Table of God's commandments (in the Catholic and Lutheran numbering, the Fourth through Tenth Commandments), which deal with human relationships rather than directly with worship of God. Unbelievers too can achieve a high level of civil righteousness and moral behavior, but this kind of righteousness cannot save or avail before God. AC XVIII 1–3 affirms:

> Our churches teach that man's will has some liberty for the attainment of civil righteousness and for the choice of things subject to reason. However, it does not have the power, without the Holy Spirit, to attain the righteousness of God—that is, spiritual righteousness—because natural man does not perceive the gifts of the Spirit of God (I Cor. 2:14); but this righteousness is wrought in the heart when the Holy Spirit is received through the Word.

Further, Ap XVIII 4 explains:

> The human will has freedom to choose among the works and things which reason by itself can grasp. To some extent it can achieve civil righteousness or the righteousness of works. It can talk about God and express its worship of him in outward works. It can obey rulers and parents. Externally, it can choose to keep the hands from murder, adultery, or theft. Since human nature still has reason and judgment about the things that the senses can grasp, it also retains a choice in these things, as well as the liberty and ability to achieve civil righteousness. This righteousness which the carnal nature—that is, the reason—can achieve on its own without the Holy Spirit, Scripture calls the righteousness of the flesh.

faith. He could well acknowledge God as the King of heaven (4:34 [ET 4:37]) without denying the existence of other gods. Thus there is no evidence that Nebuchadnezzar ever possessed true saving faith in Yahweh.[76]

Daniel, however, does demonstrate the effect of the second use of the Law in his prayer of confession in Daniel 9. Here he acknowledges his sin and throws himself and his people on God's mercy. Thus, while there are not many direct depictions of the second use of the Law, these examples allow a study in contrasts between those who hear God's Law and truly repent and those who remain unrepentant.

God's Gospel in Daniel

Daniel's emphasis on the First Commandment as his focus for God's Law is matched by his presentation of the Gospel.[77] Daniel depicts God's work for his people first and foremost through the establishing of God's eternal kingdom, of which they are and will be members. He not only prophesies this kingdom as established by the Ancient of Days through the Son of Man (7:13–14), he also depicts the humbled Nebuchadnezzar acknowledging this kingdom (3:33 [ET 4:3]; 4:31 [ET 4:34]). This depiction of the kingdom matches Jesus' teaching and the apostolic preaching of the Gospel, which is often characterized as teaching about the kingdom of God (Acts 1:3; 8:12; 19:8; 28:23, 31; Rom 14:17).[78]

This teaching about the kingdom in Daniel, however, is always focused on the King. This is implied in Daniel 2 with the stone that smashes the statue and grows into a great mountain. The implication is that the kingdom (the great mountain) begins with the work of the King—the stone (cf. Mt 21:42–44; Rom 9:32–33). This is clarified in Daniel 7, where the Son of Man is given the kingdom, and further enhanced by the depiction of the Messiah as a Leader who establishes the covenant (9:25–27). This establishment of the covenant comes at a price, however. The "Messiah will be cut off and have nothing" (9:26) "to atone for iniquity" (9:24). Without the atoning death of the Messiah, there would be no kingdom. Thus, while Daniel seldom directly addresses the atoning work of the Messiah, it is central to his view of the kingdom. *The cross and atoning death of the Messiah are the foundation of God's triumphant kingdom.* Moreover, that the Messiah continues his reign over God's kingdom forever presupposes his resurrection and ascension to the Father's right hand in power and glory (compare Dan 7:13–14 to Mt 26:64; Acts 7:56; Rom 8:34; Col 3:1).

The triumph of the king and his kingdom leads to blessings for God's people according to Daniel's final vision. They will be delivered from distress

---

[76] Note that the name "Yahweh" (יהוה) occurs in Daniel only in 9:2–20 and never in the chapters that treat the reign of Nebuchadnezzar.

[77] For other themes in Daniel that present the Gospel, see especially "The Messiah in Daniel: An Overview" and "God as the Protector of His People" in "Major Themes."

[78] For an exposition of this theme in the first Gospel, one may see "The Reign of Heaven/God in Jesus" in Gibbs, *Matthew 1:1–11:1*, 47–51.

since their names are "written in the book" (Dan 12:1; cf. Ex 32:32; Phil 4:3; Rev 13:8; 20:12). They will be resurrected to eternal life (Dan 12:2; cf. Jn 5:25; 11:25; Rev 20:12). They "will shine like the brightness of the sky ... like stars forever and ever" (Dan 12:3; cf. Mt 13:43; 2 Cor 4:6; Phil 2:15). These promises are foreshadowed in the earlier narratives in Daniel. The deliverance of the three men from the fiery furnace and the deliverance of Daniel from the lions' den are foretastes of God's everlasting deliverance of his people. The delivery of the young men from the furnace is especially a foretaste of the resurrection as they move from a place of certain death to a restored life without any permanent harm from death's flames (3:27). Moreover, they are promoted (3:30; cf. 2:48–49), a pale glimpse of the future glory of God's people.

Those who know the true God and his promises are characterized in Daniel as having insight.[d] This is an indication of the Gospel at work in their lives, since insight, wisdom, and knowledge are gifts from God (2:21; cf. 1 Cor 2:7; Eph 1:8, 17; Col 2:3). Those who know God's promise of the kingdom and who trust the messianic King whom he will send are, for Daniel, the truly wise, since God has granted them this knowledge. Their wisdom may not keep them from perishing physically in this life (Dan 11:35), but they will be preserved for God's eternal kingdom and raised on the Last Day.

(d) Dan 1:4, 17; 5:11–12, 14; 9:22; 11:33, 35; 12:3, 10

The Gospel of the kingdom of God, therefore, lies at the heart of Daniel. He encourages God's people, who will face tribulation and persecution, by directing them to the promised Messiah, the King who will deliver them through his death and resurrection so that they can reign with him in his eternal kingdom (compare 7:14 with 7:27).

Connections with Other Old Testament Books

Daniel has several prominent connections to other portions of the OT. The most important are the parallels between Daniel and Joseph in Genesis, parallels with Esther, Daniel as a prophetic book like those of the prophets, and concepts Daniel shares with the Wisdom books.

Daniel and Joseph

One of the most noticeable parallels to Daniel is the story of Joseph in Genesis. Both men are taken forcefully to a foreign country (Gen 37:12–36; Dan 1:1–7); both are condemned to punishment due to their loyalty to God, but God is with them in their punishment (Genesis 39; Daniel 6); both are servants and advisors to pagan kings (Gen 41:46; Daniel 1–6); both interpret dreams for the king (Gen 41:1–38; Daniel 2 and 4); and both are promoted to high office (Gen 41:39–45; Dan 2:48; 5:29; 6:2–3 [ET 6:1–2]).

The similarities extend beyond these common elements in the lives of the two men. The vocabulary of Daniel is similar to that of the Joseph cycle in Genesis. The similarities include the use of the term μfor"j', "magician" (Gen 41:8, 24; Dan 1:20; 2:2), an Egyptian loanword used elsewhere in Scripture only in Egyptian settings (Ex 7:11, 22; 8:3, 14–15 [ET 8:7, 18–19]; 9:11).

Another similarity is that cognate roots are used for both the noun "interpretation" and the verb "interpret": the Hebrew noun פִּתָּרוֹן, "interpretation" (Gen 40:5, 8, 12, 18; 41:11) is from the verb פָּתַר, "interpret" (Gen 40:8, 16, 22; 41:8, 12–13, 15), and the cognate Aramaic noun פְּשַׁר, "interpretation," occurs thirty-two times in Daniel, while the cognate Aramaic verb פְּשַׁר, "interpret," occurs twice (Dan 5:12, 16). This similarity is all the more remarkable because these Hebrew words (פָּתַר and פִּתָּרוֹן) occur in the OT only in Genesis 40–41, and except for Eccl 8:1 (which has the noun פֵּשֶׁר, a loanword from Aramaic), the Aramaic cognates occur in the OT only in Daniel.

Both use the verb פָּעַם with רוּחַ as its subject, one's "spirit is troubled," to describe the distress that comes upon a king because of a dream (Gen 41:8; Dan 2:1, 3). Both use the verb זָעַף, "look gaunt," to describe a downcast or gaunt look of someone's face (Gen 40:6; Dan 1:10). These are the only uses of this verb in this sense; elsewhere it means "to be angry, to rage" (see the textual note on it in 1:10). Finally, it should be noted that eunuchs (singular or plural of סָרִיס) play an important role in the early captivity of both Joseph and Daniel.[79]

Even more significant are the parallels that connect the wisdom and insight of both Joseph and Daniel with God. Both men, endowed with the Holy Spirit, are described by pagans as having a "spirit of (holy) gods" in them (Gen 41:38; Dan 4:5–6, 15 [ET 4:8–9, 18]; 5:11, 14). Both recognize God's use of dreams to reveal the future to kings (Gen 41:25, 28; Dan 2:28). Joseph and Daniel alike freely admit that their ability to interpret dreams does not come from themselves, but from God (Gen 40:8; 41:16; Dan 2:28).

These connections are far too many to be explained as mere happenstance or the result of similar incidents in the lives of these two men.[80] Very clearly Daniel has modeled his historically true composition after Genesis and is consciously drawing his readers' attention to the similarity between his situation and Joseph's. In doing so, Daniel is telling his readers that God has not lost control of the world, nor has he abandoned his people in the Babylonian captivity. Instead, when famine forced the patriarchs move from Israel to Egypt, God was present in Joseph's life and used him "to keep alive many people" (Gen 50:20). In the same way, even though the Judeans have been taken captive in Babylon, God is present with Daniel and with his people, graciously using them in his plan of salvation, which will culminate in the advent of the "Son of Man" (Dan 7:13) and "Messiah" (9:25–26).

Some scholars have seen another connection between Joseph and Daniel, however. They note that the Tale of Ahikar, the story of a court minister who

---

[79] See Gen 37:36; 39:1; 40:2, 7; Dan 1:3, 7–11, 18. This commentary's view is that סָרִיס in these passages does mean "eunuch." See the commentary on Dan 1:3–7.

[80] The assertion of some scholars that Daniel is a midrash on the Joseph stories is misguided and incorrect. A midrash is an interpretive reading of a text. Daniel is not attempting to interpret Genesis. He is presenting an entirely new and factual story. See the discussion in Collins, *Daniel*, 39–40.

is disgraced and rehabilitated, is similar to the stories of Joseph and Daniel (especially Daniel 6). The Tale of Ahikar was apparently widespread, as shown by its existence in Aramaic, Syriac, Arabic, Armenian, Slavonic, and Ethiopic versions. The story was probably originally composed in Aramaic somewhere in Mesopotamia (Ahikar is Assyrian for "brother is precious") and may be as old as the seventh century BC. The story was known in Jewish circles and was transformed and adopted by the author of Tobit for inclusion in his book, which makes Ahikar the nephew of Tobit (Tobit 1:21–22; 2:10; 11:18; 14:10).

While there are some similarities in the overall plotline of the Tale of Ahikar, the most that can be asserted is that Daniel may have been acquainted with stories of fallen and restored courtiers such as Ahikar and may have adhered to some conventions of the genre of such stories. There is little or no evidence that Daniel is dependent on Ahikar.[81] Instead, it is much more important to see the shared elements of Daniel with the Joseph story and understand the theological similarities of these two Hebrew compositions.

Daniel and Esther

The chronologically later parts of Daniel share a Persian setting with the book of Esther. Moreover, both books in their entirety share the general setting of Judean exiles living among a predominantly pagan culture. Therefore, we should not be surprised that the two books have some features in common.

Both prominently feature the intoxicating effects of wine at parties that lead to hasty and ill-advised actions on the part of kings (Esther 1; Daniel 5). Mordecai, like Daniel, is an advisor to the king who sits in the king's gate.[e] Both men are honored by the king with special garments (Esth 6:7–11; Dan 5:29). Both books refer to the unchangeable nature of royal decrees "in the laws of the Persians and the Medes" (Esth 1:19) or "in accord with the law of the Medes and the Persians" (Dan 6:9 [ET 6:8]; see also 6:13, 16 [ET 6:12, 15]). Most importantly, both books refer to professional jealousy and rivalry that leads to persecution because of the Judeans' identity, faith, and piety (Esther 3; 5:9–7:10; Daniel 3 and 6).

(e) Esth 2:19, 21; 3:2–3; 4:2, 6; 5:9, 13; 6:10, 12; Dan 2:49

While some of these similarities stem from the similar historical settings of the books, others stem from the common experience of the Judean exiles as monotheistic believers living in a polytheistic pagan environment. These similarities do not point to a reliance of one book upon the other. Instead, they point to some common experiences of God's people, including the author responsible for the composition of each book. Both books affirm that living in a pagan society is fraught with peril for believers in the one true God because of their religious beliefs and practices, which set believers apart from their neighbors and construct a barrier that prevents their complete assimilation into the society in which they live. Both books demonstrate that refusal to assimilate to heathen practices and beliefs may lead to persecution.

---

[81] Collins, *Daniel*, 41.

However, both books also demonstrate that believers can remain faithful to their identity as God's people at the same time that they serve pagan masters (cf. Eph 6:5–8; Col 3:22–25; Philemon), even pagan kings (cf. Phil 4:22). Both also demonstrate that some cultural assimilation is possible without compromising the true faith. For example, both Mordecai and Daniel were called by non–Israelite names with pagan theophoric elements from Marduk or Bel, alternate names for the patron god of Babylon: Mordecai contains a form of Marduk, and Daniel was renamed Belteshazzar, which contains Bel. Finally, and most importantly, both books emphasize that God can place his people in positions of authority even in a system that is corrupted by idolatry, although this theme is much more subtly expressed in Esther (Esth 4:14) than in Daniel.

Daniel and the Prophets

From antiquity Daniel was considered to be among the prophets God raised up for Israel. At Qumran, Dan 11:32 and 12:10 were quoted as words of a prophet.[82] Josephus reveres Daniel as a prophet.[83] In the NT, Jesus speaks of "the prophet Daniel" (Mt 24:15).

In the tripartite Jewish arrangement of the canon (Torah, Prophets, Writings), Daniel is not grouped among the Prophets but is included in the Writings. However, this should not be an impediment for understanding Daniel as a prophet, since the Jewish arrangement probably stems from liturgical developments in late antiquity[84] and is not a judgment on the prophetic content of Daniel's book. Nevertheless, Daniel contains no public proclamation of God's Word by the prophet, a leading feature that is found so frequently in the other prophets.[85] Still, Daniel has a number of features that places it squarely among the rest of the prophetic books.

One feature that Daniel has in common with previous prophets is his ministry to royalty. Just as Gad, Nathan, Ahijah, Elijah, Micaiah, Elisha, Isaiah, and Jeremiah prophesied to kings, so also on at least three occasions Daniel (in chapters 2, 4, and 5) declared God's Word to Babylonian kings. However, there is a difference between Daniel as a prophet to the kings of Babylon and the previous prophets. Unlike them, Daniel never prophesied unless God first revealed something to the king in a dream (Daniel 2 and 4) or through the mysterious handwriting on the wall (Daniel 5).

The difference, of course, is the setting. In contrast to the kings of Israel and Judah, a prophet could not assume that the kings of Babylon would have

---

[82] 4QFlorilegium, column 2, line 3 (Allegro, *Qumrân Cave 4.I*, 54). See "Evidence from Qumran" in "Date, Authorship, and Unity" above.

[83] Josephus, *Antiquities*, 10.266; 12.322; also see *Antiquities*, 10.210, 266–81; 11.337.

[84] See Steinmann, *Oracles of God*, 136–41.

[85] While most of the OT prophetic books prominently feature public preaching by the prophet, Jonah contains only five (Hebrew) words of public proclamation (Jonah 3:4), and Habakkuk contains only dialogue between the prophet and God (Habakkuk 1–2) plus a prayer (Habakkuk 3).

been familiar with the God of Israel or would have held him in respect or fear. Even a corrupt and faithless king such as Ahaz feigned respect for Israel's God when confronted by the prophet Isaiah (Is 7:12), and the evil Ahab could be moved to repentance by Elijah's prophecy (1 Ki 21:17–29). However, Babylon's kings had little familiarity and oftentimes less use for what they perceived as the peculiar God worshiped by the captive Judeans. Therefore, God prepared the way for the prophet and his message through revelation that arrested the king's attention and required the ministry of Daniel as God's spokesman to interpret and clarify.

Daniel's prophetic ministry in these instances was not limited to interpreting dreams and signs, however. In each case, Daniel used his opportunity to declare some additional truth. In Daniel 2 he tells Nebuchadnezzar that humans are unable to interpret dreams reliably, but that there is one God who reveals mysteries (2:27–28). In Daniel 4, Daniel prophesied repentance and reformation (4:24 [ET 4:27]). Before interpreting the handwriting on the wall, the prophet used the occasion to preach the Law of God to an arrogant king (5:18–23). Though brief, these prophetic messages are similar to the messages of Israel's prophets both before, during, and after the Babylonian captivity.

Visions are also another common feature of Yahweh's prophets.[86] Two of Daniel's visions (Daniel 7 and 8) involve symbolic features that call for interpretation. This type of vision is recorded as early as the eighth century in Amos (Amos 7:7–9; 8:1–3) and is also among the types of visions received by Daniel's older sixth-century contemporaries Jeremiah (Jer 1:11–19; 24:1–10) and Ezekiel (37:1–14; 40:1–48:35).[87] Later, in the postexilic period, Zechariah would also receive several symbolic visions (Zech 1:7–6:8). Thus Daniel's visions are neither a new way of God revealing his Word to a prophet nor unique in form.

Another more obvious feature of Daniel's prophecy is his frequent use of predictive prophecy, which not only is a constant feature of his visions, but also is the main thrust of his interpretation of Nebuchadnezzar's dreams (chapters 2 and 4) and of the handwriting on the wall (chapter 5). Daniel's predictive prophecies could have a short term fulfillment (Daniel 4 and 5), thereby confirming Daniel's status as a true prophet of God to his contemporaries (fulfilling the requirement in Deut 18:21–22; cf. Jer 28:1–17). However, Daniel's visions and his prophecy to Nebuchadnezzar in Daniel 2 have a decidedly long term,

---

[86] The OT references visions received by God's prophets at least fifty-seven times, including twenty-seven times in Daniel: Num 12:6; 24:4, 16; 1 Sam 3:15; 2 Sam 7:17 ‖ 1 Chr 17:15; Is 1:1; 21:2; 22:1, 5; Ezek 1:1; 7:13, 26; 8:3, 4; 11:24; 12:22, 23, 27; 40:2; 43:3 (three times); Hos 12:11 (ET 12:10); Obad 1; Nah 1:1; Hab 2:2, 3; Dan 1:17; 2:19; 7:1, 2, 7, 13, 15; 8:1, 2 (twice), 13, 15, 16, 17, 26 (twice), 27; 9:21, 23, 24; 10:1, 7 (twice), 8, 14, 16; 11:14; 2 Chr 9:29; 32:32 (cf. Jer 14:14; 23:16; Ezek 12:24; 13:7, 16; Joel 3:1 [ET 2:28]; Micah 3:6; Zech 13:4).

[87] For a discussion of the generic features associated with the prophets' report of their symbolic visions, see Niditch, *The Symbolic Vision in Biblical Tradition*, 243–48.

eschatological emphasis that is both messianic and focused on the kingdom of God.

Therefore, Daniel's book is rightly placed among the prophetic books in Christian Bibles. While his prophetic ministry was in many ways unique owing to his setting in the Babylonian court during the exile, it nevertheless was a forceful proclamation of the Word of God in ways similar to the other prophets. It continued the divine revelation first begun with the books of Moses and pointed forcefully forward to Christ and his kingdom.

Daniel and Wisdom Books

Even a casual reader of the Hebrew and Aramaic text of Daniel soon realizes that there is a high concentration of words normally associated with Wisdom books, especially Proverbs. Among these are the Hebrew verb בִּין, "understand" (twenty-two times in Daniel), and the related Hebrew and Aramaic noun בִּינָה, "understanding" (five times); the Hebrew noun דַּעַת (twice) and the cognate Aramaic noun מַנְדַּע (four times), both meaning "knowledge"; the Hebrew and Aramaic noun חָכְמָה, "wisdom" (ten times); the Hebrew verb שָׂכַל (in the Hiphil), "have insight" (nine times), and the cognate Aramaic verb שְׂכַל (in the Hithpaal), "consider" (once), and the related nouns שֵׂכֶל (Hebrew; once) and שָׂכְלְתָנוּ (Aramaic; three times), both meaning "insight." Daniel himself is not the only one described by these words; for instance, his eschatological prophecies also speak about "those who have insight" (12:3) and about how "knowledge will increase" (12:4).

Clearly, wisdom concepts are important for Daniel. Indeed, some critical scholars have sought to locate the composition of the book not in the Persian period immediately following the fall of Babylon, but in second-century Palestine among Jewish "wisdom circles." They also assert that this type of wisdom is "mantic wisdom," supposedly a distinct type in contrast to the wisdom contained in Proverbs, Ecclesiastes, and Job.[88] However, that distinction is artificial, because the wisdom in both cases is the same.

Wisdom is primarily an attribute of God. Secondarily, true wisdom is granted by God to his people and is possessed only by those who have been brought by God into his kingdom through faith. This is emphasized repeatedly in Proverbs. In addition, there are more than a few passages in the Wisdom books of the OT that speak of how a wise person acts before a king. Among these are sayings that are especially relevant to Daniel, including Job 12:18; Prov 14:35; 16:12–15; 19:12; 20:2, 28; 21:1; 22:11, 29; and Eccl 8:1–4.

The sayings in Proverbs lay out what it means to be a wise person before a king. Daniel provides a concrete example of such a wise person. His life as a wise courtier is, in effect, a case study of wisdom in action. Daniel also contrasts to the wise men of Babylon, who lack divine wisdom and are unable to interpret Nebuchadnezzar's dreams or read the handwriting on the wall. As

---

[88] Collins, *Daniel*, 49–50.

Daniel himself acknowledges, the wisdom to do such things comes only from the one true God (2:27–30). Daniel also prophesies about other wise people who have "insight" and "make many understand" (11:33), who may stumble (11:35), but in the end will be resurrected (12:3). During their time "knowledge will increase" (12:4).

Daniel's prophecy is about his fellow believers who, like him, are wise—not in the way that the world counts wisdom, but in God's ways. He looks forward to the day when knowledge of the Gospel will be increased because the Messiah will come—and beyond, to the increasing spread of the Gospel throughout the world through the church's ministry, until Christ returns. In this way, Daniel's wisdom points to Christ crucified, who is deemed foolishness by the world, but is indeed the true and saving Wisdom of God (1 Cor 1:18–30). Daniel moves from Proverbs' more abstract presentation of wisdom to the concrete example of wisdom in action in order to encourage God's people in using the wisdom of God that he grants to his people, and to encourage them to look for the coming of Wisdom in the person of Christ, at both his first and second advents. Jesus imparts the supreme revelation of the knowledge of God through his ministry, teaching, death, and resurrection.[f]

(f) Cf. 2 Cor 2:14; 4:6; Col 1:9–10; 2:2–3; 3:10; 2 Pet 1:2–8

Daniel in the New Testament

Daniel is an important book for understanding the portions of the NT that treat eschatology, specifically the first and second advents of Christ. The most important connections between Daniel and the NT are the connection between the Messiah and the coming of God's kingdom[89] and the "Son of Man" in Daniel's vision of the Ancient of Days (see the commentary on 7:13–14). While the origin of Jesus' use of the Son of Man has been endlessly debated among scholars, there can be no doubt that several passages in the NT are based on Daniel's use of this term. A quick comparison demonstrates that Jesus understood himself to be the Son of Man seen in Daniel's vision.

Daniel 7:13–14

[13]I kept looking in the visions of the night, and behold, *with the clouds of heaven one like a Son of Man* was *coming*. He came to the Ancient of Days, and he was brought before him. [14]To him was given *dominion, honor, and a kingdom* [the Old Greek includes δόξα, "glory"]. All peoples, nations, and languages will worship him. His dominion is an eternal dominion that will not pass away, and his kingdom is one that will not be destroyed.

Matthew 24:30

And then the sign of the *Son of Man* will appear in heaven, and then all the tribes of the earth will mourn, and they will see the *Son of Man coming on the clouds of heaven* with *power* and great *glory*.

---

[89] See "The Messiah in Daniel: An Overview" in "Major Themes" above.

Matthew 25:31

When the *Son of Man comes* in his *glory*, and all the angels with him, then he will sit on his glorious throne.

Matthew 26:64

Jesus said to him, "You have said so. But I tell you, from now on you will see the *Son of Man* seated at the right hand of *power* and *coming on the clouds of heaven.*"

Mark 13:26

And then they will see the *Son of Man coming in clouds* with great *power* and *glory*.

Mark 14:62

And Jesus said, "I am, and you will see the *Son of Man* seated at the right hand of *power* and *coming with the clouds of heaven.*"

Luke 21:27

And then they will see the *Son of Man coming in a cloud* with *power* and great *glory*.

John also understood Jesus to be the Son of Man from Daniel, as demonstrated by several passages in Revelation.

Revelation 1:7

Behold, he is *coming with the clouds*, and every eye will see him, even those who pierced him, and all tribes of the earth will mourn on account of him. Yes. Amen.

Revelation 1:13

And in the midst of the lampstands was *one like a Son of Man*, clothed with a long robe and with a golden sash around his chest.

Revelation 14:14

Then I looked, and behold, a white *cloud,* and seated *on the cloud one like a Son of Man*, with a golden crown on his head and a sharp sickle in his hand.

In addition to Dan 7:13–14, there is another messianic passage in Daniel that depicts the "Messiah" and "Leader who is coming": 9:25–26. This passage and 7:13–14 probably lie behind John the Baptist's question to Jesus.

Daniel 9:25–26

[25]You should know and have insight: from the going forth of a word to restore and rebuild Jerusalem until *Messiah, a Leade*r, seven weeks, and sixty-two weeks when it again will have been built [with] plaza and moat, but during the troubled times. [26]Then after the sixty-two weeks, *Messiah* will be cut off and have nothing. Both the city and the holy place will be destroyed with *a*

Leader who is coming, and its end will be with a flood. Until the end will be war, and desolations have been determined.

Matthew 11:2–3

²Now when John heard in prison about the deeds of the Christ, he sent word by his disciples ³and said to him, "Are you *he who is coming*, or shall we look for another?"

Luke 7:18–20

¹⁸Calling two of his disciples to him, John ¹⁹sent them to the Lord, saying, "Are you *he who is coming*, or shall we look for another?"

²⁰And when the men had come to him, they said, "John the Baptist has sent us to you, saying, 'Are you *he who is coming*, or shall we look for another?' "

This same connection is found in Revelation in John's threefold description of God:[90]

Revelation 1:4

John to the seven churches that are in Asia: Grace to you and peace from him who is and who was and *who is coming* and from the seven spirits who are before his throne.

Revelation 1:8

"I am the Alpha and the Omega," says the Lord God, "he who is and who was and *who is coming*, the Almighty."

Revelation 4:8

And the four living creatures, each having six wings, are full of eyes all around and within, and they do not rest day and night, saying, "Holy, holy, holy, is the Lord God, the Almighty, who was and who is and *who is coming*!"

Another connection to Daniel is in the NT descriptions of Jesus' eternal kingdom. In Daniel, the kingdom of the Son of Man is said to be an "eternal dominion that will not pass away, and his kingdom is one that will not be destroyed" (7:14). Similarly, other passages in Daniel state that God's kingdom is "eternal" (3:33 [ET 4:3]; 4:31 [ET 4:34]; 6:27 [ET 6:26]; 7:27), "forever" (2:44; 4:31 [ET 4:34]), and "will never/not be destroyed" (2:44; 6:27 [ET 6:26]). This description of God's kingdom that is found six times in Daniel is rare else-

---

[90] This commentary takes "from him who is and who was and who is coming" as a description of the Trinity rather than of the Father alone. The following phrases "from the seven spirits … and from Jesus Christ" (1:4–5) can be understood to be epexegetical references to the Spirit and to the Son, supporting the view that the preceding threefold description applies to the whole Trinity, not just to the Father. Note that Rev 1:8 affirms that "he who is and who was and who is coming" is also "the Alpha and the Omega," and in Rev 22:12–13, after Jesus declares, "I am coming soon," he affirms, "I am the Alpha and the Omega." Other verses in Revelation also describe Jesus as "coming" (the verb ἔρχομαι in the present tense in 2:5, 16; 3:11; 16:15; 22:7, 12, 20).

where in the OT.⁹¹ The NT refers to "the eternal kingdom of our Lord and Savior Jesus Christ" (2 Pet 1:11; cf. Mt 16:18; Rev 11:15). The Daniel passages are also reflected in Gabriel's words to Mary:⁹²

Luke 1:33

And he will reign over the house of Jacob *forever,* and *of his kingdom there will be no end.*

Thus Dan 7:13–14 provides the most important connection between Daniel and the NT. Moreover, the use of this passage in the NT reveals that both Jesus and his contemporaries viewed the Son of Man in Daniel 7 as the Messiah. Since Daniel 7 is the pivotal chapter in the book (see "Overview of Daniel" above) it should not be surprising that it is also *the* most important messianic chapter in Daniel.

Another messianic connection to Daniel is made by Jesus in elaborating on Ps 118:22–23 (cf. also Is 8:14; 28:16), which Jesus applies to himself. Jesus explains, "The one who falls on this stone will be broken to pieces, and the one on whom it falls will be crushed" (Mt 21:44; cf. Lk 20:18). This imagery of the stone falling on someone and crushing him is a reference to the stone that smashes the statue in the dream of Nebuchadnezzar:

Daniel 2:44–45

⁴⁴In the days of those kings the God of heaven will establish a kingdom that will never be destroyed, nor will the kingdom be left to another people. It will *crush* and end all of these kingdoms, but it will be established forever, ⁴⁵just as you saw that a *stone* was cut out of the mountain without hands, and it *crushed* the iron, the bronze, the clay, the silver, and the gold. A great God has made known to Your Majesty what will happen after this. The dream is sure, and its interpretation is certain.

This stone that crushes is found only in Daniel, and Jesus clearly identifies it with himself.

Many other concepts and phrases from Daniel are used in the NT. The highest concentration of these is in Revelation, whose apocalyptic vision and

---

⁹¹ Outside of Daniel, Ps 145:13 describes Yahweh's kingdom as eternal. All of the other OT verses that use either מַמְלָכָה or מַלְכוּת, "kingdom," with עוֹלָם, "eternity; eternal," to speak about a kingdom that endures forever are traditionally regarded by Christians as messianic, since they promise the eternal kingdom to the king from the line of David: 2 Sam 7:13, 16; 1 Ki 9:5; Is 9:6 (ET 9:7); 1 Chr 22:10; 28:7; 2 Chr 13:5. See also Ps 45:7 (ET 45:6), which calls the messianic king "God," ascribes to him a throne that is eternal (עוֹלָם), and refers to the scepter of his "kingdom" (מַלְכוּת) as uprightness; the verse is quoted in Heb 1:8. See 1 Chr 17:14, in which God promises to establish the messianic king בְּבֵיתִי וּבְמַלְכוּתִי עַד־הָעוֹלָם, "in my house and in my kingdom forever." Contrast 1 Sam 13:13, where Saul's infidelity caused his kingdom not to endure forever. (Neither מְלוּכָה nor מַמְלָכוּת, two other Hebrew nouns for "kingdom," ever occurs with עוֹלָם, "eternity; eternal.")

⁹² Note that Gabriel is mentioned in the Bible only in Daniel (8:16; 9:21) and the first chapter of Luke (1:19, 26).

eschatology draw heavily upon Daniel.[93] The following are the most important uses of Daniel in the NT:

- Dan 2:47 in Rev 17:14
- Dan 3:4 in Rev 10:11
- Dan 3:23–25 in Heb 11:34
- Dan 4:9, 18 (ET 4:12, 21) in Mt 13:32; Mk 4:32; Lk 13:19
- Dan 7:2 in Rev 7:1
- Dan 7:7 in Rev 12:3; 13:1
- Dan 7:9 in Rev 1:14; 20:4, 11
- Dan 7:9–10 in Mt 19:28[94]
- Dan 7:10 in Rev 5:11; 20:12
- Dan 7:11 in Rev 13:5; 19:20
- Dan 7:13 in Rev 1:7, 13; 14:14
- Dan 7:20 in Rev 13:5; 17:12
- Dan 7:21 in Rev 11:7; 13:7
- Dan 7:24 in Rev 12:3; 13:1; 17:12
- Dan 7:25 in Rev 12:14; 13:6–7
- Dan 8:10 in Rev 12:4
- Dan 8:26 in Rev 10:4
- Dan 9:27 (also 11:31; 12:11; cf. 8:13) in Mt 24:15; Mk 13:14[95]
- Dan 10:5 in Rev 1:13
- Dan 10:6 in Rev 1:14; 2:18; 19:1, 12
- Dan 11:36 in 2 Thess 2:4[96]
- Dan 12:1 in Rev 3:5; 7:14; 13:8; 20:12
- Dan 12:2 in Mt 25:46; Jn 5:29; Acts 24:15
- Dan 12:3 in Mt 13:43; Phil 2:15
- Dan 12:10 in Rev 22:11

The widespread use of imagery and themes from Daniel in the NT testifies to the importance of this book as a prophecy that connects the earthly kingdom

---

[93] For the more important connections between Revelation and Daniel, see Beale, "The Danielic Background for Revelation 13:18 and 17:9"; "The Interpretative Problem of Rev 1:19"; "The Origin of the Title 'King of Kings and Lord of Lords' in Revelation 17:4"; "A Reconsideration of the Text of Daniel in the Apocalypse"; "The Use of Daniel in the Synoptic Eschatological Discourse and in the Book of Revelation."

[94] Note the connection between Jesus, the Son of Man, on his throne and the throne of God the Father, the Ancient of Days.

[95] This commentary's view is that 9:27 refers to the desolation that would take place after Jesus' earthly ministry, so it is most relevant for Mt 24:15 and Mk 13:14, whereas Dan 11:31 and 12:11 (cf. 8:13) refer to the desolation accomplished under Antiochus IV Epiphanes.

[96] This passage is key to Paul's view of the "man of lawlessness," the "Antichrist." See the commentary on 7:23–25; 11:36–39; and 12:5–7.

of God's OT people, Israel, to his eternal kingdom, inaugurated by Jesus Christ at his first advent—a kingdom of grace open to all believers in Christ, Jewish and Gentile alike. Daniel begins with events in the last days of Judah as an independent kingdom, then shows the transition of the Judeans into a captive people among the nations. Yet by faith the Judeans continue to be God's people in his kingdom of grace, awaiting their Messiah (7:13–14; 9:25–26), their resurrection (12:2–3), and the consummation of the eternal kingdom in the new heavens and new earth (Isaiah 11; 65:17–25). Daniel's enduring contribution is to fill us with that same eschatological faith. While the Messiah has already come, we are still scattered and persecuted in a hostile world. Nevertheless, through faith in Christ we are already citizens of God's eternal kingdom, and we await the parousia of Christ and the consummation of all the promises that are ours because of his completed ministry.

Figure 3

Timeline of Biblical Eschatology

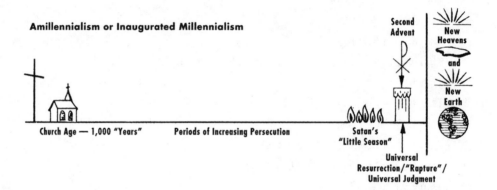

The NT Scriptures teach that Christ will one day visibly return in glory. They refer to his second advent by using several different terms: "coming" or "presence" (παρουσία, e.g., Mt 24:27), "appearance" (ἐπιφάνεια, e.g., 1 Tim 6:14), "revelation" (ἀποκάλυψις, e.g., 1 Cor 1:7), and "the day of the Lord" (ἡ ἡμέρα τοῦ κυρίου, e.g., 1 Thess 5:2). A study of the texts in which these terms occur reveals that Christ's second advent is *one event at the end of history*. The Scriptures teach the following concerning Christ's second and final coming:

1. Christ will come visibly and all people will see him (Mt 24:27, 30; Mk 13:24–26; 14:62; Lk 17:22–24; 21:27, 35; Acts 1:11; Rev 1:7).

2. Christ will come in glory surrounded by the host of his angels (Mt 13:39–43, 49; 16:27; 24:30–31; 25:31; 2 Thess 1:7; Titus 2:13; 1 Pet 4:13; Jude 14, 24; Rev 19:11–14; see also Zech 14:3).

3. When Christ returns, a bodily resurrection of all the dead will take place. Believers will be raised to salvation and unbelievers to damnation (Dan 12:1–2; Jn 5:27–29; 6:39–40, 44, 54; 1 Cor 15:12–57; Rev 20:11–15). All believers, both dead and living, will, be "caught up" to "meet the Lord in the air" (1 Thess 4:13–17). Death will be destroyed (1 Cor 15:26, 54–57; Rev 20:14).

4. When Christ returns, he will judge all people, both the living and the dead (Mt 25:31–46; Jn 5:27; Acts 10:42; 17:31; Rom 2:16, 2 Tim 4:1, 8; Jude 14–15; Rev 20:11–15). Believers will receive eternal salvation and unbelievers eternal damnation (Mt 25:31–46; 2 Cor 5:10; 2 Thess 1:6–10; Heb 9:28; 1 Pet 1:4–5, 7; 5:4; 1 Jn 3:2). Satan and the Antichrist will be destroyed (2 Thess 2:8; Rev 20:10).

5. When Christ returns, "new heavens and a new earth" will be created (2 Pet 3:10–13). Nowhere, however, do the Scriptures teach that at his return Christ will establish a this-worldly, political kingdom or "millennium."

The date of Christ's second advent is unknown. Jesus himself taught, "But of that day and hour no one knows, not even the angels of heaven, nor the Son, but the Father only" (Mt 24:36; cf. Mt 24:42, 44; 25:13; 1 Thessalonians 5; 2 Peter 3). The times or seasons fixed by the authority of the Father are "not for you to know" (Acts 1:7). Therefore, speculation concerning the time of the end is forbidden. This much *can* be said: the fact that God has delayed it now for almost two millennia is due to his patience and mercy, for "the Lord is not slow about his promise as some count slowness, but is forbearing toward you, not wishing that any should perish, but that all should reach repentance" (2 Pet 3:9).

The scriptural teaching concerning Christ's second advent has a very practical purpose. God wills that all come to believe in the Gospel, lead a holy life in service to Christ, and eagerly await the last day with patience (Rom 13:12–14; Titus 2:11–13; 1 Pet 1:13–15; 2 Pet 3:11–12; 1 Jn 3:2–3; 1 Tim 6:14; Mt 25:14–30).

Adapted from *The End Times: A Study of Eschatology and Millennialism*
(a report of the Commission on Theology and Church Relations
of The Lutheran Church—Missouri Synod, September 1989), 26–27, 45.
Used by permission of The Lutheran Church—Missouri Synod. Scripture quotations: RSV.

Figure 4

Timelines of Millennial Eschatologies

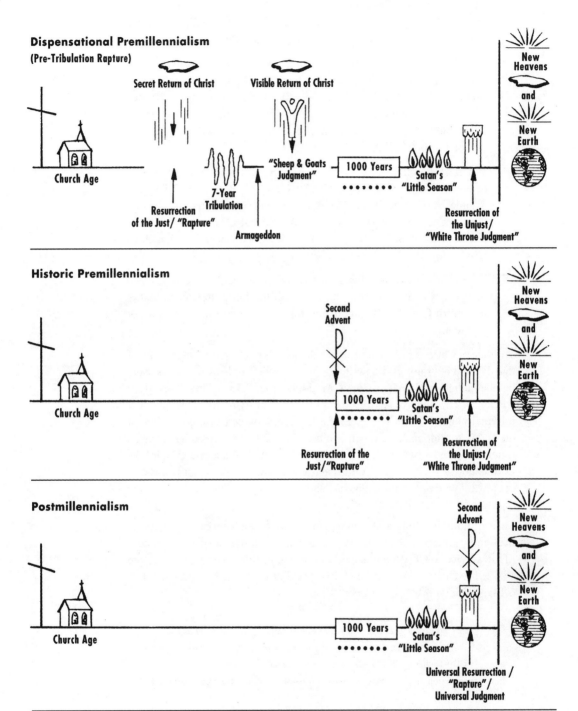

Adapted from *The End Times: A Study of Eschatology and Millennialism*
(a report of the Commission on Theology and Church Relations
of The Lutheran Church—Missouri Synod, September 1989), 45.
Used by permission of The Lutheran Church—Missouri Synod.

Eschatology and Dispensational Premillennial Interpretations of Daniel

This commentary interprets Daniel in harmony with the view of biblical eschatology that has been held by the majority of the Christian church for the last two millennia.[97] This view is that the "millennium" described in Revelation 20 is the church age, spanning the time between Christ's first and second advents. This view is usually called "amillennialism," but that term should not be misunderstood to mean that this view denies that there is a millennium. Instead, this period of time, figuratively described as a thousand years, has already begun, so "inaugurated millennialism" might be technically more accurate for it. The timeline of this view of biblical eschatology is relatively easy to illustrate, as shown in figure 3.

Another approach to understanding Revelation 20 and its thousand years (Rev 20:1–7) is dispensational premillennialism, which offers it own unique understanding of several sections of Daniel.[98] Of the various millennial understandings of the Bible, dispensational premillennialism is by far the most popular. The popularity of this hermeneutical scheme requires a discussion of its presuppositions before addressing its specific interpretations of Daniel passages.[99] Figure 4 illustrates its view of history, as well as the timelines of the less popular views of historic premillennialism and postmillennialism.

Dispensational premillennialism had its origin in the early nineteenth century among the Plymouth Brethren in England and Ireland. This system of interpretation was promoted by one of the early leaders of the Plymouth Brethren, John Nelson Darby (1800–1882), and was a reaction against the then widely held view called postmillennialism. It received its name from its view that human history is divided into "dispensations." A dispensation is defined as "a period of time during which man is tested in respect to his obedience to some specific revelation of the will of God."[100] This definition is suspect from the outset, since it elevates human obedience over the gracious work of God in Christ and makes faith humanly generated obedience to God rather than the work of the Holy Spirit (contrary to, e.g., Rom 8:7; 1 Cor 2:14; 12:3; Eph 2:8–9). The most common dispensational scheme holds that there are seven dispensations:

---

[97] For a historical survey of Jewish and Christian millennialism and how Revelation 20 has been interpreted over the centuries, one may see "The Millennium" in Brighton, *Revelation*, 533–41. Brighton advocates the historic "amillennial" view held by the majority of Christendom.

[98] An accessible book in which each of the proponents of the four main eschatological views—historic premillennialism, dispensational premillennialism, postmillennialism, and amillennialism (the view of this commentary)—presents a defense of his view is *The Meaning of the Millennium*, edited by Robert Clouse. A more thorough presentation of traditional biblical eschatology is by Hoekema, *The Bible and the Future*.

[99] See *The End Times: A Study of Eschatology and Millennialism* (a report of the Commission on Theology and Church Relations of The Lutheran Church—Missouri Synod, September 1989).

[100] Scofield, English, et al., *Oxford NIV Scofield Study Bible*, 3.

- Innocence (Gen 1:28–3:6)
- Conscience or Moral Responsibility (Gen 4:1–8:14)
- Human Government (Gen 8:15–11:32)
- Promise (Gen 12:1–Ex 18:27)
- The Law (Ex 19:3–Acts 1:26)
- The Church (Acts 2:1–Revelation 19)
- The Millennial Kingdom (Revelation 20)[101]

Dispensational premillennialism is widely held among evangelical groups in the United States and Canada, and has spread its influence throughout Christianity worldwide. The spread of dispensational theology was largely due to the influence of the *Scofield Reference Bible*, first published in 1909. While there are several schools of thought within current dispensational interpretation, their common approach to prophecy and eschatology generally dictates similar interpretations of several passages in Daniel.

Basic Dispensational Presuppositions

Dispensational premillennialism is based on three basic presuppositions: a radical distinction between Israel and the church; the "literal" fulfillment of prophecy; and the glorification of God as the purpose of history.[102]

A Radical Distinction between Israel and the Church

According to dispensationalists, God has pursued two goals throughout history. One of these goals is the preservation of an earthly people, the Jewish people or ethnic Israel. The other goal is the salvation of Gentiles through the church. According to this view, the church was not revealed in the OT because its prophecy was concerned only, or at least primarily and overwhelmingly, about God's predicted plan for Israel. The church is an unexpected "parenthesis" or detour in God's plan. During the time of the church, there may be "neither Jew nor Greek" among God's people (Gal 3:28; Col 3:11), but in the future God will again make such distinction, and this distinction will last throughout eternity. This view involves a strange reading of Paul, who insists that there is no distinction between Jew and Greek, since God is Lord of all (Rom 10:12). Paul also declares that there is only "one body … one Lord, one faith, one Baptism" (Eph 4:4–5; cf. Jn 10:16). This view also leads to seeing Christ's death and resurrection as an unfortunate series of events that could and would have been avoided had the Jewish people as a whole merely believed in Christ and allowed him to establish his earthly kingdom when he first came to them. The church was only needed—and, therefore Christ's death and resurrection were only needed—because ethnic Israel rejected the Messiah.

---

[101] *The End Times*, 4, citing Scofield, English, et al., *Oxford NIV Scofield Study Bible*, 3, 6, 13, 18, 86, 1130, 1335–36.

[102] Ryrie, *Dispensationalism Today*, 44–46.

The dispensational view that the central work of Christ's ministry[103] was peripheral to the real work of God's kingdom flies in the face of all that the NT says about Jesus and reduces OT messianic prophecy to a myopic, self-centered Israelite-focused messianism. Yet as many of the OT prophecies themselves indicate, the Messiah's work was never intended to be only for Israel, since that was "too small" for him (Is 49:6; cf. Is 42:6). Moreover, Paul follows the standard that "neither circumcision nor uncircumcision counts for anything, but a new creation," and he makes clear that *all* baptized believers in Christ (Jewish and Gentile alike) comprise "the Israel of God" (Gal 6:15–16; cf. 2 Cor 5:17; Gal 3:26–29). Elsewhere he makes clear that membership in God's true Israel is only by faith in Christ and that being Jewish carries no special entry into God's kingdom apart from Christ (Rom 9:6–23, especially 9:6–8).

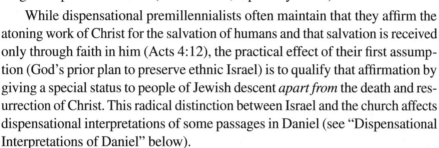

While dispensational premillennialists often maintain that they affirm the atoning work of Christ for the salvation of humans and that salvation is received only through faith in him (Acts 4:12), the practical effect of their first assumption (God's prior plan to preserve ethnic Israel) is to qualify that affirmation by giving a special status to people of Jewish descent *apart from* the death and resurrection of Christ. This radical distinction between Israel and the church affects dispensational interpretations of some passages in Daniel (see "Dispensational Interpretations of Daniel" below).

The "Literal" Fulfillment of Prophecy

Dispensational premillennialists often insist that their interpretation is correct because it understands all prophecies "literally." This often dovetails with their assumption of a plan for a new Israelite kingdom apart from the church, since they interpret many of the prophecies in the Psalms and the prophetic books to mean that before the resurrection of all flesh, God's kingdom will be a kingdom on earth in which the Messiah will rule on David's throne from Jerusalem. One example of this "literal" approach is the dispensational belief that the promise to Abraham[g] was to Abraham's physical descendants—despite clear statements to the contrary by Jesus (Mt 3:9; Lk 3:8; Jn 8:39–44) and Paul (Rom 4:16; 9:6–7; Gal 3:7–9, 13–14; 4:22–28)—and that the Jewish people will possess Canaan forever (despite Heb 11:13–16).

(g) Gen 12:1–3, 7; 13:14–17; 17:1–8; cf. Gen 26:2–5; 28:13–15; 35:9–12

Premillennial, including dispensational, interpretations of the Scriptures insist that in passages in visionary and apocalyptic books that employ numbers, those numbers must be taken as literal enumerations or quantifications.[104] The word "premillennial" comes from the "thousand years" in the well-known pas-

---

[103] Many NT passages declare that the central purpose of Jesus' incarnation and ministry was to atone for the sin of all people by his death on the cross and then to rise from the dead as testimony to his completion of the work of our redemption and to promise our own bodily resurrection. This central purpose was in fulfillment of OT prophecy (e.g., Isaiah 53). See, for example, Mt 1:18–25; 16:21; 26:54; Lk 24:25–26, 44–53; Jn 1:29; Romans 4–5; 1 Corinthians 15; Galatians 3.

[104] See Walvoord, "The Prophecy of the Ten-Nation Confederacy," 99–100.

sage in Revelation 20. Here those who were martyred for their faith in Christ reign with him for a thousand years (the millennium) while the devil is confined to the abyss (Rev 20:1–7).[105] "Millennial" comes from the Latin *mille*, "one thousand," and *annus*, "year," and the prefix "pre-" ("before") indicates that this approach believes Christ will return right "before" this period and reign on earth during it. Insisting that the thousand years must be understood literally, not symbolically, the method goes on to apply the same hermeneutic to the visionary passages in Daniel. This is true even though proponents admit that the passages under examination are highly symbolic. For example, dispensational premillennialists admit that the beasts in Daniel's vision (Daniel 7) are not real beasts, but represent kingdoms. The great sea (Dan 7:2) represents the nations, not a literal sea. The four winds (Dan 7:2) are not literal, since "in Daniel, wind is uniformly used to represent the sovereign power of God."[106] Presumably, God does not have four separate sovereign powers.

Dispensational writings contain many other cases of non-literal, symbolic interpretation of highly symbolic visions in Scripture, especially in Daniel and Revelation. Certainly no dispensationalist thinks that rivers or trees will grow hands to clap (Ps 98:8) or that hills will get voices in order to sing (Is 55:12). Nor do dispensationalists think that hills will spontaneously drip wine or have rivers of milk (Joel 4:18 [ET 3:18]; Amos 9:13). Thus the dispensational hermeneutic is quite selective in its "literal" interpretation of prophecy. Those passages that support dispensational understandings of eschatology through a "literal" interpretation are read in that way, whereas many other prophecies are not. Instead of seeking *contextual* reasons within a biblical book that has a prophecy or vision as to what is intended literally and what is intended figuratively, the dispensational hermeneutic seeks to interpret some portions of some prophecies for purely *ideological* reasons related to its view of Israel and the church, and the resulting dispensational eschatology and soteriology. Instead of affirming that Christ and his work, culminating in his cross and resurrection, are the center of the message "in all the Scriptures" (Lk 24:27), the dispensational hermeneutic of "literal interpretation" often unwittingly relegates Christ to the sidelines in order to elevate a non-scriptural distinction between Jews and Gentiles in the order of salvation and in relation to God's kingdom.

The Glorification of God as the Purpose of History

This presupposition of dispensational hermeneutics could be understood correctly. That is, one could understand it to mean that the central events in the history of God's redemptive work for humankind—the cross and empty tomb of Christ—glorify God and enable his true glory to shine forth (Jn 17:1–5; Phil 2:5–11). However, dispensational premillennialists do not view the death and

---

[105] For a historic Christian and amillennial interpretation of Rev 20:1–6, one may see Brighton, *Revelation*, 542–70.

[106] Walvoord, *Daniel*, 152.

resurrection of Christ as the central and supreme revelation of God's glory. Instead, "the soteriological or saving program of God is not the only program but one of the means God is using in the total program of glorifying Himself."[107] Thus dispensationalists believe that they need not relate every work of God to Christ and his cross in order to see God's glory; instead they focus just as much on his works that they see as being apart from Christ[108] as they do on his work in and through his Son. They hold this view despite Paul's insistence that we see God's glory in the Gospel of Christ (2 Cor 4:4, 6). Paul defines that Gospel as the preaching of the cross and resurrection of Jesus Christ, by which he "abolished death and brought life and immortality to light" (2 Tim 1:10; see also 2 Tim 2:8).

When dispensational premillennialists apply this view to Daniel, they see much of the prophecy as about God establishing his kingdom only in the eschaton, and not in the earthly ministry, death, and resurrection of Jesus. Once again, such a view denies the clear words of Christ, who time and again insists that he already brought the kingdom of God to his people during his ministry.[h] The NT contains the "now but not yet" eschatological tension since Christ established the kingdom of God at his first coming, but the full consummation of his kingdom is also yet to come.[i] Dispensational premillennialism destroys this tension by denying that Christ at his first advent actually brought the promised kingdom of God and that the Gospel of Christ crucified and risen is the definitive revelation of God's glory. Instead dispensationalism expects the kingdom of God to come only in the future. As it collapses eschatology and destroys the "now but not yet" eschatological tension, it relegates the Gospel of the death and resurrection of Christ to being one of several important works of God that contribute to his eternal kingdom rather than *the* work of God that alone creates the kingdom and brings people into it—already now through faith and in all its fullness on the Last Day.

(h) Mt 12:28; Mk 9:1; Lk 9:27; 10:9; 11:20; 17:20–21

(i) Mt 25:34; Mk 9:47; Lk 19:11; 22:18; 1 Cor 6:9–10; 15:50; Gal 5:19–21

Dispensational Interpretations of Daniel

Dispensational interpretations of Daniel mainly effect five passages: the interpretation of Nebuchadnezzar's dream (Daniel 2); Daniel's vision of four beasts (Daniel 7); Daniel's description of the little horn in his second vision (Daniel 8); the "seventy weeks" revealed to Daniel (Daniel 9); and the interpretation of predictive time periods at the end of Daniel's final vision (Daniel 12). While detailed exegesis of these passages, including refutations of dispensational understandings of them, is found in the commentary on each passage, a few general observations are in order here.

---

[107] Ryrie, *Dispensationalism Today*, 46.

[108] The NT and orthodox Trinitarian theology affirm that the Father and the Son are one (e.g., John 17), so we should not speak of the Father as performing works apart from his Son. However, dispensational interpretation often gives the impression that God carries out works in his accomplishment of his plans for humanity and the world apart from Christ and his works.

Daniel 2

The interpretation of the statue in Nebuchadnezzar's dream in Daniel 2 is a typical case of dispensational interpretation. The statue made out of four metals representing four kingdoms is interpreted in a way that enables dispensational premillennialists to delay the coming of the kingdom of God until the eschaton. The fourth metal, iron, on the lower part of the statue is interpreted as the Roman Empire. This is not unique to dispensationalists. However, dispensational interpretations often make a point of the two legs and ten toes in the iron portion of the statue. The legs are said to represent the dividing of the empire into east and west, and the ten toes are said to represent a ten-nation confederacy that is to grow out of the territory once covered by the Roman Empire. These ten toes are seen as the same as the ten horns in Daniel's vision of the frightening beast in Daniel 7. This then enables dispensational premillennialists to understand the stone that smashes the statue and grows into a great kingdom that fills the earth—Christ's coming to establish the kingdom of God—as a purely eschatological event: it does not, according to dispensationalists, depict the first advent of Christ nor the church age, but the future establishment of the millennial kingdom and the reign of God in the new heavens and new earth.[109]

However, there is a glaring problem with such exegesis. Nowhere in Daniel 2 is there any description of the statue as having two legs.[110] Thus to make an interpretive point that the two legs represent the dividing of the Roman Empire is *to read into the text a feature that is not there*, rather than to interpret the text itself. Moreover, the toes of the statue are never numbered. While it is fairly reasonable to assume that the statue probably would have ten toes, it goes well beyond the text to read some significance into the number of toes or assign them any representational value. In fact, the toes are mentioned only twice (2:41–42) without any hint that they represent separate entities; they are merely part of the lower, iron portion of the statue. Moreover, the two arms of silver both represent the second kingdom, and the two thighs of bronze both represent the third kingdom, so why should one assume that if the statue has two legs, they each represent a separate kingdom?

Clearly, dispensational interpreters are reading details into the account that are not part of the text. They do this in order to justify their view that Jesus did not establish the kingdom of God at his first coming. However, the dream and Daniel's interpretation of it simply describe the stone as smashing the statue on its feet, which are part of the fourth kingdom. The prophecy is that the kingdom of God will come during the days of the fourth empire, Rome (see the excursus

---

[109] See, for example, Walvoord, "The Prophecy of the Ten-Nation Confederacy," 101–2; *Daniel*, 68–76.

[110] From the description of the statue (Dan 2:32–33), it appears to be a human likeness. However, this is never explicitly stated. Thus the assumption that the statue had only two legs is reasonable, but not absolutely certain.

"The Four-Kingdom Schema in Daniel"). There is no hint that the fourth empire would be prolonged through a later ten-nation confederacy and that God's kingdom would only come during that later confederacy.

Daniel 7

Similar questionable hermeneutics are employed in the dispensational interpretation of Daniel 7. Two major problems present themselves for interpreters of this vision of four creatures. Neither of these problems is adequately addressed in dispensational literature. The first is the supposed gap between the fall of the fourth beast, the Roman Empire in the fifth century, and its supposed revival at a future date yet to be revealed. Daniel, as well as the rest of Scripture, is silent about any gap, especially one lasting at least sixteen centuries.

Moreover, the entire vision in Daniel 7 (as well as Nebuchadnezzar's dream in Daniel 2) assumes complete continuity from each of the four kingdoms to the next without any gap in consecutive fulfillment. The first beast gives way to the second, which gives way to the third, which gives way to the forth, followed by the rise of the ten horns and the rise of the little horn. Even dispensationalists interpret the first four kingdoms as consecutive without any gaps between them: Babylon, Persia, Greece, and Rome. Moreover, they see continuity, not a gap, between the rise of the ten-nation confederacy and the rise of the Antichrist.[111] The only place in Daniel's vision they find a gap is between the fourth beast (the Roman Empire) and the ten horns (the ten-nation confederacy). Yet neither Daniel 7 nor any of the texts they cite as speaking about the rise of this confederacy (Daniel 2; Rev 13:1–2; 17:3, 7, 12–18)[112] so much as hints at a historical gap. This gap is needed so that the "parenthesis" of the church age can be inserted and the establishment of the kingdom of God can once again be treated as purely a part of future eschatology.

A Literalistic Interpretation of Numbers Is Disproved by Daniel 1:20 and 3:19

A second problem arises from the dispensational insistence on a "literal" interpretation of details, including numbers. This requires that all numbers in visionary or apocalyptic texts be taken as literal enumerations or quantifications. In Daniel 7 this requires dispensationalists to try to identify exactly ten kingdoms that arise from the Roman Empire (Dan 7:24) and to interpret Dan 7:25 as referring precisely to three and a half years.

This artificially constructed principle fails to acknowledge that visionary texts are more likely than narratives to have figurative details, and even outside of Daniel's visions (chapters 7–12), numbers are employed in non-enumerative, metaphorically charged ways. Two examples of figurative mathematics are

---

[111] See, for example, Walvoord, "The Prophecy of the Ten-Nation Confederacy," 102–3; *Daniel*, 159–63.

[112] Walvoord, "The Prophecy of the Ten-Nation Confederacy," 99, 104.

found in Daniel's narratives (chapters 1–6). First, Daniel and his friends were "ten times [better]" than the Babylonian wise men (1:20). Second, the furnace into which Shadrach, Meshach, and Abednego were to be thrown was ordered to be heated "seven times hotter" than normal (3:19). In both instances, these numbers seem to be figurative comparisons, not literal enumerations or quantifications. There is no reason to assume that Daniel's friends scored ten times higher on some proficiency exam or that Nebuchadnezzar's servants used some type of thermodynamic measure to determine the heat of the furnace.[113] In both cases, the numbers are a rhetorical device used to point to something that was exceedingly surpassing ("ten times [better]" in 1:20) or as high as possible ("seven times hotter" in 3:19).

Failure to recognize that numbers can be and are used by Daniel with non-enumerative or non-quantifiable meanings dooms dispensational interpretations from the start. Since they begin with a false premise (numbers are never symbolic), they introduce constraints on the text that the author never intended. This leads to indefensible postulations (i.e., a historical gap where none is indicated in the text) and incorrect conclusions. One such faulty conclusion, based on Dan 7:24, is that the anti-Christ will arise from a ten-nation confederacy, and this leads to speculation about which ten nations in modern Europe will (or already do) comprise this confederacy. Such speculations in the recent past have proven to be fanciful. For example, some assumed that the European Union was the confederacy since it had ten member nations, but now it has more than ten.

Most importantly, the dispensational method of interpretation denies the central theme of the NT, especially the Gospels: that Jesus has brought and opened to us the kingdom of God through his life, death, and resurrection. It robs Christians of the comfort of knowing that they are members of God's kingdom now and replaces that comfort with an uncertain hope that they may (or may not) someday be members of God's eternal kingdom.

Daniel 8

Another dispensational hermeneutical difficulty is encountered in Daniel 8. Here, Daniel has a vision of a ram, representing Persia, and a goat, representing Greece. A little horn grows from one of the goat's horns. Everyone, except some dispensational premillennialists, agrees that this little horn represents Antiochus Epiphanes. However, since the vision mentions this little horn as arising at "the appointed time of the end" (Dan 8:19), dispensationalists take "end" in an absolute sense as the end of this present world,[114] making the need

---

[113] If one insists on taking the statement literally, one would have to assume that the temperature was measured on a scale that (like the modern Kelvin scale) begins at absolute zero (-460 degrees Fahrenheit or -273 degrees Celsius). If the normal furnace temperature were, for example, 540 degrees Fahrenheit, then the temperature seven times hotter would be 7,000 degrees Fahrenheit, something impossible to produce with the technology then available.

[114] Instead, "the appointed time of the end" should be understood contextually in this vision. It refers to the time of the end or the latter part of the period of history covered by this vision, which is the series of four world kingdoms leading up to the first advent of Christ.

for an additional eschatological interpretation. Therefore, many dispensational premillennialists speak of a double fulfillment of 8:23–26: these verses were fulfilled by Antiochus, but they will be equally fulfilled by a future Antichrist near the end of the world.

The problems inherent in such a double fulfillment view are manifold. Most seriously, it raises an entire set of troubling questions. If a prophecy in Scripture predicts one specific person or event, and nothing in the text points to a double (or multiple) fulfillment, how can an interpreter justify a view that requires two fulfillments? If, without textual basis, the interpreter posits two fulfillments, what is to keep one from hypothesizing even more? What would limit speculations about the number of fulfillments? How does this method of interpreting Scripture resist turning the text into a malleable object in the hands of a reader, so that it means anything the reader wants it to mean, regardless of the intent of the original author—both the human author and the Holy Spirit? That is to say, how does one resist practicing *eisegesis* instead of *exegesis*? These fundamental hermeneutical questions are often not asked or answered by dispensational premillennialists who advocate a double fulfillment of 8:23–26.[115]

However, some dispensational interpreters sense the inherent problems embedded in this dual-fulfillment theory. Therefore, they view Antiochus as fulfilling these prophecies, but also see Antiochus as a foreshadowing of the Antichrist. To be sure, there is good reason to view the little horn of Daniel 8 as a foreshadowing of the activity of the little horn of Daniel 7. The most obvious of these is that both are characterized as a little horn. However, one need not follow a dispensational interpretation of Scripture to adopt such a view. What is unique among dispensational premillennialists who view 8:23–26 as fulfilled in Antiochus but also as foreshadowing the Antichrist is that they insist that the "time of the end" and similar phrases point to an eschatological fulfillment that *cannot* apply to Antiochus. As a result, they often attempt to pick out details in 8:23–26 that they feel are not apt descriptions of Antiochus and, therefore, must be about the Antichrist.[116] Thus, in practice, these dispensational premillennialists do not simply see a foreshadowing of the Antichrist in these verses; that is, they do not believe that the verses simply depict Antiochus, who was a type or shadow, a shape whose general profile was similar to the future Antichrist. Instead, they are in part (and on a finer scale) following the method of those who apply the whole of 8:23–26 to a future Antichrist. Their belief that parts of 8:23–26 were *not* fulfilled in the latter days of the kings described in 8:20–22 is contrary to the clear statement of the text.

---

[115] See further the discussion of this issue of multiple fulfillment in the excursus "Dispensational Interpretations of Daniel 8."

[116] See, for example, Walvoord, *Daniel*, 197–99.

Daniel 9

In the interpretation of Daniel 9, which prophesies the "seventy weeks" (9:24–27), dispensational premillennialists once again look to postpone the coming of the kingdom of God by a peculiar understanding of the prophecy. The "seventy weeks" are understood by dispensationalists to be seventy sets of seven years. The first sixty-nine weeks are said to have been completed with the ministry of Jesus and his crucifixion (see the commentary on Daniel 9 for the details). However, the dispensationalists view the seventieth week as yet to be fulfilled. In their scheme, this postponement of the seventieth week is necessary to leave room for the church age, the so-called "parenthesis" before the final "week." That last "week" is a seven-year tribulation period that will lead up to the millennial kingdom. Thus they often speak of a "gap" between the sixty-ninth week and the seventieth week.[117] However, Daniel 9 gives no indication of such a gap. Once again, this gap is needed to postpone the coming of the kingdom, to maintain that it did not come during Jesus' earthly ministry, but will only come at his eschatological return. To support their theory, dispensationalists again read into the text a feature (here, a gap) that is not present, rather than reading the text as it stands.

Daniel 12

Finally, dispensational premillennialists, employing their theory of "literal" interpretation of numerically indicated time periods, understand the 1,290 and 1,335 days mentioned in 12:11–12 as periods of about three and a half years, making them prophecies relating to the so-called tribulation period of seven years that is supposed to immediately precede Christ's millennial reign on earth.[118] However, these periods are actually pointing to Jesus' earthly ministry, not his eschatological reign (see the commentary on 12:11–12). Once again, dispensational interpreters move the focus away from Jesus' life, death, and resurrection to his eschatological reign, which in the dispensational view is an earthly reign of a thousand years that precedes the eternal kingdom of God.

Summary

Two grave mistakes repeatedly arise in the dispensational interpretations of Daniel. One of these is primarily hermeneutical. The other is theological. The hermeneutical mistake is one of twisting the text to make it fit a preconceived eschatological timetable *despite the immediate context of the words and the wider context of the book of Daniel as a whole*. At times dispensational premillennialists do this by reading into the text details that are not in the text (i.e., the number of legs of the statue in Daniel 2; the "gap" before the seventieth week in Daniel 9) or that the text does not emphasize (i.e., the number of toes on the statue in Daniel 2). At other times, they insist on a reading of the

---

[117] See, for example, Walvoord, *Daniel*, 228–37.

[118] See, for example, Walvoord, *Daniel*, 294–96.

text apart from its context. For example, numbered time periods are always read literally, no matter what the context, and any mention of the end times or last days is always understood as an absolute reference to the future end of the world. Another example is the resorting to a double meaning or fulfillment of the "little horn" in the prophecy of Daniel 8. This distortion of the text to fit the dispensational premillennial eschatology raises serious questions that dispensational interpreters have yet to confront.

Even more troubling is the theological mistake of dispensational interpretations of Daniel. Such interpretations constantly downplay the ministry of Christ, who brought the kingdom through his life, death, and resurrection, and who, throughout the present church age, welcomes people into God's kingdom through repentance and faith. Daniel, properly understood, constantly points its readers to the coming of the kingdom of God in the ministry of Jesus, as well as to its consummation at his return and the resurrection. However, dispensational interpretations constantly deny the focus on the advent of the kingdom in Jesus' ministry in order to exalt the supposedly future millennial kingdom.[119] This, in turn, changes the focus of theology from the cross and resurrection of Christ to the glorious power of God to establish a future earthly kingdom. It clearly exchanges a theology of the cross for a theology of glory.[120] While not denying Jesus' death and resurrection for the sins of the world, dispensational premillennialism demotes these events to a sidelight or prelude to the "real" kingdom.

Thus for dispensational premillennialists, the kingdom of God in Daniel does not focus on forgiveness, salvation, and eternal life in Christ, but upon a future earthly kingdom of power and glory. This, of course, contradicts the clear teaching of the Bible: "the kingdom of God" does not consist of earthly things, but "of righteousness and peace and joy in the Holy Spirit" (Rom 14:17). Dispensational premillennialism seeks to offer Christians the comfort of knowing a timetable for the future fulfillment of God's plan for humanity, but it actually robs them of the sure and certain comfort of the cross and resurrection of Jesus by relegating his earthly ministry to secondary importance and removing it completely from the purview of Daniel's prophecies.

---

[119] The traditional Christian view is that the "thousand years" in Rev 20:1–6 are, in fact, the present church age, when Satan is bound so that the Gospel can be proclaimed throughout the world, and those brought to faith are already raised spiritually to new life (cf. Rom 6:1–11; Col 2:11–14) and have begun to reign by incorporation into the reigning Christ and his kingdom (cf. Lk 17:21; Rom 5:17, 21; Eph 2:6).

[120] The distinction between the theology of the cross and the theology of glory is set forth by Luther in theses 20–21 of the *Heidelberg Disputation*: "He deserves to be called a theologian, however, who comprehends the visible and manifest things of God seen through suffering and the cross. A theologian of glory calls evil good and good evil. A theologian of the cross calls the thing what it actually is" (AE 31:40; see also LC III 65–67).

Figure 5

Qumran Manuscripts of Daniel

Manuscript	Contents	Date of Production	DJD (Volume and Page)
1QDan^a	1:10–17 2:2–6	AD 50–68	1:150–51
1QDan^b	3:22–30	AD 50–68	1:151–52
4QDan^a	1:16–20 2:9–11 2:19–33 2:33–46 2:47–3:2 4:29–30 (ET 4:31–32) 5:5–7 5:12–14 5:16–19 7:5–7 7:25–8:5 10:16–20 11:13–16	50 BC	16:239–54
4QDan^b	5:10–12 5:14–16 5:19–22 6:8–22 (ET 6:7–21) 6:27–7:4 (ET 6:26–7:4) 7:5–6 7:11? 7:26–28 8:1–8 8:13–16	AD 50–68	16:255–67
4QDan^c	10:5–9 10:11–16 10:21 11:1–2 11:13–17 11:25–29	Late second century BC	16:269–77
4QDan^d	3:8–10? 3:23–25 4:5–9 (ET 4:8–12) 4:12–16 (ET 4:15–19) 7:15–23	25–1 BC	16:279–86
4QDan^e	9:12–14 9:15–17	Early first century BC	16:287–89
6QDan^a	8:16–17? 8:20–21? 10:8–16 11:33–36 11:38	Early first century AD	3:114–16

In addition, Dan 11:32 and 12:10 are quoted in 4QFlorilegium (4Q174; DJD 5:54). Thus some portion of all twelve chapters of Daniel is preserved in these ancient scrolls.

The Text and Other Daniel Traditions

The Hebrew and Aramaic Text

The Masoretic Text

The text of Daniel that is used as the base for this commentary is that of *BHS*, which contains the text of the Leningrad Codex B 19[A]. This codex was copied in AD 1008 or 1009. Other Masoretic manuscripts offer the same text with minor variations, including variations in pointing. Many of these variations are included in the apparatus of *BHS*. Occasionally one of the readings from the apparatus is to be preferred, as is noted in the textual notes in this commentary.

The Masoretic Text of Daniel is Hebrew for 1:1–2:4a and 8:1–12:13, but Aramaic for 2:4b–7:28. The division of the Hebrew text into chapters is different from that of standard English versions in two places: MT 3:31–33 is part of chapter 4 in English (4:1–3), and MT Dan 6:1 is included at the end of chapter 5 in English (5:31). This then causes all of the English verse numbers to be different from those of the Hebrew in chapters 4 and 6.[121]

Qumran Manuscripts

Among the ancient texts found at Qumran, eight different fragmentary manuscripts of Daniel have survived. They are shown in figure 5.

The Qumran manuscripts generally confirm the trustworthiness of the Masoretic Text. The shift from Hebrew to Aramaic in 2:4b is preserved in 1QDan[a]. The shift from Aramaic to Hebrew in 8:1 is confirmed in 4QDan[a] and 4QDan[b]. These manuscripts confirm that Daniel was originally a dual-language composition. The Prayer of Azariah and the Song of the Three Young Men found in Daniel 3 in the Greek versions is absent from 1QDan[b] and 4QDan[d], confirming that they were later additions.

These Dead Sea Scrolls generally support the consonantal text of the MT. The large majority of the variants are morphological, orthographic, or phonological. In a few cases, the scrolls offer superior readings to the MT (as noted in the textual notes), but "on the whole, the Qumran discoveries provide powerful evidence of the antiquity of the textual tradition of the MT."[122]

Daniel in the Greek Traditions

The Old Greek and Theodotion

Two ancient Greek versions of Daniel are extent in the surviving manuscripts. The Old Greek survives in a few manuscripts, but at an early time, the translation attributed to Theodotion replaced it in the church. Thus many more manuscripts of the Theodotion version survive. For a long time, the Old Greek was known only through one Greek manuscript, which was a copy of Origen's

---

[121] See "Introduction to Daniel 4" and "Introduction to Daniel 6."
[122] Collins, *Daniel*, 3.

Greek Hexapla text, Codex Chisianus (manuscript 88). To this day this manuscript is the only nearly complete copy of the Old Greek version of Daniel. More recently, pre-Hexaplaric manuscripts of the Old Greek tradition have been brought to light, enabling a critical edition of the Old Greek to be republished in revised form in the Göttingen Septuagint series in 1999.[123] However, it ought to be kept in mind that there are currently only three major witnesses to the Old Greek, with a number of minor witnesses also available.

The Greek translations of Daniel contain material not found in the MT. The Prayer of Azariah and the Song of the Three Young Men are inserted into Daniel 3 after 3:23.[124] The account of Susanna is found before Daniel 1 in the Theodotion version, but after Daniel 12 in the Old Greek version. The story of Bel and the Serpent concludes Daniel in both the Old Greek and Theodotion.[125]

The Old Greek differs from the MT most often in Daniel 4–6. The differences have led to much discussion among scholars as to the translation method used by the Old Greek in these chapters and whether the Old Greek or the MT preserves an earlier form of the text. Albertz and, later, McLay concluded that the Old Greek of Daniel 4–6 originated from a different translator than the rest of the Old Greek of Daniel.[126]

The Old Greek most probably was translated in the late second century BC.[127] This translation seems to read quite differently than the MT in many places, leading some scholars to conclude either that it was following a noticeably different Hebrew *Vorlage* or that the translator was tendentious due to his own theological biases.[128] However, recent studies by Jeansonne and McLay have concluded that neither is the case; rather, the Old Greek's *Vorlage* was not exactly the same as the MT, but it also was not wildly divergent from it. Jeansonne explains:

> The possibility that the OG [Old Greek] is faithful to its own divergent *Vorlage* must also be considered and indeed accounts for some of the variants in the OG of Daniel. …
>
> The OG tries to render faithfully the *Vorlage* into well-constructed Greek prose. However, unlike the recension of θ´ [Theodotion], the OG is not concerned with standardizing roots or grammatical forms and employs a much wider vocabulary. For these reasons, it is fair to say that the OG is a freer

---

[123] See Ziegler and Munnich, *Susanna, Daniel, Bel et Draco*.

[124] In the Greek versions, the Prayer of Azariah is 3:24–45, followed by five verses of prose (3:46–50), and the Song of the Three Young Men is 3:51–90. Greek 3:91–97 corresponds to MT/ET 3:24–30.

[125] Papyrus 967 (Old Greek) reverses the order at the end of Daniel, with Bel and the Serpent following Daniel 12 and Susanna concluding the book.

[126] Albertz, *Der Gott des Daniel*; McLay, *The OG and Th Versions of Daniel*, 212.

[127] See Collins, *Daniel*, 8; Hartman and Di Lella, *Daniel*, 78; Montgomery, *Daniel*, 38.

[128] However, Jeansonne, *The Old Greek Translation of Daniel 7–12*, has concluded that the translator followed a text close to that of the MT, but that his translation technique was less rigid due to his concern to make the text read smoothly in Greek.

translation than that of θ´. ... The OG is reasonably accurate and faithful. ... Employing a diverse vocabulary and being unconcerned with standardization of roots or of grammatical forms is simply a typical characteristic of the translation as a whole. ...

The translator did indeed err when reading the words and deciphering the letters of words in the *Vorlage*. ...

The OG translator was not attempting to depart from the meaning or implications of the Semitic *Vorlage*. ... The translator is not engaging in any particular interpretative activity.

Thus, our over-all assessment maintains that the OG translator of Daniel 7–12 attempted to translate accurately the *Vorlage* available of the day. In the attempt to translate, the OG translator was most concerned with conveying an accurate rendering in Greek of the Semitic text available. If, on occasion, this required that an antecedent be expressed, a phrase in apposition be added, a paraphrase be used, or that one particular connotation of a word be emphasized, the translator felt free to do so. However, these changes were not made to depart intentionally from the meaning of the Semitic text. The OG translator was more concerned with providing an interesting and readable Greek style than a consistent, standardized translation.[129]

McLay says:

For the most part, OG provided a faithful rendition of a *Vorlage*, which was very similar to, and, in most cases, basically identical with MT. ... OG's translation was not only faithful to the semantic content of his parent text, but also exhibited a relatively high degree of formal equivalence to MT. However, OG is usually regarded as a "free" translation, and there were particular features about his TT [translation technique] that were identified as characteristic of his dynamic approach. The most consistent characteristic of OG's dynamic approach was variety in the choice of lexical equivalents. OG also employed various methods to avoid excessive parataxis. ... OG often made small additions or introduced slight changes in the syntax in order to make something explicit that was implicit. Most of these changes should be regarded as attempts to remain faithful to the content and intention of the *Vorlage*. However, there were occasions, sometimes due to misunderstanding the parent text, that OG's theology was more evident in the translation (eg. 3:17).[130]

The translation attributed to Theodotion became the early church's version of Daniel. Although Theodotion was supposed to have lived and worked in the late second century AD, the NT occasionally quotes Theodotion readings, and Josephus seems to have known and used it.[131] Therefore, it is probably to be dated no later than the early first century AD.

---

[129] Jeansonne, *The Old Greek Translation of Daniel 7–12*, 131–33.

[130] McLay, *The OG and Th Versions of Daniel*, 211–12.

[131] For example, in Josephus, *Antiquities*, 10.190, 192–93, Nebuchadnezzar's official is called Ἀσχάνη, corresponding to Theodotion's Ασφανεζ in Dan 1:3, not the Old Greek's Αβιεσδρι.

There is disagreement among scholars as to whether Theodotion is a correction of the Old Greek,[132] a new translation by a person who knew the Old Greek,[133] or a completely independent translation. I agree with McLay, who states:

> There is ample evidence that Th [Theodotion] was translating independently from OG. ... Th has his own pattern of translation equivalents for vocabulary sharing the same domain (eg. knowing, wisdom) and his own way of resolving conflicts when two words are collocated that he normally renders by the same lexeme. That Th's translation pattern is substantially his own is also verified by the numerous HL [Hebrew language] and translation equivalents employed by Th that are not shared with OG. ... Th consistently makes his own contextual guess, rather than follow OG, when he does not understand MT. Finally, we have seen numerous omissions against MT and OG that would not be there if Th were revising OG toward MT. For these reasons, we can affirm that in the book of Daniel, the available evidence supports that Th is an independent translation of MT and not merely a revision of OG.[134]

Theodotion is generally easier to match with the Hebrew MT than is the Old Greek, but cannot always be assumed to allow accurate reconstruction of its *Vorlage*. This is a consequence of his translation technique. As McLay notes:

> Generally speaking, Th prefers to follow a consistent pattern of formal equivalence, but he deviates from that pattern when required. Th's formal equivalence is subordinated to his concern for clarity and the demands of the target language. ... Th's sensitivity to the meaning of the parent text is also exemplified by occasional renderings of lexemes with dynamic equivalents. A rather curious feature of Th's translation ... is the occasional omissions of words. Some of these omissions are due to textual problems, but not all. For these reasons, it would be completely inaccurate to assume that Th intended to provide a translation by which we could retranslate back to the semitic *Vorlage*. Th's reverence for the text is evident in his basic technique of formal equivalence, but it was an attempt to translate faithfully the meaning of the parent text.[135]

Thus the Old Greek and Theodotion are valuable from at least two perspectives: They provide some evidence for use in textual criticism of Daniel, especially when they agree.[136] They also provide us with insight into how specific passages in Daniel were understood among Jews in antiquity. Discussions of Old Greek and Theodotion readings can be found throughout the textual notes in this commentary.

The other ancient Greek translations, by Aquila and Symmachus (known from the Syriac translation of the Hexapla), reflect a Hebrew *Vorlage* nearly

---

[132] Collins, *Daniel*, 11.

[133] Hartman and Di Lella, *Daniel*, 82.

[134] McLay, *The OG and Th Versions of Daniel*, 216.

[135] McLay, *The OG and Th Versions of Daniel*, 212–13.

[136] However, these agreements must be used with caution, especially in the case of omissions against the MT. See McLay, *The OG and Th Versions of Daniel*, 213.

identical with the Masoretic Text. In a similar vein, the Vulgate and Syriac are based on texts very similar to MT. Therefore, these versions seldom contribute to text critical discussions about variant texts.

The Old Latin, Coptic, and Ethiopic versions of Daniel are daughter translations of the Greek versions (most often Theodotion), and, therefore, are of little use in textual criticism.

The Greek Additions to Daniel

It is well-known that the Greek versions of Daniel contain three major additions: (1) the story of Susanna, (2) the account of Bel and the Serpent, and (3) the Prayer of Azariah and the Song of the Three Young Men. None of these are extant in Hebrew or Aramaic, but scholars are generally agreed that they were composed in a Semitic language. They probably were part of the Greek translations from their beginning, but whether or not they were ever part of a Hebrew and Aramaic recension of Daniel is disputed. However, Moore makes a strong case that they were never incorporated into the original language text of Daniel:

> The external evidence supports and reinforces the impression drawn from the internal evidence, i.e. there are no ancient Hebrew or Aramaic texts containing any of these Additions, no indisputable instances of their being quoted in the Talmud, and no extant Greek translation of them by Aquila, the Jewish convert of the second century A.D. who translated the then-current masoretic text (MT) into slavishly literal Greek.[137]

The Jewish tradition has never considered the Greek additions to be part of the biblical canon. Roman Catholics treat these additions as part of the canon, placing them among the deuterocanonical books. Luther rejected their canonical status, but placed them, along with other books of the Apocrypha, between the Old and New Testaments in his German Bible. Since these additions to Daniel were generally known to earlier generations of Lutherans, they have had some effect on Lutheran piety and worship. Thus though it is not considered to be part of Scripture, the Song of the Three Young Men is often found in Lutheran hymnals as a canticle and still may be sung or chanted in worship.[138]

These insertions, which often attempt to enhance theological themes in the Hebrew and Aramaic Daniel, testify to the popularity of Daniel in the second century BC, if not earlier. They serve as an attempt to strengthen the book's message of commitment to monotheism and trust in deliverance by God, as he promised to Israel.

Susanna

The story of Susanna introduces us to a beautiful young woman, the wife of Joakim, a wealthy Jew living in Babylon during the exile. Two elders who were also judges lusted after Susanna. They insisted that she satisfy their lust and threatened to charge her with adultery if she did not. When she refused, out

---

[137] Moore, *Daniel, Esther, and Jeremiah*, 5.
[138] E.g., *LSB* 930 and 931 or *LW* 9.

of loyalty to God's Law and her husband, they accused her in open court. They claimed to have discovered her committing adultery with a young man. They testified that the man escaped and that they were unable to identify him. The court believed the elders and sentenced Susanna to death. However, Susanna cried to God for vindication, and God moved Daniel to intervene. Daniel caught the two elders in an inconsistency in their testimony. As a result, Susanna was spared, but the elders were executed. As a further result, Daniel's reputation was increased.

This story could serve as a kind of introduction to Daniel and his wisdom, and so it is not surprising that it is placed at the beginning of Daniel in the Theodotion tradition. However, in the Old Greek tradition it is placed after Daniel 12 and before Bel and the Serpent, though in Papyrus 967 (Old Greek), it is placed after Bel and the Serpent.

The Old Greek and Theodotion versions of the story differ quite markedly in several places.[139] There is no consensus among scholars as to whether Susanna was originally composed in either Hebrew or Aramaic. Nor is there agreement on the date or place of composition of this story, or whether or not it is a Jewish adaptation of a tale from outside the Jewish community. Since it is included in the Old Greek version, it could not have been composed later than the second century BC.

In its present form, Susanna reinforces Jewish theology, piety, and morality in harmony with the OT. While it presents an entertaining story, it also reinforces the importance of obedience to God's Law and confirms the theological themes that God eventually will vindicate the righteous and punish sinners, particularly those who persecute the faithful.

Bel and the Serpent

Bel and the Serpent is sometimes called Bel and the Dragon because the Greek for "serpent" in it is δράκων, which can be transliterated as "dragon."[140] The story consists of two episodes. In the first, the king of Babylon (Cyrus the Persian in Theodotion[141]) challenges Daniel as to why he refuses to worship Bel, the patron god of Babylon. Daniel replies that he only worships the living God, who created all things. The king maintains that Bel too is a living god, since he eats large quantities of food. Daniel, noting that Bel is made of clay and bronze, counters that Bel can eat nothing. This provokes the king into a rage in which he demands that either the priests of Bel must prove that he is a living god who eats or Daniel must prove that Bel does not eat. Whoever is wrong will be executed.

---

[139] DeSilva, *Introducing the Apocrypha*, 231–32; Moore, *Daniel, Esther, and Jeremiah: The Additions*, 78–80.

[140] In the NT, δράκων refers to Satan and so is properly translated as "dragon" (Revelation 12–13; 16:13; 20:2).

[141] The following summary follows Theodotion's translation.

The king lays food in front of Bel in his temple for the evening. Then Daniel has ashes scattered on the floor, and Daniel and the king shut the temple and seal the door. The next morning the seals are found intact, but the food is gone. Daniel points out to the king that in the ashes are the footprints of men, women, and children. The king then forces the priests to reveal that they had gained entry into the temple through a secret entrance at night and had consumed the food set before Bel. The king then executes the priests and authorizes Daniel to destroy Bel and his temple.

The second episode involves a serpent. The king invites Daniel to worship it, since it must be a living god. Daniel disproves this claim by feeding the serpent a concoction made of fat, pitch, and hair, causing its death. The Babylonians, incensed by Daniel's treatment of their gods (Bel and the snake), demand that Daniel be thrown into a den of lions. The lions, though obviously hungry, do not eat Daniel, who is in the den for a week. On the sixth day, Daniel is fed by God, who has an angel transport the prophet Habakkuk from Judea with some stew and bread. At the end of the week, Daniel is discovered to be alive. The king then acknowledges the one true God, and the Babylonians who opposed Daniel are thrown into the den and immediately devoured by the lions.

Like Susanna, there are a number of differences between the Old Greek and Theodotion versions of Bel and the Serpent. However, the differences are not as stark.[142] Scholarly consensus on the date and place of composition or the language of the original story (Hebrew or Aramaic) does not exist, though like Susanna, it could not have been composed later than the end of the second century BC. In both the Old Greek (except for Papyrus 967) and Theodotion, Bel and the Serpent concludes Daniel. Clearly, its account of Daniel in the lions' den owes much to the account in Daniel 6, but seeks to magnify both God and Daniel in the eyes of the reader since Daniel stays in the den longer (a week instead of overnight) and is implied to be part of the company of the prophets when Habakkuk visits him. Moreover, the outright declaration of monotheism by the Babylonian king (Bel 41) surpasses the praise given to God by pagan kings in the Hebrew and Aramaic text of Daniel.[j]

(j) Dan 2:47; 3:28–29; 4:31–32 (ET 4:34–35); 6:26–28 (ET 6:25–27)

Most obviously, Bel and the Serpent assertively advocates devotion to the one God and rejection of idolatry as not only contrary to reality but also as simpleminded and foolish. Unlike the accounts in the Hebrew and Aramaic text of Daniel, in the story Daniel aggressively challenges pagan beliefs and succeeds in converting the pagan king. In addition, the story reinforces the theme that God will rescue his faithful people and vindicate them, a theme already well-developed in the Hebrew and Aramaic text of Daniel.

The Prayer of Azariah and the Song of the Three Young Men

The only major addition in the Greek versions of Daniel to be inserted within the chapters of the Hebrew and Aramaic book are two liturgical pieces

---

[142] See DeSilva, *Introducing the Apocrypha*, 237–38; Moore, *Daniel, Esther, and Jeremiah: The Additions*, 129.

attributed to the young men who are thrown into the fiery furnace in Daniel 3. These are inserted following 3:23.

In Greek versions, 3:24–45, is the Prayer of Azariah. He confesses his people's sins against God and his covenant, admits that God has been just in bringing disasters upon his people and prays for vindication and deliverance for them. In its general content, it shows dependence on other prayers of corporate confession in the OT, especially Dan 9:4–19 and Neh 9:26–37.

The Prayer of Azariah is connected to the Song of the Three Young Men by five verses of prose (3:46–50). The song (3:51–90) is a psalm of praise to God, calling on all creation to bless his holy name. It shows thematic and formulaic dependence on the book of Psalms, especially Psalms 103 and 148.

The differences between the Old Greek and Theodotion versions of this insertion into Daniel are slight and mostly involve the ordering of a couple of verses in the Song of the Three Young Men. Due to the presence of several Hebraisms in Theodotion, there is general agreement among scholars that this portion of Greek Daniel was originally composed in Hebrew. It was probably composed in Palestine, and like the other additions to Daniel, it could not have been composed later than the end of the second century BC.

Theologically, the Prayer of Azariah reinforces themes found explicitly in Daniel only in Daniel 9. It serves to justify and explain God's use of pagan nations to chastise Israel, and to set forth a model for repentance and faith in God's deliverance. The Song of the Three, with its call to all creation to praise God, serves to outdo the pagan kings, who elsewhere in Daniel call on their subjects to honor and praise God (3:28–29; 6:26–28 [ET 6:25–27]).

Qumran Daniel Traditions

The Greek additions to Daniel are not the only testimony to the popularity of Daniel among Jews immediately prior to the birth of Jesus. Several compositions apparently related to Daniel were also discovered among the finds at Qumran. All of these survive in only a few fragments, and their text is difficult to reconstruct. Several other manuscripts have been proposed as relating in some way to Daniel, but are less likely to be directly related.[143]

The Prayer of Nabonidus (4QPrNab ar/4Q242)[144]

The Prayer of Nabonidus survives in several fragments from the first column of a manuscript and several fragments of a later column. Although the

---

[143] These include 4QpapApocalypse ar (4Q489), which survives in eight small scraps of papyrus and shares two words with Daniel; 4QDaniel Suzanna? ar (4Q551), which mentions a judge who is prominent in a court, and which some scholars view as a variant version of Susanna; and 4QFour Kingdoms[a–b] ar (4Q552–4Q553), which depicts four trees that represent four kingdoms. While this last composition shares with Daniel the four kingdom scheme and the characterization of God as the Most High, the kingdoms it depicts are different, and it has little else in common with Daniel. See Flint, "The Daniel Tradition at Qumran," 361–63.

[144] For details and analysis, see Collins, "4QPrayer of Nabonidus ar"; Flint, "The Daniel Tradition at Qumran," 332–38.

beginning speaks of a prayer of Nabonidus, none of the surviving fragments contain the prayer itself. The beginning of the document tells us that for seven years while living in Tema, Nabonidus suffered from a disease brought upon him by God's decree. A Jewish diviner advised the king to honor God instead of the idols he had been worshiping.

The parallel to the story of Nebuchadnezzar's madness in Daniel 4 is striking. Many critical scholars believe that the Prayer of Nabonidus is an older (and, they suppose, somewhat more accurate) version of Daniel 4. However, the prayer is most certainly a composition based on Daniel (see the excursus "Daniel 4 and the Prayer of Nabonidus"). It is significant to note that in the surviving manuscripts, Daniel is never named.

The surviving copy of the prayer was copied between 75 and 50 BC.[145] How much earlier the Prayer of Nabonidus was composed is a matter of conjecture.

Pseudo-Daniel (4QpsDan^{a-c} ar/4Q243–4Q245)[146]

Three Pseudo-Daniel manuscripts were discovered in the fourth cave at Qumran. Originally scholars assumed that these were parts of the same composition. However, subsequent analysis has led to the conclusion that while 4QpsDan^a and 4QpsDan^b are from the same source, 4QpsDan^c derives from a different composition altogether.

The first Pseudo-Daniel composition (4QpsDan^{a-b}) is a historical review with an eschatological ending depicting God's final vindication and deliverance of his people. This is a familiar type of literature, the historical apocalypse, and is an ornate development deriving its method from several biblical texts, most notably portions of Daniel and Zechariah.[147] From the period before Christ, there are several other examples of such apocalypses found at Qumran, including the Animal Apocalypse and the Apocalypse of Weeks, both of which are incorporated into the pseudepigraphal book of *1 Enoch*.

Flint outlines this Pseudo-Daniel apocalypse as follows:

The Court Setting, where Daniel addresses King Belshazzar and his court and explains a writing or book which probably contained the overview of biblical history that follows.

The Primeval History, dealing with the events or material found in Genesis 5–11 (including Enoch, the flood, and the Tower of Babel). It appears that the Creation and Fall did not feature in Daniel's survey of history.

From the Patriarchs to the Exile, including the time in Egypt, crossing the Jordan, the tabernacle, Nebuchadnezzar's conquest, and the exile.

---

[145] Collins, "4QPrayer of Nabonidus ar," 85; Flint, "The Daniel Tradition at Qumran," 332.

[146] For details and analysis, see Collins and Flint, "4Qpseudo-Daniel^{a-c} ar"; Flint, "The Daniel Tradition at Qumran," 338–60.

[147] See Steinmann, "The Shape of Things to Come," 25–47.

The Hellenistic Era, which is distinguished from the preceding ones by the presentation of events as yet to come and by the presence of Greek proper names *(Balakros*,]*rhos*, and]*s, son of)*.

The Eschatological Period, which specifies a time of oppression, but then how (God) will save them "with his great hand." Several further terms connote the destruction and restoration associated with the eschatological age.[148]

There are several connections between this work and Daniel, including the mention of Belshazzar and Daniel, and the review of Hellenistic history from a Jewish perspective (paralleling the prophecy about Hellenistic kings in Daniel 11). While its author obviously was acquainted with Daniel, this composition is not modeled on the biblical text, but takes some of Daniel's features as a point of departure for propounding its own view of history and eschatology. Its most likely date of composition is between 200 BC and the capture of Jerusalem by Pompey (63 BC),[149] although the fragments of these two manuscripts were copied in the first century AD.[150]

The third Pseudo-Daniel manuscript (4QpsDan^c) is preserved in four fragments. Two of these (fragments 3 and 4) are of little consequence, since one preserves only two words and the other only part of a single word. Fragment 1 apparently contains text from near the beginning of the work, while fragment 2 contains the final words of the composition. Apparently the work claims to be a new revelation, mentioning Daniel and a book that was given (lines 3 and 4). Then follows a list of the descendants of Levi beginning with Kohath (1 Chr 6:1 [ET 6:16]) and continuing through the Hellenistic high priest Onias and the Hasmoneans Jonathan and Simon. Next follows a list of Israel's kings. The second fragment apparently describes the eschatological conclusion of history. Since this conclusion mentions two groups, one of which is blind and has gone astray while the other is predicted to arise and return, the most probable function of the lists in fragment 1 is to demonstrate how both the priesthood and the kingship had gone astray.[151] Since fragment 2 mentions some who will arise, some scholars have seen this as reference to resurrection. However, not enough context has been preserved to draw any definitive conclusion on the matter.

This Pseudo-Daniel text is connected to Daniel only through the mention of his name and a book (see Dan 10:21; 12:1, 4) and perhaps the eschatological dividing of humanity into two groups (cf. Dan 12:2). The manuscript was copied in Herodian times (early first century AD),[152] but the reference to Simon

---

[148] Flint, "The Daniel Tradition at Qumran," 339, including n. 26, citing Collins and Flint, "4Qpseudo-Daniel^{a-c} ar," 97–151.

[149] Collins and Flint, "4Qpseudo-Daniel^{a-c} ar," 137–38.

[150] Flint, "The Daniel Tradition at Qumran," 332.

[151] Flint, "The Daniel Tradition at Qumran," 355–56.

[152] Flint, "The Daniel Tradition at Qumran," 352.

means that it dates to sometime after the beginning of his reign in 142, perhaps to the reign of his successor, John Hyrcanus (135–104 BC).[153]

The Son of God Text (4QApocalypse ar/4Q246)

This text contains two surviving columns. Half of the first column is torn. The second column is intact. Most importantly, the second column describes someone about whom it is said, "He will be called the Son of God, and they will call him Son of the Most High" (line 2). Later it is said, "[He is] a great God among the gods" (line 7), and the reader is told that "his kingdom is an eternal kingdom" (line 5) and "his dominion is an eternal dominion" (line 9). This is reminiscent of Lk 1:32–33, 35, but the language is also similar to the presentation of the Son of Man before the Ancient of Days in Dan 7:13–14. The relationship between this text and Daniel is uncertain because Daniel is not mentioned. The text may be read as if it is being spoken by a Jewish seer in the presence of a Gentile king, perhaps recalling Daniel in the court of the Babylonian kings.[154] The date of the composition of the Son of God text is uncertain, but it can be no later than the last third of the first century BC, the date of the copying of the Qumran scroll.

Summary

Thus the materials related to Daniel among the Dead Sea Scrolls testify to an ongoing fascination with Daniel and its eschatology. While these works are preserved in now fragmentary texts, they demonstrate that the hope for God's eternal kingdom was alive among Jews immediately before and during the ministry of Jesus, and that they understood Daniel to be a genuine prophet, whose work they imitated in their own eschatological writings, and whose name they adopted to give their works an appearance of divine authority.

---

[153] Collins and Flint, "4Qpseudo-Daniel^{a-c} ar," 158; Flint, "The Daniel Tradition at Qumran," 356.

[154] Flint, "The Daniel Tradition at Qumran," 361.

Daniel 1:1–21

The Judeans Are Steadfast in Practicing Their Faith

Introduction to Daniel 1

1:1–2	The Beginning of the Babylonian Captivity
1:3–7	Young Judeans from the Nobility Are Pressed into Service in the Babylonian Court
1:8–21	The Judeans Are Steadfast in Practicing Their Faith
Excursus	*Daniel's View of the Exile*

Introduction to Daniel 1

Major Emphases in Daniel 1

The first chapter of Daniel serves as an introduction to the rest of the narrative portions of Daniel (Daniel 2–6). Here we are introduced to the Babylonian exile and Daniel's experience of it. We meet Nebuchadnezzar, the king who will dominate the narrative in the next four chapters. We are told that the vessels from the temple in Jerusalem were taken captive, an important piece of information that will help explain their appearance again in Daniel 5. We are introduced to Daniel's companions Azariah, Hananiah, and Mishael. They will appear again in Daniel 2 and be the focus of attention in Daniel 3.

The chapter opens with the first capture of Jerusalem by Nebuchadnezzar in 605 BC (1:1–2), when he took the articles from the temple and the first exiles from the young Judean nobility. He brought both the articles and the first exiles to Babylon to be used as he saw fit (1:2–7). However, some of the young Judeans resolved to resist attempts to acculturate them to Babylonian ways, and the tension is resolved through the intervention of God on behalf of the faithful Judean young men. Thus we are introduced not only to Nebuchadnezzar, Daniel, and others, but we are also introduced to the gracious God of Israel and his saving work.

Moreover, the introductions to people and things, important as they are for the narratives in Daniel, are less important than the introduction to themes that will dominate the entire book of Daniel. The first of these themes is that God is in control over all things that happen among humans. This is signaled throughout this chapter, reemphasized in every subsequent narrative chapter and is clearly in focus in Daniel's visions of future events (Daniel 7–12). The readers cannot escape the conclusion that God governs all of history for the benefit of his people. Of course, ultimately, the point of this guidance of history is redemption. "But when the fullness of time had come, God sent forth his Son, born of woman, born under the Law, in order to redeem those who were under the Law, so that we might receive the adoption of sons" (Gal 4:4–5).[1]

Second, we are introduced to one of the central concerns of faithful Judeans throughout the Babylonian captivity: how does a believer deal with living in a pagan culture? Daniel and his companions have to answer this question from the start, and this chapter demonstrates that they were determined to remain faithful to God despite the pagan context in which they were forced to live.

A third theme, related to the second, is the question of how a believer deals with authorities in the context of a pagan culture. Before the captivity,

---

[1] For the theme of God's governance of history for the purpose of redemption, see further "The Messiah in Daniel: An Overview" in "Major Themes" in the introduction.

the people of Israel could assume that the covenant that Yahweh made with his people was at least officially tolerated by their Israelite authorities, even if it was not always followed in practice. However, in Babylonian society there was no understanding of the unique features of Israel's religious practices and beliefs, especially of the belief that there is only one God. In this chapter, we learn that Daniel and his companions find a way to practice their faith despite the orders of the king. Yet they do not break the Fourth Commandment (which mandates respect for human authority), but they work through the various levels of authority in Babylon, enabling them to keep both the First and the Fourth Commandments. By their behavior they acknowledge what Paul would later write: "there is no authority except from God, and those that exist have been established by God" (Rom 13:1).[2]

Finally, we are introduced to another theme that runs throughout the book: God gives gifts to his people so that they can serve him. This theme is frequently and explicitly highlighted in the narrative portions of Daniel and is the underlying assumption in the visions. Daniel and all faithful Judeans survive and even prosper in the captivity because God blesses them with the gifts that he abundantly showers on his people.[3]

---

[2] For a discussion of how the book of Daniel reflects the First and Fourth Commandments, see further "God's Law in Daniel" in "Law and Gospel in Daniel" in the introduction.

[3] For this theme, see further "God as the Protector of His People" in "Major Themes" in the introduction.

Daniel 1:1–2
The Beginning of the Babylonian Captivity

Translation

1 ¹In the third year of the reign of King Jehoiakim of Judah, King Nebuchadnezzar of Babylon came to Jerusalem and besieged it. ²The Lord gave into his hand King Jehoiakim of Judah and some of the vessels of the house of God, and he brought them to the land of Shinar, into the house of his god. He brought the vessels into the treasury of his god.

Textual Notes

1:1 נְבוּכַדְנֶאצַּר—This name is the Hebrew transliteration of the Babylonian name Nabu-kudurri-usur, "(the god) Nebo protect my offspring." "Nebuchadnezzar" is spelled this way only here in Daniel, though this is a common spelling elsewhere in the OT.[a] Elsewhere in Daniel, the spelling is נְבֻכַדְנֶצַּר (e.g., 1:18) or נְבוּכַדְנֶצַּר (e.g., 2:28). The second nun (-נ-) represents nasalization of an original *resh*. The name spelled with *resh* (נְבוּכַדְרֶאצַּר) is used frequently by Jeremiah (e.g., 21:2) and always by Ezekiel (e.g., 26:7).

(a) 2 Ki 24:11; 25:22; Jer 27:6, 8, 20; 28:3; 29:1, 3; Esth 2:6; 2 Chr 36:6–7, 10, 13

וַיָּצַר עָלֶיהָ—The third masculine singular imperfect verb (with *waw* consecutive) probably is the Qal (G) of צוּר, "besiege" (BDB, s.v. צוּר II, 2) or "lay siege to" (*HALOT*, s.v. צוּר I, 3). See Joüon, § 23 b. The form could also be the Hiphil (H) of one of the צרר verbs, which can mean "cause distress" or "attack," but which here would have to have the nuance "besiege." The prepositional phrase עָלֶיהָ could be rendered literally as "(lay siege) against her." The suffix is feminine because cities (here יְרוּשָׁלַם) are feminine.

1:2 אֲדֹנָי—Daniel seldom refers to God except as אֱלֹהִים in Hebrew (eighteen times) and אֱלָהּ in Aramaic (thirty-seven times). The title for God here, אֲדֹנָי, "Lord," occurs also in 9:3–4, 7, 9, 15–17, 19. Its Aramaic equivalent, מָרֵא, refers to God in 2:47 and 5:23. The divine name, יהוה, occurs in 9:2, 4, 8, 10, 13–14, 20.

וּמִקְצָת כְּלֵי בֵית־הָאֱלֹהִים— In the OT, only in literature of the early Persian period is the construct of the noun קְצָת, "end," used with the preposition מִן in a partitive sense (BDB, s.v. מִן, 3 b (*a*)): literally, "from the end of." Here and in Neh 7:69 (ET 7:70), the expression carries the meaning "some of." In Dan 1:5, 15, 18, it has the temporal meaning "at the end of, after." כְּלִי (plural in construct: כְּלֵי) is a general term for almost any kind of "vessel, utensil, receptacle," but is often used for those in the tabernacle and temple (see BDB, s.v. כְּלִי, 2 f).

וַיְבִיאֵם אֶרֶץ־שִׁנְעָר בֵּית אֱלֹהָיו—The antecedent of the third masculine plural suffix on the Hiphil (H) of בּוֹא, "he brought *them*," refers back to both objects of the preceding verb, וַיִּתֵּן, "(the Lord) gave" both "Jehoiakim" and the "vessels" בְּיָדוֹ, "into his [Nebuchadnezzar's] hand."

Both of the construct phrases, אֶרֶץ־שִׁנְעָר, "the land of Shinar," and בֵּית אֱלֹהָיו, "the house/temple of his god," are accusative phrases that indicate the direction or goal of motion (see Joüon, § 125 n). English requires the addition of "to" or "into."

"Shinar" is the biblical name for lower (southern) Mesopotamia.[b] Daniel probably uses it here for its connection in Genesis with the Mesopotamian warrior-king Nimrod, the first empire builder mentioned in the OT (Gen 10:8–10), as well as its connection with the scattering of people from the tower of Babel (Gen 11:2).

בֵּית אוֹצַר אֱלֹהָיו—Literally, "the house of the treasury of his god," this is a reference to storehouses or rooms adjacent to a temple (*HALOT*, s.v. אוֹצָר, b). Such sacred treasuries were common in the ancient Near East, including Israel (Josh 6:19, 24).

(b) Gen 10:10; 11:2; 14:1, 9; Josh 7:21; Is 11:11; Zech 5:11; Dan 1:2

Commentary
The Events of 605 BC (1:1)

Daniel begins by referring to activities by King Nebuchadnezzar "in the third year" of Jehoiakim. These activities occurred in the part of Jehoiakim's third year that was in 605 BC.[1] This is the first of a number of chronological notices that date major sections of the book of Daniel, as shown in figure 6.

Figure 6

Chronological Notices in Daniel

Section of Daniel	Chronological Notice
Daniel 1	Third year of Jehoiakim (1:1)
Daniel 2	Second year of Nebuchadnezzar (2:1)
Daniel 7	First year of Belshazzar (7:1)
Daniel 8	Third year of Belshazzar (8:1)
Daniel 9	First year of Darius (9:1)
Daniel 10–12	Third year of Cyrus (10:1)

However, the very first phrase of Daniel, "in the third year" of Jehoiakim, has been a historical problem for interpreters because Jer 25:1 equates the fourth year of Jehoiakim with Nebuchadnezzar's first year. The problem is easily solved, however, when it is noted that Jeremiah employs the nonaccession-year system for counting the years of a king's reign.[2] Under this system, if a king began his reign in the middle of a year, this first, partial year was counted as his

---

[1] The third year of Jehoiakim was September 19, 606–October 6, 605.

[2] The nonaccession-year system was used in the book of Kings for Jehoiakim's successors in Judah (Jehoiachin and Zedekiah). See Young, "When Did Jerusalem Fall?" 38. This is contrary to Thiele (*Mysterious Numbers*, 215), who assumed that from Amaziah onward the reigns of all the kings of Judah were reckoned according to the accession-year system. The reigns of Judean kings from Jehoram though Joash were also reckoned according to the nonaccession-year system (Thiele, *Mysterious Numbers*, 215).

first year. Daniel, however, uses the accession-year system that was current in Babylon under the Babylonian and Persian kings.[3] This system did not count the partial year at the beginning of a king's reign. Thus under the nonaccession-year system used by Jeremiah, this was Jehoiakim's fourth year, counting his partial first (accession) year as his first year. However, under the accession-year system used by Daniel, this was Jehoiakim's third year, with his accession year not counted in the total.

This first siege of Jerusalem fits well with the events of 605 BC. Sometime between the beginning of the spring campaign in Nisan (April 12–May 10)[4] and the death of Nebuchadnezzar's father, Nabopolassar, on the eighth of Ab (August 16), most likely during the month of Ziv (May 11–June 9) or Sivan (June 10–July 8), the Babylonian forces, led by Crown Prince Nebuchadnezzar, defeated the Egyptian forces of Pharaoh Neco on the border of Syria at Carchemish on the Euphrates River, then pursued them as far as Hamath on the Orontes River in central Syria, where Nebuchadnezzar finished off the Egyptian troops.[5] The Babylonian Chronicle states that following the battle, Nebuchadnezzar conquered Syria-Palestine.[6] This would mean that perhaps during the end of the month of Ziv and most certainly in the months of Sivan (June 10–July 8), Tammuz (July 9–August 7), and much of Ab (August 8–September 6), until word reached him that his father had died,[7] Nebuchadnezzar subdued Syria and Palestine—that is, from about June 1 to August 26. This was undoubtedly easy if, as the Babylonian Chronicle reports, the Egyptian army and its allies were thoroughly defeated. On the first day of Elul 605 (September

---

[3] Daniel used accession-year dating, as was common in Babylon, where he was trained in the royal court. For Jehoiakim, he reckoned the years starting in Tishri, as was the custom in Judah throughout its history (Thiele, *Mysterious Numbers*, 53). This is the only way that Daniel's reckoning matches Jeremiah's. If Daniel had used years starting in Nisan, Jehoiakim's third year would have ended on the first day of Nisan 605, before the Battle of Carchemish. The Babylonians reckoned regnal years as beginning in Nisan. This calendrical procedure in Daniel, in which a biblical author uses the method for counting regnal years in use in the country in which he resides (in this case Babylon), but mixes it with the starting month of the king's country, is also a procedure sometimes employed by the author of Kings (see Thiele, *Mysterious Numbers*, 49–50, 53; Young, "When Did Jerusalem Fall?" 32, n. 17).

[4] These dates are determined using Parker and Dubberstein, *Babylonian Chronology 626 B.C.–A.D. 75*, 27.

[5] See Wiseman, *Chronicles of Chaldean Kings (626–556 B.C.) in the British Museum*, 23–25, 46. Tablet BM 21946 describes the battle and the subsequent pursuit of the retreating Egyptian troops to Hamath in central Syria and their total defeat there (obverse, lines 3–7). After the account of the pursuit and defeat of the Egyptian troops, obverse, line 10, tells that Nabopolassar died on 8 Ab (Wiseman, *Chronicles of Chaldean Kings*, 66–69).

[6] BM 21946, obverse, line 8, says that Nebuchadnezzar conquered "all Hatti-land," which included Judah, as is obvious from reverse, lines 11–12 (see Wiseman, *Chronicles of Chaldean Kings*, 68–69, 72–73). Wiseman favors May–June (Ziv or early Sivan) for the Battle of Carchemish (Wiseman, *Chronicles of Chaldean Kings*, 25, and "Some Historical Problems in the Book of Daniel," 17).

[7] This probably took about ten days, which means that Nebuchadnezzar campaigned until toward the end of August. See Wiseman, *Chronicles of Chaldean Kings*, 26.

7), Nebuchadnezzar arrived in Babylon to claim the throne.[8] Thus he had over two months of the year 605 to subdue Syria-Palestine, including Judah, before his return to Babylon to assume the throne after his father's death.

Moreover, the Babylonian Chronicle tells us that after Nebuchadnezzar's coronation, he returned to Syria-Palestine that same year and campaigned until the month of Shebat (which began on February 2, 604).[9] Since it is almost certain that Nebuchadnezzar did not take his troops with him back to Babylon for his coronation (except for a small guard that traveled with him),[10] the entire campaign in Syria-Palestine, after the Battle of Carchemish, must have lasted some seven months or more. This is more than sufficient time for the siege of Jerusalem and the capture of Jehoiakim.[11]

During Shebat (February 2–March 2, 604), Nebuchadnezzar took the spoils of this campaign to Babylon.[12] This means that Jehoiakim and the other Judean captives probably arrived in Babylon during February 604 BC. See figure 7.

Figure 7

Nebuchadnezzar's Campaign of 605–604 BC

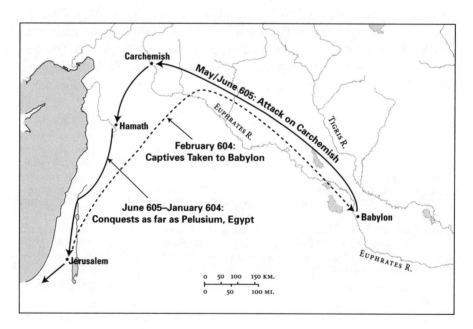

---

[8] BM 21946, obverse, line 11 (Wiseman, *Chronicles of Chaldean Kings*, 68–69).

[9] BM 21946, obverse, line 12 (Wiseman, *Chronicles of Chaldean Kings*, 68–69).

[10] See Wiseman, *Chronicles of Chaldean Kings*, 26.

[11] Since Daniel used years beginning in Tishri for Jehoiakim, Jehoiakim must have capitulated to Nebuchadnezzar before the first day of Tishri 605 (October 7, 605).

[12] BM 21946, obverse, line 13 (Wiseman, *Chronicles of Chaldean Kings*, 68–69).

That Nebuchadnezzar subdued all of Syria, including Palestine, is confirmed by Berosus and Josephus. Berosus states that Nebuchadnezzar entrusted the transportation of Judeans, Phoenicians, Syrians, and Egyptians to others, most likely because he hurriedly returned to Babylon to consolidate his grip on the throne.[13] Josephus tells us that Nebuchadnezzar took "all of Syria as far as Pelusium [at the eastern border of Egypt on the Mediterranean coast], except Judah."[14] This exception for Judah is probably an acknowledgement of Jehoiakim's capitulation, which allowed Judah to remain nominally independent as long as Jehoiakim paid tribute to Nebuchadnezzar each year (2 Ki 24:1).

While Nebuchadnezzar had time for a prolonged campaign in Judah after the Battle of Carchemish, Daniel simply states that Nebuchadnezzar besieged Jerusalem. He does not say that Jerusalem was conquered. Since "the Lord gave into his [Nebuchadnezzar's] hand King Jehoiakim of Judah" (1:2), Daniel may be indicating that Jehoiakim, an ally of the defeated Pharaoh Neco, capitulated almost immediately. Thus if Nebuchadnezzar was merely mopping up after his victory, Jerusalem may have been an easy plum to pick that year. That the Babylonian Chronicle does not specifically mention Judah as part of Nebuchadnezzar's campaign is not necessarily at variance with what Daniel says, since it is not always specific or complete.

Although this reconstruction of events is well-documented and endorsed by many commentators,[15] critical scholars often dismiss it and claim that Nebuchadnezzar never campaigned in Judah in 605 BC.[16] Instead, critical scholars often hold that the three years of subjugation of Jehoiakim to Nebuchadnezzar mentioned in 2 Ki 24:1 was somehow conflated with the account of Jehoiakim's capture in 2 Chr 36:6 and became the source of the beginning of Daniel. However, these scholars do not explain how three years of subjugation became the third year of Jehoiakim's reign, and this seems more like a feeble attempt to dismiss Daniel's data than to deal with it.

---

[13] Berosus, as quoted by Josephus, *Antiquities*, 10.220–22, and *Against Apion*, 1.135–37.

[14] Josephus, *Antiquities*, 10.86.

[15] Archer, "Daniel," 31–32; Baldwin, *Daniel*, 20–21, 77–78; Lucas, *Daniel*, 50–52; Mercer, "Daniel 1:1 and Jehoiakim's Three Years of Servitude"; Millard, "Daniel 1–6 and History," 69; Miller, *Daniel*, 56.

[16] Collins, *Daniel*, 130–32; Gowan, *Daniel*, 43–44; Hartman and Di Lella, *Daniel*, 128–29; Montgomery, *Daniel*, 113–16. Collins, in particular, argues that there is no Babylonian record of military activity in Judah before the Battle of Carchemish (which he dates as late as possible by placing it in June or July) and that there was no time between the battle and Nebuchadnezzar's coronation for him to conquer Jerusalem. He specifically discounts the evidence from Berosus as recorded by Josephus mainly because Berosus attributes the purpose of Nebuchadnezzar's campaign to the defeat a rebellious satrap in Egypt. While Berosus may have confused Pharaoh Neco with a Babylonian-appointed administrator of Egypt, this does not necessarily mean that his entire account of Nebuchadnezzar's campaign is inaccurate, as Collins assumes. Moreover, the confluence of facts in BM 21946, in Josephus' account (especially the mention of Pelusium), and in Berosus confirms that most of Berosus' account is a fairly accurate reflection of the events of 605 BC.

"He brought them to the land of Shinar, into the house of his god" (Dan 1:2) could be read as if Nebuchadnezzar brought both Jehoiakim and the vessels into the temple. However, the last clause in the verse, "he brought the vessels into the treasury of his god," clarifies that only the vessels were put into the temple treasury. Thus it would appear that Dan 1:2 agrees with 2 Chr 36:6–7, where we are told that Nebuchadnezzar "bound him [Jehoiakim] with bronze shackles to take him to Babylon" and "Nebuchadnezzar took some of the vessels of the house of Yahweh to Babylon and put them in his temple in Babylon." Apparently, Jehoiakim, who had been placed on the throne of Judah by Neco, heretofore had pursued a pro-Egyptian foreign policy. So he was taken to Babylon to make him swear a loyalty oath to Nebuchadnezzar before he was returned to his throne in Jerusalem as a Babylonian vassal.[17] The Assyrians may have done something similar with Manasseh (2 Chr 33:11–13), and to swear loyalty may also have been the reason that later Nebuchadnezzar made Zedekiah travel to Babylon (Jer 51:59–64).

Jehoiakim remained a loyal vassal of Nebuchadnezzar for three years, most likely sending him tribute each year (2 Ki 24:1). However, probably due to Nebuchadnezzar's disastrous campaign that ended in defeat at the hands of the Egyptians during Kislev of 601 BC (November 21–December 19),[18] Jehoiakim ceased his loyalty to Nebuchadnezzar. Jehoiakim died in December 598 before Nebuchadnezzar could exact vengeance. Jehoiachin succeeded him and continued to refuse tribute to Babylon. This then led to Jerusalem's fall to a resurgent Nebuchadnezzar only three months and ten days into Jehoiachin's reign after Jehoiakim's death in late 598 BC (2 Ki 24:10–12; 2 Chr 36:9).[19] At that time, Nebuchadnezzar replaced Jehoiachin with his uncle Zedekiah (2 Ki 24:17; 2 Chr 36:10).[20] Zedekiah continued to reign as a vassal until Jerusalem fell a third time in 587, when the temple was destroyed and the largest number of Judeans was exiled. See figure 8.

God's Control over the Events of 605 BC (1:2)

More importantly, Daniel makes it clear that "*the Lord* gave" Jehoiakim into Nebuchadnezzar's hand (1:2). Yahweh, the God whose temple and king were taken, is still in control. Just as he scattered humanity for its arrogance in building a tower in Babylon (Gen 11:1–9), he can and will judge the arrogance

---

[17] That Jehoiakim was returned to Jerusalem shortly after having been captured by Nebuchadnezzar is implied by the subsequent account of his reign in 2 Ki 24:1–6 and 2 Chr 36:5–8. Moreover, Jehoiakim was in Jerusalem during Kislev (November 24–December 23) 604; see Jer 36:9–26.

[18] See BM 21946, reverse, lines 6–7 (Wiseman, *Chronicles of Chaldean Kings*, 70–71).

[19] This fall of Jerusalem to Nebuchadnezzar was on 2 Adar 597 BC (March 16) according BM 21946, reverse, line 12 (Wiseman, *Chronicles of Chaldean Kings*, 72–73). This means that Jehoiakim died on 22 Bul 598 (December 10) and Jehoiachin reigned from 22 Bul 598 to 2 Adar 597 (December 10, 598–March 16, 597).

[20] That Nebuchadnezzar replaced Jehoiachin with Zedekiah is confirmed in BM 21946, reverse, line 13 (Wiseman, *Chronicles of Chaldean Kings*, 72–73).

of Babylonians again (the accounts of Daniel 3–4). God even permitted (but certainly did not cause or will) Nebuchadnezzar to profane the vessels of grace from his holy temple. Later Belshazzar too would commit sacrilege with these vessels, and God would execute judgment upon him that very night (see the commentary on 5:1–4, 30).

Dan 1:3 will say that the captives are from the nobility and the royal family, which also may signal God's control of the events as he may be fulfilling the prophecy of Is 39:7. That only the king himself and the nobility are mentioned as captives in Dan 1:2–3 points to God's longsuffering and mercy toward Judah. This deportation in 605 BC was only the first of three deportations to Babylon (see 2 Ki 24:15–16; 25:11; 2 Chr 36:20). The remaining people in Judah were given another chance to repent and turn to God. Unfortunately, the people of Judah did not repent and avail themselves of the mercy of God, leading to the catastrophe and third deportation in 587 BC. Likewise, the obduracy and rejection of the Messiah by the Jewish people as a whole would lead to the final destruction of Jerusalem in AD 70. Nevertheless, just as God's grace remained active among Daniel and the exiles and was even offered to their Babylonian captors, so also the remnant of Israel that believed in the Christ was scattered in order to bring the saving Gospel also to Gentiles, that it might be spread throughout the world, as indeed it has been to this day.

Figure 8

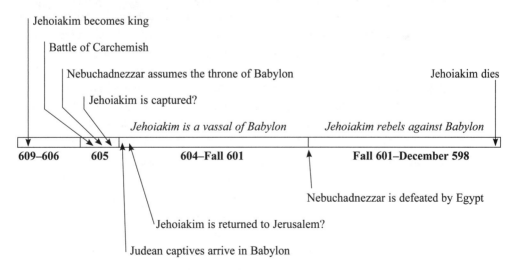

Daniel 1:3–7

Young Judeans from the Nobility Are Pressed into Service in the Babylonian Court

Translation

1 ³The king told Ashpenaz, the chief of his eunuchs, to bring from those sons of Israel who were from the royal family or from the nobility ⁴young men who had no blemish, were good looking, having insight into all kinds of wisdom, possessing knowledge, understanding learning, and who had ability for service in the king's palace—to teach them the literature and language of the Chaldeans. ⁵The king assigned them daily rations from the royal delicacies and the wine that he drank and that they should be trained for three years. At the end of their time [of training] they were to serve the king. ⁶Among them from the Judeans were Daniel, Hananiah, Mishael, and Azariah. ⁷The chief of the eunuchs gave them [new] names. He gave to Daniel [the name] "Belteshazzar," to Hananiah "Shadrach," to Mishael "Meshach," and to Azariah "Abednego."

Textual Notes

1:3 לְאַשְׁפְּנַז רַב סָרִיסָיו—There is no certain etymology for אַשְׁפְּנַז, "Ashpenaz." Some take it not as a name, but as a title derived from Old Persian *ashpinja*, "lodging," and conclude that this person was in charge of the lodgings for the captives. But it is attested as a name in at least one Aramaic inscription. It seems best to understand it as a name. He is called רַב סָרִיסָיו, "the chief of his [Nebuchadnezzar's] eunuchs." As a noun, רַב can mean "chief" (BDB, s.v. רַב II, under the root רבב I). Later he will be called by the equivalent title שַׂר הַסָּרִיסִים, literally, "the chief of the eunuchs" (1:7–11, 18). שַׂר can mean the "chief, head" over a class of officials (BDB, s.v. שַׂר, 4 a, under the root שׂרר).

מִבְּנֵי יִשְׂרָאֵל וּמִזֶּרַע הַמְּלוּכָה וּמִן־הַפַּרְתְּמִים:—Three prepositional phrases, each beginning with מִן, describe the lineage of those Judeans selected for training to serve in the Babylonian court. The first phrase, "from the sons of Israel," designates all of them as native Israelites. The second and third phrases are specific descriptions of two different elite groups within the Israelites. The second is, literally, "and from the seed of the kingdom," meaning "from the royal family," indicating direct royal lineage. The third, literally, "and from the nobles," uses פַּרְתְּמִים, a loanword from Old Persian (*HALOT*) that occurs in the OT only here in Daniel and in Esther (Esth 1:3; 6:9), books written during the Achaemenid Empire. The second and third phrases are restrictive: "*those* from the sons of Israel *who were* from the royal family or from the nobility." The restrictive phrases also indicate that after Nebuchadnezzar conquered Jerusalem (1:1–2) he especially took the royal and noble classes into captivity in Babylon to help prevent the remaining Judahites from reconstituting their government and rebelling against him.

1:4 אֵין־בָּהֶם כָּל־מאוּם—Literally, "there was not in them any blemish," this means "they had no blemish" (see Joüon, § 160 k). מוּם, "blemish," can refer to either a physical or a moral defect (*HALOT*, 1, 2). The Kethib, מְאוּם, retains the original middle root letter, א. This is the only other time in the OT besides Job 31:7 that this word is written with an א (see BDB, s.vv., מְאוּם and מוּם; *HALOT*, s.v. מוּם; GKC, § 23 c).

וּמַשְׂכִּילִים בְּכָל־חָכְמָה—The Hiphil of שָׂכַל, "have insight, discernment," is an important theological term in OT Wisdom literature. The participle recurs in 11:35 and 12:10, where it refers to God's saints (believers), and in 11:33 and 12:3, where it refers especially to those who impart the Gospel to others. Here, however, the emphasis is that the pagan Babylonians discern that these Israelites possess uncommon "wisdom" (חָכְמָה), for which, see the commentary on 1:17.

וְיֹדְעֵי דַעַת וּמְבִינֵי מַדָּע—Both of these phrases have a participle in construct with a noun as an objective genitive (Waltke-O'Connor, § 9.5.2b), literally, "knowing knowledge and discerning knowledge." All four terms are common in OT Wisdom literature. For the two cognate nouns for "knowledge," דַעַת and מַדָּע (both are from the verb יָדַע), see the commentary on 1:17.

כֹּחַ בָּהֶם—Literally, "strength was in them," this is translated as "had ability." The noun כֹּחַ can denote physical or intellectual ability (*HALOT*, 2).

לַעֲמֹד בְּהֵיכַל הַמֶּלֶךְ—Literally, "to stand in the palace of the king," this is rendered as "for service in the king's palace" (see *HALOT*, s.v. עמד, 2 d ii). The Qal (G) of עָמַד is used again in the same sense in 1:5 (יַעַמְדוּ לִפְנֵי הַמֶּלֶךְ, literally, "they were to stand before the king") and in 1:19.

סֵפֶר וּלְשׁוֹן כַּשְׂדִּים—This is one of the rare instances in the OT of a construct chain that has two words both in construct with the third word, literally, "the scroll [literature] of and the language of the Chaldeans" (see GKC, § 128 a, footnote 1; Joüon, § 129 a, footnote 5; Waltke-O'Connor, § 9.3b, footnote 6). כַּשְׂדִּים (or the Aramaic equivalent), "Chaldeans," is used several times in Daniel.(a) Here and in 3:8; 5:30; and 9:1, it is an ethnic designation for the Babylonians. In the other passages, it is used in a more specialized and derived meaning: the "diviners" who were advisors to the king.

(a) Dan 1:4; 2:2, 4, 5, 10; 3:8; 4:4; 5:7, 11, 30; 9:1

1:5 מִפַּת־בַּג הַמֶּלֶךְ—This is, literally, "from the delicacies of the king." The construct phrase פַּת־בַּג represents a loanword from Old Persian (*HALOT*) and only occurs in Daniel. In the MT it is written as one word in 1:8, 13, 15, 16, but here and in 11:26 it is written as two words joined with *maqqeph*. However, in 1QDan[a] it is written as two words in 1:13.[1]

וּלְגַדְּלָם—This is the Piel infinitive construct of גָּדַל (with preposition, suffix, and conjunction). In the Piel stem it can mean "bring up, raise (children)," but in this case it refers to education and training (*HALOT*, 1). It is translated as a passive: "and that they should be trained." Especially in later Biblical Hebrew an infinitive with לְ can have the nuance of an obligation or command (Joüon, § 124 l).

וּמִקְצָתָם—For this combination of קְצָת, "end," and מִן with the temporal meaning "at the end of, after," see the second textual note on 1:2. While the third plural suffix is

---

[1] Barthélemy and Milik, *Qumran Cave I*, 150.

masculine, it refers to the feminine noun שָׁנִים, "years" (see GKC, § 135, o), hence, "at the end of them [the three years]."

1:6 דָּנִיֵּאל—"Daniel" by etymology means "my judge [דִּינִי] is God [אֵל]." This name occurs outside of Daniel in Ezek 14:14, 20; 28:3; Ezra 8:2; Neh 10:7 (ET 10:6); and 1 Chr 3:1.

חֲנַנְיָה—"Hananiah" means "gracious [חָנָן] is Yah [יָהּ]." This name occurs twenty-six times in the Bible and in Daniel in 1:6–7, 11, 19; 2:17.

מִישָׁאֵל—"Mishael" means "who [מִי] is what [the relative pronoun שֶׁ] God [אֵל] is?" This name occurs eight times in the Bible, including five times in Daniel (1:6–7, 11, 19; 2:17).

וַעֲזַרְיָה—"Azariah" means "Yah [יָהּ] has helped [עָזַר]." This name occurs thirty-three times in the Bible, but in Daniel only in 1:6–7, 11, 19; 2:17.

1:7 שַׂר הַסָּרִיסִים—"The chief of the eunuchs" is a title of Ashpenaz. See the first textual note on 1:3.

בֵּלְטְשַׁאצַּר—There is little agreement on the derivation and meaning of the Babylonian names given to the Judeans. The first one, "Belteshazzar," is often said to derive from (*Bēl-*)*balaṭ-su-uṣur*, "(may Bel) protect his life."[2] *Bel*, "lord," in this context is a reference to the Babylonian god Marduk. However, it has also been proposed that the name derives from *Bēlet-shar-uṣur*, "Lady [referring to the consort of Bel], protect the king."[3] However, this seems less likely, since the name would have to be spelled with a ת instead of a ט, and 4:5 (ET 4:8) specifically connects this name with the name of Nebuchadnezzar's god. Shea argues that Belteshazzar is a deliberate corruption of the theophoric element in the name "Belshazzar," which derives from *Bēl-shar-uṣur*, "Bel protect the king."[4] Later in Daniel we meet a king named Belshazzar (5:1–30; 7:1; 8:1). Shea notes that throughout Daniel, for the Israelites "there is a distinct inclination to use their Hebrew names, except where strictly required by a Babylonian setting or by direct dialogue with a Babylonian personage."[5] However, in the book, King Belshazzar never uses Daniel's Babylonian name. Shea attributes this to the fact that both Belshazzar and Daniel had the same name, but the author of Daniel, for the sake of his readers, has purposely corrupted it when it refers to Daniel. Moreover, Shea notes that two Babylonian texts from the reigns of Amel-marduk (562–560 BC) and Neriglissar (559–556 BC) identify the king's chief officer as Belshazzar. Since this appears to be too early for the Belshazzar who was the son of Nabonidus, and since it was unlikely that that Belshazzar would be the king's chief officer, but his father would succeed to the throne upon the assassination of Labashi-marduk (556 BC), Shea proposes that the Belshazzar in the Babylonian texts is none other than Daniel.[6]

---

[2] Archer, "Daniel," 34–35; Baldwin, *Daniel*, 81; Hartman and Di Lella, *Daniel*, 130; P. W. Coxon, "Belteshazzar," *ABD* 1:661–62; Lucas, *Daniel*, 53; Miller, *Daniel*, 65.

[3] Berger, "Der Kyros-Zylinder," 231–34.

[4] Shea, "Bel(te)shazzar Meets Belshazzar," 74–76.

[5] Shea, "Bel(te)shazzar Meets Belshazzar," 73.

[6] Shea, "Bel(te)shazzar Meets Belshazzar," 74–80.

שַׁדְרַךְ—There is little agreement on the derivation of "Shadrach." Some derive it from *shudur-aku*, "the command of Aku."[7] Aku was the Babylonian moon god. Others derive it from *shādurāku*, "I am very frightened (of a god),"[8] but this seems less likely. The other three names given to the young men appear to be explicitly theophoric (with pagan deities), so this name is most probably explicitly, not implicitly, theophoric. If Shea's analysis of the name "Meshach" is correct (see the next textual note), then "Shadrach" is most probably a deliberate corruption of *shudur-marduk*, "command of Marduk," with the final consonant (ךְ) being the only element left from the theophoric element of the name.

מֵישַׁךְ—"Meshach" is the most obscure of the four Babylonian names. Some see it as a deliberate play on the meaning of the name "Mishael" and derive it from *mi-sha-aku*, "who is what Aku is?"[9] Others see it as deriving from *mēshāku*, "I am of little account,"[10] which seems forced and inappropriate. Shea proposes that this is a deliberate corruption of the name *Mushallim-marduk*. A person by that name appears on a clay prism from the time of Nebuchadnezzar, and Shea tentatively identifies him as this biblical Mishael/Meshach.[11]

עֲבֵד נְגוֹ:—There is general agreement that "Abednego," or "Abed-nego," is a corruption of the Aramaic name עֲבֵד נְבוֹ, "servant of Nebo."[12] The Babylonian equivalent would have been *Arad-nabu* or *Ardi-nabu*. Nebo was the Babylonian god of wisdom and agriculture, the patron of scribes and schools, and the god after whom Nebuchadnezzar was named. In the Hebrew and Aramaic of Daniel, the name is always spelled as two words. In 3:29 it is spelled וַעֲבֵד נְגוֹא. Once again, Shea proposes that the form "Abednego" contains a deliberate corruption of the pagan theophoric element.[13]

Commentary

The king instructed Ashpenaz to select certain promising captives for training. Ashpenaz is called "the chief of his [Nebuchadnezzar's] eunuchs" (רַב סָרִיסָיו, 1:3) and "the chief of the eunuchs" (שַׂר הַסָּרִיסִים, 1:7–11, 18). Commentators have debated whether or not סָרִיס means that Ashpenaz was an actual "eunuch" or whether it was a title for a high official. Eunuchs certainly did serve as officials, and it is possible that the phrases have a literal meaning.

---

[7] Archer, "Daniel," 34; Miller, *Daniel*, 65.

[8] Baldwin, *Daniel*, 81; Berger, "Der Kyros-Zylinder," 224.

[9] Archer, "Daniel," 34; Miller, *Daniel*, 65.

[10] Baldwin, *Daniel*, 81; Berger, "Der Kyros-Zylinder," 225.

[11] Shea, "Daniel 3: Extra-Biblical Texts and the Convocation on the Plain of Dura," 49–50. This identification is possible, but very controversial. Whether or not Shea's identification of the official listed on Nebuchadnezzar's prism is correct, his suggestion that the name has been purposely corrupted to obscure the Babylonian theophoric element is quite possible.

[12] Archer, "Daniel," 34; Berger, "Der Kyros-Zylinder," 225–26; Collins, *Daniel*, 141; Hartman and Di Lella, *Daniel*, 130; Lucas, *Daniel*, 53; cf. Baldwin, *Daniel*, 81.

[13] Shea, "Daniel 3," 48–49; "Mutilation of Foreign Names by Bible Writers," 114.

It is sometimes argued that since Potiphar was called a eunuch (סָרִיס, Gen 37:36; 39:1) and he was married, he was not an actual eunuch, and the term, at least in his case, simply means "official."[14] However, some literal eunuchs did marry, most notably, the eunuchs who served the Chinese emperors. Moreover, castration does not absolutely prevent a man from engaging in sexual intercourse, but it does reduce his sexual desires and of course renders him incapable of siring children. Therefore, Potiphar's marriage is not a good argument that in his case the term simply indicated a royal official. To the contrary, the fact that Potiphar's wife attempted to seduce Joseph may argue that Potiphar was a eunuch and his reduced libido prompted his wife's bold behavior.

Some also argue that the etymology of סָרִיס (*saris*, "eunuch"), from the Akkadian *sha reshi*, "of the head," indicates that originally the term simply denoted an official and that "eunuch" is a later, secondary meaning, since many court officials were eunuchs.[15] However, etymology does not determine later usage and cannot be employed to argue that in this context the word must mean "an official."

Thus we cannot be certain whether Ashpenaz was a eunuch or whether he is simply being depicted as a court official. The phrase רַב־סָרִיס, "chief eunuch" (similar to the phrase in 1:3) is used elsewhere of high Assyrian or Babylonian officials (2 Ki 18:17; Jer 39:3, 13). In those verses, some English translations transliterate it: "Rabsaris" or "Rab-saris" (e.g., KJV, RSV, ESV). However, even in those contexts it is impossible to determine whether or not the individual designated by that title was a eunuch.

This, of course, leads to speculation whether the young Judean exiles were made eunuchs. There is no indication in the text that they were, nor is there any indication that they were not. Some commentators point out that Nebuchadnezzar had specifically requested young men who had no blemish (1:4), making it unlikely that they were previously or subsequently castrated.[16] However, Herodotus reports that handsome boys captured in war were often castrated.[17] Josephus specifically reports that some of the Judean young men captured by Nebuchadnezzar were castrated, although he does not give any names.[18] Rabbinic literature often asserts that Daniel, Hananiah, Azariah, and Mishael were eunuchs.[19] Moreover, the terminology used to describe the young men's appearance as "good looking" (the adjective טוֹב in construct with the noun מַרְאֶה, 1:4) is used elsewhere only of women[b] and could be understood to be a subtle clue that the intent of the Babylonians was to emasculate these young men.

(b) Gen 24:16; 26:7; 2 Sam 11:2; Esth 1:11; 2:2–3, 7

---

[14] Archer, "Daniel," 33; Collins, *Daniel*, 134; Miller, *Daniel*, 59.

[15] Archer, "Daniel," 33; Collins, *Daniel*, 134; Miller, *Daniel*, 59.

[16] E.g., Miller, *Daniel*, 59.

[17] Herodotus, *Histories*, 8.105.1.

[18] Josephus, *Antiquities*, 10.186.

[19] Ginzberg, *The Legends of the Jews*, 4:326; 6:415.

Thus it is quite possible that these captured Judean men were made eunuchs, but we have no proof of it. If, as noted earlier (see the commentary on 1:2), Daniel is implying that the capture of these young men was a fulfillment of Is 39:7, and if סָרִיס in that passage means "eunuch" rather than "official," then it is likely that they were castrated.[20] However, we have no firm proof of this. What is much clearer is that these young men were, from all outward appearances, entirely at the disposal of the Babylonian court.

Daniel is careful in identifying those selected from all the exiles brought from Jerusalem to Babylon. He first identifies them as מִבְּנֵי יִשְׂרָאֵל, "from the sons of Israel" (1:3). The designation "Israel" is used only here and in Daniel's prayer of confession in chapter 9 (9:7, 11, 20). In both places it has a theological force. These are the people of Yahweh. It is a reminder that God has established a covenant with them that cannot be annulled by a Babylonian king. Elsewhere in the book, they are simply called "Judeans" (בְּנֵי יְהוּדָה, 1:6), "the people of Judah" (אִישׁ יְהוּדָה, 9:7), or "the exiles of Judah" (בְּנֵי גָלוּתָא דִי יְהוּד, 2:25; 5:13; 6:14 [ET 6:13]).

Next Daniel says that they were specifically "from the royal family and from the nobility" (1:3). Their exile to Babylon was likely the result of Nebuchadnezzar's attempt to rid the land of Judah of its next generation of leaders, thereby hindering the remaining Judeans from rebelling against Babylon. Nebuchadnezzar also had the opportunity to train these exiles in Babylonian customs, promote them, and make them more loyal to him than to the nation of Judah or to Israel's God.

The young men chosen for this inculcation into the Babylonian culture and hierarchy were not just any of the next generation of those who would have been Judah's leadership, but the best, both physically and intellectually. The threefold description of their intellectual abilities most probably emphasizes their fitness to be trained for service in the royal court. That training involved "the literature and language of the Chaldeans" (1:4). This required them to learn Akkadian and its cuneiform writing system. Unlike their native Hebrew or the more cosmopolitan Aramaic, which were written with alphabetic symbols, the cuneiform signs were syllabic. This complicated system that uses hundreds of signs would have taken some time to learn to read with proficiency, which accounts for the three years of training that they were to receive before they could enter into full-time service in the Babylonian court.

However, the training prescribed involved more than simply learning to read and write Akkadian and acquiring familiarity with the classic literature of Babylon. Clearly Nebuchadnezzar's orders indicate that these young men were to be acculturated into Babylon. This not only ensured that they could serve competently among other civil servants, but it was also a method to weaken their

---

[20] The Babylonian Talmud (*Sanhedrin*, 93b) counts Daniel and his companions among the eunuchs mentioned in Is 39:7 and possibly those mentioned in Is 56:4–5, but recounts differing rabbinic opinions about whether Daniel and the other Judeans were literal eunuchs.

loyalty to their native land and God. Therefore, they not only learned Babylonian literature, but they were also to eat food from the royal rations. Moreover, to complete their acculturation these young men were assigned Babylonian names that disconnected them from the God of Israel, who was honored in their Hebrew names (see the textual notes on 1:6). There were probably more than four young Judeans who were part of this training, but Daniel only names himself and three others. In two of their Hebrew names, the theophoric element was *El*, "God," while the other two contained the theophoric element *Yah*, a short form of *Yahweh*, usually translated "the LORD."

The new names they were assigned are probably all corrupted forms of Babylonian theophoric names honoring gods of the Babylonian pantheon (see the textual notes on 1:7). Commentators often make little of this and claim that Judeans in general and Daniel in particular had little objection to having pagan names.[21] They note that Joseph was given a new name in Egypt, apparently without objection (Gen 41:45), and that several exilic Judeans such as Mordecai, Esther, and Zerubbabel bore such names. However, it appears as if these names in Dan 1:7 are purposely bowdlerized by Daniel, the author of the biblical book.[22] First of all, the theophoric element in each name contains a corruption involving an addition, deletion, or change of one or more consonants. Thus "Belt-" instead of "Bel-" in "Belteshazzar," "–k" instead of "–marduk" in "Shadrach," and "–nego" instead of "-nabu" in "Abednego" (see the third textual note on 1:7 for "Meshach"). This consistent pattern points to deliberate alteration of the names.

Second, this may have been a covert and subversive way of protesting the attempted detachment of these young men from Israel's God. They had no choice in the matter, but Daniel may have been indicating that while they could not do anything about what the Babylonians were intent on calling them, they did not personally approve of having names associated with pagan gods instead of their God.

Third, the idiom Daniel uses for naming here indicates that he views the renaming by the Babylonians as an attempt to impose the will and polytheistic worldview of Babylon on these young men. Instead of using the common Hebrew idiom for naming, קָרָא ("to call") plus שֵׁם ("a name"), he uses the less common שִׂים ("to set/place") plus שֵׁם ("a name," 1:7), an idiom most commonly used of God placing his name on his people (Num 6:27) or in Jerusalem or its temple.[23] In two passages, it recalls God's naming of two of the patriarchs:

---

[21] Archer, "Daniel," 34; Baldwin, *Daniel*, 81; Collins, *Daniel*, 141; Gowan, *Daniel*, 45; Montgomery, *Daniel*, 123.

[22] Lucas is one of the few commentators that sees these names as deliberately altered to avoid the names of pagan gods (*Daniel*, 53).

[23] Arnold, "Word Play and Characterization in Daniel 1," 237–38, citing Deut 12:5, 21; 14:24; 1 Ki 9:3; 11:36; 14:21; 2 Ki 21:4, 7; 2 Chr 6:20; 12:13; 33:7.

Jacob/Israel (2 Ki 17:34) and Abram/Abraham (Neh 9:7).[24] Daniel seems to be indicating that he and his companions viewed their Hebrew theophoric names as given by Yahweh (perhaps through the agency of their parents), and now the Babylonians were attempting to impose the perceived will of their false gods on these young men. This is confirmed by noting that the Babylonian names for these men are only used in Babylonian contexts: when these men are addressed by Babylonians, when the Babylonians are taking action with regard to the men, or when there is a reference to the renaming of these men.[c]

(c) Dan 1:7; 2:26, 49; 3:12–14, 16, 19–20, 22–23, 26, 28–30; 4:5–6, 15–16 (ET 4:8–9, 18–19); 5:12; 10:1

In addition, that the names were purposely altered to disfigure the names of pagan gods is further reinforced by the play on the verb שׂים in the very next verse (1:8), where Daniel (literally) "set" his mind to undo the king's command that he and his companions eat the royal rations.[25] Just as the Babylonians "set" a pagan name on Daniel and his companions, Daniel "sets" his heart on undoing the most offensive part of Nebuchadnezzar's acculturation of these young men into Babylon's pagan society. Arnold summarizes the force of this wordplay well:

> The irony of the word play is that the Babylonians think they have changed Daniel's character, but the narrator knows otherwise. They succeeded in changing all the circumstances of his life, and the name change in verse 7 represents Daniel's complete transformation, at least from the Babylonian perspective. But the inner resolve and dedication revealed by the word play in verse 8 is the narrator's full portrait of Daniel and transcends even the description of his impressive personal and intellectual skills in verses 3–4. It is his commitment to God that sets Daniel apart, and prepares the reader for the continued conflict between aggressive world powers and God's servants.[26]

Furthermore, given the resistance to paganism shown in this chapter as these young men find a way not to eat the king's food (and in later chapters, most notably Shadrach, Meshach, and Abednego's refusal to worship the statue in Daniel 3), this may have been a more subtle form of resistance that testifies to the wisdom exercised by Daniel and his companions. They could have objected to every perceived pagan influence imposed upon them, but that would have involved them in constant confrontation with their Babylonian overlords. Instead, they chose to make a stand in the more important matters and let the matter of names pass by without comment. Yet, when Daniel writes his account of their life in Babylon, he subtly indicates their displeasure with the pagan names by disfiguring the names of the pagan gods that were embedded in the names they were given.

Thus from the very beginning, Daniel is subtly teaching his readers how to live in a pagan society and maintain a steadfast commitment to Yahweh. One

---

[24] The only other passage in which this idiom is used of a human naming another human is Judg 8:31, where Gideon names Abimelech.

[25] Arnold, "Word Play and Characterization in Daniel 1," 238–41.

[26] Arnold, "Word Play and Characterization in Daniel 1," 248.

must chose one's battles against paganism wisely and fight those battles that are most important for the preservation of the one true faith. A name containing *El*, "God," or *Yah*, for "Yahweh, the LORD," is a witness to the one true God, but not a necessity for remaining faithful to the laws of God given in the covenant mediated by Moses. Other matters, such as the dietary laws in obedience to explicit commands in the Torah, were more directly relevant to preserving faithful piety.

In many ways, Christians today face analogous issues as we live in secular cultures that seek to impose cultural norms that challenge our faithful life as God's people, redeemed in Christ. Daniel is telling us that we also need to choose wisely when taking a stand against the prevailing culture. Some matters are more important for our witness to the one true and triune God, and for our conscience and piety, and so they must be resisted, lest we be drawn away from God. Other matters may be only incidental and do not inherently draw us away from Christ.

Naming, of course, was not completely inconsequential. Throughout the OT, naming is seen as significant, and often the reason for giving a name is also mentioned. The most important naming, however, occurs in the NT. There the angel of the Lord gives specific instructions to Joseph: "She [Mary] will bear a son, and you shall call his name Jesus, because he will save his people from their sins" (Mt 1:21). Jesus' very identity as the Savior is bound up with his name, which means "Yahweh/the LORD saves."[27] In the same way, the Judeans clung to the memory of their Israelite names because their identity as people of Yahweh was bound up with their names. The corrupted Babylonian names used in Daniel are a constant reminder that the men's real identity was not as Babylonian courtiers but as the called and redeemed people of God, fellow members of the "one holy catholic and apostolic church" (Nicene Creed) consisting of all OT and NT believers.

---

[27] "Jesus" is a Greek form of the name "Joshua," which had several different Hebrew forms in the OT. See Harstad, *Joshua*, 12–13, and Gibbs, *Matthew 1:1–11:1*, 107.

Daniel 1:8–21
The Judeans Are Steadfast in Practicing Their Faith

Translation

1   ⁸Daniel made up his mind that he would not defile himself with the king's delicacies and the wine that he drank. So he sought [permission] from the chief of the eunuchs so that he would not defile himself. ⁹God gave Daniel favor and compassion before the chief of the eunuchs. ¹⁰Now the chief of the eunuchs said to Daniel, "I am afraid of my lord the king, who assigned your food and your drink. Why should he see your faces looking more gaunt than the [other] young men who are your age? You risk my life before the king."

¹¹Daniel said to the superintendent whom the chief of the eunuchs had assigned over Daniel, Hananiah, Mishael, and Azariah, ¹²"Please test your servants for ten days: give to us some of the vegetables, and let us eat [them], and water, and let us drink [it]. ¹³Observe our appearance, and the appearance of the young men who eat the royal delicacies. Then according to what you see, do with your servants." ¹⁴So he listened to them in this matter and tested them for ten days.

¹⁵At the end of ten days, their appearance was observed to be better than and they were healthier than any of the young men who had been eating the royal delicacies. ¹⁶So the superintendent permanently took away their delicacies and the wine for their drink and only gave them vegetables. ¹⁷As for these four young men, God gave to them knowledge and insight into all kinds of literature, as well as wisdom, and Daniel understood every [kind of] vision and dreams.

¹⁸And at the end of the days that the king had said to bring them, the chief of the eunuchs brought them before Nebuchadnezzar. ¹⁹The king spoke with them, and none of them were found like Daniel, Hananiah, Mishael, and Azariah. So they served the king. ²⁰In every matter of wisdom and understanding that the king sought from them, he found them ten times [better] than all the magicians and soothsayers in his entire kingdom. ²¹Now Daniel remained [there] until the first year of King Cyrus.

Textual Notes

1:8   וַיָּשֶׂם דָּנִיֵּאל עַל־לִבּוֹ—Literally, "Daniel set on his heart," this is rendered, "Daniel made up his mind." For the play on words with שִׂים between this verse and the previous verse, see the commentary on 1:7. The Hebrew word לֵב, "heart," denotes more than the seat of emotions as in English. In Hebrew, the heart (לֵב or לֵבָב) is not only the source of emotions such as joy (Is 24:7), fear (Josh 2:11), and despair (Eccl 2:20), but also the seat of intellectual capacities such as insight (Prov 2:2) and critical evaluation

(Josh 14:7), as well as the locus of the human will (2 Sam 7:3; 1 Ki 8:17). Thus in some contexts, such as this one, it is best translated "mind."

אֲשֶׁר לֹא־יִתְגָּאָל—Twice in this verse אֲשֶׁר introduces an object clause (Joüon, § 157 c) with the Hithpael (HtD) imperfect of גָּאַל, forming a negated purpose clause, "that he would not defile himself." The OT contains two different homographic verbs of גָּאַל. One means "redeem" and is used throughout the OT. The other means "defile" and is used in literature from the time of the fall of Israel (722 BC) onward.[a]

(a) Is 59:3; 63:3; Zeph 3:1; Mal 1:7 (twice), 12; Lam 4:14; Dan 1:8 (twice); Ezra 2:62; Neh 7:64

בְּפַתְבַּג—For the collective compound noun פַּתְבַּג, "delicacies" (also in 1:13, 15–16), see the first textual note on 1:5.

1:9 וַיִּתֵּן הָאֱלֹהִים אֶת־דָּנִיֵּאל לְחֶסֶד וּלְרַחֲמִים—Here the verb נָתַן is used with prepositional phrases with לְ meaning "God made Daniel an object for [a person who received] favor and compassion" (see BDB, s.v. נָתַן, 3 b).

1:10 אֲשֶׁר לָמָּה יִרְאֶה אֶת־פְּנֵיכֶם זֹעֲפִים—The relative pronoun אֲשֶׁר and the interrogative לָמָּה can introduce a question with a negative connotation that describes an undesirable situation: literally, "Why should he see your faces being gaunt?" (cf. Joüon, § 161 h; Waltke-O'Connor, § 18.3c, including example 24). The participle זֹעֲפִים, "gaunt," carries the meaning of physical demeanor that indicates a problem. In the OT it has this meaning only here and in Gen 40:6 in the story of Joseph[1] (HALOT, s.v. זעף II). All other words from this root in the OT describe (extreme) anger: the verb זָעַף, "to be angry, to rage" (HALOT; Jonah 1:15; Prov 19:3; 2 Chr 26:19); the noun זַעַף, "rage" (HALOT; Is 30:30; Micah 7:9; Prov 19:12; 2 Chr 16:10; 28:9); and the adjective זָעֵף, "furious" (HALOT; 1 Ki 20:43; 21:4). With the following מִן־, זֹעֲפִים becomes comparative: "more gaunt than …"

וְחִיַּבְתֶּם אֶת־רֹאשִׁי לַמֶּלֶךְ—Literally, "you [would] make my head guilty to the king," this is rendered, "you risk my life before the king." The hapax legomenon verb חוּב, "be guilty," has a causative meaning in the Piel (D), "inculpate" (BDB) or "make guilty." In form this Piel perfect with geminated consonantal yod (־יִּ־) may be due to Aramaic influence (so Joüon, § 80 h).

1:11 הַמֶּלְצַר—מֶלְצַר, "superintendent," is probably an Akkadian loanword denoting an official lower than the chief of the eunuchs (HALOT). In Akkadian, maṣṣāru is a "guardian," derived from the root nṣr, "to guard," cognate to the Hebrew נָצַר.[2]

1:12 נַס—This is an apocopated Piel (D) imperative of נָסָה, "to test," whose expected form would be נַסֵּה (GKC, § 75 cc). Its Piel recurs is in 1:14 (וַיְנַסֵּם, "and he tested them").

מִן־הַזֵּרְעִים—The preposition מִן is used partitively: "some of." The plural noun for "vegetables" occurs only here in the OT (like the related word זֵרְעֹנִים in 1:16). It is from the root זָרַע, "to sow," indicating that the noun refers to food from cultivated plants (rather than meat). It should not be so narrowly defined as the English word "vegetables" would imply.

---

[1] See "Daniel and Joseph" in "Connections with Other Old Testament Books" in the introduction.

[2] Baldwin, *Daniel*, 84; Collins, *Daniel*, 144; Hartman and Di Lella, *Daniel*, 130; Montgomery, *Daniel*, 134.

1:13 וְיֵרָאוּ לְפָנֶיךָ מַרְאֵינוּ וּמַרְאֵה הַיְלָדִים—The Niphal (N) of רָאָה, "see," is jussive: literally, "let our appearance … be seen before you." It has a compound subject: both מַרְאֵינוּ ("our appearance") and וּמַרְאֵה הַיְלָדִים ("and the appearance of the [other] young men"). For the sake of English, the passive Niphal (N) is rendered as an active imperative: "observe …" In form מַרְאֵינוּ could be either the singular or the plural of the noun מַרְאֶה with suffix, as also is true of מַרְאֵיהֶם in 1:15 (see GKC, § 93 ss; Joüon, § 96C e). However, the following singular וּמַרְאֵה supports the view that these forms are singular ("our appearance," 1:13; "their appearance," 1:15), implying that all the Judeans would share the same or a similar appearance.

תִּרְאֶה עֲשֵׂה—The unusual vocalization (-אֶ- instead of -אָ-) of the Qal (G) imperfect, "you will see," probably is to avoid hiatus with the following עֲ (so GKC, § 75 hh). The Qal imperative עֲשֵׂה here has the nuance of consequent action: after the observation, "(then) do/act" accordingly (see Joüon, § 114 m).

1:15 וּמִקְצָת—For the temporal sense "at the end of" (also for וּלְמִקְצָת in 1:18), see the second textual note on 1:2.

נִרְאָה מַרְאֵיהֶם טוֹב—"Their appearance was observed to be good" uses the Niphal (N) of רָאָה as in 1:13. With the following מִן־, the adjective טוֹב becomes comparative: "better … than …"

וּבְרִיאֵי בָּשָׂר—Literally, "and fat of flesh," this construct phrase with the adjective בָּרִיא indicates health as opposed to sickliness, as also in Gen 41:2, 18 (cf. Gen 41:4; Zech 11:16). With the following מִן־, it has a comparative meaning: "fatter/healthier than …"

1:16 וַיְהִי הַמֶּלְצַר נֹשֵׂא … וְנָתֵן—This construction, וַיְהִי followed by two participles (נֹשֵׂא … וְנָתֵן), forms two result clauses with durative force. As a result of the observation at the end of the trial, from that time onward the steward permanently "took away" (נֹשֵׂא) the royal delicacies and wine, and "gave" (וְנָתֵן) them only vegetables. For נָשָׂא in the sense of "take away," see BDB, Qal, 3.

זֵרְעֹנִים—This plural word for "vegetables" is a hapax, like the related word זֵרֹעִים in 1:12. See the second textual note on that verse.

1:17 נָתַן לָהֶם הָאֱלֹהִים מַדָּע וְהַשְׂכֵּל בְּכָל־סֵפֶר וְחָכְמָה—"God gave to them" faculties that the king sought in 1:4: מַדָּע, "knowledge," וְהַשְׂכֵּל בְּכָל־סֵפֶר, "insight into all kinds of literature," and חָכְמָה, "wisdom." Here הַשְׂכֵּל, "insight," is the Hiphil (H) infinitive absolute used as a noun (BDB, s.v. שָׂכַל I, Hiphil, 3) and as a direct object (Waltke-O'Connor, § 35.3.3b, including example 12). It corresponds to the Hiphil participle וּמַשְׂכִּילִים, "having insight," in 1:4. סֵפֶר, literally, "scroll," here means "literature."

וְדָנִיֵּאל הֵבִין בְּכָל־חָזוֹן וַחֲלֹמוֹת—In addition to the faculties God gave to all four of the young men (see the preceding textual note), Daniel could (literally) "discern every vision and dreams." The Hiphil (H) perfect הֵבִין, "discern," corresponds to the Hiphil participle in the phrase וּמְבִינֵי מַדָּע in 1:4, where the king sought men who were proficient at, literally, "discerning knowledge." Here God gave Daniel interpretive abilities beyond those sought by the king, involving modes of divine revelation.

1:19 וְלֹא נִמְצָא מִכֻּלָּם כְּדָנִיֵּאל—Literally, "no [one] was found from all of them like Daniel," the Niphal (N) of מָצָא, "be found," indicates the result of examination and testing. Likewise, the Qal (G) in 1:20 (וַיִּמְצָאֵם, "he found them") implies that the king evaluated the men.

וַיַּעַמְדוּ לִפְנֵי הַמֶּלֶךְ:—Literally, "and they stood before the king," this means "so they served the king." See the fifth textual note on 1:4.

1:20 וְכֹל דְּבַר חָכְמַת בִּינָה—This four-word construct chain is, literally, "and every word/matter of wisdom of understanding." There has been much debate but no satisfactory consensus about the significance of חָכְמַת being in construct with בִּינָה.[3] Most English versions follow the lead of the Old Greek (συνέσει καὶ παιδείᾳ) and Theodotion (σοφίας καὶ ἐπιστήμης),[4] which are partially supported by a Dead Sea scroll,[5] and translate as if the two nouns were coordinated with a *waw*: "wisdom and understanding" (KJV, ESV, NASB, NIV, NRSV). The initial וְכֹל דְּבַר ("every matter of …") emphasizes that the Judeans displayed a broad range of different kinds of wisdom and understanding. That militates against taking the genitive construction חָכְמַת בִּינָה in one of the many common ways that involve limiting or restricting the meaning of either noun (cf. Waltke-O'Connor, § 9.5). Similarly broad was בְּכָל־חָכְמָה in 1:4. Perhaps the construct form חָכְמַת is used merely for the purpose of linking (cf. Joüon, § 129 r).

For the meaning of חָכְמָה, "wisdom," see the commentary on 1:17. Its less common synonym בִּינָה recurs in Daniel in 2:21 (Aramaic); 8:15; 9:22; 10:1. Here it refers to the "act" or exercise of "understanding" (so BDB, s.v. בִּינָה, 1) displayed by the Judeans as they mastered their learning and responded to the king's evaluative testing.

עֶשֶׂר יָדוֹת—The idiom "ten hands" means "ten times" (*HALOT*, s.v. יָד I, 7; Waltke-O'Connor, § 15.4b, including example 14; Joüon, § 142 q). This idiomatic use of יָד as a multiplicative is also found in Gen 43:34 and 2 Sam 19:44 (ET 19:43). "Ten times" must be a figurative comparison implying a surpassing difference, rather than a literal number, for example, a test score literally "ten times" higher.

הַחַרְטֻמִּים הָאַשָּׁפִים—The first term, translated "magicians," most likely is Egyptian, since it refers to those in Pharaoh's court in Gen 41:8, 24; Ex 7:11, 22; 8:3, 14–15 (ET 8:7, 18–19); 9:11 (cf. *HALOT*). Egyptians were known to have served in Babylonian courts. The term recurs in Aramaic in Dan 2:10, 27; 4:4, 6 (ET 4:7, 9); 5:11. The second term, rendered "soothsayers," is a loanword from Akkadian *āshipu*, a person skilled in incantations (*HALOT*). In the OT, it occurs only in Daniel. It recurs in Hebrew in 2:2 and in Aramaic in 2:10, 27; 4:4 (ET 4:7); 5:7, 11, 15.

The OT and NT affirm that practitioners of occult arts and those under the influence of evil spirits are indeed able to perform supernatural feats (e.g., Ex 7:11–12; Mk 5:1–20; Acts 16:16–18). However, those same texts demonstrate the superiority of the

---

[3] Montgomery, *Daniel*, 138, includes a variety of proposed explanations.

[4] For these Greek translations, see Ziegler and Munnich, *Susanna, Daniel, Bel et Draco*, 240–41.

[5] 4QDan[a] reads חן[כמ]ה ב[ינה] (Ulrich et al., *Qumran Cave 4.XI*, 242–43). Apparently the scribe wrote the more familiar absolute form חָכְמָה in place of the construct form חָכְמַת. There is no conjunction on בִּינָה, so this scroll has only partial agreement with the Old Greek and Theodotion.

one true God, who grants his people the ability to subdue and overcome the devil and his works. That the true God grants to Daniel wisdom that is superior to the powers possessed by the Babylonian wise men and diviners will be a major theme in chapter 2.

בְּכָל־מַלְכוּתוֹ:—This is "in his entire kingdom." בְּכָל־ is missing in 4QDan[a],[6] but that is probably a mistake. It is present in the MT and the versions in general.

Commentary
Daniel Is Granted an Exemption (1:8–14)

Daniel demonstrates his leadership qualities as he alone among the four companions approaches the chief of the eunuchs to request permission to avoid the king's food and wine and the defilement that would come from eating and drinking them. Commentators have sought reasons why Daniel did not want to eat the king's food and drink his wine and instead requested only vegetables and water. Among the explanations are these:

1. These young men did not want to give the impression that they were bound to total loyalty to the king. This explanation may be partly true, as long as it is not pushed to the extreme. It seems as if Daniel had no problem with giving political loyalty to Nebuchadnezzar as long as he did not have to defile himself by worshiping pagan gods. Therefore, this explanation is probably a minor part of Daniel's motivation, if it had any part at all in his request.

2. Daniel and his companions did not want to break the dietary laws found in the Pentateuch. This would explain the request to eat only plant matter, since the Torah did not consider any edible plants to be unclean. Daniel's request to eat only vegetables would free him from the need to give a long explanation (such as that in Leviticus 11) of which types of meat he could and could not eat. However, this reason cannot provide a complete explanation since wine was permissible under the Law of Moses, and Dan 10:3 indicates that Daniel had no scruples against drinking wine (or eating meat).

3. Daniel was avoiding foods offered to idols. Eating those foods could be construed as his acceptance and endorsement of pagan worship (cf. 1 Corinthians 8–10). This reason could explain his reluctance to drink the wine, but fails to explain his willingness to eat any vegetable foods, since grains were often offered to the gods. However, as in the OT, animals were the primary or most important sacrifices, although they could be accompanied by grain offerings and libations.

Perhaps a combination of the last two reasons best explains Daniel's request. It allowed the Judeans to avoid any possibility of breaking the dietary laws of the Pentateuch and also minimized their eating of food offered to idols.

Although the chief of the eunuchs does not grant Daniel his request, we are told that God gives Daniel favor in his eyes. Therefore, the eunuch does not interpret the request as an act of rebellion against Nebuchadnezzar, and so he

---

[6] Ulrich et al., *Qumran Cave 4.XI*, 242–43.

does not punish Daniel. However, because of his fear of Nebuchadnezzar, neither does he grant the request.

Daniel approaches a lesser official with a new plan.[7] This time he does not ask for a permanent change of diet, but only for a test period. That Daniel would ask for such a short test period demonstrates his confidence that God would reward his faithfulness. At the same time, he makes clear that he is not defying the superintendent's authority or the king's order, since he suggests that the superintendent alone could be the final judge of the experiment with a vegetarian diet.

Daniel is also wise enough to recognize that authority is often divided among several individuals. Instead of defying authority, he seeks out a different official who has more limited power, and to him Daniel offers a more limited request. In this way, Daniel avoids breaking the Fourth Commandment and is able to take a step toward his goal of not having to break the First Commandment or the dietary laws.[8]

God Grants Success to the Young Judean Men (1:15–17)

Although God is not mentioned as the cause for the better health of the young Judeans, it is clear that Daniel is implying that God has rewarded the faithfulness of these four men. The diet now becomes the prescription for all of the young men in training in Nebuchadnezzar's academy—not just the four, but all the Judeans and all the others as well.

This first testing of Daniel and his friends demonstrates their ability to withstand the pressure of a foreign culture to compromise their faith. It is likely that these young men in training (1:4–5) were only young adolescents at this time, perhaps around fourteen years of age. Yet they show remarkable maturity in faith, and Daniel in particular demonstrates wisdom and tact that is not normally possessed by one so young. All of these qualities are implied to be gifts from God, not simply human characteristics produced by these young men.

Dan 1:17 specifically mentions further gifts from God to these young men that went beyond those gifts needed to request and succeed in the dietary experiment. They are given "knowledge" (מַדָּע) and "insight" (הַשְׂכֵּל) into their studies. These and cognate words occur frequently in OT Wisdom literature, and in the NT, their Greek equivalents refer to God's gifts for a wise and discerning life of faith in Christ.[b]

(b) E.g., Eph 1:8, 17; 4:13; Col 1:9–10; 2:3; 1 Jn 2:20

"Knowledge" (מַדָּע, Dan 1:4, 17; elsewhere only in Eccl 10:20; 2 Chr 1:10–12), like its common synonym and cognate דַּעַת, "knowledge" (Dan 1:4; 12:4; and eighty-six other times in the OT), signifies more than intellectual

---

[7] Despite the clear wording of 1:11 that treats the superintendent as a lesser official under the chief of the eunuchs, some commentators understand them to be the same person. See, for example, Archer, "Daniel," 36.

[8] For the way in which Daniel affirms the First and Fourth Commandments, see "God's Law in Daniel" in "Law and Gospel in Daniel" in the introduction.

knowledge in the sense of facts one has learned. It also denotes awareness of one's situation and the ability to integrate learned facts and concepts into a life of faith that prudently deals with everyday situations. A person endowed with the divine gift of knowledge can not only avoid dangers and pitfalls, but also understand how to lead a God-pleasing life that benefits others as well. Knowledge of God implies a relationship with him that guides the entirety of one's life (Prov 2:5) and that leads to eternal life (Eccl 7:12; cf. Lk 1:77; 2 Pet 1:3). In many passages, including Dan 1:4, דַּעַת, "knowledge," is used as a synonym for חָכְמָה, "wisdom."

"Insight" (הַשְׂכֵּל) also has a spiritual dimension. It and other words derived from the root שׂכל, when used in a positive sense,[9] often denote spiritual insight, the ability to understand and follow God's ways even when circumstances seem to indicate some other course of action may be desirable or prudent (Prov 19:11; Dan 11:33–35). Such a person is spiritually and morally prudent.

To these attributes God also added חָכְמָה, "wisdom" (1:17). It includes spiritual knowledge *and* the ability to apply what one knows. In some passages in the OT it denotes craftsmanship and proficiency in one's occupation (e.g., Ex 35:31). In Proverbs it has a wider sense denoting the ability to live in accordance with God's plan and will (e.g., Prov 1:1–7). It can manifest itself in practical matters and in interpersonal relationships. Wisdom depends on reasoning and the aptitude and willingness to learn, and so it was an appropriately desirable quality for God to give to these young men. It also is characterized by insight into the ways that God has ordered the world, both in creation and in his plan of redemption, as well as into the dangerous ways that sin corrupts the world. This "wisdom" served Daniel, Hananiah, Mishael, and Azariah well.

Daniel was given an additional gift: the ability to understand "every [kind of] vision and dreams" (1:17). This, of course, prepares us for Daniel's activity in chapters 2, 4, and 5. Daniel's ability to interpret dreams in the context of a foreign court has often been compared to Joseph's ability in Pharaoh's court.[10] Joseph had also experienced his own prophetic dreams (Gen 37:5–11), and it seems that his brothers (Gen 37:8) and his father (Gen 37:10) shared the ability to interpret them.[11]

This is the third time in this chapter that we are told God "gives" (נָתַן) something.[12] In 1:2 he "gives" Jehoiakim into Nebuchadnezzar's hand. In 1:9 he "gives" Daniel favor before the chief of the eunuchs. Now in 1:17, he "gives" these young men intellectual and spiritual acumen. Clearly, Daniel wants us to understand that all of the events in the lives of these young men were under God's control. He allowed his people to suffer defeat and exile, but his ultimate

---

[9] Dan 1:4, 17; 9:13, 22, 25; 11:33, 35; 12:3, 10. This root is used in a negative sense in 8:25.

[10] Archer, "Daniel," 36; Collins, *Daniel*, 144; Montgomery, *Daniel*, 132.

[11] For a comparison of Joseph and Daniel, see further "Daniel and Joseph" in "Connections with Other Old Testament Books" in the introduction.

[12] This is pointed out by Arnold, "Word Play and Characterization in Daniel 1," 247.

purpose was to bring about their salvation. It was his plan to bring them to Babylon and enable them to rise to high positions in Nebuchadnezzar's government. This blessing of God upon Daniel that brought him wisdom and favor foreshadows God's blessing upon his Son, who "grew and became strong, being filled with wisdom, and the favor of God was upon him" (Lk 2:40).

The Judeans Are Given Responsibilities in Nebuchadnezzar's Court (1:18–21)

Apparently Nebuchadnezzar reserved for himself the final examination of these young men at the end of their prescribed training period. The results of God's gift to them of knowledge and insight were obvious even to Nebuchadnezzar, though he probably did not attribute their ability to Israel's God. Dan 1:20 is probably to be understood as a general statement about their service throughout the time they were in Nebuchadnezzar's employ, rather than implying that in one interview he found them superior to all of his wise men. Instead, this statement is prospective and primes the reader to expect in later chapters further accounts of how Nebuchadnezzar learned of the Judeans' superiority.

"Ten times [better]" (1:20) is the first time in Daniel that we find the use of a number in a symbolic or metaphorical way. Such uses of numbers will become more prominent in the visions later in the book. This is one example that refutes the dispensational rule that all numbers in prophecy must be taken literally.[13] Certainly, "ten times" does not represent a quantifiable measure of the Judeans' abilities relative to the other trainees. Instead, it signifies the surpassing nature of their skill and points the reader once again to God's control over the events even in Nebuchadnezzar's government. As later chapters will affirm, all the kingdoms of this world are subservient to God's kingdom.

The surpassing knowledge of the young Daniel and his friends before the Babylonian court was a foretaste of Jesus Christ's surpassing knowledge, which he would demonstrate at the young age of twelve:

> After three days they found him in the temple, sitting in the midst of the teachers, listening to them and asking them questions. And everyone who heard him was amazed at his understanding and his answers. (Lk 2:46–47)

The final notice in this chapter tells us that Daniel served Chaldean kings in the royal court for a long time, until the first year that Cyrus, king of Persia, officially became king over Babylon, spring 538–spring 537 BC,[14] after having conquered it in 539. If we assume that Daniel was about fourteen years of age when taken into captivity in 605 BC,[15] he would have been about eighty-

---

[13] See further "A Literalistic Interpretation of Numbers Is Disproved by Daniel 1:20 and 3:19" in "Eschatology and Dispensational Premillennial Interpretations of Daniel" in the introduction.

[14] See "Introduction to Daniel 6."

[15] See the commentary on 1:1–2.

one or eighty-two years old when he finally retired from royal service. He lived until at least the beginning of Cyrus' third year (10:1, 4), spring 536,[16] when he would have been about eighty-three years old.

Moreover, this notice tells us that Daniel did not write this chapter (in its present form) until after his service had ended. Thus the book of Daniel is an early Persian period composition, as indicated at both its beginning (1:21) and near its end (10:1). This explains the Persian loanwords that appear in the book. Many of these may have already crept into the Aramaic or Hebrew used by the exiles before the fall of Babylon, but many of them may have been quickly adopted by necessity into the Aramaic used by courtiers such as Daniel because of Cyrus' accession to the throne of Babylon.

---

[16] See "Introduction to Daniel 10–12."

Excursus
Daniel's View of the Exile

Daniel offers us a unique perspective on the Babylonian exile of the Judeans. The book of Kings views the exile as a judgment by God on the people of Israel for their unfaithfulness (2 Ki 17:1–23),[1] and both Jeremiah and Lamentations condemn the unfaithfulness of Judah and call the people to repentance (e.g., Jer 3:1–4:31; Lam 2:1–22; 3:40). However, only once does Daniel portray the exile as God's judgment that calls for repentance (Dan 9:4–19), and that is in response to his reading the prophecies of Jeremiah (9:2). Nor is Daniel like his contemporary and fellow exile Ezekiel, who spends much of his time prophesying to his fellow exiles that further judgment is coming on Judah, thereby implying that the exiles should not expect to return to their homeland anytime soon. Instead of encouraging hope for a quick return to Judah, Ezekiel urges repentance and acceptance of God's just judgment on the Judeans for their sins.[2] Moreover, Daniel does not display any of the open bitterness because of the treatment he received at the hands of his captors as does the author of Psalm 137.

Instead, Daniel offers us a distinctively different Judean response to the exile. Even though his prayer in Daniel 9 picks up the themes of judgment and repentance, it is different in focus from the other works of the exilic era. Daniel contrasts God's faithfulness to his promises with the unfaithfulness of Daniel's people (Dan 9:4–11). God's great act of faithfulness that Daniel mentions in his prayer is that God shows mercy to those who love him and obey him (9:4, 9). Notice that Daniel admits that even those who love and obey God must rely on his mercy. Thus no one can be saved by obedience to the Law. Since all people remain sinners during this life, their obedience is at best only partial and never is sufficient. People can be saved only by divine mercy—by pure grace and through faith alone.

Israel not only disobeyed God, but also rebelled against him (9:11). Nevertheless, God in his mercy sent prophets to warn his people about the consequences of their rebellion and to invite them to keep his covenant in faith again. They refused, and Daniel admits this in his prayer (9:6, 10). Daniel is an exiled believer who is repentant and who confesses that it was his people's sin

---

[1] While this passage is primarily a statement of the reason for the exile of the Northern Kingdom by the Assyrians, it also anticipates Judah's exile (2 Ki 17:12, 18–20). Therefore, the writer of Kings does not have a second treatment of the reason for the Babylonian exile of Judah at the end of Kings.

[2] The bulk of the first half of Ezekiel (chapters 1–24) consists of judgment oracles against Judah. He warns that those who had not yet been exiled would soon face more severe judgment. See Hummel, *Ezekiel 1–20,* 10–12. Incidentally, Ezekiel names Daniel as a paragon of righteousness (Ezek 14:14, 20) and as extremely wise (Ezek 28:3, although the king of Tyre, as a type of Satan before his downfall, was wiser).

that led to their exile. In corporate solidarity with his fellow exiles, he prays to God penitentially for mercy.

The final section of Daniel's prayer calls on God to listen (9:17–19). In this section, Daniel repeats that he is relying on God and his compassion and forgiveness. He admits that the reason that God should act is not because Daniel or his people deserve any mercy, but because God and his honor deserve to be recognized by all people. Thus Daniel's view of the exile is that it can bring glory to God as his people confess their sins and their faith in salvation by his grace alone. While this perspective on the exile is not denied by the authors of Kings, Jeremiah, Lamentations, or Psalm 137, it is not a major emphasis in their writings, although it sometimes appears also in Ezekiel (e.g., Ezek 14:22–23; 16:53–63; 39:21–24). However, this is a major theme about the exile throughout the narrative chapters in Daniel (chapters 1–6).

One way in which the exile brings glory to God is that it emphasizes God's control over all events among humans—even when to the eyes of the world it appears as if Yahweh is impotent to keep his people from domination by a foreign power. God governs world history not only to judge sin but also to establish his kingdom of grace and to redeem his people.[3] God's control in executing judgment is emphasized when he gave Jerusalem into Nebuchadnezzar's power (1:2), but his gracious governance is evident when he grants Daniel and his companions favor in the eyes of the Babylonians (1:9). Though Nebuchadnezzar thinks he is more powerful than any god and has the ability to persecute and even kill God's saints (3:15), God's gracious reign delivers Shadrach, Meshach, and Abednego from him (3:23–28). When Nebuchadnezzar becomes prideful and arrogant about his accomplishments, God humbles him until he acknowledges that God is the sovereign Lord (4:21–34 [ET 4:24–37]). Belshazzar's defiance of God leads to Babylon's downfall, demonstrating that Yahweh, who gave Judah and Jerusalem into Babylon's clutches, could also give Babylon into the power of Persia (Daniel 5). Moreover, God's governance over events continues after Babylon's downfall, and he is able to protect Daniel from the scheming officials under the new Persian rule of Babylon (Daniel 6).

Another way that God receives glory during the exile is in the prosperity of the Judeans. Despite their status as captives, God enables Daniel and his friends to succeed and prosper in ways that outstrip even native Babylonians. Daniel explicitly gives God credit that he and his companions can deal with the Babylonians. It is God who causes the Babylonians to look with favor upon Daniel (1:9), and it is God who grants the Judeans robust health (1:15) and enables them to learn the language and literature of Babylon (1:17). By implication, it is God who makes the Babylonians perceive the abilities he gave to

---

[3] See "Theological Threats Posed by the Critical Dating of Daniel" in "Date, Authorship, and Unity," and "The Messiah in Daniel: An Overview" and "God as the Protector of His People" in "Major Themes" in the introduction. See also the commentary on 2:27–30, 34–35, 44–45 and 7:9–14.

Daniel, even though they do not acknowledge the one true God (4:5–6, 15 [ET 4:8–9, 18]; 5:11). Also by implication, Daniel commends himself to the Persians early in their rule over Babylon precisely because God is with him (6:2–6, 27 [ET 6:1–5, 26]). Daniel's contemporaries and even his opponents seem to admit this (6:5–6 [ET 6:4–5]).

Moreover, God does not simply give Daniel and his Judean friends ability to prosper, but he gives them abilities that surpass those of the Babylonians (1:20; 4:5–6, 15 [ET 4:8–9, 18]; 5:11). God receives the glory for this (2:27–28, 47). The ability of Daniel to do what the Babylonian diviners could not do is a constant testimony to God's power and glory.

God is not only glorified as he works graciously in the lives of his people, but he is also glorified when he uses those who are not his people, including the pagan powers and rulers to whom Daniel is subject. Thus he reveals the future to Nebuchadnezzar (Daniel 2) and uses Darius to punish both the insolent Belshazzar (5:30) and those who would persecute Daniel (6:25 [ET 6:24]).

Finally, God receives glory through his captive people who learn to work within a pagan system and yet retain their faith in him. Thus Daniel and his companions assimilate to Babylonian culture when possible without compromising their faith. They do not object to learning Babylonian language and literature (1:4). They work in the service of the Babylonians and the Persians (1:19–21; 2:48–49; 3:30; 6:2–4 [ET 6:1–3]). However, they also bring glory to God by refusing to assimilate when they would have to deny Yahweh their God (3:14–18; 6:8–11 [ET 6:7–10]; see commentary on 1:8).

(a) Dan 2:47; 3:28–29; 3:32–33 (ET 4:2–3); 4:31–32, 34 (ET 4:34–35, 37); 6:27–28 (ET 6:26–27)

Thus, for Daniel, the Babylonian captivity is not simply punishment by God for unfaithfulness as well as another opportunity for repentance, but it is also the continuing story of the glory of God shown in the history of his dealing with humans and his mercy toward sinners. Therefore, Daniel not only records his praise to God for what he does (2:20–23), but also records the praise ascribed to God by pagan kings who, despite their polytheism, must confront the only true God, who exercises his power and seeks to show his mercy to all people.[a]

By adopting this view of the exile in the narratives (chapters 1–6), Daniel paves the way for the visionary prophecies at the end of his book (chapters 7–12). God's glory is shown in the exile, but the greater glory of God will be demonstrated in the future, when God fulfills his promise to bring the Messiah, who is the explicit focus of Daniel's prophecies in Daniel 7 and 9. Just as God will show his glory through exiled Israel living under the domination of Babylon, so God will show greater glory through his Son, who comes to his people living under the domination of Rome in the days of Caesar Augustus (Lk 2:1–7; Jn 1:14).

Daniel 2:1–49

Nebuchadnezzar's Dream of the Statue: Four Kingdoms before the Kingdom of God

Introduction to Daniel 2

2:1–13 Nebuchadnezzar Challenges Babylon's Wise Men to Recount and Explain His Dream

2:14–23 God Reveals Nebuchadnezzar's Dream to Daniel

2:24–49 Daniel Recounts and Explains Nebuchadnezzar's Dream of the Statue

Excursus *The Four-Kingdom Schema in Daniel*

Introduction to Daniel 2

Major Emphases in Daniel 2
Divine Revelation to Daniel and His Prayer

The first mortal threat to Daniel comes in this chapter. Nebuchadnezzar has a dream so troubling that he demands that his court diviners interpret it. When they ask him to describe the dream, he refuses and adds the requirement that they must, in addition to interpreting the dream, also tell him its content. Of course no one could do such a thing without divine revelation. This extra requirement is the king's way of ensuring that the interpretation too is given by divine revelation. If the wise men of the court are unable to give both the dream and its interpretation, all the wise men, including Daniel and his three Judean friends, will be executed.

This chapter introduces the first direct divine revelation in Daniel, which becomes a common feature in the book. Of the twelve chapters, only Daniel 1, 3, and 6 do not feature some type of direct revelation from God, and God still performs miracles in those chapters. The revelation to Daniel in chapter 2 is given by God for Nebuchadnezzar, to answer his thoughts about the future (2:29) and to reveal to him for the first time that Israel's God is in control over all that happens among human kingdoms. Nebuchadnezzar's dream of a statue constructed with four metals drives this point home as Daniel interprets it to be about four great world empires that give way to God's eternal kingdom.

Though the messianic overtones of Daniel's interpretation are clear,[1] they are lost on Nebuchadnezzar, who has no interest in the theological nuances of what he considers to be the faith of a third-rate people whom he has subjugated. Though in the end Nebuchadnezzar acknowledges Daniel's God as "God of gods, Lord of kings, and Revealer of mysteries" (2:47), he does not understand the full implications of the dream, either in its messianic message or its implied monotheism.

However, the theological center of the chapter is not the dream and its interpretation, but Daniel's prayer (2:20–23). This prayer fuses the two major theological themes in the chapter: God governs all human history, and God alone grants knowledge and wisdom. This second theme is emphasized by the contrast between the inability of the Babylonian wise men to fulfill the royal demand and Daniel's ability to do what they are unable to do. Nebuchadnezzar twice demands that the wise men of Babylon tell him both the dream and its interpretation (2:5–6, 8–9). God reveals both to Daniel (2:19), whereas the Babylonians do not believe that such divine disclosure is possible because their gods' "dwelling is not with mortal flesh" (2:11). In contrast, Daniel's God does

---

[1] See further "The Messiah in Daniel: An Overview" in "Major Themes" the introduction.

interact with mortals, and indeed he would come to dwell in human flesh in the person of Jesus Christ (Mt 1:18–25; Jn 1:14; Heb 2:14; 1 Jn 4:2).

Daniel among the Wise Men

Critical scholars often allege that the beginning of chapter 2 contradicts chapter 1 in two ways. A first alleged contradiction involves the relationship between Daniel and the other kinds of wise men.[2] Daniel is not among the specific classes of wise men of Babylon that come before the king in 2:1–11, which critics interpret to mean that Daniel had not yet completed his training, thus contradicting 1:18 and also contradicting 1:19, which states that Daniel and his three compatriots "stood before/served the king." However, the circumstances of 2:1–11 do *not* mean that Daniel had yet to complete his training, nor do they mean that he had not begun his service under the king. On the contrary, 2:1–11 only shows that Daniel and the three other Judeans were not serving Nebuchadnezzar in the same capacity as the "the magicians, the soothsayers, the sorcerers, and the Chaldeans" (2:2).

Nothing in chapter 1 implies that the Judeans were in training to become persons who practiced such occult arts or who would be characterized as "wise men, soothsayers, magicians, or diviners" (2:27). That the Judeans were found to be better than those with demonic powers (1:20) does not mean that they themselves were practitioners of the demonic.[3] Similarly, in chapter 2, Daniel demonstrates his superiority over the Babylonian diviners because of his God-given wisdom, but this does not imply that Daniel ever was part of their group.

Indeed, even at the end of chapter 2, Daniel is not placed among these specific classes of diviners, but is "chief prefect" (רַב־סִגְנִין) over them (2:48). He is their supervisor, but he is never one of them. Later too, Daniel is not among them, but separate from them. He is not included among them in Daniel 4 and is brought to the king only when they cannot interpret Nebuchadnezzar's dream (4:4–5 [ET 4:7–8]). Nor is Daniel among them in chapter 5. Once again, he is called before Belshazzar only after the wise men who are specifically called "the soothsayers, the Chaldeans, and the diviners" (5:7) cannot interpret the handwriting on the wall (5:8–12).

Daniel and his companions are included among the more general class called "wise men" (Aramaic: חַכִּימִין), all of whom would have been killed if God had not revealed Nebuchadnezzar's dream and its interpretation to Daniel (2:12–14, 18).[4] That this is a more general classification is confirmed by 5:15, where the

---

[2] For the second alleged contradiction, see "Chronology and Nebuchadnezzar's Second Year" below.

[3] See the third textual note on 1:20 for a discussion of the terms "magicians" and "soothsayers" used in that verse.

[4] In Daniel, the Hebrew חָכָם, "wise man," does not occur, but the Aramaic equivalent, חַכִּים, occurs (always plural: חַכִּימִין) in 2:12–14, 18, 21, 24, 27, 48; 4:3, 15 (ET 4:6, 18); 5:7, 8, 15.

phrase חַכִּימַיָּא אָשְׁפַיָּא, literally, "the wise men, the soothsayers," has the restrictive meaning "those wise men who specifically were the soothsayers." Similar is the restrictive meaning of this phrase in 2:27: חַכִּימִין אָשְׁפִין חַרְטֻמִּין גָּזְרִין, "those wise men who specifically were soothsayers, magicians, diviners." In 2:27 Daniel is saying that no person wise in the occult arts of divination could reveal the king's mystery. Only the one true God can do that, and he works through a different kind of wise man—namely, Daniel—to reveal his mysteries.

Therefore, Daniel and his friends were classified as wise men. That is why they would have been executed, since the king's order did not distinguish among the various classes of his wise men and courtiers (2:12–14, 18). However, Daniel and the Judeans were never among those wise men who practiced pagan divination or the occult.

Chronology and Nebuchadnezzar's Second Year

Critical scholars often point to the date notice at the beginning of chapter 2 as an inaccuracy in Daniel and a sign that the author was confused over the sequence of the historical events.[5] That confusion allegedly created another contradiction between chapters 1 and 2. The second year of Nebuchadnezzar (2:1), they argue, would occur before the end of the three-year period (1:5) prescribed before the young Judean men would complete their training (1:18). Their promotion to positions of prominence in Babylon (2:48–49) would then come before their interview with Nebuchadnezzar, which completed their training (1:18–19).

However, there is no conflict here. Nebuchadnezzar's second regnal year is actually the third year in the Daniel narratives. The Babylonian system of reckoning the years of a king's reign did not count his first partial (accession) year. Nebuchadnezzar's accession year lasted from 1 Elul 605 BC to the end of Adar 604 (September 7, 605–April 1, 604). His first (full) regnal year was from 1 Nisan 604 to the end of Adar 603 (April 2, 604–March 21, 603). His second regnal year lasted from 1 Nisan 603 to the end of Adar 602 (March 22, 603–April 9, 602). Since it was normal for people in the ancient Near East to count partial years when reckoning time spans, the Judeans would have been in training during the last part of Nebuchadnezzar's accession year,[6] his entire first year, and part of his second year, making three years according to Hebrew count, fulfilling the "three years" in 1:5. Thus the notice that the events of chapter 2 took place in Nebuchadnezzar's second year (2:1) implies that it was shortly after Daniel and his companions had completed their training (1:18).

Therefore, chapter 2 immediately illustrates the statement in 1:20 that Daniel was superior in every way to Nebuchadnezzar's other wise men.

---

[5] E.g., Hartman and Di Lella, *Daniel*, 137–38; Montgomery, *Daniel*, 140–41.

[6] Daniel and his three companions probably arrived in Babylon in February 604 BC. See the commentary on 1:1, "The Events of 605 BC."

Thus the time notices in Daniel 1 and 2 imply this sequence of events:

Nebuchadnezzar's Accession Year, Which Was the First Year of Training for the Judean Captives

- Sometime between June 605 and January 604, Jerusalem capitulates to Nebuchadnezzar (Dan 1:1–2). (Nebuchadnezzar assumes the throne in September 605.)
- In February 604, captives from the Judean nobility (1:3) are taken to Babylon.
- Sometime between February 604 and April 1, 604, Daniel, Hananiah, Azariah, and Mishael begin their training (1:3–7). This is year 1 of that training.

Nebuchadnezzar's First Year, Which Was the Second Year of Training for the Judean Captives

- From April 2, 604, to March 21, 603, Nebuchadnezzar's first regnal year, the Judeans are in training to serve in Nebuchadnezzar's court (1:8–17). This is year 2 of their training.

Nebuchadnezzar's Second Year, Which Was the Third Year of Training for the Judean Captives

- Sometime between March 22, 603, and fall 603, during Nebuchadnezzar's second regnal year, the Judeans complete their training (1:18–19, fulfilling 1:5). This is year 3 of their training.
- Also during his second regnal year, in fall 603 or winter 603–602, Nebuchadnezzar dreams the dream recorded in Daniel 2; God reveals the dream and its interpretation to Daniel; and the Judeans are promoted (2:48–49).

Daniel 2:1–13

Nebuchadnezzar Challenges Babylon's Wise Men to Recount and Explain His Dream

Translation

2 ¹In the second year of the reign of Nebuchadnezzar, Nebuchadnezzar dreamt a dream. His spirit was troubled, but sleep came upon him [again]. ²The king said to summon the magicians, the soothsayers, the sorcerers, and the Chaldeans to relate to the king his dream. So they came and stood before the king. ³The king said to them, "I dreamt a dream, and my spirit was troubled to understand the dream."

⁴The Chaldeans said to the king in Aramaic, "Your Majesty, may you live forever! Tell the dream to your servants, and we will explain its meaning."

⁵The king answered and said to the Chaldeans, "The matter from me is certain: if you do not make known to me the dream and its meaning, you shall be made into body parts, and your houses will be made a pile of rubble. ⁶However, if you reveal the dream and its meaning, you will receive gifts, a reward, and great honor from me. Therefore, reveal to me the dream and its meaning!"

⁷They answered a second time and said, "Let the king tell the dream to his servants, and we will explain its meaning."

⁸The king answered and said, "For sure I know that you are buying time because you see that the matter is certain from me, ⁹because if you do not make the dream known to me, there is only one decree for you. You have devised a lying and corrupt response to say before me until the time changes. Therefore, reveal to me the dream, and I will know that you are able to reveal to me its meaning."

¹⁰The Chaldeans answered before the king, saying, "There is no person on earth who is able to reveal the king's matter, since no great and powerful king has ever requested a matter like this from any magician, soothsayer, or Chaldean. ¹¹The matter that the king requests is difficult, and there is no one else who can reveal it to the king except gods, whose dwelling is not with mortal flesh."

¹²Because of this the king became very angry and enraged, and he gave the order to destroy the wise men of Babylon. ¹³The decree was issued, and the wise men were [in the process of] being executed. So they sought Daniel and his companions to execute [them].

Textual Notes

2:1 חֲלַם נְבֻכַדְנֶצַּר חֲלֹמוֹת—The cognate accusative construction with the verb חָלַם and the noun חֲלֹמוֹת is, literally, "Nebuchadnezzar dreamt dreams." The plural noun probably refers to a single dream that had many detailed parts and extended for a long time.

Similar is the use of the plural מַרְאוֹת, "visions," for a detailed and extended vision of God in Ezek 1:1 and 8:3. The plural (חֲלֹמֹתָיו) recurs in Dan 2:2, but the king uses the singular חֲלוֹם twice in 2:3.

וַתִּתְפָּעֶם רוּחוֹ—"His spirit was troubled" has the only occurrence of the Hithpael (HtD) of the verb פָּעַם in the OT. Most often it is used in the Niphal (N) (Gen 41:8; Ps 77:5 [ET 77:4]; Dan 2:3). In this case, the Hithpael signals a reflexive or deliberative aspect of Nebuchadnezzar's thought.

וּשְׁנָתוֹ נִהְיְתָה עָלָיו—Literally, "but his sleep was upon him," this uses the unusual Niphal (N) of הָיָה. Many commentators understand this difficult clause to mean that Nebuchadnezzar was unable to sleep, and some see a parallel with the Aramaic clause in 6:19 (ET 6:18): וְשִׁנְתֵּהּ נַדַּת עֲלוֹהִי, "and his sleep fled from him."[1] Collins goes so far as to suggest emending the text here by replacing נִהְיְתָה עָלָיו with נָדְדָה.[2] However, commentators also recognize that the expression as it stands here in Hebrew means that Nebuchadnezzar fell back to sleep.[3] Nebuchadnezzar probably had his dream during "first sleep."[4] That is, in the days before widespread artificial light, the natural sleep pattern of humans was segmented: a cycle of two periods of sleep during the night, with a period of wakefulness in between, lasting for several hours and beginning around midnight.[5] The first segment was characterized by deep sleep that often included dreams. For another segmented sleep cycle with dreams, see Gen 41:4–5.

2:2 לַחַרְטֻמִּים וְלָאַשָּׁפִים—For "magicians" and "soothsayers," see the third textual note on 1:20.

וְלַמְכַשְּׁפִים—"Sorcerers" is a Piel (D) participle of the verb כָּשַׁף. This verb denotes seeking knowledge of the future by pagan occultic—and hence demonic (cf. 1 Cor 10:21)—means, apart from divinely initiated revelation by the one true God. It occurs

---

[1] Hartman and Di Lella, *Daniel*, 138; Leupold, *Daniel*, 82–83; Lucas, *Daniel*, 62; Miller, *Daniel*, 77; Montgomery, *Daniel*, 141; Walvoord, *Daniel*, 47. See also *HALOT*, s.v. היה, Niphal, 3; ESV, NASB, NIV.

[2] Collins, *Daniel*, 148.

[3] Calvin, *Daniel*, 1:117; Collins, *Daniel*, 148; Goldingay, *Daniel*, 30, 32; Lucas, *Daniel*, 62.

[4] See Holladay, "Indications of Segmented Sleep in the Bible." While the noun תַּרְדֵּמָה, "deep sleep," is not in Daniel, the cognate verb רָדַם, "sleep deeply," occurs in 8:18 and 10:9, and this sleep apparently is induced in Daniel by God or his Word. While some occurrences of תַּרְדֵּמָה, "deep sleep," in the Bible are divinely induced (Gen 2:21; Is 29:10) or divinely extended (1 Sam 26:12), Holladay notes that in other passages it seems to be a natural phenomenon that probably should be understood as "first sleep" (Job 4:13; 33:15; Prov 19:15). Note that in Abraham's case its onset is linked with sundown (Gen 15:12). Holladay discusses the following passages that probably involve the waking interval in natural, segmented sleep: Judges 7; 16:3; 1 Sam 28:8–25; Jer 6:5; Micah 2:1–2; Pss 36:5 (ET 36:4); 63:7 (ET 63:6); 77:7 (ET 77:6); 119:55, 62, 148; Ruth 3:8–13; Song 3:1–5; 5:2–8; Judith 11:17; 12:5–6; Mt 25:1–13 (especially Mt 25:9–10); Mk 14:40–43; Lk 11:5; Acts 16:11–40. I would also add the entire cycle of segmented sleep as mentioned in Gen 41:1–7 and the passage here, Dan 2:1. Holladay also proposes that Gen 28:10–17; 1 Ki 3:5; and Wisdom 18:14–19 mention the dreams that typically come at the end of first sleep.

[5] A. Roger Ekirch, "Sleep We Have Lost: Pre-industrial Slumber in the British Isles," *American Historical Review* 106 (2001): 343–86; *At Day's Close: Night in Times Past* (New York: Norton, 2005); Paul Bohannan, "Concepts of Time among the Tiv of Nigeria," *Southwestern Journal of Anthropology* 9 (1953): 251–62.

together with "wise men" describing Egyptian practitioners in Pharaoh's court (Ex 7:11). Other OT passages strongly condemn the practice (Deut 18:10; Mal 3:5; 2 Chr 33:6) and even prescribe the death penalty for it (Ex 22:17 [ET 22:18]).

וְלַכַּשְׂדִּים—See the last textual note on 1:4. In this context, "Chaldeans" seems to be a general word that covers all three classes of diviners previously mentioned. Thus in 2:4 the "Chaldeans" who reply to the king include the three other kinds of diviners ("the magicians, the soothsayers, the sorcerers") named in 2:2.

2:4 אֲרָמִית—This is an adverbial accusative: they spoke "in Aramaic."[6]

Much has been made of the fact that 1QDan[a] does not contain אֲרָמִית, but does contain a space to mark the beginning of the first line in Aramaic. However, there is sufficient space at the end of the previous line in 1QDan[a] for this word, so it probably was there, although the margin is damaged, and several words at the end of each line are illegible. Moreover, this is a Hebrew word (2 Ki 18:26; Is 36:11; Ezra 4:7), so it would make sense that it would come before the space in 1QDan[a] marking the beginning of the Aramaic.[7]

מַלְכָּא לְעָלְמִין חֱיִי—The contemporary English equivalent of מַלְכָּא is not "O King," as in most versions, but "Your Majesty." The determined state in Aramaic may be used as a vocative.[8] This is equivalent to the use of the article in Hebrew to mark a vocative, as in the address to the king as הַמֶּלֶךְ (e.g., Judg 3:19; 1 Sam 17:55).

The flattering imperative clause לְעָלְמִין חֱיִי, "(may you) live forever," will recur in 3:9; 5:10; 6:7, 22 (ET 6:6, 21), always spoken to a king (Nebuchadnezzar, Belshazzar, or Darius). The inclusion of it here by Daniel the author involves ironic satire since Nebuchadnezzar is a mere mortal, whose kingdom will end as prophesied in the dream. Later in this chapter, Daniel will assert that it is the messianic kingdom of God that truly "forever/eternally [לְעָלְמִין] will not be destroyed," but will be established "forever" (לְעָלְמַיָּא, 2:44). Daniel will also ascribe praise to God, whose name is to be blessed "forever and ever" (מִן־עָלְמָא וְעַד־עָלְמָא, 2:20).

וּפִשְׁרָא נְחַוֵּא:—A פְּשַׁר (e.g., 2:4–7, 9), *peshar*, is not simply an "interpretation," but the "meaning" that also explains the coming reality presaged by the dream. Among the Dead Sea Scrolls were *pesherim* that cited biblical passages and then offered a detailed interpretation (פֵּשֶׁר, *pesher*, in Hebrew) of the supposed meaning and expected historical fulfillment of each passage.[9] פְּשַׁר is used as the object of the Pael (D) of חֲוָה, "explain, make known, reveal," in 2:4, 24; 5:7, and as the object of the Haphel (H) of חֲוָה in 2:6–7, 9, 16; 5:12, 15.

---

[6] For the significance of the Aramaic portions of the book in its overall structure, see "Interlocked Chiasms and the Dual Language of the Book" in "Overview of Daniel" in the introduction. For a discussion of the Aramaic in Daniel in relation to the Aramaic language in general, one may see Steinmann, *Fundamental Biblical Aramaic*, 285–87.

[7] Barthélemy and Milik, *Qumran Cave 1*, 150; Mastin, "The Reading of 1QDan[a] at Daniel 2:4."

[8] See Rosenthal, *A Grammar of Biblical Aramaic*, § 43; Steinmann, *Fundamental Biblical Aramaic*, 297.

[9] See Rabinowitz, "*Pēsher/Pittārōn*: Its Biblical Meaning and Its Significance in the Qumran Literature."

2:5 עָנֵה מַלְכָּא וְאָמַר לְכַשְׂדָּאֵי—In the Aramaic portion of Daniel, the verb עֲנָה, "to answer" (here its participle, עָנֵה), frequently is used with the verb אֲמַר, "to say," as a kind of hendiadys. Sometimes, as here in 2:5 (also, e.g., 2:7–8, 10, 27; 3:16), the utterance is in response to prior speech, so both verbs can be translated, "answered and said." However, often the speaker is not responding to a prior statement, but is prompted to speak by the situation (e.g., 2:15, 20, 26) or simply takes the initiative to speak (3:9). In such cases, the two Aramaic verbs are best translated by a single English verb: "said."

הַדָּמִין תִּתְעַבְדוּן—By saying, "You shall be made (into) body parts," Nebuchadnezzar is threatening his advisors with dismemberment. See the same idiom (הַדָּמִין with the Hithpeel [HtG] of עֲבַד) in 3:29. "Body parts" is a loanword from Old Persian that means "members of the body."[10]

וּבָתֵּיכוֹן נְוָלִי יִתְּשָׂמוּן—Probably this means "your houses will be made (into) a pile of rubble." The meaning "dunghill" for נְוָלִי (*HALOT*) is only a guess based on later Jewish Aramaic. BDB derives נְוָלִי from Akkadian *namâlu* or *nawâlu*, "ruin."[11]

2:6 וּנְבִזְבָּה—This term, translated as "a reward," recurs in the plural in 5:17, and in both verses it is parallel to מַתְּנָא, "gift." It may be a loanword from Akkadian (see *HALOT*) or Persian.[12]

2:8 עִדָּנָא אַנְתּוּן זָבְנִין—This is, literally, "time you are buying." The verb זְבַן means "to buy" (*HALOT*) and is an economic term. The Aramaic matches well the English idiom "to buy time."

2:10 יַבֶּשְׁתָּא—Rendered, "earth," this literally means "dry land" (*HALOT*), as does the Hebrew יַבָּשָׁה (e.g., Ex 15:19; Josh 4:22; Jonah 1:9, 13; 2:11 [ET 2:10]). It is used here to signify the entire earth, where we might have expected אַרְעָא.

2:11 יְחַוִּנַּהּ—The (Pael [D]) imperfect of חֲוָה has the nuance of capability: no one "*can* reveal [it]."[13] Its force is similar to the combination of verbs (יְכֻל and the Haphel [H] infinitive of חֲוָה) in 2:10: יוּכַל לְהַחֲוָיָה, there is no one who "is able to reveal [it]."

2:12 בְּנַס וּקְצַף שַׂגִּיא—This has an ingressive meaning, literally, "he *became* angry and enraged—very." The two verbs probably approach a hendiadys, and so the adverb שַׂגִּיא, "very," modifies both.

2:13 וְחַכִּימַיָּא מִתְקַטְּלִין—"The wise men were being executed," with a (Hithpaal [HtD]) participle, probably indicates that the process of execution had begun, but was not yet completed. The first step would have been to round up all of the wise men. Calvin assumes that some of the wise men have already been executed.[14] However, since Daniel and his friends have not yet been seized, it may be that no one has already been executed.

---

[10] See *HALOT*; Rosenthal, *A Grammar of Biblical Aramaic*, § 189.

[11] See also Rosenthal, *A Grammar of Biblical Aramaic*, § 190.

[12] *TWOT*, § 2844; Rosenthal, *A Grammar of Biblical Aramaic*, § 190.

[13] See Steinmann, *Fundamental Biblical Aramaic*, 316.

[14] Calvin, *Daniel*, 1:135.

Commentary

Nebuchadnezzar's Challenge to Babylon's Wise Men (2:1–3)

The chapter opens with Nebuchadnezzar experiencing troubled sleep because of a dream. Although he returns to sleep, he remembers the dream and continues to be troubled by it. Then 2:3 explains the reason for his distress: he wants to know the meaning of the dream. Josephus and Calvin believe that Nebuchadnezzar, upon waking, has forgotten the dream, and that is why he asks his wise men to recount to him the dream itself, not just its meaning.[15] However, it is most likely that he remembers the gist of the dream, but because he fell back asleep (2:1), he cannot remember its details.[16] He certainly has to remember the gist of the dream in order to be able to know when his demand that the dream be recounted to him has been obeyed. Therefore, in his statement "my spirit was troubled *to know/understand* [לְדַעַת] the dream" (2:3), the verb יָדַע (Qal [G] infinitive construct) most likely does not imply that he no longer remembers the dream and will "know" it only if it is described to him, but that he wants to "understand" its meaning.[17]

Apparently, from the very beginning, Nebuchadnezzar is counting on his experts in pagan methods of divination to tell him both the dream and its interpretation. Instead of telling them what he dreamt, he stops and waits for his courtiers to apply their skills. His silence is a tacit request for them to divine the contents of his dream.

The Wise Men's Reply and Nebuchadnezzar's Response (2:4–6)

Nebuchadnezzar's diviners do not comply with his tacit request. They begin with "Your Majesty, may you live forever!" (2:4; also 3:9; 5:10; 6:7, 22 [ET 6:6, 21]), a rather common address to the king expressing a wish for his well-being. In a pagan context, it would be understood as a prayer to the gods, especially the patron god of the nation, which for Babylon was Bel (also called Marduk). The inclusion of the wish by Daniel the author may be a form of ironical satire because Nebuchadnezzar, as a mere mortal, would not live "forever." In contrast, this chapter later will introduce a theme that recurs in Daniel: God's kingdom truly is "forever" (2:44; 4:31 [ET 4:34]), "eternal" (3:33 [ET 4:3]; 4:31 [ET 4:34]; 6:27 [ET 6:26]; 7:27), and it "will never/not be destroyed" (2:44; 6:27 [ET 6:26]). This is the same kingdom of grace that the NT calls "the eternal kingdom of our Lord and Savior Jesus Christ" (2 Pet 1:11; cf. Mt 16:18; Rev 11:15).[18]

---

[15] Josephus, *Antiquities*, 10.195; Calvin, *Daniel*, 1:117.

[16] Baldwin (*Daniel*, 85) says that Nebuchadnezzar forgot the dream, but later she seems to indicate that the king forgot only the details of the dream (p. 87).

[17] Collins, *Daniel*, 156; Lucas, *Daniel*, 70; Miller, *Daniel*, 78, 80. However, Collins seems to contradict himself on this; see Collins, *Daniel*, 148.

[18] See further "Daniel in the New Testament" in the introduction.

The king's advisors ask him to recount the dream, as they would normally expect him to do. However, Nebuchadnezzar tells them in no uncertain terms that he has already made up his mind that this dream is too important for such an approach. It would be relatively easy for occult practitioners (or charlatans) to speculate about the possible meaning of a dream that was described to them. They could then make flattering predictions about the future (as did the false prophets in 1 Kings 22). Nebuchadnezzar anticipates that his advisers would concoct an interpretation that would please him, but that would be no divine revelation.

The king knows because of his troubled night that this dream is not an ordinary dream, but a communication from the supernatural realm. Therefore he wants to hear its "meaning" (פְּשַׁר): what future it actually portended. This future could only be made known by another supernatural revelation. The king's requirement that his advisors recount the dream itself to him is intended to ensure that their interpretation too, like their recounting of his dream, is the result of a divine revelation to them, not a flattering concoction. His zeal to ascertain the dream's meaning explains his threat (2:5) and promise (2:6) contingent on the performance of the wise men.

Nebuchadnezzar's threat to dismember those with whom he is displeased and to destroy their houses (2:5) will be repeated in 3:29, but there it will be issued against those who speak against the God of Shadrach, Meshach, and Abednego. The depiction of Nebuchadnezzar as having no qualms about carrying out his threat is confirmed by his earlier treatment of Shadrach, Meshach, and Abednego (3:20–21), and also by his treatment of the Judean king Zedekiah (2 Ki 25:7) and the Judean rebels Ahab and Zedekiah (Jer 29:22). Moreover, this type of punishment was not unusual in the ancient Near East.[19] Although Daniel and his companions are not part of the group currently assembled before Nebuchadnezzar, Daniel the author has skillfully begun to heighten the reader's anxiety for the Judeans at this point in the narrative.

The Wise Men's Second Reply and Nebuchadnezzar's Response (2:7–9)

The plea from the wise men is an admission that they cannot do what Nebuchadnezzar requires. Just as he began the conversation with an unspoken request for them to tell him what he dreamt, so now they concede the unspoken admission that they cannot do it (2:7).

Nebuchadnezzar's reply (2:8–9) voices the unspoken concern behind his original request: he expects that they will give him an answer that will not match the future portended by the dream. He is sufficiently bothered by the dream that he wants to ensure that he receives its real meaning. He charges them with "buying time" (2:8) and devising "a lying and corrupt response" (2:9). They are using a delaying tactic, hoping to get more information about the dream so

---

[19] For examples, see Montgomery, *Daniel*, 146.

that they can fabricate a flattering explanation to please him. Barring that, they may hope that if enough time passes ("the time changes," 2:9), Nebuchadnezzar might relent about his threat, lose interest in the dream, and forget the entire incident. But Nebuchadnezzar remains determined to carry out his threat unless they can deliver the genuine meaning.

That Nebuchadnezzar would be able to recognize the dream when it is recounted (2:9) demonstrates that he remembered the dream's major features. His wise men's request in 2:7 also assumes that he knows the dream.

The Wise Men's Third Reply and Nebuchadnezzar's Response (2:10–13)

Desperate to escape the king's wrath, the Chaldeans point out that no king, no matter how powerful, has ever made such a demand. Moreover, they assert that there is no one else (וְאָחֳרָן לָא אִיתַי, literally, "another there is not," 2:11) who can tell the king his dream—implying that he might as well recount his dream to them so they can interpret it, since no other person will be able to do any better. The only exception they give is "gods, whose dwelling is not with mortal flesh" (2:11). Their view is that the gods do not dwell among mortals nor reveal such things to people. This statement reveals more about the Babylonian view of deity than they probably intended. They believed that they could determine the gods' intentions through methods of divination, through manipulation of items or interpretation of signs,[20] but they could not communicate directly with the gods because they were remote and inaccessible to mortals.

(a) E.g., 1 Ki 8:10–13, 27; Pss 68:17, 19 (ET 68:16, 18); 76:3 (ET 76:2); 84:2 (ET 84:1); 132:7, 13; Ezra 7:15; 2 Chr 36:15

Of course, Daniel the author quotes those words to imply that their theological assumption is wrong and leads them to the wrong conclusion. In fact, there is a God who dwells among humans! He dwelt among his chosen people Israel in the tabernacle (e.g., Ex 29:45–46; 40:35; 2 Sam 15:25; 1 Chr 23:25) and then in the temple in Jerusalem.[a] Ultimately, in the fullness of time (Gal 4:4), he would come to dwell among us as the Word made flesh (Jn 1:14; Col 1:15–19; 2:9). Though God's dwelling place is in heaven (1 Ki 8:39, 43, 49; 2 Chr 6:30, 33, 39), he who fills all things dwelt in a special way among his people in Jerusalem. Had the Babylonians known this God, as Daniel knew him, they would not have made this statement. Thus by recording their assertion about the gods, Daniel helps the reader anticipate the story's climax.

While it is only the Chaldean wise men who cannot tell Nebuchadnezzar his dream, his fury is so strong that he issues the order to execute also all the other courtiers who were not part of this conversation about his dream. Daniel and his companions are about to be caught in the executioner's dragnet. Up to

---

[20] Some examples of Babylonian methods of divination are mentioned in Ezek 21:26 (ET 21:21). God, speaking through Ezekiel, prophesies that the king of Babylon (Nebuchadnezzar) will "practice divination" to decide whether to attack Rabbah or Jerusalem: "he will shake the arrows, consult the teraphim, and examine the liver." Yet in this case, the one true God has already determined that the outcome of these methods will be that Nebuchadnezzar will attack and conquer Jerusalem. For a discussion, see Hummel, *Ezekiel 21–48*, 634–36, 654–55.

this point, Daniel the author has been heightening the tension in the story by not answering the question of whether the young Judeans too are in danger. He answers that question in 2:13 where "Daniel and his companions" are mentioned for the first time in the chapter. But this leads to a greater tension, because the reader moves from suspecting that the Judeans may be in dire straights to knowing that they are in mortal danger.

Daniel 2:14–23
God Reveals Nebuchadnezzar's Dream to Daniel

Translation

2 ¹⁴Then Daniel replied with prudent judgment to Arioch, the chief of the king's executioners, who had gone out to execute the wise men of Babylon. ¹⁵He said to Arioch, the king's officer, "Why is the decree so harsh from the king?" So Arioch explained the matter to Daniel. ¹⁶Then Daniel entered [the court] and requested from the king that he would give him time so that he could reveal the meaning to the king.

¹⁷Then Daniel went to his house and explained the matter to Hananiah, Azariah, and Mishael, his companions, ¹⁸so that they might seek mercy from the God of heaven concerning this mystery, so that they might not destroy Daniel and his companions with the rest of the wise men of Babylon.

¹⁹Then the mystery was revealed to Daniel in a vision at night. Then Daniel blessed the God of heaven. ²⁰Daniel said,

"May the name of God be blessed forever and ever,
  because wisdom and power are his.
²¹He changes times and eras.
  He deposes kings and establishes kings.
He gives wisdom to wise people
  and knowledge to those who know discernment.
²²He reveals deep things and hidden things.
He knows what is in the dark,
  and the light dwells with him.
²³To you, God of my ancestors, I give thanks and praise,
  because you have given me wisdom and power.
Now you have made known to me what we requested of you,
  because you have made known to us the king's matter."

Textual Notes

2:14 דָּנִיֵּאל הֲתִיב עֵטָא וּטְעֵם—This is, literally, "Daniel returned prudence and judgment." The two nouns form a hendiadys: "prudent judgment."

רַב־טַבָּחַיָּא דִּי מַלְכָּא—This is, literally, "the chief of the executioners who belonged to the king." The noun טַבָּח, "executioner," is from the verb טְבַח, "to slaughter," usually with reference to animals. The cognate verb (טָבַח) and noun (טֶבַח) occur in Hebrew (e.g., the words occur together in Gen 43:16; Ezek 21:15 [ET 21:10]; Prov 9:2). The equivalent Hebrew title for this officer is רַב־טַבָּחִים, "chief executioner."[a]

(a) 2 Ki 25:8, 10–12, 15, 18, 20; Jer 39:9–11, 13; 40:1–2, 5; 41:10; 43:6; 52:12, 14–16, 19, 24, 26, 30

2:15 דָּתָא מְהַחְצְפָה—Daniel describes "the decree" (דָּתָא) using the Haphel (H) participle "harsh" (*HALOT*). The verb חֲצַף means "be insolent, overbearing, audacious." In an effort to soften Daniel's question, some commentators and versions translate this word as "urgent," a meaning that the equivalent Aphel (H) participle may entail at 3:22.[1]

מִלְּתָא הוֹדַע—This idiom with the noun מִלָּה as the object of the Haphel (H) of יְדַע, literally, "he made known the word," is translated, "he explained the matter" both here and in 2:17.

2:16 וְדָנִיֵּאל עַל—The verb עַל is the Peal (G) perfect of עֲלַל, "to **go in**, enter for an audience with the king" (*HALOT*, Peal). Hence it is translated, "Daniel *entered* [*the court*]." The verb recurs in 2:24–25 and chapters 4–6.

וּפִשְׁרָא לְהַחֲוָיָה לְמַלְכָּא:—While the syntax of the infinitive (Haphel [H] of חֲוָה) is simple parataxis ("and the meaning to reveal to the king"), the larger context supports translating it as a purpose clause, "*so that* he could reveal the meaning to the king." See also the first textual note on 2:18.

2:18 וְרַחֲמִין לְמִבְעֵא מִן־קֳדָם אֱלָהּ שְׁמַיָּא—This purpose clause with Peal (G) infinitive (לְמִבְעֵא) places the object noun (וְרַחֲמִין) first for emphasis: literally, "so that *mercy* [they] would seek from before the God of heaven." In Ezra too, the Judean exiles refer to their God as אֱלָהּ שְׁמַיָּא, "the God of heaven" (Ezra 5:11–12; 6:9–10; 7:12, 21, 23), but in Daniel the expression is used only in this chapter (Dan 2:18–19, 37, 44). Like its Hebrew equivalent, אֱלֹהֵי הַשָּׁמַיִם,[b] this phrase is used mainly by Israelites when they identify their God to Gentiles or by Gentiles who are speaking about Israel's God. The equivalent Greek phrase ὁ θεὸς τοῦ οὐρανοῦ occurs in the NT in Rev 11:13; 16:11.

(b) Gen 24:3, 7; Jonah 1:9; Ezra 1:2; Neh 1:4–5; 2:4, 20; 2 Chr 36:23

רָזָה—"Mystery" (רָז) is a loanword from Old Persian.[2] This word is always used in Daniel in reference to the meaning of a revelatory dream (2:18–19, 27–30, 47; 4:6 [ET 4:9]).

2:19 בְּחֶזְוָא דִי־לֵילְיָא—This is, literally, "in a vision of the night." Throughout Daniel, visions at night are consistently connected with dreams.[c] On חֱזוּ, see further the second textual note on 2:28.

(c) Dan 2:19, 28; 4:2, 6–7, 10 (ET 4:5, 9–10, 13); 7:1–2, 7, 13, 15

2:20–23 Daniel breaks into a psalm of praise whose clauses exhibit a high degree of parallelism. The first verse has a pair of clauses, while 2:21 has four clauses, 2:22 has three clauses, and 2:23 has four clauses. In 2:20 and both pairs of 2:23, the second clause begins with דִּי and is causal, "because …" Synonymous parallelism is evident in 2:21c–d:

(A) He gives wisdom (B) to wise people
   (A') and knowledge (B') to those who know discernment.

Antithetical parallelism is apparent in "the dark … the light" (2:22).

2:20 לֶהֱוֵא שְׁמֵהּ דִּי־אֱלָהָא מְבָרַךְ—The expression with the infinitive (לֶהֱוֵא) and the Pael (D) passive participle (מְבָרַךְ), literally, "to be his name—God's—blessed," forms

---

[1] So Montgomery, *Daniel*, 156. ESV, NASB, and NRSV translate it as "urgent" in both 2:15 and 3:22.

[2] *HALOT*; Rosenthal, *A Grammar of Biblical Aramaic*, § 189.

an optative expression of praise: "may the name of God be blessed." It is equivalent to the Hebrew expression יְהִי שֵׁם יְהוָה מְבֹרָךְ, with the jussive (יְהִי) and the Pual (Dp) participle (מְבֹרָךְ), in Ps 113:2 and Job 1:21. 4QDan[a] adds the word "great": להוא שמה די אלהא רבא מברך, "may the name of the great God be blessed."[3] The Old Greek reads, ἔσται τὸ ὄνομα τοῦ κυρίου τοῦ μεγάλου εὐλογημένον, "may the name of the great Lord be blessed."[4]

Commentary

Daniel Intercedes with Arioch and Then Nebuchadnezzar (2:14–16)

Two different verbs in two verses (הֲתִיב, literally, "he returned [a prudent judgment]," in 2:14, and עֲנֵה, "he answered,"[5] in 2:15) state that Daniel replied to Arioch. This implies that Arioch had announced the king's edict that the wise men should be executed. Daniel's prudence is demonstrated by his question, which does not challenge the king's authority or judgment (as the Chaldeans had in 2:10–11). Instead, Daniel inquires as to the reason for the severity of the king's decree.

It is obvious that at this time Daniel is not a high-level official, since he does not have access to information about the prior events in Nebuchadnezzar's court (2:1–13). However, he is able to obtain access to the king. Daniel is able to obtain a grace period from the king precisely for the reason that the Chaldeans were not: he does not challenge the king's insistence that his wise men must recount to him his dream itself before explaining its meaning. Instead, Daniel merely asks for time to prove that he can explain the true meaning of the dream. It is clear from the king's question in 2:26 and Daniel's subsequent reply that Daniel also sought and received from God the contents of the dream itself; it was part of the "mystery" (2:19) revealed to him.

Once again we see the skill of Daniel the author as a storyteller. He does not record his conversation with Nebuchadnezzar. The text does not even explicitly state that Daniel received a reprieve. Recording the conversation and response would have slowed down the pace of the narrative. Instead, Daniel wants his readers to move directly to his psalm of praise to God so that the focus is on God's grace in answering the Judeans' prayer. God's grace in providing the revelation is so great that it rescues not only the four young Judean men, but also the wise men of Babylon. This can be seen as at least a preliminary fulfillment of God's ancient promise to Abraham that all nations (even Gentiles) would be blessed through him and his seed (e.g., Gen 12:3; 22:18), a promise fulfilled in Christ (Galatians 3) and evident beginning on Pentecost (Acts 2) and continu-

---

[3] Ulrich, *Qumran Cave 4.XI*, 244.
[4] Ziegler and Munnich, *Susanna, Daniel, Bel et Draco*, 248.
[5] See the first textual note on 2:5.

Daniel and His Friends Pray to God for Revelation and Rescue (2:17–18)

Daniel immediately seeks out his fellow believers in Yahweh. Not only are they facing the same danger as he, but also they alone can share in prayer to God in true faith, asking that he deliver them. This seeking the company of other faithful followers of God to worship and pray, especially in times of crisis, is characteristic of the saints throughout history (e.g., Acts 4:23–31).

The young Judeans set about seeking God's "mercy" (Aramaic רַחֲמִין, Dan 2:18). Daniel and his companions know that they can only rely on God's mercy. They have no right to demand anything from him, but can only trust his promise, since he is the God to whom belong, literally, "the mercy [the Hebrew cognate הָרַחֲמִים] and the forgiveness [וְהַסְּלִחוֹת]" (9:9).

The verb in the negated purpose clause in 2:18 has a vaguely defined antecedent (דִּי לָא יְהֹבְדוּן דָּנִיֵּאל וְחַבְרוֹהִי, "so that *they* might not destroy Daniel and his companions"). This allows Daniel to move the focus of the story from Nebuchadnezzar and the Babylonians (the implied subjects of the verb) to God and his action on behalf of his people.

God's Revelation and Daniel's Response (2:19–23)

While much attention has been paid to the interpretation of Nebuchadnezzar's dream, this poetic prayer actually functions as the theological center of this chapter.[6] We learn that God answered the prayer of the four young Judeans with a vision that came to Daniel at night. This is clearly a parallel to Nebuchadnezzar's nocturnal dream.

However, there also is a contrast between God's enigmatic dealings with a pagan king, who was troubled because he did not understand what he saw (2:1–3), and God's compassion toward his people, for whose sake he gives understanding to Daniel. Nebuchadnezzar received an important revelation from God in a dream. He sensed its importance and divine origin, but he was unable to make sense of it, since God did not reveal its meaning; to him it remained a mystery. In contrast, Daniel also received a revelation from God, but this revelation explained the "mystery" (רָזָה, 2:18–19).

Another contrast is between Nebuchadnezzar's response to God's revelatory dream and Daniel's response. Nebuchadnezzar's troubled bewilderment led him to issue an impossible demand, followed by anger and the threat of death for other humans, which he was in the process of carrying out.[7] Daniel's understanding leads to praise and blessing for God.

---

[6] This point is made by Prinsloo, "Two Poems in a Sea of Prose," 100.

[7] See the textual note on 2:13.

As Prinsloo notes, Daniel's prayer serves several functions in the narrative:

1. The poetic form of the prayer brings it to the foreground, since it contrasts with the prose narrative of the rest of the chapter. The poem calls the reader's attention to what it has to say.
2. The prayer heightens the tension because in it Daniel reveals that he now knows the meaning of the king's dream, but we readers must wait until 2:24–49 to learn what the dream and its meaning are.
3. It slows the pace of the narrative, once again calling the reader's attention to the content of Daniel's prayer.
4. Precisely where the narrative pace is slowed, the psalm gives us the most important theological content in the chapter.[8]

The prayer contains three major theological themes. First, God is worthy of blessing and praise (2:20). Daniel praises God because he alone has all wisdom and power (cf. the doxologies in 1 Chr 29:11; Rom 11:33; Rev 5:12; 7:12). The wisdom given to Daniel derives from God, as the rest of the chapter will elaborate (2:24–49). Likewise, the power given to Nebuchadnezzar also derives from God. God deserves praise for these gifts of wisdom and power. Since only God's power and wisdom endure throughout all human generations, he deserves this praise forever.

Second, as God exercises and grants power and wisdom, he is in control over all human authorities and earthly history, which he governs for the sake of his redeemed people. Daniel affirms this first with respect to God's power (2:21a–b). He alone changes times and eras, including the reigns of individual kings and the longer eras of kingdoms, governments, and nations. He alone grants power to kings (Rom 13:6; 1 Pet 2:13–14) and so can also abolish rulers and their countries when he so desires for the sake of his own kingdom of grace.[9] This, of course, anticipates the dream and its interpretation in 2:24–49. The power given to Nebuchadnezzar was evident in his authority to carry out his threat of capital punishment and in his conquest of Jerusalem and its king, which "the Lord gave into his hand" (1:2). But all of the ways in which this king might exercise the power given him are under God's control and subservient to God's overarching plan for the advent of his kingdom of grace in his Son, Jesus Christ (2:34–35, 44–45).

God's control is also evident when he reveals wisdom (2:22c–23a). This divine revelation can occur because God alone is wise, and he is the only one who can know all things and shed light on all mysteries (2:23b–c). This, of course, anticipates Daniel's statement in 2:27–28. God's gift of wisdom too serves the purpose of the advent of his kingdom of grace, as Daniel shows when

---

[8] Prinsloo, "Two Poems in a Sea of Prose," 101.

[9] A major theme in Daniel (and the rest of Scripture) is that God governs world history for the sake of his own kingdom, consisting of all believers. See "The Messiah in Daniel: An Overview" and "God as the Protector of His People" in "Major Themes" in the introduction.

he employs his God-given wisdom to explain the dream's message that "the God of heaven will establish a kingdom that will never be destroyed" (2:44).

Finally, God is to be thanked and praised because of the gifts he gives in response to prayer. He granted to Daniel the wisdom and power that are his alone (2:23b; see also 2:20). Daniel uses plurals in 2:23 to include the petitions of his companions ("what *we* requested") and to acknowledge that God's revelation to him was also for their benefit ("you have made known to *us*"). God granted Daniel wisdom through a supernatural dream (cf. 1 Ki 3:3–15), but in every age he grants wisdom and understanding through his Gospel in his Word, which imparts knowledge of him and his gracious ways. He grants the requests of his people who pray to him (Dan 2:23), including prayers for wisdom (cf. Eph 1:17; James 1:5). Together with "wisdom" Daniel includes "power" as a gift he received (Dan 2:23) because the divine wisdom revealed to him also granted him a measure of influence, even over the king, and this may also refer proleptically to his promotion to be "ruler over the entire province of Babylon and chief prefect over all the wise men of Babylon" (2:48).

Thus Daniel's prayer is the theological heart and center of the entire chapter. It summarizes the reasons for what has happened to this point in the narrative, and it anticipates what follows.

Daniel 2:24–49

Daniel Recounts and Explains Nebuchadnezzar's Dream of the Statue

Translation

2 ²⁴As a result of this, Daniel went in to Arioch, whom the king had appointed to destroy the wise men of Babylon. He went and said this to him: "Do not destroy the wise men of Babylon. Bring me before the king, and I will explain the meaning to the king."

²⁵Then Arioch immediately brought Daniel before the king. This is what he said to him: "I have found a man from the exiles of Judah who will make known the meaning to the king."

²⁶The king said to Daniel (whose name was Belteshazzar), "Are you able to make known to me the dream that I saw and its meaning?"

²⁷Daniel answered before the king and said, "The mystery that the king is asking, no wise men, soothsayers, magicians, or diviners are able to reveal to the king. ²⁸However, there is a God in heaven who reveals mysteries, and he has made known to King Nebuchadnezzar what will happen in the latter days. Your dream—the visions of your head upon your bed—is this:

²⁹"You, Your Majesty—your thoughts upon your bed arose about what will be after this, and the Revealer of mysteries made known to you what will happen. ³⁰But as for me, this mystery was not revealed to me because of wisdom that is in me more than [in] any [other] living beings. Rather, [it was revealed to me] so that the meaning may be made known to Your Majesty and so that you may know the thoughts of your heart.

³¹"You, Your Majesty, were looking, and there was a very large statue. That statue, [which was] large and whose brightness was extraordinary, was standing before you, and its appearance was frightening. ³²The statue—its head was of fine gold, its chest and its arms were of silver, its abdomen and its thighs were of bronze, ³³its shins were of iron, and its feet were partly of iron and partly of clay. ³⁴You continued to look until a stone was cut, [but] not by [human] hands. It struck the statue on its feet that were of iron and clay, and it smashed them. ³⁵Then the iron, the clay, the bronze, the silver, and the gold were crushed simultaneously and became like the chaff on the summer threshing floors. The wind lifted them, and no place could be found for them. However, the stone that struck the statue became a great mountain and filled the entire earth.

³⁶"This is the dream. So we will tell its meaning before Your Majesty. ³⁷You, Your Majesty, are king of kings to whom the God of heaven has given a kingdom, power, strength, and glory. ³⁸In all the places where the sons of man, the beasts of the field, and the birds in the sky dwell, he has given them into your hand, and he has made you ruler over all of them. You are the head of gold. ³⁹Now after you

another kingdom will arise that is inferior to you. Then another, a third kingdom [will arise] that is of bronze and that will rule the entire earth. ⁴⁰A fourth kingdom will be strong as iron, since iron crushes and shatters everything. So, like iron that smashes, it will crush and smash all of these. ⁴¹And because you saw feet and toes partly of potter's clay and partly of iron, it will be a divided kingdom. It will have some of the firmness of iron, because you saw iron mixed with common clay. ⁴²Morever, the toes of the feet were partly iron and partly clay, [meaning that] part of the kingdom will be strong and part of it will be brittle. ⁴³Because you saw iron mixed with common clay, they [the different parts of the kingdom] will be mixed among the seed of man and they will not adhere to one another, just as iron does not mix with clay.

⁴⁴"In the days of those kings, the God of heaven will establish a kingdom that will never be destroyed, nor will the kingdom be left to another people. It will crush and end all of these kingdoms, but it will be established forever, ⁴⁵just as you saw that from the mountain a stone was cut but not by [human] hands, and it crushed the iron, the bronze, the clay, the silver, and the gold. A great God has made known to Your Majesty what will happen after this. The dream is sure, and its meaning is certain."

⁴⁶Then King Nebuchadnezzar fell face down and paid homage to Daniel. He commanded that a gift and incense be offered to him. ⁴⁷The king said, "Truly your God is God of gods, Lord of kings, and Revealer of mysteries because you were able to reveal this mystery."

⁴⁸The the king promoted Daniel to a high position and gave him many great gifts. He made him ruler over the entire province of Babylon and chief prefect over all the wise men of Babylon. ⁴⁹Daniel sought from the king, and he appointed over the service of the province of Babylon Shadrach, Meshach, and Abednego. Daniel [remained] in the royal court.

Textual Notes

2:24 דָּנִיֵּאל֙ עַ֣ל עַל־אַרְי֔וֹךְ—The first עַל is the verb עֲלַל, "go in, enter," often used for an audience before the king in his court (see the first textual note on 2:16), but here it refers to an audience before a royal official. The second עַל is the preposition "to," hence, "Daniel went in to Arioch." The Haphel (H) of עֲלַל, "bring in, introduce" (*HALOT*), will occur later in 2:24 (the imperative הַעֵ֙לְנִי֙, "bring me") and in 2:25 (the perfect הַנְעֵ֖ל).

לְהוֹבָדָ֥ה לְחַכִּימֵ֖י בָבֶ֑ל—Aramaic frequently uses the preposition לְ to introduce a direct object.[1] Twice in this verse לְחַכִּימֵ֖י בָבֶ֑ל ("the wise men of Babylon") is a direct object: here of the Haphel (H) infinitive לְהוֹבָדָ֥ה, "to destroy," and later of the negated Haphel imperative אַל־תְּהוֹבֵ֑ד, "do not destroy."

2:25 בְּהִתְבְּהָלָ֔ה—This is the Hithpeel (HtG) infinitive of בְּהַל, "be frightened, make haste," which is used as a substantive with the preposition בְּ, "in haste," and translated as an adverb, "immediately." The identical form recurs in 3:24 and 6:20 (ET 6:19).

---

[1] Steinmann, *Fundamental Biblical Aramaic*, 308; Rosenthal, *A Grammar of Biblical Aramaic*, § 182.

גְּבַר֙ מִן־בְּנֵ֤י גָלוּתָא֙ דִּ֣י יְה֔וּד—This is, literally, "a man from the sons of the exile of Judah." Twice more Daniel is characterized as "from the sons of the exile of Judah" (5:13; 6:14 [ET 6:13]).

2:26 דִּ֥י שְׁמֵ֖הּ בֵּלְטְשַׁאצַּ֑ר—"Whose name was Belteshazzar": for this alternate name of Daniel, see the second textual note on 1:7.

2:27 חַכִּימִין֙ אָֽשְׁפִ֔ין חַרְטֻמִּ֖ין גָּזְרִ֑ין—This phrase is restrictive: "[those] wise men [who specifically were] soothsayers, magicians, diviners." See "Daniel among the Wise Men" in "Introduction to Daniel 2."

2:28 בְּאַחֲרִ֣ית יֽוֹמַיָּ֑א—Literally, "in the latter part of the days," this is traditionally translated as "in the latter days" (KJV, NASB, ESV). The equivalent Hebrew phrase בְּאַחֲרִ֣ית הַיָּמִ֔ים occurs in Dan 10:14. Throughout the OT, the Hebrew phrase[a] nearly always has an eschatological, messianic connotation. This era begins with the coming of the Messiah. *Thus the goal of this vision is the ushering in of the messianic era.* See further the discussion of the phrase in "The Messiah in Daniel: An Overview" in "Major Themes" in the introduction.

The NT uses equivalent Greek phrases to refer to the present age as the eschatological age inaugurated with the ministry, death, and resurrection of Jesus, extending until his return.[b]

חֶלְמָ֛ךְ וְחֶזְוֵ֥י רֵאשָׁ֖ךְ עַֽל־מִשְׁכְּבָ֥ךְ דְּנָ֥ה הֽוּא׃—The *waw* in, literally, "your dream *and* the visions of your head upon your bed—this is it" is the epexegetical or explicative *waw*. This can be seen by the singular pronoun הוּא, "it," whose antecedent is חֶלְמָךְ, "your dream." Thus "the visions of your head upon your bed" elaborates "your dream," the dream that the king had. It was not an ordinary dream, but a revelatory vision from "the Revealer of mysteries" (2:29).

Throughout Daniel, the noun חֵ֫זוּ usually refers to a revelatory "vision."[c] Its Hebrew equivalent, חָזוֹן, is used for a prophetic "vision" (e.g., Is 1:1; Obad 1; Nahum 1:1), and it occurs throughout the OT, also extensively in Daniel.[d]

Usually in the OT, the organ connected with thought is לֵב, the "heart" (Aramaic לְבַב in 2:30), not רֹאשׁ (Aramaic רֵאשׁ here), the "head." However, throughout the Aramaic portion of Daniel, thought is associated with the head (רֵאשׁ, 4:2, 7, 10 [ET 4:5, 10, 13]; 7:1, 15).[2]

2:29 מַלְכָּ֗א—For "the king" as the honorific "Your Majesty," see the second textual note on 2:4.

רַעְיוֹנָךְ֙ עַל־מִשְׁכְּבָ֣ךְ סְלִ֔קוּ—The subject of the plural Peal (G) perfect סְלִ֔קוּ, "(they) arose," is the singular noun רַעְיוֹנָךְ, "your thought," which is translated as plural ("your thoughts") to match the verb and English idiom.

וְגָלֵ֥א רָזַיָּ֖א—This construct phrase with the participle גָּלֵא and the plural of רָז forms a divine title: the one true God is "the Revealer of mysteries." God receives the title "Revealer of mysteries" again in 2:47 from the lips of Nebuchadnezzar.

(a) Gen 49:1; Num 24:14; Deut 4:30; 31:29; Is 2:2 ‖ Micah 4:1; Jer 23:20; 30:24; 48:47; 49:39; Ezek 38:16; Hos 3:5; Dan 10:14

(b) Acts 2:17; 2 Tim 3:1; Heb 1:2; James 5:3; 2 Pet 3:3; 1 Jn 2:18; Jude 18

(c) Dan 2:19, 28; 4:2, 6–7, 10 (ET 4:5, 9–10, 13); 7:1–2, 7, 13, 15

(d) Dan 1:17; 8:1–2, 13, 15, 17, 26; 9:21, 24; 10:14; 11:14

---

[2] Glasson's suggestion in "'Visions of Thy Head' (Daniel 2[28])" that this association represents Greek thought is clearly influenced by critical theories that have tried to see Daniel as a Hellenistic era composition.

2:30 וַאֲנָ֗ה לָ֤א בְחָכְמָה֙ דִּֽי־אִיתַ֣י בִּ֔י מִן־כָּל־חַיַּיָּ֔א רָזָ֥א דְנָ֖ה גֱּלִ֣י לִ֑י—This verse begins with a pronoun as a *casus pendens*, וַאֲנָ֗ה, "as for me …" Then the syntax continues, literally, "not by wisdom that is in me more than [in] all [other] living beings [was] this mystery revealed to me." English idiom requires rearranging the syntax. Even though רָזָ֥א דְנָ֖ה גֱּלִ֣י לִ֑י is a positive statement, "this mystery was revealed to me," English requires negating the verb ("this mystery was *not* revealed to me") because of the negative לָ֤א in the phrase לָ֤א בְחָכְמָה֙, "not by wisdom." The implied agent of the passive verb (Peil [Gp] perfect) גֱּלִ֣י, "revealed," is God, as Daniel emphasizes in 2:28, 45.

פִּשְׁרָ֖א לְמַלְכָּ֥א יְהוֹדְעֽוּן—Here the Haphel (H) imperfect of יְדַע forms a purpose clause. God revealed the meaning of the dream to Daniel for this purpose: (literally) "so that they would make known the meaning to the king." Often in Aramaic an impersonal plural verb implies that God is the ultimate agent of the action, and the verb is best rendered as a passive, as here: "so that the meaning *may be made known* to Your Majesty."

2:31 וַאֲל֨וּ—This particle, also in 4:7, 10 (ET 4:10, 13) and 7:8, is the Aramaic equivalent of Hebrew הִנֵּה, "behold." In a narrative, it directs the attention of the hearer or reader to a change in circumstance or focus. In this instance, it introduces the statue that dominates the first part of Nebuchadnezzar's dream.

2:33 רַגְל֕וֹהִי מִנְּהֵ֥ין דִּ֥י פַרְזֶ֖ל וּמִנְּהֵ֥ין דִּ֥י חֲסַ֑ף—This use of the preposition מִן in Aramaic is partitive (*HALOT*, 4), literally, "its feet, part of them was of iron and part of them was of clay." Similar wording is in 2:41–42.

2:34 הִתְגְּזֶ֤רֶת אֶ֨בֶן֙ דִּי־לָ֣א בִידַ֔יִן—Literally, "a stone [אֶ֨בֶן֙] was hewn [הִתְגְּזֶ֤רֶת] which was not [דִּי־לָ֣א] [hewn] by hands [בִידַ֔יִן]," this sentence implies that no humans, but God himself hewed this stone. An equivalent expression occurs in 2:45. Daniel will interpret the "stone" as the one who brings and establishes God's eternal kingdom, which cannot ever be destroyed. See further the commentary on 2:44–45.

The stone was "cut, hewn": הִתְגְּזֶ֤רֶת is the Hithpeel (HtG) of גְּזַר, whose Hebrew cognate, גָּזַר, can have a similar meaning, "cut (off, in two)," resulting in death for a person: the baby in 1 Ki 3:25–26 or the Suffering Servant in Is 53:8, who was "cut off from the land of the living." This verb can be interpreted in harmony with passages such as "they have pierced[3] my hands and feet" (Ps 22:17 [Et 22:16]) and "they shall look upon me, whom they have pierced" (דְּקָרוּ, Zech 12:10) as pointing to the crucifixion of Christ.

The implication of the statement that the stone was cut "not by [human] hands" means that this action was performed by God. Similar is the implication of the NT use of ἀχειροποίητος, "not made by human hands," which refers to God's salvation accomplished in Christ without the aid of any other human (divine monergism in salvation).

---

[3] Most manuscripts have כָּאֲרִי, which could mean "like a lion," but that makes little sense in the context, which requires a verb to go with "my hands and my feet." Some manuscripts have כָּאֲרוּ and two have כָּרוּ, which are variant spellings for a verb (כָּרָה) meaning "they dug, bored, pierced." Most likely כָּאֲרִי is a textual variant for כָּאֲרוּ and the ו- was misread or miscopied as י- by a scribe. The LXX (ὤρυξαν, "they dug") and the Syriac (ܓܪܚܘ, "they pierced, bored through") both support the meaning "pierced."

It occurs in three NT passages, referring to (1) the new temple (Christ himself) raised by God (Mk 14:58); (2) the new and eternal "house" in heaven that awaits Christians (2 Cor 5:1); and (3) the new circumcision in Christ that God himself performs in Holy Baptism (Col 2:11).

2:36 וּפִשְׁרֵהּ נֵאמַר קֳדָם־מַלְכָּא:—Daniel here uses the deferential plural נֵאמַר, literally, "its meaning *we will say* before the king/Your Majesty."

2:37 מַלְכוּתָא חִסְנָא וְתָקְפָּא וִיקָרָא יְהַב־לָךְ—Daniel acknowledges that God has "given" (יְהַב) to King Nebuchadnezzar "a kingdom [מַלְכוּתָא], power [חִסְנָא], strength [וְתָקְפָּא], and glory [וִיקָרָא]." This verse, together with 1 Chr 29:11 (cf. Ps 145:11–12; Rev 12:10), may be an OT precedent for the doxology of the Lord's Prayer: ὅτι σοῦ ἐστιν ἡ βασιλεία καὶ ἡ δύναμις καὶ ἡ δόξα εἰς τοὺς αἰῶνας τῶν αἰώνων. Ἀμήν.[4] While Daniel describes gifts that God has given to a human king, the Lord's Prayer ascribes them to God as the sole possessor and originator. Throughout Daniel, these are God's to give or to take away (see, e.g., 2:21; 4:14, 22, 29 [ET 4:17, 25, 32]).

2:38 וְהַשְׁלְטָךְ—The Haphel (H) of שְׁלֵט means "to make someone the ruler over." Here God is the subject and the suffix refers to Nebuchadnezzar. The Haphel perfect recurs in 2:48 (וְהַשְׁלְטֵהּ), where Nebuchadnezzar is the subject and the suffix refers to Daniel.

2:39 אַרְעָא מִנָּךְ—The Kethib is אַרְעָא while the Qere is אֲרַע. Literally, this phrase is "earth(ward) from you," that is, "beneath you," meaning "a kingdom inferior to yours" (*HALOT*, s.v. אֲרַע, 2).

2:41 בַּחֲסַף טִינָא—Literally, "clay of the mud," this construct phrase, which recurs in 2:43, probably signifies "common clay" as opposed to an especially fine grade of clay. English translations are divided in their understanding of this phrase: "soft clay" (ESV), "common clay" (NASB), or simply "clay" (NIV, NRSV).

2:42 מִן־קְצָת—The noun קְצָת, "end," with the preposition מִן has the partitive meaning "part of" (*HALOT*, s.v. קְצָת, 2), similar to the partitive meaning of just מִן (with suffixes) in 2:33, 41–42.

2:43 מִתְעָרְבִין לֶהֱוֺן בִּזְרַע אֲנָשָׁא—Literally, "mixed they will be among the seed of man," this is usually taken to indicate intermarriage among various ethnic groups in the fourth kingdom.[5] Critical commentators who identify the fourth kingdom as the Greek domination of the eastern Mediterranean see this as a reference to the marriage alliances among the Ptolemaic and Seleucid kings (11:6, 17).[6] However, the expression is unusual, and its meaning is far from certain. Both the Greek and the Roman kingdoms included a variety of ethnic groups, and royal intermarriages occurred during both kingdoms, as indeed they have in many other kingdoms and nations throughout world history.

---

[4] Some NT manuscripts include part or all of this doxology at the end of Mt 6:13 (cf. *Didache* 8:2).

[5] Baldwin, *Daniel*, 93.

[6] Collins, *Daniel*, 170; Hartman and Di Lella, *Daniel*, 149; Lucas, *Daniel*, 76; Montgomery, *Daniel*, 177. Interestingly, Luther understood this as a reference to intermarriage and marriage alliances among royalty, but still understood the fourth kingdom as Rome, not Greece ("Preface to Daniel," AE 35:296).

Any argument that uses this clause to identify the fourth kingdom is little more than an attempt to force the meaning of the clause to fit one's own notion of its referent.[7]

2:44 מַלְכוּ דִּי לְעָלְמִין לָא תִתְחַבַּל—Literally, this says that God will establish "a kingdom that forever will not be destroyed." English idiom requires "a kingdom that will never be destroyed."

2:45 פַּרְזְלָא נְחָשָׁא חַסְפָּא כַּסְפָּא וְדַהֲבָא—The list of materials representing kingdoms is "the iron, the bronze, the clay, the silver, and the gold." It seems that חַסְפָּא, "the clay," is out of order. Some critical scholars suppose that חַסְפָּא is a secondary addition and that the original text only listed the metals.[8] However, the Syriac has the same materials and order as in the MT. The Old Greek, Theodotion, and the Vulgate have the order clay, iron, bronze, silver, gold, while papyrus 967 has the order as iron, clay, bronze, silver, gold.[9] Either of those two orders would be expected if one starts at the feet (iron mixed with clay), which are struck by the hewn stone, and moves up (back in historical order) to the head of the statue. The most likely explanation is that the harder reading in the MT is the original order and that the Greek and Latin traditions are correcting the MT.

2:46 וּלְדָנִיֵּאל סְגִד—The king "paid homage to Daniel." In other OT passages, the verb סְגִד refers to the worship of idols; see the eighth textual note on 3:5. Its use here for the veneration of a person is in harmony with the pagan perspective of the king.

2:47 אֱלָהֲכוֹן הוּא אֱלָהּ אֱלָהִין—This is "your God, he is God of gods." Hebrew equivalents of this phrase (לֵאלֹהֵי הָאֱלֹהִים, יְהוָה אֱלֹהֵיכֶם הוּא אֱלֹהֵי הָאֱלֹהִים, Deut 10:17; אֱלֹהֵי הָאֱלֹהִים, Ps 136:2; אֵל ׀ אֱלֹהִים יְהוָה, Ps 50:1; אֵל אֵלִים, Dan 11:36) are used sparingly in the OT, probably to avoid endorsing the idea that there are other gods or that Yahweh is head of a pantheon.

2:49 בִּתְרַע מַלְכָּא—Literally, "in the gate of the king," this expression is the designation for service "in the royal court."[10] Mordecai, who was a high-ranking official in the Persian royal court, is described in a similar way (Esth 2:19, 21).

Commentary
Arioch Takes Daniel to Nebuchadnezzar (2:24–26)

Daniel has the solution to the challenge that Nebuchadnezzar has posed. Since Daniel knows the matter is solved (2:20–23) and is now confident that God will rescue him from danger, he is willing to go through the proper protocol, approaching Arioch, who then approaches Nebuchadnezzar (contrast Daniel's direct conversation with the king in 2:16). Arioch takes a measure of credit for helping to solve the king's problem, claiming to have found someone who is able to do what the king has requested. However, in taking credit,

---

[7] See further the second point under "Advantages of the Roman View" in the excursus "The Four-Kingdom Schema in Daniel."

[8] E.g., Montgomery, *Daniel*, 180, suggests that as a possibility.

[9] Collins, *Daniel*, 152.

[10] For usage of similar phrases throughout the ancient Near East, see Montgomery, *Daniel*, 184.

he also puts himself at some risk, since he may be punished if this proves to be a false claim. Nebuchadnezzar first asks about the claim that Daniel can tell him both the dream and its meaning. He is cautious, taking into consideration his last conversation with those who were supposed to be able to interpret the dream (2:3–11).

Daniel Explains the Source of His Knowledge (2:27–30)

Daniel stands in sharp contrast to Arioch. Instead of seeking credit for something with which he had little to do, he disavows any credit for what he will reveal to the king (2:30). But first he offers a mild defense of the wise men of Babylon: they simply are not able to do what the king asked of them (2:27). At the same time, Daniel also contradicts the Chaldeans who asserted that the gods are too distant from people to reveal mysteries (2:28; cf. 2:11).

Daniel clearly states that the goal of the dream is to reveal "what will happen in the latter days" (2:28)—in the messianic era. This may have been lost on Nebuchadnezzar but would not be on Daniel's readers. From Daniel's words we are told to expect a message about the advent of the Messiah long promised to Israel.[11]

God revealed the mystery through two people, Nebuchadnezzar and Daniel. This is signaled by the unusual syntax employed in 2:29–30. First, 2:29 begins with the pronoun "you" (Qere אַנְתְּ, Kethib אַנְתָּה), and Daniel tells of Nebuchadnezzar's thoughts about the future as he laid upon his bed. God, "the Revealer of mysteries" (2:29), told Nebuchadnezzar about the future in a dream. Then 2:30 begins with the pronoun "me" (וַאֲנָה) as Daniel tells of his role: God revealed the mystery to him for the express purpose of explaining Nebuchadnezzar's thoughts to him. Daniel also emphasizes that, humanly speaking, he is no better than anyone else, including Babylon's wise men. He is simply the instrument through which Israel's God reveals the mystery to Nebuchadnezzar.[12]

The one true and triune God can reveal these mysteries because he has complete foreknowledge of all events, even before they happen:

> God's foreknowledge is nothing else than that God knows all things before they happen, as it is written, "There is a God in heaven who reveals mysteries, and he has made known to King Nebuchadnezzar what will be in the latter days" (Daniel 2:28). (FC Ep XI 3)

God's foreknowledge means that he knows the future completely, both the good things and the evil things that will come to pass. Yet God is by no means

---

[11] See the first textual note on 2:28 and "The Messiah in Daniel: An Overview" in "Major Themes" in the introduction.

[12] Some critical scholars speculate that 2:29–30 is an ancient duplicate of preceding verses and somehow found its way into the text (Hartman and Di Lella, *Daniel*, 140; Montgomery, *Daniel*, 162). That view clearly misses the point of these verses, which is not simply to repeat earlier material, but to emphasize the respective roles of Nebuchadnezzar and Daniel as conduits of God's revelation about the coming messianic era.

a cause of evil. Rather, evil is caused by the will of sinful people and the devil. Yet God according to his foreknowledge sets limits for such evil: how long it will endure, and when he shall punish it. "For the Lord God governs everything in such a way that it must redound to the glory of his divine name and the salvation of his elect, and thereby the ungodly are confounded" (FC SD XI 6).

God's foreknowledge is distinct from his election of his children to eternal salvation. His election "not only foresees and foreknows the salvation of the elect, but by God's gracious will and pleasure in Christ Jesus it is also a cause which creates, effects, helps, and furthers our salvation and whatever pertains to it."[13] It is never God's will that unbelievers reject his Word and perish eternally. Rather, their impenitence is the result of their sinful hearts and the influence of the devil.

This distinction helps us understand Daniel 2. Daniel and his Judean companions are believers, and so by faith they are among those elected to salvation and membership in God's eternal kingdom. Nebuchadnezzar and Arioch are unbelievers, and so they are not among the elect. God's will is for their conversion, but the king persists in his idolatry (as evidenced by the image he constructs in chapter 3). Nevertheless, God still can and does use the pagan king to help communicate the future (known to God according to his foreknowledge), both the eventual destruction of the four worldly kingdoms and the establishment of his eternal kingdom of grace in Jesus Christ.

Daniel Recounts Nebuchadnezzar's Dream (2:31–35)

The initial description of the statue as large and bright with a frightening appearance is never explicitly explained by Daniel. However, it may refer to the glory and power of the kingdoms that the statue represents (2:37–40). This initial impression could also have conveyed to Nebuchadnezzar that the ensuing vision was no ordinary dream, but a divine revelation.

Scholars have engaged in much speculation about the origins or historical precedents of the statue of four metals. Similar sequences of metals are found in other ancient literary works. The sequence of gold, silver, bronze, and iron, used to signify four ages, is found in the Greek poet Hesiod (eighth century BC) and in Ovid (43 BC–AD 17).[14] Some Zoroastrian works use a somewhat similar sequence of metals to signify four ages.[15] Many critical commentators conclude that this dream in Daniel is dependent on Zoroastrian sources through Persian influence.[16] However, the Zoroastrian sources are late (thirteenth cen-

---

[13] FC SD XI 8. For God's eternal foreknowledge in relation to his eternal election, see further the entirety of FC SD XI.

[14] Hesiod, *Works and Days*, 109–201; Ovid, *Metamorphoses*, 1.89–162.

[15] *Denkard*, 9.8; *Bahman Yasht*, 1. The sequence in both is gold, silver, steel, and one mixed with iron.

[16] Montgomery provides a succinct survey (*Daniel*, 188–89). See also Collins, *Daniel*, 167–68; Flusser, "The Four Empires in the Fourth Sibyl and in the Book of Daniel."

tury AD), and it is uncertain whether the traditions they preserve predate Daniel (sixth century BC). Hesiod clearly predates Daniel and has the same sequence of metals. However, even Hesiod shares only a few features with Daniel 2. In examining this evidence, Lucas concludes: "There is no compelling evidence of Persian influence on either the Sibylline Oracles or Daniel."[17]

More closely aligned with Daniel 2 is the so-called Dynastic Prophecy from Babylon. It was probably written in the Persian or Seleucid era.[18] Yet even here there are striking differences from Daniel 2.[19] Hasel concludes:

> In several respects Dan 2 is closer to the four world empire schema of the Babylonian "Dynastic Prophecy" than to the schemes of Roman, Hellenistic, and Persian provenance and yet the differences as noted above between the Babylonian "Dynastic Prophecy" and Dan 2 are so striking that a direct or even indirect relationship seems to be out of the question.[20]

It *may* be that God uses a motif of successive empires that was familiar throughout the eastern Mediterranean region by the time of Nebuchadnezzar to make the dream more meaningful to him.[21] However, even *if* the dream uses a preexisting motif, it clearly adapts the motif for its own purposes. Unique features of the dream include the metals in the form of a composite statue, the introduction of iron mixed with clay, the stone that smashed the statue, and the mountain that the stone becomes. Clearly, although God *may* have decided to reveal this dream to Nebuchadnezzar by using a motif that he would have found somewhat familiar, he also intended to rework the imagery for his own purposes. Yet we should keep in mind that there is no compelling evidence that such a motif was known in Babylon in Nebuchadnezzar's day.

While the dream's meaning is not apparent in Daniel's description of it (2:31–35), there are clues to important features. The stone hewn without hands points to divine activity.[22] The striking of the statue on its feet (2:34) indicates that the destruction will happen during the time signified by the iron part of the statue. While the statue's feet are crushed by the falling stone, apparently the rest of the statue is crushed by falling on the stone (2:35). Baldwin notes that the statue would have been top-heavy and fragile, prone to falling and being shattered.[23]

The wind sweeping away the remnants of the statue (2:35) points to this being a dream whose meaning is about history and eschatology. The image of chaff being swept away by the wind is a familiar one in the OT.ᵉ This meta-

(e) Is 17:13; 29:5; 40:24; 41:2, 15–16; Jer 4:11–12; 13:24; 51:2; Hos 13:3; Zeph 2:2; Pss 1:4; 35:5; 83:14 (ET 83:13); Job 13:25; 21:18

---

[17] Lucas, "The Origin of Daniel's Four Empires Scheme Re-examined," 202.

[18] Hasel, "The Four World Empires of Daniel 2 against Its Near Eastern Environment," 22.

[19] Hasel, "The Four World Empires of Daniel 2 against Its Near Eastern Environment," 23.

[20] Hasel, "The Four World Empires of Daniel 2 against Its Near Eastern Environment," 24.

[21] See Collins' comment that "the imagery had a long and widespread tradition behind it" (*Daniel*, 165).

[22] See the textual note on 2:34.

[23] Baldwin, *Daniel*, 92.

phor combines the concepts of transience and impermanence with the ease with which God can sweep away humans and their achievements. In this dream, the heavy statue that seems impressive and immovable is suddenly reduced into chaff that is easily blown away (then replaced by the permanent mountain). This transformation dramatically underscores God's almighty power to achieve his purposes despite the apparent power and might wielded by humans.

The fact that the stone *becomes* a mountain is significant. The stone enters the dream as a rock and then grows into a mountain, picturing the Messiah's first advent, then the growth of his kingdom throughout this world. Thus the vision does not end with the fourth kingdom, but depicts human history beyond the fourth kingdom as the kingdom of God grows. This is confirmed by the final statement, that the mountain "filled the entire earth" (2:35), which points to the cosmic scope of the church, far beyond Babylon and its environs.

Daniel Explains the Image Made of Four Metals (2:36–43)

Daniel begins his interpretation by a flattering, hyperbolic description of Nebuchadnezzar. This is designed to put the king at ease, since he had been troubled by the dream. Moreover, it softens the news that his kingdom will eventually fall to another. At the same time, Daniel is able to make an important theological point: the power and glory that Nebuchadnezzar enjoys are not his own doing, but the result of God's gift. This is the same point Daniel the author made in 1:2: "the Lord gave into his [Nebuchadnezzar's] hand" Jerusalem and even the temple vessels. Since Jerusalem (the capital of God's chosen people Israel) with its temple (the place of sacrifice for the forgiveness of sins) was indeed the center of God's dealings with all humanity, Nebuchadnezzar's dominion over it could be extrapolated theologically to mean that he was ruler over the whole world (2:38).

Daniel does not identify the head of gold with Nebuchadnezzar until after his description of Nebuchadnezzar's might (2:36–38). He once again is flattering by identifying Nebuchadnezzar alone, and not his kingdom, as the head of gold. Clearly, from the explanation of the statue, each metal stands for a kingdom, not merely one king. But Daniel prudently allows the implicit equation of Nebuchadnezzar with the kingdom of Babylon (2:38).

Daniel next moves to the silver part of the statue, which is said to be a kingdom that rises after Nebuchadnezzar and is inferior to him (2:39a). Daniel does not state why or in what way it is inferior. The message implied by the kinds of metals is that each is of inferior value to the preceding one. Since subsequent kingdoms, including the Persians, Greeks, and Romans, ruled over larger territory than Nebuchadnezzar's Babylonian Empire, "inferior" must not be determined by geopolitical reach.

Like the second kingdom, the third kingdom, of bronze, is given little attention (only half a verse) in Daniel's explanation (2:39b). Daniel states that this third kingdom will rule the "entire earth" (2:39b), which was also implied about Nebuchadnezzar's kingdom (2:38). There are no such explicit statements about the second (silver) or fourth (iron) kingdoms, but this is implied, since the second (silver) kingdom supplants Nebuchadnezzar's worldwide kingdom, and especially since the fourth kingdom crushes all those that came before (2:40).

The most attention is given to the iron kingdom (2:40–43). The focus is especially on the feet and the meaning of their composition, a mixture of iron and clay. The major features of this kingdom are its ability to crush, signified by the iron; its brittle nature, signified by the clay; its population of a mixture of peoples, signified the iron mixed with clay; and its inability to remain united, signified by the iron and clay failing to adhere to one another. This lack of cohesion signifies the eventual dissolution of the Roman Empire, but the continuing influence of its institutions. Thus much of the heritage of Rome lasts even to this day, especially in the West (Europe and the Americas), but all attempts in subsequent history to revive a semblance of the Roman Empire with its power have failed.

The only kingdom that Daniel identifies in his explanation of the dream is that Nebuchadnezzar (monarch of the Babylonian kingdom) is the gold head (2:38). The lack of explicit identification of the other kingdoms has led to much argument over their identity. The two main views and their chief proponents are (1) evangelical scholars who identify the four kingdoms as Babylon, Persia, Greece, and Rome and (2) critical scholars who identify them as Babylon, Media, Persia, and Greece. A detailed discussion of the identities of these kingdoms, with specific reasons to accept the evangelical view, is provided in the excursus "The Four-Kingdom Schema in Daniel."

For Christians, the determinative factor is the establishment of God's kingdom during the time of the fourth empire, which was fulfilled by the first advent of Jesus Christ during the Roman era.[f] If the fourth kingdom were Greece rather than Rome, then the kingdom of God would not have been established during the fourth kingdom, and Daniel's prophecy would be false prophecy, not to be honored or believed (Deut 18:20–22; Jer 23:9–32; 1 Jn 4:1).

Those evangelicals who hold dispensational views make much of the assumption that the statue had two legs and ten toes. They identify the (presumably two) iron shins as the division of the Roman Empire into its eastern and western parts, and they further identify the (presumably ten) toes as ten states that will arise out of the Roman Empire.[24] The impetus for these interpretations of these details is the number of the ten horns mentioned for the fourth kingdom in 7:7, 20, 24.

(f) E.g., Mt 12:28; Lk 2:1–7; 3:1–23; 11:20; 17:20–21

However, it should be noted that the legs and toes in chapter 2 are not numbered in Daniel's description of the statue (2:31–35). Neither does Daniel's interpretation (2:36–43) include any reference to the number of legs and toes or indicate that these numbers would have any significance. It is natural for us to assume that the statue had two legs and ten toes, but this is an assumption; in

---

[24] Miller, *Daniel*, 97–99; Walvoord, "The Prophecy of the Ten-Nation Confederacy," 100–2; *Daniel*, 71–76.

the text itself there is no statement about those numbers, much less any interpretation of what their significance might be. Moreover, the vision in Daniel 7 does not describe the fourth kingdom as being divided into two parts.

In chapter 2, the division of the fourth kingdom is signified by its composition of both iron and clay (2:41), not by any reference to the (presumably two) legs, and the lack of cohesion in the fourth kingdom is signified by the clay not adhering to the iron (2:43). Nothing in the interpretation suggests that the (presumably ten) toes signify states that would arise later from the fourth kingdom. Nor does the vision in Daniel 7 connect the ten horns with the (presumably ten) toes of the statue in Daniel 2. Instead, the progressive nature of the revelation in Daniel argues that the number of toes is irrelevant at this point.[25] Moreover, if we are to assume that the (presumably two) iron shins of the statue had important significance for the history of the fourth kingdom, then why should we not also assume that the (presumably two) arms of silver signify a division of the second kingdom, and that the (presumably two) thighs of bronze signify a division of the third kingdom? In the interpretation of the statue (2:36–43) Daniel ascribes no such significance to the arms, thighs, or shins.

As important as the four kingdoms are for the interpretation of the statue, the focus of the vision is not on the statue itself and the kingdoms it represents, but on the stone and the kingdom it represents. The advent of the kingdom that will endure forever is the reason why God revealed the future to Nebuchadnezzar. As Nebuchadnezzar was contemplating the future on his bed, God gave him a dream to expand his vision beyond his own future or that of Babylon. The one true God was reaching out to Nebuchadnezzar and the Babylonians and calling them to repentance and faith in him. Unfortunately, Nebuchadnezzar does not fully grasp nor believe the Gospel told to him in this dream and in its interpretation by Daniel.

Daniel Explains the Establishment of the Kingdom of God (2:44–45)

In 2:44 Daniel explains the significance of the stone that crushes the statue, and then in 2:45a, he recounts details about that stone in the dream. Once again (2:45, as in 2:34), he affirms that the stone was hewn, but not by human hands, which affirms its divine origin (see the textual note on 2:34). The metaphor that a stone is cut or hewn from a rock is used in Is 51:1–2 to say that believers are stones hewn from Abraham as their father. However, the "stone" in Daniel 2 has no human origin. This stone was cut "from the mountain" (מִטּוּרָא)—a detail added in 2:45 that was absent in Daniel's original description of the dream

---

[25] "Progressive revelation" means that in the course of history, God inspired more and more writings of sacred Scripture, and these writings progressively revealed more and more of his plan of salvation. Daniel is an individual biblical book that also displays such "progressive revelation." Earlier chapters reveal the main contours of the course of salvation history, and then later chapters add further details. We should not seek to interpret its earlier chapters as if they had the details revealed only in its later chapters.

(2:34). This too points to this "stone" as the Messiah, who has divine origins and is himself divine ("whose origins are from of old, from days of eternity," Micah 5:1 [ET 5:2]). Throughout the OT, the Hebrew cognate (צוּר, "rock") to the Aramaic term here translated "mountain" (טוּר) is used as a metaphor to describe God as a "rock" of salvation and refuge.[26] The Aramaic (and Hebrew) term אֶבֶן for the "stone" hewn from the "mountain/rock" is also used as a metaphor for God as the "rock," the stronghold and Redeemer of his people (Gen 49:24), and specifically for the Messiah as the "rock" or "stone" established by God (Is 8:14–15; 28:16; Zech 3:9; 4:7; for Ps 118:22 see further below). Therefore the assertion in Dan 2:45 that the "stone" was hewn from the "mountain" reaffirms the divine origin and divine identity of the "stone," which derives from God, the "mountain."[27] That the Messiah, God the Son, was preexistent from eternity with the Father and is eternally begotten from the Father is affirmed in other biblical passages (e.g., Ps 2:7; Jn 1:1, 14, 18; Hebrews 1) and in the Nicene and Athanasian Creeds.[28]

Siegman notes:

> Probably the most cogent consideration in the selection of this stone-symbolism was the use by previous prophets of the stone or rock to symbolize Yahweh, or the messianic kingdom, or the rock of Mt. Sion as His favorite abode.[29]

In Daniel's original description of the dream, "the stone that struck the statue became a great mountain [טוּר] and filled the entire earth" (2:35). That detail is not mentioned in Daniel's explanation. However, there can be no doubt that the "stone" that grows into a cosmic "mountain" is yet another affirmation of the divine origin and divine identity of the Messiah and the miraculous growth of his kingdom, which is God's kingdom. The Messiah will establish a kingdom that will grow to fill the entire earth. The kingdom adds rock mass as God adds to it royal subjects. The apostle Peter put it this way: "As you come to him, a living stone rejected by men but chosen and precious in the sight of God, you yourselves like living stones are being built up as a spiritual house,

---

[26] See, for example, Deut 32:4, 15, 18, 30–31; 1 Sam 2:2; 2 Sam 22:3, 32, 47 ∥ Ps 18:3, 32, 47 (ET 18:2, 31, 46); 2 Sam 23:3; Is 17:10; 26:4; 30:29; 44:8; Hab 1:12; Pss 19:15 (ET 19:14); 28:1; 31:3 (ET 31:2); 62:3, 7–8 (ET 62:2, 6–7); 71:3; 78:35; 89:27 (ET 89:26); 92:16 (ET 92:15); 94:22; 95:1; 144:1.

[27] Luther notes that some interpret the mountain out of which the rock is hewn as the Virgin Mary, but he understands it to be the Jewish people as a whole ("Preface to Daniel," AE 35:296).

[28] The Nicene Creed confesses that the Son was "begotten of his Father before all worlds, God of God, Light of Light, very God of very God, begotten, not made, being of one substance with the Father." The Athanasian Creed confesses this truth at greater length: "The Godhead of the Father and of the Son and of the Holy Spirit is one: the glory equal, the majesty coeternal. Such as the Father is, such is the Son, and such is the Holy Spirit: the Father uncreated, the Son uncreated, the Holy Spirit uncreated; the Father infinite, the Son infinite, the Holy Spirit infinite; the Father eternal, the Son eternal, the Holy Spirit eternal" (*LSB*, p. 319).

[29] Siegman, "The Stone Hewn from the Mountain (Daniel 2)," 370, citing Is 8:11–15; 28:16–17; Ps 118:22; Zech 3:9.

to be a holy priesthood, to offer spiritual sacrifices acceptable to God through Jesus Christ" (1 Pet 2:4–5). That those who become part of God's kingdom, established by the stone, become part of the growing stone itself is analogous to the NT depiction of the church as the living and growing body of Christ (Rom 12:4–5; 1 Cor 12:12–27; Col 2:19). That the mountain fills the entire earth may be compared to the cosmic Christology of Colossians (1:15–20; 2:9).

Jesus identifies himself as this crushing rock, linking Dan 2:34, 44–45 with Is 8:14–15; 28:16; and Ps 118:22:

> As he looked at them he said, "What, then, is this that is written: 'The stone that the builders rejected, it has become the head of the corner'? *Everyone who falls on that stone will be crushed, but the person on whom it falls will be crushed."* (Lk 20:17–18; cf. Mt 21:42–44)

Many early Christian fathers recognized that the stone cut without hands is a prophecy of the incarnation of Christ.[30] Justin Martyr (ca. AD 100–165) wrote:

> The expression "it was cut out without hands" signified that it is not a work of man, but [a work] of the will of the Father and God of all things, who brought Him forth.[31]

Irenaeus (died ca. AD 195) explained more fully:

> On this account also, Daniel, foreseeing His advent, said that a stone, cut out without hands, came into this world. For this is what "without hands" means, that His coming into this world was not by the operation of human hands, that is, of those men who are accustomed to stone-cutting; that is, Joseph taking no part with regard to it, but Mary alone co-operating with the pre-arranged plan. For this stone from the earth derives existence from both the power and the wisdom of God. ... So, then, we understand that His advent in human nature was not by the will of a man, but by the will of God.[32]

This view was also held into the forth and fifth centuries as witnessed by the writings of Jerome (ca. AD 345–413) and Theodoret (ca. AD 390–458).[33]

Many contemporary commentators take the stone as a reference only to the kingdom, and not directly to Christ.[34] However, it is impossible to separate the kingdom from the one who brings and establishes the kingdom that grows to fill the earth (2:35). The focus of Daniel's explanation to Nebuchadnezzar is on the kingdom since a kingdom, and not the Messiah, appealed to the king's interest. That the messianic king and his kingdom are inextricably connected

---

[30] See Collins, *Daniel*, 171; Pfandl, "Interpretations of the Kingdom of God in Daniel 2:44," 251–53.

[31] Justin Martyr, *Dialogue with Trypho*, 76 (*ANF* 1:236).

[32] Irenaeus, *Against Heresies*, 21.7 (*ANF* 1:453).

[33] Pfandl, "Interpretations of the Kingdom of God in Daniel 2:44," 252. See Jerome, *Commentary on Daniel*, on 2:40 (Archer, *Jerome's Commentary on Daniel*, 32), and Theodoret of Cyrus, *Commentary on Daniel*, on Dan 2:34–35 (trans. Hill, 50–55).

[34] Archer, "Daniel," 48; Baldwin, *Daniel*, 93; Lucas, *Daniel*, 77; Miller, *Daniel*, 99–102.

is made clear from the teaching of the apostles, who are said to proclaim Christ while at the same time teaching about the kingdom of God (Acts 8:12; 28:23, 31; cf. 2 Tim 4:1). Just as Nebuchadnezzar was inseparable from his kingdom (see commentary on Dan 2:38), so the Messiah is inseparable from the kingdom of God.

The NT teaching about the kingdom of God is directly dependent on Daniel.[35] This passage is the first in Daniel to speak directly about it. More specific details are given in Daniel's vision later in the book (7:27).

Daniel also adds some explanation that does not rest upon any specific symbolism in his preceding summary of the dream: the kingdom of God "will never be destroyed, nor will the kingdom be left to another people" (2:44). This kingdom will not be superseded by any other, and it will never be conquered and its members excluded. The crushing of the statue symbolizes that the messianic kingdom will supersede all other "worldwide" kingdoms. It will be the first and last truly universal or catholic kingdom.[36] Unlike the pretensions of the other kingdoms, it will actually fill the entire earth (2:35). Thus already in the first century, St. Paul could assert that "the Gospel that you have heard ... has been preached in all creation under heaven" (Col 1:23).

A central theme of Nebuchadnezzar's dream is the contrast between human kingdoms, which are subject to the mortality inherent in sinful human existence, and the kingdom established by the eternal God, which is itself everlasting. For God's kingdom to be everlasting, those who are its members (believers in the one true God) must be raised from death to everlasting life. That aspect of the kingdom will be revealed later in the book (Dan 12:2–3).

This messianic kingdom that struck the statue on its feet continues to crush the kingdoms of this world to this day through the preaching of the Gospel, the administration of the Sacraments, and the ingrafting of new members into

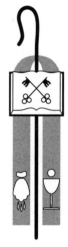

---

[35] See also "Daniel in the New Testament" in the introduction. Some scholars see the NT's dependence on Daniel as only indirect or uncertain, but Wenham ("The Kingdom of God and Daniel," 133) refutes that view when he writes:

> None of the possible alternative backgrounds [to the NT] stands out as both linguistically and conceptually superior to Daniel as an explanation of the New Testament usage [of the kingdom of God]. ...
>
> It is unnecessarily complicated to make Daniel an indirect influence on New Testament thinking and other works dependent ultimately on Daniel the direct influence, when we know that the book of Daniel itself was significant for the first Christians and when Daniel itself is a thoroughly plausible background to the Christian ideas in question [that is, the kingdom of God, the desolating sacrilege, the Son of Man, the mystery that is revealed, and resurrection to judgment and to life].

[36] "Universal" means that it will extend throughout the inhabited world, but only believers in the one true God are members of his kingdom through faith in Jesus Christ. Unbelievers are excluded. Thus "catholic," from the Greek καθολικός, "throughout the whole [world]," describes this kingdom, as confessed in the Nicene Creed: "I believe in one holy catholic and apostolic church."

the body of Christ, so that the church is spreading into all nations throughout the world.[37]

The process of ending the fourth kingdom, the Roman Empire, did not end with the fall of Rome, but continues to this day; see the commentary on 7:23–25.

The mountain into which the stone grows in Nebuchadnezzar's dream is God's kingdom, and it vividly depicts his holy mountain, which will be a place for all people to worship, the eschatological temple of God. Thus this vision also speaks about the fulfillment of the prophecy of Is 2:2–5 and Micah 4:1–5, which is fulfilled in Christ, the new temple, where God's presence dwells (Mt 12:6; Jn 1:14; 2:19–21; Col 1:19–20; Rev 21:22). From him, the cornerstone, the entire church grows to be God's everlasting temple (1 Cor 3:16–17; Eph 2:19–22; 1 Pet 2:4–9; Rev 3:12).

Nebuchadnezzar's Response to Daniel (2:46–47)

Nebuchadnezzar's reaction to Daniel's explanation is to pay homage to Daniel himself as the representative of his God. The gift and incense are religious offerings, and the particular verb for "pay homage" has pagan connotations throughout the OT.[38] These actions are consistent with the pagan religious perspective of Nebuchadnezzar. Similarly in the NT, see Acts 14:11–13. However, the reader knows that Daniel is no god; he is merely the spokesman of the one true God. Moreover, Nebuchadnezzar's words "truly your God is God of gods, Lord of kings, and Revealer of mysteries because you were able to reveal this mystery" do not indicate that he is deifying Daniel. Instead, he confirms Daniel's assertion that he, Daniel, could only reveal to the king his dream because the one true God had revealed it to Daniel (2:27–28).

God is given three titles by Nebuchadnezzar. The first is "God of gods." While this phrase may be used elsewhere in the OT without implying that there are other gods, on the lips of Nebuchadnezzar it may well signify that he is not converting to a monotheistic faith, but rather is merely accepting that the God of Israel is greater than other gods. Later verses provide evidence of the king's continuing polytheism.(g)

(g) Dan 3:12, 14, 18, 25, 29; 4:5–6, 15 (ET 4:8–9, 18)

The second title is "Lord of kings." This is an acknowledgment that God is in control of the kingdoms ruled by humans, including Nebuchadnezzar's own

---

[37] Jesus won the decisive victory over Satan by his atoning death on the cross and victorious resurrection, thus crushing Satan in fulfillment of Gen 3:15. The saving benefits of his victory are bestowed by the Gospel and received by believers. In one sense, the evil powers at work in this world are being defeated already now by the spread of the Gospel. Thus Jesus declared, "I saw Satan falling like lightning from heaven" as his seventy-two missionaries were proclaiming the Gospel and casting out demons (Lk 10:16–20). On the other hand, the final defeat of the last enemy, death, will not take place until the last day, when all believers will be raised bodily to everlasting life. Referring to that day, the apostle Paul promises, "The God of peace will crush Satan under your feet soon" (Rom 16:20).

[38] For the usage and connotation of סְגִד, "pay homage, worship," see the eighth textual note on 3:5.

kingdom and himself as its king. By using it, Nebuchadnezzar tacitly admits that the one true God has exercised his lordship over him by making him dependent on God's revelation to Daniel, who explained the dream to him. This also implies that Nebuchadnezzar acknowledges Daniel's explanation as true.

The final title, "Revealer of mysteries," is an acknowledgement of Daniel's statement that God had revealed the mystery to Daniel (2:30). Moreover, it is also a tacit admission that the Babylonian wise men were wrong in stating that no such revelation is possible (2:11). Nebuchadnezzar, therefore, used a title for God that Daniel used earlier (2:29). God has showed himself the ultimate Revealer of mysteries through the revelation of Jesus preached by the apostles. St. Paul refers to his afflictions for the sake of the body of Christ, the church, of which he was a minister:

> I became a minister according to the stewardship from God that was given to me for your sake, to make fully known the Word of God, the *mystery* hidden for ages and generations but now *revealed* to his saints. To them God chose to make known how great among the Gentiles are the riches of the glory of this *mystery*, which is Christ in you, the hope of glory. (Col 1:25–27)

Daniel and His Friends Appointed to Positions of Authority in Babylon (2:48–49)

The parallels between Daniel and Joseph have been noted by many.[39] Both are taken captive to a foreign land, where they appear before a foreign monarch and successfully interpret a dream—a divine revelation—that no one else could interpret. Both are then promoted to a high office in a foreign court. Daniel's situation is different, however, in that he is not the sole Judean in Nebuchadnezzar's court. Daniel not only remembers his companions, but he sees that they too are promoted.

However, his companions are appointed "over the service of the province of Babylon" (עֲבִידְתָּא דִּי מְדִינַת בָּבֶל), while Daniel remains "in the royal court" (בִּתְרַע מַלְכָּא; see the textual note on 2:49). That notice ties the narrative of chapter 2 with the following narrative in chapter 3. There, when the provincial officials are gathered for the dedication of Nebuchadnezzar's statue, Shadrach, Meshach, and Abednego are among them, since they are serving in the province, whereas Daniel is not, because he serves in the royal court.

---

[39] See further "Daniel and Joseph" in "Connections with Other Old Testament Books" in the introduction.

Excursus
The Four-Kingdom Schema in Daniel

Perhaps no question of interpretation better signifies the divide between scholars practicing historical-grammatical exegesis and those practicing various critical methods of exegesis than the identification of the four kingdoms that are depicted in the various dreams and visions in Daniel 2, 7, 8, and 10–12. Although there have been any number of explanations of the identity of the four kingdoms, two views predominate.[1]

The Roman View and the Greek View

The view that identifies the fourth kingdom as the Roman Empire, hence called "the Roman view," was the accepted view of Christians and Jews in antiquity and the only view among Christians until the rise of modern biblical criticism.[2] It remains the view of most evangelical Christian commentators.[3] This view presupposes that God did reveal the future to his prophets and that, in particular, Daniel reflects such divine revelation. Prophecies that extend beyond the reign of Antiochus Epiphanes (175–164 BC), such as 11:36–45, are predictions beyond the time of the Greek kingdoms and relate to troubles during the time of God's kingdom on earth. The Roman view is consistent with the NT Gospels, which firmly anchor the incarnation, birth, and ministry of Christ in Roman history (e.g., Lk 2:1), and with the Apostles' and Nicene Creeds, which confess that Jesus suffered and was crucified under Pontius Pilate, the Roman governor. It is also consistent with the prominent theme in the Gospels that Jesus himself both preached and brought the kingdom of God.[4] The NT clearly testifies that the kingdom of God was established by Jesus during the Roman Empire.[a]

(a) E.g., Mt 12:28; Mk 9:1; Lk 2:1–7; 3:1–23; 9:27; 10:9; 11:20; 17:20–21

The view that identifies the fourth kingdom as the Greek kingdoms that dominated the ancient Near East starting with Alexander, hence called "the Greek view," was first proposed by the virulent anti-Christian, Neoplatonic phi-

---

[1] For a review of the many theories proposed by the time of the early twentieth century, see Rowley, *Darius the Mede and the Four World Empires in the Book of Daniel*, 184–85. For a comparison of the dispensational view with the historic amillennial Christian view, see the discussion of Daniel 2, 7, 8, 9, and 12 in "Dispensational Interpretations of Daniel" in "Eschatology and Dispensational Premillennial Interpretations of Daniel" in the introduction.

[2] This is the oldest documented interpretation of the four kingdoms. For Jewish sources, see *4 Ezra* 12:10–12 and *2 Baruch* 39:5–6 in context, as well as Josephus, *Antiquities*, 10.276. Ancient Christian sources include the *Epistle of Barnabas* 4:1–5, Hippolytus, *Commentary on Daniel*, 1–3 (ANF 5:178–79); Eusebius, *Demonstration of the Gospel*, fragment of book 15 (PG 22:793–94); and Jerome, *Commentary on Daniel*, on 2:31, 39–40 (Archer, *Jerome's Commentary on Daniel*, 31–32). See also Luther, "Preface to Daniel," AE 35:295; Calvin, *Daniel*, 1:172–79.

[3] E.g., Leupold, *Daniel*, 115–23, 276–329; Young, *Daniel*, 275–94.

[4] For this theme in Matthew, one may see Gibbs, *Matthew 1:1–11:1*, 47–51.

losopher Porphyry (ca. AD 233–304).[5] Porphyry presupposed that there was no such thing as genuine divine revelation of the future. Instead, he argued that Daniel was written as if it were predictive prophecy, when, in actuality, it was written during the first half of the second century BC, after the events that it portrayed concerning Antiochus IV Epiphanes. The prophecies in Daniel that attempted to predict events after Antiochus (11:40–45) were inaccurate, demonstrating that there is no divinely revealed predictive prophecy. These supposedly inaccurate prophecies betrayed the author's real identity and date: a Jew in Palestine about the year 165 BC. Since genuine prediction is impossible, the fourth kingdom could not be the Roman Empire, which had not yet arrived on the scene in Palestine. The author intended the fourth kingdom to be the Greek kingdoms of his time. Though refuted by Jerome in antiquity, Porphyry's view has become the standard approach for contemporary scholars who employ higher-critical methodology.

The Greek view is a distinct minority opinion among evangelicals, though at times some will defend it while holding that Daniel is true prophecy written in the sixth century BC.[6]

The two views identify the kingdoms in the prophecies of Daniel as shown in figure 9.

Hermeneutical Issues

The Greek view stems from an antisupernaturalistic presupposition: that there can be no such thing as genuine predictive prophecy of events in the distant future. Therefore, the writer must have been writing after the events he so accurately describes, especially the events in the Seleucid and Ptolemaic kingdoms from the death of Alexander to the reign of Antiochus IV Epiphanes (11:5–35). But an even more serious problem is that this approach denies that there are any messianic features in Daniel's prophecy.[7] Thus Jesus' identification of himself as the Son of Man who comes on the clouds of heaven[b] is a misreading or reapplication of a text that was not originally intended to be about him.

This, of course, is not seen as a problem by those who do not claim to be Christian. In their estimation, Jesus was simply wrong, and Daniel was never intended to be read messianically. Or if it was to be read messianically, it expected a messiah to arise in the Greek era, not under the Roman Empire.

(b) Dan 7:13; Mt 24:30; 26:64; Mk 13:26; 14:62; Lk 21:27; cf. Rev 1:7

---

[5] Porphyry's *Against the Christians* is no longer extant, but his views on Daniel are summarized and refuted in Jerome's commentary on Daniel (see especially the prologue to Jerome's commentary [Archer, *Jerome's Commentary on Daniel*, 15–17]). A summary of Porphyry's views on Daniel is also given in Young, *Daniel*, 317–20.

[6] E.g., Armistead, "The Images of Daniel 2 and 7: A Literary Approach"; Gurney, "The Four Kingdoms of Daniel 2 and 7"; Lucas, *Daniel*, 76–77, 176–202; Walton, "The Four Kingdoms of Daniel."

[7] For the messianic features in Daniel, see "The Messiah in Daniel: An Overview" in "Major Themes" in the introduction.

Figure 9

Views on the Identity of the Kingdoms in Daniel

The Roman View

Chapter 2	Chapter 7	Chapter 8	Chapters 10–12	Identification
Gold	Lion			Babylon
Silver	Bear	Ram	11:2	Persia
Bronze	Leopard	Male goat	11:3–35	Greek kingdoms
Iron and clay	Beast		(11:36–45)	Rome
Mountain	Coming of the Son of Man		12:1–4	God's kingdom

The Greek View

Chapter 2	Chapter 7	Chapter 8	Chapters 10–12	Identification
Gold	Lion			Babylon
Silver	Bear	Ram (first horn)		Media
Bronze	Leopard	Ram (second horn)	11:2	Persia
Iron and clay	Beast	Male goat	11:3–45	Greek kingdoms
Mountain	Coming of the Son of Man		12:1–4	God's kingdom

The hermeneutical questions that the Greek view raises regarding Jesus and the NT are usually not addressed by critical scholars. Yet we must ask, If Daniel's prophecies were originally not about Jesus, was it valid for Jesus to reapply them to himself? Would it also be valid to reapply the texts to others who might claim to be messiahs? When are such reapplications valid, and when are they unfounded? Do the texts of the Gospels indicate that Jesus believed that Daniel's prophecies were originally intended to be about him, or do they indicate that Jesus was reapplying texts that were originally not about him? If "the Spirit of Christ" was at work in the OT prophets (1 Pet 1:11), leading them to write inspired Scripture (2 Tim 3:16), and if Jesus truly is God the Son, must we not agree that his application of Daniel's prophecies to himself is the authoritative interpretation that must guide our own understanding of the book?

Proponents of the Greek view are unable to answer any of these questions satisfactorily. Thus there is a certain tension among scholars claiming a Christian heritage who nevertheless advocate the Greek view. Their ability to retain both an assent to Christianity and also the critical view often requires them to issue a special pleading for one or the other, instead of consistently following defined hermeneutical principles. Indeed, critical hermeneutics are less about dealing with the text on its own terms than about explaining the text from a naturalistic worldview that has no place for direct divine intervention in human affairs.

In order to bolster the naturalistic view, critical scholars often seek the origin of Daniel's four-kingdom schema in earlier sources, either Persian or Greek.[8] In these sources, the kingdoms are in a variety of sequences, usually beginning with the Assyrian Empire. Commentators are often forced to admit that Daniel's four-kingdom schema is not the same as these supposed earlier sources, since he begins with Babylon (not Assyria, as the sources generally do), and in any case, his sequence of kingdoms is not exactly the same.[9]

Problems in Daniel for the Greek View

The text of Daniel itself poses other problems for the Greek view. We may summarize six chief difficulties, each of which also includes a factor in favor of the Roman view.

1. In Daniel 2, the coming of the Messiah and the establishing of God's kingdom is said to be "in the days of those kings" (וּבְיוֹמֵיהוֹן דִּי מַלְכַיָּא אִנּוּן, 2:44). This corresponds to the stone that strikes the statue on its feet of iron and clay (2:34). This is no problem for those who hold to the Greek view and believe that the author simply got future history wrong. He expected the kingdom of God to be established shortly after his time, still during the Hellenistic era. However, it did not arrive at that time. Therefore, the proper conclusion would be that the author of Daniel was a false prophet (cf. Deut 18:20–22). Furthermore, this

---

[8] See the commentary on 2:31–35.
[9] E.g., Collins, *Daniel*, 166–68.

eviscerates any attempt to find an enduring message for the readers of the book. Throughout Daniel, God's ability to govern history for the sake of his kingdom demonstrates his power to save his people,[10] yet according to this view, God failed to govern history and failed to save his people as promised.

Obviously, for Christians, this is hardly a viable alternative, since the NT clearly testifies that Jesus Christ established God's kingdom during the Roman Empire. Thus to hold that the fourth empire is the Greek kingdoms is also to hold that the NT is wrong about Jesus establishing the kingdom of God. Evangelicals who hold to the Greek view sense this difficulty.[11] Gurney tries to salvage his position by stating that Christ was born only about twenty years after the final obliteration of the Greek Empire.[12] However, that hardly qualifies as "*in* the days of those kings" (Dan 2:44), as Walton is forced to admit. Walton further tries to salvage this position by appealing to the slaying of the beast in Daniel 7 before the coming of the Son of Man on the clouds (Dan 7:11–13).[13] However, Walton fails to appreciate the difference between the stone in Daniel 2, which represents Christ's first advent,[14] and the coming of the Son of Man on the clouds, which is a distinctly eschatological reference that applies to Christ's second advent.[15] This corresponds to the NT tension between the "now" and the "not yet": the kingdom was established at Christ's first coming and so is here already "now" through his Word and Sacraments, but it has also "not yet" come in all its fullness. Already now we are heirs of the kingdom, but we will not fully inherit and enter it until the return of Christ, the bodily resurrection, and the entrance of all believers into the new heavens and new earth.(c)

(c) E.g., Mk 9:47; Lk 19:11–27; 22:18; 1 Cor 6:9–10; 15:50; Gal 5:21

2. The Greek view requires that three kingdoms precede the Greek kingdoms. Since Dan 2:38 specifies that the first kingdom is Babylonian, two kingdoms are needed between the Babylonians and the Greeks. This presents a problem since Babylon fell to the Persian Empire, which eventually was conquered by Alexander the Great, a Greek. Critical scholars commonly assert that Media is the needed second kingdom between Babylon and Persia. However, Babylon did not fall to the Medes. The Medes had been subsumed under the Persians eleven years before Babylon was conquered by Cyrus the Great. Cyrus had combined the Median and Persian kingdoms in himself, since he was of

---

[10] See "Theological Threats Posed by the Critical Dating of Daniel" in "Date, Authorship, and Unity," and "The Messiah in Daniel: An Overview" and "God as the Protector of His People" in "Major Themes" in the introduction. See also the commentary on 2:27–30, 34–35, 44–45 and 7:9–14.

[11] Armistead ("The Images of Daniel 2 and 7," 65–66) is an evangelical who accepts the inspiration of Daniel, but at the same time advocates the Greek view and argues that Jesus is merely reapplying a text that originally was about the Greek era.

[12] Gurney, "The Four Kingdoms of Daniel 2 and 7," 39.

[13] Walton, "The Four Kingdoms of Daniel," 35, n. 47.

[14] See the commentary on 2:31–35 and 2:44–45.

[15] Dan 7:13; Mt 24:30; 26:64; Mk 13:26; 14:62; Lk 21:27; Rev 1:7. See the commentary on Dan 7:11–14 and 7:23–27.

Persian royal descent on his father's side and of Median royal descent on his mother's side, and he solidified this with the defeat of the Median king, his grandfather Astyages, in 550 BC. It should be noted that Medes continued to play an important part in the Persian Empire, and the Greeks often called Persians "Medes" down to the fourth century BC.[16]

The Judeans in Babylon and Palestine were never ruled by the independent kingdom of the Medes. Since the emphasis of Daniel's prophecy is that God is in control of human kingdoms *for the benefit of his people*, the four successive kingdoms must be ones that ruled over God's people. This point is often ignored by those who argue that Babylon was in decline after the death of Nebuchadnezzar, so that the ascendant Median kingdom must be the second kingdom, even though it never conquered Babylon.[17] However, the Median kingdom did not arise *after* Nebuchadnezzar (as required by Dan 2:39 for the second kingdom), but was already powerful in Nebuchadnezzar's day. In fact, Nebuchadnezzar's father sought peace with the Medes by marrying him to a daughter of the Median king. Nebuchadnezzar built the famous Hanging Gardens of Babylon for his Median wife. Moreover, the Medes and the Chaldeans together were instrumental in the fall of Nineveh and the conquest of the Assyrian Empire.[18] Thus the Median kingdom does not fit the profile of the second kingdom.[19]

One solution to which critics often resort is to conclude that the author of Daniel simply did not know the correct historical sequence and made a mistake by making the Medes the second kingdom.[20] As evidence for this, critics cite the references in Daniel to the kingship of Darius the Mede.[d] Since no such person known by that name is recorded in the Babylonian annals, critics often contend that Darius was invented by the author to supply a Median kingdom between the Babylonians and Persians. Thus it is supposed that the book itself depicts this order: Babylon, Media, Persia, and Greece (see 6:29 [ET 6:28]).

(d) Dan 5:31; 6:2, 7, 10, 26, 29 (ET 6:1, 6, 9, 25, 28); 9:1; 11:1

However, in Daniel, Darius the Mede is not simply a Median king. He is clearly subject to "the law of the Medes *and the Persians*" (6:9, 13, 16 [ET 6:8, 12, 15]). This is similar to Xerxes in the book of Esther, who is subject to "the laws of the Persians and the Medes" (Esth 1:19; cf. Esth 1:3, 14, 18–19; note also "the kings of Media and Persia," in Esth 10:2, where the order is Media, then Persia, as in Daniel). Clearly, Darius is a ruler within the Persian Empire, just as surely as Xerxes was a Persian king. Thus whoever Darius was, he is

---

[16] Yamauchi, *Persia and the Bible*, 57.

[17] This is the argument of Caragounis, "History and Supra-History: Daniel and the Four Empires," 392–94.

[18] Yamauchi, *Persia and the Bible*, 53–56.

[19] Collins admits as much when he concedes this: "The inclusion of Media in the succession of world empires appears odd because Media never ruled over the Jews" (*Daniel*, 166).

[20] Rowley, *Darius the Mede and the Four World Empires in the Book of Daniel*, 147–50.

depicted in Daniel as a ruler in the Persian Empire.[21] Therefore, any claim that the figure of Darius the Mede is intended to insert a Median kingdom before the Persian one is mistaken and does not account for Darius' respect for "the law of the Medes and the Persians." Nor does it account for him receiving the kingdom of Babylon (6:1 [ET 5:31]), which was "given to the Medes *and the Persians*" (5:28).

3. A related problem with the Greek view is that it requires the ram depicted in Daniel 8 to represent two of the kingdoms in Daniel 2 and 7. While those holding to the Roman view would agree that the two horns of the ram represent Media and Persia, with the later and larger horn representing Persia (8:3), there is no precedent for equating one creature with two of the metals in the vision of Daniel 2. In Daniel 7, all commentators are agreed that the lion, bear, leopard, and fearsome beast correspond to the gold, silver, bronze, and iron of the image in Daniel 2. Similarly, all agree that the male goat in Daniel 8 corresponds to only one of the metals in the image in Daniel 2 (the bronze according to the Roman view or the iron according to the Greek view).

Thus it is in keeping with the use of the other animal imagery to view the ram as corresponding to only one of the metals of the image in Daniel 2, and there is no indication in the text to follow any other procedure. This only works if the second kingdom is the Persians and the third is the Greeks. The Greek view must see the ram as corresponding to two of the metals (silver and bronze) in order to make its case. Yet this violates the very obvious use of equivalent imagery throughout these two visions. In addition, it violates the clear statements in 8:6–7 (see also 8:20–21) that picture the goat representing Greece as breaking off *both* horns of the ram. This action can only be understood if the ram represents the combined kingdom of the Medes and the Persians, commonly called the Persian Empire.

Some critics admit this, but claim that although the ram was originally intended to represent a combined Median and Persian empire, a later editor incorporated it into the book and adapted it to Daniel 7, where critics suppose that two separate kingdoms of Media and Persia are represented.[22] Resorting to the strategy of a hypothetical earlier version of the story allegedly changed by a later editor is a tacit admission that there is an inherent problem with the Greek view. Blaming the problem on a speculative history of a supposedly changing text is not biblical scholarship, but special pleading.

4. While few clues are given in Daniel 2 to identify the second, third, and fourth kingdoms in Nebuchadnezzar's dream, subsequent chapters give greater detail. One detail that is repeated in the visions in chapters 7, 8, and 10–12 is a kingdom with a fourfold nature. In Daniel 7, the third kingdom is represented by a leopard with four wings and four heads (7:6). The four wings are probably to signify the leopard's ability to take advantage of "the four winds of heaven" (7:2). It is, therefore, even swifter than a normal leopard. Of the two kingdoms

---

[21] See the excursus "The Identity of Darius the Mede" and the commentary on 6:1 (ET 5:31).
[22] Collins, *Daniel*, 330.

mentioned in Daniel 8, the second one is symbolized by a male goat. This goat is also swift, moving across the ground without touching it (8:5). Initially this goat has one horn (8:5). However, when that horn is broken, four horns replace it, "toward the four winds of heaven" (8:8). In the vision in Daniel 10–12, the mighty king who arises will have his kingdom broken and divided "toward the four winds of heaven" (11:3–4). The parallels in the descriptions of these kingdoms is too substantial to be coincidental; it must be intentional parallelism. The four heads of the leopard do not arise sequentially, but are there simultaneously.[23] The same is true of the leopard's four wings. Similarly, the four horns on the male goat arise simultaneously. There is agreement among all scholars that the male goat of Daniel 8 and the kingdoms mentioned in 11:3–4 represent the Greeks, beginning with Alexander the Great (the single horn and the mighty king). Therefore, the third kingdom of Daniel 7 represented by the leopard must also be the Greeks. The Greek view, however, insists that it is not the third kingdom, but the fourth kingdom that is Greek, contrary to the parallels clearly present in these visions.

5. Another difficulty with the Greek view is that it must equate the little horn of Daniel 7 with the little horn of Daniel 8. Granted, these two horns are similar in some respects. Both start out small: "another horn, a little one" (7:8) and "a single horn that began small" and "became very large" (8:9). Both oppress God's people (7:21; 8:12, 24). Both are said to exercise their power over God's people or God's sanctuary for a set period of time ("a time, times, and half a time," 7:25; "two thousand three hundred evenings [and] mornings," 8:14). However, there are distinct differences between the two, as shown in figure 10.[24]

While these horns resemble one another, they are clearly not the same. The most obvious difference is that the one in chapter 7 is distinct from the other horns among which it springs up (7:8), and it overcomes other horns, while the one in chapter 8 grows out of another horn (8:9), and so is part of that other horn (see B and D in figure 10).[25]

Two other important differences are the horns' activities and the durations of those activities (see G in figure 10). The little horn in chapter 7 oppresses the saints and does so for "a time, times, and half a time" (7:25), while the little horn in chapter 8 removes the daily sacrifice at the temple and does so for

---

[23] Note that the visions are clear when indicating sequences of kings within kingdoms and also when indicating simultaneous rulers. Clear indications of sequential rulers include the following: on the ram, one horn comes up after the other (8:3); on the male goat, a little horn grows out of one of the four horns *after* the four horns have sprung up together (8:9); and likewise on the fourth beast of Daniel 7, the little horn arises later than the ten horns, and it uproots three of them (7:8). However, the four heads and four wings on the leopard are there simultaneously (7:6), just as the ten horns on the fourth beast are simultaneous, and the text gives no indication of any sequence except for the small horn, which will arise "after them" (7:24).

[24] For a similar comparison, see Young, *Daniel*, 276–77.

[25] This difference is the most difficult contrast between the two horns that needs to be reconciled by those who hold the Greek view. It is hard to see how these can be complementary views of the same horn, as claimed by Lucas, *Daniel*, 190, and Goldingay, *Daniel*, 174.

2,300 evenings and mornings (8:11–14). Many attempt to interpret these two actions and two time periods as referring to the same activity during the same time period. However, in Daniel 7, the action is oppressing the holy people, while in Daniel 8 it is the prevention of the sacrificial rites at the holy temple. While these actions may be related, they are not identical. In Daniel 8, the little horn also oppresses the holy people, but this activity is not confined to the 2,300 evenings and mornings during which he prevents the temple sacrifices, and his time of oppression should be identical to the time when the sacrifices are prevented if the action and period in chapter 7 were to be equated with those in chapter 8.

In order to equate the durations of the activities (see G in figure 10), some first interpret "a time, times, and half a time" (7:25) as meaning three and a half years, then interpret 2,300 evenings and mornings (8:14) as referring to the sum of 1,150 evening sacrifices plus 1,150 morning sacrifices, which would take only 1,150 days, slightly less than three years and two months. These commentators often say that the period 2,300 evenings and mornings is more precise, but refers to the same period as the three and a half "times," which is a round number. However, there are several problems with equating these two different time periods. Not all commentators agree that "a time, times, and half a time" is intended to be understood as three and a half years, and this commentary argues that it is not to be understood in that way (see the commentary on 7:25). In addition, not all are agreed that the period 2,300 evenings and mornings refers to the sum of 1,150 evenings and 1,150 mornings, and hence refers to just 1,150 days instead of 2,300 days, although this commentary inclines toward that view (see the commentary on 8:14). Moreover, 1,150 days is about five days short of three years and two months, so it is closer to three years than to three and a half years. To refer to the same time period, the rounded figure should have been "a time and (two) times" to indicate three years.

The most important difference may be that in Daniel 7 the removal of the little horn's dominion is followed by the kingdom that is given to the saints, while in Daniel 8 the dominion of the little horn simply comes to its end without human intervention (see H and I in figure 10). Thus while these two horns are in some ways alike, they are historically distinct from one another since they occupy different time periods in the historical sequence of earthly kingdoms, God's kingdom, and the eschaton. The Greek view, however, depends on them being identified with one another.

The Roman view distinguishes these two horns. The little horn of Daniel 7 is the Antichrist, who is active during the church age, up to the *second* coming of Christ, when he is deposed, and then the saints receive the eternal kingdom of God. In contrast, the little horn of Daniel 8 is Antiochus IV Epiphanes, who oppressed God's people prior to the *first* advent of Christ, and the arrival of the kingdom of God (at Christ's first advent) did not take place right after his reign (175–164 BC), but over a hundred and fifty years later. Yet both persecute God's people, seeking to rob them of access to God's grace. And according to the Roman view, both are treated side by side in Daniel 11. Dan 11:21–35 speaks of Antiochus IV, and 11:36–45 speaks of the Antichrist as an end-time king. The Greek view understands all of 11:21–45 as being about Antiochus, but sees 11:40–45 as the author's attempt to predict Antiochus' later career, which the author failed to predict accurately. Thus if the Greek view is correct, Daniel is false prophecy.[26]

6. Finally, the Greek view equates the male goat of Daniel 8 with the fourth kingdom of Daniel 2 and 7. However, in Daniel 2 and 7, the fourth kingdom is followed by God's eternal kingdom. This is not true in Daniel 8. Instead, what follows the dominion of the ram (and its little horn) in chapter 8 is the restoration of the sanctuary (8:14). The kingdom of God is never mentioned in the vision of Daniel 8. Clearly, the kingdom that is represented by the ram in chapter 8 is not the fourth kingdom in Daniel 2 and 7 because that fourth kingdom ushers in God's reign (at the first advent of Christ), not simply a restoration of the Jerusalem sanctuary so that the sacrifices prescribed in the OT may once again be offered.

Advantages of the Roman View

The Roman view presents none of these problems and can explain all of these difficulties. Moreover, it offers a thoroughly messianic reading of the visions of Daniel in keeping with the understanding of Daniel found in Jesus' teachings in the Gospels. Nevertheless, those who espouse the Greek view have raised some objections to it.[27] Their five main objections follow, together with reasons why the book of Daniel itself refutes their objections and requires the Roman view.

First, some interpreters object that there is nothing in the description of the fourth kingdom in Daniel 2 that requires it to be the Roman Empire. This has already been shown to be false because Daniel 2 (like Daniel 7) places the establishment of God's kingdom during the fourth kingdom, which the NT clearly defines as happening at the first advent of Jesus Christ during the Roman Empire.[28]

---

[26] Lucas (*Daniel*, 293, 308–9), an evangelical, wishes to rescue Daniel from the charge of false prophecy (which he softens by calling it "quasi-prophecy") by stating that 11:40–45 is not intended to be a detailed prediction of the end of Antiochus' reign, but simply portrays in hyperbolic terms how Antiochus' arrogance will lead him to an untimely death. However, Lucas nowhere points to a place in the text that indicates a change from detailed prediction to hyperbole. In addition, Lucas does not object to a reapplication of the text to the Antichrist or any other despotic ruler. This allowance for multiple fulfillments raises a hermeneutical problem since it makes the text subject to the whims of the interpreter and leaves an uncertainty as to when it can and should be properly reapplied or when such reapplication is an abuse of the text. (For the hermeneutical issue, see further under "Daniel 8" in "Eschatology and Dispensational Premillennial Interpretations of Daniel" in the introduction.) Moreover, Lucas sees Daniel as interested not so much in the accurate prediction of history as in the interpretation of history. However, this is a false dichotomy, since one cannot interpret history (past or future) without an accurate knowledge of it.

[27] For a summary of these objections, see Lucas, *Daniel*, 190–91.

[28] See further "The Roman View and the Greek View" above.

Figure 10

Comparison between the Little Horn in Daniel 7 and the Little Horn in Daniel 8

Daniel 7

A. While the little horn from 7:8 had an "appearance" that "was greater" (7:20) than the ten other horns, it is never described as becoming large.

B. The horn grows up among ten other horns (7:8).

C. It is different than the horns that preceded it (7:24).

D. It uproots three horns (7:8, 20, 24).

E. It has human features: eyes and a mouth that speaks (7:8, 11, 20, 25).

F. *There is no similar statement.*

G. It wages war against the saints (7:21), intends "to change times and Law" (7:25), and prevails over the saints for "a time, times, and half a time" (7:25).

H. Its dominion is taken away by the divine court (7:26).

I. Its dominion is given to the saints of the Most High (7:27).

Daniel 8

A. The "single horn that began small" eventually "became very large" (8:9).

B. The horn grows out of one of four horns (8:9).

C. *There is no similar statement.*

D. *There is no similar statement.*

E. *There is no similar statement.*

F. It understands enigmas (8:23).

G. It takes away the continual sacrifice for 2,300 evenings and mornings (8:11–14).

H. It is broken, but not by a (human) hand (8:25).

I. *There is no mention of who receives its dominion.*

Second, some argue that the iron and clay mixture that is the material for the feet (representing the fourth kingdom) of the image (2:41–43) points to marriage alliances among the Greek kings. In particular, they cite the clause "they will be mixed among the seed of man" (2:43) as pointing to marriage alliances, and connect that clause to the marriage alliances mentioned in 11:6, 17. However, as noted in the textual note on 2:43, this clause is difficult to understand. It does not necessarily refer to marriage alliances, and it is difficult to see how one Greek ruler marrying the Greek daughter of another Greek ruler means that the fourth kingdom is "mixed among the seed of man." A more likely interpretation is that the clause refers to intermarriage among ethnic groups within the kingdom. Moreover, the point of the mixed composition of the feet (2:41–43) is that the fourth kingdom will not remain united, but will crumble (2:43). The marriage alliances in Daniel 11 simply cement alliances between kingdoms, and the kingdoms and their alliances do not necessarily crumble when the marriages end. Thus it is false to argue that the marriage alliances in Daniel 11 are parallel to the mixed composition of the statue's feet in Daniel 2, and so this false parallel is no argument for the Greek view.

Third, advocates of the Greek view note that the fourth beast in Daniel 7 is said to be different than the others (7:7, 19), and they claim that this difference is that Alexander the Great was the first European to conquer the Near East. However, the fourth beast's difference is defined in the vision itself: it is more terrifying, and it crushes, devours, and tramples its victims (7:7, 19).[29] Far from being a description of Alexander and his successors, this is more in keeping with the Roman practice and policy of requiring all things in the kingdoms it conquered to bend to Rome's will.

Fourth, some object to the Roman view that the little horn in Daniel 7 has a different referent than the little horn in Daniel 8. However, as demonstrated above in number 5 in "Problems in Daniel for the Greek View," these two little horns are similar but are distinguished from one another; they point to different referents. Some claim that the two different descriptions of the horns are merely complementary and ultimately denote the same thing.[30] Yet it is difficult, if not impossible, to equate a horn that arises among ten horns and uproots three of them (7:8, 20) with a horn that grows from one of four horns and displaces none of them (8:9). In fact, some advocates of the Greek view admit that the two horns could denote different kings, although they argue that the horns probably do not since they appear in the same book.[31] However, the Greek view

---

[29] Moreover, 7:3 states that all four of the beasts were different from each other, so the fourth beast's differences should not be exaggerated.

[30] E.g., Lucas, *Daniel*, 190, claims: "If both small horns are Antiochus, the differences can be seen to produce complementary, not contradictory, portraits of him and his career."

[31] E.g., Goldingay, *Daniel*, 174, asserts: "The differences between the two chapters do not mean that at any point the portraits of the small horn are incompatible. They *could* [emphasis original] denote different kings, but—juxtaposed in the same book—this is not the natural understanding." Goldingay does not state how the "natural understanding" leads to his

itself depends on making a distinction between the leopard with four wings and four heads in Daniel 7 and the male goat with four horns, as well as the kingdom scattered to the four winds, in Daniel 8. It will hardly do to object to this perceived inconsistency in the Roman interpretation when the Greek interpretation has a greater inconsistency. Instead, the question we must ask is whether the text itself indicates that the horns (or beasts) are similar but distinct phenomena, or whether it equates one with the other. Clearly, several major differences between the two little horns are too great to be explained as complementary characteristics, especially their relationships to other horns on the same beast and the numbers of those other horns.

Fifth and finally, some protest that we must understand the fourth kingdom as Greek in order for the surveys of world history in Daniel 2, 7, 8, and 11 all to have the same terminus: the persecution of the Jews by Antiochus IV Epiphanes (175–164 BC). However, no persecution is mentioned in Daniel 2. More importantly, the terminus in both Daniel 2 and Daniel 7 is the establishment of God's kingdom (at the first advent of Christ), and chapters 8 and 11 each have a different terminus. The establishment of God's kingdom is not mentioned in Daniel 8, demonstrating that it does not have the same terminus; instead, its terminus is the reign of Antiochus IV. The survey in Daniel 11 hints at the rise of the Roman Empire (11:30). Its terminus is the end of world history at the second coming of Jesus Christ, when the bodily resurrection of all people will take place and the believers will inherit the blessing of eternal life, while unbelievers will be consigned to eternal shame and punishment (12:2–3). To be consistent with this terminus, the latter part of Daniel 11 must be referring to the Antichrist, and not to Antiochus, since Antiochus died in 164 BC, whereas the Antichrist remains until the parousia of Christ.[32] Once again, like the equating of the two little horns in Daniel 7 and 8, the problem here is one of attempting to equate items in the text that the text itself clearly distinguishes.

Thus none of the objections to the Roman view is hermeneutically sound. Instead, they are driven by the antisupernatural presupposition that God cannot and does not reveal to his prophets accurate prophecies of the distant future. For the few evangelical scholars who hold to the Greek view, it would appear as if they wish to have the respectability of the academy of critical scholars while simultaneously holding on to the accuracy of Daniel's prophecies. This, however, can only be accomplished by special pleading, not by sound hermeneutical method.

---

conclusion. Surely, within one book an author could use a metaphor two or more times to refer to two or more different things in order to highlight their similarities while also indicating key differences between them. For example, in Ecclesiastes, Solomon compares many different facets of life to "vanity, vapor" since these different aspects of life share the quality of being transitory and ephemeral (e.g., הֶבֶל in Eccl 2:1, 11, 15, 17, 19, 21, 23, 26).

[32] The Antichrist, whom Paul calls "the man of lawlessness" (2 Thess 2:3; cf. Dan 7:25), will be destroyed only at the second coming of Christ. See 2 Thess 2:8 and also the excursus "The Lutheran Confessions on the Antichrist in Daniel."

Only the Roman view takes the text of Daniel seriously as an inspired, inerrant revelation of God to the prophet Daniel. Only this view preserves the messianic interpretation of Daniel by Jesus himself in the NT, as recognized by later Christian interpreters (e.g., Jerome, Luther, Calvin).[33] It points to the reign and kingdom of God in Jesus Christ, which the book of Daniel emphasizes throughout. It affirms that God is the one who has control over world history and who has determined the course of that history even before it takes place among humans. God guided world history to prepare for the advent of his kingdom in the incarnation, birth, life, death, and resurrection of his own Son. Even now he continues to govern history to enable his kingdom of grace to come to us by his Gospel in his Word and Sacraments, preserving us in faith through all trials and tribulations, so that his church on earth will endure until our Lord returns and ushers us into his eternal kingdom of glory.

---

[33] See the citations at the beginning of "The Roman View and the Greek View."

Daniel 3:1–30

God's Faithful Servants Are Saved from Death

Introduction to Daniel 3

3:1–7	Nebuchadnezzar's Officials Obey His Command to Worship His Idol
3:8–18	Despite the Death Threat, the Judeans Remain Faithful and Entrust Themselves to God
3:19–30	The Judeans Are Thrown into the Furnace but Are Miraculously Saved by God

Introduction to Daniel 3

Major Emphases in Daniel 3
Law and Gospel in Daniel 3

The account of the three Judeans in the fiery furnace is among the best known of all the narratives in Daniel. It has a clear message of Law and Gospel.[1] Its Law message is that God requires his people to resist the pressures to compromise the one true faith by worshiping false gods. The First Commandment takes center stage in this chapter.[2] Its Gospel message is that God remains beside his persecuted believers, as shown by the appearance of the divine man with the three Judeans in the flames,[3] and God shall rescue his people from even death. For the faithful Judeans, God's rescue comes miraculously in this life so that they do not die. God does not promise always to perform such miracles in this life, but he does promise that all those who die with faith in him shall be raised to everlasting life (12:2–3). Later Daniel passages also make explicit that the basis for God's Gospel promise of resurrection to everlasting life is based on the atoning death and resurrection of the promised Messiah.[4]

While the account in chapter 3 is familiar, many readers do not appreciate how it fits into the wider context of Daniel in which it is set. Moreover, the artistry of Daniel's narrative technique throughout this chapter is often overlooked.

No Accommodation to Paganism

Throughout the first two narratives (chapters 1 and 2),[5] Daniel and his companions were able to maintain their faith without compromising it while at the same time accepting some type of accommodation to the culture of Babylon. In Daniel 1, they were willing to learn the Babylonian language and literature and accept Babylonian names[6] while maintaining their loyalty to God and the dietary laws of the Pentateuch. By requesting (not demanding) a trial exemption and by submitting to the king's examination they were also able to show loyalty to the king without compromising their ultimate loyalty to God. In Daniel

---

[1] See further "Law and Gospel in Daniel" in the introduction.

[2] See further the discussion of the First Commandment in "God's Law in Daniel" in "Law and Gospel in Daniel" in the introduction.

[3] It is likely that this divine man is the preincarnate Savior, Jesus Christ. See the commentary on 3:25.

[4] See further "God's Gospel in Daniel" in "Law and Gospel in Daniel" in the introduction.

[5] Each of the first six chapters in the book is one narrative. See "Daniel 1–6: Six Narratives" in "Overview of Daniel" in the introduction.

[6] However, Daniel the author appears to have distorted the Babylonian names as a polemic against their pagan theophoric elements. See the textual notes on 1:7.

2, Daniel is able to speak to Nebuchadnezzar about the power of the only true God in the context of a Babylonian court that believed in the existence of many gods. Daniel (and he alone) was able to comply with the king's demand that his wise men recount and interpret his dream, and afterward Daniel served the king in his court while his companions served the king in the province (2:49).

The Judeans' accommodation in chapters 1 and 2 shows that believers can and should respect and obey human authorities in the civil realm (Mt 22:21; Rom 13:1–7) as long as such obedience does not involve a compromise or denial of faith in the one true God. However, Daniel 3 (like Daniel 6) will show that believers are obligated to disobey human authorities when they require idolatry or other forms of compromise or denial of the one true faith. Taken together, chapters 1–3 therefore show the distinction between the civil realm and the religious realm, the distinction between church and state. As much as possible, believers live as law-abiding citizens of their state, but as members of the kingdom of God, their highest allegiance is to God. When required by human authorities to compromise their faith, they must "obey God rather than men" (Acts 5:29).

In Daniel 3, no accommodation is possible. Instead of having multiple choices, as in the first two narratives, the options are binary opposites: the Judeans must either worship the idol Nebuchadnezzar has erected and thereby renounce the one true God,[7] or they can confess their faith in God by refusing to engage in any idolatry and consequently face death. Their situation can be compared to that of Elijah, who gave the Israelites only two choices: "If Yahweh is God, follow him, but if Baal [is God], follow him" (1 Ki 18:21). It can also be compared to that of the apostles, who were commanded by the Jewish authorities not to preach the Gospel of Jesus Christ and who replied that they must heed the command of God to preach, rather than submit to men who forbade preaching the name of Jesus (Acts 4:18–20), because salvation is to be found only in Jesus' name (Acts 4:12).

Therefore, the most important emphasis in this account is the inviolable nature of the First Commandment, which forbids the worship of any other gods and also implicitly enjoins the worship of the one true and triune God.[8] By making an "image, statue" (צְלֵם, 3:1, etc.) and requiring worship of it, Nebuchadnezzar himself has violated the First Commandment, which prohib-

---

[7] Bowing down to this idol is an act that is equated with worshiping Nebuchadnezzar's gods (3:12, 14, 18, 28). See the first textual note and the commentary on 3:1.

[8] As Luther explained, the First Commandment not only prohibits idolatry, it also enjoins faith and trust in God (LC I 4):

> The purpose of this commandment, therefore, is to require true faith and confidence of the heart, and these fly straight to the one true God and cling to him alone. The meaning is: "See to it that you let me alone be your God, and never seek another." In other words: "Whatever good thing you lack, look to me for it and seek it from me, and whenever you suffer misfortune and distress, come and cling to me. I am the one who will satisfy you and help you out of every need. Only let your heart cling to no one else."

its the construction of "an image or any likeness" (פֶּסֶל וְכָל־תְּמוּנָה) to worship (Ex 20:4–5; Deut 5:8–9). The Judeans taken into captivity with Daniel refuse to worship or have any other gods besides the one true God. Daniel 3 highlights the difference between the Judeans from the royal court who had been taken into captivity (1:2–3) and those idolatrous Judeans who remained in Jerusalem; these two groups constitute the good figs and the bad figs, respectively, in Jeremiah 24. Furthermore, if the setting for Daniel 3 proposed below is correct (see "A Possible Historical Setting for Daniel 3"), by implication it sets the faithfulness of Shadrach, Meshach, and Abednego against the willingness of Zedekiah to bow down to idols. See Jer 51:59–64 for a possible indication that Zedekiah took part in the convocation to dedicate Nebuchadnezzar's statue.

Literary Artistry Highlights the Judeans' Resistance and Satirizes the Pagans

The utter faithfulness of the three Judeans to their God is demonstrated by their refusal to bow down to Nebuchadnezzar's statue. Their disobedience of Nebuchadnezzar's order shows their refusal to bow to the pressure exerted upon them to conform to their pagan government and cultural context. Daniel depicts this pressure through a series of literary details skillfully incorporated into the text:[9]

Literary Details	*Implication*
Impressive size of the golden statue (3:1)	Unavoidable idol
Repeated references to "the statue/image that King Nebuchadnezzar had set up" (3:2–3, 5, 7; cf. 3:10, 12, 14, 15)	Unavoidable authority of Nebuchadnezzar
Repetition of the long list of officials assembled to worship the statue (3:2–3)	Inescapable pressure from government, society, and peers
Repetition of the international scope of those assembled from "peoples, nations, and languages" (3:4, 7) to worship the idol	Universal human acceptance of idol worship
Repetition of the list of musical instruments whose music calls for worship of the idol (3:5, 7, 10, 15)	Unmistakable signal to engage in idolatry
Repeated threat of punishment in the furnace (3:6, 11, 15), which was then carried out (3:19–23)	Inescapable death penalty for insubordination
Repetition of the pagan names assigned to the accused Judeans (3:12–14, 16, 19–20, 22–23)	Intense focus on their lack of conformity to their imposed pagan names

---

[9] This list is partly based on Brensinger, "Compliance, Dissonance and Amazement in Daniel 3," especially p. 15.

The pressure on the three Judeans is made more pointed by the exclusive use of the pagan names assigned to them by the Babylonians in 1:7.[10] They are expected to act like pagans in conformity to the names imposed on them by their pagan captors. As they withstand this immense pressure to bow down to the statue, Shadrach, Meshach, and Abednego demonstrate their uncompromising faith in God and thereby become examples of faith to everyone who reads or hears of this account—examples that inspire similar saving faith through the power of the Word.[11] While these three are not named in the NT, a passage in Hebrews 11, the famous catalogue of OT saints, may well allude to them and to their deliverance from the fiery furnace (just as "shut the mouths of lions" surely alludes to Daniel 6):

> ... who through faith conquered kingdoms, enforced justice, obtained promises, shut the mouths of lions, *extinguished the power of fire*, escaped the mouth of the sword, were made strong out of weakness. (Heb 11:33–34)

A contrasting theme is skillfully interwoven with the main theme throughout this chapter: the absolute and unthinking acceptance of polytheistic idolatry among most of the participants in the convocation. Daniel emphasizes this contrasting theme through the repetition of various elements in the narrative. Often these repetitions are in the form of enumerative lists, such as the lists of officials (3:2–3) or musical instruments (3:5, 7, 10, 15). This repetition not only serves to keep this theme before the reader, but it also adds a comic effect to Daniel's satire of pagan religion. Avalos explains:

> The iteration of enumerations in Daniel 3 is comedic because it serves to expose the mechanistic and thoughtless behavior of the pagan worshippers, of the pagan government bureaucracy in particular, and because it elicits laughter in the process. ...
>
> But this court tale is also an example of Daniel's comedy at its best. The main source of satire stems from the contrast between the mechanistic and automatic behavior of the pagans and the assertive and pious behavior of Shadrach, Meshach, and Abednego. In fact, the mechanistic behavior of the pagans is a good example of what Bergson regards as one of the universal themes of comedy—the human automaton. According to Bergson, a comic character is an absentminded one. This type of character does not think much about his or her actions. He/she is a pathetic, passive, and gutless individual whose actions resemble a mindless automaton.

---

[10] Their Hebrew names, "Hananiah," "Mishael," and "Azariah," occur only in 1:6–7, 11, 19; 2:17, and never in chapter 3.

[11] The Lutheran Confessions affirm that we should honor the saints (all believers, who are righteous through faith alone) since their examples are salutary for us (Ap XXI 4–6):

> Our Confession approves giving honor to the saints. This honor is threefold. The first is thanksgiving: we should thank God for showing examples of his mercy, revealing his will to save men, and giving teachers and other gifts to the church. Since these are his greatest gifts, we should extol them very highly; we should also praise the saints themselves for using these gifts, just as Christ praises faithful businessmen (Matt. 25:21, 23). The second honor is the strengthening of our faith: when we see Peter forgiven after his denial, we are encouraged to believe that grace does indeed abound more than sin (Rom. 5:20). The third honor is the imitation, first of their faith and then of their other virtues, which each should imitate in accordance with his calling.

The officials in Daniel 3 fit this mold. ...

The four mechanical iterations of a lengthy list of musical instruments in vv 5, 7, 10, and 15 mirror the mechanistic behavior of the pagans before the image. ...

In effect, the iteration of enumerations helps to portray those pagans as a version of Pavlov's dog. ...

The worship of the lifeless image is, according to the story, one of the greatest absurdities of pagan society, and the mechanistic iteration of the enumerations is a most effective means of conveying the absurd and thoughtless behavior of pagan worship. ...

The repetition (some thirteen times within the story) of the foreign names of the three young men (Shadrach, Meshach, and Abednego) also may have struck the original Jewish readers or listeners as comical. These names, of course, were also a pagan imposition on young men who originally bore Hebrew names.[12]

Thus Daniel 3 condemns all pagan worship not by means of a direct polemic, as is often the case in other prophets, but through satire and caricature.

Literary Artistry Emphasizes God's Miraculous Power to Save

Finally, the recurring theme of God exercising his power in the world to govern history in order to defend and save his people is more openly displayed in this account than in either of the previous two in Daniel. In Daniel 1, God's control over historical events was in the form of an influence largely unobserved by most of the characters in the narrative. In Daniel 2, God's governance of the present and the future was more openly visible, but came through conventionally expected channels: a dream and a dream interpreter. However, in Daniel 3, God's power is made evident in a miraculous and completely unexpected way: the appearance of the divine man (3:25) with Shadrach, Meshach, and Abednego in the flames and the deliverance of the unscathed Judeans from the furnace. The narrative emphasizes that neither Nebuchadnezzar nor the three Judeans expect God to work this way, although the Judeans affirm that God is able to deliver them if he so desires (3:17–18).[13]

God's deliverance places an exclamation point on a theme that runs throughout every section of Daniel: the one true God alone is omnipotent, and he uses his might to accomplish salvation for the benefit of his people.[14] This is expressed in chapter 3 in a series of contrasts. A strikingly overt contrast is in the words

---

[12] Avalos, "The Comedic Function of the Enumerations of Officials and Instruments in Daniel 3," 582, 584–87, citing Henri Bergson, *Le rire* (Chartres: Durand, 1900), 17.

[13] The Judeans' statements in 3:17–18 emphasize that they do not demand or necessarily expect God to deliver them. Bloch, "Questioning God's Omnipotence in the Bible," has argued that for rhetorical purposes they state their case as if God might be unable to help them, but that is unlikely.

[14] For this theme in Daniel, see "Theological Threats Posed by the Critical Dating of Daniel" in "Date, Authorship, and Unity," and "The Messiah in Daniel: An Overview" and "God as the Protector of His People" in "Major Themes" in the introduction. See also the commentary on 2:27–30, 34–35, 44–45 and 7:9–14.

of Nebuchadnezzar himself, who first asks, "What god will save you from my hand?" (3:15), but then exclaims that he sees with the men in the furnace a fourth Man whose appearance was "like a son of gods" (3:25), and finally admits after the three men are rescued, "There is no other god who is able to save like this" (3:29). God's power to deliver is also expressed more subtly in repetitions that form contrasts. Thus the list of the pagan officials (3:2–3) is foreshortened and repeated after the three men are rescued (3:27) in order to contrast God's saving power with the impotence of these officials and of the pagan god (Nebuchadnezzar's statue) they had assembled to honor (3:2). The list "peoples, nations, and languages" (3:4, 7) is repeated (except that the words are singular) in Nebuchadnezzar's decree concerning respect for Israel's God (3:29) in order to emphasize the universal scope of God's lordship and his dominion over all peoples and human events. This contrasts with the previous verses (3:4, 7), where this list demonstrated the universal acceptance of polytheistic belief in impotent gods, a theme that pervades the beginning of the narrative. Finally, the pagan names of the three Judeans (3:12–14, 16, 19–20, 22–23) continue to be employed (3:26, 28–30) as a way for Daniel to demonstrate that the imposed renaming of God's servants after gods who do not exist (1:7) does not thereby exclude them from the power of the one true God, whom they continue to confess.

Therefore, in contrast to the literary details in the beginning of Daniel 3 that depict the pressure on Shadrach, Meshach, and Abednego to conform to pagan practices, the literary details at the end of the narrative emphasize that God never forsakes his faithful believers, but abides with them, strengthens their resolve to remain faithful and not succumb to the pressure placed upon them, and ultimately saves them, even from death.[15]

Literary Details	*Implication*
Appearance of the divine man with the Judeans in the furnace (3:25)	Demonstration of God's abiding presence with his people even when they are in deadly peril
Unharmed bodies, hair, garments (3:27)	Demonstration of God's power to effect unexpected deliverance from death
List of officials repeated (3:27)	Demonstration of God's power to save his people from the authorities who conformed to Nebuchadnezzar's order
List of international participants ordered not to speak against the one true God (3:29)	Demonstration of the universality of God's lordship and power
Continued use of the pagan names of the Judeans (3:26, 28–30)	Demonstration that God's saving power cannot be undone by human actions against his believers.

---

[15] The following list is partly based on Brensinger, "Compliance, Dissonance and Amazement in Daniel 3," 15.

A Possible Historical Setting for Daniel 3

Unlike most of the major sections of Daniel, chapter 3 contains no chronological notice for the setting of the events it relates.[16] However, a careful investigation into the book of Jeremiah and into the surviving chronicles of Nebuchadnezzar's reign suggests a date of late December 594 or January 593 BC for the convocation to dedicate the golden statue.[17]

The Babylonian Chronicle states that a rebellion took place in Babylon from the month of Kislev (December 15, 595–January 12, 594) to the month of Tebeth (January 13–February 11, 594) in the tenth year of Nebuchadnezzar's reign.[18] Nebuchadnezzar suppressed the rebellion and also purged his army of those he suspected of supporting the uprising.[19] At the end of that year (the Babylonian year ended on April 11, 594), Nebuchadnezzar made a trip to his western provinces to collect tribute from his vassals.[20] This trip was probably to enforce his authority in light of the rebellion that he recently suppressed. Moreover, he returned to those western provinces with his army in the month of Kislev the next year (December 4, 594–January 1, 593).[21]

Early in Zedekiah's fourth year as king of Judah (which corresponds to the last six months of Nebuchadnezzar's eleventh year and the first six months of his twelfth year),[22] Zedekiah made a trip to Babylon (Jer 51:59–64). Zedekiah's trip most likely took place upon the return of Nebuchadnezzar to Babylon, perhaps in late Kislev 594 (late December 594) or more likely in Tebeth 593 (January 593). Zedekiah probably was asked to make this trip to profess his loyalty to

---

[16] For the chronological notices in Daniel that begin major sections of the book, see figure 6 in the commentary on 1:1. Besides those chronological notices, some other major sections indicate a specific historical setting because of the historical events they narrate (i.e., Daniel 5 and Daniel 6). However, chapter 3 contains no such indication of its specific historical setting.

Both the Old Greek and Theodotion prefix the words ἔτους ὀκτωκαιδεκάτου to the start of 3:1 to indicate that the convocation took place in Nebuchadnezzar's "eighteenth year." However, these words probably are a secondary addition based on Jer 52:29.

[17] The specific chronicle is preserved on tablet BM 21946. See Wiseman, *Chronicles of Chaldean Kings*, 66–75. The identification of the chronological sequence that includes the convocation was first proposed by Shea, "Daniel 3." It has been favored by Dyer, "The Musical Instruments in Daniel 3," 426–27. Goldingay, *Daniel*, 69, notes Shea's work without comment. However, Miller, *Daniel*, 112, n. 24, and Collins, *Daniel*, 183, n. 47, reject this identification first proposed by Shea. Miller states that the events probably occurred earlier in Nebuchadnezzar's reign, and Collins calls the identification "unwarranted," but neither Miller nor Collins gives any reason for his position. More controversial and much less certain is Shea's identification of three officials of Nebuchadnezzar listed on a clay prism as Shadrach, Meshach, and Abednego (Shea, "Daniel 3," 37–41, 46–50).

[18] BM 21946, reverse, line 21 (Wiseman, *Chronicles of Chaldean Kings*, 72–73).

[19] BM 21946, reverse, line 22 (Wiseman, *Chronicles of Chaldean Kings*, 72–73).

[20] BM 21946, reverse, lines 23–24 (Wiseman, *Chronicles of Chaldean Kings*, 72–73).

[21] BM 21946, reverse, line 25 (Wiseman, *Chronicles of Chaldean Kings*, 74–75).

[22] Official years of Judean kings were reckoned as beginning in the fall with the beginning of the month of Tishri. Thus Zedekiah's fourth year began on 1 Tishri 594 (October 6, 594), six months after the beginning of Nebuchadnezzar's eleventh year on 1 Nisan 594 (April 12, 594).

Nebuchadnezzar. However, it appears to have had the opposite effect, since later that year, before the end of month of Shebat (February 1–March 1, 593),[23] Zedekiah, having returned to Jerusalem, plotted with emissaries from Edom, Moab, Ammon, Tyre, and Sidon to rebel against Nebuchadnezzar, even though Jeremiah advised against this rebellion (Jer 27:1–22).

This sequence of events would yield a date of late December 594 or January 593 for Zedekiah's trip to Babylon and his return. The convocation in Daniel 3 is a likely setting for the destination of Zedekiah's trip, since the trip probably was for the purpose of ensuring his loyalty to Nebuchadnezzar. Zedekiah would have been one of a number of vassals who were brought to Babylon to demonstrate their loyalty to Nebuchadnezzar by worshiping the huge statue he erected. Most commentators believe that the presupposition in the narrative of Daniel 3 is that willingness to bow down to the golden image was equated with loyalty to Nebuchadnezzar.[24] Perhaps Watts summarizes this best:

> The great golden statue they were asked to worship is not named. It could have been one of Marduk, Bel, or Nebo. Whatever its name, it represented Babylon and her king. To worship it meant total and absolute commitment to the imperial government and to the system it represented. ...
>
> Nebuchadnezzar's motivation for setting up the idol was clearly political. The [three Judean] men were accused of serving neither Nebuchadnezzar's gods nor bowing to the image (Dan 3:12). Thus the implication was that they were politically unreliable.[25]

Thus Zedekiah's trip to Babylon in late December 594 or January 593 furnishes a possible date for the convocation for the dedication of Nebuchadnezzar's golden statue. Since twice in the first three verses we are told that "all the rulers of the provinces" (וְכֹל שִׁלְטֹנֵי מְדִינָתָא, 3:2–3) came for the dedication, we should infer that it was a carefully designed ceremony to ensure the loyalty of officials outside of Babylon, as suggested by comparison to events recorded in the Babylonian Chronicle. Apparently, Nebuchadnezzar had already purged his court of those suspected of treason, and he wanted to make sure no disloyal subjects were to be found among his more distant subordinates.

While we cannot be certain that this is the occasion of this event, it is the most probable of any known verifiable date. Therefore, a possible sequence of events surrounding the dedication of the golden statue is as follows:

---

[23] Jer 28:1 dates the false prophet Hananiah's prophecy recorded in Jeremiah 28 to the fifth month (Shebat) of the same year as the events recorded in Jeremiah 27.

[24] Commentators who believe this include Archer, "Daniel," 50; Baldwin, *Daniel*, 99; Collins, *Daniel*, 183; Goldingay, *Daniel*, 73; Gowan, *Daniel*, 65; Leupold, *Daniel*, 135; Lucas, *Daniel*, 93; Miller, *Daniel*, 112; Montgomery, *Daniel*, 195; Walvoord, *Daniel*, 82; Young, *Daniel*, 88.

[25] Watts, "Babylonian Idolatry in the Prophets as a False Socio-Economic System," 120.

December 595–January 594 BC	Nebuchadnezzar suppresses a revolt in Babylon.
March–April 594	Nebuchadnezzar collects tribute from his western vassals.
December 594	Nebuchadnezzar marches west with his army.
Late December 594 or January 593	Zedekiah travels to Babylon (Jer 51:59–64) for the dedication of the golden image (Daniel 3).
Early February 593	Zedekiah plots with his western allies to rebel against Babylon (Jeremiah 27).
Late February 593	Hananiah contradicts Jeremiah's prophecy (Jeremiah 28).
Late March or early April 593	Hananiah dies (Jer 28:17).

Daniel 3:1–7
Nebuchadnezzar's Officials Obey His Command to Worship His Idol

Translation

3 ¹King Nebuchadnezzar made a statue of gold. Its height was sixty cubits and its width six cubits. He set it up in the niche in the city wall in the province of Babylon. ²King Nebuchadnezzar sent to assemble the satraps, the prefects and the governors, the counselors, the treasurers, the judges, the magistrates, and all of the rulers of the provinces to come to the dedication of the statue that King Nebuchadnezzar had set up. ³Then the satraps, the prefects and the governors, the counselors, the treasurers, the judges, the magistrates, and all of the rulers of the provinces assembled for the dedication of the statue that King Nebuchadnezzar had set up. They stood before the statue that Nebuchadnezzar had set up.

⁴The herald called out loudly, "To you peoples, nations, and languages, it is said, ⁵'When you hear the sound of the horn, the flute, lyre, the harp, triangular harp, drum, and all kinds of musical instruments, you will fall down and worship the statue of gold that King Nebuchadnezzar set up. ⁶Whoever does not fall down and worship will immediately be thrown into the flaming furnace of fire.' " ⁷Therefore, when all the peoples heard the sound of the horn, the flute, lyre, the harp, triangular harp, and all kinds of musical instruments, all the peoples, nations, and languages fell down, worshiping the statue of gold that King Nebuchadnezzar set up.

Textual Notes

3:1 אֲקִימֵהּ ... עֲבַד צְלֵם—The "statue, image" (צְלֵם) that Nebuchadnezzar constructed probably was of a god (see the commentary on 3:1). The verbal statements that Nebuchadnezzar "made" (עֲבַד) it and "set up/erected it" (אֲקִימֵהּ) emphasize that it was a manmade, handmade god, in contrast to the one true God and his Messiah, the stone hewn from the mountain "not by [human] hands" (2:34, 45). Nebuchadnezzar will use first person forms of these same verbs to describe the statue that "I set up" (הֲקֵימֵת, 3:14) and that "I made" (עַבְדֵת, 3:15). These verbs also imply that the statue represents Nebuchadnezzar's royal authority. To reinforce this point, the Haphel (H) of קוּם will be repeated frequently in this chapter in the clauses "the statue (of gold) that (King) Nebuchadnezzar had set up" (3:2, 3 [twice], 5, 7) and "the statue of gold that you/I set up" (3:12, 14, 18). In the religions of the ancient near East, kings were believed to rule on behalf of the patron god(s) of the state. Therefore venerating the statue expressed loyalty to the king as well as worship of the pagan god it represented.

רוּמֵהּ אַמִּין שִׁתִּין פְּתָיֵהּ אַמִּין שֵׁת—The dimensions of the statue are "sixty cubits" (אַמִּין שִׁתִּין) for "its height" (רוּמֵהּ) and "six cubits" (אַמִּין שֵׁת) for "its width" (פְּתָיֵהּ).

A cubit was normally the length of one's forearm, including the hand and fingers, and therefore varied from person to person. For the average Israelite, whose height was seldom more than five and a half feet, a cubit would have been about 45 centimeters or 17.5 inches as signified by the ordinary cubit (אַמַּת־אִישׁ) of Deut 3:11. By that measure, the statue would be about 27 meters or 87.5 feet tall and about 2.7 meters or 8.75 feet wide. However, throughout the ancient Near East, kings and other important officials often adopted longer cubits. (This practice may have started to emphasize the majesty of the king, who by implication was taller, more handsome, and mightier than commoners. Compare Saul as an example in 1 Sam 9:2.) One of these official cubits may have been the long cubit referred to in Ezek 40:5 (אַמָּה וָטֹפַח, "an [ordinary] cubit and a handbreadth"). Similar measures were sometimes used in Egypt and Babylon. The long cubit probably was about 52 centimeters or 20.3 inches. If the measure here is the long cubit, the statue would have been about 31.2 meters or 101.5 feet tall and about 3.1 meters or 10 feet wide.

בְּבִקְעַת דּוּרָא—This is often translated as "in the Plain of Dura." However, no certain identification has been made of a plain or valley by this name. Instead of a proper place name, some have proposed that דוּר is a loanword from Akkadian meaning "wall, enclosure."[1] If this is the case, then Nebuchadnezzar set up his statue in "in the cleft/niche in the city wall," that is, in a niche in the outer wall surrounding the city of Babylon. That explains why the next phrase adds that this convocation takes place בִּמְדִינַת בָּבֶל, "in the province of Babylon," outside the city proper. This explanation also makes sense because a statue that was some ninety feet high but only about nine feet wide may have needed the support of the city wall to keep from falling. Since the city wall of Babylon is thought to have been about two hundred ninety-five feet high and seventy-nine feet thick, it could easily have helped support such a statue.

3:2 לַאֲחַשְׁדַּרְפְּנַיָּא—"The satraps" renders an Old Persian loanword (*HALOT*) adopted into Aramaic for an administrator over a large territory.

סִגְנַיָּא וּפַחֲוָתָא—"Prefects" and "governors" are the only two terms for officials in this list that are undoubtedly Semitic terms borrowed from Akkadian at an early time (*HALOT*). In this chapter, they are always paired (3:2–3, 27), and וּפַחֲוָתָא is the only term in the middle of the list with a *waw*, so the *waw* may be epexegetical or explicative. If so, this may be a kind of hendiadys, with the second term further defining the first: perhaps "those prefects who were governors." The translation pairs them without an intervening comma. (In 6:8 [ET 6:7] the two terms are separated by other terms, and in 2:48 סִגְנִין occurs alone.)

אֲדַרְגָּזְרַיָּא—"Counselors" renders what is probably an Old Persian loanword (*HALOT*).

גְדָבְרַיָּא דְתָבְרַיָּא תִּפְתָּיֵא—"Treasurers," "judges," and "magistrates" render three terms that probably are Old Persian loanwords (see *HALOT*).

לַחֲנֻכַּת צַלְמָא—The noun חֲנֻכָּה, "dedication" (3:2–3), used also in Hebrew for the dedication of the tabernacle appointments (e.g., Num 7:10–11) and of the tem-

---

[1] See Cook, " 'In the Plain of the Wall' (Dan 3:1)."

ple (Ps 30:1 [ET: superscription]), later was transliterated as the name of the holiday commemorating the rededication of the temple in the Maccabean era, Hanukah.

3:4 וְכָרוֹזָא—It was once widely claimed that the Aramaic כָּרוֹז, "herald," derived from Greek κῆρυξ. However, more recent evidence suggests that it derives from the Old Persian *xrausa* and that the Greek may be dependent upon the Old Persian as well.[2]

קָרֵא—This participle, as well as those in 3:7, could have iterative force, denoting repeated action. If so, קָרֵא means "would call out," and in 3:7, שָׁמְעִין ... נָפְלִין ... סָגְדִין mean that whenever all the peoples "would hear," they "would fall, worshiping."

לְכוֹן אָמְרִין—Literally, this is "to you they are saying." Aramaic frequently uses an impersonal plural verb as a passive. Hence this is translated, "to you ... it is said." This must refer to an edict spoken by Nebuchadnezzar.

3:5 קָל—This Aramaic cognate to the Hebrew קוֹל, "voice, sound," is in construct with all the musical instruments that follow.

קַרְנָא—Both the Aramaic קֶרֶן, "horn," and its Hebrew cognate (also קֶרֶן) can refer to a horn on an animal (e.g., Aramaic: 7:7–8; Hebrew: 8:3, 5), but here קֶרֶן refers to a hollowed animal's horn used as an instrument (like the Hebrew שׁוֹפָר).

מַשְׁרוֹקִיתָא—This instrument is usually understood to be some type of woodwind since it follows קַרְנָא. The cognate verb in Hebrew, שָׁרַק, means "to hiss, whistle," and there are other Semitic cognates meaning "to play a pipe" (*HALOT*, s.v. [Aramaic] שׁרק). Several studies suggest it is either a "flute" (so translated) or a double-reed pipe.[3]

קַיתָרוֹס—The Qere is קַתְרוֹס, while the Kethib probably is to be vocalized קִיתָרוֹס or קִיתָרוֹס. Most interpreters agree that either spelling (the Qere or the Kethib) is a transliteration of the classical Greek word κίθαρας, an instrument that is a type of "lyre."[4] Probably the same instrument is called a κιθάρα in the NT (1 Cor 14:7; Rev 5:8; 14:2; 15:2).

סַבְּכָא—This instrument probably is a "harp" with four strings (*HALOT*, s.v. שַׂבְּכָא). This spelling occurs only here. Later in the chapter, it is spelled שַׂבְּכָא (3:7, 10, 15). The variation in spelling may indicate that the Aramaic is a loanword, probably from another Semitic language. Several studies have suggested that the related Greek σαμβύκη was a term borrowed from some Semitic source.[5]

---

[2] E.g., Goldingay, *Daniel*, 65; Hartman and Di Lella, *Daniel*, 157; Walvoord, *Daniel*, 83.

[3] Dyer, "The Musical Instruments in Daniel 3," 429–30; Mitchell, "The Music of the Old Testament Reconsidered," 138; Mitchell and Joyce, "The Musical Instruments in Nebuchadrezzar's Orchestra," 23–24.

[4] Dyer, "The Musical Instruments in Daniel 3," 430–31; Mitchell, "The Music of the Old Testament Reconsidered," 136; Mitchell and Joyce, "The Musical Instruments in Nebuchadrezzar's Orchestra," 24.

[5] Dyer, "The Musical Instruments in Daniel 3," 431–32; Mitchell, "The Music of the Old Testament Reconsidered," 138; Mitchell and Joyce, "The Musical Instruments in Nebuchadrezzar's Orchestra," 24–25.

פְּסַנְתֵּרִין—This appears to be a transliteration of the Greek ψαλτήριον, a triangular-shaped harp or lyre.[6] In 3:7 it is spelled פְּסַנְטֵרִין, and the variation in Aramaic spelling indicates that most probably it is a loanword.

סוּמְפֹּנְיָה—This (translated "drum") is the most difficult instrument to identify. It is spelled differently in 3:10, where the Qere is סוּפֹּנְיָה and the Kethib is סִיפֹּנְיָה. The variations in spelling indicate that it is a loanword, most likely from Greek συμφωνία. The Greek word can refer to music and harmony produced by several instruments together (hence its English transliteration, "symphony"). However, since the word here is in a list of instruments (the preceding terms) and is followed by the phrase וְכֹל זְנֵי זְמָרָא, "and all kinds of musical instruments" (see *HALOT*, s.v. זְמָר), it appears to indicate an instrument. An instrument called συμφωνία is first attested in Greek in the fourth century BC and was probably a type of bagpipe. Some English versions translate it here as "bagpipe" (e.g., ESV, NASB), but bagpipes were unknown in Nebuchadnezzar's Babylon. Another argument against "bagpipe" is that wind instruments were enumerated first ("the horn, the flute") and were followed by stringed instruments ("lyre, the harp, triangular harp"), so a wind instrument would be unexpected here at the end of the list. Some have suggested that this instrument is a drum and that it originally derived its name from the Semitic *tp*, which became the Greek τύμπανον (hence "tympani") and then this Aramaic word, סוּמְפֹּנְיָה.[7] The change in sounds and spellings from Greek to Aramaic can be explained as follows:

1. The exchange of "t" for "s" before either "l" or "y" is a feature of East Greek dialects, and the syllables "si" and "ti" sometimes interchange in Mycenaean Greek.
2. The Greek τύμπανον sometimes appears as τύπανον, which would explain the readings סוּפֹּנְיָה and סִיפֹּנְיָה (both without מ) in 3:10.
3. The changed vowel in the second syllable (Greek "a" versus Aramaic "o") is paralleled by the Ionic γλᾶσσα for γλῶσσα.[8]

A drum makes the most sense in this context. The order of instruments in the list would then be wind instruments first, then string instruments, and finally percussion.

תִּפְּלוּן וְתִסְגְּדוּן לְצֶלֶם דַּהֲבָא—The imperfect verbs "*you will fall down and you will worship* the statue of gold" have the force of injunctions or imperatives. The verb סְגִד means to "worship, pay homage" by physical prostration, as shown by the preceding verb נְפַל, "fall down." נְפַל accompanies סְגִד in most of its other occurrences in Daniel 3. In the OT, the Aramaic verb סְגִד is only used for worshiping this idol (3:5–7, 10–12, 14–15, 18, 28) except in 2:46, where pagan King Nebuchadnezzar pays homage to Daniel. The Hebrew cognate סָגַד occurs only in Is 44:15, 17, 19; 46:6 and always refers to "worship" of an idol.

---

[6] *HALOT;* Dyer, "The Musical Instruments in Daniel 3," 432–33; Mitchell, "The Music of the Old Testament Reconsidered," 137; Mitchell and Joyce, "The Musical Instruments in Nebuchadnezzar's Orchestra," 25.

[7] Dyer, "The Musical Instruments in Daniel 3," 434–36; Mitchell, "The Music of the Old Testament Reconsidered," 136; Mitchell and Joyce, "The Musical Instruments in Nebuchadnezzar's Orchestra," 25–26.

[8] Mitchell and Joyce, "The Musical Instruments in Nebuchadnezzar's Orchestra," 26.

3:6 בַּהּ־שַׁעֲתָא יִתְרְמֵא—This clause with the preposition בְּ (with proleptic suffix), the noun שָׁעָה, "moment, instant," and the Hithpeel (HtG) of רְמָה, "be thrown," is, literally, "in it—the instant—he will be thrown." A similar clause recurs in 3:15. בַּהּ־שַׁעֲתָא also recurs in 4:30 (ET 4:33) and 5:5, and it is translated by the adverb "immediately" (3:6, 15; 4:30 [ET 4:33]) or "at that moment" (5:5).

לְגוֹא־אַתּוּן נוּרָא יָקִדְתָּא:—This phrase, repeated in 3:11, 15, 21, 23 (similarly in 3:17, 20, 26), is, literally, "into the midst of the furnace of fire, burning." יָקִדְתָּא is the feminine Peal (G) participle of יְקַד, "burn." Since both of the nouns, אַתּוּן, "furnace," and נוּר, "fire," can be construed as either masculine or feminine, the participle could modify either noun. Probably יָקִדְתָּא modifies the immediately preceding word, נוּרָא, so the meaning is "a furnace of blazing fire" (NASB). However, many English translations render both the participle יָקִדְתָּא and the noun נוּרָא as adjectives modifying אַתּוּן, "a burning fiery furnace" (KJV, RSV, ESV).

3:7 פְּסַנְטֵרִין וְכֹל זְנֵי זְמָרָא—This conclusion of the list ("... triangular harp, and all kinds of musical instruments") omits סוּמְפֹּנְיָה, "drum" (see the seventh textual note on 3:5). Both the Old Greek (apparently) and Theodotion (according to most manuscripts) agree with the MT by omitting any translation of סוּמְפֹּנְיָה. However, many Hebrew manuscripts include סוּמְפֹּנְיָה, and a translation of it is present in the Lucian recension of the Greek and Greek codices Alexandrinus and Marchalianus as well as the Vulgate. The most likely explanation is that those manuscripts and translations that include it in 3:7 have harmonized this verse with the other three verses (3:5, 10, 15) that have the full list of the instruments.

Commentary

Nebuchadnezzar Constructs a Statue and Summons His Civil Servants (3:1–3)

While the text does not state Nebuchadnezzar's motive, we can almost be certain that he wanted to impress his officials with the golden statue and ordered that they worship it as a demonstration of their fealty to him as their king.[9] We are not told what the statue represented. Since it was gold, some commentators have speculated that it was a statue of Nebuchadnezzar himself, since he was the head of gold in the dream in Daniel 2.[10] However, the statements of the officials, Nebuchadnezzar, and the three Judeans later in this narrative equate veneration of the statue with worship of Nebuchadnezzar's "gods" (3:12, 14, 18; see also 3:28).[11] These statements appear to indicate that this statue was of one of Nebuchadnezzar's Babylonian gods, probably his patron god, who would also be a representative of the entire Babylonian pantheon. The statue may have

---

[9] For historical circumstances that may have prompted Nebuchadnezzar to seek this affirmation of loyalty, see "A Possible Historical Setting for Daniel 3" in "Introduction to Daniel 3."

[10] This is the view of, for example, Walvoord, *Daniel*, 81. Leupold suggests that it could have been a statue of Nebuchadnezzar or of one of his gods (*Daniel*, 135).

[11] In Aramaic, the plural אֱלָהִין (3:12, 14, 18, 25) always has a plural meaning, "gods," in contrast to the Hebrew אֱלֹהִים, which can have a singular meaning or a plural meaning.

been of Marduk (also called Bel) or the god after whom Nebuchadnezzar was named, Nabu.

The statue may not have been constructed from solid gold, but may simply have had an overlay of gold. Its height is impressive, but not unprecedented in the ancient world. The Colossus of Rhodes, another ancient statue with a metal exterior, was said to be higher: about seventy cubits,[12] or one hundred ten feet (thirty-four meters) high. The Egyptian stone sphinx at Giza, which is far older, is about sixty-six feet (twenty meters) high and two hundred forty feet (seventy-three meters) long.

The dimensions of the statue are somewhat out of proportion: about ninety feet tall, but only about nine feet wide (see the second textual note on 3:1). This would have made a figure that appeared much thinner in proportion to its height than a normal person. Some commentators have doubted whether what is described here is an actual statue.[13] Others have attempted to explain the height as including a pedestal on which the statue stood, which could make the dimensions of the statue itself more realistic and proportional.[14] However, there is no mention of a pedestal, so this is speculation. If, as proposed in the third textual note on 3:1, this statue was set up in a niche in the city wall, then Daniel may be describing a statue that was not viewed face-on, as is often assumed, but one that was viewed in profile. Since the city wall is thought to have been about two hundred ninety-five feet high, the statue in a niche in the wall could only be viewed from one side and only when facing the city wall from outside the city. If the statue was in such a niche in the city wall, then the statue's dimensions are not at all unrealistic.

The list in 3:2 (repeated in 3:3) of the officials summoned is arranged from the most important to the least important. Only the words for "prefects" and "governors" are Semitic; the others appear to be Persian loanwords (see the textual notes on 3:2). The Persian words point to Daniel having composed his book after the Persians came to power when Cyrus assumed the throne in 539 BC.[15] He identifies Nebuchadnezzar's officials by the Persian terms that were historically precise and that would have been understood by his contemporary audience. While some critics have seen these terms as an indication that Daniel

---

[12] Pliny, *Natural History*, 34.18.

[13] Montgomery, *Daniel*, 196, suggests that what is being described is "a stele only partly sculptured." Collins, *Daniel*, 181, who does not consider this a historical event, simply states that the dimensions "cannot be taken realistically." Gowan, *Daniel*, 65, also doubts the authenticity of the story and simply states that the statue does not represent anything. However, if this story simply were fiction, we must wonder why the author would include such enormous dimensions instead of more realistic numbers that would make the scene more believable for his readers.

[14] Goldingay, *Daniel*, 69; Miller, *Daniel*, 110; Young, *Daniel*, 84–85.

[15] Daniel likely composed his book in its final form in or within a few years of 536 BC. See "Date and Authorship according to the Book" in "Date, Authorship, and Unity" in the introduction.

cannot have been written during the sixth century,[16] these terms actually testify to the antiquity of this chapter. The terms דְּתָבְרַיָּא and תִּפְתָּיֵא, translated "the judges," and "the magistrates," occur only in Aramaic documents from the sixth and fifth centuries BC, not in later texts.[17] Moreover, the Old Greek version failed to translate four of the terms accurately, probably because by Hellenistic times they had ceased to be intelligible, demonstrating that this chapter cannot be a Hellenistic composition.[18] Instead, this chapter appears to be a composition from the early part of the Persian era. This fits well if Daniel wrote his book in or soon after the third year of Cyrus, which began in spring 536 BC, since that is the date of the final vision in chapters 10–12 (Dan 10:1, 4).

The pagan officials automatically obey the summons to assemble for idolatrous worship. The initial scene closes with the officials from the provinces of Babylon standing in front of the statue, ready to prostrate themselves when the dedication ceremony begins (3:3). The Aramaic idiom וְקָיְמִין לָקֳבֵל, "stand before," corresponds to the Hebrew עָמַד לִפְנֵי, which can mean to "stand before" God in worship and readiness to serve (e.g., Lev 9:5; 2 Ki 5:16; cf. Jer 7:10). The repetition of the long list of officials in Dan 3:3, so soon after its introduction in 3:2, serves to emphasize the solemnity of this ceremony and also the universal obedience by all of Nebuchadnezzar's provincial officials. They respond mindlessly and automatically, almost as if they were robots programmed to obey the god. This point is reinforced by the repetitious references to the god itself: "the statue that King Nebuchadnezzar had set up. ... They stood before the statue that Nebuchadnezzar had set up" (3:3). These repetitions caricature the pagan worshipers and provide a dramatic contrast to the faithful Judeans (3:8–12), who will be the only ones who do not conform to the royal edict and peer pressure.[19]

The noun "province," מְדִינָה, which occurs in the plural in 3:2–3, emphasizes the human authorities' universal obedience to the king's summons to idolatry (cf. the singular in 3:1, 12, 30). It also shows that this is primarily a ceremony involving officials in outlying territories. The officials of the Babylonian court from the city of Babylon are not mentioned. Thus the beginning of this chapter picks up where the previous chapter ended: with officials of the provinces, which include Shadrach, Meshach, and Abednego (2:49).

The Herald's Proclamation and the Obedience of the Civil Servants (3:4–7)

The herald's proclamation is addressed universally to Nebuchadnezzar's administrators from all "peoples, nations, and languages" (3:4). The proclamation

---

[16] Collins, *Daniel*, 182–83; Montgomery, *Daniel*, 198.
[17] Baldwin, *Daniel*, 101.
[18] Kitchen, "The Aramaic of Daniel," 43.
[19] See "Literary Artistry Highlights the Judeans' Resistance and Satirizes the Pagans" in "Introduction to Daniel 3."

both explains what is expected of the participants (3:5) and also sets forth the punishment for not participating as expected (3:6). This worship at the dedication of the statue is intended to impress upon the provincial administrators that they are required to demonstrate unquestioning loyalty to Nebuchadnezzar. In the ancient Near Eastern milieu, loyalty to the king also often required, and was expressed by, veneration of the king's god(s).

The list of instruments has been the subject of much discussion among scholars, especially the presence of three instruments whose names have Greek origins. Interestingly, the three instruments whose names have Semitic origins are in the determined state (קַרְנָא מַשְׁרוֹקִיתָא ... סַבְּכָא, "*the* horn, *the* flute, ... *the* harp," 3:5) as one would expect. The three instruments whose names are of Greek origin are in the absolute state (קַתְרוֹס ... פְּסַנְתֵּרִין סוּמְפֹּנְיָה, "lyre, ... triangular harp, drum"), indicating their status as loanwords that are, at this stage of Aramaic, still viewed as foreign words and therefore indeclinable. They are the only indisputably Greek words in Daniel. Older historical critics maintained that these three Greek loanwords indicated that Daniel was composed in Hellenistic times.[20] However, there is now ample evidence of Greek interaction with the Near East as early as the ninth century BC, making it quite possible that a few Greek loanwords, especially of musical instruments brought by Greeks to Babylon, could have been incorporated into sixth-century Aramaic and hence included in a composition such as Daniel.[21] Contemporary historical critics no longer use the Greek words in Daniel 3 as evidence for a Hellenistic date of composition.[22]

Furnaces in ancient Mesopotamia included not only small household ovens for baking food but also much larger furnaces used for firing bricks (brick kilns) and refining metals (smelters). Brick kilns and smelters often were very large, with room enough for several people. They had openings at the top through which material could be added to the furnace as well as entrances at the bottom through which finished products could be extracted.

Burning as a method of execution (3:6) is attested throughout the ancient world, including among Babylonians,[23] Persians,[24] and Greeks.[25] Note that

---

[20] E.g., Montgomery, *Daniel*, 22–23.

[21] Yamauchi, "The Greek Words in Daniel in the Light of Greek Influence in the Near East"; "Daniel and Contacts between the Aegean and the Near East before Alexander," especially pages 44–47; *Persia and the Bible*, 379–82; see also Coxon, "Greek Loan-Words and Alleged Greek Loan Translations in the Book of Daniel"; Kitchen, "The Aramaic of Daniel," 44–48.

[22] E.g., Collins, *Daniel*, 20.

[23] Alexander, "New Light on the Fiery Furnace," cites a royal decree, possibly issued by Rim-Sin, king of Larsa, a contemporary of Hammurabi, king of Babylon, ordering that a slave be burned to death in a furnace.

[24] Herodotus, *Histories*, 1.86, relates a case of Cyrus burning captives on a pyre.

[25] 2 Maccabees 7; 13:4–8.

Jeremiah, Daniel's older contemporary, specifically mentions burning as a punishment employed by Nebuchadnezzar (Jer 29:22).

Dan 3:7 essentially repeats the language of 3:5 to highlight the instant and total obedience of the gathered officials. They do not question the proclamation, nor do they appear to have any qualms about worshiping Nebuchadnezzar's idol. By portraying all the other provincial officials as flat, colorless, mindless characters who have no individual religious loyalty, but blindly follow the pagan religion of their king, Daniel sets up a powerful contrast to the uncompromising loyalty of Shadrach, Meshach, and Abednego to the one true God.[26]

---

[26] For this literary contrast, see further "Literary Artistry Highlights the Judeans' Resistance and Satirizes the Pagans" in "Introduction to Daniel 3."

Daniel 3:8–18

Despite the Death Threat, the Judeans Remain Faithful and Entrust Themselves to God

Translation

3 ⁸Then at that time [some] Chaldean men approached and maliciously accused the Judeans. ⁹They said to King Nebuchadnezzar, "Your Majesty, may you live forever! ¹⁰You, Your Majesty, gave an order that every man who hears the sound of the horn, the flute, lyre, the harp, triangular harp, drum, and all kinds of musical instruments, should fall down and worship the statue of gold, ¹¹and whoever does not fall down and worship will be thrown into the flaming furnace of fire. ¹²There are Judean men whom you appointed over the service of the province of Babylon: Shadrach, Meshach, and Abednego. These men do not pay attention to you, Your Majesty. Your gods they do not serve, and the statue of gold that you set up they do not worship."

¹³Then Nebuchadnezzar in a furious rage said to bring Shadrach, Meshach, and Abednego. Then these men were brought before the king. ¹⁴Nebuchadnezzar said to them, "Is it true, Shadrach, Meshach, and Abednego, that my gods you do not serve and the statue of gold that I set up you do not worship? ¹⁵Now, if you are ready at the time when you hear the sound of the horn, the flute, lyre, the harp, triangular harp, drum, and all kinds of musical instruments, you will fall down and worship the statue I made. But if you do not worship, immediately you will be thrown into the flaming furnace of fire. Then what god will save you from my hand?"

¹⁶Shadrach, Meshach, and Abednego answered and said to King Nebuchadnezzar, "We have no need to answer you about this [matter]. ¹⁷If our God whom we serve exists, he is able to save us from the flaming furnace of fire. So let him save [us] from your hand, Your Majesty. ¹⁸But if not, let it be known to you, Your Majesty, that we will not serve your gods, and we will not worship the statue of gold that you set up."

Textual Notes

3:8 וַאֲכַלוּ קַרְצֵיהוֹן דִּי יְהוּדָיֵא—Literally, "and they ate pieces of the Judeans," this is translated, "and (they) maliciously accused the Judeans." The idiom "eat [אֲכַל] pieces of [־קַרְצֵי]" is a figure of speech for malicious accusation or slander (*HALOT*, s.v. קְרַץ). It is used again in 6:25 (ET 6:24). English versions range from "maliciously accused" (ESV) to the milder "brought charges against" (NASB) and "denounced" (NIV, NRSV).

3:9 מַלְכָּא לְעָלְמִין חֱיִי—For the flattering acclamation "Your Majesty, (may you) live forever!" see the second textual note on 2:4.

3:10 שָׂמְתָּ טְעֵם֙—This idiom with the active form of the verb שִׂים and noun טְעֵם means that the king "issued a command," "established a law," or "gave an order." The corresponding idiom with a passive form of שִׂים and the noun טְעֵם will be used for a "command, order" that is "issued, established" by the king in 3:29; 4:3 (ET 4:6); 6:27 (ET 6:26).

3:12 מַנִּ֣יתָ יָתְה֔וֹן—This clause (literally, "you appointed them") has the sole OT occurrence of the Aramaic particle יָת (with suffix), which is equivalent to the Hebrew אֵת, the sign of the direct object.[1]

לָֽא־שָׂ֧מֽוּ עֲלָ֣יךְ מַלְכָּ֛א טְעֵ֖ם—This is, literally, "they did not place upon you, Your Majesty, attention." The idiom שִׂים טְעֵם here (and in 6:14 [ET 6:13]) has a completely different meaning than it did in 3:10 (see the textual note there). Here the noun טְעֵם means "attention, care, regard." The Judeans did not "shew proper deference to" (BDB, s.v. טְעֵם, 2) the king. They paid no attention to and did not heed the king's decree.

3:13 בִּרְגַ֣ז וַחֲמָ֔ה—Literally, "in rage and anger," this is a kind of hendiadys. Therefore, instead of two separate nouns, many translations use an adjective modifying a noun in expressions such as "in a furious rage."

לְהַיְתָיָ֖ה לְשַׁדְרַ֥ךְ מֵישַׁ֖ךְ וַעֲבֵ֥ד נְג֑וֹ—The verb לְהַיְתָיָה is the Haphel (H) infinitive construct of אֲתָה, "come," whose Haphel has the causative meaning "bring." Of the three names that comprise the compound direct object, the first (לְשַׁדְרַךְ) is introduced by the preposition לְ and the other two have no indicator; both constructions are common in Aramaic.[2]

גֻּבְרַיָּ֣א אִלֵּ֔ךְ הֵיתָ֖יוּ—The verb הֵיתָיוּ is the Hophal (Hp, or passive causative) perfect of אֲתָה, "come," hence, "these men were brought."

3:14 הַצְדָּ֗א—This is the noun צְדָא, "truth," with the interrogative הֲ, hence, "is it true?"

3:15 בַּה־שַֽׁעֲתָ֡ה תִתְרְמ֣וֹן—See the first textual note on 3:6, which has a similar clause.

וּמַן־ה֣וּא אֱלָ֔הּ דִּ֥י יְשֵֽׁיזְבִנְכ֖וֹן מִן־יְדָֽי׃—After the interrogative מַן, "who?" the emphatic pronoun הוּא, "he," before אֱלָהּ, "a god," could be reflected literally by "who is he who is a god (who will save you)?" The verb שֵׁיזִב appears to be a Shaphel (H) conjugation and probably is a loanword from the Akkadian *šūzubu* (*HALOT*, s.v. שֵׁיזִב). Its meaning is "to save, rescue, deliver." For the force of the imperfect form here, see the commentary on 3:15. Its imperfect recurs in 3:17b; 6:17 (ET 6:16); its infinitive is in 3:17a; 6:15, 21 (ET 6:14, 20); its perfect is in 3:28; 6:28b (ET 6:27b); and its participle is in 6:28a (ET 6:27a). These Daniel passages have the word's only occurrences in the OT. However, it also occurs in rabbinic literature meaning "to release, save; be delivered" and in passive forms meaning "to be saved, spared" (Jastrow, s.v. שֵׁיזִב). The cognate nouns שֵׁיזָבָא ("escape, safety, refuge") and שֵׁיזָבוּ ("safety, refuge") also occur in rabbinic literature (Jastrow).

---

[1] See Steinmann, *Fundamental Biblical Aramaic*, 308.

[2] See Steinmann, *Fundamental Biblical Aramaic*, 308; Rosenthal, *A Grammar of Biblical Aramaic*, § 182.

Despite the Death Threat, the Judeans Remain Faithful and Entrust Themselves to God

3:16 לָא־חַשְׁחִין אֲנַחְנָה עַל־דְּנָה פִּתְגָם לַהֲתָבוּתָךְ:—Literally, this is "we are not needing about this [matter] a word to give back to you." חַשְׁחִין is the Peal (G) participle of חֲשַׁח, "to need, have need of." The idiom with the Haphel (H) of תּוּב, "to return, give back," with the object פִּתְגָם, "a word," means "to answer, respond." פִּתְגָם is an Old Persian loanword (*HALOT*). It also occurs with the meaning "command, edict," both in Aramaic (Dan 4:14 [ET 4:17]; Ezra 6:11) and in Hebrew (Esth 1:20).

3:17 הֵן אִיתַי אֱלָהֲנָא דִּי־אֲנַחְנָא פָלְחִין—The hypothetical particle הֵן, "if," is equivalent to the Hebrew אִם (*HALOT*). אִיתַי is the particle of existence, "there is, there exists" (cf. *HALOT*, 3 a and c), equivalent to the Hebrew יֵשׁ. By saying, "If our God exists," the Judeans do not express doubt about whether their God exists; God's existence is not the question. Rather, the question is whether their God is able to save them. The conditional sentence is of the form "if … then," and the "then" clause (see the next textual note) gives their answer to the disputed question: their God *is able* to save them.

The issue Nebuchadnezzar raises by his taunting question (3:15) is slightly different: whether their God *will* save them (see the commentary on 3:15). The Judeans do not directly answer that question because they do not know the mind of God and cannot say whether or not he will save them from persecution that results in their physical death. But they affirm his power to save them and entrust themselves wholly to their God.

By describing "our God" as דִּי־אֲנַחְנָא פָלְחִין, literally, the one "whom we are serving," they declare that they will continue to serve their God in faith regardless of whether they are saved from death or are put to death for their faith. Likewise in 3:18, לָא־אִיתַנָא פָלְחִין, literally, "we are not serving," implies that even until death they will not worship Nebuchadnezzar's gods.

יָכִל לְשֵׁיזָבוּתַנָא—This construction, the participle of יְכִל, "to be able," and an infinitive (of שֵׁיזִב, "to save, deliver," with לְ and first plural suffix, "us"), is the regular way throughout Daniel to express that someone "is able to do (some action)." See the second textual note and the commentary on 3:15.

וּמִן־יְדָךְ מַלְכָּא יְשֵׁיזִב:—These words, literally, "and from your hand, Your Majesty, may he/let him save," should be understood as one thought. The *waw* on וּמִן introduces the clause as conclusive: "so …" The form of the verb יְשֵׁיזִב (see the second textual note on 3:15) could be either imperfect ("he will save") or jussive ("may he/let him save"), but the context demands the jussive meaning. Jussives express the desire of the speaker. When the speaker is in a subordinate position, as the Judeans are to God, then the desire is best understood as a petition or prayer. For such jussives in Hebrew, see Joüon, § 114 h; Waltke-O'Connor, § 34.3b.

3:18 וְהֵן לָא—The conditional clause that begins this verse, "and if not … ," is the converse of the immediately preceding clause: the prayer in 3:17b that God would save the Judeans from temporal death. Therefore the beginning of this verse means "but if [God chooses] not [to save us from temporal death] …" This verse is *not* the converse of the conditional sentence in 3:17a. (If it were, the thought then would be this: "If our God … exists [3:17a] … or if [he does] not [exist] … [3:18].")

יְדִיעַ לֶהֱוֵא־לָךְ מַלְכָּא—"Let it be known to you, Your Majesty," uses the Peal (G) passive participle of יְדַע, "to know," and the jussive of הֲוָה, "to be." יְדִיעַ לֶהֱוֵא occurs also in Ezra 4:12–13; 5:8. Some scholars have suggested that it represents the Old

Persian *avaθātaiy azdā biya*.³ If this is true, it is another testimony to the antiquity of Daniel and Ezra.

Commentary

The Threefold Accusation against Shadrach, Meshach, and Abednego (3:8–12)

The Aramaic phrase כָּל־קֳבֵל דְּנָה, literally, "all because of this," here signals a change in circumstances within the narrative, so it is translated "then" (3:8).⁴ It draws attention to the "Chaldean men" first mentioned here, at the start of this new scene within the chapter. By emphasizing that they are "*Chaldean* men" and by using the idiom rendered "maliciously accused" (see the textual note on 3:8), Daniel the author is implying that their motives are not simply to protect the king's interests, but also to attack the Judeans out of jealousy. These Chaldeans may have felt the Judeans were given positions that should not have gone to conquered foreigners, but to native Babylonians.⁵

Their accusation against the Judeans in 3:12 consists of three related charges:

1. They do not heed the king's royal authority. ("These men do not pay attention to you, Your Majesty.")
2. They do not serve the king's gods. ("Your gods they do not serve.")
3. They do not bow down to the gold statue. ("The statue of gold that you set up they do not worship.")

The first charge focuses on the civil authority of the king, and the second and third charges focus on his religious authority. In the ancient Near East, the king was expected to be the highest authority in both the realms of the government and the national religion, which were inseparably intertwined (the opposite of the modern Western idea of the separation of church and state). The second and third charges are coordinated and illustrate the first charge: by their religious disobedience, the Judeans disregard the king's royal authority and decree. In order to emphasize the two particular religious infractions as affronts to the king, they place the direct objects at the beginning of the clauses: literally, "*your gods* they do not serve, and *the statue of gold that you set up* they

---

³ Benveniste, "Eléments perses en araméen d'Egypte," 305; Coxon, "The Syntax of the Aramaic of *Daniel*," 109.

⁴ All the other times in the Aramaic portions of the OT when this phrase is used, it draws attention to an action that is dependent on or the result of the immediately preceding events (Dan 2:12, 24; 3:7, 22; 6:10 [ET 6:9]; Ezra 7:17).

⁵ Note the contrasting parallel phrases "Chaldean men" (גֻּבְרִין כַּשְׂדָּאִין, 3:8) and "Judean men" (גֻּבְרִין יְהוּדָאִין, 3:12). Since "Judean" here has a national and ethnic meaning, the parallel "Chaldean" is used here in its ethnic sense, and not with the professional meaning "pagan diviners" it had in 2:2, 4, 5, 10. Several commentators agree that "Chaldean" is an ethnic identification here (Archer, "Daniel," 53; Goldingay, *Daniel*, 70; Young, *Daniel*, 88). Others, however, disagree (Collins, *Daniel*, 186; Gowan, *Daniel*, 66; Hartman and Di Lella, *Daniel*, 157; Leupold, *Daniel*, 147; Lucas, *Daniel*, 90; Miller, *Daniel*, 116; Walvoord, *Daniel*, 86).

do not worship" (3:12). Their appeal is directly to Nebuchadnezzar's person and authority in order to ensure that their accusation would not be simply dismissed as politicking motivated by jealousy. This is reinforced by their appeal to the exact wording of the royal decree (3:10–11), so that they could show a basis for their accusation in royal law.

The emphatic placement of "your gods" in the accusation in 3:12 highlights that what is at stake is not simply civil authority (the king's royal power), but religious loyalty and theological belief. This emphasis will become even more prominent in the king's interrogation of the men in 3:14–15 (see the commentary there).

Interpreters long have noted that Daniel is not mentioned as one of the Judeans accused of insubordination by the Chaldeans. Critical scholars generally hold that Daniel 3 originally was a narrative independent from the Daniel traditions and that when it was added to Daniel, the names of Shadrach, Meshach, and Abednego were added to Daniel 1–2 (1:7; 2:49) in anticipation of Daniel 3.[6] According to this theory, the story in chapter 3 may have been added because it aided the complier of Daniel in demonstrating to his readers that they could resist the efforts of Antiochus IV Epiphanes (175–164 BC) to Hellenize the Jews of Palestine.[7] This, of course, assumes that Daniel 3 does not represent an actual historical event. Ford's observation is a good argument against such an approach:

> Had the story been the invention that many have suggested, had it originated in the days of the Maccabees to nerve the faithful against Gentile oppression, it is unlikely that the chief hero would have been omitted. … The very "incompleteness" of this account testifies to its fidelity.[8]

It could be added that even if the narrative in Daniel 3 had its origin long before the days of Antiochus and was added by a Maccabean editor, and if such an editor was capable of adding the names of Shadrach, Meshach, and Abednego to chapters 1 and 2, he also would have been capable of adding Daniel's name to chapter 3. Since Daniel is the main protagonist throughout the rest of the book, it would have been strange for such an editor (if he had existed) not to have added Daniel's name to this account.

Those who understand Daniel 3 to be a true narrative of actual events have found several ways to explain Daniel's absence.[9] However, the text of Daniel indicates why Daniel is not present and why the accusation is brought against Shadrach, Meshach, and Abednego. The setting is a convocation for officials *from*

---

[6] Collins, *Daniel*, 179; cf. Gowan, *Daniel*, 62.

[7] Hartman and Di Lella, *Daniel*, 159.

[8] Ford, *Daniel*, 108.

[9] For a list of attempts to explain Daniel's absence, all of them rather speculative, see Archer, "Daniel," 55. Goldingay's observation is partly correct, though not complete in its explanation. He simply states that the accusations relate to the Judeans' office and that Daniel holds a different office that is not included in the accusation (*Daniel*, 70).

the provinces, as is stated twice (3:2–3). Shadrach, Meshach, and Abednego are officials in the province of Babylon (2:49; 3:12, 30). Although Daniel is administrator over the province of Babylon (2:48), he does not serve in the province, but in the king's court (2:49). There is no indication in Daniel 3 that members of Nebuchadnezzar's administration who serve in the royal court at Babylon are required to attend the convocation or worship the statue. The administrators in the royal court are under the more direct supervision of Nebuchadnezzar himself, and apparently they are assumed to have unquestioned loyalty to him. Perhaps in purging his army during the rebellion, Nebuchadnezzar had already purged his court of anyone suspected of disloyalty.[10] But whatever the reason, the members of the royal court in Babylon are not required to attend the dedication of the statue. Thus Daniel is not present and cannot be accused along with the other faithful Judeans.

The Enraged Nebuchadnezzar Threatens the Judeans with Death (3:13–15)

Nebuchadnezzar's fierce anger is depicted for a second time in Daniel (the first was in 2:12). His fury demands that he confront the Judeans. His prestige depends on his being able to obtain obedience from everyone whom he has appointed. Therefore, instead of simply having Shadrach, Meshach, and Abednego executed, he is willing to give them an opportunity to demonstrate their loyalty. At the same time, he repeats the threat of execution for disobedience. His offer is an attempt to demonstrate in public, in full view of the other assembled officials, that his appointment of these men (2:49) was not bad judgment on his part. Instead, he is attempting to demonstrate bad judgment on their part.

Note that the king does not repeat the first of the three related charges that were brought against them. That first charge directly involved his civil authority (see the commentary on 3:8–12). He does not ask a theoretical question about whether they respect his royal power, or even a more specific one like "will you obey my command?" Instead, he simply demands a physical act of worship that will show their obedience. Earlier the Chaldean accusers had placed the direct objects first in their clauses for emphasis in their charges: "*your gods* they do not serve, and *the statue of gold that you set up* they do not worship" (3:12). Now the king repeats that same emphasis in his first question: "Is it true, Shadrach, Meshach, and Abednego, that *my gods* you do not serve and *the statue of gold that I set up* you do not worship?" (3:14). Since "my gods" is in the emphatic position in both 3:12 and 3:14 and one of the accusations is that they have failed to "worship" the idol, the focus of the intense pressure now brought to bear on the three Judeans is religious and theological—a matter of faith and worship.

---

[10] See "A Possible Historical Setting for Daniel 3" in "Introduction to Daniel 3."

This religious emphasis is heightened even further by Nebuchadnezzar's final question. Many translations and commentators understand Nebuchadnezzar as asking something like this: "then what god *is/will be able* to save you from my hand?" (3:15).[11] While an imperfect verb form (here יְשֵׁיזְבִנְכוֹן) can express ability, that is a less likely force here. Throughout Daniel, the normal construction for expressing ability is a finite form of the verb יְכֵל, "to be able," followed by an infinitive for the capability "to do" something.[a] Daniel includes two verses (3:29; 6:20 [ET 6:19]) where a finite form of יְכֵל, "to be able," is used with the infinitive of the verb used in this sentence, שֵׁיזִב, "to save." When Shadrach, Meshach, and Abednego affirm that their God does indeed possess the ability to deliver them, that is the construction they use (3:17). Darius also uses it in 6:20 (ET 6:19) to ask Daniel whether his God has been able to save him from the lions.

(a) Dan 2:10, 27, 47; 3:17, 29; 4:15, 34 (ET 4:18, 37); 5:16 (twice); 6:5, 21 (ET 6:4, 20)

Therefore, in 3:15 Nebuchadnezzar is asking, "Then what god *will* save you from my hand?" He is not stating that no god can rescue, but that he does not believe any (lesser) god is willing to rescue the Judeans, since they have refused to honor his (more powerful) gods. Thus Nebuchadnezzar is implicitly asserting the superiority of his own gods. They are more powerful than the God of the Judeans, as has already been proven (in his estimation) by his conquest of Jerusalem and his plundering of the temple of the Judeans' God (1:1–2). He is implicitly affirming his belief that his (victorious) gods have made him absolute monarch, and his will is the will of his gods.

The intent of this question is to taunt the Judeans' faith. It is designed to dissuade them from trusting that their God will save them. Similarly, opponents taunted Christ to mock his faith that God the Father would eventually save him (Mt 27:43). Those Jewish opponents did not deny that God *could* save, but they believed God took no pleasure in the one who claimed to be his Son, and so God *would* not save him. Subsequent events proved both Nebuchadnezzar and those opponents wrong (Dan 3:24–27; Mt 28:1–20).

The Judeans Refuse Idolatry and Entrust Themselves to God (3:16–18)

The three faithful Judeans begin their response by declaring that they have "no need" to answer the king (3:16). Their prior defiance of the king's decree speaks for itself: they have not and will not worship the idol. Their refusal to explain their actions to the king may be an implicit appeal to a higher authority: their God. In the same way, Jesus refused to supply an answer when he was accused before human authorities (Mt 26:62–63; 27:12–14). While the refusal to do evil is a passive form of disobedience toward human leaders, it is a form of obedience to God and a testimony of trust in him (as Nebuchadnezzar will admit about the Judeans "who trusted" in their God [3:28]). He is the final

---

[11] See, for example, NIV; Goldingay, *Daniel*, 64; Hartman and Di Lella, *Daniel*, 155; Lucas, *Daniel*, 82.

Judge who will vindicate his oppressed people who have trusted in him (cf. Deut 32:36; Pss 26:1; 43:1).

The conditional sentence that begins 3:17 has been a problem for interpreters and translators since antiquity.[12] The most straightforward translation is this: "if our God whom we serve exists, he is able to save us." However, most English versions (e.g., ESV, NASB, NIV, NRSV) avoid a literal translation, probably because they view it as calling God's existence into question. The Old Greek, Theodotion, the Peshitta, and the Vulgate avoided this problem by not translating it as a conditional sentence. Others have tried to understand the particle of existence (אִיתַי) as forming a periphrastic present tense with the verb יָכֵל, resulting in "if our God whom we serve is able to deliver us … let him deliver us" (NRSV).[13] However, this is unlikely to be the meaning of the text because the phrase אֱלָהַנָא דִּי־אֲנַחְנָא פָלְחִין ("our God whom we serve") intervenes between the particle of existence (אִיתַי) and the verb יָכֵל. In other passages in biblical Aramaic that have that periphrastic construction (2:26; 3:14, 18), the trailing participle always immediately follows the particle of existence, with no intervening phrase.

Nor is it likely that the first two words (הֵן אִיתַי) form some type of idiom meaning "if it be so" (KJV, NASB; ESV is similar).[14] The unexpressed antecedent of "it" would most likely be the men's lack of need to answer the king. It makes little logical sense, however, for them to say that if it is true that they have no need to answer the king, then God will be able to save them.

Thus the Judeans are simply stating a conditional thought: if their God exists—the God of Israel, who had revealed his Law and spoken his gracious Gospel words of promise through Moses and the Prophets—then it follows that he has the power to save them. The conditional sentence does not (contrary to the perception of many) call into question the premise of God's existence. It simply draws the conclusion—that God can save them—based on the premise that their saving God exists. The larger context certainly shows that the Judeans do believe that their God exists. The uncertainty is not in the heart or mind of the Judeans, but in Nebuchadnezzar. Since the God of Israel did not save Judea, Jerusalem, and even vessels from his own temple from Nebuchadnezzar's "hand" (Dan 1:1–2), how can these Judeans presume to hope that their God shall save them from the king's "hand" now (3:17)?

Moreover, the words of Shadrach, Meshach, and Abednego are a subtle criticism of Nebuchadnezzar's gold image. They are implying that in contrast to their God, Nebuchadnezzar's pagan gods do not exist, and his statue is no

---

[12] For a review of attempts to deal with the problems presented by this verse, see Coxon, "Daniel III 17: A Linguistic and Theological Problem."

[13] See also Bloch, "Questioning God's Omnipotence in the Bible," whose translation is "If our God whom we serve is able to deliver us, he will deliver us" (p. 176).

[14] So also Baldwin, *Daniel*, 104.

god. This implication is in harmony with the polemic against idolatry by earlier prophets (e.g., Is 40:19–20; 44:8–20; see also 1 Cor 10:20).

The concluding thought of the Judeans in 3:17, while spoken to the king, contains their prayer to their God: "so let him save [us] from your hand, Your Majesty." They are not demanding that God save them, nor are they stating that it is a certainty that God will save them from execution (as an imperfect verb would imply; their verb is a jussive[15]). Instead, they are entrusting themselves to God's powerful hand, for he—and he alone—is able to save them from Nebuchadnezzar's hand.

Their firm trust in God, whether or not he rescues them from physical death, is evident in the Judeans' final statement (3:18). Even if God should choose not to save them ("but if not"), they will worship him alone. Thus Shadrach, Meshach, and Abednego demonstrate the same faith that godly martyrs have had throughout the millennia: only God can save them, and indeed, he will save them eternally.

Ultimately God will save the Judeans, and all who die in the faith, from an end far worse than temporal death. In 12:2–3 God will explicitly reveal to Daniel that God will raise all believers to eternal life. The hope of life after death is what enables the Judeans here to express their resolute determination to continue to serve God even if the penalty is (temporal, physical) death. They will gladly suffer death in this life in order to gain the promised life of the world to come.

The perfect expression of such unwavering faith is by Jesus himself, God the Son, who, during his state of humiliation on earth, was completely obedient to his Father's will, even unto death on a cross, then rose on the third day and was exalted at the right hand of his Father (Phil 2:6–11).

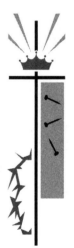

> In the days of his flesh, he [Jesus] offered prayers and petitions, with loud cries and tears, to him who was able to save him from death, and he was heard because of his reverence. (Heb 5:7; cf. Heb 11:32–35, especially 11:34)

Jesus' cruciform life of suffering in faith sets the pattern for all believers throughout the ages, who are encouraged with his promise "be faithful until death, and I will give you the crown of life" (Rev 2:10).

---

[15] See the third textual note on 3:17.

Daniel 3:19–30

The Judeans Are Thrown into the Furnace but Are Miraculously Saved by God

Translation

3 ¹⁹Then Nebuchadnezzar was filled with rage, and the expression of his face changed toward Shadrach, Meshach, and Abednego. He said to heat the furnace seven times hotter than was normal to heat it. ²⁰And he ordered some men, soldiers from his army, to bind Shadrach, Meshach, and Abednego in order to throw [them] into the flaming furnace of fire. ²¹Then these men were bound in their coats, their pants, their turbans, and their clothes, and they were thrown into the midst of the flaming furnace of fire. ²²Because the king's order was urgent and the furnace was heated excessively, those men who carried Shadrach, Meshach, and Abednego— the flame of the fire killed them. ²³But these three men, Shadrach, Meshach, and Abednego, fell into the flaming furnace of fire bound.

²⁴Then King Nebuchadnezzar was startled and immediately stood up. He said to his counselors, "Didn't we throw three men into the midst of the fire bound?"

They answered the king, "Certainly, Your Majesty."

²⁵He said, "Look! I see four men loosed and walking around in the midst of the fire with no injury. Moreover, the appearance of the fourth is like a son of gods."

²⁶Then Nebuchadnezzar approached the door of the flaming furnace of fire. He said, "Shadrach, Meshach, and Abednego, servants of the Most High God, come out!" Then Shadrach, Meshach, and Abednego came out of the midst of the furnace. ²⁷The satraps, the prefects and the governors, and the royal counselors gathered and looked at these men. The fire had no power over their bodies: the hair on their head was not singed, their coats were not different, and the smell of fire had not come on them.

²⁸Nebuchadnezzar said, "Blessed be the God of Shadrach, Meshach, and Abednego, who sent his angel and saved his servants who trusted in him and changed the king's command. They gave their bodies so that they would not reverence or worship any god except their God. ²⁹So from me is issued an order that every people, nation, and language that speaks any blasphemy against the God of Shadrach, Meshach, and Abednego shall be dismembered and his house shall be turned into a pile of rubble because there is no other god who is able to save like this." ³⁰Then the king promoted Shadrach, Meshach, and Abednego in the province of Babylon.

Textual Notes

3:19 הִתְמְלִי חֱמָא—The verb is the Hithpeel (HtG) of מְלָא, "be filled, full," whose Hebrew cognates have the same meaning. The noun חֱמָא, "rage," was also in 3:13, where too it was Nebuchadnezzar's. As in Hebrew (Waltke-O'Connor, § 10.2.1h), in Aramaic an intransitive verb can be followed by a complementary accusative noun indicating the material or substance, hence "filled *with* rage."

וּצְלֵ֨ם אַנְפּ֤וֹהִי אֶשְׁתַּנּ֨וּ—This is, literally, "the image [צְלֵם] of his face [אַנְפּוֹהִי] changed." The verb is the Ithpaal (HtD) of שְׁנָא, "to change," with metathesis of שׁ and the preformative ת. The Qere, אֶשְׁתַּנִּי, is the singular, while the Kethib, אֶשְׁתַּנּוּ, is the plural. The subject, אַנְפּוֹהִי, grammatically is dual (with suffix), agreeing in number with the Kethib.

לְמֵזֵא לְאַתּוּנָ֗א חַד־שִׁבְעָ֔ה עַ֛ל דִּ֥י חֲזֵ֖ה לְמֵזְיֵֽהּ—Literally, this is "to heat the furnace one [to] seven above what it was seen to heat it." The two Peal (G) infinitives (לְמֵזֵא … לְמֵזְיֵהּ) are of the verb אֲזָא, "to heat." (Its passive participle, אֵזֵה, "was heated," will be in 3:22.) The idiom חַד־שִׁבְעָה, "one-seven," is a ratio (one to seven) that serves as a multiplicative, meaning "seven times." The Peal (G) passive participle of חֲזֵה, "to see," has the idiomatic meaning of "be customary, usual" (cf. BDB, Peal, 4, and *HALOT*, Peal, 3).

3:21 (כְּפִ֗תוּ … וּרְמִ֛יו) כְּפִ֗תוּ בְּסַרְבָּלֵיה֔וֹן פַּטְּשֵׁיהוֹן֙ וְכַרְבְּלָתְה֔וֹן וּלְבֻשֵׁיה֑וֹן וּרְמִ֕יו—The verbs are Peil (passive): "they were bound ... and they were thrown." The terms for their various garments are translated as "their coats, their pants, their turbans, and their clothes," but their exact meanings are unknown.[1] It is likely that they are all Persian terms. סַרְבָּל, which will recur in 3:27, probably refers to a garment that covered the upper part of the body. פַּטַּשׁ (Kethib פַּטִּישׁ) may refer to clothing for the lower part of the body. כַּרְבְּלָא is some type of head covering. לְבוּשׁ (also in Hebrew) is a general word for "clothing."

3:24a בְּהִתְבְּהָלָה—For this infinitive, translated as the adverb "immediately," see the first textual note on 2:25.

לְהַדָּבְרֽוֹהִי—This term for Nebuchadnezzar's "state counsellors" (*HALOT*, s.v. הַדָּבַר) is probably a Persian loanword. It occurs four times in Daniel (also 3:27; 4:33 [ET 4:36]; 6:8 [ET 6:7]). It may refer to a group from the royal court in Babylon, but we cannot be certain of this.

3:24b–25a גֻּבְרִ֣ין תְּלָתָ֔א … מְכַפְּתִ֑ין … גֻּבְרִין֙ אַרְבְּעָ֔ה שְׁרַ֖יִן מַהְלְכִ֥ין—The description of the Judeans as, literally, "men, three ... bound" in 3:24 sets up a direct contrast to 3:25, where the king sees "men, four, loosed, walking."

3:25b וַחֲבָ֖ל לָא־אִיתַ֣י בְּה֑וֹן—This is, literally, "an injury was not upon them." A similar negated phrase with the noun חֲבָל, "injury," will describe Daniel as unscathed in the lions' den in 6:24 (ET 6:23). Both verses refer to miraculous preservation from harm.

וְרֵוֵהּ֙ דִּ֣י רְבִיעָאָ֔ה דָּמֵ֖ה לְבַר־אֱלָהִֽין—Literally, this is "his appearance, which is of the fourth, is like a son of gods." It is common syntax in Aramaic to use a proleptic and redundant pronominal suffix (here on רֵוֵהּ). In Aramaic, אֱלָהִין is strictly plural, "gods" (unlike Hebrew, where אֱלֹהִים can mean "gods," but is most commonly a plural of majesty referring to the one true "God"). However, even though Nebuchadnezzar's reference to "a son of gods" is true to his pagan perspective, his phrase affirms the divinity of the fourth man in the furnace. See the commentary on 3:25 for further discussion.

---

[1] Collins, *Daniel*, 188–89, provides a discussion of the possibilities.

The Old Greek, apparently seeking to avoid the designation of this man as divine, translated, ὁμοίωμα ἀγγέλου θεοῦ, "a likeness of an angel of God," probably based on 3:28, where Nebuchadnezzar says that the God of the Judeans sent מַלְאֲכֵהּ, "his angel." The Old Greek translated אֱלָהִין, "gods," by ἄγγελος, "angel," also in 2:11, and by εἴδωλον, "idol," in 3:12, 18 (cf. 5:4, 23). Here in 3:25, Theodotion has a more literal translation of the MT with ὁμοία υἱῷ θεοῦ, "like a son of God." In other passages, where pagan Nebuchadnezzar refers to the Holy Spirit as רוּחַ־אֱלָהִין, "the spirit of gods," Theodotion avoids the appearance of endorsing pagan polytheism by translating אֱלָהִין with the singular θεός, "God" (4:5–6, 15 [θ´/ET 4:8–9, 18]; 5:11, 14), since it refers to the one true God.

3:26 אֱלָהָא עִלָּאָה—This phrase with the adjective עִלָּי, "the Most High God," is repeated in 3:32 (ET 4:2); 5:18, 21.

פֻּקוּ וֶאֱתוֹ—The two imperatives (of נְפַק and אֲתָה), "come out and come," form a hendiadys, "come out!"

3:27 לְגֻבְרַיָּא אִלֵּךְ דִּי לָא־שְׁלֵט נוּרָא בְּגֶשְׁמְהוֹן—The Aramaic has a relative clause, literally, "these men, whom the fire had not ruled over their body." For the sake of English the relative clause is translated as the start of a new sentence: "the fire had no power over their bodies."

3:28 בְּרִיךְ אֱלָהֲהוֹן—"Blessed be their God" in Aramaic is similar to Hebrew blessing formulas (בָּרוּךְ אֵל in Gen 14:20; בָּרוּךְ אֱלֹהִים in Pss 66:20; 68:36 [ET 68:35]) that express prayers of faith. However, the pronoun on אֱלָהֲהוֹן, "*their* God," indicates that Nebuchadnezzar does not consider God to be his own God.

דִּי־שְׁלַח מַלְאֲכֵהּ וְשֵׁיזִב לְעַבְדוֹהִי דִּי הִתְרְחִצוּ עֲלוֹהִי—"Their God" (אֱלָהֲהוֹן) is the subject of שְׁלַח, the one "who sent" his angel. Probably "their God" is also the subject of וְשֵׁיזִב, "and saved" (for the verb, see the second textual note on 3:15). Yet grammatically, and also in light of OT passages that depict "the Angel of Yahweh" as a divine hypostasis of God himself, it is possible that "his angel" (מַלְאֲכֵהּ) is the subject of וְשֵׁיזִב, "and saved." "His angel" must refer to the fourth man, whom Nebuchadnezzar described as "like a son of gods" in 3:25. However, most likely God is the subject of "saved," and "his angel" is the agent of salvation, the one through whom God saved these faithful people. This is in keeping with the larger picture of biblical theology: God has saved his people by sending his Son, Jesus Christ, who fulfills the divine plan of salvation by his perfect life, atoning death, and glorious resurrection.

Nebuchadnezzar describes the Judeans who were saved as עַבְדוֹהִי, "his [God's] servants," and as דִּי הִתְרְחִצוּ עֲלוֹהִי, those "who trusted in him." The Aramaic verb רְחַץ occurs only here in the OT, but it (in the Hithpeel [HtG]) clearly means to "trust" (BDB; *HALOT*). It occurs in other forms in rabbinic literature, meaning "to lean on; to trust; to be safe" (Jastrow, s.v. רְחַץ).

3:29 יֵאמַר שָׁלָה—The expression "speaks [יֵאמַר] blasphemy [שָׁלָה]" probably is equivalent to the Akkadian *šillata qabû*.[2] The Kethib probably is to be vocalized שִׁלָּה as a loanword from the Akkadian *šillatu*, "blasphemy, sacrilege (against gods)" (*CAD*, 1

---

[2] Paul, "Daniel 3:29—A Case Study of 'Neglected' Blasphemy," 292–93.

a).³ The forceful translation "speaks (any) blasphemy" is appropriate in this context, as recognized by some translations (NRSV) and scholars.⁴ It is supported by both the Old Greek, ὃς ἂν βλασφημήσῃ εἰς τὸν κύριον τὸν θεὸν Σεδραχ ... , "whoever *blasphemes* against the Lord, the God of Shadrach, ..." and by Theodotion, who translates the MT more literally by using a noun instead of a verb, ἣ ἂν εἴπῃ βλασφημίαν κατὰ τοῦ θεοῦ Σεδραχ ... ,"which speaks *blasphemy* against the God of Shadrach ..."

The Qere, שָׁלוּ, might also derive from the Akkadian *šillatu*, in which case it too would mean "blasphemy."⁵ However, BDB and HALOT connect שָׁלוּ with the Aramaic שָׁלוּתָא, which occurs in the Targumim meaning "neglect, error, forgetfulness" (Jastrow, s.v. שָׁלוּתָא). On that basis, they define שָׁלוּ as "neglect" (BDB) or "negligence" (*HALOT*). Most English translations follow that line of interpretation and give a broader and weaker rendering: to speak "anything against" God (RSV, NIV, ESV). The Aramaic שָׁלוּ recurs in Dan 6:5 (ET 6:4) and also in Ezra 4:22 and 6:9, but in those verses it refers to a human fault rather than speech against God. See further the second textual note on Dan 6:5.

הַדָּמִין יִתְעֲבֵד וּבַיְתֵהּ נְוָלִי יִשְׁתַּוֵּה—The punishments, "shall be dismembered and his house shall be turned into a pile of rubble," use the same vocabulary as in 2:5. See the second and third textual notes on 2:5.

לָא אִיתַי אֱלָהּ אָחֳרָן דִּי־יִכֻל לְהַצָּלָה כִּדְנָה:—"There is no other god who is able to save like this" uses לְהַצָּלָה, the Haphel (H) infinitive of נְצַל, "save, deliver, rescue," whose Hebrew cognate (the Hiphil [H] of נָצַל) commonly refers to God saving his people (e.g., Ex 6:6; 18:10).

Commentary

An Enraged Nebuchadnezzar Orders the Judeans to Be Thrown into the Furnace (3:19–23)

Nebuchadnezzar's anger, shown to be explosive and vindictive already in 2:12, is on display yet again. The same Aramaic term for "rage" (חֱמָא) that was in 3:13 recurs in 3:19. The refusal of the three men to bow down to the idol was a personal affront as well as a public defiance of Nebuchadnezzar's authority. The Aramaic literally says that "*the image* of his face changed toward Shadrach, Meshach, and Abednego" (3:19). This is a play on the same noun used for the "image, statue" (צְלֵם, 3:1, etc.) that Nebuchadnezzar had erected. Daniel the author is once again showing a subtle, but unmistakable, criticism of pagan gods. They are even less than mortals. Nebuchadnezzar's image can change, but the image he set up for others to worship cannot. The god is less animated than its human creator! In contrast, the one true God—and his Son,

---

³ In its entry for שָׁלוּ, *HALOT* wrongly gives a milder definition of the Akkadian *šillatu* as meaning "negligence."

⁴ See Paul, "Daniel 3:29—A Case Study of 'Neglected' Blasphemy."

⁵ Cf. Paul, "Daniel 3:29—A Case Study of 'Neglected' Blasphemy," 293–94, who argues that שָׁלוּ in Dan 6:5 (ET 6:4) is to be connected with the Akkadian *šillatu*, which in 6:5 would refer to improper speech.

Jesus Christ—always remains constant and faithful to his Word, and so he does not change (Mal 3:6; cf. Num 23:19; 1 Sam 15:29; Heb 13:8; James 1:17).

Nebuchadnezzar's rage leads him to order the furnace heated as hot as possible in order to emphasize the penalty for ignoring his demands. The phrase "seven times hotter" (3:19) is not to be understood literally, as if the Babylonians had some type of gauge to measure the temperature in the furnace and increased it by this exact multiple. Instead, the number is used symbolically to signal that the furnace is heated as hot as possible.[6] This is the second instance of a symbolic use of a number in Daniel, and it prepares the reader for more extensive use of numbers in the symbolism of the visions later in the book.[7]

The urgency of the royal command is demonstrated by the binding of the three men while they were still in their clothes. No time was taken to strip them before throwing them into the furnace. The urgency is compounded by the deaths of the choice men of Nebuchadnezzar's army who were overcome by the heat of the furnace as they rushed to throw Shadrach, Meshach, and Abednego into the fire. However, their deaths did not stop the order from being fulfilled, since apparently the Judeans were being thrown into the furnace from above.[8] The escaping heat must have been intense as the Judeans tumbled into the furnace, bound and clothed.

God Sends His Son and Saves the Judeans (3:24–27)

The transition from 3:23 to 3:24 is abrupt. With no smooth transition, the text moves from the fall of the three men into the furnace to Nebuchadnezzar's bewilderment. This is precisely the point where both the Old Greek and Theodotion versions add the Prayer of Azariah and the Song of the Three Young Men (with a short prose introduction to each and a short prose account between them).[9] It would appear as if the Greek versions represent an attempt to deal with the abrupt transition.[10] Yet the abrupt transition serves a purpose.

---

[6] This is recognized by many commentators, who often cite Prov 24:16 and 26:16 as having parallel figurative uses of the number seven. See, for example, Baldwin, *Daniel*, 105; Goldingay, *Daniel*, 66; Hartman and Di Lella, *Daniel*, 162; Miller, *Daniel*, 121; Young, *Daniel*, 92.

[7] The first symbolic use of a number was in 1:20. See "A Literalistic Interpretation of Numbers Is Disproved by Daniel 1:20 and 3:19" in "Eschatology and Dispensational Premillennial Interpretations of Daniel" in the introduction.

[8] See the commentary on 3:6.

[9] In the Greek versions, the Prayer of Azariah is 3:24–45 (with a short prose introduction in 3:24–25), followed by five verses of prose (3:46–50), and the Song of the Three Young Men is 3:51–90 (with a short prose introduction in 3:51). Greek 3:91–97 corresponds to MT/ET 3:24–30.

[10] Hartman and Di Lella, *Daniel*, 163, argue that the description of the events in the furnace contained in Theodotion 3:46–50 (the Old Greek is similar) may be original to the story, since Theodotion has no account of deaths of the men who threw Shadrach, Meshach, and Abednego into the furnace. (The Old Greek may include a notice of their deaths in 3:23 [see also Old Greek 3:46].) Instead, these men stoke the fire in the furnace, and it is nearby Chaldeans who are burned. However, the author of this version probably eliminated the notice of their deaths in order to make his expansion of the account consistent. In addition, these verses read as

Instead of concentrating on the events in the furnace, the account emphasizes the miraculous protection of the three Judeans by immediately moving to the king's observation.

The text includes four indications of the miraculous deliverance of the Judeans. The first indication is anticipated by Nebuchadnezzar's question to his advisors: "Didn't we throw three men into the midst of the fire *bound*?" (3:24). Note the emphatic position of "bound" (מְכַפְּתִין) at the end of the question in Aramaic. After his advisors assure him that "certainly" the Judeans had been bound, he then states, "I see four men *loosed* and walking around" (3:25). Apparently the bonds had fallen off (cf. Acts 12:6–7; 16:25–26) or had been destroyed by the fire, so that the men could walk around—a clear indication that something miraculous has happened.

A second indication is that the men were unscathed, as proven by the king's observation that they were "walking around in the midst of the fire with no injury" (3:25). Further details about their miraculous preservation from the deadly power of the fire will be given in 3:27.

The third indication of the miraculous is the observation of a fourth person in the fire. Nebuchadnezzar immediately recognizes him as looking like "a son of gods" (3:25).[11] The Aramaic unmistakably quotes the words of Nebuchadnezzar as true to his pagan view. In the larger context, Nebuchadnezzar had constructed a statue that represented his "gods" (3:12, 14, 18), and he required his subjects to worship it, so he lacked faith in the one true and triune God, nor was he even a monotheist. Thus it would be wrong for us to expect Nebuchadnezzar to describe the identity of the fourth person in language consistent with biblical theology and the full revelation of God the Son in the NT.

However, it is quite possible that the fourth man he observed was the preincarnate Christ, since the second person of the Trinity existed from eternity (Micah 5:1 [ET 5:2]; Jn 1:1) and could manifest himself in OT times, before he took on flesh and was born of the Virgin Mary in "the fullness of time" (Gal 4:4; cf. Mt 1:18–25; Lk 1:26–56; 2:1–20). Many scholars recognize that Nebuchadnezzar's words affirm the divinity of the fourth person.[12] To highlight his divinity, a few versions translate freely, for example, "the fourth has the appearance of a god" (NRSV) or even "the form of the fourth is like the Son of God" (KJV, NKJV), a translation as old as the Vulgate (*similis filio Dei*, "like the Son of God," 3:92).

---

if they were added to make a transition from the Prayer of Azariah to the Song of the Three Young Men and contain an explanation of the reason why the three survive the furnace (3:50). It is this explanation, more than any other feature, that makes the account in the Greek versions suspect.

[11] "A son of the gods" is the rendition favored by most translations (e.g., RSV, NIV, ESV, NASB).

[12] E.g., Archer, "Daniel," 57; Collins, *Daniel*, 190; Goldingay, *Daniel*, 71; Miller, *Daniel*, 123; Young, *Daniel*, 94.

Many of the church fathers interpreted Nebuchadnezzar's words as indicating that the person he saw was the Son of God, Jesus Christ, or else an angel. Hippolytus, writing in the third century AD, explains the fourth man as the preincarnate Christ and Nebuchadnezzar's recognition of him as a prefiguration of the faith of Gentiles who would believe in Christ:

> "And the form of the fourth is like the Son of God." Tell me, Nebuchadnezzar, when didst thou see the Son of God, that thou shouldst confess that this is the Son of God? And who pricked thy heart, that thou shouldst utter such a word? And with what eyes wert thou able to look into this light? And why was this manifested to thee alone, and to none of the satraps about thee? But, as it is written, "The heart of a king is in the hand of God:" the hand of God is here, whereby the Word pricked his heart, so that he might recognise Him in the furnace, and glorify Him. And this idea of ours is not without good ground. For as the children of Israel were destined to see God in the world, and yet not to believe on Him, the Scripture showed beforehand that the Gentiles would recognise Him incarnate, whom, while not [yet] incarnate, Nebuchadnezzar saw and recognised of old in the furnace, and acknowledged to be the Son of God. … [Nebuchadnezzar called to the three Judeans by name] but he found no name by which to call the fourth. For He was not yet that Jesus born of the Virgin.[13]

Writing about AD 400, Jerome refers to the majority opinion and also to his own view when he comments:

> Either we must take him to be an angel, as the Septuagint has rendered it, or indeed, as the majority think, the Lord our Savior. Yet I do not know how an ungodly king could have merited a vision of the Son of God. … We are to think of angels here, who after all are very frequently called gods as well as sons of God. So much for the story itself. But as for its typical significance, this angel or son of God foreshadows our Lord Jesus Christ, who descended into the furnace of hell, in which the souls of both sinners and of the righteous were imprisoned, in order that He might without suffering any scorching by fire or injury to His person deliver those who were held imprisoned by the chains of death.[14]

The Lutheran theologian Martin Chemnitz (1522–1586) argues against the Docetic view that God the Son did not become incarnate truly or fully. He cites a Docetic opinion that misused Dan 3:25 and argued that "an angel in the form of a specter, or in the appearance of a human body, or as a phantom could have carried out the ministry which had been committed to him [Christ] by God so that it would not have been necessary that he actually assume human flesh. … since indeed the Son of God had manifested Himself to the fathers in the Old Testament in appearances of this kind, in Gen. 32:24–30 [MT 32:25–31], Dan. 3:25 and 7:13." Chemnitz first affirms that it is a "mystery … what the Son of

---

[13] Hippolytus, "Scholia on Daniel," on Theodotion 3:92 (MT/ET 3:25) (*ANF* 5:188).

[14] Jerome, *Commentary on Daniel*, on Theodotion 3:91–92 (MT/ET 3:24–25) (Archer, *Jerome's Commentary on Daniel*, 43–44).

God in His absolute omnipotence seems to be able to do" and then he shows how "the Savior Himself at various times clearly refutes this delirium which regards Him as being only a phantom or an apparition" without a true human body.[15]

Johann Gerhard (1621–1668), in a Lutheran study Bible that was widely used during the seventeenth through the nineteenth centuries, gives a brief identification of the man and an explanation for his wording, both of which are in parentheses within Luther's translation of the verse:

> **And the fourth** (which was the Son of God, who thus appeared at that time in human form with these three men in the furnace) **appeared just as if he were a son of the gods** (adorned with great lordship and beautiful radiance, "as if he were one of our gods," which the king says according to [his] erroneous heathen impression).[16]

Even though Nebuchadnezzar himself, lacking faith, could not have had true spiritual comprehension of the identity of this person, his words may have expressed more than he himself fully understood, and Daniel the author may well have included his words as a form of irony. Similarly, John the apostle records the words of the high priest Caiaphas, who said it was better for Jesus to die for the people so that they would not perish, and his words express a theological truth far greater than he realized (Jn 11:49–52). Indeed, though Nebuchadnezzar could not recognize that there is only one God (and he therefore used the plural "gods"), he did recognize something about this man that set him apart as divine. Thus it is possible that Nebuchadnezzar is describing a preincarnate appearance of Christ in terms that he, a pagan, would use. Therefore, the church fathers and Christian theologians may well have been correct in their contention that the fourth man was indeed the Savior. (See also the commentary on 3:28, where Nebuchadnezzar describes the fourth man as "his [God's] angel.")

In the OT era, God manifested his salvation by accompanying his people in various forms, such as the pillar of cloud and fire during the exodus redemption(a) and the Captain of Yahweh's army (Josh 5:13–15), traditionally understood as an appearance of the preincarnate Christ.[17] That God would save these three faithful believers in Daniel by sending his Son to accompany them and preserve them from all harm is consistent with the larger biblical context. God has

(a) E.g., Ex 13:20–21; 14:19, 24; 33:9–10; Num 12:5; 14:14

---

[15] Chemnitz, *The Two Natures in Christ*, 50.

[16] Gerhard, "Daniel," 1035. The German reads as follows:

> **Und der vierte** (welcher war der Sohn GOttes, so dazumal in menschlicher Gestalt diesen drei Männern im Feuerofen erschien) **ist gleich, als wäre er ein Sohn der Götter** (mit großer Herrlichkeit und schönem Glanz gezieret, als wäre er einer von unsern Göttern, welches der König nach heidnischem Wahn redete).

A footnote then adds an alternate interpretation: "Therefore some [interpreters] would rather understand [the man to be] only a common angel. See Job 1:6–7; 38:7," which are verses that refer to angels as "sons of God." The German is *Daher auch einige lieber nur einen gemeinen Engel verstehen wollen. S. Hiob 1, 6 f. c. 38, 7.*

[17] See Harstad, *Joshua*, 249–55.

fully revealed his salvation in the sending of his Son to be our Savior and the propitiation for our sins (1 Jn 4:9–14).

The fourth and most direct evidence of a miraculous deliverance is that the three men were able to escape from the furnace without any harm. They are able to obey the king's command to "come out!" (Dan 3:26) so that he and his advisers could carefully observe them up close. (The text does not say why Nebuchadnezzar only addresses the three men in 3:26; perhaps he discerned that the fourth, divine man was not under his authority and could not be made to obey his command.) Not only were the three not harmed, but Daniel is careful to tell us of the observation by the king and his courtiers that their hair and clothes were intact and that they did not even smell of smoke (3:27). The power of God to protect his servants was made clear to all of Nebuchadnezzar's chief administrators, including his royal counselors. This may indicate that not only the high provincial officials, but also the men in the court at Babylon (including Daniel; see 2:49) witnessed the deliverance.

Finally, we should note how Nebuchadnezzar addresses the men when he calls them out of the furnace. They are "servants of the Most High God" (3:26). Nebuchadnezzar is forced to acknowledge indirectly that they serve God first and that they were right in placing God's commands (especially the First Commandment) above his demands. Moreover, his description of Yahweh, the God of Israel, as "the Most High God" is a way of referring to God that both the Judeans and the pagan Nebuchadnezzar can accept.[b] Nebuchadnezzar acknowledges this God as above all other gods, even though he himself has not become a monotheist. At the same time, the Judeans can agree with the title and understand it to mean that the one true and triune God is Most High because all other gods are nothing.

(b) Cf. Dan 3:32 (ET 4:2); 4:14, 21–22, 29, 31 (ET 4:17, 24–25, 32, 34); 5:18, 21; 7:25

Nebuchadnezzar Praises God and Promotes Shadrach, Meshach, and Abednego (3:28–30)

God's Salvation in Two Actions (3:28a)

Nebuchadnezzar is now forced to recognize God's supremacy. He can no longer maintain that he is an absolute monarch, with power above that of any god (see the commentary on 3:15). Nebuchadnezzar's acclamation of praise confesses that God did two things. First, he "sent his angel" (שְׁלַח מַלְאֲכֵהּ). Note that earlier Nebuchadnezzar described this angel's appearance as "like a son of gods" (3:25). There is no contradiction here, since the Aramaic מַלְאַךְ, like the Hebrew מַלְאָךְ, normally means "angel, messenger" (see the second textual note on 3:28). In Nebuchadnezzar's pagan worldview, a god can be a messenger (e.g., the Babylonian Girru, similar to the Roman god Mercury or the Greek god Hermes).

Neither is there a contradiction between Nebuchadnezzar's description here and the likelihood that the person he saw was the preincarnate Christ.[18] There

---

[18] See "God Sends His Son and Saves the Judeans (3:24–27)."

are, of course, many accounts in the OT of angels sent by God as his messengers. However, in some passages, God sends a particular Angel or Messenger, often called "the Angel of Yahweh" (מַלְאַךְ יהוה), who is revealed to be divine, a hypostasis or person of the Godhead, or even Yahweh himself. Especially since this Angel often displays human characteristics, we can, in light of the fuller revelation of the Trinity in the NT, infer that this divine Angel or Messenger who appeared in the OT is the second person of the Trinity, God the Son.[19] This inference is consistent with the testimony of Jesus himself, who declared to his Jewish hearers, "Your father Abraham rejoiced that he would see my day. He saw it and was glad." Then after being asked, "Have you seen Abraham?" Jesus declared, "Truly, truly, I say to you, before Abraham was, I am" (Jn 8:56–58 ESV).[20]

The second divine accomplishment that Nebuchadnezzar recognizes in his praise is that God "saved his servants who trusted in him" (3:28). By using the same verb, שֵׁיזִב, "to save," that he used in 3:15 when he had taunted the Judeans, "Then what god will *save* you from my hand?" here the king admits that he was wrong. There is a God who is able to save his people from the most powerful ruler and even from death, and he is none other than the God of Israel. As in 3:26, where the king called Shadrach, Meshach, and Abednego "servants of the Most High God," here he calls them "his servants." He thereby acknowledges that they have a higher loyalty than to him. They are first of all God's servants, and God made this plain by rescuing them.

Moreover, by using the descriptive relative clause "who trusted in him," the king perceives that God's salvation came to the Judeans simply through their trust in God, that is, through faith. While the pagan king could not be expected to have a complete understanding of the biblical doctrine of justification, his words support what Daniel the author and the believing reader know from the rest of the Scriptures. The patriarch Abraham was reckoned as righteous through faith alone (Gen 15:6; Romans 4), as were all believers in the OT era. Likewise in the NT era, all believers in Christ are justified through faith alone (Romans 5; Galatians 3–5). The essence of faith is simple trust in God for salvation.[21]

---

[19] Consider the following passages that identify מַלְאַךְ יהוה, "the Angel of Yahweh," as Yahweh or God himself: Gen 16:7–10 with 16:11; Ex 3:2 with 3:4–6; Judg 2:1a with the statement that the angel makes in Judg 2:1b; Judg 6:11–12 with 6:14; Judg 13:3, 13–21 with 13:22.

[20] These words of Jesus may refer to the remarkable Trinitarian revelation of God in Genesis 18–19. First, the narrator (Moses) states that "Yahweh/the LORD appeared to him [Abraham]" (Gen 18:1), and "three men were standing before him" (Gen 18:2). One of the three turns out to be Yahweh himself in human form, whom we can identify as the preincarnate Christ. In this form, Yahweh speaks a Gospel promise to Abraham (Gen 18:10–14) about the son (Isaac) who will continue the line of human ancestry leading to the incarnation of Christ (cf. Gen 3:15; Rom 9:5; Galatians 3), and Abraham offers a lengthy intercessory prayer to Yahweh (Gen 18:22–33).

[21] Thus the Lutheran Confessions affirm: "To believe means to trust in Christ's merits, that because of him God wants to be reconciled to us" (Ap IV 69). Again, after quoting St. Paul in 1 Cor 15:56–57, "The sting of death is sin, and the power of sin is law. But thanks be to God, who gives us the victory through our Lord Jesus Christ," they affirm: "We conquer

The Judeans received dramatic salvation from temporal death, but they and all who trust in God shall receive everlasting salvation from eternal death through the resurrection to eternal life (Dan 12:2–3).

Two Acts of Faith by the Judeans (3:28b)

Shadrach, Meshach, and Abednego are credited with two acts of faith by Nebuchadnezzar. These good works flowed from their faith in God, since they "trusted in him" (3:28a). Saving faith always yields the fruit of good works.[22]

First, Nebuchadnezzar concedes that the faithful Judeans "changed the king's command" (3:28b). They refused to obey his order to break the First Commandment and participate in idolatry, and as a result of their rescue by the one true God, the king will abrogate his prior command (3:4–6) and replace it with a prohibition against blaspheming their God (3:29).

The second act of faith by the Judeans is that "they gave their bodies so that they would not reverence or worship any god except their God" (3:28b). They faced certain death because they refused to engage in idolatry, and in that way they offered their bodies to God. This was a good work because they did so in faith and love for God. Perhaps with them in mind as positive examples of faith, St. Paul declared negatively, "If I give over my body so that I am burned, but do not have love, I gain nothing" (1 Cor 13:3; cf. Phil 1:20). All Christians are called to offer their bodies as "a living sacrifice" to the one true God (Rom 12:1; cf. Mk 12:33; 1 Cor 6:15–20; Phil 4:18; Heb 13:16).

Nebuchadnezzar's Two Actions (3:29–30)

After his praise of God (3:28), Nebuchadnezzar undertakes two actions. Some believe that his praise and actions show that Nebuchadnezzar was brought to saving faith in the one true God.[23] However, the text does not include any personal expression by Nebuchadnezzar of repentance (contrition over his sin), nor any confession of personal faith in the one true God or trust in him for salvation. The miracle has, in effect, reprimanded the king for persecuting the Judeans for their refusal to participate in idolatry, and he has been impressed by God's power to save his servants who trust in him (3:28), but Nebuchadnezzar gives no indication that he himself trusts in God or desires to serve him exclusively.

---

through Christ. How? By faith, when we comfort ourselves by firm trust in the mercy promised because of Christ" (Ap IV 79).

[22] The Lutheran confessors assert: "It is also taught among us that such faith should produce good fruits and good works and that we must do all such good works as God has commanded, but we should do them for God's sake and not place our trust in them as if thereby to merit favor before God" (AC VI 1).

[23] This seems to have been the view of Melanchthon. In a discussion about salvation through faith alone, he cites Daniel's sermon to the king in 4:24 (ET 4:27) and declares:

> Daniel proclaimed many things to the king about the one God of Israel and converted him not only to the giving of alms but rather to faith. For there is the king's excellent confession about the God of Israel, "There is no other God who can save this way" (Dan. 3:29). (Ap IV 261)

For a discussion of this view in the Apology, see further the commentary on 4:24.

Instead, it would seem that Nebuchadnezzar merely considers the God of Israel to be a powerful god who could be added to the pantheon of gods reverenced by the Babylonians—a god whom they should not offend, but not a god whom they should worship and trust to the exclusion of all other gods as required by the First Commandment.[24]

Thus Nebuchadnezzar has been brought under the Law partially, but the effects here fall in the category of the first use of the Law: as a curb against sinful actions. Nebuchadnezzar ceases to require idolatrous worship of his statue and stops persecuting the Judeans. His subsequent command (3:29) also intends to prevent blasphemy against God. However, the king does not repent of his sins as offenses against the only true God; such repentance would have been the result of the second and most important use of the Law.[25]

Nebuchadnezzar gives no evidence of the God-given righteousness that comes only through faith in the one true God, which is the only righteousness that avails before God. Instead, he is brought to a measure of civil righteousness: law-abiding, respectful, and even reverent conduct in the realm of human relationships.[26] Although civil righteousness is not sufficient to render the sinner forgiven and righteous before God, it is good for society, as Nebuchadnezzar implicitly affirms by his decree commanding respect for the Judeans' God. He does not want his people to speak against and so anger this God who has shown such power. His decree threatens the same punishments he held over the wise men in 2:5 when they could not tell Nebuchadnezzar his dream or its interpretation.

Nebuchadnezzar does not command his people to worship Israel's God, nor does he prohibit them from continuing to worship their other gods. Yet his order does prohibit his people from blaspheming this God, and so it would also command a measure of respect for those Judeans in captivity who worship only their God. This order should prevent malicious accusations (see 3:8) and persecutions against faithful worshipers.

Finally, we are told that Nebuchadnezzar "promoted Shadrach, Meshach, and Abednego in the province of Babylon" (3:30). This chapter ends where it began, with a focus on provincial officials (3:2–3). Clearly, Daniel the author is demonstrating the virtue of worshiping only the true God. The pagans who

---

[24] See further "God's Law in Daniel" in "Law and Gospel in Daniel" in the introduction. We can both compare and contrast the edict of Nebuchadnezzar here with the edict of the king of Nineveh in Jonah 3:7–9. That king successfully exhorted his people to turn from their evil ways and to call upon the one true God, implying that both the king and the people turned away from idolatry and to God in repentance and faith (so Lessing, *Jonah,* 268–69, 299–316). Nebuchadnezzar, however, does not exhort his people to turn to and call upon the one true God, nor to turn from their other gods. He merely prohibits blasphemy against the one true God. Therefore neither he nor his people (in response to his edict) seem to have repented of idolatry or to have believed in the one true God.

[25] For the three uses of the Law, see FC Ep and SD VI.

[26] For the distinction between righteousness through faith and civil righteousness, see AC XVIII 1; Ap IV 33–35, 142; XVIII 4–10.

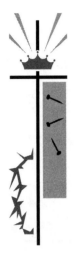

automatically bowed to the gold image worshiped gods who were not alive and could not deliver them. The Judeans, however, worshiped the only living God. They prospered because only their God is able to save (cf. Acts 4:12).

However, we should not draw the conclusion that loyalty and faithfulness to God always bring deliverance and prosperity in this life. Certainly, these three Judeans did not assume that God would save them from persecution and physical death ("but if not … ," 3:18). Their theology is the same as the theology of the cross in the NT: followers of Christ crucified cannot expect to be treated any better than was their Lord (cf. Mt 10:14–25; Acts 14:22; Rev 11:7–8). God may or may not choose to give his people promotion and prosperity in this life, but his certain promise is his gift of eternal life and glory far beyond anything this world can offer (Dan 12:2–3). Because Shadrach, Meshach, and Abednego focused on eternal life and were able to see that life in this world is not worth anything in comparison to the eternal life God promises to his people, they defied the king at the risk of their lives in the fiery furnace. Thus by faith they "extinguished the power of fire" (Heb 11:34).

Daniel 3:31–4:34 (ET 4:1–37)

Nebuchadnezzar Is Judged for His Arrogance against God

Introduction to Daniel 4 (MT 3:31–4:34; ET 4:1–37)

3:31–33	The Greeting of Nebuchadnezzar's Letter (ET 4:1–3)
Excursus	*Daniel 4 and the Prayer of Nabonidus*
4:1–15	Nebuchadnezzar Seeks the Meaning of His Dream of the Tree (ET 4:4–18)
4:16–24	Daniel Explains Nebuchadnezzar's Dream of the Tree (ET 4:19–27)
4:25–34	Nebuchadnezzar's Dream of the Tree Is Fulfilled (ET 4:28–37)

Introduction to Daniel 4
(MT 3:31–4:34; ET 4:1–37)

Major Emphases in Daniel 4

Virtually every chapter of Daniel emphasizes the certainty of God's sovereign control over all events among humans.[1] This is no less true of the account of Nebuchadnezzar's dream in Daniel 4. However, this account is unique in that it is the only record in Daniel of God dealing graciously with a Gentile in order to reform him.[2] Previously Nebuchadnezzar witnessed God's control over history and his guidance of events in the training of the Judean captives, who providentially thrived (chapter 1); in revealing the future kingdoms that will lead up to the establishment of God's kingdom (chapter 2); and in God's rescue of Shadrach, Meshach, and Abednego from the king's own power (chapter 3). In chapter 4, which is the last account in the book of an event from Nebuchadnezzar's reign, God reveals his power over Babylon and its ruler, and furthermore God takes action to reform the ruler.

Law Themes in Daniel 4

Therefore, in Daniel 4, the Law plays an important role, particularly the First Commandment.[3] In his hubris, Nebuchadnezzar ascribes power and majesty to himself, as if he himself were a god (4:27 [ET 4:30]). The dream that Nebuchadnezzar has in this account metes out judgment on the king. Like the tree in the dream, he will be cut down. Clearly, this involves both the first and the second uses of the Law. The first use is evident since God is attempting to curb Nebuchadnezzar's pride and arrogance and to lead him to be a more just and merciful ruler of his people (4:24 [ET 4:27]). However, God is also seeking to move Nebuchadnezzar to repentance and faith. The second use of the Law is evident as God judges him in order to convict him of his sins and move him to repent before he dies; he must turn away from his other gods and seek forgiveness from the only true God. Such Law-produced repentance is a necessary prerequisite for one to believe the Gospel and thus be saved through faith. (For the Gospel in Daniel 4, see below).

---

[1] For this theme in the book, see "Theological Threats Posed by the Critical Dating of Daniel" in "Date, Authorship, and Unity," and "The Messiah in Daniel: An Overview" and "God as the Protector of His People" in "Major Themes" in the introduction. See also the commentary on 2:27–30, 34–35, 44–45 and 7:9–14.

[2] While unique in Daniel, the OT contains many other examples of God dealing graciously with Gentiles, many of whom were brought to saving faith. For a survey, one may see "Mission in the Old Testament" in Lessing, *Jonah*, 151–69.

[3] See further "God's Law in Daniel" in "Law and Gospel in Daniel" in the introduction.

The Law is effectual in its first and second uses. Nebuchadnezzar does curb his pride and arrogance and admit that "the Most High God" is the ultimate power on earth (3:32–33 [ET 4:2–3]; 4:31–32 [ET 4:34–35]). Moreover, Nebuchadnezzar recognizes that he must not express hubris in the future (as he had in the past; see 4:27 [ET 4:30]) and that God was just in disciplining him (4:34 [ET 4:37]). He is moved to praise God as the one who has sovereign authority over all people; God has demonstrated his power to humble the proud (4:34 [ET 4:37]).

However, the results of the Law evident in the words and deeds of Nebuchadnezzar in Daniel 4 all are in the realm of civil righteousness.[4] Nebuchadnezzar acknowledges God's ultimate power, but he does not seek from him the forgiveness of sins. The wording of 4:5–6 (ET 4:8–9), written after his restoration, shows that the king stubbornly clings to his pagan polytheism, since he calls Bel his "god" and refers to other "gods." He does not abandon his idolatry; he has not heeded the First Commandment. Neither does the king give any indication that he had heard the Gospel of God's forgiveness and believed it. He does not seem to have been brought to faith in the only true God as his Savior from sin and its consequences, death and God's eternal judgment.[5]

The spiritual state of Nebuchadnezzar in chapter 4 is consistent with his condition in chapter 3. The commentary on 3:29–30 points out that Nebuchadnezzar's decree merely prohibited blasphemy against the one true God, but did not prohibit continuing worship of other gods, and it also failed to exhort the people to turn to the one true God in repentant faith (as did the king of Nineveh's exhortation in Jonah 3:7–9).

God has dealt with Nebuchadnezzar on four separate occasions, recorded in the first four chapters of the book. Each time God has demonstrated his power in contrast to the powerlessness of the Babylonian gods. However, Nebuchadnezzar never repents of his pagan beliefs. The most he will concede is that God is greater than all other gods. By recording these narratives, Daniel the author is reminding his readers just how difficult it is for a pagan Gentile to turn to the true God and renounce all pagan practices. His readers living in a pagan culture would have to realize that even if many of their Gentile neighbors would tolerate their religious beliefs, few would embrace them. That message is just as relevant today for us Christians who read the book. We thank God if

---

[4] For the distinction between righteousness through faith and civil righteousness, see AC XVIII 1; Ap IV 33–35, 142; XVIII 4–10. Ap IV 261–68 takes the view that Nebuchadnezzar was converted to saving faith. See the commentary on 4:24.

[5] Daniel 4 can be both compared and contrasted with Jonah 3, where the prophet preaches a message of judgment (Jonah 3:4) calling for repentance, and a Gentile king repents, calls upon God in faith, and commands his people likewise to desist from evil and to call upon God in repentant faith (Jonah 3:7–9). The Ninevites and their king were saved through faith, and they will be raised to everlasting life on Judgment Day (Mt 12:41; Lk 11:32), whereas Nebuchadnezzar is moved to contrition but apparently not to faith. For an exposition of the view that the Ninevites were indeed saved through faith and will inherit eternal life, one may see Lessing, *Jonah*, 12, 56–57, 284–85, 296–316.

Christianity gains or retains a measure of acceptance in our society, and even more if neighbors acknowledge the triune God to be supreme. But we must continue to pray and proclaim God's Word of Law and Gospel until our neighbors are brought to repentance and faith in "our great God and Savior, Jesus Christ" (Titus 2:13).

Another theme of the Law that runs throughout Daniel and is especially prominent in chapter 4 is the Fourth Commandment, especially that commandment's implication that authority in this world is established by God alone.[6] Repeated explicit statements point the reader to this theme (4:14, 22–23, 31–33 [ET 4:17, 25–26, 34–36]). This theme has two emphases. First, it emphasizes to all rulers that they are accountable to God. Just as God humbled Nebuchadnezzar, so he can humble any human authority who fails to acknowledge that God has granted him all of the authority he possesses (cf. Jn 19:11). Second, it emphasizes to readers that human authority is to be respected and that rebellion against lawful authority is rebellion against God, a theme found here through narrative and developed in a detailed exposition later by the apostle Paul:

> Let every person be subject to the governing authorities. For there is no authority except from God, and those that exist have been ordered by God. Therefore whoever opposes the authority resists what God has appointed, and those who resist will incur judgment upon themselves. For rulers are not a terror to good conduct, but to bad. Do you wish not to fear the authority? Then do what is good, and you will receive approval from it, for he is God's servant for your good. But if you do wrong, be afraid, for he does not bear the sword in vain. He is a servant of God, an avenger for [executing God's] wrath on the wrongdoer. Therefore it is necessary to be in subjection, not only because of [avoiding God's] wrath but also for the sake of conscience. For this same reason you also pay taxes, for they [the authorities] are ministers of God, attending to this very thing. Pay to all what is owed to them: taxes to whom taxes [are owed], revenue to whom revenue [is owed], respect to whom respect [is owed], honor to whom honor [is owed]. (Rom 13:1–7)

Gospel Themes in Daniel 4

However, Daniel 4 is not simply a chapter about God's Law. It is also a chapter that has Gospel themes. God's graciousness is evident in his dealings with Nebuchadnezzar. God does not simply judge and destroy the Babylonian king for his arrogance (cf. Acts 12:21–23). He first reveals to him what will happen if he does not repent by giving him a dream as a warning. Moreover, he uses Daniel to articulate a call to repentance and faith so that there can be no mistaking God's invitation to believe and be saved from both temporal and eternal punishment. When Daniel exhorts him, "break away from your sins with righteousness" (4:24 [ET 4:27]), Daniel intends more than the civil righteousness Nebuchadnezzar will display; he invites the king to receive theological

---

[6] See further under "God's Law in Daniel" in "Law and Gospel in Daniel" in the introduction.

"righteousness," the forgiveness of sins and everlasting life, which come purely by God's grace and simply through faith (Gen 15:6). That Gospel invitation spoken by God through Daniel is also intended for all who read the book and hear its message. It is basically the same as other Gospel invitations to receive salvation freely by grace alone, invitations found in the OT (e.g., Is 55:1–3) and NT (e.g., Acts 2:38–40; 16:31; Rev 22:17).

In addition, when Nebuchadnezzar finally admits his arrogance and glorifies God (Dan 3:32–33; 4:31–34 [ET 4:2–3, 34–37]), God graciously restores him to his throne. This is all the more remarkable because Nebuchadnezzar's repentance leads only to civil righteousness and not to turning from the sin of idolatry to embrace the triune God, who is the Creator and Redeemer of all. Nevertheless, God is gracious and deals kindly with Nebuchadnezzar, as the king himself acknowledges (4:31–34 [ET 4:34–37]).

There is yet another audience for the Gospel in this chapter. Daniel is conveying to his readers the power of God to keep his promises. In Daniel 2, the promise of the advent of God's eternal kingdom is linked to the removal of one Gentile power after another until they are all replaced by the kingdom of God. In Daniel 4, God demonstrates his power to remove a Gentile king from his throne, at least temporarily, and offers a foretaste of God's eventual use of his sovereignty over the world to remove Gentile kings in order to clear the way for the coming of the Messiah and the establishment of his eternal kingdom in Jesus Christ. The promise that God made via Nebuchadnezzar's dream in Daniel 2 is reinforced by the dream in Daniel 4 and its fulfillment.

God's gracious provision for his OT people as they await the establishment of his kingdom in Christ is also part of Nebuchadnezzar's dream. This Gentile king is the tree that provides abundant fruit and food for all. Under it creatures find shelter, and in its branches birds nest (4:9, 18 [ET 4:12, 21]). Here the reader is reminded that God provides for his creation, and especially for his people, through governments and authorities, all of whom he has established, even if they consist of unbelievers. The Judeans in Babylon were among those people who found earthly shelter within Nebuchadnezzar's realm. So too, later readers could know that even under despotic rulers, God still had and would provide for their earthly needs, and though the despotism might lead to persecutions and trials for believers, God would not abandon them to the kingdoms of this world, but would ultimately bring them into his eternal kingdom.

Finally, Daniel 4 is a specific example of the great reversal theme that extends throughout the Scriptures and is common in the Prophets. In the NT, this theme is expressed by Mary in her Magnificat in words that apply literally to Nebuchadnezzar:

> He [God] has brought down rulers from thrones
>   and exalted the humble. (Lk 1:52)

In the Beatitudes, Jesus repeatedly expresses this Law and Gospel theme of judgment for the proud but eschatological rescue for his lowly and oppressed believers (Matthew 5–7). Jesus himself is the epitome of this theme:

Christ Jesus, ... though being in the form of God, did not consider equality with God something to be seized, but emptied himself. ... He humbled himself, becoming obedient unto death, death on a cross. Therefore God highly exalted him. (Phil 2:5–9)

His incarnation, state of humiliation, atoning death, glorious resurrection, and session at the right hand of the Father are the basis for the hope of all believers for deliverance and resurrection to eternal life (Dan 12:2–3). In fact, the angelic decree of the "watchers" from heaven portends the great reversal in Jesus:

The Most High rules the human kingdom,
    and he gives it to whomever he wishes,
and he appoints the lowliest of humans over it. (4:14 [ET 4:17])

In Daniel 4, Nebuchadnezzar is debased, then restored to his throne. However, Jesus truly became "the lowliest of humans" on the cross as he bore the sin of the world and was abandoned by his Father, but then he was raised, exalted, and seated in power at the right hand of "the Most High," appointed with authority over the entirety of the "human kingdom" (see Mt 28:18). He now governs world history for the purpose of bringing all who believe in him to everlasting salvation (cf. Mt 24:22; Eph 1:20–23; Heb 1:3).

As a final Gospel theme, we should not fail to note that Daniel 4 contributes to the biblical understanding of God the Holy Spirit as the third person of the Trinity, even though the testimony is filtered through the words of the pagan king. In the letter Nebuchadnezzar composed after his restoration, he acknowledges that "a spirit of holy gods dwells" in Daniel (4:5–6, 15 [ET 4:8–9, 18]; cf. also 5:11, 14). Of course, Daniel's original Judean audience knew—and believing readers today know—that there are no other "gods" besides the one true God. It is his Spirit who indwelt Daniel, just as he indwelt and gave faith to all OT believers. Even so, he dwells in all baptized believers during the NT era and creates saving faith in Christ.[a] At various times in the OT, the indwelling of the Spirit was manifested in certain people by particular gifts and abilities that they could employ for the benefit of others,[b] as also in the NT era (e.g., 1 Corinthians 12). Nebuchadnezzar had learned in chapter 2 that unlike his occult diviners, Daniel possesses the ability to interpret divine revelations from the supernatural realm, and here Nebuchadnezzar rightly acknowledges (although with inadequate wording) that this is no mere human faculty, but a spiritual gift.

(a) E.g., Acts 2:17–18, 38–39; Rom 5:5; 7:6; 8:2, 14–16; Eph 1:13; 4:4–5, 30

(b) E.g., Ex 31:2–5; Num 11:25–29; 27:18; Judg 3:10; 6:34; 11:29

A Possible Historical Setting for Daniel 4

There is no chronological information in the text for the setting of the events in Daniel 4. The only thing we are told is that Nebuchadnezzar had his dream when he was at home in his palace and was at ease and flourishing (4:1 [ET 4:4]). Twelve months later he was struck with insanity (4:26–29 [ET 4:29–32]) and did not occupy the throne for a period of "seven times" (4:13 [ET 4:16]), which is usually interpreted to mean "seven years," but instead probably refers to a shorter period of complete reformation for the king.[7]

The parts of the Babylonian Chronicle extant for the reign of Nebuchadnezzar end in his tenth year, which extended from Nisan 595 to the end of Adar II 594 BC.[8] The only other records of Nebuchadnezzar's activity are the siege and fall of Jerusalem (589–587), the thirteen-year siege of Tyre (586–573), and a campaign in Egypt in 568/567 BC to quash a revolt by the regent he had placed in charge of that part of the empire.[9] Nebuchadnezzar died in 562 BC. Thus it would appear as if Nebuchadnezzar had his dream sometime between 573 BC and his death in 562 BC. Since he was in Babylon and "at ease" and "flourishing" (4:1 [ET 4:4]) when he had the dream, he was in Babylon twelve months later at the fulfillment of the dream, and he was insane for some period afterwards, Nebuchadnezzar could not have had the dream during the years 570–565, since in 568/567 he was in Egypt and sane enough to lead his troops in battle. Thus Nebuchadnezzar could not have dreamt this dream any earlier than 573 BC nor any later than 560 BC.

From this data we can conclude that there are two possible spans of years for the events of Daniel 4: either 573–569 BC or 564–562 BC. Since there is hardly enough time for all of the events to have taken place in the last two years of his reign, it is most likely that Daniel 4 is set sometime during 573–569. Perhaps the rebellion in Egypt was prompted by Nebuchadnezzar's return to power; the vassal king in Egypt may have perceived that it was a good time to assert his independence (of which he might have had a taste during Nebuchadnezzar's insanity). If this was the case, then a date sometime in the late 570s is to be preferred for the events of Daniel 4.

Chapter Division and Verse Numbering in Daniel 4

The first three verses in this section of Daniel (MT 3:31–33; ET 4:1–3) clearly are the introductory part of Nebuchadnezzar's letter, and so they belong with the rest of chapter 4 (MT 4:1–34; ET 4:4–37). Originally the inspired Hebrew and Aramaic manuscripts of OT books had no system of numbering for verses and chapters. The system of vowels and accents added by the Masoretes (Jewish scribes) during the sixth through the ninth centuries AD divided the text into verses (without numbering them).[10] (The system of indicating verse numbers in the text or in the margin was first employed in Latin Bibles in the sixteenth century.)

---

[7] For the meaning of the phrase, see the commentary on 4:13 (ET 4:16). The phrase is also used in 4:20, 22, 29 (ET 4:23, 25, 32).

[8] BM 21946 (Wiseman, *Chronicles of Chaldean Kings*, 72–75).

[9] See Wiseman, *Nebuchadrezzar and Babylon*, or Weisberg, *Texts from the Time of Nebuchadnezzar*.

[10] See Tov, *Textual Criticism of the Hebrew Bible*, 50–53, 211.

In the Middle Ages, when the Vulgate was divided into chapters, these three verses of Daniel (MT 4:1–34; ET 4:4–37) were assigned to the end of Daniel 3. (The chapter divisions in the Vulgate are attributed to Stephen Langton, archbishop of Canterbury, in the thirteenth century.) Probably the reason why these verses were assigned to the end of Daniel 3 is because they include praise of God, which normally comes at the end of sections of Daniel (as in 4:31–34 [ET 4:34–37]). Subsequently the Hebrew text was divided into chapters according to the Vulgate's system.[11] During the Reformation, both Luther[12] and Calvin[13] corrected this mistake, with the result that current English versions include these verses as the beginning of Daniel 4. However, contemporary printed editions of the MT retain the Vulgate's older chapter division.

The Genuineness of Nebuchadnezzar's Letter

The opening verse of Nebuchadnezzar's letter (3:31 [ET 4:1]) signals that it is a personal missive to all of his subjects. Therefore, it is written from a first person point of view, except for a short section, probably inserted by Daniel, that is written about Nebuchadnezzar in the third person (4:25–30 [ET 4:28–33]).[14] The first person portions of the letter exhibit some signs of biblical thought, which presumably would have been foreign to Nebuchadnezzar. For these reasons, many critical scholars view the letter as a redaction of several sources. For support of that view, some appeal to the Old Greek version, which differs substantially in its arrangement and contents.[15] However, both the third person section and the reflections of biblical thought may be explained as legitimate features that actually support the genuineness of Nebuchadnezzar's letter as recorded by Daniel, the inspired author of the book. Once again, Daniel demonstrates his skill as a writer.

The brief third person narrative inserted by Daniel into the letter in 4:25–30 (ET 4:28–33) serves at least four purposes:

1. It furnishes the reader with an account of the period of Nebuchadnezzar's insanity even though the king himself may not have retained any personal knowledge of his condition during that period.[16]

2. By saying, toward the end of the letter, "my reason returned to me" (4:31, 33 [ET 4:34, 36]), Nebuchadnezzar acknowledges that he had a prior period of insanity. However, it would have been embarrassing for him to relate his insan-

---

[11] See Tov, *Textual Criticism of the Hebrew Bible*, 52–53.

[12] WA DB 11/2.144–45. Luther keeps the MT verse numbering, but puts MT 3:31–33 (ET 4:1–3) at the beginning of chapter 4.

[13] Calvin, *Daniel*, 1:243.

[14] Dan 4:16–24 (ET 4:19–27) is also third person speech about Nebuchadnezzar. However, since these verses are part of *Nebuchadnezzar's* account of Daniel's words, they properly belong to the first person narrative.

[15] E.g., Collins, *Daniel*, 216–21.

[16] Hartman and Di Lella, *Daniel*, 174.

ity personally (in the first person). The third person form of the section (inserted by Daniel) spares him that embarrassment.[17]

3. While Nebuchadnezzar is substantially responsible for relating the events surrounding his insanity, by means of this third person insertion the viewpoint of Daniel the author becomes the reader's viewpoint, the perspective from which the account is to be understood.[18] We are led to view this account with the assumption that there is only one God—the God of Israel, who rules over all events among humans—rather than having the account filtered through the polytheistic lens that continues to characterize Nebuchadnezzar's thought. (Even when writing the letter after his restoration, the king in 4:5–6 [ET 4:8–9] still refers in pagan fashion to "gods" and to his own "god," Bel.)

4. Daniel the author chose to place the third person insert (4:25–30 [ET 4:28–33]) immediately after Nebuchadnezzar's report of Daniel's interpretation of the dream (4:17–24 [ET 4:20–27]). By doing so, Daniel has produced a large central section of the account that is primarily related in the third person (4:16–30 [ET 4:19–33]). This serves to produce the appearance of a more objective narrative, allowing the reader to see the interpretation and meaning of the events presented here as more reliable than a first person account by Nebuchadnezzar, a pagan, which would have had an inherent air of subjectivity.

The biblical thought exhibited in the letter may well be due to Daniel's influence. He interpreted the dream for Nebuchadnezzar (4:17–23 [ET 4:20–26]) and also advised him to repent and receive God's gift of "righteousness" (4:24 [ET 4:27]). Given that Daniel was the only one of Nebuchadnezzar's courtiers who understood the dream, Daniel may have also been called upon to help in the drafting of the letter, including the offering of advice on its wording.[19]

At the same time, pagan elements appear throughout the letter (4:5–6, 10, 14–15, 20 [ET 4:8–9, 13, 17–18, 23]).[20] For example, "watcher(s)" (4:10, 14, 20 [ET 4:13, 17, 23]) may be a pagan term for angels, even though in the vision it must refer to angels of the one true God. These too are evidence for its genuineness, since the king retained his polytheism. If the letter were merely a fiction composed much later (in the Maccabean era) by a pious Jew, it is difficult to explain these pagan elements, which ring true to the historical setting of Nebuchadnezzar's Babylon.

Therefore, no good reason exists to view Daniel 4 as a highly redacted tradition. Instead, we have a letter by Nebuchadnezzar with material inserted by Daniel that explains the period of the king's insanity. As Goldingay observes:

> The alternating [of first person narrative] with third person narrative ... is dramatically appropriate and parallels that in Ezra-Nehemiah and Tobit; it hardly gives grounds for identifying two versions or recensions of the chapter. ...

---

[17] Meadowcroft, "Point of View in Storytelling," 34.
[18] See Meadowcroft, "Point of View in Storytelling," 34–35.
[19] Keil, *Daniel*, 134–35.
[20] Young, *Daniel*, 98.

Thus whereas chaps. 2, 3, and 6 [of Daniel] are narratives that close with proclamation, chap. 4 is a proclamation that incorporates a narrative; and whereas Daniel has considerable prominence in chap. 2, here he is a role rather than a personality, Nebuchadnezzar having more of the focus.[21]

---

[21] Goldingay, *Daniel*, 82.

Daniel 3:31–33 (ET 4:1–3)

The Greeting of Nebuchadnezzar's Letter

Translation

3 ³¹King Nebuchadnezzar

To all people, nations, and languages that dwell in the entire earth:

May your prosperity grow great!

³²It seemed good to me to declare the signs and wonders that the Most High God did with me.

³³How great are his signs!

How mighty are his wonders!

His kingdom is an eternal kingdom,

and his dominion is from generation to generation.

Textual Notes

3:32 אָתַיָּא וְתִמְהַיָּא דִּי עֲבַד עִמִּי אֱלָהָא עִלָּאָה—This entire clause, "the signs and wonders that the Most High God did with me," is the direct object of the last verb in the final clause of the verse, שְׁפַר קָדָמַי לְהַחֲוָיָה, "it seemed good to me *to declare*." Nebuchadnezzar had referred to the God of Israel as "the Most High God" (אֱלָהָא עִלָּאָה) also in 3:26. See the first textual note and the commentary on 3:26 and the commentary on 3:32 (ET 4:2).

The Aramaic noun אָת, "sign" (3:32–33 [ET 4:2–3]; 6:28 [ET 6:27]) is cognate to the Hebrew noun אוֹת, "sign." The Aramaic noun תְּמַהּ, a "wonder, as wrought by God" (BDB), has rare Hebrew cognates, the noun תִּמָּהוֹן, "bewilderment," and verb תָּמַהּ, "be astounded." However, תְּמַהּ is used here as an Aramaic equivalent of מוֹפֵת, "a wonder, portent," which often occurs together with אוֹת, "sign," in the OT. When they occur together in the OT, the plurals of אוֹת and מוֹפֵת ("signs and wonders") usually refer to the ten plagues God performed against Egypt as proof of his power and his will to save his people (e.g., Ex 7:3; Deut 4:34; 6:22; Jer 32:20–21; Ps 78:43). Together the words also refer to Isaiah's prophetic sons (Is 8:18 [plural]) and his prophetic actions (Is 20:3 [singular]). Yet they can also refer to misleading signs performed by a false prophet (Deut 13:2–4 [ET 13:1–3]).

3:33 אָתוֹהִי כְּמָה רַבְרְבִין וְתִמְהוֹהִי כְּמָה תַקִּיפִין—These exclamations are, literally, "His signs—how great! His wonders—how mighty!" As in 3:32 (ET 4:2), English translation requires rearranging the syntax.

מַלְכוּתֵהּ מַלְכוּת עָלַם וְשָׁלְטָנֵהּ עִם־דָּר וְדָר׃—This second half of the verse, literally, "his kingdom is a kingdom of eternity, and his dominion is with generation and generation," is basically repeated but with a different word order in 4:31 (ET 4:34): שָׁלְטָנֵהּ שָׁלְטָן עָלַם וּמַלְכוּתֵהּ עִם־דָּר וְדָר, "his dominion is a dominion of eternity, and his kingdom is with generation and generation." Both 3:33b (ET 4:3b) and 4:31 (ET 4:34) are close to being Aramaic equivalents of David's prayer to God in Ps 145:13: מַלְכוּתְךָ מַלְכוּת כָּל־עֹלָמִים וּמֶמְשַׁלְתְּךָ בְּכָל־דּוֹר וָדוֹר, "your kingdom is a kingdom of all eternities, and your dominion is in every generation and generation."

Commentary

Nebuchadnezzar's Opening Greeting and Praise of God

The opening of this section[1] is clearly epistolary in form. The author identifies himself ("King Nebuchadnezzar") and his recipients ("to all people, nations, and languages that dwell in the entire earth") and offers a standard greeting, "may your prosperity grow great!" The opening praise to God indicates that something has happened that caused the king to rejoice. The letter will next recount the history of a series of events, following them in chronological order, and the readers or hearers will not learn the reason for the king's praise until the very end of the letter, where the same expression of praise will be repeated and elaborated (4:31–34 [ET 4:34–37]). Therefore the opening of the letter arouses interest to follow the narrative and learn the reason for the praise. Literarily it also balances the concluding praise, and together the two doxologies form an inclusio around the letter.

The preamble in 3:32 (ET 4:2) and doxology that follows in 3:33 (ET 4:3) prepare the reader for the content of the letter by enunciating the general topic.[2] Within that general topic, two particular themes are mentioned. First, Nebuchadnezzar speaks about the surpassing might of God as shown by his "signs" and "wonders" (3:32–33 [ET 4:2–3]), specifically in the "signs" and "wonders" he has done with Nebuchadnezzar. The phraseology of "signs" and "wonders" is frequent in the OT (see the textual note on 3:32 [ET 4:2]). Some critical scholars cite this as evidence that Daniel 4 is a later Jewish composition. However, this may simply demonstrate Daniel's influence upon Nebuchadnezzar or Nebuchadnezzar's recognition that God's miraculous actions toward him are consistent with his miraculous dealings with Israel.

The second topic is the enduring nature of God's kingdom: "his kingdom is an eternal kingdom" (3:33 [ET 4:3]). In contrast, the events related in this chapter teach Nebuchadnezzar just how impermanent human kingdoms are, including his own. Although he does not directly admit the transient nature of the Babylonian Empire that he has built, Nebuchadnezzar does concede that God's kingdom is different.[3]

---

[1] These three verses belong with chapter 4. See "Chapter Division and Verse Numbering in Daniel 4" in the "Introduction to Daniel 4."

[2] See further "Introduction to Daniel 4."

[3] This dual theme had already appeared in chapter 2. Despite the desire that a human king would live forever (2:4), human kingdoms come and go, as shown by the succession of the four parts of the statue. However, God's kingdom, and his alone, is eternal (2:44–45).

The second textual note on 3:33 points out that 3:33b (ET 4:3b), which is echoed again at the end of this letter (4:31 [ET 4:34]), is almost an Aramaic equivalent of Ps 145:13. However, this does not necessarily mean that these doxologies in Daniel composed by Nebuchadnezzar are directly drawing upon that psalm by David. The topic they express—that God's kingdom is eternal—is a common one. Daniel had proclaimed this truth to Nebuchadnezzar in 2:44–45, and the king could be reflecting that proclamation. The recognition of God's eternal and surpassing sovereignty might be difficult to express succinctly in words other than these. The letter both begins and ends on this note to emphasize that Nebuchadnezzar has come to recognize God's kingdom as far greater than his own.

Excursus
Daniel 4 and the Prayer of Nabonidus[1]

After the publication of the Nabonidus Chronicle in 1882, scholars began to speculate that the historical incident that had inspired Daniel's tale of Nebuchadnezzar's insanity was Nabonidus' ten-year sojourn in Tema, where he suffered from an illness.[2] Then in 1956 the fragmentary remains of a Dead Sea scroll were published that contained a prayer by King Nabonidus.[3] Scholars were quick to assume that the manuscript fragments of that scroll, 4Q242 (4QPrNab ar), confirmed the long-suspected history of the tradition behind Daniel 4. The text of the Prayer of Nabonidus preserved in the scroll fragments clearly is related to Daniel 4. This fragmentary scroll has been labeled "the missing link" between the Babylonian traditions expressed in the Nabonidus Chronicle and Daniel 4.[4] Although no one would claim direct literary dependence of Daniel 4 on the Prayer of Nabonidus, discussions of their relationship in scholarly and popular publications during the past fifty years are nearly unanimous in assuming that the Prayer of Nabonidus preserves a tradition older than Daniel 4.[5]

The Prayer of Nabonidus Compared to Daniel 4

The text of 4QPrNab ar is as follows:[6]

---

[1] This excursus is a slightly modified version of Steinmann, "The Chicken and the Egg: A New Proposal for the Relationship between the *Prayer of Nabonidus* and the *Book of Daniel*."

[2] The Nabonidus Chronicle indicates that Nabonidus, the last king of the Neo-Babylonian Empire (556–539 BCE), sojourned in Tema during the last ten years of his reign. For the text of the Nabonidus Chronicle, see Pinches, "On a Cuneiform Inscription Relating to the Capture of Babylon by Cyrus and the Events Which Preceded and Led to It," or *ANET*, 305–7.

Scholars generally assume that the Nabonidus Chronicle, which covers events from 556 to 539 BC, was finished early in the reign of Cyrus, whose conquest of Babylon is one of the last events recorded in the chronicle. It has all the hallmarks of official Babylonian royal archival material. Yamauchi, *Persia and the Bible*, 76–77, simply states: "Quite invaluable is the Chaldean Chronicle of the Neo-Babylonian king Nabonidus. The Chronicle is a relatively objective contemporary [to Nabonidus] account."

[3] Milik, " 'Prière de Nabonide' et autres écrits d'un cycle de Daniel."

[4] Collins, "4QPrayer of Nabonidus ar," 86.

[5] For example, see Collins, "Nabonidus, Prayer of," *ABD* 4:976–77; Eshel, "Possible Sources of the Book of Daniel"; Flusser, "Psalms, Hymns and Prayers," 554; Freedman, "The Prayer of Nabonidus"; García Martínez, "The *Prayer of Nabonidus*," 136.

[6] This reconstruction follows that of Collins, with the exception of line 2 in section 2, where Collins reads, [מנה אחן]ל[ף שלם שלו]ותי יתוב עלי] ("4QPrayer of Nabonidus ar," 88, 91). Collins' placement of the fragments is largely dependent on the reconstruction first proposed by Cross ("Fragments of the Prayer of Nabonidus"), though he admits that the placement proposed by García Martínez ("The *Prayer of Nabonidus*") may be preferable at several points (Collins, "4QPrayer of Nabonidus ar," 84). Several different reconstructions have been proposed. For a convenient discussion of the major differences, see Flint, "The Daniel Tradition at Qumran," 332–38. Many of the reconstructions propose wordings based on relevant portions

Section 1 (Fragments 1, 2a, 2b, 3)

1 מלי צול[ת]א די צלי נבני מלך בב[ל] מלכ[א] רבא כדי כתיש הוא]
2 בשחנא באישא בפתגם אל[ה]א בתימ[ן] אנה נבני בשחנא באישא]
3 כתיש הוית שנין שבע ומן [די] שוי א[ל]הא עלי אנפוהי ואסא לי
4 וחטאי שבק לה גזר והוא יהודי מן בני גלותא על לי ואמר]
5 החוי וכתב למעבד יקר ורבון לשם א[ל]הא עליא וכן כתבת אנה]
6 כתיש הוית בשחנא ב[נ]אישא] בתימן [בפתגם אלהא עליא]
7 שנין שבע מצלא חוי[ת קדם] אלהי כספא ודהבא [נחשא פרזלא]
8 אעא אבנא חספא מן די [הוית סב]ר די אלהין תנמין
   [ ] שלי° ד או
9 ת [ ][מיהון]

Section 2 (Fragment 4)

1 [לבר תמון אחלמת
2 [מנה אחן]ו[ף שלם של]ותי נשא מן קדמי]
3 [ ]°[ ]נו רחמי לא יכלת]
4 [כמה דמא אנתה ל °]
5 [° °°]

This may be translated as follows:

Section 1

1 The words of the prayer that King Nabonidus of [Baby]lon, [the great] king prayed [when he was smitten]

2 with a serious skin disease by a decree of G[o]d in Teman: ["I, Nabonidus by a serious disease]

3 was smitten for seven years and wh[en] G[od turned his face to me, I was healed]

4 and my sin was forgiven by him. A diviner, a Judean fr[om the exiles came to me and said,]

5 'Write a declaration to give honor and exalt[ation] to the name of G[od Most High.' So I wrote as follows:]

6 'I was smitten with a ser[ious] skin disease in Teman [by a decree of God Most High.]

7 I had bee[n] praying [before] the gods of silver and gold, [bronze, iron,]

8 wood, stone, clay because [I had thou]ght that [they were] gods […

9 …] their […]

---

of Daniel 4. For instance, Cross ("Fragments of the Prayer of Nabonidus," 263) reconstructs the last part of line 3 in section 1 to read, "I was like [unto a beast and I prayed to the Most High]," a reading clearly based on Dan 4:22, 29 ([ET 4:25, 32]; cf. 4:12–13, 20 [ET 4:15–16, 23]). I will discuss only those differences in reconstruction that are relevant for the issue of literary dependence involving the Prayer of Nabonidus and Daniel.

Section 2

1 ...] apart from them. You gave me a dream
2 ...] from it he made to pass. The peace of [my] restfulness [he took from me]
3 ...] my friends. I was not able [...
4 ...] how you have an appearance like [...] "
5 ...] [...

The parallels between Daniel 4 and the Prayer of Nabonidus are too striking to be coincidental. They seem to demand some type of explanation for the relationship between the two texts. The more obvious parallels are as follows:

Parallels between Daniel 4 and the Prayer of Nabonidus

Daniel 4	*The Prayer of Nabonidus*
First person account by Nebuchadnezzar (except 4:25–30 [ET 4:28–33]).	First person account by Nabonidus.
Nebuchadnezzar is stricken by God (4:26–29 [ET 4:29–32]).	Nabonidus is stricken by God (section 1, lines 2, 6).
Nebuchadnezzar is smitten for "*seven* times" (שִׁבְעָה עִדָּנִין, 4:29 [ET 4:32]).	Nabonidus is smitten for "*seven* years" (שנין שבע, section 1, line 3).
Daniel ministers to Nebuchadnezzar (4:5–24 [ET 4:8–27]).	A Judean diviner ministers to Nabonidus (section 1, lines 4–5).
Daniel advises Nebuchadnezzar to take actions toward God that will prevent his illness (4:24 [ET 4:27]).	A Judean diviner advises Nabonidus to take actions toward God that (apparently) led to the cure of his disease (section 1, line 5).

However, the two texts also exhibit a number of significant differences, including the different names of the kings, Nebuchadnezzar (Daniel 4) versus Nabonidus.

Significant Differences between Daniel 4 and the Prayer of Nabonidus

Daniel 4	*The Prayer of Nabonidus*
Takes place in Babylon.	Takes place in Teman.
Nebuchadnezzar was stricken with insanity (4:22, 29–30 [ET 4:25, 32–33]).	Nabonidus was stricken with a skin disease (שחן, section 1, lines 2, 6).
Nebuchadnezzar was smitten for "seven *times*" (שִׁבְעָה עִדָּנִין, 4:29 [ET 4:32]).	Nabonidus is smitten for "*seven* years" (שנין שבע, section 1, line 3).
Daniel is mentioned by name (4:5, 16 [ET 4:8, 19]).	The Judean diviner is unnamed (section 1, line 4).
Daniel advises Nebuchadnezzar to repent of his sins and show mercy to the oppressed (4:24 [ET 4:27]).	The Judean diviner advises Nabonidus to glorify God (section 1, line 5).

Excursus

Although there has been widespread acceptance of the theory that the Prayer of Nabonidus represents an earlier and somewhat more accurate version of the events related in Daniel 4, it has also been recognized that the Prayer of Nabonidus is hardly an accurate picture of the events of Nabonidus' reign, based on what we know of it from other ancient sources.[7] According to the Nabonidus Chronicle, Nabonidus spent ten years in Tema, whereas the Prayer of Nabonidus mentions only seven years in Teman. No mention of Nabonidus being afflicted with a chronic skin disease in known from other ancient sources that refer to him. In 4QPrNab ar the place of Nabonidus' sojourn is Teman instead of Tema.[8] Even the name Nabonidus is spelled in a peculiar manner in the prayer: נבני (*Nabunay*, section 1, line 1) instead of something more expected such as נבנד (Akkadian: *Nabû-na'id*).[9] If the Prayer of Nabonidus does preserve an earlier, more accurate Babylonian tradition about Nabonidus, it is nevertheless clear that it is a garbled and inaccurate preservation of that tradition.

Flint summarizes the differences between Daniel 4 and the Prayer of Nabonidus. He also suggests that the other ancient accounts of Nabonidus' reign underwent a transformation that resulted in the Prayer of Nabonidus:

> In many respects the Qumran text differs both from the Babylonian accounts and from Daniel 4. The Babylonian records do not say that the king suffered from a disease, and make no mention of a Jewish diviner. Moreover, the *Verse Account* accuses Nabonidus of impiety towards the Babylonian gods, whereas in the *Prayer of Nabonidus* he is misguidedly devoted to idols. In the *Harran Inscription* Nabonidus attributes his deliverance to the moon-god Sin, while the *Prayer* attributes this to the Most High God, or the God of the Jews. It is clear that Babylonian source-material has undergone a Jewish transformation, with Nabonidus' absence from Babylon being associated with a kind of sickness, and this sickness becoming an occasion for manifesting the power of the God of Israel.[10]

---

[7] For other ancient sources besides the Prayer of Nabonidus and the Nabonidus Chronicle that refer to Nabonidus, including the Persian Verse Account of Nabonidus, see *ANET*, 308–15, and Gadd, "The Harran Inscriptions of Nabonidus."

[8] Milik suggests this may have arose from confusion with the Teman in Edom ("Prière de Nabonide," 410, n. 2). Teman as a place in Edom is mentioned in the Bible (Jer 49:20; Obad 9) and may have been more familiar to a Palestinian Jew than Tema as a place in Arabia (Is 21:14; Jer 25:23; Job 6:19), making such confusion possible if the author of the Prayer of Nabonidus was a Palestinian Jew, as I propose below. Meyer suggests that the "-an" suffix is a local variant (*Das Gebet des Nabonid*, 20–21). This is a creative solution, but unprovable. García Martínez suggests that Teman is the older form of Tema, because LXX always translates תֵּימָא or תֵּמָא as Θαιμαν and because the Aramaic gentilic form תימניא preserves a (presumably) older form that protected the נ from being elided ("The *Prayer of Nabonidus*," 122). Given the problems with establishing the *Vorlagen* of the LXX texts and the problems of establishing the methods of the LXX translators, it is not sound methodology to rely on the LXX to establish the actual form of an Aramaic or Hebrew proper noun.

[9] García Martínez offers two explanations for the form נבני: it may show assimilation to the final "-ai" typical of Aramaic names, or it may represent scribal confusion of י for ד. ("The *Prayer of Nabonidus*," 120–21).

[10] Flint, "The Daniel Tradition at Qumran," 334.

The oft-mentioned theory that Nabonidus' peculiar devotion to the moon god Sin gave rise to the legend of Nebuchadnezzar's insanity in Daniel 4 requires a radical transformation of the historical occurrences behind the narrative.[11] However, there exists another possibility that most scholars have not seriously considered or have dismissed as unlikely: that the Prayer of Nabonidus is based upon Daniel 4.[12] After all, the lone fragmentary scroll of the Prayer of Nabonidus (75–50 BC)[13] is younger than the earliest known manuscripts of Daniel.[14] Could it be that since scholars had already proposed that a tradition about Nabonidus lay behind Daniel 4, they seized upon the discovery of 4QPrNab ar as a vindication of that proposal without a critical look at evidence that points to the Prayer of Nabonidus as younger than Daniel 4 and derivative from it? Given the garbled nature of the tradition about Nabonidus in the Prayer of Nabonidus, it would be prudent to examine this other possibility.

Indications That the Prayer of Nabonidus Is Dependent on Daniel 4

The major stumbling block that prevents many scholars from viewing the prayer as a composition based on Daniel 4 is the character of Nabonidus himself. Scholars assume that no Palestinian author in the Maccabean era would have known about Nabonidus (which is why they think that the well-known Nebuchadnezzar was substituted for Nabonidus sometime in the pre-history of Daniel 4). However, Nabonidus was not completely forgotten in the centuries after his reign. Scholars have long been aware that Greek historians, including Herodotus, knew of some traditions about Nabonidus.[15] Josephus, a Palestinian Jew who lived in the first century AD, knew of Nabonidus through the writings of Berosus.[16] Certainly it is not beyond the range of possibility that another, earlier Palestinian Jew—the one responsible for authoring the Prayer of Nabonidus—knew of Nabonidus through a Greek author.

Perhaps such a Palestinian Jew, upon learning of some facts about the reign of Nabonidus, composed a narrative roughly based on the plot of Daniel 4. The purpose of this narrative would be to supplement the book of Daniel and fill in a perceived and embarrassingly wide historical gap in Daniel: the era between the reign of Nebuchadnezzar and the fall of Babylon to the Persians. (That is

---

[11] For a thorough treatment of Nabonidus' devotion to Sin, see Bealieu, *The Reign of Nabonidus, King of Babylon (556–539 B.C.)*.

[12] A few scholars have argued that the Prayer of Nabonidus derives from Daniel, but they are a distinct minority. One example is Dommershausen, *Nabonid im Buche Daniel*, 85. Flint ("The Daniel Tradition at Qumran," 334–35) appears to take no position on the relationship between Daniel and the prayer.

[13] Cross, "Fragments of the Prayer of Nabonidus," 260.

[14] See "The Text and Other Daniel Traditions" in the introduction.

[15] Herodotus, however, calls him "Labynetus" (e.g., *Histories*, 1.74.3). See the discussion in Gruenthaner, "The Last King of Babylon," 409.

[16] Josephus, *Against Apion*, 1.149–53.

the historical gap between the end of Daniel 4 and the beginning of Daniel 5.) Such supplements to the book of Daniel are evident in Greek versions of Daniel.[17] The supplement called Susanna tells us of Daniel's precocious childhood and justifies Nebuchadnezzar's choice in selecting Daniel to be trained to serve in his court (Daniel 1). The Prayer of Azariah and the Song of the Three Young Men supplements Daniel 3 because it explains in more detail the mysterious survival of Azariah and his companions in the midst of the furnace and also demonstrates their piety.

In the same way, the Prayer of Nabonidus may have been intended by its author to offer a history of activity by a wise Jew in order to demonstrate a continuity of activity during the years about which the text of Daniel is silent, but which were described in the author's other historical sources. I propose that he drew upon the Aramaic text of Daniel as we know it today in order to compose a narrative that would appear to fit into the perceived gap between Daniel 4 and Daniel 5. The resulting story, the Prayer of Nabonidus, fits in this gap, both because of its historical setting and because of its thematic and verbal similarity to Daniel 4 and Daniel 5.

A number of features of the Prayer of Nabonidus logically point to it being based upon Daniel rather than it being composed from traditions that predate Daniel. These features include the following:

בִּפְתְגָם אֱ[לָהָ]א, "By a Decree of God" (בפתגם א[לה]א, Section 1, Line 2)

The superscription of the Prayer of Nabonidus states that the king's affliction was the result of a decree of God. Compare the decree that led to Nebuchadnezzar's affliction: בִּגְזֵרַת עִירִין פִּתְגָמָא, "the decree is an edict of the watchers" (4:14 [ET 4:17]). While Daniel gives some responsibility to the watchers for the judgment on Nebuchadnezzar that leads to his affliction (though the cause is ultimately ascribed to God in 4:21 [ET 4:24]), in the prayer the decree comes only from God. This appears to be a theological hypercorrection on the part of the author of the prayer. While the prayer adopts the term פִּתְגָם, "decree," from Daniel, its author also removes any perceived hint that God shares with other heavenly beings (watchers, angels) his power to issue a decree. In doing so, the prayer removes any perceived tendency toward polytheism.

But if one follows the reconstruction of García Martínez, בפתגם א[לה]א על[י]א[18] ("by a decree of the Most High God," בִּפְתְגָם אֱ[לָהָ]א עֶלְיָ[א]), the prayer has another close parallel to Daniel, since "the Most High God" occurs in Dan 3:26; 3:32 (ET 4:2); 5:18, 21. Since 5:18 and 5:21 refer to the events of Daniel 4, this divine title would indicate that the author of the prayer is drawing on the material about Nebuchadnezzar's insanity in both Daniel 4 and Daniel 5, making

---

[17] See "The Greek Additions to Daniel" in "The Text and Other Daniel Traditions" in the introduction.

[18] García Martínez, "The *Prayer of Nabonidus*," 119.

it more than likely that the prayer was composed on the basis of Daniel rather than being an independent, earlier form of the tradition that eventually produced Daniel 4.

גָּזֵר, "Diviner" (גזר, Section 1, Line 4)

In the biblical book, Daniel himself is frequently associated with the גָּזְרִין, "diviners" (the Peal [G] participle of גְּזַר in 2:27; 4:4 [ET 4:7]; 5:7, 11). In Daniel 4, he comes before the king after the "diviners" (4:4–5 [ET 4:7–8]), and in Daniel 5 he is described as their leader (5:11). His association with the diviners is significant because his superiority to the other diviners is the reason why Daniel is brought before the king in Daniel 5, which leads to his explanation of the handwriting on the wall (5:22–28). Daniel's prologue (5:18–21) to his explanation of the handwriting contains a recapitulation of the events of Daniel 4. Thus it appears as if the author of the prayer was familiar with both Daniel 4 and also Daniel 5 and drew on the account of Nebuchadnezzar's insanity in Daniel 4 and the recapitulation of that account by Daniel in Daniel 5.

Yet, even the presence of גָּזֵר, "diviner," in the Prayer of Nabonidus presents a problem for the standard theory of the genesis of the prayer. It, like most of Daniel 4, is a first person account spoken by the king as the narrator. Since both are first person accounts, the proponents of the current theory would have us believe that in the early history of this account someone, probably a Jew writing for a Jewish audience, composed an (apparently fictional) account based loosely on the sojourn of Nabonidus in Tema. This account eventually produced at least two literary offspring: the Prayer of Nabonidus (the older work) and Daniel 4 (a younger work).

But let us ask whether the word גָּזֵר, "diviner," is needed in the prayer. Why not simply state, "A Judean from the exiles came to me and said, 'Write ... ' "? Is the reference to a "diviner" needed for a Jewish audience? Would they place more credence in the character of the Judean who aids Nabonidus if he is characterized as a "diviner"? Given the strong condemnation of divination in the Torah and the rest of the OT,[a] and the radical monotheism of the writer of the prayer,[19] this seems unlikely.

However, unlike in the prayer, גָּזֵר, "diviner," fits perfectly in the book of Daniel as a term applied to Daniel himself since the book is a historically accurate depiction of how Daniel was viewed by the pagan Babylonian king in relation to his occult diviners. We can understand why the author or editor of Daniel[20] placed Daniel among the גָּזְרִין, "diviners," and included the king's statement "I know that a spirit of holy gods dwells in you" (4:6 [ET 4:9]). Daniel

(a) E.g., Lev 19:26; Deut 18:10–14; Josh 13:22; 2 Ki 17:17; Jer 14:14; Ezek 12:24; 13:6–7, 23

---

[19] See "By a Decree of God," "Honor and Exalt[ation]," and "Gods of Silver and Gold, [Bronze, Iron,] Wood, Stone, Clay."

[20] This commentary's view is that Daniel himself is the author of the book. See "Date and Authorship according to the Book" in "Date, Authorship, and Unity" in the introduction.

was presented in a similar way in chapters 1 and 2, and this wording makes the narrative of Daniel 4 fit into the rest of the book.

Since גָּזֵר, "diviner," fits well in Daniel, but not in the prayer, it would appear that the author of the prayer included the term because he was drawing on Daniel.

יְהוּדִי, "Judean" (יהודי, Section 1, Line 4)

As noted above, in the prayer the diviner remains unnamed in the text that is extant. Some scholars assume as a foregone conclusion that this diviner in the prayer is to be identified as Daniel.[21] Other scholars have argued that because the Judean diviner is unnamed in the prayer, it reflects a stage of the Nabonidus tradition before the seer was identified as Daniel in the strand of tradition that became the biblical book (an argument that presupposes that the prayer is older than the book of Daniel).[22] Still others are more cautious. It is noteworthy that the adjective יְהוּדִי, "Judean," never occurs in Daniel in reference to Daniel himself. Its only occurrences in the book are when his companions Azariah, Hananiah, and Mishael are called יְהוּדָיֵא, "the Judeans" (3:8), and גֻּבְרִין יְהוּדָאִין, "Judean men" (3:12). For Daniel himself, the noun יְהוּד, "Judah," is used when he is called גְּבַר מִן־בְּנֵי גָלוּתָא דִּי יְהוּד, "a man from the exiles of Judah" (2:25; similar are 5:13 and 6:14 [6:13]).

We should bear in mind that line 4 of the prayer is partially reconstructed: "a Judean fr[om the exiles]." While this reconstruction is quite plausible, it is based on a certain placement of the surviving fragments of 4QPrNab ar, and "from the exiles" is also based on the phrase in Dan 2:25; 5:13; 6:14 (ET 6:13). Therefore this reconstruction supports the view that the prayer is dependent on Daniel. However, many scholars want to avoid a reconstruction that suggests that the prayer is dependent on Daniel, and so they prefer to follow Milik's original placement of the fragments and include the word גְּבַר, "man," in their reconstruction,[23] resulting in "a Judean man fr[om the exiles]," although that reconstruction is still similar to Dan 2:25; 5:13; 6:14 (ET 6:13).

Perhaps the scholarly assumptions and reconstructions are actually pointing us to what the author of the prayer had in mind. If, as I propose, he was basing his work on Daniel 4, he may have sought to call to mind both Daniel 4 and its recapitulation in 5:18–21. However, if the Aramaic Daniel stories in Daniel 2–6 were well known in his circles, he may have felt that he could not name the diviner in his own story, since that would have immediately made his account suspect as a forgery. Therefore he made the diviner very much like Daniel (and

---

[21] E.g., Flusser, "Psalms, Hymns and Prayers," 554.

[22] Jongeling, Labuschagne, and van der Woude, *Aramaic Texts from Qumran with Translations and Annotations*, 124.

[23] Milik, "'Prière de Nabonide' et autres écrits d'un cycle de Daniel," 408, followed by Fitzmyer and Harrington, *A Manual of Palestinian Aramaic Texts*, 2; García Martínez, "The *Prayer of Nabonidus*," 119; Grelot, "La prière de Nabonide (4 Q Or Nab)," 485 (cf. Collins, "4QPrayer of Nabonidus ar," 91).

his story very much like Daniel 4), but he described his leading character as "a Judean" to be even more like one of Daniel's three friends, who are so described in Dan 3:8, 12. He did this to lead his readers to the conclusion that his prayer was a valid account of God's power over pagan kingdoms, since it is very much like Daniel 4 with a hint of Daniel 3. This may suggest that the author of the Prayer of Nabonidus did not intend for his readers to assume that the Jewish diviner in the prayer was Daniel, but rather that he was one of Daniel's three friends: Azariah, Hananiah, or Mishael.

יְקָר וּרְ[בוּ], "Honor and Exalt[ation]" (יקר ור[בו], Section 1, Line 5)

The only verses in Daniel in which these two words occur in close proximity are 4:33 (ET 4:36) and 5:18, which is part of the recapitulation of Daniel 4. In both biblical verses, both nouns are attributed to Nebuchadnezzar or his kingdom as gifts that were given to him by God. However, in the prayer, the king is urged to recognize "honor and exaltation" as qualities belonging to God. As elsewhere,[24] it appears that the author of the Prayer of Nabonidus drew on Daniel but composed a theological hypercorrection so that these qualities belong to God and not to a pagan king. The author of the Prayer of Nabonidus may be attempting in his own way to suggest a reading of Daniel that coincides with his understanding of theological orthodoxy.

Once again, if we follow the reconstruction of García Martínez, יקר ורנבו והד]ר,[25] ("honor, exalt[ation, and glory]," יְקָר וּרְ[בוּ וַהֲדַ]ר), the likelihood that the author of the prayer was drawing on Dan 5:18 is even greater, since all three words occur in Dan 5:18 as a group (although in a different order). This plausible alternative reconstruction lends further confidence to the view that the Prayer of Nabonidus is a later, modified tradition based on the earlier, canonical book of Daniel.

אֱלָהֵי כַסְפָּא וְדַהֲבָא [וְנְחָשָׁא פַּרְזְלָא] אָעָא אַבְנָא חַסְפָּא "Gods of Silver and Gold, [Bronze, Iron,] Wood, Stone, Clay" (אלהי כספא ודהבא [נחשא פרזלא] אעא אבנא חספא, Section 1, Lines 7–8)

Scholars widely recognize that this phrase is similar to Dan 5:4 and 5:23.[26] The sequence כַּסְפָּא־וְדַהֲבָא, "silver and gold," is found in Dan 5:23, whereas the reverse order is in 5:4. A striking feature of this formula is that it occurs in no other texts (of which I am aware) in ancient Judean writings in Aramaic or Hebrew up to the Herodian period. This would seem to argue for some dependence of one text upon the other. Surely it defies the odds (and logic) to assume

---

[24] See also "By a Decree of God" and "Gods of Silver and Gold, [Bronze, Iron,] Wood, Stone, Clay."

[25] García Martínez, "The *Prayer of Nabonidus*," 120.

[26] See, for example, Collins, "Nabonidus, Prayer of," *ABD* 4:977; "4QPrayer of Nabonidus ar," 91.

that two garbled versions of a tradition about Nabonidus' insanity were handed down and diverged into Daniel 5 and the Prayer of Nabonidus but the two managed to retain nearly identical wording for a rare formula naming types of pagan gods. The remarkable similarity between the phrases in both texts requires that one text was copying and modifying the other.

Moreover, an important element of the list of gods in the prayer is missing in Daniel 5, since it nowhere mentions gods of "clay." However, "clay" is mentioned as a constituent element in the statue seen by Nebuchadnezzar in Daniel 2 (2:33, 34, 35, 41 [twice], 42, 43 [twice], 45). The elements that make up this statue are gold, silver, bronze, iron, and clay. Therefore, lines 7 and 8 of the prayer appear to be a conflation of the elements in the statue and of the gods mentioned in Daniel, since gold, silver, bronze, and iron are materials in the statue in Nebuchadnezzar's dream and materials out of which pagan idols were made. Clay is only an element of the statue in the dream, whereas wood and stone are only mentioned as elements from which pagan gods were made. Once again,[27] the prayer appears to be a theological hypercorrection of Daniel. By conflating all the elements of the statue and of the gods, the author of the prayer affirms his radical monotheism and denies that pagan gods possess any power, since they are composed of inert earthly elements. This conflation argues that the direction of borrowing is from Daniel to the Prayer of Nabonidus.

שְׁנִין שְׁבַע, "Seven Years" (שנין שבע, Section 1, Line 3)

One of the striking parallels between Daniel 4 and the Prayer of Nabonidus is the period of the illness of both kings. However, this parallel is not as exact as it might first appear in English translation. In Daniel, Nebuchadnezzar's insanity is said to last וְשִׁבְעָה עִדָּנִין, "seven times" (4:13, 20, 22, 29 [ET 4:16, 23, 25, 32]). While many translations[28] and interpreters[29] have understood this to mean "seven *years*," the text is not necessarily intended to be understood in that way. Throughout Daniel, many predictive time periods are given in general terms,[30] which may indicate that the book did not intend a facile equation of the general time "times" with the specific length "years." We find general predictive periods such as וּבְיוֹמֵיהוֹן דִּי מַלְכַיָּא אִנּוּן, "in the days of those kings" (2:44); זְמָן וְעִדָּן, literally, "a time and a time" (7:12); עִדָּן וְעִדָּנִין וּפְלַג עִדָּן, "a time, times, and half a time" (7:25); שָׁבֻעִים שִׁבְעִים, "seventy weeks" (9:24; in contrast, שָׁבְעִים יָמִים,

---

[27] See also "By a Decree of God" and "Honor and Exalt[ation]."

[28] Beginning with the Old Greek, which has "seven years" in 4:16, 32 (MT 4:13, 29).

[29] For example, Collins interprets the phrase in Daniel 4 as "seven years" and lists Josephus, Jerome, and medieval Jewish commentators as also espousing this interpretation. However, he notes that some patristic writers understood the phrase as "seven seasons" (*Daniel*, 228). See Josephus, *Antiquities*, 10.217, and Jerome, *Commentary on Daniel*, on 4:1 (ET 4:4; Archer, *Jerome's Commentary on Daniel*, 46).

[30] Exceptions are the 1,290 days and 1,335 days in Dan 12:11–12 and the report of Jeremiah's prophecy that the exile would last seventy years (Dan 9:2), a prophecy that certainly did not originate from Daniel.

"weeks days," meaning "seven-day weeks," is used in 10:2–3 for actual time, rather than general predictive time); שָׁבֻעִים שִׁבְעָה וְשָׁבֻעִים שִׁשִּׁים וּשְׁנָיִם, "seven weeks, and sixty-two weeks" (9:25; cf. 9:26); שָׁבוּעַ אֶחָד וַחֲצִי הַשָּׁבוּעַ, literally, "one week and half of a week" (9:27); וּבְיָמִים אֲחָדִים, "in a few days" (11:20); יָמִים, "for some time" (11:33). Thus the prediction and, later, the fulfillment of Nebuchadnezzar's period of insanity lasting "seven times" (4:13, 20, 22, 29 [ET 4:16, 23, 25, 32]) may not be intended specifically as "seven years," but as a general characterization of "seven times" representing a divinely determined time of punishment.[31] Therefore, the "seven years" in the Prayer of Nabonidus bears the telltale sign of being an interpretation and reapplication of Daniel 4 by the author of the prayer.

4QPrNab ar contains only about seventy words, some of them only partially preserved. If one excludes fragment 4, whose preserved lines are all too short to enable sound conclusions, only fifty-six words remain. Of those, the fourteen words discussed above (comprising twenty-five percent of the total intelligible text) have striking parallels with similar wordings and thematic employment in Daniel 2–5. I find it almost impossible to deny that one text must depend on another. While the narrative of the Prayer of Nabonidus is most closely parallel to the account in Daniel 4, the prayer appears to draw on language from a total of four chapters in Daniel. This is strong evidence that the prayer is dependent on Daniel—indeed, that its author actively borrowed from Daniel.

Thus there are a number of indications that the Prayer of Nabonidus was composed in imitation of Daniel, reemploying Danielic vocabulary, hyper-correcting its theology, and interpreting its prophecies. The author of the prayer employed vocabulary and motifs from Daniel 2, 3, 4, and 5, which are all of the Aramaic Babylonian narrative chapters. He refrained from using motifs from Daniel 6, perhaps because it is a narrative concerning a Persian king. If no scholar had already posited the theory that Daniel 4 originated in traditions about Nabonidus, then the Prayer of Nabonidus (4QPrNab ar), when it was discovered, likely would have been seen for what I am proposing it is: a composition that, like the additional material in the Greek versions of Daniel, extended and expanded the Aramaic Daniel narrative.[32] However, scholars with the desire to vindicate the theory that Daniel 4 originated in traditions about Nabonidus (a

---

[31] Note the use of "seven" to signify an ultimate amount in Dan 3:19: "he said to heat the furnace seven times hotter than was normal to heat it." Surely we are not to understand (nor did the ancients understand) that some type of thermodynamic measurement of the heat of the furnace was being taken so that the resulting heat in the furnace was actually seven times that of its normal operating energy. Instead, "seven times" must signify something like "as hot as possible."

[32] Note that most of the major Greek expansions to Daniel—the Prayer of Azariah, the Song of the Three Young Men, and Susanna, which takes place when Daniel was a youth—are also set in the Neo-Babylonian kingdom or are concerned with discrediting Babylonian gods. The concern to discredit Babylonian gods is also evident in Bel and the Dragon, even though it is set in the Persian period. The Prayer of Nabonidus conforms to this tradition of expanding the condemnation of Babylonian (but not Persian) religion in Daniel 2–5.

theory with little hard evidence to support it) quickly seized upon 4QPrNab ar for that purpose. This rush to judgment has blinded scholars to the distinct possibility that the Prayer of Nabonidus does not stem from an earlier tradition that predated Daniel 4, but in fact had its genesis as an adaptation from Daniel.

Additional Implications for Understanding the Prayer of Nabonidus

The second section of 4QPrNab ar is much more difficult to read and interpret because of its more fragmented state. One of the most controverted words is אחלמת ("you gave me a dream") in line 1. This is obviously an Aphel (H) perfect verb form. The corresponding Hebrew Hiphil (H) conjugation of the verb חָלַם, "to dream," occurs in Jer 29:8, where its participle with a pronoun apparently means "you [the unfaithful Judeans] cause [false prophets] to dream." In the Prayer of Nabonidus, Milik translates אחלמת as "I had a dream,"[33] and Meyer zealously defends that meaning.[34] However, Collins, noting that in Syriac the Aphel verb is used in the sense of "to heal," translates the word as "I was made strong."[35] (The Hebrew Hiphil of חָלַם in Is 38:16 is understood by many to mean "heal, make strong.") Collins seems to be assuming that section 2 of 4QPrNab ar narrates the end of Nabonidus' story, when he has already been healed of his affliction.

Given the strong dependence of the prayer on Daniel—especially Daniel 4, where a dream is at the center of the narrative—the meaning "cause to dream" fits best. However, אחלמת is not necessarily a first person form, as previous attempts to read it have assumed. Although the prayer is primarily in the first person, not all of the verbs are first person verbs.[36] אחלמת could be a second person masculine singular form or even a third person feminine singular form. As reflected in my translation above, "you gave me a dream," I propose that it is a second person form, and at this point Nabonidus is addressing God, perhaps as part of his prayer. This would mean that this section of the text is not the end of Nabonidus' story of his affliction (as Collins would have it). Instead, he is relating the effects of his affliction. Such a reading fits better with לא יכלת, "I was not able," in line 3, where Nabonidus may have been speaking of some disability caused by his illness. This would also mean that Collins' reconstruction of the end of line 2 as "the peace of [my] repo[se returned to me]"[37] is mistaken, because he is assuming the wrong context for this line. I propose reconstructing the line as שלם של[ו]תי נשא מן קדמי], "the peace of [my] restfulness [he took from me]."

---

[33] Milik, "Prière de Nabonide," 409.

[34] Meyer, *Das Gebet des Nabonid*, 28.

[35] Collins, "4QPrayer of Nabonidus ar," 92.

[36] Note that Daniel 4, while primarily narrated in the first person, has a short section narrated in the third person (4:25–30 [ET 4:28–33]) and contains some verbs in the second person.

[37] [מנה אחן]לף שלם של[ו]תי יתוב עלי] (Collins, "4QPrayer of Nabonidus ar," 91–92).

Conclusion

An old conundrum asks, "Which came first: the chicken or the egg?" In many ways, the relationship between Daniel 4 and the Prayer of Nabonidus is exactly this kind of conundrum. However, the examination of this particular manifestation of the riddle has been complicated by a prior theory about the origin of Daniel 4. This theory and the desire to vindicate it have prejudiced the discussion of the relationship between Daniel 4 and the prayer ever since the discovery of 4QPrNab ar. However, a close look at the Prayer of Nabonidus reveals a number of features that can fairly be argued to derive from Daniel. I would argue that the weight of the evidence favors the theory that the prayer was written by an author who drew from Daniel as his primary source. Yet we cannot determine whether this author intended to write an independent story similar to those in Daniel, or whether he sought to supplement Daniel and supply a story to fill in the gap between the reign of Nebuchadnezzar and the Persian conquest of Babylon (the gap between Daniel 4 and Daniel 5).

It is not remarkable that Daniel is not mentioned in the surviving fragments of 4QPrNab ar. Perhaps he was mentioned in parts of the document that did not survive. Once again the author may have drawn his inspiration from Daniel 5, where Daniel is first described anonymously (5:11) before being named (5:12). Or perhaps the prayer is not a story about Daniel at all. It may well be a story about one of Daniel's friends, as suggested above.[38] This also would be in harmony with the book of Daniel, since an entire chapter contains a narrative that does not mention Daniel even once (Daniel 3).

García Martínez notes about Daniel 4 and the Prayer of Nabonidus that "apart from the common story the aim of the two narratives is identical, to show the recognition of the uselessness of the false gods and the power of the true God."[39] However, could this not also be said to be the theme of other narratives in Daniel, especially chapters 3, 5, and even 6 (cf. 6:26–28 [ET 6:25–27])? To a lesser extent it could well be said to be a theme in Daniel 1 and 2 (see 1:2, 9, 17, 20 as a group and 2:11, 18–23, 28, 44–45, 47 as a group). Therefore, this theme runs throughout the narrative portions of Daniel (chapters 1–6). The author of the prayer likely recognized this, and (if I am correct) used these narratives, with special focus on Daniel 4, as the primary guide for shaping his story about Nabonidus, even though the initial inspiration for his story may have been an extrabiblical tradition about Nabonidus gleaned from other sources.

This conclusion calls into question the practice of scholars who cite the Prayer of Nabonidus to corroborate their theory that an incident in the life of Nabonidus gave rise to the account of Nebuchadnezzar's insanity in Daniel 4. The more logical conclusion is that Daniel 4 is an independent, original composition that has no relationship to any incident in the life of Nabonidus.

---

[38] See "Judean" above.
[39] García Martínez, "The *Prayer of Nabonidus*," 129.

Excursus

Finally, the evidence suggests that the Prayer of Nabonidus is partly based on Daniel 4 and other texts from Daniel. This is a more likely scenario than the one currently accepted by most scholars. It best explains why a small, fragmented, incomplete text of only seventy words (many of them only partially preserved) has many verbal parallels to Daniel 2–5.

Daniel 4:1–15 (ET 4:4–18)
Nebuchadnezzar Seeks the Meaning of His Dream of the Tree

Translation

4 ¹I, Nebuchadnezzar, was at ease in my house and flourishing in my palace. ²I saw a dream, and it frightened me. The images upon my bed and the visions of my head alarmed me. ³So from me was issued a decree to bring before me all of the wise men of Babylon so that they might make known to me the meaning of the dream. ⁴Then the magicians, the soothsayers, the Chaldeans, and the diviners came, and I told them the dream. However, its meaning they could not make known to me. ⁵Afterward Daniel came before me (whose name is Belteshazzar, like the name of my god, and a spirit of holy gods dwells in him), and I told the dream to him.

⁶"Belteshazzar, chief magician, because I know that a spirit of holy gods dwells in you, and no mystery is too difficult for you, look at my dream that I saw and tell [me] its meaning. ⁷I was seeing the visions of my head upon my bed:

"Behold, a tree [was] in the midst of the earth, and its height was great.

⁸The tree grew and became strong,
    and its height reached to heaven,
    and it was visible to the end of the entire earth.
⁹Its leaves were beautiful and its fruit abundant,
    and food for all was in it.
Under it the beasts of the field had shade,
    and in its branches the birds of the sky dwelt,
    and from it all living creatures fed.
¹⁰"I was watching in the visions of my head upon my bed,
    and behold, a watcher who was a holy one came down from heaven.
¹¹He called out loudly, and this is what he said:
'Chop down the tree and cut off its branches.
    Strip its leaves and scatter its fruit.
Let the beasts flee from under it,
    and the birds from its branches.
¹²However, the stump of its root in the earth leave,
    with a band of iron and brass, with the grass of the field;
and with the dew from the sky let it be wet,
    and with the beasts will be its portion, among the plants of the earth.
¹³Let its heart be changed from that of a human,
    and let a heart of a beast be given to it,
and let seven times pass over it.

¹⁴The decree is an edict of watchers,
   and the matter is a command of holy ones,
so that the living people may know that the Most High rules the human
      kingdom,
   and he gives it to whomever he wishes,
and he appoints the lowliest of humans over it.'

¹⁵"This is the dream that I, King Nebuchadnezzar, saw. Now, you, Belteshazzar, tell me the meaning because none of the wise men of my kingdom are able to make known to me the meaning. But you are able, because a spirit of holy gods is in you."

Textual Notes

4:1 שְׁלֵה הֲוֵית בְּבֵיתִי וְרַעְנַן בְּהֵיכְלִי:—The poetic-style parallelism of these two clauses, "at ease was I in my house, and flourishing [was I] in my palace," emphasizes Nebuchadnezzar's prosperity, tranquility, and apparent security. The adjective רַעְנַן, "flourishing" (*HALOT*), is cognate to the Hebrew רַעֲנָן, which occurs nineteen times in the OT and often describes a verdant tree (e.g., Deut 12:2; 1 Ki 14:23), sometimes as a metaphor for a person (e.g., Pss 52:10 [ET 52:8]; 92:15 [ET 92:14]; cf. Hos 14:9 [ET 14:8]). It may be used here in anticipation of Nebuchadnezzar's depiction as a tree in the dream.

4:3 דִּי־פְשַׁר חֶלְמָא יְהוֹדְעֻנַּנִי:—This purpose clause, literally, "so that the meaning of the dream they might make known to me," uses the noun פְּשַׁר, "meaning," which was common in chapter 2, where Nebuchadnezzar sought the meaning of his dream of the statue. It recurs in 4:4, 6, 15–16, 21 (ET 4:7, 9, 18–19, 24). For it, see the third textual note on 2:4.

4:4 חַרְטֻמַיָּא אָשְׁפַיָּא—For these terms, rendered as "the magicians" and "the soothsayers," see the third textual note on 1:20.

כַּשְׂדָּאֵי—For "the Chaldeans" as a professional term for diviners in the service of the king, see "Daniel among the Wise Men" in "Introduction to Daniel 2," and also the third textual note on 2:2.

וְגָזְרַיָּא—This participle, "(the) diviners," occurred in 2:27 and will recur in 5:7, 11.

4:6 וְכָל־רָז לָא־אָנֵס לָךְ—Literally, "every mystery does not oppress you," this clause with the participle of אֲנַס, "to oppress," is translated as an elliptical comparison: "no mystery is too difficult for you" (so *HALOT*, s.v. אנס; cf. Joüon, § 141 i). For רָז, "mystery," which in Daniel always refers to a revelatory dream, see the second textual note on 2:18.

חֶזְוֵי חֶלְמִי דִי־חֲזֵית וּפִשְׁרֵהּ אֱמַר:—The MT is, literally, "the visions of my dream that I saw, and its meaning—tell." The translation assumes that instead of חֶזְוֵי (the plural of the noun חֱזוּ in construct), the correct reading is the Peal imperative חֲזִי, "look at, see, behold," which is partially supported by Theodotion, which translates, ἄκουσον τὴν ὅρασιν τοῦ ἐνυπνίου οὗ εἶδον καὶ τὴν σύγκρισιν αὐτοῦ εἰπόν μοι, "hear the vision of the dream that I saw, and tell me its meaning." Perhaps חֶזְוֵי here is an assimilation to

וְחֶזְוֵי] at the start of the next verse (4:7 [ET 4:10]).[1] אֱמַר, "tell," could be translated as a purpose clause: "look at my dream that I saw *so that* you can tell [me] its meaning."

4:8: וַחֲזוֹתֵהּ לְסוֹף כָּל־אַרְעָא—If the noun חֲזוֹת, which recurs in the similar clause in 4:17, is derived from the verb חֲזָה, "to see," then it is a synonym of חֵזוּ (e.g., 4:2, 6–7, 10 [ET 4:5, 9–10, 13]), and like it means "appearance, vision." Then this clause is, literally, "its appearance was to the end of all the earth," meaning "it was visible to the end of the entire earth." Another possibility, which has some support from the versions and older interpreters, is that חֲזוֹת refers to the "branches" or "crown" of the tree (*HALOT*, 2).

4:9 חֵיוַת בָּרָא ׀ תְּחֹתוֹהִי תַּטְלֵל—The Haphel (H) verb תַּטְלֵל probably means "find shade," in harmony with the Old Greek (*HALOT*, s.v. טלל II, Haphel, a). The verb is cognate to the common Hebrew noun צֵל, "shade." However, Theodotion and the Vulgate support the meaning "dwell, seek protection" (*HALOT*, s.v. טלל II, Haphel, b), which agrees with the parallel use of the verb שְׁכַן in 4:18 (ET 4:21).[2]

4:10: עִיר וְקַדִּישׁ מִן־שְׁמַיָּא נָחִת—This is, literally, "a watcher and a holy one from heaven came down." The noun עִיר is from the verbal root עוּר, "be awake, alert, aroused," and probably means "a watchman, one who is awake." It occurs in the OT only in Dan 4:10, 14, 20 (ET 4:13, 17, 23). Since the term is used first (and twice) by King Nebuchadnezzar, and Daniel merely repeats it after the king has used it, it may have been a pagan term for angels. Later it became a popular term for angels in Jewish literature from the Hellenistic and Roman periods, including *1 Enoch* 1–36 (especially chapters 10–16; cf. 39:12–13; 71:7); *Testament of Reuben* 5:6–7; *Testament of Naphtali* 3:5; *Jubilees* 4:15, 22; 7:21; 10:5; and several documents from Qumran including the *Genesis Apocryphon* (see Jastrow, s.v. עִיר I). Its English translation survives in Christian usage most notably in J. Athelstan Riley's hymn "Ye Watchers and Ye Holy Ones" (*LSB* 670). Here the term is further defined by וְקַדִּישׁ, "and a holy one." The *waw* is epexegetical, so the phrase means "a watcher *who was* a holy one," and it could also be rendered, "a holy watcher." The angelic identity of this "watcher" is further confirmed by his descent מִן־שְׁמַיָּא, "from heaven," implying that he is a heavenly being.

4:12: בַּעֲשַׂב אַרְעָא—Literally, this is "with the plants of the land." The collective noun עֲשַׂב is often translated "grass," but like its Hebrew cognate עֵשֶׂב, it can refer to a variety of "plants" or "herbage" (*HALOT*, s.v. עֲשַׂב), especially those eaten by people or animals. It recurs in 4:22, 29–30 (ET 4:25, 32–33); 5:21.

Commentary

Nebuchadnezzar Seeks the Meaning of His Dream (4:1–5 [ET 4:4–8])

The notice of Nebuchadnezzar's ease and prosperity is set in contrast to his reaction to the dream: it upset his ease by causing him fear and dread. Note the contrast to his reaction to the dream in Daniel 2. Here the verbs signal fear, whereas in 2:1, 3, the verb פָּעַם indicates consternation, but not fear. This may

---

[1] Collins, *Daniel*, 223; Montgomery, *Daniel*, 228; Goldingay, *Daniel*, 80.

[2] Note that Rosenthal, *A Grammar of Biblical Aramaic*, § 157, equivocates on the meaning.

be the reason why in this case the king does not demand that his wise men first tell him the dream and then its interpretation (as he had demanded in Daniel 2). He is so frightened that he wants to know the meaning immediately, and so he does not challenge his diviners with the task of telling him the contents of the dream first.

"The wise men" in 4:3 (ET 4:6) are further defined as "the magicians, the soothsayers, the Chaldeans, and the diviners" in 4:4 (ET 4:7). This list of occult practitioners is similar to the list in 2:2, except that "the sorcerers" (מְכַשְּׁפִים) there are replaced by "the diviners" (גָּזְרַיָּא) here. The change may simply be due to the difference between Hebrew (2:2) and Aramaic (4:4 [ET 4:7]). In any case, just as in Daniel 2, the "wise men" of Babylon are unable to interpret the dream (cf. 1 Cor 1:19). They may indeed have been able to contact the powers of darkness and attempt to utilize them for their purposes, as the wise men and sorcerers of Egypt did initially (cf. Ex 7:11–12, 22; 8:3, 14–15 [ET 8:7, 18–19]). However, as in Daniel 2, this dream is a revelation from a far higher power: the one true and triune God ("the Most High," 4:14, 21–22, 29, 31 [ET 4:17, 24–25, 32, 34]). His thoughts and plans are inaccessible to the demonic powers, who nevertheless often hold sway over fallen sinners on earth. But God grants his people surpassing wisdom,[a] deliverance from bondage to those powers, and victory over the devil.[b]

Here Daniel does not come before the king together with the pagan diviners who comprise the "wise men" (4:3 [ET 4:6]) of Babylon. Instead, just as in chapter 2, he comes before Nebuchadnezzar only after the wise men fail to interpret the dream. While he is later described as the leader of the wise men (5:11), he is never presented before royalty as merely part of their group.[3]

Nebuchadnezzar gives two pieces of information about Daniel when introducing him to the readers of this letter. First, he tells his readers that Daniel is called "Belteshazzar," after the name of Nebuchadnezzar's god, who was Bel (also called Marduk).[4] Daniel is only called by his Hebrew name twice in this chapter (4:5, 16a [ET 4:8, 19a]), and each time his Babylonian name immediately follows. Elsewhere in the chapter, Daniel is only called by his Babylonian name (4:6; 4:15; twice in 4:16b [ET 4:9, 18, 19b]). In the quotations of Nebuchadnezzar's speech in the chapter, he uses Daniel's Babylonian name exclusively. However, it is clear throughout the book that Daniel prefers his Hebrew name. The fact that his Hebrew name is used twice in this chapter (4:5, 16a [ET 4:8, 19a]) probably demonstrates that Daniel had a great influence on the composition and editing of this letter by Nebuchadnezzar. Daniel, as author of the book that bears his name,[5] could also have been selective in his

(a) Acts 6:10; 1 Cor 1:30; Col 1:9, 28; 2:3

(b) Cf. Mt 10:8; 12:28; Mk 16:17; Rom 16:20; Heb 2:14; 1 Jn 3:8; Revelation 12

---

[3] See further "Daniel among the Wise Men" in "Introduction to Daniel 2," and also the commentary on 2:1–3.

[4] For the meaning of "Belteshazzar," see the second textual note on 1:7.

[5] See further "Date and Authorship according to the Book" in "Date, Authorship, and Unity" in the introduction.

choices of wording and of what portions of the king's speech and decrees to include in the biblical book.

Second, Nebuchadnezzar describes Daniel as a man in whom "a spirit of holy gods dwells" (4:5 [ET 4:8]).[6] None of the pagan king's previous experiences with God's power (evident in chapters 1, 2, and 3) had yet convinced him that the one true God was the only god who existed. Neither had he been led to believe in this God for his salvation.[7] However, his prior experiences did convince him that some divine spirit dwelt in Daniel so that he could solve any mystery and interpret the dream.

The only other person so characterized in Scripture is Joseph, whom Pharaoh says is "a man in whom is a spirit of gods" (אִישׁ אֲשֶׁר רוּחַ אֱלֹהִים בּוֹ, Gen 41:38). That Daniel preserves this comment signals that he is drawing a parallel between Joseph and himself. Both were taken to a foreign land against their will. Both were called before the king to interpret a dream. Both had been successful at dream interpretation when the native wise men failed. Both served in high positions under pagan kings.[8]

Why would Daniel draw this comparison? He wants to emphasize that the God of Israel—who protected Joseph, enabled him to prosper in Pharaoh's court, and eventually led his own people out from bondage in Egypt—was still with his people exiled in Babylon, and eventually would deliver them from bondage there. God's protection of Daniel and Daniel's prosperity demonstrates that, despite the captivity, God is still powerful and effective on behalf of those whom he has chosen to be his own. Ultimately, this points to the "new exodus" theme throughout the OT, which is fulfilled in the "exodus" redemption accomplished by Jesus Christ through his death and resurrection (ἔξοδος, Lk 9:31).

In addition, there is another connection between the account of Joseph's interpretation of Pharaoh's dream and Daniel's interpretation of Nebuchadnezzar's dream: disaster brought by God comes in sevens. Joseph told of "seven years" of low harvests and famine (Genesis 41). Daniel speaks of "seven times" during which God will judge Nebuchadnezzar (Dan 4:13 [ET 4:17]).

Nebuchadnezzar Describes to Daniel the Tree in His Dream (4:6–9 [ET 4:9–12])

A tree was a common symbol of cosmic life and well-being in the ancient Near East. Moreover, a tree is a common metaphor for persons or nations in the OT.[c] The closest parallel is the cedar tree that represents Assyria and to

(c) 2 Ki 14:9–10; Pss 1:3; 37:35–36; 52:10 (ET 52:8); 92:13–16 (ET 92:12–15); Ezek 17:1–4

---

[6] In biblical Aramaic, אֱלָהִין is always a true plural, "gods," and is never understood to be singular. In 4:5, the following plural adjective קַדִּישִׁין, "holy," demonstrates that "gods" is plural here.

[7] See "Literary Artistry Emphasizes God's Miraculous Power to Save" in "Introduction to Daniel 3," and the commentary on 3:24–27 and on 3:28–30.

[8] See further "Daniel and Joseph" in "Connections with Other Old Testament Books" in the introduction.

which the Egyptian pharaoh is compared in Ezekiel 31.⁹ That tree also grew and was tall, was a nesting place for birds, had beasts under it, and provided shade. Like the tree in Nebuchadnezzar's dream, it was cut down because of its pride. Ezekiel's preaching appears to have taken place in mid-587 BC (Ezek 31:1). Since Nebuchadnezzar's dream took place no earlier than 573, it would be possible that Daniel knew of his fellow exile Ezekiel's use of the tree image and understood the parallel to Nebuchadnezzar when interpreting the dream. However, there are significant differences between the descriptions and final outcomes for the trees in Ezekiel and Daniel, so it would be overreaching to state that Daniel was dependent on Ezekiel.

The tree "reached to heaven" (Dan 4:8 [ET 4:11]). To Daniel's original audience of Judean exiles, this would have signaled that the tree represented Babylon and its hubris, since this is parallel to the description of the plan for the tower of Babel (Gen 11:4). Moreover, since the tree "was visible to the end of the entire earth" (Dan 4:8 [ET 4:11]), it represented the prominence of Babylon as a world power. The various nationalities that came under Babylonian dominance are symbolized by the creatures for which it provides food and shelter.

"In its branches the birds of the sky dwelt" (4:9 [ET 4:12]) is similar to the description of the shelter afforded by the kingdom of God in Jesus' parable of the mustard seed (Mt 13:31–32 and parallels). However, Nebuchadnezzar's kingdom merely provided temporal security and physical necessities for earthly life, whereas the kingdom of God brought by Jesus provides eternal life.¹⁰

Nebuchadnezzar Describes the Decree of the Angels in His Dream (4:10–14 [ET 4:13–17])

The second part of Nebuchadnezzar's dream is signaled by a short prose sentence (4:10 [ET 4:13]) that repeats both the phrase "the visions of my head upon my bed" and the interjection וַאֲלוּ, "(and) behold," from 4:7 (ET 4:10), the verse that introduced the first part of the dream.¹¹ Apparently the angelic herald (4:10 [ET 4:13]) addresses other "watchers" (the plural in 4:14 [ET 4:17]) with the decree, since the imperatives "chop down ... strip ... leave" (4:11–12 [ET 4:14–15]) are plural, indicating that other angels are to carry out the decree.¹² The judgment is to fall on every aspect of the tree's majesty: its height, its leaves and fruit, and the creatures that had taken refuge in and under it.

---

⁹ For its interpretation and the cosmic tree motif in the ancient Near East, one may see Hummel, *Ezekiel 21–48*, 909–10, 918–21.

¹⁰ For the kingdom of God in Matthew, one may see Gibbs, *Matthew 1:1–11:1*, 47–51.

¹¹ "The visions of my head" and "upon my bed" were also in 4:2 (ET 4:5).

¹² Compare Genesis 19, where two angels destroy Sodom, and OT passages that refer to destroying angels, such as Ex 12:23; 2 Sam 24:16; Ezek 9:1–8. In the NT, compare Rev 6:1–8; 8:7–9:21; 14:15–16:21.

However, unlike the total destruction of the tree representing Babylon in Ezekiel 31, a special command is given to "leave" the stump (Dan 4:12 [ET 4:15]). This is a sign of hope that the tree might once again sprout and grow (see Is 6:13; 11:1; Job 14:7). Yet, the tree is to be bound "with a band of iron and brass" (Dan 4:12 [ET 4:15]). It is difficult to discern what the purpose of the binding is. Some commentators view it as a reference to the physical or psychological restraints that would be placed on Nebuchadnezzar during his insanity,[13] while others see it as a reassurance to Nebuchadnezzar that he would be preserved through his trial.[14]

At first the decree merely states that the stump will be with the grass, drenched with dew and among the wild animals (4:12 [ET 4:15]). This is clarified in the following verse (4:13 [ET 4:16]), where we are now told that the human mind that the tree originally possessed will be changed to an animal mind. (In the OT, the Hebrew and Aramaic terms for "heart" often refer to mental faculties and so correspond in meaning to the English "mind"; see the textual note on 1:8.) The type of mental illness in which a person thinks he is an animal and behaves accordingly is often called lycanthropy or zoanthropy.[15] The specific malady here is more properly called boanthropy, a human behaving like a bovine.[16] The best known case of this kind of insanity in the modern era was that of King George III of Great Britain.

The change in the main character addressed by the watcher's announcement from a tree (4:11–12 [ET 4:14–15]) to a human (4:13a [ET 4:16a]; cf. also "the human kingdom" in 4:14 [ET 4:17]) to a beast (4:13b [ET 4:16b]) is seen by some critics as the sign of a redactor who wove together two or more traditions and at this point has mistakenly been inconsistent.[17] However, Lucas notes:

> The weakness of such a source-critical solution to a perceived problem is that it fails to explain why a redactor should be more prone to commit a "lapse in literary consistency" than an author would. It seems more likely that the "lapse" here is in fact the result of the author's moving from the image to the actuality (real or imagined) that it portrays.[18]

---

[13] Goldingay, *Daniel*, 89; Hartman and Di Lella, *Daniel*, 176; Keil, *Daniel*, 152; Leupold, *Daniel*, 184; Walvoord, *Daniel*, 103; Young, *Daniel*, 104. This is also, apparently, the interpretation of the Old Greek, which has additional material following 4:14 (ET 4:17) that says that Nebuchadnezzar "was delivered into prison and was bound with chains and bronze handcuffs" (εἰς φυλακὴν παρεδόθη εἰς φυλακὴν παρεδόθη καὶ ἐν πέδαις καὶ ἐν χειροπέδαις χαλκαῖς ἐδέθη).

[14] Baldwin, *Daniel*, 112; Miller, *Daniel*, 133.

[15] Etymologically, "lycanthropy" refers to the illness of a human who behaves like a wolf or dog. It is derived from the Greek λύκος, "wolf," plus ἄνθρωπος, "man, human being." The illness in which a person displays more general behavior like that of any animal is "zoanthropy," from the Greek ζῷον, "animal, creature," plus ἄνθρωπος, "man, human being."

[16] This term derives from the combination of βοῦς, "head of cattle, ox, bull," plus ἄνθρωπος, "man, human being."

[17] E.g., Collins, *Daniel*, 227.

[18] Lucas, *Daniel*, 111.

The "seven times" (וְשִׁבְעָה עִדָּנִין, 4:13 [ET 4:16]) decreed for Nebuchadnezzar is most often understood as seven years.[19] However, there many who hold that the period is purposely vague and ill-defined or, at least, indeterminate.[20] There are at least seven good reasons to think that the simple equation of "times" with "years" is mistaken.

1. It is instructive to note that Daniel has already used "seven" as a number representing completeness or thoroughness (3:19) without it being literal.[21]

2. The duration of the seven times is defined later in this chapter not in terms of years, but in terms of the time it will take for Nebuchadnezzar to acknowledge that God is sovereign over the affairs of humans (4:23 [ET 4:26]).

3. Thus it appears as if "seven" represents the time taken by God to create anew or re-create Nebuchadnezzar's mind and spiritual disposition. This could allude to Genesis 1, in which God accomplished the first creation of the world (and rested) in seven days. This would also be in harmony with biblical themes that describe a spiritual new creation on the eighth day, the first day of a new week (since days were counted inclusively), such as circumcision (incorporation into the redeemed covenant people) on the eighth day (Gen 17:12; Lev 12:3) and Jesus' resurrection on the first day of the new week (Mt 28:1; Mk 16:2; Lk 24:1; Jn 20:1), marking the start of the new creation in Christ (cf. 2 Cor 5:17).

4. When relating the actual events during Nebuchadnezzar's insanity, Daniel tells us that the king was insane "until his hair grew long like [the feathers of] eagles and his nails like [the claws of] birds" (4:30 [ET 4:33]). This did not require a period of seven years, but could easily have transpired within a much shorter period, even within seven months.

5. The Aramaic word "time" (עִדָּן) used in 4:13 (ET 4:16) is used elsewhere by Daniel in an undetermined (but finite) sense (2:8–9, 21; 7:12).

6. Since there are many parallels between Daniel in this account and Joseph, who interpreted Pharaoh's dream as portending two periods of "seven years" (see Genesis 41),[22] we might expect Daniel too to refer to "seven years" when he interprets Nebuchadnezzar's dream. However, when Daniel interprets Nebuchadnezzar's dream, he continues to use the phrase "seven times" (4:22, 29 [ET 4:25, 32]) from 4:13 (ET 4:16), and not "seven years," which we would have expected if the "times" in 4:13 (ET 4:16) really represented years. It seems that Daniel purposely avoids the term "year" (absent from Daniel 4)

---

[19] In antiquity this was the interpretation of the Old Greek version, Josephus, Jerome, and most medieval Jewish commentators (Collins, *Daniel*, 228). See Josephus, *Antiquities*, 10.217; Jerome, *Commentary on Daniel*, on 4:1 (ET 4:4; Archer, *Jerome's Commentary on Daniel*, 46). Among contemporary interpreters it is endorsed by Archer, "Daniel," 61; Collins, *Daniel*, 228; Miller, *Daniel*, 134–35.

[20] Baldwin, *Daniel*, 112; Keil, *Daniel*, 152–53; Leupold, *Daniel*, 185–86 (cf. Calvin, *Daniel*, 1:261, 293–94).

[21] See the commentary on that verse.

[22] For parallels between Daniel in chapter 4 and Joseph, see the commentary on 4:4–8.

when interpreting the dream. By doing so he draws a distinction between his situation and Joseph's.[23]

7. Finally, if the prophecy of "seven times" referred to an exact time period, we might expect Daniel's record of Nebuchadnezzar's letter to refer to this same exact time period that elapsed during his insanity, to confirm that the prophecy was fulfilled. Instead, the king uses the vague phrase (literally) "at the end of the days" (וְלִקְצָת יוֹמַיָּה, 4:31 [ET 4:34]).

For all these reasons, the "seven times" are best taken to refer to an indeterminate, but clearly delimited period of time that was sufficient for God to accomplish his purpose to reform Nebuchadnezzar. It could have been seven years, but it just as easily could have been seven seasons, seven months, or seven periods in an unknown divine reckoning of time needed to re-create Nebuchadnezzar as a contrite and more humble monarch.[24]

The announcement of the watcher states that the judgment on the king is "an edict of watchers" (4:14 [ET 4:17]). The watcher does not explicitly say that the edict came from God. Some critical interpreters construe the announcement to mean that the edict originated independently from that group of angels and not from God. That construal fits the larger assumption by some critics that parts of the book were of pagan origin. Evidence that the announcement was perceived as a problem already in antiquity is furnished by the ancient document called the Prayer of Nabonidus, since it seems to have changed it to "by a decree of God."[25]

However, the OT occasionally depicts God as presiding over a heavenly council and conversing with the angels who are present (Ps 82:1; 1 Ki 22:19–23; cf. Job 1–2). Evidently, the decree came from this council of watchers, which is understood to be under God's authority. It is clear in 1 Ki 22:19–23 that angels may express various proposals, but God has the final authority and makes the final decision about what history shall transpire, and he then decrees what the angels are to do to carry out his will (cf. Heb 1:7, 14). In Job 1–2 Satan enters the company of "the sons of God" (angels; Job 1:6) and proposes malicious actions, but God issues the final decree about what Satan is permitted to do and what he must not do.

---

[23] The only times that Daniel refers to specific numbers of years is with respect to the regnal years of kings (1:1, 21; 2:1; 7:1; 8:1; 9:1–2; 10:1; 11:1), the seventy years prophesied by Jeremiah (9:2), the time he and his companions were assigned to be trained (1:5), and Darius' age (6:1 [ET 5:31]). When Daniel prophesies about periods of "years," the prophecy does not give an exact number, but instead is always vague and ill-defined, requiring שָׁנִים to be translated, "*some* years" (11:6, 8, 13).

[24] See also "שְׁנִין שְׁבַע, 'Seven Years' " in the excursus "Daniel 4 and the Prayer of Nabonidus." The prayer, unlike Daniel 4, refers to a period of "seven years."

[25] See "בִּפְתָגָם אֱלָהָ[א], 'By a Decree of God' " in the excursus "Daniel 4 and the Prayer of Nabonidus."

The assumption that the "watcher" in Dan 4:10 (ET 4:13) and "watchers" in 4:14 (ET 4:17) are merely carrying out a decree that originated with God himself is consistent with the stated purpose of the decree:

> So that the living people may know that *the Most High rules* the human kingdom,
> and *he* gives it to whomever he wishes. (4:14 [ET 4:17b])

It is also consistent with Daniel's explanation of the dream to Nebuchadnezzar, since he explains that "it is a decree of the Most High" (4:21 [ET 4:24]).

The final statement that God appoints "the lowliest of humans" over the human kingdom (4:14 [ET 4:17b]) finds a striking fulfillment in Jesus Christ.[26]

The Wise Men Were Unable to Interpret the Dream (4:4, 15 [ET 4:7, 18])

When we read Nebuchadnezzar's description of his dream (4:7–14 [ET 4:10–17]), we may find it difficult to understand why the Babylonian wise men could not interpret it (4:4, 15 [ET 4:7, 18]). From the king's description, it is clear that the tree represents a person (4:13 [ET 4:16]) who has great influence throughout the world and dominance over others (4:8–9 [ET 4:11–12]). The person depicted by the tree must be a king, since he will be forced by his experience to acknowledge that God, not the king himself, is sovereign and gives kingdoms to whomever he wishes (4:14 [ET 4:17]).

All this pointed to the dream as a prediction of judgment on Nebuchadnezzar. He is the one whom the tree represents. So why did the wise men not understand the dream? Part of the reason may be that they were not familiar with the preaching of Ezekiel to the Judean exiles (as Daniel may have been), since Ezekiel twice used a tree as a symbol for royalty in a lengthy prophecy of judgment (Ezekiel 17 and 31). Nor would they have been familiar with the symbol of a stump as hope for the future that remains despite divine judgment (Is 6:13; 11:1; Job 14:7). Yet, even without this knowledge, it should have been possible for them to piece together the clues in the description of the dream itself.

By recording their failure (as stated by Nebuchadnezzar), Daniel the author is implying that God blinded the pagan wise men so that they were unable to see what was obvious (cf. 1 Sam 2:9; Prov 4:19; 2 Cor 4:4). This leads to another parallel between Daniel and Joseph. The Joseph narratives in Genesis draw a clear distinction between the ability of God's chosen people (Jacob and his children) to interpret dreams and the inability of pagans to do so. When Joseph recounts his dream about sheaves in the field, his brothers do not need anyone to interpret it for them; they immediately recognize its meaning (Gen 37:5–8). Likewise, when Joseph has his dream of the sun, moon, and eleven stars, his father Jacob immediately discerns its meaning without needing any interpreter (Gen 37:9–10).

---

[26] See further "Gospel Themes in Daniel 4" in "Introduction to Daniel 4."

When Joseph arrives in Egypt, he is the only one there who can understand dreams. The metaphorical dreams of the royal cupbearer and baker are not difficult to decipher, but the men cannot understand them (Genesis 40). Similarly, the two dreams of Pharaoh are simple comparisons, but only Joseph can discern their meanings (Genesis 41). In Daniel 4, the dream of Nebuchadnezzar is full of clues as to its meaning, but of all the people in Nebuchadnezzar's court, only the lone Judean who trusts Yahweh can interpret them, because he alone has been enlightened by God instead of blinded by living in darkness and being trained in occult methods of divination. Only Daniel can see the light of God's glory in this dream, because only he is part of the new creation of God. True spiritual knowledge and enlightenment comes only by the grace of the one true and triune God, and simply through faith in him. Christians now see this glory fully in Christ, as Daniel foresaw him from afar (2:44–45; 7:13–14). "For God, who said, 'From darkness let light shine,' has shone in our hearts to give the enlightenment of the knowledge of the glory of God in the face of Jesus Christ" (2 Cor 4:6).[d]

(d) Cf. 2 Sam 22:29 ‖ Ps 18:29 (ET 18:28); Is 50:10; 60:2–3; Ps 112:4; Jn 8:12; 12:46; Eph 5:8; Col 1:13–14; 1 Thess 5:5; 1 Pet 2:9; 1 Jn 1:5

Nebuchadnezzar's Charge to Daniel (4:15 [ET 4:18])

Much of 4:15 (ET 4:18) reproduces information from earlier in the narrative. Although the reader has already been told these things (see the commentary on 4:4–5 [ET 4:7–8]), this is the first time that Daniel was told that the wise men could not interpret the dream and the first time that Nebuchadnezzar states his reason for trusting that Daniel can explain its meaning.

Daniel 4:16–24 (ET 4:19–27)

Daniel Explains Nebuchadnezzar's Dream of the Tree

Translation

4 ¹⁶Then Daniel, whose name was Belteshazzar, was appalled for a moment, and his thoughts alarmed him. The king said, "Belteshazzar, do not let the dream and its meaning alarm you."

Belteshazzar answered, "My lord, [if only] the dream were about your enemies and its meaning about your foes!

¹⁷"The tree that you saw, which grew and became strong,
 and its height reached to heaven,
 and it was visible to the entire earth,
¹⁸and its leaves were beautiful and its fruit abundant,
 and food for all was in it;
under it the beasts of the field dwelt,
 and in its branches the birds of the sky dwelt—
¹⁹you are it, Your Majesty,
 for you have grown, and you have become great,
and your greatness has grown and reached to heaven,
 and your dominion to the end of the earth.
²⁰And because you saw, Your Majesty,
 a watcher and a holy one coming down from heaven,
and he said, 'Chop down the tree and destroy it;
however, the stump of its root in the earth leave,
 with a band of iron and brass, with the grass of the field;
and with the dew from the sky let it be wet,
 and with the beasts of the field will be its portion,
until seven times pass over it,'

²¹this is the meaning, Your Majesty: It is a decree of the Most High that has come upon my lord, Your Majesty. ²²So you will be driven away from humans, and your dwelling with be with the beasts of the field. And you will be fed plants like bulls [are fed], and you will be wet with the dew from the sky. And seven times will pass over you until you know that the Most High rules the human kingdom, and he gives it to whomever he wishes. ²³And because they said to leave the stump of the root of the tree, your kingdom will remain yours when you know that Heaven rules.

²⁴"Therefore, Your Majesty, let my advice be pleasing to you: break away from your sins with righteousness and from your iniquities by showing mercy to the poor. Perhaps your prosperity will be prolonged."

Textual Notes

4:16 אֶשְׁתּוֹמַם֙ כְּשָׁעָ֣ה חֲדָ֔ה—The Hebrew verb שָׁמֵם is common in forms meaning "be devastated" or "be appalled." This cognate Aramaic verb, שְׁמַם, occurs only here in the OT, and its Ithpoel (HtG) stem likewise means "be appalled" (*HALOT*). The NIV's rendering, "perplexed," is not correct. We are not being told that Daniel was perplexed by the dream, but that he was appalled that he had to tell the powerful Nebuchadnezzar that God was going to judge him. The following clause in 4:16 (ET 4:19), וְרַעְיֹנֹ֖הִי יְבַהֲלֻנֵּ֑הּ, "and his thoughts alarmed him," clarifies this. Daniel uses the corresponding Hebrew Hithpoel (HtD) וָאֶשְׁתּוֹמֵ֖ם, "I was appalled," in 8:27, when he sees the vision that reveals the coming persecution of his people by Antiochus IV Epiphanes (175–164 BC).

4:17 וַחֲזוֹתֵ֖הּ לְכָל־אַרְעָֽא—See the textual note on 4:8 (ET 4:11), where Nebuchadnezzar's description had the similar but longer clause וַחֲזוֹתֵ֕הּ לְס֖וֹף כָּל־אַרְעָֽא. ס֖וֹף ("end") is absent here in Codex Leningradensis (the base text for *BHS*), and it is not reflected in Theodotion. However, many other Masoretic manuscripts have the same reading here as in the king's description. While it is difficult to decide, the shorter reading in Codex Leningradensis is probably to be preferred, and the longer reading is probably the result of assimilation to 4:8 (ET 4:11) and perhaps also to the last clause of 4:19, which includes לְס֖וֹף.

4:20 The end of this verse condenses and omits some of the clauses that were in the king's longer description in 4:12b–13. See the commentary on 4:20 (ET 4:23).

4:22 וְלָ֣ךְ טָֽרְדִ֣ין מִן־אֲנָשָׁ֗א—Literally, "(to) you they are driving away from men," this clause illustrates the common Aramaic use of the preposition לְ to introduce what semantically is the direct object ("you")[1] and the typical Aramaic use of an impersonal plural verb (the participle טָֽרְדִ֣ין) that is best rendered as a passive, with the object as its subject: "you will be driven away."[2] Such impersonal plural verbs are especially common when there is an implication that the action is done ultimately by God or in accord with his will. See also the next textual note.

וְעִשְׂבָּ֤א ׀ כְתוֹרִין֙ לָ֣ךְ יְטַעֲמ֔וּן—Literally, "and grass like bulls to you they will feed," this is best translated as a passive: "you will be fed plants like bulls [are fed]." The Aramaic תּוֹר, like its Hebrew cognate שׁוֹר, denotes a "bull" (*HALOT*). Many translations have "ox," but that can be misleading since "ox" in English often denotes a castrated male bovine, and castration is not in view here.

4:24 וַחֲטָאָךְ֙ בְּצִדְקָ֣ה פְרֻ֔ק—Literally, "and your sin with righteousness break off," this is translated, "break away from your sins with righteousness." Based on the cognate Hebrew verb פָּרַק, the Aramaic verb פְּרַק probably has the more forceful meaning "tear away, break off" (BDB) or even "destroy" (*HALOT*, 1) instead of just "remove, wipe away" (*HALOT*, Peal). The בְּ on בְּצִדְקָה is instrumental. Instead of rendering בְּצִדְקָה with a term for "righteousness," both the Old Greek (which has a much longer text) and Theodotion have ἐν ἐλεημοσύναις, "by almsgiving," an interpretation followed by the

---

[1] See Steinmann, *Fundamental Biblical Aramaic*, 308; Rosenthal, *A Grammar of Biblical Aramaic*, § 182.

[2] See Rosenthal, *A Grammar of Biblical Aramaic*, § 181.

Syriac and the Vulgate. The following parallel phrase, including "mercy to the poor" (see the next textual note), probably influenced the Greek translations. In the Hebrew OT, the cognate צְדָקָה usually refers to "righteousness," that is, a holy and acceptable condition before God as he imputes his own holiness and righteousness to the believer through faith. By metonymy it can also refer to "righteous deeds" done by God that display his righteousness or done by believers as the fruit of faith (see BDB, s.v. צְדָקָה, 7). Such righteous actions can include almsgiving, and in postbiblical Hebrew צְדָקָה often has that more specific meaning (see Jastrow). Here, however, it must mean *righteousness in the heart that leads to good deeds*. Biblical and Christian theology affirms that God's gift of righteousness imputed through faith has the result that the believer does good works pleasing to God (Ap IV 262; see also, e.g., AC VI; Ap IV 122–82; FC Ep and SD IV and VI).

Ben Sira 3:30 seems to be a paraphrase of Daniel's counsel to Nebuchadnezzar in Dan 4:24 (ET 4:27), and its dependence on Daniel helps confirm the antiquity of the biblical book of Daniel. See further "Ben Sira 3:30 (from Daniel 4:24 [ET 4:27])" in "Date, Authorship, and Unity" in the introduction, which also gives further attention to the way Ben Sira and the Greek versions handled the verb פְּרֻק.

וַעֲוָיָתָךְ בְּמִחַן עֲנָיִן—The imperative פְּרֻק in the preceding clause carries over to this one: "[and break away from] your iniquities by showing mercy [to] poor people." The preposition בְּ on מִחַן (the infinitive of חֲנַן) indicates means: "by showing …"

Commentary

Daniel's Reaction (4:16 [ET 4:19])

Daniel's reaction to the dream is immediate and apparently is visible to Nebuchadnezzar. Daniel knows that the dream portends judgment on the king for his arrogance, but he is reluctant to inform the monarch. Considering Nebuchadnezzar's volatile temper and violent punishments of those who anger him (2:12; 3:19–22), this is understandable. However, Nebuchadnezzar, sensing Daniel's unease, coaxes him to reveal the meaning of the dream.

Even when prevailed upon by the king to divulge the significance of the dream, Daniel is cautious to distance himself from its message of judgment. He demonstrates his loyalty to the king by wishing the judgment had fallen on Nebuchadnezzar's enemies. This kind of wish, used elsewhere in the OT (1 Sam 25:26; 2 Sam 18:32), is a subtle signal that the dream does not bear good news for the Babylonian ruler.

Daniel Explains the Meaning of the Tree (4:17–19 [ET 4:20–22])

Daniel begins by repeating almost word for word the king's description of the tree in 4:7–9. The only differences are these:

1. The tree is visible "to the entire earth" instead of "to the end of the entire earth" (see the textual note on 4:17 [ET 4:20]).
2. The addition of a *waw* that connects "leaves" to the previous material (4:18 [ET 4:21]; cf. 4:9 [ET 4:12]).

3. The animals dwelt (תְּדוּר, 4:18 [ET 4:21]) under the tree instead of finding shade (תַּטְלֵל, 4:9 [ET 4:12]) there.
4. A different verb is used for the birds "living" in the tree: יִשְׁכְּנָן in 4:18 (ET 4:21) instead of יְדוּרָן in 4:9 (ET 4:12).
5. The final clause of Nebuchadnezzar's description, "and from it all living creatures fed" (4:9 [ET 4:12]), is omitted.

It would appear as if Daniel is being careful to follow the king's description to help ensure that the king regards his interpretation as valid. Daniel's attention to detail might reflect his experience in chapter 2, where the king required him first to recount the dream itself (which he had not told Daniel) to guarantee that the interpretation too (as well as the contents of the dream) was given to Daniel by divine revelation.

Just as Nebuchadnezzar inserted the repetitious "I was watching in the visions of my head upon my bed, and behold" (4:10a [ET 4:13a]) between his description of the tree and the decree of the watchers, so Daniel, after his third-person description of the tree, begins his second-person address with "you are it, Your Majesty," and identifies the tree as representing the king (4:19 [ET 4:22]) before he elaborates the divine decree (4:20–23 [ET 4:23–26]). Daniel includes enough complimentary explanation in 4:19 (ET 4:22) so as to avoid unnecessarily arousing the king's wrath. Unlike his description of this event years later, when he will describe this tree as representing not only Nebuchadnezzar but also his arrogance (5:20), here he does not refer directly to Nebuchadnezzar's hubris, but leaves that part of the description implied by the tree imagery (cf. Is 2:12–13; 10:33–34; Ezekiel 31).[3] Daniel's diplomatic language enables him to continue to speak with Nebuchadnezzar, to challenge him to repent and reform (Dan 4:24 [ET 4:27]), and ultimately to lead the king to appreciate (to some degree) God's sovereignty.

---

[3] Collins notes that at this point the Old Greek version contains a condemnation of the king for his arrogance and for the destruction of the temple in Jerusalem. Given Belshazzar's condemnation by Daniel in Daniel 5, Collins finds it remarkable that Nebuchadnezzar is not condemned in the MT at this point in chapter 4. Collins takes this as an indication that behind Daniel 4 lay a story about Nabonidus (*Daniel*, 229). However, Collins fails to appreciate the difference between Daniel 4 and Daniel 5.

In chapter 4, Daniel is dealing with a king whom God had used to execute his righteous judgment on Jerusalem. This king had promoted Daniel to serve within his royal court (Daniel 2), and he would continue to serve this king loyally, yet without compromising God's Word and message to the king. These are reasons why Daniel shows respect for Nebuchadnezzar and avoids arousing his anger. The way in which Daniel interacts with the king in chapter 4 is no indication that behind the text lay an account about Nabonidus. Instead, the biblical text shows that chapter 4 is a narrative about a king with whom Daniel had a close and respectful relationship. Nebuchadnezzar is the only Babylonian king with whom Daniel had such a relationship.

In chapter 5, Daniel is dealing with a king who has no relationship with him and who (Daniel knows) will not be ruling over him for long. This king has openly flaunted his contempt for Israel's God. For these reasons Daniel expresses more direct condemnation toward Belshazzar than he did toward Nebuchadnezzar.

Daniel Recounts the Decree of the Holy Watcher (4:20 [ET 4:23])

As he did with the description of the tree, Daniel also repeats Nebuchadnezzar's description of the decree of the watcher (4:10b–14) in 4:20 (ET 4:23). He expounds its meaning for the king in 4:21–23 (ET 4:24–26). However, in recounting the watcher Daniel omits much more of Nebuchadnezzar's description than he did for the tree. While a few of the omissions are minor, there are two major omissions and changes:

1. Instead of describing in detail the destruction of the tree—its branches, leaves, and fruit—and the scattering of the animals and birds (4:11 [ET 4:14]), Daniel simply substitutes "destroy it" (4:20 [ET 4:23]).
2. Nebuchadnezzar's transformation from having a human mind to an animal mind (4:13 [ET 4:16]) is omitted.
3. Daniel, in his explanation of the decree, will tell Nebuchadnezzar that he will be restored to his rule when he acknowledges God's rule (4:22–23 [ET 4:25–26]), but Daniel does not mention the additional revelation to Nebuchadnezzar in 4:14 (ET 4:17) that God appoints "the lowliest of humans" to rule over the human kingdom.[4]

Daniel is, therefore, continuing his diplomatic language. He avoids repeating some things whose application should now be obvious to the king. A lack of tact by Daniel at this point could cause the king to refuse to listen to Daniel's exhortation to repentance (4:24 [ET 4:27]) or cause him to become infuriated. Therefore, Daniel abbreviates the long description of the tree's destruction, sparing the king as much embarrassment before his courtiers as possible. Probably for the same reason Daniel mentions that the king will live with the animals, but he omits a direct reference to his insanity (the loss of his human mind). Finally, by not repeating that God gives the kingdom to the lowliest of humans, Daniel avoids the equation of Nebuchadnezzar with a lowly person, thereby preserving Nebuchadnezzar's royal honor.

Daniel Explains the Meaning of the Decree of the Watcher (4:21–23 [ET 4:24–27])

Daniel begins his interpretation with another change that subtly reinforces a key theological point: God is in charge.[5] Instead of referring to the singular "watcher" in 4:10 (ET 4:13) or the plural "watchers" in 4:14 (ET 4:17), Daniel directly tells Nebuchadnezzar that the judgment "is a decree of the Most High" (4:21 [ET 4:24]; cf. also 4:22 [ET 4:25]). Daniel thus confesses the truth that there is only one God. He speaks from his monotheistic viewpoint without offending the king, while at the same time hoping to move him away from his

---

[4] See "Gospel Themes in Daniel 4" in "Introduction to Daniel 4."

[5] This is a major theme of the book as a whole. See "Theological Threats Posed by the Critical Dating of Daniel" in "Date, Authorship, and Unity," and "The Messiah in Daniel: An Overview" and "God as the Protector of His People" in "Major Themes" in the introduction. See also the commentary on 2:27–30, 34–35, 44–45 and 7:9–14.

pagan assumptions. The king may have interpreted the "watcher" and "watchers" not as angelic beings, but as gods. Unfortunately, however, it is clear from Nebuchadnezzar's references to the "gods" (in the letter that he composed after his restoration to sanity and to his throne) that he did not abandon his pagan beliefs. He equated the third person of the Trinity, God the Holy Spirit, with "a spirit of holy gods" (4:5–6, 15 [ET 4:8–9, 18]).[6]

The interpretation continues with a brief description of Nebuchadnezzar's coming insanity and a reminder that it will last until the king acknowledges God's absolute rule instead of his own. The time of Nebuchadnezzar's insanity is once again said to be "seven times" (4:22 [ET 4:25]). Here Daniel had an opportunity to clarify what was meant by "times" but did not, reinforcing the notion that the period is ordained by God for reforming the king—an indeterminate but finite length of time (see the commentary on 4:10–14 [ET 4:13–17]).

Finally, Daniel interprets the stump and gives Nebuchadnezzar some hope by telling him that it means that he can retain the kingdom when he knows that Heaven rules (4:23 [ET 4:26]). It should be noted that Daniel does not mention the iron and brass band on the stump (4:12 [ET 4:15]). Since Daniel has avoided details that would embarrass Nebuchadnezzar, this may indicate that the metal band represented physical restraints that would have to be used on the king to control him during his insanity (see the commentary on 4:10–14 [ET 4:13–17]). Daniel conveniently avoids the subject of the band on the stump, and Nebuchadnezzar is not anxious to explore its meaning with him.

Daniel's Exhortation to Nebuchadnezzar (4:24 [ET 4:27])

Daniel's exhortation to the king is designed to bring him to repentance. It is a forceful word of Law and Gospel. The prophet does not shrink from forthrightly calling the king's attention to "your sins" and "your iniquities" and his need to "break away from" them. These indicate the second use of the Law: to convict the sinner of his sin and need for forgiveness by God. Daniel states that the cure by which this sin can be removed is God's gift of imputed "righteousness."[7] This gift would bring about a change in his arrogant attitude that would be demonstrated by righteous deeds, especially with "showing mercy to the poor." Throughout Scripture, God calls his people to give evidence of their repentance and faith by caring for the poor and disadvantaged.[a] Indeed, Jesus issued such a call to a rich man who wanted to follow him (Mt 19:21). Showing mercy to the poor reflects God's own generosity toward all. If the king would do this, it would be a tacit acknowledgement that he himself is no better before God than the lowliest of the poor. Indeed, all people are mere beggars before God.[8]

(a) E.g., Ex 23:11; Deut 15:11; Zech 7:10; Prov 14:21; 19:17; Lk 14:13; Rom 15:26; Gal 2:10; cf. Amos 8:4–6; Ps 41:2 (ET 41:1); Esth 9:22; Lk 19:8

---

[6] See further "Gospel Themes in Daniel 4" in "Introduction to Daniel 4."

[7] See the first textual note on 4:24 (ET 4:27) and also "Gospel Themes in Daniel 4" in "Introduction to Daniel 4."

[8] This was acknowledged by Luther on his deathbed (see AE 54:476).

The exhortation to repentance, the offer of righteousness through faith, and the call for resulting good works are accompanied by a possible (but not certain) temporal reward: "perhaps your prosperity will be prolonged" (4:24 [ET 4:27]). The prophets often include the offer of a reprieve from punishment if people repent (e.g., Amos 5:15; Joel 2:14). However, the king persisted in his arrogance (Dan 4:24 [ET 4:27]), and the prophecy of judgment in his dream was fulfilled. Nevertheless, God displays the enormity of his mercy when he later does restore the king to his throne and glory (4:33–34 [ET 4:36–37]). This does not necessarily mean that Nebuchadnezzar was converted to saving faith. God can bestow temporal rewards on unbelievers through their exercise of human reason, as the Lutheran Confessions affirm (Ap IV 24–25). What is evident from the king's letter is that God humbled the monarch so that he recognized that even kings are lowly before God, "the Most High … who lives forever" (4:31 [ET 4:34]). Just as God has the authority to exalt the lowliest of people (4:14 [ET 4:17]), so also no one can question or thwart his ability to humble the arrogant (4:32, 34 [ET 4:35, 37]).

The Apology of the Augsburg Confession cites Daniel 4 as a Scripture passage that shows that salvation is through faith. It also takes the view that Nebuchadnezzar was brought to saving faith through the prophetic preaching of Daniel. Its discussion of Daniel's ministry and theology is worth quoting at length (Ap IV 261–68):

> In Daniel's sermon [4:24 (ET 4:27)] faith is required. Daniel did not only mean to say that the king should give alms, but he includes all of penitence when he says, "Redeem your iniquities by showing mercy to the oppressed," that is, redeem your sins by changing your heart and works. This presupposes faith. Daniel proclaimed many things to the king about the one God of Israel and converted him not only to the giving of alms but rather to faith. For there is the king's excellent confession about the God of Israel, "There is no other God who can save this way" (Dan. 3:29). Daniel's sermon [4:24 (ET 4:27)] contains two parts. One part instructs about the new life and its works. In the other part Daniel promises the king forgiveness of sins. This promise of the forgiveness of sins is not the preaching of the law, but a truly prophetic and evangelical voice which Daniel surely wanted to be received by faith. Daniel knew that the forgiveness of sins in the Christ was promised not only to the Israelites but to all nations. Otherwise he could not have promised the king forgiveness of sins. … In his own language Daniel's words speak even more clearly about complete penitence and bring out the promise, "Redeem your sins by righteousness and your iniquities by favor to the poor." These words deal with the total scope of penitence. They command him to become righteous, then to do good and to defend the poor against injustice, as was the king's duty.
>
> Righteousness is faith in the heart. Sins are redeemed by penitence, that is, the obligation or debt is removed because God forgives those who are penitent, as is written in Ezek. 18:21, 22. We are not to reason from this that God forgives because of the works that follow or because of alms, but because of his promise he forgives those who take hold of that promise. They do not

take hold of it unless they truly believe and by faith conquer sin and death. Reborn in this way, they bring forth fruits worthy of penitence, as John the Baptist says (Matt. 3:8). The promise is therefore added (Dan. 4:27 [MT 4:24]), "Behold, there will be a healing of your offenses." ...

[The word "redeem"] signifies that the forgiveness of sins is possible, that sins can be redeemed, that the obligation or debt can be removed, that the wrath of God can be stilled. Everywhere our opponents omit the promises and look only at the commandments, adding to them the human theory that forgiveness depends upon works. The text does not say this, but rather requires faith. Wherever there is a promise, there faith is required. Only faith can accept a promise.

In human eyes, works are very impressive. Human reason naturally admires them; because it sees only works and neither looks at nor understands faith, it dreams that the merit of these works brings forgiveness of sins and justification. This legalistic opinion clings by nature to the minds of men, and it cannot be driven out unless we are divinely taught. The mind must be turned from such fleshly opinions to the Word of God. We see that the Gospel and the promise of Christ are presented to us. We must not reject the promise of Christ when the law is preached and works are enjoined. We must first take hold of the promise so that we may be able to do good and that our works may be pleasing to God, as Christ says (John 15:5), "Apart from me you can do nothing." If Daniel had said, "Redeem your sins by penitence," our opponents would have passed over this passage. He uses other words to express this same thought, and our opponents immediately twist his words to mean the very opposite of the teaching of grace and faith, while Daniel most emphatically wants to include faith.

This, then, is how we reply to the words of Daniel: Since he is preaching penitence he is teaching not only about works but about faith as well, as the narrative in the text shows. Secondly, because Daniel clearly sets forth a promise, he necessarily requires faith, which believes that God freely forgives sins. Although he mentions works in connection with penitence, therefore, Daniel does not say that by these works we merit the forgiveness of sins. Daniel is not speaking about remission of punishment alone, because it is vain to seek remission of punishment unless the heart first receives remission of guilt. If our opponents understand Daniel as referring only to remission of punishment, this text proves nothing against us, because then they will have to grant that first come forgiveness of sins and justification without works. Afterwards, as we readily admit, the punishments that chasten us are lightened by our prayers and good works, indeed by our complete penitence, according to the words, "If we judged ourselves, we would not be judged by the Lord" (I Cor. 11:31); "If you are converted, I will convert you" (Jer. 15:19); "Return to me and I will return to you" (Zech. 1:3); "Call upon me in the day of trouble" (Ps. 50:15).

Daniel 4:25–34 (ET 4:28–37)

Nebuchadnezzar's Dream of the Tree Is Fulfilled

Translation

4 ²⁵(All this came upon King Nebuchadnezzar. ²⁶At the end of twelve months he was walking on the palace of his kingdom in Babylon. ²⁷The king said, "Isn't this the great Babylon that I built for a royal residence by the might of my power and for the glory of my majesty?" ²⁸While the word was still in the king's mouth, a voice came down from heaven, "It is spoken to you, King Nebuchadnezzar: The kingdom has passed away from you. ²⁹You will be driven away from humans, and your dwelling will be with the beasts of the field. Grass will be fed to you like [grass is fed to] bulls, and seven times will pass over you until you know that the Most High rules the human kingdom, and he gives it to whomever he wishes." ³⁰Immediately the word was fulfilled against Nebuchadnezzar, and he was driven from humans. So he ate grass like bulls, and his body was wet with the dew of the sky until his hair grew long like [the feathers of] eagles and his nails like [the claws of] birds.)

³¹At the end of the time, I, Nebuchadnezzar, lifted my eyes to heaven, and my reason returned to me.

So I blessed the Most High,
and I praised and glorified the One who lives forever,
because his dominion is an eternal dominion
and his kingdom [lasts] forever and ever.
³²All of the inhabitants of the earth are considered nothing,
and he does as he wishes with the army of heaven and the inhabitants of the earth.
So there is no one who can stay his hand and say to him, "What have you done?"

³³At that time my reason returned to me, and for the honor of my kingdom my splendor and glory returned to me. So my counselors and nobles sought me, I was reinstated over my kingdom, and surpassing greatness was added to me. ³⁴Now, I, Nebuchadnezzar, praise, exalt, and honor the King of heaven, because all his works are true and his ways are just. All who walk in arrogance he is able to humble.

Textual Notes

4:29–30 Most of the vocabulary in these verses is repeated from 4:12–13, 20, 22 (ET 4:15–16, 23, 25).

4:29 וּמִן־אֲנָשָׁא לָךְ טָרְדִין ... עִשְׂבָּא כְתוֹרִין לָךְ יְטַעֲמוּן—The impersonal plural verbs are, literally, "from men *they are driving* away ... grass like bulls to you *they will* *feed*," but they are rendered as passives: "You will be driven away from humans. … Grass will be fed to you like [grass is fed to] bulls." Aramaic often uses impersonal plurals as passives,[1] especially when divine agency is implied: God is the ultimate cause of the actions.

In 4:30 (ET 4:33), the fulfillment of the first clause is described by the singular passive form of the same verb as used here: וּמִן־אֲנָשָׁא טְרִיד, literally, "and from men *he was driven*." The fulfillment of the second clause is described with a singular active form of a different verb: וְעִשְׂבָּא כְתוֹרִין יֵאכֻל, literally, "and grass like bulls *he ate*."

4:30 בַּהּ־שַׁעֲתָא—This phrase, literally, "in it—the moment," is also used in 3:6, 15 and 5:5. Here, as in 3:6, 15, it is translated by the adverb "immediately."

כְּנִשְׁרִין—This is "like eagles." The noun נְשַׁר, like its Hebrew cognate נֶשֶׁר, signifies any large soaring bird of prey or carrion eater. While the majority of translations have "eagles," as does the translation above, the word also includes vultures of various kinds.[2]

4:31 וְלִקְצָת יוֹמַיָּה—Literally, "at the end of the days," this refers to the conclusion of the "seven times" (see the commentary on 4:13 [ET 4:16]) that constituted the appointed time period, so it is translated, "at the end of the time."

דִּי שָׁלְטָנֵהּ שָׁלְטָן עָלַם וּמַלְכוּתֵהּ עִם־דָּר וְדָר׃—This doxology is similar to 3:33b (ET 4:3b). See the second textual note on 3:33.

4:32 וּכְמִצְבְּיֵהּ עָבֵד בְּחֵיל שְׁמַיָּא—Literally, this is "and as he wishes he does with the army of heaven." וּכְמִצְבְּיֵהּ is the Peal (G) infinitive of צְבָה, "to desire, wish, will," and the form here with כְּ and the third masculine singular suffix can be rendered, "according to his will" (*HALOT*, s.v. צבה, 2).

The Aramaic construct phrase חֵיל שְׁמַיָּא is often translated, "the host of heaven," as is the equivalent Hebrew phrase צְבָא הַשָּׁמַיִם (e.g., Dan 8:10). While "host" derives from Latin *hostis*, "stranger, enemy," modern English speakers may not recognize its military connotation, so "army" is preferable. The Aramaic noun חַיִל, like its Hebrew cognate חַיִל, can mean "strength, might," and by extension, "army" (*HALOT*, 2). This is the only OT verse that uses חַיִל in reference to "the army of heaven," whereas צְבָא הַשָּׁמַיִם is common in the OT (see the commentary on 8:10).

4:33 וְעַל־מַלְכוּתִי הָתְקְנַת—The Aramaic verb תְּקַן occurs only here in the OT but is common in rabbinic literature in active forms meaning "establish" and "set in order," and passive forms meaning "be established" (Jastrow). Likewise, its Hebrew cognate, תָּקַן occurs in Rabbinic Hebrew with active meanings that include "repair" and "establish" and passive meanings that include "restored" (Jastrow). As pointed in the MT, הָתְקְנַת is the Hophal (Hp) third feminine perfect, "she was established, restored." The (suffixed) feminine noun מַלְכוּתִי, "my kingdom," could be the grammatical subject ("my kingdom was restored"), but that would leave unexplained the initial preposition וְעַל־, "and over …" Some interpreters propose adding a suffix to the preposition to form וְעֲלַי, yielding "and *to me* my kingdom was restored." The alternative followed by the

---

[1] See Rosenthal, *A Grammar of Biblical Aramaic*, § 181.

[2] *Fauna and Flora of the Bible*, 82–84.

translation above is to repoint the final syllable of the verb to הָתְקְנֵת, a first person singular Hophal (Hp) perfect, literally, "and over my kingdom *I* was restored."

Commentary
Daniel's Insertion in the Letter (4:25–30 [ET 4:28–33])

Nebuchadnezzar's letter quotes Daniel's recounting of and interpretation of the dream (4:17–23 [ET 4:20–26]) and his exhortation for the king to repent and receive righteousness (4:24 [ET 4:27]). Now Daniel the narrator inserts into the king's letter a short description of how the dream was fulfilled (4:25–30 [ET 4:28–33]). In general, the official writings of ancient Near Eastern monarchs were intended to glorify the throne. It would have been completely out of character for arrogant King Nebuchadnezzar to relate such an embarrassing period in his life. Even if he, after being humbled (4:34 [ET 4:37]), had wished to relate it, he may well have not remembered it once he recovered. For all these reasons, it is not surprising that Daniel had to supply the facts for his readers by means of an insertion into this letter.[3]

Nebuchadnezzar's insanity strikes one year after the dream (4:26 [ET 4:29]). Daniel emphasizes that the king was in Babylon, a detail that seems unneeded. (Where else would the palace be?) However, this is Daniel's way of tying the setting of the fulfillment of the dream to the place where the dream was first received (4:1 [ET 4:4]), implying that Nebuchadnezzar had twelve more months during which he continued to be "at ease … and flourishing" (4:1 [ET 4:4]) in his palace in Babylon. At any time during this full year, he could have followed Daniel's exhortation to repent and receive righteousness (4:24 [ET 4:27]). God was more than patient with the king!

However, Nebuchadnezzar retained his arrogance. His rhetorical question to himself demonstrates his self-centered hubris: "Isn't this the great Babylon that *I* built for a royal residence by the might of *my* power and for the glory of *my* majesty?" (4:27 [ET 4:30]).[4] Nebuchadnezzar is known to have built and beautified Babylon and is credited with the construction of the famous Hanging Gardens, which were a present to his Median wife to remind her of her mountainous homeland. The problem with Nebuchadnezzar was his arrogance in taking credit for this without acknowledging that God had given him the office of king and had also given him all the power and abilities he possessed.[5] He did not undertake these projects for the good of his people, much less for the glory of the God whose surpassing power to save his people had been demon-

---

[3] See further "The Genuineness of Nebuchadnezzar's Letter" in "Introduction to Daniel 4."

[4] Mastin, "The Meaning of $H^a l\bar{a}$’ at Daniel IV 27," argues that הֲלָא (traditionally understood as "isn't … ?") does not introduce a rhetorical question but marks an exclamation. If so, it would be an even stronger expression of Nebuchadnezzar's arrogance.

[5] See further the discussion of the Fourth Commandment in "Law Themes in Daniel 4" in "Introduction to Daniel 4."

strated to him on several occasions.[6] Instead, he did them for the glory of *his own* majesty.

Although God had been patient, Nebuchadnezzar's words were too much, and Daniel tells us that the king had barely finished speaking them when the judgment fell upon him. For a similar judgment in the NT, see Acts 12:21–23. The voice from heaven (Dan 4:28–29 [ET 4:31–32]) not only signals the gravity of the situation in a miraculous form, but it repeats key elements from the dream (4:12–13, 20, 22 [ET 4:15–16, 23, 25]) so that there could be no misunderstanding as to who was judging Nebuchadnezzar. It was "the Most High,"[a] the God of Israel, who had also given both dreams (chapters 2 and 4) to the king and who had enabled his prophet Daniel to provide the interpretations.

(a) Dan 3:26; 3:32 (ET 4:2); 4:14, 21–22, 29, 31 (ET 4:17, 24–25, 32, 34)

Daniel's description of Nebuchadnezzar's insanity initially follows the description of the dream by Nebuchadnezzar. However, instead of referring to "seven times" as the duration of Nebuchadnezzar's insanity (4:13, 20, 22, 29 [ET 4:16, 23, 25, 32]), Daniel tells us that the king's insanity lasted until he had long hair and nails (4:30 [ET 4:33]). Therefore, the "seven times" could not have been as short as seven days, but could well have been less than the often-assumed seven years.[7]

Nebuchadnezzar Praises God for His Power (4:31–32 [ET 4:34–35])

"At the end of the time" (see the first textual note on 4:31 [ET 4:34]) appointed for his insanity, Nebuchadnezzar acknowledges God by lifting his eyes "to heaven." In this case, "heaven" may be a circumlocution for God, as it is elsewhere in this chapter (4:23 [ET 4:26]), and frequently in Matthew's Gospel.[8] Immediately after the return of his sanity, he confesses God's sovereignty. His acknowledgment fulfills the condition specified by God for lifting the curse (4:14, 22–23 [ET 4:17, 25–26]). Moreover, Nebuchadnezzar continues his acknowledgement of God by implicitly admitting that he is nothing before God (since he is one of the inhabitants of the earth), and that God does whatever he wishes (4:32 [ET 4:35]). Although not directly stating that all he had previously accomplished was a result of God's blessing, Nebuchadnezzar admits he was wrong to glorify himself for his accomplishments (4:27 [ET 4:30]). God's power is absolute and beyond challenge—something that Nebuchadnezzar previously maintained about his own power (3:15).

Nebuchadnezzar's affirmation that God "lives forever" and his kingdom is "eternal" and "forever" (4:31 [ET 4:34]) reinforces a theme from chapter 2,

---

[6] See especially 3:15, 24–29. See also 2:44–47. Daniel's ability to interpret Nebuchadnezzar's earlier dream was a demonstration of the one true God's power and superiority over the gods and occult powers upon which the Babylonian diviners relied (2:10–11).

[7] For the meaning of the "seven times," see the commentary on 4:13 (ET 4:16).

[8] Matthew characteristically refers to "the kingdom of heaven," whereas the other Synoptics usually refer to "the kingdom of God." See Gibbs, *Matthew 1:1–11:1*, 47–51.

where the four world kingdoms in succession are destroyed by the advent of God's eternal kingdom (2:44–45). The same theme is prominent in chapter 7 (especially 7:14, 27), which describes how God's kingdom is given to the Messiah, the one "like a Son of Man" (7:13).[9]

The king's acknowledgement that God "does as he wishes with the army of heaven and the inhabitants of the earth" (4:32 [ET 4:35]) may be part of the OT background of the Third Petition of the Lord's Prayer (Mt 6:10), in which Jesus teaches us to pray:

> Let your will be done,
>   as in heaven, also on earth.[10]

The Result of Nebuchadnezzar's Experience (4:33–34 [ET 4:36–37])

Like he did in the previous section, here Nebuchadnezzar indirectly acknowledges God's power over him. In this case, he states that his reason and the glory of his kingdom "returned" to him, and he was "reinstated" (see the textual note on 4:33 [ET 4:36]) over his kingdom, in keeping with the promise God gave to him when Daniel interpreted the dream (4:23 [ET 4:26]). The unstated agent behind those verbs is God: since the kingdom, power, and glory belong to him, they are his gifts to those privileged to hold a high office on earth.

The king continues by confessing that "all" God's "works are true and his ways are just. All who walk in arrogance he is able to humble" (4:34 [ET 4:37]). The reader of the letter is to conclude that since all of God's ways are just and God can humble everyone who is arrogant, his ways with Nebuchadnezzar were just and Nebuchadnezzar was among the arrogant, but now is humbled. However, by casting these thoughts in a doxology, the king is able to confess this without directly admitting his faults to his subjects.

Christian commentators have debated whether Nebuchadnezzar was brought to true saving faith in God through this incident.[11] Those who favor the view that Nebuchadnezzar in this passage expresses true repentance and faith cite the follow details from Daniel:[12]

1. Nebuchadnezzar demonstrates progress in his knowledge about God.
    a. In 2:47 he knows that God can reveal mysteries.
    b. In 3:28 he knows that God can rescue his servants and that they worship only one God.

---

[9] See further "God's Gospel in Daniel" in "Law and Gospel in Daniel," and "Daniel in the New Testament" in the introduction.

[10] For this translation and an exposition, see Gibbs, *Matthew 1:1–11:1*, 314–15, 324–30.

[11] Among those who believe that Nebuchadnezzar was brought to genuine saving faith are Young, *Daniel*, 114, and Walvoord, *Daniel*, 112. Melanchthon in Ap IV 261–68 states that Daniel preached true repentance to Nebuchadnezzar, who was converted; see the commentary on 4:24 (ET 4:27). Those who disagree include Baldwin, *Daniel*, 116; Calvin, *Daniel*, 1:304; and Keil, *Daniel*, 162.

[12] See, for example, Young, *Daniel*, 114.

c. In 3:29 he confesses that "there is no other god who is able to save like" the God of Israel saves.

  d. In 4:31–32 (ET 4:34–35), he makes his most complete statement about God's sovereignty, acknowledging his absolute authority, the lowliness of humans in comparison to him, and his unsurpassed power.

2. Nebuchadnezzar acknowledges God's sovereignty over him (4:34 [ET 4:37]).
3. Nebuchadnezzar acknowledges God's omnipotence (4:32 [ET 4:35]).
4. The king ascribes praise and honor to God (4:34 [ET 4:37]), which could be understood as an act of worship.

As much as these demonstrate that Nebuchadnezzar has grown in his knowledge about the God of Israel, they fall short of true saving faith. The revelatory dreams, their interpretations by Daniel, God's miraculous rescue of his servants in chapter 3, and the fulfillment of Nebuchadnezzar's dream in chapter 4 clearly have expanded the king's awareness of God's knowledge, sovereignty, power, and desire for righteous behavior. Nebuchadnezzar interprets his experiences using human reason and draws logical conclusions. However, his expressions of knowledge of God and his sovereignty do not demonstrate a personal trust in or reliance on God as the gracious God who forgives sins and grants eternal life through faith alone.

Moreover, Nebuchadnezzar never even makes a clear monotheistic confession. He could well acknowledge God as "the Most High"[b] and "the King of heaven" (4:34 [ET 4:37]) while still believing in the existence of other gods, who (in his mind) would be (less) high and in heaven. In fact, even in this letter composed after Nebuchadnezzar's restoration he refers to other gods in his description of the Holy Spirit in pagan terms as "a spirit of holy gods" (4:5–6, 15 [ET 4:8–9, 18]). He also implies that Bel remains his personal deity when he refers to the name he assigned Daniel: "Daniel … whose name is Belteshazzar, like the name of my god" (4:5 [ET 4:8]).

Thus there is no evidence that Nebuchadnezzar ever possessed true saving faith in the one true and triune God. As we draw to the close of the narratives concerning Nebuchadnezzar (chapters 1–4), we must conclude that the king probably remained a thoroughgoing pagan to the end, despite the clear opportunities presented to him to repent and rely on the one true God for forgiveness and salvation.

This same reluctance of pagan Gentile rulers to believe in the true God is reflected in the NT in the accounts concerning Paul's interactions with Felix (Acts 24:22–26) and Agrippa (Acts 26:28–31). It continues to this day as those in positions of political, cultural, intellectual, or institutional power may be the ones least able to recognize their need for the forgiveness of sins, and most reluctant to acknowledge that all they possess has been given to them by God and is to be used for his glory. After all, they have the most to lose if they forsake it all to follow the Lord (cf. the "ruler" in Lk 18:18–23). As we proclaim the Gospel, we must bear in mind how subversive it truly is and how great a threat it may appear to be to those who hold power in this world.

(b) Dan 3:26; 3:32 (ET 4:2); 4:14, 21–22, 29, 31 (ET 4:17, 24–25, 32, 34)

Daniel 5:1–6:1 (ET 5:1–31)

Belshazzar Is Judged for His Arrogance against God

Introduction to Daniel 5

5:1–12	Writing on the Wall at Belshazzar's Banquet
5:13–6:1	Daniel Interprets the Writing and Darius Receives the Kingdom (ET 5:13–31)
Excursus	*The Identity of Darius the Mede*

Introduction to Daniel 5

Major Emphases in Daniel 5

The account of Belshazzar's feast, his foolish decree that he and his guests drink out of the vessels Nebuchadnezzar had taken from Yahweh's temple (see 1:2), the mysterious and frightening hand that wrote a message on the wall, and Daniel's divinely revealed, clever, and artful interpretation of the message is one of the most dramatic narratives in all of Scripture. As he did to Nebuchadnezzar in chapter 4, God judges and humbles another Babylonian king because of his arrogance.

There are other connections between Daniel 4 and Daniel 5 as well:

1. The insanity of Nebuchadnezzar is retold by Daniel (5:20–21).
2. Daniel is once again said to have "a spirit of holy gods" in him (5:11; similar is 5:14; cf. 4:5–6, 15 [ET 4:8–9, 18]).
3. Just as the wise men could not interpret Nebuchadnezzar's second dream (4:4, 15 [ET 4:7, 18]),[1] so too they were unable to read the handwriting on the wall (5:8, 15).

But the most important item these chapters share is the theme of royal arrogance that incurs God's judgment. Just as Nebuchadnezzar had refused to acknowledge God or give him glory (4:27 [ET 4:30]), so in this chapter, Belshazzar refuses to acknowledge God or honor the vessels dedicated to his service in the Jerusalem temple. Instead of learning from his predecessor's experience, Belshazzar defied Israel's God and used the vessels to praise pagan gods, despite the fact that Nebuchadnezzar had learned that Israel's God was "the King of heaven" (4:34 [ET 4:37]) and had acknowledged him as the Most High God (4:31 [ET 4:34]). Belshazzar's drunken praise of the pagan pantheon in effect subordinated Yahweh to the gods of Babylon. The great deeds of God that Nebuchadnezzar had witnessed in chapters 2 and 3 and especially God's ability to humble even the most powerful monarch (as he did to Nebuchadnezzar in chapter 4) are lost on Belshazzar. He did not learn the lesson from the embarrassment of Babylon's greatest king. Now as Babylon's most petty ruler, he would be judged.

Judgment for Belshazzar and the Neo-Babylonian dynasty meant that God was fulfilling his promise. Already in Jeremiah God had prophesied that the captivity of his people in Babylon would last seventy years (Jer 25:11–12; 29:10). Babylon's fall to the Persians some sixty-six years after Jerusalem was first given into the hand of Nebuchadnezzar in 605 BC (Dan 1:1–2) and the first captives (including Daniel) were taken to Babylon was the first step in keeping this promise. Jeremiah had promised that the Medes would be God's instrument for punishing Babylon (Jer 51:11, 28), and Daniel dutifully records the fall of

---

[1] Neither could the Babylonian wise men interpret Nebuchadnezzar's first dream (2:1–11).

the city and kingdom to the Medes and Persians (Dan 5:28), who were led by "Darius the Mede" (6:1 [ET 5:31]).[2] God can keep these promises because he is the God who governs all earthly history for the sake of his redeemed people, the church.[3] He deposes and raises up worldly kings, as exemplified by the succession of the four kingdoms in chapter 2 (see also 4:14, 29 [ET 4:17, 32]). He does this to suit his own redemptive purposes, culminating in the advent of his everlasting kingdom of grace (2:44–45) given to the "Son of Man" (7:13), the "Messiah" (9:26–27), Jesus Christ. Moreover, the fall of Babylon is the first step in corroborating Daniel's interpretation of Nebuchadnezzar's dream of the image of four metals in Daniel 2.

Finally, Daniel 5 reinforces and brings to a climax a theme from Daniel 2 and 4: God reveals mysteries to his people that unbelievers cannot understand. These mysteries center on the kingdom of God and its King, Jesus Christ, the cut stone (2:34, 45), who became "the lowliest of humans" (4:14 [ET 4:17]) but now is enthroned at the right hand of the Father and reigns over all humanity (cf. 4:14 [ET 4:17]; 7:13). As in chapters 2 and 4, again in chapter 5, only Daniel can understand God's mysterious revelation, and he does this by the power of the indwelling Holy Spirit.[4] As in the previous chapters, again the failure of the wise men of Babylon with their occult methods of divination proves them to be servants of false gods (ultimately, the devil), and this time it also seals the doom of Babylon.

God's revelation of mysteries to his people far outstrips the humanly devised wisdom of pagan diviners. In this way, God's revelation to Daniel is but a foretaste of his ultimate revelation of his grace in Christ, which is the mystery revealed to all of God's people by the power of the Holy Spirit, who works through the Gospel to grant and sustain saving faith in Christ.[a]

(a) 1 Cor 2:7–16; 2 Cor 3:14–18; Eph 1:7–9; 3:4–6; Col 1:26–27; 2:2; 1 Tim 3:9, 16

The Historical Setting of Daniel 5

According to Dan 5:30, Babylon fell to the Persian army shortly after the disastrous end of Belshazzar's banquet. The Persians marched into Babylon on October 12, 539 (16 Tishri 539). Therefore the banquet that is the historical setting of Daniel 5 must have been on the evening of October 11, 539.

---

[2] See the excursus "The Identity of Darius the Mede."

[3] On this purpose, see "Theological Threats Posed by the Critical Dating of Daniel" in "Date, Authorship, and Unity," and "The Messiah in Daniel: An Overview" and "God as the Protector of His People" in "Major Themes" in the introduction. See also the commentary on 2:27–30, 34–35, 44–45 and 7:9–14. Contrary to the view of dispensational premillennialism, the church is the one people of God consisting of all OT and NT believers (see the refutation of the dispensational view that there is a radical distinction between Israel and the church in "Eschatology and Dispensational Premillennial Interpretations of Daniel" in the introduction).

[4] As in chapter 4, again in chapter 5, this is affirmed by a pagan king, who describes the Holy Spirit from his polytheistic perspective as "a spirit of holy gods" in Daniel (5:11 [similar is 5:14], as in 4:5–6, 15 [ET 4:8–9, 18]). Nevertheless, this description is an OT affirmation of the Holy Spirit as the third person of the Trinity. See the final Gospel theme in "Gospel Themes in Daniel 4" in "Introduction to Daniel 4."

At the end of chapter 4, Nebuchadnezzar had recovered from his insanity and regained his throne. He then died in 562 BC. If the final events of Daniel 4 occurred during the last year of Nebuchadnezzar's reign, then Daniel 5 begins twenty-three years later, in 539 BC. However, if Nebuchadnezzar's insanity ended about 570 BC,[5] then about thirty years has passed between the end of Daniel 4 and the events in Daniel 5.

Much had happened in the years between Nebuchadnezzar's death and Belshazzar's feast. Nebuchadnezzar was succeeded by his son Amel-marduk, who reigned two short years from 562–560.[6] Amel-marduk was assassinated, and his brother-in-law, Neriglissar (Nergal-shar-uṣur), one of the conspirators in the assassination plot, seized the throne and ruled from 560 until 556.[7] Neriglissar was succeeded by his young son Labashi-marduk, who reigned only a few months in 556. He was deposed in a rebellion that brought one of the members of the coup, Nabonidus (Nabu-naʾid), to the throne.

Nabonidus reigned from 556 BC until the fall of Babylon to the Persians in 539. He proved to be singularly unpopular in Babylon because of his devotion to the god Sin instead of the patron god of Babylon, Marduk (also called Bel).[8] In response to this unpopularity, Nabonidus installed his son Belshazzar as coregent and voluntarily exiled himself to Tema in the Arabian Desert for some ten years. The commonly accepted date for the beginning of Belshazzar's coregency is 553, although there is good evidence that it did not begin until 550.[9] Nabonidus was in Babylon again in 539. With the Persian army approaching Babylon, Nabonidus left the city and met Cyrus in battle at Sippar two days before the fall of Babylon. The Babylonian troops were routed by the Persians, and Nabonidus fled. He later returned to Babylon after its fall to the Persians and surrendered himself. Cyrus allowed him to live the remainder of his life in Carmania according to Berosus.[10] Therefore the sequence of Babylonian rulers after Nebuchadnezzar's death in 562 to the fall of Babylon in 539 is as follows:

- Amel-marduk (562–560)
- Neriglissar (560–556)
- Labashi-marduk (556)
- Nabonidus (556–539), with coregent Belshazzar (553–539 or 550–539)

---

[5] See "A Possible Historical Setting for Daniel 4" in "Introduction to Daniel 4."

[6] Amel-marduk is the "Evil-merodach" who freed Jehoiachin from prison (2 Ki 25:27–30).

[7] Neriglissar is mentioned in Jer 39:3, 13 as one of Nebuchadnezzar's officials when Jerusalem fell to Babylon in 587 BC.

[8] "Bel" was reflected in the pagan name "Belteshazzar," which was assigned to Daniel (4:5 [ET 4:8]). For the meaning of Daniel's Hebrew name, see the first textual note on 1:6. For the meaning of "Belteshazzar," see the second textual note on 1:7.

[9] See Hasel, "The First and Third Years of Belshazzar (Dan 7:1; 8:1)," and Shea, "Nabonidus, Belshazzar, and the Book of Daniel," 135.

[10] Cited by Josephus, *Against Apion*, 1.153.

The Person and Office of Belshazzar

Until the 1860s no historical source except the book of Daniel and works dependent on Daniel (e.g., Baruch 1:11) could provide independent confirmation of the existence of Belshazzar. Since he is not mentioned in any of the Greek historians, many nineteenth-century critical scholars viewed Daniel 5 as a purely fictional account about a fictional king. Following the lead of Josephus,[11] defenders of the historicity of Daniel often countered that "Belshazzar" might have been another name for Nabonidus.[12]

However, beginning in the 1860s, Babylonian sources came to light that named Belshazzar as the son of Nabonidus. They also stated that Belshazzar was made coregent over Babylon.[13] These texts vindicated the historical nature of Daniel's account. Furthermore, since these texts had been buried and forgotten and all memory of Belshazzar had been lost to history outside of the Bible and works dependent on it, they furnished proof positive that the writer of Daniel 5 must have been a contemporary who lived during the events recorded in the chapter. Since writers in later centuries, including writers during the Maccabean era, would have had no knowledge of Belshazzar based on the forgotten Babylonian texts, Daniel 5 could not have been composed in later centuries, disproving the long-held critical view that Daniel was written during the Maccabean era.[14]

Nevertheless, critical scholars continue to dismiss the story as largely fictionalized. In particular, they challenge two statements about Belshazzar in Daniel 5: that he was a son of Nebuchadnezzar (5:2, 11, 13, 18, 22) and that he was king (e.g., 5:1–3).[15] Critical scholars often dismiss the entire chapter as legendary based on their assumption that these two statements are false. Therefore we must give further attention to them.

Belshazzar Was a Son of Nebuchadnezzar

The claim that Nebuchadnezzar was the father of Belshazzar is found in Daniel 5 on the lips of the queen (5:11), Belshazzar himself (5:13), and Daniel (5:18), and Daniel addresses Belshazzar as Nebuchadnezzar's son (5:22). Moreover, Daniel the author calls Nebuchadnezzar the father of Belshazzar in

---

[11] Josephus, *Antiquities*, 10.231.

[12] E.g., Keil, *Daniel*, 169.

[13] See Hasel, "The First and Third Years of Belshazzar (Dan 7:1; 8:1)."

[14] See further "Date and Authorship according to the Book" and "Critical Theories about Date, Authorship, and Unity," both in "Date, Authorship, and Unity," in the introduction.

[15] Collins, *Daniel*, 32–33; Grabbe, "The Belshazzar of Daniel and the Belshazzar of History," 62–64; Hartman and Di Lella, *Daniel*, 186. However, note that Hartman and Di Lella concede that "Belshazzar was, for all practical purposes, ruler of the Neo-Babylonian empire. It is also historically true that he had this position when the city of Babylon was captured by a foreign ruler in 539 b.c." They also concede that "at best, he may have been a descendant of Nebuchadnezzar on his mother's side, ... although this is based on legendary, rather than historical evidence."

his narration of the events (5:2). Critical scholars see this as evidence that the author was either mistaken or never concerned about historical accuracy in the first place.[16]

Scholars who defend the historicity of Daniel offer two replies. The first is to note that in Semitic languages words for "father" and "son" have a wide range of meanings.[17] While they may indicate a genetic or adoptive relationship between one generation and the immediately following generation, they can also indicate relationships that extend across many generations. For example, Jesus is called "the son of David" and "the son of Abraham" (Mt 1:1) even though his ancestor King David lived a millennium earlier and the patriarch lived some two millennia earlier (cf. also Lk 19:9). When a text refers to relationships that span generations, "father" and "son" could be translated "grandfather" and "grandson" or even "ancestor" and "descendant." Moreover, they can also indicate other types of relationships. For instance, the disciples of a prophet are called his "sons" and he is their "father."[b] On the Black Obelisk erected by the Assyrian king Shalmaneser III about 830 BC, a contemporary king of northern Israel, Jehu, is called "son of Omri" even though Jehu had exterminated the descendants of Omri (885–874),[18] an earlier king of northern Israel. Shalmaneser, who conducted several campaigns in Syria and Israel between 859 and 841, could hardly have been unaware that Jehu was not a descendant of Omri. Instead, it appears as if he used "son" to mean "successor."

Therefore it is likely that Nebuchadnezzar is called the "father" of Belshazzar in the historical sense of "predecessor." The normal formula to indicate a father-

(b) 1 Sam 10:12; 1 Ki 20:35; 2 Ki 2:3, 5, 7, 12, 15; 4:1, 38; 5:22; 6:1; 9:1

---

[16] E.g., Collins, *Daniel*, 33. The argument of Collins demonstrates the circularity of critical reasoning. He states that Daniel 5 gives the false impression that Belshazzar was the immediate successor to Nebuchadnezzar. That might have been true if Daniel 5 had originally been written for a third- or second-century-BC audience, who would not have known about the intervening history of the Neo-Babylonians, but it would not have been true for a late sixth-century-BC audience. Collins, like most critical scholars, assumes that Daniel was written for a third- or second-century audience. Thus the assumption about the audience dictates the conclusion that Daniel 5 gives a false impression and therefore is fictional.

However, if Daniel 5 was written (by Daniel himself) in the sixth century only a few years after the events it relates, the audience would have known that the author skipped over several kings in the line of succession between Nebuchadnezzar and Belshazzar. They would not have made the false assumption that Daniel was claiming that Belshazzar was a first-generation son of Nebuchadnezzar, especially since Daniel 5 never uses the formula "Belshazzar, son of Nebuchadnezzar." The audience would rightly conclude that Daniel did not write about the intervening kings because that did not serve the purpose of the inspired author.

Critical scholars often claim that there is no historical truth to the tales in Daniel because they are skeptical of any evidence to the contrary and have adopted a method of purposely and prejudicially disharmonizing the biblical text with historical data. Critics often claim that those who defend the historicity of Daniel are too eager to harmonize Daniel with historical data. However, that claim appears unfair in light of the critical predisposition to do the exact opposite.

[17] Archer, "Daniel," 16; Baldwin, *Daniel*, 22; Miller, *Daniel*, 149.

[18] 2 Ki 10:1–17 records the massacre of the descendants of Ahab son of Omri by Jehu.

son relationship would be "Belshazzar, son of Nebuchadnezzar," but that formula never occurs in Daniel. Instead, Nebuchadnezzar is called "his father" (5:2), "your father" (5:11, 18), or "my father" (5:13), and Belshazzar is called "his son" (5:22). Since the formal father-son designation is never used, it is quite probable that the term "father" here signifies "predecessor," and "son" means "successor."

However, most evangelical scholars dismiss this likely meaning of the terms because of the emphasis placed on them by repetition. Nebuchadnezzar is called Belshazzar's "father" six times (5:2, 11 [three times], 13, 18), and Belshazzar is called Nebuchadnezzar's "son" once (5:22). Therefore most evangelicals, who tend to favor literal interpretation, assume that the terms signal a familial connection between the two men.[19] Nevertheless, this assumption does not necessarily fit the theological emphasis in the chapter.

The theological connection between the two men that is being emphasized in the chapter may well be one of spiritual predecessor and sinful successor. *Belshazzar should have known better than to challenge Israel's God based on the historical experiences of Nebuchadnezzar, his predecessor.* The chapter brings out this emphasis by indicating that *Belshazzar was aware of that history, particularly since Daniel summarizes the events of chapter 4 for the benefit of Belshazzar in 5:18–22.*

One theological point of the chapter is that even though Belshazzar was the genetic son of the usurper Nabonidus, in his office as king Belshazzar was the true spiritual "son" of Nebuchadnezzar since he repeats the hubris of the earlier king. Belshazzar abused the vessels from God's temple (5:2–3, 23) just as did Nebuchadnezzar (1:2). He referred to Daniel and the indwelling Holy Spirit in the same pagan way as Nebuchadnezzar did (4:5–6, 15 [ET 4:8–9, 18]; 5:11, 14). Perhaps most importantly, he arrogantly defied the one true God, the God of Israel, just as Nebuchadnezzar did. He should have learned from the humiliation that Nebuchadnezzar described in his letter (4:21–24, 31–34 [ET 4:24–27, 34–37]) that God can and will judge any king and that God can also raise up anyone to be king, no matter what his parentage (as Nebuchadnezzar himself was told in his dream and related in 4:14 [ET 4:17]).

In conclusion, the terms "father" and "son" are probably used to indicate the historical positions of the kings as "predecessor" and "successor." Theologically, the terms make the point that both Nebuchadnezzar and Belshazzar held the same office of authority and responsibility before God, but ironically Belshazzar the pagan "son" resembled and repeated the hubris and idolatry of his pagan "father," Nebuchadnezzar.

Evangelical scholars often postulate that Belshazzar may have been a descendant of Nebuchadnezzar through his mother. They often speculate that Nabonidus may have married a daughter of Nebuchadnezzar to legitimate his

---

[19] Archer, "Daniel," 16; Baldwin, *Daniel*, 23; Miller, *Daniel*, 149–50.

claim on the throne.[20] Often the wife of Nabonidus is identified as Nitocris, the daughter of an Egyptian princess who married Nebuchadnezzar according to Herodotus.[21] While this theory is attractive because it makes Belshazzar a genetic descendant of Nebuchadnezzar, the theory is based as much on supposition as it is on hard evidence. Much of the information Herodotus gives about Nitocris appears to be legendary, and much of his information about the last years of the Neo-Babylonian kings is inaccurate. We have no reliable source for information about Belshazzar's mother, so any speculation about a genetic relationship with Nebuchadnezzar through Belshazzar's mother remains conjectural.

Belshazzar Was King Since He Was Coregent with His Father, Nabonidus

A second key assertion in Daniel 5 about Belshazzar is that he was king (e.g., 5:1–3). Critical scholars concede that Belshazzar exercised considerable power as coregent, but deny that he was king. They point to the following as evidence that he did not have all the prerogatives of a king:

1. The Babylonian records never call him *šarru* ("king").
2. In the Babylonian records, the regnal years of subsequent kings were reckoned from the time of his father, Nabonidus, and never from the time of Belshazzar.
3. The Babylonian New Year Festival was not celebrated during the ten years when Nabonidus was in Tema. Critics construe this as evidence that Belshazzar could not take the part of the king in the festival.
4. The Babylonian building inscriptions unearthed so far by archaeologists do not mention Belshazzar.
5. Contract tablets mention Nabonidus but not Belshazzar.

However, none of these points demonstrate that Belshazzar could not have been called king by the Babylonians who dealt with him on a daily basis for most of his father's reign. They may indicate that Nabonidus reserved certain royal prerogatives only for himself, but they do not necessarily preclude Belshazzar from functioning as king in all other respects and from having been addressed as king.

Scholars who defend the historicity of Daniel point to evidence that Belshazzar was indeed treated and regarded as king.[22] The main points are these:

---

[20] Archer, "Daniel," 16; Baldwin, *Daniel*, 23; Miller, *Daniel*, 149–50 (cf. Leupold, *Daniel*, 211).

[21] Herodotus, *Histories*, 1.188. The case for this was first made by Dougherty, *Nabonidus and Belshazzar*, 29–70.

[22] The classic argument, which has not been superseded, is by Gruenthaner, "The Last King of Babylon." Shea proposes that the banquet in Daniel 5 was Belshazzar's coronation banquet because Nabonidus was presumed lost after the battle two days earlier and that the chronologically earlier references to him as king in 7:1 and 8:1 are either prospective or reflect his position as coregent during Nabonidus' absence ("Nabonidus, Belshazzar, and the Book of Daniel," 136, 140–43). As clever as Shea's argument is regarding the banquet in Daniel 5, there is no firm evidence for it. The closest one can come to finding support for it is the statement

1. The Persian Verse Account states that Nabonidus "entrusted the kingship" to Belshazzar.[23]
2. Several documents from Nabonidus' reign indicate that Belshazzar was entitled to royal prerogatives, including the same tribute received by his father and the power to settle religious disputes. He was also served by a subordinate official who had a title usually reserved for an officer of the king and by a special messenger with a title similar to the messenger of the king.
3. Some documents treat Nabonidus and Belshazzar together as lords of the land. These include an astrologer's report in Nabonidus seventh year that claims that the stars show favor toward Nabonidus, the king, his (the astrologer's) lord, and Belshazzar, son of the king, his (the astrologer's) lord.
4. Some documents state that oaths were sworn by the decrees of Nabonidus the king and Belshazzar, son of the king. Similar documents dating as early as Hammurapi (1792–1750 BC) demonstrate that oaths were always sworn by the gods and the king. Therefore, those who swore oaths by Nabonidus and Belshazzar must have considered both of them to be king.

Moreover, Gruenthaner notes that a sub-king under Nebuchadnezzar was treated similarly to the way Belshazzar was treated in relation to Nabonidus:

> We know from the inscriptions of Nergal-shar-uṣur that Bel-shem-iskun was king of Babylon during the reign of Nebuchadnezzar. Still his name does not appear upon any contract tablet. Nergal-shar-uṣur calls him "King of Babylon" without adding any qualification whatever to indicate that he was only a sub-king under Nebuchadnezzar.[24]

All this would seem to indicate that, with the exception of a few privileges that were reserved for Nabonidus alone, Belshazzar was functioning as king and was honored as sovereign. It would have been natural for others to refer to him as king and even address him in that manner. This is especially true given the semantic range of the Aramaic noun מֶלֶךְ (*melek*, or with the article, *malkaʾ*), "king," used for Belshazzar throughout Daniel 5. Lucas has noted that the semantic range of Aramaic מֶלֶךְ is much wider than the Akkadian word *šarru*:

> A semantic resolution to this debate is suggested by a bilingual (Aramaic and Assyrian) inscription on a statue discovered at Tell Fakhariyeh, in Syria near the border with Turkey. The statue is that of a ninth-century BC ruler of Guzan. In the Assyrian text he is styled *šakin Guzani* (governor of Guzan), whereas in the Aramaic text he is styled *mlk gwzn* (king of Guzan). … This suggests that *mlk* in Aramaic had a wider meaning, or was used more loosely, than *šarru* in Akkadian. It would be no more wrong to use it of Belshazzar, the *de facto* "king" in Babylon even if not the *de jure* one, than of the governor of Guzan. So the use of *malkaʾ* in Dan. 5 is neither inaccurate nor unhistorical.[25]

---

in the superscription to Daniel 5 in the Old Greek that says that the banquet was held "in the day of the dedication of his [Belshazzar's] palace" (ἐν ἡμέρᾳ ἐγκαινισμοῦ τῶν βασιλείων αὐτοῦ).

[23] *ANET*, 313.

[24] Gruenthaner, "The Last King of Babylon," 416.

[25] Lucas, *Daniel*, 126.

Conclusion

The references in Daniel 5 to Belshazzar as the "son" of Nebuchadnezzar (5:22), his "father" (5:2, 11, 13, 18), and the references to Belshazzar as "king" (e.g., 5:1–3) fit well with what we know of the history and politics of the period in sixth-century Babylon, and with Semitic linguistic usage of such terms. In addition, Daniel 5 has theological reasons for emphasizing the connection between Nebuchadnezzar and Belshazzar. Daniel 5 is historically accurate and depicts Belshazzar as he would have been viewed by the subjects over whom he had ruled since becoming coregent. These accurate references to Belshazzar in this account, combined with its knowledge that he was coregent over Babylon (a knowledge that was later lost to all other ancient sources), indicate that Daniel 5 must have been written by an eyewitness to the events, most likely by Daniel himself.

Daniel 5:1–12

Writing on the Wall at Belshazzar's Banquet

Translation

5 ¹King Belshazzar made a great feast for a thousand of his nobles, and in front of the thousand he drank wine. ²When he had tasted the wine, Belshazzar said to bring the vessels of gold and silver that his father Nebuchadnezzar had taken from the temple in Jerusalem, so that the king and his nobles, his wives and his concubines could drink from them. ³Then they brought the vessels of gold that they had taken from the temple that is the house of God in Jerusalem, and the king and his nobles, his wives and his concubines drank from them. ⁴They drank wine and praised the gods of gold and silver, bronze, iron, wood, and stone.

⁵At that moment the fingers of a human hand appeared and wrote opposite the lampstand on the plaster of the wall of the palace of the king, and the king saw the back of the hand that wrote. ⁶Then the king's cheerful appearance changed, and his thoughts alarmed him. His hip joints were loosed, and his knees knocked together.

⁷The king called out loudly to bring the soothsayers, the Chaldeans, and the diviners. The king said to the wise men of Babylon, "Whoever is able to read this writing and explain its meaning will be clothed in purple with a chain of gold around his neck, and he will rule as third in the kingdom."

⁸Then all the king's wise men came in, but they were not able to read the writing and make known its meaning to the king. ⁹Then King Belshazzar was greatly alarmed. His appearance changed [even more], and his nobles were perplexed.

¹⁰The queen came to the banquet hall because of the words of the king and his nobles. The queen said, "Your Majesty, may you live forever! Do not let your thoughts alarm you, and do not let your appearance be changed. ¹¹There is a man in your kingdom in whom is a spirit of holy gods, and in the days of your father, light and insight and wisdom like wisdom of gods was found in him. So King Nebuchadnezzar, your father, your father the king, appointed him chief of the magicians, soothsayers, Chaldeans, [and] diviners ¹²because an outstanding spirit and knowledge and insight in interpreting dreams and explaining riddles and solving knotty problems were found in this Daniel, whom the king named Belteshazzar. Now let Daniel be summoned, and he will explain the meaning."

Textual Notes

5:1 בֵּלְשַׁאצַּר—"Belshazzar" derives from the Akkadian Bēl-shar-uṣur, "Bel protect the king" (*HALOT*). Bel was another name for Marduk, the chief god of Babylon. "Belshazzar" probably was the same pagan name imposed on Daniel himself, although he as the author deliberately corrupted its spelling to "Belteshazzar" when it applied to him. See the second textual note on 1:7.

5:2 בֵּלְשַׁאצַּ֣ר אֲמַ֣ר ׀ בִּטְעֵ֣ם חַמְרָ֗א—The noun טְעֵם in Daniel usually means "understanding" (*HALOT*, 1, citing 2:14; 3:12; 6:14 [ET 6:13]) or a "command" (*HALOT*, 2 a, citing 3:10, 29; 4:3 [ET 4:6]; 6:27 [ET 6:26]). Only here does it mean "taste," although this meaning is supported by the Aramaic verb טְעֵם, whose Pael (D) means "to feed, give to eat" (4:22, 29 [ET 4:25, 32]; 5:21), and by Hebrew cognates. בִּטְעֵם חַמְרָא, literally, "in the taste of the wine," could refer to all the guests and mean "while they were enjoying it" (BDB, s.v. טְעֵם, 1). Or it could mean "under the influence of the wine" (*HALOT*, 2 b) and refer mainly to Belshazzar. Since the context is about him and the rest of the verse describes his foolish order (see the next textual note), the translation renders it as a temporal clause referring to Belshazzar, "when he had tasted the wine." See further the commentary.

לְהַיְתָיָה֙ לְמָאנֵי֙ דַּהֲבָ֣א וְכַסְפָּ֔א—"To bring the vessels of gold and silver" uses the Haphel (H) infinitive of אֲתָה, לְהַיְתָיָה, "to bring," as the object complement of the preceding אֲמַר, "he said/commanded." In the OT, the Aramaic noun מָאן, "vessel," always refers to the vessels from the Jerusalem temple (Dan 5:2–3, 23; 7:19; Ezra 5:14–15; 6:5; 7:19). Here its plural in construct takes the preposition לְ because it is the direct object of the infinitive לְהַיְתָיָה.

דִּ֤י הַנְפֵּק֙ נְבוּכַדְנֶצַּ֣ר אֲב֔וּהִי מִן־הֵיכְלָ֖א דִּ֥י בִירוּשְׁלֶ֑ם—This Aramaic reference to the vessels "that Nebuchadnezzar his father had taken from the temple in Jerusalem" recalls 1:2, where Daniel first recorded (in Hebrew) that Nebuchadnezzar took the vessels from the Jerusalem temple to Babylon. This historical recollection is reinforced in 5:3, which repeats much of the vocabulary here and adds that "the temple" (הֵיכְלָא) in Jerusalem was "the house of God" (בֵּית אֱלָהָא).

וְיִשְׁתּ֣וֹן בְּה֔וֹן—The Peal (G) imperfect with *waw* (וְיִשְׁתּוֹן) forms a purpose clause: "so that they could drink with them."

5:3 מָאנֵ֣י דַהֲבָ֑א—The MT refers only to "the vessels of gold." Theodotion adds "and silver," probably by assimilation to 5:2, which referred to "the vessels of gold and silver" (מָאנֵי דַהֲבָא וְכַסְפָּא).

5:5 בַּהּ־שַׁעֲתָ֗ה—Literally, "in it—the moment," this is the same phrase that was translated by the adverb "immediately" in 3:6, 15; 4:30 (ET 4:33). This requires the participle to be translated in the past tense.[1]

נֶבְרַשְׁתָּ֔א—This term for "the lampstand" may be either a Persian or Akkadian loanword.[2]

פַּ֚ס יְדָ֣ה דִּ֣י כָתְבָ֔ה—Here פַּס probably means that the king saw "the *back* of the hand that wrote" on the wall (see *HALOT*, s.v. פַּס, 2). The palm of the hand would have been facing the wall as the hand wrote. פַּס denotes the flat part of the hand, as distinguished from the fingers, or the flat part of the foot, as distinguished from the toes. Most translations and lexicons consider it to refer to the "palm" of the hand or the "sole" of

---

[1] Rosenthal, *A Grammar of Biblical Aramaic*, § 177.
[2] Millard, "The Etymology of *Neḇraštāʾ*, Daniel 5:5."

the foot, based on the use of its Hebrew cognate, פַּס, which in the OT always refers to a long garment whose sleeves extend to the flat part of the hand and whose hem extends to the foot (Gen 37:3, 23, 32; 2 Sam 13:18–19).

5:6 אֱדַיִן מַלְכָּא֙ זִיוֺ֣הִי שְׁנ֔וֹהִי—English requires smoothing out the Aramaic syntax, which is, literally, "then the king, his cheerful appearance changed." The Aramaic noun זִיו means "brightness, radiance" (*HALOT*) in 2:31 and 4:33 (ET 4:36). Here and in 5:9–10, it refers to the king's face and gestures, which were changed so that he no longer showed the bright cheer of the feasting, but instead fright and alarm. It refers to Daniel's changed features in 7:28. It is plural, perhaps after the pattern of the Hebrew plural פָּנִים for "face." In all these verses (5:6, 9–10; 7:28), a parallel clause includes the verb בְּהַל (see the next textual note).

וְרַעְיֹנֹ֖הִי יְבַהֲלוּנֵּ֑הּ—Literally, this is "his thoughts terrified him." The plural of רַעְיוֹן, "thought," is the subject of the Pael (D) imperfect of בְּהַל, "to frighten, terrify." Similar clauses refer to Daniel in 4:16 (ET 4:19) and 7:28 and to the king in 5:10 (where the jussive is negated).

וְקִטְרֵי֙ חַרְצֵהּ֙ מִשְׁתָּרַ֔יִן—Literally, "the knots/joints of his loin were loosed/untied," this is usually understood as a reference to the hips, which is a logical inference because of the following reference to the king's knees (see the next textual note). KJV has "the joints of his loins were loosed," but most other translations are more general, for example, "his limbs gave way" (ESV). מִשְׁתָּרַיִן is the Hithpaal (HtD) of שְׁרָה, whose Peal (G) can mean "loosen" (cf. 3:25; 5:16). The loins may represent human strength,[a] which here fails. Some have suggested that this is a reference to incontinence caused by extreme fear.[3]

(a) Cf. Deut 33:11; 1 Ki 12:10; Ps 69:24 (ET 69:23); Job 40:16

וְאַ֨רְכֻבָּתֵ֔הּ דָּ֥א לְדָ֖א נָֽקְשָֽׁן׃—This is, literally, "his knees, this one to this one knocked." The noun אַרְכֻבָּה, "knee," attested also in Rabbinic Aramaic and Syriac, probably is cognate to the Hebrew בֶּרֶךְ, "knee," with a transposition of the consonants (from the order ברך to the order -רכב-).

5:7 לְאָֽשְׁפַיָּא֙—For "the soothsayers," see the third textual note on 1:20.

כַּשְׂדָּאֵ֔י—For "the Chaldeans" as a professional term for diviners in the service of the king (5:7, 11, 30), see "Daniel among the Wise Men" in "Introduction to Daniel 2," and also the third textual note on 2:2. Before this term, 4QDan[a] adds חרטמיא,[4] "the magicians," in apparent agreement with the Old Greek (φαρμακούς). This is probably due to assimilation to other passages in Daniel that include the Hebrew or Aramaic חַרְטֹם in lists of the various types of wise men. See the third textual note on 1:20.

וְגָזְרַיָּ֑א—This term for "(the) diviners" was also in 2:27 and 4:4 (ET 4:7) and recurs in 5:11. See "Daniel among the Wise Men" in "Introduction to Daniel 2."

וּפִשְׁרֵהּ֙ יְחַוִּנַּ֔נִי—For the noun פְּשַׁר, "meaning" (also in 5:8, 12, 15–17, 26), see the third textual note on 2:4. The Pael (D) of חֲוָה, "declare, make known," was also used for the interpretation of Nebuchadnezzar's first dream in 2:4, 11, 24.

וְתַלְתִּ֥י בְמַלְכוּתָ֖א יִשְׁלַֽט׃—Literally, this is "and third in the kingdom he will reign." Many commentators connect תַּלְתִּי with the Akkadian *šalšu* and the Hebrew שָׁלִישׁ and

---

[3] Wolters, "Untying the King's Knots: Physiology and Wordplay in Daniel 5."

[4] Ulrich et al., *Qumran Cave 4.XI*, 249.

argue that תַּלְתִּי simply denotes a high official. The word may originally have meant "third (in rank)," but later lost its numerical meaning and so here simply refers to a high rank.[5] The Hebrew שָׁלִישׁ is thought originally to have designated the "third" man in a chariot (*HALOT*, s.v. שָׁלִישׁ III, A, B), as might be evident in Ex 14:7. Later, however, שָׁלִישׁ simply came to mean a military "officer."[b] If that were the meaning of the term here, then the king would merely be promising to confer a mid-level military rank upon the person who could interpret the writing.

However, there are several problems with that view. First, the Aramaic use of *taw* in place of the Hebrew *shin* is reserved for native Aramaic words, for example, Hebrew שׁוֹר, Aramaic תּוֹר, "bull." Akkadian loan words, especially those that designate officials, are always transliterated directly from Akkadian and preserve Akkadian *shin*, for example, אָשַׁף, "soothsayer" (e.g., 2:10; not אָתַף*). Also note שָׁלָה, "blasphemy" (3:29 Kethib; not תְּלָה*), and even *shin* in the names בֵּלְטְשַׁאצַּר (e.g., 5:1) and בֵּלְשַׁאצַּר (e.g., 1:7). Second, later in this chapter, the form תַּלְתָּא (5:16, 29) is used as an equivalent of תַּלְתִּי here, and this later form can only be analyzed as a determined state ordinal adjective, "the third" in rank. Compare תְּלָתָא, the determined cardinal numeral "three," in, for example, Dan 3:24 and Ezra 6:4. Finally, it is difficult to reconcile the bestowal of royal honors (represented by the purple robe and gold chain) with the offer to bestow a mid-level military rank.[6]

Therefore this word in Belshazzar's promise ought to be understood as offering the person who can read and interpret the writing a royal position with the "third" highest authority. Only the two coregents, Nabonidus and Belshazzar, would have higher authority.[7]

5:8 כֹּל חַכִּימֵי מַלְכָּא—"All the king's wise men" is the reading of Leningradensis and hence *BHS*, which is supported by Theodotion. Some Masoretic manuscripts read כֹּל חַכִּימֵי בָבֶל, "all the wise men of Babylon." Instead of either reading, the Old Greek lists three kinds of diviners.

5:9 וְזִיוֹהִי שָׁנַיִן עֲלוֹהִי—This is the same idiom as used in 5:6 (see the first textual note on 5:6) but with the addition of עֲלוֹהִי, "upon him," rendered, "his appearance changed *even more*."

5:10 מַלְכָּא לְעָלְמִין חֱיִי—The queen addresses the king with the same flattering acclamation, "Your Majesty, may you live forever!" addressed to Nebuchadnezzar earlier. See the second textual note on 2:4.

(b) 1 Ki 9:22; 2 Ki 7:2, 17, 19; 9:25, 10:25; 15:25; Ezek 23:15, 23; 2 Chr 8:9

---

[5] See, for example, Collins, *Daniel*, 247, and Lucas, *Daniel*, 130, who follow Montgomery, *Daniel*, 254, 56–57.

[6] The suggestion by Grabbe, "The Belshazzar of Daniel and the Belshazzar of History," 65 (cf. Hartman and Di Lella, *Daniel*, 184), that the offer of being one of three rulers was related to Daniel being one of three supervisors under Darius (6:3 [ET 6:2]) is far-fetched. The three supervisors are nowhere depicted as having royal honor, and they are selected as supervisors over the satraps. The office held by these three supervisors does not allow them to rule over the entire kingdom; that was an honor that Darius contemplated giving to Daniel only *after* he made him one of the three supervisors (6:4 [ET 6:3]).

[7] For Nabonidus and Belshazzar as coregents, see "The Historical Setting of Daniel 5" in "Introduction to Daniel 5."

5:11 רוּחַ אֱלָהִין קַדִּישִׁין בֵּהּ—The queen's description of Daniel, literally, "a spirit of holy gods is in him," is the same as in 4:5 (ET 4:8). The expression also occurs with בָּךְ, "in you," instead of בֵּהּ in 4:6, 15 (ET 4:9, 18). The king will repeat the phrase in the second person (בָּךְ, "in you") but without קַדִּישִׁין ("holy") in 5:14. In the Aramaic portions of the OT, אֱלָהִין is always a true plural, "gods," and not a reference to the one true "God" (as the Hebrew אֱלֹהִים usually is). Nevertheless, this expression spoken by a pagan affirms the indwelling Holy Spirit (see "Gospel Themes in Daniel 4" in "Introduction to Daniel 4").

נַהִירוּ וְשָׂכְלְתָנוּ וְחָכְמָה כְּחָכְמַת־אֱלָהִין הִשְׁתְּכַחַת בֵּהּ—The queen ascribes divine qualities to Daniel: "light and insight and wisdom like wisdom of gods was found in him." The noun נַהִירוּ, "illumination" (*HALOT*) or "light," is similar to the Aramaic noun נְהִיר, "light," which Daniel ascribed to God himself in 2:22 in his psalm of praise after God revealed to Daniel Nebuchadnezzar's first dream. The Aramaic noun שָׂכְלְתָנוּ, "insight" (*HALOT*), which the queen will repeat in 5:12, is a wisdom term cognate to the Hebrew verb שָׂכַל, which refers to the faculty or exercise of God-given insight (see the second textual note on 1:4 and the first textual note on 1:17). חָכְמָה, "wisdom," also occurs in the Hebrew portions of Daniel (see the commentary on 1:17).

The king repeats almost the same phrase to Daniel in 5:14 but weakens the divine quality וְחָכְמָה כְּחָכְמַת־אֱלָהִין to merely וְחָכְמָה יַתִּירָה, "outstanding wisdom." Compare 5:12, where the queen ascribes to Daniel רוּחַ ׀ יַתִּירָה, "an outstanding spirit."

רַב חַרְטֻמִּין אָשְׁפִין כַּשְׂדָּאִין גָּזְרִין—For Daniel as the "chief" (רַב) of these pagan diviners, see "Daniel among the Wise Men" in "Introduction to Daniel 2." For חַרְטֻמִּין and אָשְׁפִין, see also the third textual note on 1:20.

אֲבוּךְ מַלְכָּא:—Many commentators regard "your father the king" as awkward and superfluous at the end of this verse, and propose deleting the words as a scribal error.[8] Both Theodotion and the Syriac omit them, probably in an effort to resolve the difficulty. However, they stand here at the end of the sentence to emphasize that Belshazzar's relationship to Nebuchadnezzar is not by blood, but by office. Nebuchadnezzar is Belshazzar's "father" only because he was Belshazzar's predecessor on the throne.[9]

5:12 וּמַנְדַּע—Daniel in his psalm in 2:21 used this noun for "knowledge" that God gives to those who have understanding. It was also used by Nebuchadnezzar in 4:31, 33 (ET 4:34, 36) when God returned to him his "knowledge" after his period of insanity.

מְפַשַּׁר חֶלְמִין—That Daniel "interpret[s] dreams" was shown in chapters 2 and 4, where he provided the meaning of Nebuchadnezzar's two dreams. The Pael (D) participle מְפַשַּׁר, "interpreting, explaining the meaning," is cognate to the noun פְּשַׁר, "meaning" (see the fourth textual note on 5:7 and the third textual note on 2:4).

וַאֲחַוָיַת אֲחִידָן—The verb is the Haphel (H) infinitive of חֲוָה in construct, here meaning "to interpret."[10] Some parse it as a feminine noun (cf. BDB, s.v. אַחֲוָיָה, under the

---

[8] E.g., Montgomery, *Daniel*, 260; Young, *Daniel*, 122.
[9] See "The Historical Setting of Daniel 5" in "Introduction to Daniel 5."
[10] *HALOT*, 2; Rosenthal, *A Grammar of Biblical Aramaic*, § 111.

root חוה). The noun אֲחִידָה, "riddle," is cognate to Hebrew חִידָה, "riddle" (8:23). The phrase here is similar to לְהַגִּיד הַחִידָה in Judg 14:14.

וּמְשָׁרֵא קִטְרִין—Literally, "loosening knots," this is translated, "and solving knotty problems." The king will use the same vocabulary when he addresses Daniel in 5:16. The Pael (D) participle of שְׁרָא literally means "loosening, untying." Its Peal (G) passive participle was used in 3:25 for the three "unbound, loosed" men in the furnace. Its Hithpaal (HtD) participle in 5:6 referred to the king's "loosed" (wobbly) hip joints, and 5:6 also used the plural of קְטַר in reference to those hip "joints." The Syriac cognate ܩܛܪܐ can refer to a "knot."

כְּעַן דָּנִיֵּאל יִתְקְרֵי וּפִשְׁרָה יְהַחֲוֵה:—This is a jussive clause, "now let Daniel be called/summoned," followed by a purpose clause, literally, "so that its meaning he can explain." יִתְקְרֵי is the Hithpeel (HtG) of קְרָא, "to call; read," and יְהַחֲוֵה is the Haphel (H) imperfect of חֲוָה, meaning "to make known," as in, for example, 2:6–7. 4QDan^a is fragmentary but has … וכתבא יקרא,[11] probably meaning "he will read the writing [and explain the meaning]." This appears to be a scribal change of the Hithpeel (HtG) יִתְקְרֵי to the Peal (G) imperfect יִקְרָא influenced by similar passages in Daniel 5 (Peal forms of קְרָא occur in 5:7 [twice], 8, 15–17).

Commentary

Belshazzar's Banquet (5:1–4)

Daniel begins his account of the last night in Babylon under Neo-Babylonian rule without a hint that the Persian army has advanced upon the city. The first-time reader has no idea that grave danger lurks outside the city's famed walls. This adds to the drama that unfolds in the chapter. Belshazzar's actions, which look foolish even without this knowledge, seem even more foolish when we learn that Babylon fell that night (5:30–6:1 [ET 5:30–31]). Why would a king hold a drunken feast when the defense of the city should be his first and only priority? Yet Herodotus and Xenophon both report that there was feasting and celebrating in Babylon when it fell to the Persians.[12]

Daniel the author tells us that Belshazzar ordered the sacred vessels from God's temple to be brought and used for drinking "when he had tasted the wine" (5:2). Some interpreters suggest that he did this after the first taste of wine following a meal.[13] Others have understood this to be a euphemism for drunkenness.[14] Either way, it demonstrates an incredible arrogance and lack of judgment. Earlier, in 605 BC, God had allowed Nebuchadnezzar to take captives from Judah, including Daniel, and to seize "some of the vessels of the house of God," which Nebuchadnezzar brought "to the land of Shinar, into the house of his god" (1:2). The redundant statement "he brought the vessels into the treasury

---

[11] Ulrich et al., *Qumran Cave 4.XI*, 250.
[12] Herodotus, *Histories*, 1.191; Xenophon, *Cyropaedia*, 7.5.15, 21, 25.
[13] E.g., Montgomery, *Daniel*, 251.
[14] E.g., Baldwin, *Daniel*, 120; Miller, *Daniel*, 152.

of his god" (1:2) highlights the hubris of Nebuchadnezzar, who assumed that his pagan gods had triumphed over Israel's God. To be sure, God had allowed the heathen Babylonians to execute his judgment on his apostate people Israel, but the Babylonians too would come under divine judgment, as indeed will all unbelievers. The OT prophets make this point abundantly clear.[15]

The temple and its liturgical rites had been the means of grace through which God bestowed the forgiveness of sins and salvation on his OT people. The abuse of the temple vessels by Nebuchadnezzar and now Belshazzar could be likened by analogy to a modern incident if unbelievers were to seize the vessels (chalice and paten) used for distributing Holy Communion in a church and use them for some profane purpose. Surely this would incur God's judgment, even as the NT warns about abuses of the Lord's Supper itself (cf. 1 Cor 10:16–22; 11:27–31).

In the preceding chapters of Daniel, the one true God demonstrated his power to judge and depose kings (chapters 2 and 4) and also his power to save his faithful people (the Judean exiles in chapter 1 and the three Judeans in chapter 3). Those historical events took place earlier, during the reign of Nebuchadnezzar, but Belshazzar must have been familiar with them and should have learned from them. Daniel the author leaves us a clue as to why Belshazzar may have issued his order to bring the temple vessels. In 5:2, Daniel states in narrative form that Nebuchadnezzar is "his [Belshazzar's] father," a relationship repeated in the quotations in 5:11, 13, 18. Daniel seems to be making the point that Belshazzar is purposely seeking to outshine his predecessor and to demonstrate that he is greater than Nebuchadnezzar, Babylon's greatest king, when in fact he is following his predecessor on the same path of arrogance that will surely incur divine judgment.[16] Perhaps Belshazzar also does this to bolster the morale of his leaders and troops in Babylon in the face of the impending Persian attack.

Daniel immediately reports that Belshazzar's order is obeyed (5:3). His use of repetition, one of his favorite literary devices, emphasizes the almost mechanical way in which the pagan subjects obey the order of their heathen king.[17] By the end of 5:3, the reader has come to see the king as foolish and sacrilegious.

---

[15] For example, Daniel's contemporary Ezekiel first pronounces judgment on Israel (Ezekiel 1–24) then on the heathen nations (Ezekiel 25–32). But God's purpose is to bring all sinners under his judgment and move them to repentance so they can then receive through faith alone his salvation, promised for the sake of Jesus Christ. This is the theme of Ezekiel 33–48, which promises Christ as the new David and Prince (e.g., Ezek 34:23–24; 37:24–25; 44:3; 45:7, 16). For the purpose of the classical prophetic outline of the book of Ezekiel, see Hummel, *Ezekiel 1–20*, 10–12, who cites 1 Pet 4:17 and Rom 3:22–24 as NT statements of this same purpose: God brings all sinners under judgment and then promises his grace to all in Christ.

[16] For the relationship between Nebuchadnezzar and Belshazzar, see further "The Person and Office of Belshazzar" in "Introduction to Daniel 5."

[17] Similarly, extensive repetitions in Daniel 3 emphasized the blind obedience of pagans to the royal order to commit idolatry. See "Literary Artistry Highlights the Judeans' Resistance and Satirizes the Pagans" in "Introduction to Daniel 3."

Even from a pagan point of view, his hubris would call for divine retribution. His wives and nobles are painted as dutiful followers of a fool.

Then the profane revelers add another insult to the one true and triune God: "they praised the gods of gold and silver, bronze, iron, wood, and stone" (5:4, recounted in 5:23). These are the gods in whom they trust. They give these gods credit for their defeat of Israel and for their ability to humiliate Israel's God by means of their abuse of his temple vessels. While the pagans understand their gods to be more than mere metal, wood, or stone, Daniel heightens the sense of their foolishness by the implicit comparison of their real identity (only lifeless metal, wood, or stone) with the true, living God, who had demonstrated his power over all idols during Nebuchadnezzar's reign (especially in Daniel 3). The praising of these pagan gods is a direct affront to Israel's God by implying that he is subordinate to gods of gold, silver, bronze, iron, wood, and stone. This is a more direct insult to God than Nebuchadnezzar, despite his arrogance, had ever made.[18]

Daniel's description of the constitutive elements of these gods is itself a satire of them (cf. Is 37:19; 40:18–20; 44:9–20). The reader may also recall that Nebuchadnezzar had dreamt of a statue consisting of most of these same elements (gold, silver, bronze, iron, clay), but the advent of God's kingdom in the Messiah shattered them all (2:35, 44–45). In the modern age, few may still openly venerate such idols. Nevertheless, unbelievers may revel in a false sense of triumph over Christians, thinking that Christ was defeated by his crucifixion and burial and is unable to save those who trust in him. Yet the vindication of all believers shall come on the Last Day (cf. Ps 25:3; 2 Tim 1:12; Rev 11:7–12).

The Handwriting on the Wall and Belshazzar's Reaction (5:5–6)

Daniel's description of the pagan gods as lifeless metal, stone, and wood (5:4) imply that they cannot hear the praise lavished upon them. He makes this more explicit later, in 5:23. However, the God whom the king and his followers are insulting and defying can hear their words, and he immediately reacts.

The vision of a hand writing on the wall is the most eerie of all phenomena described in the OT.[19] However, instead of dwelling on it, Daniel focuses the narrative on Belshazzar. When he sees the hand, he becomes alarmed, and his hips and knees are weakened and trembling. While this may have been true of the other guests, Daniel wants his readers to see God's judgment as falling specifically on Belshazzar as the one whom God holds responsible for the fool-

---

[18] Nebuchadnezzar had openly challenged Israel's God by doubting his power to save Shadrach, Meshach, and Abednego from the furnace (3:15). In that way, he implicitly subordinated God to his idol, which all his subjects were to worship. For the significance of his idol, see the commentary on 3:1–3.

[19] Some commentators describe the hand as "detached" (e.g., Collins, *Daniel*, 246; Lucas, *Daniel*, 129), but the text does not necessarily imply that. The hand may have been attached to an arm or even a whole being (God in human form, or perhaps an angel), but only the hand was visible.

ish sacrilege during the banquet. The king's thoughts "alarmed him" (5:6), a clause that is used elsewhere of Daniel's reaction to God's revelation (4:16 [ET 4:19]; 7:18). However, Daniel's alarm never leads to pure fright as Belshazzar's does. The difference, of course, is that Daniel knows the gracious God of Israel, whereas Belshazzar only knows God's wrath.

Belshazzar's Offer to Anyone Who Can Interpret the Writing (5:7)

Belshazzar in his panic screams for his wise men to be brought to him. He then makes an offer that betrays his desperate situation: anyone who can read and interpret the writing will receive royal honor and serve as "third" ruler in the kingdom (see the fifth textual note on 5:7). Since Belshazzar himself was only second in rank under his coregent father, Nabonidus, "third" would be the highest possible rank for someone under Belshazzar.[20] The historical accuracy of this statement as recorded by Daniel the author is another indication that this is an eyewitness account. The suggestion by some that Belshazzar does not have the authority to offer such a position without Nabonidus' permission[21] overlooks the urgency of the situation. Either Belshazzar has already been informed of his father's defeat on the battlefield, in which case Belshazzar cannot obtain permission from him, or Belshazzar is so frightened that at this point he is not overly concerned about scrupulously observing protocol. In any event, he offers the successful interpreter the highest honor and rank that he can bestow. His offer of this immediate promotion emphasizes the grave importance of knowing what has been written on the wall.

The Failure of the Wise Men to Read the Writing (5:8–9)

The failure of the wise men to read—much less interpret—the writing has led to speculation as to why they could not decipher what was written. From Daniel's interpretation (5:25–28), it seems that the inscription was in Aramaic, a language with which the wise men would have been familiar. Over the centuries, interpreters have proposed a number of explanations for the wise men's failure, including these:

- The words were written vertically in columns instead of horizontally.[22] This interpretation was adopted by Rembrandt in his famous painting of this scene.
- The words were written in code, perhaps *atbash*.[23]

---

[20] See "The Historical Setting of Daniel 5" in "Introduction to Daniel 5."

[21] Grabbe, "The Belshazzar of Daniel and the Belshazzar of History," 65.

[22] Talmud, *Sanhedrin*, 22a.

[23] Talmud, *Sanhedrin*, 22a. *Atbash* means that the first letter of the alphabet is replaced by the last letter (Hebrew/Aramaic *a*leph is replaced by *t*aw, hence "at-"), the second letter of the alphabet is replaced by the second-to-last letter (Hebrew/Aramaic *b*eth is replaced by *sh*in, hence "-bash"), and so on.

- The words were written in cuneiform marks signifying weights.[24] Daniel's interpretation of the meaning is based on the equivalent Aramaic words.
- The wise men could read the words, but they could not interpret their meaning.[25] However, this explanation is contrary to the plain words in 5:8.

As ingenious as these suggestions are, there is a simpler explanation for the wise men's difficulty. While longer Aramaic inscriptions were usually written with word dividers (spaces, dots, or lines that indicated which consonants go together to form the individual words), short inscriptions were often written without these dividers. Moreover, ancient Aramaic was not written with vowels. (The vowels in modern printed editions of the biblical Aramaic text, like those of the biblical Hebrew text, were added by the Masoretic scribes in the sixth–ninth centuries AD.) From Daniel's interpretation (5:25–28), it appears as if the three words are written together as follows:

מנאתקלפרס (transliterated: *mn'tqlprs*)

Daniel divided these consonants into three words of three letters each, מנא תקל פרס, which are vocalized (supplied with vowels) as *mᵉnē, tᵉkēl, pᵉrēs* (5:25). However, there are many other ways in which the inscription could have been read, depending on the word division and the vocalization. Another possible word division would be this:[26]

מן אתקל פרס (transliterated: *mn 'tql prs*)

However, even with this word division, the consonants could be vocalized in different ways. One way, with the Aphel (H) perfect of the verb תְּקַל, "stumble," is this:

מַן אַתְקֵל פָּרַס (*man a'tqel paras*), "Who caused Persia to stumble?"

Yet another vocalization of those same consonants, with the Peal (G) imperfect of the verb תְּקַל, "weigh," is this:

מַן אֶתְקַל פָּרַס (*man e'tqal paras*), "What shall I weigh, a half mina?"

Still another possible division into words would be this:

מַן אַת קַל פָּרַס (*man 'at qal paras*), "Whoever you are, Persia is insignificant."

There are still other possibilities.[27] In fact, there are so many possibilities that dividing the consonants into words and then vocalizing them could be used as a parlor game for Aramaic scholars. Most probably the wise men were attempting to divide the inscription into words that would form a sentence, whose meaning they could then interpret. However, because of the ambiguity of the unvocalized consonants that ran together, they could not be certain about how to read the inscription, and they also may have disagreed with each other

---

[24] Instone Brewer, "*Mene Mene Teqel Uparsin*: Daniel 5:25 in Cuneiform."
[25] Collins, *Daniel*, 248; Montgomery, *Daniel*, 264.
[26] The following suggestions are found in Wolters, "The Riddle of the Scales in Daniel 5," 159.
[27] See Wolters, "The Riddle of the Scales in Daniel 5," 159–60.

about the likelihood of the different possibilities. Since they could not offer a convincing interpretation, they failed to provide what the king demanded.

Daniel will read the inscription as three words and then interpret them as a play on the words. Even if the word division and vocalization were certain, arriving at the correct interpretation intended by God required a huge step that required divine revelation (see commentary on 5:25–28).

The wise men's failure resulted in an intensifying of Belshazzar's panic as well as total bewilderment on the part of his nobles (5:9). The wise men were supposed to be good at interpreting riddles and esoteric signs by means of their occult methods.[28] However, they had no way of reading this riddle written by the one true God. Just as in chapters 2 and 4, where God gave Nebuchadnezzar prophetic dreams that only Daniel could interpret, the correct interpretation could only be given by the inspiration of the same God who authored the writing.

Similarly, the Holy Scriptures are the written Word of God, but they remain opaque to unbelievers. The proper interpretation of Scripture requires humility, prayer, and above all, the guidance of the same Spirit by whom God inspired the Scripture writers.[c]

(c) Cf. Jn 6:63; 1 Cor 2:7–16; 2 Tim 3:16; 1 Pet 1:10–11; 2 Pet 1:19–21

The Queen Mother Informs Belshazzar about Daniel (5:10–12)

Because the queen has knowledge of events involving Daniel in the reign of Nebuchadnezzar (before Belshazzar's time), and because the king's wives were already at the banquet (5:2–3), commentators are generally agreed that the woman characterized here as "queen" was the queen mother: the mother of Belshazzar and the wife of Nabonidus, Belshazzar's father.[29] That she was the grandmother of Belshazzar is an interpretation as ancient as Josephus, and many of the rabbis held that she was Belshazzar's mother.[30] The queen entered the banquet uninvited, a definite breach of protocol. The Old Greek version seeks to correct this by having the king summon her.[31]

The queen seeks to reassure Belshazzar that the inscription on the wall can be read. She describes Daniel in terms similar to those used in earlier chapters of the book (2:48; 4:5–6 [ET 4:8–9]). She also adds some information about Daniel: he can interpret dreams (as demonstrated in Daniel 2 and 4) and explain riddles, a skill that he will employ when summoned before Belshazzar. In an

---

[28] See the third textual note on 1:20, the textual notes on 2:2, and "Daniel among the Wise Men" in "Introduction to Daniel 2."

[29] See "The Historical Setting of Daniel 5" in "Introduction to Daniel 5." Commentators who hold that she was the queen mother include Archer, "Daniel," 72; Baldwin, *Daniel*, 121–22; Collins, *Daniel*, 248; Hartman and Di Lella, *Daniel*, 188; Lucas, *Daniel*, 130; Miller, *Daniel*, 159–60; Montgomery, *Daniel*, 257; Walvoord, *Daniel*, 123; Young, *Daniel*, 122.

[30] Josephus, *Antiquities*, 10.237; Ginzberg, *The Legends of the Jews*, 6:431.

[31] The Old Greek has an almost completely different text in 5:9: "Then the king summoned the queen concerning the sign and showed her how great it was and that no man was able to declare to the king the interpretation of the writing" (τότε ὁ βασιλεὺς ἐκάλεσε τὴν βασίλισσαν περὶ τοῦ σημείου καὶ ὑπέδειξεν αὐτῇ ὡς μέγα ἐστί καὶ ὅτι πᾶς ἄνθρωπος οὐ δύναται ἀπαγγεῖλαι τῷ βασιλεῖ τὸ σύγκριμα τῆς γραφῆς).

ironic twist that to the reader seems like a satirically humorous comment, she also says that Daniel is adept at "solving knotty problems" or, more literally, "untying knots" (see the fourth textual note on 5:12). Readers of the Aramaic text would immediately note that this is exactly what Belshazzar does not need, since "the knots/joints of his loin" are already untied (see the third textual note on 5:6)! This use of biting satirical humor prepares Daniel's readers for the interpretation of the handwriting on the wall. Its message for the king and his officials will not be good.

It is not surprising that Belshazzar (drunk with wine and in a panic) needs to be reminded of Daniel's abilities as an interpreter of dreams and signs. At this time, Daniel would have been well-advanced in years.[32] He may have been retired from royal service. More importantly, there had been two palace coups since Nebuchadnezzar's death. The new kings may have demoted or forcefully retired many of Nebuchadnezzar's advisors in order to appoint new ones whom they thought would be more loyal to them. Therefore, Daniel could have been living in Babylon even if his abilities were unfamiliar to Belshazzar.

The queen's words provide a firm link between this account and especially Daniel 4. She calls Daniel a man "in whom is a spirit of holy gods," echoing Nebuchadnezzar's words (4:5–6, 15 [ET 4:8–9, 18]; see the first textual note on 5:11). She refers to Nebuchadnezzar, first as Belshazzar's "father" and then by name. Finally, she notes that Daniel can interpret dreams, as he did for Nebuchadnezzar. By quoting the words of the queen, Daniel the author is gradually drawing his readers' attention to the parallel between Nebuchadnezzar's arrogance and Belshazzar's arrogance, between God's judgment on Nebuchadnezzar and his coming judgment on Belshazzar. This parallel will be made more explicit by Daniel's own words to the king in 5:18–21.

Chapter 4 ended with Nebuchadnezzar humbled and praising the one true God (4:31–34 [ET 4:34–37]). This chapter ends with the opposite result: the death of Belshazzar (5:30). However, that judgment prepares for the accession of Darius the Mede (6:1 [ET 5:31]), who should be identified with Cyrus the Great,[33] who would issue the edict permitting the Judeans to return to the land, rebuild the temple, and return the temple vessels to their rightful location and divine use (Ezra 1:1–11, especially Ezra 1:7–11; 2 Chr 36:22–23). Therefore this narrative ends on a far stronger Gospel note that rectifies the sacrilegious tragedy that began the book (Dan 1:1–2) and set the stage for this narrative (5:2–4).

---

[32] If Daniel was fourteen years old when he was taken into captivity in 605, he would have been eighty years old when Babylon fell to the Persians. See "Date and Authorship according to the Book" in the introduction, and the commentary on 1:18–21.

[33] See the excursus "The Identity of Darius the Mede."

Daniel 5:13–6:1 (ET 5:13–31)

Daniel Interprets the Writing and Darius Receives the Kingdom

Translation

5 ¹³Then Daniel was brought before the king. The king said to Daniel, "Are you Daniel who is one of the exiles of Judah whom my father the king brought from Judah? ¹⁴I have heard about you that a spirit of gods is in you, and light and insight and outstanding wisdom is found in you. ¹⁵Now, those wise men who were the soothsayers were brought before me to read this writing and to make its meaning known to me, but they were not able to explain the meaning of the message. ¹⁶Yet I have heard about you that you are able to clarify meanings and to solve knotty problems. Therefore, if you are able to read the writing and make its meaning known to me, you will be clothed in purple with a chain of gold around your neck, and you will rule as the third in the kingdom."

¹⁷Then Daniel answered the king, "Keep your gifts for yourself, or give your rewards to someone else! Nevertheless, I will read the writing to the king, and I will make known to him its meaning. ¹⁸You, Your Majesty—the Most High God gave the kingdom, greatness, splendor, and glory to Nebuchadnezzar, your father. ¹⁹So because of the greatness that he gave him, all peoples, nations, and languages trembled and were afraid in his presence. He killed whomever he wanted, and he let live whomever he wanted. Also, he promoted whomever he wanted, and he demoted whomever he wanted. ²⁰But when his mind was lifted up and his spirit grew strong so that he acted presumptuously, he was deposed from the throne of his kingdom, and [his] splendor was taken away from him. ²¹He was driven away from humans, and his mind was changed to that of a beast. So his dwelling was with the wild donkeys. He was fed grass like bulls [are fed], and his body was wet with dew from the sky until he knew that the Most High God rules the human kingdom and whomever he desires he raises up over it.

²²"But you, his son, Belshazzar, did not humble your heart although you knew all this. ²³Instead, you lifted yourself against the Lord of heaven. The vessels of his house were brought before you, and you and your nobles, your wives and your concubines drank wine from them. Then you praised the gods of silver and gold, bronze, iron, wood, and stone who do not see and do not hear and do not know. But you did not honor the God in whose hand is your breath and who owns all your ways. ²⁴Then from him was sent the back of the hand, and this writing was inscribed.

²⁵"Now this is the writing that is inscribed: Mene ... Mene, Tekel, and Parsin [a mina, a shekel, and half-minas].

²⁶"This is the meaning of the message: A mina [means that] God has counted your kingdom and paid it out. ²⁷A shekel [means that] you have been weighed in

the scales, and you have been found lacking. ²⁸A half-mina [means that] your kingdom has been broken in two and given to the Medes and the Persians."

²⁹Then Belshazzar spoke, and they dressed Daniel in purple with a chain of gold around his neck, and they proclaimed about him that he was the third ruler in the kingdom. ³⁰In that very night, King Belshazzar the Chaldean was killed. ⁶:¹And Darius the Mede received the kingdom, being about sixty-two years old.

Textual Notes

5:15 חַכִּימַיָּא אָשְׁפַיָּא—This phrase, literally, "the wise men, the soothsayers," is restrictive: "those wise men who were soothsayers." See "Daniel among the Wise Men" in "Introduction to Daniel 2."

דִּי־כְתָבָה דְנָה יִקְרוֹן וּפִשְׁרֵהּ לְהוֹדָעֻתַנִי—Literally, "so this writing they would read and its meaning to make known [to] me," the Peal (G) imperfect יִקְרוֹן and the Haphel (H) infinitive (with לְ and suffix), לְהוֹדָעֻתַנִי form a purpose clause: the diviners were brought "to read this writing and to make its meaning known to me." The identical infinitive recurs in 5:16. Its suffix (תַנִי-) serves as an indirect object with datival meaning: "*to* me."

5:16 פִּשְׁרִין לְמִפְשַׁר—Literally, "to give the meaning of meanings" or "to interpret interpretations," such cognate accusative constructions (a verb and a noun as its direct object from the same root) are relatively rare in Daniel's Aramaic, though common in Biblical Hebrew.

וְקִטְרִין לְמִשְׁרֵא—For this vocabulary (but here the Peal [G] infinitive of שְׁרָא), see the fourth textual note on 5:12.

וְתַלְתָּא בְמַלְכוּתָא תִּשְׁלַט׃—See the fifth textual note on 5:7.

5:17 מַתְּנָתָךְ לָךְ לֶהֶוְיָן—Aramaic does not have separate forms of the imperfect and jussive. The context indicates that the Peal (G) לֶהֶוְיָן (third feminine plural of הֲוָה) is jussive, meaning "*let* your gifts [מַתְּנָתָךְ] be to you/yours [לָךְ]." The phrase is translated in idiomatic English as "keep your gifts for yourself."

וּנְבָזְבְּיָתָךְ—For this term (here plural with suffix), translated, "or your rewards," see the textual note on 2:6.

5:18 אַנְתָּה מַלְכָּא—Daniel starts to address Belshazzar with "you, Your Majesty," but recounts the history of Nebuchadnezzar in the rest of 5:18–21. Then in 5:22 he returns to Belshazzar and again addresses him with the pronoun "you." In both verses, the Kethib is אַנְתָּה, but the Qere is אַנְתְּ.

5:19 הֲווֹ זָיְעִין וְדָחֲלִין מִן־קֳדָמוֹהִי—Literally, "they were trembling and fearing from before him," the construction with a perfect verb (הֲווֹ) and two participles (זָיְעִין וְדָחֲלִין) has durative force, implying that the people trembled and were afraid during Nebuchadnezzar's reign until he was humbled. The Qere, זָיְעִין, and the Kethib, זָאֲעִין, are alternate spellings of the Peal (G) participle of זוּעַ, "to tremble" (*HALOT*). The same participles (with the same Qere/Kethib variation) occur in an almost identical clause in 6:27 (ET 6:26).

דִּי־הֲוָה צָבֵא הֲוָא קָטֵל וְדִי־הֲוָה צָבֵא הֲוָה מַחֵא—Literally, these two clauses are "whom he was willing he was killing, and whom he was willing he was making alive." The construction with the Peal (G) perfect הֲוָה and participles (מַחֵא ... צָבֵא ... קְטֵל ... צְבָא) has durative and also iterative force, denoting frequent (and apparently capricious) actions by Nebuchadnezzar. The participles קְטֵל, "kill," and מַחֵא (Aphel [H] of חָיָא), "make alive, let live," are antonyms, forming a merism.

וְדִי־הֲוָה צָבֵא הֲוָה מָרִים וְדִי־הֲוָה צָבֵא הֲוָה מַשְׁפִּיל:—The same construction used in the previous two clauses is employed for these clauses, which have the antonymous (Aphel [H]) participles מָרִים, "lift up, exalt," and מַשְׁפִּיל, "bring down, make lowly." They are translated idiomatically as "promoted ... demoted." Causative forms of the cognate Hebrew verbs (רוּם and שָׁפֵל) occur together as antonyms in 1 Sam 2:7 and Ps 75:8 (ET 75:7), referring to actions by God.

5:20 רָם לִבְבֵהּ—Literally, "his heart was lifted up," this could be translated, "his mind became haughty." The Hebrew and Aramaic terms for "heart" often refer to mental faculties and so correspond in meaning to the English "mind" (see the first textual note on 1:8). The Peal (G) passive participle רָם, "be lifted up," corresponds in meaning to the stative Hebrew Qal in the similar phrase in 11:12, וְרָם לְבָבוֹ, "his heart will become high/arrogant." Compare also הִתְרוֹמַמְתָּ, the Hithpolel (HtD) of רוּם in 5:23, where Daniel tells Belshazzar, "you lifted yourself up" against God.

וְרוּחֵהּ תִּקְפַת לַהֲזָדָה—Literally, "and his spirit became strong to act presumptuously," this is translated, "and his spirit grew strong so that he acted presumptuously." The Peal (G) perfect תִּקְפַת is the same verb (תְּקֵף) used for the tree that was a metaphor for Nebuchadnezzar that "grew strong" (4:8, 17 [ET 4:11, 20]; also 4:19 [ET 4:22]). The Haphel (H) infinitive לַהֲזָדָה, "to **act presumptuously** ... behave sinfully" (*HALOT*, s.v. זוּד), is translated as a result clause (cf. NASB: "his spirit became so proud that he behaved arrogantly"). The cognate Hebrew verb זִיד can refer to insolent action against God (Deut 1:43; 18:20; Jer 50:29; Neh 9:10, 16, 29).

5:21 See the textual notes on 4:12–13, 20, 22, 29–30 (ET 4:15–16, 23, 25, 32–33), which contain most of the same vocabulary here.

5:24 שְׁלִיחַ פַּסָּא דִי־יְדָא—Literally, this is "the back of the hand was sent." The language is phenomenological: the king only saw the "back" of the hand (5:5), and so that is what Daniel says "was sent." For פַּס, "back," see the third textual note on 5:5. The Peal (G) passive participle שְׁלִיחַ, "was sent," has peculiar pointing in Codex Leningradensis, upon which *BHS* is based. Many other Masoretic manuscripts and printed editions have the conventional pointing שְׁלִיחַ.

5:25 מְנֵא מְנֵא—This repeated Aramaic word means "mina," a unit of weight. It is cognate to the Hebrew מָנֶה and is a loanword from Akkadian and Sumerian (*HALOT*, 1). Many commentators assume that its repetition is an indication of dittography.[1] When Daniel quotes and explains this first part of the inscription in 5:26, he quotes only one מְנֵא. However, 5:25 represents the way Daniel initially read the inscription to the king. The inscription itself likely was unpointed and lacked word dividers, and so probably read, מנאתקלפרס. However, when reading it aloud Daniel probably read the first word, paused, and repeated it before moving to the second and third words. He may have paused and repeated the first word to reinforce to the king how the unpointed conso-

---

[1] See Collins, *Daniel*, 250.

nants in the inscription were to be divided and vocalized to form the first word. He may have repeated the first word for emphasis, since the first word, מְנֵא, a three-consonant word in the Aramaic *qᵉtēl* pattern signifying a weight (a mina), set the pattern for how the rest of the inscription was to be read: also as weights. Thus the inscription probably was to be pronounced as *mᵉnē, tᵉkēl, pᵉrēs*.

For a further explanation of the ambiguity caused by the inscription lacking word dividers and pointing, see the commentary on 5:8–9, "The Failure of the Wise Men to Read the Writing." For Daniel's inspired interpretation of מְנֵא, see the commentary on 5:26.

תְּקֵל—This Aramaic term for "shekel," another unit of weight, is cognate to the Hebrew שֶׁקֶל (*HALOT*) and similar terms in other Semitic languages. For Daniel's inspired interpretation of this term, see the commentary on 5:27.

וּפַרְסִין:—This word with conjunction is the Aramaic plural of פְּרַס, a weight that was half of a mina (*HALOT*), so it could be translated "and half minas." In 5:28 Daniel quotes the written inscription as having the singular פְּרַס, *pᵉrēs*. When reading the inscription aloud, Daniel probably converted the singular into the plural וּפַרְסִין, *ūpharsīn*, to signal that this word would have a double play: on the Aramaic word for "broken in two" and also on the Aramaic word for "Persians." See the textual note and commentary on 5:28.

5:28 פְּרֵס פְּרִיסַת מַלְכוּתָךְ וִיהִיבַת לְמָדַי וּפָרָס—Daniel explains פְּרֵס, "half a mina," with two phrases, each of which contains a play on the word. The first is פְּרִיסַת מַלְכוּתָךְ, "your kingdom has been broken in two." פְּרִיסַת is the Peal (G) passive perfect of פְּרַס, "to divide" (*HALOT*) or "break in two" (BDB). Wolters argues that this verb only means "break in two" in Hebraized Aramaic.[2] However, it is clearly a play on פְּרַס, "half a mina," a mina divided in two, so the meaning "broken in two" is clearly what is intended here.

The second phrase, וִיהִיבַת לְמָדַי וּפָרָס, "it has been given to the Medes and the Persians," uses another Peal passive (Gp) perfect verb, וִיהִיבַת, from יְהַב, "to give." It is feminine because the feminine noun (with suffix) מַלְכוּתָךְ, "your kingdom," is its subject. פָּרָס is the pausal form of פְּרַס, which can refer to either the territory of "Persia" or as here, to its inhabitants, "the Persians" (*HALOT*).

5:30 קְטִיל בֵּלְאשַׁצַּר—The MT states, "Belshazzar was killed." However, the Old Greek version does not state that Belshazzar was killed. Instead it says, καὶ τὸ σύγκριμα ἐπῆλθε βαλτασαρ τῷ βασιλεῖ καὶ τὸ βασίλειον ἐξῆρται ἀπὸ τῶν Χαλδαίων καὶ ἐδόθη τοῖς Μήδοις καὶ τοῖς Πέρσαις, "and the judgment came upon King Baltasar, and the kingdom was removed from the Chaldeans and given to the Medes and the Persians."

Commentary
Belshazzar's Offer to Daniel for Interpreting the Writing (5:13–16)

When Daniel is brought before the king, it is obvious from Belshazzar's words that he is already acquainted with Daniel. The queen did not tell him

---

[2] Wolters, "The Riddle of the Scales in Daniel 5," 168–70.

about Daniel's ethnic background, but Belshazzar already knows about it. Since Belshazzar calls Daniel "one of the exiles of Judah whom my father the king brought from Judah," he makes a clear connection between the vessels brought from Judah and Daniel, who was also brought from Judah. (This same connection was in Dan 1:2–7.) This may explain why the king, though he knew about Daniel, did not summon him with the rest of the wise men (5:7–8): the king had shown contempt for Judah's God, and he did not want to hear from a Judean who worshiped that God.

However, Belshazzar is so desperate, and his nobles, whom he may have sought to encourage (see the commentary on 5:1–4), were so perplexed, that he was now forced to acknowledge and resort to Daniel. However, the king seems to express his contempt for Daniel's God by his treatment of Daniel himself. He merely claims to have heard of Daniel's ability from others, but he refuses to state directly that such ability actually resides in Daniel. Contrast his qualified words in 5:14 with Nebuchadnezzar's direct affirmation in 4:6 (ET 4:9). Unbelieving Belshazzar's arrogance has made him cynical and reluctant to acknowledge Daniel's God-given ability to read and interpret the divine writing. Also note that the pagan queen gave a higher appraisal of Daniel than Belshazzar does. She characterized the Holy Spirit dwelling in Daniel as "a spirit of *holy* gods" (5:11), whereas Belshazzar refers to the Spirit in Daniel only as "a spirit of gods" (5:14).[3] This too also signals Belshazzar's resentment at Daniel's prowess as a wise man.

This contempt continues after Belshazzar describes the inability of the Babylonian wise men to read the writing (5:15). He continues by saying, "Yet *I have heard* about you that you are able to clarify meanings and to solve knotty problems. Therefore, *if you are able* ..." (5:16). This phraseology is a doubting challenge to Daniel to demonstrate that he is indeed wiser than the Babylonians who failed. Still, Belshazzar offers Daniel the same reward (5:16) that he promised the other wise men (5:7), perhaps thinking that at this point he will not have to honor his promise, since this aged Judean[4] cannot possibly be as wise as his own advisors.

Daniel Reminds Belshazzar of Nebuchadnezzar's Arrogance against God (5:17–21)

Daniel's reply to Belshazzar is direct and forceful. He does not greet the king with a salutation, as was customary (e.g., as the queen did in 5:10). Daniel had always been respectful of Nebuchadnezzar because God had used the heathen

---

[3] These descriptions by pagans, like those in 4:5–6, 15 (ET 4:8–9, 18), nevertheless refer to the Holy Spirit, the third person of the Trinity. See the final Gospel theme in "Gospel Themes in Daniel 4" in "Introduction to Daniel 4."

[4] If Daniel was fourteen years old when he was taken into captivity in 605, he would have been eighty years old when Cyrus the Great conquered Babylon. For the view that "Darius the Mede" in 6:1 (ET 5:31) is Cyrus the Great, see the excursus "The Identity of Darius the Mede."

king to judge his unfaithful people Israel (1:1–2) and had determined that Daniel should serve under him.[5] However, Daniel knows the coming judgment on Belshazzar and that God has given his kingdom to others. Therefore, he feels no obligation to engage in pleasantries. In this way, Daniel demonstrates God's disapproval of Belshazzar and God's impending judgment on his impious act of drinking from the temple vessels and honoring pagan gods with them.

Furthermore, Daniel refuses the king's reward (5:17) to demonstrate that his wisdom is not for sale, nor is his God. Moreover, Daniel could not be accused of tailoring his interpretation merely to gain a reward. Later, Daniel will receive the gifts from Belshazzar (5:29), but by then he has proven that he is not a prophet for hire nor is his God's wisdom capable of being bought. However, Belshazzar is in no position to object, so he allows Daniel to continue with his scathing condemnation of the king.

Daniel's words to the king that preface the interpretation of the writing on the wall are divided into two sections, each beginning with the pronoun אַנְתְּ, "you." The first section (5:18–21) is a short recapitulation of the events of Daniel 4. The description of Nebuchadnezzar's greatness here (5:18) combines four words, "kingdom," "greatness," "splendor," and "glory," that occur together elsewhere only at the end of those events, when Nebuchadnezzar was restored (4:33 [ET 4:36]). In this way, Daniel emphasizes for his readers that the greatness of Nebuchadnezzar both before (5:18) and after (4:33 [ET 4:36]) his bout of insanity was a gift from God.

The description of Nebuchadnezzar's glory is primarily from Daniel 4. However, the description of Nebuchadnezzar's use of his authority in killing and pardoning, promoting and demoting (5:19) is unique to Daniel 5 and is intended to demonstrate that Nebuchadnezzar was given divine authority from the only source that could grant it: the God of Israel (cf. 5:21).[6]

Nebuchadnezzar's insanity is also described in clauses drawn from Daniel 4. Daniel adds a detail not found elsewhere when he states that Nebuchadnezzar lived "with the wild donkeys" (5:21). In the final clause of 5:21, Daniel makes the point that it is the God of Israel, "the Most High God" (see the commentary on 3:27), who controls human kingdoms. This is the God whom Belshazzar has insulted and treated with contempt. Although Daniel does not contrast the one true God with the lifeless, powerless gods of Babylon until later (5:23), that comparison is implicit already here in the appellation "the Most High God" (5:21).

---

[5] For Daniel's respect toward Nebuchadnezzar, see the commentary on 1:8–14 and also, for example, 4:16 (ET 4:19).

[6] For government authority as established by God, see further the discussion of the Fourth Commandment in "God's Law in Daniel" in "Law and Gospel in Daniel" in the introduction.

By this point in Daniel's words, Belshazzar must have known that the inspired interpretation that Daniel would give about the words written by God would not be favorable.

Daniel Accuses Belshazzar of Arrogance against God (5:22–24)

After the recollection of Nebuchadnezzar's insanity (5:20–21), Daniel's speech turns its attention directly to Belshazzar. He connects the two kings by calling Belshazzar "his [Nebuchadnezzar's] son" (5:22), the only time in Daniel 5 that this description is used of the king. Daniel's connection "your father … his son" (5:18, 22) drives home his twofold accusation: Belshazzar knew what had happened to Nebuchadnezzar, but did not learn from it and humble himself. Instead, he did the opposite and lifted himself against God (5:23). This makes Belshazzar the "son" of Nebuchadnezzar and a forerunner of the great eschatological king, the Antichrist, who will lift himself against God (11:36).[7]

Daniel's description of the way that Belshazzar exalted himself against God lists three steps of the king's action (5:23):

1. He and his guests drank from the vessels of grace seized from God's temple.[8]
2. He praised lifeless gods.
3. He did not honor the God who controls Belshazzar's future.

Daniel's description of the false gods repeats his description of them in the narration of the events of the banquet (5:4),[9] but he now adds his contempt for them because they do not see, hear, or have any knowledge (5:23). This is a traditional biblical condemnation of idols (Deut 4:28; Pss 115:4–7; 135:15–17; Rev 9:20). Although the pagans thought of their gods, represented by the idols, as living and perceiving, the gods in fact do not exist and are no more alive than the materials of which their representations are made. As Paul declares, "We know that 'an idol in this world is nothing,' and that 'there is no God but one' " (1 Cor 8:4). Yet Paul also adds that worship of such idols really is worship of demons, who exist and are powerful evil spirits, so believers must refrain from all such idolatry (1 Cor 10:20–21; cf. 1 Jn 5:21).

Part of the reason that Daniel emphasizes to Belshazzar that the idols cannot see or hear or know is so that he can contrast these gods to the one true God, who holds Belshazzar's breath in his hand and who is ruler over all the king does (5:23). Daniel is telling the king that he got it backwards: he praised lifeless, powerless gods while profaning the vessels of the living, almighty God. It is this God whom Belshazzar holds in contempt who sent the hand to write the message on the wall. If Belshazzar did not understand that the message was

---

[7] For the relationship between Nebuchadnezzar and Belshazzar, see "The Person and Office of Belshazzar" in "Introduction to Daniel 5." For the antichrist in 11:36, see the excursus "The Lutheran Confessions on the Antichrist in Daniel."

[8] For this outrage, see further the commentary on 5:1–4.

[9] However, 5:23 inverts the order of the first two materials, "silver and gold," instead of "gold and silver" (5:4).

going to be one of judgment and condemnation before this, he surely must have been prepared for it now.

Daniel Interprets the Writing on the Wall (5:25–28)

After taking the opportunity to reproach the king for his sin, Daniel read and interpreted the inscription on the wall. His reading begins with the first word, *mᵉnē*. Daniel's repetition of the first inscribed word in his oral reading here, "Mene … Mene," is no mistake (see the first textual note on 5:25). By dividing the consonants of the inscription so that the first word has three consonants and by vocalizing the first word in the Aramaic *qᵉtēl* pattern, Daniel reveals the pattern for how the entire inscription is to be read. It consists of three words, each having three consonants and each in the *qᵉtēl* pattern: *mᵉnē, tᵉkēl, pᵉrēs*.[10] Moreover, his repetition of the first word shows that he is reading aloud somewhat freely; he is orally reading the entire inscription with a hint of its interpretation. That explains why, when reading the third word aloud, he converts the singular *pᵉrēs* to the plural *ūpharsīn*, to signal that it will have a double play on words in his interpretation (see the third textual note on 5:25).

Based on findings from Aramaic inscriptions, Clermont-Ganneau first proposed in 1886 that Daniel read the three words as weights: the mina, the shekel, and the half-mina.[11] This interpretation has been accepted by most commentators.[12] However, some scholars have been bothered by the order of the weights, since they do not proceed from heaviest to lightest. A Babylonian mina was equivalent to sixty shekels. Some have suggested that the final weight, *pᵉrēs*, the half-mina, is actually a half-shekel.[13] Others have proposed that the original order was *mᵉnē, pᵉrēs, tᵉkēl*.[14] However, part of the reason that the Babylonian

---

[10] That these were the three words of the actual written inscription (as distinct from what Daniel *said* in 5:25 when he read them aloud to the king) is indicated by the use of each of these three words at the beginning of each verse of the interpretation (5:26–28). See also the commentary on 5:8–9.

[11] Clermont-Ganneau, "Mané, thécel, pharès et le festin de Balthasar" (ET: "Mene, Tekel, Peres, and the Feast of Belshazzar"). Sometimes commentators refer to these weights as "money" or "coins." However, coinage had not been invented and first became widespread later under the Persian Empire.

[12] E.g., Baldwin, *Daniel*, 123–24; Collins, *Daniel*, 251–52; Goldingay, *Daniel*, 110–11; Hartman and Di Lella, *Daniel*, 189–90; Montgomery, *Daniel*, 263–64; Young, *Daniel*, 126. The older suggestion that the three words are passive participles is still advocated by some (e.g., Miller, *Daniel*, 165). However, the second and third words would have to be changed in order for them to be the passive participles תְּקִיל and פְּרִיס. Miller (*Daniel*, 165, n. 84) contends that the words appear to be participles nevertheless, since they are accented on the second syllable (תְּקֵל, 5:25, 27, פְּרַס, 5:28). However, that contention is not convincing. It is true that the second syllables of those words are accented, but the first syllables have *shewa* and in Aramaic a syllable with *shewa* is never accented.

[13] Goldingay, *Daniel*, 111. Although etymologically *pᵉrēs* means "divided," there is no extant text that uses it to refer to half of a shekel. Whenever it is used to signify a weight, it refers to a half-mina.

[14] This is the order given in the preface to Daniel 5 in the Old Greek version (Collins, *Daniel*, 241–42).

wise men were unable to interpret the inscription (and did not realize that it refers to three weights) is that the weights are not in a logical order.

Since a passage in the Talmud equates weights with an evaluation of the quality of persons,[15] some scholars have proposed that the three weights represent certain Babylonian kings.[16] However, the text of Daniel 5 gives no indication that the inscription applies to anyone other than Belshazzar and his kingdom.

Daniel's interpretation of each of the three weights involves a play on words. He gives both an explicit and an implicit play on the words for the first two weights. He makes two explicit plays on the word for the third weight. In each case, the first wordplay is accomplished by converting the noun for the weight into a verb from the same root. These verbs indicate God's evaluation of Belshazzar and his kingdom. In each case, the second play on words (implicit for the first two weights; explicit for the third weight) states God's action based on his evaluation.

Daniel interprets the first inscribed word as this:

מְנֵא מְנָה־אֱלָהָא מַלְכוּתָךְ וְהַשְׁלְמַהּ:

Mina [$m^e n\bar{e}$]: God has counted [$m^e n\hat{a}$] your kingdom and paid it out. (5:26)

The spelling of the first verb, מְנָה ($m^e n\hat{a}$), "counted," clearly is a play on the spelling of the noun for the weight, "mina" ($m^e n\bar{e}$). The second verb, וְהַשְׁלְמַהּ ($w^e hashl^e mah$, Haphel [H] of שְׁלַם with suffix), is not related to the spelling of either "mina" or of the first verb. The second verb could mean "and brought it to an end" (see *HALOT*). However, it can also mean "to pay out,"[17] that is, to pay a debt or bill, which a buyer would do in order to take or reclaim possession of something. The application here would be that God was repossessing the kingdom, taking it away from Belshazzar and giving it to someone else. That is most probably the meaning here, since the first verb, מְנָה, can also convey this meaning: "to count (out)" a commodity (money) in the process of buying something.[18] Therefore, the second verb, "to pay out," is an implicit play on the noun for "mina." This play is implicit or indirect because it involves a possible meaning of the first verb, and only the first verb is obviously related to "mina" by means of its spelling.

Since we have no evidence that coinage was used at this time in Babylon, "counting" and "paying out" would have been accomplished by weighing quantities of a precious metal in scales.

The second word is interpreted as this:

תְּקֵל תְּקִילְתָּה בְמֹאזַנְיָא וְהִשְׁתְּכַחַתְּ חַסִּיר:

---

[15] Talmud, *Ta'anith*, 21b.

[16] For examples of these suggestions, see Collins, *Daniel*, 251; Hartman and Di Lella, *Daniel*, 190; Lucas, *Daniel*, 133.

[17] *HALOT*, citing Montgomery, *Daniel*, 262–63, 65.

[18] Wolters, "The Riddle of the Scales in Daniel 5," 172.

Shekel [*tᵉkēl*]: You have been weighed [*tᵉkîltah*] in the scales, and you have been found lacking. (5:27)

Once again, the spelling of the first verb, "you have been weighed" (*tᵉkîltah*), is an explicit play on the spelling of the noun for the weight, "shekel" (*tᵉkēl*). Here too there is a second, implicit wordplay that depends on meaning. The adjective חַסִּיר, "lacking," in this context means "lacking in weight" and hence "too light." That meaning could also be expressed by forms of the verb קָלַל (*kᵉlal*), including תִּקַּל (*tikkal*), "you are light," which would result from a different vocalization of the same consonants in תְּקֵל (*tᵉkēl*), "shekel."[19] Those same consonants are also present in the first verb, תְּקִילְתָּה (*tᵉkîltah*), "you have been weighed."

Finally, Daniel interprets the third word as this:

פְּרֵס פְּרִיסַת מַלְכוּתָךְ וִיהִיבַת לְמָדַי וּפָרָס׃
Half-mina [*pᵉrēs*]: Your kingdom has been broken in two [*pᵉrîsat*] and given to the Medes and the Persians [*paras*]. (5:28)

For this third word, which supplies the ultimate judgment of God on Belshazzar, Daniel provides a double explicit play on words. The spelling of "half-mina" (*pᵉrēs*) is similar to the spelling of the verb "has been broken in two" (*pᵉrîsat*) and also to the spelling of "Persians" (*paras*). The interpretation of this third word unambiguously describes how God will execute his judgment: he destroys Babylon's power by breaking it in two and then delivers it to the rising empire of the Medes and Persians.

Thus Daniel's inspired interpretation involves an elaborate wordplay with a three-part interpretation of each of the three words, each of which consists of three consonants:

	Interpretation Part 1	Interpretation Part 2	Interpretation Part 3
Word 1	Mina מְנֵא	Counted מְנָה	Paid out [מְנָה] הַשְׁלְמַהּ
Word 2	Shekel תְּקֵל	Weighed תְּקִילְתָּה	Light [תִּקַּל] חַסִּיר
Word 3	Half-mina פְּרֵס	Broken in two פְּרִיסַת	Persians פָּרָס

This masterful, complex interpretation with its multiple plays on words expressed concisely in the original Aramaic could only have been given to Daniel by divine inspiration. It was so convincing to Belshazzar that he had no doubt whatsoever that Daniel had indeed given the correct reading of the handwriting on the wall. As in chapters 2 and 4, Daniel once again provided the means through which God demonstrated that he was superior to the Babylonian gods and sovereign over all human kingdoms. Moreover, by beating the Babylonian

---

[19] Wolters, "The Riddle of the Scales in Daniel 5," 173–74.

wise men at their own game, God used Daniel to demonstrate that even "the foolishness of God is wiser than (that of) humans and the weakness of God is stronger than (that of) people" (1 Cor 1:25).

Daniel Is Rewarded, Belshazzar Is Slain, and Darius Receives the Kingdom (5:29–6:1 [ET 5:29–31])

Although Daniel had spurned the king's offer of rewards for reading and interpreting the handwriting on the wall (5:17), Belshazzar still orders that he be given the promised honors. Though Daniel's interpretation might have been deemed worthy of death under other circumstances, the fright of the king and the promise he had made in front of his guests probably forced him into honoring Daniel.

The transition of world powers from the Chaldean kings to the Medo-Persian kings is signaled by the contrast between "King Belshazzar the Chaldean" (5:30) and "Darius the Mede" (6:1 [ET 5:31]).[20] Interestingly, Darius' age is given as "about sixty-two." This is a way of identifying who this Darius is.[21] Darius is the only person whose age is given in Daniel.[22] Moreover, Darius would have been born about 601 BC, at the height of Babylonian power and just after Daniel was taken into captivity with the first wave of exiles from Judah in 605 BC. Thus Daniel signals that even at the beginning of Israel's captivity, God had already begun to implement his plan to bring it to an end, as he promised through his prophets (e.g., Is 44:24–45:8; Jer 25:11–12; 29:10; Ezek 34:11–16).

This narrative ends with powerful Law and Gospel. The swift death of Belshazzar (Dan 5:30) is the ultimate judgment of God upon him (cf. 1 Sam 25:37; Acts 5:5, 10; 12:23). According to the interpretation of the handwriting, God's plan also included the transfer of the kingdom to Darius. Daniel the author signals that both of these are the work of God. In the case of Belshazzar's death, he uses a passive verb, קְטִיל, "was killed" (5:30), which does not require the naming of the human killer,[23] thereby pointing to this act as carried out to fulfill God's judgment proclaimed by Daniel (cf. Gen 2:17; Ezek 3:18–19; Rom 1:32; 6:23a).

---

[20] This is the only time in Daniel where a Babylonian king is referred to as a Chaldean. Darius is called a Mede here and in 9:1 and 11:1.

[21] See further the excursus "The Identity of Darius the Mede."

[22] Goldingay (*Daniel*, 112) suggests that Belshazzar's age, sixty-two, is a fulfillment of the message of the handwriting. To get a total of sixty-two shekels, Goldingay adds one mina (which equals sixty shekels) to one shekel and two half-shekels. Goldingay argues that *pᵉrēs* was equivalent to a half-shekel rather than a half-mina (p. 111), and he counts two of them since Daniel in 5:25 used the plural *parsîn*. However, his argument fails on two counts. First, there is no evidence that *pᵉrēs* was ever used to signify a half-shekel. Second, in every other instance where Daniel gives a specific year or number of years, it is intended literally, not symbolically. See 1:1, 5, 21; 2:1; 7:1; 8:1; 9:1–2; 10:1; 11:1. (While some translations give "seven years" in 4:13, 20, 22, 29 [ET 4:16, 23, 25, 32], the Aramaic does not have the word for "years" there and instead refers to "seven times.")

[23] The only source outside of Daniel that records Belshazzar's death is Xenophon, who states that Cyrus' general Gobryas (Gubaru) executed him. According to Xenophon, the soldiers entered

Yet Daniel also states that Darius "received" (קְבֵל) the kingdom (Dan 6:1 [ET 5:31]), implying that he would not have ruled unless God had granted him this authority. God rules all world kingdoms for the sake of his kingdom of grace, the one church of Jesus Christ. God had made that point in Daniel 2 via the dream of four world kingdoms represented by the statue that is shattered at the advent of God's eternal kingdom (2:44–45). Even Nebuchadnezzar acknowledged God's unique ability to save (3:29) and that human kingdoms are transitory; God deposes and enthrones rulers for the sake of his own everlasting kingdom (4:28, 31–34 [ET 4:31, 34–37]).

Gospel is latent in the statement that Darius received the kingdom (6:1 [ET 5:31]). Even though Darius (Cyrus) did not believe in the one true God (Is 45:4), he was God's instrument to release his chastised and repentant people Israel from captivity (Is 44:28; 45:1–6; 2 Chr 36:22–23; Ezra 1:1–11). His edict in 538 BC would permit the Judeans to return to the promised land and begin the rebuilding of Jerusalem and the temple, where God would once again dwell. Then in the fullness of time, God's own Son would come to dwell there and redeem all who stood under the condemnation of the Law, gaining for them redemption through the forgiveness of sins by his unblemished life, atoning death, and bodily resurrection (Gal 4:4; Eph 1:7; Col 1:14).

---

the palace, where they found the king holding a dagger, about to take his own life. They overpowered him and "avenged themselves upon the wicked king" (*Cyropaedia*, 7.5.29–32 [trans. Walter Miller, *Xenophon's Cyropaedia* (Loeb Classical Library; Cambridge, Mass.: Harvard University Press, 1914), 2:273, 275]).

Excursus
The Identity of Darius the Mede

Darius the Mede in Daniel

(a) Dan 6:1, 2, 7, 10, 26, 29 (ET 5:31; 6:1, 6, 9, 25, 28); 9:1; 11:1

(b) Is 44:28; 45:1; Ezra 1:1–2, 7–8; 3:7; 4:3, 5; 5:13–14, 17; 6:3, 14; 2 Chr 36:22–23

No person mentioned in the book of Daniel is more obscure and controversial than Darius the Mede.[a] No person by this name is known from extrabiblical records as having taken over the rule of Babylon following the fall of Nabonidus and Belshazzar. Daniel records the name of Cyrus (1:21; 6:29 [ET 6:28]; 10:1), the Persian king who defeated Babylon, and Cyrus is named in other biblical books too.[b] The person called "Darius the Mede" in Daniel (6:1 [ET 5:31]; 11:1) is unknown by that name in any other record.

Daniel tells us the following facts about Darius:

1. He was about sixty-two years of age when Babylon was conquered (6:1 [ET 5:31]).
2. He appointed one hundred twenty satraps over the kingdom of Babylon (6:2 [ET 6:1]).
3. He had the authority to write to "all the peoples, nations, and languages that dwelt in the entire earth" (6:26 [ET 6:25]).
4. He reigned at least part of one year (9:1; 11:1).
5. He was a Median (6:1 [ET 5:31]; 9:1; 11:1), descended from a certain Ahasuerus (9:1).
6. He "received the kingdom" of Babylon (6:1 [ET 5:31]) and "was made king" (9:1).
7. His conquest of Babylon ended Daniel's service to the Chaldean kings (1:21).

Critical Scholars Suppose Darius Is a Fictional Construct

Critical scholars assert that Darius was not a historical person. Often they simply declare that Darius is a fictional construct and Daniel 6 is a fictional account.[1] They note that there is no extant extrabiblical record that states that a man named Darius ruled Babylon immediately following its fall. However, that is merely an argument from silence and may simply reflect that such historical records of Darius have not survived or come to light yet. The discovery during the nineteenth century of extrabiblical historical records that name Belshazzar[2] should lead scholars to be more cautious about denying the historicity of Darius, another person from antiquity named in Daniel.

Some critics refine the crassly skeptical view of Darius by stating that the story, while fictional, originally was set in the reign of a historical person named Darius: the Persian king Darius I (Darius the Great, 522–486 BC). Later, when this story was incorporated into the book of Daniel, the description of Darius was changed so that he became the conqueror of Babylon (6:1 [ET 5:31]) and

---

[1] E.g., Montgomery, *Daniel*, 63–65, 268.

[2] See "The Person and Office of Belshazzar" in "Introduction to Daniel 5."

was called a Mede in order to fulfill the prophecies of Isaiah and Jeremiah (Is 13:17; 21:2; Jer 51:11, 28).[3] However, these critical scholars too make no effort to reconcile the biblical statements about Darius with other historical records because they believe Daniel's accounts about him are fictional and unhistorical.

Attempts to Identify Darius with Another Known Historical Person

Evangelical scholars who defend the historicity of Daniel have sought to identify Darius with a historical person known from other ancient historical records in addition to the book of Daniel. They have offered several suggestions. Two men are most often identified as the person who could be the one Daniel calls Darius the Mede:[4] the commander Gubaru, who captured Babylon, and Cyrus II (Cyrus the Great), who ruled Persia from 559 BC until his death in 530.

Gubaru

Throughout the nineteenth and early twentieth centuries, Gubaru was often put forward as the most likely person known to Daniel as Darius. Gubaru was the general of the Persian army that conquered Babylon, and he briefly served as governor or perhaps vassal king of Babylon under Cyrus.[5] This could explain

---

[3] See, for example, Collins, *Daniel*, 30–32; Hartman and Di Lella, *Daniel*, 35–36, 196–201. See also the comments of Grabbe, "Another Look at the *Gestalt* of 'Darius the Mede,' " 211–12, who cites with approval Sparks ("On the Origin of 'Darius the Mede' at Daniel V. 31"). Sparks argues that that the name "Darius the Mede" was a result of the author of Daniel 6 consulting the books of Zechariah and Haggai and identifying the Darius mentioned there with the conqueror of Babylon.

A few other scholars propose that Cambyses, Cyrus' son and successor on the throne of Persia, was the Darius named in Daniel (e.g., Boutflower, *In and around the Book of Daniel*, 142–55). A number of cuneiform texts indicate that Cyrus installed Cambyses as king of Babylon while Cyrus was king of Persia. These texts date to "the first year of Cyrus, king of lands, Cambyses, king of Babylon." According to Yamauchi (*Persia and the Bible*, 95), most scholars assume that this refers to Cyrus' first year as king, which was spring 538–spring 537 BC. However, Shea argues that it refers to Cambyses' first year as coregent with Cyrus, near the end of Cyrus' life ("An Unrecognized Vassal King of Babylon in the Early Achaemenid Period," part 2). Shea's position is difficult to maintain, since it is clear that Babylon was governed by a "governor" named Gubaru from no later than Cyrus' fourth year until Cambyses' fifth year. Yamauchi (*Persia and the Bible*, 95) notes that many scholars believe that Gubaru was made governor as early as the end of Cyrus' first year. But either way, Cambyses can hardly be Darius. Cambyses could not have been sixty-two years of age in 538 BC, when his father was sixty-three years old.

[4] A few evangelical scholars hold that Darius was a historical person, but offer no opinion as to whether he should be identified with a particular person known from extrabiblical historical records. See, for example, Walvoord, *Daniel*, 134, and Young, *Daniel*, 131. Miller holds that Darius could be either Gubaru or Cyrus, but he does not favor one over the other (*Daniel*, 177).

[5] This man is also called Ugbaru, since the cuneiform signs for "ug" and "gu" are similar. In the past there was some confusion because there were two men named Gubaru who were governors over Babylon. The first Gubaru was the general who captured the city in 539 BC

why Daniel states that Darius "received the kingdom" (6:1 [ET 5:31]) and "was made king" (9:1), according to this view, by Cyrus. Though this view is not as popular as it once was, it has had defenders in recent times.[6]

Though the Persian army conquered Babylon on 16 Tishri 539 (October 12, 539), Cyrus did not enter the city until he arrived with other Persian troops on 3 Heshvan 539 (October 29, 539).[7] Thus Gubaru ruled Babylon until Cyrus arrived. Upon his arrival, Cyrus apparently appointed Gubaru as governor of Babylon because the Nabonidus Chronicle notes that Gubaru, "his [Cyrus'] governor," appointed (sub)governors for Babylon (cf. Dan 6:2–3 [ET 6:1–2]). However, Gubaru died on 11 Heshvan (November 6), having ruled only twenty-five days from the fall of Babylon and only one week after having been appointed governor of Babylon by Cyrus.

While Shea has proposed a clever chronology to synchronize all of the data about Gubaru from the Babylonian sources and Daniel,[8] the twenty-five days of his rule are barely enough time to encompass the events of Daniel 6 and 9 (cf. 9:1). Daniel 6 refers to thirty days during which no one could pray to any god except to Darius (6:8, 13 [ET 6:7, 12]), and that time period would have expired after the death of Gubaru/Darius. Moreover, Shea's chronology requires that Gubaru appointed all one hundred twenty satraps (6:2 [ET 6:1]) in one day,[9] a highly unlikely scenario unless he merely reappointed a great number of officials who had already served under Nabonidus—also highly unlikely. In addition, Shea's chronology requires that Gubaru had come to the conclusion that Daniel should be appointed head of the satraps on the same day that he appointed all the other satraps, despite the impression given by Dan 6:4 (ET 6:3) that it took some time for Daniel to distinguish himself sufficiently above the others so that Darius planned to appoint him as head of the satraps. Moreover, the account in Daniel 6 depicts Darius as favorably disposed toward Daniel, implying that the king had had time to develop a relationship that expressed a warm affection for him. Probably it would have required at least a few months for such a relationship to develop.

---

and died one month later. The other was governor over Babylon from at least Cyrus' fourth year (spring 535–spring 534) to Cambyses' fifth year (spring 525–spring 524). Many scholars hold that this second Gubaru became governor at the end of Cyrus' first year (Yamauchi, *Persia and the Bible*, 95). Failure to distinguish these two men led some scholars to make claims about Gubaru being Darius that could not be sustained. For example, see the now discredited study by Whitcomb, *Darius the Mede*.

[6] Most notable is a series of articles by Shea, "An Unrecognized Vassal King of Babylon in the Early Achaemenid Period," parts 1–4; "Darius the Mede: An Update"; "The Search for Darius the Mede (Concluded), or, The Time of the Answer to Daniel's Prayer and the Date of the Death of Darius the Mede." For a time Shea abandoned this view in favor of identifying Darius as Cyrus ("Darius the Mede in His Persian-Babylonian Setting").

[7] These events are recorded in the Nabonidus Chronicle (*ANET*, 306).

[8] Shea, "The Search for Darius the Mede (Concluded)," 104.

[9] Shea, "The Search for Darius the Mede (Concluded)," 99–100, 104.

There are other problems with the identification of Darius as Gubaru. For instance, why would a governor or vassal king have the authority to write to "all the peoples, nations, and languages that dwelt in the entire earth" and command them to honor Daniel's God (6:26–28 [6:25–27])? Why would Gubaru have authority to order that no one pray to any god but to himself (6:8, 13 [ET 6:7, 12]) if he were merely a vassal of Cyrus? Would not this be seen in the Persian court as an attempt to elevate himself above Cyrus? Moreover, advocates of this theory offer no hard evidence for Gubaru's age or his Median descent. Therefore, while it is possible that Gubaru could have been the man known to Daniel as Darius (perhaps as his throne name), the probability of this identification is low.

Cyrus the Great

Some ancient Jewish texts identify Darius as the Persian king Cyrus the Great. The oldest is Theodotion's version of Bel and the Serpent (Bel 1).[10] This identification was proposed again in modern times by the British scholar D. J. Wiseman and has been adopted by others.[11] This identification interprets the *waw* on וּבְמַלְכוּת in Dan 6:29 (ET 6:28) as epexegetical or explicative:

וְדָנִיֵּאל דְּנָה הַצְלַח בְּמַלְכוּת דָּרְיָוֶשׁ וּבְמַלְכוּת כּוֹרֶשׁ פָּרְסָאָה׃
So this Daniel prospered in the reign of Darius, *that is*, in the reign of Cyrus the Persian.

This kind of use of the conjunction *waw* is common in Daniel.[12] It also occurs in Chronicles in a reference to an Assyrian king by his shorter and longer names:

וַיָּעַר אֱלֹהֵי יִשְׂרָאֵל אֶת־רוּחַ ׀ פּוּל מֶלֶךְ־אַשּׁוּר
וְאֶת־רוּחַ תִּלְּגַת פִּלְנֶסֶר מֶלֶךְ אַשּׁוּר
The God of Israel aroused the spirit of Pul, king of Assyria, *that is*, the spirit of Tiglath-pileser, king of Assyria. (1 Chr 5:26)

That is similar to the reference to the foreign king(s) in Dan 6:29 (ET 6:28). Thus this interpretation of the *waw* in 6:29 (ET 6:28) is altogether reasonable.

Could Darius be another name for Cyrus? Several examples of kings having more than one name are known. Moreover, Herodotus twice notes that the original name of the great Persian ruler was not Cyrus, since his mother had given

---

[10] Both the Old Greek and Theodotion read "Cyrus" instead of the MT's "Darius" in Dan 11:1.

[11] Wiseman proposed this hypothesis in 1957 in "The Last Days of Babylon." See also Wiseman, "Some Historical Problems in the Book of Daniel," 9–16. Later advocates of this view include Baldwin, *Daniel*, 26–28; Bulman, "The Identification of Darius the Mede"; and Lucas, *Daniel*, 136–37. This hypothesis was adopted for a time by Shea ("Darius the Mede in His Persian-Babylonian Setting"). Although Colless ("Cyrus the Persian as Darius the Mede in the Book of Daniel") does not affirm the historicity of Daniel, he believes that the author called Cyrus Darius because he wished to provide an alternate name for this historical person, just as the author does for some other historical characters in Daniel (e.g., 1:7).

[12] For examples see the second textual note on 2:28 and the second textual note on 3:2.

him a different name at birth.[13] It is possible, then, that Darius was Cyrus' actual name given by his mother, who was a Mede, and that he took the name Cyrus later, perhaps as a throne name. This would explain why he is called "Darius *the Mede*," a name bestowed on him by his Median mother.

Certainly the prerogatives enjoyed by Darius according to Daniel 6 would have been appropriate for Cyrus: appointing satraps (6:2 [ET 6:1]) and issuing a letter to "all the peoples, nations, and languages that dwelt in the entire earth" (6:26–28 [6:25–27]). Moreover, the practice of praying to a king (6:8, 13 [ET 6:7, 12]) bestowed on him a special connection to the divine, which is central to the plot of Daniel 6. The inauguration of this practice was traced by Arrian (in the second century AD) to Cyrus the Great.[14] The portrait of Darius in Daniel 6 matches well with the theory that Darius the Mede is Cyrus the Great.

Darius' age at the conquest of Babylon was "about sixty-two" (6:1 [ET 5:31]). Cyrus died in 530 BC at the age of seventy. Therefore, Cyrus would have turned sixty-two in 539 BC, the year that Babylon fell to his armies.

Darius is called a Mede in Daniel, but never "king of the Medes." Instead, Daniel uses "the Mede" to refer to Darius' descent from Median ancestors (9:1). This matches what was known of Cyrus. On his father's side he was a Persian: he was descended from his great-great-grandfather Achaemenes (ca. 700–ca. 675), his great-grandfather Teispes (ca. 675–ca. 640), his grandfather Cyrus I (ca. 640–600), and his father Cambyses I (ca. 600–559), all of whom were Persian rulers. However, Cyrus' father, Cambyses, was a vassal of the Medes and married Mandana, the daughter of the Median king Astyages (Old Persian: *Arštivaiga*; 585–550). Cyrus became ruler of Persia in 559 BC. He rebelled against his grandfather Astyages and deposed him in 550. Thus Cyrus united the Medes and the Persians in his dual heritage as a Persian and a Mede, and he eventually became ruler of the combined kingdoms of the Medes and the Persians. Herodotus knew that Cyrus was the son of a daughter of Astyages, and Xenophon noted that he was born to a daughter of a Median king.[15] In Dan 9:1 Darius the Mede is called "son of Ahasuerus," which may refer to his Median grandfather, since "Ahasuerus" could be a Hebrew rendition of the Median name (translated into English as) Astyages. Alternately, "Ahasuerus" may be an ancient Achaemenid royal title bestowed on one of Cyrus's ancestors.[16]

Some might object that the statements that Cyrus "received the kingdom" (6:1 [ET 5:31]) and "was made king" (9:1) are inaccurate because they depict Cyrus as having a passive role. It would have been more accurate to describe him as the active conqueror, since he defeated the Babylonians and seized the throne that had been occupied by Chaldean kings. However, these statements

---

[13] Herodotus, *Histories*, 1.113–14.

[14] Arrian, *Anabasis Alexandri*, 4.11.

[15] Herodotus, *Histories*, 1.112; Xenophon, *Cyropaedia*, 8.5.19; see also Wiseman, "Some Historical Problems in the Book of Daniel," 13–14.

[16] Wiseman, "Some Historical Problems in the Book of Daniel," 15.

by Daniel should be read as theological in nature. Daniel often uses passive constructions that imply that God is the real agent of the action.[17] The statements in 6:1 (ET 5:31) and 9:1 do not focus on human actions but instead imply that behind all human authority is God, who makes kings of whomever he pleases—a point made repeatedly in Daniel.[c]

(c) Dan 1:2; 2:21, 37; 4:14, 22, 29, 32 (ET 4:17, 25, 32, 35); 5:21

Conclusion

There is strong correlation of evidence between Daniel's depiction of Darius and the facts known about Cyrus, making the identification of Darius the Mede as Cyrus the Great highly probable. Therefore, Daniel knows this king both by his more familiar name Cyrus (1:21; 6:29 [ET 6:28]; 10:1) and as Darius.[d] Daniel equates the two in 6:29 (ET 6:28) by means of the epexegetical *waw*.

(d) Dan 6:1, 2, 7, 10, 26, 29 (ET 5:31; 6:1, 6, 9, 25, 28); 9:1; 11:1

Daniel's use of the name "Darius" may be his way of emphasizing the fulfillment of the words of the prophets who spoke of the Medes as the ones who would bring about Babylon's fall (Is 13:17; 21:2; Jer 51:11, 28). Daniel himself speaks about the fall of Babylon to "the Medes and the Persians" (Dan 5:28).

Yet Daniel also presents Cyrus the Persian. By tying the names Darius and Cyrus together in (6:29 [ET 6:28]), Daniel makes the point that Babylon fell to "*the Medes and the Persians*" (5:28), a point reinforced by constant reference to "the law of the Medes and the Persians" in Daniel 6 (6:9, 13, 16 [ET 6:8, 12, 15]). In this way, Daniel also emphasizes the fulfillment of the prophecy of Isaiah that Babylon would fall to the Persians (Elam) and the Medes (Is 21:2).

Finally, it should be noted that three of the eleven references to Cyrus/Darius in Daniel are to his first full regnal year as king over Babylon.[18] The first of these three references records that Daniel served Chaldean kings from the time of his exile from Judah in 605 BC until Cyrus' first year (1:21). The second such reference tells us that Daniel was moved to pray about the end of Judah's exile in Babylon during Darius' first year (9:1). The third such reference is in the statement of an angel to Daniel that he strengthened Michael, the archangel of God's people (12:1), during Darius' first year (11:1). Each of these is related to the fulfillment of the prophecy of the end of Israel's captivity (Is 44:28; 45:1; Jer 25:11–12). In Daniel 1, Daniel himself remains subservient to Chaldean kings until the first year of Cyrus, just as the vessels from the Jerusalem temple were taken captive (Dan 1:2) and would be freed from Babylonian bondage in Cyrus' first year (2 Chr 36:22–23; Ezra 1:1–11). Daniel in chapter 9 is concerned about the restoration of the temple in Jerusalem, which is begun through Cyrus' decree in his first year (2 Chr 36:22–23; Ezra 1–3). In Daniel 11, the

---

[17] See, for example, the textual notes on 4:22, 29 (ET 4:25, 32). In other passages, Daniel the author states outright that God is the true agent who enables even a foreign and pagan king to conquer: for example, "the Lord gave into his [Nebuchadnezzar's] hand King Jehoiakim of Judah" (1:2).

[18] Babylon's fall in 539 commenced Cyrus' accession year. His first full regnal year as king began on 1 Nisan 538 (March 24, 538).

Excursus

angel speaking with Daniel stood to strengthen Michael, the angel of God's people, in the first year of Darius the Mede. The angel then tells Daniel that there will be three more kings of *Persia* before a fourth, rich king arises (11:2). Clearly Darius is treated in this passage as a king of Persia, implying that he is, indeed, Cyrus the Great. Thus the events on earth were reinforced by spiritual warfare in heaven. This understanding of the strengthening of Michael so that the Judeans could return to the land and rebuild Jerusalem and the temple is clearly the understanding of 11:1 in the Old Greek and Theodotion versions, which change the name from *Darius* to *Cyrus*.

In sum, Darius is most likely another name for Cyrus the Great. While the evidence for this hypothesis is not ironclad, it is strong and fits well with both the book of Daniel and the rest of Scripture. Moreover, there are extrabiblical sources about Cyrus that correlate well with what Daniel says about Darius. Therefore, unless other evidence surfaces to shed further light on Darius, it is best to consider him the same historical person as Cyrus the Great.

Daniel 6:2–29 (ET 6:1–28)

God's Faithful Servant Daniel Is Rescued from Death

Introduction to Daniel 6

6:2–29　　　God's Faithful Servant Daniel Is Rescued from Death (ET 6:1–28)

Introduction to Daniel 6

Major Emphases in Daniel 6

The story of Daniel in the lions' den is probably the best known of the narratives[1] in Daniel, along with the account of the three Judeans in the fiery furnace (Daniel 3). The two accounts are clearly parallel in many ways. Both are narratives of faith in the face of persecution and of miraculous deliverance by God's almighty power to save his people. Both narratives present accusations by pagan officials against Judeans who refuse to compromise their faith and worship of Yahweh alone. Both even employ the same Aramaic idiom, "to eat pieces of" someone, signifying malicious accusations, and these are the only two times this expression occurs in Daniel (3:8; 6:25 [ET 6:24]). Both accounts end with a decree of the king to all peoples, nations, and languages in all the earth, proclaiming God's power and commanding respect for the God of the Judeans (3:29–30; 6:26–28 [ET 6:25–27]).

However, two important differences in the two accounts point to the unique emphases in the narrative of Daniel's persecution in contrast to the persecution of Shadrach, Meshach, and Abednego. In Daniel 3, the faithfulness of the Judeans is demonstrated by their unwillingness to break the First Commandment: they would not bow down to an idol. However, Daniel was not required by Darius' decree in Daniel 6 to worship any particular god. Instead, he was forbidden to pray to his God, the only true God. Therefore, the emphasis in this account is on the First and Third Commandments and the truth that a believer must not neglect to worship God in order to try to avoid persecution. The failure to worship the one true God is not compatible with affirming belief in him. The contrast between the two chapters is from a negatively worded command (Daniel 3: *do not* worship other gods) to a positively worded one in Daniel 6: *do* worship the true God.[2]

Daniel could have avoided any accusation against himself simply by not worshiping God for a month. However, Daniel felt an obligation to worship

---

[1] Daniel 1–6 consists of narratives while Daniel 7–12 is comprised of visions. See "Organization of the Book: The Clearly Defined Sections" in "Overview of Daniel" the introduction.

[2] The First Commandment (Ex 20:3; Deut 5:7) prohibits the worship of any other god. Especially in light of God's redemption in the immediately preceding prologue (Ex 20:2; Deut 5:6), the First Commandment also means that "we should fear, love, and trust in God above all things" (Luther, SC I 1–2 [*LSB*, p. 321]), and so it also implies a positive command to worship the one true God (and him alone).

While the Third Commandment (Ex 20:8–11; Deut 5:12–15) specifically mandates observance of the Sabbath, it also applies more generally to the proper worship of God every day, including worship by means of prayer as practiced by Daniel in chapter 6.

For an explanation of how the commandments are evident in the book of Daniel, see further "God's Law in Daniel" in "Law and Gospel in Daniel" in the introduction.

God. Moreover, his trust in God as the only source of life, forgiveness, comfort, and aid drew him to prayer three times each day. He could not give this up, even for the sake of obeying a decree of the king, a violation of which was punishable by death. Therefore, this account supplements the message of Daniel 3 by reminding readers that not only is it imperative to avoid idolatry even in the face of persecution, but believers also cannot compromise the one true faith by neglecting the worship of God, even when that worship exposes believers to persecution and death. Neglecting to worship God is as much a denial of the true God as bowing down to idols. As Jesus said, "Everyone who acknowledges me before people, I also will acknowledge before my Father, who is in heaven. But whoever denies me before people, I also will deny before my Father, who is in heaven" (Mt 10:32–33; cf. Lk 12:8–9; Rom 10:9–11; 2 Tim 2:11–13).

Related to this theme is a second one: the contrast between the new Persian policy and attitude toward Judeans and the old Babylonian policy and attitude. The policy of the Babylonians (under whom the Judeans lived in Daniel 1–5) assumed that everyone was a polytheist and so everyone could and would worship the Babylonian gods, perhaps in addition to their own favorite deities. Since the Babylonian rulers assumed that everyone believed that there were many gods, they presumed that subjugated peoples would willingly incorporate into their religion the worship of the gods of Babylon, who had proved their superiority by granting Babylon military victory over those peoples.[3] This assumption lay behind the account in Daniel 3: Nebuchadnezzar pursued the policy of religious indoctrination linked with loyalty to the crown as he set up the statue he expected all his officials to worship. Although it probably was jealousy that prompted certain officials to bring charges against Shadrach, Meshach, and Abednego, what drives the account in Daniel 3 is also the insistence of Nebuchadnezzar that they worship his god, and his anger when they refuse to obey.

However, the Persian policy depicted in Daniel 6 is different. Here the initiative that led to the decree that no one could pray to any god except to Darius came from the king's advisors as a plot hatched specifically to entrap Daniel. The king did not pursue this policy and tried to circumvent it (6:15 [ET 6:14]). Darius remains favorably disposed to Daniel throughout the account (6:17, 21, 24 [ET 6:16, 20, 23]).

This contrast between Babylonian and Persian policy is intended to mirror the changed status of the Judean captives in general. Under Babylon they were exiled from the land (1:1–2). Under Persia they will be allowed to return (2 Chr 36:22–23; Ezra 1:1–11). Under Babylon the temple in Jerusalem was destroyed (1:1–2). Under Persia it would be rebuilt (Ezra 3:8–6:15). By depicting this change via the contrast between Nebuchadnezzar and Darius, Daniel

---

[3] This assumption is evident already in Daniel 1. After Babylon conquered Judah (1:1–2), the Babylonians assigned new names to the captive Judeans—pagan names that honored Babylonian deities. See the textual notes on 1:7.

the author is demonstrating that God has brought about a change for his people. He used the captivity to bring his unfaithful people to repentance and to refine them so that they would gladly worship the gracious God who preserved them throughout their time in Babylon (cf. Ezek 11:16). Now under the Persians, God will grant the Judean exiles prosperity (Dan 6:29 [ET 6:28]) and freedom from captivity so that may return to the land, rebuild the temple in Jerusalem, and worship him joyfully there, awaiting the advent of the promised Messiah.[4]

The Christian reader of Daniel 6 may notice a number of parallels between Daniel and the life of Jesus Christ. Both prayed regularly (Dan 6:11 [ET 6:10]; Lk 5:16). Malicious accusers sought to entrap each by means of his worship practice and fidelity to God's Word (Dan 6:6 [ET 6:5]; Mt 4:6–10; 22:15–46). An unruly crowd brings him to a pagan ruler and accuses him of violating the law (Dan 6:12–14 [ET 6:11–13]; Mt 26:47–50; 27:1–2, 11–14; Jn 18:1–19:15).[5] The ruler, deeming him innocent, seeks to set him free, but eventually gives in to the crowd's desire and condemns him to death (Dan 6:15–17 [ET 6:14–16]; Mt 27:18–26; Jn 19:8–16). Both Daniel and Jesus are said to have "trusted in (his) God" (Dan 6:24 [ET 6:23]; Mt 27:43). A rock is placed over the opening of the pit or tomb and sealed with a royal seal (Dan 6:18 [ET 6:17]; Mt 27:66). At dawn the king hurries to the pit (Dan 6:20 [ET 6:19]), as the women did to the tomb on Easter dawn (Mt 28:1). Both emerge alive: Daniel, who served "the living God" (Dan 6:21, 27 [ET 6:20, 26]; cf. Mt 26:63), and the risen Jesus, who is himself "the living one" (Lk 24:5).

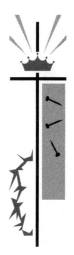

These parallels may indicate that Jesus endured the sum total of the world's hatred and persecution of all believers in God (cf. Jn 15:18–19; 1 Jn 3:13). The rescue of Daniel from death was a sign pointing to the eternal salvation won for all by Jesus' suffering, death, and bodily resurrection. Thus Heb 11:33 speaks of OT saints "who through faith ... stopped the mouths of lions" (cf. Dan 6:23 [ET 6:22]) as testimony to salvation through faith in Jesus Christ.

The Historical Setting of Daniel 6

The other narrative accounts in Daniel (chapters 1–5) have a clean break between each. Unlike them, the account of Daniel 5 flows seamlessly into Daniel 6. In 6:1 (ET 5:31), Darius the Mede (Cyrus the Persian)[6] "received the kingdom," and in 6:2 (ET 6:1), Darius decides to place satraps over the conquered kingdom of Babylon. It is obvious that Daniel 6 took place shortly after the fall of Babylon to the Persians.

The city of Babylon was entered by the Persian commander Gubaru on 16 Tishri 539 BC (October 12, 539). The Persian king Cyrus arrived in Babylon

---

[4] See "The Messiah in Daniel: An Overview" in "Major Themes" in the introduction.

[5] One might even compare the citation of Darius' law in order to get Darius to condemn Daniel (6:14 [ET 6:13]) to the citation of Caesar by Jesus' opponents in order to get Pilate to condemn Jesus (Jn 19:15–16).

[6] See the excursus "The Identity of Darius the Mede."

on 3 Heshvan 539 (October 29, 539). He appointed Gubaru governor and other officials were appointed under Gubaru. However, Gubaru died on 11 Heshvan (November 6, 539).[7] Babylonian records do not reveal who was ruler of Babylon under Cyrus between 11 Heshvan 539 and the beginning of Cyrus' first official year on 1 Nisan 538 (March 24, 538). However, almost thirty cuneiform tablets from Cyrus' first year speak of "Cyrus, king of lands, Cambyses, king of Babylon," indicating that Cyrus' son Cambyses was placed on the throne of Babylon as coregent with his father. Moreover, Cambyses took part in the New Year's festival honoring the patron god of Babylon, Marduk (Bel)—a privilege reserved for Babylon's king. However, probably due to the difficulty Cambyses had working with Babylonian officials, he was removed from the throne nine months later and replaced by a governor named Gubaru (a different man than the now-deceased Persian commander by the same name).[8] Beginning with the tenth month of his first year, Cyrus is called "king of Babylon, king of lands." Gubaru remained governor beyond Cyrus' death until Cambyses' fifth year as king over the Persian Empire.

We should note that Daniel was Cyrus' presumptive choice to be the person placed over the entire kingdom of Babylon (6:3 [ET 6:2]). However, nowhere does Daniel 6 say that he was placed in that position. Instead, we are only told that Daniel "prospered" during the reign of Cyrus (6:29 [ET 6:28]) and lived until at least Cyrus' third year (10:1). Given the trouble Cyrus had with jealousy among officials in Babylon (as evidenced by the account in Daniel 6), it appears that he decided instead to place his son Cambyses in charge. Therefore, Daniel was probably not promoted to the position of governor, though he appears to have retained important influence in the affairs of the kingdom.

Thus the events of Daniel 6 take place between Cyrus' arrival in the city of Babylon in October 539 and the naming of Cambyses as king of Babylon in late March 538. We can construct a possible chronology for the events in Daniel 6 as follows:

3 Heshvan (October 29) 539 BC	Cyrus arrived in Babylon and appointed Gubaru governor.
4–10 Heshvan (October 30–November 5) 539	Gubaru began appointing satraps.
11 Heshvan (November 6) 539	Gubaru died.
12–29 Heshvan (November 7–24) 539	Cyrus completed the appointing of satraps and placed three overseers (including Daniel) over the satraps (instead of a new governor; Dan 6:2–3 [ET 6:1–2]).

---

[7] These events are recorded in the Nabonidus Chronicle (*ANET*, 306).

[8] Yamauchi, *Persia and the Bible*, 95. Shea notes that Gubaru's name (or the name of any other governor) does not appear on contract tablets until Cyrus' fourth year, indicating that he was not governor until then ("A Further Note on Daniel 6: Daniel as 'Governor,'" 170). However, most scholars are convinced that Gubaru was made governor at the earlier date.

Kislev 539–Shebat 538 (November 25, 539–February 21, 538)	Daniel distinguished himself; Cyrus planned to appoint him as governor of the kingdom of Babylon (6:4 [ET 6:3]).
Late Shebat–Adar 538 (Late February–March 23, 538)	The plot against Daniel was hatched: no one was allowed to pray to any god other than Darius/Cyrus. Daniel was rescued from the lions' den.
1 Nisan (March 24) 538	At the beginning of Cyrus' first official year, Cambyses was made king of Babylon and took part in New Year's festival in Babylon.

This fits well with what is known of the religious disruption in and around Babylon following the fall of the city to the Persians. In order to rally the gods in defense of the city, Nabonidus had brought their images from the surrounding cities to Babylon. After the city's fall, Cyrus ordered the gods to be returned to their temples. This repatriation of the gods took place from Kislev 539 to Adar 538 (November 25, 539–March 23, 538), so that they were in place by the beginning of the new year on 1 Nisan 538 (March 24, 538). During the time when the gods were not in their temples, formal worship of them may have been suspended in many places. Thus the request made by those who plotted against Daniel would have made good sense: since many people could not pray to their local patron gods, Darius became the one to whom they prayed until the repatriation could be completed. This would suggest that the thirty-day period when prayers to other gods were proscribed (6:8, 13 [ET 6:7, 12]) was near the end of the repatriation.

The plot was hatched against Daniel. Although Daniel was rescued from the lions and his accusers were executed (6:24–25 [ET 6:23–24]), Darius (Cyrus) may have decided that putting the Persian crown prince in charge of Babylon would prevent further infighting among officials in Babylon. Thus Cambyses was made king at the new year. However, he seemed to have offended and dealt poorly with the Babylonians and was deposed after nine months to be replaced by another official, Gubaru.

We may conclude, therefore, that Daniel 6:2–3 (ET 6:1–2) probably took place in Heshvan 539 BC (late October–late November 539). Daniel 6:4 (ET 6:3) describes Daniel's rise to Darius' attention starting in Kislev 539 (late November–late December 539). By late Shebat 538 (late February 538), Darius had decided to place Daniel in charge of Babylon (6:4 [ET 6:3]), but in late Shebat or in Adar 538 (late February–late March 538), some officials plotted against Daniel, and so instead of being promoted, he was thrown to the lions, rescued, and saw his accusers executed (6:5–29 [ET 6:4–28]).

Chapter Division and Verse Numbering in Daniel 6

The first verse to mention Darius the Mede is numbered as 6:1 in the MT and Vulgate, but 5:31 in English translations. This verse was assigned to the beginning of Daniel 6 when the Vulgate (the Latin translation produced by Jerome ca. AD 400) was divided into chapters. The Vulgate chapter divisions were introduced in the Middle Ages, and they are attributed to Stephen Langton, archbishop of Canterbury, in the thirteenth century. This chapter division kept all of the references to Darius in the same chapter. When the Hebrew text was divided into chapters, the Vulgate chapter divisions were used. However, in Luther's German translation of the Bible[9] and in subsequent English translations, the verse was assigned to the end of Daniel 5 in order to demonstrate the complete fulfillment of the message of the handwriting on the wall.

Since the narrative of Daniel 5 flows without interruption into Daniel 6, either chapter division makes sense. However, the two chapters are separate accounts. In content, Daniel 5 is parallel to Daniel 4 (in both chapters Daniel interprets a divine revelation of judgment on a pagan king), whereas Daniel 6 is parallel to Daniel 3 (persecuted believers are delivered from death). Just as Daniel 3 and Daniel 4 are separate accounts, so too Daniel 5 and Daniel 6 need to be viewed as separate accounts.

Throughout Daniel 6, verse numbers are one number higher in printed Hebrew texts than in English Bibles. Starting with 7:1, the Hebrew and English chapter divisions and verse numbering again align with each other and continue that way throughout the remainder of the book.

---

[9] WA DB 11/2.154–55. Luther keeps the MT verse numbering, but puts MT 5:31 (ET 6:1) at the beginning of chapter 6.

Daniel 6:2–29 (ET 6:1–28)

God's Faithful Servant Daniel Is Rescued from Death

Translation

6 ²It seemed good to Darius to set over the kingdom one hundred twenty satraps who would be throughout the kingdom. ³Over them would be three overseers (Daniel was one of them) who would be the ones to whom these satraps would give a report, and the king would not suffer [any] loss. ⁴Then this Daniel distinguished himself above the overseers and satraps because an outstanding spirit was in him. So the king intended to promote him over the entire kingdom.

⁵Then the overseers and satraps kept seeking to find an accusation concerning Daniel with regard to the kingdom. However, they were unable to find an accusation or corruption because he was trustworthy and no neglect [of duty] or corruption could be found concerning him. ⁶Then these men said, "We will not find concerning this Daniel any accusation unless we find [something] against him in the law of his God."

⁷Then these overseers and satraps came as a crowd to the king and said this to him, "Darius, Your Majesty, may you live forever! ⁸All the overseers of the kingdom, the prefects and the satraps, the counselors and the governors advise the king to establish a statute and to ratify a decree that whoever prays a prayer to any god or person for thirty days except to you, Your Majesty, he will be thrown into the pit of lions. ⁹Now Your Majesty, please establish a decree and sign the document that cannot be changed, in accord with the law of the Medes and the Persians that cannot be revoked." ¹⁰Therefore King Darius signed the written decree.

¹¹Now, when Daniel knew the document had been signed, he went to his house. It had open windows on its upper story facing Jerusalem. Three times each day he would kneel on his knees and pray and offer praise before his God, just as he had been doing before this. ¹²Then these men came as a crowd and found Daniel praying and seeking favor from his God.

¹³Then they came and said to the king concerning the decree, "Your Majesty, did you not sign a decree that any man who prays to any god or man for thirty days except to you, Your Majesty, would be thrown into the pit of lions?"

The king answered, "Certainly. The matter is like the law of the Medes and the Persians that cannot be revoked."

¹⁴Then they answered the king, "Daniel, who is from the exiles of Judah, does not pay attention to you, Your Majesty, nor to the decree that you signed. Instead, three times each day he is praying his prayers."

¹⁵Then the king, when he heard this matter, was very upset about him, and he set his mind to save Daniel. So until sunset he worked hard to rescue him. ¹⁶Then

these men (came as a crowd to the king and) kept saying to the king, "Understand, Your Majesty, that it is the law of the Medes and the Persians that every decree or statute that the king establishes cannot be changed."

¹⁷Then the king spoke, and Daniel was brought and thrown into the pit of lions. The king said to Daniel, "May your God, whom you serve continually, save you." ¹⁸A stone was brought and placed over the mouth of the pit, and the king sealed it with his signet ring and the signet rings of his nobles so that nothing could be changed with regard to Daniel. ¹⁹Then the king went to his palace. He spent the night without food, and no entertainment was brought before him, and his sleep fled from him.

²⁰Then at dawn the king arose in the daylight and hurriedly came to the pit of lions. ²¹As he came near the pit, he cried out in a troubled voice. The king said to Daniel, "Daniel, servant of the living God, your God whom you serve continually: Was he able to save you from the lions?"

²²Then Daniel spoke with the king, "Your Majesty, may you live forever! ²³My God sent his angel and shut the mouth of the lions, and they have not hurt me because he found me innocent before him. Also before you, Your Majesty, I have committed no crime." ²⁴Then the king was very glad, and said for Daniel to be brought up from the pit. So Daniel was brought up from the pit, and no harm was found in him, because he trusted in his God.

²⁵The king spoke, and these men who maliciously accused Daniel were brought and thrown into the pit of lions—they, their children, and their wives. They had not reached the bottom of the pit when the lions overpowered them and crushed all their bones.

²⁶Then King Darius wrote to all the peoples, nations, and languages that dwelt in the entire earth:

"May your peace increase! ²⁷From me is given an order that throughout my royal dominion, [people] should continually tremble and be afraid before the God of Daniel.

"For he is (the) living God,
    enduring forever.
His kingdom will not be destroyed,
    and his dominion is eternal.
²⁸He saves and rescues,
    and he works signs and wonders in heaven and on earth,
    as he saved Daniel from the hand of the lions."

²⁹So this Daniel prospered during the reign of Darius, that is, during the reign of Cyrus the Persian.

Textual Notes

6:2 לַאֲחַשְׁדַּרְפְּנַיָּא—For אֲחַשְׁדַּרְפְּנַיָּא, "(the) satraps," see the first textual note on 3:2. As is customary in Aramaic, the preposition לְ is used to introduce the direct object, here of וַהֲקִים, literally, "he set, established."

6:3 וְעֵלָּא מִנְּהוֹן סָרְכִין—Literally, this is "and above from them [would be] overseers." The adverb עֵלָּא, "above," occurs only here in Biblical Aramaic. סָרְכִין is a loanword from the Old Persian *sāraka*, "to stand at the ready" (*HALOT*). It recurs in 6:4–5, 7–8 (ET 6:3–4, 6–7) but nowhere else in the OT.

וּמַלְכָּא לָא־לֶהֱוֵא נָזִק:—Literally, this is "and the king would not be injured." The Peal (G) imperfect לֶהֱוֵא is combined with נָזִק, the Peal (G) passive participle of נְזַק, "injure, inflict damage," or perhaps "suffer loss" (see *HALOT*, s.v. נזק). Apparently the arrangement of the subordinate officials was designed to protect the well-being of the king and the efficiency of his administration. Ironically, however, the king does suffer agony in 6:15, 19–21 (ET 6:14, 18–20) because of the punishment of Daniel, which was the result of infighting among these officials, since Daniel was one of the three overseers (6:3 [ET 6:2]).

6:4 מִתְנַצַּח—This Hithpaal (HtD) participle means that Daniel "distinguished himself" (see *HALOT*, s.v. נצח) by his God-given, Spirit-endowed wisdom, talent, and industriousness. It can be contrasted with the Hithpolel (HtD) הִתְרוֹמַ֫מְתָּ in 5:23, where Daniel accuses Belshazzar: "you *lifted yourself* against the Lord of heaven."

6:5 הֲווֹ בָעַיִן עִלָּה—The construction with the perfect of הֲוָה and the participle of בְּעָה denotes durative, ongoing action: they "*kept seeking ... an accusation*." In Aramaic, עִלָּה (twice in 6:5 [ET 6:4]) or עִלָּא (6:6 [ET 6:5]) means "ground for complaint, reason for accusation" (*HALOT*, which compares it to αἰτία, "charge," in Mt 27:37). The Old Greek renders the second occurrence in this verse with ἄγνοια, "ignorance, ... sin, mistake" (LEH), while Theodotion translates all three occurrences with πρόφασις, "pretext, excuse" (see LEH). The opponents sought any matter concerning Daniel's service that could be construed as the basis of an accusation.

וְכָל־שָׁלוּ וּשְׁחִיתָה לָא הִשְׁתְּכַחַת עֲלוֹהִי:—This is, literally, "any neglect or corruption could not be found concerning him." The noun שָׁלוּ is usually regarded as a masculine equivalent of Aramaic שָׁלוּתָא, which occurs in the Targumim meaning "neglect, error, forgetfulness" (Jastrow, s.v. שָׁלוּתָא). Therefore שָׁלוּ probably means "neglect" (BDB) or "negligence" (*HALOT*). However, שָׁלוּ was the Qere in 3:29, where the context called for the stronger meaning "blasphemy," since it referred to speech against God (see the first textual note on 3:29). The Akkadian *šillatu* probably is cognate to the Kethib שלה in 3:29 and possibly also is cognate to the Qere in 3:29, שָׁלוּ, the same word as here. Akkadian *šillatu* can refer to "blasphemy" against a god (*CAD*, 1 a), "blasphemous talk (against the king or an official)" (*CAD*, 1 b), or an "insult, insolence (against a superior)" (*CAD*, 1 c). Such a sin of speech by Daniel against the king or high officials would be a suitable meaning here as the basis for an accusation against Daniel.[1] Elsewhere in the Aramaic portions of the OT, שָׁלוּ occurs in Ezra 4:22 and 6:9, where, as here, it refers to a human fault rather than speech against God.

6:6 בְּדָת אֱלָהֵהּ:—The opponents resolved to find a pretext against Daniel "in (the matter of) the law of his God" (see BDB, s.v. Aramaic בְּ, 7). דָּת is the same noun for

---

[1] Paul, "Daniel 3:29—A Case Study of 'Neglected' Blasphemy," 293–94, who proposes that שָׁלוּ in 6:5 (ET 6:4) should be read as שָׁלָה and understood as referring to the verbal offence of "improper speech."

"law" used to refer to royal edicts (2:9, 13, 15; 6:9, 13, 16 [ET 6:8, 12, 15]). In 7:25 it refers to God's "Law" in a context that also refers to worship "times," the Sabbath and other worship occasions specified in the OT, which the Antichrist will seek to change. Here "the law of his God" refers to Daniel's faith and worship practices based on God's Word. Daniel's accusers may not have had access to the written Law of Moses and the other OT books that had been composed by this time (539–538 BC). They may have understood little or nothing of the content of the written OT books. However, they did perceive that Daniel based his own faith and worship practices on God's written Word. For a discussion of pertinent OT passages, see further the commentary on 6:11–12 (ET 6:10–11).

6:7 הַרְגִּשׁוּ עַל־מַלְכָּא—The Haphel (H) of רְגַשׁ probably means "come thronging" (BDB) or "come as a crowd," but it may have negative connotations because some Semitic cognates mean "start a rebellion, disturbance, uprising" (see *HALOT*). It recurs in 6:12, 16 (ET 6:11, 15).

מַלְכָּא לְעָלְמִין חֱיִי—This is the same flattering salutation addressed to Nebuchadnezzar and Belshazzar. See the second textual note on 2:4.

6:8 אִתְיָעַטוּ ... לְקַיָּמָה קְיָם מַלְכָּא—The syntax of this long clause is complicated. The Ithpaal (HtD) verb אִתְיָעַטוּ, "take counsel together" (*HALOT*, s.v. יעט, Ithpaal) or "advise" is followed by the long compound subject listing the different kinds of officials (see the next textual note). The direct object of "advise" is מַלְכָּא, "the king." That direct object is preceded by an object complement, an infinitive with a cognate accusative noun, stating what the officials advise the king to do: לְקַיָּמָה קְיָם, literally, "to establish an establishment/statute." The noun קְיָם, "statute" (*HALOT*), will recur in 6:16 (ET 6:15).

כֹּל ׀ סָרְכֵי מַלְכוּתָא סִגְנַיָּא וַאֲחַשְׁדַּרְפְּנַיָּא הַדָּבְרַיָּא וּפַחֲוָתָא—For אֲחַשְׁדַּרְפְּנַיָּא, "the satraps," see the first textual note on 3:2. For סִגְנַיָּא, "the prefects," and פַחֲוָתָא, "the governors," see the second textual note on 3:2. For הַדָּבְרַיָּא, "the counselors," see the second textual note on 3:24a.

וּלְתַקָּפָה אֱסָר—This is a second object complement, also using an infinitive (Pael [D] of תְּקַף, which in Peal [G] means "be strong") that restates the first object complement[2] in other words, describing what the officials advise the king to do: "to ratify a decree." Shalom Paul argues that the Pael infinitive of the verb תְּקַף when used in a legal context is the semantic equivalent of the Assyrian verb *dunnunu*, "to strengthen." In legal contexts, causative forms of that Assyrian verb can mean "to make valid or binding."[3] By analogy, then, the causative and transitive Pael (D) of תְּקַף means "to ratify." He also suggests a similar meaning for the Piel (D) infinitive construct of קוּם in Esth 9:29.

כָּל־דִּי־יִבְעֵה בָעוּ מִן־כָּל־אֱלָהּ וֶאֱנָשׁ עַד־יוֹמִין תְּלָתִין לָהֵן מִנָּךְ מַלְכָּא—The officials request a law that states, literally, "Everyone who requests a request from any god or man for thirty days except from you, Your Majesty," will be thrown into the pit of lions. The reiteration of the law in 6:13 (ET 6:12) is almost identical to its wording here. In

---

[2] For the first object complement with infinitive, see the first textual note on this verse.

[3] Paul, "Dan 6,8: An Aramaic Reflex of Assyrian Legal Terminology," 108–10.

other contexts, the verb בְּעָא, "to seek, request," and the preposition מִן, "from," were used when Daniel "requested/sought" something "from" the king (2:16, 49). They were also used for prayer: Daniel exhorted his Judean companions to "seek mercy from the God of heaven" (2:18), and after God granted that prayer, Daniel recalled how he had "requested from/of" God the revelation of Nebuchadnezzar's first dream (2:23). Compare also 7:16, where Daniel (literally) "sought from" (בְּעָה and מִן) an angel or divine figure the meaning of the vision he received from God.

Here, to "request" a "request, petition, prayer" (the verb בְּעָה and the cognate noun בָּעוּ) "from" (מִן) "a god" (אֱלָהּ) must mean "to utter a prayer" (*HALOT*, s.v. בעה, Peal, 2). Similarly, בְּעָה means "to pray" also in 6:12–14 (ET 6:11–13), where it describes Daniel as praying to God. The same cognate accusative construction (the verb בְּעָה and cognate noun בָּעוּ) are used at the end of 6:14 (ET 6:13). (Different vocabulary is used in 6:11 [ET 6:10] to describe Daniel's praying.) The preposition מִן, "from," that stands before כָּל־אֱלָהּ, "any god," is then repeated with a suffix referring to the king: מִנָּךְ, "from you." For the sake of English idiom, this is translated, "prays a prayer to …"

Thus the law prohibits prayer to any deity or person "except" (לָהֵן) to the king. This implies that the king serves, at the very least, as the high priest and mediator of all the pagan gods venerated in Babylon. Yet more than that, the law requires that he be treated as a god, and as the only god who may receive prayers during the thirty days. See further the commentary on 6:8 (ET 6:7).

6:9 תְּקִים אֱסָרָא וְתִרְשֻׁם כְּתָבָא—Two imperfect verbs are used instead of imperatives to show deference to the king. To indicate this, the translation includes "please." The Haphel (H) imperfect תְּקִים could also be rendered, "may you establish." The Peal (G) of רְשַׁם was used in 5:24–25 for the writing on the wall and meant "write, inscribe." Here, however, the king would have dictated the law to a scribe, who would write "the writing/document" (כְּתָבָא), and the king would simply "sign" it. Hence רְשַׁם is translated, "sign(ed)" in 6:9–11, 13–14 (ET 6:8–10, 12–13).

6:10 רְשַׁם כְּתָבָא וֶאֱסָרָא:—Literally, "he wrote the writing and the decree." The two nouns joined by the conjunction form a hendiadys. The first noun is translated adjectivally: "the written decree."

6:11 הוּא ׀ בָּרֵךְ עַל־בִּרְכוֹהִי וּמְצַלֵּא וּמוֹדֵא קֳדָם אֱלָהֵהּ—These three participles (בָּרֵךְ … וּמְצַלֵּא וּמוֹדֵא) describing Daniel are iterative: three times daily "he *would kneel* on his knees and *pray* and *offer praise* before his God." צְלָא, whose Pael (D) means "to pray" (*HALOT*), recurs elsewhere in the OT only in Ezra 6:10, where it refers to intercessory prayer for the king and his sons. The Aramaic יְדָא, whose Haphel (H) means "to praise" (*HALOT*) or "offer praise," recurs elsewhere only in Dan 2:23, where Daniel praised God. However, the Hebrew cognate, the Hiphil of יָדָה, "to praise," is common in the OT, especially the Psalms.

Instead of the pronoun הוּא in הוּא ׀ בָּרֵךְ, "he would kneel," a number of Masoretic manuscripts and printed editions have the perfect verb הֲוָה, "he was," resulting in הֲוָה בָּרֵךְ, "he was kneeling," a periphrastic construction for repeated past action. (Similar is הֲוָא עָבֵד, "he had been doing," later in 6:11 [ET 6:10].) The pronoun הוּא (the reading of Codex Leningradensis and hence *BHS*) would make the subject emphatic, since it is not needed here. Daniel was already emphasized at the beginning of 6:11 (ET 6:10), since his name, וְדָנִיֵּאל, is the first word of the verse. Therefore it may be preferable to follow the manuscripts that read הֲוָה instead of הוּא.

6:13 עַל־אֱסָר מַלְכָּא—The accents indicate that these words go together: the men spoke to the king "concerning the decree of the king." While some translations (e.g., KJV, NIV, NASB) follow that syntax, other English translations consider מַלְכָּא to be the first word of the quotation, as in the translation above: "Your Majesty …"

אַרְיָוָתָא—Elsewhere in Daniel this word for "the lions" is pointed with a *qamets* under the *waw*: אַרְיָוָתָא. The peculiar pointing here is unique to Codex Leningradensis. Other Masoretic manuscripts as well as printed editions point this word normally.

6:14 לָא־שָׂם עֲלָךְ מַלְכָּא טְעֵם—The same idiom, "not to pay attention to," with the negated verb שִׂים, "set, place," the preposition עַל, "to," and the noun טְעֵם, "attention, heed," was used in 3:12 for the accusation against Shadrach, Meshach, and Abednego. For a similar idiom with שִׂים, see the next textual note. However, the idiom שִׂים טְעֵם can also mean "give an order"; see the first textual note on 6:27 (ET 6:26).

6:15 וְעַל דָּנִיֵּאל שָׂם בָּל לְשֵׁיזָבוּתֵהּ—Literally, "upon Daniel he set his mind to save him," the noun בָּל, "mind" occurs only here in the OT. For the verb שֵׁיזִב, "to save," see the second textual note on 3:15. It recurs in 6:17, 21, 28 (ET 6:16, 20, 27).

6:16 בֵּאדַיִן גֻּבְרַיָּא אִלֵּךְ הַרְגִּשׁוּ עַל־מַלְכָּא וְאָמְרִין לְמַלְכָּא—This is, literally, "then these men came as a crowd to the king and kept saying to the king …" For the verb רְגַשׁ, see the first textual note on 6:7 (ET 6:6). Theodotion, which usually follows the MT fairly closely, omits most of this clause and reads only τότε οἱ ἄνδρες ἐκεῖνοι λέγουσιν τῷ βασιλεῖ, probably indicating that the Hebrew text before the translator only read as follows: בֵּאדַיִן גֻּבְרַיָּא אִלֵּךְ אָמְרִין לְמַלְכָּא. Some manuscripts in the Theodotion tradition, especially those of the Lucianic recension, have additional words that align the Greek text with the MT. The words הַרְגִּשׁוּ עַל־מַלְכָּא may have been added by a Hebrew scribe to align this verse with 6:7, 12 (ET 6:6, 11), but if so, the scribal insertion is very ancient, since these words appear in 4QDan[b].[4] They are also represented in other ancient versions, including the Syriac and Vulgate. However, because of their absence in Theodotion, they are in parentheses in this commentary's translation above.

The MT states that after the men spoke to the king in 6:14 (ET 6:13), he "worked hard to rescue him [Daniel]" (מִשְׁתַּדַּר לְהַצָּלוּתֵהּ, 6:15 [ET 6:14]) until sundown. That may imply that throughout the rest of the day, the accusers continued to press their case and remind the king of the immutability of the law. If so, the actions described in 6:16 (ET 6:15) would have continued throughout the day. However, in the MT, the participial clause beginning with וְאָמְרִין, which here signals repeated action ("kept saying"), follows הַרְגִּשׁוּ עַל־מַלְכָּא, with a perfect verb. The absence of a translation of הַרְגִּשׁוּ עַל־מַלְכָּא in Theodotion makes it clearer that throughout the time that the king was working to rescue Daniel from the decree (from the time the officials spoke in 6:14 [ET 6:13] until sundown), they kept reminding him that the decree could not be altered. They did not simply crowd around him at the end of the day to state this, but they said

---

[4] Ulrich et al., *Qumran Cave 4.XI*, 261.

it repeatedly, pressing the issue. This would help explain the king's complete annoyance at them that led to their condemnation (6:25 [ET 6:24]).

6:17 אֱלָהָךְ דִּי אַנְתְּ פָּלַח־לֵהּ בִּתְדִירָא הוּא יְשֵׁיזְבִנָּךְ:—Literally, this is "your God, whom you are serving in continuance, he—may he save you." The participle פָּלַח connotes durative action, "(constantly) serving," which is reinforced by the noun תְּדִיר with the preposition בְּ serving as an adverb: "continually." The phrase אֱלָהָךְ דִּי אַנְתְּ פָּלַח־לֵהּ בִּתְדִירָא is repeated in 6:21 (ET 6:20) with a different form of שֵׁיזִב following. For שֵׁיזִב, "to save," see the second textual note on 3:15. Grammatically, the resumptive or emphatic pronoun הוּא and the imperfect verb יְשֵׁיזְבִנָּךְ could express confidence that "he will save you." However, in light of the king's question in 6:21 ("was he able to save you ... ?" [ET 6:20]), the verb here is best understood as a jussive expressing a hope or prayer: "may he save you."

6:19 וְדַחֲוָן לָא־הַנְעֵל קָדָמוֹהִי—Literally, this is "and entertainment (?) he did not cause to come before himself." The derivation and meaning of the noun דַּחֲוָה is unknown. Some suggestions include "woman," "concubine," "dancing girl," "food," "music," "musician," and "servant."[5]

6:22 דָּנִיֵּאל—"Daniel" is pointed peculiarly in Codex Leningradensis (with -ִיֵּ- instead of -ִיֵּ-) only here. Many other Masoretic manuscripts and printed editions have the usual pointing here.

6:23 אֱלָהִי שְׁלַח מַלְאֲכֵהּ וּסֲגַר פֻּם אַרְיָוָתָא—Literally, "my God sent his angel and he shut the mouth of the lions," the subject of וּסֲגַר, "and he shut," could be either "God" or "his angel." Probably God performed this action through his angel, who performed a supernatural feat of redemption. Similarly, a fourth "man" with divine characteristics, a Christ figure, appeared with the three Judeans when God saved them from the furnace (see the commentary on 3:25).

6:24 הֵימִן בֵּאלָהֵהּ:—"He trusted in his God" uses the Haphel (H) perfect of אָמַן. The Haphel (H) participle of the same verb describes Daniel as "faithful, trustworthy" in 6:5 (ET 6:4). These verses support the biblical doctrines of salvation through faith alone (6:24 [ET 6:23]) and of sanctification, as saving faith leads to faithful conduct in life (6:5 [ET 6:4]). Here God performs an act of physical deliverance to demonstrate his grace toward Daniel, but God does not promise always to do this. Contrast Mt 27:43, where the Jewish leaders mock Christ with similar words: "he trusted in God; let him save him now if he delights in him" (πέποιθεν ἐπὶ τὸν θεόν, ῥυσάσθω νῦν εἰ θέλει αὐτόν). Jesus was not spared from death, but remained faithful even unto death, and then was raised on the third day, earning the promise of resurrection for all believers (Dan 12:2–3).

6:25 אֲכַלוּ קַרְצוֹהִי דִּי דָנִיֵּאל—These men literally "ate his pieces, which were Daniel's." The idiom is translated, "maliciously accused Daniel." The same idiom was used for the malicious accusation against the three Judeans; see the textual note on 3:8.

---

[5] See the discussion in *HALOT* and also Collins, *Daniel*, 270; Goldingay, *Daniel*, 121; Montgomery, *Daniel*, 277–78.

שְׁלִ֣טוּ בְה֗וֹן אַרְיָוָתָא֙ וְכָל־גַּרְמֵיה֖וֹן הַדִּֽקוּ׃—This fate of the malicious unbelievers, "the lions overpowered them and crushed all their bones," contrasts with 3:27, where the same verb, שְׁלַט, was negated: the fire "had no power" over the faithful Judeans in the furnace. The fate of the unbelievers here also resembles the fate of the worldly kingdoms in 2:34–35, 44–45, where the same verb, דְּקַק, was used to state that the advent of the kingdom of God in the Messiah (the "stone") will "crush" the statue representing the four world kingdoms.

6:27 מִן־קֳדָמַי֙ שִׂ֣ים טְעֵ֔ם—Literally, this is "from before me is given an order." For this idiom with שִׂים טְעֵם, see the textual note on 3:10. Contrast the meaning of שִׂים טְעֵם ("pay attention, give heed") in 3:12 and 6:14 (6:13).

לֶהֱוֹ֤ן זָיְעִין֙ וְדָ֣חֲלִ֔ין מִן־קֳדָ֖ם—This is almost identical to a clause in 5:19, which denoted continuing action in the past (see the first textual note on 5:19). However, 5:19 had the perfect of הֲוָה, but this clause uses its imperfect (לֶהֱוֹן) with jussive force, and the two participles (זָיְעִין וְדָחֲלִין) denote action continuing into the future, literally, "they should be trembling and fearing before …"

דִּי־ה֣וּא ׀ אֱלָהָ֣א חַיָּ֗א—Since the noun and adjective are determined, this clause is, literally, "for he is *the* living God." However, the articles are absent in 4QDan[b], which reads אלה חי, "*a* living god."[6] Therefore the translation above has "the" in parentheses. Without the articles, Darius could merely be acknowledging that Daniel's God is one living god among other deities, so that this Gentile ruler does not necessarily express saving faith in the only true God. Might the Jewish Qumran sectarians have omitted the articles to weaken the portrayal of Darius? Both the Old Greek (αὐτὸς γάρ ἐστι θεὸς μένων καὶ ζῶν, "for he is a God who endures and lives") and Theodotion (αὐτός ἐστιν θεὸς ζῶν καὶ μένων, "he is a God who lives and endures") lack any articles, although their Greek construction is such that including articles might confuse the subject and predicate (cf. καὶ θεὸς ἦν ὁ λόγος in Jn 1:1). However, the articles are in the Syriac (ܐܠܗܐ ܚܝܐ). Darius used the articles in 6:21 (ET 6:20) when he called Daniel עֲבֵד֙ אֱלָהָ֣א חַיָּ֔א, "servant of the living God," before he knew that God had saved Daniel. His opinion about Daniel's God probably would not be lower now, but higher and stronger after seeing that this God did save Daniel.

עַד־סוֹפָֽא׃—Literally "until the end," this idiom means that God's dominion is "eternal." Similarly in 7:26, it means "forever."

6:28 מְשֵׁיזִ֣ב וּמַצִּ֗ל—These two synonymous participles describe God as "saving and rescuing." Darius will explain מְשֵׁיזִב by using a finite form of the verb in the next line: "he saved [שֵׁיזִיב] Daniel from the hand of the lions." The Haphel of נְצַל, here translated as "rescue" to distinguish it from שֵׁיזִב, was also used by Nebuchadnezzar in 3:29 to express God's unique ability "to save."

וְעָבֵ֤ד אָתִין֙ וְתִמְהִ֔ין בִּשְׁמַיָּ֖א וּבְאַרְעָ֑א—Nebuchadnezzar's praise also used the verb עֲבַד with the plurals of the nouns אָת and תְּמַהּ as direct objects: "the signs and wonders that the Most High God did" (3:32 [ET 4:2]; see also 3:33 [ET 4:3]). See the textual note on 3:32. "In heaven" may allude to the angel (6:23 [ET 6:22]) sent from heaven to perform

---

[6] Ulrich et al., *Qumran Cave 4.XI*, 263.

the miracle "on earth." Nebuchadnezzar spoke of God governing those in heaven and on earth (4:32 [ET 4:35]). Compare the chorus of the heavenly angelic host in Lk 2:14.

6:29 וְדָנִיֵּאל דְּנָה הַצְלַח—The Haphel (H) of צְלַח can have the causative and transitive meaning "cause someone to prosper," as in 3:30. However, like its Hebrew cognate (the Hiphil of צָלַח), it can also have the intransitive meaning "to prosper, be successful."

בְּמַלְכוּת דָּרְיָוֶשׁ וּבְמַלְכוּת כּוֹרֶשׁ פָּרְסָאָה:—The *waw* on וּבְמַלְכוּת probably should be understood as epexegetical or explanatory: "during the reign of Darius, *that is*, during the reign of Cyrus the Persian." See the excursus "The Identity of Darius the Mede."

Commentary
Darius Appoints Administrators over Babylon (6:2–4 [ET 6:1–3])

One of the first items following a conquest is to set up a government apparatus for administering the new king's rule. Darius, we are told, has decided to appoint one hundred twenty officials throughout the kingdom. Some interpreters have objected that the Persian Empire was never organized into as many as one hundred twenty satrapies, but usually had between twenty and thirty.[7] However, nearly all commentators are agreed that the term "satrap" was often used in a loose sense to denote lower officials, so one hundred twenty governors or similar officials is not an unreasonable number.[8] It compares well to the one hundred twenty-seven provinces of the Persian Empire under Xerxes, as reported in Esther (1:1; 8:9; 9:30).

Commentators often point out that the establishment of the office of the three overseers (Dan 6:3 [ET 6:2]) is without parallel in the history of the Persian Empire. However, if the historical setting of this chapter follows the death of Gubaru,[9] this office may have been a temporary arrangement until Darius could determine whom he would appoint as governor of Babylon. Since Darius probably lacked firsthand knowledge of the capabilities and reliability of those leaders already in Babylon who may have been equipped for government service when he took control, he may have used the temporary arrangement of three overseers who could keep each other in check until he found someone he could trust. Indeed, this seems to have been the case according to 6:4 (ET 6:3). Daniel's faithful service comes to the attention of Darius after some time, and so Darius intends to appoint him as governor of the kingdom of Babylon.

The narration tells us that Daniel commended himself to Darius because "an outstanding spirit was in him" (רוּחַ יַתִּירָא בֵּהּ, 6:4 [ET 6:3]). This recalls earlier phrases used to refer to the Holy Spirit dwelling in Daniel, although he was described by pagan Babylonian kings, who used the phrase "a spirit of (holy)

---

[7] E.g., Montgomery, *Daniel*, 269, who calls the one hundred twenty "an exaggeration, or at least an inaccuracy."

[8] Collins, *Daniel*, 264–65; Goldingay, *Daniel*, 127; Hartman and Di Lella, *Daniel*, 197–98; Leupold, *Daniel*, 247–48; Lucas, *Daniel*, 148; Miller, *Daniel*, 177–78; Montgomery, *Daniel*, 269.

[9] See "The Historical Setting of Daniel 6" in "Introduction to Daniel 6."

gods" in earlier accounts (4:5–6, 15 [ET 4:8–9, 18]; 5:11, 14). In contrast, Daniel the author, when writing the narration here, avoids that polytheistic terminology ("gods") and adopts the same phrase (רוּחַ יַתִּירָא, "an outstanding spirit") used by the Babylonian queen in 5:12 to refer to the Holy Spirit in Daniel. This enables him to imply that his accomplishments were a result of God's gifts and blessing instead of his own prowess.[10] Similarly, the NT exhorts Christians to serve in their vocations faithfully and joyfully by the power of the Spirit, knowing that they are not just serving human masters (employers, bosses), but ultimately are serving the Lord (e.g., Rom 12:11; Eph 6:1–9; Col 3:16–24).

The Other Administrators Conspire to Eliminate Daniel (6:5–6 [ET 6:4–5])

The other officials seek to have Daniel removed from office out of ambition and jealousy. There is no mention of whether they are also motivated by ethnic or religious bigotry. However, since Daniel is faithful in his vocation, they decide that Daniel's monotheism and his devotion to his God are the only means to effect his downfall. They decide to use "the Law of his God" against him (see the textual note on 6:6 [ET 6:5]).

This decision by the Babylonian officials tells us that Daniel's religious practices are known to those around him. Daniel does not hide his faith. Moreover, they understand that Daniel's dedication to worship Israel's God means that he will not neglect God's command to worship. Whether or not they are familiar with the First and Third Commandments, they understand that Daniel's commitment to worship is based on the laws and customs of Israel.[11]

This chapter contrasts the "Law" (דָּת) of God (6:6 [ET 6:5]) with the "law" (דָּת) of the Medes and the Persians (6:9, 13, 16 [ET 6:8, 12, 15]). Daniel is perfectly willing to obey Persian law, as demonstrated by his faithful service in 6:2–5 (ET 6:1–4), even as he had submitted to the Babylonian law and king in chapters 1–2, 4–5, since they had not required him to compromise faithfulness to God's Word (as the Babylonian edict required the three Judeans to do in chapter 3). However, even his enemies know that his ultimate commitment is to the Law of his God.[12]

---

[10] For these references to the Spirit, see further "Gospel Themes in Daniel 4" in "Introduction to Daniel 4."

[11] Regarding the First and Third Commandments, see further "Major Emphases in Daniel 6" in "Introduction to Daniel 6."

[12] The assertion by Collins (*Daniel*, 263, 265) that 6:6 (ET 6:5) is a Maccabean redactional insertion misses the contrast between "the Law of his God" 6:6 (ET 6:5) and "the law of the Medes and the Persians" (6:9, 13, 16 [ET 6:8, 12, 15]). Collins offers the following reasons for his conclusion: First, the Old Greek version does not mention the Law of Daniel's God. Second, there is no evidence that the Jewish Torah was ever grounds for an accusation before the Maccabean period. Third, the king's edict did not conflict with Jewish law, since Daniel could have simply avoided keeping any command to worship, as allowed by Jewish halakah (for this point Collins cites Ginzberg, *The Legends of the Jews*, 4:348; 6:435). However, Collins' argument fails on all three points. First, the Old Greek version of Daniel 6

The Administrators Persuade Darius to Issue a Decree (6:7–10 [ET 6:6–9])

By using the verb רְגַשׁ in the Haphel (H) stem, "came as a crowd" (6:7, 12, 16 [ET 6:6, 11, 15]), Daniel depicts the Persian officials as a thronging tumult that crowd around the king.[13] They present the essence of their plot as the consensus of all the officials of Babylon. The decree they propose has been seen by some interpreters as deifying the king.[14] In the ancient Near East, kings could be deified, as were the Egyptian pharaohs. Daniel's contemporary Ezekiel condemned the king of Tyre for claiming to be God or a god (Ezek 28:2, 9). Nebuchadnezzar had claimed to be so powerful that no god could save the Judeans from his hand (Dan 3:15). The grammar of 6:8 (ET 6:7) construes prayer to Darius ("to you, Your Majesty") in the same way as praying "to any god" (see the fourth textual note on 6:8 [ET 6:7]). However, since the decree was to be in force for only thirty days, Darius would at most be honored as a temporary deity. Moreover, the decree specifically forbids prayer to "any god *or person*," which implies that prayers might be offered to the king as a person and not necessarily to him as a god.

It would appear that the decree, in effect, makes Darius the sole priest of the gods, the only one through whom prayer can be offered to any god. It would therefore also make prayer or requests to any god that come through any other priest illegal for a month. This decree would make sense if the thirty days are during the time when the images of the gods, which had earlier been removed from their temples and brought to Babylon, are being returned.[15] During this period, the priests are not able to offer prayers or sacrifices in the temples. The decree makes Darius the high priest, through whom all prayers are brought to the gods.

This proposed decree not only allows worship to continue while the gods are absent from their temples, it also appeals to Darius' ego. He would perceive the counsel of the officials as aimed at a positive goal: to allow worship of the gods while they are being repatriated. However, the reader knows the sinister

---

never mentions any "law," not even that of the Medes and the Persians. Clearly, there must have been something more complicated behind the Old Greek rendering of this story than Collins' suggestion that what it omits here was an editorial insertion. Second, lack of evidence is not the same as evidence to the contrary. There may well have been unrecorded cases before Maccabean times of accusations against Judeans or (later) Jews based on their keeping of the Torah. Finally, the halakah in the Talmud preserves old rabbinic opinions, but it was written much later (third through sixth centuries AD) than the book of Daniel (sixth century BC). Although the halakah offers an excuse for not keeping the commands of the Torah or other traditions, and some rabbis may have approved of that practice, already in the first century AD, that rabbinic provision was controversial, and Jesus condemned it (Mt 15:1–9; Mk 7:5–13).

[13] For a thorough discussion of the evidence for this meaning, see Collins, *Daniel*, 265–66.

[14] This is the view of, for example, Hartman and Di Lella, *Daniel*, 198.

[15] See "The Historical Setting of Daniel 6" in "Introduction to Daniel 6."

twist in the plot. The goal is actually a negative one: to deny Daniel permission to worship his God.

That "the law of the Medes and the Persians … cannot be revoked" (6:9, 13 [ET 6:8, 12]) is also mentioned in Esth 1:19 and 8:8. It is confirmed by Diodorus Siculus, who reports that Darius III could not revoke a death sentence even though he later found out that the condemned man was innocent.[16] Ironically, however, the same verb (עֲדָה) here translated "revoked" is used in other passages that describe how God "deposes" kings (2:21) and makes their kingdom and glory "pass/be taken away" from them (4:28 [ET 4:31]; 5:20; cf. 7:12, 26). But it is also used to state that the kingdom and dominion given the Son of Man, the Messiah, "will not pass away" (7:14).[17]

Daniel Is Caught Disobeying Darius' Decree (6:11–12 [ET 6:10–11])

Daniel's upper story room has windows facing Jerusalem. Apparently, he prays facing west in the direction of Jerusalem. Praying toward the temple in Jerusalem was first mentioned in Solomon's prayer at the dedication of the temple as he asked God always to hear prayers directed toward the city and the temple, the place of sacrificial atonement for the forgiveness of sins, the place where God promised to dwell among his people in grace (1 Ki 8:27–53). God heard Solomon's prayer and promised to be attentive to that place (1 Ki 9:3; 2 Chr 7:12, 15). Therefore, the direction of Daniel's prayer is not simply custom, nostalgia, or superstition but is based on God's promise. While God can hear a prayer prayed in any direction, he promised to hear prayers directed toward Jerusalem. Therefore, Daniel relies on God's promise as he prays. This promise continued to be honored among Jews, as attested in 1 Esdras 4:58 and perhaps Tobit 3:11.

Jesus Christ is the new temple (Jn 2:18–22), the incarnate dwelling place of God with humanity (Jn 1:14), the one who offered the sacrificial atonement to forgive the sins of all through his blood (Eph 1:7). He has given us the model prayer (Mt 6:9–13; Lk 11:2–4). The corresponding way in which NT believers pray is not toward any place, but calling upon God in the name of Jesus Christ, relying on his grace and with faith in him.[a] These are the prayers that are heard by God and acceptable to him.

(a) Jn 14:13–14; 15:16; 16:23–27; 1 Thess 5:16–18; 2 Thess 1:11–12; James 5:14–15; Jude 20–21

There is no command in Scripture concerning the number of times one should pray each day. In Ps 55:18 (ET 55:17), David mentions prayers at morning, noon, and evening, while in Ps 119:164, the psalmist tells of prayers he offers seven times each day. Josephus describes prayer twice daily, in the morn-

---

[16] Diodorus Siculus, *Library*, 17.30, cited in Montgomery, *Daniel*, 270.

[17] See further "The Messiah in Daniel: An Overview" in "Major Themes" in the introduction.

ing and evening.[18] Some early Christians prayed three times each day,[19] and the same practice was known among Jews of the Mishnaic period.[20] Later rabbis based threefold daily prayer on this passage in Daniel[21] and the practices of Abraham (morning), Isaac (afternoon), and Jacob (evening).[22] In the NT, St. Paul encourages continual prayer: "rejoice always, pray ceaselessly" (1 Thess 5:16–17).

Praying on one's knees is attested elsewhere in Scripture,[b] though other postures for prayer are also mentioned (see, e.g., 2 Sam 12:16). The custom is still followed by many Christians, particularly for confessional prayer.[23]

(b) 1 Ki 8:54; 2 Chr 6:13; Ezra 9:5; Lk 22:41; Acts 7:60; 9:40; 21:5; Eph 3:14

Daniel, we are told, knows about the king's decree but continues his habit of prayer "just as he had been doing before this" (Dan 6:11 [ET 6:10]). While Daniel normally is a scrupulous follower of all laws of the governing authorities, he understands that his first loyalty is to God. When a human authority establishes a regulation that conflicts with God and his Word, then, as the apostles declares, "We must obey God rather than men" (Acts 5:29). Daniel could have tried to rationalize that simply refraining from prayer for thirty days would not deny the one true God nor his own faith in him. However, he knows that God has commanded prayer and graciously invited his people to bring their requests to him. Prayer expresses his communion with God in faith and also is a testimony to others about his trust in God (cf. 6:24 [ET 6:23]). Therefore, God's command and promise to hear and answer compel Daniel to continue his custom of praying. Thus Daniel understands that refraining from practicing his faith is as good as denying his faith in God. He refuses to abandon his practice of daily prayer and praise. Moreover, we are told that after Darius issued his command, the men found Daniel "praying and *seeking favor* from his God" (6:12 [ET 6:11]). This implies that Daniel has specifically requested that God look upon him with favor and save him, even if he suffers the consequences of disobeying the king's command. While Daniel's enemies rely on Persian law to rid them of Daniel, Daniel relies on God to rid him of all trouble.

Daniel's enemies are already prepared to accuse him and simply come together outside Daniel's house to see him praying as he faces out of his upper-story window toward Jerusalem. They observe that Daniel is praying—an indisputable conclusion since he is kneeling. He may also have his hands outstretched toward heaven, according to the ancient custom for prayer found elsewhere in Scripture[c] and throughout the Near East.

(c) Pss 28:2; 63:5 (ET 63:4); 134:2; 141:2; Lam 2:19; 3:41; Neh 8:6; 1 Tim 2:8

---

[18] Josephus, *Antiquities*, 4.212. Compare God's command that incense be burned on the altar of incense every morning and every evening (Ex 30:7–8; see also Ps 141:2; Lk 1:8–10; Rev 5:8; 8:3–4).

[19] *Didache* 8.

[20] Mishnah, *Berakoth* 4:1.

[21] Talmud, *Berakoth*, 31a.

[22] Talmud, *Berakoth*, 26b, citing Gen 19:27; 24:63; 28:11.

[23] The Mishnah prescribes standing as the normal prayer posture for Jews in *Berakoth* 5:1.

Charges against Daniel Are Brought to Darius (6:13–14 [ET 6:12–13])

When the officials come to the king, they immediately remind him of the decree's content (6:13 [ET 6:12]). They are attempting to back the king into a corner, and their question betrays a suspicion that Darius will favor Daniel over them. Therefore, to ensure that the decree will be applied to Daniel, the officials make Darius commit himself to the decree once again. They state the terms of the decree so they can later pressure the king to enforce the terms against Daniel. Indeed, Darius steps into their trap not only by affirming the decree and its terms but also by stating that it cannot be changed.

Daniel's accusers spring their surprise on the king (6:14 [ET 6:13]). Their strategy is to accuse Daniel of disobeying Darius, then attempt to place distance between Darius and Daniel, hoping to alienate Darius from his favored official whom he was intending to promote (6:4 [ET 6:3]). The first way they attempt to lower Darius' opinion of Daniel is by referring to him as "from the exiles of Judah" (6:14 [ET 6:13]). Daniel is suspect, they imply, because he is not a Mede or Persian, nor does he obey "the law of the Medes and the Persians" (6:13 [ET 6:12]), and his loyalty to Judah might lead him to betray Darius. Second, they try to widen the split between Darius and Daniel by claiming that Daniel "does not pay attention to you, Your Majesty" (6:14 [ET 6:13]). In fact, they place this charge before the accusation that Daniel is ignoring the decree. While they have evidence that Daniel has ignored the decree, their first charge, that he is in the habit of ignoring Darius, is unwarranted. In the months since Darius (Cyrus) had assumed power over Babylon, Daniel has distinguished himself as faithful under Darius (6:4 [ET 6:3]). Thus the officials use Daniel's one area of disobedience to overgeneralize about him so that they can attack him politically.

Daniel's accusers make their point about Daniel's disobedience by noting that he continues to pray "*three times* each day" (6:14 [ET 6:13], echoing 6:11 [ET 6:10]). They have conducted a thorough investigation into Daniel's piety. Their observation is not of a single prayer but of his regular practice. His prayer is not a simple lapse or oversight; he has repeatedly violated the king's order. They are claiming that because of its repetition, Daniel's disobedience is not accidental, but willful rebellion.

Darius' Unsuccessful Attempt to Dismiss the Charges against Daniel (6:15–16 [ET 6:14–15])

When Darius learns of the real intent of the decree he has issued at his officials' request, he is upset. He has been deceived by his officials. Moreover, he is at risk of losing a highly valued lieutenant, and he may well have a strong personal affection for Daniel.[24] The text does not explain what methods Darius

---

[24] The suggestion of Goldingay (*Daniel*, 132) that Darius may have also been vexed with Daniel for ignoring the decree is without contextual support and runs counter to the king's subsequent actions.

attempts to use to free Daniel from the charges against him. He may have consulted experts in the law, looked for a plausible alternate interpretation of the decree, or sought a way to annul the decree. However, Daniel's accusers press their advantage by reminding Darius that the law of the Medes and the Persians is supreme and will not allow any alteration of the decree. This must have appeared to them to be a good strategy at the time, but by angering the king, they have given him added incentive to carry out the punishment on themselves after Daniel is proven innocent by the miracle (6:25 [ET 6:24]). In the end, the king gives in to their request even though he knows that Daniel does not deserve condemnation (cf. Jn 19:8–16).

Darius' Favor toward Daniel Militates against Critical Theories about Daniel

Critical scholars often suppose that the narrative accounts in Daniel 1–6 were incorporated into the book in Hellenistic times. These scholars imagine that the compilers of the final form of the book included the accounts of Daniel and his Judean friends overcoming oppression because they believed these accounts would encourage Jews to oppose Hellenism and its tendency to alienate Jews from their historic faith.[25] Supposedly, the compilers of the book viewed the kings in the narratives as metaphors for the oppression of the Jews in Palestine under Antiochus Epiphanes in the second century.

However, the portrayal of Darius as well-disposed toward Daniel (6:4, 15 [ET 6:3, 14]) and even toward Daniel's God (6:17 [ET 6:16]) cannot be reconciled with the actions of Antiochus.[26] Collins is one critical scholar who has admitted that Darius cannot be construed as representing Antiochus.[27] Therefore Collins speculates that this account originated among upper-class Jews in the second century BC who eschewed rebellion and sought instead to advance in society by using the system in place under their Greek rulers.[28] This speculation begs the question of how and why such an account would be incorporated among the other narratives that appear to support resistance to Hellenism and look forward to the downfall of Gentile kingdoms. Nor does it explain the inclusion of Daniel 6 immediately before visions (Daniel 7–12) that critical scholars say are intended to encourage the Maccabean rebellion and active resistance to Greek rulers.

Darius Carries Out the Terms of His Decree (6:17–19 [ET 6:16–18])

Darius has no choice but to condemn Daniel to the lions. If he had refused to enforce his own decree, he would have undermined his own authority and

---

[25] Many critical scholars hypothesize that the narratives themselves came from the Eastern Diaspora. See the discussion in Collins, *Apocalyptic Vision*, 54–59.

[26] Lucas, *Daniel*, 151.

[27] Collins, *Daniel*, 270; *Daniel with an Introduction to Apocalyptic Literature*, 72.

[28] Collins, *Daniel with an Introduction to Apocalyptic Literature*, 72–73.

encouraged others in Babylon to ignore the law of the Medes and the Persians—a risky example for a new king to set for his newly conquered people. Yet he does not abandon all hope, but expresses the desire that Daniel's God would save him (see the textual note on 6:17 [ET 6:16]).

Darius notes that Daniel continually serves God. This does not mean that he does not serve the king, but that in serving the king, he is also serving God through his vocation (cf. Rom 13:1–10). Daniel's service to God is so faithful that he has no question about the choice between abandoning his worship of God for thirty days in order to obey the royal decree or continuing to worship God and place his service to God above all other responsibilities. Faith, worship, and service to God are continual throughout the life of a believer and should not be abandoned at any time (cf. Jn 8:31–32; 15:4–6; 1 Cor 13:8, 13; 1 Thess 5:17; 1 Jn 2:24). Service in one's job or occupation normally is not continual, but only required when one is performing the duties of a vocation.

The sealing of the pit with the signet rings of the king and his nobles (Dan 6:18 [ET 6:17]) ensures that neither party can tamper with the judgment on Daniel. The king will not be able to rescue Daniel, and Daniel's accusers will not be able to kill him if the lions do not. We are told that Darius has the pit sealed with the rings (6:18 [ET 6:17]), indicating not only that he will abide by the decree but also that he does not trust Daniel's enemies (cf. Mt 27:66).

Darius' night without food and sleep are a consequence of the severe anxiety he is experiencing. It would be torturous for a ruler to be pressured into condemning an innocent man whom he has regarded favorably (cf. Dan 6:4 [ET 6:3]; Mt 27:19). With a guilty conscience, Darius is not able to enjoy entertainment or pleasures, and so he refrains from them (see the textual note on 6:19 [ET 6:18]).

Daniel Survives a Night in the Lions' Den (6:20–24 [ET 6:19–23])

Darius seems to have displayed some hope that God would be able to deliver Daniel from the lions. He repeats most of his wish or prayer from 6:17 (ET 6:16) in the form of his hopeful question in 6:21 (ET 6:20). He hurries to the sealed pit at dawn (cf. Mt 28:1) and calls out to Daniel, which he would not have done if he were certain Daniel was dead. He characterizes Daniel as "servant of the living God" (6:21 [ET 6:20]). God is often called "the living God" in Scripture.[29] However, these (6:21, 27 [ET 6:20, 26]) are the only passages in the entire OT where the divine title appears on the lips of a Gentile (non-Israelite). It demonstrates that Darius has at least some small hope that it is possible for Daniel yet to live if his God favors him. Since Daniel worships a God who

---

[29] Deut 5:26; Josh 3:10; 1 Sam 17:26, 36; 2 Ki 19:4, 16 ‖ Is 37:4, 17; Jer 10:10; 23:36; Mt 16:16; 26:63; Acts 14:15; Rom 9:26; 2 Cor 3:3; 6:16; 1 Tim 3:15; 4:10; Heb 3:12; 9:14; 10:31; 12:22; Rev 7:2; see also 1 Thess 1:9; Rev 15:7.

is "living," unlike the gods of metal, stone, and wood (5:4, 23), his God might be able to preserve and save life.[30]

In the NT, Jesus builds on the fact that God is "the God ... of the living" in order to support the biblical doctrine of the resurrection and that believers who have died still live to God (Mk 12:18–27). Moreover, after his bodily resurrection from the dead, Jesus himself is acclaimed as "the living one" (Lk 24:5).

Daniel's reply from the pit begins with a formal greeting for the king with another reference to life: "Your Majesty, may you live forever!" (6:22 [ET 6:21]). He then explains why he has been able to survive among the lions overnight: God sent an angel, who shut their mouths. Occasionally in both Testaments God sends an angel to deliver his faithful people from harm and bring them to safety (e.g., 1 Ki 19:5–7; Mt 2:13, 19–20). Earlier Nebuchadnezzar saw the divine man (Dan 3:25) whom he described as God's "angel" (3:28), yet who probably was the preincarnate Christ, the Son of God, who is the "stone" who brings God's kingdom in 2:34–35, 44–45 and who also appears as the "Son of Man" who receives God's kingdom in 7:13–14; the "Prince of the army" in 8:11; the "Messiah" and "Leader" in 9:25–26; and the heavenly man in 10:4–21.[31] It is possible that the "angel" here in 6:23 (ET 6:22) might be the preincarnate Christ, who sometimes appears in the OT as "the Angel of Yahweh/the Lord."[32]

Here Daniel is the only one who perceived the angel (though possibly the lions saw him; cf. Num 22:23–31), but Darius and his officials certainly witness the result of the miracle. The miraculous preservation of Daniel confirms that the usual purpose for which God sends his "ministering spirits" is to aid believers as part of his larger plan of bringing them to eternal life (Heb 1:14; cf. Heb 1:7). The deliverance of believers can give them further opportunities to proclaim the Gospel and so lead unbelievers to salvation (cf. Acts 5:19; 8:26; 10:22; 12:7–11).

Daniel declares that he was saved because he is righteous before God, who "found me innocent before him" (Dan 6:23 [ET 6:22]). His faith was evident in his faithfulness in worship and prayer, even when threatened with the penalty of death. He was confident that not even death would separate him from his loving God. Later God will reveal more to Daniel about the resurrection to eternal life (Dan 12:2–3; cf. Rom 8:31–39). The portrayal of Daniel in this chapter is consistent with the probable allusion to him in Heb 11:33 that saints by faith "stopped the mouths of lions."

Danicl has honored God as the ultimate King and Savior. God has regarded faithful Daniel as having fulfilled the First and Third Commandments, which

---

[30] Collins (*Daniel*, 270) comments that the title "the living God" is premature here and possibly redactional (a scribal gloss copied from 6:27 [ET 6:26]). However, that misses the point of the title here in the narrative.

[31] See further the textual notes and commentary on 2:34–35, 44–45; 3:25, 28; 7:13–14; 8:11; 9:25–26; and 10:4–21. See also "The Messiah in Daniel: An Overview" in "Major Themes" in the introduction.

[32] See the commentary on 3:28a.

address the believer's proper worship of God.³³ Moreover, God did not regard Daniel as having violated the Fourth Commandment, which addresses proper conduct toward human authority; Daniel confirms this when he adds, "Also before you, Your Majesty, I have committed no crime" (6:23 [ET 6:22]). Daniel is not claiming that he did not disobey the royal decree. Instead, he is claiming that his act of praying, though a violation of the decree, was not a demonstration of disloyalty to Darius. (Darius had known this, and that is why he had intended to promote Daniel in 6:4 [ET 6:3] and tried to keep Daniel from being condemned in 6:15 [ET 6:14].)

Daniel's dual statement that he was "found ... innocent" by God and also "committed no crime" against the king (6:23 [ET 6:22]) affirms the two kinds of righteousness that each believer has by grace.³⁴ The saving righteousness before God (*coram Deo*) that each believer has through faith is normally hidden from other people, but God has publicly revealed his favor toward Daniel by saving him from the lions. The believer's righteousness before other people (*coram hominibus*) is demonstrated by good works, that is, deeds of love and fidelity motivated by the Gospel. Daniel's civil righteousness was already evident to the king (6:4, 15 [ET 6:3, 14]) and even to his opponents (6:5–6 [ET 6:4–5]).

By suffering because of his righteousness, Daniel serves as a fine example of a believer who lives out the apostle's exhortation in 1 Pet 2:12–25.

Darius' reaction to Daniel's reply (Dan 6:24 [ET 6:23]) reveals that he has been well-disposed toward Daniel all along. When Daniel is lifted out of the pit, he is found to be unharmed, demonstrating that he has received divine protection. The parallel to the account of Shadrach, Meshach, and Abednego in the fiery furnace is striking. In both cases, God demonstrated his power by providing complete protection from harm. The preservation of his faithful followers from physical harm and temporal death affords a glimpse of the salvation from eternal death and resurrection to eternal life that all God's people have through faith (12:2–3).

Darius Punishes Daniel's Accusers (6:25 [ET 6:24])

The punishment for Daniel's accusers is the fate they had designed for him. The legal practice of imposing upon those who make a false accusation the penalty that would have been imposed on the accused was common in the ancient Near East (see Esth 7:10) and was even endorsed in OT Law.³⁵ The punishment of the entire families of the offenders, however, was forbidden in the Law of Moses (Deut 24:16; see also 2 Ki 14:6; Ezekiel 18). In Israel, families were

---

³³ For the commandments in relation to Daniel, see further "God's Law in Daniel" in "Law and Gospel in Daniel" in the introduction.

³⁴ For the distinction between righteousness through faith and civil righteousness, see AC XVIII 1; Ap IV 33–35, 142; XVIII 4–10.

³⁵ Deut 19:16–21; Ps 7:15–17 (ET 7:14–16); Prov 19:5, 9; 21:28; see also Luther, "Preface to Daniel," AE 35:298–99.

punished together with the offender only when they appear to have been complicit accomplices (Num 16:27–33; Josh 7:24–25).

The ravenous appetite of the lions is demonstrated in the way that they pounce upon their prey before the bodies have reached the floor of the pit. Daniel includes this detail to highlight the miraculous intervention of God that saved Daniel from the lions. This was a vivid demonstration of what the absence of God's protection means. It is also a foreshadowing of the resurrection to eternal death, "contempt," and "everlasting abhorrence" awaiting all who die as unbelievers (12:2; see also the second textual note on 6:25 [ET 6:24]).

Darius Issues a New Decree (6:26–28 [ET 6:25–27])

Darius' decree has three parts. It begins with a greeting, "may your peace increase!" (שְׁלָמְכוֹן יִשְׂגֵּא, 6:26 [ET 6:25]). Compare Paul's standard Christianized greeting at the start of his epistles: "grace to you and peace" (χάρις ὑμῖν καὶ εἰρήνη, e.g., Rom 1:7; 1 Cor 1:3; Philemon 3).[36] Next follows the decree's command to reverence Daniel's God. Similar to the decrees of Nebuchadnezzar in Dan 3:29 and in 3:31–4:34 (ET 4:1–37), this decree is addressed to "all the peoples, nations, and languages that dwelt in the entire earth" (6:26 [ET 6:25]; see 3:29; 3:31 [ET 4:1]). However, this decree goes beyond the first decree of Nebuchadnezzar, a negative decree that only commanded punishment for blasphemy against the God of the Judeans (3:29).[37] This positive decree commands respect for God: all people "should continually tremble and be afraid before the God of Daniel" (6:26 [ET 6:25]). The vocabulary is Law-based and stops short of using Gospel language of faith and trust for salvation. This is what one would expect among syncretistic polytheists who might recognize the supremacy of Israel's God without trusting in him alone for salvation and without renouncing the existence of all other gods. Yet this fear of God could lead to repentance and be important preparation for believing the message of salvation through faith in this God alone.[38]

The longest section of the decree is a poetic rationale for the command (6:27b–28 [ET 6:26b–27]). The rationale's first and last lines identify God as "(the) living God … [who] saved Daniel from the hand of the lions." Between these lines, God and his work are described.

Darius' praise of God in his decree echoes the praise in Nebuchadnezzar's decrees. He acknowledges that God's kingdom endures forever (6:27 [ET 6:26]; see also 3:33 [ET 4:3]; 4:31 [ET 4:34]; cf. 7:14, 18, 27) and will never be destroyed (cf. 2:44). He agrees with Nebuchadnezzar's statement that "there is

---

[36] For the view that Paul has adapted a standard secular greeting but incorporated and emphasized God's "grace" in Jesus Christ and the resulting "peace" with God (cf. Rom 5:1), see Nordling, *Philemon*, 153, 176–84.

[37] Nebuchadnezzar's second decree (3:31–4:34 [ET 4:1–37]) does not issue any overt command for the peoples it addresses, but recounts the narrative of God's punishment and restoration of Nebuchadnezzar, which elicited his praise of God.

[38] See further "Law and Gospel in Daniel" in the introduction.

no other god who is able to save like this" (3:29) and that Daniel's God is the one who works signs and wonders (3:32–33 [ET 4:2–3]).

The inclusion of Darius' decree by Daniel the author allows him to summarize the lessons learned by pagan rulers throughout the narrative section of Daniel (chapters 1–6) before moving on to the section of the book that will relate his visions (chapters 7–12). The visions presuppose the actions and attributes of God set forth in the decrees of Nebuchadnezzar and Darius. The visions go on to relate how God will bring his eternal kingdom to his people and save them for eternity.

Daniel's Prosperity (6:29 [ET 6:28])

The narrative concludes by telling us that Daniel prospered during the reign of Darius (Cyrus). He lived until at least Cyrus' third year (10:1). However, this sentence does not say that Daniel was promoted to the position Darius had intended to give him (6:4 [ET 6:3]). There is no record here or elsewhere that he became governor or top official of Babylon. Perhaps after the infighting among his officials described in chapter 6, Darius decided that it would be politically expedient not to appoint a Judean to such a high position. Perhaps Daniel, who by this time was probably into his eighth decade of life,[39] desired to go into retirement or semi-retirement and remain only as an advisor to the king without having responsibility for the day-to-day duties that would normally be required of a palace official. Whatever the case, God enabled Daniel to prosper as a further sign of his grace, which no doubt was evident to the competing pagans among whom Daniel served.

---

[39] See the commentary on 1:18–21.

Daniel 7:1–28

Daniel's Vision of Four Kingdoms and the Establishment of the Kingdom of God

Introduction to Daniel 7

7:1–14   Daniel's Vision of Four Beasts and the Coming of the Son of Man

7:15–28   An Angel Explains the Four Beasts and the Establishment of the Kingdom of God

Introduction to Daniel 7

Major Emphases in Daniel 7

Daniel's dream vision in this chapter is obviously parallel to Nebuchadnezzar's dream in Daniel 2. Both portray a series of four world empires followed by the establishment of God's kingdom.[1] However, the perspectives on the world empires are different, and the two chapters reveal different details about the world kingdoms, God's kingdom, and the way in which God's kingdom comes.

In Daniel 2, God gave a revelatory dream to pagan King Nebuchadnezzar of Babylon. Then Daniel was given a divine revelation of the contents of the dream and its meaning, which he explained to the king. Therefore, the chapter is intended to communicate to unbelievers as well as believers, and its depiction of the world kingdoms was more neutral. Chapter 2 presented a statue composed of metals that signifies the world empires. This imagery appealed to Nebuchadnezzar, whose kingdom was symbolized by gold, the most precious of the four metals. God's kingdom was not assigned any metal, but was represented by a stone (2:34–35, 44–45). God's kingdom shattered and crushed the metals and grew into a great mountain, but chapter 2 gave little detail about the personal Messiah who brings God's kingdom or the judgment of God against the human kingdoms. While God revealed to Nebuchadnezzar the future up to the establishment of God's kingdom, he did it in a diplomatic way that appealed to the king's ego and made the king receptive to Daniel's interpretation of the dream (see 2:36–38). This enabled Daniel to be promoted to an influential position (2:48). God continued to work through Daniel as he held prominent positions in the government under Babylon kings and then under Darius/Cyrus.[2]

Daniel 7 is a divine revelation given directly to Daniel alone. He states, "I kept the matter to myself" (7:28), but recorded it in the book. It is intended primarily for the "saints" (7:18, 21–22, 25, 27), that is, all believers, who are righteous through faith alone. Therefore, it reveals the sinister nature of the world kingdoms under whom the persecuted saints must live, but it also offers greater comfort than the dream in Daniel 2 by its fuller presentation of their personal Messiah and the eternal kingdom he establishes for them. In these respects, it resembles the NT book of Revelation.[3]

In Daniel 7, the four world kingdoms are represented by strange beasts. The first three are compared to animals; the first and third are composite creatures.

---

[1] For an explanation of the world history that these chapters prophesy and the identification of the four world kingdoms they depict, see the excursus "The Four-Kingdom Schema in Daniel."

[2] See the excursus "The Identity of Darius the Mede."

[3] The commentary on 7:1–14 notes many parallels to Revelation.

Introduction to Daniel 7

The fourth beast is different and not readily comparable to any natural animal. While Daniel 2 portrays the splendor of the four human empires (especially the first), Daniel 7 does not glorify the four kingdoms, but instead portrays them as beastly, fearsome, and destructive. Moreover, this chapter devotes much more detail to the establishment of God's kingdom through the person of God and his personal Messiah. It portrays both "the Ancient of Days" (7:9, 13, 22), God the Father, and "one like a Son of Man" (7:13), the Messiah, God the Son, who receives God's kingdom and grants God's saints membership in it. God's judgment is executed on the beasts, particularly on the fourth one, whose little horn has waged war and prevailed over the saints. It is destroyed, and God's kingdom, as well as the dominion and greatness of the worldly kingdoms, are given to "the saints of the Most High" (7:22, 27; cf. 7:18). Clearly, this vision portrays human kingdoms in a much less favorable light than Nebuchadnezzar's dream in Daniel 2. It also depicts their warfare against the saints and gives greater detail about the advent of God's kingdom in order to give persecuted saints greater faith and hope as they await God's final victory and their entrance into the eternal kingdom of glory.

Four major emphases emerge in Daniel 7. They are in sharper focus and are developed more fully in Daniel 7 than in Daniel 2.

First, God governs all world history for the sake of his kingdom of grace, consisting of his redeemed people.[4] Daniel 2 reveals the same succession of four kingdoms, but Daniel 7 includes much more characterization of each kingdom. The beasts each have distinctive features that will characterize the kingdoms, including those that will arise after Daniel's day. This demonstrates God's foreknowledge of human events and implies that God is in control of history. This assurance of God's governance comforts the saints, who live in circumstances beyond their own control and who may feel that the world is spinning out of control. Persecuted saints experience evil in the world, but God is guiding all events ultimately for the sake of their redemption (cf. Jn 16:33; Rom 8:28, 35–39; Rev 1:1, 9).

A second emphasis is that God's kingdom comes through the ministry of the personal Messiah, who establishes and receives the authority over this eternal kingdom (Dan 7:13–14).[a] The "one like a Son of Man" who "was coming" (7:13) is clearly a messianic figure.[5] He receives the kingdom from the Ancient of Days. He is clearly human since he is called the "Son of Man." At the same time, he has divine attributes, especially as one who rides on the clouds (Is 19:1; Ezek 1:4; Pss 97:2; 104:3) or more generally is enveloped in clouds (2 Sam

(a) Cf. Mt 28:18; Lk 1:31–33; 4:43; 6:20; 11:2; 23:42

---

[4] See "Theological Threats Posed by the Critical Dating of Daniel" in "Date, Authorship, and Unity," and "The Messiah in Daniel: An Overview" and "God as the Protector of His People" in "Major Themes" in the introduction. See also the commentary on 2:27–30, 34–35, 44–45 and 7:9–14.

[5] See further "The Messiah in Daniel: An Overview" in "Major Themes," and "Daniel in the New Testament" in the introduction.

22:12 ‖ Ps 18:12 [ET 18:11]; Job 22:14). God's kingdom is his kingdom, and it will never be destroyed (Dan 7:14). The passing away of the world kingdoms and their replacement by the eternal kingdom of God in Jesus Christ is summarized in Rev 11:15: "The kingdom of the world has become the kingdom of our Lord and of his Christ, and he will reign forever and ever."

The third emphasis is the benefit God's people receive from the personal Messiah and the establishment of his kingdom. The kingdom that is given to the Son of Man becomes the possession inherited by the "saints" (7:18, 22). In NT language, all baptized believers in Christ receive what properly belongs to Christ himself: his righteousness and the forgiveness of sins he earned by his sacrificial death on the cross (hence they are repeatedly called "saints, holy ones" in Daniel 7); the promise of resurrection to eternal life (Dan 12:2–3) guaranteed by his own resurrection; and the promise to reign with him for eternity (Rom 5:17; Rev 22:3–5). All this is summarized in the acclamation of the Lamb in Rev 5:9–10: "Worthy are you to take the scroll and to open its seals, for you were slain, and by your blood you ransomed for God [a people] from every tribe and language and people and nation, and you have made them a kingdom and priests to our God, and they shall reign on the earth." Although now they are oppressed, God passes judgment in their favor (Dan 7:22), and all other dominions will be subject to them (7:27).

Therefore, although Daniel 7 covers much the same ground as Daniel 2, it is designed to be much more encouraging for God's people, especially when they face persecution. They are assured that God is in control over all events among humans, that he has a plan for their redemption carried out by his Messiah, and that that plan is designed for their eternal glorification (Rom 8:30).

A fourth emphasis is eschatology, which is more developed in Daniel 7. The biblically literate Christian can read Daniel 2 as a straightforward prediction of four world kingdoms (Babylon, Medo-Persia, Greece, and Rome) in the era before Christ (the OT and intertestamental periods) that give way to the establishment of God's eternal kingdom at the first advent of Christ. Similarly, the four beasts in 7:1–8 depict the same four world empires that precede the birth of Christ, which takes place during the time of the fourth empire, Rome, symbolized by the fourth beast. However, the careful reader of the rest of Daniel 7 will see connections to the NT depictions of both the first and second advents of Christ. Dan 7:9–27 has parallels to Revelation 4–5, a vision of the enthronement of the Lamb after his victory on the cross, which has already been fulfilled by his ascension and session at the right hand of the Father. Yet it also has parallels to Revelation 19–20, including the final judgment at the end of the world upon Christ's return, which still lies in the future.[6]

It seems that the vision given Daniel in 7:9–14, which is interpreted in 7:15–28, pictures in one scene the entire sweep of salvation history that includes

---

[6] See further "Eschatology and Revelation Parallels" in the commentary on Dan 7:9–10.

Christ's first advent, the church age, and Christ's second advent.[7] Daniel sees this whole span of history as the advent of the Son of Man, who receives the kingdom from the Ancient of Days (God the Father), and in turn gives the kingdom to his saints, his church consisting of all believers. During the time from Christ's first advent to his return, the little horn that arose from the fourth beast wages war against God and his saints, but upon Christ's return, the final judgment takes place and the little horn (the Antichrist) is destroyed forever in a fiery judgment. God's saints then take possession of the eternal kingdom in the new heavens and new earth (Revelation 21–22, foreseen in, e.g., Isaiah 11; 65:17–25; Ezekiel 40–48; Dan 12:2–3).

Christians read Daniel 7 knowing that the four world kingdoms depicted by the beasts have already passed away. Christ has already established the eternal kingdom of God by his incarnation, life, ministry, suffering, death, and resurrection, and he has granted us membership in it through faith alone. Yet we also know that we live in a world that still is dominated by aggressive nations and sinister powers not unlike the four beasts in Daniel 7 and that war shall continue until the return of Christ (Mt 24:6–31). We will continue to experience persecution from anti-Christian forces and the Antichrist, who speaks against God and his saints, seeking to pervert the Gospel and divine worship (Dan 7:21, 25). Final deliverance will be ours only at the second coming of Christ, when Satan and his minions will be judged. Then all the dead will be raised bodily, all unbelievers will be condemned to eternal perdition, and all God's saints (believers) will inherit eternal life in the new creation (Dan 12:2–3).

The Historical Setting of Daniel 7

Daniel records that he had his dream sometime "in the first year of King Belshazzar" (7:1). Belshazzar ruled as coregent with his father Nabonidus, who reigned from 556 until the fall of Babylon to the Persians in 539. Nabonidus proved to be singularly unpopular in Babylon, however, because of his devotion to the god Sin instead of the patron god of Babylon, Marduk. In response to this unpopularity, in either 553 or (more probably) 550, Nabonidus installed his son Belshazzar as coregent and voluntarily exiled himself to Tema in the Arabian Desert for some ten years.[8]

Daniel received this revelation in Daniel 7 at an important time. 550 BC was the year that Cyrus the Persian defeated his Median grandfather and took over the Median Empire, and so he became the ruler of the Medo-Persian Empire.

---

[7] This compressed sweep of history is similar to that in 2:34–35 and 2:44–45, where the rock, representing the kingdom of God brought by the Messiah, smashes the worldly kingdoms and grows into a worldwide kingdom that shall endure forever. See the textual note on 2:34 and the commentary on 2:34–35, 44–45.

[8] See further "The Historical Setting of Daniel 5" in "Introduction to Daniel 5" and the commentary on 5:1–4. The coregency of Nabonidus and Belshazzar explains why Belshazzar promised that whoever interpreted the writing would become the "third" in authority (5:7, 16, 29) since he would be under the two kings.

Thus Daniel's dream of the future kingdoms took place around the time when Cyrus positioned the Medo-Persian Empire as Babylon's new rival for dominance in the Near East. About a decade after Daniel received the vision in Daniel 7 (in 553 or 550 BC), Cyrus would defeat Babylon (in 539 BC), and then his empire would become the second world kingdom depicted in both Daniel 2 and Daniel 7.

The Importance of Daniel 7 in the Book of Daniel

Daniel 7 unites the narratives of the Babylonian court in first part of the book (Daniel 1–6) with the other eschatological visions that comprise the last part of the book (Daniel 8–12). It connects the preceding and following parts of the book in several ways.

First, it connects to the preceding because Daniel 7, like Dan 2:4b–6:29 (ET 2:4b–6:28), is written in Aramaic (while Daniel 8–12 is in Hebrew, as is 1:1–2:4a). Second, Daniel receives this vision during the Neo-Babylonian period, the same general historical setting as Daniel 1–5 and Daniel 8, whereas the other chapters are on the eve of Cyrus' conquest of Babylon (Daniel 6) or soon after that conquest (Daniel 9–12).[9] Third, the content of this vision is, in general terms, parallel to Nebuchadnezzar's vision in Daniel 2.[10] Fourth, a key concept in the chapter is expressed with the noun שָׁלְטָן, "dominion" (7:6, 12, 14, 26–27). Previous accounts in Daniel emphasize that "dominion" belongs to God and that he gives it to rulers (3:33 [ET 4:3]; 4:19, 31 [ET 4:22, 34]; 6:27 [ET 6:26]). Daniel 7 repeats that emphasis (7:6) but then adds that God will take away the "dominion" of the worldly kingdoms (7:12, 26) and give everlasting "dominion" to the Son of Man (7:14) and to his now-persecuted saints (7:27). Daniel 7 is the last chapter of the book that uses this term. Fifth and finally, Daniel 7 forms the final panel of a chiastic arrangement of major sections of the first part of the book.[11] Daniel 2–7 can be called an Aramaic chiasm preceded by a Hebrew introduction (Daniel 1). Thus in some ways, Daniel 7 closes out the first part of the book.

However, Daniel 7 has ties to the visions that follow. Most obvious is its visionary character. It is the first of four visions received by Daniel. Its general span of prophetic concern, the history that will affect God's people until God has fully established his eternal kingdom, is also identical to the concern of the final three visions (Daniel 8, Daniel 9, and Daniel 10–12). The three final Hebrew-language visions, like the Aramaic narratives (chapters 2–6) and the Aramaic

---

[9] See figure 1, "Timeline of Daniel and Related Events."

[10] See "Major Emphases in Daniel 7" above. Certain parts of Daniel 7 also have parallels in later chapters. See "The Roman View" in figure 9, "Views on the Identity of the Kingdoms in Daniel." Compare also figure 10, "Comparison between the Little Horn in Daniel 7 and the Little Horn in Daniel 8."

[11] See figure 2, "The Interlocked Chiastic Structure of Daniel," and also "Interlocked Chiasms and the Dual Language of the Book" in "Overview of Daniel" in the introduction.

vision (chapter 7) earlier in the book, are arranged chiastically.[12] In addition to being the final part of the Aramaic chiasm in Daniel 2–7, Daniel 7 serves as an Aramaic introduction to the Hebrew chiasm that follows, much like Daniel 1 is the Hebrew introduction to the Aramaic chiasm that follows it.

Thus Daniel 7 is the pivot around which the entire book turns, the interlocking device that unites historical narratives (chapters 1–6) and eschatological visions (chapters 7–12).[13] It simultaneously closes out the Aramaic chiasm while introducing the visions that continue in subsequent chapters in Hebrew. This careful arrangement of the divinely inspired book points to this chapter as the book's most important section.

It is no accident, then, that more scholarly papers, essays, and discussions have been produced about Daniel 7 than about any other major section of the book. It is this chapter that introduces the Son of Man, an important messianic title that is adopted by Jesus himself as his favorite self-designation in the Gospels. It is this chapter that first discusses the role of the "saints" in God's eternal kingdom. Therefore, Daniel 7 is the key to understanding the major themes that run throughout the book: God's governance of history, the eschatological kingdom of God, the promise of the Messiah, the protection God affords his people even during the darkest hours of persecution, and eternal salvation he promises to all who are members of his kingdom already now through faith.

Whether a Babylonian or Canaanite Mythic Background Influenced Daniel 7

Daniel's strange vision of animals arising from the churning sea, the frightful little horn, the coming of the Son of Man to the Ancient of Days, and the establishment of God's eternal kingdom are pieces in one of the most challenging hermeneutical puzzles in all of Scripture. What does the sea represent? What is the source of the strange composite animal imagery? Who is the Son of Man? What historical time period and events is the vision about?

With the discovery in the nineteenth century of ancient Babylonian myths, followed by the discovery in the twentieth century of ancient Canaanite myths, scholars began to propose that the imagery in Daniel 7 was modeled on ancient pagan mythology. In 1895 Hermann Gunkel became the first to propose that the background to Daniel 7 lay in the Babylonian myth *Enuma Elish*.[14] Although many scholars have dismissed Gunkel's theory, it has had its adherents and advocates since then.[15] Parallels include the four winds of heaven, the churning of the

---

[12] Again, see figure 2, "The Interlocked Chiastic Structure of Daniel," and also "Interlocked Chiasms and the Dual Language of the Book" in "Overview of Daniel" in the introduction.

[13] This has been observed by others. See Collins, *Apocalyptic Vision*, 7–19; Patterson, "The Key Role of Daniel 7"; Raabe, "Daniel 7: Its Structure and Role in the Book."

[14] Gunkel, *Schöpfung und Chaos in Urzeit und Endseit*, 323–35. For the text of *Enuma Elish*, see *ANET*, 60–72.

[15] Recently, Gardner, "Daniel 7,2–14: Another Look at Its Mythic Pattern."

sea (the goddess Tiamat in the Babylonian myth), and beasts from the sea (from Tiamat). In addition, Gunkel claimed that the Son of Man who comes before the Ancient of Days to receive eternal dominion is parallel to Marduk coming before Anshar to receive everlasting dominion in the Babylonian myth.

Despite these alleged parallels, there is much in the *Enuma Elish* that has no parallel in Daniel 7, and there is much in Daniel 7 that had no parallel in the myth. In addition, even the parallels are not as close as they might seem at first blush. In the Babylonian myth, the sea is represented by the goddess Tiamat. If Daniel 7 were parallel, we would expect that the sea would be called by some cognate word such as "the deep," for example, the Hebrew תְּהוֹם, *tehom*.[16] Instead, the sea is simply called יַמָּא רַבָּא, "the great sea" (7:2). In *Enuma Elish*, eleven beasts rise from the sea, whereas only four arise from the sea in Daniel 7. The beasts represent kingdoms in Daniel, but in *Enuma Elish* they are gods. Daniel 7 presents the Son of Man before the Ancient of Days after the beasts are judged and slain. In the Babylonian myth, Marduk receives the kingdom before the beasts are punished.

Therefore, we must question whether the parallels between *Enuma Elish* and Daniel 7 are due to the influence of the myth upon Daniel or whether the parallels are more the perception of the scholars who are seeking a Babylonian influence on the Judean prophet in exile. Even the advocates of the parallels admit that (in their view) the myth has been highly transmuted by the author of Daniel.[17] Given that admission, it is just as probable that the perceived parallels are nothing more than distant similarities in two texts that are unrelated.

More recently, some have proposed that Daniel 7 is dependent upon the Akkadian Vision of the Netherworld.[18] However, most scholars have rejected that view with good reason:

> The similarities between Daniel 7 and the *Vision of the Netherworld* are limited to some common features of Near Eastern dream imagery—supernatural figures in hybrid form, a human figure, a throne vision. There is no reason to posit any relationship between these texts. The Akkadian *Vision* is helpful precisely in illustrating Near Eastern dream imagery and is of considerable interest for the milieu in which the genre apocalypse developed. It does not, however, provide the specific background to Daniel 7.[19]

After the discovery of Canaanite texts at Ugarit in Syria in 1928, many scholars began to examine the myths they contain for parallels to biblical pas-

---

[16] Gen 1:2; 7:11; 8:2; 49:25; Ex 15:5, 8; Deut 8:7; 33:13; Is 51:10; 63:13; Ezek 26:19; 31:4, 15; Amos 7:4; Jonah 2:6 (ET 2:5); Hab 3:10; Pss 33:7; 36:7 (ET 36:6); 42:8 (ET 42:7); 71:20; 77:17 (ET 77:16); 78:15; 104:6; 106:9; 107:26; 135:6; 148:7; Job 28:14; 38:16, 30; 41:24 (ET 41:32); Prov 3:20; 8:24, 27–28.

[17] Gardner, "Daniel 7,2–14: Another Look at Its Mythic Pattern," 250.

[18] Kvanvig, "An Akkadian Vision as Background for Dan 7?"; *Roots of Apocalyptic*, 389–459. For the text of the Vision of the Netherworld, see Kvanvig, *Roots of Apocalyptic*, 390–92, or *ANET*, 109–10.

[19] Collins, *Daniel*, 286.

sages. Aage Bentzen first proposed that the author of Daniel 7 drew upon the Canaanite Baal myth as found in the Ugaritic texts.[20] This thesis became more popular when J. A. Emerton reformulated Bentzen's theory in an attempt to demonstrate a parallel between the portrayal of Baal in the Canaanite myth and the Son of Man as portrayed in Daniel 7.[21] Several scholars have followed his theory.[22] The Baal myth speaks of Baal overcoming the gods Yam ("sea"), Nahar ("river"), and Mot ("death") and receiving dominion from the head of the Canaanite pantheon, El ("god"). However, the only similarities it has with Daniel 7 are these:

1. The sea appears in both texts.
2. Both Baal and the Son of Man ride on the clouds and receive dominion.
3. El is described as "Father of Years," while in Daniel 7, God the Father is called "the Ancient of Days."

Yet none of the other features of Daniel 7 are part of the Baal myth. It has no winds of heaven, no strange beasts from the sea, no slaying of Baal's enemy Yam with fire (in Dan 7:11 the horned beast, not the sea, is slain and burned). Moreover, as Arthur Ferch has pointed out, the relationship of the characters and the tenor of the scene in the Baal myth are completely different than in Daniel 7.[23] In addition, the Canaanite myths from Ugarit are from the second millennium BC, whereas Daniel was written in the sixth century BC. Even the advocates of the view that Canaanite myth is the background of Daniel 7 have been hard pressed to demonstrate how the myth would have been transmitted and then adapted among the Israelites over this period of time.[24] Thus the supposed Canaanite background of Daniel 7 is as doubtful as the proposed Babylonian background.

If there are real and not simply perceived parallels between ancient pagan myths and Daniel 7, it is highly unlikely that the myths provided the genesis of the imagery in Daniel's vision. Instead, the vision may include purposeful polemic against a few chosen pagan commonplaces, such as those that appear in *Enuma Elish*, to demonstrate that Israel's God, not the pagan gods, is in control of human events.[25] Yet even this proposal is speculative at best.

In conclusion, Daniel the author presents his vision as a divine revelation given to him by the God of Israel. There are no persuasive reasons to doubt that assertion of the text. If we must seek literary sources for Daniel 7, the most likely origins for the imagery and thought in Daniel 7 are previously written

---

[20] Bentzen, *King and Messiah*, 74–75.

[21] Emerton, "The Origin of the Son of Man Imagery."

[22] Beasley-Murray, "The Interpretation of Daniel 7"; Collins, *Apocalyptic Vision*, 96–106; *Daniel*, 286–94; "Stirring Up the Great Sea: The Religio-Historical Background of Daniel 7"; Mosca, "Ugarit and Daniel 7: A Missing Link."

[23] Ferch, "Daniel 7 and Ugarit: A Reconsideration."

[24] See Collins, *Daniel*, 291–94.

[25] Lucas, "The Source of Daniel's Animal Imagery," especially p. 185.

OT books. The depiction of the Babylonian Empire as a lion with eagles' wings appears to be based on biblical characterizations of Nebuchadnezzar as a lion (Jer 4:7; 50:17; cf. Jer 49:19; 50:44) and he, his armies, or his nation as eagles (Jer 4:13; 48:40; 49:22; Ezek 17:3; Hab 1:8; Lam 4:19). The three beasts identified in Daniel 7, the lion, the bear, and the leopard, occur together in Hos 13:7–8. Other OT books have precedents for the depiction of God as King, the use of symbolism in visions, the ferociousness of lions and bears (1 Sam 17:34–35; Amos 5:19; Prov 28:15), the imagery of the four winds of heaven (Jer 49:36; Ezek 37:9), and, above all, the Messiah as the one who brings and reigns over God's kingdom forever (Gen 49:10; 2 Sam 7:12–16, 29; Is 9:5–6 [ET 9:6–7]; Psalms 2 and 110). Thus one has to look no further than the OT itself for parallels to the language and imagery in Daniel 7.

Daniel 7:1–14

Daniel's Vision of Four Beasts and the Coming of the Son of Man

Translation

7 ¹In the first year of King Belshazzar of Babylon Daniel saw a dream and visions of his head upon his bed. Then he wrote the dream; he related the main words.

²Daniel said, "I was looking in my vision in the night, and behold, the four winds of heaven were churning the great sea. ³Four large beasts were coming up from the sea, each one different from the others.

⁴"The first was like a lion, and it had wings of an eagle. I kept looking until its wings were plucked off. Then it was lifted up from the earth and was made to stand on its feet like a man, and a man's mind was given to it.

⁵"And behold, another, second beast resembled a bear, and on one side it was raised up. Three ribs were in its mouth between its teeth. And this is what was being said to it: 'Arise, devour much flesh.'

⁶"After this, I continued looking, and behold, another was like a leopard, and it had four bird wings on its back. The beast had four heads, and dominion was given to it.

⁷"After this I continued looking in the visions of the night, and behold, a fourth beast was frightening and terrible and exceedingly strong. It had large iron teeth. It devoured and crushed, and what was left it trampled with its feet. Now it was different from all the beasts that were before it in that it had ten horns.

⁸"I was considering the horns when, behold, another horn, a little one, came up among them, and three of the previous horns were uprooted in front of it. And behold, eyes like human eyes were in that horn and a mouth speaking great things.

⁹"I continued to look until thrones were set up,
 and the Ancient of Days was seated.
His clothes were white as snow,
 and the hair of his head was like pure wool.
His throne was flames of fire;
 its wheels were burning fire.
¹⁰A river of fire flowed and came out from before him.
Thousands upon thousands attended to him,
 and ten thousands upon ten thousands stood before him.
The court was seated,
 and books were opened.

¹¹"I kept looking then because of the sound of the great words that the horn was speaking. I kept looking until the beast was killed and its body was destroyed

and it was given to the burning fire. ¹²As for the rest of the beasts, their dominion had been taken away, but an extension of life was given to them for a period of time.

¹³"I kept looking in the visions of the night,

> and behold, with the clouds of heaven one like a Son of Man was coming.

He came to the Ancient of Days,

> and he was brought before him.

¹⁴To him was given dominion, honor, and a kingdom.

> All peoples, nations, and languages will worship him.

His dominion is an eternal dominion that will not pass away,

> and his kingdom is one that will not be destroyed."

Textual Notes

7:1 בִּשְׁנַת חֲדָה לְבֵלְאשַׁצַּר מֶלֶךְ בָּבֶל—"In the first year of Belshazzar, king of Babylon," could have been 553 BC but more likely was 550 BC. See "The Historical Setting of Daniel 5" and also "The Person and Office of Belshazzar" in "Introduction to Daniel 5" as well as "The Historical Setting of Daniel 7" in "Introduction to Daniel 7." For the meaning of the name "Belshazzar," see the textual note on 5:1.

וְחֶזְוֵי רֵאשֵׁהּ עַל־מִשְׁכְּבֵהּ—"And the visions of his head upon his bed" was also used to describe the divine revelations to Nebuchadnezzar through dream visions (2:28; 4:2, 7, 10 [ET 4:5, 10, 13]).

7:2 בְּחֶזְוִי עִם־לֵילְיָא—"In my vision in the night" is similar to בְּחֶזְוֵי לֵילְיָא, "in visions of [during] the night" in 7:7, 13 (see also 2:19). However, some manuscripts in the Theodotionic tradition lack a translation of the phrase here, and all Theodotionic manuscripts lack one in 7:7 but have one in 7:13. Some critical scholars have suggested that the phrase is original in 7:13, but secondary in 7:2, 7. However, the Old Greek translates the Aramaic phrases in all three verses (by καθ' ὕπνους νυκτός in 7:2 and by ἐν ὁράματι τῆς νυκτός in 7:7, 13). In 4QDan[b], ב]חזוי עם is extant in 7:2,[1] making it likely that the Theodotionic translator simply omitted a translation here and in 7:7.

אַרְבַּע רוּחֵי שְׁמַיָּא מְגִיחָן לְיַמָּא רַבָּא—The Hebrew verb גִּיחַ has the intransitive meaning "burst forth" and is used for the birth of the sea in Job 38:8 (cf. also for the Jordan in Job 40:23). Some propose that the Aramaic cognate here, מְגִיחָן, the Haphel (H) participle of גּוּחַ or גִּיחַ, also has intransitive meaning. However, it more likely has the transitive meaning "to churn up, stir up" (*HALOT*, b), and the preposition לְ (on לְיַמָּא) indicates the direct object: "the four winds of heaven were churning the great sea."

7:3 וְאַרְבַּע חֵיוָן רַבְרְבָן—"Four large beasts" uses the plural of the adjective רַב, which is reduplicated (רַבְרְבָן), as also in 7:7–8, 11, 17, 20. The adjective can also mean "many" or "great" or have other nuances depending on the context. Compare the textual note on 7:8.

---

[1] Ulrich et al., *Qumran Cave 4.XI*, 263.

שָׁנְיָן דָּא מִן־דָּא—This phrase with the plural participle שָׁנְיָן is, literally, "being different, this one from that one."

7:4 קַדְמָיְתָא כְאַרְיֵה וְגַפִּין דִּי־נְשַׁר לַהּ—"The first one was like a lion, and wings of an eagle [belonged] to it." The Aramaic noun נְשַׁר, like its Hebrew cognate נֶשֶׁר, signifies any large soaring bird of prey or carrion eater. While the majority of translations have "eagle," as does the translation above, the word can include vultures of various kinds.[2]

וּלְבַב אֱנָשׁ יְהִיב לַהּ—"And a heart/mind of a man was given to it." The Aramaic לְבַב, like its Hebrew cognates לֵב and לֵבָב, can signify the organ of thought (hence "mind") as well as emotions. See the first textual note on 1:8.

7:5 וּתְלָת עִלְעִין בְּפֻמַּהּ—Probably this means the second beast had "three ribs in its mouth." עֲלַע is a "rib" (*HALOT*) and is cognate to Hebrew צֵלָע. The Jewish scholar Saadia Gaon (AD 882–942) suggests that when used with reference to the mouth here, the plural denotes large teeth that appear to be like shaped like ribs.[3] Luther follows this interpretation and identifies the ribs as the three most important Medo-Persian kings: Cyrus, Darius, and Xerxes.[4] Equating the ribs with teeth is a clever suggestion, but cannot be demonstrated to be a meaning of this term in Imperial Aramaic. More likely the "ribs" are from the carcass of a victim, in harmony with the command given to this beast later in the same verse, קוּמִי אֲכֻלִי בְּשַׂר שַׂגִּיא, "arise, devour much flesh."

וְכֵן אָמְרִין לַהּ—Literally, this is "thus they were saying to it." The verb אָמְרִין is the Peal (G) plural participle. Biblical Aramaic frequently uses plural forms that are impersonal (with no stated subject) but that imply God as the ultimate cause of the action. Usually they are best translated as passives, hence "this is what *was being said* to it." See further the commentary.

Compare Rev 6:7–8, where an angelic being summons a horseman who is given authority (permission ultimately from God) to kill part of humanity by wild beasts. Compare Dan 6:25 (ET 6:24) but contrast Dan 6:23 (ET 6:22).

7:6 וְשָׁלְטָן יְהִיב לַהּ—"Dominion was given to it." This is the first occurrence of the noun שָׁלְטָן, "dominion," in Daniel 7. It is an important word in previous accounts in the book, which stress that dominion belongs to God, and he gives it to rulers (3:33 [ET 4:3]; 4:19, 31 [ET 4:22, 34]; 6:27 [ET 6:26]). It is also a key word in this chapter. Later in Daniel 7, we are told that all four beasts had "dominion" (7:12) and that "dominion" will be taken away from rulers in this world (7:12, 26). Total "dominion" will be given to the Son of Man, who will secure it for God and his saints (7:14, 27).

7:7 וְהִיא מְשַׁנְּיָה מִן־כָּל־חֵיוָתָא דִּי קָדָמַיהּ ... וְקַרְנַיִן עֲשַׂר לַהּ—The pronoun הִיא ("it") is emphatic and draws attention to the final statement, which describes the beast's unique feature: "it was different from all the beasts that were before it ... *in that* it had

---

[2] *Fauna and Flora of the Bible*, 82–84.

[3] Frank, "The Description of the 'Bear' in Dn 7,5," citing the Rabbinic Bible (Venice: 1568), translated in A. F. Gallé, *Daniel avec commentaires de R. Saadia, Aben Ezra, Raschi ...* (Paris, 1900), 72–73.

[4] Luther, "Preface to Daniel," AE 35:299.

ten horns." The *waw* on וְקַרְנַיִן is used in an epexegetical or explicative sense, as also in, for example, 1:3; 2:28; 3:2; 4:10 [ET 4:13]; 6:29 [ET 6:28]; 7:1. The statement that "it had ten horns" explains how this beast was different from the others. No other beast in this vision has any horns. קָדָמַיהּ ("before it") is the only instance in the OT where the preposition קֳדָם has a temporal meaning.[5]

7:8 וּפֻם מְמַלִּל רַבְרְבָן—The translation above agrees with those that give the literal "and a mouth speaking great things" (KJV, RSV, ESV). רַבְרְבָן is the reduplicated feminine plural of the adjective רַב, "great, large, many." There is a contrast between the horn itself being "a little one" (זְעֵירָה) and the "great things" that it speaks, showing that the horn has grandiose ideas and aggressive ambitions that it does not have the ability to achieve. A number of translations render רַבְרְבָן more specifically as arrogant or boastful statements: e.g., "great boasts" (NASB) or "pompous words" (NKJV). Later 7:20–22 and 7:25 reveal that the "great things" the little horn speaks are polemical words against God and his saints. The Old Greek anticipates 7:21 by its longer reading here: καὶ στόμα λαλοῦν μεγάλα καὶ ἐποίει πόλεμον πρὸς τοὺς ἁγίους, "and a mouth speaking great things, and it was making war against the saints."

7:9 כָּרְסָוָן רְמִיו—"Thrones were set up." The Aramaic noun כָּרְסֵא is cognate to the Hebrew כִּסֵּא, "throne." רְמִיו is the Peal passive (Gp) perfect of רְמָא. This verb has occasioned much discussion. Normally רְמָא means "throw" (*HALOT*, s.v. רמה, 1), so the passive would mean "be thrown," as does the identical form in 3:21. However, most commentators agree that the meaning in this context is that thrones were "placed" or "set up" (see *HALOT*, 2) for seating members of the divine court. Similarly, the Hebrew יָרָה in Qal (G) usually means "throw," but occasionally it can mean "place, set up" (Gen 31:51; Job 38:6).

7:10 וְסִפְרִין פְּתִיחוּ—Literally, "scrolls were opened" to reveal their contents for the purpose of rendering judgment, as also in Rev 20:12. Most translations render סִפְרִין as "books," but the codex or book (as we think of it) was not invented until the early Christian era. Christians quickly adopted the codex for biblical manuscripts, whereas Jews have continued to use scrolls for biblical texts.

7:12 עַד־זְמַן וְעִדָּן—Literally, "until a time and a time," this is translated, "for a period of time." זְמַן is probably a loanword from Persian and is used in Daniel[a] as an equivalent of the native Aramaic עִדָּן.[b] Both words are used also in 2:21 and 7:25. Here they are connected by an epexegetical *waw* to form a pleonasm. Some scholars assume that עִדָּן, "time," has the more specific meaning "year," but that is unwarranted (see the commentary on 4:13 [ET 4:16] and on 7:25).

7:13 כְּבַר אֱנָשׁ—"(One) like a Son of Man" uses the preposition כְּ on בַּר, "son," the Aramaic equivalent of the Hebrew בֵּן, "son." כְּבַר is in construct with אֱנָשׁ, "a man," cognate to the Hebrew אִישׁ. The phrase means that this person possesses a true human nature and human appearance. At the same time, כְּ, "like," implies that he is far greater than an ordinary man. Similar is the frequent use of כְּ, "like," in the Hebrew of Ezek 1:26–28, where Ezekiel describes a divine vision of the brilliant, enthroned human figure who is

(a) Dan 2:16, 21; 3:7–8; 4:33 (ET 4:36); 6:11, 14 (ET 6:10, 13); 7:12, 22, 25

(b) Dan 2:8–9, 21; 3:5, 15; 4:13, 20, 22, 29 (ET 4:16, 23, 25, 32); 7:12, 25

---

[5] Rosenthal, *A Grammar of Biblical Aramaic*, § 84.

"the Glory of Yahweh." He describes the Glory as having דְּמוּת כְּמַרְאֵה אָדָם, "an image like the appearance of a man" (Ezek 1:26).[6] The comparison affirms the human form and nature of the divine figure while also implying that he is so majestic that he can only be described as being "like" a man.

Similar to the Aramaic phrase here in Dan 7:13 is the Hebrew כִּדְמוּת בְּנֵי אָדָם, literally, "(one) like the form of sons of man/men," describing the one who appears to Daniel in 10:16. See also the description of the same man in 10:18: כְּמַרְאֵה אָדָם, literally, "[one whose appearance was] like the appearance of a man." And compare בֶּן־אָדָם, "a son of Adam/man," in, for example, Pss 8:5 (ET 8:4); 80:18 (ET 80:17).

Daniel is called בֶּן־אָדָם in Dan 8:17, and that phrase often refers to Ezekiel (e.g., Ezek 2:1, 3, 6, 8). Compare also בְּנֵי־אָדָם, "sons of man" (e.g., Is 52:14) and בְּנֵי־אִישׁ "sons of man" (Pss 4:3 [ET 4:2]; 49:3 [ET 49:2]; 62:10 [ET 62:9]; Lam 3:33). However, those Hebrew phrases often are used in contexts that stress sinfulness, mortality, and frailty, which are the opposite of the characteristics of the Son of Man portrayed in Dan 7:13–14.

7:14 שָׁלְטָנֵהּ שָׁלְטָן עָלַם דִּי־לָא יֶעְדֵּה—"His dominion is an eternal dominion that will not pass away" uses the construct phrase שָׁלְטָן עָלַם ("dominion of eternity"), and the genitive is adjectival, hence "eternal dominion." The verb עֲדָה, "to go away" (*HALOT*, 2) or "pass away," is negated here, in contrast to 2:21; 4:28 (ET 4:31); 5:20; 7:12, 26, where forms of the same verb are used to state that earthly kingdoms and their glory did (or will) pass away.

וּמַלְכוּתֵהּ דִּי־לָא תִתְחַבַּל:—"And his kingdom is one that will not be destroyed" recalls the promise made with the same verb, the Hithpaal (HtD) of חֲבַל, "be destroyed," in 2:44: "the God of heaven will establish a kingdom that will never be destroyed." The same verb was also in Darius' acknowledgement about God's kingdom after God rescued Daniel from the lions' den: "his kingdom will not be destroyed" (6:27 [ET 6:26]). See also the negated cognate noun חֲבָל, used to say that "no injury/destruction" befell the Judeans in the furnace (3:25) or Daniel in the lions' den (6:24 [ET 6:23]).

Like the preceding clause (see the first textual note on 7:14), this clause contrasts with another Daniel verse that uses a form of the same verb to refer (metaphorically) to the destruction of a worldly kingdom. The command was given to "destroy" (Pael [D] of חֲבַל) the tree that represented Nebuchadnezzar and his kingdom (4:20).

Commentary
Daniel as Author (7:1)

Dan 7:1 contains the first direct reference in the book to Daniel's activity as an author. It clearly states that the account of this dream comes from Daniel's pen. Moreover, this verse and indeed this entire chapter exhibit literary tendencies that are characteristic of the earlier chapters. The use of the epexegetical

---

[6] For the view that the Glory seen by Ezekiel is the preincarnate Christ, see Hummel, *Ezekiel 1–20*, 13, 49, 64–67. Hummel (pp. 70–72) cites as a parallel the vision in Daniel 7, "Son of Man" as Jesus' favored self-designation in the Gospels, and the description of the exalted Christ in Revelation 4.

or explanatory *waw* in connecting phrases such as "saw a dream *and* visions of his head" (7:1) is common throughout Daniel (e.g., 1:3; 2:28; 3:2; 4:10 [ET 4:13]; 6:29 [ET 6:28]) and is used several times in Daniel 7 (also in 7:7, 12). The repetition of thought in חֶלְמָא כְתַב רֵאשׁ מִלִּין אֲמַר, literally, "he wrote the dream, and he related⁷ the head of [main] words" (7:1), is a common thought pattern in Daniel (e.g., 2:23b, 28b; 5:17, 20; 6:5 [ET 6:4]). Therefore, there is ample evidence to conclude that Daniel, the author of this chapter, is the author of the entire book.⁸

Introduction to the Vision (7:2–3)

Daniel's vision begins with "the four winds of heaven ... churning the great sea" (7:2). While commentators have discussed various proposals about the identity of "the four winds," throughout Scripture this phrase is used when referring to the entire earth and especially the farthest reaches of the earth.ᶜ Compare the four angels "standing at the four corners of the earth, holding back the four winds of the earth" in Rev 7:1. Presumably the number of winds derives from the cardinal compass points (north, south, east, and west), making the number four symbolic of the entire earth. Hence the whole world is in turmoil.

More controversial is the identity of "the great sea" (7:2). Some scholars understand the Aramaic phrase יַמָּא רַבָּא, "the great sea," to be equivalent to the Hebrew phrase הַיָּם הַגָּדוֹל, "the Great Sea."⁹ The Hebrew phrase usually refers to the Mediterranean Sea (Num 34:6–7; Josh 1:4; 9:1; 23:4; cf. Jonah 1:12), also in Ezekiel's eschatological vision of the new creation (Ezek 47:10, 15, 19–20; 48:28).¹⁰ However, while some of the world powers described later in Daniel 7 arise out of the Mediterranean basin, not all of them do, and there is no evidence that Daniel's Aramaic phrase is intended to be the equivalent of the Hebrew phrase.

Interpreters who favor a mythological background for Daniel 7 argue that the raging sea is the primordial chaos of ancient Near Eastern creation myths.¹¹ However, the theories that a Babylonian or Canaanite mythic background influenced Daniel 7 are problematic.¹² The Genesis creation account refers to the Spirit (interpreted by some as "wind") of God hovering over the primordial

(c) Jer 49:36; Ezek 37:9; Zech 2:6; 6:5; Dan 7:2; 8:8; 11:4; Mt 24:31; Mk 13:27; Rev 7:1

---

⁷ Normally the verb אֲמַר means "say, speak," but in this context after the verb כְתַב, "write," it too refers to written communication and so is translated, "he related."

⁸ See further "Date and Authorship according to the Book" in "Date, Authorship, and Unity" in the introduction.

⁹ Goldingay, *Daniel*, 160; cf. Archer, "Daniel," 85. Goldingay notes that the Aramaic phrase occurs in 1QapGen 21:16 and denotes the Mediterranean Sea. However, this only proves that in the first century BC, someone used the Aramaic phrase to correspond to the Hebrew phrase as used in the Pentateuch.

¹⁰ For this eschatological vision, see Hummel, *Ezekiel 21–48*, 1149–60.

¹¹ Collins, *Daniel*, 294–95; Gardner, "The Great Sea of Dan VII 2."

¹² See "Whether a Babylonian or Canaanite Mythic Background Influenced Daniel 7" in "Introduction to Daniel 7."

waters (Gen 1:1–2), but that scene lacks the violent action ("churning") and evil (the emerging beasts) present here (Dan 7:2–3). A mythological view is also contradicted by 7:17, which states that the beasts will arise "from the earth." In contrast, the mythological language of the Near Eastern creation texts pictures beasts arising from the sea goddess, the Babylonian Tiamat.

Instead, the great sea in Daniel signifies something coextensive with the earth (7:17). Some commentators note that the sea is sometimes a metaphor for the nations.[13] In Is 57:20 the sea is a metaphor for wicked people, and in Is 17:12 the thunder of many peoples is likened to the thunder of the sea. In Jer 6:23 the sea denotes the armies of Babylon.

Since the sea in Dan 7:2 is churned up by the four winds, which encompass the entire earth, the sea most likely represents all the peoples of the earth.

Daniel sees four beasts ascending from the sea and notes that they are different from one another (7:3). The most obvious difference is that each of the first three is described as resembling a different animal or as composed of parts of different animals, while the last beast does not resemble any natural animal. These differences signify the differences between the various kingdoms the beasts represent. Each represents a dominant world power, but each nation has its own particular character, way of spreading, and method of defeating its foes.

Revelation contains some rough parallels. In Rev 12:18–13:10 (ET 12:17b–13:10), Satan stands on the shore of the sea and conjures out of the sea a beast that he will use in his warfare against the church.[14] This first beast continues to appear in later chapters of Revelation until it is finally thrown into the lake of fire after the return of Christ; compare its judgment in Rev 19:20 to Dan 7:11 (cf. also Rev 20:10). Then in Rev 13:11–18, Satan conjures a second beast from the earth.[15] Another rough parallel to the four beasts in Daniel 7 is the four symbolic horsemen who are summoned in Rev 6:1–8 and given permission to ravage humanity. However, the horsemen are not kingdoms, but agents of destruction that can range over the entire world throughout history until the return of Christ.[16]

The First Beast: A Lion with Eagle's Wings (7:4)

The kingdom represented by the first beast, the creature "like a lion" with "wings of an eagle" (7:4), is Babylon, as commentators of all stripes have acknowledged. Nebuchadnezzar, king of Babylon, is compared to a lion in Jer 4:7 and 50:17 (cf. Jer 49:19; 50:44). The Babylonian king, nation, or armies are compared to eagles in Jer 4:13; 48:40; 49:22; Ezek 17:3; Hab 1:8; and Lam

---

[13] Baldwin, *Daniel*, 138; Miller, *Daniel*, 195; Young, *Daniel*, 142; Zevit, "Structure and Individual Elements of Daniel 7."

[14] For an interpretation, see Brighton, *Revelation*, 341–57.

[15] For an interpretation, one may see Brighton, *Revelation*, 347–48, 357–63.

[16] For an interpretation, one may see Brighton, *Revelation*, 160–69.

4:19. The specific description of the wings as "of an eagle" (דִּי־נְשַׁר, Dan 7:4) probably combines the concepts of swiftness in flight with the ability to attack like a bird of prey.

The time when the lion still has its wings and can travel quickly represents the rapid expansion of the Neo-Babylonian Empire under Nabopolassar and Nebuchadnezzar. During Nebuchadnezzar's reign that expansion slowed, as signified by the plucking of the wings from the lion. Eventually, however, the lion was made to stand upright and given "a man's mind" (לְבַב אֱנָשׁ, 7:4). This is an obvious reversal of the transformation of Nebuchadnezzar, whose human "mind/heart" was taken away, and he was given the "mind/heart" of an animal (לְבַב twice in 4:13 [ET 4:16]).

Some commentators see here a reference to the restoring of Nebuchadnezzar's sanity ("my reason returned to me," 4:31, 33 [ET 4:34, 36]).[17] However, the only time that the Aramaic noun for "mind" (לְבַב) in 7:4 is mentioned in reference to Nebuchadnezzar (besides 2:30) is when he loses his sanity (4:13 [ET 4:16], recalled in 5:20–21). Other vocabulary is used for the restoration of his sanity in 4:31, 33 (ET 4:34, 36). The transformation of the lion is an ironic twist on the earlier narrative, since an animal is given a human "mind," the exact opposite of Nebuchadnezzar's experience. Moreover, the detail about the lion being made to stand on its feet is not mentioned at all in Daniel 4.

Instead of recalling Nebuchadnezzar in chapter 4, the humanizing of this beast represents the lessening ferocity of the Babylonian Empire under its later kings.

The Second Beast: A Bear (7:5)

In the Scriptures, bears are often associated with lions as fierce and dangerous predators.[d] "On one side" this bear "was raised up" (Dan 7:5). Some commentators have seen this posture as meaning that it was ready to lunge down on its prey.[18] However, that posture would mean the bear would rear up and stand on its hind legs, and so we would expect the text to say that its "front" (Aramaic אַף or קְדָם)[19] would be raised up. However, the noun שְׂטַר denotes a lateral "side," left or right, and so the clause וְלִשְׂטַר־חַד הֲקִמַת means "and to/on one side [left or right] it was raised up." In confirmation of this, שְׂטַר, "side," with the preposition בְּ means "next to, beside."[20] Therefore, this bear was higher on one side than on the other. This has led some commentators to surmise that

(d) 1 Sam 17:34–37; Hos 13:8; Amos 5:19; Prov 28:15; Lam 3:10

---

[17] In ancient times, this view was held by Hippolytus and Jerome (Collins, *Daniel*, 297). See Hippolytus, *Commentary on Daniel*, 1 (*ANF* 5:178); Archer, *Jerome's Commentary on Daniel*, 73. Archer, "Daniel," 86, lists this as a possibility, and Miller, *Daniel*, 197, advocates it.

[18] Baldwin, *Daniel*, 139; Montgomery, *Daniel*, 288.

[19] *CAL*, s.vv. אַף and קְדָם.

[20] *CAL*, s.v. בִּשְׂטַר.

the bear was disfigured.[21] However, the Hophal (Hp) perfect verb הֳקִמַת indicates that the side of the bear was "raised up" by someone.

This is a reference to God granting greater dominion to the Persians in the empire consisting of both the Medes and the Persians—the Medo-Persian Empire created by Cyrus.[22] The raised side is a strong indication that this beast represents Media-Persia, and not simply Media, as critical scholars claim. The difference is of great importance. If the beast only represents Media (the second kingdom), then Persia and Greece would be the third and fourth kingdoms, and God's kingdom should have arrived during the Greek era (which it did not). If this second animal represents Medo-Persia, then the third represents Greece and the fourth Rome, during whose era the kingdom of God did arrive in the person of Jesus Christ.[23] The two-sided nature of this second beast corresponds with the two horns on the ram that represents Media-Persia in 8:3. Its raised side corresponds to the larger horn representing Persia in 8:3.

The three ribs in the bear's mouth represent conquests by the Medo-Persian Empire. One is tempted to identify them as the major conquests of Lydia (in ca. 547 BC), Babylon (in 539), and Egypt (in 525).[24] If the Aramaic term meant "teeth" instead of "ribs" (see the first textual note on 7:5), they could represent three particularly prominent kings of Persia. However, these kinds of attempts at specific identifications are mere speculations and cannot be proven with any certainty. Instead, the number should be understood as symbolic in import.[25] The three ribs represent the substantial but limited power of the bear to devour. The Medo-Persian Empire will not devour the entire world, so the bear does not have an entire set of ribs in its mouth. Since ribs occur in pairs, a full set would require an even number. But the Medo-Persian Empire will dominate a good part of the world, so its power is to be feared.

While Daniel is looking at the bear, it is being commanded, "Arise, devour much flesh" (7:5). This command denotes divine authorization for the Medo-Persian dominion over the ancient Near East. God allows this warfare as part of his plan of preparation for the coming of his kingdom through the Son of Man (7:13; cf. Mt 24:6–31).

Many commentators view the order of events within 7:5 as sequential, as if the bear first appears to Daniel, then he observes its traits, and only afterward does he hear the command for the bear to arise and devour. However, the

---

[21] This opinion is reported, but not necessarily endorsed, by Goldingay, *Daniel*, 162, and Lucas, *Daniel*, 179.

[22] Archer, "Daniel," 86; Leupold, *Daniel*, 291; Walvoord, *Daniel*, 156; Young, *Daniel*, 145.

[23] See the excursus "The Four-Kingdom Schema in Daniel."

[24] Archer, "Daniel," 86; Miller, *Daniel*, 199. However, Calvin objects that identifying the three ribs as three kingdoms is defining the text too narrowly (*Daniel*, 2:16).

[25] See "A Literalistic Interpretation of Numbers Is Disproved by Daniel 1:20 and 3:19" in "Eschatology and Dispensational Premillennial Interpretations of Daniel" in the introduction.

participle אָמְרִין, literally, "they (were) saying," indicates that Daniel hears the command simultaneously as he sees the bear in his dream. The assumption that the bear has already received the command explains why the bear already has ribs in its mouth. No subject is used with the participle (see the second textual note on 7:5). This leaves unstated whether God or an intermediary spoke the command, and thereby it preserves a proper distance between God himself and the command that allows warfare and death.[26]

The Third Beast: A Leopard with Four Wings and Four Heads (7:6)

The third beast resembles a four-winged, four-headed leopard. The leopard, known as a swift animal, is made more swift by a double set of wings. Unlike the lion's wings, which were described more specifically as "wings of an eagle" (7:4), the wings on this third creature are simply called "bird wings" (7:6). Since it has the unnatural number of "four" bird wings, the implication is that these four wings could take advantage of "the four winds of heaven" (7:2). Thus Daniel saw a vision of a speedy and mobile animal.

While the rise of both the Neo-Babylonian and Medo-Persian Empires was relatively fast, the speedy rise of Alexander's Greek empire was without equal in the ancient Near East. Alexander began his conquest of Persia in May 334 BC and continued to conquer territory until the revolt of his troops at Opis in August 324. In one short decade, the Macedonian king had established an empire more vast than any that preceded it. The four wings able to fly on the four winds in all four compass directions (north, south, east, west) on an already swift animal predict and symbolize this stunning achievement by Alexander the Great.

Many interpreters who rightly understand this third creature to represent the Greek domination of the ancient Near East view its "four heads" (7:6) as the four major kingdoms into which Alexander's empire was split by the Greek rulers who followed him.[27] The later Greek rulers and their territories were Antigonus (or later Cassander) in Greece and Macedon, Lysimachus in Thrace and Asia Minor, Seleucus I Nicator in Syria and Babylon, and Ptolemy I Soter in Egypt and Palestine. This interpretation seems to be influenced by Dan 8:8, 21–22, where the goat representing Greece has four horns that represent four

---

[26] Similarly, Revelation quotes commands that express God's permission for warfare and other calamities to take place on earth (e.g., Rev 6:1–8). Some of the commands are spoken by angels (e.g., Rev 7:2; 14:15, 18; 19:17–18), no doubt at God's bidding. The commands in Rev 6:1–8 come from the living creatures (angelic beings) who support God's throne. Other commands come from God himself, although usually this is expressed obliquely, for example, "a voice from the temple" in heaven (Rev 16:1). God's antecedent will is to save all people (1 Tim 2:4). Yet when people do not repent, even after suffering warnings of God's judgment (cf. Rev 9:20; 16:9, 11), his consequent will is to judge and punish sin. See Pieper, *Christian Dogmatics*, 1:454–55. The final judgment will take place at the return of Christ.

[27] E.g., Archer, "Daniel," 86; Calvin, *Daniel*, 2:18–20; Leupold, *Daniel*, 294; Miller, *Daniel*, 200; Walvoord, *Daniel*, 158. This view of the four heads was also held by Hippolytus (died ca. AD 236), Jerome (died AD 420), and Rashi (died AD 1105), who are cited by Collins (*Daniel*, 298). See Hippolytus, *Commentary on Daniel*, 1 (*ANF* 5:178); Archer, *Jerome's Commentary on Daniel*, 75.

kings who succeed one great horn (Alexander). However, here in 7:6, the "four heads" do not replace one head, so the heads in Daniel 7 are not parallel to the horns in Daniel 8. Moreover, Daniel 7 never states the symbolic meaning of the heads. Therefore, it is more probable that the "four heads" (like the leopard's "four" wings [7:6]) derive their symbolism from "the four winds of heaven" (7:2). Thus the leopard's four heads probably indicate that it has ambition and vision for conquest in all four directions, toward all corners of the earth. While the four heads may also anticipate the later breakup of Alexander's kingdom into four pieces, it is premature to speak about the heads as four separate kingdoms, since this detail will not be revealed until the following vision in Daniel 8, and there it is symbolized by four horns (not heads).

In the visions in Daniel (chapters 7–12), the number "four" is consistently and exclusively (except for 7:2–3) associated with the Greek dominance of the Near East. In the vision of Daniel 7, the Greek dominance is represented by a leopard with "four bird wings" and "four heads" (7:6). Of the two kingdoms mentioned in Daniel 8, the second one is symbolized by a male goat, which is explained as Greece (8:21). Initially this goat had one horn (8:5). However, when that horn is broken, it is replaced by "four" horns "toward the four winds of heaven" (8:8; see also 8:22). In the vision in Daniel 10–12, the mighty king (Alexander the Great) who arises will have his kingdom broken and divided "toward the four winds of heaven" (11:3–4).

Some critics who hold that the third beast represents Persia identify the four heads as the only four Persian kings mentioned in the Bible (Cyrus, Ahasuerus/Xerxes, Artaxerxes, and Darius II/III),[28] and some claim that the four heads are the four Persian kings prophesied in 11:2.[29] However, the four kings prophesied in 11:2 are Cambyses, Gaumata, Darius I, and Xerxes, whose campaign against Greece is prophesied there,[30] and as a result, the biblical authors refer to at least seven Persian kings. The mistaken identification of the four heads of the leopard in 7:6 with the four Persian kings in 11:2 is one of many reasons why the widely accepted critical theory about the second, third, and fourth beasts (that the bear symbolizes Media, the leopard symbolizes Persia, and the fourth beast symbolizes Greece) is untenable.[31]

The third beast is the only one that is said to be given "dominion" (7:6). This is a foreshadowing of the Greek kingdom's use and abuse of its dominion described in later visions (Daniel 8, 10–12), especially the abuse of dominion by Antiochus IV Epiphanes (175–164 BC), who viciously persecuted the Jewish people. Just as the command to the bear-like beast, "arise, devour much

---

[28] E.g., Hartman and Di Lella, *Daniel*, 213.

[29] See Collins, *Daniel*, 298; Montgomery, *Daniel*, 290.

[30] See the commentary on 11:2.

[31] The critical theory is called the Greek view since it supposes that the book of Daniel promised that God's kingdom would arrive during the Greek era. See further the excursus "The Four-Kingdom Schema in Daniel."

flesh" (7:5), was an anonymous command, so too the impersonal passive construction "dominion was given to it" does not state the agent and cause (who the giver is) nor the source of this beast's dominion.

Thus the verse only implies that this beast receives its dominion from God. This is because the beast (like the other beasts) is not a direct agent of God in bringing his kingdom of grace and salvation through faith. Rather, the worldly kingdoms are servants of God (cf. Rom 13:1–7) in the realm of the created order and the Law, a common theme throughout Daniel,[32] but not in the order of redemption, the church and the Gospel. They are to maintain civil order and prepare for the advent of God's kingdom in Christ, but they cannot implement God's kingdom.

In contrast, when the Son of Man is "given dominion" in 7:14, it is clear from the context that "the Ancient of Days" (7:13) is the one who gives dominion to him. Moreover, he uses this dominion to establish the eternal kingdom of God and to give it to the saints by his grace (7:18, 27).

The Fourth Beast: Different from the Other Beasts (7:7)

Daniel does not describe the fourth beast he sees as resembling any natural animal. Instead, he describes it by its effect on him (דְּחִילָה וְאֵימְתָנִי, "frightening and terrible") and its strength (וְתַקִּיפָא יַתִּירָא, "exceedingly strong"). The same adjective for "strong" (תַּקִּיפָה) describes the fourth kingdom represented by the statue in Nebuchadnezzar's dream (2:40, 42). The fourth beast's "iron" teeth (7:7) are reminiscent of the fourth metal, "iron," in the shins and feet of the statue (2:33–35, 40–45). This beast also "crushed" (the verb דְּקַק) and "trampled with its feet" (7:7), just as the fourth kingdom represented by Nebuchadnezzar's statue had the ability to "crush" (the verb דְּקַק twice) and "shatter" (2:40). Therefore, the fourth beast represents the same kingdom—Rome—as the fourth part of the statue: the iron shins and iron and clay "feet."[33]

This beast is the only one described as recklessly destructive. The bear would "devour" (7:5), and the leopard had "dominion" (7:6), but only the fourth beast was so destructive that "it devoured and crushed, and what was left it trampled with its feet" (7:7). This is an apt description of cruel Roman power and Rome's willingness to use that power ruthlessly to subdue conquered peoples.

Daniel notes one major difference between this fourth animal and the others: it has horns. A natural horned animal would have only two. The "ten horns" (7:7) mark this beast as exceedingly powerful. Already in 1:20, the number "ten" is used in a symbolic manner to indicate a quality that surpasses all others: the

---

[32] See further the discussion of the Fourth Commandment in "God's Law in Daniel" in "Law and Gospel in Daniel" in the introduction.

[33] While 7:4 mentions the "feet" or "legs" (plural of רְגַל) of the first beast, all the other references in Daniel to feet (רְגַל) are for the fourth part of the statue (2:33–34, 41–42) or the fourth beast (7:7, 19).

king deems the wisdom of the Judeans to be "ten times" better than that of his occult diviners.[34] The horns of an animal signify its power (Deut 33:17; cf. 1 Ki 22:11; Ps 75:11 [ET 75:10]) just as a "horn" can represent God's power to save his people (e.g., Pss 18:3 [ET 18:2]; 132:17; Lk 1:69). Therefore, the unnatural number of ten horns signifies the unique character of this animal that sets it apart from the others: it surpasses them all in its power.

A Little Horn (7:8)

Daniel's attention has shifted from the beast as a whole to its ten horns, which caught his attention because they made the beast different from the others (7:7). As he is contemplating the horns, a little horn arises on the beast, and "three of the previous horns [are] uprooted in front of it" (7:8). The passive verb once again implies divine action.[35] The uprooting is done with God's permission, and it also demonstrates the power of the little horn. Interpreters often assume that by uprooting the three horns, the little horn inherits their former power.[36] However, the fact that only three of the ten horns are uprooted implies that only part of the power of the beast is exercised by the little horn.

The little horn's eyes and mouth reveal that the horn represents a human institution (just as the other horns represent human kings or kingdoms). The eyes denote the ability to observe and may also imply intelligence.[37]

The "great things" the little horn speaks (7:8) are polemical words against God and his saints according to the subsequent explanation in the vision (see the commentary on 7:21, 25). This little horn is the only entity in the entire chapter that is depicted as specifically attacking God's people.

The beast with the ten horns and then the little horn is the OT background for the second beast, the beast from the earth, conjured by Satan in Rev 13:11–18. In Revelation, this beast has horns like a lamb (imitating the Lamb of God) but speaks like a serpent or dragon (Rev 13:11)—its ultimate master, Satan![38] Later in Revelation, this beast mutates into the harlot (Rev 17:1, 15–16; 19:2) and into the false prophet (Rev 16:13), who, with the first beast, is finally cast into the lake of fire (Rev 19:20; cf. Rev 20:10). Therefore, the fourth beast in Daniel 7, and in particular its little horn, represents the Antichrist.[39] This little

---

[34] See the commentary on 1:20 and also "A Literalistic Interpretation of Numbers Is Disproved by Daniel 1:20 and 3:19" in "Eschatology and Dispensational Premillennial Interpretations of Daniel" in the introduction.

[35] Goldingay, *Daniel*, 164.

[36] E.g., Baldwin, *Daniel*, 140.

[37] Baldwin, *Daniel*, 140; Miller, *Daniel*, 202.

[38] For the second beast, the beast from the earth in Rev 13:11–18, see Brighton, *Revelation*, 357–63. The first beast was conjured out of the sea by Satan (Rev 12:18–13:10 [ET 12:17b–13:10]), and it remains the "beast" throughout the rest of Revelation. The second beast serves as a puppet of the first beast, but Satan is the mastermind and the real power behind them both.

[39] See also the commentary on 7:19–22 and the excursus "The Lutheran Confessions on the Antichrist in Daniel."

horn is not to be equated with the one in Daniel 8, which represents Antiochus IV Epiphanes.[40]

The Ancient of Days Convenes a Court (7:9–10)

Daniel's description of his vision changes to the tight parallelism of poetry in 7:9–10, 13–14 when describing the vision of the Ancient of Days and Son of Man.

Eschatology and Revelation Parallels

The imagery of this vision is taken up again in two main places in Revelation. Revelation 4–5 views the coronation and enthronement of the Lamb after he has completed his atonement and thereby opened the kingdom of God to all who believe. The Lamb once slain "won the victory" (Rev 5:5) by completing his mission through his incarnation, perfect life, atoning death, bodily resurrection, and ascension. All baptized believers in Christ are already now members of his eternal kingdom of grace. Through faith, the OT saints too are equal members of this kingdom; they are represented by twelve of the twenty-four elders gathered around the throne. (See further below under "Who Is to Be Seated on the Thrones?")

This scene also has parallels to the final judgment in Revelation 19–20 at the end of the world upon the return of Christ. These parallels include the worshiping throng around the throne (Dan 7:10, 14 and Rev 19:1–10); the fiery judgment of the fourth beast and its little horn (Dan 7:11) and the casting of the beast and false prophet into the lake of fire (Rev 19:19–20; cf. Rev 19:3; 20:9–10); the opening of books for judgment (Dan 7:10 [cf. 12:1–3] and Rev 20:12); and the coming of the Son of Man on the clouds of heaven to receive the kingdom (Dan 7:13–14) and the opening of heaven for the second coming of Christ with the hosts of heaven to execute the final defeat of God's foes (Rev 19:11–16).

The sequence of events in Dan 7:9–14 is relatively simple and smooth. However, as one can see from the verse references cited (not in biblical order) from Revelation, the parallels in Revelation do not follow the same simple sequence of events as in Dan 7:9–14. The most likely explanation is that Daniel, from his perspective as a prophet in the sixth century BC, is shown from afar a brief glimpse of all that God would accomplish through the first advent of Christ; his ascension, session, and reign over the church throughout the present church age; and his eventual second coming in power and glory to bring this world to its close, vanquish all of God's foes, and inaugurate the eternal salvation of the saints in the new heavens and new earth. Daniel sees all these events from a great distance, which makes it appear as if the events follow one another smoothly, much as mountain peaks appear close together when one views the

---

[40] See problem 5 and figure 10 in "Problems in Daniel for the Greek View" in the excursus "The Four-Kingdom Schema in Daniel."

range of mountains from a distance out on the plains. Revelation gives much more detail about those events, but its cyclical or spiral structure does not present those events in a simple, linear chronological order.[41]

The Divine Court Is in Session (7:9–10)

The setting of 7:9–10 is the convening of the divine court, as is clear in 7:10.[42] The court would make its judgment based on what God has recorded in his records, which are opened for the judges to consult. These record books are mentioned occasionally in Scripture[e] and will be mentioned again in Daniel (12:1). God's record books are mentioned extensively in Revelation. Especially comforting are the references to the book of life belonging to the Lamb since it records the names of all believers.[f] Unbelievers are judged based on their deeds recorded in the (plural) "books" (Rev 20:12); they are condemned because of their works. However, believers are neither condemned or acquitted based on their works. Instead, they are saved simply because their names are written in the Lamb's book of life (Rev 20:15), that is, by grace alone, through faith in the Lamb's atonement.

(e) Ex 32:32–33; Pss 56:9 (ET 56:8); 69:29 (ET 69:28); 139:16; Phil 4:3

(f) Rev 3:5; 13:8; 17:8; 20:12, 15; 21:27

Who Is to Be Seated on the Thrones? (7:9)

The first thing Daniel mentions is that "thrones were set up" (7:9). The plural has attracted much discussion. Some modern commentators understand the "thrones" to be for the angelic host and appeal to other OT passages that speak of a heavenly court convened by God at which angels are present (1 Ki 22:19; Is 6:1–7; Job 1:6; 2:1).[43] However, in none of these passages do the angels sit on thrones. They stand in 1 Ki 22:19, and the seraphim fly in Isaiah 6. Therefore, it is unlikely that the thrones are for angels.

Already in ancient times, Rabbi Akiba explained the thrones as "one for Him [the Ancient of Days] and one for David."[44] This has a definite messianic coloring and implies that the Son of Man (7:13) is the coming Davidic king who will occupy a throne beside God the Father. This is already promised in Ps 110:1, where David says, "Yahweh/the Lord said to my Lord, sit at my right hand." In

---

[41] For the structure of Revelation, see Brighton, *Revelation*, 9–11, 150–54. See also Steinmann, "The Tripartite Structure of the Sixth Seal, the Sixth Trumpet, and the Sixth Bowl of John's Apocalypse (Rev 6:12–7:17; 9:13–11:14; 16:12–16)." Due to the cyclical nature of Revelation, chapter 19 depicts the final judgment and the defeat of God's foes, but then Rev 20:1–6 returns to the binding of Satan at Christ's first advent and during the present church age, when Christians are already raised spiritually and begin to reign with Christ for the "thousand years" of the church age. See the excursus "The Millennium" and the commentary on Rev 20:1–6 in Brighton, *Revelation*, 533–41 and 546–70. Then Rev 20:7–15 returns to the final battle against God's saints on earth, the defeat of the enemies of God and his saints at the second coming of Christ, the final judgment, the banishment of unbelievers to hell and the deliverance of all whose names are recorded in the Lamb's book of life.

[42] For other glimpses of the heavenly court in the OT, see Job 1:6–12; 2:1–6; and 1 Ki 22:19–22.

[43] E.g., Hartman and Di Lella, *Daniel*, 217; Young, *Daniel*, 150–51.

[44] Talmud, *Ḥagigah*, 14a; *Sanhedrin*, 38b.

Mt 22:42–44, Jesus explains that Psalm 110 is about himself as David's "Lord." In Mt 25:31 Jesus declares, "When the Son of Man comes in his glory, and all the angels with him, then he will sit on his glorious throne." By saying that, Jesus implies that one of the "thrones" here in Dan 7:9 is for him. Jesus also testified to the high priest, "From now on you will see the Son of Man seated at the right hand of the Power and coming on the clouds of heaven" (Mt 26:64; cf. Mt 24:30). Jesus connects Psalm 110 with Daniel 7 by stating that he will sit at the right hand of the Power (Ps 110:1) and that he will come on the clouds of heaven (Dan 7:13). In addition, Jesus states that he will sit on his throne of judgment (Mt 25:31), both to mete out punishment to the wicked and to show mercy to all who believe in him. See also the references to the enthronement of God the Son in Heb 1:8; 4:16; 8:1; 12:2.

However, Jesus goes even farther in his Gospel promises. In addition to the thrones for him and his Father, after he is seated on his throne, his disciples will also sit on thrones, and the apostles will judge the twelve tribes of Israel from their thrones (Mt 19:28; Lk 22:30). When the apostle John is shown the scene of the heavenly court, in addition to the throne of God shared by the Lamb (Rev 5:13; cf. Rev 7:17; 22:1, 3), there are twenty-four thrones for twenty-four elders who represent all the saints (those who are righteous through faith), the entire church of both Testaments: twelve for the tribes of Israel and twelve for the apostles of the Lamb (Rev 4:4; 11:16; cf. Rev 20:4).[45]

We can interpret Daniel's vision in light of the fuller revelation to come in the NT. Therefore, as the court convenes, Daniel sees thrones set up that are for the Ancient of Days (7:9), the Son of Man (7:13), and the saints of the Most High (7:18). This interpretation is consistent with Daniel's own words. Even though the only individual he mentions as being seated on a throne is the Ancient of Days, at the end of the initial scene he notes that "the [entire] court was seated" (דִּינָא יְתִב, 7:10), and the Son of Man would naturally be enthroned as King after he receives God's eternal kingdom (7:14).

The Identity of the Ancient of Days (7:9; Also 7:13, 22)

From antiquity, the identity of the Ancient of Days has been debated. Many church fathers identify him as God the Father. These include Hippolytus, Eusebius of Caesarea, Cyril of Jerusalem, John Chrysostom, and Jerome.[46] This appears to be the most natural reading for Christians, since the Son of Man, traditionally identified as Christ, appears before the Ancient of Days.

---

[45] See Brighton, *Revelation*, 116–20.

[46] Royer, "The Ancient of Days: Patristic and Modern Views of Daniel 7:9–14," 138–42. See Hippolytus, "Scholia on Daniel," on 7:13 (*ANF* 5:189); Eusebius, *Ecclesiastical Theology*, 3.17 (PG 24:1037–38); Cyril of Jerusalem, *Catechetical Lectures*, 15 (*NPNF*[2] 7:104–14); e.g., John Chrysostom, *On the Incomprehensible Nature of God*, 11 (trans. Paul W. Harkins [Washington, D.C.: Catholic University of America Press, 1982], 279); Archer, *Jerome's Commentary on Daniel*, 73.

However, some church fathers identified the Ancient of Days as Christ, usually on the principle that all OT theophanies are manifestations of the preincarnate Son of God. This is the view of Cyril of Alexandria, John of Damascus, and Andrew of Caesarea.[47] Still other church fathers, such as Theodoret of Cyrus and Pseudo-Dionysius, do not identify the Ancient of Days with a particular person of the Trinity, preferring to view him simply as the triune God.[48]

Even if contemporary Christian interpreters take different positions as to the identity of the Son of Man (see the commentary on 7:13–14), all agree that the Son of Man is not the same person as the Ancient of Days. In general, contemporary Christian interpreters understand the Ancient of Days as God the Father or as God without specifying which person of the Trinity. If we identify the Son of Man as God the Son, Jesus Christ (as argued in this commentary; see on 7:13–14), then the Ancient of Days must be God the Father. All three persons of the one triune God have existed from eternity,[49] as affirmed about the Son in, for example, Micah 5:1 (ET 5:2); Jn 1:1; Col 1:17, so it is possible that "the Ancient of Days" could refer to the Son. However, it is particularly appropriate as a title for "the Father of our Lord Jesus Christ" (Col 1:3), since the Son is begotten of the Father and the Spirit proceeds from the Father and the Son. The order of the persons in the NT Trinitarian formulation is Father, Son, and Holy Spirit (Mt 28:19), and the ecumenical Creeds (Apostles', Nicene, and Athanasian) reflect that order.

The Description of the Ancient of Days (7:9–10)

The description of the Ancient of Days involves three aspects: his personal appearance, his throne, and his surroundings.

In personal appearance, the Ancient of Days has clothes "white as snow" and hair that is like "pure wool" (7:9). Given the poetic parallelism, we are to understand the pure wool hair as being brilliant white like his clothes. Both his clothes and hair are features that speak of God's holiness, a holiness that his justified people reflect by his grace (Dan 11:35; 12:10). Thus through the prophet Isaiah, God promises that if his people repent, their scarlet sins shall become "white as snow ... like wool" (Is 1:18; cf. Is 61:10; 2 Cor 5:4; Gal 3:27). This same symbolism, partly adopted from Daniel, is used extensively in Revelation. The exalted Christ has hair that is "white like wool, as white as

---

[47] Royer, "The Ancient of Days: Patristic and Modern Views of Daniel 7:9–14," 142–44. See Cyril of Alexandria, *Commentary on Daniel* (PG 70:1461–62); John of Damascus, *On the Divine Images* (trans. David Anderson [Crestwood, N.Y.: St. Vladimir's Seminary Press, 1980], 80); Andrew of Caesarea, *Commentary on the Apocalypse*, 1:12–16 (PG 106:227–28, 517–18).

[48] Royer, "The Ancient of Days: Patristic and Modern Views of Daniel 7:9–14," 144–45. See Theodoret of Cyrus, *Commentary on Daniel* (trans. Hill, 186–87); Pseudo-Dionysius, *The Divine Names* (trans. Colm Luibheid, *Pseudo-Dionysius: The Complete Works* [New York: Paulist, 1987], 120–21).

[49] The Athanasian Creed affirms that the Father, Son, and Spirit are "coeternal," "uncreated," and "eternal," "and yet there are not three Eternals, but one Eternal," the one triune God (*LSB*, p. 319, vv. 6, 8, 10–11).

snow" (Rev 1:14) and is seated on a white cloud (Rev 14:14) and white horse (Rev 19:11; cf. the "white throne" in Rev 20:11). His redeemed saints are promised or have received "white" garments (Rev 3:4–5, 18; 4:4; 6:11; 7:9, 13–14) and will receive a "white" stone (Rev 2:17).

God's throne and its wheels are flaming fire (Dan 7:9). Fire too represents the holiness of God, especially as he reveals himself in theophany.[g] By fire he can mete out judgment upon sinners (Dan 7:11).[h] Yet by fire he can also refine and purify his people (Zech 13:9; Mal 3:2–3; cf. 1 Cor 3:11–15). Once again, this symbolism, drawn at least partially from Daniel, is common in Revelation. Christ has eyes of fire (Rev 1:14; 2:18; 19:12; cf. Rev 10:1), and he can purify his people as if by fire (Rev 3:18; cf. Rev 15:2). Fire characterizes God's theophany (Rev 4:5) and his judgments.[i]

The wheels on the throne recall Ezekiel's vision of the wheeled cherubim who form a living throne of God (Ezek 1:15–21). This is significant in Daniel because he, like Ezekiel, ministers among the exiled Judeans in Babylon. Elsewhere, the OT pictures the place of God's throne as Jerusalem (Ps 9:8, 12 [ET 9:7, 11]) and particularly the cherubim over the ark of the covenant (e.g., 1 Sam 4:4; 2 Sam 6:2; 2 Ki 19:15; Pss 80:2 [ET 80:1]; 99:1), but to these two prophets in exile God revealed that his throne is supported by wheels. This implies mobility: God on his throne of grace can accompany his people wherever they go (cf. Is 66:1; Pss 11:4; 103:19). This anticipates the new covenant in Christ, when the people of God will worship in Spirit and truth (Jn 4:23–24) in all places where they gather around his Word and Sacraments.

As for his surroundings, from the Ancient of Days flows a river of fire (Dan 7:10), showing that his holy judgment emanates outward from him. Around him are attendants. Their ascending number is first given as, literally, "a thousand of thousands" and then as "a myriad of myriads," or "ten thousands upon ten thousands" (7:10). Neither of the two increasing numbers is a precise calculation, and so not even the larger one is intended to give a literal maximum count. Rather, these increasing powers of ten refer to the surpassing numbers of God's angels who wait on him. On the other hand, the numbers are finite, not infinite (as numbers for God might be). Angels are creatures, and God has created a limited number of them, even if it is a very large number. (Since they are creatures, they also have a beginning and do not exist from eternity, in contrast to "the Ancient of Days.")

A similar expression of angels numbering thousands upon thousands and ten thousands upon ten thousands, all gathered around the throne of God and the Lamb, is in Rev 5:11. Also parallel is the rejoicing throng of angels and saints around the throne in Rev 19:1–10.

It should be noted that the angels stand before God to attend him and to be ready to do his bidding (cf. 1 Ki 22:19). They are not the ones for whom the thrones were set in place. (Contrast the throne of God the Son in Heb 1:8 with the unenthroned angels in Heb 1:7, 13–14.)

(g) E.g., Ex 3:2; 13:21–22; 19:18; Pss 18:9, 13–14 (ET 18:8, 12–13); 50:3

(h) Also, e.g., Gen 19:24; Lev 10:2; 2 Ki 1:10–14; Pss 21:10 (ET 21:9); 78:21; 89:47 (ET 89:46); 97:3

(i) Rev 8:5, 7–8; 9:17–18; 11:5; 14:10, 18; 16:8; 17:16; 18:8; 19:20; 20:9–10, 14–15; 21:8

The Judgment of the Beasts (7:11–12)

In the dream, Daniel's attention is drawn back to the little horn "because of the sound of the great words" (7:11) that it is still speaking (the "great things" in 7:8). The implication of the attention now given the little horn in the setting of the divine court in session is that the horn is judged by the court. The fourth beast is slain, and then its body is completely destroyed by the fire emanating from God's throne (7:10–11). As in 7:5 and 7:8, passive verbs ("was killed ... was destroyed ... was given," 7:11) indirectly indicate divine action as a result of the verdict of God in his heavenly court.

This scene is expanded in Revelation, where the beast and the false prophet, who corresponds to the little horn who speaks "great things/words" (Dan 7:8, 11), are thrown into the lake of fire (Rev 19:20). That scene in Revelation is of the final judgment of Satan's agents at the end of the world, after the return of Jesus Christ.[50] The judgment scene here can also be compared to the crushing of the four OT worldly kingdoms (2:44–45) by the arrival of God's kingdom. The crushing of the kingdoms that precedes the first advent of Christ sets the pattern for the final and permanent destruction of Satan and all his minions at the second advent of Jesus Christ.

Daniel now tells us the doom of the three earlier beasts that he saw (7:12). Previously in the vision, he simply told us about the succession of beasts (7:4–7) without telling us what happened to each of them. Some commentators understand 7:12 to be saying that the three other beasts survive the slaying of the fourth beast and its little horn.[51] However, that understanding ignores the force of the verb in its context: הֶעְדִּיו, a Haphel (H) perfect in וּשְׁאָר֙ חֵיוָתָ֔א הֶעְדִּ֖יו שָׁלְטָנְה֑וֹן, literally, "as for the rest of the beasts, they took away their dominion," translated as a passive, "their dominion *had been taken away*," with God as the implied agent of the action. The perfect aspect in Aramaic, as in Hebrew, usually indicates a completed act or state. In this context, it indicates that the dominion of each beast has already been taken away when it is succeeded by the subsequent beast; the first beast has lost its dominion when it is succeeded by the second beast, and so forth. Therefore, in this case, the Aramaic perfect aspect corresponds to the English past perfect (pluperfect) tense.

---

[50] Brighton, *Revelation*, 522, n. 61, explains in this way the relationship between Satan and the (first) beast and the false prophet who are judged in Rev 19:20:

> The relationship among the three members of the unholy trinity is revealed in chapters 12–13. Satan, the dragon, wars against the church (12:13–18). He conjures up two beasts to help him in this warfare (chapter 13). The second beast serves the first beast (13:11–18), who in turn is a henchman for Satan. The second beast mutates into the harlot (chapter 17) and into the false prophet (16:13; 19:20; 20:10)—into whatever form is most expedient for deceptively carrying out the schemes of the lord of the two beasts, Satan himself.

Rev 19:17–21 describes the final judgment of the (first) beast, the false prophet, and the unbelievers who followed them. Then Rev 20:10 describes the final judgment of Satan himself.

[51] Baldwin, *Daniel*, 142; Montgomery, *Daniel*, 302.

However, the verse also states the following about the three earlier beasts: וְאַרְכָה בְחַיִּין יְהִיבַת לְהוֹן, literally, "a length/extension in life was given to them" (7:12). After their dominion is taken away, they are allowed to live on for a while—alive but powerless—until the judgment of the heavenly court is handed down and executed. Thus these kingdoms survive in some form, but without dominion, until the fourth beast and its little horn are slain.

This corresponds to the events in the dream of Nebuchadnezzar in Daniel 2. In that dream, all four metals of the statue are destroyed simultaneously (2:35, 44).

One may also compare NT passages such as Mt 13:24–43, where God does not immediately root out the weeds, but allows them to continue to live until the judgment.

The judgment on the first three beasts is their eventual loss of life at the judgment. The more severe punishment of the fourth beast and its horn corresponds to its actions.[52] None of the first three beasts spoke words for which it had to be judged by the divine court. Further detail about the diabolical words and actions of the fourth beast and its horn will be given in 7:21, 25. Its eternal judgment will be elaborated in 7:26.

The Coming of the Son of Man (7:13–14)

When Daniel's vision shifts back again to the heavenly court, his style again shifts from prose (7:11–12, as in 7:1–8) back to poetic parallelism (7:13–14, as in 7:9–10). The heightened literary style of poetry highlights that his attention is turned from observing events among human kingdoms (7:1–8, 11–12) to divine actions.

The Identity of the Son of Man

Perhaps no phrase in Daniel has elicited more comment by scholars than כְּבַר אֱנָשׁ, "one like a Son of Man" (see the textual note on 7:13).[53] Jesus

---

[52] Collins, *Daniel*, 304; Lucas, *Daniel*, 183; Young, *Daniel*, 153.

[53] The following is but a short list of works on the identity of the Son of Man that include a study of Daniel 7: Bauckham, "The Son of Man: 'A Man in My Position' or 'Someone' "; Beale, "The Problem of the Man from the Sea in IV Ezra 13 and Its Relation to the Messianic Concept in John's Apocalypse"; Beasley-Murray, "The Interpretation of Daniel 7"; Casey, "General, Generic and Indefinite: The Use of the Term 'Son of Man' in Aramaic Sources and in the Teaching of Jesus"; Adela Yarbro Collins, "The Origin of the Designation of Jesus as 'Son of Man' "; "Daniel 7 and Jesus"; "The Apocalyptic Son of Man Sayings"; John J. Collins, "The Son of Man and the Saints of the Most High in the Book of Daniel"; "The Son of Man in First-Century Judaism"; Dunn, " 'Son of God' as 'Son of Man' in the Dead Sea Scrolls? A Response to John Collins on 4Q246"; Emerton, "The Origin of the Son of Man Imagery"; Ferch, *The Son of Man in Daniel 7*; Gelston, "Sidelight on the Son of Man"; Hindley, "The Son of Man: A Recent Analysis"; Horbury, "The Messianic Associations of 'The Son of Man' "; Kee, "Messiah and the People of God"; Lacocque, "The Vision of the Eagle in 4 Esdras, a Rereading of Daniel 7 in the First Century C.E."; Longenecker, " 'Son of Man' as a Self-Designation of Jesus"; Morgenstern, " 'Son of Man' of Daniel 7:13 f.: A New Interpretation"; Muilenburg, "Son of Man in Daniel and the Ethiopic Apocalypse of Enoch"; Stuckenbruck, " 'One Like a Son of Man as the Ancient of Days' in the Old Greek Recension of Daniel 7,13: Scribal Error or Theological Translation?" "The Throne-Theophany of the

(j) Mt 24:30; 25:31; 26:64; Mk 13:26; 14:62; Lk 21:27

(k) Num 23:19; Is 51:12; 56:2; Jer 49:18, 33; 50:40; 51:43; Pss 8:5 (ET 8:4); 80:18 (ET 80:17); Job 16:21; 25:6; 35:8

appropriates this term and the imagery of 7:13 for himself in the Gospels.[j] The equivalent Hebrew phrase, בֶּן־אָדָם, "son of man," is used one hundred seven times in the OT. From its uses, it is clear that it is a way of referring to a person as human. This is shown by the times it occurs in parallel to another word for a human, such as אִישׁ, אֱנוֹשׁ, or גֶּבֶר,[k] as well as its ninety-three uses by God to refer to Ezekiel. Therefore, in his vision, Daniel sees someone whose person and appearance is "like" that of a human; he has a human appearance and nature, yet in this context, he obviously is more than an ordinary human.

Three primary suggestions find support among scholars for the identification of the Son of Man: (1) a collective figure for the people of God; (2) a representative angel from among God's angels (such as Michael); or (3) a messianic figure.[54] The identification of the Son of Man as the Messiah is the most ancient interpretation among both Christians and Jews, and it is the position taken by this commentary. However, it is seldom held among critical scholars today. We will discuss each of the three views in turn.

A Collective Figure

Since the nineteenth century, many critical scholars have regarded the Son of Man as a collective figure for the whole people of God.[55] The main argument for this is that in the vision in 7:14, the Son of Man is given the kingdom, whereas in the explanation of the vision, "the saints of the Most High" are given the kingdom (7:22, 27). However, it is somewhat simplistic to equate the Son of Man with the saints on that basis. The implication of the text could well be that the Messiah himself receives the kingdom for the sake of the saints and then gives it to them. Moreover, the saints are a separate entity from the Son of Man. This can be seen in 7:21–22, where the little horn wages war against the saints and defeats them until the coming of the Ancient of Days, and then the saints receive the kingdom. Daniel 7 pictures no such suffering and defeat for the Son of Man; in this chapter, he is depicted exclusively as a triumphal figure whose enthronement accompanies the defeat of the little horn. The destruction of the little horn is not accomplished by the saints, but by the divine court (7:26; cf. 7:11), of which the Son of Man is an enthroned member. The collective interpretation fails to account for these features in Daniel 7 and therefore is untenable.

An Angel

The angelic interpretation[56] is primarily based on the identification of the "saints/holy ones of the Most High" (7:22, 27) as angels. Angels can be called

---

Book of Giants: Some New Light on the Background of Daniel 7"; Zevit, "Structure and Individual Elements of Daniel 7."

[54] A good summary of the history of these positions is found in Collins, *Daniel*, 304–10. Collins adopts the angelic interpretation.

[55] E.g., Montgomery, *Daniel*, 317–24. The collective interpretation dates to late antiquity. See the discussion in Collins, *Daniel*, 304–10.

[56] A representative of this view is Collins, "The Son of Man and the Saints of the Most High in the Book of Daniel"; *Daniel*, 304–10. See also Dequeker, "The 'Saints of the Most High' in Qumran and Daniel"; Zevit, "Structure and Individual Elements of Daniel 7."

"holy ones," as Daniel does elsewhere (8:13 twice). However, even in Daniel, this identification is not certain, since God's people are also called holy (עַם־קֹדֶשׁ, literally, "a people of holiness," 12:7). As argued in the commentary on 7:18, the saints must be understood as God's people and not as angels.[57] Therefore, the Son of Man is not an angelic figure.

The Messiah

This leaves the messianic interpretation. This is the oldest documented interpretation of the Son of Man. In this interpretation, the Son of Man is the Messiah, who comes to reign as the Davidic King and is enthroned beside the Ancient of Days. The Son of Man figure in the Similitudes of Enoch (usually dated to the first century AD, before AD 70) is based on Daniel 7 and is specifically identified as the Messiah (*1 Enoch* 46:1–5; 48:3–7, 10; 52:4). In *4 Ezra* 13 (late first century or early second century AD), the man who rises from the sea and flies with the clouds is definitely a messianic figure. Among the rabbis, this is the majority view well into the Middle Ages.[58] Even Ibn Ezra, who advocates the collective interpretation of the Son of Man, acknowledges the prevalence of the messianic view among the rabbis.[59]

The messianic interpretation is definitely that of Jesus, since he applies the vision of the Son of Man coming with the clouds to himself.[1] In addition, the Gospels quote other people whose words allude to the "coming" one in Dan 7:13–14 and assume that he is the Messiah (e.g., Mt 3:11; 8:29; 11:3; Jn 1:30; 4:25). Finally, there are several clear allusions in Revelation to Dan 7:13–14, and they all understand this to be a messianic passage fulfilled in Jesus (Rev 1:7, 13; 14:14). The most important of these are Rev 1:13 and 14:14, both of which use the phrase "one like a Son of Man" (ὅμοιον υἱὸν ἀνθρώπου), an exact Greek translation of the Aramaic כְּבַר אֱנָשׁ, "one like a Son of Man" in Dan 7:13. Rev 1:13 uses this Greek phrase to describe the exalted person John sees at the beginning of his vision. This person is Jesus, the one who died but who is now risen and lives forever (Rev 1:18). Moreover, the portrait of his glorified person (Rev 1:13–18) is clearly drawn from Daniel's vision of a person in Dan 10:4–6, 10. Rev 14:14 describes John's vision of "one like a Son of Man" seated on a cloud, using imagery drawn directly from Dan 7:13.

(1) Mt 24:30; 25:31; 26:64; Mk 13:26; 14:62; Lk 21:27

"The Son of Man" is a title that Jesus applies to himself frequently in the Gospels. The way he uses it indicates that he is deliberately fulfilling OT prophecy concerning it, for example, "the Son of Man goes as it is written concerning him" (Mt 26:24; Mk 14:21; cf. Lk 22:22). Of the OT passages that use this title, only a few could be understood as messianic, such as "the son of man" (בֶּן־אָדָם) in Ps 8:5 (ET 8:4; cf. Heb 2:6–8) or Ps 80:18 (ET 80:17). However,

---

[57] See "The Identity of the Holy Ones/Saints of the Most High" in the commentary on 7:18.
[58] Talmud, *Sanhedrin*, 98a; *Midrash Rabbah Numbers* 13:14; *'Aggadat Berešit* 14:3; 23:1 according to Casey, *Son of Man*, 80.
[59] Ferch, *The Son of Man in Daniel 7*, 10–11, 21.

(m) See Mt 24:30; 25:31; 26:64; Mk 13:26; 14:62; Lk 21:27

(n) See Is 19:1; Ezek 1:4; Pss 97:2; 104:3; cf. 2 Sam 22:12 ‖ Ps 18:12 (ET 18:11); Job 22:14

when referring to himself in the Gospels as the "Son of Man," the passage Jesus directly connects with this title for himself is Dan 7:13–14, since Jesus cites his coming on the clouds of heaven with power and attending angels, and his session on his throne beside God.[m] Thus despite the skepticism of many who have sought in vain to find some other source for Jesus' self-designation as Son of Man,[60] it is probably best to understand Jesus' use of this term as deriving primarily, if not exclusively, from Dan 7:13–14.[61]

The biblical teaching that Jesus Christ is both true man and true God, possessing a human nature (without sin) and a divine nature, is implicit in 7:13–14.[62] Granted, as many scholars have pointed out, the title "one like a Son of Man" is a comparison, not a direct identification of this figure as a human.[63] The first three beasts are likened to animals: "*like* a lion ... *resembled* a bear ... *like* a leopard" (כְּאַרְיֵה ... דָּמְיָה לְדֹב ... כִּנְמַר, 7:4–6). They share some qualities with those natural animals, but also are far greater. The Messiah is likened to "a Son of Man," meaning that he is not like a beast, but a human. However, the context also clearly signals that he is much more than a human. In fact, since he possesses an eternal kingdom (7:14), he is God, who alone has a kingdom that does not end (2:44–45; 6:27 [ET 6:26]; 7:27). His divine nature is signaled as soon as he is introduced as one who rides on the clouds (Dan 7:13).[n] He rules as a human and over all humanity since elsewhere in Daniel, phrases like "all peoples, nations, and languages" are used in royal communications from a human king to his human subjects (3:4, 7, 29; 3:31 [ET 4:1]; 6:26 [ET 6:25]; cf. 5:19). Yet the divine vision reveals that "all peoples, nations, and languages *will worship him*" (7:14). The book of Daniel consistently condemns worship of any person or thing other than the one true God.[64]

---

[60] See the discussions in the works listed above on the identity of the Son of Man.

[61] This is also the conclusion of Longenecker, " 'Son of Man' as a Self-Designation of Jesus," 158, quoting Gustaf Dalman, *The Words of Jesus* (trans. D. M. Kay; Edinburgh: T&T Clark, 1902), 259:

> Contrary to much of current thought on the subject, the evidence strongly suggests that Son of Man was a distinct self-designation of Jesus used by Him to indicate His understanding of the nature of His Messiahship. In so doing, He reached back to the enigmatic figure of Daniel 7 and in fulfillment of the prophet's vision sought thereby to explicate His person and redemptive ministry in terms of glorification through suffering. "In using the title," as Dalman has said, "He purposely furnished them with a problem which stimulated reflection about His person, and gave such a tendency to this reflection that the solution of the problem fully revealed the mystery of the personality of Jesus."

[62] For a classic and extensive presentation of this teaching based on the OT and NT, see Chemnitz, *The Two Natures in Christ*. Chemnitz expounds Dan 7:13 (and 3:25) on page 50 and Dan 7:13–14 on pages 316–17.

[63] Baldwin, *Daniel*, 142; Goldingay, *Daniel*, 168; Young, *Daniel*, 154.

[64] This is the theme of Daniel 3 and 6. In chapter 6, the king's edict required the king to be the recipient of prayers (see the fourth textual note and the commentary on 6:8 [ET 6:7]). Daniel 6 implicitly condemns that edict since God overturned the condemnation of Daniel for violating it.

Thus the portrayal of the Son of Man in 7:13–14 is of a Messiah who is both human and divine. This matches the claims about Jesus in the NT both in respect to the use of this passage and in respect to the two natures in the Christ.[65]

The Vision of Daniel 7 as Enactment of Psalms 2 and 110

Daniel's vision climaxes with the installation of the Son of Man as eternal king. The vision is essentially ended with 7:14. Therefore, at this point, it is appropriate to compare the enthronement of the Son of Man in Daniel 7 with other passages in the OT that speak of the enthronement of the Messiah.

Two psalms are particularly relevant, and they follow much the same pattern as Daniel's vision: Psalms 2 and 110. Both of these psalms speak of the decree of God concerning the Messiah's installation as king. While not every element in Daniel is present in these two psalms nor is every element in the psalms present in Daniel, these three passages present complementary pictures of the enthronement of the Messiah. Jesus explicitly connects Psalm 110 and Daniel 7 in Mt 26:64 and Mk 14:62. The heavenly vision of Christ shown to Stephen at his martyrdom (Acts 7:55–56) probably reflects a combination of Psalm 110 and Daniel 7.

Figure 11 shows the pattern of the Messiah's enthronement.

Some items in this messianic enthronement sequence are unique to each particular text. The heavenly court is found only in Daniel 7, though the decrees in Psalms 2 and 110 assume it. The declaration of the Messiah as Priest is found only in Psalm 110. Two elements appear in both Psalm 2 and Daniel 7: in both, the nations prompt the divine decree concerning the Messiah, and both mention the blessed result of the Messiah's gracious reign for God's people. These shared elements make Daniel 7 and Psalm 2 closer to each other than either is to Psalm 110.

One major variation appears in Daniel 7: the Messiah is not pictured as ruling until after the beasts are shorn of their power, whereas in these two psalms, the Messiah's reign begins the process of defeating the nations. However, the difference is one of emphasis. The psalms wish to emphasize that the Messiah's

---

[65] The Lutheran Confessions cite Dan 7:14 to support the communication of attributes, and specifically the *genus maiestaticum*. Through the personal union of the two natures in Christ, his human nature shares the divine attributes he possesses according to his divine nature (FC SD VIII 54–55):

> The statement is, of course, correct and true that Christ's human nature in and by itself possesses all the created gifts which have been given to it. But these do not measure up to the majesty which the Scriptures, and the ancient Fathers on the basis of Scriptures, ascribe to the assumed human nature in Christ. For to give life, to execute all judgment, to have all authority in heaven and on earth, to have all things given into his hands, to have all things under his feet, to cleanse from sin, and so forth are not created gifts but divine and infinite qualities. Yet according to the statement of the Scriptures these properties have been given and communicated to the man Christ (John 5:21, 27; 6:39, 40; Matt. 28:18; Dan. 7:14; John 3:31, 35; 13:3; Matt. 11:27; Eph. 1:22; Heb. 2:8; 1 Cor. 15:27; John 1:3, 10).

reign with God has already begun. Daniel, by contrast, is emphasizing the eschatological dimensions of the kingdom that the saints will inherit.

The same two themes can be found in the NT. They correspond to the "now" but "not yet" tension that characterizes all biblical eschatology. Jesus rules already now,° and his kingdom of grace is now present among his people.ᵖ Yet Jesus has not yet returned in power. At some time in the future, he will come on the clouds of heaven to reign in power and glory.ᵍ His people still on earth look forward to inheriting the kingdom in the future when they finally shall be delivered from all suffering and persecution (Mt 25:34; Rev 21:1–8; cf. 1 Cor 6:9–10; 15:50; Gal 5:19–21; Rev 7:13–17).

(o) Lk 22:69; Acts 2:33; 5:31; 7:55–56; Rom 8:34; 1 Cor 15:25; Eph 1:20–23; Col 2:10; 3:1; Rev 1:5

(p) Mt 12:28; Mk 1:15; 9:1; Lk 9:27; 10:9, 11; 11:20; 17:21; 21:31

(q) Mt 24:30; 26:64; Mk 13:26; 14:62; Lk 21:27; Rev 1:7; cf. Mt 25:31; Rev 11:15

Figure 11

The Messiah's Enthronement in Daniel 7 and Psalms 2 and 110

Daniel 7	*Psalm 2*	*Psalm 110*
A. Four beasts (nations) emerge from the sea to rule oppressively over God's people before the advent of the Messiah (7:1–8, 17, 19–21, 23–25).	A. Nations oppose God and his Messiah (2:1–3).	
B. The Ancient of Days convenes his heavenly court (7:8–10).		
C. Decree of the heavenly court: the Son of Man is installed as eternal king over all nations (7:13–14).	C. God's decree: God mocks the rebels and installs his Messiah as King to rule the nations (2:4–9).	C. God's decree: God installs David's Lord as King at his right hand to rule over his enemies (110:1–3).
		D. God's decree: the Messiah is Priest forever (110:4).
E. Decree of the heavenly court: the beasts are shorn of power and slain (7:11–12, 26).	E. Admonition to the nations: serve the Lord and kiss the Son or you will perish (2:10–12a).	E. The Lord and his Messiah crush kings and fill nations with corpses (110:5–6).
F. The Ancient of Days comes and decrees in favor of his saints; they receive the kingdom for eternity (7:18, 22, 27).	F. Those who take refuge in the Son are blessed (2:12b).	

Daniel 7:15–28
An Angel Explains the Four Beasts and the Establishment of the Kingdom of God

Translation

7 ¹⁵"I, Daniel—my spirit was distressed within [my] body, and the visions of my head disturbed me. ¹⁶I approached one of those standing [there], and I asked him the truth about all this. So he spoke to me and made known to me the meaning of the words.

¹⁷" 'These great beasts that are four are four kings [who] will arise from the earth. ¹⁸But the saints of the Most High will receive the kingdom, and they will possess the kingdom forever—forever and ever.'

¹⁹"Then I desired to be certain about the fourth beast that was different from all of them. It was very frightening. Its teeth were of iron, and its claws were of bronze. It devoured and crushed, and what was left it trampled with its feet. ²⁰[I also desired to be certain] about the ten horns on its head and the other [horn] that came up and three fell before it. Moreover, that horn had eyes and a mouth speaking great things, and its appearance was greater than its companions. ²¹I kept looking, and that horn made war with the saints and prevailed over them ²²until the Ancient of Days came, and judgment was given in favor of the saints of the Most High. Then the time came, and the saints took possession of the kingdom.

²³"This is what he said: 'The fourth beast is the fourth kingdom that will be on the earth. It will be different from all the kingdoms. It will devour the entire earth, trample it, and smash it. ²⁴And as for the ten horns, from it—the kingdom—ten kings will arise, and another will arise after them. It will be different from the previous ones, and it will humble three kings. ²⁵It will speak words against the Most High so that it will wear out the saints of the Most High. Moreover, it will intend to change times and Law. So they will be given into his hand for a time, times, and half a time.

²⁶" 'Then the court will be seated, and his dominion will be taken away in order to destroy and annihilate [it] forever. ²⁷But the kingdom and the dominion and the greatness of the kingdoms under all the heavens will be given to the people, the saints of the Most High. His kingdom is an eternal kingdom, and all dominions will worship and obey him.'

²⁸"This was the end of the matter. I, Daniel—greatly did my thoughts alarm me, my appearance changed, and I kept the matter to myself."

Textual Notes

7:15 אֶתְכְּרִיַּת רוּחִי אֲנָה דָנִיֵּאל בְּגוֹא נִדְנֶה—Literally, "my spirit was distressed—I, Daniel—in the midst of sheath (?)." The broken syntax conveys Daniel's alarm, as also in 7:28. The Ithpeel (HtG) of כָּרָה means "be distressed" (*HALOT*). נִדְנֶה is of uncertain meaning. It may be related to the suffixed Hebrew noun נְדָנָהּ, "its sheath" (for a sword), in 1 Chr 21:27. The Hebrew word occurs nowhere else. Both the Hebrew and Aramaic words are possibly loanwords from Old Persian. Many interpreters repoint נִדְנֶה to נִדְנַהּ with a feminine suffix, yielding "my spirit ... in the midst of its sheath" (see *HALOT*, s.v. נְדַן, A). The "sheath" of Daniel's spirit is his body.

וְחֶזְוֵי רֵאשִׁי יְבַהֲלֻנַּנִי—An identical clause was in 4:2. Compare also the first textual note on 7:2.

7:16 וְיַצִּיבָא אֶבְעֵא־מִנֵּהּ—Literally, "certainty I sought from him." The noun יַצִּיב means "what is certain, what is reliable," as in 2:45 and 6:13 (ET 6:12). It (with the article) is translated as "the truth" here. The Pael (D) infinitive of the cognate verb יְצַב is used in 7:19: צְבִית לְיַצָּבָא, "I desired to make sure, be certain."

וּפְשַׁר מִלַּיָּא יְהוֹדְעִנַּנִי—Literally, "and the meaning of the words he made known to me." For פְּשַׁר, see the third textual note on 2:4. Here the plural of מִלָּה, "word," is used for "the content or object of a vision, the thing that is seen" (*HALOT*, 2 b). Thus the revelatory vision is described as "words" from God.

7:18 קַדִּישֵׁי עֶלְיוֹנִין—Literally, this is "the holy ones of the Most High." The identical phrase will recur in 7:22, 25, 27. The adjective קַדִּישׁ, "holy, sacred," is used as a substantive noun, "saint, holy person," one who is righteous through faith. Compare זָכוּ, "innocence, righteousness," in 6:23 (ET 6:22). See further the commentary. The Aramaic plural עֶלְיוֹנִין refers to God as "Most High" in 7:18, 22, 25, 27. These are the only times עֶלְיוֹן is used in the Aramaic portions of the OT. The use of the plural for the one true God may be patterned after the Hebrew plural אֱלֹהִים, "God" (*HALOT*, s.v. עֶלְיוֹן).

עַד־עָלְמָא וְעַד עָלַם עָלְמַיָּא—Literally, "until eternity and until eternity of eternities," this is rendered, "forever—forever and ever." The Aramaic עָלַם, like its Hebrew cognate עוֹלָם, does not always mean "forever." In some contexts, it means a long time, either in the past or into the future. For the Hebrew עוֹלָם with that sense, see Deut 32:7; 1 Sam 27:8; Is 51:9; 58:12; 61:4; 63:9, 11; Jer 6:16; 18:15; 28:8; Micah 7:14; Mal 3:4; Job 22:15; Prov 22:28; 23:10. For the Aramaic עָלַם, see Ezra 4:15, 19. At times, the word may be repeated to make the point that the reader or hearer should understand the speaker to mean "forever." The threefold repetition here makes that point emphatically.

7:19 The description of the fourth beast repeats vocabulary from 7:7. See the textual note and commentary on 7:7.

7:20 The description of the little horn recalls 7:8, 11. See the textual note and commentary on 7:8.

7:22 וְדִינָא יְהִב לְקַדִּישֵׁי עֶלְיוֹנִין—Literally, "judgment was given to the holy ones/saints of the Most High." The preposition לְ has the nuance of advantage, "in favor of, for the benefit of" the saints. This means that judgment was executed upon their foes (described in 7:21) and the saints received a judgment of justification, vindication. While יְהִב is the Peal passive (Gp) perfect, "was given," the Greek versions, the Syriac, and the Vulgate have an active verb, indicating that they vocalized the verb as יְהַב. Since the translators were working with unpointed texts, this reading is understandable. However, the passive is more likely, since God's acts frequently are portrayed in the passive voice elsewhere in Daniel 7.

7:25 וּלְקַדִּישֵׁי עֶלְיוֹנִין יְבַלֵּא—"The saints of the Most High" are introduced as the direct object with the preposition לְ, as is common in Aramaic. The verb יְבַלֵּא is the Pael (D) of בְּלָא, literally, "wear out," which BDB interprets as "harass continually." The Aramaic verb occurs only here in the OT, but is common in later Aramaic (see Jastrow, s.vv. בלי and בְּלֵי). It is cognate to the Hebrew verb בָּלָה, "be old, worn out" (Qal [G]) or transitively, "wear out" (Piel [D]), and the Hebrew adjective בָּלֶה, "worn out," applied to sacks, wineskins, sandals, and clothes in Josh 9:4–5.

Since the preceding clause says the horn "will speak words against the Most High" (וּמִלִּין לְצַד עִלָּאָה יְמַלִּל), this may be a result clause: "*so that* it will wear out the saints of the Most High." See further the commentary.

וְיִסְבַּר לְהַשְׁנָיָה זִמְנִין וְדָת—"It will intend to change times and Law." The verb סְבַר, "to intend" (*HALOT*), occurs only here in OT Aramaic, though it occurs in later Aramaic with this meaning as well as the related meanings "plan," "expect," and "hope" (see *CAL* and Jastrow, s.v. סְבַר I). Its Hebrew cognate שָׂבַר is used twice in the OT in the Qal (G), meaning "examine," and six times in the Piel (D), meaning "hope, wait."

An infinitive clause is the object of וְיִסְבַּר and states what the little horn intends to do: "to change [לְהַשְׁנָיָה] times [זִמְנִין] and Law [וְדָת]." דָּת was also used in 6:6 (ET 6:5) for the "Law" of Daniel's God, meaning the extant OT books and Daniel's worship practices in accordance with them. Therefore, it is likely that the זִמְנִין, "times," refers to the worship times appointed in the OT, such as the Sabbath, festival days, and morning and evening sacrifices (when the temple stood). Hence the little horn seeks to prevent worship practices ordained by God in his Word.

עַד־עִדָּן וְעִדָּנִין וּפְלַג עִדָּן:—"Until a time, times, and half a time." The MT points וְעִדָּנִין as plural, "times," not dual. However, some commentators argue that it should be pointed as dual, עִדָּנַיִן, "two times," which would make a total of three and a half times.[1] Other commentators follow that interpretation even without the emendation since the plural עִדָּנִין could refer to two times, making a total of three and a half times.[2] The similar Hebrew expression in 12:7, לְמוֹעֵד מוֹעֲדִים וָחֵצִי, literally, "for a time, times, and a half," has a plural (rather than a dual) and probably means "three and a half times," the same as the Aramaic expression used here.

7:26 עַד־סוֹפָא—Literally "until the end," this idiom means that the fourth beast will be destroyed "forever." עַד־סוֹפָא was also used in 6:27 (ET 6:26) to say that God's dominion is "eternal." In 7:28, סוֹף will have its usual meaning, "end": עַד־כָּה סוֹפָא דִי־מִלְּתָא, literally, "as far as here—the end of the word/matter."

---

[1] Lucas, *Daniel*, 163, 194; Miller, *Daniel*, 214; Montgomery, *Daniel*, 312–15; Walvoord, *Daniel*, 176. Baldwin, *Daniel*, 146, also seems to advocate this. For a contrary opinion, see Leupold, *Daniel*, 326.

[2] *HALOT*, s.v. עִדָּן, 2, although *HALOT* wrongly defines the length as "years" (see the commentary on 7:25); Archer, "Daniel," 94; Collins, *Daniel*, 322; Young, *Daniel*, 162.

7:27 יְהִיבַת לְעַם קַדִּישֵׁי עֶלְיוֹנִין—All earthly dominion "will be given to the people, the saints of the Most High." The Peal passive (Gp) perfect יְהִיבַת is a prophetic perfect that envisions the action as already completed because God's Word surely will come to pass. Hence it is translated as a future tense. The indirect object is לְעַם, given "to the people." The *ṭiphḥah* accent on לְעַם is disjunctive, reflected in the translation by the comma after "people." The following construct phrase קַדִּישֵׁי עֶלְיוֹנִין, "the saints of the Most High," is in apposition to לְעַם and is epexegetical in that it explains who the "people" are. "The people" consist of "the saints of the Most High." See further "The Identity of the Holy Ones/Saints of the Most High" in the commentary on 7:18.

7:28 אֲנָה דָנִיֵּאל שַׂגִּיא ׀ רַעְיוֹנַי יְבַהֲלֻנַּנִי—As in 7:15, the disjointed syntax conveys Daniel's distress. The *casus pendens* אֲנָה דָנִיֵּאל is followed by the adverb שַׂגִּיא preceding (instead of following) the verbal clause: literally, "I, Daniel—greatly my thoughts alarmed me." The same expression with the plural of רַעְיוֹן, "thought," as subject of the Pael (D) of the verb בְּהַל, "to alarm, terrify," was in 4:16 (ET 4:19); 5:6, 10.

וְזִיוַי יִשְׁתַּנּוֹן עֲלָי—Literally, "my expressions changed upon me." Similar clauses with the plural of זִיו, "appearance, facial expression," occur with the verb שְׁנָה, "to change," in the Peal (G) in 5:6, 9 and in the Hithpaal (HtD) in 5:10, as here. The expression has the preposition עַל in 5:9, as here. See the first textual note on 5:6.

Commentary

The vision itself was completed with 7:14. The final part of the chapter consists of explanations of what Daniel has seen in the vision. Distressed, Daniel asks an angel (7:15–16), who explains the vision as a whole (7:17–18). Then Daniel asks for clarification about the fourth beast with the little horn and its judgment by the heavenly court (7:19–22). He restates what he has seen (7:19–20), but adds the new information that the "horn made war with the saints and prevailed over them until the Ancient of Days came" (7:21–22). Then Daniel repeats that God has judged the beast, but adds the further detail that God has given the kingdom to his "saints" (7:22). Finally, the angel gives Daniel a further explanation of the beast and its judgment and the establishment of God's kingdom (7:23–27).

Daniel Asks for an Explanation of the Vision (7:15–16)

Daniel's distress at the vision demonstrates the psychological and physical stress that come with receiving a vision from God. Ezekiel has similar reactions (Ezek 1:28; 3:14–15, 25–26). Daniel also experiences similar things when he receives later visions (Dan 8:27; 10:10–11, 15–18).

Daniel seeks out "one of those standing" in God's court (7:16), who probably was one of the angelic attendants of the Ancient of Days, since the angels "stood" before God (7:10).[3] Daniel's request for an interpretation of the vision takes place within the vision itself. In visions received by earlier OT prophets,

---

[3] In contrast, the "thrones" are for God the Father, God the Son, and the saints. See "Who Is to Be Seated on the Thrones?" in the commentary on 7:9.

God himself acts as the interpreter (i.e., the visions in Isaiah 6; Jeremiah 1; or Amos 7–8). Beginning with the exile, God uses angels to serve as guides and interpreters in visions (e.g., Ezekiel 40–48;[4] Zechariah 1–6). Daniel has angelic guides or interpreters in all of his visions (chapters 7–12), beginning with this one. In Revelation, angels interpret various features of the vision shown to the apostle John (e.g., Rev 1:1; 10:5–11; 17:1–18; 21:9–22:6).

In extrabiblical literature, the angelic interpreter will become a standard figure in Jewish and Christian visionary and apocalyptic texts written during the intertestamental period and beyond.

This particular angel is not identified, but in later visions "Gabriel" speaks with Daniel (8:16; 9:21). Dan 9:21 may imply that Gabriel spoke with Daniel in this vision as well.

An Angel Explains the Vision (7:17–18)

The angel's explanation is short and provides only a summary of the meaning of the vision without any details of interpretation. Dan 7:2–8 is summarized by 7:17. Dan 7:9–14 is summarized by 7:18.

The four beasts are said to be "four kings [who] will arise from the earth" (7:17). The concepts of king and kingdom are nearly interchangeable in the dreams and visions in Daniel. Thus in Nebuchadnezzar's dream, he, the king, is the head of gold (2:38). However, the head is also his kingdom, and indeed the Babylonian Empire ruled by a succession of kings, since it is succeeded by three consecutive kingdoms (2:39–40). In the visions following Daniel 7, the ram has two horns representing "the kings of Media and Persia" (8:20). From the context, these "kings" obviously represent the Medo-Persian kingdom. The goat seen in the vision in Daniel 8 is "the king of Greece" (8:21a), yet the single horn on its forehead is "the first king" (8:21b), so the goat is not a single king, but a kingdom.

For this reason, when a beast or a horn is identified as a king, it is best to remember that the king and his kingdom are melded into one. This is also true in Daniel's final vision (chapters 10–12) since in 11:5–35, "the king of the north" and "the king of the south" each represent an entire succession of kings. The same is true in this chapter. While in 7:17 the four beasts are said to represent four kings, in 7:23 the fourth beast is said to be a kingdom.

This interchangeability of kings and kingdoms was recognized in ancient times as shown by the way both the Old Greek and Theodotion translate 7:17. Both identify the four beasts as "four kingdoms" (τέσσαρες βασιλεῖαι) instead of "four kings" (אַרְבְּעָה מַלְכִין).

These kingdoms will arise "from the earth" (7:17), though in the vision, the beasts came from the sea (7:3). This demonstrates that the interpretation of

---

[4] Hummel, *Ezekiel 21–48*, 1195–96, entertains the possibility that the gleaming man in Ezek 40:3, who subsequently serves as Ezekiel's guide and interpreter, is the preincarnate Christ.

the "meaning"[5] goes beyond stating what the vision represents to its practical consequences for Daniel and his readers. The sea in the vision is not simply the earth, but most likely represents the peoples of the earth (see the commentary on 7:3). The practical consequence of this is that the kingdoms arise on earth. The beasts are not symbolic of spiritual entities that remain in heaven. Rather, they are earthly manifestations in the form of human kings and kingdoms.

The same is true about the kingdom of God, which Matthew calls "the kingdom of heaven" (e.g., Mt 3:2; 4:17): it comes to earth in the Messiah, God incarnate in human flesh, who is the King over his kingdom of grace, consisting of all flesh-and-blood believers (see, e.g., Mt 4:17; 5:3, 10; cf. Mt 6:10).

The beasts described as "coming up from the sea" (סָלְקָן מִן־יַמָּא, 7:3) but that represent kingdoms that will "arise from the earth" (יְקוּמוּן מִן־אַרְעָא, 7:17) form the OT background for the two beasts in Revelation 13. The first one is seen "arising from the sea" (ἐκ τῆς θαλάσσης … ἀναβαῖνον, Rev 13:1) and the second one "is arising from the earth" (ἀναβαῖνον ἐκ τῆς γῆς, 13:11). Those two beasts represent spiritual forces of evil that are manifest in concrete ways through people and human institutions.[6]

The interpretation of the second part of the vision (Dan 7:9–14) is that "the saints of the Most High will receive the kingdom" and "possess" it "forever and ever" (7:18). This statement has led some interpreters to equate the "one like a Son of Man" who receives the kingdom in 7:13–14 with "the saints" in 7:18. These interpreters consider the Son of Man merely to be a collective figure for the saints. However, this is a simplistic reading of the angel's interpretation, and it contradicts details in the chapter (see "The Identity of the Son of Man" in the commentary on 7:13–14). Instead, this is another instance where the angel skips over some steps in the interpretation and states the practical consequences for the readers: the result of the Son of Man receiving the kingdom (7:13–14) is that "the saints" receive and possess the kingdom forever (7:18). This implies that the Son of Man alone is worthy to receive the kingdom (see Rev 5:9), but he in turn graciously grants membership in the kingdom to all who believe in him ("you have made them a kingdom," Rev 5:10).

The Identity of the Holy Ones/Saints of the Most High (7:18; Also 7:22, 25, 27)

The longstanding traditional identification of "the holy ones/saints of the Most High" (see the first textual note on 7:18) is that they are God's holy people, the saints. This identification is supported by a variety of OT and NT passages. God is the one who already in the OT era redeemed and sanctified his people, rendering them holy through his means of grace.[7] Likewise the NT calls bap-

---

[5] For פְּשַׁר in 7:16, see the third textual note on 2:4.

[6] For the interpretation of these two beasts, see Brighton, *Revelation*, 348–63.

[7] Lev 11:45; 20:8; 21:8, 23; 22:9, 16, 32. For the theology of God's holiness imparted to his people, see Kleinig, *Leviticus*, 3–13.

tized believers in Christ, who are members of God's kingdom, the "saints" (ἅγιοι, e.g., Rom 1:7; 8:27; 12:13).

However, this traditional view is held by only a minority of modern critical scholars. Instead, most of them favor identifying the holy ones as angels. This thesis was first advanced by Procksch in 1927, but did not receive wider support until it was taken up by Noth in 1955.[8] These are the main arguments for this interpretation:

1. Elsewhere in Daniel (outside chapter 7), the Aramaic term קַדִּישׁ, "holy (one)," and its Hebrew cognate קָדוֹשׁ, "holy (one)," are used only for gods or celestial beings. The Aramaic adjective קַדִּישׁ modifies אֱלָהִין and refers to "holy gods" in 4:5–6, 15 (ET 4:8–9, 18); 5:11. The term by itself used as a substantive refers to "holy" angels in 4:10, 14, 20 (ET 4:13, 17, 23), who are also called "watcher(s)." The Hebrew קָדוֹשׁ used as a substantive refers to a "holy" angel in 8:13. (But Hebrew קָדוֹשׁ is used as a substantive for the saints in 8:24; see number 1 in the refutation below.)

2. The Hebrew adjective קָדוֹשׁ, "holy (one)," when used as substantive in the OT usually refers to angels (Ps 89:6, 8 [ET 89:5, 7]; Job 5:1; 15:15; Zech 14:5; Dan 8:13).

3. The literature from Qumran and other intertestamental literature support this meaning.

4. Dan 7:21–22, which clearly refer to God's people as "saints," was not originally part of the book, but was added by a later editor who reinterprets the vision by applying it to God's people.

5. The Son of Man (7:13–14) is a heavenly figure. Since there is a close connection between the Son of Man and "the holy ones," they too must be heavenly beings.

6. The noun עַם, "people," in the phrase לְעַם קַדִּישֵׁי עֶלְיוֹנִין, "to the people, the saints of the Most High" in 7:27 should be translated "host" rather than "people," as supported by documents from Qumran that use עַם in reference to angels.

7. The phrase לְעַם קַדִּישֵׁי עֶלְיוֹנִין, "to (the) people, the saints of the Most High" (7:27) can be interpreted as a possessive, "to a people associated with the holy ones [angels] of the Most High," rather than appositional and epexegetical, "to people *who are* the holy ones of the Most High."

---

[8] The history of this thesis is presented in Hasel, "The Identity of 'The Saints of the Most High' in Daniel 7," 173–76, citing, for example, O. Procksch, "Der Menschensohn als Gottessohn," *Christentum und Wissenschaft* 3 (1927): 429, and Noth, "Die Heiligen des Höchsten." However, Hasel disagrees with that thesis and affirms the traditional view.

These seven arguments seem to present a strong case, especially when considered together. However, each one of them is problematic or wrong.

1. The Hebrew term קָדוֹשׁ, "holy," is used in וְעַם־קְדֹשִׁים in 8:24, referring to "the people of the saints," that is, the people of God, who are saints.[9]

2. The Hebrew adjective קָדוֹשׁ, "holy (one)," is used in some passages as a substantive for God's holy people, his saints. Ps 34:10 (ET 34:9) uses the substantive קְדֹשָׁיו, "his saints," to refer to God's people. Ps 16:3 probably uses the substantive adjective לִקְדוֹשִׁים, "to saints," to refer to God's people, not to angels. In Deut 33:3 כָּל־קְדֹשָׁיו, "all his holy ones," may be understood as a reference to angels, but probably it refers to God's people. The plural adjective קְדֹשִׁים in Prov 9:10; 30:3; Hos 12:1 (ET 11:12) probably refers to God, but perhaps it might refer to God's people.

Thus of the eleven uses of the adjective as a substantive outside of Daniel, at least one, but probably three, and perhaps as many as six refer to God's people. Given the small number of examples, one cannot make any conclusions about the meaning of this term in Dan 7:18 based on statistics. Indeed, even if there were many more examples and the overwhelming majority of them demonstrated that the referent normally was angels, we would still have to ask, based on context, whether a less common meaning was intended by the author in 7:18, 22, 25, 27. The evidence must be weighed, not counted.

3. Early investigations of literature from Qumran revealed a number of instances where קָדוֹשׁ, "holy (one)," was used of angels. However, subsequent research has yielded an equal or greater number of places where it refers to human "saints." These two uses can be found in intertestamental literature as well.[10] Thus there is support for both meanings in the extrabiblical literature subsequent to Daniel.

4. Attributing 7:21–22 to a later editor is a convenient way to discount its witness to the traditional interpretation. However, there is no extant manuscript evidence that supports this conjecture, and even among critics it is controversial.

---

[9] Noth sought to eliminate this phrase in 8:24 on textual grounds ("Die Heiligen des Höchsten," 146, n. 7). However, no manuscript tradition gives convincing evidence for omitting the phrase. The Old Greek reads, δῆμον ἁγίων, "an assembly of holy ones," while Theodotion reads, λαὸν ἅγιον, "a holy people." Both reflect the presence of וְעַם־קְדֹשִׁים, "a people [consisting] of holy ones/saints."

[10] Goldingay, *Daniel*, 176, lists the following passages as favoring the meaning "angel": Ben Sira 42:17; Wisdom 10:10; *Jubilees* 17:11; *Testament of Levi* 3:3; *1 Enoch* 12:2; 14:23; 1QapGen 2:1; 1QM 15:14. He also lists the following passages as favoring the meaning "human": Tobit 12:15; 1 Macc 1:46; *Testament of Levi* 18:11, 14; *Testament of Issachar* 5:4; *1 Enoch* 93:6; 1QM 3:4–5; 10:10. Hasel, "The Identity of 'The Saints of the Most High' in Daniel 7," 183–85, reports tallies of the uses in Qumran and intertestamental literature. From Qumran he reports thirteen occurrences that refer to angels, eleven to humans, and two that could be taken either way. Among intertestamental literature, he reports seventeen occurrences that refer to angels, twenty-five to humans, and five that could be taken either way.

5. As argued above, the Son of Man is not simply a heavenly figure.[11] In fact, the phrase "son of man" is normally used in the OT to emphasize someone's humanity.

6. There are no uses of עַם, "people," as referring to angels in the OT. Neither are there any clear and unambiguous examples from Qumran. The two most plausible instances (1QH 3:21–22; 1QM 12:8) more likely should be read as עִם, "with," instead of עַם, "people."[12]

7. The phrase לְעַם קַדִּישֵׁי עֶלְיוֹנִין (7:27) has a construct chain (קַדִּישֵׁי עֶלְיוֹנִין) in apposition to the first word (לְעַם), so it must mean "to (the) people, the saints of the Most High" (see the textual note on 7:27). The critical construal that it means "to a people associated with the holy ones [angels] of the Most High" would only be possible if one were to change the Hebrew Masoretic Text by changing the disjunctive *ṭiphḥah* accent on לְעַם into a conjunctive accent to form a three-word construct chain. This change is obviously a rather transparent attempt to rescue the angelic thesis; based on the Hebrew text as it stands, the angelic thesis fails.

Nowhere else in all of the Scriptures are the people who receive God's kingdom called a people associated with or of angels. The heirs of God's kingdom are always God's people. The critical construal would make 7:27 a unique and strange case. The passages that come closest to associating God's people with an angel are 10:21 and 12:1, where Michael is called "your [Daniel's] prince" (10:21) and "the great prince who stands over your people" (12:1). However, these passages refer to only one angel, and the plural term "holy ones" in 7:18, 22, 25, 27 requires more than one. In addition, the relationship between the people and the angel in 10:21 and 12:1 is the opposite of the relationship critics propose for 7:18. That is, in 10:21 and 12:1, the people of God are not associated with Michael. Rather, Michael is associated with the people. God has assigned him to protect and fight for the people.

Thus some of the support offered for the angelic interpretation is false (numbers 1, 4, 6), some is inconclusive at best (numbers 2, 3, 5), and some requires changing the Hebrew text and the relationships it depicts (number 7). For these reasons, there remain scholars of all stripes who support the traditional understanding of "the holy ones" in 7:18, 22, 25, 27 as referring to God's people as "saints."[13] In addition, several more arguments support this understanding.

1. When God established the nation of Israel as his people by redeeming them from bondage and revealing himself to them at Sinai, he promised that they would be "a *kingdom* of priests and a *holy* [קָדוֹשׁ] nation" (Ex 19:6).

---

[11] See "The Identity of the Son of Man" in the commentary on 7:13–14.

[12] Poythress, "The Holy Ones of the Most High in Daniel VII," 210–11.

[13] See, for example, Hasel, "The Identity of 'The Saints of the Most High' in Daniel 7"; Poythress, "The Holy Ones of the Most High in Daniel VII"; Baldwin, *Daniel*, 151–52; Casey, *Son of Man*, 40–48; Hartman and Di Lella, *Daniel*, 89–102.

Throughout the OT, he continued to preserve Israel as his kingdom and promise a greater, future kingdom.

2. Israel is often described as "holy" (קָדוֹשׁ) in the OT. See especially Deut 7:6; 14:2, 21; 26:19; 28:9. Even if the substantive use of this word as "holy ones" is rare when referring to Israel, the frequent adjectival use of the term lends strong secondary support to understanding "the holy ones" in Daniel 7 as God's people.

3. The depictions of the oppression and defeat of "the holy ones" in Daniel 7 would be inexplicable if they were angels. In 7:21–22 they are oppressed and defeated until the advent of the Ancient of Days. In 7:25 they are persecuted by the little horn, especially by his attempts to change God's Law and times, neither of which apply to angels! Also in 7:25 they are given into the little horn's power for a period of time.[14] Yet no passages in Scripture depict God allowing his holy angels to be defeated or given into the power of evil temporarily.[15]

4. There is a direct connection between "the holy ones/saints" in Daniel 7 and עַם־קֹדֶשׁ, "the people of holiness/a holy people" in 12:7.[16] In 7:25 Daniel is told that "the holy ones" are given into the power of the little horn for "a time, times, and half a time," an Aramaic expression corresponding to the Hebrew expression for the same span of time that the holy people are persecuted in 12:7.[17]

For these reasons, the traditional view that the holy ones in Daniel 7 are God's people, his saints, is the correct understanding of the term "the holy ones of the Most High" (7:18, 22, 25, 27).

Daniel Asks for Further Explanation of the Fourth Beast and the Little Horn (7:19–22)

Daniel's desire for more detailed interpretation centers on the fourth beast and the horns on its head because these parts of the vision directly affect the saints. These verses summarize and comment upon 7:7–14. At first Daniel simply repeats elements of his description of his earlier vision with some abbreviations. He states that the beast is "very frightening" (7:19) without mentioning that it is "terrible" or "exceedingly strong" (7:7). He calls the eleventh horn simply "the other [horn]" (7:20) without mentioning that it is "little" (7:8). It

---

[14] Sensing this problem with his angelic thesis, Noth proposed that the verb יְבַלֵּא in 7:25 did not mean "he/it will wear out." Noth based his proposal on a supposed Arabic cognate ("Die Heiligen des Höchsten," 153–54). However, well-attested Hebrew and Akkadian cognates of this verb both mean "wear out," and the ancient translations of 7:25 also support the meaning "wear out." See the first textual note on 7:25 and the discussion in Hasel, "The Identity of 'The Saints of the Most High' in Daniel 7," 185–86.

[15] The angels who followed Satan in his rebellion against God (cf. Lk 10:18; 1 Pet 3:19–20; Rev 12:4) became agents of evil permanently. As soon as they fell, they ceased being "holy" and became "unclean" (Mt 10:1) and "evil" (Mt 12:45; Lk 7:21).

[16] Hasel, "The Identity of 'The Saints of the Most High' in Daniel 7," 190–91.

[17] See the textual notes on those expressions in 7:25 and 12:7.

has eyes (7:20), but they are not characterized as "like human eyes" (7:8). The three horns simply fall (7:20) before the eleventh (little) horn instead of being "uprooted" (7:8)

Daniel gives one major addition in his description of the fourth beast: the detail that it has "claws ... of bronze" (7:19). This added detail makes the beast even more fierce. We cannot be certain why Daniel did not relay this detail when he first described the vision for his readers. However, he may have left it out of the initial description in 7:7 so that the reader would focus instead on the fourth beast's "iron teeth" (7:7, repeated in 7:19), which indicates that the fourth beast represents the same kingdom (Rome) as the "iron" section of the statue in Nebuchadnezzar's dream in Daniel 2.[18]

The Spiritual Warfare of the Little Horn, the Antichrist, Part 1 (7:20–21)

About halfway through his recapitulation of 7:7–14, Daniel begins to add new information about what he has seen. He also substitutes for words that simply described his vision other words that describe the practical outcome of what he has seen. This begins in 7:20, where the last clause adds that the little horn's "appearance was greater than its companions" (וְחֶזְוַהּ רַב מִן־חַבְרָתַהּ), that is, more important or larger than the other horns, even though it was "little" (7:8) in comparison to them. This horn's prominence was due to its eyes and mouth and its effect on the saints.

The effect of the horn speaking "great things" (see the textual note on 7:8) was that it "made war with the saints and prevailed over them" (7:21). This horn's primary weapon against the saints is its words. It fights against the saints, whose primary weapon is "the sword of the Spirit, which is the Word of God" (Eph 6:17; cf. Heb 4:12). This statement about the verbal warfare waged by the little horn in Daniel 7 is a key indication that it does not represent Antiochus IV Epiphanes.[19] The historical sources about Antiochus' actions against the Jews, primarily 1 and 2 Maccabees, make abundantly clear that his war against them was conducted with physical force. There is only one passing reference to any speech by Antiochus, and it scarcely figures into his acts against the Jews.[20]

This horn in Daniel 7 is the Antichrist, who perverts the Gospel by speaking things that contravene the Word of God. He was already present in the apostolic age, as St. Paul reports about "the man of lawlessness," and he will continue his warfare throughout the church age until the second coming of Christ, who shall slay him "with the breath of his mouth" (2 Thess 2:1–10), that is, with

---

[18] See the commentary on 7:7.

[19] Instead, Antiochus is represented by the little horn in Daniel 8. See problem 5 and figure 10 in "Problems in Daniel for the Greek View" in the excursus "The Four-Kingdom Schema in Daniel."

[20] 1 Macc 1:24 states this about Antiochus: "He departed to his own land. He committed deeds of murder, and spoke with great arrogance [ἐλάλησεν ὑπερηφανίαν μεγάλην]" (RSV). In context, this refers to Antiochus's speech back in Syria, "his own land."

the Word of God (Rev 19:15).²¹ This identification of the horned fourth beast, and in particular its little horn, is confirmed by the parallel description of the second beast in Revelation 13. The second beast, which Satan conjures from the earth, had horns like a lamb (a false imitation of the Lamb of God!) but "was speaking like a serpent/dragon" (ἐλάλει ὡς δράκων, Rev 13:11), meaning that he is Satan's mouthpiece or spokesman.²² This second beast is the one that later in Revelation mutates into the harlot (Rev 17:1, 15–16; 19:2) and into the false prophet (Rev 16:13), which again confirms that he wages war against the church by means of speaking words—false doctrine that leads people away from Christ. This second beast in his disguise as "the false prophet" will finally be cast (together with the first "beast," from Rev 13:1–10) into the lake of fire after the second coming of Christ (Rev 19:20).²³ Then Satan himself will be cast into the lake containing them (Rev 20:10).

The Advent of the Ancient of Days and the Judgment of the Little Horn (7:22)

The scene of the Ancient of Days in the vision (7:9–10) is reduced to a clause: "until the Ancient of Days came" (7:22). In the earlier vision, the sequence was the appearance of the Ancient of Days (God the Father) for the purpose of judging the beasts (particularly the fourth beast and its little horn [7:11–12]) and to give the eternal kingdom to the Son of Man, God the Son, who comes on the clouds of heaven (7:13–14). The same basic sequence is present here in 7:22. The advent of "the Ancient of Days" here represents, in NT terms, the appearance of God the Father as Judge immediately after the second advent of Jesus Christ. Rev 19:11–21 and Rev 20:7–10 are parallel accounts of the final battle and defeat of all the forces of evil by Christ at his second advent, and then Rev 20:11–15 pictures the final judgment before the throne of God the Father.

The slaying of the fourth beast and especially of its little horn according to the divine judgment (Dan 7:11–12) is described here in terms of the authorization for this slaying. "Judgment was given in favor of the saints of the Most High" (7:22) means that the little horn that waged war against the saints is vanquished, together with all forces of evil and all who are outside the kingdom of God.

Finally, in place of repeating the enthronement of the Son of Man (7:13–14), here Daniel describes the effect on the saints of his enthronement at his second coming: "then the time came, and the saints took possession of the kingdom" (7:22).

---

²¹ See also the commentary on 7:8 and the excursus "The Lutheran Confessions on the Antichrist in Daniel."

²² For the beast in Rev 13:11–18, see Brighton, *Revelation*, 357–63. Brighton calls him the "religious beast" since he operates within the church to corrupt the Gospel and persecute faithful believers.

²³ See Brighton, *Revelation*, 522. In contrast, the first beast conjured out of the sea by Satan (Rev 12:18–13:10 [ET 12:17b–13:10]) remains the "beast" throughout the rest of Revelation.

An Angel Explains the Fourth Beast (7:23–25)

In explaining the fourth beast, the angel once again affirms that it represents a kingdom (cf. "kings" in 7:17) and that it is different from the others. This difference was originally implied by the beast's horns, which no other animal possesses ("different … in that it had ten horns"; see the commentary on 7:7). The angel also confirms the viciousness of this beast as it devours and tramples the earth (7:7, 19). The angel then focuses on the horns. For the first time, he defines the ten horns as ten kings that come from this beast. This reinforces the unique character of this beast. Whereas the previous three beasts/kingdoms are replaced by other kingdoms, this beast is succeeded by kingdoms that grow out of it.

This fits well the Roman Empire. Unlike the Babylonian, Medo-Persian, or Greek Empires that dominated the world, the Roman Empire was not replaced by another empire, but it fell and its power was divided among various rulers. The number of horns—ten—points to the surpassing power of the beast, since ten is used metaphorically with this significance elsewhere in Daniel (1:20; see the commentary on 7:7). This surpassing power will be fragmented and passed on to others.

In keeping with the general symbolic nature of the features of the beasts in this chapter, and the symbolic meaning of "ten," we ought not look for a literal ten kingdoms to succeed the Roman Empire.[24] In modern times, some dispensational premillennialists have speculated that a ten-member confederacy of nations will arise that will reincarnate the Roman Empire and fulfill Daniel 7 (and other prophecies) in some literal way, but the changing number of nations belonging to the European Common Market and its failure to provide the Antichrist have shown that such interpretations are misguided.[25]

The eleventh horn, the little horn of 7:8, is said to "humble" three kings (7:24). The variation in the verbs used to describe what happens to the three horns, which are "uprooted" (7:8), "fell" (7:20), and now are humbled (7:24), cautions against pressing the meaning of any one of them. Instead the thrust seems to be that some significant portion of the power and influence of the beast will eventually pass to the little horn.

The Spiritual Warfare of the Little Horn, the Antichrist, Part 2 (7:25)

Twice previously the little horn was depicted as "speaking great things" (7:8, 20). The angel now explains the content of the horn's words. The most general characterization is that they are polemical "words against the Most High"

---

[24] Curiously, Luther lists ten areas into which the Roman Empire was broken, but also adds "etc.," indicating that he did not view the ten as a literal number (Luther, "Preface to Daniel," AE 35:300).

[25] See the critique of dispensational premillennialism in "Eschatology and Dispensational Premillennial Interpretations of Daniel" in the introduction. For "ten" as a symbolic number, see "The 'Literal' Fulfillment of Prophecy" in that section in the introduction.

(7:25). Moreover, the effect of the words is that they "wear out the saints" like one wears out a garment (see the first textual note on 7:25). The picture here is not of a short, violent attack on the saints, but of a prolonged campaign of verbal warfare that wears them down like the fabric of a garment breaks down and eventually frays or tears because of constant abuse. The horn's false teachings, heresies, and blasphemies against God have the effect of wearing down the saints until they become exhausted in their attempt to resist and remain steadfast to God's Word.

The angel then adds a more specific evil purpose: through his words, the little horn "will intend to change times and Law" (7:25). The expression "times" probably refers to the appointed religious festivals of Israel, and "Law" is a reference to God's Law, the OT (see the second textual note on 7:25). This way in which the little horn will attack God and his saints is expressed in terms that Daniel and his readers could readily understand, since the appointed worship occasions and liturgical rituals specified in the Torah and the OT itself were foundational for Israel's faith and life.

The little horn will seek the prerogatives of God. The horn's words and teaching will usurp God's authority by seeking to change the worship and piety of God's people. The little horn will attempt to replace God's Word with his own "great words" (7:11). This matches what Paul says about "the man of lawlessness ... who opposes and exalts himself above all that is called God or [above] what is worshiped so that he seats himself in the temple of God, displaying himself as God" (2 Thess 2:3–4). Paul's triple reference to divine worship and God's gracious presence in the divine service (what is "called God ... what is worshiped ... in the temple of God") expands upon "intend to change times and Law" in Dan 7:25.

The little horn seeks to change the worship life of the saints by corrupting their understanding of God's Word. His sinister method is to substitute human words for God's Word to get the saints to change their faith, worship, and life to match those deceptive words presented as words from God. In the Christian church, the central feature of divine worship is that God works through his proclaimed Word of Law and Gospel and the proper administration of his Sacraments to produce repentance, to forgive sins for Christ's sake, to strengthen faith in Christ as the only and all-sufficient Savior, and to preserve the saints steadfast in this true faith unto life everlasting. The little horn (in NT terms, the man of lawlessness, the Antichrist) seeks to pervert the central message of the Scriptures: the Gospel of justification by grace alone, through faith in Christ alone. He intends to substitute "another gospel" (Gal 1:6) and make his false message the focus of the worship and life of the saints. There can be a great variety of false gospels, but the main feature they all share is that they are forms of works-righteousness that present salvation as something that can be achieved through human effort or ingenuity (human "power" or "wisdom"; see 1 Cor 1:18–31), rather than as the free and gracious gift of God in Christ.[26]

---

[26] See further the excursus "The Lutheran Confessions on the Antichrist in Daniel."

The Duration of the Little Horn's Warfare: Three and a Half Times (7:25)

Finally, the angel adds a chronological notice about the warfare of the little horn. It will last for three and a half "times" (עִדָּנִין; see the third textual note on 7:25). Both critical scholars and evangelical scholars who adopt millennialist interpretations of Daniel usually assume that this equals three and a half *years*. They often appeal to 4:13, 20, 22, 29 (ET 4:16, 23, 25, 32), which refer to the "seven times [עִדָּנִין]" that will pass over Nebuchadnezzar until his sanity is restored, and they assume that the time period in those passages is equal to seven years.[27] However, this is a circular argument, since it assumes that the "times" in Daniel 4 are years and then uses that assumption as support for the same assumption about the "times" in Daniel 7.[28]

There is no good reason to assume that the "times" in Daniel 4 are years.[29] Neither is there any good reason to make that assumption here.[30] Elsewhere in the Aramaic portion of the book, Daniel the author uses the Aramaic term שְׁנָה, "year" (and not עִדָּן, "time") when he wants to refer to a year or years (Dan 6:1 [ET 5:31]; 7:1). Neither the Old Greek nor Theodotion gives any indication that it understood the "times" to be years; both translate 7:25 using καιρός, "time," not ἔτος, "year."[31] As with the "seven times" in Nebuchadnezzar's dream (4:13, 20, 22, 29 [ET 4:16, 23, 25, 32]), the emphasis is not on the word "time" but on the symbolic number.

In this case, that symbolic number is three and a half. What do these three and a half "times" represent? Already in Daniel the number seven has been used to denote completeness or thoroughness (see the commentary on 3:19 and 4:13 [ET 4:16]). This probably derives from the creation account in Genesis 1–2, where God created the entire world then rested on the seventh day. This is reemphasized when God commands the weekly and yearly sabbatical observances (Ex 20:8–11; 23:11–12; Lev 25:3–4). Since three and a half is half of seven, *the period of oppression is depicted as one-half of a divinely determined complete period for the world.*

The Scriptures depict this divine dividing of human history into two great periods by the use of phrases such as "the latter/last days," which implies an

---

[27] E.g., Walvoord, *Daniel*, 176, who is a chief proponent of dispensational premillennialism.

[28] If proponents of such an approach were consistent, they would also have to insist that after the authority of the first three beasts was stripped from them, they were allowed to live for two years (זְמַן וְעִדָּן, literally, "a time and a time," 7:12). However, proponents do not make that assumption for 7:12. They usually explain that the three earlier beasts are given an extension of life that apparently lasts for centuries.

[29] See the commentary on 4:13 (ET 4:16). The commentary there presents seven reasons why the "times" should not be assumed to represent years.

[30] Goldingay, *Daniel*, 181, notes that עִדָּן, "time," is not simply a substitute for שְׁנָה, "year."

[31] The Old Greek rendered the phrase as ἕως καιροῦ καὶ καιρῶν καὶ ἕως ἡμίσους καιροῦ, "until a time and times and until half a time." Theodotion rendered it, ἕως καιροῦ καὶ καιρῶν καὶ ἥμισυ καιροῦ, "until a time and times and half a time."

earlier period, "the former/first days." The latter or last days commence with the (first) coming of the Messiah and his kingdom.[32] The reference to the messianic era as commencing "in the latter days" is also found twice in Daniel (בְּאַחֲרִית יוֹמַיָּא, 10:14; בְּאַחֲרִית הַיָּמִים, 2:28).

The NT clarifies this. Both Peter and the writer to the Hebrews understood that "the last days" had already begun with the first advent of Christ. They confirm that they and their hearers and readers were already "in the last days" (Acts 2:17; Heb 1:2). The apostles' use of the phrase "last days" to describe conditions that were already present as they wrote is further confirmation of this (2 Tim 3:1; James 5:3; 2 Pet 3:3). The same is true of their use of equivalent phrases such as "the last hour," in which antichrists have already arrived (1 Jn 2:18), and "the last time(s)," in which scoffers are present (Jude 18) but also in which God has already revealed his salvation in Christ (1 Pet 1:20).[33]

Therefore, the three and a half times in Daniel's vision represent the period from the first coming of the Messiah to the final judgment of the fourth beast's little horn immediately after the Messiah's second coming, that is, *from Jesus' first advent to his triumphant parousia and the final judgment.* It is during this period of time that the little horn, the Antichrist, is attacking God and his people. Paul confirms this when he notes that "the mystery of lawlessness is *already* at work" (2 Thess 2:7). The Antichrist, the little horn of Daniel 7, has been present on earth since the NT age, and he will continue to be present and will wage war against the saints until the second coming of Christ. Though he is present now, he is being restrained and is partially hidden so that he is a "mystery" (2 Thess 2:6–7). But at the return of Christ, the Antichrist will be fully revealed and killed by the Lord Jesus (2 Thess 2:8).[34]

Critical Interpretations of the Little Horn

Critical scholars generally deny that God can predict the future through his inspired prophets. (That presupposition, of course, flatly contradicts the message of Daniel 2, 4, and 5.) Consequently they maintain that Daniel 7, like other biblical predictions, is a prophecy *ex eventu*, "after the fact." It is allegedly a kind of pseudo-prophecy written at best immediately before, but more likely during or after the events, then attributed to an author who lived long before the events. Critics suppose that the author accurately portrays current and past events, but places them in a fabricated context, as if they were accurately predicted long

---

[32] Num 24:14; Is 2:2 ‖ Micah 4:1; also see Jer 48:47; 49:39; Ezek 38:16; Hos 3:5. One may see the study of the prophetic use of the phrases "the latter years" (Ezek 38:8) and "the latter days" (Ezek 38:16) in Hummel, *Ezekiel 21–48*, 1109, 1119–20.

[33] The discussion above emphasizes the "already now" aspect of NT eschatology. Other passages use the same or related vocabulary to emphasize the "not yet" aspect of NT eschatology. Thus Jesus repeatedly promises that on "the last day" he will raise up all who believe in him (Jn 6:39, 40, 44, 54; cf. Jn 11:24–25). Peter states that believers are now being guarded for the salvation that will be revealed "in the last time," after Christ returns (1 Pet 1:5).

[34] See further the excursus "The Lutheran Confessions on the Antichrist in Daniel."

before they happened. The author supposedly constructs this deceit to convince his audience of the accuracy and divine origin of his message.[35]

Most critical scholars assume that the author of Daniel 7 wrote sometime in the first half of the second century BC, during the Greek era.[36] These scholars identify the fourth kingdom as Greek, rather than Roman, because they suppose that the author could not have predicted any subsequent kingdoms.[37] They believe that the author is describing the persecution of God's people under Antiochus IV Epiphanes, the Seleucid (Greek) king who reigned from 175 to 164 BC. The ten horns represent kings who were predecessors or contemporaries of Antiochus. The vision of the little horn describes Antiochus' persecution of the Jews living under his rule in Palestine.

However, in addition to the problems caused by identifying the fourth kingdom as Greek, there are several more problems with viewing the little horn as Antiochus. First and most important is the nature of Antiochus' persecution. It was accomplished by violent military force (1 Macc 1:20–24, 29–40). In contrast, Daniel depicts the little horn as waging war by means of speech and words (Dan 7:8, 11, 20, 25), not by force.

Second, the identification of the ten horns is uncertain.[38] At least three of the kings would have to be contemporaries of Antiochus in his earlier years, since three other horns are uprooted after the little horn sprouts (7:8). Some interpreters hold that the ten horns represent ten Hellenistic kings who were contemporaries of Antiochus. However, they cannot agree about which ten are meant. They find it impossible to offer any proof for any proposed set of ten kings.

Instead of all ten being contemporary kings, it is somewhat more common for interpreters to propose that at least seven of the ten horns represent predecessors of Antiochus. Only seven Seleucid kings preceded Antiochus IV.[39] Many interpreters, therefore, hold that the other three horns represent three kings overthrown by Antiochus, but there is little agreement on which three kings they would be. Some interpreters include Ptolemaic kings of Egypt, but they offer no satisfactory explanation for why Ptolemaic kings should be rep-

---

[35] Of course, it raises all kinds of moral, ethical, and theological problems to suppose that biblical writers portray a false and deliberately deceptive historical setting for the context of their "prophecies" in order to convince readers that what they wrote is the Word of God! But critical scholars hardly ever address these kinds of questions.

[36] See "Critical Theories about Date, Authorship, and Unity" in "Date, Authorship, and Unity" in the introduction.

[37] See the excursus "The Four-Kingdom Schema in Daniel."

[38] For details about various identifications of the ten horns, see the discussions in Collins, *Daniel*, 320–21; Goldingay, *Daniel*, 179–80; and Lucas, *Daniel*, 193.

[39] They were Seleucus I Nicator, Antiochus I Soter, Antiochus II Theos, Seleucus II Callinicus, Seleucus III Soter Ceraunos, Antiochus III the Great, and Seleucus IV Philopater. Opinions vary as to whether Alexander the Great should be considered an eighth preceding king represented by one of the horns.

resented by any of the three horns when the other seven horns exclusively represent Seleucid kings.[40]

This uncertainty as to which kings are represented by the ten horns undermines the entire theory that the little horn represents Antiochus. It would have been easy for an author writing during or after the events to describe them in strikingly accurate historical terms. However, the fact that modern scholars cannot convincingly demonstrate the accuracy of the symbolism of the ten horns (or even of the three uprooted horns) during the Greek era undermines their entire premise that Daniel 7 depicts the Greek era and is *ex eventu* prophecy. Some scholars resort to the defense that the original author and his audience both knew which ten kings he meant, but we simply cannot reconstruct the history that would reveal which they were. However, that defense really is a case of desperate speculation rather than evidence that would support the plausibility of the theory that Daniel 7 is *ex eventu* prophecy about the Greek era.

Sensing this weakness in their argument, some proponents of this view hold that ten is simply a round number that does not intend to give an accurate count of Hellenistic kings.[41] However, this once again undermines the contention that Daniel 7 is *ex eventu* prophecy, since one of the signs of such prophecy is the ability to accurately portray past events (which are construed as if they were future prophecies). Approximate, round numbers would hardly serve the purpose of *ex eventu* prophecy, since they would not convince readers that the purported predictions were accurate. Instead, they would instill doubt or even elicit opposition from readers who would require accurate details to be convinced that the author was functioning as a prophet inspired by God.

Finally, we encounter a similar problem with the critical interpretation of the time period of three and a half times in 7:25. Critics generally hold that this is intended to correspond to the time period during which the temple lay desecrated by Antiochus, which they assert was three and a half years long. However, that assertion is not accurate. 1 Macc 1:54 states that Antiochus desecrated the altar of the temple on 15 Kislev in the one hundred forty-fifth year of the Seleucid era (December 6, 167 BC). 1 Macc 4:52–53 states that Judas Maccabaeus and his companions were able to offer sacrifices on a newly consecrated altar for the first time on 25 Kislev in the one hundred and forty-eighth year (December 14, 164 BC). Therefore, the temple was desecrated for three years and ten days (reckoned according to the soli-lunar calendar) or three years and eight days (reckoned according to the Julian calendar). In either case, if 7:25 were a prophecy of that desecration, it would have been in error by over five months (more than eleven percent). It is inexplicable why the author would not instead have

---

[40] Goldingay, *Daniel*, 179, lists six possible historical figures for the three uprooted kings, including some Ptolemaic kings of Egypt.

[41] Collins, *Daniel*, 321; Goldingay, *Daniel*, 179.

referred to just three years, which would have been quite accurate if he were referring to this time when the temple was desecrated by Antiochus. We should expect that an *ex eventu* prophecy would have been much more accurate.

Once again critics, sensing a problem with their own view, have suggested that the three and a half times were merely symbolic of the time of the desecration.[42] Another suggestion is that 7:25 is a case of genuine but inaccurate prophecy before the fact (before the completion of the time period), indicating perhaps that the author was writing before the retaking of Jerusalem by Judas Maccabaeus. Proponents of that suggestion argue that the fact that the author got the time period wrong indicates that he attempted true prophecy (but failed!). With either of these suggestions, the argument undermines itself. Symbolic numbers are no better than round numbers in furthering the goals of an author of *ex eventu* prophecy who wishes to convince readers that he is a true prophet. Moreover, if this were an attempt at genuine prophecy that fell far short in its prediction, we would have to ask why the book of Daniel was accepted so readily among Jews in the two centuries before Christ,[43] when it should have been rejected as false prophecy.

Therefore, the critical argument that the little horn of Daniel 7 represented Antiochus Epiphanes has several major flaws. When added to the other weaknesses of the larger critical approach of identifying the fourth beast as representing the Greek kingdoms, this interpretation is highly suspect.

The Critical View Nullifies the Gospel

Yet the greatest danger of the critical approach to Daniel 7 is that it mutes the vision's message concerning the grace of God in his Messiah. The vision becomes an *ex eventu* prophecy by a Maccabean-era author who expected the kingdom of God to be established in his day. God's people were to receive the kingdom, but the Son of Man is not the messianic savior. Instead, critics believe he is either a collective figure for God's people or an angel. The focus is on the promise of a temporal kingdom, which the author saw as divinely decreed. This kingdom failed to materialize, and so according to the critical view of Daniel 7, the vision becomes the failed expectation of a long-dead Jewish author. Instead of pointing to the true, everlasting kingdom of God won by Christ on the cross and secured by his empty tomb—but a kingdom still yet to be revealed in its full glory—the critical approach reduces Daniel 7 to another example of misplaced faith and misguided hope as its author and audience supposedly looked for a kingdom that never arrived.

---

[42] E.g., Lucas, *Daniel*, 194.

[43] See "Evidence—An Argument for the Traditional Date of Daniel" in "Date, Authorship, and Unity" in the introduction.

Dispensational Premillennial Interpretations of the Little Horn

Of the variety of kinds of millennial interpretations of Daniel, by far the most popular is dispensational premillennialism.[44] That framework for interpreting the Scriptures insists that passages in visionary and apocalyptic books must be taken as literal enumerations or quantifications.[45] The "millennialism" part of the name for the approach comes from the thousand years in the well-known passage in Revelation 20. Here the devil is confined to the abyss for a thousand years, and during this time those who have been beheaded on account of the testimony of Jesus are raised and reign with Christ (Rev 20:1–6).[46] Insisting that the thousand years must be understood literally as a prophecy of some future era, not symbolically about the present era, the method goes on to apply the same hermeneutic to the visionary passages in Daniel.

Dispensational premillennialists insist on the same kind of literal interpretation of Daniel even though they admit that the passages under examination are highly symbolic. For example, dispensational premillennialists admit that the beasts in Daniel's vision (Daniel 7) are not real beasts, but represent kingdoms. The great sea (7:2) represents the nations, not a literal sea. The four winds (7:2) are not literal, since "in Daniel, wind is uniformly used to represent the sovereign power of God."[47] Presumably, God does not have four separate sovereign powers, so "four" must be a symbolic number. Many other cases of non-literal, symbolic interpretation of highly symbolic visions in Scripture (especially in Daniel and Revelation) can be found in dispensational premillennialist writings.

These interpreters rightly adopt the Roman view of the four kingdoms presented in Daniel.[48] Moreover, they correctly agree that the little horn of Daniel 7 represents the Antichrist.

However, their insistence on literal enumeration or quantification as the proper interpretation of numbers in visions leads them to postulate a quite different fulfillment of Daniel 7 than is advocated in this commentary. Because ten distinct kingdoms did not arise from the fall of the Roman Empire, and because their hermeneutical assumption requires a fulfillment of the prophecy

---

[44] For illustrations of the three main millennial conceptions of eschatology, see figure 4, "Timelines of Millennial Eschatologies," in the introduction. For dispensational premillennialism in particular, see further "Eschatology and Dispensational Premillennial Interpretations of Daniel" in the introduction.

[45] Walvoord, "The Prophecy of the Ten-Nation Confederacy," 99–100. Walvoord is a highly influential author who has shaped contemporary pretribulational dispensational premillennialism.

[46] The traditional amillennial Christian interpretation of this passage is that it describes the spiritual death and resurrection (cf. Rom 6:1–4; Col 2:11–13) and reign of all believers in Christ during the present church age, which has already lasted some two millennia and which will continue until the return of Christ. See figure 3, "Timeline of Biblical Eschatology." For a detailed interpretation of Rev 20:1–6 that is in harmony with biblical eschatology, see Brighton, *Revelation*, 542–70.

[47] Walvoord, *Daniel*, 152.

[48] See the excursus "The Four-Kingdom Schema in Daniel."

of Daniel 7 that involves the literal number ten, they believe that in the future, near the time of the parousia, a ten-nation confederacy will arise from the territory of the historic Roman Empire. The Antichrist will arise from within this confederacy and establish a worldwide empire, deceive the nations, and ultimately be judged by Christ at his parousia.[49]

Dispensational premillennialists treat the three and a half "times" in 7:25 in a similar manner. These are interpreted as three and a half years, the first half of the supposed seven-year tribulation period, the persecution of God's people under the Antichrist.[50] Immediately after this seven-year tribulation Christ will return visibly, establish his earthly kingdom, and reign over it for a thousand years. That is to be followed by the eternal state in the new heavens and new earth.[51]

Two major problems are present in this conception of history and eschatology advocated by dispensational premillennialism. Neither of these problems is adequately explained in their literature.

The first major problem is the supposed gap between the fall of the Roman Empire in the fifth century AD and its supposed revival at a future date yet to be revealed. Daniel, as well as the rest of Scripture, is silent about any such long gap, which has now lasted sixteen centuries. Instead, Daniel 7 pictures a smooth and continuous transition from the fourth beast to its ten horns and then to its little horn. Moreover, the entire vision in Daniel 7 (as well as Nebuchadnezzar's dream in Daniel 2) assumes complete continuity from one kingdom to another without any gap in between the consecutive fulfillments of the various features. The first beast gives way to the second, which gives way to the third, which

---

[49] Walvoord, "The Prophecy of the Ten-Nation Confederacy." Dispensational premillennialists interpret other pericopes using similar imagery in the same way. Other passages that they believe prophesy a ten-nation confederation include Daniel 2; Rev 13:1–2; 17:3, 7, 12–18 (Walvoord, "The Prophecy of the Ten-Nation Confederacy," 99, 104).

[50] Dispensational premillennialists disagree with each other about whether or for how long Christians may have to endure the seven-year tribulation. Many believe that the "rapture" (at a secret, invisible return of Christ, ostensibly based on 1 Thess 4:17) will take all Christians out of this world immediately before the seven-year tribulation, so the only Christians who will have to endure the tribulation are those unbelievers who are converted to Christianity during the tribulation. That is the view that is illustrated and labeled "Dispensational Premillennialism" in figure 4. Others believe that Christians will have to endure the first three and a half years of the tribulation, but then the "rapture" halfway through it will take all Christians out of this world. Still others believe that Christians will have to endure the full seven years of the tribulation unless they are martyred during it.

[51] This view of the "tribulation" is based on the belief that "the great tribulation" (τῆς θλίψεως τῆς μεγάλης) mentioned in Rev 7:14 is a reference to this seven-year period of time, even though there is no indication of that length in the immediate context. Rather, "the great tribulation" in Rev 7:10–17 lasts during the entire church age, whose total length we do not know. Throughout this time, Christians suffer various trials and persecutions during their lives on earth, but John sees them "coming out [note the present participle: ἐρχόμενοι ἐκ] of the great tribulation" (Rev 7:14) as they die and join the church triumphant in heaven. See Brighton, *Revelation*, 197–201.

gives way to the fourth, followed by the rise of the ten horns and the rise of the little horn.

Even dispensational premillennialists rightly interpret the first four kingdoms as consecutive without any gaps between them: Babylon, Medo-Persia, Greece, and Rome. Moreover, they see continuity, not a gap, between the rise of the ten-nation confederacy and the rise of the Antichrist. The only place in Daniel's vision they find a gap is between the fourth beast (the Roman Empire) and the ten horns (the ten-nation confederacy). Yet Daniel 7 and also all of the other texts they cite as speaking about the rise of this confederacy (Daniel 2; Rev 13:1–2; 17:3, 7, 12–13) give absolutely no hint of such a historical gap. We must conclude that their insistence on using a peculiar, artificially constructed hermeneutical principle forces them to postulate a historical gap that is not indicated anywhere in any of the biblical texts.

The second major problem arises from their insistence that all numbers in visionary or apocalyptic texts must be taken as literal enumerations or quantifications.[52] They fail to acknowledge that even outside of visions, in narrative prose (normally a more literal genre of literature), numbers are employed in non-enumerative, metaphorically charged ways, as with "ten" in 1:20 and "seven" in 3:19.[53] Failure to recognize that numbers can be and are used by Daniel with non-enumerative or non-quantifiable meanings dooms millennial interpretations from the start. Since they begin with a false premise (numbers are never symbolic), they introduce constraints on the text that the author never intended. This leads to indefensible postulations, for example, a historical gap where none is indicated in the text, and incorrect conclusions.

The Gospel Nullified by the Dispensational View

Like the critical approach to Daniel 7, the most serious error of dispensational premillennialism is that it distorts the scriptural view of messianic deliverance and deprives readers of the chapter's Gospel message. By placing the last part of the vision only at the very end of history, it fails to see that Daniel's message is that the messianic kingdom breaks into earthly history in the time of the Roman Empire, through the incarnation, birth, and ministry of the Son of Man, and that the last days began with Christ's crucifixion and resurrection.[54] The kingdom of God was established at that time by Christ's first advent, in harmony with the message of Daniel 2 (especially 2:34–35, 44–45);

---

[52] However, they are inconsistent in following this procedure. For example, as noted earlier, Walvoord interprets the "four" winds in Dan 7:2 symbolically (*Daniel*, 152).

[53] See further the discussion in "The 'Literal' Fulfillment of Prophecy" in "Eschatology and Dispensational Premillennial Interpretations of Daniel" in the introduction, and the commentary on 1:20 and 3:19.

[54] This is clearly seen in John 11, for example. Martha expresses the confidence that Lazarus, her dead brother, would rise "in the resurrection on the *last day*" (Jn 11:24). Jesus responds, "I am the resurrection" (Jn 11:25), then raises Lazarus from the dead (11:43–44), showing that the last day has already arrived proleptically in Christ. That is made even more evident by Jesus' own bodily resurrection.

Daniel 7; and the entire NT. At the same time, Daniel 7 (like Daniel 2) also sets forth the basis of our hope for the future as we await our bodily resurrection and final inheritance of that kingdom, with the promise that on the Last Day we "will possess the kingdom forever—forever and ever" (7:18; cf. 7:22).

This means that the kind of persecution that is most dangerous for the saints is not some future worldwide political ruler who could deprive them of earthly goods, limit commerce, require a numerical mark on their bodies, or even take their physical lives.[55] Instead, the most dangerous persecution is the insidious corruption of the Gospel of justification through Christ alone and its replacement by a false gospel that mixes faith with works and false spirituality. It is this kind of spiritual warfare that can cause saints to shift their trust from the atonement of Christ to themselves and human or demonic teachings. If they compromise the exclusive claims of God in Christ in order to accommodate other religions, they will lose their relationship with the loving, merciful God who accomplished their full redemption in Jesus Christ.

This is precisely the kind of persecution experienced by God's saints in chapters 3 and 6 of the book of Daniel. The vision in Daniel 7 focuses on the little horn's persecution through its words and speech. This persecution is directed at severing God's people from him by changing the basis for their faith, God's Word and his means of grace in divine worship (7:25). This is a constant danger for all God's saints throughout the ages and is the mark of all antichrists. They are present already now (1 Jn 2:18), not simply in the future.[56]

Daniel is offering comfort for all of God's people from his time forward by demonstrating that, despite appearances to the contrary, God knows the trials of his people and continually governs the events of this world, from Daniel's day to the end. There is no gap in his control or knowledge of history, nor is he ignorant of his people's plight throughout history. Instead, no matter where they are in history, God has provided for them in Christ. The decree of God in favor of the saints (7:22) is the verdict of justification because of the Son of Man (7:13–14), which ensures the final victory and eternity in God's kingdom. This is just as certain for those believers living today as it was when Daniel first received this vision.

The vision of Daniel is not intended to focus readers on the era directly before the final establishment of God's eternal kingdom to the exclusion or minimizing of their present situation, as the millennial interpretations tend to do. It is not intended to excite them to fervent faith and piety because they see the

---

[55] Rev 13:11–18 is often misinterpreted as meaning that the Antichrist (represented by the beast from the earth) will require some sort of tattoo or electronic code mark on each person (perhaps including the number 666) in order to regulate all financial transactions. For a biblical view, see Brighton, *Revelation*, 357–63.

[56] See further the excursus "The Lutheran Confessions on the Antichrist in Daniel."

future unfolding in some precisely predefined fashion, which is supposed to make them confident that they will not be left behind by their God.[57]

Instead, Daniel 7 focuses our vision on the kingdom that is ours already now because of the cross and empty tomb of Christ, and on the time of the final establishment of the kingdom when Christ shall return for us. We were not left behind or excluded when Christ died for all on Calvary (cf. Rom 5:6–8), so we are confident that we who trust in him will not be left behind when Christ returns (cf. Rom 5:9–10). Daniel 7 is designed to give hope and comfort to us in our present situation, in these last days that began with the first advent of Christ, because Christ has already triumphed in the cross and resurrection. The parousia of the Son of Man on the clouds of heaven will be the final revelation of that triumph for all to see—the time of most bitter grieving for unbelievers but the day of final redemption for all believers (Dan 7:13–14; Mt 24:30–31; 1 Thess 4:16–18; Rev 1:7).

An Angel Explains the Establishment of God's Kingdom (7:26–27)

The angel's explanation continues in a brief summary of the convening of the court by the Ancient of Days (7:9–10), followed by the judgment on the fourth beast and its little horn (7:11–12). Neither of these is given expanded explanation, indicating that Daniel already understands that part of the vision. Instead, the angel expands the implications of the enthronement of the Son of Man (7:13–14). When he receives the eternal kingdom and dominion over the entire universe (cf. Phil 2:10–11), the saints will reign with him (cf. Lk 22:30; 2 Tim 2:12), and so "the kingdom ... will be given to the people, the saints of the Most High" (Dan 7:27).

Note that the language about the kingdom of the Most High is a paraphrase of the dominion given to the Son of Man (7:14). "All dominions will worship" the Most High (7:27), a paraphrase of the worship rendered to the Son of Man by "all peoples, nations, and languages" (7:14). Thus the Son of Man receives the same honor and worship that the Most High receives (see Jn 5:22–23). This is an implicit affirmation of the divinity of the Son of Man—God the Son, the second person of the Trinity.[58]

The Unfolding of History as Depicted in the Fourth Beast

Thus the sequence of the events foreseen in this vision is that the fourth kingdom, Rome, will eventually dissolve and its power will be distributed

---

[57] The immensely successful and best-selling Left Behind series of novels by Jerry Jenkins and Tim LaHaye (Carol Stream, Ill.: Tyndale, 1995–2007) is a popular presentation of the events predicted by dispensational premillennialism. "Left behind" alludes to the rapture of Christians into heaven, so that non-Christians are "left behind" to live during the horrible conditions of the seven-year tribulation.

[58] The Athanasian Creed confesses about the Trinity that the "three persons are coeternal with each other and coequal, so that in all things ... the Trinity in Unity and Unity in Trinity is to be worshiped" (*LSB*, p. 320, v. 25).

among several dominions. A portion of its power (symbolized by three of the ten horns) will eventually pass to another authority, as represented by the little horn. This little horn will be brought to an end (the slaying of the fourth beast) with the coming of Jesus, the Son of Man. This sequence is what Paul has in mind in his discussion of "the man of lawlessness" in 2 Thess 2:3–8. The term "the man of lawlessness" itself may be based on Dan 7:25, where the little horn will demonstrate his lawlessness by his intent to change, among other things, "*Law*." Concerning this man, Paul sets forth this sequence:

2 Thessalonians	Daniel	Comment
Paul's readers knew what was restraining the man of lawlessness (2 Thess 2:6).	The fourth beast has dominion (Dan 7:7a, 19, 23).	The Roman Empire was ruling the world in Paul's day.
The man of lawlessness will only be revealed "in his time" (2 Thess 2:6).	Only after the rise of the fourth beast and then of its ten horns does the little horn arise later in the vision (Dan 7:7b–8, 20, 24).	In Paul's day, this time had not yet come.
The mystery of lawlessness is already at work in Paul's day, but the restraining power will continue to restrain the man of lawlessness until that power is out of the way (2 Thess 2:6–7).	The fourth beast dominated the world for some time before the rise of the ten horns and then the little horn (Dan 7:7a, 19, 23).	The Roman Empire would continue for a while, and the Antichrist would not be revealed during this time.
When the restraining power is removed, the man of lawlessness will be revealed (2 Thess 2:7–8).	The ten horns cannot restrain the little horn. It uproots three of them and then wages war against God and his saints (Dan 7:7b–8, 20–21, 24–25).	When the empire falls, the Antichrist will arise. After the fall of the Roman Empire in the fifth century BC, the Roman papacy grew in power and prominence.
The man of lawlessness will be killed and annihilated by Jesus at his parousia (2 Thess 2:8).	The beast is slain and its little horn is destroyed forever at the coming of the Son of Man (Dan 7:11–14, 22, 26–27).	The Antichrist remains throughout the church age until the return of Christ, when it will be destroyed forever.

Daniel's Reaction to the Vision (7:28)

This vision takes a great physical and mental toll on Daniel, an experience that will be repeated with future visions (8:27; 10:10–11, 15–18). Daniel tells us that he kept the matter to himself. He probably was pondering its meaning and fulfillment (1 Pet 1:10–11). Future visions will reveal more details about the matters revealed in this vision. In the meantime, he reveals it to no one.

Similarly, toward the end of the final vision Daniel is told, "Now you, Daniel, close up the words and seal the scroll until the time of the end" (12:4). It would take over five centuries until the first advent of the Messiah and the inauguration of the last days.[59] From then on, believers would rightly consider the fulfillment of the rest of the vision to be imminent. Therefore, at the end of the last book of the NT canon, John the Seer is told, "Do not seal up the words of the prophecy of this book, for the time is near" (Rev 22:10).

---

[59] See the commentary on 7:25, "The Duration of the Little Horn's Warfare: Three and a Half Times."

Daniel 8:1–27

Daniel's First Vision of Post-Babylonian Kingdoms

Introduction to Daniel 8

8:1–14   Daniel's Vision of the Ram and the Goat

8:15–27   Gabriel Explains the Vision of the Ram and the Goat

Excursus   *Dispensational Interpretations of Daniel 8*

Introduction to Daniel 8

Major Emphases in Daniel 8

Like Daniel 7, this vision is about animals that represent kingdoms. However, only two animals appear to Daniel in this vision: a ram and a goat. The second animal, a goat that initially has one horn but eventually has four, is the real focus of the vision. Out of one of the goat's four horns comes a little horn that causes great harm.

Of the visions in Daniel, which make up chapters 7–12, this second vision is probably the most neglected by scholars. Some of this neglect is due to that fact that it is not so controversial. Both critical and evangelical scholars agree on the interpretation of many (but not all) of the details of this vision. Moreover, the explanation of his vision given by the angel to Daniel makes the identification of the events it prophesies indisputable and easy compared to the other visions. In addition, this vision emphasizes a theme that runs throughout Daniel: God governs history for the benefit of his people, and he even uses evil rulers and their persecution of believers as part of his plan to bring his people to salvation in his eternal kingdom.[1] This shared theme makes it difficult to find any particular theological distinction that sets this vision apart from the other visions in Daniel.

Added to all this is the truncated span of history that this vision treats as compared to Nebuchadnezzar's dream in Daniel 2 and Daniel's vision in chapter 7. This vision of the ram and the goat covers only two of the four kingdoms portrayed in those chapters. The ram represents the second kingdom, Medo-Persia, and the goat represents the third kingdom, Greece. Unlike the narrative of chapter 2 and the vision of chapter 7, this vision does not depict either the first kingdom, Babylon, or the fourth kingdom, Rome, during which God establishes his eternal kingdom through the Messiah, who is the "stone" (2:34–35, 44–45) and the "Son of Man" (7:9–14). Since this vision does not extend to the time of the fourth kingdom, it does not picture the advent of God's eternal kingdom. Thus there seems little unique about this vision and little that is new.

However, there is one feature of this vision that makes it memorably distinctive: its depiction of the oppression of the Jews under Antiochus IV Epiphanes (175–164 BC). There are similarities between the depiction of this persecution by Antiochus and the warfare against the saints by the Antichrist depicted in Daniel 7. Most obvious is that both are depicted as little horns. Moreover, both persecute God's people and seek to corrupt divine worship (7:25; 8:11–14). Yet

---

[1] For this theme, see "Theological Threats Posed by the Critical Dating of Daniel" in "Date, Authorship, and Unity," and "The Messiah in Daniel: An Overview" and "God as the Protector of His People" in "Major Themes" in the introduction. See also the commentary on 2:27–30, 34–35, 44–45 and 7:9–14.

these horns are distinct from one another and ought not to be identified with one another.[2]

The little horn in Daniel 8, representing Antiochus, who would persecute God's people during the Greek era, is a foretaste of the greater persecution by the little horn in Daniel 7, representing the Antichrist, who wages war against the saints throughout the church age until Christ returns.[3] By demonstrating how God would deliver his people from Antiochus Epiphanes, the vision in Daniel 8 offers hope to Christians throughout the church age, who must face the Antichrist's persecution and corruption of the Gospel. God demonstrates that his salvific plans cannot be thwarted. Antiochus' persecution would not stop the coming of Christ to redeem humanity from sin and bring the kingdom of God into the world. So too the Antichrist's persecution will not be able to eradicate the Gospel, deprive the saints of salvation through faith alone, or prevent the consummation of Christ's glorious kingdom at his parousia.

Daniel 8 returns to the Hebrew language that Daniel used to begin his book (1:1–2:4a) as well as for the remainder of the book. Daniel 7 (in Aramaic) and Daniel 8 are in chronological order (see immediately below), and chapters 9–12 also will follow in historical order, although the events narrated in Daniel 5 and 6 transpired after the reception of Daniel 7 and 8 and before the reception of chapter 9 and chapters 10–12. The switch back to Hebrew in Daniel 8 and the chronological order of the visions both contribute to the interlocking structure of the book as a whole.[4]

The Historical Setting of Daniel 8

Daniel tells us that this is his second vision, since it came "after the one that appeared to me previously" (8:1), that is, after chapter 7.

This vision came "in the third year of the reign of King Belshazzar" (8:1), two years after Daniel 7, which was revealed "in the first year of King Belshazzar" (7:1). Since Daniel received his first vision in either 553–552 or, more likely, in 550–549, this vision was received in 551–550 or, more likely, 548–547.[5] If the earlier date is accepted, it was around the time that Cyrus defeated his grandfather Astyages and began to reign over a united kingdom of Media and Persia. If the later date is correct, Daniel had this vision around the time that Cyrus defeated the Lydian king Croesus. This was Cyrus' last major

---

[2] See problem 5 and figure 10 in "Problems in Daniel for the Greek View" in the excursus "The Four-Kingdom Schema in Daniel." See also the commentary on 8:9, 11–14, 23–25.

[3] For the little horn in Daniel 7 as the Antichrist, who was present already in the NT era and who will remain until the second coming of Christ and who seeks to pervert the Gospel and divine worship, see the commentary on 7:8, 20–21, 25 and the excursus "The Lutheran Confessions on the Antichrist in Daniel."

[4] See further figures 1 and 2 and "Interlocked Chiasms and the Dual Language of the Book" in "Overview of Daniel" in the introduction.

[5] See "The Historical Setting of Daniel 5" in "Introduction to Daniel 5," and "The Historical Setting of Daniel 7" in "Introduction to Daniel 7."

conquest before taking Babylon.[6] Either of these dates might explain why this vision begins with a ram that represents Medo-Persia.

Unlike the revelations in Daniel 2 and 7, this vision does not begin with a symbol representing the Babylonian Empire. The reason could be that Babylon's downfall, predicted in those earlier chapters, is certain. The Persians would soon turn their military might toward Babylon, which would fall to Cyrus in 539 BC, about a decade after the date of Daniel 8. Therefore, the Babylon Empire is no longer deserving of attention. The focus turns to those kingdoms that are closer to the arrival of God's kingdom in the Messiah, Jesus Christ.[7]

---

[6] See "The Historical Setting of Daniel 6" in "Introduction to Daniel 6."
[7] See "The Messiah in Daniel: An Overview" in "Major Themes" in the introduction.

Daniel 8:1–14

Daniel's Vision of the Ram and the Goat

Translation

8 ¹In the third year of the reign of King Belshazzar, a vision appeared to me—me, Daniel—after the one that appeared to me previously.

²I saw in the vision, and when I saw, I was in the fortress-city Susa, which is in the province of Elam. I saw in the vision, and I was beside the Ulai Canal. ³I lifted up my eyes and I saw, and behold, a ram was standing beside the canal. He had two horns, and the two horns were large. However, the one was larger than the other, but the larger one had come up later. ⁴I saw the ram pushing toward the west, north, and south, and no beast was able to stand in his way, and nothing could rescue [anyone] from his power. So he did as he pleased and magnified himself.

⁵I was pondering [this], when behold, a male goat came from the west over the face of the entire earth, but he was not touching the ground. The goat had a conspicuous horn between his eyes. ⁶He came up to the ram with the two horns I saw standing beside the canal, and he ran at him in his powerful anger. ⁷I saw him coming beside the ram, and he was enraged at him. He struck the ram and broke his two horns. The ram had no power to stand before him, so [the goat] threw him to the ground and trampled on him. There was no one who could rescue the ram from his power.

⁸The male goat magnified himself exceedingly. But as he became strong, the large horn was broken, and four conspicuous [horns] came up in its place toward the four winds of heaven.

⁹Then from one of them came a single horn that began small, but it became very large toward the south and the east and the beautiful [land]. ¹⁰It magnified itself against the army of heaven and made some of the army and some of the stars fall to earth, and it trampled them. ¹¹It magnified itself against the Prince of the army, from whom the continual sacrifice was taken, and the place of his sanctuary was thrown down. ¹²The army will be given [to it] together with the continual sacrifice during the transgression, and it will throw truth to the ground. It will succeed in doing this.

¹³Then I heard a holy one speaking, and another holy one said to the one speaking, "How long is the vision about the continual sacrifice and the transgression causing desolation—the giving over of both the Holy Place and the army for trampling?"

¹⁴He said to him, "Until two thousand three hundred evenings [and] mornings, and then the Holy Place will be consecrated."

Textual Notes

8:1 חָזוֹן נִרְאָה אֵלַי ... אַחֲרֵי הַנִּרְאָה אֵלַי בַּתְּחִלָּה:—The masculine noun חָזוֹן, "vision," is the subject of the Niphal (N) masculine singular perfect (of רָאָה), נִרְאָה, "appeared." The identical verb form then recurs with a definite article, הַנִּרְאָה, which serves as a relative pronoun, "*the one that* appeared." Some grammarians are unjustifiably skeptical of the perfect verb with the article and propose repointing it to a Niphal masculine participle with the article, which would be הַנִּרְאֶה (Joüon, § 145 e).

אֵלַי אֲנִי דָנִיֵּאל—The pronoun אֲנִי and the author's name, דָנִיֵּאל, are in apposition to the suffix in the prepositional phrase אֵלַי: "to me—me, Daniel" (see Joüon, § 146 d). The superfluous pronoun adds emphasis.

8:2–3 וָאֶרְאֶה בֶחָזוֹן ... וָאֶרְאֶה בֶחָזוֹן ... וָאֶרְאֶה—Literally, "and I saw in the vision ... and I saw in the vision ... and I saw." The verb וָאֶרְאֶה appears three times in these two verses. In keeping with Classical Hebrew style, the full (long) form of the imperfect (אֶרְאֶה) is retained for the first person singular with *waw* consecutive, וָאֶרְאֶה (GKC, § 49 e). The Old Greek omits the second "and I saw in the vision," while Theodotion omits the first instance of that clause. 4QDan[a] seems to agree with the MT: it has the first clause (ואראה בחזון) and the last part of the second (בחזון), and there is room in the lacunae for the second and third occurrences of ואראה.[1] In the more fragmentary 4QDan[b], only the last three letters of the second clause are extant, but there seems to be room in the lacunae for the rest of that clause as well as the other two clauses.[2] Therefore, all three should be retained. The repetition may signal Daniel's attempt to orient himself during the initial phase of the vision. The omissions in the Greek versions may simply reflect the translators' preference to avoid repetition.

8:2 עַל־אוּבַל אוּלָי:—This is, literally, "beside the canal of Ulai." The noun אוּבַל, "canal," recurs in 8:3, 6, where it is spelled defectively, אֻבָל. It may be a variant spelling of יָבָל, "canal," in Is 30:25; 44:4 and of יוּבָל, "canal," in Jer 17:8. All three are derived from the verb יָבַל, which in the Hiphil (H) means "to bring, carry along," and all refer to an artificial stream.

8:3 וָאֶשָּׂא עֵינַי וָאֶרְאֶה וְהִנֵּה ׀ אַיִל אֶחָד—Literally, "and I saw, and behold, one ram." The adjectival numeral "one" can function as an indefinite pronoun (Joüon, § 137 u), hence "*a* ram." (See also קָדוֹשׁ אֶחָד, "one/a/another holy one," twice in 8:13.) The MT is rendered precisely by Theodotion: εἶδον καὶ ἰδοὺ κριὸς εἷς. However, 4QDan[a] and 4QDan[b] have the word גדול ("large") after אחד ("one/a"),[3] and the Old Greek too has the word "large": εἶδον κριὸν ἕνα μέγαν, "I saw a large ram." It is hard to decide between the MT and the inclusion of "large" as attested by those ancient witnesses.

קְרָנַיִם—This dual form of the feminine noun קֶרֶן, whose dual means "two horns," has assumed some of the characteristic pointing of a masculine plural (קְרָנִים). The normal dual pointing would be קַרְנַיִם. See GKC, § 93 n.

---

[1] Ulrich et al., *Qumran Cave 4.XI*, 252.

[2] Ulrich et al., *Qumran Cave 4.XI*, 266.

[3] Ulrich et al., *Qumran Cave 4.XI*, 252, 266.

וְהַגְּבֹהָה עֹלָה בָאַחֲרֹנָה:—Literally, this is "and the larger arising afterward." The participle עֹלָה denoting ongoing action ("arising") indicates that Daniel has seen the horn as it was sprouting. By necessity for English in this context, the participle is translated as a past perfect (pluperfect): "the larger one *had come up* later." The feminine form of the adjective אַחֲרוֹן, "after," is used adverbially with בְּ in a temporal sense, "in [the time] afterward, later."

8:4 מְנַגֵּחַ יָמָּה וְצָפוֹנָה וָנֶגְבָּה—The verb נָגַח, in both the Qal and the Piel (here the Piel participle, מְנַגֵּחַ), means "push, thrust, gore" (BDB) and is used for animals butting and goring with their horns. It is used figuratively for people behaving like aggressive animals also in, for example, Deut 33:17 and Ezek 34:21. To the three directions, literally, "seaward, northward, and southward," 4QDan^a adds ומזרחה,[4] "and to the east." That reading is supported by Greek papyrus 967, which adds πρὸς ἀνατολάς. That has led some to favor this reading. The Persian Empire did expand eastward also.[5] However, no other ancient manuscript tradition adds "east" to the other directions. "East" seems to have been added to include all four cardinal directions, and so it is most probably a secondary addition. The main expansion of the Persian Empire was to the north to include Media, south to include Babylon and Egypt, and west to encompass Lydia.

וְהִגְדִּיל:—The Hiphil (H) of גָּדַל will recur in 8:8, 11, 25. Normally its Hiphil is transitive and causative, "to make [something] great." However, in Daniel 8 it is used absolutely, with no direct object. It could be rendered "do great things" (BDB, 3). More likely it is an example of an inwardly transitive or internal Hiphil, in which "the subject causes himself to be regarded as great" (Waltke-O'Connor, § 27.2f; cf. example 19 b). *HALOT*, 2, proposes that it has a reflexive meaning, "magnify oneself," but notes that a middle meaning, "become great," is in harmony with the way the ancient versions translate it. In context, it is clear that the ram (Persia) expanded by defeating other peoples and nations. The ram is a metaphor for a human empire. When the Hiphil (H) of גָּדַל has a human subject in the OT, it almost always implies arrogance.[6] This arrogance becomes hubris in 8:10, which uses the Qal (G). To convey arrogance, the Hiphil in 8:4, 8, 11, 25 is translated as "magnified himself/itself." A reflexive translation is used also for the Qal of גָּדַל in 8:10 (but not for the Qal in 8:9; see the second textual note on 8:9).

8:5 וַאֲנִי | הָיִיתִי מֵבִין—Literally, "and I, I was pondering." The Hiphil participle of בִּין here may have a conative force: "I was *trying* to discern, understand." Compare 8:15, where Daniel uses the cognate noun בִּינָה when he says he sought an "understanding" of the vision.

צְפִיר־הָעִזִּים—Literally, "a male goat of the goats," this construct phrase recurs in 8:8 and, without the article, in 2 Chr 29:21. It is the equivalent of the common construct phrase שְׂעִיר־עִזִּים (e.g., Gen 37:31; Lev 4:23; Num 7:16). See also the textual note on Dan 8:21, where the uncommon noun צָפִיר, "male goat," occurs together with שָׂעִיר, the usual noun for a "male goat." Besides 8:5, 8, 21, the Hebrew צָפִיר occurs only in Ezra 8:35; 2 Chr 29:21, and the cognate Aramaic צְפִיר occurs only in Ezra 6:17.

---

[4] Ulrich et al., *Qumran Cave 4.XI*, 252.

[5] Collins, *Daniel*, 330.

[6] E.g., Jer 48:26; Joel 2:20; Zeph 2:10; Pss 35:26; 55:13 (ET 55:12). No arrogance is connoted when the subject is God (e.g., 1 Sam 12:24; Ps 126:2–3).

וְהַצָּפִיר קֶרֶן חָזוּת בֵּין עֵינָיו:—The syntax with *casus pendens* is, literally, "and the goat—a horn of conspicuousness [was] between its eyes." The construct phrase קֶרֶן חָזוּת has an adjectival genitive and means "a conspicuous horn."

8:6 הָאַיִל בַּעַל הַקְּרָנָיִם—In apposition to הָאַיִל, "the ram," is the noun בַּעַל in the sense of "owner, possessor." בַּעַל is joined by the conjunctive accent to the dual noun with article, הַקְּרָנָיִם, "the two horns." The whole phrase is translated as "the ram with the two horns." The whole phrase (but with a relative clause inserted) is repeated in 8:20.

8:7 וַיִּתְמַרְמַר—This is the rare Hithpalpel conjugation of מָרַר, "be bitter," meaning "be enraged" (BDB). It is related to the Hithpael (HtD) conjugation, but instead of doubling the middle root letter, the biliteral root itself (מר) is repeated (cf. Waltke-O'Connor, § 26.1.1c, example 36). Many grammarians assume that geminate verbs originally consisted of a bilateral root, which was expanded to the normal three letters by repetition of the second letter, hence מר to מרר. The Hithpalpel of מָרַר recurs in 11:11 with the same meaning.

8:8 וַתַּעֲלֶנָה חָזוּת אַרְבַּע תַּחְתֶּיהָ—Since the noun קֶרֶן, "horn," is feminine, its plural is the implied subject of the feminine plural verb, וַתַּעֲלֶנָה, "came up" (normally spelled וַתַּעֲלֶינָה [Joüon, § 80 b, note 3]). The syntax of חָזוּת אַרְבַּע, "conspicuousness four" is unusual, but חָזוּת was used for the single "conspicuous" horn (see the third textual note on 8:5), so it must function adjectivally here too, referring to "four conspicuous [horns]."

8:9 וּמִן־הָאַחַת מֵהֶם יָצָא קֶרֶן־אַחַת מִצְּעִירָה—Literally, "from the one of them came out one horn, from small." The masculine suffix is used on מֵהֶם even though its antecedent is the four (grammatically feminine) horns in 8:8 (GKC, § 135 o). It is possible that מִצְּעִירָה ("from small") could be in apposition to וּמִן־הָאַחַת ("from the one"). If so, the new horn sprouted "from the one" of the four horns that was "small." However, in light of the "little horn" described by the cognate adjective (קֶרֶן ... זְעֵירָה) in 7:8, and because of the contrast between this clause and the next clause, which states that the horn that sprouted "became very large," it is more likely that מִצְּעִירָה modifies קֶרֶן־אַחַת. If so, the "one horn" that sprouted was "little, small." Almost all English translations assume that is the meaning. To simply say, "one small horn arose," the Hebrew could have been יָצָא קֶרֶן־אַחַת צְעִירָה (with no prefixed preposition מִן on צְעִירָה). The force of the prefixed preposition מִן may be temporal, indicating the starting point (see BDB, s.v. מִן, 4 a). Therefore, it is translated, "a single horn *that began small*."

וַתִּגְדַּל־יֶתֶר אֶל־הַנֶּגֶב—The Qal (G) of גָּדַל can mean "grow up" (BDB, 1), "become strong" (so *HALOT*, 1, for 8:9–10; cf. NIV: "grew in power"), or "become great" in some respect such as "importance" (so BDB, 2 e, for 8:9–10). The noun יֶתֶר is used adverbially, "very, exceedingly" (cf. הִגְדִּיל עַד־מְאֹד in 8:8). Within the metaphor here, the three following prepositional phrases with אֶל mean that the horn grew larger "toward" the directions indicated. However, applied to the referent of the metaphorical little horn, the bellicose king, they could indicate his warfare "into, against" the surrounding peoples. See the next textual note.

8:10 וַתִּגְדַּל עַד־צְבָא הַשָּׁמָיִם—As in 8:9 (see the preceding textual note), the Qal (G) of גָּדַל could simply mean "become great," and the preposition עַד could merely mean "until" and indicate the extent of the horn's expansion. However, the rest of the verse shows that the intent of the horn was to exalt itself through warfare. To express this hubris, the verb is translated reflexively, "magnified itself," as are the Hiphils in 8:4, 8, 11, 25. The prepositional phrase with עַד is rendered "*against* the army of heaven." This clause is parallel to the clause with the Hiphil that begins 8:11 (see the next textual note).

8:11 וְעַד שַׂר־הַצָּבָא הִגְדִּיל—Literally, "and against the Prince of the army it magnified itself." The construct phrase שַׂר־צְבָא can be used for a commander of an ordinary human military force (e.g., Gen 21:22, 32; Judg 4:2, 7; 2 Ki 5:1). However, Dan 8:10 states that the reference is to צְבָא הַשָּׁמַיִם, "the army of heaven," so its "Prince" (שַׂר) must be a heavenly figure. See the commentary.

וּמִמֶּנּוּ הוּרַם הַתָּמִיד—Following the Qere, this is, literally, "from him [from the Prince] is removed the continual sacrifice." The Qere is the masculine Hophal (Hp) הוּרַם, and its subject must be the masculine noun הַתָּמִיד, which agrees with it in gender. The Kethib is the masculine Hiphil (H) הֵרִים, which could express the same thought with an active verb: "from him [the Prince] it [the horn] removes the continual sacrifice." However, the meaning of the Kethib requires the feminine noun "horn" to be the implied subject of the masculine verb. Therefore the Qere is preferable.

The Torah of Moses prescribed that each day two sacrifices were to be offered to God. The morning sacrifice was a lamb that burned on the altar until the afternoon, when another lamb, the evening sacrifice, was offered, and it burned until morning. Thus there was a continual sacrifice before God. This came to be seen as the most essential sacrifice. Whenever it was not able to be offered, as during the exile, the worship of the temple had ceased. This sacrifice was called the עוֹלַת תָּמִיד "the burnt offering of continuity, continual burnt offering" (Ex 29:38–42; Num 28:3–8). It is mentioned several times in Daniel as simply הַתָּמִיד, "the continual (sacrifice)" (8:11–13; 11:31; 12:11), the name it often bears in postbiblical literature.

The references to "the continual sacrifice" in Daniel (8:11–13; 11:31; 12:11) are themselves a prophecy that the Jerusalem temple, which was destroyed by Nebuchadnezzar in 587 BC and still lay in ruins during the time when Daniel composed his book, would be rebuilt and the sacrifices specified by Moses would resume there before they would be halted by the little horn. Similarly, the references to the "sanctuary" (see the next textual note) and "the Holy Place" (see the second textual note on 8:13) also presuppose that the profaned and ruined temple would be rebuilt and reconsecrated. After the return from exile allowed by Cyrus' edict in 538 BC, the rebuilding of the temple began, but it was not finished until 515. Daniel himself lived (in Babylon) long enough to hear of the start of the rebuilding, but he probably died no later than about 530, before the second temple was finished.[7]

---

[7] See "Date and Authorship according to the Book" in "Date, Authorship, and Unity" in the introduction.

וְהֻשְׁלַךְ מְכוֹן מִקְדָּשׁוֹ׃—The construct phrase מְכוֹן מִקְדָּשׁוֹ, "the place of his sanctuary," is the subject of the Hophal (Hp) verb וְהֻשְׁלַךְ, "was thrown down." While this might refer to a heavenly sanctuary, as does מָכוֹן in, for example, 1 Ki 8:39, 43, 49, it more likely refers to the Jerusalem temple, so this prophecy predicts that it will first be rebuilt before it is debased. The pronominal suffix on מִקְדָּשׁוֹ, "*his* sanctuary," must refer back to the "Prince."

8:12 וְצָבָא תִּנָּתֵן עַל־הַתָּמִיד בְּפָשַׁע—Literally, "the army will be given [into the power of the little horn] together with the continual sacrifice during the transgression." The translation of this clause has caused much discussion, since its syntax is unusual.[8] This translation understands צָבָא as a feminine noun here (as also in Is 40:2), instead of its normal masculine gender. It is the subject of the feminine Niphal imperfect verb, תִּנָּתֵן. The preposition עַל is taken in the sense of "together with," as in, for example, Num 28:10 and 1 Sam 12:19. This is supported by Dan 8:13, where an angel says that both the army and the sacrifice are given to be trampled (by the little horn). Most English versions offer similar understandings of this clause. In addition, the preposition בְּ on בְּפֶשַׁע is understood to be temporal: "during the transgression."

Some interpreters would emend the text at by omitting "army," since no equivalent for it appears in the Old Greek or Theodotion. However, the Greek versions make "transgression" the subject, which would require further emendation. Others have tried several creative solutions. However, without any manuscript evidence or support from the versions, they must remain highly speculative.[9] Some take the word "army" in a different sense from the previous verses and translate "a host was appointed against the continual sacrifice." This solution is creative, but doubtful, since it requires a different meaning for צָבָא in this verse alone and then a reversion to the previous meaning for it in 8:13.

וְתַשְׁלֵךְ אֱמֶת אַרְצָה—The shortened, jussive form of the Hiphil (H) of שָׁלַךְ, "throw, hurl," is used even though the meaning must be an indicative prophetic statement, "it will throw truth to the ground," not a wish or prayer for the horn to do this. Compare Joüon, 114 l.

וְעָשְׂתָה וְהִצְלִיחָה׃—The verbs "it will do and it will succeed" are coordinated, forming a loose hendiadys, meaning "it will succeed in doing this" (cf. Waltke-O'Connor, § 32.3b). The second verb could also be rendered adverbially: "it will successfully do this." The same expression, but with masculine verbs (in the reverse order) referring to the Greek king, is in 8:24: וְהִצְלִיחַ וְעָשָׂה.

8:13 עַד־מָתַי הֶחָזוֹן הַתָּמִיד וְהַפֶּשַׁע שֹׁמֵם—The loose, uncoordinated syntax is, literally, "until when the vision the continual sacrifice and the transgression desolating?" In light

---

[8] See the extended discussion in Collins, *Daniel*, 334–35.

[9] Perhaps the most plausible of these is put forward by Ozanne, "Three Textual Problems in Daniel," 445–46. He would redivide and repoint the words וְצָבָא תִּנָּתֵן as וּצְבָאֹת נָתַן and read them with the previous verse: "and he cast down [reading וְהִשְׁלִךְ instead of וְהֻשְׁלַךְ] the place of his sanctuary, and hosts he delivered up [וּצְבָאֹת נָתַן]." He would then understand the rest of 8:12 by supplying a verb and reading it like this: "it rose up against the continual burnt-offering in transgression …"

of 8:11–12, הֶחָזוֹן הַתָּמִיד must mean "the vision [about] the continual sacrifice [being taken away]." וְהַפֶּשַׁע שֹׁמֵם must mean that the vision also is of "the transgression causing desolation." We would expect the Qal (G) participle שֹׁמֵם to have the article if it modifies the noun with article וְהַפֶּשַׁע: "the transgression *that* causes desolation." GKC, § 126 z, comments that "without any apparent reason the article is omitted in Dn 8¹³ and 11³¹." However, the participle may be construed as a predicate verb with וְהַפֶּשַׁע as its subject: "the transgression (is) causing desolation."

Participles of שָׁמַם, "cause to be desolate," will be used again in 9:27; 11:31; and 12:11 in connection with "detested thing(s)." These form the background for Jesus' citation of "the detested thing of/causing desolation spoken through the prophet Daniel" (Mt 24:15; cf. Mk 13:14). Forms of שָׁמַם also occur without "detested thing" in Dan 8:27; 9:18, 26.

תֵּת וְקֹדֶשׁ וְצָבָא מִרְמָס:—The syntax is difficult here too: literally, "to give and Holy (Place) and army, trampling," but the parallel use of vocabulary helps clarify the meaning. The Qal (G) infinitive תֵּת is of נָתַן, whose Niphal was used in 8:12 to express the parallel idea that the army "will be given" over to the power of the horn. The noun מִרְמָס, "trampling," derives from the verb רָמַס used in 8:7 when the goat "trampled" the ram, and so here it must refer to the goat's little horn "trampling" God's Holy Place and army. The two nouns that are the direct objects are coordinated with repeated וְ (וְקֹדֶשׁ וְ), meaning "both ... and." This use of וְ is rare, but it occurs several other times in Daniel's visions (8:25; 9:25; 10:3, 6).

The noun קֹדֶשׁ can have the abstract meaning "holiness" but often is used for "the temple and its precincts" (BDB, 2 d). This is its first occurrence in Daniel, and it will recur in reference to the Jerusalem temple in 8:14; 9:16, 20, 24, 26; 11:45 (but with different meanings in 11:28, 30; 12:7). Like הַתָּמִיד, "the continual sacrifice" (see the second textual note on 8:11), the references in Daniel to "the Holy Place" are prophecies that the Jerusalem temple, which lay in ruins during the exile, would be rebuilt and the Torah sacrifices would be resumed there.

Some interpreters speculate that an error in dividing words crept into the text, which might have originally read, תִּתּוֹ קֹדֶשׁ וְצָבָא מִרְמָס,[10] "his [God's] giving over the Holy Place and the army for trampling." However, since there is no manuscript or versional evidence for that, this commentary follows the MT.

8:14 וַיֹּאמֶר אֵלַי—The MT reads, "and he said *to me*," which would refer to Daniel. However, the Syriac has ܠܗ, "to him," which is supported by the Old Greek and Theodotion and is followed by this commentary.

Commentary
Daniel's Vision in Belshazzar's Third Year (8:1)

On the setting of this vision in the third year of Belshazzar, see "The Historical Setting of Daniel 8" in "Introduction to Daniel 8."

---

[10] Collins, *Daniel*, 336; Montgomery, *Daniel*, 341.

A Ram (8:2–4)

Although some have read 8:2 as saying that Daniel was in Susa when he had his vision, the great majority of commentators follow the more natural reading of the text, which implies that in the vision he saw himself in Susa.[11] Babylon ruled Susa for a while, but it eventually was taken by the Persians. It is not known which of these kingdoms ruled it when Daniel had his vision. Susa, however, is an important starting point for the vision, since it would become the winter capital of the Persian Empire. The opening verses of the vision are signaling the ascendancy of the Persians. The Ulai Canal ran near the city to the northeast.

The image of the ram with two horns is rather simple for modern readers with knowledge of history to understand, even without Gabriel's explanation (8:20). The ram is the Medo-Persian Empire, and the two horns are the Median and Persian kingdoms, which this empire included. The longer horn that came up second represents Persia, which dominated the Medo-Persian Empire. Before Cyrus came to the throne of Persia, the Medes had dominated the Persians. When Cyrus came to the throne he overthrew his Median grandfather Astyages and took over the united kingdoms of Media and Persia. Thus Cyrus and his successors are the longer, second horn that came up later and overshadowed the Median kingdom (the smaller but older horn).

Persia's major conquests of Media, Babylon, Egypt, and Lydia are depicted by the ram pushing north, south, and west. It is significant that "no *beast* was able to stand in his way" (8:4). This is a signal that this vision will continue the imagery in the previous vision (Daniel 7), where animals represented kingdoms.

Because the ram had power over all other kingdoms, it could do what it pleased. The power of the Medo-Persian Empire was such that it was the unquestioned authority in the Near East for about two centuries (550–331 BC). This is why the ram "magnified himself" or "made himself great" (see the second textual note on 8:4). Chapters 3, 4, and 5 of Daniel show that the arrogance of a king was an ominous sign calling for divine punishment. The seeds of the fall of Medo-Persia were sown in its success. Therefore, the appearance of another animal to defeat the ram is already implied in this characterization.

A Male Goat Attacks and Defeats the Ram (8:5–7)

While the meaning of the imagery of the ram may be obvious to many modern readers, it was not obvious to Daniel, since its fulfillment was about a decade in the future. Therefore, he tells us that he was "pondering" or "trying to discern" the vision of the ram (see the first textual note on 8:5). However, his thoughts were interrupted by a new creature: a goat.

This male goat came from the west. Its movement was so swift that it did not touch the ground. This swiftness corresponds to the wings of the leopard in

---

[11] E.g., Goldingay, *Daniel*, 208; Hartman and Di Lella, *Daniel*, 233; Montgomery, *Daniel*, 325–26.

7:6 and serves to identify the goat in this vision with the leopard in the previous one. Therefore, the goat, like the third beast in chapter 7 and the third part of the statue in Daniel 2, represents the kingdom of Greece.

The goat had "a conspicuous horn between his eyes" (8:5). By noting that the horn was placed in the center of the forehead of the goat, Daniel is signaling to us that the horn is symbolically associated with the entire goat. This is in contrast to the two horns on the ram, each of which symbolize one part of the ram (8:3), or the one raised side of the bear in 7:5. Both of those were depictions of the Medo-Persian Empire, formed by the combination of Media and Persia (as well as other conquered territories).

Goats are more powerful and aggressive than sheep (Jer 50:8; Zech 10:3), so it is no accident that Daniel saw the goat defeating the ram. Without any allies to help the ram (8:7), the goat was favored to win any conflict between the two.

Once again, the goat is easy to interpret, even without Gabriel's explanation (8:21). The goat comes from the west, representing the Greek invasion of the Near East by Alexander the Great, who is the goat's single horn. The ram's rage refers to the animosity of the Greeks against the Persians that was a result of Persian incursions into Europe, especially under Darius I (490 BC) and Xerxes I (480 BC). Alexander's attacks on Asia began as a campaign to liberate the Greek cities in Anatolia from the Persians.

Both the description of the swiftness of the goat and of the ram's inability to stand up to the goat fit well the rise of Alexander's empire. None of the subjugated peoples of the Medo-Persian Empire offered significant aid to help it combat the Greeks (8:7). The Persians never won a major battle against Alexander. His three decisive victories at Granicus (334 BC), Issus (333 BC), and Arbela (331 BC) destroyed Persian dominance in only three years.

The Horns on the Male Goat (8:8)

Just as the ram elicited divine judgment when he "magnified himself" (8:4), so the even greater arrogance of the goat, which "magnified himself exceedingly" (8:8, using the same Hebrew verb as 8:4 plus an adverbial phrase), signals the imminent downfall of his single horn. Alexander died in Babylon in June 323 BC, at the height of his power. He had no mature male successor, and his two young sons, Alexander IV and Herakles, were subsequently murdered. After several years of battles and contention, his empire was divided among four of his generals. Macedonia and Greece came under the control of Cassander. Thrace and Asia Minor were ruled by Lysimachus. Seleucus gained control of Syria and Mesopotamia, and Ptolemy ruled Egypt. These four became known as the Diadochi, the "successors."

The four new horns of the goat, representing four rulers with dominion in four different areas ("toward the four winds of heaven," 8:8), match the four wings and four heads of the leopard in 7:6, which likewise represents the Greek Empire. It is also represented by the empire of the mighty king that is broken and scattered to the four winds of heaven in 11:4. All three represent the Greek dominance of the Near East as first established by Alexander.[12]

A Little Horn on One of the Goat's Horns (8:9–12)

While the little horn of Daniel 7 is distinct from the little horn in this vision,[13] the two are connected. Since each is called by a cognate adjective (Aramaic in 7:8; Hebrew in 8:9) meaning "little, small," we are alerted to some similarities made evident by their contexts. They both attempt to take divine prerogatives, and they both persecute God's people. The similarities are intentional, because the little horn in this vision is a foreshadowing of the little horn of Daniel 7. Antiochus IV Epiphanes' persecution of the Jews in the second century BC was a precursor of the greater persecution of God's people by the Antichrist throughout the church age. However, the two remain distinct, as shown by their different origins in these two visions. The little horn of Daniel 7 arose on the *fourth* beast, representing the Roman Empire; that beast had ten horns, and then the little horn uprooted three of the ten. The little horn of Daniel 8 arose on the goat, which corresponds to the *third* beast in Daniel 7 (and the third metal, bronze, in the statue of Daniel 2), representing the Greek Empire.[14] This goat had four horns (not ten), and the little horn sprouted from one of four horns without displacing any of the four.

The small horn in Daniel 8 symbolizes Antiochus IV, who took the surname Epiphanes, Greek for "divine manifestation" (reflected by Epiphany, the name for the season of the church year that celebrates the revelation of God in Christ to all peoples). During his reign, coins were stamped ΒΑΣΙΛΕΥΣ ΑΝΤΙΟΧΟΣ ΘΕΟΣ ΕΠΙΦΑΝΗΣ, "King Antiochus, God Manifest." This arrogance is especially pictured in 8:11, as he magnified himself against "the Prince of the army," God himself (especially God the Son), and sought to take away the sacrifice, defile God's temple, and destroy God's truth. Just as the arrogance of the Persians and Alexander was depicted by the way they "magnified" themselves (8:4, 8), so also Antiochus is depicted as the most arrogant of all.

Daniel observed that the horn "began small, but it became very large" (8:9). Antiochus was not the heir to the throne that had been occupied by his brother, Seleucus IV. However, after his brother's death, he usurped the throne from his nephew through bribery and flattery. During his reign, he attacked Egypt (1 Macc 1:16–19) in the south; Persia (1 Macc 3:31; 6:1, 5, 56; 2 Macc 9:1–2), Parthia, and Armenia in the east; and Palestine (1 Macc 1:20–62; 2 Maccabees 5–6). Daniel calls Palestine, "the beautiful [land]" (Dan 8:9), a term he will use again (11:16, 41; cf. 11:45), and which had previously been used by his older contemporary prophet in exile, Ezekiel (Ezek 20:6, 15).

---

[12] See further the excursus "The Four-Kingdom Schema in Daniel."

[13] See the comparison of the two in figure 10 in the excursus "The Four-Kingdom Schema in Daniel" and the discussion that follows.

[14] See "Introduction to Daniel 8" as well as the excursus "The Four-Kingdom Schema in Daniel."

Daniel's prophecy does not list Antiochus' military campaigns in chronological order. Instead, he names the attack on "the beautiful [land]" last (Dan 8:9) so that he can continue by focusing on the king's atrocities toward the Jews in and around Jerusalem. The little horn magnified itself and attacked "the army of heaven … and some of the stars" (8:10). Some commentators take these two synonymous terms to be angels, gods, or astral bodies,[15] while others see them as mythic.[16] However, the interpretation given to Daniel later in the vision identifies them as "the people of the saints" (8:24). This accords with passages where Israel is called "the Lord's army" (Ex 7:4; 12:41). Moreover, "heaven" in this passage may be a circumlocution for God, as it is in 4:26. This would make "the army of heaven" equivalent to "the army of God." In Daniel, God is often explicitly called "the King of heaven" (4:34 [ET 4:37]), "the Lord of heaven" (5:23), or "the God of heaven" (2:18–19, 37, 44). Nebuchadnezzar had confessed that God "does as he wishes with the army of heaven [בְּחֵיל שְׁמַיָּא]" (4:32).

The "stars" (Dan 8:10) can also represent God's people. This draws on the imagery of God's promise to Abraham that he would have descendants as numerous as the stars in heaven (Gen 15:5; 22:17). God also promises through Daniel that "those who bring many to righteousness [will shine] like the stars forever and ever" (Dan 12:3).

Like much of the imagery in Daniel's visions,[17] the casting down of the stars is used again in Revelation. There Satan is a dragon who sweeps one third of the stars down from heaven (Rev 12:4).

The trampling of the army of God aptly describes the persecution of the Jews under Antiochus. He sacked the temple in Jerusalem (1 Macc 1:20–24). He forbade under penalty of death practices commanded in the Law of Moses (1 Macc 1:41–51) and forced Jews to adopt Greek customs and religious practices (2 Macc 6:1–11). However, Antiochus' outrage was not simply against the Jewish people, but also against "the Prince of the army" (Dan 8:11), God himself. Israel was God's army (Ex 7:4; 12:41), so he is the Prince of his army.[18] Later in the vision he is identified as "the Prince of princes" (8:25).

The term "Prince" is used to focus especially upon the second person of the Trinity. Josh 5:14–15 uses an extended form of the phrase here, "the Prince of the army" (שַׂר־הַצָּבָא, Dan 8:11), to refer to "the Prince of the army of Yahweh" (שַׂר־צְבָא־יְהוָה), a divine figure who commands Joshua to remove his sandals because his presence hallows the ground, just as Yahweh commanded Moses

---

[15] See Montgomery, *Daniel*, 333–35.

[16] See Collins, *Daniel*, 331–32.

[17] See especially "Eschatology and Revelation Parallels" in the commentary on 7:9–10.

[18] Some have proposed that the prince was the high priest Onias III, who was assassinated in 170 BC, or the angel Michael, who is called "prince" in 10:13, 21; 12:1. See the discussion in Collins, *Daniel*, 334, and Lucas, *Daniel*, 216. However, the majority of scholars agree that the "Prince" here refers to God (e.g., Archer, "Daniel," 100; Baldwin, *Daniel*, 157; Goldingay, *Daniel*, 210; Hartman and Di Lella, *Daniel*, 236; Leupold, *Daniel*, 346–47; Montgomery, *Daniel*, 335; Walvoord, *Daniel*, 187; Young, *Daniel*, 172).

from the burning bush (Ex 3:5). That Prince who manifested himself on earth to facilitate Israel's divinely mandated warfare is traditionally identified as the preincarnate Christ, the Word not yet made flesh.[19] He is also called "the Prince of peace" in the famous messianic prophecy of Is 9:5–6 (ET 9:6–7).

The identification of the "Prince" here too as the preincarnate Christ fits the context of the temple and sacrifice. He is the one to whom the daily sacrifice was offered until it was removed ("from whom the continual sacrifice was taken," Dan 8:11), and the temple is called "the place of his sanctuary" (8:11). This is an implicit affirmation that in the OT era, the Jerusalem temple (to be rebuilt) along with its sacrifices (to be reinstituted) represented Christ and anticipated his own perfect, all-availing sacrifice and his resurrection as the new temple (Jn 2:18–22).

On the fifteenth day of Kislev in the one hundred forty-fifth year of the Seleucid era (December 6, 167 BC), Antiochus specifically defied Israel's God by erecting "a detested thing of desolation [βδέλυγμα ἐρημώσεως] on the altar" of the temple (1 Macc 1:54). Most likely this was an idol to Zeus (cf. 2 Macc 6:1–2) made to resemble Antiochus himself. Thus the continual sacrifice was taken away from the Prince of the army. Since the continual sacrifice on the altar signified the once-for-all, all-sufficient sacrifice of Christ that paid for the sins of all people at all times, the abolishing of this sacrifice was a direct offense against Christ.

The attack on God is seen in the removing of the sacrifices God had commanded and the throwing down of the sanctuary (Dan 8:11). Antiochus not only forbade sacrifices to Israel's God (1 Macc 1:44–46), but on the twenty-fifth day of Kislev (December 16), he also defiled the altar with the first pagan sacrifices (1 Macc 1:59), which probably included pigs (1 Macc 1:47; cf. 2 Macc 6:4).

Daniel then tells his readers that God's people ("the army") and the continual sacrifice will be given over to the little horn, who will "throw truth to the ground" (8:12). The specific truth in view here is the Law of Moses. Not only were Jews forbidden to practice their faith according to the strictures of the Pentateuch (1 Macc 1:41–51; 2 Macc 6:1, 6), but any scrolls of the Torah were destroyed, and anyone found in possession of the Torah was executed (1 Macc 1:56–57). Yahweh reveals himself in his Torah to be a God "abounding in grace and truth" (Ex 34:6; cf. Gen 24:27; 32:11 [ET 32:10]), the same "truth" to be embodied and fully revealed in the incarnate Messiah (Jn 1:14, 17; 14:6).

Daniel makes it clear to his readers that Antiochus will be successful in this persecution—at least for a while: "during the transgression," he "will succeed in doing this" (8:12). Thus 8:12 depicts Antiochus' initial success in his time of "transgression"—defying God, defiling the Jerusalem temple and its sacrifices, and persecuting the Jews.

---

[19] So Harstad, *Joshua*, 250–55.

An Angel Inquires about the Length of the Little Horn's Activity (8:13–14)

In the vision, Daniel overheard two angels conversing, probably about the meaning of the vision. Each is called "a holy one" (8:13), the Hebrew equivalent of the Aramaic "holy one" used for the angel in Nebuchadnezzar's dream vision (4:10, 20 [ET 4:13, 23]). One angel inquired about the length of time that it will take to fulfill the part of the vision concerning the sacrifice and the transgression in the last part of the vision that Daniel related (8:10–12). This is further defined in the angel's question as "the giving over of both the Holy Place and the army for trampling," the desecration of the temple and the trampling of God's people by the little horn.

The reply is, literally, "evening, morning, two thousand and three hundred" (עֶרֶב בֹּקֶר אֲלָפַיִם וּשְׁלֹשׁ מֵאוֹת, 8:14). The syntax is unusual, since the words "evening" and "morning" are not joined by any conjunction (but see 8:26, where both have articles and are connected by a conjunction). The placement of "evening" before "morning" is consistent with the Jewish way of reckoning a day as beginning at evening (sundown), based on Genesis 1, where each of the days of creation is marked by "evening" and then "morning."

Two interpretations have been suggested for this time period. One views the expression as meaning 2,300 days, a little over six years and three months. This interpretation was favored by Jerome, Luther, and Calvin,[20] and has adherents among more recent scholars.[21] Among those who take this view, there several ways of explaining how it applied to Antiochus' persecution. They include these:

1. The 2,300 days fall somewhat short of seven years.[22] Since seven is a divine number, the meaning is symbolic: the number symbolizes a period slightly short of a full period of divine judgment (seven years).[23] The problem with this view is that it does not explain why the expression "evening, morning" was used (without a conjunction) instead of "days." In some other passages, Daniel uses symbolic numbers of "days" (12:11–12). Moreover, elsewhere in the vision of Daniel 8, numbers are used with literal significance, and there is no other place in the chapter where numbers associated with times or kingdoms are used symbolically. The numbers of horns on the ram (two, for Media and Persia) and on the goat (four, for the kings who succeeded Alexander) represent actual numbers, and even the four winds of heaven (8:8) refer to the four geo-

---

[20] Archer, *Jerome's Commentary on Daniel*, 86–87; Luther, "Preface to Daniel," AE 35:302; Calvin, *Daniel*, 2:108–10.

[21] Goldingay, *Daniel*, 213; Keil, *Daniel*, 2:302–8; Walvoord, *Daniel*, 190; Young, *Daniel*, 174.

[22] This, apparently, was the way Theodoret of Cyrus (ca. AD 393–ca. 460) calculated the period, arriving at six and a half years by Hebrew reckoning. See Theodoret of Cyrus, *Commentary on Daniel* (trans. Hill, 214–15).

[23] Keil, *Daniel*, 306–8; Leupold, *Daniel*, 356–57; cf. Goldingay, *Daniel*, 213.

graphical directions. The specification of "evening" and "morning" (8:14) is quite different from the cryptic use of "times" and the symbolic numbers used with it: the three and a half "times" (7:25; 12:7) or the seven "times" (4:13, 20, 22, 29 [ET 4:16, 23, 25, 32]) in other visions, which leave the time period indefinite and thereby imply that the significance is to be found in the symbolic number associated with it.

2. It represents the period from the assassination of the high priest Onias III in 171 BC to the rededication of the temple and the restoration of the sacrifices by Judas in 164.[24] The problem with this view is that 8:13–14 portrays the period as coextensive with the taking away of the continual sacrifice and the "trampling" of the temple (the time when it was used as a pagan temple). Even after the death of Onias, sacrifices continued for several years, and Antiochus' decree forbidding sacrifice to Israel's God (1 Macc 1:41–51) came at least two years (1 Macc 1:29) after he sacked the temple (1 Macc 1:20–24).

3. A slightly different interpretation reckons the period to be from 171 BC until Antiochus' death in 164.[25] As with the previous interpretation, this is problematic because the sacrifices were not stopped for several years after 171. An additional problem is posed by the fact that they were restored in 164 by Judas before Antiochus' death.

Another approach is to interpret the 2,300 evenings and mornings as 2,300 evening and morning sacrifices, which would take place over 1,150 days, since one evening sacrifice and one morning sacrifice were performed each day. This would explain the unusual syntax of "evening, morning" in 8:14. Moreover, this is confirmed by 8:26, which calls this, literally, "the vision of *the* evening and *the* morning." In addition, the vision is about הַתָּמִיד (8:11–13), which is the term for "the continual sacrifice" offered twice daily (see the second textual note on 8:11).

This interpretation was endorsed by Ephraim of Syria and seems to have been held by Hippolytus as well.[26] It has support among many contemporary scholars.[27] 1 Macc 1:54 states that Antiochus desecrated the altar of the temple on 15 Kislev in the one hundred forty-fifth year of the Seleucid era (December 6, 167 BC). 1 Macc 4:52–53 states that Judas Maccabaeus and his companions were able to offer sacrifices on a newly consecrated altar for the first time on 25 Kislev in year 148 (December 14, 164). Thus from the time that the temple altar was desecrated to its rededication was 1,106 days (365 days + 365 days + 366 days + 10 days; 164 BC was a Julian leap year).

---

[24] Luther, "Preface to Daniel," AE 35:302; see the discussion in Keil, *Daniel*, 302–6.
[25] Walvoord, *Daniel*, 190; Young, *Daniel*, 174–75.
[26] Young, *Daniel*, 173. See Hippolytus, *Commentary on Daniel*, 10 (*ANF* 5:180).
[27] E.g., Archer, "Daniel," 103; Baldwin, *Daniel*, 158; Collins, *Daniel*, 336; Montgomery, *Daniel*, 343.

Since this falls slightly short of 1,150 days, some critical scholars suggest that this was an attempt at genuine prophecy by a Judean author writing about 165 BC and that his prediction was close, but not exact.[28] However, 1 Macc 1:41–53 suggests that Antiochus' order banning sacrifices to Israel's God was in force *before* the desecration of the altar on 15 Kislev (December 6; 1 Macc 1:54). If the sacrifices were stopped forty-four days earlier, on 28 Tishri (October 22), then the prediction is exact.

However, we should keep in mind that OT prophecies concerning time periods are usually given in round numbers. Abraham was told that his descendents would live in Egypt for four hundred years (Gen 15:13), but the actual time was four hundred thirty years (Ex 12:40–41). In a similar way, Jeremiah prophesied that the captivity would last for seventy years (Jer 25:11–12; 29:10). However, the captivity lasted from 605 BC, when the first wave of Judean exiles was taken captive and subsequently hauled to Babylon, to the first return of the exiles in 538 BC, or almost 68 years.

Prophecy is intended to demonstrate God's governance of history for his gracious purposes and thus strengthen faith in him. It is not intended to promote a shallow, deterministic understanding of God's accounting of time. Therefore, the time of the cessation of the evening and morning sacrifices probably was *approximately* 1,150 days. It most certainly included the period from the desecration of the altar until its rededication, and perhaps it included a few weeks before the desecration.

This interpretation is confirmed in the next vision, where Daniel's concern for the temple and its cultus is so important that he notes that Gabriel arrived to tell him about it "about the time of the evening sacrifice" (see the commentary on 9:21).

The Festival of Hanukkah

Daniel's prophecy of an end to the profanation of the temple was fulfilled when Judas Maccabaeus recaptured Jerusalem, cleansed the temple, and erected a new altar. This led to the establishment of a new religious observance for Jews from that time onward. Judas and the assembly in Jerusalem established an eight-day festival to commemorate the dedication of the altar, which is known as חֲנֻכָּה, Hanukkah, meaning "dedication" (the term used in the Aramaic of 3:2–3 for the "dedication" of Nebuchadnezzar's idolatrous statue). This festival was celebrated by Jesus, who went to Jerusalem at its time (Jn 10:22–39). John specifically tells us that it was winter, the traditional time for Hanukkah, which is celebrated by Jews every December to this day.

The Millerite Tradition and Daniel 8:14

The prophecy of the 2,300 evenings and mornings also led to the rise of the Seventh Day Adventists and other denominations in the Millerite tradition. In

---

[28] Collins, *Daniel*, 336.

the nineteen century, William Miller, a Baptist layman, predicted the return of Christ, based on his peculiar belief that all biblical prophecies that give a time period in days are actually predicting one year for each day. He based his theory on Ezek 4:6 and Num 14:34, where such equations are made. However, those passages do not purport to set down a general principal about prophecy.

Nevertheless, Miller believed that the 2,300 years began in 457 BC and therefore Jesus would return to earth in 1844. When this did not happen, he and his followers experienced the "Great Disappointment." Those who remained in the Millerite movement reinterpreted the disappointment in various ways. One of these led to the founding of the Seventh Day Adventist denomination, which still defends Miller's questionable hermeneutical theory of equating a day with a year.[29]

---

[29] Shea, "Supplementary Evidence in Support of 457 B.C. as the Starting Date for the 2300 Day-Years of Daniel 8:14." Miller and the Seventh Day Adventists began at 457 BC as the starting point for the 2,300 years based on a rather complicated calculation involving questionable assumptions about the seventy weeks of Dan 9:24–27 and their supposed relationship to the 2,300 evenings and mornings of Daniel 8. The interpretations involved in relating Daniel 8 to Daniel 9 in this scheme are speculative and highly questionable, and discussion of them is well beyond the scope of this commentary.

Daniel 8:15–27

Gabriel Explains the Vision of the Ram and the Goat

Translation

8 ¹⁵When I, Daniel, had seen the vision, I sought an understanding [of it]. And behold, standing in front of me [was someone] like the appearance of a man. ¹⁶I heard a human voice between [the banks of] the Ulai, and it called out and said, "Gabriel, make this man understand the vision."

¹⁷So he came beside the place where I stood, and when he came, I was terrified and fell facedown. He said to me, "Understand, son of man, that the vision concerns the time of the end." ¹⁸When he had spoken with me, I fell into a deep sleep facedown on the ground. He touched me and made me stand on the place where I stood.

¹⁹He said, "Behold, I am about to make known to you what will happen in the latter part of the indignant anger, because it concerns the appointed time of the end. ²⁰The ram that you saw had two horns, the kings of Media and Persia. ²¹The male goat is the king of Greece, and the large horn between his eyes is the first king— ²²the one that was broken and four arose in its place. Four kingdoms from [his] nation will arise, but not with his [same] strength.

²³"In the latter part of their kingdom, when the transgressors are completed, there will arise a merciless king who understands enigmas. ²⁴His power will be mighty, but not by his own power. He will destroy wonderful things, and he will succeed in doing this. He will destroy mighty men and the people of the saints. ²⁵Through his cunning, he will both cause deception to succeed by his power and magnify himself in his heart. He will destroy many who are at ease, and he will arise against the Prince of princes. However, he will be broken, but not by human power. ²⁶The vision of the evenings and the mornings that was spoken is true. But you—close up the vision, because it concerns many days [in the future]."

²⁷I, Daniel, was exhausted and sick for days. Then I got up and did the king's business. I was appalled by the vision and did not understand it.

Textual Notes

8:15 : כְּמַרְאֵה־גָבֶר—To fill out the thought completely in English would require adding these bracketed words: "[was someone whose appearance was] like [כְּ] the appearance [מַרְאֵה] of a man." This is similar to the elliptical expression כְּבַר אֱנָשׁ, "(one) like a Son of Man" (7:13). Also similar is the wording of the two descriptions of the divine figure who appears to Daniel in chapter 10: וּפָנָיו כְּמַרְאֵה בָרָק, "his face had the appearance of lightning" (10:6), and especially כְּמַרְאֵה אָדָם, literally, "[one whose appearance was] like the appearance of a man" (10:18). Likewise, the descriptions of the angels (or the preincarnate Christ) in Judg 13:6 and Ezek 40:3 both use כְּמַרְאֵה.

8:17 וַיָּבֹא אֵצֶל עָמְדִי—The uncommon noun עֹמֶד, "standing place," recurs in 8:18. In the OT it always occurs after a preposition (here אֵצֶל, "beside," and in 8:18, עַל, "on") and always with a suffix.

לְעֶת־קֵץ הֶחָזוֹן:—The statement that "the vision concerns the time of the end" is the first Daniel passage with קֵץ, "end," which recurs in 8:19; 9:26; 11:6, 13, 27, 35, 40, 45; 12:4, 6, 9, 13. In each case, its meaning needs to be determined from the context. We must not isolate it from its context and always assume that in every passage it must refer in an absolute sense to the end of this earth at the return of Christ. In other OT passages, similar phrases refer to the ends of particular eras still in the OT period. For example, in Gen 6:13, "the end [קֵץ] of all flesh" refers to the end of the antediluvian period, brought to its "end" by the flood in the time of Noah. In Amos 8:2, "the end [קֵץ] has come" refers to the end of the Northern Kingdom of Israel, which was conquered by Assyria in 722 BC. Also, קֵץ in Ezek 7:2–3, 6 and "the time of iniquity's end [קֵץ]" in Ezek 21:30, 34 (ET 21:25, 29); 35:5 refer to the end of the Southern Kingdom of Judah in 587 BC, when Babylon conquered Jerusalem. So also do the clauses with קֵץ in Lam 4:18. However, עֶת־קֵץ, "the time of the end," does refer to the final eschatological events preceding the return of Christ in Dan 11:35, 40; 12:4, 9. See the commentary for the meaning of the phrase here.

8:18 נִרְדַּמְתִּי עַל־פָּנַי אָרְצָה—Literally, "I fell into a deep sleep on my face to the ground." The Niphal (N) of רדם denotes a very heavy sleep (see *HALOT*, 1), often induced by God. Both here and in 10:9, which repeats the vocabulary of this clause, the purpose of this sleep induced by God is to impart a revelation. Jonah fell into a deep sleep denoted by this verb so that he slumbered during a storm on the high seas (Jonah 1:5–6),[1] which led to the repentance and salvation of the sailors through faith in Yahweh (Jonah 1:16). Sisera was in this kind of sleep, perhaps induced by God to facilitate his defeat, when Jael drove a tent peg through his temples (Judg 4:21). The related noun תַּרְדֵּמָה describes the "deep sleep" God imposed on Adam when he took a rib from his side to make Eve (Gen 2:21). תַּרְדֵּמָה is induced for a divine revelation in Gen 15:12. Compare also 1 Sam 26:12 and Job 4:13; 33:15.

8:19 הִנְנִי מוֹדִיעֲךָ—This construction, the interjection הִנֵּה with suffix ("behold, I") and a participle (מוֹדִיעֲךָ, the Hiphil of יָדַע with datival suffix, "making known to you") is a *futurum instans* (GKC, § 116 p) denoting imminent action: "I am *about to* make known to you."

8:20 בַּעַל הַקְּרָנָיִם—See the textual note on 8:6.

8:21 וְהַצָּפִיר הַשָּׂעִיר מֶלֶךְ יָוָן—Literally, "the male goat, the male goat (is) king of Greece." Both the rare noun צָפִיר (also in 8:5, 8) and the common noun שָׂעִיר (only here in Daniel) denote a "male goat." Probably the combination of the two here is a pleonasm. Some English translations ignore the repetition and simply translate with something like "the he-goat" (RSV) or "the male goat" (NKJV), or they ignore the

---

[1] For a brief study of רדם in this and other passages, see Lessing, *Jonah*, 104–5.

gender of both nouns and translate just with "the goat" (ESV). Others take שָׂעִיר to be a plene spelling of the adjective שָׂעִר, "hairy" (elsewhere only in Gen 27:11, 23), and translate וְהַצָּפִיר הַשָּׂעִיר as "the shaggy goat" (NIV, NASB; cf. KJV, "the rough goat"). The problem with this interpretation is that the goat is not called shaggy or hairy elsewhere in Daniel 8, and in 8:5, 8, צָפִיר was used in place of שָׂעִיר to mean "male goat." See the second textual note on 8:5.

While יָוָן is often simply transliterated as *Javan*, it means "Greece." Etymologically it is related to Greek Ἴων, "(an) Ionian," and Ἰωνία, "Ionia," consisting of the Greek islands. Compare Is 66:19, where יָוָן is associated with "far away islands." Here and also in Dan 10:20 and 11:2, it is a general designation for Greece as a whole. Both the Old Greek and Theodotion translate מֶלֶךְ יָוָן here as βασιλεὺς (τῶν) Ἑλλήνων, "king of (the) Greeks," and they also translate יָוָן in 10:20 and 11:2 as (τῶν) Ἑλλήνων, "of (the) Greeks."

8:22–23 וַתַּעֲמֹדְנָה אַרְבַּע תַּחְתֶּיהָ אַרְבַּע מַלְכֻיוֹת מִגּוֹי יַעֲמֹדְנָה ... יַעֲמֹד מֶלֶךְ—Three times in these two verses the verb עָמַד, which usually means "to stand" (as in 8:15, 18), is used with the meaning "arise, appear, come on the scene" (BDB, Qal, 6 a). It will be so used also in 11:2–4, 7; 12:1.

8:23 כְּהָתֵם הַפֹּשְׁעִים—The Hiphil (H) infinitive of תָּמַם (with the preposition כְּ in a temporal sense, "when") has a causative meaning, "to finish, complete, bring to an end." The implied subject is God, but since no subject is given, the verb can be translated as a passive, "are completed, ended," with the understanding that God is governing history. The verb's direct object is the participle הַפֹּשְׁעִים used as a substantive, "the transgressors." The participle is cognate to the noun פֶּשַׁע, "transgression," in 8:12–13 and in the similar phrase in 9:24, "to end transgression." Instead of vocalizing the consonants as the participle, the translators who made the Old Greek, Theodotion, Vulgate, and perhaps the Syriac apparently vocalized the word as the noun הַפְּשָׁעִים, "the transgressions." Since this verse appears to be the angel's explanation for 8:12–13, where the noun פֶּשַׁע, "transgression," is used twice, this different vocalization is understandable and does not change the meaning significantly. However, the sin of "transgression" must be perpetrated by human "transgressors." It certainly is possible that in the explanation here Gabriel has supplied the perpetrators ("transgressors") of the deeds ("transgression") Daniel saw earlier. Most English translations follow the MT but render the verb freely, for example, "when the transgressors have reached their full measure" (RSV), "when the transgressors have run their course" (NASB), "when rebels have become completely wicked" (NIV).

יַעֲמֹד מֶלֶךְ עַז־פָּנִים—Literally, "there will arise a king (who is) strong of face," that is, "merciless." The phrase גּוֹי עַז פָּנִים (literally, "a nation strong of face") occurs in Deut 28:50 in a context (Deut 28:15–68) that describes merciless brutality by a nation God will use to punish Israel and remove his people from the land when they prove unfaithful.

וּמֵבִין חִידוֹת:—"Who understands enigmas" uses the same Hiphil (H) participle of בִּין that Daniel used for himself in 8:5 when he was "pondering, trying to understand" the vision, and in 8:27, when he admits he "did not understand" it. The noun חִידָה, "riddle, enigmatic, perplexing saying or question" (BDB [under the root חוד I]), is used seventeen times in the OT.ᵃ It refers to sayings that present a challenge that requires wisdom or cleverness to solve. In this context, it seems to signify the crafty and deceptive nature of the king, who uses his intelligence for evil purposes (8:25). The translation "enigmas" follows the two oldest interpretations of this word in this context: αἰνίγματα, "enigmas," in the Old Greek and προβλήματα, "problems," in Theodotion.

8:24 וְנִפְלָאוֹת יַשְׁחִית—"He will destroy/corrupt wonderful/miraculous things" uses the Niphal (N) participle of the verb פָּלָא, "be surpassing, extraordinary, miraculous." The cognate noun פֶּלֶא can refer to a salvific miracle (e.g., Ex 15:11; Is 9:5 [ET 9:6]). The Niphal participle of this verb occurs forty-six times in the OT. In most of these instances, it is used as a noun referring to "the wonderful acts of [Yahweh] in judgment and redemption" (BDB, 4). In Dan 11:36 it is used as a noun referring to wondrous words. Three times it is used adjectivally ("wonderful" in Job 42:3; Ps 131:1; "difficult [?]" in Deut 30:11). Twice it is used adverbially ("wonderfully, miraculously" in Job 37:5; Ps 139:14). Most English versions understand it to be used adverbially here, for example, "he will destroy to an extraordinary degree" (NASB); "he shall cause fearful destruction" (ESV). However, since it is used as a noun in the overwhelming majority of cases, including its only other occurrence in Daniel, the translation above assumes it is used nominally here too, as the indefinite direct object of the verb.

This is supported by the parallel clauses in 8:24 and 8:25 that use the same verb, the Hiphil (H) of שָׁחַת, "to destroy, corrupt, ruin," with nominal direct objects (see the third textual note on 8:24). In both clauses, the direct objects pertain to God and his people. "Wonderful/miraculous things" in 8:24a is an especially appropriate term for God's means of grace through sacrificial worship at the temple, where God bestowed his salvation. To "destroy, corrupt, ruin" the divine service is the greatest act of violence possible against God and his people.

וְהִצְלִיחַ וְעָשָׂה—See the third textual note on 8:12.

וְהִשְׁחִית עֲצוּמִים וְעַם־קְדֹשִׁים:—"He will destroy mighty men and the people of saints." "The people of saints" means "the people consisting of the saints, holy ones." The genitive is epexegetical. For the "saints," see the commentary on 7:18, 21, 22, 25, 27.

8:25 וְעַל־שִׂכְלוֹ—This could be rendered literally by supplying "relying," "[relying] on his cunning," but it is translated, "through his cunning."

וְהִצְלִיחַ מִרְמָה בְיָדוֹ וּבִלְבָבוֹ יַגְדִּיל—The two clauses each beginning with וְ mean that he will do "both ... and ..." (see the second textual note on 8:13). Whereas the Hiphil verb הִצְלִיחַ was intransitive ("to succeed") in 8:12, 24, here it is causative, "to cause deception [מִרְמָה] to succeed." בְיָדוֹ, literally, "by his (own) hand," means "by his own power." For the Hiphil of גָּדַל, "magnify himself," see the second textual note on 8:4.

וּבְשַׁלְוָה יַשְׁחִית רַבִּים—The noun שַׁלְוָה, "quietness, ease," or "peace" (BDB), implies that the people were at peace among themselves and also with God (as the word connotes in Ps 122:7) when they came under attack by the little horn. The Aramaic cognate was used in 4:24 (ET 4:27) for a possible lengthening of Nebuchadnezzar's "prosperity," that is, his reign, if he repented before God. בְּשַׁלְוָה recurs in 11:21 and 11:24, which prophesy that Antiochus Epiphanes will attack God's peaceful people. (Later in Daniel 11, the prophecy in 11:36–45 predicts the Antichrist as the one who will attack God's

(a) Num 12:8; Judg 14:12–19; 1 Ki 10:1; Ezek 17:2; Hab 2:6; Pss 49:5 (ET 49:4); 78:2; Prov 1:6; Dan 8:23; 2 Chr 9:1

people.) ESV renders בְּשַׁלְוָה "without warning" (8:25; 11:21, 24), implying suddenness. That translation points toward Antiochus' attack "suddenly" (ἐξάπινα) as recorded after the event in 1 Macc 1:30. BDB (s.v. שַׁלְוָה) also notes the possibility that בְּשַׁלְוָה in 8:25; 11:21, 24 means "suddenly, unawares," which may be supported by the Syriac translation of it as ܡܢ ܫܠܝ. While the Old Greek and Theodotion translate it with δόλῳ, "by deceit," in 8:25, the Old Greek translates it with ἐξάπινα, "suddenly," in 11:21, 24. See the textual note on 11:21, 24.

וְעַל־שַׂר־שָׂרִים יַעֲמֹד—The unique title "Prince of princes" is a Christological term for God similar to "Prince of the [divine] army" (8:11). See the commentary on 8:11 (cf. Dan 2:37; 1 Tim 6:15; Rev 17:14; 19:16).

וּבְאֶפֶס יָד יִשָּׁבֵר—Just as בְּיָדוֹ earlier in the verse meant "by his (own human) hand/power," וּבְאֶפֶס יָד, literally, "and by no hand," means the opposite, "not by human power," meaning that the king will be "broken" (יִשָּׁבֵר) miraculously by God alone.

8:26 כִּי לְיָמִים רַבִּים—Translation requires supplying the words in brackets: "because it concerns many days [in the future]." The identical phrase לְיָמִים רַבִּים is used once elsewhere in the OT, where it has the same meaning. In Ezek 12:27 the exiles mistakenly say that Ezekiel's prophecies were about the distant future, but that is true here for Daniel.

8:27 וַאֲנִי דָנִיֵּאל נִהְיֵיתִי וְנֶחֱלֵיתִי יָמִים—Daniel recorded similar reactions to his first vision (see the commentary on 7:15, 28). נִהְיֵיתִי is the Niphal (N) of הָיָה, which is rare, but does occur once elsewhere in Daniel. See the textual note on 2:1, where the Niphal meant that Nebuchadnezzar's sleep "came upon him [again]." Given the context, "exhausted" seems to be the meaning here. Unconvincing are attempts to derive this verb form from the root הוה, "fall" or possibly "ruin" (cf. הַוָּה, "ruin," Job 6:2 Qere), or that see it as a dittograph of the following Niphal verb וְנֶחֱלֵיתִי,[2] whose well-attested meaning is "be/become sick, weak."

Commentary
Gabriel Is Told to Explain the Vision to Daniel (8:15–18)

Daniel's vision had ended in 8:14, and he "sought an understanding" of it (8:15), probably through prayer. Note the similarity to the previous vision, where Daniel requested an explanation (7:16). The result here was a resumption of visionary experience, in which he saw someone whose appearance was "like the appearance of a man" (8:15). In the NT too, angels are sometimes described as human in appearance, a "man" or "young man" (Mk 16:5; Lk 24:4). The human voice that Daniel heard came from "between [the banks of] the Ulai" (Dan 8:16), on or above the water, where no mortal man could be standing (cf. Mt 14:25–29 and the voice from heaven in Mt 3:17 when Jesus was being baptized in the Jordan). Therefore, it is probably God who commands

---

[2] See Montgomery, *Daniel*, 355–56, who suggests the meaning "was befallen" for the Niphal here, and the discussion in Collins, *Daniel*, 342.

the angel. Yet God speaks in "a human voice" (Dan 8:16) so that his words will be intelligible to Daniel.

God addresses the angel by name, "Gabriel" (8:16), the first time an angel is named in the Scriptures. The name itself, גַּבְרִיאֵל, *Gabriel*, forms a play on the noun for "a man," גֶּבֶר, *geber*, describing the angel's appearance in 8:15. The noun גֶּבֶר denotes a "man as strong" in contrast to women and children, "non-combatants whom he is to defend" (BDB). It is also related to the noun גִּבּוֹר, "warrior." Therefore, "Gabriel" probably means "God is my warrior." Gabriel is named again in 9:21, and he is the angel sent for the annunciation of the birth of John the Baptist (Lk 1:11–19) and the annunciation of the incarnation of God the Son by the Virgin Mary (Lk 1:26–33). His primary function seems to be the delivery of the most important messages from God, confirming that the voice Daniel heard emanating from the canal was God's.

Gabriel reveals to Daniel that the vision "concerns the time of the end" (8:17). This phrase must be interpreted according to the context of the vision in which it occurs. Here the construct phrase עֶת־קֵץ, "the time of the end," is not intended to be taken in an absolute sense as if the vision is only about the final eschatological events preceding the return of Christ (see the second textual note on 8:17). Instead, Daniel is told that the vision's emphasis is on the time period spoken of earlier at the end of this vision, the 2,300 evenings and mornings (8:14).[3] This is confirmed in 8:19, where this time period is called "the latter part of [God's] indignant anger" and "the appointed time of the end." It is also confirmed in 8:26, where the Daniel's vision is called "the vision of the evenings and the mornings." In terms of history, the vision of chapter 8 focuses on the persecution inflicted by Antiochus IV Epiphanes in the second century BC, although in some ways he foreshadows the Antichrist's persecution throughout the church age, which intensifies before Christ's return.

Daniel's fright at being in close proximity to God's messenger is similar to the reaction of his contemporary prophet, Ezekiel, at the vision of God enthroned over angels that he received beside a canal in Babylon earlier but also in the sixth century BC (Ezek 1:28; cf. Ezek 3:23; 44:4). In keeping with the similarity to Ezekiel, whom God always addresses as "son of man," Gabriel addresses Daniel with that title, which emphasizes Daniel's humanity.[4] Daniel's reaction is to fall into a deep sleep and lie prone on the ground facedown, demonstrating his terror as a sinner and his unworthiness to be in God's presence, as he also does in 10:9 (cf. Is 6:5).

However, that posture was not appropriate for him as he would receive the divine revelation. Gabriel touches him and makes him stand (similar to 10:10). In Ezekiel's prophetic call, the Spirit entered him and enabled him to stand and

---

[3] This is the consensus of the majority of commentators. See Baldwin, *Daniel*, 159; Collins, *Daniel*, 338; Walvoord, *Daniel*, 191; Young, *Daniel*, 176.

[4] See the textual note and commentary on 7:13, including "The Identity of the Son of Man." For the use of the title for Ezekiel, see Hummel, *Ezekiel 1–20*, 74, 83.

receive the divine Word (Ezek 2:1–3). The touch represented the conferral of forgiveness and strength to carry out the prophetic role. The mouths of Isaiah (6:7) and Jeremiah (1:9) were touched to enable their ministry of preaching. Daniel is not called to be a preacher, but a seer and author (7:1; 8:26; 12:4).

Gabriel Explains the Ram and the Male Goat (8:19–22)

The brief statement in 8:17 about the time horizon of the vision is expanded. Daniel is told that the explanation will center on "the latter part of the indignant anger" (8:19), that is, the 2,300 evenings/mornings (8:14), since the vision emphasizes "the appointed time of the end" (8:19). This becomes evident in the following explanation of the vision. Gabriel quickly and concisely explains the ram and the goat (8:21–22), but then he slows down to concentrate on the explanation of the little horn (8:23–25).

The noun זַעַם, "indignant anger" (8:19), denotes furious judgment in a strong reaction to human sin. With the possible exception of Hos 7:16, it always refers to God's wrath. The indignant anger that God would have at Antiochus is not only a sign of his wrath against the king's sins but also the result of his zeal for defending and saving his people. This is confirmed by Gabriel's use of the term מוֹעֵד, "appointed time" (8:19), which indicates that God would not ignore the evil oppressor or his people's suffering, but would bring both to an end at a time that he has already determined. The same implication is in other Daniel verses with מוֹעֵד, "appointed time" (11:27, 29, 35; 12:7). Speaking eschatologically, Jesus affirms the same thing about God's administration of history for the sake of the elect (Mt 24:22; cf. Lk 18:7; 2 Pet 3:1–10).

As in Daniel 7, the explanation in Daniel 8 sometimes uses "king" by metonymy to denote a kingdom. Gabriel's explanation of the ram and the goat are precise:

Symbol in the Vision	Explanation
Ram with two horns	Medo-Persian Empire
Goat	Greek kingdoms
Large horn	First Greek king (Alexander)
Four horns	Four later Greek kingdoms

In addition, Gabriel adds two other pieces of information that were implied in the vision: the four kingdoms would arise from the first king's nation, meaning that Alexander's successors were also Greek kings, and these kingdoms would be less powerful than Alexander's. All this is consistent with the depictions of the second (Medo-Persian) and third (Greek) kingdoms in chapters 2 and 7, but chapter 8 gives finer details about them.[5]

---

[5] See the excursus "The Four-Kingdom Schema in Daniel."

Gabriel Explains the Little Horn (8:23–26)

Starting with 8:23, Gabriel's explanation of the vision slows down to give particular attention to the persecution of God's people under the (Greek) Seleucid king Antiochus IV Epiphanes (175–164 BC). This king would arise "in the latter part of their kingdom" (8:23). If the starting point of the Greek kingdoms is dated from Alexander's first year as king after he defeated Darius III, the last Medo-Persian king, in 331 BC, and the endpoint is dated to the capture of Egypt by Octavian (who later received the title Caesar Augustus) following the Battle of Actium in 31 BC, the period of Greek dominance prophesied in this vision lasted three hundred years. If "the latter part" (Dan 8:23) means "the second half," it would begin one hundred fifty years after 331 BC, hence 181 BC. Antiochus came to the throne in 175 BC and first began his persecution of the Jews in Jerusalem when he sacked the temple in 169 BC.

This king would arise when "the transgressors are complete" (8:23). This may refer to those Jews who transgressed the Law of Moses by voluntarily leading Jerusalem's inhabitants in adopting Hellenistic customs. They urged Jews to abandon the OT covenant and instead make a covenant with the Gentiles (1 Macc 1:11–15). They built a gymnasium in Jerusalem and obliterated the circumcision of Jews.[6] They are even called παράνομοι, "law violators" (1 Macc 1:11). They are seen here as aiding and abetting Antiochus.

Antiochus is described as "merciless" and one "who understands enigmas" (see the second and third textual notes on 8:23). Polybius affirms Antiochus' craftiness: "King Antiochus was a man of ability in military practice and daring in tactics and showed himself worthy of the royal name."[7] However, his ability to discern enigmas has an ominous tone in this context. Like the serpent in Gen 3:1, he would use his shrewdness to perceive how to deceive and seduce God's people into sin and apostasy. Thus it implies that he would use his insight in sinister and duplicitous ways, as affirmed in 8:25.

Antiochus would be mighty and successful, but "not by his own power" (8:24). Because this phrase is missing in some Theodotionic manuscripts, some scholars would omit it as a secondary intrusion, repeated from 8:22, which has the identical words (וְלֹא בְכֹחוֹ).[8] However, it is a reminder that all the earthly power of governing authorities derives ultimately from God (Dan 2:21; 4:32 [ET 4:35]; Rom 13:1). God's will is always for them to do good, and so evil rulers are abusing their God-given authority. Nevertheless, God may permit them to do evil for a period of time when this serves his overarching plan of salvation,

---

[6] Greek custom was for athletes in a gymnasium to perform nude (γυμνός, the root of "gymn-"). 1 Macc 1:15 states: ἐποίησαν ἑαυτοῖς ἀκροβυστίας, literally, "they made for themselves foreskins," which the RSV paraphrases, "[they] removed the marks of circumcision."

[7] Polybius, *Histories*, 28.18: ὅτι Ἀντίοχος ὁ βασιλεὺς ἦν καὶ πρακτικὸς καὶ μεγαλεπίβολος καὶ τοῦ τῆς βασιλείας προσχήματος ἄξιος.

[8] Scholars who would omit it include Collins, *Daniel*, 340; Hartman and Di Lella, *Daniel*, 223; and Montgomery, *Daniel*, 350, 354. Lucas notes the issue but takes a neutral position (*Daniel*, 221).

as Jesus affirmed about Pilate (Jn 19:11). God's will is always to drive people to repentance and bring his faithful believers to everlasting salvation.

One of the acts of Antiochus is that "he will destroy wonderful/miraculous things" (see the first textual note on 8:24). This likely is a reference to the sacking of the Jerusalem temple and the removal of its vessels in 169 BC (1 Macc 1:20–24). The items he stole, including "the golden altar, the lampstand … the table for the bread of the Presence, the cups for drink offerings, the bowls, the golden censers, the curtain" (1 Macc 1:21–22), were essential for the sacrificial divine worship God had instituted to bestow the forgiveness of sins and everlasting salvation on his OT people, all foreshadowing the sacrifice of Christ (see Hebrews 9). Thus the sacrilege of Antiochus can be compared to the theft of the Eucharistic vessels and liturgical appointments from a church in the attempt to deprive a congregation of God's Word and Sacraments, his means of bestowing his saving grace on his people.

The wicked king would succeed in doing this (Dan 8:24) for a while. Antiochus' deceit came to the fore two years later when he sent his tribute collector with a large military force to Jerusalem and its people (1 Macc 1:29). He "spoke to them peaceful words in deceit, and they believed him" (ἐλάλησεν αὐτοῖς λόγους εἰρηνικοὺς ἐν δόλῳ καὶ ἐνεπίστευσαν αὐτῷ, 1 Macc 1:30). But then he "attacked the city suddenly … and destroyed many people of Israel" (ἐπέπεσεν ἐπὶ τὴν πόλιν ἐξάπινα … καὶ ἀπώλεσεν λαὸν πολὺν ἐξ Ισραηλ, 1 Macc 1:30). In this way, Antiochus fulfilled the prophecy "through his cunning, he will … cause deception to succeed by his power" and "destroy many who are at ease" (Dan 8:25).[9]

It is well-known that Antiochus did "magnify himself in his heart" (8:25), taking the title θεὸς Ἐπιφάνης, "God Manifest," which he had stamped on the coins he issued (see the commentary on 8:9–12). Antiochus' high opinion of himself was manifest in some of his antics as king, which seemed so outlandish to his subjects that in their private speech they derisively changed his title from Ἐπιφάνης, *epiphanes*, "Manifest," to Ἐπιμανής, *epimanes*, "the Madman."[10]

Antiochus defied "the Prince of princes" (8:25), God himself, not only by claiming to be God Manifest but also when he defiled the temple and converted it into a place for worship of the Greek gods (1 Macc 1:54; 2 Macc 6:1–2). This, however, lasted only a short time in God's calculation, since Antiochus died a little over three years later, in late December 164.[11] He died "not by human power" (8:25). Accounts of his death vary as to the cause, but they all agree that he died of (what we would call) natural causes and was not killed or murdered by a person.[12]

---

[9] See the third textual note on 8:25 for the possibility that the Hebrew translated "at ease" in 8:25 could mean "suddenly," as ἐξάπινα does in 1 Macc 1:30.

[10] See Polybius, *Histories*, 26.1.

[11] See also the commentary on 8:13–14, which discusses events in this general time period.

[12] 1 Macc 6:1–16; 2 Macc 9:1–28; Polybius, *Histories*, 31.11.

When Gabriel finishes his explanation, he assures Daniel that the vision "is true" (8:26), meaning that what he had been shown would indeed happen as predicted. Gabriel's reference to the vision as "the vision of the evenings and the mornings" (8:26) emphasizes the short duration of the persecution and defilement of the temple in Jerusalem, giving hope and comfort to Daniel and his readers who would endure the suffering foretold.

Despite its hopeful message, Daniel is told to "close up" (the imperative סְתֹם) the vision because its fulfillment is many days away from Daniel's time (8:26). The identical imperative is used in this way again in 12:4, where the context indicates that it refers to physically rolling up the scroll that contains the written record of the revelation and sealing it to prevent unauthorized opening. The Hebrew verb carries the connotation of prohibiting the use of an item so that it can be kept from use or kept safe or protected from abuse.[b] The passive participle in 12:9 has the corresponding meaning, "closed up."

The purpose of this closing of the vision is so that the wise—those who have faith in God—will be able to understand and use Daniel's vision, but others will not. See 12:10, and compare Jesus' explanation of his use of parables (Mt 13:10–17).[13]

(b) Gen 26:15, 18; 2 Ki 3:19, 25; Ezek 28:3; Ps 51:8 (ET 51:6); Neh 4:1 (ET 4:7); 2 Chr 32:3–4, 30

Daniel's Reaction to the Vision (8:27)

Daniel's reaction to the vision is similar to the toll the previous vision took on him (7:15, 28). However, his reaction here is more extreme, perhaps because he understood that this vision predicted severe persecution against his people.

When Daniel recovered, he went about the king's business. Daniel may have been serving the royal court in a reduced capacity due to his advanced age.[14]

Daniel not only was appalled by the vision, since it predicted dire times ahead, but he admits that he did not understand it. This is not to be taken in the absolute sense that he understood nothing about the vision. Instead, it probably indicates that he did not understand how it would be fulfilled in future history. While it is possible to obtain a good understanding of the past, it is much harder to understand what the future will be like. Daniel was telling us that the vision was closed up for him at this time (8:26). It is now open to us, mainly because we can look at it in hindsight, which is always easier than trying to view the future with foresight.

---

[13] See also the commentary on Dan 7:28. Compare Revelation 5, where Jesus alone has the right to break the seals and open the scroll, showing that he alone has authority to govern world history for the sake of those he has redeemed.

[14] See "Date and Authorship according to the Book" in "Date, Authorship, and Unity" in the introduction.

Excursus
Dispensational Interpretations of Daniel 8

Dispensational premillennialism is the radically literalistic interpretation of eschatological prophecy in the Bible—including the visions in Daniel—that is popular among many fundamentalist and evangelical Christian groups.[1] Proponents of this view often see in Daniel 8 an eschatological prophecy of history some of which still lies in the future, instead of an OT prophecy that was completely fulfilled at the time of Antiochus Epiphanes (175–164 BC).[2] The impetus for this approach is the phrase "the time of the end" (8:17), which dispensationalists read absolutely, as if it applied to the end of all earthly history, without regard for the contextual clues that indicate that it refers to the end of the period covered by this vision of Daniel (see the commentary on 8:17). Once this misinterpretive step is made, dispensationalists are forced to find some application to their particular eschatological interpretation of biblical prophecy.

Some simply attempt to interpret all of 8:23–26 as applying to a future Antichrist and not at all to Antiochus. This, of course, is difficult to maintain, since the king described in these verses arises in the latter part of the time of the Greek kingdoms spoken about in 8:20–22 (see 8:23 and "Greece" in 8:21). Therefore, many dispensationalists speak of a double fulfillment of 8:23–26: these verses were fulfilled by Antiochus, but they will be equally fulfilled by a future Antichrist.

However, the problems inherent in a double fulfillment view are manifold. The vision in Daniel 8 adds further detail about part of the sequence of the four kingdoms in both chapter 2 and chapter 7 of Daniel,[3] and those four kingdoms lead up to the arrival of the kingdom of God at the first advent of Jesus Christ,[4] a unique, one-time event in history. While Christ will come again, his second advent will be in power and glory to bring this world to its close, quite unlike his first advent. A double fulfillment theory of 8:23–26 risks blurring the distinction between the first and second advents of Christ by confusing the historical circumstances that led to his first advent with the historical circumstances prior to his return.[5] It also risks blurring the distinction between Daniel 8 and Daniel

---

[1] See further "Eschatology and Dispensational Premillennial Interpretations of Daniel" in the introduction.

[2] For a summary of dispensational interpretations of Daniel 8, see Walvoord, *Daniel*, 194–96.

[3] See "Major Emphases in Daniel 8" in "Introduction to Daniel 8."

[4] See "The Messiah in Daniel: An Overview" in "Major Themes" in the introduction.

[5] Granted, the fact that God preserved his people through the persecution under Antiochus Epiphanes can encourage Christians that God will also preserve them through the persecution

7, which depicts the Antichrist as a little horn that is not to be confused with the little horn in Daniel 8.[6]

A double-fulfillment theory raises an entire set of troubling questions. If a predictive prophecy in Scripture speaks of one fulfillment and neither it nor its context indicates two fulfillments, what is the justification for positing them? If we suppose there are two fulfillments, how do we know there are not more? How could we then set any limit on the number of fulfillments? How does this method of interpreting Scripture resist turning the text into a malleable object in the hands of a reader who chooses a second (or third or fourth) fulfillment to suit a personally held ideology or theology, so that Scripture means anything the reader wants it to mean, regardless of the intent of the original author (both the human author and the Holy Spirit)? That is to say, how does one resist practicing *eisegesis* instead of *exegesis*?

These fundamental hermeneutical questions are often not asked nor answered by dispensationalists who advocate a double fulfillment of 8:23–26. The root of the question that is never addressed by dispensationalists is whether one may understand a prophecy that predicts a specific person or event to be fulfilled several times by multiple persons or events *when there is no indication in the text to that effect*.

By way of illustration, consider the following two NT passages, the first of which indicates multiple fulfillments of prophecy, the second of which does not:

> Children, it is the last hour, and as you have heard that an antichrist is coming, and now *many* antichrists have come. Therefore, we know that it is the last hour (1 Jn 2:18)

> And every spirit that does not profess Jesus is not from God. This is *the* spirit of the Antichrist, that you have heard was coming and now is already in the world. (1 Jn 4:3)

1 Jn 2:18 indicates that there are many antichrists. The prophecy is fulfilled multiple times in multiple people, as John clearly states. However, in 1 Jn 4:3 the apostle speaks of "the [one and only] spirit of the Antichrist," which is characterized by a specific attribute: no profession of Jesus.[7] Thus the text of 1 Jn 2:18 predicts multiple fulfillments, and each of the "many antichrists" will

---

instigated by the Antichrist (see "Major Emphases in Daniel 8" in "Introduction to Daniel 8"). But this *pastoral application* of 8:23–26 as encouragement for those who live during the historical period of the Antichrist is quite different from interpreting 8:23–26 as an OT prophecy that God will fulfill a second time.

[6] For the little horn in Daniel 7 as the Antichrist and for reasons why it is not to be confused with the little horn in Daniel 8, see figure 10 in the excursus "The Four-Kingdom Schema in Daniel," the commentary on 7:8, 20–21, 25, and the excursus "The Lutheran Confessions on the Antichrist in Daniel."

[7] 1 Jn 2:22–24 expands this in Trinitarian terms: he who denies that Jesus is the Christ is the Antichrist, who denies both the Father and the Son, because whoever denies the Son also does not have the Father.

manifest the one "spirit of the Antichrist" by not professing Jesus (1 Jn 4:3). That one manifestation may occur in multiple people; there may be many antichrists, but they share the one spirit that fails to profess Jesus.

When we turn to Dan 8:23–26 we read of only one "merciless king." There is no indication that there will be several of them. We should note that it is true that the merciless king that fulfilled the prophecy of 8:23–26, Antiochus Epiphanes, is clearly depicted in terms similar to ones used to describe the Antichrist later in 11:36–39. Thus it would be appropriate to argue that the merciless king of Daniel 8 foreshadows the Antichrist.[8] However, it would be improper to hold that Daniel 8 was only partially fulfilled by Antiochus and so Daniel 8 remained unfulfilled until the time of the Antichrist. Since there is no indication in the text itself of a second "merciless king," the chapter was fulfilled by Antiochus without any need to posit a second such king.

Moreover, if an interpreter requires two fulfillments of the prophecy of Daniel 8, what is to stop the interpreter from requiring this prophecy to be fulfilled in others who have persecuted Jews (as an ethnic group) or have persecuted God's people (OT and NT believers)? Did it also find fulfillment in Haman in the book of Esther? Or in any of the Roman emperors who persecuted Christians? Or in Adolf Hitler? Or in anyone who simply opposes Christianity? If not, why not? The dispensationalist hermeneutic of double (or multiple) fulfillment has no controlling mechanism to rule out any of these possible fulfillments. Therefore, carried to the extreme, dispensational hermeneutics render this prophecy virtually meaningless in its details since so many of the details in Daniel 8 clearly and specifically apply to Antiochus, but do not in any meaningful way apply to other persecutors. Thus the dispensationalist multiple fulfillment scheme, if taken to its logical extreme, simply transforms the text into a cipher that can be used to brand anyone who persecutes God's people as a fulfillment of Daniel 8. While dispensationalists often stop short of seeing more than two fulfillments of a prophecy such as 8:23–26, their method contains no safeguards against such an excessive approach.

We should note, however, that some dispensational interpreters sense the inherent problems embedded in a dual fulfillment theory for Daniel 8. Therefore, they view Antiochus as fulfilling these prophecies, but also see Antiochus as a foreshadowing of the Antichrist, who is symbolized by the little horn in Daniel 7. There is good reason to view the little horn of Daniel 8 as a foreshadowing of the activity of the little horn of Daniel 7. The most obvious of these is that both are characterized as little horns. However, one need not follow a dispensational interpretation of Scripture to adopt such a view.

What is unique among dispensationalists who view 8:23–26 as fulfilled in Antiochus but also foreshadowing the Antichrist is that they insist that "the (appointed) time of the end" (8:17, 19) and similar phrases point to an

---

[8] See further the commentary on 11:36–39.

eschatological fulfillment that cannot apply to Antiochus. As a result, they often attempt to pick out details in 8:23–26 that they feel are not apt descriptions of Antiochus and therefore must be about the Antichrist.[9] In practice, these dispensationalists do not see a foreshadowing of the Antichrist in these verses; they do not consider Antiochus to be merely a shadow or shape whose general profile is similar to that of the later Antichrist. Instead, they are simply attempting to do on a finer scale what is done by those who simply apply the whole of 8:23–26 to a future Antichrist. They deny, despite the clear statements of the text, that some portions of 8:23–26 were fulfilled in the latter days of the Greek kings described in 8:20–22.

The theological problem with these dispensational approaches to Daniel 8 is that they deny the comfort that the vision is intended to offer readers. For the original readers in the sixth century BC and for all those who lived before or during the persecution of Antiochus in the second century BC, Daniel offered hope and comfort that God had already determined an end to the fierce persecution before it happened. If the chapter only partially applied to Antiochus, the original readers or those who lived during the persecution could not know what actions of Antiochus God would or would not stop, since only some of the things prophesied applied to him.

For later readers of Daniel 8, including Christians today, the vision offers comfort through the complete fulfillment of its words. Since God fully kept his promise to overcome Antiochus, the chapter gives comfort to those facing persecutions throughout the church age, including persecution by the Antichrist, whom Antiochus foreshadowed. We too will be completely delivered by God on the Last Day, when the Antichrist and his puppeteer, Satan, shall be judged (2 Thess 2:8; Rev 19:20; cf. Rom 16:20; Rev 20:10).[10]

In contrast, dispensational interpretation either makes the text an easily manipulated script in the hands of the interpreter, or it makes the text a thicket of interwoven near-fulfillment and far-fulfillment prophecies that invite speculation instead of offering comfort. In the end, the view that the prophecy was not adequately or completely fulfilled in Antiochus raises doubts about whether God actually fulfilled his promises about the past and whether he will completely fulfill his promises about the present and the future.

---

[9] Walvoord, *Daniel*, 197–99.

[10] The Antichrist is called "the man of lawlessness" by St. Paul in 2 Thessalonians 2. He is pictured as the beast from the earth in Rev 13:11–18, and the false prophet in Rev 16:13; 19:20; 20:10. See further the commentary on Dan 7:8, 20–21, 25.

Daniel 9:1–27

Daniel's Prayer and Vision concerning Jerusalem during the Post-Babylonian Kingdoms

Introduction to Daniel 9

9:1–19   Daniel's Prayer

9:20–27   Gabriel Explains Jerusalem's Future

Introduction to Daniel 9

Major Emphases in Daniel 9

Daniel's vision in chapter 9 (9:20–27) is different in several respects from the other visions in chapters 7–12. The most obvious is that it comes in response to a prayer. The narrative introduction to the prayer (9:1–4a) is followed by the text of Daniel's prayer (9:4b–19), which takes up most of the chapter, sixteen of twenty-seven verses. The chapter is a remarkable demonstration of God's gracious responsiveness to prayer in faith. Daniel's prayer was answered by God sending Gabriel to console and instruct him. Moreover, his prayer apparently elicited the divine decree (the "word" that went forth [9:23, 25]) that prompted Cyrus to issue his edict permitting the Judeans to return home and rebuild Jerusalem with its temple, fulfilling Is 44:28. Thus Daniel's prayer helped shape world history and momentous events in the redemption of Israel.[1]

Daniel's prayer is one of repentance.[2] As such, it is a fine example of the application of Law and Gospel to the life of a believer.[3] In the first part, Daniel contrasts God's faithfulness to his promises with the unfaithfulness of Daniel's people (9:4b–6). God's great act of faithfulness that Daniel mentions in his prayer is that God keeps "mercy for those who love him and keep his commands" (9:4). By saying this, Daniel admits that even those who (like himself) believe in and obey God must rely on his mercy, grace, and favor. This is reinforced by his preceding statement that he besought God with "a plea for grace" (תַּחֲנוּנִים, 9:3, also in 9:17–18) and by his later tragic confession that "we did not entreat [וְלֹא־חִלִּינוּ] the face" of God (9:13), as well as by his final plea for God to act for his own sake and for the sake of his name (9:19). All of these implicitly affirm that salvation is purely by God's grace, not by striving to keep God's commands (Rom 9:30–31).

However, Israel not only disobeyed God, but also rebelled against him. In his mercy, God sent prophets to warn his people about the consequences of their rebellion and to invite them to keep his Law again. They refused, as Daniel admits in his prayer (Dan 9:5–6).

The second part of Daniel's prayer contrasts God's compassion and forgiveness with his people's rejection of God's forgiveness (9:7–14). Note that according to Daniel's prayer, faith in God's forgiveness is lived out by obeying God. The person who has received God's forgiveness *wants* to live the way

---

[1] See further the commentary on 9:25: "The First Phase of the Seventy Weeks: From the Word to Restore Jerusalem to the Advent of the Messiah."

[2] A portion of the following discussion is adapted from Steinmann, *Is God Listening? Making Prayer a Part of Your Life*, 69–70.

[3] The first of Luther's Ninety-Five Theses is that the Christian life is characterized by repentance (AE 31:25).

God's Word teaches us humans to live. Saving faith in God manifests itself in good works prescribed in the Scriptures.

However, Daniel had to admit, "We did not listen to the voice of Yahweh our God by walking in his teachings that he set before us by the hand of his servants, the prophets. All Israel transgressed your teaching and turned away by not listening to your voice" (9:10–11). The phrase translated as "in his teachings" is בְּתוֹרֹתָיו, using the plural of the Hebrew noun תּוֹרָה, *torah*, and the singular is used in "your teaching" (תּוֹרָתֶךָ). This word is often translated "law." However, the Hebrew word denotes more than the idea of laws that tell us what to do and what not to do. It involves more than a rigid way for people to determine what they should do in each situation by applying a set of rules. The verbal root of תּוֹרָה is יָרָה, whose Hiphil (H) can mean "to instruct" and is used for God instructing his people in the way of life, forgiveness, and redemption.[a] Through the Scriptures, God's people did not merely receive laws. They first received salvation from God, then received his laws in the context of instructions to show to each other love, mercy, and forgiveness—the very things that God had already showed them in his actions toward them. When they did not show these things toward others, they showed that they had also rejected God's forgiveness (cf. Jn 14:24; 1 Jn 3:6–10). Daniel's prayer admits that the Israelites received God's punishment because they rejected God's mercy and forgiveness.

The third part of Daniel's prayer is a request (9:15–16). He asks God to forgive his people once again. He bases his request on God's great act of redemption in the OT: leading his people out of bondage in Egypt. Throughout the OT, this one great act of Yahweh is the defining moment of Israel's relationship with him. When they were totally helpless with the mightiest army in the world bearing down on them, God parted the Red Sea and saved them. They did nothing, and God did everything (Ex 14:13–14; cf. 1 Cor 10:1–4). By citing this paradigmatic action by God, Daniel is again relying on God to do everything needed to grant his request and save his people.

The final section of Daniel's prayer calls on God to listen (9:17–19). In this section, he repeats that he is relying on God and his compassion and forgiveness. He admits that the reason that God should act is not because Daniel or his people are deserving, but because God and his honor deserve to be recognized by all people. Already in the OT, God's salvation had this evangelistic purpose, which intensifies in the NT as the Gospel of Jesus Christ spreads to all nations and peoples (Acts 1:8).

Daniel's prayer relies on another great theme that runs through this chapter: God always keeps his promises. God had promised through the prophet Jeremiah that he would restore his people to the homeland he had given them (Jer 16:14–15; 25:11–12; 29:10; see also Deut 30:1–5; Is 11:11–16). Daniel in 9:2 cites Jeremiah by name and explains that it was this promise that moved Daniel to pray. After Daniel's prayer, God reaffirms his promise "to restore and rebuild Jerusalem" (9:25). God's promise to forgive, redeem, and restore his people is Daniel's great hope.

(a) E.g., Ex 4:12, 15; 1 Ki 8:36; Is 2:3; Pss 27:11; 86:11; 119:33, 102; Prov 4:4, 11

God's promise leads to the last great theme in this chapter: the messianic salvation to be fulfilled when God puts an end to sin, atones for wickedness, and brings in everlasting righteousness (9:24). This chapter is the only one in Daniel where the word מָשִׁיחַ, "Messiah," occurs.[4] Gabriel appears to Daniel and brings him a message concerning the city of Jerusalem that culminates with the promised Savior (9:24–27), who is called מָשִׁיחַ נָגִיד, "Messiah, a Leader" (9:25). This messianic theme ties all of Daniel 9 together. God hears the repentant sinner's prayer because of the merit and atonement of the Messiah, Jesus Christ. God keeps his promises most vividly in the ministry of Christ, who fulfilled them all (2 Cor 1:20). God has redeemed his people through the work of Christ. Through faith alone in Christ alone, believers are credited with his own divine righteousness.[b]

The Unity of Daniel 9

It is common for critical scholars to view the prayer (9:4b–19) as a late editorial addition to this chapter.[5] They commonly cite the use of the name "Yahweh," which is present in the book of Daniel only in the introduction to the prayer (9:2, 4a) and the prayer itself (9:8, 10, 13–14, 20). They also commonly observe that the prayer presents "a Deuteronomistic theology" with its heavy emphasis on Israel's punishment by God because Israel abandoned him to follow the ways of the surrounding nations.[6] This theology supposedly marks this section as foreign to the context and out of place in the rest of the book. However, even some critical scholars have defended the authenticity of the prayer,[7] and some evangelical scholars have rejected the assertion that it is specifically "Deuteronomistic" in its theological outlook.[8] The dual theme of Israel's infidelity and God's mercy despite his people's unworthiness was articulated by Moses in Deuteronomy. Yet it is part of the divine message of Law and Gospel, sin and grace, which extends throughout the OT and NT. Its pres-

(b) Rom 1:17; 3:21–26; 4:3–6; 5:17; 2 Cor 5:21; Phil 3:9; 2 Pet 1:1

---

[4] However, other references to the Messiah are found in other parts of the book. See further "The Messiah in Daniel: An Overview" in "Major Themes" in the introduction.

[5] E.g., Montgomery, *Daniel*, 362.

[6] See, for example, van Deventer, "The End of the End, or, What Is the Deuteronomist (Still) Doing in Daniel?" and Collins, *Daniel*, 359–60, who notes that some scholars would include the entire chapter, not simply the prayer, as having connections to Deuteronomistic themes.

[7] Jones, "The Prayer in Daniel IX."

[8] Young, *Daniel*, 185–87, notes that in 9:6–10 Daniel is referring to the OT prophets and that "the law/teaching of Moses" in 9:11, 13 refers to the entire Pentateuch (not just Deuteronomy or its theology). Leupold, *Daniel*, 382, also considers the prayer to reflect the OT Scriptures in general, not simply Deuteronomy. He states on the basis of the prayer:

> Daniel appears as a man who is deeply rooted in the knowledge of God's dealings with His people in the past and one who is thoroughly familiar with the sacred Scriptures. As a result his understanding of the way of salvation is soundly evangelical. He solemnly disavows every thought that might savor of work-righteousness and builds his every petition on the mercies of his God.

ence (or absence) cannot be used as an argument for the authorship or date of a particular biblical text.

A number of indications in Daniel's prayer mark it as one with the surrounding context in the book he authored.[9] A prime indication is the name of God. Throughout the book of Daniel, the particular name used for God is appropriate for the specific context. The use of God's proper name, "Yahweh," is most appropriate in chapter 9 since it is a prayer by Daniel, a believer in Yahweh, based on the promises made by the prophets in the name of Yahweh. Besides the divine name, some of the other vocabulary of the prayer is repeated in the vision at the end of the chapter, while several wordplays flow from the prayer into the vision, making the prayer and its concerns closely tied to the rest of the chapter. These links include the following, which are obvious in Hebrew even though some of them are obscured in English translations:[10]

Prayer	*Vision*
So you poured out ... and the oath	The week[11] ... is poured out
וַתִּתַּךְ ... וְהַשְּׁבֻעָה, 9:11	הַשָּׁבוּעַ ... תִּתַּךְ, 9:27
To acquire insight	To give you insight
וּלְהַשְׂכִּיל, 9:13	לְהַשְׂכִּילְךָ, 9:22
To turn ... to acquire insight	Have insight ... again[12]
לָשׁוּב ... וּלְהַשְׂכִּיל, 9:13	וְתַשְׂכֵּל ... לְהָשִׁיב, 9:25
Our desolations	Desolator ... desolator
שֹׁמְמֹתֵינוּ, 9:18	מְשֹׁמֵם ... שֹׁמֵם, 9:27

Since Daniel is fond of such repetition and wordplay elsewhere,[13] these examples serve to demonstrate that the prayer was not a late addition, but is part of the fabric out of which Daniel constructed the chapter.

Moreover, Daniel's prayer is prompted by his reading of Jeremiah (Dan 9:2). Jeremiah was an older contemporary sixth-century prophet who was able to remain in Jerusalem when Daniel and Ezekiel were exiled to Babylon. Daniel's prayer fits well into the opening context of Daniel 9 because the prayer contains a wealth of allusions to Jeremiah's prophecies, demonstrating that Daniel had prayed this prayer not on the basis of one or two passages in Jeremiah, but based on the entire book (see the commentary on 9:1–19).

---

[9] See further "Date and Authorship according to the Book" in "Date, Authorship, and Unity" in the introduction.

[10] Jones, "The Prayer in Daniel IX," 491.

[11] The Hebrew word for "week" is very similar to that for "oath."

[12] The Hebrew verb translated adverbially as "again" in 9:25 is a different form of the same verb translated "to turn" in 9:13.

[13] See, for example, the third textual note on 5:6 and the fourth textual note and the commentary on 5:12.

In turn, Nehemiah's later prayer about Jerusalem (446 BC) draws much of its language from Daniel's prayer (Neh 1:5–11), and Nehemiah's prayer in Nehemiah 9 (445 BC) is similar to Daniel's prayer but expanded.

Therefore, Daniel's prayer fits well within the time period after Jeremiah's prophecies but before the ministry of Nehemiah, that is, in the latter part of the life of Daniel himself.[14] The setting of Daniel 9 is "in the first year of Darius" (9:1), that is, Cyrus,[15] whose first full regnal year began on 1 Nisan 538 (March 24, 538). The events of Daniel 9 occurred shortly before Cyrus issued his edict in 538 that permitted the exiles to return to Jerusalem (see the commentary on 9:1–2).

---

[14] See further "Date and Authorship according to the Book" in "Date, Authorship, and Unity" in the introduction.

[15] See the excursus "The Identity of Darius the Mede."

Daniel 9:1–19
Daniel's Prayer

Translation

9 ⁱIn the first year of Darius, son of Ahasuerus, a Mede by descent, who was made king over the kingdom of the Chaldeans, ²in the first year of his reign, I, Daniel, understood in the scrolls the number of years that was the Word of Yahweh to the prophet Jeremiah for fulfilling the devastations of Jerusalem: seventy years.

³I turned my face to the Lord God to seek [him in] prayer and a plea for grace with fasting, sackcloth, and ashes. ⁴I prayed to Yahweh, my God, and made confession. I said, "Please, Lord, the great and feared God who keeps the covenant and mercy for those who love him and keep his commands. ⁵We have sinned, committed iniquity, acted wickedly, rebelled, and turned aside from your commands and standards. ⁶We did not listen to your servants the prophets who spoke in your name to our kings, princes, and fathers, and to all the people of the land.

⁷"Righteousness is yours, Lord, but we are shamefaced this day—the people of Judah, the inhabitants of Jerusalem, and all Israel, both near and far in all the lands where you have banished them because of their wrongdoings that they wrongly committed against you. ⁸Yahweh, we are shamefaced—our kings, our princes, and our fathers, who sinned against you. ⁹Acts of compassion and forgiveness belong to the Lord our God, because we have rebelled against him. ¹⁰We did not listen to the voice of Yahweh our God by walking in his teachings that he set before us by the hand of his servants the prophets. ¹¹All Israel transgressed your teaching and turned away by not listening to your voice. So you poured out upon us the curse and the oath that is written in the teaching of Moses, the servant of God, because we sinned against him.

¹²"He has fulfilled his words that he spoke against us and against our rulers who ruled us by bringing upon us a great disaster that has not been done under all of heaven as that which was done in Jerusalem. ¹³As written in the teaching of Moses, all this disaster came upon us, but we did not entreat the face of Yahweh our God in order to turn from our iniquity and to acquire insight into your truth. ¹⁴Therefore, Yahweh watched over the disaster and brought it upon us, because Yahweh our God is righteous according to all his works that he does, and we did not listen to his voice.

¹⁵"And now, Lord our God, you who brought your people out of the land Egypt with a mighty hand and made for yourself a name as to this day, we have sinned, we have acted wickedly. ¹⁶Lord, according to all your righteous acts, may your anger and wrath turn from your city Jerusalem, your holy mountain, for by our sins and the iniquities of our fathers, Jerusalem and your people have become an object of contempt to everyone around us.

¹⁷"Now listen, our God, to the prayer of your servant and to his plea for grace, and let your face shine upon your desolate sanctuary for the sake of my Lord. ¹⁸Incline, my God, your ear and hear. Open your eyes and see our desolations and the city that is called by your name. For it is not because of our righteous acts that we are casting down our plea for grace before you, but because of your great compassionate acts. ¹⁹Lord, listen! Lord, forgive! Lord, pay attention and act, and do not delay—for your sake, my God, because your city and your people are called by your name."

Textual Notes

9:1–2 בִּשְׁנַת אַחַת ... בִּשְׁנַת אַחַת—The OT usually prefers a cardinal number for counting years, as here, literally, "in the year of one," meaning "in the first year" (see Joüon, § 142 o).

9:2 אֲנִי דָּנִיֵּאל בִּינֹתִי—"I, Daniel, understood" uses a rare form of the Qal perfect of בִּין (Joüon, § 81 d).[1] The expected form would be בַּנְתִי. A similar Qal perfect, וָבִין, occurs in 10:1. Often in the OT, the Hiphil stem of בִּין is used for "understand, comprehend." The Hiphil can also have a causative meaning, as in 8:16; 9:22; 10:14; 11:33. See also the last textual note on 9:23.

לְמַלֹּאות לְחָרְבוֹת יְרוּשָׁלַםִ—Literally, "to fulfill the devastations of Jerusalem," this is an ellipsis meaning "to fulfill [the time allotted for] the devastations of Jerusalem" or "to fulfill [the prophecy] about [the restoration of] the devastations of Jerusalem." The Piel (D) of מָלֵא can mean "to fulfill, complete" a period of time (e.g., Gen 29:27–28; Ex 23:26; Is 65:20; Job 39:2; 2 Chr 36:21 [second occurrence]) or "to fulfill" a word, promise, or plan (e.g., 1 Ki 8:15, 24; Ps 20:5–6 [ET 20:4–5]; 2 Chr 6:4, 15; 36:21 [first occurrence]). Either meaning would be suitable here since Daniel is referring to "the Word of Yahweh" that promises restoration after a period of time: seventy years (see the commentary). The noun חָרְבָּה, "ruin, devastation," often refers to the ruins of a city (e.g., Lev 26:31, 33; Is 44:26; 52:9). It comes from the verb חָרַב, "to be dry," implying lack of water and hence of vegetation and life in general. Here it describes the devastation, destruction, and depopulation of Jerusalem under Nebuchadnezzar and his successors.

9:3 אֲדֹנָי הָאֱלֹהִים—This exact divine title, literally, "(my) Lord the God," occurs only here in the OT. The most similar titles are אֲדֹנָי אֱלֹהֵינוּ, "(my) Lord our God," in Dan 9:9, 15 and Ps 90:17, and אֲדֹנָי אֱלֹהַי, "(my) Lord my God," in Pss 38:16 (ET 38:15); 86:12. In reference to God, the suffix on אֲדֹנָי is always pointed with final *qamets* (-ָ-) instead of the normal *patach* for a plural noun (אֲדֹנַי, "my lords"). The plural-like form of the suffix probably indicates that אֲדֹנָי is a plural of majesty, as is אֱלֹהִים when it refers to the one true "God." While the suffix may retain its semantic value ("*my* Lord,"

---

[1] Joüon states that normally the Hiphil (H) is used for the meaning "understand." That statement is based on Joüon's assumption that the imperfects of the form יָבִין are Hiphil and not Qal (G). However, many lexicons, including BDB, assume that many of the imperfects of the form יָבִין are Qal. In any event, the imperfects of the Qal and the Hiphil would have identical forms.

as translated in 9:17), English translations normally omit the suffix and simply render אֲדֹנָי as "Lord." אֲדֹנָי is the most frequent title in the prayer of Daniel (9:4, 7, 9, 15–17, 19 [three times]), who in some of those cases uses it as a vocative to address God. He uses אֱלֹהִים, "God," without a suffix in again in 9:11 and with first person suffixes in 9:4, 9–10, 13–15, 17–19. While Daniel will use God's name, יהוה, "Yahweh," fairly frequently in this prayer (9:8, 10, 13, 14 [twice]), he clearly shows a preference for calling God "Lord," especially in vocative expressions. He uses "Yahweh" as a vocative only once (9:8). Daniel may be giving evidence of the beginning of the practice of avoiding the use of God's proper name and substituting אֲדֹנָי, "Lord," in its place. That substitution became standard Jewish practice in the intertestamental period and was nearly universal by Jesus' day, as shown by the NT use of κύριος, "Lord," in place of God's proper name.

9:4 לַיהוָה אֱלֹהַי—Daniel addresses God as "Yahweh my God" also in 9:20. This address occurs thirty-nine times in the OT, eleven times in the Psalms (e.g., Pss 7:2, 4 [ET 7:1, 3]; 13:4 [ET 13:3]; 30:3, 13 [ET 30:2, 12]).

אָנָּא—This strong particle of entreaty, translated, "please," could also be rendered, "I (or we) beseech thee!" (BDB). The actual entreaty or petition does not begin until 9:16 (Joüon, § 105 c, note 4).

9:5 וְסוֹר מִמִּצְוֹתֶךָ—After four perfect verbs, each first person plural, the Qal (G) infinitive absolute וְסוֹר, "to turn aside, apostatize," is used as the equivalent of the preceding forms (Joüon, § 123 x), and so it is translated as if it were an inflected perfect too: "we ... turned aside." Daniel uses the same infinitive in a similar way in 9:11. The suffix on the plural noun מִמִּצְוֹתֶךָ, "from your commands," is written defectively for ־ֶיךָ (GKC, § 91 n).

9:7 לְךָ אֲדֹנָי הַצְּדָקָה וְלָנוּ בֹּשֶׁת הַפָּנִים כַּיּוֹם הַזֶּה—The initial position of the two prepositional phrases (לְךָ ... וְלָנוּ) with לְ indicating possession is emphatic: literally, "*to you*, Lord, belongs the righteousness, but *to us* belongs the shame of face as this day." The construct phrase בֹּשֶׁת הַפָּנִים, "the shame of face," recurs in 9:8 and (with לָנוּ) is translated as "we are shamefaced." It also occurs (sometimes with a pronominal suffix) in Jer 7:19; Ps 44:16 (ET 44:15); Ezra 9:7; 2 Chr 32:21.

9:9 לַאדֹנָי אֱלֹהֵינוּ הָרַחֲמִים וְהַסְּלִחוֹת—Literally, "to the Lord our God belong acts of compassion and forgiveness." Both nouns are determined and plural, indicating that they refer to concrete actions rather than abstract concepts.

כִּי מָרַדְנוּ בּוֹ׃—A causal כִּי clause can be based on an implied thought that justifies it (see BDB, s.v. כִּי, 3 c). There is an implied reason why "because we rebelled against him" proves that God has performed acts of compassion and forgiveness. The implied reason is that Israel deserved to be obliterated, not just exiled. Therefore, the continuing existence of Israel in exile shows that God has been merciful to his people.

9:10 לָלֶכֶת בְּתוֹרֹתָיו—"By walking in his teachings" uses the Qal (G) infinitive construct of הָלַךְ with לְ to explain what the result would have been if the Israelites had "listened to, obeyed" (שָׁמַע) God's voice. Faith would have been demonstrated by faithful actions.

The noun תּוֹרָה, "teaching," occurs in Daniel only in 9:10–11, 13. Its plural (9:10) occurs twelve other times in the OT,[a] often with the plural of the noun חֹק, "statute," in the same context (Ex 18:16, 20; Lev 26:46; Ps 105:45; Neh 9:13; חֹק is singular in Is 24:5). The plural of תּוֹרָה refers to God's "teachings," "instructions," "laws," or similar strictures or mandates. The root of תּוֹרָה is the verb יָרָה, whose Hiphil (H) can mean "to instruct" and is used for God instructing his people in the way of life, forgiveness, and redemption. See the discussion of the second part of Daniel's prayer in "Introduction to Daniel 9." The singular of תּוֹרָה in 9:11, 13 in the phrase "written in the teaching of Moses" includes the entire Torah or Pentateuch authored by Moses, but the context refers specifically to the curses in the covenant with Israel established through Moses at Sinai. See further the commentary,

[a] Gen 26:5; Ex 16:28; 18:16, 20; Lev 26:46; Is 24:5; Jer 32:23; Ezek 43:11; 44:5, 24; Ps 105:45; Neh 9:13

9:11 : כִּי חָטָאנוּ לוֹ—The Leningrad codex and hence *BHS* reads, לוֹ, "because we sinned against *him*," which grammatically could refer to Moses. A number of other Masoretic manuscripts read לָךְ, the pausal form of לְךָ, "against *you*," referring to God. Both the Old Greek and Theodotion retain the harder reading ὅτι ἡμάρτομεν αὐτῷ, "because we have sinned against him." The verb חָטָא, "to sin," can be used for sinning against a person or people (see BDB, s.v. חָטָא, Qal, 2 a). Because of the ministerial office of Moses, the covenant mediator, sinning against him would be tantamount to sinning against God. See Num 12:1–15. Both the verb חָטָא and noun חַטָּאת are used in Num 12:11.

9:12 וַיָּקֶם אֶת־דְּבָרָיו—The Hiphil (H) of קוּם means "to fulfill" as also in Deut 9:5. Its direct object in the translation, "his words," follows the Kethib, דְּבָרָיו, which is supported by the Old Greek (τὰ προστάγματα αὐτοῦ) and Theodotion (τοὺς λόγους αὐτοῦ). The Qere reads the singular דְּבָרוֹ, "his word."

9:13 אֵת כָּל־הָרָעָה הַזֹּאת בָּאָה עָלֵינוּ—The subject (כָּל־הָרָעָה הַזֹּאת) of the Qal (G) perfect verb בָּאָה, "came," is introduced by אֵת, which normally is the sign of the direct object. אֵת would be understandable if the verb were Hiphil (הֵבִיא), meaning that God "brought" upon Israel all the evil written in the Torah. (The Hiphil לְהָבִיא was in 9:12, and וַיְבִיאֶהָ is in 9:14.) However, this is one of several examples in the OT where אֵת is used for emphasis when introducing a subject (GKC, § 117 m; Joüon, § 125 j (7)).

וְלֹא־חִלִּינוּ אֶת־פְּנֵי ׀ יְהוָה אֱלֹהֵינוּ—The verb חָלָה II occurs only in the Piel (D) and often means "entreat the favour of" God (BDB, 1 b). Like other vocabulary (see especially 9:3–4), this shows that a right relationship with God is obtained only by his gracious favor and mercy. The idiom with this verb and פָּנִים, "face," as its object occurs fourteen times in the OT[b] and always denotes seeking someone's favor or mercy even though the seeker has no legal right to demand it and does not deserve it.

9:15 וְעַתָּה ׀ אֲדֹנָי אֱלֹהֵינוּ—"And now, Lord our God," uses וְעַתָּה to signal the beginning of Daniel's first petition (9:15–16). His second petition (9:17–19) begins similarly (see the textual note on 9:17).

9:16 כְּכָל־צִדְקֹתֶךָ—"According to all your righteous acts" uses the plural of the noun צְדָקָה for actions, similar to the plurals הָרַחֲמִים וְהַסְּלִחוֹת (see the first textual note on 9:9). These "righteous acts" manifest God's innate attribute of "righteousness," denoted by the singular of צְדָקָה in 9:7. The plural is used again in 9:18, but there Daniel

[b] Ex 32:11; 1 Ki 13:6 (twice); 2 Ki 13:4; Jer 26:19; Zech 7:2; 8:21–22; Mal 1:9; Ps 119:58; Job 11:19; Prov 19:6; Dan 9:13; 2 Chr 33:12

denies that he and Israel have performed any meritorious deeds that they could claim as צִדְקֹתֵינוּ, "our righteous acts."

יָשָׁב־נָא אַפְּךָ וַחֲמָתְךָ—This is a classic use of the shorter jussive form יָשָׁב (of שׁוּב) in contrast to the longer imperfect form, יָשׁוּב. Its modal, jussive meaning, "*may/let* your anger and your wrath turn from …" is strengthened by the particle of entreaty, נָא, left untranslated. The masculine singular jussive agrees with the suffixed masculine noun אַפְּךָ, "your anger," as its subject although the compound subject also includes the suffixed feminine noun וַחֲמָתְךָ, "and your wrath."

9:17 וְעַתָּה ׀ שְׁמַע אֱלֹהֵינוּ—"And now, listen, our God" uses וְעַתָּה to signal the beginning of Daniel's second petition (9:17–19).

9:18 וְהָעִיר אֲשֶׁר־נִקְרָא שִׁמְךָ עָלֶיהָ—Literally, "the city which your name is called over her," this is translated, "the city that is called by your name." Similar is Daniel's final appeal for God to act for the sake of his name: כִּי־שִׁמְךָ נִקְרָא עַל־עִירְךָ וְעַל־עַמֶּךָ (literally, "because your name is called over your city and over your people," 9:19).

כִּי ׀ לֹא עַל־צִדְקֹתֵינוּ אֲנַחְנוּ מַפִּילִים תַּחֲנוּנֵינוּ לְפָנֶיךָ—Literally, "because not on the basis of our righteous actions (are) we casting down our plea for grace before you." The negated causal clause ("because not …") is placed first for emphasis. Since that clause precedes, the pronoun אֲנַחְנוּ is then placed before the participle מַפִּילִים (Joüon, § 154 f e; without a preceding clause, the usual order is for a participle to be followed by its pronoun subject [Joüon, § 154 f d]). For the idiom מַפִּילִים תַּחֲנוּנֵינוּ, see the commentary on 9:18.

9:19 אֲדֹנָי ׀ שְׁמָעָה ׀ אֲדֹנָי ׀ סְלָחָה אֲדֹנָי הַקְשִׁיבָה—Three times after a vocative אֲדֹנָי, "O Lord," the lengthened form of imperative (with ־ָה) is used (GKC, § 48 i): "listen … forgive … pay attention."

Commentary

Daniel's Understanding of Jeremiah's Prophecies concerning the Length of the Captivity (9:1–2)

Daniel begins recounting his prayer by giving us the setting and reason for it. The first year of Darius (Cyrus the Great)[2] refers to his first full regnal year, which began on 1 Nisan 538 (March 24, 538). This is shortly after Daniel survived the lions' den (Daniel 6).[3] Sometime during this year, Daniel was reading "in the scrolls" (9:2). While the OT canon was not complete at this point in time, this phrase indicates that Daniel and his contemporaries recognized a group of scrolls as authoritative writings inspired by God. These included the prophecies of Jeremiah. It is unmistakable from the context that Daniel regarded these writings to be inerrant and infallible since without any reservation he believed what they said.

---

[2] On the identity of Darius and his ancestor Ahasuerus, see the excursus "The Identity of Darius the Mede."

[3] See "Introduction to Daniel 6."

For the first time in his book, Daniel the author records God's proper name, Yahweh, used only in this chapter. There are several other chapters in Daniel that confine themselves to particular names or titles for God. Daniel 4 and 7 use the title "the Most High" (cf. "the Most High God" in 3:26; 3:32 [ET 4:2]; 5:18, 21), whereas Daniel 2 uses "the God of heaven."[4] In each case, the particular name or title is appropriate for the context. This chapter calls for God's covenant name. Purely by his grace, he had bestowed his sacred name upon his chosen people. Priests at his holy temple invoked his name in blessing, and so his name was pronounced over his holy city (see further the commentary on 9:17–19).

There are two passages in Jeremiah that speak of the "seventy years" of captivity. The first is Jer 25:11–12, a prophecy given by Jeremiah in Jerusalem in 605 BC,[5] the year Daniel was taken captive and subsequently hauled to Babylon with the first wave of exiles.[6] There Jeremiah states that the land would become a "devastation" (the same noun, חָרְבָּה, as in Dan 9:2) for seventy years and that Judah and other captive nations (see Jer 25:19–26) would serve Babylon for seventy years. The second passage, Jer 29:10, is part of a letter that Jeremiah in Jerusalem wrote to captives in Babylon in 597 BC (see Jer 29:1–2). It urges the exiles to settle in Babylon and seek to prosper there because they will not return to Jerusalem until the seventy years are completed. This second passage indicates that since the seventy years Jeremiah prophesied earlier were not yet ended, the exiles were to take seriously his previous prediction of the duration of the captivity.

Daniel saw that according to both of these prophecies, God would bring the captivity to an end with the punishment of Babylon (Jer 25:12), that is to say, when seventy years were completed for Babylon (Jer 29:10). The time of Daniel's prayer is shortly after Babylon's fall to Cyrus the Great in 539 BC. Daniel perceived that the event he read about in Jeremiah—the trigger that would bring the exile to an end and begin the restoration of Jerusalem—had happened. The date notice in Dan 9:1–2 therefore explains the reason for his prayer about the restoration of Jerusalem. It was some sixty-seven or sixty-eight years after he had been taken into captivity. Daniel was now calling on God to keep his promise made through Jeremiah. Probably it was a matter of weeks or months after his prayer that Cyrus issued his edict in 538 BC permitting the return. Thus the total duration of the exile (605–538 BC) can easily be rounded up to seventy years.[7]

---

[4] Collins, *Daniel*, 348–49.

[5] The prophecy came to Jeremiah in "the fourth year of Jehoiakim" (Jer 25:1).

[6] See the commentary on 1:1 and "Date and Authorship according to the Book" in "Date, Authorship, and Unity" in the introduction.

[7] Some scholars interpret 2 Chr 36:21 and Zech 1:12 to be indications that other biblical writers calculated the seventy-year period differently (e.g., Grabbe, " 'The End of the Desolations of Jerusalem': From Jeremiah's 70 Years to Daniel's 70 Weeks of Years," 67–68). However, their interpretation is based on a misreading of both of those passages. They take 2 Chr 36:15–21

Daniel's Confession of His People's Sins against God (9:3–6)

Daniel signals to the reader from the start that his prayer was penitential by stating that he sought God with "a plea for grace" (תַּחֲנוּנִים, 9:3; also in 9:17–18). This noun derives from the verb חָנַן, "be gracious, show favor," used for God in the Aaronic Benediction (Num 6:25) and other passages. The noun (an abstract plural translated as a singular) almost always refers to a supplication made by a person to God. Daniel also states that he "made confession" (9:4). He demonstrated his penitence by fasting, wearing sackcloth, and covering himself with ashes (9:3), all three of which are signs of mourning and repentance. While each of these three signs is familiar to readers of the OT, all three are mentioned together in only two other places (Is 58:5; Esth 4:3). By these actions and by using first person verbs in the body of the prayer (e.g., "we have sinned … we did not listen," 9:5–6), Daniel joins himself in corporate solidarity with the people, sharing in the blame for his people's sins.

Daniel begins his prayer with a description of God. He describes God as "great and feared" and one "who keeps the covenant and mercy" (9:5). The covenant of Moses includes Yahweh's own declaration that he remains faithful to his promise to show abundant mercy (חֶסֶד) toward his faithful people (Ex 34:6–7), and this language was incorporated into later OT creeds about Yahweh, Israel's God.[8] That Yahweh "keeps" (שָׁמַר) his "covenant" (בְּרִית) and "mercy" (חֶסֶד) toward "those who love him and keep his commandments" (Dan 9:4) is language found already in Deut 7:9–12. That Yahweh "keeps" (שָׁמַר) his "covenant" (בְּרִית) and "mercy" (חֶסֶד) is also expressed in 1 Ki 8:23; Ps 89:29 (ET 89:28); Neh 1:5; 9:32; 2 Chr 6:14 (cf. Is 54:10; 55:3; Pss 25:10; 106:45).

---

as indicating that the seventy-year captivity began with the fall of Jerusalem under Zedekiah in 587 BC. However, this passage is in fact a summary of all of the reasons for the captivity and all of the steps leading to the destruction of Jerusalem and the temple; it is not simply an account of the fall of Jerusalem in 587. This fact can be seen in 2 Chr 36:15–16, which is not simply a summary of what happened in Zedekiah's time, but of what transpired throughout the time of the monarchy. Furthermore, some of the events mentioned in 2 Chr 36:17–20 happened before Zedekiah's reign, including the capture of vessels from the temple, which happened in 605 BC (Dan 1:1–2; 2 Chr 36:5–7) and again in 597 (2 Chr 36:9–10). Therefore, the Chronicler is calculating from the beginning of Babylon's actions against Jerusalem (2 Chr 36:17), which started in 605 BC, and he concludes by relating this to Jeremiah's prophecies (2 Chr 36:21).

Zech 1:12 mentions that God had been angry at Jerusalem and Judah for seventy years. However, Zechariah does not connect the seventy years with Jeremiah's prophecies about the duration of the exile or the time of the return to the land. Instead, Zechariah's prophecy has the goal of encouraging the completion of the rebuilding of the temple. The time of God's anger refers (in a round number) to the length of time that the temple had lain in ruins. Zechariah began to prophesy in 520 BC (Zech 1:1) and received his night visions in 519 (Zech 1:7), sixty-eight years after the destruction of the temple in 587 BC. The temple was being rebuilt, but it would not be completed until 515 BC.

[8] See, for example, Jonah 4:2. A discussion of the covenant background of this creedal language is provided by Lessing, *Jonah*, 367–70. While this commentary follows KJV and others who render חֶסֶד as "mercy," others prefer "faithfulness," for example, Wilch, *Ruth*, 30–37, 87–88, who bases his discussion on חֶסֶד in Ruth 1:8; 2:20; 3:10.

This language that Daniel uses in 9:4 demonstrates that in addition to Jeremiah, he had also read the Torah and other books of Scripture, and he is able to appropriate what he learned from them in his prayer. Nehemiah's later prayer follows Daniel's opening nearly word for word (Neh 1:5), and the same phraseology is also found in Neh 9:32.[9] Daniel's description of God as keeping his covenant and "mercy for those who love him and keep his commands" (Dan 9:4) is drawn from Ex 20:6, where God first gave his covenant to his people from Mount Sinai. It should be noted that God's attributes described here as they are revealed in his interactions with people involve both his wrath and his grace. He is "feared" by sinners because of his holiness, but he also demonstrates his faithfulness as he "keeps" his covenant promises of grace and mercy. The first drives Daniel to repentance, while the second leads him to trust in God's love.

Daniel's description of his people's sin begins with five verbs for their wayward actions. The first three ("we have sinned, committed iniquity, acted wickedly") are quoted from Solomon's prayer at the dedication of the temple (1 Ki 8:47).[10] Solomon had asked God to have compassion on his people when they find themselves captives in a foreign land and pray to him, confess their sins, and turn toward his temple—his dwelling place and the site of sacrificial atonement for the forgiveness of sins, anticipating the cross of Christ. Daniel trusted God's promise that he would do what Solomon had asked (1 Ki 9:3). Daniel purposely repeats Solomon's words and adds other descriptions of the sin of his people to emphasize his contrition.

Next Daniel adds a specific charge against his people: "we did not listen to your servants the prophets" (9:6). Jeremiah describes the prophets as God's "servants" more often than any other OT book.[c] A further parallel is that Daniel notes how the prophets "spoke in your name to our kings, princes, and fathers, and to all the people of the land" (9:6), and Jeremiah similarly characterizes the people of Judah as consisting of "your fathers, your kings, your princes, and the people of the land" (Jer 44:21; cf. Jer 1:18). These parallels between Daniel's prayer and Jeremiah demonstrate that Daniel had carefully read and studied Jeremiah's prophecies. He was not merely searching around in them for prophecies about the duration of the captivity. Instead, he had taken to heart Jeremiah's call for repentance and faith in the Lord.

(c) Jer 7:25; 25:4; 26:5; 29:19; 35:15; 44:4

God's Righteousness Contrasted with Israel's Sinfulness (9:7–11)

Daniel's prayer began with an invocation of God, who "keeps the covenant and mercy" (9:4), and immediately moved to confess the corporate sins

---

[9] Young, *Daniel*, 185, who states that "since the prayer in Neh. 9 is more expanded in form than that of Dan. 9, the dependence, if any, is on the part of Neh. and not of Dan."

[10] The three verbs are first person plural in 1 Ki 8:47 as in Dan 9:5, Solomon used Qal (G) forms of the first and third verbs and a Hiphil (H) form of the second (חָטָאנוּ וְהֶעֱוִינוּ רָשָׁעְנוּ), whereas Daniel used Qal forms for the first two and a Hiphil form of the third (חָטָאנוּ וְעָוִינוּ הִרְשַׁעְנוּ). However, there is no significant difference in meaning between the Qal and Hiphil forms of the second verb ("commit iniquity") and third verb ("act wickedly") since their Hiphil forms are internally transitive.

of Israel (9:5–6). He now develops this contrast between the faithful God and his unfaithful people.

The first contrast is between God's own intrinsic "righteousness" (צְדָקָה, 9:7) and Israel's wrongdoing. This contrast will be strengthened when Daniel calls God צַדִּיק, "righteous" (9:14), and refers to צִדְקֹתֶךָ, "your righteous acts" of judgment (9:16), then denies that he and his fellow Israelites have any righteous deeds (צִדְקֹתֵינוּ, "our righteous acts," 9:18) that could avail before God. Because of Israel's wrongdoing, Daniel confesses, "We are shamefaced" (9:7), a phrase adopted from Jer 7:19. This shame applies to all Judeans. Once again, Daniel borrows a common expression from Jeremiah to describe his countrymen: "the people of Judah, the inhabitants of Jerusalem" (Dan 9:7).[d]

(d) See Jer 4:4; 11:2, 9; 17:25; 18:11; 32:32; 35:13

Daniel specifically extends his prayer to include all Israel, "both near and far in all the lands where you have banished them because of their wrongdoings" (9:7). This is not simply a prayer for Judeans in exile and back home in Judah, but for all of the twelve tribes. Daniel once again demonstrates his diligent study of Jeremiah by his use of the phrase "in all the lands where you have banished them" (see Jer 16:15; 23:3, 8; 32:37). Some nine centuries before the era of Jeremiah and Daniel, even before Israel took possession of the land, God had threatened their banishment in the words of Moses (Deut 30:1; cf. Lev 26:33; Deut 28:36–37), which Daniel also echoes here. The greatest sin against God was, of course, idolatry. Daniel may be hinting at this by again mentioning the kings, princes, and fathers (Dan 9:8), all of whom were involved in promoting idolatry according to Jer 44:17.

Daniel then notes that God remains a gracious God who repeatedly performed "acts of compassion and forgiveness" (הָרַחֲמִים וְהַסְּלִחוֹת) despite Israel's rebellion against him (9:9). One of God's attributes mentioned throughout Scripture is his graciousness despite human sinfulness (2 Ki 13:23; Ps 25:6; 2 Chr 30:9). He saves his people purely by his grace, which they receive through faith. Were it not so, no one could be saved (Pss 14:1–3; 53:2–4 [ET 53:1–3]; and other OT verses quoted in Rom 3:10–18).

God expects his people to obey his voice (Ex 15:26; 19:5; Deut 4:30), but Daniel three times admits that Israel had failed to do this (Dan 9:10–11, 14). This led them to fail to live, or "walk," according to God's laws (9:10). They had these laws constantly brought to their attention through the prophets, but Israel refused to listen. Jeremiah frequently condemned Judah for this.[e]

(e) Jer 25:3–4; 26:4–5; 29:19; 32:23; 35:15; 44:4–5

Daniel acknowledges God's just action in pouring out upon his people the punishment he had sworn to use on them if they persistently ignored his Word. The foundational Word of God came through the greatest OT prophet, Moses, who is called "the servant of God" here (9:11).[11] The Torah of Moses contains

---

[11] Moses is called "the servant of Yahweh" (Deut 34:5; Josh 1:1, 13, 15; 8:31, 33; 11:12; 12:6 [twice]; 13:8; 14:7; 18:7; 22:2, 4–5; 2 Ki 18:12; 2 Chr 1:3; 24:6) or " the servant of God" (Dan 9:11; Neh 10:30 [ET 10:29]; 1 Chr 6:34 [ET 6:49]; 2 Chr 24:9) twenty-two times in the OT.

covenant blessings and curses predicated on whether or not the people continue in faith or apostatize from the God who had redeemed them (Leviticus 26; Deuteronomy 27–28). Daniel's declaration that God had fulfilled "the curse and the oath that is written in the teaching of Moses" (Dan 9:11) refers specifically to the curses listed in Lev 26:14–39 and Deut 28:15–68. Daniel's knowledge of these curses demonstrates that, in addition to the prophecies of Jeremiah, he had also studied the books of Moses. The Mosaic covenant not only predicted the apostasy of the people (Deut 31:16–29; 32:15–35), but also held out the hope that after the curses would be fulfilled, the people would repent and again turn in faith to their God, who would remember his ancient covenant promises of grace and blessing (Lev 26:40–45; Deut 30:1–10; 32:36).

God's Judgment on Israel's Sin (9:12–14)

Daniel's prayer progresses from the words of Moses and the prophets to the fulfilling of those words. God brought on Jerusalem "a great disaster" (רָעָה גְדֹלָה, 9:12), a phrase modeled on "all the disaster I spoke to them" in Jer 35:17 and 36:31 and similar Jeremiah passages.[12] Daniel notes that all of this was already "written in the teaching of Moses" (Dan 9:13), in the books held to be sacred. Phrases like "as is written" (כַּאֲשֶׁר כָּתוּב, 9:13; cf. אֲשֶׁר כְּתוּבָה, 9:11) became a standard way of quoting from canonical books.[13] Daniel notes that even after the disaster was inflicted on Jerusalem by Nebuchadnezzar's armies, still "we did not entreat the face of Yahweh our God" (see the second textual note on 9:13).

Daniel expresses the goal of entreating God: "in order to turn from our iniquity and to acquire insight into your truth" (9:13). The thought is that Israel should seek from God the ability to repent and to understand the teachings of Moses and the prophets. Repentance and faith are prerequisites for understanding God's truth (see 1 Cor 2:14). The verb "to acquire insight" (לְהַשְׂכִּיל, Dan 9:13) is from the root (שׂכל) that provides Daniel's favorite wisdom-related family of words.[f] Its use here affirms what true insight and wisdom are: knowledge and faith obtained from the teachings of God's Word.[14] God imparts both the power to repent and the ability to understand his Word. Repentance, faith, and wisdom are works and gifts of God, not the result of human volition or strength.[g]

(f) Dan 1:4, 17; 5:11–12, 14; 8:25; 9:13, 22, 25; 11:33, 35; 12:3, 10

(g) Rom 8:7; 1 Cor 12:3; Eph 2:1, 8–9; AC V; Ap IV 250; SC II 6

---

[12] Besides Dan 9:12, "a great disaster/evil" (רָעָה גְדֹלָה) occurs in the OT only in Jer 26:19; 44:7; Jonah 4:1; Neh 1:3; 2:10. The phrase with definite articles, הָרָעָה הַגְּדֹלָה, "the great evil," occurs in Jer 16:10; 32:42 as well as Gen 39:9; 1 Sam 6:9; 2 Sam 13:16; Neh 13:27.

[13] In the OT, the similar phrase כַּכָּתוּב, "as it is written," is used exclusively for reference to the books of Moses (Josh 8:31; 1 Ki 2:3; 2 Ki 14:6; 23:21; Ezra 3:2, 4; Neh 8:15; 10:35, 37 [ET 10:34, 36]; 2 Chr 23:18; 25:4; 30:5, 18; 31:3; 35:12, 26). See also the Greek ὡς γέγραπται, "as it stands written" (the Greek perfect tense referring to past action that continues to remain in force during the present time) in LXX 2 Chr 35:12; Neh 10:35, 37 (ET 10:34, 36); Mk 7:6; Lk 3:4, and the much more frequent use in the LXX and the NT of simply γέγραπται, "it stands written."

[14] For its use as a negative attribute denoting cunning, see 8:25.

Daniel concludes this recitation of God's judgment by noting that Yahweh "watched over [וַיִּשְׁקֹד] the disaster and brought it upon" Israel (9:14). This concept of God watching over a judgment in order to bring it to pass is drawn once again from Jeremiah (שָׁקַד in Jer 1:12; 31:28; 44:27; cf. Jer 5:6). Moreover, Daniel affirms that Yahweh's judgment of Israel demonstrates that "our God is righteous according to all his works," since the people's refusal to listen to his voice through the prophets demanded his righteous punishment (9:14).

That God Would Avert His Anger from Jerusalem (9:15–16)

Daniel in 9:15–16 offers the first of his two petitions to God. Knowing that he and his people have no right to appeal to God on the basis of their actions or merit, he instead appeals to God's ultimate act of salvation in the OT: the exodus from Egypt. He employs a common Pentateuchal expression for God's power applied to deliver his people from their slavery: "with a mighty hand" (בְּיָד חֲזָקָה, 9:15, as in Ex 3:19; 6:1; 13:9; 32:11; Deut 4:34; 5:15; 6:21; 7:8, 19; 9:26; 26:8). However, both it and the rest of Daniel's phraseology derives most closely from Jer 32:20–21, where the prophet confesses this about God: "you made for yourself a name to this day" (וַתַּעֲשֶׂה־לְּךָ שֵׁם כַּיּוֹם הַזֶּה), "and you brought your people out of the land Egypt ... with a mighty hand" (וַתֹּצֵא אֶת־עַמְּךָ אֶת־יִשְׂרָאֵל מֵאֶרֶץ מִצְרָיִם ... וּבְיָד חֲזָקָה). While Daniel reverses the order of those two statements, his wording follows Jeremiah almost verbatim.

His appeal to God's foundational OT act of redemption as the basis for his plea for God now to be gracious toward his people is equivalent to the Christian practice of appealing to the perfect life, atoning death, and glorious resurrection of Jesus Christ as the basis for our prayer for God to be gracious and merciful to us now. In fact, in the NT the apostles implored God, "Enable your servants to speak your Word with all boldness by stretching out your hand to heal and by performing signs and wonders through the name of your holy servant Jesus" (Acts 4:29–30, alluding to Is 53:1 as well as the Exodus and Deuteronomy verses cited above; cf. Acts 11:21). Thus it is in Jesus that God reveals his "mighty hand," his power to redeem and save.

While appealing to God's salvation, Daniel in 9:16 once again unequivocally confesses the sins of his people. He emphasizes that he has no right to ask God for deliverance. Instead, he invokes God's "righteous acts" and pleads that God would act again in keeping with his redemptive activity in the past. He begs for God to turn his wrath away from Jerusalem and the people in order to fulfill the prophecy of Jeremiah, in which God had promised to forgive and restore his people and his holy city. He asks that God would remove the contempt from Israel, a contempt that was also prophesied by Jeremiah (Jer 23:40; 24:9; 29:18; 51:51). The destruction of Jerusalem was a sign, obvious even to the pagan nations surrounding Israel, that this people had betrayed their God and so had incurred his righteous fury. The restoration of Jerusalem would remove that contempt by showing all nations that God once again was treating his people with forgiving grace and love. Even so in the NT, the resurrection of Christ is the divine act that vindicated him from the contempt he had endured, and the promise of resurrection is what enables Christians to endure contempt and reproach as we suffer for his sake.[h]

(h) Pss 22:7 (ET 22:6); 69:7 (ET 69:8); 119:22; Mt 5:11–12; Lk 6:22; 23:11; 1 Tim 4:10; Heb 10:13; 13:13

That God Would Shine His Face on His City and Sanctuary (9:17–19)

Daniel's second petition is a request for God's favor. He begs God to listen to his "plea for grace" (9:17–18) concerning Jerusalem and its temple in terms that are strikingly similar to Solomon's prayer at the temple's dedication (1 Ki 8:28). Daniel's appeal that God would "let [his] face shine" on the sanctuary is reminiscent of the Aaronic Benediction (Num 6:25), which uses the same verb (Hiphil of אוֹר) followed by the verb "be gracious" (חָנַן) that is the root of the noun "plea for grace" Daniel uses in 9:3, 17–18). This benediction (Num 6:24–26) was the great OT blessing the priests were to use to place God's name on his people, so that he would bless them (Num 6:27). This blessing must have been used often while the temple stood. Many of Israel's prayers allude to it.[i]

(i) Pss 31:17 (ET 31:16); 67:2 (ET 67:1); 80:4, 8, 20 (ET 80:3, 7, 19); 119:35

Daniel once again draws on Jeremiah (Jer 14:7, 21) in his appeal to God to act for his own sake (Dan 9:17, 19) on behalf of the city and the people that are called by his name (9:18–19). In NT theology, the baptized believer in Christ bears the triune name of God (Mt 28:19; cf. Acts 2:38; 10:48; 1 Cor 6:11) and is sealed with the Holy Spirit (2 Cor 1:22; Eph 1:13) and so belongs to Christ and God (Gal 3:29; 2 Tim 2:19; cf. 1 Pet 4:14). Thus like OT saints (Pss 79:9; 115:1), Christians too can appeal to God to forgive and deliver based on God's name, which they bear, and for Christ's sake (Rom 1:5; 15:9; 1 Cor 1:2; cf. Eph 4:32). The adjective "Christian" (1 Pet 4:16; also Acts 26:28) of course derives from the name of Christ.

Daniel's pleas "incline, my God, your ear and hear" and "open your eyes and see" (9:18) are nearly identical to Hezekiah's plea for Judah's deliverance from the Assyrians (2 Ki 19:16 ‖ Is 37:17). Like that prayer, Daniel's petition is spoken in urgency and with the acknowledgement that only God can rescue his people from the grave situation in which they find themselves.

Daniel now makes explicit what he has implied throughout his prayer: he cannot ask God for anything because of his people's acts, since they merit nothing but God's wrath. However, he can ask because of God's compassionate acts in the past, which have demonstrated his forgiveness and love toward Israel. Daniel uses a rare idiom, literally, "we are causing our plea for grace to fall before you" (אֲנַחְנוּ מַפִּילִים תַּחֲנוּנֵינוּ לְפָנֶיךָ, 9:18). The image is of casting a request on the ground before the king, showing abject humility and reliance entirely on his good will.[15] This exact wording occurs nowhere else, but in 9:20 Daniel uses the singular of the same participle (מַפִּיל), "causing to fall/cast-

---

[15] Compare Rev 4:10, where the twenty-four elders, who represent the church of both Testaments, cast their crowns before the throne of God.

ing," with the object תְּחִנָּתִי, "my prayer for grace," a noun from the same verb (חָנַן, "be gracious") as the noun here. Besides 9:20, idioms with Qal and Hiphil forms of the verb נָפַל, "fall," and the noun תְּחִנָּה, "prayer for grace," occur only in Jeremiah (Jer 36:7; 37:20; 38:26; 42:2, 9), once again demonstrating Daniel's thorough knowledge of that book by his prophetic contemporary.

Daniel's final urgent plea begins with requests for God to listen and forgive (9:19), requests that were frequently joined together in Solomon's prayer at the dedication of the temple (1 Ki 8:30, 34, 36, 39), making them most appropriate for Daniel's prayer for the restoration of the temple. Daniel asks God not to delay in granting his request because God's reputation is at stake, since he made a promise to his people about his city.

Daniel is bold in asking God to keep his promise. When praying for things God has promised, his people can always boldly request him to grant them because God's promises are never broken. The Lutheran Confessions approvingly cite Daniel's prayer to support several key doctrines (Ap IV 328–38):

> In the Lord's Prayer the saints pray for the forgiveness of sins; therefore saints have sins, too. ...
>
> Therefore Daniel prays (9:18, 19), "For we do not present our supplications before thee on the ground of our righteousness, but on the ground of thy great mercy. O Lord, hear; O Lord, forgive; O Lord, give heed and act; delay not, for thy own sake, O my God, because thy city and thy people are called by thy name." So Daniel teaches us to take hold of mercy when we pray, that is, to trust the mercy of God and not our merits before him. ...
>
> Prayer relies upon the mercy of God when we believe that we are heard because of Christ the high priest, as he himself says (John 16:23), "If you ask anything of the Father, he will give it to you in my name." "In my name," he says, because without the high priest we cannot draw near to the Father.
>
> Here Christ's statement (Luke 17:10) also applies, "When you have done all that is commanded you, say, 'We are unworthy servants.'" These words clearly say that God saves through mercy and because of his promise, not as a payment which he owes to us for our good works. ...
>
> Indeed, this confession that our works are worthless is the very voice of faith, as is evident from the example of Daniel referred to above. ... Faith saves because it takes hold of mercy and the promise of grace, even though our works are worthless.

Daniel 9:20–27
Gabriel Explains Jerusalem's Future

Translation

9 ²⁰While I was still speaking and praying and confessing my sin and the sin of my people Israel and casting my prayer for grace before Yahweh my God concerning the holy mountain of my God, ²¹while I was speaking in prayer, the man Gabriel whom I had seen in the first vision touched me in [my] complete exhaustion about the time of the evening sacrifice. ²²He instructed me, "Daniel, now I have gone out to give you insight [with] understanding. ²³At the beginning of your plea for grace, a word went forth, and I came to declare [it to you], because you are highly prized. So understand the word and discern the vision.

> ²⁴"Seventy weeks are determined concerning your people and your holy city
> to end transgression,
>> to finish sin,
>>> and to atone for iniquity;
> to bring everlasting righteousness,
>> to seal up vision and prophet,
>>> and to anoint a Most Holy One.
>
> ²⁵You should know and have insight:
> from the going forth of a word to restore and rebuild Jerusalem until
>> Messiah, a Leader,
> seven weeks, and sixty-two weeks when it again will have been built [with]
>> plaza and moat,
>> but during the troubled times.

²⁶"Then after the sixty-two weeks, Messiah will be cut off and have nothing. Both the city and the holy place will be destroyed with a Leader who is coming, and its end will be with a flood. Until the end will be war, and desolations have been determined.

²⁷"He will confirm a covenant for the many [during] one week. In the middle of the week, he will cause sacrifice and offering to cease. On the wing of detested things (is) a desolator, until the decreed end is poured out on the desolator."

Textual Notes

9:20 וּמַפִּיל תְּחִנָּתִי לִפְנֵי יְהוָה אֱלֹהָי—Literally, "causing my prayer for grace to fall before Yahweh my God," this idiom is similar to the one in 9:18 and seems to have been borrowed by Daniel from Jeremiah, his contemporary. See the commentary on 9:18.

9:21 בֶחָזוֹן בַּתְּחִלָּה—Literally, this is "in the vision, in the first." The noun תְּחִלָּה can refer to the "first in a series" (BDB [under the root חלל III]). This phrase refers to Daniel

7, which was the first of the visions Daniel received and recorded in chapters 7–12 (cf. 8:1). This verse may imply that the angel to whom Daniel spoke in 7:16 was Gabriel.

מֻעָף בִּיעָף נֹגֵעַ אֵלָי—Probably this means, literally, "exhausted in exhaustion, he was touching me." Daniel is telling us that he was exhausted from his period of fasting in prayer (9:3). Gabriel then touched Daniel to strengthen and reassure him, as is done in other visions (8:18; 10:10, 16, 18). Elsewhere in the OT, the verb יָעַף occurs in Qal (G) and means "be weary, tired."[a] This is the only instance where it is not Qal, and מֻעָף is the Hophal participle, meaning "wearied" (BDB). The related noun יְעָף, "weariness, exhaustion," occurs only here in the OT and is derived from the verb יָעַף. The combination of the verb and the noun forms an absolute superlative (cf. Waltke-O'Connor, § 14.5b): Daniel was, literally, "utterly weary" or "completely exhausted." Some translations and commentators interpret the phrase in such a way.[1]

(a) Is 40:28, 31–32; 44:12; Jer 2:24; 51:58, 64; Hab 2:13; cf. Judg 8:15; 2 Sam 16:2; Is 40:29; 50:4

Most translations and commentators interpret the first phrase as something like "flying in flight," meaning "swiftly flying," in which case it must refer to Gabriel, not Daniel.[2] According to this view, מֻעָף would be the Hophal participle of עוּף, "to fly," a verb that elsewhere usually occurs in Qal, once in Hiphil (the Qere in Prov 23:5), and never in Hophal. The Polel (D) is used for the flying Seraphim in Is 6:2. However, it is difficult to derive the noun form יְעָף from the verb עוּף, "to fly." This view is also less likely because Daniel has just described Gabriel as "the man" (וְהָאִישׁ, 9:21), and Gabriel is never depicted in Daniel or elsewhere in Scripture as having wings or flying. This view seems to be reading into this passage about Gabriel the description of winged cherubim (Ex 25:18–20; 1 Ki 6:23–28) or flying seraphim (Is 6:2). Many of those translations and commentators who interpret the first phrase as Gabriel flying take the participial phrase נֹגֵעַ אֵלָי as meaning that Gabriel "came to me [Daniel]" (RSV, ESV, NIV; cf. NKJV: "reached me"). However, the verb נָגַע in the Qal (G) stem normally means "touch" (8:5, 18; 10:10, 16, 18). It is the Hiphil (H) stem of the verb that can mean "approach, come to" (8:7; 12:12).

The Old Greek has τάχει φερόμενος προσήγγισέ μοι, "swiftly coming he approached me," which clearly has influenced many later translations. Theodotion has πετόμενος καὶ ἥψατό μου, "flying, and he touched me," with no translation for בִּיעָף. The Vulgate has *cito volans tetigit me*, "quickly flying he touched me." The Syriac has a longer reading: ܦܪܚ ܣܚܦ ܘܛܣ ܡܢ ܫܡܝܐ, "he flew, flew, and soared, and came from heaven."

9:22 וַיָּבֶן וַיְדַבֵּר עִמִּי—Literally, "he instructed and he spoke with me," the two verbs form a hendiadys: "he (verbally) instructed me." The Hiphil of בִּין has the causative meaning ("instruct, cause to understand") that corresponds to the Qal of בִּין, "to understand," Daniel uses in 9:2 and 10:1.

לְהַשְׂכִּילְךָ בִינָה:—The Hiphil (infinitive construct) of שָׂכַל has the causative meaning "give insight, teach" (BDB, 4) and takes two accusative objects, the pronominal

---

[1] So NASB; Goldingay, *Daniel*, 228; Keil, *Daniel*, 335; Leupold, *Daniel*, 401.

[2] So KJV; RSV; NKJV; ESV; NIV; Archer, "Daniel," 111; Collins, *Daniel*, 345; Hartman and Di Lella, *Daniel*, 243; Montgomery, *Daniel*, 370–71; Walvoord, *Daniel*, 214–15; Young, *Daniel*, 190.

suffix ("you") and the noun בִּינָה, "understanding" (see the commentary on 1:20), which here refers to what Gabriel teaches Daniel.

9:23 תַחֲנוּנֶיךָ—See the commentary on 9:3.

כִּי חֲמוּדוֹת אָתָּה—"For you are highly prized." The noun חֲמוּדָה denotes something that is precious or valuable (BDB). Its abstract plural denotes a quality (Joüon, § 136 g; Waltke-O'Connor, § 7.4.2a). Its plural is applied to Daniel two other times (10:11, 19). Most often it denotes something of rarity and great cost.[b]

(b) Gen 27:15; Dan 10:3; 11:38, 43; Ezra 8:27; 2 Chr 20:25

וּבִין בַּדָּבָר וְהָבֵן בַּמַּרְאֶה:—Here the imperatives of the Qal (G) and the Hiphil (H) of בִּין are used as synonyms: "to understand, discern." The parallelism of the two clauses also suggests that the "word" consists of the content of the "vision" now shown Daniel.

9:24 שָׁבֻעִים שִׁבְעִים נֶחְתַּךְ—Literally, "weeks, seventy, are determined." Elsewhere in the OT outside of Daniel, שָׁבוּעַ denotes "a week, seven days."[c] Outside of Daniel, its plural is always feminine, שָׁבֻעוֹת. Daniel alone has the masculine plural form of the noun (9:24–26; 10:2–3), and he uses the singular in 9:27. When Daniel uses it to refer to an ordinary, regular week of seven days, he adds יָמִים, "days," yielding שָׁבֻעִים יָמִים, "weeks of days, seven-day weeks" (10:2–3). The absence of יָמִים, "days," in 9:24–27 signals that it is being used in an unusual way. Instead of a literal week, in Daniel 9 it refers to a sevenfold period of some kind, but not consisting of just seven ordinary days.

(c) Gen 29:27–28; Ex 34:22; Lev 12:5; Num 28:26; Deut 16:9 (twice), 10, 16; Jer 5:24; Ezek 45:21; 2 Chr 8:13

The verb חָתַךְ occurs only here in the OT, but it is used in Rabbinic Hebrew in the Qal, meaning "to cut" and sometimes "to decree, determine," and in the Niphal, meaning "to be severed" and also "to be decided, decreed."[3] Therefore, the Niphal (N) here likely means "decreed" or "determined" as it sometimes does in rabbinic literature.

לְכַלֵּא הַפֶּשַׁע—This is "to end transgression." The Piel infinitive construct of כָּלָה, meaning to "complete, bring to an end, finish" (BDB, Piel, 1 a), is spelled with final א in the Leningrad Codex. This form may be an Aramaism that arose from the frequent interchange of quiescent ה and א in Aramaic. However, even older Hebrew includes some interchange of verb forms with final ה and final א (Joüon, § 79 l). In many Masoretic manuscripts, the form is spelled לְכַלֵּה. Both the Old Greek and Theodotion translate it with συντελεσθῆναι, "to be completed, ended," confirming the meaning. The verb כָּלָא, "to withhold, refrain, forbid" (which does not occur in Piel), is not intended here.

For פֶּשַׁע, "transgression," see the same noun in 8:12–13. See also the first textual note on 8:23, which has the participle or the noun in a clause similar to the one here.

וּלְהָתֵם חַטָּאת—"And to finish sin" is the Qere reading of both words in Leningradensis and the sole reading in many Masoretic manuscripts. "To finish" is also supported by the translations of the verb in the Old Greek (καὶ τὰς ἀδικίας σπανίσαι), Aquila, the Syriac, and the Vulgate. The Kethib in Leningradensis is וּלְחְתֹּם חַטָּאוֹת, "and to seal up sins." "To seal up" is supported by Theodotion (καὶ τοῦ σφραγίσαι ἁμαρτίας), which indicates that the confusion of these two words stems from early times. The Kethib of the verb is probably due to confusion with וְלַחְתֹּם later

---

[3] See Jastrow, s.v. חָתַךְ; *TWOT*, § 778; Collins, *Daniel*, 353.

in the verse (see the next textual note). Both the Old Greek and Theodotion support the plural noun "sins."

וְלַחְתֹּם֙ חָז֣וֹן וְנָבִ֔יא—Literally, this is "to seal up vision and prophet." The two nouns can be understood as a kind of hendiadys, "to seal up prophetic vision," that is, divine revelation given through a prophet by means of a vision. The noun חָזוֹן denotes a prophetic "vision" in, for example, 1:17; 8:1–2; as well as Is 1:1; Obad 1; Nah 1:1. The Qal (G) verb חָתַם denotes sealing, blocking, or otherwise stopping the use or function of something (Lev 15:3; Job 14:17; 24:16; 37:7; Song 4:12). Most often it is used of sealing a scroll or document, with the result that it cannot be read unless the seal is broken, as in Dan 12:4, 9.[d] In Dan 6:18 (ET 6:17), the mouth of the den or cave of the lions was occluded with a stone and sealed with the seal of the king and his officials to prevent anyone from opening it. In the NT, the scroll of world history has seven seals, which only the Lamb has the authority to open (Rev 5:1–8:1).

(d) Also 1 Ki 21:8; Is 8:16; 29:11; Jer 32:10–11, 14, 44; Esth 3:12; 8:8 (twice), 10; Neh 10:1–2 (ET 9:38–10:1)

9:25 עַד־מָשִׁ֣יחַ נָגִ֔יד—"Until Messiah, a Leader," clearly calls the "Messiah" a "Leader." Therefore, when נָגִיד recurs in 9:26, it must again refer to the Messiah as a "Leader." The only other occurrence of נָגִיד in Daniel is in 11:22, where again it refers to the Messiah. מָשִׁיחַ too recurs in 9:26, and these are the only two instances of "Messiah" in Daniel. The noun מָשִׁיחַ is a passive formation from the verb מָשַׁח, "anoint," so "Messiah" means "Anointed One." The Greek equivalent is χριστός, "Christ, Anointed One," from the verb χρίω, "anoint." Jesus first received this title at his birth (Lk 2:11) from "an angel of the Lord" (Lk 2:9), who was most likely Gabriel, the angel named in Lk 1:19, 26, as well as in Daniel.[4]

תָּשׁוּב֙ וְנִבְנְתָ֔ה—Both verbs are feminine because their subject is the preceding name יְרוּשָׁלִַ֗ם, "Jerusalem." Hebrew city names are always feminine. Neither of the masculine nouns that follow (רְח֣וֹב וְחָר֔וּץ) can be the subject of the verbs. The verb שׁוּב is often used adverbially, meaning "again," in combination with another verb, which is the main verb. Here the main verb is the Niphal perfect with *waw* consecutive וְנִבְנְתָה, "will be built." Thus the verbs literally say that Jerusalem "again will be built," but this could be conveyed by saying, "it will be rebuilt." In such adverbial constructions, often both verbs have or do not have *waw*, but here only the second verb does (Joüon, § 177 b).

9:26 הַשָּׁבֻעִים֙ שִׁשִּׁ֣ים וּשְׁנַ֔יִם—This is, literally, "the weeks, sixty and two." The counted unit (הַשָּׁבֻעִים) is plural and precedes the numerals (Waltke-O'Connor, § 15.2.4a, including example 10). While הַשָּׁבֻעִים has the article, the numerals do not since they seem to be definite in themselves (Waltke-O'Connor, § 15.2.6a, including example 6).

יִכָּרֵ֥ת מָשִׁ֖יחַ וְאֵ֣ין ל֑וֹ—Literally, "Messiah is cut off, and there is nothing (belonging) to him." The Niphal (N) of כָּרַת, "cut," may recall the stone—the Messiah, who brings the kingdom of God—that was הִתְגְּזֶרֶת, "hewn, cut out" (2:34; cf. 2:45). The crucifixion of Christ is similarly prophesied by other OT passages: he is "cut off from the land of the living" (Is 53:8) and "pierced" (Zech 12:10; Ps 22:17 [Et 22:16]; see further the first textual note on Dan 2:34).

---

[4] For other references to the Messiah in Daniel, see "The Messiah in Daniel: An Overview" in "Major Themes" in the introduction.

Here the preposition לְ is used in the sense of possession (see BDB, s.v. לְ, 5 b (a), and s.v. אַיִן, 3). Normally אֵין לְ- is used as a nominal predicate with another noun as its subject ("*something* does not belong to someone"), but here and in Ex 22:2 (ET 22:3), אֵין לוֹ has no subject and simply means "nothing/no one belongs to him." When the Messiah is "cut off" he possesses or owns nothing and is completely abandoned by everyone. For the fulfillment in Christ, see, for example, Mt 27:31, 35, 46; Jn 16:32; 2 Cor 8:9.

וְהָעִיר וְהַקֹּדֶשׁ יַשְׁחִית עַם נָגִיד הַבָּא—Almost all Hebrew manuscripts have this reading. The subject is the construct chain עַם נָגִיד הַבָּא, "the people of the Leader who is coming." Usually an attributive relative participle (הַבָּא) agrees with its noun (נָגִיד) in being definite or indefinite, but exceptions occur in later Hebrew, as here (Waltke-O'Connor, 37.5b, including example 14). The compound direct object, וְהָעִיר וְהַקֹּדֶשׁ, precedes the Hiphil verb, יַשְׁחִית. Therefore, the meaning is this: "the coming Leader's people will destroy the city and the holy place." (That construal of the syntax would be unmistakable if the direct object marker אֶת were used with the object, but it is not.) Most English translations reflect that understanding (e.g., KJV, RSV, ESV, NIV, NASB, NKJV). That understanding is partially supported by the Old Greek, καὶ βασιλεία ἐθνῶν φθερεῖ τὴν πόλιν καὶ τὸ ἅγιον μετὰ τοῦ χριστοῦ, "and the king of the peoples will destroy both the city and the holy place with the Christ."

However, one Masoretic manuscript reads the verb as a Niphal, יִשָּׁחֵת, making וְהָעִיר וְהַקֹּדֶשׁ the compound subject: "the city and the holy place will be destroyed." One might expect the verb to be plural, and עִיר is feminine, but the masculine singular verb יִשָּׁחֵת agrees in gender and number with its immediately preceding subject, וְהַקֹּדֶשׁ. The Niphal reading is supported by the Syriac translation and is commended by Baumgartner, the editor of Daniel in *BHS*, and some other scholars.[5] Moreover, that one Hebrew manuscript also points the next word as the preposition עִם, "with," instead of the noun עַם, "people," resulting in "… with a Leader who is coming." That reading is partially supported by Theodotion: καὶ τὴν πόλιν καὶ τὸ ἅγιον διαφθερεῖ σὺν τῷ ἡγουμένῳ τῷ ἐρχομένῳ, "he [the Messiah] will destroy both the city and the holy place with the leader who is coming."

Both Hebrew readings predict that the city of Jerusalem and the temple will be destroyed at the time of the coming Leader. The Hiphil reading says the destruction will be inflicted by the Leader's people, while the Niphal reading emphasizes the role of the Leader himself. Both readings predict the fulfillment in Christ. The Hiphil reading would blame the destruction of Jerusalem and the temple in AD 70 and AD 135 on the infidelity of the Jewish people, the ethnic kin (Rom 9:4–5) of the Messiah, Jesus, the Leader. This would be in harmony with, for example, Jn 2:19, where Jesus challenges his Jewish opponents, "Destroy this temple" (then promises to raise up the temple of his body). The Niphal reading attributes the destruction of Jerusalem and the temple to the Leader himself. This would be in harmony with, for example, the assertion by Jesus' opponents that he said, "I will destroy this temple" (Mk 14:58). To be sure, it was the

---

[5] This reading is also adopted by Payne, "The Goal of Daniel's Seventy Weeks," 106; Rosenberg, "The Slain Messiah in the Old Testament," 260, including note 2.

sin of the Jewish people who rejected their Messiah that precipitated the destruction of Jerusalem and the temple. Yet the ministry, atoning death, and resurrection of Christ also rendered the temple obsolete, requiring its destruction.

Yet another possible view could be that the coming "leader" is a pagan Gentile who destroys Jerusalem and the temple. That view is expressed by the Old Greek translation of 9:26 quoted above. Hence the "leader" could refer to the Roman general Titus, whose troops destroyed Jerusalem and the temple in AD 70. Eschatologically, it could refer to the Antichrist, who wars against the church in the end times. However, 9:26a refers to the first advent of the Messiah (only at his first coming was Christ "cut off," crucified), so the implication of 9:26b must be that the destruction happens at the time of the first advent of the Messiah. Moreover, the term נָגִיד, "Leader," clearly refers to the Messiah in 9:25 (see the first textual note on that verse) and 11:22, so it is most consistent with the surrounding context to regard נָגִיד in 9:26 as referring to the "Leader" who is the Messiah.

וְקִצּוֹ בַשֶּׁטֶף—The masculine suffix on וְקִצּוֹ, "his end," could refer to one of the immediately preceding masculine words, the coming "Leader" (נָגִיד) or his "people" (עַם). However, since the preceding clause speaks of the destruction of the city and temple, most translations and interpreters render וְקִצּוֹ as "*its* end," which would refer to "the holy place" (הַקֹּדֶשׁ) and "the city" (possible even though עִיר is a feminine noun). The noun שֶׁטֶף can refer to a "flood" of water (Job 38:25), but it usually is metaphorical for sudden destruction as a divine judgment, which fits the biblical descriptions of the destruction of Jerusalem and the temple. Yet it could also refer to the death of the Leader, who suffers the entirety of God's judgment against the sin of all humanity (2 Cor 5:21; cf. Mt 27:46) and so is suddenly "cut off" (Dan 9:26).

וְעַד קֵץ מִלְחָמָה נֶחֱרֶצֶת שֹׁמֵמוֹת:—The syntax indicated by the Masoretic accents is, literally, "until (the) end of war, destructions are decreed," as reflected in KJV. However, this implies that "to the end there shall be war" (ESV; similar is NASB). קֵץ, "end," can refer to the end of an era, such as the OT era or the era during which the temple stood, and does not necessarily refer to the end of the world at the second coming of Christ. See the second textual note and the commentary on 8:17. The Qal (G) participle שֹׁמֵמוֹת means "desolations" (BDB, Qal, 1) or "destructions." The feminine plural participle is used for devastated land, ruined cities, and desolated places in Dan 9:18 (שֹׁמְמֹתֵינוּ, "our desolations," referring to Judah) and Is 49:8, 19; 61:4; Ezek 36:4 (see the verb also in Ezek 33:28; 35:12; Lam 1:4; 5:18).

The feminine plural might be understood to have a (singular) abstract meaning, "destruction," which could explain why its feminine Niphal predicate participle נֶחֱרֶצֶת, "decreed, determined," is singular. This same participle, but spelled נֶחֱרָצָה, meaning "determined, decided (by God)," refers to exterminating divine judgment also in 9:27 as well as Is 10:23; 28:22. In Dan 11:36 it refers to the hubris of the Antichrist, which God allows until he is destroyed.

9:27 וְהִגְבִּיר בְּרִית לָרַבִּים שָׁבוּעַ אֶחָד—The subject of "he will confirm a covenant for the many [during] one week" is the "Messiah" and "Leader" in 9:25–26. The Qal of גָּבַר means "be strong, prevail." Its Hiphil (H), which occurs only here and in Ps 12:5 (ET 12:4), both times means "confirm a covenant" (BDB), as is made clear here by the direct object, בְּרִית. The preposition לְ on לָרַבִּים serves as a dative of advantage, "for the benefit/sake of the many." "Many" does not imply a limited atonement. Rather, it points to the messianic covenant as one that will include many peoples from many nations, not just Israel. Similarly רַבִּים, "many," occurs five times (Is 52:14, 15; 53:11, 12 [twice]) in the fourth Suffering Servant Song (Is 52:13–53:12) and designates the beneficiaries of the Servant's sacrificial atonement and resurrection.[6] Jesus alludes to those verses in Isaiah and Dan 9:27 when he speaks of giving his life as "a ransom *for many*" (Mt 20:28) and of his blood "poured out *for many* for the forgiveness of sins" (Mt 26:28; see also Rom 5:15).

וְעַל כְּנַף שִׁקּוּצִים מְשֹׁמֵם—"And on the wing of detested things (is) a desolator." The noun שִׁקּוּץ, "detested thing" (BDB), can refer to an idol, an image or symbol of a pagan deity, and more generally to something loathsome, "an object to abhor" or "horror" (*HALOT*). In Daniel, it occurs in similar phrases also in 11:31 and 12:11. The phrase שִׁקּוּצִים מְשֹׁמֵם is challenging. Some interpreters cite the similar expressions about "the detested thing causing desolation" in 11:31 (הַשִּׁקּוּץ מְשׁוֹמֵם) and 12:11 (שִׁקּוּץ שֹׁמֵם) and construe the singular Poel participle מְשֹׁמֵם, "desolator, one causing desolation," as modifying the plural noun שִׁקּוּצִים even though that is grammatically problematic.[7] The Old Greek and Theodotion translations of 9:27 read, βδέλυγμα τῶν ἐρημώσεων, "a detested thing of the desolations," which could reflect a Hebrew text that read, שִׁקּוּץ־הַשֹּׁמְמִים or שִׁקּוּץ־הַמְשֹׁמְמִים.

In the NT, Jesus refers to τὸ βδέλυγμα τῆς ἐρημώσεως, "the detested thing of/causing desolation" (Mt 24:15; Mk 13:14), which is a fairly literal translation of the Hebrew phrases in 11:31 and 12:11, and probably also expresses the sense of 9:27 too. Collins argues that "the desolating abomination" is the best reading, considering the parallel expressions in 11:31 and 12:11, the singular noun in the Greek versions, and the evidence from other ancient versions.[8] However, the literal meaning of 9:27, "on the wing of detested things (is) a desolator," could easily be paraphrased (in harmony with 11:31; 12:11) as speaking of "the detested thing of/causing desolation" (Mt 24:15; Mk 13:14).

וְעַד־כָּלָה וְנֶחֱרָצָה תִּתַּךְ עַל־שֹׁמֵם:—Literally, "and until the end decreed is poured out on a desolator." The feminine noun כָּלָה, "complete destruction" (BDB, 2) or "end," is modified by the feminine participle נֶחֱרָצָה (see the fifth textual note on 9:26) joined to it by *waw*, forming a hendiadys:[9] "a decreed end" of destruction. This feminine hendiadys is then the subject of the feminine Qal imperfect (of נָתַךְ), תִּתַּךְ, which has the intransitive meaning, "is poured out." The same Qal verb was also in 9:11, where it had a transitive meaning: Daniel stated that God "poured out" the covenant curse on disobedient Israel. The Qal participle שֹׁמֵם, "desolator, one who causes desolation," has

---

[6] One may see Mitchell, *Our Suffering Savior*, 137–38.
[7] Goldingay, *Daniel*, 230.
[8] Collins, *Daniel*, 346–47, 357.
[9] Collins, *Daniel*, 346. So also ESV, NIV, NRSV.

the same meaning and referent as the Poel participle מְשֻׁמֵּם in the preceding clause (see the preceding textual note).

Commentary

Gabriel Comes to Explain Jerusalem's Future (9:20–23)

Daniel begins his account of Gabriel's appearance with a summary of his prayer, in which he confesses his sin, that of Israel, and concern for "the holy mountain of my God" (9:20). This last phrase emphasizes that Daniel's concern for Jerusalem stems from the desire to reinstitute worship of God at the temple on Mount Zion. This concern is echoed in 9:21, where Daniel notes that Gabriel appeared "about the time of the evening sacrifice," about 3:00 pm (also "the ninth hour" after sunrise, when Christ died [Mt 27:45–50]). This phrase connects Daniel 9 with Daniel 8, "the vision of the evenings and mornings" (8:26), and confirms that "the evenings and mornings" in that vision refer to the evening and morning sacrifice (see the commentary on 8:14).

Daniel's vision begins with Gabriel touching him while he is praying (9:21). He identifies "Gabriel" as "the man ... whom I had seen in the first vision" (cf. 8:1). His first vision was Daniel 7. After seeing the coming of the "Son of Man" (7:13), Daniel had approached an unidentified member of the heavenly court and requested an explanation of the vision (7:16). This reference seems to identify Gabriel as that angel who had explained the prior vision. It also links chapter 9 with chapter 8, since Daniel named Gabriel also in 8:16. These connections affirm that Daniel is the author of these three visionary accounts, Daniel 7, 8, and 9.[10] The only other Scripture passages that name Gabriel are Lk 1:19, 26, in the infancy narratives of John the Baptist and Jesus. Gabriel was the angel sent to announce both births and explain the momentous significance of each.

Daniel was exhausted from his fervent prayer and time of fasting. Gabriel's arrival was signaled by his touching Daniel. In Daniel's visions in chapters 8, 9, and 10–12, a divine messenger or God himself (Gabriel in 8:18; God in human form in 10:10, 16, 18)[11] touches Daniel to strengthen him when he is weak or overwhelmed, thereby providing him with the vigor needed to receive divine revelation.

Gabriel tells Daniel he was sent "to give" him "insight [with] understanding" (9:22). God gave these two gifts to Daniel and his friends when they were first in Nebuchadnezzar's court: "insight" was given in 1:17 and "understanding" was evident in 1:20. In chapter 1, these faculties, which are related to wisdom, allowed the Judeans to discern how to be spiritually and morally faithful and also prudent.[12] Here these faculties will allow Daniel to discern God's

---

[10] Cf. Baldwin, *Daniel*, 167.

[11] For the view that the heavenly man who touches Daniel in chapter 10 is God the Son, the preincarnate Christ, see the commentary on 10:4–6.

[12] See the first textual note and the commentary on 1:17 and the first textual note and the commentary on 1:20.

unfolding plan of salvation, which will shape future history. Gabriel is giving Daniel a message designed to inculcate insight, understanding, and faith in God's plan for Jerusalem and its temple, culminating in the advent of the "Messiah" (9:25–26), Jesus Christ. A further result of these divine gifts is that Daniel will be able to author his book, one of the inspired Scriptures, "which are able to make you wise unto salvation" (2 Tim 3:15).

Gabriel also informs Daniel that "a word went forth" even as he began his prayer, and now that answer to his prayer has arrived (Dan 9:23). This shows that "your Father knows what you need before you ask him" (Mt 6:8). Daniel received this particular answer because he was "highly prized" by God (Dan 9:23). Thus Gabriel reminds Daniel of God's grace in favoring him and forgiving his sin, which he had confessed in 9:20. Daniel was well aware of his sin, as his prayer confirms multiple times. However, God pronounced him forgiven and precious in his sight, as he does every believer, whose precious treasure is Christ himself (cf. 2 Cor 4:7; 1 Pet 1:7, 19; 2:4, 6; 3:4).

Jerusalem's History as Seventy Weeks (9:24–27)

As can be seen from the quantity of textual notes on this passage, it is one of the most difficult and enigmatic portions of the OT.[13]

Daniel 9:24 and Jeremiah's Seventy Years

Gabriel reveals to Daniel that God has already determined the future of his people in their holy city Jerusalem. He begins with the same number Daniel discerned in the prophecy of Jeremiah: seventy (see the commentary on 9:2). Many commentators believe that Gabriel is reinterpreting Jeremiah's seventy years and that Daniel's prayer was about the meaning of the seventy years.[14] However, Gabriel is not interpreting the meaning of Jeremiah's prophecies of the duration of Jerusalem's desolation by Babylon. Daniel had clearly understood Jeremiah's prophecies, as he stated in 9:2. Instead, God through Gabriel uses the number seventy as a motif to explain a future desolation that will occur during the "seventy weeks" (9:24) instead of a desolation lasting "seventy years" (9:2). God's intent is not to interpret Jeremiah, but to answer the concerns of Daniel's prayer: forgiveness needed for his own sin and for the sin of his people, a turning of God's wrath from Jerusalem, and the rebuilding of the city, which, however, will then be destroyed along with its holy place. This destruction will be prompted by the cutting off of the Messiah, who will nevertheless confirm a covenant for the many and cause the OT sacrifices to cease.

---

[13] One critical scholar has dubbed the history of the exegesis of this passage "the Dismal Swamp of O.T. criticism" (Montgomery, *Daniel*, 400).

[14] E.g., Avalos, "Daniel 9:24–25 and Mesopotamian Temple Rededications," 507; Collins, *Daniel*, 352.

The Meaning of "Seventy Weeks" (9:24)

The interpretation of Gabriel's message to Daniel cannot be discussed without determining what is meant by seventy "weeks" and the following references to seven, sixty-two, and one "week" that add up to that total (the plural שָׁבֻעִים and singular שָׁבוּעַ) in 9:24–27. All commentators agree that here שָׁבוּעַ does not carry its normal meaning of a seven-day "week." We will first discuss what we believe is the proper understanding of the weeks and the messianic interpretation of the passage, even though this understanding is a minority view among modern commentators. Then we will critique the common competing views offered by critical commentators.

A "Week" Is a Symbolic Period of Time

In Deut 18:21–22 God declares that a prophecy that does not come true is a false prophecy, not spoken by Yahweh, and not to be revered. However, even after the era of Antiochus, Jews continued to preserve the book of Daniel, believing it to be sacred Scripture. After the advent of Christ, his followers too continued to regard Daniel as the inspired Word of God. These Jews and Christians must have understood it to be an accurate prophecy. The likely reason is that they understood the "weeks" to be symbolic periods of time.

Some scholars who hold that the seventy weeks are intended as 490 years nevertheless believe that it is only a schematic calculation and that the sub-groupings ("seven weeks … sixty-two weeks" in 9:25 and "one week" and "the middle of the week" in 9:27) were intended by the author to be understood symbolically and not literally.[15] That is a move in the right direction, but we must go farther and consider the possibility that the weeks were never meant to be equated with groups of seven years. Some faithful and evangelical commentators agree.[16]

Clearly, "week(s)" is being used in a metaphorical manner in 9:24–27. No interpreter would suggest that Gabriel, speaking to Daniel in 538 BC, was stating that Jerusalem would be rebuilt within seventy literal weeks, less than a year and a half. Since the meaning is clearly metaphorical, we should ask why "weeks" (instead of months or years or some other time specification) were chosen. It is probable that the choice had to do with the relationship between the Hebrew words שָׁבוּעַ, "week," and שִׁבְעָה, "seven." Seven, of course, is a number that has figured prominently in numerical symbolism in earlier chapters of Daniel.[17] Since these seventy weeks include the time during which Jerusalem will be rebuilt, the choice was probably made so that this could be seen as Jerusalem's re-creation, patterned after the seven days or one week for the

---

[15] Baldwin, *Daniel*, 168–71; Goldingay, *Daniel*, 257–58; Lucas, *Daniel*, 248.

[16] Commentators who view the seventy weeks as symbolic include Keil, *Daniel*, 336–39, 373–75; Leupold, *Daniel*, 417–18; and Young, *Daniel*, 203.

[17] See the commentary on 3:19; 4:13 (ET 4:16); 7:25; and the excursus "Daniel 4 and the Prayer of Nabonidus."

original creation (Genesis 1). Similarly, "seven times" were the period for the re-creation (repentance and restoration) of Nebuchadnezzar (see the commentary on 4:13 [ET 4:16]). "Seventy" (9:24) draws on the "seventy years" in Jeremiah (see 9:2) to signifying that desolated Jerusalem would be rebuilt, and the "weeks" draw on Genesis 1 to signify re-creation.

"Seventy" and "weeks" are commonly used for symbolic time in apocalypses written after Daniel, and many of these apocalypses represent a kind of commentary on how their authors understood these terms in Daniel.[18] For example, according to *1 Enoch* 10:11–12, the evil watchers are imprisoned for "seventy generations" until the judgment. *1 Enoch* 91:12–19; 93:1–10, often called "the Apocalypse of Weeks," divides history into ten "weeks." The *Pesher on the Periods* (4Q180, 4Q181) seems to divide the time when Israel was led astray into seventy weeks. The *Apocalypse of Thomas*, composed no later than the fifth century AD, divides the time of eschatological judgment into periods of hours and days. In none of these works are the time periods to be understood as literal, whether they be years, weeks, days, or hours.[19] The book of Revelation pictures world history in terms of seven seals, seven trumpets, and seven censers, which clearly do not represent measurable time periods, but are symbolic.

The "seventy weeks" in Daniel should be understood as having only symbolical import. They and their subdivisions ("seven weeks ... sixty-two weeks" in 9:25; "one week ... the middle of the week," 9:27) do not predict an exact chronology. Instead, "week" has a symbolical significance that implies re-creation and the passing of the length of time determined by God to accomplish his re-creation.

The Messianic Interpretation of the Seventy Weeks

The traditional Christian interpretation of 9:24–27 is that the Messiah in 9:25–26 is Jesus Christ and that the seventy weeks culminate in the first advent of Christ. A common expression of this view is illustrated as the first view in figure 12. This is the view of Luther and Calvin, and many modern conservative and evangelical Christian scholars have adopted this view.[20] A messianic interpretation has also been held by a few Jewish interpreters.[21] This interpretation understands the seventy weeks as commencing with the end of the captivity (the exact date is debated; see the discussion below) and climaxing at the sixty-ninth

---

[18] Although Collins, *Daniel*, 352–53, considers the seventy weeks to be 490 years, he admits that later apocalypses use "seventy" and "weeks" in purely symbolic portrayals of time.

[19] For a discussion of how such works divide history into periods, see Steinmann, "The Shape of Things to Come," 25–147.

[20] Luther, "Preface to Daniel," AE 35:303–5; Calvin, *Daniel*, 2:195–231; Newman, "Daniel's Seventy Weeks and the Old Testament Sabbath-Year Cycle"; Payne, "The Goal of Daniel's Seventy Weeks"; Young, *Daniel*, 191–221. This view is summarized in *The End Times: A Study on Eschatology and Millennialism* (a report of the Commission on Theology and Church Relations of The Lutheran Church—Missouri Synod, September 1989), 50–51, which presents it as one of two salutary views of the passage.

[21] See further "The Purpose of the Seventy Weeks (9:24)."

Figure 12

The Seventy Weeks (Daniel 9:24–27)

THE TRADITIONAL MESSIANIC INTERPRETATION

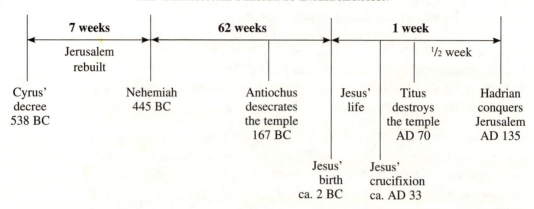

THE TYPOLOGICAL MESSIANIC INTERPRETATION

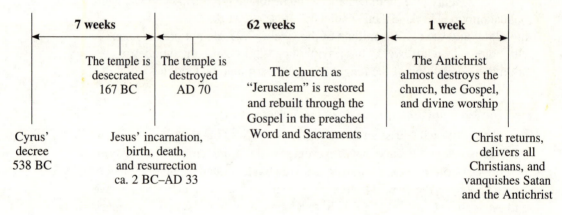

week with the coming of the Messiah. The seventy weeks are often interpreted (e.g., by Luther and Calvin) as ending with the destruction of Jerusalem by the Romans under Titus (AD 70) or Hadrian (AD 135).[22] According to this view, Daniel 9 was fulfilled in its entirety by those events soon after the first advent of Christ. This agrees with the words of Jesus, who taught that the detested thing of desolation prophesied by Daniel (in the second half of the seventieth week [9:27]) would occur after his ministry (Mt 24:15; Mk 13:14), although he did not indicate how long afterward.

A typological messianic interpretation held by notable Lutherans of the nineteenth and twentieth centuries (Kliefoth, Keil, Leupold) is that the vision covers the entire time between the time of Daniel and the second coming of Christ.[23] This is the second view illustrated in figure 12. The first seven weeks represent the time between the edict of Cyrus (538 BC) and the first advent of Christ. The sixty-two weeks represent the church age, when the Christian church, "the spiritual Jerusalem,"[24] the antitype[25] of OT Israel, is built up through the preaching of the Gospel and administration of the Sacraments. However, the church will often endure "troubled times" (9:25). The persecution of the church began already with Christ's own suffering and death. It will continue, especially by means of the Antichrist, who is already present now,[26] until the Lord returns in glory to save his suffering followers and vanquish all his enemies (Mk 13:1–26; also Mt 24:1–31; Lk 21:5–28). This persecution reaches its climax during the seventieth week, which is Satan's "little" season (Rev 20:3).[27] The typological view agrees with the traditional view that "Messiah, a

---

[22] Luther, "Preface to Daniel," AE 35:305; Calvin, *Daniel*, 2:229; Payne, "The Goal of Daniel's Seventy Weeks." Payne provides an interesting exception as a premillennialist who views this prophecy as fulfilled with Titus' destruction of the temple.

[23] This view is summarized in (but not adopted by) Young, *Daniel*, 193–94, citing Kliefoth and Keil. See Kliefoth, *Übersetzung des Buches Daniel*, and Keil, *Daniel*, 336–402. It is also endorsed by Leupold, *Daniel*, 404–5, and advocated by him on pages 409–40. It is summarized in *The End Times: A Study on Eschatology and Millennialism*, 51, which presents it as the second of two salutary views of the passage.

[24] Leupold, *Daniel*, 424. NT passages that would support this view of the church and Jerusalem include Gal 4:26; Heb 12:22; and eschatologically, Rev 3:12 and Revelation 21.

[25] Typology involves both similarities and differences, and the OT type is surpassed by the greater NT antitype. Here "antitype" emphasizes similarity and continuity. The NT church is the continuation of OT Israel as the elect, redeemed people of God, bound to him by his covenant of grace. The church is the heir of God's Gospel promises in the OT (see, e.g., Romans 4–5; Galatians 3) as well as those in the NT.

[26] The little horn in Daniel 7 is a visionary prophecy of the future Antichrist, who was present but hidden in the apostolic era, then was revealed after the fall of the Roman Empire, fulfilling 2 Thess 2:6–7. In the fourth and fifth centuries AD, the Roman papacy began to openly claim supremacy over all Christendom and confound the Gospel. For the length of the Antichrist's persecution of the church, see "The Duration of the Little Horn's Warfare: Three and a Half Times" in the commentary on 7:25. For more description of the Antichrist, his identity, and his persecution, see also figure 10 in the excursus "The Four-Kingdom Schema in Daniel," the commentary on 7:8, 20–21, 25, and especially the excursus "The Lutheran Confessions on the Antichrist in Daniel."

[27] See the diagram of amillennialism in figure 3, "Timeline of Biblical Eschatology."

Leader" in 9:25 is Jesus Christ. But the typological view considers the "leader who is coming" in 9:26 to be the Antichrist, who is also the one in 9:27 who "will confirm a covenant for the many," a wicked covenant of allegiance to Satan (cf. Mt 24:5, 11; 2 Thess 2:9–12; Rev 13:4, 12–18), and who "will cause sacrifice and offering to cease," that is, will prevent Christian worship with God's means of grace, the faithful proclamation of the Gospel and administration of the Sacraments. The Antichrist, the antitype of Antiochus IV Epiphanes,[28] succeeds in cutting off the Messiah (Dan 9:26) by all but silencing his Gospel and eradicating believers in Christ, who comprise the true church. The Antichrist makes a covenant with many and hinders divine worship. However, he and the last week are brought to an end by the glorious return of Christ.[29]

The typological interpretation has some advantages but also suffers from weaknesses. First, it requires a change in the referent of the same Hebrew title, נָגִיד, "leader," in 9:25 (Christ) versus 9:26 (the Antichrist).[30] (Dispensational interpretations share that same weakness.) Second, throughout Daniel, "Jerusalem" refers to the physical city. Even in Daniel 9 every occurrence of "Jerusalem" in the prayer (9:2, 7, 12, 16) refers to the city. The typological interpretation requires that "Jerusalem" in 9:25 and the reference to "the city" in 9:26 all of a sudden become references to the church without any contextual clues to this change. Third, it requires that the "destruction" of the city and the holy place (representing the church) to be only partial or incomplete, although the text does not qualify the destruction as partial or otherwise less than complete. Participles of the verb שָׁמֵם are used once in 9:26 (שֹׁמְמוֹת) and twice in 9:27 (מְשֹׁמֵם ... שֹׁמֵם) to describe this destruction. This verb means "to be desolate" or "to be devastated," and when referring to places it means that they become uninhabited or deserted (see *HALOT*, Qal, 1). The text of the vision indicates full destruction, something the typological interpretation and its understand-

---

[28] See figure 10, "Comparison between the Little Horn in Daniel 7 and the Little Horn in Daniel 8." The little horn in Daniel 8 represents Antiochus, and the little horn in Daniel 7 represents the Antichrist. The Antichrist is the "antitype" of Antiochus in the sense of continuity: both fiercely persecute God's people and seek to prevent divine worship. In keeping with typology, the antitype is greater than the OT type. Antiochus reigned for a relatively short time and persecuted God's people in a limited geographic area. The Antichrist is active throughout the church age and seeks to corrupt the church throughout the world.

When compared to Christ himself, the Antichrist is an "antitype" in a negative sense that stresses their oppositeness. The Antichrist is a religious leader who commands allegiance and claims to guide his followers in the way of truth and life, but he usurps the role of Christ and leads people away from saving faith in Christ, into death. He operates by false imitation and deception, as do all of Satan's agents. See, for example, Mt 7:15; 2 Cor 11:14; 1 Jn 2:18–22; 2 Jn 7.

[29] The defeat and damnation of the Antichrist at the return of Christ is described in, for example, 2 Thess 2:8 and Rev 19:20. The Antichrist is described by Paul in 2 Thess 2:1–12 as "the man of lawlessness." In Revelation 13, Satan conjures two beasts. The Antichrist is represented by the second beast (13:11–18) and also by the "false prophet" (Rev 19:20) defeated in the last battle at the return of Christ (Rev 19:11–21).

[30] However, those who hold to this view maintain that calling the Antichrist a נָגִיד, "leader," in 9:26 indicates that the Antichrist is a false imitation who mimics the נָגִיד, "Leader," in 9:25, who is Christ.

ing of Jerusalem as the church cannot admit, since the NT clearly indicates that the church will never be completely wiped out like an uninhabited or deserted city (e.g., Mt 16:18; 24:22). The Lutheran Confessions concur in teaching the church's persistence in this world even through the fiercest persecutions.[31]

Some interpreters equate the final half week (half of a seven) in Daniel (9:27) with the three and a half "times" in Dan 7:25 and with the three and a half "times" in 12:7, and also with the time period in Revelation called "forty-two months" (Rev 11:2; 13:5) and "1,260 days" (Rev 11:3; 12:6), both of which are half of seven years, and "time, times, and half a time" (Rev 12:14).[32] The contexts of each of those passages in Revelation depict the era in which Satan and his minions attempt to silence the Gospel and destroy the church. Brighton comments:

> In both Daniel [7:25; 12:7] and Revelation this time period is that period of time when God's people on earth will be trodden underfoot by the pagan nations. Daniel sees this time of suffering and persecution prophetically in the future, while John sees it as the time in which he is living, a time that will also continue until the end of the present world at Christ's return. ... The entire church age is a time of tribulation, though toward the end of it, persecution shall increase to the point where it becomes a great tribulation.[33]

Dispensational premillennialists usually view the first sixty-nine weeks as ending with Christ's earthly ministry and consider the seventieth week (or sometimes only the last half of the seventieth week) to still be in the future. The last "week" will be a seven-year period of tribulation immediately before the return of Christ to set up his millennial kingdom on earth. During this future time of tribulation, the Antichrist will be the desolator of which 9:27 speaks.[34] Dispensationalists too equate the final half week in Daniel with the time period in Rev 11:2–3; 12:6, 14; 13:5. However, they believe this time period did not begin in the apostolic age. Rather, it still lies entirely in the future.

The dispensational view that the seventieth week consists of seven literal years and that it (or at least the last half of it) lies in the future, immediately before the return of Christ, suffers from grave exegetical problems. First, it must

---

[31] The Augsburg Confession begins its article on the church by saying: "It is also taught among us that one holy Christian church will be and remain forever" (AC VII 1). See also Ap VII/VIII 9.

[32] This is especially common among dispensational premillennialists. See Miller, *Daniel*, 271–72, and Walvoord, *Daniel*, 175–76, 235–37, 293–96.

[33] Brighton, *Revelation*, 289. Brighton has a fuller discussion of this time period on pages 287–91. As to why the entire church age should be described by numbers in Revelation that amount to half of seven years (years that are figurative, not literal), Brighton believes that the NT age is being depicted as the second half of a seven. He believes the OT era of God's gracious covenant with Israel could described by an equal number, so that the OT and NT eras of God's grace together would add up to a complete seven (p. 291).

[34] Archer, "Daniel," 117–18; McComiskey, "The Seventy 'Weeks' of Daniel against the Background of Ancient Near Eastern Literature," 32–35; Miller, *Daniel*, 269; Walvoord, *Daniel*, 236–37.

propose a gap of at least two millennia between the sixth-ninth and seventieth weeks, although there is no textual support for any gap in the seventy weeks.[35] Second, the dispensational interpretation understands the "Leader" in 9:25 to be Christ while holding that the "leader" in 9:26 is the Antichrist.[36] This too is without support in the text, which gives no indication that such a distinction ought to be made. The most natural way to read the text is to understand "Messiah, a Leader" in 9:25 to be the same "Messiah" and "Leader" in 9:26.

Further details about the traditional Christian messianic interpretation, which is followed by this commentary, are given below in the exposition of the individual verses in 9:24–27. But first it is necessary to address some invalid views and their invalid objections to the messianic interpretation.

These are the chief criticisms raised against the messianic interpretation:[37]

1. The "messiah/anointed one" (9:25–26) in this passage cannot be messianic since there is no interest in a messianic figure elsewhere in Daniel. This objection is circular reasoning since critical scholars discount the messianic meaning of Daniel 2 and 7 and other passages. If those passages are indeed about the Messiah, as argued in this commentary,[38] then this objection is baseless. Moreover, even some critics admit that 9:24–27 is messianic.[39]

2. The "going forth of a word" in 9:25 most likely refers to the prophecies of Jeremiah, which rules out a messianic interpretation. However, it is unclear why critics reason that this interpretation of 9:25 rules out a messianic interpretation of the passage. A messianic interpretation would only be impossible if the seventy weeks started during the ministry of Jeremiah and spanned 490 literal years, since in that case they would end some time during the second century BC. Moreover, there is no good reason to assume that 9:25 refers to Jeremiah's prophecies. As argued below in the commentary on 9:25, it refers to Gabriel being sent forth by God to Daniel (in 538 BC) with the word that Jerusalem would be restored (9:23).

3. It reads the "seven weeks" and "sixty-two weeks" in 9:25 as a unit, contrary to a Masoretic accent, the *athnach* on שָׁבֻעִים שִׁבְעָה in 9:25. This objection exaggerates the *athnach*. It also distorts the fact that conservatives do follow the meaning of the Hebrew text. This commentary will argue below that the

---

[35] This supposed gap was unknown prior to the rise of the Plymouth Brethren and their peculiar hermeneutics propounded most notably by J. N. Darby in the 1830s.

[36] This is an exegetical slight-of-hand similar to that of the Antiochene interpretation. See "The Seventy Weeks Do Not Refer to the Oppression by Antiochus" below.

[37] Lucas, *Daniel*, 246, provides a convenient list of these objections.

[38] In Daniel, Christ appears as the "stone" in 2:34–35, 44–45; "a son of gods" in 3:25; possibly the "angel" in 6:23 (ET 6:22); the "Son of Man" in 7:13–14; and the divine man in 10:4–21. See the textual note on 2:34; the second textual note on 3:25b; the second textual note on 3:28; and the commentary on 2:44–45; 3:25, 28; 7:13; and 10:4–6. See also "Daniel in the New Testament," and "The Messiah in Daniel: An Overview" in "Major Themes" in the introduction.

[39] E.g., Rosenberg, "The Slain Messiah in the Old Testament," 260.

Masoretic pointing is correct and that the text presents the "seven weeks" and the "sixty-two weeks" as consecutive periods (adding up to a total of sixty-nine weeks) that span the time period from Daniel until the advent of the Messiah. This understanding of the Hebrew text is at least as old as Theodotion's Greek translation.[40]

4. The introduction of a gap in time between the sixty-ninth and seventieth week is unwarranted. This objection is valid, but it applies only to the dispensational premillennial variation of the messianic interpretation. It does not apply to either of the traditional, amillennial Christian messianic interpretations.

A "Week" Does Not Mean Seven Years

Most modern critical commentators and also some evangelicals believe that a "week" means seven literal years, so that the "seventy weeks" (9:24) are a total of 490 years.[41] Their common assumption is that since the source of the expression "seventy weeks" is Jeremiah's prophecies of "seventy years," each week must represent a set of seven years.[42] However, that assumption is without warrant. The only thing that is clear is that through Gabriel, God is transforming the "seventy years" (9:2) he spoke of to Jeremiah into "seventy weeks" (9:24). Daniel 9 gives no indication that the "weeks" are intended to mean groups of seven years. A transformation has taken place in the meaning of the temporal noun, but the text does not explicitly describe the extent of the transformation. For example, it does not say, "seventy weeks of years."

Another line of argumentation given by scholars who support the theory that the weeks are groups of seven years is that the word spoken through Gabriel is patterned after the sabbatical year reckoning as presented in Leviticus (Lev 25:8; 26:27–35).[43] Some note that 2 Chr 36:18–21 specifically connects Leviticus 26 with the seventy-year prophecy of Jeremiah. However, there is no evidence in Daniel 9 that Gabriel is connecting the seventy-year prophecy of Jeremiah with the sabbatical cycle. The passages in Leviticus that command the sabbatical-year cycle do not use the term "week" to describe the period from one sabbatical year to another. Instead, the seven-year periods are described as "Sabbaths of years" (שַׁבְּתֹת שָׁנִים, Lev 25:8) and "Sabbaths" (שַׁבְּתֹת, Lev 26:34–35). Gabriel, on the

---

[40] See further "The Relationship between the Seven Weeks and the Sixty-Two Weeks" in the commentary on 9:25.

[41] Baldwin, *Daniel*, 168; Calvin, *Daniel*, 2:196–97; Collins, *Daniel*, 352; Dimant, "The Seventy Weeks Chronology (Dan 9,24–27) in the Light of New Qumranic Texts"; Goldingay, *Daniel*, 257–58; Gruenthaner, "The Seventy Weeks," 47; Hartman and Di Lella, *Daniel*, 244; Hasel, "The Hebrew Masculine Plural for 'Weeks' in the Expression 'Seventy Weeks' in Daniel 9:24"; Lucas, *Daniel*, 241; Luther, "Preface to Daniel," AE 35:303; Miller, *Daniel*, 257–58; Montgomery, *Daniel*, 373; Newman, "Daniel's Seventy Weeks and the Old Testament Sabbath-Year Cycle." The medieval Jewish scholar Saadia Gaon also understood the seventy weeks as 490 years (Chazan, "Daniel 9:24–27: Exegesis and Polemics," 146).

[42] E.g., Goldingay, *Daniel*, 257.

[43] Baldwin, *Daniel*, 168; Collins, *Daniel*, 352; Lucas, *Daniel*, 241; Lurie, "A New Interpretation of Daniel's 'Sevens' and the Chronology of the Seventy 'Sevens' "; Montgomery, *Daniel*, 373.

other hand, never describes the weeks as "Sabbaths." Moreover, Daniel's other visions contain many time-conditioned references, but there is no evidence that his other prophecies were influenced by sabbatical cycles. Therefore, there is no support in Daniel 9 or in the rest of the book for this argument.

In addition, all of the historical calculations based on the assumption that the seventy weeks represent 490 years have failed to arrive at a satisfactory conclusion. For instance, Luther assumes that the weeks correspond to groups of seven years. He claims that the sixty-nine weeks (the seven weeks plus sixty-two weeks in 9:25, which would total 483 years) extend from the time of the prophecies of Haggai and Zechariah to the coming of the Messiah, ending on the date of Jesus' Baptism.[44] Unfortunately, Luther is relying on a faulty historical calculation; the actual span of time is about 550 years. In a similar vein, Calvin understands the weeks to be groups of seven years and believes that the sixty-nine weeks in 9:25 span the time from Cyrus' decree (2 Chr 36:22–23; Ezra 1:1–4) to the Baptism of Jesus. However, Calvin is unable to propose a specific reckoning that proves his point.[45] The actual time between those two historical events would be about 568 years.

Many modern critical scholars assume that the "seventy weeks" are a prediction of 490 years between Jeremiah's prophecies of a seventy-year captivity and the defilement of the temple by Antiochus Epiphanes (see further "The Seventy Weeks Do Not Refer to the Oppression by Antiochus" below).[46] However, the actual span of time between those two events was about 438 years. Critics then explain the error in the alleged prediction as demonstrating a lack of real historical knowledge by the author of Daniel. The problem with this approach is that it uses a modern mistake (the assumption that a "week" is seven years) to "prove" an ancient mistake (the miscalculation of 490 instead of 438 years) that in turn "proves" another modern mistake (the assumption that the author of Daniel portrayed history falsely). We might have reason to believe that the author had intended a "week" to mean "seven years" if his prediction (interpreted to mean 490 years) were accurate, but that is not the case.

Evangelical scholars who hold that the weeks are to be understood as groups of seven years generally attempt to find a more congenial starting point for the "going forth of a word to restore and rebuild Jerusalem" (9:25), so that the end of the sixty-ninth week coincides with a date during Jesus' earthly life and ministry. Frequently, they pick Artaxerxes' permission to Nehemiah to return to Jerusalem in 445 BC, since it mentions rebuilding Jerusalem (Neh 2:4–6).[47] However, there are two main problems with this calculation. First, the permis-

---

[44] Luther, "Preface to Daniel," AE 35:303–4.

[45] Calvin, *Daniel*, 2:203–14.

[46] E.g., Hartman and Di Lella, *Daniel*, 250–53. Collins, *Daniel*, 354–55, understands the period to be from the time of Daniel's prayer to the time of Antiochus, which would be about 372 years.

[47] E.g., Walvoord, *Daniel*, 228.

sion given Nehemiah to rebuild Jerusalem is set in the context of rebuilding its walls and gates (Neh 1:3; 2:3, 8, 13, 15, 17), and the ruin and lack of rebuilding in Jerusalem *only* refers to its walls and gates, not to its temple. Moreover, the rebuilding of the wall had already been started many years before (Ezra 4:12). The rebuilding of Jerusalem as a whole had begun long before Nehemiah, with houses and the temple in Jerusalem (Ezra 1–7; Hag 1:4, 14). The concern for Jerusalem in Dan 9:24–27 centers on the temple, whose rebuilding was started in 536 and completed in 515 BC.

The second problem with starting the seventy weeks in 445 BC is that the sixty-nine weeks in 9:25 (483 years) would end in AD 39, at least six years and perhaps nine years after Jesus' crucifixion (when he was "cut off," 9:26) and resurrection in AD 33 or AD 30. If one "week" represented seven years, then Daniel's prophecy should have said that the events in 9:26 would occur after seven plus sixty-*one* weeks, not the seven plus sixty-*two* weeks given in 9:25.

To solve this dilemma supporters of this theory often suppose that Gabriel is speaking about "prophetic years" which are 360 days long, about five days shorter than a normal year.[48] Proponents of this supposed prophetic year claim support from Revelation, where 1,260 days appear to correspond to forty-two months, yielding exactly thirty days for each month (Rev 11:2–3; 12:6; 13:5; cf. Rev 12:14).[49] These foreshortened years allow the terminal date to be AD 32, which is supposed to be the exact year of Jesus' triumphal entry into Jerusalem and subsequent crucifixion.[50] Yet the weakness of this scheme is the concept of the "prophetic year." There is no evidence in Scripture for the use of calculations with such years outside of Revelation, and Revelation itself is probably using time periods symbolically.[51] Certainly, Daniel's use of the word "year" elsewhere in his book is understood according to the soli-lunar calendar used throughout the ancient Near East. These years varied in length due to the insertion of intercalary months in some years, but their average length was just over 365 days, a normal solar year. If Daniel was to "know and have insight" (9:25) that the seventy weeks were weeks of years, there would have been no way

---

[48] The use of so-called prophetic years was popularized by Sir Robert Anderson in his book on the seventy weeks in Daniel 9, *The Coming Prince* (first published in 1881), 67–75, 99–100, 127–28, who mistakenly claims that 360 days was the length of the lunisolar year used by the Israelites. On the Israelite calendar, see Finegan, *Handbook of Biblical Chronology*, 29–33, and Archer, "Daniel," 115, 120. The concept of prophetic years has become a mainstay for many dispensational premillennial interpreters.

[49] E.g., Anderson, *The Coming Prince*, 73–75; Walvoord, *Daniel*, 228.

[50] This date for Jesus' crucifixion was first proposed at the end of the nineteenth century (Anderson, *The Coming Prince*, 97, 122).

[51] The fact that forty-two months is reckoned as 1,260 days in Revelation is a clue that the apostle John intended these months to be symbolic, since the calendars commonly used in antiquity contained months of varying length. Whether one uses the ancient Near Eastern soli-lunar calendar, the later Gregorian calendar, or the Julian calendar, the length of forty-two months is about 1,278 days, since all of these calendars closely approximate the average solar year of 365.24 days.

for him to perceive that the years were intended as shorter "prophetic years," whose length would not be revealed until half a millennium later, in the book of Revelation. The "prophetic year" calculation is nothing more than special pleading and cannot be seriously considered. Moreover, the year of Jesus' triumphal entry, crucifixion, and resurrection probably is either AD 30 or (more probably) AD 33.[52] The choice of AD 32 for Jesus' entry into Jerusalem seems to be designed to fit the calculation based on Daniel, and the starting point seems to be chosen to fit a possible ending date that yields an important event in Jesus' life.

An alternate dating scheme used by some evangelicals is to claim that the "going forth of a word to restore and rebuild Jerusalem" (9:25) is the decree of Artaxerxes to Ezra in 458 BC (Ezra 7:11–26).[53] The problem with this is that Artaxerxes' "word" did not include any mention of rebuilding Jerusalem, so it cannot be characterized as "a word to restore and rebuild."[54] Moreover, as noted above, rebuilding in Jerusalem had begun long before that time, with houses and the temple in Jerusalem (Ezra 1–7; Hag 1:4, 14). If one follows this proposal, the coming of the Messiah at the end of sixty-nine weeks would have taken place in AD 26, a possible date for Jesus' Baptism and the beginning of his ministry. However, the most likely date for Jesus' Baptism is AD 29.[55]

Moreover, while "until Messiah, a Leader" (9:25) could be a reference to Jesus' Baptism, it could also be a reference to his incarnation, his birth, or his triumphal entry into Jerusalem. "Until Messiah" (9:25) most likely is a reference to Jesus' birth, since at his birth Jesus was first called χριστός, "Christ" (Lk 2:11), the Greek equivalent of Hebrew מָשִׁיחַ, "Messiah" (see the first textual note on 9:25). This title was given by "an angel of the Lord" (Lk 2:9), who most likely was Gabriel (since he is named in Lk 1:19, 26). Like the previous proposal (starting in 445 BC), the choice of Jesus' Baptism for the end date seems to be designed to fit the calculation, and the starting point seems to be chosen to fit a possible ending date that yields an important event in Jesus' life.

In conclusion, none of the proposals that view the weeks as groups of seven literal years can adequately explain Gabriel's words and the fulfillment of the prophecy.

---

[52] Finegan, *Handbook of Biblical Chronology*, 361–62.

[53] Archer, "Daniel," 114; Miller, *Daniel*, 266; Payne, "The Goal of Daniel's Seventy Weeks," 101.

[54] Miller, *Daniel*, 266, n. 85, admits as much in this concession: "The only real problem with the 458 B.C. date is that this decree did not specifically refer to the building of the city as did the later proclamation to Nehemiah." Miller seeks to rescue his position by saying, "Evidently, permission to rebuild was implied in earlier decrees." However, if it was implied in earlier decrees, then should not one of them be viewed as the "going forth of a word to restore and rebuild Jerusalem" (9:25)?

[55] Finegan, *Handbook of Biblical Chronology*, 329–49.

The Seventy Weeks Do Not Refer to the Oppression by Antiochus

The standard critical view (favored also by a few evangelicals) is that the "seventy weeks" (9:24–27) culminate in the persecution of the Jews in Jerusalem by Antiochus IV Epiphanes. This view often alleges that 9:24–27 was written after the persecution, but worded as if it were a prophecy before the events it describes (*ex eventu* prophecy).[56] The primary reason why critics favor it is their bias against any genuine predictive prophecy.

According to a typical expression of this interpretation, the "word" that goes forth (9:25) is one of Jeremiah's prophecies, most likely the Book of Consolation (Jeremiah 30–31, especially 30:18; 31:38–39). The coming anointed one in 9:25 is Cyrus or one of the postexilic leaders mentioned in the OT: Zerubbabel or Joshua. This would make the exile equivalent to the first seven "weeks," about forty-nine years, from about 587/586 to 538/537. The anointed one who is cut off after the next sixty-two weeks (9:26) is supposed to be the high priest Onias III, who was murdered in 171 BC. The middle of the final week (9:27) saw the desecration of the temple by Antiochus, about three and a half years after the death of Onias. The final part of the seventieth "week" led to the Maccabean victory and the cleansing of the temple. This interpretation assumes that שִׁקּוּצִים מְשֹׁמֵם, literally, "detested things, a desolator," in 9:27 is to be equated with the events related in 11:31 and 12:11 and that 1 Macc 1:54 (βδέλυγμα ἐρημώσεως) is a reference to Dan 9:27 (as well as to 11:31; 12:11).

Though critical scholars often treat this view as the self-evident meaning of Gabriel's words, it has several problems:

1. The messiah (מָשִׁיחַ) who is defined as a leader (נָגִיד) in 9:25 must be seen as a different individual than the messiah (מָשִׁיחַ) in 9:26a and the leader (נָגִיד) in 9:26b. This is a doubtful proposition, considering the close proximity of these words within a single oracle.[57]

2. Within 9:25 the "seven weeks" must be separated from the "sixty-two weeks" in order to find two anointed ones. Critical scholars often appeal to the Masoretic pointing, which places an *athnach* accent at the end of the "seven weeks" (שָׁבֻעִים שִׁבְעָה), so that a new clause begins with the "sixty-two weeks."[58]

---

[56] Collins, *Daniel*, 352–58; Dimant, "The Seventy Weeks Chronology (Dan 9,24–27) in the Light of New Qumranic Texts"; Goldingay, *Daniel*, 260–63; Gruenthaner, "The Seventy Weeks"; Hartman and Di Lella, *Daniel*, 250–53; Lucas, *Daniel*, 246–48; Montgomery, *Daniel*, 378–90. Note also Baldwin, *Daniel*, 173, who understands the seventieth week to refer to Antiochus' persecution, but she cannot reconcile this with Jesus' words in the NT (Mt 24:15; Mk 13:14). Therefore, she takes them as historically fulfilled in Antiochus, but also with future implications.

[57] Montgomery's objection that the second occurrence of נָגִיד, "leader," should have had an article if it referred to the first occurrence (*Daniel*, 384) misses the fact that it is being treated as a title and so it needs no article. This is demonstrated by the use of the arthrous participle הַבָּא, "who is coming," which immediately follows it in 9:26 and modifies it.

[58] Pierce, "Spiritual Failure, Postponement, and Daniel 9," 213–15. Goldingay notes the pointing and speculates that the accent may have been adopted by the Masoretes for anti-messianic (anti-Christian?) reasons (*Daniel*, 229).

However, the phrases "seven weeks" and "sixty-two weeks" are still adjacent to one another in the Hebrew and obviously are part of the same verse. Hebrew verses normally have an *athnach* that marks the end of the first half of the verse. If the two phrases referred to separated time periods, we might have expected the second phrase to begin a new verse, but the Masoretes did not divide the verse between the phrases. Moreover, the two phrases are framed by the mention of the Messiah immediately before the "seven weeks" in 9:25 and again immediately after the repeated mention of "sixty-two weeks" in 9:26, making it likely that they are to be understood consecutively. Therefore, a total of sixty-nine "weeks" transpire from the going forth of the word to the coming of the Messiah.

3. The "sixty-two weeks" that are supposed to transpire from the return from exile to the messiah should be 434 years. However, since the edict of Cyrus permitting the return was issued in 538 BC, this would place Onias' murder at about 104 BC, not 171 BC.[59] This has led some to understand the weeks to be only schematic or symbolic time periods. Others simply claim that the writer was confused or misinformed about the actual time.[60] However, we would have to ask how the writer knew the actual time of the exile and the actual time from the death of Onias to the oppression by Antiochus, but did not know the time between those events. Jewish writers during the second century BC were not as ignorant of chronology as critics often assume.[61]

4. The half week that follows the desecration of the temple (9:27) should have lasted three and a half years according to this interpretation. However, in fact it lasted just over three years.[62] To solve this inconsistency, critics propose that the original writer of this *ex eventu* prophecy was writing after Antiochus' desecration of the temple, but before the Maccabean victory. They allege that his prediction of the imminent victory constituted his only real prophecy, but the author fell short by some six months.[63] Blaming the author of the text is an ingenious but unconvincing way to explain why the text does not support this modern theory of interpretation.

5. The text of 9:24–27 does not match what we know from other sources about Antiochus' activities and what was accomplished during the Maccabean era. McComiskey summarizes the problems:

---

[59] Pierce, "Spiritual Failure, Postponement, and Daniel 9," recognizes this problem. He proposes an idiosyncratic interpretation that the events relate not to Antiochus, but the Hasmoneans. The death of Aristobulus I ends the sixty-nine weeks, and the persecution of fellow Jews by Alexander Jannaeus took place during the seventieth week. However, Pierce's chronology requires gaps between the first seven weeks and the sixty-two weeks, and between the sixty-two weeks and the final week. His proposal has not found support from others.

[60] E.g., Montgomery, *Daniel*, 393.

[61] Laato, "The Seventy Yearweeks in the Book of Daniel," 213–19, compellingly argues for the accurate knowledge of history by second-century Jewish writers.

[62] See the commentary on 8:13–14.

[63] E.g., Hartman and Di Lella, *Daniel*, 253–54.

The view that holds that this figure [the "messiah" in 9:26] is Onias III and that the *nāgîd* ["leader"] is Antiochus Epiphanes has several weaknesses. The most significant is that Antiochus did not fulfill the total range of the prophecy. J. Baldwin notes, "Commentators who argue that Antiochus Epiphanes fulfilled this prophecy are at a loss to account for the fact that he destroyed neither the Temple nor the city of Jerusalem, though undoubtedly much damage was done (1 Macc. 1:31, 38)." And J. A. Montgomery, who holds this view, acknowledges, "To be sure, a similar objection may be made against our identification of the final Week of the Seventy with the period of Ant[iochus]'s tyranny, for the 62 Weeks would then take us down some 65 years too far." However, he meets this objection by positing "a chronological miscalculation on part of the writer." The "strong covenant" of [9:]27 has always been difficult to find within the scope of Antiochus' political activity. And, the ultimacy of such statements as "to put an end to sin" and "to bring in everlasting righteousness" [9:24] seems to strike a discordant note when one places them against the background of the Hasmonean struggle.[64]

Therefore, the interpretation that sees 9:24–27 as fulfilled in Antiochus' persecution fails on chronological and historical grounds. It also does violence to the text by claiming different referents for each of the two instances of "Messiah" and "Leader" (9:25–26) when the text itself contains no hint of such a rapid shift of referent.

The Purpose of the Seventy Weeks (9:24)

Gabriel in 9:24 uses six infinitive phrases to describe God's purpose for the seventy weeks. They are arranged in two groups of three with the third in each group being the climax. The first three are these:

> to end transgression,
>> to finish sin,
>>> and to atone for iniquity

These three assure Daniel that his sin and the sin of his people are forgiven through the coming Messiah. He will bring an end to sin's power by atoning for all sin.[65] These infinitives point to the atoning death and resurrection of Jesus Christ as the purpose and goal of the seventy weeks. They view it from a negative perspective: our need for the forgiveness of our sin.

The second group of three infinitives focuses on the same thing, but in a positive sense:

> to bring everlasting righteousness,
>> to seal up vision and prophet,
>>> and to anoint a Most Holy One

---

[64] McComiskey, "The Seventy 'Weeks' of Daniel against the Background of Ancient Near Eastern Literature," 31, quoting Baldwin, *Daniel*, 171; Montgomery, *Daniel*, 393.

[65] Some critical scholars view the "sin" mentioned here as Antiochus' desecration of the altar (Collins, *Daniel*, 354, referring back to pp. 339–40; Goldingay, *Daniel*, 259). However, it is difficult to see how Daniel could call that act "my sin," or how the subsequent cleansing of the temple by Judas Maccabaeus could have been viewed as an atonement for Daniel's sin.

The righteousness that the Messiah will bring will be everlasting. This implies that there will be no further need of righteousness obtained by repeated sacrifices at the temple; Christ's once-for-all sacrifice atones for all sins committed by all people (Heb 7:27; 9:12; 10:11–14). Therefore, the advent and atonement of the Messiah toward the end of the seventy weeks will bring an end to the temple and its system of sacrifices instituted by Moses.

The seventy weeks will also see the sealing of "vision and prophet" (9:24). While some commentators view this as a witness to the authenticity of the words of the prophets,[66] a seal not only witnesses to the authenticity of the words on a scroll, but it also prevents further words from being written on it (see the fourth textual note on 9:24). Thus the sealing of "vision and prophet" is an affirmation that no further prophecy will be needed once the seventy weeks are ended.[67]

The final infinitive states this purpose: וְלִמְשֹׁחַ קֹדֶשׁ קָדָשִׁים, "to anoint a Most Holy One" (9:24). This phrase has been understood in two ways. Most critical scholars and some evangelicals understand it to be a reference to the rebuilt second temple in Jerusalem.[68] The superlative phrase קֹדֶשׁ קָדָשִׁים, "holy of holies, most holy," is always used in association with the tabernacle or temple: It describes objects used in the tabernacle or temple, including the altar, utensils, basin, and incense (Ex 29:37; 30:10, 29, 36; 40:10). More often it refers to the sacrifices offered there.[69] Once it describes Aaron (1 Chr 23:13; see NASB), and once it is used for the Most Holy Place (Holy of Holies) in Ezekiel's temple (Ezek 45:3). The related phrase with the article, קֹדֶשׁ הַקֳּדָשִׁים, is used most often to denote the Most Holy Place in the tabernacle or temple;[70] it is also used to describe the most holy offerings or things.[71] However, the only other verse besides Dan 9:24 that refers to "anointing" (מָשַׁח) and "most holy" (קֹדֶשׁ קָדָשִׁים) is Ex 40:10.

Many other interpreters have understood the anointing to point to the "Anointed One, Messiah" (מָשִׁיחַ) mentioned in Dan 9:25–26. Since Aaron as high priest and the temple appointments could be called "most holy," how much more appropriately does it apply to the Messiah, "the Holy One of God"

---

[66] Baldwin, *Daniel*, 169; Collins, *Daniel*, 354; Goldingay, *Daniel*, 260; Lucas, *Daniel*, 242; Miller, *Daniel*, 261.

[67] See also the commentary on 12:4 and 12:9, which use the same verb as here, חָתַם, "to seal." Compare Zech 13:1–6, which connects the cleansing of the inhabitants of Jerusalem from sin with the cessation of prophecy. See also 1 Cor 13:8.

[68] Collins, *Daniel*, 354; Lucas, *Daniel*, 242; Montgomery, *Daniel*, 375. Keil, *Daniel*, 348–49, views it as the dwelling of God with his people in the new Jerusalem. Archer, "Daniel," 113, and Miller, *Daniel*, 261–62, see in it a likely reference to a future earthly millennial temple. Meadowcroft, "Exploring the Dismal Swamp: The Identity of the Anointed One in Daniel 9:24–27," views it as the people of God, but few have adopted his view.

[69] Lev 2:3, 10; 6:10, 18, 22 (ET 6:17, 25, 29); 7:1, 6; 10:12, 17; 14:13; 24:9; 27:28; Num 18:9 (cf. Ezek 43:12; 48:12).

[70] Ex 26:33–34; 1 Ki 6:16; 7:50; 8:6; Ezek 41:4; 1 Chr 6:34 (ET 6:49); 2 Chr 3:8, 10; 4:22, 5:7. See also Heb 9:3.

[71] Lev 21:22; Num 4:4, 19; 18:9–10; Ezek 42:13; 44:13; Ezra 2:63; Neh 7:65; 2 Chr 31:14.

(Mk 1:24; Jn 6:69; see also Acts 2:27; 13:35; Rev 3:7)? A messianic interpretation was adopted by some older Jewish commentators, including Ibn Ezra and Nachmanides (Rabbi Moshe ben Nachman or Ramban).[72] The Christian messianic interpretation is the traditional view held by Hippolytus, Tertullian, Theodoret, and Calvin, as well as contemporary evangelical scholars.[73] In the NT, the equivalent Greek verb "anoint" (χρίω, from which "Christ" is derived) refers to the anointing of Jesus (Lk 4:18; Acts 4:27; 10:38; Heb 1:9). It is also applied to baptized believers in Christ (2 Cor 1:21), who "have the anointing from the Holy One" (χρῖσμα ἔχετε ἀπὸ τοῦ ἁγίου, 1 Jn 2:20; cf. 1 Jn 2:27).

The OT and intertestamental literature support the view that the phrase means "to anoint a Most Holy One" and refers to the Messiah. For the tabernacle constructed under Moses, holy oil was used to anoint Aaron and his sons, the priests, as well as the altar of burnt offering and all its utensils (Ex 30:23–32; 40:10). However, no anointing is ever mentioned in connection with Solomon's temple. Neither is there any mention in the OT of anointing for the second temple, rebuilt after the exile (Ezra). Moreover, 1 and 2 Maccabees say nothing about anointing the second temple when it was rededicated by Judas Maccabaeus (164 BC). Therefore, the fulfillment of Dan 9:24 must be the anointing of the Messiah, not any anointing of the second temple. It is clear in Dan 9:25–26 that the "Messiah, Anointed One" is a person, and the phrase "most holy" is applied to a person at least once elsewhere in the OT (1 Chr 23:13, as accurately translated by the NASB).

It is noteworthy that the temple is *not* called "the Most Holy Place" (קֹדֶשׁ קָדָשִׁים) in Dan 9:26, but simply "the holy place" (הַקֹּדֶשׁ). While this could be seen as an abbreviation of the longer phrase, it more likely distinguishes the temple, which "will be destroyed," from the "Most Holy One" in 9:24, who, though "cut off" (9:26), will be raised and live forevermore.

However, we do not simply have to choose between either the temple or the messianic interpretation, since Jesus himself is the new temple, both destroyed and risen (Jn 2:18–22).[74] He is where heaven meets earth, the abiding presence of God incarnate for and among his people (Jn 1:14). This concept of God as the temple for his people was already expressed about fifty years earlier by Ezekiel, a contemporary of Daniel also in exile in Babylon. In Ezek 11:16 God promises to be his people's sanctuary even while they are exiled among the nations, when no sanctuary remains in Jerusalem.

Jesus is the ultimate sanctuary for his people. In Mt 12:6 he compares himself to the temple and declares that he is greater. He is the Word who became

---

[72] Montgomery, *Daniel*, 376.
[73] See Hippolytus, *Commentary on Daniel*, 17 (*ANF* 5:181); Tertullian, *Against the Jews*, 8 (*ANF* 3:160); Theodoret of Cyrus, *Commentary on Daniel* (trans. Hill, 242–43); Calvin, *Daniel*, 2:203; Young, *Daniel*, 201.
[74] Baldwin, *Daniel*, 169, is not far from this when she states that the Most Holy is both the temple and the Messiah.

flesh and dwelt or tabernacled (ἐσκήνωσεν) among us (Jn 1:14). His body is the temple that will be destroyed and raised in three days, since in his body dwells the fullness of God (Jn 2:18–22; Col 1:19–20). In the new Jerusalem, the eternal state of the redeemed, he, along with the Father, will be the temple (Rev 21:22). Moreover, Jesus is the cornerstone of the temple, which is his church (1 Cor 3:16–17; Eph 2:19–22; 1 Pet 2:4–9; Rev 3:12) and his body (Rom 12:5; 1 Cor 12:27; Eph 4:12).[75]

Gabriel's words look beyond the history of the city of Jerusalem to the eternal temple, the Messiah himself. That is why a finite time of "seventy weeks" (Dan 9:24) is given for Jerusalem. The prophecy points Daniel beyond the temple as a building to the heavenly reality that the earthly temple represented (Acts 7:44–50; Heb 8:1–9:28). That heavenly reality was embodied on earth in the incarnate Messiah, who is the anointed "Most Holy" temple of Dan 9:24. This ties Gabriel's words to the fulfillment of the other messianic passages in Daniel.[76]

The First Phase of the Seventy Weeks: From the Word to Restore Jerusalem to the Advent of the Messiah (9:25)

After telling Daniel about the purpose of the seventy weeks, Gabriel begins to describe the events of these weeks. The first subdivision mentioned is "from the going forth of a word to restore and rebuild Jerusalem until Messiah" (9:25). The beginning of this period has been controversial. Proposals for the starting point include the following:

1. God's sending of word to Daniel through Gabriel (9:23), in 538 BC.[77]

This identification has strong contextual support, since it refers to the statement by Gabriel only two verses previously and apparently refers to a divine command that was sent. According to this view, the word was sent when Daniel began to pray in 9:23, and in 9:25 Gabriel now explains that word: it is a positive answer by God to Daniel's request that Jerusalem be rebuilt, as God had also promised through Jeremiah (the prophecies Daniel was reading in Dan 9:2). Some object to this view by asserting that the focus of 9:24–27 is not the

---

[75] Some commentators understand the "most holy" (9:24) to be God dwelling with his people in the new Jerusalem (Keil, *Daniel*, 348–49) or an earthly temple in a millennial kingdom (Archer, "Daniel," 113). However, Christ's first advent is the main focus of this prophecy. Yet it is true that the result of Christ's redemption for his people will be the presence of God and the Lamb as the temple in the new Jerusalem (Revelation 21), which is the eternal state. Meadowcroft, "Exploring the Dismal Swamp: The Identity of the Anointed One in Daniel 9:24–27," is on the right track when he claims that the anointed "most holy" in 9:24 is the holy people, but he misses the crucial messianic significance: it is only in Christ that people are God's and are holy. The reference in 9:24 is first of all to Christ. Then only secondarily does it apply to his people, who become holy through faith in his atoning work and by his baptismal anointing (2 Cor 1:21; 1 Jn 2:20, 2:27).

[76] See "The Messiah in Daniel: An Overview" in "Major Themes" in the introduction.

[77] Collins, *Daniel*, 355. Collins (p. 355, n. 68) notes that Jerome reports that this view was held by Jewish scholars and that the view is attested in Tertullian. See Archer, *Jerome's Commentary on Daniel*, 108; Tertullian, *Against the Jews*, 8 (ANF 3:159).

rebuilding of Jerusalem, but its desolation.⁷⁸ However, the rebuilding of the city is a prerequisite for its future desolation, and the rebuilt city is the focus of sixty-two of the seventy weeks (9:25b).

2. The royal decree of Cyrus in 538 BC allowing the Judeans to return and rebuild the temple in Jerusalem (2 Chr 36:22–23; Ezra 1:1–4; reiterated in Ezra 6:1–5). This is the most commonly held position.⁷⁹ While the decree of Cyrus only specifically mentions the rebuilding of the temple, not the city as well, Is 44:28 emphasizes that God used Cyrus to accomplish his purpose of rebuilding both Jerusalem and its temple (see also Is 45:13). And Josephus connects Cyrus' command with the rebuilding of both the temple and the city of Jerusalem as prophesied by Isaiah.⁸⁰

3. One of Jeremiah's prophecies about exile and return: Jer 25:11–12 (605 BC); 29:10 (597 BC); or 30:1–31:40 (587 BC).⁸¹

Based on Jeremiah's promise of a return to Judah (Jeremiah 30–31), many Jewish interpreters, including Saadia Gaon and Nachmanides, understand the starting point of the seventy weeks to be the destruction of the first temple in 587.⁸² This view has the advantage of tying Daniel's original concern with Jeremiah's prophecies (Dan 9:2) to the starting date of the seventy years. Proponents of this view often note that "the going forth of a word" (מֹצָא דָבָר, 9:25) is similar to the idiom for a word (דָּבָר) that goes out (יָצָא) from God, used for a divine decree (Gen 24:50; Is 2:3 ‖ Micah 4:2; Is 55:11; Ezek 33:30). However, this is not decisive, since this idiom can also be used for a word that goes out from a king or other person, that is, for human declarations, including royal edicts.ᵉ

Proponents of this view also note that Jeremiah refers to the word (דָּבָר) or words of his prophecies (Jer 25:13; 29:1). Moreover, the word that goes forth in Dan 9:25 is the promise "to restore" (לְהָשִׁיב) Jerusalem, and in Jeremiah, God promises "to restore" (לְהָשִׁיב) the captives (Jer 29:10; see also, e.g., Jer 29:14; 30:3). However, "word" (דָּבָר) and "to restore" (שׁוּב) are common Hebrew words, and Jeremiah and the other prophets use them in other passages. Therefore, they do not make a strong case for a tie between Gabriel's "word" that went forth and those particular Jeremiah verses. Moreover, this view is dependent on the assertion that the seventy weeks are a reinterpretation of Jeremiah's seventy years, an assertion that is false (see "A 'Week' Does

(e) Josh 6:10; Jer 44:17; Eccl 5:1; Esth 1:17, 19; 3:15; 7:8; Neh 6:19

---

⁷⁸ Goldingay, *Daniel*, 260; Lucas, *Daniel*, 243.

⁷⁹ Baldwin, *Daniel*, 169; Calvin, *Daniel*, 2:209; Grabbe, " 'The End of the Desolations of Jerusalem': From Jeremiah's 70 Years to Daniel's 70 Weeks of Years," 68; Keil, *Daniel*, 352; Leupold, *Daniel*, 418; Lurie, "A New Interpretation of Daniel's 'Sevens' and the Chronology of the Seventy 'Sevens'," 307–9; Young, *Daniel*, 203.

⁸⁰ Josephus, *Antiquities*, 11.1–18.

⁸¹ Gruenthaner, "The 70 Weeks," 48; Hartman and Di Lella, *Daniel*, 250–51; Lucas, *Daniel*, 243; Montgomery, *Daniel*, 378; Pierce, "Spiritual Failure, Postponement, and Daniel 9," 212–13.

⁸² Chazan, "Daniel 9:24–27: Exegesis and Polemics," 147, 152–53.

Not Mean Seven Years" above). Another difficulty with Jer 25:11–12 (605 BC) and 29:10 (597 BC) is that it is contextually difficult to understand the decree as having gone forth before Jerusalem's destruction (in 587),[83] and, one might add, some sixty-seven or fifty-nine years before Daniel began to pray his prayer in Daniel 9.

4. The prophecies of Haggai (Hag 1:1–15) and Zechariah (Zech 1:1–17) and the subsequent decree of Darius I Longimanus (Ezra 6:6–12) in 520 BC. Luther holds this view, mainly on the grounds of the strong connection between these passages and the rebuilding of the temple.[84] The weakness of this argument is that Gabriel's words in Dan 9:24–27 do not explicitly mention the rebuilding of the temple itself, and Ezra 1:1–5 and 6:1–5 show that the first decree allowing the temple to be rebuilt was issued by Cyrus.

5. The decree of Artaxerxes to Ezra (Ezra 7:12–26) in 458 BC.[85] This decree is often proposed by premillennial dispensational evangelicals who seek to view the seventy weeks as a period of 490 years. However, the chronological calculations for dating this decree to 458 BC are not convincing.[86] This date suffers from the fact that the rebuilding of Jerusalem had already begun eighty years earlier with houses and the temple (Ezra 1–7; Hag 1:4, 14). Cyrus' decree had already allowed the restoration and rebuilding of the temple (Ezra 1:1–5; cf. Ezra 6:1–5). Also, Artaxerxes' decree did not explicitly include the rebuilding of Jerusalem.[87]

6. The permission given by Artaxerxes to Nehemiah (Neh 2:1–9) in 445 BC. This decree is also favored by some dispensational evangelicals[88] and suffers from the same problems as identifying the beginning of the seventy years with the earlier decree of Artaxerxes.

In light of the discussion above, it seems that "the going forth of a word to restore and rebuild Jerusalem" (9:25) is a reference either to God's decree through Gabriel to Daniel (number 1) or to God prompting the royal decree of Cyrus (number 2). Both take place in 538 BC, and both are a response to Daniel's prayer. If we understand the divine response to Daniel's prayer (9:23) as the starting point, then Cyrus' decree is the manifestation of God's decree, in keeping with the prophecy of Isaiah:

---

[83] Collins, *Daniel*, 354–55.

[84] Luther, "Preface to Daniel," AE 35:303–4. This possibility is also explored by Doukhan, "The Seventy Weeks of Dan 9: An Exegetical Study," 15–16, who rejects it in favor of Artaxerxes' decree (Ezra 7:12–26).

[85] Archer, "Daniel," 114; Doukhan, "The Seventy Weeks of Dan 9," 15–16; Miller, *Daniel*, 263; Payne, "The Goal of Daniel's Seventy Weeks," 101.

[86] A major motive for choosing this decree is the possibility that it could have been issued in 458 BC.

[87] See further "A 'Week' Does Not Mean Seven Years" above.

[88] Anderson, *The Coming Prince*, 58–64, 121–22; Newman, "Daniel's Seventy Weeks and the Old Testament Sabbath-Year Cycle," 233; Walvoord, *Daniel*, 227–28.

Thus says Yahweh, your Redeemer, … I am Yahweh … who fulfills the word of his servant, … who says to Cyrus, "He is my shepherd, and he will complete all my desire, saying to Jerusalem, 'It shall be rebuilt,' and of the temple, 'Its foundation will be laid.' " (Is 44:24–28)

The Relationship between the Seven Weeks and the Sixty-Two Weeks

Another thorny issue is the relationship between the "seven weeks" and the "sixty-two weeks" in 9:25. Critical scholars often argue that the *athnach* (a Hebrew accent) that occurs at the end of the phrase "seven weeks" (שָׁבֻעִים שִׁבְעָה) implies that the verse is saying that the Messiah will arrive at the end of the "seven weeks," and then after the Messiah comes Jerusalem will be rebuilt during the following sixty-two weeks. They would translate the verse like this:

> From the going forth of a word to restore and rebuild Jerusalem until Messiah, a Leader, [will be] seven weeks. [Then during] sixty-two weeks it will again be built [with] plaza and moat, but during the troubled times.

The *athnach* is a strong disjunctive accent normally used to divide a Hebrew verse into its two halves. Sometimes it does warrant ending a sentence, then beginning a new one with the following words.[89] However, it often does not justify making such a strong division between clauses. Sometimes a comma is the most appropriate way to reflect it in translation.[90] In some verses, the preceding and following words go together so closely that no English punctuation is appropriate for the *athnach*.[91] It certainly would be an exaggeration to claim that the *athnach* requires translating the verse as immediately above.

On the other hand, Christians who adopt the messianic interpretation of these verses often place a major break after the "sixty-two weeks" (instead of after the "seven weeks") and read the remainder of the verse as a separate sentence, following the reading found in Theodotion.[92] They would translate the verse like this:

> From the going forth of a word to restore and rebuild Jerusalem until Messiah, a Leader, (will be) seven weeks and sixty-two weeks. It will be rebuilt …

However, placing the major break after the sixty-two weeks is syntactically more difficult. We would have to ask why the text did not simply give the length of time as "sixty-nine weeks" instead of "seven weeks, and sixty-two weeks."

---

[89] This is the case in 9:26, where וְאֵין לוֹ is translated, "and have nothing." A new sentence then follows.

[90] For example, in 9:24 the *athnach* is on עֹלָמִים, "everlasting righteousness," represented in the translation by a comma.

[91] For example, in 9:2 the *athnach* is on בַּסְּפָרִים, "in the scrolls," but the context requires connecting this prepositional phrase with the immediately following words, using no comma or other intervening punctuation: "I, Daniel, understood in the scrolls the number of years that was the Word of Yahweh to the prophet Jeremiah."

[92] This Greek translation dates from about the early first century AD. The Old Greek translation, which dates from the late second century BC, omits both the seven weeks and the sixty-two weeks in its rendition of 9:25.

The syntax indicated by the Masoretic accents is the most natural way to read the verse, and it is followed by this commentary's translation, which places a comma after the "seven weeks" to reflect the *athnach*:

> From the going forth of a word to restore and rebuild Jerusalem until Messiah, a Leader, seven weeks, and sixty-two weeks when it again will have been built [with] plaza and moat, but during the troubled times. ²⁶Then after the sixty-two weeks, Messiah will be cut off and have nothing.

This does not mean that the text says the Messiah will come immediately after the "seven weeks." Note that the "Messiah" immediately precedes the seven weeks, and then "Messiah" also immediately follows the description of the sixty-two weeks. This framing device indicates that there will be a seven week period and also a sixty-two week period before the coming of the Messiah. Observe too that the text states that it is only "*after* the sixty-two weeks" that the "Messiah will be cut off."

The "seven weeks" refer to the period of the restoration of Jerusalem from the time of Cyrus' decree in 538 BC authorizing the return to Jerusalem and the rebuilding of its temple to the completion of Jerusalem's walls by Nehemiah in 445 BC. The "sixty-two weeks" represent the period from Nehemiah to the life and ministry of Jesus, beginning with Jesus' incarnation and birth in about 2 BC.[93] These sixty-two weeks follow Jerusalem's restoration, as indicated by the perfect aspect of the Niphal verb וְנִבְנְתָה, translated by the English future perfect tense, "will have been built" (9:25). The Hebrew perfect aspect can denote completed action; in this case, it means that the rebuilding will be completed by the time the "sixty-two weeks" start. Therefore, Gabriel's words to Daniel speak of it as an action completed in the future.

The Events Predicted by Gabriel (9:25–26)

Having cleared most of the problems associated with this difficult and enigmatic prophecy, the events of 9:25–26 can now be identified in summary:

Gabriel's Words	*Fulfillment*
"Seven weeks" (9:25).	Rebuilding of Jerusalem (538–445 BC).
"Sixty-two weeks when it will again have been built [with] plaza and moat" (9:25).	From Nehemiah to Jesus (445–2 BC).
"Troubled times" (9:25).	The Hellenistic era (Daniel 11), especially the persecution of Antiochus (ca. 167–164 BC).
"Messiah will be cut off" (after the sixty-ninth week and during the seventieth week; 9:26).	Jesus' crucifixion (ca. AD 33).

---

[93] Jesus' arrival on earth through his incarnation and birth is the most likely reference point of "until Messiah" (עַד־מָשִׁיחַ, 9:25) for both historical and linguistic reasons since that is when he was first called "Christ" (Lk 2:11). See the first textual note on 9:25.

| "The city and the holy place will be destroyed with a Leader who is coming," the risen Messiah who will return (9:26) | Roman devastations of Jerusalem under Titus (AD 70) and Hadrian (AD 135), which portend the end of the world at the return of Christ. |

The description of the seventieth week is given in general terms in 9:26. After the seven weeks and the sixty-two weeks, "Messiah will be cut off and have nothing." This is a reference to Jesus' crucifixion and abandonment by all his disciples and even by the Father (see the second textual note on 9:26). Since Jesus was, by and large, rejected among his own people (Is 53:3; Jn 1:11), his earthly life appeared to end in failure—until his resurrection on Easter.

"Both the city and the holy place will be destroyed, ... and its end will be with a flood" (Dan 9:26). The destruction of the city and the holy place took place with the two conquests of Jerusalem by the Romans, in AD 70 and AD 135, both of which were preceded by Jewish revolts with false messianic hopes. Elsewhere Daniel uses the noun שֶׁטֶף, "flood" (11:22), and its cognate verb שָׁטַף, "to flood" (11:10, 22, 26, 40), to denote the destruction caused by an army overwhelming its opponent. Here the noun denotes total victory over Jerusalem.

"Until the end will be war, and desolations have been determined" (9:26). The plural "desolations" (שֹׁמֵמוֹת) points to more than one destruction. The coming of the Messiah will put into motion the end of the connection between the earthly city of Jerusalem and God's chosen people through the coming "desolations" of the city. Jesus mentioned these to his disciples in his Olivet Discourse and warned them to leave the city with all haste, for it was to be desolated (Mt 24:15–23; Mk 13:14–20; Lk 21:20–24). His use of the phrase "the detested thing of/causing desolation" (τὸ βδέλυγμα τῆς ἐρημώσεως, Mt 24:15; Mk 13:14) is a direct reference to Dan 9:26–27 (and echoes the similar phrases in 11:31; 12:11).[94] Gabriel warns of an overwhelming force that will inundate ("with a flood," 9:26) Jerusalem and warns of war "until the end" of the seventy weeks, references to the Roman legions that twice conquered Jerusalem.

In 9:26 Jesus is once again referred to as both "Messiah" and "Leader," as he was in 9:25. This is a reference to his dual office as Priest and King, since both terms are used primarily to refer to priests and kings.[95] As priest, he brings

---

[94] Although the phrase Jesus uses in Mt 24:15 and Mk 13:14 is a fairly literal translation of the Hebrew phrases in Dan 11:31 and 12:11, those verses refer to the desolation accomplished under Antiochus IV Epiphanes (cf. also 8:13), whereas 9:27 refers to the desolation that would take place after Jesus' earthly ministry, so it is the most relevant for Mt 24:15 and Mk 13:14. See the second textual note on Dan 9:27.

[95] Anointed persons most often in the OT are priests (Ex 29:7; 30:30; 40:13, 15; Lev 7:36; 8:12; 16:32; Num 3:3; 35:25; 1 Chr 29:22) or kings (Judg 9:8, 15; 1 Sam 9:16; 10:1; 15:1, 17; 16:3, 12–13; 2 Sam 2:4, 7; 3:39; 5:3, 17; 12:7; 19:11 [ET 19:10]; 1 Ki 1:34, 39, 45; 5:15 [ET 5:1]; 19:15; 2 Ki 9:3, 6, 12; 11:12; 23:30; 1 Chr 11:3; 14:8; 29:22; 2 Chr 22:7; 23:11). Only once is a prophet anointed (1 Ki 19:16). Of the forty-four occurrences of נָגִיד, nineteen are to kings (1 Sam 9:16; 10:1; 13:14; 25:30; 2 Sam 5:2; 6:21; 7:8; 1 Ki 1:35; 14:7; 16:2; 2 Ki 20:5; Ezek 28:2; Ps 76:13 [ET 76:12]; 1 Chr 11:2; 17:7; 28:4; 29:22; 2 Chr 6:5; 11:22) and six to priests (Jer 20:1; Neh 11:11; 1 Chr 9:11, 20; 12:28 [ET 12:27]; 2 Chr 31:13). There

an end to the sacrifices by establishing the new and everlasting covenant in his blood, shed for many for the forgiveness of sins ("confirm a covenant for the many," 9:27; "my blood of the covenant, which is poured out for many for the forgiveness of sins," Mt 26:28). As king, he brings the end to the old Jerusalem as the city of God's people. Instead of ruling in Jerusalem, he will reign at the right hand of the Father in heaven, over all the earth (cf. Psalm 110).

The "Leader who is coming" (נָגִיד הַבָּא, Dan 9:26) uses same term for "Leader" that refers to the Messiah in 9:25. It also uses a participle with article: הַבָּא, "who is coming." The same participle with article is found in the messianic passage Ps 118:26: "Blessed is he *who is coming* in the name of Yahweh." It is the Hebrew equivalent of the Aramaic participle and perfect used in Dan 7:13 for the "one like a Son of Man" who "was coming" (אָתֵה הֲוָה) "with the clouds of heaven." Jesus appropriated this language for himself already during his earthly ministry, looking past his death to his resurrection, ascension, session at the right hand of the Father, and second coming.[96]

The abomination of Roman (Gentile) defilement and destruction of Jerusalem and its temple in AD 70 (and of the city in AD 135) serves as a kind of pattern of the Antichrist attacking the church. His attacks will intensify toward the end of the world, but he will finally be defeated and vanquished forever at the return of Christ, "who is coming" (9:26).[97]

Gabriel Further Explains the Seventieth Week and the Work of the Messiah (9:27)

Gabriel finally relates details about the seventieth week. They were fulfilled in this way:

Gabriel's Words	*Fulfillment*
The Messiah "will confirm a covenant for the many" (9:27).	Jesus establishes the new covenant in his blood, shed for many (Jer 31:31–34; Mt 26:28; Mk 14:24; Lk 22:20; 1 Cor 11:25; 2 Cor 3:6; Heb 7:22; 8:8, 13; 9:15; 12:24; 13:20).
In the middle of the week, the Messiah "will cause sacrifice and offering to cease" (9:27)	Titus conquers Jerusalem and destroys the temple, ending its sacrifices (AD 70).
At the end of the seventieth week, there will no longer be a connection between Daniel's people and the holy city (cf. 9:24).	Hadrian conquers Jerusalem and bans Jews from entering the city (AD 135).

---

are two references to Levites (2 Chr 19:11; 31:12) and sixteen to those holding other offices. (The occurrence in Prov 8:6 is an abstract plural meaning "princely things" [BDB, 5].)

[96] Mt 24:30; 25:31; 26:64; Mk 13:26; 14:62; Lk 21:27. See further "The Messiah" in the commentary on Dan 7:13–14 as well as "Daniel in the New Testament" in the introduction.

[97] For the Antichrist in Daniel, see figure 10 in the excursus "The Four-Kingdom Schema in Daniel," the commentary on 7:8, 20–21, 25, and the excursus "The Lutheran Confessions on the Antichrist in Daniel."

There will be desolation until the final decree is poured out on the desolator (the end of the seventieth week and beyond; 9:27).	The Roman Empire falls (as predicted in Daniel 2 and 7). The Antichrist continues to persecute the church until he falls at Christ's return.

The main characteristic of the final week is that during it the Messiah "will confirm a covenant for the many" (see the first textual note on 9:27). This is a reference to Jesus fulfilling Jeremiah's prophecy of a new covenant in which God will "forgive their *iniquity* and remember their *sins* no more" (Jer 31:34). Thus the covenant in Dan 9:27 is a reference to the fulfilling of the purpose of the seventy weeks: "to finish *sin,* and to atone for *iniquity*" (9:24). The covenant was confirmed during the last "week" (9:27) of the fulfillment of the prophecy, when "Messiah" was "cut off" and had "nothing" (his death on the cross; 9:26).

The temple in Jerusalem would continue to be the center of Jewish worship for several decades, but sacrifice and offering would cease "in the middle of the [last] week" (9:27; the temple was destroyed in AD 70). Never again has the temple been rebuilt, nor will it ever be according to God's plan, because the perfect sacrifice of Christ rendered all of the OT sacrifices obsolete. In contrast, the new covenant confirmed by the Messiah endures to this day, and the Gospel shall continue to be proclaimed throughout the earth until the Messiah comes on the clouds of heaven.

Today Jerusalem, despite a large Jewish presence, continues to be a city occupied by others, with a Palestinian presence and one of the most important mosques in Islam, the Dome of the Rock, an idolatrous shrine located on the former site of the temple. Thus Jesus connected the fulfilling of the seventy weeks with its aftermath: "Jerusalem will be trampled by the Gentiles until the times of the Gentiles are fulfilled" (Lk 21:24).

The Messiah's coming also brings an end to sacrifices: "on the wing of detested things (is) a desolator, until the decreed end is poured out on the desolator" (Dan 9:27). Jesus speaks of "the detested thing of/causing desolation" (τὸ βδέλυγμα τῆς ἐρημώσεως) in Mt 24:15 and Mk 13:14, echoing Dan 9:27. Luke records Jesus saying, "When you see Jerusalem surrounded by armies, then know that its desolation [ἐρήμωσις] has drawn near" (Lk 21:20). This helps explain the difficult phrase "on the wing of detested things" (Dan 9:27). "Wing" (כָּנָף) brings to mind (by synecdoche of a part for the whole) a swift raptor such as an eagle or falcon. "Wing" is used several times in the Prophets in connection with swiftly attacking armies (Is 8:8; Jer 48:40; 49:22; Ezek 17:3, 7). The "desolator" (Dan 9:27) or "detested thing of/causing desolation" (Mt 24:15; Mk 13:14) is the pagan Roman legions that conquered Jerusalem in AD 70 and again in AD 135.

The Roman general Titus quelled the Jewish revolt in AD 70. Jews were still allowed to live in the city after it was conquered and the temple destroyed. However, in 132 a Jewish messianic revolt arose. It was led by Simon bar Kozibah, called "Bar Kochba," meaning "son of the star," in reference to the messianic prophecy in Num 24:17. This revolt was sparked by the Emperor Hadrian's plan to build a temple dedicated to Jupiter on the ruins of the Jewish temple. For a short time, Jews took control of Jerusalem, but in 135 AD, they were defeated by Hadrian's legions. He razed the city, renamed it Aelia Capitolina,[98] and erected a temple to Jupiter. Jews were forbidden to enter the city. This marks the end of the seventieth week, according to the traditional messianic interpretation.

However, the typological messianic interpretation sees the detested thing of desolation (Dan 9:27; 11:31; 12:11) as the false religion and worship promoted by the Antichrist (2 Thess 2:1–12; Rev 13:11–18), whose destruction at the return of Christ marks the end of the seventieth week (Rev 19:11–21). This view seems to be supported by a passage in the Lutheran Confessions. Apparently the Lutherans were accused of desolating the churches, but they in turn identified the "desolation" as "ignorance of the Gospel" caused by false teachings of the Roman Church, in line with the view that the papacy is the Antichrist.[99] They state in Ap XXIV 44–47:

> In the Confutation our opponents wring their hands over "the desolation of the temples" and the altars standing unadorned, without candles or statues. They call these trifles the ornament of the churches. Daniel describes a vastly different desolation, ignorance of the Gospel. The people were swamped by the many different traditions and ideas and could not grasp the sum of Christian doctrine. Who among the people has ever understood our opponents' doctrine of penitence? Yet this is the principal doctrine of the Christian faith.
>
> Satisfactions and the enumeration of sins were a torture for consciences. Our opponents never mentioned faith, by which we freely receive the forgiveness of sins. All their books and sermons were silent about the exercise of faith in its struggle with despair and about the free forgiveness of sins for Christ's sake. In addition, they horribly profaned the Mass and introduced much wicked worship into the churches. This is the desolation that Daniel describes.

Gabriel adds one final note, the notice that a final decree will be poured out on the desolator (Dan 9:27). Following the end of the seventieth week, the desolator, Rome, will also have judgment poured out on it. This, of course, was already spoken of in Daniel 2 and 7, both of which predict the fall of the Roman Empire.[100] Likewise, final judgment shall be poured out on Satan and his minions, including the Antichrist, at the end of the world (Rev 19:20; 20:10).

The seventy weeks also had the purpose "to seal up vision and prophet" (Dan 9:24). Indeed, all the books of the NT were written in the first century, most before AD 70. Likewise, most or all of the apostles except for John passed from the scene before AD 70. Thus the apostolic era and the canonical NT books were completed long before Hadrian's conquest of Jerusalem in AD 135. There has been no authoritative, inspired revelation from God since that time, as has been universally recognized by Christians (and Jews).

---

[98] The name comes from Hadrian's clan name Aelius combined with the name of the triad of gods associated with the Capitoline Hill in Rome.

[99] See the excursus "The Lutheran Confessions on the Antichrist in Daniel."

[100] See the excursus "The Four-Kingdom Schema in Daniel."

Daniel 10:1–12:13

The Divine Man Explains Daniel's Second Vision of Post-Babylonian Kingdoms Plus the Antichrist, the Resurrection, and the End

Introduction to Daniel 10–12

10:1–11:1	Daniel's Vision of a Divine Man
11:2–35	The Divine Man Explains the First Two Post-Babylonian Kingdoms
11:36–45	The Divine Man Explains the Antichrist and the Time of the End
Excursus	*The Lutheran Confessions on the Antichrist in Daniel*
12:1–4	After the End, the Resurrection to Eternal Life or to Everlasting Abhorrence
12:5–13	The Divine Man Concludes His Revelation to Daniel about the Time of the End

Introduction to Daniel 10–12

Major Emphases in Daniel 10–12

Daniel's final vision spans the last three chapters of his book. This vision mainly prophesies events during the Persian Empire and, in much greater detail, the Greek dominance of the ancient Near East, especially under the Ptolemaic and Seleucid kingdoms. It begins with a rather lengthy introduction (10:1–11:1) in which Daniel has a vision of a heavenly man who was engaged in a cosmic battle against forces of evil. The Son of God, the Messiah before his incarnation,[1] then reveals to Daniel future events that will affect his people. The events are related in 11:2–12:4, which depicts Persian and Greek kings but ends with an eschatological prophecy of the resurrection of the dead. This is the clearest of the passages in the OT that teach the bodily resurrection on the Last Day, and it covers the resurrection both of believers to eternal life and of unbelievers to everlasting perdition. Finally, 12:5–13 forms an epilogue to the vision. The epilogue contains the only numerically described chronological prophecy in the vision. It also contains an epilogue for the book as a whole (12:13) that anticipates the end of Daniel's life.

Three major themes occupy this vision. The first one is found frequently in Daniel: God's foreknowledge of history and his ability to communicate the future through revelatory dreams, visions, and his inspired prophets.[2] However, the emphasis on God's foreknowledge is greater in this vision than in any other portion of Daniel. The great detail given about the Hellenistic era even reveals which king will subdue others and which kings will intermarry with other dynasties. This amount of detail drives home this theme in a way that no other prophecy in Scripture does.

In fact, the prophecy in these chapters is so specific that the Neo-Platonist philosopher Porphyry (ca. AD 233–304) used it in his virulent attack against the Christian faith, claiming that it must not be genuine prophecy by Daniel, but a forgery by a Maccabean-era author written after the events it details.[3] This same approach is characteristic of contemporary critical biblical scholars. However, this approach rests on the interpreter's presupposition that God

---

[1] For this identification of the glorious man as Jesus, see the commentary on 10:4–6. For God the Son elsewhere in the book of Daniel, see "The Messiah in Daniel: An Overview" in "Major Themes" in the introduction. See also the textual notes and commentary on the "stone" in 2:34–35, 44–45; "a son of gods" in 3:25; the "angel" in 6:23; the "Son of Man" in 7:13–14; the "Prince of the army" in 8:11; and the "Messiah" and "Leader" in 9:25–26.

[2] See further "Theological Threats Posed by the Critical Dating of Daniel" in "Date, Authorship, and Unity," and "God as the Protector of His People" in "Major Themes" in the introduction. God's foreknowledge of history and his ability to communicate it in advance is the basic presupposition of chapters 2, 4, 5, 7, 8, and 9:24–27.

[3] See Archer, *Jerome's Commentary on Daniel*, 15.

cannot inspire predictive prophecy. This method not only seeks to neutralize the message of this vision, but also attempts to inflict a mortal blow against the book itself. If the prophecies in Daniel were not genuine predictive prophecy, then their message that God guides history for the benefit of his people would be without any basis in Daniel. Instead, the book would only show that people were "inspired" to write about God's control of history after events happened, something that could be accomplished without divine intervention. Such after-the-fact "predictions" would not demonstrate God's governance of history nor testify to the trustworthiness of this God who promises to save and raise those who believe in him. Surely the same type of "prophetic vision" could have been received by a follower of one of Babylon's gods, who are powerless to control history or save their adherents.

Daniel's message is that only the God of Israel can predict the future because he is the only living and omniscient God. He alone has inerrant foreknowledge and the ability to communicate the future through his inspired prophets. Moreover, there is a reason that this vision contains many details of the Hellenistic era: it is explaining the "troubled times" that were predicted in 9:25 for the second temple period. In this vision, the latter part of Daniel 11 even extends into the time of the Antichrist and his sinister persecution of the true church.[4]

The second, related theme is that in addition to having foreknowledge, God governs world events as part of his plan to protect and save his people.[5] He exercises control over history for the good of those who believe in him and for the sake of his Messiah. This is especially evident in chapters 2, 7, and 9, where the goal of history is the advent of the Messiah.[6] Daniel 10–12 reinforces this redemptive goal and extends it more clearly past the first advent of Christ through the church age, during which the Antichrist persecutes the church, and finally to the resurrection after the second coming of Christ.

The third theme, spiritual warfare, emerges as a major topic in Daniel only in chapters 10–12. This vision makes explicit for the first time in the book that while God's people are fighting the good fight of faith on earth, at the same time, God and his angels also are fighting Satan and his forces in the heavenly realms, and the spiritual battles affect earthly outcomes. It reveals to us that

---

[4] See the commentary on 11:36–45. Also, the little horn in Daniel 7 represents the Antichrist. See figure 10 in the excursus "The Four-Kingdom Schema in Daniel," the commentary on 7:8, 20–21, 25, and the excursus "The Lutheran Confessions on the Antichrist in Daniel."

[5] See "God as the Protector of His People" in "Major Themes" in the introduction.

[6] See the commentary on 2:27–30, 34–35, 44–45; 7:9–14; and 9:24–27. Daniel 2 focuses mainly on the first advent of Christ. Dan 7:9–14 encompasses the first and second advents of Christ. The traditional interpretation of 9:24–27 sees it as culminating in the first advent of Christ, but the typological interpretation considers it to extend through the church age (the sixty-two weeks) to the second advent of Christ.

behind human history lies a profound spiritual war in which the heavenly host (army), led by the Son of God himself, defends God's people.[7]

Only brief hints of this theme are in earlier chapters, such as the passing reference to the Son of God as "the Prince of the army" in 8:11. The heavenly man in 10:4–21 is Christ, the captain and champion of God's army. For the second time in Daniel,[8] we are told a name of one of the angels in God's service: "Michael" (10:13, 21; 12:1), who is given the charge of defending God's holy people.

The concept of heavenly warfare linked to the theological warfare of believers on earth is not unique to Daniel.[a] Many more passages depict the involvement of God and his angels in the defense of his people in their earthly battles[b] as well as when they are attacked by Satan and his demons.[c] But it is rare that we are given such a clear glimpse of spiritual warfare as in Daniel 10–12. The warfare in heaven is not just revealed to Daniel; it affects him personally as the divine man, delayed by his fight against demonic powers, comes to strengthen and instruct him about God's plan and about the angel Michael's battle on behalf of God's people.[9]

This window into spiritual realities normally hidden from us serves as a kind of retrospective revelation for the readers. As we read this chapter, we realize that the spiritual attacks and challenges that Daniel and his friends endured in captivity were not fought on an earthly plain alone since God's angels have been fighting for God's people against their foes (seen and unseen) all along. We therefore recognize that these believers who lived during the OT era are fellow members of the church militant commanded by Yahweh Sabaoth, the Lord of hosts (his heavenly and earthly armies). These saints of old, righteous through faith (Hebrews 11), were led to victory and now have joined the church triumphant in heaven.[10]

The ultimate outcome of the heavenly battle is the same as the conclusion of the earthly struggles of God's people since our eternal salvation has already been won by Christ, now risen and enthroned above all principalities and powers (Col 2:9–15; 1 Pet 3:18–22). He is victorious over our sin and death and also over Satan and his minions, who are the true enemies we must battle (Eph 6:10–18). While this salvation has been present in the background of every narrative and vision in Daniel, it is brought to the foreground at the end of Daniel's vision, where the bodily resurrection and the eternal glory that God will grant his people are revealed more clearly than in any other OT passage.

(a) E.g., Josh 5:13–15; 2 Ki 6:14–17; Mk 13:25; Lk 10:18; Rev 12:7–12

(b) E.g., Ex 13:21–22; 14:19–31; 23:23; 32:34; Heb 1:14

(c) E.g., Zech 3:1–2; Job 1:6–2:7; Mt 4:1–11; 8:28–32; Jude 9; Rev 12:13–17

---

[7] See also the commentary on 10:12–14.

[8] The first angel named in Daniel or anywhere in Scripture is "Gabriel" in 8:16 and 9:21.

[9] The angel Gabriel too had comforted and instructed Daniel in 8:15–27 and 9:20–27.

[10] In Revelation (e.g., 4:4, 10; 5:5–14), John sees twenty-four elders in heaven gathered in worship around God's throne. Twelve represent the OT saints and twelve stand for the NT believers. See also Rev 7:1–8, where the church on earth is described in OT terms, and Rev 7:9–17 and 14:1–5, which depict the church in heavenly glory.

Thus Dan 12:2–3 is the climax of the book. It tells the reader that all the glory, honor, and prosperity that earthly kings bestowed on Daniel and his Judean companions[d] pale in comparison to the eternal glory, honor, and prosperity God has reserved not only for Daniel but for all of his redeemed people.

(d) Dan 1:19–20; 2:46–49; 3:30; 5:16, 29; 6:29 (ET 6:28)

In addition, this chapter reveals that this eternal glory comes in the person of the heaven-sent Messiah, God the Son not yet incarnate in human flesh. He is the glorious man who reveals this vision to Daniel (see the commentary on 10:4–6), including the promise of resurrection. The similarity between his brilliant radiance (10:6) and those raised to be shining stars (12:3) suggests in visionary form the Gospel promise articulated by St. Paul: the "Savior, the Lord Jesus Christ … will transform our lowly body to be like his glorious body" (Phil 3:20–21; cf. 1 Cor 15:47–57).

"The Third Year of Cyrus, King of Persia" (10:1)

This is the date when the entire vision of chapters 10–12 was revealed. The third year of Cyrus (Darius the Mede)[11] is counted from his conquest of Babylon in October 539 BC. His first full regnal year began the following spring, in 538. This third year, then, began in the spring of 536. In 10:4 we are told that the exact date of the vision was 24 Nisan, or April 23, 536.[12] This places Daniel's last vision just a few weeks before work began to rebuild the foundation of the temple in Jerusalem (Ezra 3:8). The warfare depicted later in Dan 10:20–11:1 most probably concerned efforts by Christ and his angels to defend the work on the temple from evil spirits, who naturally would oppose the reestablishment of God's dwelling place on earth as the site of sacrifice for the forgiveness of sins and the salvation of all who believe. Daniel is told in this vision that the rebuilding of the temple will not be an easy task and that even after it is completed, there will be "troubled times" (9:25), described in 11:2–35.

Some critical scholars have charged that Daniel's reference to Cyrus as "king of Persia" (10:1) is anachronistic since they believe that title was not used

---

[11] See 6:1–2 (ET 5:31–6:1) and the excursus "The Identity of Darius the Mede," which argues that Darius is another name for Cyrus.

[12] Shea, "Wrestling with the Prince of Persia: A Study on Daniel 10," 225–32, proposes that the year was actually 535 BC. He reasons that Daniel as a Judean would have reckoned Cyrus' regnal years as beginning in the fall month of Tishri because that was the month for reckoning the beginning of regnal years in Judah. According to Shea's proposal, Cyrus' first full regnal year would have begun in Tishri 538 and his third regnal year in Tishri 536, making the first month of that year (reverting for the calculation of the month to the system of starting the year in the spring) Nisan 535.

However, Shea's proposal is without merit. The procedure used by Daniel of reckoning the reigns of a foreign king using the current Judean system of reckoning the number of years (accession-year or nonaccession-year dating) while at the same time using the foreign country's system for reckoning the beginning of the regnal year (in this case, Nisan rather than Tishri) is sometimes employed by the author of Kings (see Thiele, *Mysterious Numbers*, 49–50, 53; Young, "When Did Jerusalem Fall?" 32, n. 17). Compare the commentary on 1:1, "The Events of 605 BC."

for him until Hellenistic times.[13] They allege that this reference is evidence that Daniel was a Maccabean composition. It is true that the surviving Babylonian documents do not show that Cyrus used this title for himself. However, we should note that Cyrus is called "king of Persia" in the Nabonidus Chronicle, a composition that was likely composed during Cyrus' reign.[14] In addition, "king of Persia" is a title used for Cyrus in the postexilic books of the OT,[15] all which were written in the Persian era. Therefore, the claim by some scholars that no one referred to him this way until much later is a false claim.

The Content of Daniel's Vision in Daniel 10–12[16]

Of all of Daniel's visions, Daniel 10–12 offers the most fertile ground for critical scholars who view Daniel as *ex eventu* prophecy. It only mentions that four Persian kings will follow Cyrus (11:2), while we know from other historical sources that there were six more Persian kings (plus several insurgents who briefly seized the throne). Critical scholars assume that all of the kings of the north and of the south (11:4–40) are the Seleucid kings from Syria (to the north of Israel) and the Ptolemaic kings from Egypt (to the south of Israel), respectively. A king of the north and a king of the south are mentioned late in the chapter in 11:40, almost immediately before the eschatological climax of the vision in 12:1–4. However, the description of the kings in the last section of the chapter (11:36–45) does not correspond to what is known from other historical sources about any Seleucid or Ptolemaic king. The lack of correspondence is evidence that the critical assumption about the identity of the kings in 11:36–45 is wrong. Nevertheless, critics construe the lack of correspondence as evidence that the author of 11:36–45 attempted to prophesy future history but failed to predict it accurately.

The critical view that chapter 11 is about Seleucid and Ptolemaic kings does not leave room in it for the Roman Empire, which should come before the end of the world and the resurrection, described in 12:1–4. The visions in chapters 2 and 7 both portray the Roman Empire as the fourth kingdom, during which the kingdom of God arrives in the Messiah.[17]

Thus critical scholars allege that the author of Daniel 10–12 was historically inaccurate at times (e.g., he mentions only four Persian kings in 11:2) and at other times attempted genuine predictive prophecy but got it wrong (e.g., 11:36–45). They suppose that chapters 10–12 were written during the reign of Antiochus IV Epiphanes (who is described in 11:21–35) and allege that 11:36–

---

[13] E.g., Hartman and Di Lella, *Daniel*, 277; Montgomery, *Daniel*, 405.

[14] *ANET*, 306. On the Nabonidus Chronicle, see further the excursus "Daniel 4 and the Prayer of Nabonidus."

[15] Ezra 1:1–2, 8; 3:7; 4:3, 5; 2 Chr 36:22–23. See Collins, *Daniel*, 372.

[16] This discussion is drawn from Steinmann, "Is the Antichrist in Daniel 11?"

[17] See the excursus "The Four-Kingdom Schema in Daniel."

12:4 shows that the author expected God's eschatological kingdom to arrive soon, still during the era of Antiochus, but it did not arrive then.

However, a careful look at the structure of the vision clears up these apparent problems. The vision begins with someone like a man who appears to Daniel (10:4–21), and after Daniel's initial reaction to him, the man explains that he has been involved in heavenly warfare that affects human historical events as recorded in "the Book of Truth" (10:21). He has been embroiled in warfare with "the [demonic] prince of Persia" (10:20) since the fall of Babylon (see the commentary on 11:1). When that battle finally ends, he will have to engage in a new battle with "the prince of Greece" (10:20). Thus the opening section of the vision tells Daniel the author (and through him, the reader) that the events to be revealed are the earthly manifestations of this heavenly warfare waged by the Son of God.[18]

The historical events as they will play out on earth are related in the main body of the revelation, which begins with 11:2 and ends in 12:4. The epilogue (12:5–13) reveals a few more details, including some cryptic chronological information. Thus the structure of this vision is as follows:

I. Introduction: a divine man appears to Daniel to reveal events in "the Book of Truth" (10:1–11:1).

II. Events from "the Book of Truth" (11:2–12:4).

   A. 11:2: Three more kings for Persia with a fourth stirring up everyone against *Greece*.

   B. 11:3–4: A warrior (*Greek*) king whose kingdom will "be divided toward the four winds of heaven" (11:4), the four *geographic directions*.

   C. 11:5–35: The history of the kings of the *north* and the *south*, culminating in the purification of "*those who have insight*" until "*the time of the end*" (11:35; cf. 11:33).

   D. 11:36–12:4: The king who does as he pleases at "*the time of the end*" (11:40) along with events that will happen when Michael arises, and "*those who have insight*" will be raised to shine (12:3).

III. Epilogue: further explanation of "*the time of the end*" (12:5–13).

The events of the main body of this revelation are related by a variation of a Wisdom technique: the *catchword*. This technique is used at times in Proverbs to string together seemingly unrelated sayings or groups of sayings.[19] In this case, the sections are bound together by concepts that link one section to the next as shown in figure 13.

---

[18] For this identification of the man, see the commentary on 10:4–6.

[19] A good example is Prov 6:1–19. It contains four sections linked to one another by catchwords or phrases. Another example is Prov 11:3–11, nine sayings bound together by several catchwords.

Figure 13

Catchwords and Catch-Concepts in Daniel 11:2–12:4

Characteristic King(s)	Biblical Section	Catchwords and Catch-Concepts
"Kings ... for Persia" מְלָכִים ... לְפָרַס	Section 1 11:2	"Greece"
"A warrior king" מֶלֶךְ גִּבּוֹר	Section 2 11:3–4	A Greek king "Four winds of heaven" (directions)
"The king of the south" מֶלֶךְ־הַנֶּגֶב "The king of the north" מֶלֶךְ הַצָּפוֹן	Section 3 11:5–35	Kings of two directions "The time of the end"; "those who have insight"
"The king" הַמֶּלֶךְ	Section 4 11:36–12:4	"The time of the end"; "those who have insight"

Thus section 1 (11:2), the section on Persian kings, only progresses until a king who interacts with Greece (Xerxes I) is encountered. Then the revelation continues immediately in section 2 (11:3–4) with a discussion of the Greek king Alexander without mentioning any subsequent Persian kings. This section ends with Alexander's kingdom being split "toward the four winds of heaven" (11:4). Once again details of the split, a description of the struggles of the Diadochi for domination of Alexander's empire, or any mention of two (east and west) of the four winds are skipped so that section 3 (11:5–35) can concentrate only on kings of the north and the south (Seleucid and Ptolemaic, respectively). This section continues down to one particularly evil king of the north (Antiochus IV Epiphanes), during whose activity many "who have insight" (11:33, 35) will be purified for "the time of the end" (11:35). After the mention of "the time of the end," the revelation skips the rest of the Seleucids and Ptolemies, as well as the Roman Empire, in order to arrive at "the time of the end" (11:40; 12:4) and its surrounding events in section 4 (11:36–12:4). These events include the activity of the eschatological king who does as he pleases: he is the Antichrist, who is active throughout the church age.

Once we understand the method used to link the various persons and events in the main body of the revelation, we can recognize that what appears to be historical inaccuracies or failures in predictive prophecy are instead intentional gaps. These gaps are necessary for the revelation to move from one era to another by means of *catchwords* and *catch-concepts*.

Moreover, each section begins with the introduction of a king or kings whose characterization is unique to that section. In section 1, the kings are "kings … for Persia" (11:2). In section 2, the king is "a warrior king" (11:3). In section 3, the kings are "the king of the south" and "the king of the north" (11:5–6). In section 4, the king is simply "*the* king" (11:36).

This also explains the similarities and differences between the little horn in Daniel 7 and the little horn in Daniel 8.[20] Antiochus Epiphanes (the little horn in Daniel 8; also the "contemptible person" in 11:21–35) is a foreshadowing of the Antichrist (the little horn in Daniel 7; also "the king" in 11:36–45).[21] This revelation clarifies that the two resemble each other yet are distinct from one another. This is why the revelation links one to the other and skips over some history to make a seamless transition from one to the other.

---

[20] See problem 5 and figure 10, "Comparison between the Little Horn in Daniel 7 and the Little Horn in Daniel 8," in "Problems in Daniel for the Greek View" in the excursus "The Four-Kingdom Schema in Daniel."

[21] For the Antichrist, see the commentary on 7:8, 20–21, 25 and on 11:36–45. See also the excursus "The Lutheran Confessions on the Antichrist in Daniel."

Daniel 10:1–11:1

Daniel's Vision of a Divine Man

Translation

10 ¹In the third year of Cyrus, king of Persia, a divine message was revealed to Daniel, whose name was Belteshazzar. Now the divine message was true, and [it was about] a great war. He understood the divine message, and understanding [came] to him in the vision.

²In those days I, Daniel, was mourning for three whole weeks. ³I ate no expensive food, and no meat or wine entered my mouth, nor did I anoint myself at all until the completion of three whole weeks.

⁴On the twenty-fourth day of the first month, I was beside the Great River, that is, the Tigris. ⁵I lifted up my eyes and I saw, and behold, a man dressed in linen garments, and he was wearing a belt of gold from Uphaz around his waist. ⁶His body was like jasper, and his face had the appearance of lightning. His eyes were like burning torches, and his arms and feet were like polished bronze. The sound of his words was like the sound of an army.

⁷I, Daniel, alone saw the vision. The men who were with me did not see the vision. Rather, a great trembling fell over them, and they ran away to hide. ⁸I was left alone, and I saw this great vision. No strength was left in me, my appearance changed for the worse, and I had no strength. ⁹I heard the sound of his words, and as I heard the sound of his words I was in a deep sleep face down with my face to the ground.

¹⁰Then a hand touched me and caused me to tremble on my knees and hands. ¹¹He said to me, "Daniel, a man highly prized, understand the words that I am speaking to you. Stand up in your place, because now I have been sent to you." When he spoke this word to me, I stood up shaking.

¹²He said to me, "Do not be afraid, Daniel, because from the first day that you began to set your heart to understand and to humble yourself before your God, your words have been heard, and I have come in response to your words. ¹³However, the prince of the kingdom of Persia was standing against me twenty-one days. Yet Michael, one of the chief princes, came to help me, for I had been left there against the kings of Persia. ¹⁴I have come to explain to you what will happen to your people in the latter days, because [the] vision concerns days still [to come]."

¹⁵As he spoke these words to me, I placed my face to the ground and was silent. ¹⁶Then someone whose form was like a Son of Man was touching my lips. So I opened my mouth and spoke and said to the one standing before me, "Lord, pains have come upon me in the vision, and I have retained no strength. ¹⁷How can this servant of my Lord speak with my Lord? And I, from now on—no strength remains in me, and no breath is left in me."

18The one whose appearance was like a man touched me again and strengthened me. **19**He said to me, "Do not be afraid, highly prized man. Peace to you. Be strong! Be strong!"

As he spoke with me I was strengthened, and I said, "Let my Lord speak, because you strengthen me."

20He said, "Do you know why I have come to you? Now I will return to fight with the prince of Persia. But after I leave [that battle], the prince of Greece will come. **21**Nevertheless, I will tell you what is inscribed in the Book of Truth. No one is supporting me against these except Michael, your prince. **11:1**In the first year of Darius the Mede I stood up to strengthen and protect him."

Textual Notes

10:1 בִּשְׁנַת שָׁלוֹשׁ לְכוֹרֶשׁ מֶלֶךְ פָּרַס—As in 9:1–2, a cardinal number is used for counting a year, literally, "in the year of three," meaning "in the third year" (see Joüon, § 142 o). Theodotion correctly reads, ἐν ἔτει τρίτῳ. However, the Old Greek reads, ἐν τῷ ἐνιαυτῷ τῷ πρώτῳ, "in the first year," which may be an attempt to harmonize this verse with 1:21.

דָּבָר נִגְלָה לְדָנִיֵּאל—Literally, "a word was revealed to Daniel." דָּבָר in the Prophets and the historical books often refers to a *"word of God ... a divine communication"* (BDB, I 2), here translated as "divine message." The message in chapters 10–12 is partly visionary (seen) and partly verbal (heard), so it can be described both as an auditory "word" here and as a "vision" (מַרְאֶה) later in 10:1. Similarly, Gabriel described the divine revelation he would impart in 9:24–27 as both a "word" (דָּבָר, 9:23) and a "vision" (מַרְאֶה, 9:23).

בֵּלְטְשַׁאצַּר—For this deliberately corrupted spelling of the pagan alternate name imposed on Daniel, see the second textual note on 1:7.

וֶאֱמֶת הַדָּבָר וְצָבָא גָדוֹל—The noun הַדָּבָר with the article is the subject, and the anarthrous noun אֱמֶת is its predicate, literally, "the word (was) truth." אֱמֶת often refers to "truth ... *as spoken*" (BDB, אֱמֶת, 4 a, under the root אמן), especially by God. Most English translations render the predicate noun as the adjective "true."

The syntax of the adjectival clause וְצָבָא גָדוֹל, "and a great war," within the verse is difficult. Most likely it is a second predicate of הַדָּבָר that describes the content of the revelation: "the divine message was truth and (was about) a great war." Medieval Jewish authorities, based on their understanding of צָבָא in Job 7:1, understand the word here to mean "appointed time."[1] That translation is followed by Calvin[2] and KJV, which both translate וְצָבָא גָדוֹל as "but the time appointed was long." Some commentators understand וְצָבָא גָדוֹל to mean "great/hard service," in harmony with the likely meaning of צָבָא in Job 7:1; 14:14; and possibly Is 40:2, and think it refers to the great toll that the vision took on Daniel (10:8, 15–17). However, the more common meanings of צָבָא are the concrete "army, host" (BDB, 1) and the extended abstract meaning "war, warfare" (BDB, 2). Here it most likely refers to the warfare depicted in the vision,

---

[1] Montgomery, *Daniel*, 405.

[2] Calvin, *Daniel*, 2:231, 233.

both the spiritual warfare described in Daniel 10 (see the third major theme in "Major Emphases in Daniel 10–12" in the introduction to Daniel 10–12) and the earthly warfare predicted throughout Daniel 11.

וּבִין אֶת־הַדָּבָר—In form בִּין could be the Qal (G) imperative, the command to "understand!" But most likely בִּין is a rare Qal perfect form of בִּין (Joüon, § 81 d), so this clause means "he understood the word." A similar Qal perfect occurred in 9:2. The perfect is confirmed by the following parallel clause with the cognate noun בִּינָה (see the commentary on 1:20), וּבִינָה לוֹ בַּמַּרְאֶה, "and understanding [came] to him in the vision."

10:2–3 שְׁלֹשָׁה שָׁבֻעִים יָמִים ... שְׁלֹשֶׁת שָׁבֻעִים יָמִים—The repeated phrase "three weeks, days," means "three weeks consisting of days" or "three literal weeks." The addition of יָמִים, "days," clarifies that these are literal weeks instead of symbolic weeks as in 9:24–27. The addition of יָמִים after a description of time also indicates a complete (not partial) time period, such as an entire month (Deut 21:13; 2 Ki 15:13) or two full years (Gen 41:1; 2 Sam 13:23; 14:28; Jer 28:3, 11). This is confirmed in Dan 10:13, where these three weeks are called עֶשְׂרִים וְאֶחָד יוֹם, "twenty-one days." Therefore Daniel was fasting during the same time that the divine man (Jesus) was hindered by his warfare from coming to Daniel.

10:3 לֶחֶם חֲמֻדוֹת לֹא אָכַלְתִּי—Literally, "food of expense I did not eat." The abstract plural noun חֲמֻדוֹת refers to costly commodities also in 11:38, 43 (there, precious metals and gems). In 9:23 and 10:11, 19, it is used to call Daniel "highly prized, valued."

וְסוֹךְ לֹא־סָכְתִּי—The infinitive absolute (וְסוֹךְ) precedes the negated perfect (סָכְתִּי) of the same verb, סוּךְ, "anoint." The infinitive serves to strengthen the negation: "I did not anoint myself at all" (cf. Waltke-O'Connor, § 35.3.1i, example 34). סוּךְ, "anoint," denotes the use of oil for grooming and hygiene (see *HALOT*, s.v. סוּךְ II, Qal). In contrast, the verb מָשַׁח, "anoint," signifies the liturgical and theological use of oil to induct someone into a holy office, as in 9:24, "to anoint a Most Holy One," who is the מָשִׁיחַ, "Messiah, Anointed One," in 9:25–26.

10:4 חִדֶּקֶל—"Tigris" is the river's more specific proper name. It occurs elsewhere in the Scriptures only in Gen 2:14. הַנָּהָר הַגָּדוֹל, "the Great River," here refers to the Tigris, but elsewhere it refers to the parallel Euphrates (Gen 15:18; Deut 1:7; Josh 1:4), as do the corresponding Greek phrases in Rev 9:14; 16:12.

10:5 אִישׁ־אֶחָד—The numeral אֶחָד, "one," sometimes serves as an indefinite article (Joüon, § 137 u), hence "*a* man."

לָבוּשׁ בַּדִּים—"Dressed/vested (in) linen garments" uses the Qal passive (Gp) participle of לָבַשׁ, "to wear, clothe," with the noun בַּד, "white linen" (BDB), as a direct object (Joüon, § 121 o). The noun בַּד is usually used in the singular, almost always for the material of priestly vestments, including the ephod.[a] Its plural can be considered a plural of composition, referring to "linen garments" composed of linen material (Joüon, § 136 b). It is used in the plural only in this phrase, לָבוּשׁ (הַ)בַּדִּים, which in the OT only refers to this divine, priestly man in Daniel (10:5; 12:6–7) and to the Christ figure in Ezek 9:2–3, 11; 10:2, 6–7. For the identity of this man as the Son of God, see the com-

(a) Ex 28:42; 39:28; Lev 6:3 (ET 6:10); 16:4, 23, 32; 1 Sam 22:18

mentary on Dan 10:4–6. The textual notes on 10:6 point out several other phrases in Daniel that have affinities with Ezekiel's visionary prophecies.

וּמָתְנָיו חֲגֻרִים בְּכֶתֶם אוּפָז—Literally, "his loins (were) girded with fine gold of Uphaz." The noun כֶּתֶם refers to refined, highest quality "gold" associated with royalty in Ps 45:10 (ET 45:9) and Song 5:11, where it alludes to the crown of Solomon as a type of Christ.[3] No other person in Scripture wears a gold belt or sash except the exalted Christ in Rev 1:13.

The location of the distant land "Uphaz" (אוּפָז) is unknown. It is mentioned elsewhere only in Jer 10:9 (וְזָהָב מֵאוּפָז), where too it is a source of "gold," there denoted by the more common noun זָהָב. Here in place of אוּפָז, a few Masoretic manuscripts have אוֹפִיר, "Ophir," which is the source of כֶּתֶם in Is 13:12; Ps 45:10 (ET 45:9); Job 28:16. The variant reading here is probably a scribal substitution of the more familiar "gold of Ophir" for "gold of Uphaz." Some commentators suggest deleting the א on אוּפָז to make וּפָז, "and fine gold," since the noun פָּז is a synonym for "fine gold" that occurs with כֶּתֶם in Song 5:11. The emendation would eliminate the rare place name here, but the emendation would not work in Jer 10:9, where the preposition מִן on מֵאוּפָז requires a place name to follow. Another proposed emendation is to separate אוּפָז into a construct phrase, אִיֵּ־פָז, "coasts of fine gold."[4] This involves no change in the consonantal text and could work both here and in Jer 10:9. However, it requires (1) a spelling of the plural of אִי in construct (normally אִיֵּי־) that is unattested elsewhere and (2) that in both verses the Masoretes misconstrued the word division, a very unlikely coincidence. Therefore, it is best to retain the difficult reading "Uphaz."

10:6 וּגְוִיָּתוֹ כְתַרְשִׁישׁ—"His body was like *tarshish*" probably is a reference to yellow jasper (see BDB, s.v. תַּרְשִׁישׁ I; *TWOT*, § 2546). It has also been identified as topaz (*HALOT*, s.v. תַּרְשִׁישׁ II), chrysolite (NIV), and beryl (RSV, NRSV, NASB). In the centuries immediately before Christ, when the OT was translated into Greek, some translators apparently did not know which gemstone it designated since they sometimes simply transliterated it as θαρσις (Ezek 1:16; Song 5:14; Dan 10:6).[5] In some other verses, it is translated as χρυσόλιθος (Ex 28:20; 36:20 [MT/ET 39:13]) or ἄνθραξ (Ezek 10:9). This semi-precious gem is mentioned several times in the OT. The breastpiece worn by the high priest included this gem representing one of the twelve tribes before God (Ex 28:20; 39:13). Like כֶּתֶם (Dan 10:5 and Song 5:11), תַּרְשִׁישׁ too characterizes Solomon as a type of Christ (Song 5:14).[6] In Ezekiel, it describes the wheels under God's throne (Ezek 1:16; 10:9) and was a gem found in the Garden of Eden (Ezek 28:13).

וּפָנָיו כְּמַרְאֵה בָרָק—That, literally, "his face (was) like the appearance of lightning" suggests that he is divine, since lightning often accompanies theophany (e.g., Ex 20:18;

---

[3] One may see Mitchell, *The Song of Songs*, 921–22, 944–61. On page 960, Mitchell suggests that the man in Dan 10:5–6 and the figure in Revelation 10 could be Christlike angels but that most likely they both are depictions of the same person called the "Son of Man" in Dan 7:13, who is Jesus, the Messiah/Christ.

[4] Dahood, "Egyptian *'iw*, 'Island,' in Jeremiah 10,9 and Daniel 10,5."

[5] See Mitchell, *The Song of Songs*, 930, n. 57.

[6] So Mitchell, *The Song of Songs*, 929–32.

Job 36:30, 32; Ps 144:6; Ezek 1:13–14; Rev 4:5; of Christ's parousia in Mt 24:27). Similar are the descriptions of glorified Christ in Mt 17:2; Rev 1:16; 10:1.[7]

וְעֵינָיו֙ כְּלַפִּ֣ידֵי אֵ֔שׁ—Literally, "his eyes were like torches of fire." This language is applied to the exalted Christ in Rev 1:14; 2:18; 19:12. It states that the figure does not simply reflect divine light, but is himself the source of intensely powerful light (cf. Jn 8:12).

וּזְרֹעֹתָ֣יו וּמַרְגְּלֹתָ֔יו כְּעֵ֖ין נְחֹ֣שֶׁת קָלָ֑ל—Literally, "his arms and his feet (were) like the appearance of burnished/polished bronze." The feet of the four angels supporting God's throne are described in identical terms in Ezek 1:7 (כְּעֵין נְחֹשֶׁת קָלָל). Equivalent Greek terms for burnished bronze are appropriated for the glorified Christ's feet in Rev 1:15; 2:18. Less similar is Song 5:14–15, which uses similes of gold for Solomon's arms and feet.

וְק֥וֹל דְּבָרָ֖יו כְּק֥וֹל הָמֽוֹן:—"The sound of his words (was) like the sound of an army." הָמוֹן often refers to a "great army" (BDB, s.v. הָמוֹן, 3 a, under the root המה, as in 11:10–13 and also, e.g., Judg 4:7; 1 Ki 20:13, 28; Is 29:5). The combination of קוֹל and הָמוֹן is used for battle tumult (1 Sam 4:14; Is 13:4) and for theophany (Is 33:3). The expression resembles the thundering sounds of theophany in, for example, Ex 20:18; Is 66:6; Ezek 1:24; 10:5.

10:7 וְרָאִ֩יתִי֩ אֲנִ֨י דָנִיֵּ֤אל לְבַדִּי֙ אֶת־הַמַּרְאָ֔ה—The syntax makes the subject emphatic: literally, "I saw—I, Daniel, only I—the vision." He alone saw the glorious figure; his companions did not. Compare the distinction between Saul and his companions at the Christophany described in Acts 9:3–7; 22:9–11.

אֲבָל—This adverb restricts the preceding clause: the other men "did not see the vision. *Rather*, a great trembling fell over them" (see Waltke-O'Connor, § 39.3.5e, including example 19). See also the first textual note on 10:21, where אֲבָל recurs.

10:8 וְהוֹדִי֙ נֶהְפַּ֤ךְ עָלַי֙ לְמַשְׁחִ֔ית—Literally, "my splendor changed on me to disfigurement." The first part of the Hebrew idiom is similar to the Aramaic idioms in 3:19; 5:6, 9; 7:28. The noun הוֹד usually refers to the "splendor, majesty" of God or his king. Here it may refer to "manly *vigour* … as displayed in outward appearance" (BDB, 3 c) since the next clause refers to Daniel's loss of כֹּחַ, "strength." The noun מַשְׁחִית usually refers to physical "destruction." However, the cognate noun מִשְׁחַת refers to the "disfigurement" of the Suffering Servant in Is 52:14, its only OT occurrence.

10:9 וָאֶשְׁמַ֖ע אֶת־ק֣וֹל דְּבָרָ֑יו—This clause, "I heard the sound of his words," is absent in the translations of the Old Greek and the Syriac. The omission could be due to parablepsis (the translator's eyes skipped from וָאֶשְׁמַע to the following וּכְשָׁמְעִי), or it could be the translator's attempt to simplify the repetitious verse.

וַאֲנִ֗י הָיִ֛יתִי נִרְדָּ֥ם עַל־פָּנַ֖י וּפָנַ֥י אָֽרְצָה:—The combination of a form of הָיָה and the Niphal participle נִרְדָּם has durative force: "I was sleeping/continued to sleep on my face." The textual note on 8:18, which includes most of the same vocabulary, points out

---

[7] For the significance of this feature for the identity of the figure in Revelation 10, see Brighton, *Revelation*, 259–61, and for this figure's identity in general, see pages 274–78.

that the verb רָדַם and the cognate noun תַּרְדֵּמָה often refer to sleep induced by God for a divine purpose. That purpose is for divine revelation in 8:18 and here.

10:11 אִישׁ־חֲמֻדוֹת—Literally, "a man of high value," the construct phrase has an adjectival genitive and means "a highly prized man." This phrase for Daniel recurs in 10:19. For the abstract plural חֲמֻדוֹת, see the second textual note on 9:23, where too it refers to God's estimation of Daniel.

10:12 מִן־הַיּוֹם הָרִאשׁוֹן אֲשֶׁר נָתַתָּ אֶת־לִבְּךָ—In the context here, the perfect verb נָתַתָּ has an ingressive nuance: "from the first day that you *began* to set your heart" (see Waltke-O'Connor, § 30.5.1b, including example 3).

וַאֲנִי־בָאתִי בִּדְבָרֶיךָ:—The redundant, emphatic pronoun וַאֲנִי and the perfect verb בָאתִי are part of a telic clause (Waltke-O'Connor, § 30.2.1d, including example 7) that could be rendered, "I myself/personally have come in response to your words."

10:13 וְשַׂר ׀ מַלְכוּת פָּרַס—"The prince of the kingdom of Persia" uses the noun שַׂר, "prince, chief." It is used for human authorities in 1:7–11, 18; 9:6, 8; 11:5. However, it refers to the Son of God as "the Prince of the army/host" in 8:11 and as "the Prince of princes" in 8:25. In 10:13, 20–21 and 12:1, שַׂר refers to angelic powers. It refers to the archangel Michael in 10:13b (see the next textual note); 10:21; and 12:1. But in 10:13a, 20, it refers to fallen angels, demons who are the spiritual leaders of pagan countries: Persia in 10:13a, 20 and Greece in 10:20. Modern commentators of all stripes are generally agreed that angels, not humans, are the princes of various nations mentioned in this vision (chapters 10–12).[8] Calvin and a few later scholars have attempted to explain these "princes" as human kings,[9] but this explanation is improbable given the context here (an opponent against whom the Son of God fights) and the unique phrase "the prince of the kingdom" (10:13), which is never used elsewhere for a human ruler. Later in 10:13, the Son of God refers to his battle against "the kings of Persia" (מַלְכֵי פָרָס), which refers to demons stationed over Persia during the reigns of its human kings. See also the third textual note on 10:21, where אֵלֶּה, "these," refers to the demons mentioned in 10:13, 20.

מִיכָאֵל אַחַד הַשָּׂרִים הָרִאשֹׁנִים—"Michael, one of the foremost/chief princes" describes this archangel stationed over the Israelites. שַׂר, "prince," again refers to an angelic being (see the preceding textual note). He is named again and described by similar phrases in 10:21 and 12:1. His name is a rhetorical question: "Who [מִי] is like [כְּ] God [אֵל]?" The answer is that no one is like God. God is unique: he alone is omniscient, omnipotent, and able to save his people.[b] His kingdom is the only eternal kingdom (2:34–35, 44–45; 7:13–14). Michael is named in the NT in Jude 9, where he fights against the devil and is called "the archangel" (ὁ ἀρχάγγελος), and in Rev

(b) Dan 2:11, 20–23; 3:29; 4:34 (ET 4:37); 5:21–23; 6:23, 27–28 (ET 6:22, 26–27)

---

[8] See, for example, Baldwin, *Daniel*, 181; Bampfylde, "The Prince of the Host in the Book of Daniel and the Dead Sea Scrolls," 131; Collins, *Daniel*, 375; Goldingay, *Daniel*, 291–92; Lucas, *Daniel*, 275–76; Miller, *Daniel*, 284; Montgomery, *Daniel*, 411; Stevens, "Daniel 10 and the Notion of Territorial Spirits"; Walvoord, *Daniel*, 246; Young, *Daniel*, 228.

[9] Calvin, *Daniel*, 2:252; Shea, "Wrestling with the Prince of Persia: A Study on Daniel 10," 234.

12:7–11, where he and his angels fight against the dragon (Satan) and his forces and throw them out of heaven.

Some critics claim that "Michael" derives from the name of the Canaanite god Mikal, which probably meant "the powerful one." However, this derivation is quite doubtful as several recent critical commentators note.[10]

10:14 בְּאַחֲרִית הַיָּמִים—For "in the latter days" as a phrase that refers to the ushering in of God's eschatological kingdom at the first advent of Christ, see the first textual note on 2:28 and "The Messiah in Daniel: An Overview" in "Major Themes" in the introduction.

10:16 כִּדְמוּת בְּנֵי אָדָם—Literally, "(one) like the form of sons of man/men," this is the reading of Leningradensis and most Masoretic manuscripts. However, even if one follows that plural reading ("sons"), the context requires that the phrase must refer to *one* person whose form was "like the form of sons of men." The rest of this verse refers to this person in the singular, for example, the singular participles נֹגֵעַ, "touching," and הָעֹמֵד, "the *one* standing." The singular phrase in 10:18, כְּמַרְאֵה אָדָם, "one whose appearance was like a man," refers to the same person described here in 10:16. He is the same divine man, the Son of God, described in 10:5–6. He is also described in 7:13 by the singular Aramaic phrase כְּבַר אֱנָשׁ, "one like a Son of Man."

The plural construct phrase בְּנֵי־אָדָם, "sons of men," is common in the rest of the OT but does not occur elsewhere in Daniel. In Daniel, the singular Hebrew phrase בֶּן־אָדָם occurs only in 8:17, where God uses it for Daniel himself.

For all these reasons, the translation "whose form was like a Son of Man" follows the reading of one Masoretic manuscript, which has the singular בֶּן. That singular reading is supported by the singular in the translations of Theodotion (ὡς ὁμοίωσις υἱοῦ ἀνθρώπου) and the Vulgate (*quasi similitudo filii hominis*).

The Old Greek (ὡς ὁμοίωσις χειρὸς ἀνθρώπου) apparently read יָד in place of בֶּן or בְּנֵי. The Syriac (ܘܐܝܟ ܕܡܘܬܐ) lacks any translation of either בֶּן or בְּנֵי.

בַּמַּרְאָה נֶהֶפְכוּ צִירַי עָלָי—Literally, "in the vision, my pangs were turned upon me." The noun צִיר here refers to "physical effects of mental distress" (BDB, s.v. צִיר IV), but it often refers to a mother's pangs or writhing in childbirth. Its plural is used with that meaning in 1 Sam 4:19, where it is the subject of the Niphal of הָפַךְ and is used with the preposition עַל, as here.

10:18 וַיֹּסֶף וַיִּגַּע־בִּי—Literally, "he again touched me." The Hiphil (H) of יָסַף often is used adverbially ("again") with a following infinitive, or sometimes with a following imperfect with *waw* consecutive, as here (BDB, s.v. יָסַף, Hiphil, 2 b).

כְּמַרְאֵה אָדָם—The subject is a person whose appearance is "like the appearance of a man." This refers to the same divine man described similarly in 10:16a (see the first textual note on 10:16) and portrayed more fully in 10:5–6.

וַיְחַזְּקֵנִי—The Piel (D) of חָזַק has the causative meaning "to strengthen" that corresponds to the stative Qal (G) meaning, "to be strong." The Piel again refers to the divine

---

[10] See, for example, the discussion in Collins, *Daniel*, 375, including n. 45; Hartman and Di Lella, *Daniel*, 282.

man strengthening Daniel at the end of 10:19, which also uses Qal and Hithpael (HtD) forms of חָזַק (see the third and fourth textual notes on 10:19). Its Hiphil (H), also meaning "strengthen," occurs in 11:1.

10:19 אִישׁ־חֲמֻדוֹת—For this construct phrase, here used as a vocative referring to Daniel, see the textual note on 10:11.

שָׁלוֹם לָךְ—"Peace to you!" "Peace to …" (-לְ שָׁלוֹם) is a salutation from God also in Judg 6:23; Is 57:19; Zech 9:10. In the NT, Christ speaks the salutation εἰρήνη ὑμῖν in Lk 24:36; Jn 20:19, 21, 26. Compare Eph 2:17, alluding to Is 57:19. לָךְ here is the pausal form of לְךָ.

חֲזַק וַחֲזָק—The repeated Qal (G) imperative has the stative meaning: "Be strong! Be strong!" A few other OT passages have an identical imperative repeated adjacently[c] or even a pair of repeated adjacent imperatives.[d] Here a few Masoretic manuscripts substitute the imperative of אָמֵץ for the second imperative of חָזַק, producing the reading חֲזַק וֶאֱמָץ, "be strong and courageous," which occurs in Deut 31:7, 23; Josh 1:6–7, 9, 18; 1 Chr 22:13; 28:20. That reading that may be reflected in the Old Greek and Theodotion, which have ἀνδρίζου καὶ ἴσχυε, "be virile and strong." That reading appears to be an adaptation to a more familiar phrase. According to the text-critical rule *lectio difficilior melior est*, "the harder reading is better" and to be preferred.

(c) 2 Sam 16:7; 20:16; Is 40:1; 51:9, 17; 52:1, 11; 57:14; Ezek 3:1; 33:11; Nah 2:9 (ET 2:8); Ps 137:7; Prov 30:15; Lam 4:15

(d) Judg 5:12; Is 62:10; Song 7:1 (ET 6:13)

וּכְדַבְּרוֹ עִמִּי הִתְחַזָּקְתִּי—"As he spoke with me I was strengthened" affirms the power of God's spoken Word to calm, comfort, alleviate fear, and strengthen faith (cf. Is 55:10–11; Rom 10:8–17), which Daniel confirms in his response in 10:19b. The Piel (D) infinitive construct of דָּבַר, "speak," with the preposition כְּ forms a temporal clause: "*as/when* he spoke." Here the Hithpael (HtD) of חָזַק, הִתְחַזָּקְתִּי, has the passive meaning "be strengthened." It is the passive of the causative Piel (D) of חָזַק, "to strengthen," at the end of 10:18 and 10:19. But its Hithpael (HtD) in 10:21 has a transitive meaning (see the third textual note on 10:21).

10:20 וַאֲנִי יוֹצֵא וְהִנֵּה שַׂר־יָוָן בָּא—Literally, "and I leaving, behold, the prince of Greece comes." The two Qal (G) participles, יוֹצֵא and בָּא, are vivid ways of picturing consecutive actions: "but after I leave, the prince of Greece will come." יוֹצֵא refers to the Son of God "leaving" his battle against the prince of Persia, a battle he had been fighting (10:13) and which he will soon resume (10:20a). Since he is the protector of Daniel and his people, he will leave this battle only after he is victorious, after his combat has allowed the divine plan for Israel during the Persian era (including the rebuilding of the temple) to be accomplished on earth. However, even after he wins that battle, his spiritual warfare must continue because God's people will face new threats from the prince of Greece and his forces. For יָוָן, "Greece," see the textual note on 8:21.

10:21 אֲבָל אַגִּיד לְךָ—"Nevertheless, I will tell you" uses the adverb אֲבָל to restrict the preceding statement in 10:20 (Waltke-O'Connor, § 39.3.5e, example 21). The divine man said he was about to return to the battle (10:20). Nevertheless, he would first reveal contents from the Book of Truth.

הָרָשׁוּם בִּכְתָב אֱמֶת—Literally, "the [things] inscribed in the writing of truth," this refers to a written document: "the Book of Truth." הָרָשׁוּם is the Qal passive (Gp) participle of the Hebrew verb רָשַׁם, "to inscribe, write," which occurs only here in the OT, but the cognate Aramaic verb רְשַׁם, which has the same meaning, is in 5:24–25;

6:9–11, 13–14 (ET 6:8–10, 12–13). The Hebrew noun כְּתָב, "a writing, inscription, mode of writing" occurs only here in Daniel but is common in Esther and is found also in Ezekiel, Ezra, Nehemiah, and Chronicles. The cognate Aramaic noun כְּתָב, "a writing, inscription," is in 5:7–8, 15–17, 24–25; 6:9–11 (ET 6:8–10). The noun אֱמֶת often refers to God's revealed "truth" (BDB, s.v. אֱמֶת, 4 c, under the root אמן), as in its other Daniel occurrences (8:12, 26; 9:13; 10:1; 11:2). Compare 12:1, where the names of God's people are "written in the book" (כָּתוּב בַּסֵּפֶר), and also 12:4, where הַסֵּפֶר refers to "the book/scroll" of Daniel.

וְאֵין אֶחָד מִתְחַזֵּק עִמִּי עַל־אֵלֶּה—Literally, "there was no one supporting me against those" uses the Hithpael (HtD) stem of חָזַק with the preposition עִם. This combination, which occurs also in 1 Chr 11:10 and 2 Chr 16:9, means "to support, aid" (cf. BDB, s.v. חָזַק, Hithpael, 4). אֵלֶּה, "these," must refer to the demons who are called the "prince" (10:13, 20) and "kings" (10:13) of Persia and "the prince of Greece" (10:20). The Son of God must fight these demons especially during the Persian and Greek eras, when the Israelites were subject to Persian and then Greek kings.[11]

מִיכָאֵל שַׂרְכֶם:—For the name "Michael" and his designation as a שַׂר, "prince," see the second textual note on 10:13. שַׂרְכֶם, "your prince," has the plural (second masculine) suffix, indicating that Michael is the prince of all the Israelites, not just Daniel. This is confirmed by the fuller descriptions of Michael in 10:13 and 12:1.

11:1 וַאֲנִי ... עָמְדִי לְמַחֲזִיק וּלְמָעוֹז לוֹ—Most English translations (e.g., "I stood up to strengthen and protect him") smooth over the broken syntax. The pronoun begins the verbal clause, which is interrupted by a temporal phrase (see the next textual note), then resumed by the pronominal suffix on the infinitive construct: וַאֲנִי ... עָמְדִי, literally, "I ... my standing up." When a verse begins with such a pronoun as a *casus pendens*, it is usually resumed by a finite verb form, so many commentators propose emending עָמְדִי to the perfect עָמַדְתִּי, but the emendation is not necessary. The preposition לְ (twice) on לְמַחֲזִיק וּלְמָעוֹז indicates purpose: literally, "for strengthening and for (being) a refuge." See עָמַד לְ in Is 11:10 (cf. BDB, s.v. לְ, 4 a). The Hiphil (H) of חָזַק can mean "strengthen" (BDB, 1 a), as the Piel (D) often does. Since the Hiphil can also mean "grasp, take hold of," here it may mean "sustain, support" as in Is 42:6; 45:1 (so BDB, Hiphil, 6 c). The noun מָעוֹז often refers to God as the "refuge" of his people, though here the Son of God provides protection for Michael. The last use of the preposition, לוֹ, "for him," must refer to Michael (10:21), indicating that the Son of God strengthened Michael even as he had strengthened Daniel (the Piel [D] of חָזַק at the end of 10:18–19).

בִּשְׁנַת אַחַת לְדָרְיָוֶשׁ הַמָּדִי—The Hebrew reads, "in the first year of Darius the Mede." The gentilic adjective מָדִי, "Mede," occurs only here in the OT. Instead of "Darius," both the Old Greek and Theodotion have "Cyrus," which may be an attempt to harmonize this verse with 10:1. However, it may also reflect the view that Darius was another name for Cyrus. See the excursus "The Identity of Darius the Mede." For the use of the cardinal number in the date notice, see the textual note on 9:1–2.

---

[11] These eras are the second and third eras, respectively, depicted in Daniel 2 and Daniel 7. See the excursus "The Four-Kingdom Schema in Daniel."

Commentary

Daniel's Vision during Cyrus' Third Year (10:1)

For the historical setting and date (536 BC) of this vision, which comprises chapters 10–12, see "The Third Year of Cyrus, King of Persia" (10:1) in "Introduction to Daniel 10–12."

Daniel begins his account of the vision by identifying himself as the one who had been renamed Belteshazzar. This, plus the reference to Cyrus, is a direct tie to the beginning of the book (1:7, 21). Thus Daniel is claiming his authorship of the entire book and is giving us notice that the book in the form that we have it was probably composed during the early years of Cyrus' reign.[12]

Three times in 10:1 Daniel refers to the content of this vision as a "divine message" (דָּבָר; see the second textual note on 10:1). This message is a further explanation of the previous visions (chapters 7–9), which Daniel now understands to be part of a "great war" (צָבָא גָדוֹל) fought in heaven as well as on earth. He specifically tell us that he now "understood" the message which had been revealed to him progressively in four visions and that he acquired this understanding "in the vision" itself, referring to this fourth vision.[13] This does not mean that Daniel understood the meaning of every detail of the fourth vision nor of the three preceding ones. In fact, he states that he did not (12:8). Instead, it means that Daniel now understood in broader terms that this vision, like the preceding ones, was about the future of his people leading up to the coming of the Messiah[14] and that it explained in more detail some features of the previous visions.

Daniel's Activity at the Beginning of Cyrus' Third Year (10:2–3)

Daniel's mourning that led to fasting was probably due to his continued concern for Jerusalem (see 9:3 and his prayer in 9:4–19). Now in 536 BC, two years had passed since Cyrus' edict in 538 BC that allowed the first Judean exiles in Babylon to return to Jerusalem. Daniel was now at an advanced age, and so he did not return with them. Perhaps he had received word that the returnees had not yet begun the rebuilding of the temple.

Daniel's note that he did not eat any meat or wine means that in his mourning he did not partake of the Passover lamb that year, since Passover would have

---

[12] See further "Date and Authorship according to the Book" in "Date, Authorship, and Unity" in the introduction.

[13] The four visions in Daniel are chapter 7, chapter 8, chapter 9, and chapters 10–12. See further "Daniel 7–12: Four Visions" in "Overview of Daniel" in the introduction. The divine message is not limited to these visions however. The revelatory dream in Daniel 2 portrays the same sequence as the vision in Daniel 7: four world kingdoms followed by the advent of the Messiah, who brings God's eternal kingdom.

[14] "The coming of the Messiah" includes both the first and the second advents of Christ. Daniel 10–12 envisions history leading up to Christ's first advent and then the subsequent church age, when the Antichrist persecutes God's people, until the second advent of Christ, whereupon the resurrection takes place (12:2–3). Similarly, 7:9–14 and possibly 9:24–27 encompass both the first and second advents of Christ.

been celebrated on 14–15 Nisan as commanded in Ex 12:1–6, and the date of the vision was 24 Nisan (Dan 10:4). Celebrating the deliverance of Israel by means of the Passover pilgrimage (celebrated in conjunction with the Feast of Unleavened Bread), one of the three annual pilgrimages to the Jerusalem temple (Ex 23:14–17; 34:24; Deut 16:16), was out of the question, since the temple still lay in ruins and its sacrifices were on hold. Yet he could still hope for the future deliverance through the Messiah, the Passover Lamb without blemish (cf. Gen 22:8; Ex 12:5; Is 53:7, quoted in Acts 8:32; Jn 1:29, 36; 1 Cor 5:7; 1 Pet 1:19; Rev 5:6, 12).

Daniel's neglect of anointing was a sign of mourning, as seen in 2 Sam 14:2. When mourning ceased, one resumed the use of oil (2 Sam 12:20; Judith 10:3), which was seen as part of normal daily hygiene (Eccl 9:8; Amos 6:6; Mt 6:17). Because this use of oil was associated with the end of mourning, it was called "the oil of gladness" (Ps 45:8 [ET 45:7]; Is 61:3).

Daniel's fast was apparently accompanied by prayer and study of God's Word, including requests for understanding the previous vision he had received (10:12; cf. 9:2, where he indicates he had been reading Jeremiah). Thus his concern seems to be for his people and the city of Jerusalem, including the temple. In later apocalypses, fasting often preceded the reception of a vision.[e]

(e) 4 *Ezra* 5:13; 9:24–25; 2 *Baruch* 9:2–10:1; 12:5–13:1; 20:5–22:1; 47:2–48:1, 25–28

A Divine Man Appears to Daniel (10:4–6)

Daniel's reference to the day he received this vision ("on the twenty-fourth day of the first month," 10:4) dates it to 24 Nisan 536, or April 23, 536 BC. This is the only vision that Daniel received after the exile had officially ended with Cyrus' decree in 538 BC that allowed the Judeans to begin to return to Jerusalem.[15] Later, two postexilic prophets, Haggai and Zechariah, each received a revelation from God on the twenty-fourth day, but of different months (Hag 2:10, 18; Zech 1:7).

Daniel also tells us the location of his vision (10:4). What brought him to the banks of the Tigris is a matter of speculation, though it may have been royal business, if he was still serving in some official capacity in Babylon.

Daniel's vision begins with his description of someone in human form. He was "dressed in linen garments," which refers to priestly vestments (see the second textual note on 10:5). The identical phrase is used for him again in 12:6–7, and elsewhere in the OT only for the divine, priestly man in Ezekiel's vision who saves the faithful remnant from Jerusalem's destruction. While six angels were assigned to slaughter the apostate Israelites, the Christ figure "clothed in linen garments" (Ezek 9:2–3, 11; 10:2, 6–7) was to mark a cross-shaped *taw* on the foreheads of the repentant people who mourned over Jerusalem's apostasy so that the marked believers would be saved.[16]

---

[15] See figure 1, "Timeline of Daniel and Related Events."

[16] See Hummel, *Ezekiel 1–20*, 268, and especially 275–79. This man's action was similar to the sealing of Christian believers in Rev 7:3–8. Compare also the sealing with the Spirit in 2 Cor 1:22; Eph 1:13; 4:30, which allude to the Sacrament of Holy Baptism (cf. Acts 2:38–39). However, the sealing in Rev 7:3–8 may refer not just to Baptism, but to the ongoing work of

The description of the individual in Daniel 10 also has points of contact with Ezekiel's vision of God and his cherubim in Ezekiel 1 and with John's vision of the exalted Christ in Revelation 1. See figure 14.[17]

Some scholars identify this person in Dan 10:5–6 as an angel, perhaps Gabriel (8:16; 9:21), who spoke to Daniel in previous visions.[18] In favor of this identification is that Daniel fell face down and went into a deep sleep before Gabriel (8:17–18), and he does the same here in response to the sound of this divine man's words (10:9). In both cases, he is revived by a touch (8:18; 10:10). Some also view the divine man's reference to Darius the Mede (11:1) as an indication that the person speaking to Daniel is Gabriel, since Gabriel spoke with Daniel in a previous vision that was received in the first year of Darius (9:1).[19] However, the reference to "Darius the Mede" in 11:1 does not match the phraseology in 9:1 ("Darius, son of Ahasuerus, a Mede by descent"), but it does match the phraseology of Daniel's narrative description of him in 6:1 (ET 5:31): "Darius the Mede." Moreover, Gabriel is primarily a messenger angel. The person who appears to Daniel in this vision is primarily a warrior (as confirmed by 10:13; 10:20–11:1) and only secondarily a divine messenger.

Others identify this person as God, with Christian commentators identifying him as the preincarnate Christ,[20] who appears in other Daniel passages.[21] The parallels with Ezekiel and Revelation clearly favor this identification. The later descriptions of him in Daniel 10 as one "whose form was like a Son of Man" (see the first textual note on 10:16) and "whose appearance was like a man" (10:18) are expressions that are similar to the one "like a Son of Man" (כְּבַר אֱנָשׁ) in 7:13.[22]

God the Holy Spirit, who is active through God's Word and Sacraments preserving believers in the faith despite persecution and afflictions (so Brighton, *Revelation*, 183–87).

[17] His description in Daniel 10 also bears similarities to the "mighty angel" in Revelation 10, whose face shines like the sun, who has legs like pillars of fire, and whose voice was like a roaring lion (cf. Rev 5:5) prompting the seven thunders. Some interpreters (cited in Brighton, *Revelation*, 274–78) regard that angel to be the exalted Christ.

[18] E.g., Calvin, *Daniel*, 2:240–43; Montgomery, *Daniel*, 420. Bampfylde, "The Prince of the Host in the Book of Daniel and the Dead Sea Scrolls," identifies him as the supreme arch-angel, the commander of God's heavenly army.

[19] Lucas, *Daniel*, 278.

[20] E.g., Miller, *Daniel*, 282; Young, *Daniel*, 225.

[21] He appears in 3:25; possibly as God's "angel" in 6:23 (ET 6:22); in visions in 7:13–14; 8:11, 25; and in 9:24–27. See further "The Messiah in Daniel: An Overview" in "Major Themes" in the introduction.

[22] Dan 10:5 uses אִישׁ, "man," which is cognate to the Aramaic term אֱנָשׁ, "man," in 7:13. Dan 10:16 and 10:18 use אָדָם, "man." However, for the angel Gabriel in 8:15, "like the appearance of a man" uses גֶּבֶר for "man," a Hebrew term not used in the descriptions in Daniel 10 and also not cognate to the Aramaic term אֱנָשׁ in 7:13. In fact, the Hebrew גֶּבֶר is not used in any Daniel verse besides 8:15, although it is cognate to the Aramaic term גְּבַר, "man," used for people in Daniel 2–3, 5–6 (e.g., 2:25; 3:8, 12–13).

Figure 14

Comparison of the Divine Figures in Daniel 10; Ezekiel 1; and Revelation 1

Daniel 10:5–6: *The Divine Man*	*Ezekiel 1:4–28:* *God and His Cherubim*	*Revelation 1:13–16:* *The Glorified Jesus Christ*
Appearance like a man, a Son of Man (10:5, 16, 18; cf. 7:13)	God's appearance is like a man (1:26–27)	Like a Son of Man (1:13)
Clothed in linen garments (10:5)	No reference to clothing	Clothed in long robe (1:13)
A gold belt around his waist (10:5)	Appearance of gleaming metal above God's waist and fire below his waist (1:27)	A gold belt around his chest (1:13)
Body like jasper (10:6)	Appearance of gleaming metal and fire (1:27)	No reference to his body
Face like lightning (10:6)	Flashes of lightning from the cherubim (1:13)	Face shining like the sun (1:16)
Eyes like burning torches (10:6)	God's presence like fire (1:4); torches flash between the cherubim (1:13); from the waist down, God appeared like fire (1:27)	Eyes like flames of fire (1:14)
Arms and feet like polished bronze (10:6)	God's presence like glowing metal (1:4); the cherubim had feet like polished bronze (10:7); from the waist up, God appeared like glowing metal (1:27)	Feet like polished bronze refined in a furnace (1:15)
Voice like an army (10:6); compare 12:6–7, where he is "above the waters of the river"	The wings of the cherubim made the sound of many waters, like the voice of the Almighty, like battle tumult and an army camp (1:24)	Voice like many waters (1:15), that is, ocean breakers or a large waterfall

The primary objection to this identification of the man as the preincarnate Christ is that this person receives support from the archangel Michael (10:13, 21), and some commentators think that God the Son should not need such support.²³ The Son of God shares with the Father the divine attributes of omnipotence and omniscience. Strictly speaking, God does not need anyone, angels or humans, to accomplish his will. The Almighty can merely will things to happen. At times, however, he chooses to use the work of angels or humans to further his will. Sometimes he himself revealed things directly to his prophets, while at other times he used angels to deliver his message. He uses the support and aid of humans and angels as he sees fit.²⁴ Thus this objection is less than persuasive.

In fact, this observation may actually support the view that the divine man is Christ. His apparent weakness in receiving help hints at the theology of the cross: in his warfare against our spiritual enemies, Christ became weak for us, even to the point of suffering death on the cross (cf. 2 Cor 13:4; Phil 2:6–8). That no one helps him except Michael (Dan 10:13, 21) shows that he is the champion of God's people; no angel or other person can take his place. It seems that he can carry out the battle single-handedly, unassisted by any except this archangel. That Michael, an archangel (Jude 9), assists him shows his superiority to the angels (cf. Heb 1:3–14). During Christ's earthly ministry, angels announced his birth (Lk 2:8–15) and ministered to him (Jn 1:51), for example, after his temptation (Mt 4:11) and in Gethsemane (Lk 22:43). At the end of the world, the Son of Man will come in glory with his angels, whom he will send out to do his bidding (Mt 13:41; 16:27; 24:31).

Given the fact that this person also has knowledge of the future (Dan 12:6–11); that in addition to Michael, other angels are subservient to him (12:5–6); that he takes a divine oath (12:7); and that he pronounces a blessing (12:12), this person should be identified as the preincarnate Christ who appears to Daniel and later appears to the apostle John on Patmos in a remarkably similar visionary form. His warrior role in Daniel 10 is consistent with the defeat of the beast and its little horn (the Antichrist) in Dan 7:11, 19–27 at the advent of the Son of Man (7:13–14). It is also consistent with his titles in Daniel 8, where he is called "the Prince of the army" (8:11) and "the Prince of princes" (8:25).²⁵ Thus he is the conquering King (cf. Rev 17:14; 19:16).

---

²³ Miller, *Daniel*, 281–82, following G. Coleman Luck, *Daniel* (Chicago: Moody, 1958), 109, seeks to overcome this objection by positing that there are two heavenly figures in this vision. According to Miller, the first one, in 10:5–9, is God, and the second one, in the rest of the vision, is an angel. However, this is unlikely since the text makes no obvious distinction between the two men in the vision.

²⁴ Compare Genesis 18–19, where Yahweh appeared to Abraham. Of the three "men," one turns out to be the LORD himself, probably the preincarnate Christ, while the other two are angels whom he dispatches to carry out his will in Sodom.

²⁵ Although not equating this heavenly man with Christ, Bampfylde, "The Prince of the Host in the Book of Daniel and the Dead Sea Scrolls," 130–31, does agree that this man is to be identified with "the prince of the army" in 8:11.

This divine man declares to Daniel, "I have been sent to you" (Dan 10:11), a clear indication that this is the second person of the Trinity, whom the Father sends.[26] His appearance to Daniel emphasizes his divinity, his royal dignity (the gold belt), his holy power (lightning), his holy wrath (eyes of fire), and the power of his Word (like the sound of an army). In addition to his office as King, his linen vesture (cf. Lev 6:3 [ET 6:10]; 16:32; 1 Sam 22:18) is probably meant to signify that he is the great High Priest (Heb 4:14). Yet he does not use his power to terrify or judge Daniel; rather, he touches and speaks to him to strengthen and console him (Dan 10:18–19), just as the exalted Christ will do for John (Rev 1:17–18).

Daniel's Reaction to Seeing the Man (10:7–9)

Seldom in the Scriptures are we told that a prophet had a vision while he was in the company of other people. When Elisha had a vision of protecting angels, he alone saw it until the Lord opened the eyes of Elisha's servant (2 Ki 6:15–17). The appearance of Christ to Paul on the road to Damascus is similar to Daniel's account here (Acts 9:7; 22:9). In that case, the men who were near Paul heard (but did not understand) the voice and saw the light, but did not know what Paul was seeing and hearing.

Daniel's reaction at the vision is similar to his reaction to the vision in Daniel 8 (8:16–18), though less severe. In this case, Daniel is probably much weaker, since he has fasted for a long time. In addition, the appearance of the divine man in this vision is more splendorous and overwhelming than Gabriel was in chapter 8.

Daniel Is Reassured and Strengthened by the Man (10:10–11)

As in previous visions, Daniel is touched, strengthened, and given the ability to understand by the one speaking with him (8:18; 9:21–22). Daniel is also specifically identified as the one to whom this man was sent. The reason that he but not the others saw the vision is hinted at in the title "highly prized" (10:11). God chose Daniel as his prophet, and this faithful believer was cherished and valued by God, as are all his believers (cf. Pss 72:14; 116:15; 2 Cor 4:7; 1 Pet 1:7; 3:4).

The Man Explains the Delay in His Arrival (10:12–14)

The divine man's greeting, "do not be afraid" (10:12), serves as a comforting benediction and absolution that was often spoken by God and his angels to believers (Gen 15:1; 26:24; Judg 6:23; Lk 1:13, 30; Acts 27:24). Christ spoke the equivalent of אַל־תִּירָא, "do not be afraid," when he appeared in a very similar form to John (Rev 1:17), and he uttered the same words on other

---

[26] Is 61:1; Mt 10:40; Mk 9:37; Lk 4:18; 9:48; 10:16; Jn 4:34; 5:23–24, 30, 36–38; 6:29, 38–39, 44, 57; 7:16, 28–29, 33; 8:16, 18, 26, 29, 42; 9:4; 10:36; 11:42; 12:44–45, 49; 13:20; 14:24; 15:21; 16:5; 17:3, 8, 18, 21, 23, 25; 20:21; 1 Jn 4:9–10, 14.

(f) E.g., Mt 14:27; 17:7; 28:10; Lk 5:10; 12:32; Acts 18:9

occasions.ᶠ The holy divine power that accompanies God and his angels is so overpowering that this reassurance was designed to calm the fear that would naturally come over a sinful human being on these occasions.

The man's words in Dan 10:12 show that Daniel's fasting and seeking to understand God's Word was accompanied by prayer, as is often the case in the OT. The humbling of oneself is often connected with fasting and the offering of prayers and sacrifice (Lev 16:29, 31; 23:27, 32; Ps 35:13; Ezra 8:21). Daniel's prayer was heard and answered from the very first day he began praying, although three weeks elapsed before Daniel received the audible answer from the man. This shows the need for perseverance in prayer with confidence that God is hearing and answering even though we may not be aware of his response (cf. Lk 18:1–8; 1 Thess 5:17).

There was a delay in the arrival of the divine man for the twenty-one days of Daniel's fast (Dan 10:13). The delay was caused by the divine man's battle against "the prince of the kingdom of Persia." The phrase "the prince of the kingdom" (שַׂר מַלְכוּת) is unique in the OT. It expresses that a fallen angel, a demon (see the first textual note on 10:13) had taken a special interest in thwarting God's salvific purposes, which God would accomplish partly through using the pagan kingdom of Persia.²⁷ This particular demon took up his position over Persia to attempt to foil God's plans involving this nation.

The NT describes the demonic possession of certain individuals, and declares that worship of pagan gods and idols really is demon worship (1 Cor 10:20–21), but this passage shows that a demon can gain a position of influence over an entire pagan nation or people. This is also one of the clearest portrayals in Scripture of opposition by the devil and his evil angels to God, his holy angels, and his salvific purpose, which ultimately is to redeem all people through his Son, Jesus Christ. Luther notes:

> The tenth chapter is a prologue to the eleventh. Yet in it Daniel writes something special about the angels, the like of which we find nowhere else in the Scriptures, namely, that the good angels do battle with the evil angels in defense of men. Besides Daniel calls also the evil angels princes, as when he speaks of "the prince of Greece" [10:20]. Hence we may understand why things are so wild and dissolute at the courts of kings and princes, and why they hinder the good and bring on war and unhappiness. For there are devils there, hounding and goading, or hindering to such an extent that nothing goes as it should. For example, though the Jews were supposed to get out of Babylon by the help of the Persian kings, nothing happened despite the willingness of the kings; as a result this [good] angel here says that he has his hands full and must fight against the prince of Persia, and expresses the concern on departing that the prince of Greece will come in the meanwhile. It is as if he

---

²⁷ Both Daniel 2 and Daniel 7 showed that Persia, the second kingdom, figured in God's plan for world history culminating in the advent of the Messiah. In particular, after Cyrus the Persian conquered the kingdom of Babylon in 539 BC, he issued the edict in 538 BC that permitted the exiled Judeans to return to Jerusalem and begin to rebuild it and the temple.

were to say, "Where we parry one misfortune the devil produces another; if you get liberated from Babylon, then the Greeks will bedevil you."[28]

Heavenly warfare involving Christ as the commander of his angels is mentioned throughout the Scriptures, though in less detail than here. Already in Exodus, God had promised that his angel would go before Israel into the land of Canaan to fight for them (Ex 32:34; 33:2). This was fulfilled in Joshua's day, as confirmed by the appearance of the preincarnate Christ to Joshua in the form of "the Prince of the army of Yahweh" (Josh 5:14). The battle of Barak against Sisera was also fought in heaven (Judg 5:19–20, where "stars" likely refers to angels, as in Job 38:7; Rev 1:20; 12:4). The demonic army that opposes God will be punished at the final judgment (Is 24:21), and Paul reminds us that our most significant struggles in this life are against the spiritual powers of darkness who fight on the heavenly plane (Eph 6:12). The most explicit NT passage to depict this warfare is Rev 12:7–11, where the archangel Michael and the angels under his command fight Satan and his angels; Michael and his troops expel the fallen angels from heaven after the first advent of Christ.

The divine man told Daniel, "I had been left there against the kings of Persia" (Dan 10:13), which refers to demons who had stationed themselves over Persia during the reigns of past Persian kings. The verb "left" (נוֹתַרְתִּי) probably means that God the Son was left alone,[29] repelling the enemy by himself until Michael came to his aid. This is similar to the temptation of Christ: he alone fought against Satan (Mt 4:1–10), then after his victory over the devil, angels attended him (Mt 4:11). Jesus was also abandoned on the cross (Mt 27:46, quoting Ps 22:2 [ET 22:1]), where he alone defeated the devil (Heb 2:14; 1 Jn 3:8) by atoning for humanity's sins, then angels accompanied his resurrection (Mt 28:2–3; Mk 16:5; Lk 24:4).

Presumably after the divine man and Michael won the most recent battle against the prince of the kingdom of Persia, Michael remained stationed in the Persian court to thwart further attacks while the divine man visited Daniel. After the Son of God would complete his visit to reveal the divine message to Daniel, he would return to continue his spiritual warfare along with Michael against "the prince of Persia," and after that, against "the prince of Greece" (10:20). His statement "I had been left there against the kings of Persia" (10:13) emphasizes that spiritual attacks had come throughout the reigns of several past Persian kings. It also suggests that spiritual assaults would continue in the future under the Persian kings who would succeed Cyrus. The divine man would have to continue to wage spiritual war to ensure that the Judeans who returned to Israel would have a heavenly warrior who would defend them as they would struggle to rebuild the temple in Jerusalem.[30] The opposition they

---

[28] Luther, "Preface to Daniel," AE 35:305–6.

[29] The Niphal of יָתַר sometimes means "be left alone" (BDB), as in Gen 32:25 (ET 32:24); 1 Ki 18:22; 19:10, 14.

[30] Keil, *Daniel*, 419, espouses a similar view.

would face and eventually overcome (recorded in Ezra 1–6) was a reflection of the ebb and flow of the battles that the divine man and Michael would fight on their behalf in the spiritual realm.

Michael is called "one of the chief princes" (10:13), the equivalent of ἀρχάγγελος, "archangel" (Jude 9). Thus it is possible that in addition to Michael himself, other angels under his command (Rev 12:7) were posted at the Persian court.

The Son of God characterizes his revelation to Daniel as "what will happen to your people in the latter days" (10:14). The phrase בְּאַחֲרִית הַיָּמִים, literally, "in the latter part of the days," can be used simply as a reference to the future (e.g., Deut 31:29; Jer 23:20; 30:24). However, it most often refers to the future as it culminates in the advent of the Messiah and his kingdom.^g The corresponding Aramaic phrase (בְּאַחֲרִית יוֹמַיָּא) was used with that meaning already in Dan 2:28,³¹ and that is also the meaning here. These OT verses often compress into this phrase the whole span of Christ's first advent, the church age, and his second advent. Similarly, the NT uses "the last days" to refer to the era that began with Christ's first advent and continues throughout the church age until Christ returns (Acts 2:17; Heb 1:2; cf. also 2 Tim 3:1; 2 Pet 3:3), though sometimes the emphasis of that phrase is on the return of Christ and Judgment Day (James 5:3).

The revelation to Daniel will relate the coming events that will affect God's people and will culminate in the resurrection of all the dead (Dan 12:2–3) on the Last Day, after the return of Christ. This eschatological perspective is confirmed when the divine man says, עוֹד חָזוֹן לַיָּמִים, literally, "yet [the] vision is concerning the days [to come]" (10:14). Thus the vision is not simply about future world history, but about the eschatological and theological future that culminates in the promised eschatological kingdom of God in Christ,³² which arrived at his first advent (Mk 1:14–15; 9:1; Col 1:13) and will be consummated at his second advent (1 Cor 6:9–10; 15:24; 2 Tim 4:1, 18).

(g) Gen 49:1; Num 24:14; Is 2:2 ‖ Micah 4:1; Jer 48:47; 49:39; Hos 3:5

Daniel Is Reassured and Strengthened a Second Time (10:15–19)

Despite receiving some consolation and strength earlier (10:10–12), the words of the man in Daniel's vision were so powerful and overwhelming, "like the sound of an army" (10:6; see also 10:9, 16b–17), that he was again weakened and fell to the ground unable to speak (10:15). So the man touched him again (10:16), as he had earlier (10:10). This time Daniel describes the one standing before him as having a "form … like a Son of Man" (see the first textual note on 10:16), which is probably a reference to the "Son of Man" he saw in his first vision (7:13). Daniel was beginning to realize that this person speaking with him was the focus of revelation in his inaugural vision: the Son of Man who would receive God's eternal kingdom (7:13–14).

---

³¹ See the first textual note on 2:28.
³² Hartman and Di Lella, *Daniel*, 284; Miller, *Daniel*, 287.

God or a seraph touched the lips of the prophets Isaiah and Jeremiah in their visions that called them into the prophetic office, consecrating their mouths and granting them the power to preach God's Word (Is 6:6–7; Jer 1:9; cf. Ezek 3:1–3). The touch on his lips from the Son of God enabled Daniel to speak to him, but he still had "pains" and lacked "strength" (Dan 10:16–17). A third healing touch was needed to strengthen him (10:18).

Then the divine man spoke further encouragement (10:19). The combination of "do not be afraid" and "peace to you" was also pronounced by the Lord, who earlier in the account is called "the Angel of Yahweh" (Judg 6:11–12, 21–22), most likely the preincarnate Christ, when he appeared to Gideon (Judg 6:23).[33] Daniel received strength through the powerful Word of the divine man, as he acknowledged ("as he spoke with me I was strengthened," Dan 10:19). The Word of God has the power to accomplish God's will (Is 55:10–11; Rom 1:16), especially to strengthen God's people (LC, Preface, 11).

Similarly, God speaking his Word enabled other prophets to carry out their vocation (e.g., Is 6:8; 8:11; Jer 1:4–10; Ezek 2:1–2; Amos 7:15). The divine man's double imperative "Be strong! Be strong!" (Dan 10:19) uses the same verb (חֲזַק) as in the pair of imperatives "be strong and courageous" repeatedly spoken to Joshua by Moses (Deut 31:7) and by God (Deut 31:23; Josh 1:6–7, 9, 18) and spoken to God's people by Moses (Deut 31:6) and by Joshua (Josh 10:25).

The Man's Spiritual Battles (10:20–11:1)

The divine man continues by asking Daniel a rhetorical question, "Do you know why I have come to you?" (10:20), which expects no answer, and so he does not wait for one. Instead, he informs Daniel that he will return to continue the battle against the demonic power that seeks to undermine God's purpose in the Persian Empire. However, he also tells Daniel that when that particular battle is over, the demon who will be the prince of Greece will come, implying that a new battle will begin against him (10:20). Satan's spiritual warfare shall continue for the rest of the OT era, intensify against Christ in his earthly ministry (Mt 4:1–11; Jn 13:27), and persist throughout the church age as Satan, both directly and through his agents, seeks to destroy the followers of Jesus (e.g., 1 Thess 2:18; 1 Pet 5:8; Rev 12:13–13:18), but Christ's conquest on the cross has secured eventual and eternal victory over Satan for all believers (Rom 16:20).

Before returning to war, the Son of God is going to tell Daniel what is contained in "the Book of Truth" (10:21). This book is only mentioned here in the Scriptures. (It should not be confused with the "books" opened in the judgment in 7:10 or with "the book" in Dan 12:1 in which the names of God's saints are written.) From the content of the remainder of the vision, it appears as if this book contains the true course of history as recorded by God in his

---

[33] The combination was also spoken by the man in charge of Joseph's house to Joseph's brothers in Gen 43:23.

foreknowledge of all things. Daniel used the same noun, אֱמֶת, "truth," in 10:1 to describe the entire fourth vision (chapters 10–12), and the divine man will use it again in 11:2 to characterize the content of the later portion of the vision. Both of those other uses of אֱמֶת, "truth," reinforce that the content of the "Book of Truth" is God's "truth," which the divine man now reveals. Compare the revelation of "truth" in and by Christ in Jn 1:14, 17; 8:32, 40; 14:6; 18:37.

The only heavenly support that the Son of Man receives is from Michael (and probably also Michael's angelic soldiers), but that is sufficient (10:21). Michael here is called "your prince," signifying that Michael's permanent assignment is the defense of God's people, which will be confirmed when he is called "the great prince who stands over your people" (12:1). This explains why Michael is engaged in the battle. He is the holy counterpart to the demonic princes who take up positions over Persia and Greece.

The divine man then goes on to tell Daniel that he "stood up to strengthen and protect" Michael in his battle already in "the first year of Darius the Mede" (11:1). This is a direct reference to 6:1 (ET 5:31) and the fall of Babylon, which was conquered by Darius/Cyrus.[34] The heavenly war with the prince of Persia began at that time. As soon as God moved Darius/Cyrus to fulfill his gracious promise to return his people to Jerusalem and rebuild the temple,[35] the devil and his angels began a war to impede God's plan. The heavenly war had been raging for almost three years at the time Daniel received this final vision.[36]

Some critical scholars who find (the first part of) 11:1 difficult seek to label it as a gloss.[37] However, this is a failure to understand the logic of the text and an attempt to make sense of it by a radical cut-and-paste procedure.[38] Instead, the logic of the text is clear, but nonlinear (11:1 is about events three years previous). In addition, most of 10:21b and all but the first word of 11:1 are extant in 4QDan^c, a manuscript from the late second century BC, testifying to the antiquity of the verses.[39] Therefore, the text should be read as it stands.

---

[34] Dan 6:1 (ET 5:31) is the only other place in the book where the phrase "Darius the Mede" occurs. For his identity as Cyrus, see the excursus "The Identity of Darius the Mede."

[35] See the commentary on 9:2, where Daniel meditates on God's promise of "seventy years" through Jeremiah.

[36] This incidentally is another indication that Daniel does not view a separate Median kingdom coming between the Babylonian and Persian kingdoms. The war with the prince of *Persia* (not Media) began at Babylon's downfall, and Darius the Mede was the ruler in the new Persian realm. Therefore the four kingdoms in Daniel 2 and 7 are Babylon, Medo-Persia, Greece, and Rome, in whose era the Messiah brings the kingdom of God. See the excursus "The Four-Kingdom Schema in Daniel."

[37] E.g., David, "Daniel 11,1: A Late Gloss?" (who sees 11:1 as a gloss, but not a "late" gloss and one that makes sense in the present arrangement of the text); Montgomery, *Daniel*, 416–17 (who views 11:1a as a gloss).

[38] Montgomery, *Daniel*, 416–17, not only views 11:1a as a gloss but also discusses rearranging the rest of the parts of 10:20–11:1.

[39] Ulrich, *Qumran Cave 4.XI*, 274.

The rather awkward chapter division is due to the date formula in 11:1. Apparently when Daniel was divided into chapters by Stephen Langton, archbishop of Canterbury, in the thirteenth century, he started a new chapter here by analogy to the previous visionary chapters, each of which begins with a date formula (7:1; 8:1; 9:1; 10:1).

Daniel 11:2–35

The Divine Man Explains the First Two Post-Babylonian Kingdoms

Translation

11 ²"Now I will tell you truth: behold, three more kings will arise for Persia, then the fourth one will gain great riches, more than anyone else. As he becomes strong by his riches he will awaken everyone, [especially] the kingdom of Greece.

³"A warrior king will arise and will rule a great dominion and will do as he pleases. ⁴But as he rises, his kingdom will be broken and be divided toward the four winds of heaven, but not to his descendants and not according to his dominion that he ruled, because his kingdom will be uprooted and [given] to others besides these.

⁵"The king of the south will become strong, but one of his commanders will become stronger than he and rule a dominion greater than his.

⁶"At an end of some years, they will make an alliance. The daughter of the king of the south will come to the king of the north to make an equitable agreement. However, she will not retain her strength of arm, and his descendant will not endure. She will be given up—she, those who brought her, the one who fathered her, and the one who strengthened her during the times.

⁷"But one from a branch of her root will arise in his place. He will come against the army and come into the fortress of the king of the north. He will make [war] with them and prevail. ⁸He will also take captive to Egypt their gods with their cast images and with their valuable vessels of silver and gold. For some years he will leave the king of the north alone. ⁹But he will come into the kingdom of the king of the south, then will return to his own land.

¹⁰"His sons will be stirred up and will gather a multitude of many armies, which will keep coming, flood, pass through, and again be stirred up as far as his fortress.

¹¹"The king of the south will be enraged, will go out and fight with him—with the king of the north. He [the king of the north] will raise up a great army, but the army will be given into his [the king of the south's] hand. ¹²When the [king of the north's] army is taken away, his [the king of the south's] heart will become arrogant, and he will cause myriads to fall, but he will not prevail.

¹³"The king of the north will again raise an army, (which will be) greater than the first [army], and after some years he will keep coming with a great army and many supplies. ¹⁴In those times, many will rise up against the king of the south; violent men of your people will lift themselves up to fulfill [this] vision, but they will stumble. ¹⁵The king of the north will come and build siege works and capture a fortified city. The forces of the south will not stand, nor will his best troops,

because there will be no strength to stand. ¹⁶The one who comes against him will do as he pleases, and no one will stand before him. He will stand in the beautiful land, and it will be completely in his power. ¹⁷He will set his face to come with the power of his entire kingdom, and [bring] a treaty with him, which he will enforce. He will give him a daughter of men to destroy it [the southern kingdom]. But it [his plan] will not stand or be to his advantage. ¹⁸He will set his face toward the coastlands and capture many. However, a commander will put an end to his insolence. Moreover, he will repay him for his insolence. ¹⁹Then he will turn his face toward the fortresses of his land. He will stumble and fall, and not be found.

²⁰"Then will arise in his place one who will send an exactor of tribute for the glory of his kingdom. However, in a few days he will be broken, but not in anger or battle.

²¹"A contemptible person will arise in his place, and they will not confer upon him the majesty of the kingdom. He will come when it is at ease and seize the kingdom through intrigue. ²²An overwhelming force will be overwhelmed before him and broken, together with a leader of a covenant. ²³After an alliance is made with him [with the leader of a covenant], he [the contemptible person] will act deceitfully. He will rise up and become powerful with a small nation. ²⁴He will come to the richest parts of the province when it is at ease and do what his fathers and fathers' fathers did not do. He will distribute spoil, plunder, and property to them. He will devise plans against strongholds, but [only] until a time.

²⁵"He will awaken his power and his heart against the king of the south with a great army. The king of the south will stir himself up for battle with an exceedingly great and strong army, but he will not stand because plots will be plotted against him. ²⁶Those who eat his delicacies will break him, and his army will be swept away. Many slain people will fall. ²⁷The two kings will have hearts [inclined] toward evil. At one table they will speak a lie, but it will not succeed, because an end is yet for an appointed time. ²⁸He will return to his land with a great number of goods and his heart [set] against a holy covenant. He will take action and then return to his own land.

²⁹"At the appointed time he will return and come into the south, but this later [invasion] will not be like the first [invasion]. ³⁰But ships from Kittim will come against him, and he will be humbled.

"Then he will turn and become indignant against a holy covenant, take action, return and favor those who abandon a holy covenant. ³¹Forces from him will arise and profane the temple fortress and abolish the continual sacrifice and set up the detested thing causing desolation. ³²So he will defile wicked men of a covenant with smooth talk, but a people who know their God will be strong and take action.

³³"Those of the people who have insight will make many understand, but they will stumble by sword, flame, captivity, and plunder for some time. ³⁴However, when they stumble they will be aided by a little help, and many will join them insincerely. ³⁵Some of those who have insight will stumble in order to refine them, purify [them], and make [them] white until the time of the end, for it is still for an appointed time."

Daniel 11:2–35

Textual Notes

11:2 וְעַתָּ֕ה אֱמֶ֖ת אַגִּ֣יד לָ֑ךְ—Literally, "and now truth I will declare to you" uses the same noun, אֱמֶת, for God's revealed truth that Daniel used in 10:1 to characterize the entire fourth vision (chapters 10–12) and that the divine man used in naming the source of the vision, "the Book of Truth" (10:21). See the fourth textual note on 10:1 and the second textual note and the commentary on 10:21.

עֹמְדִים—The Qal (G) of עָמַד occurs sixteen times in 11:2–31 with a variety of meanings. The seven occurrences of עָמַד in 11:2–4, 7, 20–21, 31 mean that a person will "arise, appear, come on the scene" (BDB, Qal, 6 a), as also in 8:22–23; 12:1. The context of this prophecy requires the participle here to be translated as a future tense: "will arise." For other meanings of עָמַד, see the fourth textual note on 11:6, the second textual note on 11:8, the first textual note on 11:14, and the first textual note on 11:16.

יַעֲשִׁ֧יר עֹֽשֶׁר־גָּד֛וֹל מִכֹּ֖ל—The Hiphil (H) of עָשַׁר, "be rich," can have the internally transitive meaning "gain riches" (BDB, 2) or "make oneself rich." With this meaning, it can be used absolutely, but here it is followed by an adverbial accusative cognate noun עֹשֶׁר, "riches," which, together with the adjective גָּדוֹל and comparative מִכֹּל, "more than all/everyone else," indicates extreme wealth.

יָעִ֣יר הַכֹּ֔ל אֵ֖ת מַלְכ֥וּת יָוָֽן:—Literally, "he will arouse everyone, the kingdom of Greece." The Hiphil (H) verb יָעִיר, "awaken, arouse," has the direct object הַכֹּל, "everyone." Probably אֵת מַלְכוּת יָוָן is a second direct object of the verb יָעִיר, marked with the definite object marker אֵת, giving this object special emphasis: "[especially] the kingdom of Greece." For יָוָן, "Greece," see the textual note on 8:21. It is also possible that אֵת could be the preposition "with," which is often used with the Niphal (N) of לָחַם, "attack, wage war against." Most English translations construe the syntax to mean "he will stir up everyone against the kingdom of Greece" (NIV; similar are KJV, ESV, NASB). That construal still captures most of the sense of the verse and is supported by the Vulgate, but not by the Old Greek or Theodotion. See further the commentary.

11:5 וְיֶחֱזַ֥ק מֶֽלֶךְ־הַנֶּ֖גֶב וּמִן־שָׂרָ֑יו—The syntax of this verse is difficult. Following the Masoretic accents (especially the *athnach* on שָׂרָיו), the meaning could be "the king of the south will be strong and more than [stronger than] his princes," taking the preposition מִן in a comparative sense. However, the rest of the verse seems to describe someone who usurps and surpasses the king. Therefore, most English translations (e.g., NIV, ESV, NASB) take the prepositional phrase וּמִן־שָׂרָיו as partitive, "[one] from/of his princes," disregard the *athnach*, and take "one of his princes" as the subject of the following verbs, וְיֶחֱזַ֥ק עָלָ֖יו וּמָשָֽׁל, "will be strong over him [the king] and will rule."

11:6 וּלְקֵ֤ץ שָׁנִים֙ יִתְחַבָּ֔רוּ—The simple plural of שָׁנָה can mean "some years," as again in 11:8 (GKC, § 139 h). The indefinite time span "at an end of some years" refers to literal (not symbolic) years but does not specify how many. קֵץ and שָׁנִים occur in a similar sense in 11:13. קֵץ, "end," also recurs in 11:27, 35. In all these verses, קֵץ refers to the "end" of time spans lasting a few years during the intertestamental period. It does not have the eschatological meaning of the end times, a meaning it can have elsewhere in the book. See the second textual note and the commentary on 8:17. The Hithpael (HtD) of חָבַר, "unite, be joined," has the reciprocal meaning "join themselves together" (KJV) or "make an alliance ... league together" (BDB). An Aramaic form of the Hithpael occurs in 11:23.

לַעֲשׂוֹת מֵישָׁרִים—Literally, this is "to make equity." The noun מֵישָׁר can be used as an abstract plural for justice or uprightness, and here it refers to "an equitable arrangement" (BDB, 2).

וְלֹא־תַעְצֹר כּוֹחַ הַזְּרוֹעַ—Literally, "she shall not retain strength of the arm." Daniel had used עָצַר and כֹּחַ in 10:8, 16 to say that he had no strength. The noun זְרוֹעַ, "arm," often is a metaphor or "symbol of *strength*," either divine or human (BDB, 2), as also in the next clause (see the next textual note).

וְלֹא יַעֲמֹד וּזְרֹעוֹ—Literally, "and he will not endure and his arm," this could be translated, "he and his strength will not endure." Here the Qal (G) of עָמַד means to "endure" (BDB, 3 d) or "remain, last, survive." Instead of "arm" Theodotion reads, τὸ σπέρμα αὐτοῦ, "his seed/descendant." That meaning requires repointing וּזְרֹעוֹ as וְזַרְעוֹ without any change in the consonants. This commentary's translation follows Theodotion.

וְתִנָּתֵן—The Niphal (N) of נָתַן can mean "be given into the power of" in the negative sense of being given over to death or destruction (BDB, Niphal, 1 e).

וְהַיֹּלְדָהּ—"And the one who fathered her" is the masculine Qal (G) participle of יָלַד with the article and a feminine suffix. When a participle has the article, its suffix is always its accusative object (Joüon, § 121 k; cf. GKC, §§ 116 f; 127 i). Most often the Qal of יָלַד is used in feminine forms with the mother as its subject, meaning "give birth." However, masculine forms, like the participle here, can be used for a father who "begets" or "fathers" a child (see BDB, Qal, 2 a).

11:7 כַּנּוֹ—The noun כֵּן, "base, pedestal, office" (BDB, s.v. כֵּן III, under the root כון I), occurs with a third masculine singular suffix in 11:7, 20–21, 38. It is preceded by the preposition עַל in 11:20–21, 38. In all four verses, it means "*in his* [or: its] *place* ... in his stead, as his successor" (BDB, כֵּן III, 2).

וְיָבֹא בַמָּעוֹז—"He will come into the fortress" is the first of six occurrences of מָעוֹז in the chapter referring to an earthly military "fortress." It recurs in 11:10, 19, 31, 38–39. It also occurs in 11:1 but metaphorically: the divine man was a "refuge" for the archangel Michael in their war against the prince of Persia (see the first textual note on 11:1).

וְעָשָׂה בָהֶם וְהֶחֱזִיק—Literally, "he will make [war] with them and be strong," the two Hebrew verbs could be combined as a hendiadys: "he will prevail over them." The Qal (G) of עָשָׂה often is used in clauses that mean "make war" (BDB, II 1 e). The Hiphil (H) of חָזַק can mean to "prevail" (BDB, 5). A similar expression with the same two verbs occurs in 11:32: יַחֲזִקוּ וְעָשׂוּ, "they will be strong and take action" (cf. BDB, s.v. חָזַק, Hiphil, 1 c). Compare also וְלֹא יָעוֹז, "he will not be strong/prevail," at the end of 11:12.

11:8 בַּשְּׁבִי יָבִא מִצְרַיִם—Literally, "in captivity he will bring (to) Egypt," this is translated, "he will also take captive to Egypt." English requires placing this verbal clause first in translation, but in the Hebrew the long compound object precedes this verbal clause.

יַעֲמֹד מֶלֶךְ הַצָּפוֹן:—Here the Qal (G) of עָמַד means that he will "*stand off/far* from the king of the north" (cf. BDB, Qal, 1 f), that is, leave him alone. It probably implies that he will refrain from waging war, as in 2 Chr 20:17 (cf. BDB, Qal, 2 b).

11:10 וּבָנָיו יִתְגָּרוּ וְאָסְפוּ הֲמוֹן חֲיָלִים רַבִּים—"His sons" (וּבָנָיו) is the reading of the Qere as well as Theodotion (οἱ υἱοὶ αὐτοῦ), the Syriac, and the Vulgate. The plural is consistent with the following two plural verbs. The Kethib, וּבְנוֹ, "his son," is also the reading of the Old Greek (ὁ υἱὸς αὐτοῦ). The Old Greek reading is suspect, however, since it also reads the following two verbs as singular, whereas they are plural in the MT and the other ancient versions. יִתְגָּרוּ is the Hithpael (HtD) of גָּרָה, meaning "be stirred up" (*TWOT*, § 378) or "wage war" (BDB, 2). It recurs later in the verse (see the next textual note) and also in 11:25.

The object of "gather" (וְאָסְפוּ) is הֲמוֹן חֲיָלִים רַבִּים, "a multitude of many armies." The noun הֲמוֹן by itself often refers to a "great army" (BDB, s.v. הָמוֹן, 3 a, under the root המה). The context certainly supports that meaning for the four additional occurrences of הָמוֹן in 11:11–13.

וּבָא בוֹא וְשָׁטַף וְעָבַר וְיָשֹׁב וְיִתְגָּרֶה—These singular finite verbs (with the infinitive בּוֹא) must have as their subject the preceding noun (in construct) הָמוֹן, the "multitude of" the many amassed armies. Usually an infinitive absolute precedes a finite verb, but here and again in 11:13, the Qal (G) infinitive absolute בוֹא follows a finite form of the same Qal verb, וּבָא here and יָבוֹא in 11:13. Probably the nuance is durative, "will keep coming," or perhaps iterative, "will repeatedly come," even though Joüon, § 123 l (4), is doubtful about the nuance in these verses.

The second occurrence in the verse of the Hithpael (HtD) of גָּרָה is preceded by וְיָשֹׁב, which may have the adverbial meaning: "*again* be stirred up" (see BDB, s.v. שׁוּב, Qal, 8; in 11:13 וְשָׁב also has that adverbial meaning). For the first occurrence of "stirred up," see the preceding textual note. The singular וְיִתְגָּרֶה is the Qere in Leningradensis (and the form in 11:25). It is also the sole reading in many Masoretic manuscripts and is supported by the Old Greek, Theodotion, and the Vulgate. The plural Kethib, וְיִתְגָּרוּ, is supported by the Syriac. The plural verb would have either וּבָנָיו, "his sons," or חֲיָלִים רַבִּים, their "many armies," as its subject.

In form וְיָשֹׁב is jussive, but it has the meaning of an imperfect. Throughout the rest of chapter 11, we find other jussive forms with *waw* used as imperfects, for example, וְיָבֹא beginning 11:15, וְיֵשֵׁב beginning 11:17–18, וְיָשֵׁב beginning 11:19, וְיָעֵר beginning 11:25, וְיָשֹׁב beginning 11:28, and וְיָבֵן in 11:30. These and other imperfects are used as a future tense instead of the Classical Hebrew sequence of an imperfect followed by perfects with *waw* consecutive to refer to the future. See the discussion in Joüon, § 119 zb.

עַד־מָעֻזּוֹ:—"As far as his fortress" uses the noun מָעוֹז (see the second textual note on 11:7). The Qere, מָעֻזּוֹ, has the normal form of the third masculine singular suffix. The Kethib probably is to be vocalized מָעֻזֹּה, with an archaic form of the same suffix. Theodotion has τῆς ἰσχύος αὐτοῦ, supporting either form. The Old Greek has ἐπὶ πολύ, "upon many."

11:11 וְיִתְמַרְמַר—For this Hithpalpel (HtD) of מָרַר, to be "enraged" (BDB), see the textual note on 8:7, which has the only other occurrence of this stem of this verb in the OT.

עִמּוֹ עִם־מֶלֶךְ הַצָּפוֹן—"With him—with the king of the north" is somewhat repetitious, but clarifies which king is being attacked "to prevent any possible misunderstanding" (GKC, § 131 k; see also § 131 n). Such repetition of a preposition is common when the first instance of the preposition has a pronominal suffix (Joüon, 146 e, including observation 2). עִמּוֹ is not reflected in the Old Greek or Theodotion, so some interpreters speculate that it is the result of an accidental duplication of the following עִם. However, the Hebrew is clear and ought to be retained. When translating this sentence, the Greek versions probably smoothed out the syntax, a procedure followed by most English translations here.

In 11:11b–12, this commentary's translation is forced to supply in brackets which kings are the subjects and objects, but the repetitions phrase here makes such an insertion unnecessary. Most English translations also supply words in 11:11b–12 to help indicate who attacks whom and who is victorious.

11:12 וְנִשָּׂא הֶהָמוֹן וְרָם לְבָבוֹ—Most translations and commentators take וְנִשָּׂא as the Niphal (N) of נָשָׂא with הֶהָמוֹן as its subject: "the [king of the north's] army will be taken/swept away" (see BDB, s.v. נָשָׂא, Niphal, 4). However, the form could also be the Piel (D) of נָשָׂא, which can have the corresponding active meaning, "take away" (BDB, Piel, 4). A few translations (KJV, NKJV) and apparently the Old Greek, Theodotion, and the Vulgate take it as the Piel (D), in which case the king of the south is its subject and הֶהָמוֹן is its object: "he [the king of the south] takes away the army [of the king of the north]." However, the lack of the marker אֶת before (what would be) the definite direct object הֶהָמוֹן favors taking the verb as Niphal.

The first verbal clause (וְנִשָּׂא הֶהָמוֹן) serves adverbially in a temporal sense, "*when* the army …" and the second verbal clause (וְרָם לְבָבוֹ) is the main clause. The idiom with לֵבָב (or לֵב) as the subject of רוּם, literally, "his heart will be high," means "he will become arrogant," as in, for example, Hos 13:6. The Qere, וְרָם, is the Qal (G) perfect with *waw* consecutive, matching the form of the previous (Niphal [N] or Piel [D]) perfect with *waw* consecutive, וְנִשָּׂא. The Kethib is יָרוּם, the Qal (G) imperfect without *waw*.

וְהִפִּיל רִבֹּאוֹת—"He will cause myriads to fall" uses the plural of רִבֹּא, "myriad," as an indefinite number expressing great magnitude (Waltke-O'Connor, § 15.2.5, including example 8).

וְלֹא יָעוֹז:—The Qal (G) of עָזַז, "be strong," often means to "prevail" (BDB). That the king of the south "will not prevail" refers to him losing the battles to be described in 11:13–16a.

11:13 וּלְקֵץ הָעִתִּים שָׁנִים—Literally, "and to the end of the times, years," this means "and after some years." It does not refer to symbolic periods of time, but literal years, without specifying how many. A similar phrase with קֵץ and שָׁנִים began 11:6. See the first textual note on 11:6.

11:14 יַעַמְדוּ—Here the Qal (G) of עָמַד means "to rise up" in rebellion against a reigning king in the attempt to overthrow his power.

יְנַשְּׂאוּ—This form traditionally has been explained as the Hithpael (HtD) of נָשָׂא with the prefixed ת assimilated and marked by the *daghesh* in the *nun*, -נּ- (GKC, § 54 c). Others explain it as an example of a נ-reflexive conjugation or of a Hippael (HtD) conjugation (see Waltke-O'Connor, § 21.2.3c). In any case, it has a reflexive or middle meaning: the violent men "will lift themselves up" or "elevate themselves" in rebellion against higher authority.

וְנִכְשָׁלוּ:—The Niphal (N) of כָּשַׁל, "to stumble," occurs in Daniel in 11:14, 19, 33–35, 41. It refers to those who are attacked and persecuted, even to the point of physical death for some. In most cases, it refers to believers, some of whom are martyred: OT believers in 11:33–35 and NT believers oppressed by the Antichrist in 11:41. However, in 11:19 it clearly refers to the death of an evil unbeliever, Antiochus III. Here in 11:14 it probably refers to a Jewish party punished by a Gentile conqueror because of its political loyalty to a rival power. See further the commentary.

11:15 וּזְרֹעוֹת הַנֶּגֶב—Literally, "the arms of the south," this is translated, "the forces of the south." זְרוֹעַ recurs in 11:22, 31 with the same meaning of military forces or troops. Compare also כֹּחַ הַזְּרוֹעַ, "strength of arm," in 11:6.

11:16 וְיַעֲמֹד בְּאֶרֶץ־הַצְּבִי—Literally, "he will stand in the land of beauty" uses עָמַד with the connotation of conquest. אֶרֶץ־הַצְּבִי will recur in 11:41, and צְבִי also occurs in 8:9; 11:45, always referring to the Holy Land or more specifically to Mount Zion, the temple mount (11:45). Other OT books use it for the land of Israel (e.g., Ezek 20:6, 15) or the temple (Ezek 7:20), or even for the Messiah (Is 4:2).

וְכָלָה בְיָדוֹ:—The MT probably means "and complete destruction is in his hand/power" (see BDB, s.v. the noun כָּלָה, 2 b), meaning that he would be able to (or actually would) completely destroy the beautiful (Holy) Land. That is the sense of the translations by KJV, NIV, ESV, NASB. The noun כָּלָה could also be adverbial (cf. BDB, 1), in which case the land would be "completely in his hand." Another possibility is that וְכָלָה is the Qal (G) masculine singular perfect verb, meaning "it will be finished/destroyed," but we would expect the verb to be feminine if its subject were אֶרֶץ, although its subject might be הַצְּבִי. Theodotion translates with a verb, καὶ συντελεσθήσεται ἐν τῇ χειρὶ αὐτοῦ, "and it will be ended/finished off by his hand." The Old Greek translates, καὶ ἐπιτελεσθήσεται πάντα ἐν ταῖς χερσὶν αὐτοῦ, "and everything will be completed/accomplished by his hands," so it may have vocalized the consonants וכלה as וְכֻלָּה, "*and all of it* [the land] shall be in his power" (RSV [emphasis added]; NRSV is similar).

11:17 וְיָשֵׂם ׀ פָּנָיו—The Qal (G) of שִׂים with the object פָּנִים, "to set one's face," implies steely determination to go somewhere (see BDB, s.v. שִׂים, Qal, 2 c). The verb has the shortened form of the jussive, but its meaning is the same as an imperfect (וְיָשִׂים). The identical idiom is repeated as the Qere at the start of 11:18. The Semitic idiom was incorporated into the NT: Jesus "set his face to go to Jerusalem" (Lk 9:51), which begins the long Lukan travel narrative of Jesus' journey to Jerusalem and the cross (Lk 9:51–19:28).

וִישָׁרִים עִמּוֹ וְעָשָׂה—The noun is the plural of יָשָׁר, which usually means "honesty, uprightness," but here means an "agreement" (*HALOT*, 3) or "treaty" that he will forcibly "make" (וְעָשָׂה), that is, impose and enforce. The Old Greek has συνθήκας, "agreements, pacts." English translations include "terms of an agreement" (ESV) and "a proposal of peace" (NASB).

וּבַת הַנָּשִׁים יִתֶּן־לוֹ לְהַשְׁחִיתָהּ—The MT is, literally, "and *a daughter of women* he will give to him to destroy it." This is followed by Theodotion's θυγατέρα τῶν γυναικῶν. However, 4QDan^c has ובת אנשים, to be vocalized as וּבַת אֲנָשִׁים, "and a daughter of men,"[1] supported by the Old Greek's θυγατέρα ἀνθρώπου, "a daughter of a man." The MT may have resulted from a confusion of the letters א and ה. At any rate, both readings are ancient. The implied referent of the feminine suffix on לְהַשְׁחִיתָהּ, "to destroy *it*," is the southern kingdom. Hebrew words for "kingdom" (מַלְכוּת, מַמְלָכָה) are feminine, and the northern king naturally would intend to ruin the southern kingdom. Several English versions supply "kingdom" (RSV, NIV, ESV). The KJV took the antecedent as the daughter (וּבַת) whom the northern king gives, "corrupting her," but that seems unlikely in this context.

וְלֹא תַעֲמֹד וְלֹא־לוֹ תִהְיֶה:—The subject of the two feminine verbs most likely is the abstract idea of the northern king's plan to destroy the southern kingdom by giving the daughter to its king. Abstract ideas often are treated as feminine in Hebrew. Thus, literally, "it [his plan] will not stand/endure, and it will not be for him [to the advantage of the northern king]." That is the sense of the RSV, ESV, and NIV. However, NASB takes the subject as the daughter (בַּת), who does not stay loyal to the northern king: "she will not take a stand for him or be on his side" (KJV is similar). Either interpretation of the grammar is in harmony with the historical fulfillment, for which see the commentary.

11:18 וְיָשֵׂם ׀ פָּנָיו—The Qere repeats the idiom "and he will set his face" found at the start of 11:17. See the first textual note on 11:17. The Kethib is וְיָשֵׁב פָּנָיו, "and he will turn his face," which is the sole reading at the start of 11:19.

11:20 מַעֲבִיר נוֹגֵשׂ הֶדֶר מַלְכוּת—Literally, "one making travel an oppressor, glory of kingdom," this means the new leader will send an exactor of tribute to travel about the land. The tribute he collects will be for the glory of the kingdom. הֶדֶר is an unusual construct form of הָדָר, whose usual construct form is הֲדַר (GKC, § 93 dd).

11:21, 24 בְשַׁלְוָה ... בְשַׁלְוָה—Both 11:21 and 11:24 use שַׁלְוָה, "ease, peace," with the preposition בְּ in a temporal sense: "when [it is] at ease, peaceful." In both verses, Theodotion translates it by ἐν εὐθηνίᾳ, which also has a temporal meaning, "when [it is] in prosperity." In both verses, the Old Greek translates בְשַׁלְוָה with the adverb ἐξάπινα, "suddenly," as also in 8:25 (see the third textual note on 8:25).

11:21 וְהֶחֱזִיק מַלְכוּת בַּחֲלַקְלַקּוֹת:—Literally, "he will take hold of kingdom by means of slippery things," this is translated, "he will ... seize the kingdom through intrigue." חֲלַקְלַקּוֹת is a reduplicated noun form from the root חלק. It is an abstract plural meaning "slipperiness, flattery, fine promises" (BDB). It recurs with the same preposition (בַּחֲלַקְלַקּוֹת) in 11:34, where the context requires the adverbial meaning "insincerely."

---

[1] Ulrich, *Qumran Cave 4.XI*, 274.

Basically synonymous is בַּחֲלַקּוֹת, the abstract plural of the non-reduplicated noun חֲלָקָה, which occurs in the OT only in 11:32 and is translated "smooth talk."

11:22 וּזְרֹעוֹת הַשֶּׁטֶף יִשָּׁטְפוּ—Literally, "arms of the flood/sweep will be flooded/swept away." For the noun שֶׁטֶף see the fourth textual note on 9:26. The cognate verb, שָׁטַף, "flood, sweep away," occurs in active Qal (G) forms in 11:10, 26, 40. The form here is Niphal (N) with a passive meaning. Some propose that the Masoretes incorrectly pointed it as a Niphal and that it really is a Qal passive (Gp; Waltke-O'Connor, § 22.6b, including n. 31).

11:23 וּמִן־הִתְחַבְּרוּת אֵלָיו—This means "after an alliance is made with him." The preposition מִן is used in a temporal sense: "after." הִתְחַבְּרוּת is an Aramaic-form Hithpael (HtD) infinitive (GKC, § 54 k; Joüon, §§ 53 f; 88M j) of חָבַר, "unite," meaning "make an alliance" (BDB). The regular Hebrew form of its Hithpael (HtD) in 11:6 had a similar meaning. A high priest, "a leader of a covenant," makes the alliance with Antiochus, the "contemptible person." See further the commentary.

11:26 פַּת־בָּגוֹ—For this expression for "delicacies," see the first textual note on 1:5.

וְחֵילוֹ יִשְׁטוֹף—Normally the Qal (G) of שָׁטַף when referring to an army means that it will "flood" or "sweep across" a land in victory. The Qal of שָׁטַף can refer to a river and have the intransitive meaning "flow, run" (BDB, 2), so this clause might mean "his army will flow away." Many manuscripts have the *ḥaser* spelling יִשְׁטֹף, and the Syriac and Vulgate apparently vocalized the consonants as the Niphal (N) imperfect יִשָּׁטֵף, "will be swept away," which is the reading followed in this commentary.

11:27 וּשְׁנֵיהֶם הַמְּלָכִים לְבָבָם לְמֵרָע—The syntax is, literally, "the two of them, the kings, their heart is toward evil." מֵרָע is pausal for מֵרַע, which in form could be the Hiphil (H) participle of רָעַע, "do evil," with the participle used as a noun. It might also be a noun, meaning "evil," that occurs only here in the OT (see *HALOT*).

כָּזָב יְדַבֵּרוּ וְלֹא תִצְלָח—"A lie they will speak, but it will not succeed." The feminine imperfect תִצְלָח is used as a generic impersonal (GKC, §144 b–c), referring to the plan hatched at table. Grammatically its subject is not the masculine noun כָּזָב, "a lie," but that noun describes the content of the plan that will fail.

כִּי־עוֹד קֵץ לַמּוֹעֵד:—"Because an end is yet for an appointed time" is similar to the clause that ends 11:35. See the first textual note on 11:6.

11:29 וְלֹא־תִהְיֶה כָרִאשֹׁנָה וְכָאַחֲרֹנָה:—Literally, "it will not be like the first and like the later," the Hebrew idiom with repeated preposition כְּ means "the later will not be like the first." See Joüon, § 174 i (cf. § 133 h). Since the context is referring to invasions, the translation supplies "invasion" after "later" and after "first."

11:30 צִיִּים כִּתִּים—The rare noun צִי, "ship," is an Egyptian loanword (*HALOT*). Elsewhere in the OT, it only occurs in Num 24:24 (see the commentary); Is 33:21; and Ezek 30:9. כִּתִּים, "Kittim," occurs eight times in the OT.[a] It first refers to descendants of Javan (Gen 10:4; 1 Chr 1:7), son of Japheth (Gen 10:2), who apparently fathered the Greek and Roman peoples. In most of the other OT passages, it is a place name of the area where those descendants of Javan settled (Num 24:24; Is 23:1, 12; Ezek 27:6). כִּתִּים may come from Kition, the ancient capital of Cyprus. Here in this phrase כִּתִּים is used as a gentilic adjective, literally, "Kittim ships," but the attributive adjective indicates the country of

(a) Gen 10:4; Num 24:24; Is 23:1, 12; Jer 2:10; Ezek 27:6; Dan 11:30; 1 Chr 1:7

origin, so the phrase is translated as "ships from Kittim."[2] It refers to the Roman fleet that thwarted Antiochus IV's second war against Egypt (see the commentary).

וְיָבֵן עַל־עֹזְבֵי בְּרִית קֹדֶשׁ:—Here and in 11:37, the Qal (G) of בִּין with the preposition עַל has the nuance "*give heed to ... consider* (with attention)" (BDB, s.v. בִּין, Qal, 3 e), and is translated here as "*favor* those who abandon a holy covenant."

11:31 הַמִּקְדָּשׁ הַמָּעוֹז—The two nouns in apposition, "the temple, the fortress," serve as a hendiadys, "the temple fortress." It refers to a fortress erected on the temple mount, "the city of David" (1 Mac 1:33). See further the commentary.

הַשִּׁקּוּץ מְשׁוֹמֵם:—For the noun שִׁקּוּץ, "detested thing" (BDB), see the second textual note on 9:27. The participle probably is adjectival, "the detested thing causing desolation," even though we would expect the Polel (D) participle מְשׁוֹמֵם to have a definite article to match that on הַשִּׁקּוּץ. The construction is similar to וְהַפֶּשַׁע שֹׁמֵם, "the transgression causing desolation," in 8:13, where too the noun is definite and the Qal (G) participle lacks an article. The phrase here has the same Polel participle that was in 9:27, וְעַל כְּנַף שִׁקּוּצִים מְשֹׁמֵם, "on the wing of detested things (is) a desolator." See the second textual note on 9:27. In the NT, Jesus refers to "the detested thing of/causing desolation" (Mt 24:15; Mk 13:14). Jesus is echoing Dan 9:27 (as well as the phrase in 11:31; 12:11) and is referring to events that took place after his earthly ministry.[3] That later desolation is a different historical event, but also involved a desecration of the temple by a Gentile invader, like the desolation that had been accomplished under Antiochus IV Epiphanes in the second century BC, which is the desolation predicted in 8:13; 11:31; and 12:11.

11:32, 34 בַּחֲלַקְלַקּוֹת ... בַּחֲלָקוֹת—For these two synonyms, each with the preposition בְּ, see the textual note on 11:21.

11:32 וְעַם יֹדְעֵי אֱלֹהָיו יַחֲזִקוּ וְעָשׂוּ—Literally, "a people of knowers of his God will be strong and will act." The singular collective noun עַם, "people," is followed by a plural participle in construct, יֹדְעֵי, because the "people" consist of many individuals (Joüon, § 148 a). The suffix on אֱלֹהָיו, "his [the people's] God," is singular, referring back to עַם, "people," but English translation requires "their God." The individuals indicated by the plural participle are then the subjects of the following plural verbs, יַחֲזִקוּ וְעָשׂוּ. The Hiphil (H) of חָזַק can be causative, "strengthen," but here and occasionally elsewhere it is internally transitive, "be strong" (see BDB, Hiphil, 1 c).

11:33 וּמַשְׂכִּילֵי עָם יָבִינוּ לָרַבִּים—Hiphil (H) forms of the verbs שָׂכַל and בִּין can have causative, transitive meanings: for בִּין, "make [others] understand," and for שָׂכַל, "impart insight" as in 9:22. They each can also have intransitive (technically called internally transitive) meanings: for בִּין, "to understand," and for שָׂכַל, "to have insight" as in 1:4; 9:13, 25; 12:3, 10. The construct phrase מַשְׂכִּילֵי עָם could have the causative meaning, "those who give insight to the people," with עָם as the direct object of the participial verb

---

[2] English too can use an attributive adjective to indicate source or origin, as in "Idaho potatoes," meaning "potatoes from/grown in Idaho."

[3] See the commentary on 9:24–27, especially 9:26–27, and "Daniel in the New Testament" in the introduction.

(see GKC, § 116 g). But more likely it has the intransitive meaning, "those of the people who have insight," with "of the people" serving as a partitive genitive. (The same participle but in the absolute state in 11:35, הַמַּשְׂכִּילִים, has the same intransitive meaning.) The construct phrase is then the subject of the following verb יָבִינוּ, which must be transitive and causative since it has the indirect object לָרַבִּים, hence "those of the people who have insight will make many understand."

11:35 לִצְרוֹף בָּהֶם וּלְבָרֵר וְלַלְבֵּן—The three infinitives construct with לְ are purpose clauses, expressing God's plan. The Qal (G) of צָרַף usually has the literal meaning to "melt, refine" metal, but here with בָּהֶם as its object ("with them," referring to the believers "who have insight"), it has the metaphorical meaning "*refine* (men, by trials)" (BDB, s.v. צָרַף, 1). See also its Piel (D) participle in Mal 3:2. The Piel of בָּרַר occurs only here in the OT, but has the same meaning as the Qal, "purify." וְלַלְבֵּן, "to make white," is a doubly unusual form of the Hiphil (H) infinitive construct, whose expected form would be וּלְהַלְבִּין (GKC, § 53 q). The ה prefix has been elided and the *hireq* vowel has become *tsere*, the stem vowel of the Hiphil (H) infinitive absolute.

עַד־עֵת קֵץ כִּי־עוֹד לַמּוֹעֵד:—"Until the time of the end, for it is still for an appointed time" does refer eschatologically to the period of time leading up to the return of Christ. See the second textual note on 8:17.

Commentary

The Next Four Kings of the Persian Empire (11:2)

Daniel sees this vision "in the third year of Cyrus, king of Persia" (10:1), also called Darius the Mede (11:1). He is told that three more kings would arise in Persia before a fourth, wealthy king (11:2). These were the three kings who followed Cyrus:

- Cambyses (530–522 BC)
- Gaumata (Pseudo-Bardiya/Pseudo-Smerdis; 522 BC)
- Darius I (522–486 BC)

The fourth king was Xerxes (486–465), who by all accounts was very rich.[4] He is called Ahasuerus in the book of Esther. The prophecy given Daniel states that Xerxes "will awaken everyone, [especially] the kingdom of Greece" (11:2), which is a reference to him arousing and enlisting people from all parts of his vast kingdom to join his army and invade Greece. However, Xerxes was unable to conquer Greece because the various Greek city-states managed to forge an effective coalition and repel his attacks. It has sometimes been noted that there was no "kingdom of Greece" in Xerxes' day. However, the point of the revelation is that Xerxes will "awaken … [especially] the kingdom of Greece." That is, his invasion caused the Greeks to realize that they could be a unified force.

---

[4] Jerome first identified the fourth king as Xerxes (Archer, *Jerome's Commentary on Daniel*, 119). Others who agree include Calvin, *Daniel*, 2:270; Keil, *Daniel*, 430; Leupold, *Daniel*, 477; Luther, "Preface to Daniel," AE 35:306; Miller, *Daniel*, 291; Walvoord, *Daniel*, 256; Young, *Daniel*, 232.

This eventually led to a united Greece under Philip of Macedon, whose son was Alexander the Great, whose conquests made Greece a world empire.

The subsequent kings of Persia are not mentioned. They were these:

- Artaxerxes I Longimanus (465–424 BC)
- Darius II (423–405 BC)
- Artaxerxes II Mnemon (404–359 BC)
- Artaxerxes III Ochus (358–338 BC)
- Arses (337–336 BC)
- Darius III Codomannus (335–330 BC)

Since there were more Persian kings and because the *catch-concept* organizing principle of this revelation is not always understood (see "Introduction to Daniel 10–12"), some commentators have proposed other identifications. Some critical scholars identify the first three Persian kings as the three mentioned elsewhere in the OT: Cyrus, Xerxes, and Artaxerxes I. Then the fourth, rich king would be Darius III, who fell to Alexander the Great. According to this view, Xerxes could not be the king who stirred up Greece, since it is thought that Jews in the second century would not have had knowledge of Xerxes' invasion of Greece.[5] This, of course, involves a certain amount of circular reasoning. First, it assumes that Daniel is a second-century composition. Then, second, on the basis of that assumption, it surmises that a second-century Jew could not have referred to Xerxes' campaign against Greece. In addition, the critical view also contends that the stirring up refers to Alexander's campaign against Darius III. However, the text does not say that Greece will stir up (or fight against) the fourth Persian king. Instead, it says that the fourth Persian king will stir up the kingdom of Greece. Therefore, the text cannot be describing the Persian king Darius III since he did not initiate action against the Greeks. Rather, the Greek king Alexander the Great invaded territory controlled by the Persians.

Some evangelical scholars, bothered by the fact that the later Persian kings named above are not mentioned in Daniel, propose that the sequence "three more kings ... the fourth one" (11:2) indicates a complete set of something, like the graded numerical sayings in Proverbs and Amos.[6] They believe the text is merely indicating a complete set of Persian kings and that the numbers are not to be taken literally. However, there are two problems with this proposal. First, the sequence in Proverbs and Amos is always "three ... four," never "three ... fourth." Second, when this saying is used in Proverbs 30, four items are always listed (Prov 30:15–16, 18–19, 21–23, 29–31). In fact, graded numerical sayings occur elsewhere with other numbers, where there is a list of items equal to the greater number, for example, "six ... seven" (Prov 6:16–19).[7] Therefore,

---

[5] Collins, *Daniel*, 377; Montgomery, *Daniel*, 423.
[6] Prov 30:15, 18, 21, 29; Amos 1:3, 6, 9, 11, 13; 2:1, 4, 6. See Baldwin, *Daniel*, 185; Goldingay, *Daniel*, 294–95; cf. Lucas, *Daniel*, 279.
[7] See also Steinmann, "The Graded Numerical Saying in Job."

the presence of the pattern "three ... the fourth" in Daniel can and should be understood as referring to the numbers literally.

The Kingdom of Alexander the Great (11:3–4)

There is no dispute about the application of these verses. The mighty "warrior king" is Alexander the Great (10:3). He "will do as he pleases," a description also used of the Persian ram in 8:4. This signifies that he will conquer a large amount of territory quickly and easily.

Yet the demise of Alexander's kingdom was also swift. He began his conquests in 334 BC and died in 323 BC at the age of thirty-two. The fourfold division of his kingdom matches the description of it in 7:6 and 8:8, 22. "The four winds of heaven" (11:4) signify the four cardinal compass points. Although the four parts into which the Greek Empire was divided did not exactly correspond to the compass points, that is not the intent of the text here. Instead, it emphasizes the breakup of the kingdom into four parts. However, the use of "the four winds" will enable two of the kingdoms resulting from this split to be referred to as "north" and "south." These two were in fact geographically northern and southern (in Syria-Mesopotamia and in Egypt, respectively) in relation to each other.

The last part of 11:4 makes two points. First, the kingdoms that succeed Alexander's will not be as vast as his. Second, his descendants will not rule. Alexander's deranged half-brother Philip Arrhidaeus and Alexander's infant son Alexander IV were nominal rulers of his kingdom after his death, but they wielded no real power. Both were eventually murdered. Alexander's generals fought over the kingdom and eventually split it into four parts: (1) Greece and Macedon, ruled by Antigonus and, later, Cassander; (2) Thrace and Asia Minor, ruled by Lysimachus; (3) Syria and Mesopotamia, ruled by Seleucus I Nicator; and (4) Egypt and Palestine, ruled by Ptolemy I Soter.

Just as 11:2 skipped over the last kings of the Persian Empire to get to the Greek king Alexander, 11:3–4 skips any detailed description of the four kingdoms. Beginning in 11:5, only two of them are treated.

The Rebellion of Seleucus I against Ptolemy I (11:5)

The Ptolemaic and Seleucid Kingdoms

It is universally agreed that 11:5–35 is a description of various Greek kingdoms that were successors to Alexander's empire. "The king of the north" is used to designate various kings who ruled the Seleucid kingdom of Syria and Mesopotamia, while "the king of the south" designates various kings who ruled Ptolemaic Egypt. Figure 15 shows the Ptolemaic and Seleucid kings mentioned in Daniel 11.

Figure 15

The Ptolemies and the Seleucids

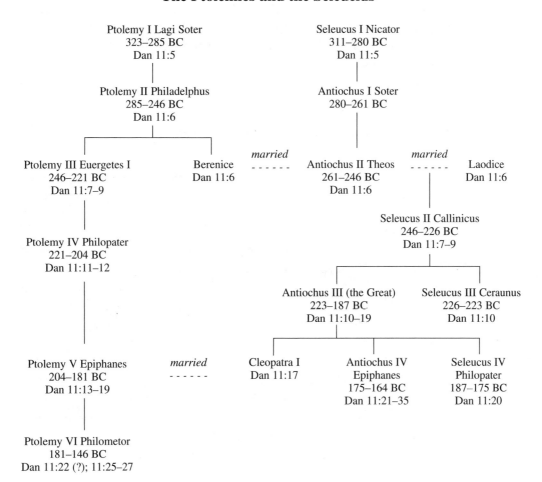

Shortly after the death of Alexander the Great in 323 BC, Ptolemy I was made satrap of Egypt and later took the title "king." In 11:5 he is called "the king of the south." In 321 BC, Seleucus I was designated the satrap of Babylon. But when attacked by Antigonus in 316 BC, Seleucus fled to Egypt, where Ptolemy made him one of his generals. In 312 Ptolemy and Seleucus defeated Antigonus at Gaza. Seleucus returned to Babylon and later took the title "king." After Antigonus was killed in battle at Ipsus in 301, Seleucus gradually took control of Antigonus' territory, which he expanded into a greater kingdom than Ptolemy's.

The Marriage of Berenice, Daughter of Ptolemy II, to Antiochus II (11:6)

Succeeding Ptolemaic and Seleucid kings fought each other in attempts to expand and defend their kingdoms. About 250 BC, Ptolemy II agreed to a peace treaty with Antiochus II. Part of the treaty involved a marriage alliance: Berenice, Ptolemy's daughter, married Antiochus, who thereby was forced to leave his first wife, Laodice. Berenice's offspring was to become the next Seleucid ruler. However, in 246 BC, Antiochus took back Laodice, but died shortly thereafter, allegedly poisoned by Laodice. She also arranged for the murder of Berenice and her child to insure her son's succession to the throne as Seleucus II. Many of Berenice's attendants who came from Egypt also perished, and her father died that same year. This is all accurately predicted by 11:6: "She [Berenice] will be given up—she, those who brought her [her attendants], the one who fathered her [Ptolemy II], and the one who strengthened/supported her during the times [Antiochus II]." Since the Hiphil (H) of בוֹא usually means "to bring," the Hiphil participle וּמְבִיאֶיהָ literally means "those who brought her" (NKJV), but some translations render it as "her attendants" (RSV, ESV) or "her royal escort" (NIV) to link the wording of the prediction more closely to its fulfillment.

Conflict between Ptolemy III and Seleucus II (11:7–9)

Berenice's brother Ptolemy III succeeded their father, Ptolemy II. To retaliate for the murder of his sister Berenice, Ptolemy III invaded Syria, captured the Syrian capital of Antioch, and campaigned far to the east (11:7). He captured Laodice and executed her. Ptolemy captured many spoils of war, including the idols that the Persian king Cambyses had carried off from Egypt to Persia in 525 BC. Thus he took "captive to Egypt their gods" (11:8). The mention of Egypt as the destination of the spoils identifies the king of the south as a Ptolemaic king. The Egyptians gave Ptolemy the name Euergetes, "benefactor," because he returned their idols. However, Ptolemy was unable to solidify his control over Seleucid territory because he had to return to Egypt to deal with a rebellion. Therefore, Seleucus II was able to reestablish his authority. Two years later, in 242 BC, Seleucus attempted to invade Egypt, but was unsuccessful (11:9).

Military Campaigns of Seleucus III and Antiochus III (11:10)

Seleucus II was succeeded by his son Seleucus III, who reigned only three years before being murdered during a military campaign in 223 BC. He was succeeded by his brother Antiochus III, who became known as "the Great" because of his military success. At first he had to suppress rebellions in Media and Asia Minor. When the weak Ptolemy IV became the southern king in 221, Antiochus saw an opportunity to regain territory in Syria that his father had lost to the southern kingdom. In 219–218, Antiochus campaigned in Syria and Palestine. Palestine had been under the control of Egypt until this time. This is probably what is meant that Antiochus was "stirred up as far as his [the king of the south's] fortress" (cf. "the temple fortress" in 11:31).

Conflict between Ptolemy IV and Antiochus III (11:11–12)

In 217 BC, in response to Antiochus' military actions, Ptolemy launched a counterattack. The decisive battle was fought at Raphia in Palestine. Polybius reports that the Egyptian forces numbered "seventy thousand infantry, five thousand cavalry, and seventy-three elephants" while the Syrians had "sixty-two thousand infantry, six thousand cavalry, and one hundred and two elephants."[8] Despite the "great army" (11:11) raised by Antiochus, he was soundly defeated, losing seventeen thousand troops as opposed to Ptolemy's loss of twenty-two hundred troops. Thus "he [the king of the north] will raise up a great army, but the army will be given into his [the king of the south's] hand" (11:11). Ptolemy regained Palestine and southern Syria, but did not press his advantage.

Ptolemy returned to Egypt where he "abandoned all noble pursuits and gave himself up to the life of debauchery,"[9] fulfilling the prophecy that "his heart will become arrogant" (11:12). How "he will cause myriads to fall" (11:12) is described by Polybius, when Ptolemy suppressed rebellions in Egypt:

> Ptolemy however immediately after these events became involved in a war with his Egyptian subjects. For in arming them for his campaign against Antiochus he had taken a step which, while it served his immediate purpose sufficiently well, proved eventually disastrous. Elated with their victory at Rhaphia they refused any longer to receive orders from the king; but looked out for a leader to represent them, on the ground that they were quite able to maintain their independence. And this they succeeded in doing before very long.[10]

Relations between Ptolemy V and Antiochus III (11:13–19)

Antiochus campaigned in the eastern part of his empire from 212 to 205 BC. Then in 204, Ptolemy IV and his queen died under mysterious circumstances. Sensing an opportunity to wrest territory away from the young Ptolemy V, who was only five years old, Antiochus attacked Egypt and took back southern Syria.

---

[8] Polybius, *Histories*, 5.79 (trans. Shuckburgh, 1:430–31).
[9] Polybius, *Histories*, 14.12 (trans. Shuckburgh, 2:135).
[10] Polybius, *Histories*, 5.107 (trans. Shuckburgh, 1:453).

The Egyptian general Scopas managed to drive Antiochus back for awhile. However, in a decisive battle at Paneas (called Caesarea Philippi in the NT) in 200, Antiochus gained control of southern Syria and Palestine. Neither would again come under Ptolemaic control.

During the last years of Ptolemy IV and the early years of Ptolemy V, many provinces of the Egyptian kingdom rebelled or otherwise asserted a measure of independence (11:14). However, commentators disagree about which exact circumstances are described by the "violent men" who "lift themselves up to fulfill [this] vision." It is known that during this time there were pro-Ptolemaic and pro-Seleucid parties among the elite Jews in Jerusalem. Perhaps the "violent men" are one or both of these parties as they vied for power during this time of transition. "They will stumble" may refer either to the conquest of Jerusalem by Antiochus,[11] which would have brought punishment against the pro-Ptolemaic party of Jews, or to the previous subduing of the Jewish nation by Scopas,[12] who may have punished the pro-Seleucid party. The "vision" to which 11:14 refers is this part of the last vision of Daniel (chapters 10–12).

After being defeated at Paneas, Scopas retreated to the city of Sidon, where Antiochus besieged him and forced his surrender in 198 BC (11:15). The phrase "his best troops" probably refers to Scopas' Aeolian mercenaries. "There will be no strength to stand" may refer to the famine caused by the siege; the famine forced Scopas to surrender.

Antiochus, like Alexander (11:3), "will do as he pleases" (11:16) since he is now in complete control, having bested his enemies. This arrogance would lead to his downfall. His victory over Scopas led to permanent Seleucid control of all of Palestine, "the beautiful land" (11:16). He also seized coastal areas in Asia Minor and some of the Greek islands.

Since Rome's power was beginning to assert itself from the west, Antiochus did not invade Egypt. Instead, he entered into a marriage alliance by giving his daughter Cleopatra to Ptolemy V as his wife. Apparently, he hoped she would undermine Ptolemy's realm from within; thus "he will give him a daughter of men to destroy it [the southern kingdom]" (11:17). However, Cleopatra became steadfastly loyal to her husband, so that Antiochus' scheme was thwarted; thus "it [his plan] will not stand or be to his advantage" (11:17).

Antiochus turned to campaign in the west, taking islands in the Aegean and campaigning in Thrace in 196 BC, fulfilling 11:18. Rome warned him not to attack Greece itself, but Antiochus did not listen and did as he pleased, invading Greece in 192 BC. The Romans and their Greek allies defeated him at Thermopylae in 191. The Romans then drove him eastward and defeated him soundly at the Battle of Magnesia in 190. By this act, the Roman commander Lucius Cornelius Scipio fulfilled "a commander will put an end to his insolence.

---

[11] Polybius, *Histories*, 16.39.
[12] Polybius, *Histories*, 16.39, quoted by Josephus, *Antiquities*, 12.135.

Moreover, he will repay him for his insolence" (11:18). In 188 BC, Antiochus was forced to accept the Treaty of Apamea in which he became a Roman vassal and was forced to send twenty hostages, including his son Antiochus IV, to Rome.

Having no options to campaign in the west, he turned eastward to Syria, Mesopotamia, and beyond (11:19). In 187, desperate for funds to pay his tribute to Rome, he attempted to pillage the temple of Zeus/Bel in Elymaïs. The local population rose up in indignation to defend the sanctuary, killing Antiochus and many of his followers.

The Reign of Seleucus IV (11:20)

Antiochus III was followed on the throne by his son Seleucus IV. In order to secure more funds to pay the obligation to Rome inherited from his father, Seleucus IV sent his finance minister, Heliodorus, to Jerusalem in order to seize the wealth of the temple treasury. Thus Heliodorus is the "exactor of tribute" (11:20). 2 Maccabees 3 reports that Heliodorus was turned back by an attack of God's angelic forces. Seleucus IV's inconsequential reign ended in 175. He did not die in an angry attack of the populace, as had his father, nor in battle (11:20). Instead, he was poisoned by Heliodorus, who may have been in league with Seleucus IV's brother, Antiochus IV. Antiochus IV was returning to Syria from Rome when his brother was killed.

Antiochus IV Seizes Control of Syria and Palestine (11:21–24)

The "contemptible person" (11:21) who took the place of Seleucus IV was his brother Antiochus IV Epiphanes. Antiochus had been a prisoner in Rome as required by the terms of the Treaty of Apamea. However, in late 176 or early 175, he was released in exchange for Seleucus IV's elder son Demetrius. Antiochus IV was in Athens when his brother was murdered. With the assistance of Eumenes II of Pergamum, he acquired an army and marched eastward to Babylon. After the death of Seleucus IV, Heliodorus had briefly seized the throne even though Demetrius was the rightful heir. When Antiochus IV and his army arrived, Heliodorus fled. Antiochus took the throne, ostensibly as regent in place of his nephew Demetrius, and with his younger nephew Antiochus (an infant) as coregent. (The younger nephew was murdered in 170.) Thus "the majesty of the kingdom" was not rightfully conferred on Antiochus IV. Instead, he seized the throne "through intrigue" (11:21).

The portrait of Antiochus IV that follows in 11:22–24 is a general description of his reign. Some interpreters take the "overwhelming force" that "will be overwhelmed ... and broken" (11:22) to be a reference to the Egyptian forces defeated by Antiochus IV (as described in 11:25–26).[13] However, the text does not mention the king of the south, making this unlikely. It is most probably a description of the forces Antiochus defeated in his ascent to the throne.

---

[13] E.g., Miller, *Daniel*, 299.

"A leader of a covenant" (11:22) refers to the Jewish high priest, the liturgical leader of God's covenant people. However, the text leaves ambiguous which high priest is being described. The one who is "broken" in 11:22 is usually understood to be the high priest Onias III. Antiochus III had confirmed the Jewish right to internal self-government according to traditional Jewish laws. This meant that the high priest was the local ruler in Jerusalem. Antiochus IV, however, was at odds with Onias III because this high priest was opposed to the growing influence of Hellenism in Palestine. Soon after Antiochus IV took the throne, Onias' brother Jason offered to Antiochus IV a large bribe along with the promise that he would pursue the Hellenization of Jerusalem. Antiochus accepted Jason's offer, deposed Onias, and named Jason to be the high priest (2 Macc 4:7–10). In 172 BC, Menelaus, who was not from the traditional high-priestly family, offered Antiochus IV an even larger bribe and was made high priest instead of Jason (2 Macc 4:23–26). When Onias learned that Menelaus had stolen some of the gold vessels from the temple, he made a public protest (2 Macc 4:32–33). Then Onias took refuge in the sanctuary at Daphne near Antioch, but he was lured out of the sanctuary and murdered (2 Macc 4:34). Dan 11:22b–23 may refer to this incident.

Thus "an alliance is made with him" (11:23) probably refers to either Jason or Menelaus (or both) making an agreement with Antiochus IV. "He will act deceitfully" (11:23) refers to Antiochus, whose treachery was evident in his dealings with three high priests: he deposed Onias, then deposed Jason, and wrongfully installed Menelaus. Then 11:23b–24 goes on to describe further outrages by Antiochus, who "will rise up and become powerful with a small nation." The "small nation" consists of those Jewish people in Jerusalem and Judea who apostatized from God and the true faith, and aided and abetted Antiochus.

Others understand the "leader of a covenant" (11:22) to be Ptolemy VI, with whom Antiochus made a treaty, then broke it.[14] In favor of this is that the text says נְגִיד בְּרִית, "a leader of a covenant," not נְגִיד הַבְּרִית, "*the* leader of *the* covenant," as might be expected if the high priest were in view. However, this cannot explain the "small nation" in the next verse, which seems to be a direct reference to Jerusalem and Judea.

The indefinite "*a* leader of a covenant" (11:22) may be a subtle prediction that there would be two or three competing occupants of the high priestly office, none of whom could rightly be called by the more definite "*the* leader of the covenant." Jason and Menelaus both bribed their way into the office. Supporting the view that "a covenant" is God's covenant with Israel (not a covenant by Antiochus with Ptolemy VI) is the fact that when "covenant" is mentioned later, the article is never used, but it still most certainly refers to the holy covenant of God with Israel (בְּרִית in 11:28, 30 [twice], 32). See also 9:27,

---

[14] E.g., Miller, *Daniel*, 299.

where it lacks the article even though it refers to the new covenant established by the Messiah.

Throughout his time as king, Antiochus plundered provincial and temple treasuries in his realm,[15] acting more rapacious than any of his predecessors, fulfilling 11:24. He also lavishly distributed gifts (1 Macc 3:30). Polybius recounted his unusual habits:

> In regard to making presents, too, his behaviour was on a par with this. Some he presented with dice made of gazelle horn, some with dates, others with gold. There were even instances of his making unexpected presents to men whom he met casually, and whom he had never seen before. In regard to public sacrifices and the honours paid to the gods, he surpassed all his predecessors on the throne; as witness the Olympieium at Athens and the statues placed round the altar at Delos. He used also to bathe in the public baths, when they were full of the townspeople, pots of the most expensive unguents being brought in for him; and on one occasion on some one saying, "Lucky fellows you kings, to use such things and smell so sweet!" without saying a word to the man, he waited till he was bathing the next day, and then coming into the bath caused a pot of the largest size and of the most costly kind of unguent called *stacte* to be poured over his head, so that there was a general rush of the bathers to roll themselves in it; and when they all tumbled down, the king himself among them, from its stickiness, there was loud laughter.[16]

Antiochus also devised "plans against strongholds, but [only] until a time" (11:24), which is probably a reference to his campaigns against Egypt, which are treated in more detail in the text that follows.

Antiochus IV Campaigns against Ptolemy VI and against Jerusalem (11:25–28)

Antiochus undertook his first campaign against Egypt in 169 BC, probably provoked by aggression on the part of Ptolemy VI. While Ptolemy was a youth, his mother, Cleopatra, who was also Antiochus' sister, acted as regent. When she died, Ptolemy came under the influence of two advisors, Eulaeus and Lenaeus. They gave him bad advice and encouraged him to attempt to wrest Palestine back from Seleucid power. Antiochus learned of the plan and prepared for battle at Pelusium on the Egyptian border. Ptolemy was captured as he attempted to flee, following the advice of his courtiers. Thus Ptolemy was not able to succeed, since word of his plans was leaked to his opponent. Counterplots were "plotted against him," and in Antiochus' victory over him "many slain people" fell (11:25–26).

Antiochus now controlled most of Egypt, except Alexandria, where the leaders declared Ptolemy's younger brother Ptolemy VII to be king. Under the guise of support for Ptolemy VI's rightful claim to the throne, Antiochus made

---

[15] Antiochus even died shortly after or while looting a temple or temples (Polybius, *Histories*, 31.11; 1 Macc 6:1–17; 2 Macc 1:11–17; 9:1–29).

[16] Polybius, *Histories*, 26.1 (trans. Shuckburgh, 2:354).

an alliance with him, setting Ptolemy VI up as king in Memphis. Yet neither of these "two kings," Ptolemy and Antiochus, intended to observe the terms of the treaty they made "at one table" (11:27). Each was using the other in an attempt to enhance his own control over Egypt. The alliance between Ptolemy VI and Antiochus unraveled when Ptolemy VI and Ptolemy VII were reconciled through the efforts of their sister Cleopatra II, and they became joint rulers of Egypt. Thus the "lie" between Ptolemy and Antiochus did "not succeed" (11:27).

The divine man[17] speaking to Daniel includes a reminder that God is ultimately in control of these events when he states, "But it will not succeed, because an end is yet for an appointed time" (11:27). The plots of humans cannot undo the plans of God.

Antiochus was unable to capture Alexandria, so he stationed a garrison at Pelusium and returned to Syria (11:28). On his way, he stopped at Jerusalem, sacked the temple, and seized its valuables. 1 Macc 1:20–24 describes this sacrilege:

> After subduing Egypt, Antiochus returned in the one hundred forty-third year [of the Seleucid era, which was spring 169–spring 168 BC]. He went up against Israel and came to Jerusalem with a strong force. He arrogantly entered the sanctuary and took the golden altar, the lampstand for the light, and all its utensils. He took also the table for the bread of the Presence, the cups for drink offerings, the bowls, the golden censers, the curtain, the crowns, and the gold decoration on the front of the temple; he stripped it all off. He took the silver and the gold, and the costly vessels; he took also the hidden treasures that he found. Taking them all, he went into his own land. He shed much blood, and spoke with great arrogance. (NRSV)

Antiochus IV Campaigns against Ptolemy VI Again but Is Blocked by the Roman Fleet (11:29–30a)

God's "appointed time" for the "end" (11:27) of Antiochus' campaigns against Egypt came in 168 BC with Antiochus' second invasion of Egypt. This invasion was not successful because of the intervention of a Roman fleet ("ships from Kittim," 11:30), a hint of the fourth kingdom that will dominate the world.[18] As Antiochus moved to attack Alexandria, a Roman delegation arrived in response to Egypt's request for help. Polybius relates the events that followed:

> When Antiochus had advanced to attack Ptolemy in order to possess himself of Pelusium, he was met by the Roman commander Gaius Popilius Laenas. Upon the king greeting him from some distance, and holding out his right hand to him, Popilius answered by holding out the tablets which contained

---

[17] For his identity, see the commentary on 10:4–6.

[18] The Greek kingdoms are part of the third world empire, and the Roman Empire is the fourth kingdom depicted in Daniel 2 and Daniel 7. See the excursus "The Four-Kingdom Schema in Daniel."

the decree of the Senate, and bade Antiochus read that first: not thinking it right, I suppose, to give the usual sign of friendship until he knew the mind of the recipient, whether he were to be regarded as a friend or foe. On the king, after reading the despatch, saying that he desired to consult with his friends on the situation, Popilius did a thing which was looked upon as exceedingly overbearing and insolent. Happening to have a vine stick in his hand, he drew a circle round Antiochus with it, and ordered him to give his answer to the letter before he stepped out of that circumference. The king was taken aback by this haughty proceeding. After a brief interval of embarrassed silence, he replied that he would do whatever the Romans demanded. Then Popilius and his colleagues shook him by the hand, and one and all greeted him with warmth. The contents of the despatch was an order to put an end to the war with Ptolemy at once. Accordingly a stated number of days was allowed him, within which he withdrew his army into Syria, in high dudgeon indeed, and groaning in spirit, but yielding to the necessities of the time.[19]

The phrase "ships from Kittim" (11:30) is a deliberate reference to Balaam's prophecy in Numbers 24. The phrasing is similar, and these are two of only four OT passages with this particular rare Hebrew noun (צִי) for "ship" (see the first textual note on 11:30). These are the only two passages in the Scriptures to connect "ships" with "Kittim":

- וּבָאוּ בוֹ צִיִּים כִּתִּים, "ships from Kittim will come against him" (Dan 11:30).
- וְצִים מִיַּד כִּתִּים, "ships [will come] from beside Kittim" (Num 24:24).

Balaam's prophecy concerns a star rising out of Jacob and a scepter rising out of Israel (Num 24:17), a vision of the Messiah. In this prophecy uttered in 1407 BC, before mentioning the ships that will come from Kittim, Balaam asks the question "Who will be alive when God does this?" (Num 24:23), implying that from his standpoint it is in the distant future. Num 24:24 itself predicts that the ships from Kittim will afflict Assyria, a chief enemy of Israel during the first half of the first millennium BC, and the Kittim will also afflict the Hebrew people themselves, but the Kittim people will eventually be destroyed. By including the arrival of ships from Kittim, the divine man speaking to Daniel is hinting that the demise of the Greek domination of the Near East will be near its end when Antiochus IV reigns. He is also implying that the Messiah foreseen by Balaam will come shortly thereafter (in the era of the Kittim, the Roman era).

This is the only hint of the Messiah in Daniel 11.[20]

Antiochus IV Attempts to Hellenize the Jews in Judea (11:30b–32)

These verses describe the actions of Antiochus IV against Jerusalem in 167 BC when he sent his collector of revenue, Apollonius, to Jerusalem. 1 Macc 1:29–35 describes what happened:

---

[19] Polybius, *Histories*, 29.27 (trans. Shuckburgh, 2:405–6).

[20] For other references to the Messiah in the fourth vision (chapters 10–12), see the commentary on 10:4–21 and 12:2–3. See also "The Messiah in Daniel: An Overview" in "Major Themes" in the introduction.

Two years later the king sent to the cities of Judah a chief collector of tribute, and he came to Jerusalem with a large force. Deceitfully he spoke peaceable words to them, and they believed him; but he suddenly fell upon the city, dealt it a severe blow, and destroyed many people of Israel. He plundered the city, burned it with fire, and tore down its houses and its surrounding walls. They took captive the women and children, and seized the livestock. Then they fortified the city of David with a great strong wall and strong towers, and it became their citadel. They stationed there a sinful people, men who were renegades. These strengthened their position; they stored up arms and food, and collecting the spoils of Jerusalem they stored them there, and became a great menace. (NRSV)

Thus Antiochus began his suppression of the Jewish religion. Circumcision, possession of the Scriptures, sacrifices, feast days, and other practices were forbidden on penalty of death (1 Macc 1:41–51, 56–57). The ultimate act of desecration is described by the divine man as "the detested thing causing desolation" (Dan 11:31). 1 Maccabees describes the fulfillment of this prophecy: On 15 Kislev 167 (December 6, 167), "a detested thing of desolation" (βδέλυγμα ἐρημώσεως) was erected on the altar of the temple (1 Macc 1:54). Most likely this was an idol of Olympian Zeus (cf. 2 Macc 6:1–2). On 25 Kislev (December 16), sacrifices, probably including pigs, were offered on the altar (1 Macc 1:47, 59; 2 Macc 6:4).

"He will defile wicked men of a covenant" (Dan 11:32) refers to the high priest Menelaus and his followers who readily acquiesced to the abominable policies imposed by Antiochus. However, many Jews resisted this forced Hellenization. So the divine man says, "A people who know their God will be strong and take action" (11:32). The writer of 1 Maccabees understood the fulfillment of this prophecy as the resistance offered by many Jews: "But many in Israel stood firm and were resolved in their hearts not to eat unclean food. They chose to die rather than to be defiled by food or to profane the holy covenant; and they did die" (1 Macc 1:62–63 NRSV).

Foremost among those who resisted Antiochus was a priest named Mattathias of Modein and his five sons, John, Simon, Judas, Eleazar, and Jonathan. They led the Maccabean rebellion (named after his son Judas Maccabaeus) that led to the recapture of Jerusalem and the temple and the reestablishment of worship there in accordance with the Law of Moses.

The phrases "abolish the continual sacrifice [הַתָּמִיד]" and "causing desolation" (11:31) connect the events described here with the events described in 8:9–14, especially 8:13. Daniel has now been given more details about the vision he had seen in chapter 8 concerning the persecution of faithful Jewish people by Antiochus IV. His termination of sacrifice and desolation were a forerunner of the greater events to come through the activity of the "Messiah, a Leader" (9:25), described in 9:27: "he will cause sacrifice and offering to cease," and after the completion of his ministry, "a desolator" will come "on the wing of detested things" (see Mt 24:15; Mk 13:14; Lk 21:20). However, the desolation by Antiochus was limited to 1,150 days (Dan 8:14), but the later one that came with the Messiah will last "until the times of the Gentiles are fulfilled" (Lk 21:24), that is, until the parousia of the Christ (Rom 11:25–32).[21]

Faithful Jews Resist Antiochus IV (11:33–35)

There has been much speculation as to the identity of those who "have insight" (11:33, 35), and commentators often seek to equate them with some party among the Jews in Antiochus' day.[22] However, in light of the use of the same verb in 1:4 and other verses in Daniel (see the textual note on 11:33), Daniel himself and his faithful Judean companions serve as examples of such people. Therefore, those who "have insight" are those who have faith in and are faithful to God, who study and understand his Word, and who rely upon it to respond to the challenges they face in living committed lives of faith in his promises, even when persecuted to the point of death (see Daniel 3 and Daniel 6). Therefore, Daniel is told that such people will respond to the grave conditions under Antiochus by instructing others and encouraging them to remain faithful in the face of persecution. However, they themselves will not be immune from persecution, as the divine man makes clear to Daniel. "They will stumble by sword, flame, captivity, and plunder" (11:33). This does not mean that they will fall from faith. Rather, it means that they will be persecuted. Some will die and be martyred ("by sword, flame") while others will survive but be taken captive ("captivity, and plunder").

When these faithful believers are persecuted, they "will be aided by a little help" (11:34). Many commentators have taken this as a reference to the Maccabees. However, the Maccabees probably were only the best known of many who resisted Antiochus' measures to Hellenize the Jews. This verse is most likely a reference to all who remained steadfast in obedience to God's Word and mounted some type of armed or passive resistance to the Seleucids. These allied believers who help those facing martyrdom are called "a little help" because human encouragement to remain faithful to God, though important, pales in comparison to God's faithfulness to his people. He is their real "help" (עֵזֶר or עֶזְרָה), their only true refuge in times of trouble.[b] Moreover, Daniel and his readers are warned that "many will join them insincerely" (11:34), so believers should be cautious in depending on mere human help when suffering persecution.

The divine man's words also give an indication as to God's purpose in allowing the persecution: it will refine and purify the faithful with an eye to the true end that God has appointed for a future time (11:35). This future is ultimately the resurrection of all flesh (12:2–3). These people will be made white (11:35) like Christ himself (Rev 1:14) and God the Father (Dan 7:9). This imagery is taken up again in John's vision of those who survive great tribulation and wash their robes and make them white in the blood of the Lamb (Rev 7:9, 13–14; cf.

(b) Pss 40:18 (ET 40:17); 46:2 (ET 46:1); 70:6 (ET 70:5); 121:1–2; 146:5

---

[21] See further the commentary on 9:24–27.

[22] See the discussion in Lucas, *Daniel*, 287–89.

Rev 3:4–5, 18; 4:4; 6:11; 19:14). Thus the persecution of Antiochus ultimately served God's purpose as it refined among the Jewish people those who would faithfully cling to his promise of deliverance in the Messiah, so that many would be looking for his coming (Mk 15:43; Lk 2:25–38; 3:15; 23:50–51; Jn 6:14) even as we look for his return (Titus 2:13; Jude 21).

Daniel 11:36–45

The Divine Man Explains the Antichrist and the Time of the End

Translation

11 ³⁶"The king will do as he pleases. He will exalt himself and magnify himself over every god, and against the God of gods he will speak wonderful things. He will prosper until indignant anger is completed because what has been determined will be done. ³⁷He will not favor the God of his fathers. He also will not favor desire of women nor any god because he will magnify himself above all [of them]. ³⁸He will honor a god of fortresses in their place. A god whom his fathers did not know he will honor with gold, silver, precious stones, and highly prized things. ³⁹He will deal with fortified fortresses with [the help of] a foreign god. To whoever acknowledges [him] he will give great honor and make them rule over many. Moreover, he will parcel out land at a price.

⁴⁰"Then, at the time of the end, the king of the south will engage in war with him, and the king of the north will storm out against him with chariots, horsemen, and many ships. He will enter countries, flood, and pass through. ⁴¹He will enter the beautiful land, and many will stumble. However, these will be delivered from his power: Edom, Moab, and the chief part of the Ammonites. ⁴²He will seek to harm countries, and the land of Egypt will not be one that escapes. ⁴³He will rule over the treasures of gold and silver and all of the highly prized things of Egypt, and Libyans and Cushites will be within his grasp. ⁴⁴However, reports from the east and from the north will terrify him. He will go out in great anger to destroy and to annihilate many. ⁴⁵He will pitch his royal tents between the seas toward the beautiful holy mountain. Yet he will come to his end, and there will be no one to help him."

Textual Notes

11:36 אֵל אֵלִים—This exact title for "the God of gods" is unique in the OT. However, there are three similar phrases to be translated the same way: (1) אֵל אֱלֹהִים in Josh 22:22; Ps 50:1; (2) אֱלֹהֵי הָאֱלֹהִים in Deut 10:17; Ps 136:2; and (3) the Aramaic אֱלָהּ אֱלָהִין in Dan 2:47. Like those other phrases, this phrase too refers to the one true God, Israel's God. In the NT, compare "King of kings" and "Lord of lords" applied to God and Christ in 1 Tim 6:15; Rev 17:14; 19:16.

נִפְלָאוֹת—For this Niphal (N) participle meaning "wonderful/miraculous things," see the textual note on 8:24. There Antiochus IV destroys God's "wonderful" salvific things, namely, his OT means of grace: the temple, divine worship, and sacramental rites, including circumcision (as described in the commentary on 11:31). Here the escha-

Daniel 11:36–45

tological king (the Antichrist) utters his own fake "wonderful things" to replace God's salvific Word and Sacraments instituted by Christ.

עַד־כָּלָה זַעַם—"Until indignant anger is completed" uses the Qal (G) perfect כָּלָה as a future perfect, referring to future time from the perspective of the speaker (Waltke-O'Connor, 30.5.2b, including example 7). It could be translated, "will have been accomplished" (see Joüon, § 112 i).

נֶחֱרָצָה נֶעֱשָׂתָה:—The Niphal (N) feminine participle נֶחֱרָצָה, "determined, decided (by God)," refers to what God has determined for the future. It refers to divine judgment in 9:26 (spelled נֶחֱרֶצֶת; see the fifth textual note on 9:26); in 9:27; and also in Is 10:23; 28:22. Here in Dan 11:36, it refers to the hubris of the Antichrist, which God has determined he will allow until Christ returns and destroys the Antichrist (2 Thess 2:8). The participle is the subject of the Niphal feminine perfect נֶעֱשָׂתָה, which in context must be a prophetic perfect, referring to the future, hence translated, "will be done."

11:37 וְעַל־אֱלֹהֵי אֲבֹתָיו לֹא יָבִין—For the Qal (G) of בִּין with the preposition עַל meaning "favor" (here negated by לֹא), see the second textual note on 11:30. The same idiom is repeated in the second clause of this verse (see the second textual note below).

חֶמְדַּת נָשִׁים—Grammatically this construct phrase could have a subjective genitive: "women's desire, desire by women" for a male. The genitive could also be an objective genitive: "desire for women," referring to the natural desire of men for women. Compare the phrase τὴν φυσικὴν χρῆσιν, "the natural use/relation," used both for the natural desire of women for men (Rom 1:26) and for the natural desire of men for women (Rom 1:27). Some commentators take the genitive here as subjective, but in the larger context here it is preferable to see it as an objective genitive: the eschatological king abstains from marriage and also frustrates the natural desire of some men to marry women. See further the commentary and the excursus "The Lutheran Confessions on the Antichrist in Daniel."

וְעַל־כָּל־אֱלוֹהַּ לֹא יָבִין—The noun אֱלוֹהַּ is a less common term for "God" or "a god," and it is used in that latter, profane sense in 11:37–39, its only occurrences in Daniel.

11:38 וְלֶאֱלֹהַּ מָעֻזִּים עַל־כַּנּוֹ יְכַבֵּד—Literally, "to the god of fortresses in its place he will show honor." עַל־כַּנּוֹ, "in its place," is translated, "in their place" because the singular pronoun refers to כֹּל, "all [of them]," in the last clause of 11:37. For כַּנּוֹ, see the first textual note on 11:7.

וּבַחֲמֻדוֹת:—Literally, this is "and with highly prized things." The abstract plural noun חֲמֻדוֹת refers to costly commodities (precious metals and gems) here and in 11:43. It refers to expensive bread in 10:3. It also refers to Daniel as "highly prized" by God in 9:23; 10:11, 19.

11:39 אֲשֶׁר יַכִּיר יַרְבֶּה כָבוֹד וְהִמְשִׁילָם בָּרַבִּים—The relative clause "whoever recognizes/acknowledges him," with the singular Hiphil (H) of נָכַר (the Qere is the imperfect: יַכִּיר; the Kethib is the perfect: הִכִּיר), is translated, "to whoever ..." because it must be the indirect object of the following clause, יַרְבֶּה כָבוֹד, literally, "he [the king] will multiply glory," that is, "will give great glory/honor." Even though the relative clause has a singular verb, it must be the antecedent of the plural pronoun on the third Hiphil verb, וְהִמְשִׁילָם, "and he [the king] will make *them* rule over many."

11:40 וּבְעֵת קֵץ—In this context, "at the time of the end" refers to the church age eschatologically, emphasizing that it is the time preceding the return of Christ, who will bring this world to its end. See also the second textual note on 12:4 as well as the second textual note on 8:17.

יִתְנַגַּח עִמּוֹ—The Qal (G) of נָגַח is used for animals, meaning "to gore, butt." So is the Piel (D), as for the ram in 8:4. The Hithpael (HtD) occurs only here in the OT and has a reciprocal meaning, "*engage in thrusting with*" someone else, metaphorically meaning "wage war with" someone (BDB).

וְיִשְׂתָּעֵר—This Hithpael (HtD) of שָׂעַר is cognate to nouns for "a storm" and can be translated, "the king shall storm out against him" (see BDB, s.v. שָׂעַר II, Hithpael).

וְשָׁטַף וְעָבָר—The identical pair of verbs, "flood/sweep away" and "pass through," were in 11:10.

11:41 וּבָא בְּאֶרֶץ הַצְּבִי—Literally, "and he will come into the land of beauty," this refers to the Holy Land. See the first textual note on 11:16. צְבִי recurs in 11:45 referring specifically to Mount Zion, the temple mount.

11:42 וְיִשְׁלַח יָדוֹ בַּאֲרָצוֹת—Literally, "he will stretch out his hand against the lands," the construction שָׁלַח plus יָד and the preposition בְּ means to attempt to harm or steal.[a] It is translated, "he will seek to harm."

11:43 בְּמִצְעָדָיו—Literally, "in his steps," this is understood in various ways by commentators and English versions. It seems to be indicating that conquest of Libya and Cush would only be a step away after the conquest of Egypt. Therefore it is translated, "within his grasp."

11:44 וּשְׁמֻעוֹת יְבַהֲלֻהוּ מִמִּזְרָח וּמִצָּפוֹן—Literally, "things heard will terrify him from the east and from the north." The noun שְׁמוּעָה has the form of a Qal passive (Gp) participle of שָׁמַע, "to hear," and it means "a report, news, a message." The verb בָּהַל in the Piel (D) stem usually means "to terrify" (*HALOT*, 1)[b] or sometimes "to hasten" (see *HALOT*, 2).[c]

11:45 וְיִטַּע אָהֳלֵי אַפַּדְנוֹ—The idiom of the verb נָטַע, "stretch out," with the object אֹהֶל, "tent," means "to pitch/set up a tent." The construct phrase אָהֳלֵי אַפַּדְנוֹ is, literally, "the tents of his palace," which serves as an adjectival genitive, "his royal tents." The noun אַפֶּדֶן, "palace," is a loanword from Old Persian (BDB, *HALOT*).

(a) Gen 37:22; Ex 22:7, 10 (ET 22:8, 11); 1 Sam 24:7, 11 (ET 24:6, 10); 26:9, 11, 23; Ps 55:21 (ET 55:20); Esth 2:21; 3:6; 6:2; 8:7; 9:2; Neh 13:21

(b) Pss 2:5; 83:16 (ET 83:15); Job 22:10; Ezra 4:4; 2 Chr 32:18

(c) Eccl 5:1; 7:9; Esth 2:9; 2 Chr 35:21

Commentary

The Identity of the King in 11:36–45[1]

Virtually every commentator recognizes that a new section in the divine man's explanation begins in 11:36.[2] This has been recognized from antiquity. The medieval Jewish scholar Ibn Ezra saw these verses as fulfilled in Constantine the Great.[3] At the time of the Reformation, Calvin thought they applied to the

---

[1] The following discussion is drawn from Steinmann, "Is the Antichrist in Daniel 11?"

[2] For the identity of the divine man who speaks to Daniel in chapters 10–12 as the preincarnate Christ, see the commentary on 10:4–6.

[3] Keil, *Daniel*, 461.

Roman Empire.[4] Although there have been any number of suggestions, there are two main interpretations of the evil king depicted in these verses: they could continue the description of Antiochus IV Epiphanes (the "contemptible person" and king of the north in 11:21–35), or they are a description of an eschatological figure who is to be equated with the Antichrist in the NT.

Antiochus IV

Most critical scholars as well as a few evangelicals interpret 11:36–45 as applying to Antiochus.[5] According to this interpretation, 11:36–39 depicts in general terms Antiochus' religious hubris. Then 11:40–45 is an attempt by the Maccabean-era author of Daniel to write genuine predictive prophecy concerning the end of Antiochus' reign. Since 11:36–45 does not mention Antiochus' eastern campaign in 165 BC, the rededication of the temple in Jerusalem in 164, or Antiochus' death in 164, critics often hold that this passage's unsuccessful attempt at accurate predictive prophecy serves to date Daniel 10–12 to about 165 BC.

There are a few verbal connections between the description of the king in 11:36 and the description of Antiochus IV in Daniel 8 and 11:21–35. The word נִפְלָאוֹת in "against the God of gods he will speak wonderful things" (11:36) is also used in 8:24 ("he will destroy wonderful things") to describe Antiochus' attacks against the Jewish religion, most probably his sacking of the temple in Jerusalem. In 11:36 it is used to describe the king's verbal attacks against God. Likewise, זַעַם, "indignant anger," is used in 8:19 to refer to God's wrath against Antiochus, and here too in 11:36 it refers to God's anger against the king. In 11:30 the related verb זָעַם describes how Antiochus "became indignant" against God's holy covenant with Israel. Thus there are some indications of parallels between the king described in 11:36 and earlier passages that clearly apply to Antiochus.

Yet there are several problems with a simple identification of the king in 11:36–45 with Antiochus IV. First of all, there is no indication that Antiochus exalted and magnified "himself over every god," did "not favor the god of his fathers," or honored "a god whom his fathers did not know" (11:36–38). Antiochus had his coins inscribed ΒΑΣΙΛΕΥΣ ΑΝΤΙΟΧΟΣ ΘΕΟΣ ΕΠΙΦΑΝΗΣ, "King Antiochus, God Manifest," so he did claim to be a god. However, at the same time, some of these coins bore the likeness of Zeus on the reverse, while other coins depicted Apollo, so he venerated some other gods. Moreover, Antiochus was known for his devotion to the Greek gods in general, and in Jerusalem he most likely had erected a statue of Olympian Zeus and ordered sacrifices to be offered to it.[6] He also promoted the worship of Dionysius in

---

[4] Calvin, *Daniel*, 2:339–45.

[5] E.g., Collins, *Daniel*, 386–90; Goldingay, *Daniel*, 304–5; Hartman and Di Lella, *Daniel*, 301–5; Lucas, *Daniel*, 289–93; Montgomery, *Daniel*, 460–67.

[6] See the commentary on 11:30b–32: "Antiochus IV Attempts to Hellenize the Jews in Judea."

Jerusalem (2 Macc 6:7). Polybius reports that (in 166 BC) Antiochus held a festival at Daphne where he honored "all the gods or spirits mentioned or worshiped by people."[7] In addition, Apollo was honored on the festival's coinage.[8]

Second, there is no agreement by critics as to what the phrase חֶמְדַּת נָשִׁים, "desire of women," refers (see the second textual note on 11:37). Critics generally take it to refer to one of the pagan gods whose cult was especially popular with women. Since the late nineteenth century, critics have tended to view this as a reference to Tammuz/Adonis (cf. Ezek 8:14),[9] although some have claimed Dionysius was intended.[10] The problem with this is that there is no evidence that Antiochus ever discouraged women from expressing their natural affection for men or suppressed the cult of either of these gods. He promoted Dionysius in Jerusalem itself (2 Macc 6:7).[11]

Given these problems, a recent critical commentator has claimed that the author engaged in "deliberate polemical distortion, to depict the impiety of the king in the most extreme terms possible" and was "probably indulging in polemical exaggeration."[12] However, that "solution" raises a problem of its own. If the text is an inaccurate distortion or exaggeration, how can we know that is what the author intended and that the modern interpreter is correct in assuming that the text was about Antiochus? Could it be that instead of the text distorting the facts about Antiochus, it is the modern interpretation that is wrong and that distorts the text?

An evangelical scholar who holds that these verses are about Antiochus admits: "Although the chapter finds its first fulfillment in the character and reign of Antiochus IV, the matter does not stop there."[13] However, this too raises another problem. If the text is not adequately fulfilled by Antiochus, could it be that this "first fulfillment" is more in the perception of the interpreter than the intention of the author of Daniel? How can we assume that the author has engaged in hyperbolic polemic that only partially applies to Antiochus when it is also possible that there is no extreme distortion or exaggeration in the text and that it instead refers to someone else? How does one distinguish between some type of double application intended by the author and a mistake by the interpreter in attempting to have a passage apply to more people than the author intended?

---

[7] Polybius, *Histories*, 30.25.

[8] Collins, *Daniel*, 387.

[9] E.g., Collins, *Daniel*, 387; Montgomery, *Daniel*, 461–62.

[10] See Lucas, *Daniel*, 290.

[11] For the likely meaning of the phrase in 11:37, see further below "The Eschatological King as a Religious Figure (11:36–39)" and also the excursus "The Lutheran Confessions on the Antichrist in Daniel."

[12] Collins, *Daniel*, 387–88.

[13] Baldwin, *Daniel*, 199.

It is most likely that the author never intended 11:36–45 to be about Antiochus. Even scholars who apply these verses to Antiochus admit that 11:40–45 do not fit what is known about Antiochus from other historical sources. So it is very probable that it is the Antiochene theory, and not some distortion of him by the author of Daniel, that is the cause of these problems. The attempt to rescue the Antiochene interpretation of 11:36–45 by resorting to the theory that extreme polemics distort its depiction of Antiochus is more special pleading than reasoned exegesis. The author accurately predicts historical facts about other Greek rulers in his polemics against them elsewhere (e.g., 11:11–12, 17–18 about Antiochus III). Those other polemics do not distort the depiction of the other kings so as to make the identifications of those kings problematic for scholars of any stripe. Even though Antiochus IV was the most reviled Hellenistic king among Jews because of his blasphemous actions and sacrilegious policies, the polemic against him in 11:21–35 does not distort the portrait of him. The identity of the king of the north in 11:21–35 clearly was Antiochus IV, as all scholars easily conclude.

Therefore the view that 11:36–45 depicts Antiochus IV is far from being proved and depends more on assumptions and assertions by interpreters than on evidence in the text.

An Evil Eschatological King

The traditional Christian interpretation understands 11:36–45 as applying to an eschatological king, which in NT terms is the Antichrist or "the man of lawlessness" (2 Thess 2:3–12). This was the position of the early church fathers, including Chrysostom, Hippolytus, Theodoret, and Jerome.[14] Luther and the sixteenth-century Lutheran reformers also adopted this interpretation.[15] During the last two centuries, Lutheran[16] and evangelical[17] scholars have often advocated it.

There are two plain indications in the text that the king who is the focus in 11:36–45 is not the same as the king of the north in 11:21–35. First, 11:35 ends with the notice that the persecution of Antiochus will refine God's people "until the time of the end" (עַד־עֵת קֵץ). From that, it is reasonable to infer that the

---

[14] Jerome sees some application to the Antichrist starting in 11:21, but sees 11:36–45 as exclusively applying to the Antichrist. See Jerome's commentary on 11:21–45 in Young, *Daniel*, 306–17, or Archer, *Jerome's Commentary on Daniel*, 129–44. Hippolytus and Theodoret understand 11:36 as the beginning of the prophecy about the Antichrist, while Chrysostom seems to merge the ages of Antiochus and the Antichrist (cf. the discussion in Montgomery, *Daniel*, 468–70). See Hippolytus, *Commentary on Daniel*, 38–44 (*ANF* 5:184–85); Theodoret of Cyrus, *Commentary on Daniel* (trans. Hill, 304–15); Chrysostom, *Discourses against Judaizing Christians*, 5.7 (trans. Paul W. Harkins [Washington, D.C.: Catholic University of America Press, 1977], 120–24; see especially p. 124, n. 86).

[15] See Luther, "Preface to Daniel," AE 35:313, and the excursus "The Lutheran Confessions on the Antichrist in Daniel."

[16] Keil, *Daniel*, 463–74; Leupold, *Daniel*, 510–25.

[17] Walvoord, *Daniel*, 270–80; Young, *Daniel*, 246–53.

next part of the prophecy will begin a discussion about "the time of the end," in keeping with the catch-concept organizing principle that is evident elsewhere in this fourth vision (chapters 10–12).[18] In fact, three more times in the final part of the vision the timeframe is called "the time of the end" (עֵת קֵץ, 11:40; 12:4, 9). Nowhere else besides these four verses (11:35, 40; 12:4, 9) does the fourth vision refer to "the time of the end."[19] Earlier examples of a sudden shift to a later time support this view of the shift between 11:35 and 11:36. Earlier the prophecy skips from a Persian emperor who stirred up Greece to a Greek king (11:2–3) and from the breakup of the Greek Empire into four kingdoms ("toward the four winds of heaven") to only two of those kingdoms and their kings, the king of the north and the king of the south (11:4–6).

Second, 11:36 introduces the king in a unique way. He is simply referred to as הַמֶּלֶךְ, "*the* king." No Hellenistic king prior to 11:36 is ever referred to simply as "the king," even when he has been recently mentioned. For example, 11:25 refers to the northern king's designs "against the king of the south" (עַל־מֶלֶךְ הַנֶּגֶב), and then the next clause in the same verse does not refer to the southern king as "the king," but instead as "the king of the south" (מֶלֶךְ הַנֶּגֶב) again. Alexander the Great is called "a warrior king" (מֶלֶךְ גִּבּוֹר). Various Seleucid kings are always called "the king of the north" (מֶלֶךְ הַצָּפוֹן, 11:6–8, 11, 13, 15). Various Ptolemaic kings are always called "the king of the south" (מֶלֶךְ הַנֶּגֶב, 11:5–6, 9, 11, 14, 25 [twice]). The kings of the north and the south together are once called, literally, "the two of them, the kings" (וּשְׁנֵיהֶם הַמְּלָכִים, 11:27), and that is the only other verse in Daniel 10–12 where מֶלֶךְ has the definite article, but there מֶלֶךְ is plural, whereas it is singular in 11:36.

Therefore, there are good indicators that there is a change of both timeframe and subject between 11:35 and 11:36. When "the king" is introduced at 11:36, it is after the transition to the end times (11:35b), and he is introduced in a unique, dramatic way. This signals that this king is not a Hellenistic king, but an eschatological king who will arise at "the time of the end" (11:35, 40; 12:4, 9).

But what about the verbal ties between the king in 11:36 and the descriptions of Antiochus in chapter 8 and earlier in chapter 11? As this commentary suggests elsewhere, Antiochus is depicted throughout the visions in Daniel as foreshadowing the Antichrist.[20] Thus Antiochus is prophesied as attacking the

---

[18] See "The Content of Daniel's Vision in Daniel 10–12" in "Introduction to Daniel 10–12."

[19] The only other verse in the entire book of Daniel with the phrase "the time of the end" (עֵת קֵץ) is 8:17.

[20] The excursus "The Four-Kingdom Schema in Daniel" compares the little horn in chapter 7, representing the Antichrist, with the little horn in chapter 8, representing Antiochus IV (see problem 5 and figure 10 in "Problems in Daniel for the Greek View" in that excursus). See also "Major Emphases in Daniel 8" in "Introduction to Daniel 8"; the commentary on 8:9–12 and 8:15–18; the excursus "Dispensational Interpretations of Daniel 8"; the commentary on 9:24–27, which depicts Christ and the Antichrist; and the excursus "The Lutheran Confessions on the Antichrist in Daniel."

Daniel 11:36–45

"wonderful things" of God in his temple (8:24), and the Antichrist is prophesied to attack God by speaking "wonderful things" that he designs to replace God's words (11:36). The actions of Antiochus perverted the Jerusalem temple of God and turned it into a pagan shrine (8:24–25; 11:31).[21] The actions of the Antichrist seek to pervert the church and turn it into a temple for himself (Dan 11:36–39) instead of letting the church be the spiritual temple of God (Eph 2:19–21; 1 Pet 2:4–6). He attacks "the beautiful land" (Dan 11:41) and sets his encampment "toward the beautiful holy mountain" (11:45), that is, in the church, which is the new holy land. Therefore, by these actions both Antiochus and the Antichrist will arouse God's indignation and anger, prompting their well-deserved destruction (Antiochus in 8:19, 25; 11:30; the Antichrist in 11:36, 45).

The Eschatological King as a Religious Figure (11:36–39)

An ominous note is sounded by the opening sentence, "the king will do as he pleases" (11:36). The identical wording for this arrogance (עָשָׂה, "do," and כִּרְצוֹנוֹ, literally, "according to his pleasure") was also used for the characteristic arrogance of the kingdom of Persia, represented by the ram (8:4), of Alexander the Great (11:3), and of Antiochus III (11:16). However, those statements came within the descriptions, but this is the very first statement about the eschatological king. He is chiefly characterized by his willful arrogance. Unlike those other kings, his arrogance is characterized as primarily religious in nature (11:36–39). This king will be a religious figure, and his power will be exercised in ways that pervert and profane what is godly, instead of challenging the geopolitical order as the other kings' actions did. Antiochus IV was a foreshadowing of this eschatological king because Antiochus IV was the only one of the Hellenistic kings whose actions directly corrupted and prevented the biblically based worship of the God of Israel. However, the other acts of Antiochus IV mentioned in 8:9–14, 23–25 and 11:21–35 were primarily geopolitical in nature.

The main characteristic of this end-time king is that he elevates himself over every other god. To usurp the one true God, he speaks "wonderful things" (נִפְלָאוֹת)—ostensibly divine words—against God (11:36), making him the same as the little horn in the vision in Daniel 7 (7:25). This Niphal (N) participle occurs in Daniel only in 8:24 and 11:36 (see the textual notes on it in those verses). The Niphal feminine plural participle occurs a total of forty-four times in the OT. In thirty-nine of these instances, it is used as a noun for the wonderful, miraculous, salvific acts of God. In 8:24 it refers to God's salvific actions through his OT means of grace, the temple and its liturgical rites. But here it refers to the Antichrist's deceptive words, which are crafted to supplant God's Word, through which salvation comes to his believing people. Clearly, this figure's words against the true God are designed to replace the wonderful acts of God that redeem his people and which are God's alone.[d] Interestingly, Theodotion translates this word in 11:36 with ὑπέρογκα, "arrogant things," a

(d) E.g., Pss 40:6 (ET 40:5); 72:18; 86:10; 98:1; 136:4

---

[21] See the commentary on those verses.

word used by both Peter and Jude in their descriptions of the false teachers that will arise among Christians. Peter warns:

> Also false prophets arose among the people, just as also among you there will arise false teachers, who will secretly introduce destructive heresies, even denying the Master who bought them, bringing upon themselves swift destruction. ... For by speaking arrogant things [ὑπέρογκα] of futility, they entice by desires of the flesh, by sensuality, those who barely escape from the ones who live in error. (2 Pet 2:1, 18)

Jude uses similar language to speak about such people:

> For certain men sneak in secretly, who were written about long ago for this condemnation, ungodly persons who turn the grace of our God into licentiousness and deny our only Master and Lord, Jesus Christ. ... These men are grumblers, malcontents, following their own lusts. Their mouths speak arrogant things [ὑπέρογκα], flattering people for the sake of gaining an advantage. (Jude 4, 16)

The prophecy given to Daniel by the divine man predicts the coming of an eschatological figure whose words will be the epitome of such arrogant, false teaching that is disguised as divine words.

Daniel is also told that this king will prosper until God's anger against him is completed, since God has determined that his actions should run their course (11:36). St. Paul calls this eschatological figure "the man of lawlessness," describes him in terms parallel to 11:36–37, and notes that it will be Christ who ends his power. The apostle expands the prophecy given to Daniel:

> Let no one deceive you in any way. For that day ["the Day of the Lord," 2:2] will not arrive until the apostasy comes first and the man of lawlessness is revealed, the son of destruction. He opposes and *exalts himself above everything called God* [see Dan 11:36a] or that is worshiped, so that he takes his seat in God's temple, *displaying himself as if he is God* [see Dan 11:37]. ... Then that lawless one will be revealed, *whom the Lord will slay with the spirit/ breath of his mouth and bring to an end by the epiphany of his parousia* [cf. Dan 11:36b]. His [the man of lawlessness's] coming is by Satan's working with every kind of *miracle and signs and false wonders* [δυνάμει καὶ σημείοις καὶ τέρασιν ψεύδους; see Dan 11:36a]²² and with all deception of wickedness for those who are perishing. (2 Thess 2:3–4, 8–10a)

This king "will not favor the God of his fathers" (Dan 11:37). The phrase "the God of his [or: our, your, their] fathers" occurs forty-five times in the OT and is always a description of Yahweh.²³ Therefore, this king will come

---

²² The Greek plural of τέρας, "a (miraculous) wonder," can be used to translate Hebrew נִפְלָאוֹת, "wonderful things" (Dan 11:36), as in LXX 1 Chr 16:12. It can also translate the Hebrew cognate פֶּלֶא, "a wonder, miracle," as in LXX Ex 15:11. Moreover, the Greek σημεῖον, "a sign," is used often in the LXX to translate the Hebrew word אוֹת ("sign"), and τέρας, "a (miraculous) wonder," is often used to translate מוֹפֵת ("wonder, portent"). These Hebrew words are synonyms of the Hebrew נִפְלָאוֹת, "wonderful things."

²³ Ex 3:13, 15–16; 4:5; Deut 1:11, 21; 4:1; 6:3; 12:1; 26:7; 27:3; 29:24 (ET 29:25); Josh 18:3; Judg 2:12; 2 Ki 21:22; Dan 11:37; Ezra 7:27; 8:28; 10:11; 1 Chr 5:25; 12:18 (ET 12:17); 29:20; 2 Chr 7:22; 11:16; 13:12, 18; 14:3 (ET 14:4); 15:12; 19:4; 20:6, 33; 21:10; 24:18, 24; 28:6, 9, 25; 29:5; 30:7, 19, 22; 33:12; 34:32–33; 36:15. In addition to Dan 11:37, only 1 Chr

(e) See also Ex 6:7; 29:46; Deut 4:35, 39; 7:9; 28:64

from among the people of God. Similar is the implication of the statement "he will honor a god ... whom his fathers did not know" (11:38) since "a people who know their God" in 11:32 refers to believers in the one true God of Israel.ᵉ Some commentators see this as an indication that the Antichrist will be Jewish.[24] However, this phrase is not an ethnic identification, but a religious one. It indicates that the eschatological king will come from those whose ancestral tradition is to worship the one true God. Thus in Paul's terms, "he takes his seat in God's temple" (2 Thess 2:4), arising from among the faithful believers (cf. 1 Jn 2:19).

The king will not favor normal human marital relations[25] nor any god because he will make himself greater than all (11:37). His arrogance renders him incapable of the loving devotion that is required by both marriage and true piety. He personally is not married and does not rightly honor the one true God, and as a king, he imposes this disdain for marriage and this dishonorable view of God upon his subjects.

Some interpreters claim that "desire of women" refers to Jewish women's desire to bear and give birth to the Messiah. To support this theory they note that in the other occurrences of the noun חֶמְדָּה in construct, the following genitive is always subjective ("desired by ... "), not objective ("desire for ..."), and that it is used in what may be a messianic designation in Hag 2:7: חֶמְדַּת כָּל־הַגּוֹיִם, "the desire of [the person desired by] all the nations."[26] However, there are only three other uses of the noun in construct (1 Sam 9:20; Hag 2:7; 2 Chr 36:10), which is hardly enough to establish any restricted pattern of usage, and there are many examples of other nouns in construct that are followed by both subjective and objective genitives. Contextually, one might argue that "desire of women" could be a designation for some divinity revered by women. However, the wider context suggests something else: the king will not have an intimate loving relationship with God or with a woman because he relates to others only on the basis of power (Dan 11:39). He will honor something else: "a god of fortresses" (11:38). Moreover, note that another noun of the same root, the plural of חֲמוּדָה, "desirable/highly prized things," is used in 11:38 to describe the

---

5:25; 12:18 (ET 12:17); and 2 Chr 20:33 do not explicitly identify "the God of his/their/our fathers" with Yahweh. The suggestion by most commentators that this phrase should be translated "the gods of his fathers" in Dan 11:37 is grammatically possible, but is unsupported by the rest of the OT, where it always means "the God of his fathers." Those who advocate the translation "the gods of his fathers" include Archer, "Daniel," 144–45; Calvin, *Daniel*, 2:346; Collins, *Daniel*, 386–87; Hartman and Di Lella, *Daniel*, 301; Keil, *Daniel*, 463; Leupold, *Daniel*, 515; Walvoord, *Daniel*, 274; and Young, *Daniel*, 248.

[24] Young, *Daniel*, 249; cf. Walvoord, *Daniel*, 273–74.

[25] The excursus "The Lutheran Confessions on the Antichrist in Daniel" identifies this as the papal prohibition of clergy marriage. Luther suggests that "desire of women" (11:37) is a reference to the love of women in marriage ("Preface to Daniel," AE 35:313). This interpretation is followed by Calvin, *Daniel*, 2:345–46; Keil, *Daniel*, 464–65; Leupold, *Daniel*, 515–16; Young, *Daniel*, 249 (cf. Archer, "Daniel," 144). See also the second textual note on 11:37.

[26] E.g., Walvoord, *Daniel*, 274; see also Miller, *Daniel*, 307.

things the king uses to honor his god, indicating that he gives what he desires to "a god of fortresses," which then must be the object of his own desire.[27] Thus this eschatological king has no enduring relationship with God or a woman. Instead, he has a relationship with "a god of fortresses."

What is this "god of fortresses ... a god his fathers did not know" (11:38)? It is temporal power as signified by fortresses.[28] This will be the thing that he values above all else, making it his "god."[29] He will honor temporal power because it will provide him with the things that fortresses provide: a way to project his power, a means of defense, and a place of security. Ironically, מָעוֹז, "fortress," is used most often in the OT as a metaphor for God himself as the strength, protection, and salvation of his people.[f] When the king rejects the God of his fathers, he will seek to use temporal power to replace what only God can supply.

Therefore, this eschatological king will deal with other temporal threats ("fortified fortresses") with the help of "a foreign god" (11:39), which is the "god of fortresses," the god whom his fathers did not know (11:38). That is, instead of relying on God and his Word as a fortress to protect him—the means of grace, through which Christians find security and victory—he will rely upon temporal power to deal with the powers of this world. Therefore, he will honor those who acknowledge him and his power, and for that price he will give them power in this world over people and territory (11:39).

Thus the eschatological king will be like Antiochus IV, who foreshadowed him. Both use temporal power, and both attack God, his people, and divine worship, through which God grants salvation and eternal security to his people. However, Antiochus was primarily a geopolitical figure who used his status to attack the religious institutions and practices of the Jews. The eschatological king primarily will be a religious figure who will use his religious position to wield temporal power. This is exactly how Paul describes the Antichrist, "the man of lawlessness" in 2 Thess 2:3–12. It also fits the description of the Antichrist as the beast in Rev 13:11–18.[30]

With this understanding of the eschatological king, it is now possible to see the type of parallel that the revelation to Daniel draws between Antiochus and the Antichrist: they are mirror images of each other, the first being a geopolitical figure who stirs up problems of a religious nature, the second being a religious figure who stirs up problems of a geopolitical nature.

(f) E.g., 2 Sam 22:33; Is 17:10; 25:4–5; Jer 16:19; Joel 4:16 (ET 3:16); Nah 1:7; Pss 27:1; 28:8; 31:3, 5 (ET 31:2, 4); 37:39; 43:2; Prov 10:29

---

[27] The plural of חֲמוּדֹת, "desirable/highly prized things," is also used in 11:43 for the treasures of Egypt, which the king covets and seizes. In contrast, the same plural is used to describe God's estimation of a believer who is precious in his sight: Daniel is called "highly prized" (9:23; 10:11, 19).

[28] Miller advocates "his overwhelming military power" as the king's god (*Daniel*, 308). Similar are Keil, *Daniel*, 466; Leupold, *Daniel*, 517; Walvoord, *Daniel*, 276; Young, *Daniel*, 249. The identification of this god as military warfare is partly true but too narrow.

[29] "A god is that to which we look for all good and in which we find refuge in every time of need" (Luther, LC I 2).

[30] For an interpretation, see Brighton, *Revelation*, 357–63.

Antiochus IV (11:21–35)	*Eschatological King (11:36–45)*
1. A geopolitical figure occupied in warfare (11:21–30a).	1. A religious figure preoccupied with temporal power (11:36–39).
2. Uses his political power to attack God's people and prohibit and pervert God's ordained worship institutions and practices (11:30b–32).	2. Because of his abuse of religious authority, which he wields in geopolitical affairs, he is attacked and becomes involved in warfare (11:40–45).

The King's Final Days: The End of the Eschatological King (11:40–45)

"The time of the end" is an expression that occurs four times in this vision (11:35, 40; 12:4, 9). Just as it was used in 8:17 to signify the time when the period prophesied in that vision would end, so it is also used here to indicate the end of the period covered by the divine man's words. In the case of this vision, it is the end of the world at the return of Christ, since the timeframe of this vision ends with the resurrection (12:1–3). Therefore, 11:40–45 speaks of the end of the eschatological king immediately before the parousia of Christ, to be followed by the bodily resurrection. Thus Dan 11:40–45 is parallel to Rev 20:7–10, and Dan 12:1–3 is parallel to Rev 20:11–15.

The end is played out as a great military conflict. However, the words here are symbolic. There are several indications of this. First of all, Moab (11:41) had ceased to be an independent nation with a distinct identity after its conquest by Tiglath-pileser III in 733 BC. Already in Daniel's day it no longer existed. Instead, it, along with Ammon and Edom, represents enemies of God's people. Second, with the coming of the Roman Empire (the fourth kingdom predicted in Daniel, during whose era is the first advent of the Messiah[31]), the kings of the north and the south, the Seleucid and Ptolemaic dynasties, ceased to exist. The rise of this fourth kingdom is hinted at in 11:30. Here in 11:40–45, the eschatological king assumes the identity of the king of the north, and his main rival is the king of the south.[32] This is appropriate, since the last king of the north

---

[31] See the excursus "The Four-Kingdom Schema in Daniel."

[32] Some commentators see three kings in this conflict: the eschatological king, the king of the north, and the king of the south. This view is common among dispensationalists (e.g., Harton, "An Interpretation of Daniel 11:36–45"; Tanner, "Daniel's 'King of the North': Do We Owe Russia an Apology?"; Walvoord, *Daniel*, 277). Leupold, *Daniel*, 520–21, also takes this position.

However, there are good reasons to understand the king of the north in 11:40 as the eschatological king, the Antichrist. First, the king of the south "will engage in war with him" (11:40a), that is, with the eschatological king. He then must be "the king of the north" (11:40b), who launches a counterattack at Egypt from the north. The same eschatological king (of the north) then goes through the Holy Land ("the beautiful land," 11:41) before he reaches Egypt (11:42), and then lands to the south (Cush) and west (Libya) of Egypt are "within his grasp" (11:43). Second, throughout Daniel, Antiochus IV is a foreshadowing of the Antichrist, and

discussed in Daniel 11 was Antiochus IV, who foreshadows this eschatological king.

In fact, the description of the eschatological king in 11:36–45 is parallel to the description of Antiochus IV as set forth in 11:21–35. Both begin with a general description of his reign and events largely unrelated to warfare (for Antiochus, 11:21–24; for the eschatological king, 11:36–39). This is followed by descriptions of warfare. Twice Antiochus engages with war in Egypt and then enters Palestine (11:25–28 and 11:29–35). The same pattern holds true for the eschatological king in 11:40–45. In 11:40 he battles the king of the south, followed in 11:41 by an invasion of Palestine, "the beautiful land." Then he conquers Egypt (11:42–43) and once again enters Palestine, the area "between the seas" (the Mediterranean Sea and the Dead Sea), "toward the beautiful holy mountain" (11:45). Therefore, the text draws a tight parallel between Antiochus IV as the oppressor of God's people in the Hellenistic era and the eschatological king's oppression of God's people in the end times.

The final acts of the eschatological king are difficult to interpret in detail. Here we find ourselves in the same situation as Daniel himself (12:8): looking at a prophecy of the future and seeking to understand its interpretation. We must keep in mind that there are several indications that the words of the divine man in 11:40–45 are symbolic and metaphorical. Nevertheless, the general picture drawn in the revelation is clear:

1. The king will engage in a power struggle with a rival power and overcome him, appearing to be on the verge of a sweeping victory (11:40, 42–43).

2. This power struggle will affect God's people. "The beautiful land" (11:41) is a metaphor for God's people, the Christian church, the new Israel, residents of the "Jerusalem above" (Gal 4:26; see also Heb 12:22). Many will "stumble" (Dan 11:41). This verb was used earlier in Daniel 11 to refer to believers who were persecuted even to the point of martyrdom (see the third textual note on 11:14). Here these Christian believers will be willing to suffer death rather than fall away from the faith or the visible church because of the king's actions. However, the king will spare enemies of the Gospel. "Edom, Moab, and the chief part of the Ammonites" (11:41) are metaphors for the theological enemies of Christ who contribute to the persecution of God's people.

3. Something will alarm him, and he will turn to persecute many while strengthening his position as a religious figure among God's people; "he will

---

Antiochus IV was a king of the north earlier in the prophecy (11:21–35). Third, earlier still it was a king of the north (Antiochus III) who entered "the beautiful land" (11:16), and in an earlier vision, Antiochus IV, pictured as the little horn, also entered "the beautiful [land]" (8:9), so the eschatological king who enters the "beautiful land" (11:41) is also a king of the north (11:40b). Finally, the tight parallel between the actions of Antiochus IV and the eschatological king supports the view that both are characterized as the king of the north. Therefore, many commentators (e.g., Keil, *Daniel*, 469–70; Young, *Daniel*, 251), including some dispensationalists (e.g., Archer, "Daniel," 147–48), see only two kings here, the kings of the north and the south.

pitch his royal tents between the seas [the Mediterranean Sea and the Dead Sea] toward the beautiful holy mountain" (11:44–45).

4. This final act will not save him, and in the end, he will have no aid since no one can stand against God's judgment (11:45; cf. 2 Thess 2:8).

More than this cannot be reliably determined because searching for a future fulfillment of a prophecy is not as easy as determining the way a prophecy was fulfilled after it has come to pass (cf. 1 Pet 1:10–12).

Excursus
The Lutheran Confessions on the Antichrist in Daniel

The Antichrist is depicted in Daniel as the little horn in chapter 7 and as the evil eschatological "king (of the north)" in 11:36–45. The Antichrist is foreshadowed by Antiochus IV Epiphanes (175–164 BC), the Seleucid king who fiercely persecuted the Jewish people in the second century BC. Antiochus IV is depicted as the little horn in Daniel 8 and as a "king of the north" in 11:21–35. He has some similarities to the Antichrist, but also significant differences, and so he should not be equated or confused with the Antichrist.

In Daniel 7, the prophet sees the Antichrist as the little horn on the fourth beast. This horn speaks "great things" against the Most High, wages war against the saints and wears them out, and seeks to change "times and Law," that is, God's Word and means of grace in divine worship (7:8, 20–21, 25). At the coming of the Son of Man (the second advent of Christ), this beast with its horn suffers a fiery judgment and is destroyed forever (7:11, 22, 26). This visionary depiction of the little horn is in harmony with NT passages about the Antichrist. He was present already in the apostolic age, remains active throughout the church age, intensifies his warfare against the church as the time of the end draws near, and is destroyed at the return of Christ.[1]

In 11:36–45 the divine man[2] describes to Daniel the Antichrist as the eschatological "king (of the north)" (11:36, 40), who considers himself to be divine: he will "exalt himself and magnify himself over every god" (11:36). Similar to the little horn (7:8, 11), "he will speak wonderful things" that are polemical "against the God of gods" (11:36). He will prohibit marriage and "not favor desire of women" (11:37). Instead of honoring God and scriptural truth, he will value temporal power and "honor a god of fortresses" (11:38). He will carry out this quest for temporal power by means of great wealth, "with gold, silver, precious stones, and highly prized things" (11:38), and to those who obey him "he will give great honor and make them rule over many" (11:39). He will set himself up in the church, represented by "the beautiful land" (11:41) and "the beautiful holy mountain" (11:45). Yet at the return of Christ "he will come to his end, and there will be no one to help him" (11:45).

---

[1] See further the commentary on 7:8, 20–21, 25, and especially "The Unfolding of History as Depicted in the Fourth Beast" in the commentary on 7:26–27, which includes a table comparing Daniel 7 and St. Paul's portrait in 1 Thessalonians 2 of "the man of lawlessness," another guise of the Antichrist. See also the timeline of "Amillennialism or Inaugurated Millennialism" in figure 3; in it Satan's "little season" is the period leading up to the return of Christ when the Antichrist intensifies his warfare against the church.

[2] For his identity as the preincarnate Christ, see the commentary on 10:4–6.

The history of the interpretation of these and other OT texts about the Antichrist begins in the intertestamental period. Already in the medieval period, some Roman Catholics interpreted the Antichrist as the papacy. The Lutheran confessors agreed with this view, which was over three hundred years old by the time of the Reformation.³

The Lutheran Confessions speak several times of the Antichrist, with most of the references clustered in the Apology of the Augsburg Confession (Articles VII/VIII, XV, XXIII, and XXIV), the Smalcald Articles (mainly Part II, Article IV), and the Treatise on the Power and Primacy of the Pope (especially paragraphs 39–59). The Confessions include references and connections to Daniel's prophecy. We might have expected that they would refer to the depiction of the Antichrist as the little horn in 7:8, 11, 20–21, 24–25, but they include no citations of the little horn. This may be due to Luther's explanation of the little horn as "Mohammed or the Turk."⁴ The Confessions instead focus on 11:36–45 and refer specifically to 11:36–39 (in Ap VII/VIII 24); 11:37 (in Ap XXIII 25); and 11:38 (in Ap XV 19, 21; XXIV 51). They probably also allude to 11:38, 43 (in SA III III 25). However, most biblical interpreters have understood that there is a close connection between the little horn in Daniel 7 and the king described in 11:36–45. The confessors may have been aware of that connection even though they do not explicitly cite the little horn.

Another likely reason why the Confessions concentrate on Daniel 11 rather than Daniel 7 is that the little horn's activity is described in more general terms in Daniel 7, whereas Daniel 11 is much more specific in its description of the eschatological king. The Lutheran Confessions recognize that the NT speaks of one particular "man of lawlessness" (2 Thess 2:3–12; see Ap VII/VIII 4; Treatise 39) who opposes God, whom the Confessions often call "*the* Antichrist," and that the NT also speaks of multiple antichrists (1 Jn 2:18). The Apology defines these antichrists as false teachers (Ap VII/VIII 48). However, that in itself does not adequately explain either the Confessions' use of Daniel 11 or their identification of the Antichrist as the office of the papacy. To understand these, we must first understand what the Confessions view as the primary characteristics of the Antichrist as set forth in Scripture. These are set forth by Philip Melanchthon in the Treatise ("The Marks of the Antichrist" in Treatise 39–40):

1. The Antichrist promotes false doctrine that conflicts with the Gospel of Christ, especially the central article of the true faith: justification for Christ's sake by grace

---

³ For the history of interpretation, see McGinn, *Antichrist*, especially "Counterfeit Holiness: The Papal Antichrist (1200–1335)" (pp. 143–72), "Antichrist on the Eve of the Reformation (1335–1500)" (pp. 173–99), and "Antichrist Divided: Reformers, Catholics, and Puritans Debate Antichrist (1500–1660)" (pp. 200–30).

⁴ Luther, "Preface to Daniel," AE 35:300. However, Ap XV 18 seems to consider "the kingdom of Mohammed" as well as the papacy to be parts of "the kingdom of Antichrist" because both Islam and Roman Catholicism hold that sinners can be justified by performing human rites and works. See the quotation of Ap XV 18–19 below.

alone and through faith alone. He claims the right to change doctrine established by Christ.
2. The Antichrist institutes forms of worship that conflict with the Gospel.
3. The Antichrist rules in the church. He assumes the supreme right to forgive or retain sins in this life and even claims jurisdiction over the fate of souls after this life. He is primarily a ruler in the church, although he claims to exercise temporal power as well.[5]
4. The Antichrist makes himself out to be God by usurping the authority and prerogatives of God himself. He is unwilling to be judged by the church or anyone else and fiercely persecutes any who dissent.

The first two of these marks of the Antichrist are often treated together in the Confessions, since the altering of doctrine and the altering of worship go hand in hand. Thus the papacy is characterized as the Antichrist because it alters worship in ways that turn the focus away from Christ and his merits, by which sinners are justified through faith alone, to human efforts to merit God's favor (Ap XV 18–21; XXIV 51, 98; SA II IV 4). This change simultaneously promotes false doctrine and false worship. Luther singles out the papal encouragement of the invocation of the saints as a particular abuse by the Antichrist because it undermines the true knowledge of Christ (SA II III 25).

In Ap XXIV 44–48, Melanchthon cites Daniel as he responds to the Roman criticism that the reformers were desolating the churches by minimizing the use of statues and other adornments not mandated in Scripture:

> In the Confutation our opponents wring their hands over "the desolation of the temples" and the altars standing unadorned, without candles or statues. They call these trifles the ornament of the churches. Daniel describes a vastly different desolation, ignorance of the Gospel. The people were swamped by the many different traditions and ideas and could not grasp the sum of Christian doctrine. Who among the people has ever understood our opponents' doctrine of penitence? Yet this is the principal doctrine of the Christian faith.
>
> Satisfactions and the enumeration of sins were a torture for consciences. Our opponents never mentioned faith, by which we freely receive the forgiveness of sins. All their books and sermons were silent about the exercise of faith in its struggle with despair and about the free forgiveness of sins for Christ's sake. In addition, they horribly profaned the Mass and introduced much wicked worship into the churches. This is the desolation that Daniel describes.
>
> By the blessing of God, the priests in our churches pay attention to the ministry of the Word, they teach the Gospel of the blessing of Christ, and they show that the forgiveness of sins comes freely for Christ's sake. This teaching really consoles consciences. They add to it the teaching of the good works which God commands, and they talk about the value and use of the sacraments.

Apparently the Roman Catholics were applying Daniel's descriptions of the desolation of the temple to the effects of the Reformation. Exegetically, this commentary showed that Daniel in fact refers to two different desolations: the

---

[5] For his exercise of temporal power too, see also Ap VII/VIII 23–24.

desecration of the temple by Antiochus IV in 167 BC (Dan 11:31; 12:11) and, after the advent of the Messiah, the destruction of the temple by the Romans in AD 70 (9:26–27).[6] It is clear from the contexts that Daniel is speaking of the cessation of the sacrifices on the altar of the Jerusalem temple (9:26–27; 11:31; 12:11) and to the complete destruction of the Jerusalem temple (9:26–27). Both the Roman Catholics and the Lutherans applied those passages in a spiritual, metaphorical way: the Catholics to Reformation churches in the sixteenth century and the Lutherans to the Roman Catholic Church as a whole. Melanchthon's theological point is sound: the loss of a physical temple and its adornments pales in comparison to the loss of the Gospel in both theology and worship. That loss creates the worst kind of desolation among God's people.

The papal insistence on clerical celibacy could also be included under these first two characteristics of the Antichrist as described in Daniel 11 and by the Confessions. In the Confessions, both Luther and Melanchthon mention the papal ban against clergy marriage as antichristian. Luther says in SA III XI ("The Marriage of Priests") 1–3:

> The papists had neither authority nor right to prohibit marriage and burden the divine estate of priests with perpetual celibacy. On the contrary, they acted like antichristian, tyrannical, and wicked scoundrels, and thereby they gave occasion for all sorts of horrible, abominable, and countless sins, in which they are still involved. As little as the power has been given to us or to them to make a woman out of a man or a man out of a woman or abolish distinctions of sex altogether, so little have they had the power to separate such creatures of God or forbid them to live together honestly in marriage. We are therefore unwilling to consent to their abominable celibacy, nor shall we suffer it. On the contrary, we desire marriage to be free, as God ordained and instituted it, and we shall not disrupt or hinder God's work, for St. Paul says that to do so is a doctrine of demons [1 Tim 4:1–3].

In the Apology, Melanchthon makes specific reference to Daniel. He declares that this teaching of the papacy fulfills Daniel's prophecy that the Antichrist "will not favor desire of women" (Dan 11:37) and explains: "Daniel says that it is characteristic of Antichrist's kingdom to despise women (11:37)" (Ap XXIII ["The Marriage of Priests"] 25). The prohibition of marriage is contrary to the Scriptures, which portray the marriage of believers as a holy estate within which the mutual love of Christ and his bride, the church, is displayed (e.g., Song of Songs; Psalm 45; Eph 5:21–33; cf. also 1 Tim 5:14; Heb 13:4). St. Paul prophesied that in the last days those who follow "deceiving spirits and teachings of demons" will forbid marriage (1 Tim 4:1–3). Prohibiting the natural, God-created desire consummated in the holy estate of marriage can lead to sexual sins, including homosexuality, contrary to the express will of God (Rom 1:24–28; 1 Cor 6:9–11). The Confessions recognize that the requirement of

---

[6] The commentary on 9:24–27 notes that the (alternate) typological view considers the desolation of the temple in 9:26–27 to be the persecution and destruction of the church by the Antichrist, especially during the final period shortly before the return of Christ.

clergy celibacy is contrary to God's order of creation and can lead to all manner of unmentionable sins.[7]

In regard to the promotion of false doctrine and worship, Melanchthon in the Apology cites Dan 11:38 thrice. In the first instance, he cites the papacy's invention of rites that are counter to the Gospel and says that this is what Daniel is describing in 11:38 when he says that the Antichrist will honor "a god whom his fathers did not know." Ap XV 18–19 states:

> What need is there for words in a matter so clear? If our opponents defend the notion that these human rites merit justification, grace, and the forgiveness of sins, they are simply establishing the kingdom of Antichrist. The kingdom of Antichrist is a new kind of worship of God, devised by human authority in opposition to Christ. Thus the kingdom of Mohammed has rites and works by which it seeks to be justified before God, denying that men are freely justified before God by faith for Christ's sake. So the papacy will also be a part of the kingdom of Antichrist if it maintains that human rites justify. They take honor away from Christ when they teach that we are not justified freely for his sake but by such rites, and especially when they teach that for justification such rites are not only useful but necessary. The Confutation condemns our statement in the article on the church that for the true unity of the church it is not necessary that rites instituted by men be everywhere alike. In his eleventh chapter Daniel says that the invention of human rites will be the very form and constitution of the kingdom of Antichrist. This is what he says (11:38): "He shall honor the god of fortresses instead of these: a god whom his fathers did not know he shall honor with gold and silver, with precious stones and costly gifts." Here he is describing the invention of rites, for he says that a god will be worshiped whom the fathers did not know.

Shortly thereafter, in the second instance, he specifically critiques the Roman claim that such humanly invented rites can merit God's grace and the forgiveness of sins. He then quotes again the last part of Dan 11:38. Ap XV 21–22 states:

> We are amazed when our opponents maintain that traditions have another purpose, namely, to merit the forgiveness of sins, grace and justification. What is this but honoring God "with gold and silver and precious stones" [Dan 11:38], believing that he is reconciled by a variety of vestments, ornaments, and innumerable similar observances in the human traditions.
>
> In Col. 2:23 Paul writes that traditions "have an appearance of wisdom," and indeed they have. This good order is very becoming in the church and is therefore necessary. But because human reason does not understand the righteousness of faith, it naturally supposes that such works justify men and reconcile God.

---

[7] The article "The Marriage of Priests" begins (AC XXIII 1–2): "Among all people, both of high and of low degree, there has been loud complaint throughout the world concerning the flagrant immorality and the dissolute life of priests who were not able to remain continent and who went so far as to engage in abominable vices."

In the third instance, he notes that the papacy promotes worship of things rather than the proclamation of the Gospel. Apparently he again has in mind the "gold, silver, precious stones, and highly prized things" at the end of Dan 11:38. Ap XXIV 51 says:

> The real adornment of the churches is godly, practical, and clear teaching, the godly use of the sacraments, ardent prayer, and the like. Candles, golden vessels, and ornaments like that are fitting, but they are not the peculiar adornment of the church. If our opponents center their worship in such things rather than in the proclamation of the Gospel, in faith, and in its struggles, they should be classified with those whom Daniel (11:38) describes as worshiping their God with gold and silver.

With regard to the third characteristic of the Antichrist, the Apology first cites the NT teaching that the Antichrist will rule in the church: "Paul also predicts that Antichrist will 'take his seat in the temple of God' (II Thess. 2:4), that is, that he will rule and hold office in the church" (Ap VII/VIII 4). Later it references the whole of Dan 11:36–39 to demonstrate that the Scriptures depict the Antichrist as a ruler who exercises power in both the church and the world (Ap VII/VIII 23–24):

> Perhaps our opponents demand some such definition of the church as the following. It is the supreme outward monarchy of the whole world in which the Roman pontiff must have unlimited power beyond question or censure. He may establish articles of faith, abolish the Scriptures by his leave, institute devotions and sacrifices, enact whatever laws he pleases, excuse and exempt men from any laws, divine, canonical, or civil, as he wishes. From him the emperor and all kings have received their power and right to rule, and this at Christ's command; for as the Father subjected everything to him, so now this right has been transferred to the pope. Therefore the pope must be lord of the whole world, of all the kingdoms of the world, and of all public and private affairs. He must have plenary power in both the temporal and the spiritual realm, both swords, the temporal and the spiritual. Now, this definition of the papal kingdom rather than of the church of Christ has as its authors not only the canonists but also Dan. 11:36–39.

The fourth characteristic of the Antichrist is mentioned by Luther in the Smalcald Articles. Luther refers to St. Paul's statement in 2 Thess 2:4. He could just as easily have cited the OT background for that passage, Dan 11:36–37, which states that the eschatological king "will exalt himself and magnify himself over every god. … He also will not favor desire of women nor any god because he will magnify himself above all." In SA II IV 10–13, Luther states:

> This is a powerful demonstration that the pope is the real Antichrist who has raised himself over and set himself against Christ, for the pope will not permit Christians to be saved except by his own power, which amounts to nothing since it is neither established nor commanded by God. This is actually what St. Paul calls exalting oneself over and against God [2 Thess 2:4]. Neither the Turks nor the Tartars, great as is their enmity against Christians, do this; those who desire to do so they allow to believe in Christ, and they receive bodily tribute and obedience from Christians.

However, the pope will not permit such faith but asserts that one must be obedient to him in order to be saved. This we are unwilling to do even if we have to die for it in God's name. All this is a consequence of his wishing to be the head of the Christian church by divine right. He had to set himself up as equal to and above Christ and to proclaim himself the head, and then the lord of the church, and finally of the whole world. He went so far as to claim to be an earthly god and even presumed to issue orders to the angels in heaven.

Intriguingly, the Confessions do not use other descriptions in the prophecies of Daniel that would have been helpful for making the case that the papacy fulfills the biblical portrait of the Antichrist. There are at least five of these.

First, Daniel depicts the Antichrist as having "a mouth speaking great things" (7:8; see also 7:11), speaking "words against the Most High" (7:25) and "against the God of gods ... wonderful things" (11:36). These descriptions fit well with the assertion that the pope has attacked Christ by claiming that his own words and doctrines have divine authority and by teaching another gospel contrary to the Gospel.

Second, neither do the confessors mention that the papal attack on the Gospel could be what Daniel prophesied: he will make "war with the saints" (7:21) and "wear out the saints of the Most High" (7:25).

Third, the confessors also could have pointed out that the pope's attempts to change the Gospel by imposing upon Christians rites and customs foreign to the Gospel could be what Daniel was told about the little horn: "it will intend to change times and Law" (7:25).

Fourth, given the widespread practice of simony in the medieval church and at the time of the Reformation, the confessors could have noted that this was an abuse of temporal power mixed with ecclesiastical prerogatives, fulfilling the third mark of the Antichrist listed above and the words to Daniel about the eschatological king: "To whoever acknowledges [him] he will give great honor and make them rule over many. Moreover, he will parcel out land at a price" (11:39).

Fifth and finally, the Antichrist is to endure throughout the church age, and he will only be destroyed at the second coming of Christ (2 Thess 2:8). Thus "he will come to his end" (Dan 11:45) just before the resurrection on the Last Day (12:2–3). Many other identifications of the Antichrist have been proposed, but the papacy is the only one that has continued to exist throughout the church age. In the early centuries of the Christian era, the bishop of Rome did not claim authority over the other bishops or over all the churches. He was restrained until the demise of the Roman Empire in the fifth century AD.[8] Subsequently, the bishop of Rome claimed authority over all Christendom and began to pro-

---

[8] This fulfills the prophecy in 2 Thess 2:6–8 that the man of lawlessness would not be revealed until what was restraining him (in St. Paul's day) was removed. See further "The Unfolding of History as Depicted in the Fourth Beast" in the commentary on Dan 7:26–27.

mote false doctrines and practices openly. In many respects, that abuse of power continues today.

Those omissions suggest that the confessors were not seeking to thoroughly analyze and comprehensively include all of the biblical evidence from all of the passages in Scripture that speak about the Antichrist. That could be left to exegetes or dogmaticians writing other kinds of works besides the Confessions. Instead, the confessors thought it sufficient to cite only representative verses and enough biblical evidence to make a convincing case for the opinion that the papacy fulfills the primary marks of the Antichrist as he is described in the Scriptures.

The judgment of the Lutheran Confessions that the office of the papacy is the Antichrist is a historical one. That is, there is no passage in Scripture that explicitly equates the papal office and system in the Roman Catholic Church with the Antichrist. Instead, this equation remains a judgment that the portrait of the Antichrist in Scripture fits the events of history subsequent to the writing of the books of the Bible involving the teachings of the pontiff of the Roman Catholic Church. Thus this identification is not the unassailable and explicit teaching of Scripture. Rather, it is a conclusion based on Scripture and subsequent history. This commentary concurs with that conclusion, which is based in part on the book of Daniel.

The confessors' identification of the papacy as the Antichrist is often dismissed as Reformation-era anti-Catholic polemic. However, a sensitive reading of the Confessions reveals that the confessors felt compelled to make this identification because of the testimony of the Scriptures themselves. Moreover, the confessors did not seek to overthrow or abolish the Roman Catholic Church or the papacy, but to reform the church body, calling for it to return to biblical teaching and practice. They desired to remain within it; only after they were expelled did they form a separate church body.

Their identification of the papacy as the Antichrist is actually intended as a constructive criticism for the Roman Catholic Church in at least two ways. First, by identifying the papacy as a mortal threat to Christian faith, the Confessions are seeking to warn brothers and sisters in Christ of the grave danger they face from the tyranny of papal rule. Far from being anti-Catholic polemic, the motivation is Christian love and concern for fellow believers and for the good of the church as a whole. To use an analogy, God's love and human compassion would move us to be concerned about our fellow citizens if our state or country were seized by a ruthless and abusive tyrant. We would speak out against him and take action to save others from his tyranny, to alleviate his oppression of others as well as of ourselves. So the Confessions were concerned about the papal abuses that oppressed people redeemed by Christ, abuses that in many cases continue unabated in the Roman Catholic Church today.

Second, by acknowledging that the Scriptures teach that the Antichrist will arise within the church, the Confessions implicitly acknowledge that the pope and the Roman Catholic Church are part of the "one holy Christian and apostolic church" (Nicene Creed). Many individual members of the Roman Catholic Church are Christians, and genuine saving faith in Christ exists among its members. Moreover, it is the institution and office of the papacy—specifically as it has mandated false teachings and practices—that the confessors identify as the Antichrist, not the person of any pope or popes. Many of the individual popes may well have been Christians—justified through faith in Christ as the sole source of salvation—and may well be in heaven today.

Daniel 12:1–4

After the End, the Resurrection to Eternal Life or to Everlasting Abhorrence

Translation

12 ¹"Then at that time, Michael, the great prince who stands over your people, will arise. There will be a time of distress that has not happened from the time there was a nation until that time.

"At that time your people will be delivered,
everyone who is found written in the book.
²Many of those sleeping in the dusty earth will awake,
some to everlasting life,
and some to contempt, to everlasting abhorrence.
³Those who have insight will shine
like the brightness of the sky,
and those who bring many to righteousness
like the stars forever and ever.
⁴"Now you, Daniel, close up the words and seal the scroll until the time of the end. Many will run back and forth, and knowledge will increase."

Textual Notes

12:1 יַעֲמֹד—Here again the Qal (G) of עָמַד, usually "to stand," means "to arise." See the second textual note on 11:2.

מִיכָאֵל הַשַּׂר הַגָּדוֹל הָעֹמֵד עַל־בְּנֵי עַמֶּךָ—Literally, "Michael, the great prince who stands over the sons of your people" describes this archangel in terms similar to those used for him in 10:13, 21. See the textual notes and commentary on 10:13.

12:2 וְרַבִּים מִיְּשֵׁנֵי אַדְמַת־עָפָר יָקִיצוּ—The plural adjective רַבִּים, here used as a substantive, "many," is the subject of יָקִיצוּ, the Hiphil (H) of קִיץ, "to awaken." This verb can be used for awakening from ordinary sleep (BDB, 1). It can also be used in promises of the bodily resurrection, described as awakening from the "sleep of death" (BDB, 2), as here and also in Is 26:19 and Ps 17:15. "Many" (רַבִּים) refers to all the dead, not just some, just as the Messiah establishes a covenant that is open to "many" (Dan 9:27) and atones for the sin of "many" (Is 52:15; 53:11–12), meaning everyone. See the first textual note on Dan 9:27 and the commentary on 12:2.

The prepositional phrase מִיְּשֵׁנֵי אַדְמַת־עָפָר is, literally, "from sleepers of earth of dust." The adjective יָשֵׁן, "asleep, sleeping," is used here as a substantive, "sleeping persons." It is cognate to the verb יָשֵׁן, used for the sleep of death in Ps 13:4 (ET 13:3). The expected form with the preposition מִן would be מִיְשֵׁנֵי (GKC, § 102 b).

The construct phrase אַדְמַת־עָפָר, "earth of dust," has an adjectival genitive: "dusty earth," not "the dust of the earth" as in many English translations.

אֵלֶּה ... וְאֵלֶּה—אֵלֶּה לְחַיֵּי עוֹלָם וְאֵלֶּה לַחֲרָפוֹת לְדִרְאוֹן עוֹלָם׃ The repeated אֵלֶּה ... וְאֵלֶּה indicates two distinct groups: "these ... those" (BDB, s.v. אֵלֶּה, b) or "some ... others." Both of the construct phrases לְחַיֵּי עוֹלָם and לְדִרְאוֹן עוֹלָם have adjectival genitives: "life of eternity" means "eternal/everlasting life," and "abhorrence of eternity" means "eternal/everlasting abhorrence." The noun דִּרְאוֹן, "abhorrence, an object of horror, something horrible," occurs only here and in Is 66:24. In both verses, it refers to the horror of the eternal damnation of those who rejected God. Is 66:24 emphasizes that after the bodily resurrection, those who rebelled against God will be afflicted with unending fire and worm. Preceding לְדִרְאוֹן עוֹלָם here is the parallel prepositional phrase לַחֲרָפוֹת, literally, "to contempts, reproaches." The plural form of חֶרְפָּה may be intensive, "(utter) contempt" (GKC, § 124 e), or an abstract plural (Joüon, § 136 g; Waltke-O'Connor, § 7.4.2a). In either case, it is appropriately translated as a singular: "contempt."

12:3 וְהַמַּשְׂכִּלִים יַזְהִרוּ כְּזֹהַר הָרָקִיעַ—The Hiphil (H) participle הַמַּשְׂכִּלִים could have the transitive, causative meaning, "those who made others have insight, taught insight to others," but more likely it has the intransitive (internally transitive) meaning, "those who have insight." See the textual note on 11:33. Similarly, the Hiphil (H) verb יַזְהִרוּ is intransitive, "to shine." Waltke-O'Connor, § 27.4a, including example 10, explains both verbs as inwardly transitive. This clause has the only OT occurrence of this verb זָהַר (BDB, זָהַר I).[1] It is followed by the cognate noun זֹהַר, "shining, brightness," which occurs only here and in Ezek 8:2, and which seems to be a description of God himself, since it is parallel to the description of God in Ezek 1:27. The implication is that risen believers in glory will reflect the divine glory of God himself (cf. Lk 9:30–31; 1 Cor 15:41, 43; Col 3:4). רָקִיעַ, "sky, firmament of heaven," refers to the expanse in which the sun, moon, and stars are set and shine (Gen 1:6–8, 14–17; Ps 19:2 [ET 19:1]), above which God resides (Ezek 1:22–23, 25–26; 10:1; Ps 150:1). This celestial imagery is reinforced by כַּכּוֹכָבִים, "like the stars" (see the next textual note).

וּמַצְדִּיקֵי הָרַבִּים כַּכּוֹכָבִים לְעוֹלָם וָעֶד׃—Unlike הַמַּשְׂכִּלִים (see the previous textual note), this Hiphil (H) participle, of צָדַק, "be justified, reckoned as righteous," has a causative, transitive meaning, "turn many others to righteousness" (see BDB, s.v. צָדַק, Hiphil, 4), "bring many to righteousness." It is not the believers themselves who justify others. Rather, they proclaim the Gospel of justification by God's grace alone and through faith alone. The Hiphil (H) participle is in construct with its direct object (GKC, § 116 g), הָרַבִּים, "the many," which here only refers to some: those who hear and believe the Gospel. The construction כְּ ... יַזְהִרוּ, "will shine like ... ," in the preceding clause (see the previous textual note), is continued in this clause by כַּכּוֹכָבִים, "[will shine] like the stars."

12:4 סְתֹם הַדְּבָרִים וַחֲתֹם הַסֵּפֶר—The imperative סְתֹם, "close up," was also used in 8:26 (see the commentary there). Here "close up the words [of this prophecy]" is parallel and essentially synonymous with "seal the scroll [of this prophecy]," referring

---

[1] There is a homograph that in the Hiphil (H) means "instruct, teach, warn" (BDB, זָהַר II).

to the book of Daniel. The same two verbs (סָתַם and חָתַם) whose Qal (G) imperatives are used here are used as Qal passive (Gp) participles in 12:9 in a similar context: סְתֻמִים וַחֲתֻמִים הַדְּבָרִים, "the words [of the prophecy given Daniel] are closed up and sealed." Compare other nuances of "to seal" in 6:18 (ET 6:17; the Aramaic חֲתַם) and in 9:24 (the Hebrew חָתַם).

עַד־עֵת קֵץ—In the context of this verse and in 12:9, where this phrase is repeated, "until (the) time of (the) end" does refer eschatologically to the period of time leading up to the return of Christ. See the second textual note on 8:17.

יְשֹׁטְטוּ רַבִּים—The Polel (D) stem of שׁוּט can have the nuances "go eagerly, quickly, to and fro" (BDB). It could be rendered with an iterative meaning, "many will repeatedly/continue to go back and forth."

וְתִרְבֶּה הַדָּעַת:—The feminine noun דַּעַת (in pause: דָּעַת), "knowledge," is the subject of the feminine Qal (G) imperfect תִּרְבֶּה, "will increase." The article on הַדָּעַת, "*the* knowledge," indicates a specific kind of knowledge, which in this context must be justifying faith, knowledge of God through his Gospel. In the OT, especially the Wisdom literature, דַּעַת often refers to faith-based "knowledge" of God (see BDB, s.v. דַּעַת, 2, under the root ידע). This understanding of the Wisdom term "knowledge" is in harmony with the preceding verse, which referred to believers as "those who have insight" and who bring others to "righteousness" through faith in the Gospel (12:3).

Some interpreters propose alternate understandings of this clause that change it from Gospel to condemning Law. First, a proposed emendation is to change the noun הַדָּעַת to הָרָעָה, "(the) evil," claiming this as is an example of the common graphic confusion of ר with ד. To support this claim, they cite the Old Greek translation, καὶ πλησθῇ ἡ γῆ ἀδικίας, "and the earth is full of evil/unrighteousness."[2] However, the Old Greek obviously is significantly different from the MT in other ways (the meaning of the verb and the addition of "the earth").

The second alternate understanding does not emend the text. It proposes that the noun הַדָּעַת does not derive from יָדַע, "to know," but from a second, homographic root, יָדַע II (which has no firm attestation in the OT), meaning "become still, quiet, at rest." The noun derived from it supposedly would mean "being reduced to humiliation or submission by means of discipline or punishment," and it would occur in the OT here and in Is 53:11. The clause then would mean "and great shall be the humiliation (punishment)."[3]

However, neither of those suggested emendations is particularly convincing. The passage makes good sense if we follow the well-attested meaning of the common noun דַּעַת, "knowledge," as the majority of commentators do.[4]

---

[2] Collins, *Daniel*, 369; Hartman and Di Lella, *Daniel*, 261, 274.

[3] Thomas, "Note on הַדָּעַת in Daniel XII. 4," followed by Day, "*Daʿat* 'Humiliation' in Isaiah LIII 11 in the Light of Isaiah LIII 3 and Daniel XII 4, and the Oldest Known Interpretation of the Suffering Servant," 98–99; Goldingay, *Daniel*, 281.

[4] E.g., Archer, "Daniel," 154; Baldwin, *Daniel*, 207; Keil, *Daniel*, 486; Lucas, *Daniel*, 258; Miller, *Daniel*, 321; Montgomery, *Daniel*, 474; Walvoord, *Daniel*, 291; Young, *Daniel*, 258.

Commentary

Michael Defends God's People, Who Will Be Raised to Eternal Life (12:1–3)

The divine man[5] continues his explanation of the end times begun in 11:36–45, and this eschatological perspective extends to the end of the book. The end times or "latter days" (2:28; 10:14) begin with the first advent of Christ, last throughout the church age, and conclude with Christ's return, followed by the resurrection (12:2–3).[6]

Michael is the guardian archangel of God's people (see the commentary on 10:13, 21). He will arise "at that time" to defend them (12:1). The time to which the divine man refers is the time of the eschatological king (11:36–45), the Antichrist. Michael "stands over" Daniel's people (12:1). This is generally taken to mean that Michael is in charge of heavenly warfare in defense of the saints, based on Rev 12:7–8. Some have argued that Michael's role is that of a judicial defender of God's people.[7] This would make him the defender of Israel in front of the heavenly court, which was convened in 7:9–14. While this is an intriguing suggestion of a parallel with a previous vision, this interpretation runs counter to the portrayal of Michael in this fourth vision (chapters 10–12) as a warrior (10:13, 21).

The rule of the eschatological king will bring "a time of distress" (12:1). This phrase (עֵת צָרָה) occurs five other times in the OT (Is 33:2; Jer 14:8; 15:11; 30:7; Ps 37:39; cf. Judg 10:14; Neh 9:27), and God is always the source of deliverance from this distress. Jesus refers to this worldwide eschatological distress as existing immediately before his parousia (Mt 24:29–30; Mk 13:24–27; Lk 21:25–27). This distress will be unique, because nothing can be compared to it since nations first came into existence (Dan 12:1). This is similar to Jesus' description of the distress in Jerusalem before its fall to the Romans (Mt 24:21; Mk 13:19). Therefore, the fall of Jerusalem and its great distress foreshadow the distress at the end of time.

Despite this distress, Daniel is assured that his people—all who, like Daniel, believe in the one true God and thereby are heirs of his eternal kingdom—"will be delivered" (12:1). This promise extends to "everyone who is found written in the book" (12:1). This is a reference to the book of life, which is mentioned several times in the OT (Ex 32:32–33; Is 4:3; Ps 69:29 [ET 69:28]). Already before the foundation of the world, God recorded the names of the people whom he elected to salvation by his grace alone, as is revealed more fully in the NT (e.g., Mt 24:22–24; 25:34; Lk 10:20; Eph 1:4; Rev 13:8; cf. 2 Tim 2:10, 19). This record is the same as the Lamb's "book of life," which plays an important role in Revelation, especially in the judgment on the Last Day.[a] Through

(a) Rev 3:5; 13:8; 17:8; 20:12, 15; 21:27

---

[5] For the identity of the divine man, see the commentary on 10:4–6.

[6] For this view of the end times or latter/last days, see the commentary on 2:28; 7:25; and 10:14 and the second textual note and the commentary on 8:17.

[7] Collins, *Daniel*, 390; Goldingay, *Daniel*, 306.

his Word and Sacraments God calls people into his kingdom, sustains them in saving faith until death, and preserves them until the Last Day, when all the elect shall be resurrected to everlasting life (see FC Ep and SD XI, "Election").

The clearest teaching about the resurrection in the entire OT is found in Dan 12:2. This verse is so clear in its teaching that there is near universal agreement among scholars on this. However, some argue that the passage does not teach a universal resurrection of all humanity, but only a resurrection of some. They note that Daniel is not told that "all" (כֹּל) who sleep will be resurrected; instead, he is told that "many of" (-מִ רַבִּים) those sleeping will awake. Based on the word "many" and the following preposition מִן, "of," whose use here definitely is partitive,[8] some hold that only Israel or some portion of humanity will be resurrected.[9] However, this is clearly contradicted by Jesus, who teaches that believers will be resurrected to eternal life and that unbelievers too will be resurrected but to damnation.[b]

(b) Mt 12:41–42 ‖ Lk 11:31–32; Mt 25:31–46; Jn 5:28–29; see also Rev 20:12–15

Other scholars hold that "many" here means "all."[10] While there is no clear case in the OT where רַב, "many," means כֹּל, "all," in Is 2:2–3, the two words are used in parallel: the eschatological promise first states that "all the nations" (כָּל־הַגּוֹיִם) will stream to the temple mount and then states that "many nations" (עַמִּים רַבִּים) will come to it. It could be argued that כֹּל, "all," is used to stress entirety, while רַב, "many," is used to stress a large number. Yet what cases such as Is 2:2–3 demonstrate is that "many" does not exclude "all" as a possibility.[11] That is, by using "many," the divine man is not saying, "not all, but only many, most of." Instead, he is saying "a great number" without excluding the possibility that the great number covers all of the dead.[12] Thus some commentators correctly understand "many" here simply to signify a large number, with no upper limit on how large that number is.[13] Therefore, there is no conflict

---

[8] "Partitive" is a grammatical term that specifies a subset of items from a more generally defined group, as in, for example, "half *of* those present were men."

[9] Alfrink, "L'idée de résurrection d'après Dan 12,1–2"; Collins, *Daniel*, 392; Gardner, "The Way to Eternal Life in Dan 12:1e–2 or How to Reverse the Death Curse of Genesis 3"; Hartman and Di Lella, *Daniel*, 308; Lucas, *Daniel*, 295; Miller, *Daniel*, 317; Montgomery, *Daniel*, 471; Walvoord, *Daniel*, 307–8.

[10] Calvin, *Daniel*, 2:374; Baldwin, *Daniel*, 204.

[11] Another passage that supports the view that "many" can in fact encompass "all" is the fourth Suffering Servant Song, Is 52:13–53:12. רַבִּים, "many," occurs five times in Is 52:14–15; 53:11–12. Four of those are in verses (Is 52:15; 53:11–12) that describe how the Servant will atone for, justify, and bear the sin of "many" (see Mitchell, *Our Suffering Savior*, 102–3, 137–43). The NT, of course, affirms that the sacrifice of Christ was not a limited atonement only for many but not for all. Rather, Christ died for the sins of all people.

[12] The partitive use of מִן does not imply that "the many" are simply a smaller subset of "those who sleep." To use an English example, the phrase "some of the dead" is partitive since it designates a subset of those who are dead. However, the phrase "all of the dead" is also partitive, and it designates a subset that is of the same size as the primary set; it includes everyone who is dead.

[13] Keil, *Daniel*, 481; Young, *Daniel*, 256.

between 12:2 and biblical passages that teach the universal bodily resurrection of all humanity (e.g., Mt 25:31–46; Jn 5:28–29; 1 Cor 15:52; Rev 20:12–15). The words of the divine man emphasize the great number of those who will be resurrected without denying that all who have died will be resurrected.

Sleep is a common metaphor for death in the Scriptures.[14] That the dead are "sleeping" (Dan 12:2) implies that they are in a temporary state and that they shall be awakened when their bodies are raised. "Dust" (עָפָר) is often pictured as the location of the sleep of death.[c] The closest background passages for Dan 12:2 are Gen 3:19 and Is 26:19; 66:24:[15]

(c) Is 26:19; Pss 22:16 (ET 22:15); 104:29; Job 7:21; 21:26; 34:15

> Many of those sleeping in the *dusty earth* will *awake*, some to everlasting life, and some to contempt, to everlasting *abhorrence*. (Dan 12:2)

> By the sweat of your face you will eat food until you return to the *earth*, because out of it you were taken, since you are *dust*, and to *dust* you will return. (Gen 3:19)

> Your dead will come back to life; your corpses will *rise*. *Awake* and shout joyfully, those who lie in *dust*! For your dew is a dew of lights [like plants drenched with the morning dew], and the land will give birth to its dead spirits. (Is 26:19)

> They will go out and see the corpses of those who rebelled against me, for their worm [the maggots that eat them] will not die, and their fire [that torments them] will not go out. They will be an *abhorrence*[16] to all flesh. (Is 66:24)

After the dead are raised each person will experience one of two outcomes. Believers, justified by God's grace alone, will be raised "to everlasting life," while unbelievers, damned because of their sins, will be raised "to contempt, to everlasting abhorrence" (12:2). These two eternal states, the first for the faithful and the second for the unfaithful, are also emphasized by Jesus in the NT (e.g., Mt 25:46; Jn 5:28–29). Here the punishment is described as God's everlasting contempt and abhorrence. Those banished away from God's gracious presence enjoy no blessing, only suffering under the wrath of the Almighty.

Dan 12:2 is the only place in the OT where the expression חַיֵּי עוֹלָם, "eternal/everlasting life," occurs. However, the expression for it in Ps 133:13 is similar: חַיִּים עַד־הָעוֹלָם, "life for eternity." The concept is expressed in other wordings in other OT passages.[d] In the NT, (ἡ) ζωὴ (ἡ) αἰώνιος or ἡ αἰώνιος ζωή, "eternal life," occurs forty-three times.

(d) Pss 21:4 (ET 21:3); 28:9; 37:18, 27–28; 41:13 (ET 41:12); Prov 10:25, 30

Daniel is told more in 12:3 about the everlasting glory God's people will inherit by his grace. "Those who have insight" indicates those who have faith, spiritual wisdom, and the ability to trust and follow God's ways even when

---

[14] Jer 51:39, 57; Pss 13:4 (ET 13:3); 76:6 (ET 76:5); 90:5; Job 14:12; Mt 9:24 ‖ Mk 5:39 ‖ Lk 8:52; Jn 11:11–13; 1 Cor 15:51; Eph 5:14.

[15] See Bailey, "The Intertextual Relationship of Daniel 12:2 and Isaiah 26:19: Evidence from Qumran and the Greek Versions"; Gardner, "The Way to Eternal Life in Dan 12:1e–2 or How to Reverse the Death Curse of Genesis 3," 5–10.

[16] In the OT, the noun דֵּרָאוֹן, "abhorrence, an object of horror, something horrible," occurs only in Is 66:24 and Dan 12:2. See the second textual note on 12:2.

circumstances seem to indicate some other course of action may be desirable or prudent (Prov 19:11; Dan 11:33–35). Words from the root שׂכל occur in 1:4, 17; 5:11–12, 14; 9:13, 22, 25; 11:33, 35; 12:10,[17] and the same Hiphil (H) participle as used here, מַשְׂכִּילִים, is also in 11:33, 35, where it denotes those who have insight granted by God and who are faithful even in times of persecution. In 12:3 the preincarnate Christ promises that they will shine like the sky, a reflection of Christ's own shining righteousness (10:5–6), which is ours through faith in him (Jer 23:6; 33:16; 1 Cor 1:30; 2 Cor 5:21).

Moreover, "those who bring many to righteousness" (Hiphil of צָדַק, 12:3) are also a reflection of Christ, who will "bring everlasting righteousness" (צֶדֶק, 9:24) and who "justifies many, renders many as righteous" (Hiphil of צָדַק in Is 53:11). These believers have imputed righteousness since they are justified through faith, and they demonstrate their faith and spiritual insight by proclaiming the Gospel, thereby leading others to justifying faith (Dan 12:3). The same truth was expressed earlier in Wisdom terms: those "who have insight will make many understand" (11:33). For this faithful use of God's gift to them, they will be rewarded with the brightness of stars, a promise repeated by Jesus when he speaks of the glory given to the righteous in the resurrection (Mt 13:43; see also Phil 2:15). This also fulfills the ancient promise to Abraham and his descendants that his spiritual descendants, who are justified by faith just as he was (Gen 15:6), will be as numerous as the stars in the sky.[e] All baptized believers in Christ are children of Abraham and heirs of God's OT promises (Gal 3:26–29).

(e) Gen 15:5; 22:17; 26:4; Ex 32:13; Deut 1:10; Heb 11:12

Daniel Is Told to Seal the Book (12:4)

Daniel is instructed is to "close up the words and seal the scroll until the time of the end" (12:4). Both commands signify the cessation of further divine revelation to Daniel. No more words can be added to a scroll that has been sealed. In addition, these commands indicate that Daniel's vision will not be understood "until the time of the end," since the words on the scroll cannot be read as long as the seal remains unbroken.[18]

"The time of the end" is also the time of the activity of the eschatological king, the Antichrist (11:36–45). He was present but hidden in the apostolic age and was not fully revealed until several centuries later.[19] This means that

---

[17] This root is used in a negative sense in 8:25 for the cunning of Antiochus IV.

[18] See the fourth textual note and the commentary on 9:24 and the commentary on 12:9. Both 9:24 and 12:9 have חָתַם, "to seal." Compare also 7:28, where Daniel says he kept the vision of Daniel 7 to himself.

[19] For the presence of the Antichrist already in the NT era, see 2 Thess 2:6–8 (cf. 1 Jn 2:18, 22; 4:3; 2 Jn 7). 2 Thess 2:7 states that the Antichrist is not fully revealed until "the restrainer … is out of the way." The "restrainer" was the Roman Empire. In the fourth and fifth centuries AD, the Roman papacy began to openly claim supremacy over all Christendom and to confound the Gospel. For more description of the Antichrist, his identity, and his persecution, see figure 10 in the excursus "The Four-Kingdom Schema in Daniel," the commentary on 7:8, 20–21, 25, and especially the excursus "The Lutheran Confessions on the Antichrist in Daniel."

the sealed scroll began to be opened with the first advent of Christ. The victorious Lamb who was slain is the only one with authority to unseal the scroll, and he began to do that in Rev 5:1–8:1 because he had inaugurated "the time of the end" (Dan 12:4) by his suffering, death, resurrection, ascension, and session in power at the right hand of the Father.[20] Thus the end times had arrived before John received his vision. In John's vision, the scroll is opened by Christ (Rev 5:1–8:1), who has authority over all world history and governs it for the sake of his church.

The second sentence of Dan 12:4 describes the time of the end when the meaning of Daniel's visions will be more clearly understood by those who have insight (12:10): "many will run back and forth, and knowledge will increase." "Run back and forth" is not simply a prediction about advances in transportation. Instead, the verb שׁוּט often indicates going back and forth in order to investigate and gain knowledge (Jer 5:1; Zech 4:10; Job 1:7; 2:2; 2 Chr 16:9). Amos 8:12 is the closest parallel to the use of שׁוּט in Dan 12:4 since it speaks of looking for God's Word:

> [People] will stagger from sea to sea and from north to east. They will go back and forth looking for a revelation from Yahweh, but they will not find any.

Thus Daniel is told that many will investigate the meaning of this vision, and knowledge about it will increase. With the coming of Christ, much of the prophecy given to Daniel was fulfilled, making it easier to understand. This increased understanding is possible because of the revelation of the fullness of the Gospel in Jesus, and this increased understanding is especially given to those who have the gift of God's Holy Spirit, who dwells in all who trust in Christ.

Therefore, in contrast to Dan 12:4, the opposite instruction is given to the apostle John at the end of the last book of the NT canon: "*Do not* seal up the words of the prophecy of this book, for the time is near" (Rev 22:10). The last days began already with the first advent of the Messiah, and believers always rightly regard his return as imminent (cf. 2 Pet 3:4–13).

---

[20] See the commentary on 7:25: "The Duration of the Little Horn's Warfare: Three and a Half Times."

Daniel 12:5–13

The Divine Man Concludes His Revelation to Daniel about the Time of the End

Translation

12 ⁵I, Daniel, saw, and there were two others standing [there], one on this bank of the river and the other on that bank of the river. ⁶He said to the man dressed in linen garments who was above the waters of the river, "How long until the end of the wonderful things?" ⁷Then I heard the man dressed in linen garments who was above the waters of the river. He raised his right hand and left hand to heaven and swore by him who lives forever that it was for a time, times, and half [a time], and when the rejection of a holy people is finished, all these things would be finished.

⁸I myself heard, but I did not understand. So I said, "Lord, what will be the latter part of these things?"

⁹He said, "Go, Daniel, because the words are closed up and sealed until the time of the end. ¹⁰Many will be purified, be made white, and be refined, but the wicked will behave wickedly. The wicked will not understand, but those who have insight will understand.

¹¹"From the time the continual offering is removed and a detested thing of desolation is set up, [there will be] one thousand two hundred ninety days. ¹²Blessed is the one who waits and reaches one thousand three hundred thirty-five days.

¹³"But you, go to the end. You will rest and rise to your allotted portion at the end of the days."

Textual Notes

12:6–7 לְבוּשׁ הַבַּדִּים ... לְבוּשׁ הַבַּדִּים—For "dressed in linen garments," see the second textual note on 10:5. This vesture connotes priesthood. In the OT, this phrase is used only for the divine man who appears to Daniel in chapters 10–12 and for the Christ figure seen by Ezekiel in Ezekiel 9–10. For his identity as the Son of God, see the commentary on Dan 10:4–6.

אֲשֶׁר מִמַּעַל לְמֵימֵי הַיְאֹר ... אֲשֶׁר מִמַּעַל לְמֵימֵי הַיְאֹר—"Who was above the waters of the river," repeated in 12:6 and 12:7, reinforces that the man "dressed in linen garments" is the Son of God, since no ordinary person could stand above water. See Mt 14:25–26 and the disciples' conclusion, "Truly you are the Son of God" (Mt 14:33).

12:6 קֵץ הַפְּלָאוֹת—"The end of the wonderful/miraculous things" uses קֵץ, "end," in an eschatological sense. The phrase looks toward the final events of history and the end of the world at the return of Christ. The same is true for עֵת קֵץ, "the time of the end" (12:9; see the second textual note on that verse). For קֵץ, see the second textual note on

8:17. The noun פֶּלֶא has both masculine and (as here) feminine plural forms. Usually it means a miracle or "wonder" and refers to "God's acts of judgment and redemption" (BDB, 2). It occurs only here in Daniel, but it is cognate to the feminine plural Niphal (N) participle of the verb פָּלָא, "wonderful/miraculous things," which occurs twice: in 8:24 it refers to the "wonderful things" of God (the temple and its divine worship) that Antiochus IV destroyed, and in 11:36 it refers to the fake "wonderful things" that the Antichrist speaks to replace God's Word. Since 11:36 is part of the same fourth vision (chapters 10–12) and it is only sixteen verses prior to this verse (while 8:24 is almost four chapters earlier), most likely הַפְּלָאוֹת refers to the same phony "wonderful things" spoken by the Antichrist denoted by נִפְלָאוֹת in 11:36.

12:7 וַיִּשָּׁבַע בְּחֵי הָעוֹלָם—The Niphal (N) of שָׁבַע, "to swear, take an oath," can take the preposition בְּ attached to "Yahweh" (e.g., Gen 24:3) or his "name" (e.g., Lev 19:12) to indicate that the oath invokes God by name as the guarantor and enforcer of the oath. Here בְּ is attached to what is probably the construct form of the adjective חַי, which often refers to "God, as the living one" (BDB, 1 a).[1] Here the adjective is used as a substantive verbal noun, "him who lives." Therefore הָעוֹלָם in the construct phrase חֵי הָעוֹלָם, literally, "the living one of eternity," is translated adverbially: "him who lives forever."

לְמוֹעֵד מוֹעֲדִים וָחֵצִי—"For a time, times, and half [of a time]," this Hebrew phrase is equivalent to the Aramaic phrase in 7:25. See the third textual note on 7:25. מוֹעֵד often denotes an "appointed time" (BDB, 1; *HALOT*, 3). For the second unit of time, both 7:25 and this verse use a true plural, here מוֹעֲדִים, "times," rather than a dual, מוֹעֲדַיִם, "two times." Nevertheless, it is likely that the intended total in both 7:25 and 12:7 is three and a half times (so BDB, s.v. מוֹעֵד, 1 b, under the root יעד).

וּכְכַלּוֹת נַפֵּץ יַד־עַם־קֹדֶשׁ—This clause with כְּ in a temporal sense ("when") and two Piel (D) infinitive constructs (of כָּלָה and נָפַץ) is, literally, "and when [he/they] finish shattering (the) hand of a people of holiness." Many take "hand" in the sense of "power" and translate the clause as something like this: "when he/they finish breaking the power of the holy people" (similar are KJV, RSV, NIV, ESV, NASB). The meaning would then be that when the power of the Christian church ("the holy people") is finally broken by the Antichrist (11:36–45) and his minions, Christ will return and forever end the persecution of his people. This would be consistent with NT passages that depict Satan and his Antichrist as almost destroying the Christian church shortly before Christ returns (Mt 24:22; Rev 20:7–9).

However, one scholar has noted the similar Akkadian phrase *qāta napāṣu*, literally, "to thrust away the hand," which means "to refuse, reject" in contexts where someone rejects a covenant with or the allegiance of someone else. This scholar interprets the phrase to mean that God will reject the Jewish people for some time, but "when the appointed time arrives, God will renew his covenant with Israel and all the 'awful

---

[1] GKC, § 93 aa, footnote 1, considers 12:7 to be the only OT occurrence of the construct form of the adjective חַי. It considers the other (about fifteen) OT occurrences of חֵי in oaths to be contracted forms of the absolute state of the adjective חַי. However, other grammarians consider חֵי to be the construct state of the abstract plural noun חַיִּים (Joüon, § 165 e, including footnote 2; Waltke-O'Connor, § 40.2.2b).

things' (הַנִּפְלָאוֹת) will come to an end."[2] However, this interpretation fails to explain how the Jewish people could still be called "a holy people" (12:7) during the time when God has rejected a covenant relationship with them. Israel was elected to be God's "holy nation" (Ex 19:6), but by their unbelief they forfeited that status, and the NT affirms that all believers in Christ are God's "holy nation" (1 Pet 2:9; cf. Is 62:12). Nevertheless, if the Hebrew idiom is, literally, "thrust away the hand," meaning that God will "reject a covenant relationship with" the Jewish people, then it would refer to the time during which they reject the Messiah. As long as the Jewish people as a whole reject the Messiah, God's covenant will not be established with them. The new covenant in Christ includes all who believe in Christ, Jew and Gentile alike (Rom 1:16–17; Gal 3:22–29).

12:9 סְתֻמִים וַחֲתֻמִים הַדְּבָרִים—"The words [of the prophecy given Daniel] are closed up and sealed." The Qal passive (Gp) participles are of the same verbs used in imperatival form in 12:4. The imperative סְתֹם was also spoken to Daniel in 8:26. See the commentary on 8:26 and the first textual note on 12:4.

עַד־עֵת קֵץ׃—This phrase is repeated from 12:4. In the context of both verses, "until (the) time of (the) end" does refer eschatologically to the period of time leading up to the return of Christ. See the second textual note on 8:17.

12:10 יִתְבָּרֲרוּ וְיִתְלַבְּנוּ וְיִצָּרְפוּ רַבִּים—The plural רַבִּים is the subject of the three plural verbs, which can be translated as passives: "many will be purified, be made white, and be refined," emphasizing that justification and sanctification are God's actions, not human actions. For Hithpael (HtD) verb forms, older lexicons, notably BDB, generally prefer to give reflexive or middle meanings instead of passive meanings. Thus BDB defines the Hithpael of בָּרַר, "purify," as "purify oneself" (Hithpael, 1). However, for the Hithpael of לָבֵן, "be white," which occurs only here in the OT, BDB gives the passive meaning "be purified." Newer lexicons tend to include more passive meanings for Hithpael verbs. For the Hithpael forms of בָּרַר and לָבֵן, *HALOT* gives "be sifted, sorted out" and "be cleansed," respectively. The passive meanings "will be purified" and "will be made white" are consistent with the third, Niphal (N) verb, וְיִצָּרְפוּ, "will be refined." These three passive meanings, with God as the implied agent who does the actions to "the many" (רַבִּים), are also consistent with 11:35, which uses active Qal (G), Piel (D), and Hiphil (H) forms of the same three verbs to state that God's purpose is לִצְרוֹף בָּהֶם וּלְבָרֵר וְלַלְבֵּן, "to refine them [those who have insight], purify [them], and make [them] white." God accomplishes that purpose through his Word and Sacraments and by allowing their faith to be tested and purified through suffering and persecution (cf. Rom 5:3–5; James 1:2–4). The passive meanings here are also consistent with the end of Dan 12:10, which clarifies that the "many" are וְהַמַּשְׂכִּלִים, "those who have insight," since insight is a gift given by God, not something a person can produce for himself (see 1:17; 9:22; and the next textual note). That said, other Scripture passages

---

[2] Tawil, "Hebrew נָפֵץ יָד = Akkadian *qāta napāṣu*: A Term of Non-Allegiance." The quote is on page 82. In the quote, Tawil cites הַנִּפְלָאוֹת, which does not occur in Daniel. The Niphal participle נִפְלָאוֹת occurs, but without the definite article, in 8:24 and 11:36. Presumably the Hebrew Tawil cites is an error for הַפְּלָאוֹת, a term in 12:6, which Tawil translates as "awful things" on page 79.

The Divine Man Concludes His Revelation to Daniel about the Time of the End

can speak of Christians as those who have "washed their robes and made them white in the blood of the Lamb" (Rev 7:14; cf. Rev 7:9, 13). See further the commentary on Dan 11:35.

וְהַמַּשְׂכִּלִים יָבִינוּ—Here the Hiphil (H) participle הַמַּשְׂכִּלִים has the intransitive meaning, "those who have insight," as also in 11:33, 35; 12:3. See the textual note on 11:33 and the first textual note on 12:3. Similarly, יָבִינוּ, which in form could be either the Qal (G) or Hiphil (H) of בִּין, here is the Qal with the intransitive meaning "understand, know" (BDB, 2 a), as also in the preceding clause of 12:10 (וְלֹא יָבִינוּ כָּל־רְשָׁעִים). The Hiphil of בִּין has that same intransitive meaning in, for example, 1:4, 17; 8:17; 9:23. The transitive Hiphil, "cause others to understand," occurs in, for example, 8:16 and 9:22. For בִּין, see the textual note on 11:33.

12:11 הוּסַר הַתָּמִיד—"The continual offering is removed" is the Hophal (Hp) perfect of סוּר with the definite noun הַתָּמִיד as its subject. Similar clauses about the removal of the continual offering were in 8:11 and 11:31. See the second textual note on 8:11.

וְלָתֵת שִׁקּוּץ שֹׁמֵם—The Qal (G) infinitive construct of נָתַן with *waw* and לְ continues the preceding finite verb, הוּסַר, "is removed," and the infinitive can be translated as a corresponding finite verb, "is set up" (see Joüon, § 124 p). For the noun שִׁקּוּץ, "detested thing" (BDB), see the second textual note on 9:27. Literally, "a detested thing desolating" is similar to וְהַפֶּשַׁע שֹׁמֵם, "the transgression causing desolation" in 8:13, and to הַשִּׁקּוּץ מְשׁוֹמֵם, "the detested thing causing desolation" in 11:31. It is less similar to a statement in 9:27, וְעַל כְּנַף שִׁקּוּצִים מְשֹׁמֵם, "on the wing of detested things (is) a desolator." When Jesus refers to "the detested thing of/causing desolation" (Mt 24:15; Mk 13:14), the most direct OT background verse is Dan 9:27 since Jesus is referring to events that would take place after his earthly ministry.[3] That later desolation would also be a desecration of the temple by a Gentile invader, like the desolation that had been accomplished under Antiochus IV Epiphanes in the second century BC, which is the desolation predicted in Dan 8:13; 11:31; 12:11.

12:13 וְאַתָּה לֵךְ לַקֵּץ—"But you, go to the end" refers to the "end" of Daniel's earthly life, whereas לְקֵץ הַיָּמִין, "at the end of the days," at the end of the verse (see the next textual note) refers to the end of world history at the return of Christ. Many commentators would omit לַקֵּץ here since it is not reflected in the translations of the Old Greek or Theodotion,[4] although the Greek translations do reflect the imperative לֵךְ. These commentators allege that לַקֵּץ is a dittograph from the last phrase in the verse, where the same sequence of five consonants as here (לֵךְ לַקֵּץ) occurs in (לְיֹרֶל)לְךָ לְקֵץ הַיָּמִין).

וְתָנוּחַ וְתַעֲמֹד לְגֹרָלְךָ לְקֵץ הַיָּמִין—"You will rest" refers to the time between Daniel's death and his resurrection on the Last Day. See ἀναπαύομαι, "to rest," in Rev 6:11 and 14:13, referring to the rest after death that believers enjoy with God as they await their resurrection on the Last Day. Contrast the lack of "rest" (ἀνάπαυσις) for dead unbelievers in Rev 14:11. וְתַעֲמֹד, "you will stand up/rise" refers to Daniel awakening and

---

[3] See the commentary on 9:24–27, especially 9:26–27, and "Daniel in the New Testament" in the introduction.

[4] Collins, *Daniel*, 370, 402; Goldingay, *Daniel*, 281; Hartman and Di Lella, *Daniel*, 261; Lucas, *Daniel*, 263; Montgomery, *Daniel*, 477.

rising to eternal life on the Last Day (Dan 12:2). This will be his גּוֹרָל, "*allotted portion, share*, in the Messianic consummation" (BDB, 3), granted to him by God's grace. The same word was used in Joshua 14–21 for the portions in the promised land allotted by God in his grace to the tribes of Israel (e.g., Josh 15:1; 16:1; 17:1). Here קֵץ refers eschatologically to the "end": the world's end at the parousia of Christ, followed by the resurrection. The form of הַיָּמִין, the plural of יוֹם, is unusual since it has the Aramaic plural ending ִין- (GKC, § 87 e). About twenty examples of this Aramaic plural ending on Hebrew nouns are found in the OT (see Joüon, § 90 c; Waltke-O'Connor, § 7.4b).

Commentary

The Length of the Eschatological King's Activity (12:5–7)

The divine man who first appeared to Daniel in 10:5–6 and has been revealing to Daniel the contents of his fourth vision (chapters 10–12) now concludes the revelation to the prophet. For the identity of this man, see the commentary on 10:4–6. Now as the divine man finishes the revelation, Daniel sees two others, presumably angels (12:5). Some propose that the two angels appear to serve as witnesses to the oath that the divine man will swear (12:7). However, witnesses were required by the Law of Moses (Deut 17:6; 19:15) only in the case of criminal prosecutions.[5] Even though the two others are angels, the three together in a theophany to Daniel hint at the Trinity, the three persons of the one Godhead, as in Genesis 18–19, where "Yahweh appeared to" Abraham (Gen 18:1), and of the three persons who appeared to him, one turned out to be Yahweh himself (e.g., Gen 18:13) and the two others were angels (Gen 19:1).

"The river" (Dan 12:5) is probably the Tigris, mentioned at the start of this fourth vision (10:4), although the term here is הַיְאֹר (12:5–7), which is usually used for the Nile (e.g., Gen 41:1–3; Ex 1:22; 2:3, 5). The two angels here may be the same two angels who appeared in one of Daniel's previous visions (Daniel 8). There the two angels conversed with each other (8:13–14) so that Daniel could overhear their question and answer, and then God commanded one of them, who was Gabriel, to explain the vision further to Daniel (8:16–26). In 8:16 God spoke with "a human voice between [the banks of] the Ulai," that is, on or above the water of that canal.[6] That parallel is further confirmation that in 12:5–13 the divine man dressed in linen "who was above the waters of the river" (12:6–7) and who speaks to Daniel from that location is God the Son, the preincarnate Christ.

One of the angels asks the Son of God about the time until "the wonderful things" would end (12:6). This is a reference to the "wonderful things" spoken by the eschatological king, things disguised as substitutes for God's Word, but which in fact militate against God's Word and deceive people away from the

---

[5] Keil, *Daniel*, 487–88. For two or three witnesses in the NT, see Mt 18:16; 2 Cor 13:1; 1 Tim 5:19; Heb 10:28; Rev 11:3.

[6] For the Ulai Canal, see the textual note on 8:2. For the identity of the speaker who was above that canal and for the significance of his location, see the commentary on 8:16.

truth of the Gospel (see the commentary on 11:36). Therefore, the question is about the length of the activity of the eschatological king, the Antichrist.[7]

In giving his reply, the divine man poised above the water raises both hands to swear his oath (12:7). Since normally only one hand was raised when taking an oath, the raising of two hands may signal the great solemnity attached to this oath.[8] The wording of the oath suggests that it is a purposeful duplication of God's oath in Deut 32:40 to avenge the shed blood of his persecuted people and to take vengeance on his enemies (see Deut 32:40–43). There God says, "I lift up my hand to heaven, and I say, 'As I am alive/live forever'" (Deut 32:40). God raises one hand in the normal gesture for swearing an oath and describes himself with the same verbal adjective חַי, "alive, do live," and noun עוֹלָם, "eternity," used adverbially, "forever," as in Dan 12:7.

Here the divine man raises two hands to confirm again the oath God swore of old. The second hand signals a recommitment to the ancient oath, now given with a timetable for its fulfillment.[9] He swears by "him who lives forever." Both of these oaths, but especially Dan 12:7, since it is spoken about the length of time until the end, are the likely OT background for the oath taken by the mighty angel in Rev 10:5–7, who spoke about the consummation of God's "mystery"—his plan of salvation—at the return of Christ:

> The angel ... raised his right hand to heaven and swore by him who lives forever and ever [ὤμοσεν ἐν τῷ ζῶντι εἰς τοὺς αἰῶνας τῶν αἰώνων] ... that there would be no more time [delay], but in the days of the sound of the seventh angel, when he is about to blow the trumpet, the mystery of God would be fulfilled, just as he evangelized [made the Gospel promise to] his servants the prophets.[10]

In his oath in Daniel, the divine man states that the length of time until the end will be "a time, times, and half [a time]" (12:7). The Hebrew here matches the time period expressed in Aramaic in Dan 7:25, where it denotes the period during which the little horn (the Antichrist) is active. It also matches "a time, times, and half of a time" (καιρὸν καὶ καιροὺς καὶ ἥμισυ καιροῦ) in Rev 12:14, the period when the woman representing the church is persecuted by but

---

[7] See "The Identity of the King in 11:36–45" in the commentary on 11:36–45.

[8] See Collins, *Daniel*, 399.

[9] McGarry, "The Ambidextrous Angel (Daniel 12:7 and Deuteronomy 32:40): Inner-Biblical Exegesis and Textual Criticism in Counterpoint," argues that the raising of both hands by this angel is actually a misunderstanding of the parallelism of the (presumed) version of the Hebrew text reflected in LXX Deut 32:40, which has ὅτι ἀρῶ εἰς τὸν οὐρανὸν τὴν χεῖρά μου καὶ ὀμοῦμαι τῇ δεξιᾷ μου, "for I will lift to heaven my hand, and I will swear by my right hand." Both Dan 12:7 and Deut 32:40 contain the lifting of a hand in an oath sworn by God as the one who lives forever. They are the only verses in the OT to combine those elements. McGarry is on the right track. However, the two-handed oath is not based on a misunderstanding of Deut 32:40, but a duplication of the posture there for solemn emphasis.

[10] For an interpretation of the oath in Rev 10:5–7, one may see Brighton, *Revelation*, 269–70. For the question of whether the mighty angel who swears it is Christ himself or a created angel, one may see Brighton, *Revelation*, 252–62, 274–78.

also protected from the serpent, representing the devil. What do these three and a half times represent? Already in Daniel the number "seven" has been used to denote completeness or thoroughness (see the commentary on 3:19 and 4:13 [ET 4:16]). Moreover, 9:24–27 prophesied seventy "weeks" (sevens) as the time in which God would complete his plan of salvation.[11] "Seven" as a complete period for God to finish his activity is probably based on the creation account in Genesis 1–2, where in seven days God creates the entire world and rests. This significance of "seven" is reemphasized when God commands the weekly and yearly sabbatical cycles (Ex 20:8–11; 23:10–12; Lev 25:3–4). Three and a half is half of a full seven. Therefore, the period during which the Antichrist oppresses the church, three and a half times, is depicted as half of a divinely determined complete period for the world. The first half of the complete period was the OT era, from the creation until the first advent of Christ. The second half of the complete period—the three and a half times in Dan 7:25 and 12:7—is the NT era, or the church age, from the first advent of Christ until his return.[12]

The Scriptures depict this divine dividing of human history into two great periods by the use of the phrase "the latter/last days," which implies an earlier period, "the former/first days." The latter or last days commence with the coming of the Messiah and his kingdom.[a] The reference to the messianic era as the latter days is also found twice in Daniel (2:28; 10:14). The NT affirms this understanding of the phrase. Both Peter and the writer to the Hebrews understood that the last days began with the first advent of Christ and confirm that they and their hearers or readers were already in the last days (Acts 2:17; Heb 1:2). The apostles' use of the phrase "in the last days" to describe conditions that were already present as they wrote is further confirmation of this (2 Tim 3:1; James 5:3; 2 Pet 3:3; see also "it is the last hour" in 1 Jn 2:18).

Therefore, the three and a half times in Daniel's visions (7:25; 12:7) is a symbolic period representing the time from the first advent of the Messiah to the final judgment of the Antichrist, who is represented by the beast with its little horn (7:7–8, 11, 21–26) and by the eschatological king (11:36–45).[13] It is the same as "the latter days" (2:28; 10:14) and the end times: the NT era or the church age, from Jesus' earthly ministry to his parousia.[14] It is during this period of time that the eschatological king, the Antichrist, is present on earth and

(a) Num 24:14; Is 2:2 ‖ Micah 4:1; also see Jer 48:47; 49:39; Ezek 38:16; Hos 3:5

---

[11] See the first textual note and the commentary on 9:24, especially "A 'Week' Is a Symbolic Period of Time." Compare also the "seventy years" prophesied by Jeremiah (25:11–12; 29:10), cited by Daniel in 9:2. In the NT, the scroll that covers the history of the world has seven seals (Rev 5:1–8:1). Later in Revelation, two more sets of seven, the seven trumpets (Rev 8:2–11:19) and the seven censers (Rev 15:1–16:21), each also cover world history until the return of Christ.

[12] See also the commentary on 7:25: "The Duration of the Little Horn's Warfare: Three and a Half Times." The little horn in Daniel 7 represents the Antichrist.

[13] See the commentary on 7:7–8, 11, 21–26 and 11:36–45 as well as the excursus "The Lutheran Confessions on the Antichrist in Daniel."

[14] See also the commentary on 2:28; 7:25; and 10:14 and the second textual note and the commentary on 8:17.

continues to attack God and his people, and his persecution will escalate as the return of Christ draws nearer (Rev 20:7–9). St. Paul confirmed that the Antichrist was already present in the apostolic era when he wrote that "the mystery of lawlessness is already at work" (2 Thess 2:7). This mystery of lawlessness operates through "the man of lawlessness" (2 Thess 2:3), who was restrained while the Roman Empire lasted, but emerged clearly after it fell in the fifth century AD (see 2 Thess 2:6–8). "The man of lawlessness" in 2 Thessalonians 2, the little horn in Daniel 7, and the eschatological king in Dan 11:36–45 all refer to the Antichrist. He will continue to utter his "wonderful things" against God (Dan 11:36; also 12:6) until Jesus slays him at this second coming (2 Thess 2:8).

It is during this time that there will be "rejection by a holy people" (see the third textual note on 12:7). The Jewish people, elected in the OT to be God's treasured possession, will as a nation reject Jesus as the Messiah.[b] However, the Jewish apostles and disciples in the Gospels and the Jewish apostle Paul remind us that there will always be a remnant of Jewish people who believe in the Messiah God promised and sent for them and for all (Rom 11:1–6). The hardness of heart among the Jewish people as a whole (Rom 11:7, 25) signals a time of grace when the Gospel is preached to all peoples and God offers salvation in Christ to all, Jew and Gentile alike (Rom 1:16–17; 11:7–10, 25–27; Gal 3:26–29). When the "time, times, and half [a time]" (Dan 12:7) end, all members of the true Israel—all believers in Christ from among Jews and Gentiles alike—will be saved (Rom 11:26) and will inherit God's eternal kingdom at the resurrection (Dan 7:18, 22, 27; Mt 8:11; 25:34; 1 Cor 15:50–52).

(b) E.g., Is 53:3; Ps 118:22, quoted in Mt 21:42; Mt 23:37 ‖ Lk 13:34; Lk 9:22; 17:25; Jn 1:11; Rom 11:7–10, 25–27

Daniel Is Told the Outcome of the Vision (12:8–10)

As in a previous vision, Daniel did not understand (8:27). Therefore, he asks for an explanation of "the latter part of these things" (12:8). This refers to the latter part of "all these things" that will "be finished" at the return of Christ (12:7). Daniel wants to understand the events of the church age, which will last "a time, times, and half [of a time]" (12:7), during which the Antichrist, the eschatological king in 11:36–45, will be active. It is not surprising that Daniel did not understand these things since they were to begin centuries later than his lifetime, upon the first advent of the Messiah, and they would not be revealed in any more detail until the divine revelations recorded in the inspired writings of the NT.

Daniel is not given any specific dates about the time of the first or second advent of Christ. (He will receive symbolic chronological information in 12:11–12.) The divine man reminds him that "the words are closed up and sealed until the time of the end," that is, until the first advent of Christ, which marks the beginning of the end times and latter days (12:9; cf. 12:4). But Daniel is told what will happen during the church era: "many will be purified, be made white, and be refined" (12:10) through the work of the coming Messiah, through faith in him, and through suffering and persecution (see the first textual note on 12:10). This purification of Christians throughout the church age, starting

about 560 years after Daniel's lifetime, will be parallel to the refining of believers that would come first, about 360 years after Daniel's lifetime, through their persecution at the time of Antiochus IV. That first persecution was described in 11:35 with different forms of the same three verbs used in 12:10, "purify," "make white," and "refine." Therefore, the divine man is implying that the church era, lasting three and a half times (12:7), is a time of persecution for God's faithful people.[c]

Also during this era, "the wicked will behave wickedly" (Dan 12:10). The ultimate display of wickedness will be the rejection and crucifixion of the promised Messiah,[15] followed by the persecution and martyrdom of the saints. The contrast between the wicked who do not understand and the understanding possessed by those who have insight reveals that even after the words of this vision are unsealed with the first coming of Christ, only those who are given insight by God through faith in the Messiah will truly understand and grasp with faith the meaning of the divine man's words (cf. Lk 24:45; 2 Cor 3:7–16).

(c) Mk 10:30; Lk 21:12; Jn 15:20; 2 Tim 3:12; Rev 12:6–17

Daniel Is Told How Long It Will Be before the Last Day (12:11–12)

Daniel is given some further chronology to answer his question in 12:8. That question asked about "the latter part of these things," the end of the end times as described in 12:1–3, which (in NT terminology) involves the last battle of the Antichrist against the church, the return of Christ, and the resurrection. The answer Daniel is given contains two numerical totals of days, one of which extends from the persecution by Antiochus IV to the return of Christ and the other of which extends from Daniel's own time to the return of Christ. Unfortunately, the interpretation of these two periods of days has caused much controversy.

These Are Not Literal Numbers of Days

Critical scholars, who view Daniel as a Maccabean-era work, understand the two periods as successive attempts to utter predictive prophecy about the time of the temple's desecration by Antiochus IV in 167 BC and its restoration in 164. Supposedly the original attempt was the 2,300 evenings and mornings, totaling 1,150 days, in 8:14. But when that prediction proved to be inaccurate, someone wrote a gloss attempting a second prediction of 1,290 days in 12:11. When this second attempt too failed, yet a third prediction of 1,335 days was made in 12:12.[16]

However, that critical explanation defies logic.[17] All extant copies of Daniel, both in Hebrew/Aramaic and in the ancient translations (the Greek versions, the

---

[15] Peter declares to his fellow Jews, alluding also to the role of the Gentile Romans, "You, with the help of *wicked men*, put him to death by nailing him to the cross" (Acts 2:23).

[16] Collins, *Daniel*, 401; Hartman and Di Lella, *Daniel*, 313; Montgomery, *Daniel*, 477. This was first proposed by Gunkel, *Schöpfung und Chaos in Urzeit und Endzeit*, 269, n. 1.

[17] See the discussion of this in Lucas, *Daniel*, 297.

Vulgate, and the Peshitta) agree about the numbers in each of the three verses (8:14; 12:11; and 12:12). If the author circulated his (shorter) book with the first number (and without 12:11–12), how could a second attempt (12:11)—after subsequent history proved that first number incorrect—be added to all the extant copies of the book, and then after that number turned out to be wrong, could a third prediction (12:12) be added to all copies of the book already in circulation? On the other hand, if the subsequent additions in 12:11 and 12:12 were added before the book was circulated, why were the first and second numbers retained when they had already been proven to be wrong? Why weren't the first and second numbers changed to agree with the third number? Moreover, if these numbers represent successive predictions and at least the first two proved to be wrong, how did the book gain acceptance so rapidly as a genuine prophecy? Why was it not immediately rejected as a sham?

The other extreme of literalistic interpretation is espoused by dispensational premillennialists, who also take these numbers as literal periods of time. They view the three and a half times in 12:7 as three and a half literal years and as the same time period described in Revelation as forty-two months (Rev 11:2; 13:5) and as 1,260 days (Rev 11:3; 12:6). The three and a half years (or forty-two months or 1,260 days) are the second half of a seven-year "tribulation" just before the establishment of a thousand-year earthly kingdom by Christ. Then dispensationalists usually explain the slightly higher numbers of days in Dan 12:11–12 as follows. The 1,290 days in 12:11 include thirty additional days (compared to 1,260 days or forty-two months or three and a half years) to clean up the aftermath from Christ's victory over his enemies when he returns to earth. Then the 1,335 days in 12:12 include forty-five more days (compared to the 1,290 days in 12:11, a total of seventy-five more days than the 1,260 days) as the time Christ needs to take to set up his earthly millennial kingdom after cleaning up the aftermath of his victory.[18]

These dispensational interpretations fail to recognize that the three and a half *times* in 7:25 and 12:7 are not a literal equivalent of three and a half *years*. Instead, they represent a symbolic time period.[19] Furthermore, their explanations for the additional thirty days in 12:11 and the additional thirty plus forty-five days in 12:12 are quite fanciful and based on conjecture. No passage in Scripture mentions such numbers of days needed by Christ or his followers to do these things.[20] Dispensationalists use these rationalistic explanations to fit these pas-

---

[18] See, for example, Archer, "Daniel," 156–57; Miller, *Daniel*, 325–26; Walvoord, *Daniel*, 295–96.

[19] See further below, and see also the commentary on 7:25: "The Duration of the Little Horn's Warfare: Three and a Half Times." For other time periods that are symbolic, but which dispensationalists wrongly assume are literal numbers of years, see "The Meaning of 'Seventy Weeks' (9:24)" in the commentary on 9:24–27.

[20] Dispensational premillennialists often interpret Ezekiel 38–39 as a depiction of the last battle against the Antichrist before Christ sets up his millennial kingdom, which they suppose is described in Ezekiel 40–48. Ezek 39:9–16 mentions that after the battle, the Israelites will

sages into their false assumption that Christ will establish an earthly millennial kingdom.[21]

In addition, the dispensational view is not in harmony with the context of 12:5–13. The two numbers of days given in 12:11–12 are an answer to Daniel in response to his question about "the latter part of these things" (12:8), that is, the latter part of the end times, which conclude with the second coming of Christ. It would be foreign to the context for the answer to be about periods of time before a supposed millennial kingdom, which (according to premillennialists, including dispensationalists) would last for a thousand years before the end of the world at the return of Christ. Those periods of time would not be "the latter part" but a much earlier, preliminary part of the end times.

Moreover, a description of those hypothetical periods of time would not furnish an answer to Daniel's question. Daniel conceded in 12:8 that he did not understand the vision, and 12:11–12 is intended as an explanation for Daniel of what he did not understand. The coming of Christ, who brings God's kingdom, had been revealed to Daniel (2:34–35, 44–45; 7:9–10, 13–14) and so had the Antichrist and his warfare in the end times (7:11–12, 20–27; 11:36–45). But Daniel had not been told anything about an earthly millennium (as defined by dispensationalists, which they believe would be revealed some six hundred years later in Rev 20:1–7). Therefore, a description about time periods leading up to the millennium would not be an answer to Daniel's question.

These Are Symbolic Time Periods That Conclude with the Second Coming of Christ

Therefore, we must adopt a different line of interpretation to arrive at a satisfying explanation. In keeping with the use of "a time, times, and half (a time)" as a symbolic period (7:25; 12:7), the periods of days in 12:11–12 also should be understood as symbolic.[22] The only time period to which Daniel could have related these numbers of days is the three and a half times. Since these days are an explanation in response to his request for further information about "the

---

collect the weapons of their defeated foes, and those weapons will provide enough fuel for fires for seven years. It also says that it will take the Israelites seven months to bury all their slain foes. However, both seven months and especially seven years are considerably longer time periods than the extra thirty days (one month) in Dan 12:11 and the extra seventy-five days (two and a half months) in 12:12. The "seven" months and years in Ezek 39:9, 12, 14 are symbolic time periods. Moreover, the victory depicted in Ezekiel 38–39 may well be the final battle by Christ and his church against the Antichrist, but it is followed by the eternal state, depicted in Ezekiel 40–48 (which is parallel to Revelation 21–22), not by an earthly millennial kingdom. See Hummel, *Ezekiel 21–48*, 1099–1103 and 1149–58.

[21] The period of the "thousand years" depicted in Rev 20:1–7, during which Satan is bound and Christians are spiritually resurrected, represents the NT era, lasting from Christ's advent until shortly before his second advent, when Satan is released for a brief time. See the illustration "Amillennialism or Inaugurated Millennialism" in figure 3, "Timeline of Biblical Eschatology." One may also see "The Millennium" in Brighton, *Revelation*, 533–41, and the interpretation of Rev 20:1–10 in Brighton, *Revelation*, 542–79.

[22] So Keil, *Daniel*, 502–3; Young, *Daniel*, 263; cf. Lucas, *Daniel*, 298.

latter part of these things" (12:8)—the things that will take place during the three and a half times, the era of the new covenant in Christ—the natural way to interpret the passage is to relate 12:11–12 to 12:7–8. Both numbers of days in 12:11–12 are a little longer than three and a half years, but it is clear that the days were meant to be related to the symbolic three and a half times *as if the times were symbolic years*.

Three and a half solar years consists of 1,278 days. However, on the basis of the soli-lunar calendar used in the ancient Near East, the calculation of three and a half years would have been 1,269 days or 1,284 days.[23] Therefore, 1,290 days is perhaps six days longer, but probably twenty-one days longer, than three and a half years. Moreover, 1,290 is an exact multiple of 30. It would appear to be the total number of days in forty-three months, each consisting of thirty days, since 43 x 30 = 1,290. This is a further indication that the number is indeed symbolic since not all months are thirty days long. Instead, the calculation is the same that would be used later in Revelation to equate forty-two months (Rev 11:2; 13:5) with 1,260 days (Rev 11:3; 12:6) since 42 x 30 = 1,260.

The divine man tells Daniel what event will begin the symbolic period of the 1,290 days. It starts "from the time the continual offering is removed and a detested thing of desolation is set up" (12:11). This is a reference to the desecration of the temple by Antiochus IV in 167 BC, prophesied earlier in this same vision with similar language in 11:31.[24] Thus Daniel is told that the time from the desolation by Antiochus to "the latter part of these things" (12:8)—the end of the NT era at the return of Christ—is *longer* than the 1,260 days or three and a half times, which represent the duration of the activity of the eschatological king (the Antichrist), beginning with the birth of Jesus and ending with his parousia. Thus both the 1,290 days and the 1,260 days or three and a half times end at the same time, at the return of Christ. However, the 1,290 days begin earlier, before the birth of Jesus and the church age.

The second number, 1,335 days (12:12), then relates directly to Daniel, as the divine man suggests in the next verse, where he addresses Daniel personally ("but you ... ," 12:13). It symbolizes the time from Daniel's own life to "the

---

[23] The lunar calendar had 354 days in a year. Four times in eleven years a thirteenth month of thirty days was added to a year to keep the solar and lunar cycles aligned. A typical three and a half year period would have had one year consisting of thirteen months. Therefore, three and a half years would have been 354 + 354 + 354 + 177 + 30 = 1,269 days. If the beginning year and the final half year both were years consisting of thirteen months (a less typical scenario), the final half year would have had an extra fifteen days (half of the extra, thirteenth month), making it 1,284 days long. The average of these two ways of calculating three and a half soli-lunar years is 1,276.5 days, almost the same as three and a half standard solar years: 1,278.3 days.

[24] Daniel's fourth vision comprises chapters 10–12. The similar expression "on the wing of detested things (is) a desolator" was also used earlier, in 9:27, to describe the later Roman destruction of the temple in AD 70. However, Daniel 9 is a different vision, and the intended referent here is different. Nevertheless, the desecration of the temple by Antiochus IV in 167 BC (11:31; 12:11) was a foreshadowing of the destruction of the temple by the Romans in AD 70 (9:27).

latter part of these things" (12:8), to the return of Christ. It is forty-five days (one and a half months) longer than the 1,290 days. In turn, the 1,290 days were thirty days (one month) longer than the 1,260 days or three and a half times. The implication is that the period of time from Daniel's own life to the desecration by Antiochus (one and a half symbolic months) will be *longer* than the time from Antiochus to the coming of the Messiah (one symbolic month).

Subsequent history confirms that this predictive prophecy was accurate and that this is the correct interpretation of the numbers of days. Elderly Daniel received this final vision in 536 BC.[25] If he lived to 530 BC, then it would be another 363 years until Antiochus desecrated the temple in 167 BC. A shorter period of time, another 165 years, would transpire from the time of Antiochus until the birth of Christ in about 2 BC. Moreover, both of those periods of years are much shorter than the time between the birth of Christ and his return, which at the time of this writing has been about 2,010 years. How much longer it will be until the end of the 1,260 symbolic days or three and a half times, only God knows (Mk 13:32).

Therefore, the symbolic periods in Dan 12:7, 11–12 can be diagrammed as in figure 16.

Figure 16

The Symbolic Periods of Time in Daniel 12:7, 11–12

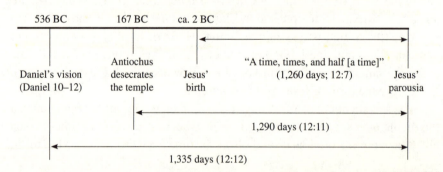

The divine man pronounces a benediction: "blessed is the one who waits and reaches one thousand three hundred thirty-five days" (12:12). The Piel (D) participle הַמְחַכֶּה, "who waits," could also be translated, "who longs for, who hopes for" since the verb can refers to waiting in faith and hope for God himself, who will fulfill all his promises (e.g., Is 8:17; 64:3 [ET 64:4]; Zeph 3:8; Ps 33:20). Those who believe in God and wait for his promises, particularly Christ's promise to return and deliver all his saints, are blessed (1 Thess 1:10; Titus 2:13; Heb 9:28). This blessing applies especially to those who are living

---

[25] See 10:1, 4 and "'The Third Year of Cyrus, King of Persia' (10:1)" in "Introduction to Daniel 10–12."

at the end of the time because they (along with all the dead in Christ) will see the consummation of the long awaited eschatological kingdom of God at Jesus' parousia (1 Thess 4:13–18).

A Final Blessing for Daniel (12:13)

The command given to Daniel at the beginning of the divine man's clarification of the time of the end (לֵךְ in 12:9) is repeated here (לֵךְ in 12:13): "go!" Moreover, Daniel is told that he will "rest" (see the second textual note on 12:13), a synonym for the sleep of death (12:2). Daniel will not live to see most of the events he prophesied. However, Daniel is also given a promise that he will be among those who will participate in the resurrection to eternal life on the Last Day (12:2). Since God has granted him wisdom and insight (e.g., 1:17, 20; 9:22), he will be among "those who have insight," who "will shine like the brightness of the sky," and since God has worked through him and the book God inspired him to write to "bring many to righteousness," he will shine "like the stars forever and ever" (12:3). This will be his "allotted portion" (12:13), his eternal reward by grace. This is the same glorious award described by Paul as "the portion of the inheritance of the saints in light" (τὴν μερίδα τοῦ κλήρου τῶν ἁγίων ἐν τῷ φωτί, Col 1:12). Finally, Daniel is told that he will receive this "at the end of the days" (Dan 12:13). The resurrection of all believers to eternal life (and of all unbelievers to eternal damnation [12:2]) will occur at end of the time periods described by symbolic days in 12:11–12, which is also the end of the time period in 12:7 and covered by this entire fourth vision (chapters 10–12): "the blessed hope and epiphany of the glory of our great God and Savior, Jesus Christ" at his parousia (Titus 2:13).

Index of Subjects

Aaron, 466

Abhorrence, 557, 561

Abomination of desolation. *See* Desolation, detested thing causing

Abraham, 93, 402

Accusation
    against Daniel, 307, 318–19
    against God's people, 299
    against Judean youths, 179–80, 182–84

Accusers
    punishment of, 321–23

Actium, Battle of, 415

Adam, 409

Advent of Christ. *See* Jesus Christ, advent of

Aelia Capitolina, 476. *See also* Jerusalem

Ahab, 41, 118

Ahasuerus. *See* Xerxes

Ahaz, 41

Ahijah, 40–41

Akiba, Rabbi, 350

Akkadian loanwords, 9

Aku, 89

Alexander IV, 400, 520

Alexander the Great
    and vision of divine man, 485
    and vision of four beasts, 345–47
    as horn of goat, 400
    as warrior king, 539
    death of, 522
    in dream of statue, 145, 148, 155
    reign of, 415, 519–20

Alliance, 516, 526

Amel-marduk, 2, 259

Amillennialism, 48–49, 51. *See also* Eschatology; Jesus Christ, return of; Last days, church age as

Ammon, 544

Ancient of Days
    and little horn of Daniel 7, 372
    as Anshar, 333
    court of, 349–51
    description of, 352–53
    God as, 26, 328, 330, 354
    identity of, 351–52
    throne of, 350–51, 353
    vision of, 43

Angel, 231, 234–38, 350, 568. *See also* Divine man; Gabriel; Michael; Seraphim; Watchers
    and fiery furnace, 196–97
    and vision of ram and goat, 404
    appearance of, 412
    as holy one, 367–69
    as interpreter, 365
    as son of man, 356–57
    divine man as, 498
    in lions' den, 311, 321
    Messiah as, 26
    numbers of, 353
    of Yahweh, 190, 197, 321, 505
    preincarnate Christ as, 321
    warfare of, 480–81, 502–4

Anger, 414
    of Antiochus IV Epiphanes, 534
    of God against evil king, 541
    of Nebuchadnezzar, 180, 184, 188–89, 191–92

Animal Apocalypse, 71

Animals. *See* Beasts

Anointing, 489, 497

Anshar, 333

Antichrist. *See also* Evil king
    activity of, 569–70
    and Antiochus IV Epiphanes, 543–45
    and Rome, 474
    and vision of divine man, 485
    and vision of ram and goat, 59, 418–20
    as evil king, 535–36, 538–44
    as leader, 448, 456, 458
    as little horn of Daniel 7, 152–53, 348–49, 371–72
    dispensationalism on, 380–82
    end of, 544–46
    judgment on, 476, 570–71
    Lutheran Confessions on, 547–55
    power of, 565
    pride of, 448, 534, 552–53
    reign of, 57, 376, 571
    time of, 562–63

Antigonus, 520, 522
    in vision of four beasts, 345–46

Antiochus I, 17, 521

Antiochus II, 521–22

Antiochus III, 521
    and Ptolemy IV, 523
    and Ptolemy V, 523–25

and Seleucus III, 523
death of, 514
Antiochus IV Epiphanes, 17, 183, 521. *See also* North, king/kingdom of
    abuses of, 346–47
    alliance with, 516
    and Antichrist, 456, 539–40, 543–45, 547
    and Daniel's visions, 3
    and Darius, 319
    and desolation, 567
    and dream of statue, 144–45, 156
    and Hellenization of Judea, 529–32
    and means of grace, 533–34
    and Ptolemy VI, 527–28
    and seventy weeks, 460, 463–65
    and vision of divine man, 483–84
    and vision of ram and goat, 58–59, 389–90, 413
    as appalling, 241
    as evil king, 536–38
    as little horn of Daniel 8, 152–53, 390, 401–3
    duration of, 575–70
    God's wrath at, 414
    not as little horn of Daniel 7, 371, 377–79
    persecution under, 29, 415–17, 572
    reign of, 404–6, 525–29
    warfare of, 412
Apamea, Treaty of, 525
Apocalypse of Week, 71
Apocrypha, 67–70
Apollo, 536–37
Apollonius, 529–30
Aramaic
    and date of Daniel, 8–9
    and structure of Daniel, 21–25
    and unity of Daniel, 5–6
    and vision of four beasts, 331
Arbela, Battle of, 400
Archangel. *See* Angel; Gabriel; Michael
Archer, Gleason, 7, 9
Arioch, 132
Arm, 511
Army
    gathering of, 512
    of heaven, 249, 396–98, 402
    sound of, 491

Arses, 519
Artaxerxes, 462, 470
Artaxerxes I Longimanus, 519
Artaxerxes II Mnemon, 519
Artaxerxes III Ochus, 519
Ashpenaz, 86, 89–90
Astyages, 149, 399
Athnach, 458–59, 471
Atonement, 27, 465. *See also* Forgiveness; Sacrifice
Authority. *See also* Commandment(s), Fourth; Dominion; Sovereignty of God
    and God, 205
    honoring of, 34
    respect for, 77–78
Authorship of Daniel, 1–6, 340–41
Azariah, Hananiah, and Mishael. *See* Shadrach, Meshach, and Abednego
Azariah, Prayer of, 69–70, 220
    and fiery furnace narrative, 192
    and textual tradition, 64

Baal, 334
Babel, tower of, 80, 234
Babylon
    and Persia, 5, 271, 300–301, 313–14, 399
    and vision of ram and goat, 391
    as a lion with eagles' wings, 335, 342–43
    as tree, 235
    fall of, 2, 257–59, 286–87, 301–3, 399, 506
    in dream of statue, 136–37, 144–57
    in vision of four beasts, 144–57, 342–43, 365
    officials of, 175–76
    punishment of, 435
    submission to, 34
Babylonian captivity, 31, 77–78, 80–85, 300–301
    accommodation to, 161–63
    and narratives of Daniel, 20
    and sovereignty of God, 85
    Daniel on, 104–6
    duration of, 435
    Judean experience of, 39–40

Bahman Yasht, 134
Balaam, 4–5, 12, 27, 529
Banquet of Belshazzar, 271–73
Baptism, 460, 462. *See also* Sacraments
Bar Kochba, 475
Bear, 146, 343–45. *See also* Persia, in vision of four beasts
  imagery of, 335
  significance of, 150
Beasts. *See also* Antichrist; Babylon, in vision of four beasts; Fourth beast; Greece, in vision of four beasts; Persia, in vision of four beasts; Rome, in vision of four beasts; Vision of four beasts; Vision of ram and goat
  of Revelation, 342, 348, 354, 372
Bel. *See* Marduk
Bel and the Serpent, 64, 68–69
Believers. *See* Saints
Belshazzar, 2, 11, 88
  and Daniel, 277
  and First Commandment, 32
  and first use of the Law, 34–35
  and handwriting on wall, 273–74
  and Nebuchadnezzar, 257, 260–63, 270, 272, 284
  and Pseudo-Daniel, 72
  and vision of four beasts, 330
  and vision of ram and goat, 390–91
  banquet of, 271–73
  coregency of, 21, 259, 263–65
  death of, 288
  fear of, 268
  judgment of, 106, 281, 283
  name of, 266–67
  queen mother of, 276–77
Belteshazzar. *See* Daniel
Ben Sira, 13–17
Benediction, 576–77
Berenice, 521–22
Berosus, 83, 219
Beryl, 490
Blasphemy, 190–91
  as charge against Daniel, 307
  prohibition of, 199, 204
Blessing, 577
Boanthropy, 235, 241, 249. *See also* Insanity of Nebuchadnezzar
Boast
  of beast with ten horns, 339
  of little horn of Daniel 7, 348, 363, 371
  of papacy, 553

Book of life, 350, 559–60
Book of Truth, 484, 494–95, 505–6
Bronze, 491
  claws of, 371
  gods of, 223–24, 273
  in dream of statue, 132
  significance of, 134, 136, 150
Burnt offering, 396. *See also* Sacrifice

Caesar Augustus, 415
Cambyses, 302, 518
Canonization, 17–18
Cassander, 520
  and vision of four beasts, 345–46
  and vision of ram and goat, 400
Castration, 90
Catchwords, 484–85
Cedar tree, 233–34
Celibacy, 550–51. *See also* Eunuch
Chaldeans. *See also* Diviners; Magicians; Occult; Wise men
  and dream of tree, 232
  before Nebuchadnezzar, 119
  diviners as, 87, 115
  jealousy of, 182–83
Chaos, 341
Chemnitz, Martin, on preincarnate Christ, 194–95
Chiasm
  and structure of Daniel, 21–25
  and vision of four beasts, 331
Christ. *See* Jesus Christ; Messiah
Christians. *See* Church; People of God; Saints
Chronology
  and Antiochus IV Epiphanes, 378–79
  and fiery furnace narrative, 167–69
  and historicity of Daniel, 12
  and Nebuchadnezzar's reign, 111–12
  and vision of divine man, 482–83
  in Daniel, 1–3, 80–85
  of Daniel in lions' den, 302–3
  of fall of Babylon, 258–59
  of last days, 572–77
  of Nebuchadnezzar's humbling, 207–8
  of vision of ram and goat, 390–91
Chrysolite, 490
Church. *See also* Kingdom of God; People of God; Saints
  age of, 571
  growth of, 139–42
  in dispensationalism, 52–53

Clay
- gods of, 223–24, 273
- in dream of statue, 132, 155
- significance of, 137

Cleopatra I, 521, 524

Cleopatra II, 528

Colossus of Rhodes, 175

Commandment(s). *See also* Law of God
- First, 31–34, 36, 78, 100, 161–63, 196, 198–99, 203–4, 299, 314, 321–22
- Fourth, 34, 78, 100, 205, 250, 283, 322, 347
- Fourth through Tenth, 35
- Ninth and Tenth, 34
- Second, 32
- Third, 33–34, 299, 314, 321–22

Communion, Holy. *See also* Sacraments
- abuse of, 272

Companions of Daniel. *See* Shadrach, Meshach, and Abednego

Confession
- of God by Darius, 312, 323–24
- of Nebuchadnezzar, 212
- of sin, 104–5, 425–26, 432–33, 436–39

Constantine, 535

Control, God's. *See* Authority; Dominion; Sovereignty of God

Conversion. *See* Faith; Repentance; Salvation

Counselors, 171

Court of Ancient of Days. *See* Ancient of Days, court of

Covenant
- confirmation of, 448–49, 456, 475
- leader of, 526

Coxon, Peter, 9–11

Criticism. *See* Higher criticism; Source criticism

Cyrus, 2. *See also* Darius the Mede
- and Belshazzar, 259
- and Daniel's prayer, 429
- and dream of statue, 148–49
- and Gubaru, 291–93
- and rebuilding of temple, 396
- and seventy weeks, 460
- and vision of divine man, 482–83, 496–98
- and vision of four beasts, 330–31, 344
- as anointed one, 463
- as Darius the Mede, 293–96
- as ram, 399
- decree of, 469–70
- edict of, 425, 455, 464
- in vision of ram and goat, 390–91
- reign of, 102–3, 518–19

Damnation, 557

Daniel (person), 1, 270, 276, 340–41, 567. *See also* Daniel in lions' den; Daniel's prayer
- accusation against, 318–19
- age of, 102–3, 576
- and Belshazzar, 281–83, 288
- and Darius, 324
- and dream of statue, 133–36
- and dream of tree, 242
- and fate of accusers, 312, 322
- and fiery furnace narrative, 183–84
- and interpretation of statue, 136–42
- and Jeremiah, 434–35, 437–39
- and Jesus Christ, 301
- and Joseph, 37–39, 143
- and Mordecai, 39–40
- and Nebuchadnezzar, 142–43, 239
- and Nebuchadnezzar's letter, 210–11, 232–33, 250–51
- and prophets, 40–42
- and psalm of praise, 123–24
- and Pseudo-Daniel, 72
- and vision of divine man, 491–92
- and vision of four beasts, 364, 385–86
- and vision of ram and goat, 417
- and wise men, 42–43, 110–11, 221–23
- as court official, 102–3
- as governor of Babylon, 302, 313
- as highly prized, 445
- as interpreter of dreams, 238–39
- as leader, 99–100
- as possible eunuch, 90–91
- as prophet, 17–18, 147–48
- blessing for, 577
- concern of for Jerusalem, 450
- diet of, 93, 96–97, 99–100
- exhaustion of, 444
- faith of, 30–31
- faithfulness of, 93–94
- gifts of, 29
- honor of, 132
- in Babylonian captivity, 105–6, 129
- mourning and fasting of, 496–97
- name of, 88, 92–93, 129
- plot against, 303, 307–8, 314–18
- strengthening of, 501, 504–5
- testing of, 97–98
- training of, 91–92, 94
- wisdom of, 97–98, 100–101

Daniel in lions' den, 319–22
- and fiery furnace, 299
- historical setting of, 301–4

581

Index of Subjects

Daniel's prayer, 104–5, 109–10, 124–26, 502
   and confession of sin, 436–39
   and wrath of God, 440–41
   as petition for grace, 441–42
   practice of, 309–10
   setting of, 434–35
   theology of, 427–29
Daphne, 537
Darby, John Nelson, 51
Darius I, 518
Darius II, 519
Darius III Codomannus, 519
Darius the Mede, 5, 290–96, 318–23. *See also* Cyrus
   and confession of God, 312, 323–24
   and Daniel, 300, 310–11, 324, 434–35
   and dream of statue, 149–50
   and fall of Babylon, 258, 288–89
   and proscription of prayer, 33
   and vision of divine man, 498
   God's use of, 106
   prayer to, 315
   reign of, 21, 301–4, 313–14
Date
   of Christ's return, 571–72
   of Daniel in lions' den, 303–4
   of Daniel's prayer, 429
   of events in Daniel, 80–85
   of fall of Babylon, 258–59
   of fiery furnace, 167–69
   of Nebuchadnezzar's reign, 111–12, 207–8
   of vision of divine man, 482–83
   of vision of ram and goat, 390–91
Date of book of Daniel, 1–3, 6–18, 103
   critical theories on, 3–6, 18–19
   traditional view of, 6–18
Daughter, 515
David, 350
Day of the Lord, 48, 541
Days, 445. *See also* Last days
Death
   sleep of, 556, 561
   victory over, 481 (*See also* Resurrection)
Decalogue. *See* Law of God
Decree
   of Cyrus, 469–70
   of God, 445
   of king, 122
Dedication
   of statue as idol, 171–72

Deliverance. *See also* Salvation
   and God, 299
   from fiery furnace, 181
   of Daniel, 311–12
   of Judean youths, 185, 193, 195–96
Demetrius, 525
Demons, 492, 502. *See also* Antichrist; Evil spirits; Satan
Denkard, 134
Desire, 534, 537, 542, 550–51
Desolation
   and little horn of Daniel 8, 397–98
   detested thing causing, 449–50, 473, 475–76, 517, 530–31, 567
   of temple, 403–4
Diet, 93, 96–97, 99–100
   and First Commandment, 32
Dionysius, 536–37
Discernment, 87
Disciples, 351
Dismemberment, 116, 118
Dispensationalism, 50–55. *See also* Eschatology; Last days; Millennium
   and interpretation of Daniel, 55–61
   on chronology of last days, 573–74
   on dream of statue, 137–38
   on fourth beast, 373
   on little horn of Daniel 7, 380–84
   on seventy weeks, 456–58
   on vision of ram and goat, 418–21
Distress, 361–62
Divination. *See also* Diviners
   and Nebuchadnezzar's dream, 117
Divine man. *See also* Jesus Christ; Messiah; Son of Man; Vision of divine man
   and spiritual warfare, 481
   appearance of, 484
   as preincarnate Christ, 161, 165–66, 193–97, 321, 497–501, 568
   benediction of, 576–77
   Daniel's reaction to, 491–92
   delay of, 501–4
   description of, 489–91, 493, 497, 499, 501
   identity of, 498–501
   vision of, 479
Diviners, 115. *See also* Chaldeans; Magicians; Occult; Wise men
   and interpretation of dreams, 109, 232
   and Nebuchadnezzar's dream, 117
   and Prayer of Nabonidus, 221–23
   as advisors, 87

Doctrine, altering of, 549–51
Dome of the Rock, 475
Dominion, 331. *See also* Authority; Sovereignty of God
    as gift of God, 338
    given to Greece, 346–47
    of God, 363
    of saints, 364
    of Son of Man, 340, 384
    removal of, 354
Dream of statue, 113–14, 117
    and eschatology, 129
    and vision of four beasts, 327–28, 347
    as mystery, 122
    interpretation of, 56–57, 117–20, 136–42, 144–57
    revelation of, 123–26, 133–34
    stone in, 130–31
Dream of tree
    content of, 233–38
    interpretation of, 230–33, 242–45
Dreams
    interpretation of, 32, 38, 41, 101, 270–71
    visions in, 337
Driver, S. R., 5–6
Drum, 173
Dust, 556–57, 561

Eagles, 249, 335, 338
Earth, 365–66
Edom, 544
Egypt, 511
    magicians of, 98
    Persian conquest of, 399
Elders, 351
Election, 134. *See also* Foreknowledge of God
Elijah, 40–41
Elisha, 40–41, 501
Emerton, J. A., 334
End, time of, 409, 413, 518, 535, 544, 558, 562–63. *See also* Last days
Enigma. *See* Mystery
Enuma Elish, 332–35
Eschatology, 43, 47–50. *See also* Antichrist; Dispensationalism; End, time of; Jesus Christ, advent of; Jesus Christ, return of; Last days; Millennium; 1,335 days; 1,290 days; Seventy weeks; Time, times, and half a time
    and dream of statue, 129

and interpretation of Daniel, 51–61
and messianic theme, 26
and vision of four beasts, 349–50
Esther, 39–40, 92
Eternity, 362. *See also* Everlasting life; Kingdom of God, as eternal; Resurrection
Ethnic diversity, 155
Eulaeus, 527
Eumenes II, 525
Eunuchs, 89–90
Euphrates, 489
European Common Market, 373
Evenings and mornings, two thousand three hundred, 152, 404–7, 417
Everlasting life, 561. *See also* Resurrection
Evil, 133–34
Evil king. *See also* Antichrist
    and persecution, 559
    as Antichrist, 547–48
    as religious figure, 540–44
    end of, 544–46
    identity of, 535–40
    reign of, 568–71
Evil spirits, 98–99. *See also* Demons
Exhaustion of Daniel, 444
Exhortation to repentance, 245–47. *See also* Repentance
Exile. *See* Babylonian Captivity
Extrabiblical evidence and historicity of Daniel, 11–12
Exultation, gift of, 223
Eyes
    of divine man, 491
    of little horn, 348
Ezekiel
    and Babylonian captivity, 104
    and Daniel, 17, 428
    and Son of Man, 339–40, 356
Ezra, 462, 470

Faith, 19, 30–31. *See also* Forgiveness; Gospel; Prayer; Salvation
    and Daniel's prayer, 439
    and Gospel, 31
    and Nebuchadnezzar, 203–5, 252–53
    and salvation, 246–47
    narratives of, 299
    of Judean youths, 187, 197–98
Faithfulness
    of Daniel, 311, 314, 316–18, 321–22

Index of Subjects

of God, 104–6
of Judean youths, 93–94, 99–100, 176

False gods, 19, 29–30. *See also* Idolatry; Marduk; Paganism; Polytheism; Zeus
and Belshazzar, 257, 284
and diviners, 119
and God, 196
and Nebuchadnezzar, 184–85, 204, 245, 253
and Prayer of Nabonidus, 223–24
and public policy, 300
and renaming of Judean youths, 93
and Son of God, 193
and temple vessels, 273
criticism of, 191–92
prayer to, 315
worship of, 174–75, 177, 303

False prophet, 348, 354, 372. *See also* Antichrist

False teachers, 541, 548

Fasting, 450, 489, 496–97

Father, 261–62

Fear, 535
of Belshazzar, 268
of Daniel, 413
of fourth beast, 347, 370
of Nebuchadnezzar, 279

Fiery furnace
and Daniel in lions' den, 299
and Law and Gospel, 161
and paganism, 161–63
historical setting of, 167–69
narrative structure of, 163–66
temperature of, 189, 192
threat of, 177–78, 184–85

Fire, 353, 491

Flute, 127

Foreknowledge of God, 133–34, 479, 505–6. *See also* Election

Forgiveness, 438, 465. *See also* Grace; Salvation
and Daniel's prayer, 432
and obedience, 425–26
of sins, 206
prayer for, 104–15

Fortress, 511

Four, 346

Fourth beast. *See also* Antichrist; Beasts; Rome, in vision of four beasts
and kingdom of God, 384–85
destruction of, 363
explanation of, 370–71, 373
judgment on, 372, 384

Gabriel, 365
and birth of Jesus Christ, 446
and Daniel, 444–45
and vision of ram and goat, 412–17
divine man as, 498
ministry of, 450–51
on seventy weeks, 465–76
predictions of, 472–76

Gad, 40–41

Gaius Popilius Laenas, 528–29

Gaumata, 518

Gentiles
and trampling of Jerusalem, 475
salvation of, 52–53, 123–24

George III, 235

Gerhard, Johann, 195

Glory
gift of, 534, 561–62
of God, 54–55, 105–6
of saints, 482

Goat, 146, 394–95. *See also* Greece, in vision of ram and goat
and leopard, 156
and ram, 395, 400
as kingdom, 389
description of, 399–400
explanation of, 414
Greece as, 409–10
horns of, 400–401
identity of, 153
significance of, 150–51

God. *See also* Ancient of Days; Holy Spirit; Jesus Christ; Sovereignty of God
acts of, 565
address to, 431–32
and authority, 205
and Belshazzar, 283
and dominion, 338, 363–64
and evil king, 541–44
and false gods, 29–30, 196, 272
and Gabriel, 413
and Judean youths, 185, 190
and justification, 242
and little horn of Daniel 7, 374
and transgressors, 410
and watchers, 237–38
as Ancient of Days, 26, 328, 330, 354
as God of heaven, 122
as Most High, 33, 212, 362
as protector of people, 19, 28–29
as revealer of mysteries, 129–30, 258
as rock, 139
as source of knowledge, 133–34
attributes of, 100–101

Daniel's confession of, 320–21
Daniel's praise of, 123–24
Darius' confession of, 312, 323–24
decree of, 220–21, 445
devotion to, 161–65
dwelling of, 119
existence of, 186
faithfulness of, 104–6, 206
foreknowledge of, 133–34, 479, 505–6
gifts of, 78, 101–2, 126, 131
glory of, 54–55, 105–6
grace of, 441–42
mercy of, 30–31, 124
name of, 32–33, 79, 123, 435
Nebuchadnezzar's confession of, 142–43, 198–99, 213, 251–52
of gods, 533
of Joseph and Daniel, 233
patience of, 250–51
power of, 29–30, 165–66, 181
prayer to, 316–17, 425–27
revelation from, 232
righteousness of, 437–39
salutation from, 494
salvation of, 195–96, 299, 311
sins against, 436–37
throne of, 350–51, 353
wisdom of, 42
worship of, 125, 299–300, 450
wrath of, 414, 434, 437, 440–41, 561

God of fortresses, 534
and evil king, 543

Gold
and statue of idol, 174–75
belt of, 490
gods of, 223–24
in dream of statue, 132, 138
proclamation of, 475
significance of, 134, 136, 150
vessels of, 267

Gospel, 31. *See also* Jesus Christ; Law and Gospel; Revelation; Salvation; Word of God
altering of, 553
and Nebuchadnezzar, 205–7
in Daniel, 36–37
nullification of, 379, 382–84
perversion of, 371–72
proclamation of, 141, 562

Göttingen Septuagint, 64

Governors, 171

Grace, 561–62. *See also* Forgiveness; Salvation
and prayer, 443
and salvation, 425–27, 438

kingdom of, 327–30
of God, 441–42
praise for, 123–24

Granicus, Battle of, 400

Grass, 231

Great Disappointment, 407

Great River, 489

Greece
and invasion of Persia, 518–19
as fourth beast, 377–79
in dream of statue, 136–37, 144–57
in vision of divine man, 144–57, 479, 485–86, 520–32
in vision of four beasts, 144–57, 345–47, 365
in vision of ram and goat, 58–59, 144–57, 389–90, 399–407, 409–10, 414
prince of, 484, 494–95
rise of, 510

Greek additions to Daniel. *See* Apocrypha; Azariah, Prayer of; Bel and the Serpent; Song of the Three Young Men; Susanna

Greek loanwords, 5, 10–11

Gubaru (Persian commander)
as Darius, 291–93
as governor of Babylon, 302
death of, 313

Gubaru (second governor of Babylon), 302

Gunkel, Hermann
on vision of four beasts, 332–33

Hadrian, 475–76

Hair, 352

Half-mina. *See* Mina

Hand, 267–68, 565–66

Handwriting on the wall
and Belshazzar's fear, 273–74
and First Commandment, 32
interpretation of, 274–76, 279, 284–88

Hanging Gardens of Babylon, 149, 250

Hanukkah, 172, 406

Harlot, 348, 372

Harp, 172–73

Hasmoneans, 72

Heart, Hebrew concept of, 95–96

Heaven
firmament of, 557
four winds of, 150–51
wind of, 341

585

Hebrew language
  and date of Daniel, 6–8
  and structure of Daniel, 21–25
  and unity of Daniel, 5–6
  and vision of four beasts, 332
  and vision of ram and goat, 390
Heliodorus, 525
Hellenization, 526, 529–32
Herakles, 400
Herald, 172, 176–77
Hermeneutics, 144, 157, 380. *See also* Dispensationalism; Higher Criticism; Interpretation
Hezekiah, 441
High priest, 526
Higher criticism, 3–6, 18–19. *See also* Source criticism
  on chronology of last days, 572–73
  on Daniel in lions' den, 301–4
  on Darius the Mede, 290–91
  on dream of statue, 144–45
  on Jehoiakim's reign, 83
  on little horn of Daniel 7, 376–79
  on seventy weeks, 463–65
  on Son of Man, 356
  on vision of divine man, 479–80, 483–84
  on vision of four beasts, 330–31
Historical setting
  of Belshazzar's banquet, 258–65
  of Daniel in lions' den, 301–4
  of fall of Babylon, 258–59
  of fiery furnace, 167–69
  of first deportation to Babylon, 80–85
  of Judeans' training, 111–12
  of Nebuchadnezzar's humbling, 207–8
  of vision of four beasts, 330–31
  of vision of divine man, 482–83
  of vision of ram and goat, 390–91
Historicity, 11–12, 18–19
History, 54–55
Holiness, 398. *See also* Most Holy One
Holy Land, 514, 535, 540, 545
Holy place, 398, 473–74. *See also* Most Holy Place; Temple
Holy Spirit. *See also* God
  working in Daniel, 233, 270, 277, 282, 313–14
Honor, 223, 482
Horns
  of beast with ten horns, 339
  of goat, 151–54, 395
  of ram, 150–54, 393–94

Hosts. *See* Army, of heaven
Hyrcanus, John, 73

Ibn Ezra, 467, 535
Idolatry, 132, 170–71, 174–78, 284, 438, 449. *See also* Demons; False gods; Marduk; Paganism; Polytheism; Zeus
  and demons, 502
  and fiery furnace, 161–63
  and Judean youths, 164, 185–87, 198
  and Nebuchadnezzar, 199
  of Babylon, 303
  of Nebuchadnezzar, 31, 184–85
  vanity of, 29–30
Illumination, 270. *See also* Insight
Incarnation, 26–27
Iniquity, 465, 475
Insanity of Nebuchadnezzar, 209–11, 215, 235–36, 244–45, 250–51, 259, 283, 375. *See also* Boanthropy
Insight, 557. *See also* Knowledge; Understanding; Wisdom
  and Gabriel's ministry, 450–51
  of Judean youths, 97–98, 100–101
  of people, 518
  of saints, 562, 567
Inspiration, 157
Intermarriage, 155
Interpretation
  of Babylonian captivity, 104–6
  of dream of statue, 56–57, 115, 117–20, 136–42, 144–57
  of dream of tree, 231–33, 238–39, 242–45
  of dreams, 32, 38, 109, 270–71
  of eschatology, 51–61
  of evenings and mornings, two thousand three hundred, 404–7
  of handwriting on wall, 274–76, 284–88
  of little horn of Daniel 7, 370–84
  of Nebuchadnezzar's insanity, 210
  of numbers, 57–58
  of prophecy, 53–54
  of vision of four beasts, 364–70, 384–85
  of watchers, 244–45
Irenaeus, 140
Iron, 224
  gods of, 273
  in dream of statue, 132, 155
  significance of, 134, 137, 150
  teeth of, 371

Isaiah, 17, 40–41
Islam, 475
Israel
    and kingdom of God, 47–48
    in dispensationalism, 52–53
    judgment on, 439–40
    sins of, 437–39
    unfaithfulness of, 104–6, 425
Israelites. *See* Jews; Judeans; Sons of Israel
Issus, Battle of, 400

Jacob, 93
Jason, 526
Jasper, 490
Javan. *See* Greece
Jehoiachin, 2
Jehoiakim, 2
    and siege of Jerusalem, 4
    capitulation to Nebuchadnezzar, 83
    reign of, 80, 85
Jeremiah, 40, 458
    and Daniel, 428, 434–35, 437–38
    and Daniel's prayer, 440
    dating of, 81
    on Babylonian captivity, 104
    seventy years of, 435, 451, 459, 469–70
Jerome
    on dream of statue, 140
    on Porphyry, 145
    on preincarnate Christ, 194
Jerusalem. *See also* Temple
    and Antiochus IV Epiphanes, 528
    and seventy weeks, 451
    as Aelia Capitolina, 476
    as eschatological city, 468
    capture of, 77
    Daniel's concern for, 450
    destruction of, 447–48, 455, 473–74
    devastations of, 431
    future of, 34
    identity of, 456
    judgment on, 439
    rebuilding of, 460–61, 472
    restoration of, 435, 468–71
    siege of, 4, 81
    trampling of, 475
Jesus Christ. *See also* Divine man; Messiah; Son of Man
    advent of, 26, 366, 418–19, 471–72
    and Antichrist, 371–72
    and Daniel, 301
    and dream of statue, 137, 144–48
    and Gospel, 206–7
    and kingdom of God, 47–48, 56–57, 382–84
    and last days, 129, 376
    and new covenant, 475
    and salvation, 440
    and seventy weeks, 453–59
    and vision of divine man, 481
    as angel in lions' den, 321
    as divine man, 498–501, 568
    as Leader, 446–49, 455–56
    as Messiah, 26–27, 329–30, 360, 473–74
    as Prince, 403
    as Son of Man, 43–45, 356–59
    as stone, 46, 140
    as temple, 467–68
    as warrior, 502–7
    Baptism of, 460, 462
    death of, 450
    dispensationalism on, 52–53
    faith of, 187
    in fiery furnace, 193–95, 197
    knowledge of, 102
    on detested thing, 449
    return of, 48–50, 349, 384, 390, 409, 531, 544, 568, 570–72, 574–77
    throne of, 350–51
    triumphal entry of, 461
Jews. *See also* Israel; Judeans
    and vision of ram and goat, 389–90
    persecution of, 402–4, 415–17, 530–32
    salvation of, 52–53
Jonah, 409
Joseph
    and Daniel, 37–39, 143, 233
    as interpreter of dreams, 238–39
    name of, 92
Josephus
    and Nabonidus, 219
    and Theodotion Daniel, 65
    on Belshazzar, 4
    on Daniel, 17, 40
    on Nebuchadnezzar, 83
Joshua (postexilic leader), 463
Joshua and Prince of army, 402–3, 503
Judas Maccabaeus, 379. *See also* Maccabean rebellion
    and Hanukkah, 406
    and rededication of temple, 467
    and reinstitution of sacrifices, 405

Judea, Hellenization of, 529–32
Judean youths. *See* Shadrach, Meshach, and Abednego
Judeans. *See also* Israel; Jews
   as sons of Israel, 91
   in Babylonian captivity, 105–6
   training of, 111–12
Judges
   in Babylonian Empire, 171
Judgment, 565. *See also* Desolation; Sin; Wrath of God
   against sin, 414
   and Ancient of Days, 353
   and record books, 350
   and vision of four beasts, 354–55, 372
   final, 349
   for saints, 362–63
   on Antichrist, 476, 544–46, 570–71
   on Babylon, 272, 281
   on Belshazzar, 257–58, 277, 283–88
   on Israel, 104, 439–40
   on Nebuchadnezzar, 238, 241, 244–45, 250–51
   on tree in dream, 234–35
Jupiter, 475–76
Justification, 32, 242. *See also* Forgiveness; Salvation
   Gospel of, 383
Justin Martyr
   on dream of statue, 140

King. *See also* Alexander the Great; Artaxerxes; Belshazzar; Cyrus; Darius the Mede; Nebuchadnezzar; Xerxes
   address to, 115, 117, 269
   and human kingdoms, 131
   as merciless, 420
   audience before, 128
   authority of, 182 (*See also* Authority; Commandment(s), Fourth)
   Belshazzar as, 263–65
   decree of, 122, 310, 315–16, 323–24
   deference to, 309
   Messiah as, 27
   of Greeks, 410
   protection of, 307
   service to, 87
King (evil). *See* Evil king
King(s) of Persia, 516–20
   and spiritual warfare, 503–4
   title of, 482–83
   versus Son of God, 492

Kingdom of God, 43, 117, 152–53. *See also* Church; Messianic kingdom
   and Babylonian captivity, 31
   and Darius, 312–13
   and dream of statue, 136, 138–42
   and dream of tree, 206, 234
   and Gospel, 36–37
   and human kingdoms, 32
   and Israel, 47–48
   and last days, 570–71
   and Messiah, 446
   and saints, 369
   and Son of Man, 382–84
   and vision of ram and goat, 389
   as eternal, 45–46
   coming of, 56, 366
   dispensationalists on, 52–53
   establishment of, 384–85
   in dream of statue, 147–48, 156
   in vision of four beasts, 327–30
   indestructibility of, 340
   mystery of, 258
   Nebuchadnezzar on, 212–14, 251–52
Kingdoms (human). *See also* Babylon; Greece; Medo-Persia; Persia; Rome
   and dream of statue, 136–37, 144–57
   and Fourth Commandment, 34
   and messianic kingdom, 141–42
   and sovereignty of God, 149
   and vision of four beasts, 144–57, 327–31
   and vision of ram and goat, 144–57, 389–90
   animals as, 146, 399
   judgment on, 354–55
   kings of, 365
Kings
   and human kingdoms, 365
   in vision of divine man, 485–86
   prophetic ministry to, 40
   rash acts of, 39
Kitchen, Kenneth, 8–10
Knowledge. *See also* Insight; Understanding; Wisdom
   as gift of God, 109
   increase of, 558, 563
   of Daniel, 102, 270
   of Judean youths, 97–98, 100–101
   source of, 133
Kohath, 72

Labashi-marduk, 2, 259
Lamb
   continual offering of, 396
   enthronement of, 349

Langton, Stephen, 209, 304, 507

Last days, 375–76, 493, 568–77. *See also* Antichrist; Church, age of; End, time of; Eschatology; Latter days
and evil king, 538–39
and vision of ram and goat, 409, 413
chronology of, 572–77
church age as, 535

Latter days, 26

Law and Gospel, 31–37, 245. *See also* Gospel; Law of God
and Antichrist, 374
and Daniel's prayer, 425
and fiery furnace, 161
and handwriting on wall, 288–89

Law of God, 31–36. *See also* Commandment(s); Law and Gospel; Word of God
altering of, 363
and Antiochus IV Epiphanes, 403
and Babylonian captivity, 78
and Daniel in lions' den, 299
and plot against Daniel, 307–8, 314
and reform of Nebuchadnezzar, 203–5
dietary code of, 99
first use of, 34–35, 199
on sacrifices, 396
Second Table of, 35
second use of, 35–36, 199, 203, 245
third use of, 34

Law of Medes and Persians, 39, 149–50, 295, 314–16, 318–20

Leader
dispensationalism on, 458
identity of, 456
Jesus Christ as, 473–74
Messiah as, 27, 446–49

Lenaeus, 527

Leopard, 146. *See also* Beasts; Greece, in vision of four beasts
and goat, 156, 400
imagery of, 335
significance of, 150–51
with four wings and four heads, 345–47

Letter of Nebuchadnezzar, 209–11, 213–14, 250–52

Lightning, 408, 490

Lion, 146, 310, 320–21. *See also* Babylon, in vision of four beasts
and Daniel's accusers, 312
imagery of, 335
significance of, 150
with eagle's wings, 342–43

Lions' den, Daniel in, 319–22

Literary style
of fiery furnace narrative, 163–66

Little horn of Daniel 7, 348–49
and higher criticism, 376–79
and little horn of Daniel 8, 151–56, 390, 419–21
as Antichrist, 547–48
boast of, 363
dispensationalism on, 380–84
explanation of, 370–71
judgment on, 372, 384
spiritual warfare of, 371–76

Little horn of Daniel 8
and army of heaven, 397–98
and little horn of Daniel 7, 151–56, 390, 419–21
and temple sacrifice, 396–97
as Antiochus IV Epiphanes, 390, 401–3
attack of, 411–12
duration of, 404–6
explanation of, 414–17
growth of, 395–96

Lord's Supper. *See* Communion, Holy

Lucius Cornelius Scipio, 524

Lydia, 399

Lyre, 173

Lysimachus, 520
and vision of ram and goat, 400
in vision of four beasts, 345–46

Maccabean era and composition of Daniel, 5–6

Maccabean rebellion, 530–32. *See also* Judas Maccabaeus

Maccabeans and seventy weeks, 464–65

Magicians, 37–38, 115. *See also* Chaldeans; Diviners; Occult
and interpretation of dream of tree, 232
in Babylonian court, 98–99

Magistrates, 171

Male goat. *See* Goat

Man of lawlessness. *See* Antichrist

Many, 557, 560–61
covenant with, 449
purification of, 566–67

Marduk, 88–89, 175, 259, 302, 330
and Belshazzar, 266
and First Commandment, 32
as false god, 29
as Son of Man, 333

Nebuchadnezzar's devotion to, 204
prayer to, 117

Marriage
and evil king, 542
between ethnic groups, 131–32
prohibition of, 550–51

Martin, W. J., 6–7

Martyrdom, 545

Masoretic Text of Daniel, 63

Mattathias of Modein, resistance of, 530

Means of grace. *See also* Gospel; Sacraments; Word of God
and Antiochus IV Epiphanes, 533–34
destruction of, 411, 540
Word of God as, 543

Medes, 258, 281, 390–91

Media
and dream of statue, 137, 148–50
and vision of four beasts, 344, 365
Persian conquest of, 399

Mediterranean Sea, 341

Medo-Persia, 389, 391, 399. *See also* Kingdoms (human), and vision of four beasts; Persia

Melanchthon, Philip, 548–49

Mene. *See* Mina

Menelaus, 526, 530

Mercy
lack of, 410, 415, 420
of God, 425–26, 436
prayer for, 124, 433

Messiah, 26–27, 38, 105, 480, 542. *See also* Divine man; Jesus Christ
and dream of statue, 136, 139–40, 145–48
and kingdom of God, 141
and last days, 376
and salvation, 465
and seventy weeks, 453–59, 468
and ships from Kittim, 529
and vision of four beasts, 327–30
and wisdom, 43
anointing of, 466–67
as cut off, 473
as divine man, 479
as God's gift, 29
as King, 366
as Leader, 446–49, 458
as Son of Man, 357–59
coming of, 471–72
enthronement of, 359–60
era of, 129
glory of, 106, 482

Jesus Christ as, 43, 473–74
mystery of, 258
reign of, 570–71
revelation of, 31
worship of, 34

Messianic kingdom, 18–19, 328–30, 358–60, 382–84. *See also* Kingdom of God
and human kingdoms, 141–42
and last days, 570–71
as eternal, 340
coming of, 366

Messianic psalms and vision of heavenly court, 359–60

Micaiah, 40–41

Michael, 556. *See also* Angel
and assistance of divine man, 500
and Son of God, 495
and vision of divine man, 481
as prince, 492–93, 506
as protector of God's people, 559–62
as warrior, 503–4

Millennium. *See also* Dispensationalism; Eschatology; Jesus Christ, return of; Last Days
timelines of, 48–50
views of, 51–52

Miller, William, 407

Millerite tradition, 406–7

Mina, 280–81, 285–87

Moab, 544

Mohammed, 548

Mordecai, 132
and Daniel, 39–40
name of, 92

Moses, 438–39

Most Holy One, 27

Most Holy Place, 466–67. *See also* Temple

Mountain, 136, 138–40, 142

Mourning, 496–97

Mouth of little horn. *See* Little horn of Daniel 7

Mystery, 122
dream as, 230
of kingdom of God, 258
of understanding, 410–11
revelation of, 123, 129–30, 133–34, 143

Myth, 332–35
Mythology, 332–35

Nabonidus, 2
    and Belshazzar, 260, 263–65, 330
    and Gubaru, 292
    and Nebuchadnezzar, 219
    as Belshazzar, 4
    idolatry of, 303
    illness of, 224–25
    reign of, 218, 259
    wife of, 276
Nabonidus Chronicle, 215
Nabonidus, Prayer of, 70–71, 215–28, 237
Nabopolassar, 81
Nabu, 175
Nachmanides, 467
Narratives
    and structure of Daniel, 20
    and unity of Daniel, 5–6
    and visions, 106–7
    chronology of, 1
    introduction to, 77–78
Nathan, 40–41
Nations, 342
Naturalism, 145, 147, 156–57
Nebo, 89
Nebuchadnezzar, 2
    and Belshazzar, 257, 260–63, 270, 272, 284
    and Daniel, 41, 142–43, 239
    and deliverance of Judean youths, 165–66
    and destruction of temple, 396
    and dream of statue, 26, 113–14, 117, 124, 149, 327
    and dream of tree, 231–33, 238, 243
    and fall of Jerusalem, 77
    and God's people, 28–29
    and Jerusalem, 431, 439
    and Judean youths, 102, 199–200
    and kingdom of God, 138
    and Law, 34–36, 199
    and Nabonidus, 219
    and persecution of God's people, 28–29
    and siege of Jerusalem, 4, 80–84
    and temple vessels, 267
    and vision of four beasts, 365
    and wise men, 117–02
    anger of, 180, 184, 188–89, 191–92
    approach to, 132
    as lion, 343
    authority of, 182–83
    bewilderment of, 192
    command of, 180
    confession of, 212, 251–52
    humiliation of, 105
    idolatry of, 29–31, 162–63, 174–78
    insanity of, 209–11, 215, 224–25, 259
    judgment on, 238, 241, 250–51
    kingdom of, 131
    letter of, 209–11, 213–14
    name of, 79
    on man in fiery furnace, 193–96
    pride of, 282–83
    prosperity of, 230
    reform of, 203–11, 237, 245–47, 252–53
    reign of, 21, 111–12, 136, 167–69, 207–8, 279–80, 283
    restoration of, 259
    revelation to, 106, 109
Neco (Pharaoh), 81
Nehemiah
    and seventy weeks, 460–61, 470
    prayer of, 429, 437
Neriglissar, 2, 259
New covenant, 475
New Testament, 17, 43–49. *See also* Gospel; Jesus Christ; Messiah
    Son of Man in, 357–59
Nile, 568
Nimrod, 80
Noah, 409
Nobility, 86, 91
North, king/kingdom of, 520–32, 538, 544–45. *See also* Seleucid king/kingdom; Seleucus I–IV
Numbers
    interpretation of, 57–58, 98, 102, 192, 382, 519–20, 572–73
    meaning of, 404
    of angels, 353
    use of, 488

Oath, 569
Obedience, 425–26
Occult, 98–99, 114–15. *See also* Chaldeans; Diviners; Magicians; Satan; Wise men
Octavian. *See* Caesar Augustus
Official
    audience before, 128
    of Babylonian Empire, 175–76
    promotion to, 269

Index of Subjects

Oil
  anointing with, 497
  use of, 489
Old Greek version of Daniel, 63–67
Old Testament
  and Daniel, 37–43
1,335 days, 575–76. *See also* Eschatology
1,290 days, 575–76. *See also* Eschatology
Onias
  and Pseudo-Daniel, 72
  assassination of, 405, 464, 526
Ophir, 490
Organization of Daniel, 20–25
Origen, and text of Daniel, 63–64

Paganism. *See also* False gods; Idolatry
  and fiery furnace, 161–63
  satire of, 164–65
Papacy. Antichrist as, 548–55
Parents, 34. *See also* Authority;
  Commandment(s), Fourth
Parousia. *See* Eschatology; Jesus Christ,
  return of
Parsin. *See* Mina
Passover, 496–97
Patience, 250–51
Paul, 501
Peace, 411–12, 515
People of God, 447, 517. *See also* Church;
  Israel; Kingdom of God; Saints
  and evil king, 542
  and spiritual warfare, 481
  as collective son of man, 356
  as saints, 367–70
  comfort of, 383–84
  persecution of, 402–4, 415, 545–46
  protection of, 28–29, 506, 559–62
  purification of, 571–72
  sins of, 436–39
Persecution, 151–52
  and Babylonian captivity, 39–40
  and First Commandment, 32
  and Third Commandment, 33
  narratives of, 299
  of God's people, 29, 402–4, 415, 572
  of Jews, 530–32
Persia. *See also* Medo-Persia
  and Babylonian Empire, 271, 300–301
  and Belshazzar's kingdom, 281
  and fall of Babylon, 301–2
  as setting for Daniel, 39
  expansion of, 394
  in dream of statue, 136–37, 144–57
  in vision of divine man, 144–57, 479,
    485–86, 517–20
  in vision of four beasts, 144–57,
    343–45, 365
  in vision of ram and goat, 58–59,
    144–57, 390–91, 399, 414
  kings of, 516–20
  organization of, 313–14
  prince of, 492, 502
Persian loanwords, 5
Persians
  and date of Daniel, 9–11
  and fall of Babylon, 258
  submission to, 34
Peter, 139–40
Petition, 432
Philip Arrhidaeus, 520
Pigs, sacrifice of, 403
Plot against Daniel, 303, 307–8, 314–18
Plymouth Brethren, 51
Polytheism. *See also* False gods; Idolatry
  and public policy, 300
  of Nebuchadnezzar, 142
Porphyry
  on dream of statue, 144–45
  on historicity of Daniel, 3
  on vision of divine man, 479
Potiphar, as possible eunuch, 90
Power
  of God, 19, 28–30
  quest for, 543
Praise of God
  by Daniel, 122–26
  by Darius, 323–24
  by Nebuchadnezzar, 142–43, 190,
    196–98, 206, 212–14, 251–52
Prayer, 308–9. *See also* Azariah, Prayer of;
  Daniel's prayer; Faith; Nabonidus,
  Prayer of
  and Daniel in lions' den, 299–300
  and grace, 441–43
  and practice of Daniel, 309–10
  and Third Commandment, 33–34
  answer to, 492, 502
  of Daniel, 104–5, 109–10, 316–18,
    425–27, 434–42, 450, 497
  of Darius, 320
  of Judean youths, 124–26, 187
  proscription of, 303, 315–17
Predestination. *See* Election;
  Foreknowledge of God
Predictive prophecy, 3–4, 12, 28–29,
  41, 144–45, 472–74, 479–80,

576. *See also* Foreknowledge of God; Revelation

Prefects, 171

Preincarnate Christ. *See* Angel, preincarnate Christ as; Divine man; Jesus Christ; Prince, of army of heaven; Prince, of princes

Premillennial dispensationalism. *See* Dispensationalism; Eschatology; Millennium

Pride
- of Antichrist, 448, 534, 552–53
- of Antiochus IV Epiphanes, 401
- of Belshazzar, 257, 277, 284
- of evil king, 540–41
- of goat, 400
- of king of south, 513
- of Nebuchadnezzar, 203–4, 243, 246, 250–52, 280, 282–83

Priest, 359

Prince
- Michael as, 506
- of army of heaven, preincarnate Christ as, 27, 396, 402–3, 481, 500
- of Greece, 494–95, 505
- of Persia, 492–95, 502–4
- of princes, preincarnate Christ as, 412, 416, 500

Prophecy, 376–77. *See also* Predictive prophecy; Revelation
- and divine foreknowledge, 479–80
- and historicity, 18–19
- and vision of divine man, 483
- dispensationalism on, 53–54
- *ex eventu,* 3–4, 12, 17, 378–79
- sealing of, 446, 466

Prophet, Daniel as, 452

Prophetic years, 461–62

Prosperity, 482

Prostration of officials, 176–78. *See also* Idolatry

Protection, 559–62. *See also* Salvation

Providence, 28–29, 77

Pseudo-Daniel, 71–73

Ptolemaic king/kingdom, 539. *See also* South, king/kingdom of
- and dream of statue, 145
- and fourth beast, 377–78
- and Seleucid kingdom, 479, 485, 520–32
- and vision of divine man, 479, 485
- as symbol, 544

Ptolemy I Soter, 345–46, 400, 520–21

Ptolemy II, 521–22

Ptolemy III, 17, 521

Ptolemy IV, 521, 523

Ptolemy V, 521, 523–25

Ptolemy VI, 17, 521, 526–28

Ptolemy VII, 528

Queen mother of Belshazzar, 269–70, 276–77

Qumran
- Daniel traditions in, 40, 70–73
- manuscripts of Daniel, 17–18, 62–63

Ram, 146, 393–94. *See also* Beasts; Persia, in vision of ram and goat
- and goat, 395, 400
- as kingdom, 389
- description of, 399
- dominion of, 153
- explanation of, 414
- horns of, 365
- interpretation of, 58–59
- significance of, 150

Rapture. *See* Dispensationalism; Eschatology; Last days; Millennium

Record books, 350. *See also* Book of life

Redemption. *See* Salvation

Reformation, Lutheran, 549–50

Repentance
- and Babylonian captivity, 104
- and Daniel's prayer, 425, 439
- and Nebuchadnezzar, 198, 203–6, 252–53
- exhortation to, 245–47

Resistance
- to pagan society, 93–94

Rest, 567–68

Restoration
- of Jerusalem, 431
- of Nebuchadnezzar, 249–50, 252, 259

Resurrection, 49, 556–57, 560–62
- promise of, 27
- prophecy of, 479

Revelation. *See also* Predictive prophecy; Word of God
- and Word of God, 488
- from God, 232
- given to Daniel, 109, 327
- of dream of statue, 133–34
- of dreams, 118
- of future events, 479

of mysteries, 129–30
of vision of four beasts, 334–35
of vision of ram and goat, 409
Ribs in vision of four beasts, 338, 344
Riches, 510
Righteousness
and Daniel's prayer, 432
and judgment, 440
as everlasting, 465–66
bringing others to, 558, 562
of God, 433–34, 437–39
of Jesus Christ, 329
of Nebuchadnezzar, 199, 204–6, 241–42, 245
of saints, 362
River of fire, 353
Roman Catholic Church, 554–55
Rome, 524–25
abomination of, 473–74
and Antiochus IV Epiphanes, 528–29
and desolation of Jerusalem, 475–76
and little horn of Daniel 7, 380–81
as evil king, 536
in dream of statue, 56–57, 136–38, 142, 144–57
in vision of divine man, 144–57, 483, 485
in vision of four beasts, 57, 144–57, 347–48, 373
judgment on, 476
Royal family, 86, 91

Sabbath, 33
Sabbatical year, 459–60
Sacraments, 141. *See also* Baptism; Communion, Holy
Sacrifice
and little horn of Daniel 8, 396–97
reinstitution of, 403, 405
removal of, 151–52, 396, 416, 530–31, 567
Saints. *See also* Church; People of God
and judgment, 362–63
and kingdom of God, 366
and little horn of Daniel 7, 373–76
as stars, 402
as stones, 138
dominion of, 364
identity of, 366–70
of Most High, 363
Salvation. *See also* Forgiveness; Gospel; Grace
acts of, 411
and book of life, 559–60
and divine man, 497
and faith, 246–47
and grace, 425–27, 438
and Jesus Christ, 440
and last days, 571
and Messiah, 465
and Nebuchadnezzar, 252–53
and sovereignty of God, 181
and spiritual warfare, 481–82
and suffering, 101–2
as deliverance, 37
history of, 328–30, 480
of Daniel, 312
of God, 195–96, 565
of Judean youths, 165–66, 187, 197
plan of, 451
Satan. *See also* Demons; Evil spirits; Magicians; Occult
and beasts in Revelation, 342, 348, 354, 372
and little horn of Daniel 7, 372
and Michael, 503
and stars, 402
binding of, 380
judgment on, 476
little season of, 48, 50, 455
power of, 565
spiritual warfare against, 480–81, 505
Satraps, 171
Schechter, Solomon, 13–15
Scofield Reference Bible, 52. *See also* Dispensationalism
Scopas, 524
Scrolls
opening of, 339
sealing of, 557–58, 562–63, 566
Sea
in vision of four beasts, 337, 341–42
nations as, 365
Second coming of Christ. *See* Eschatology; Jesus Christ, return of; Last days
Second temple, 3
Seleucid king/kingdom, 539
and dream of statue, 145
and fourth beast, 377–78
and Ptolemaic kingdom, 479, 485, 520–32
as symbol, 544

Seleucus I Nicator, 345–46, 400, 520–22
Seleucus II, 521–22
Seleucus III, 521, 523
Seleucus IV, 521, 525
Seraphim. *See also* Angel
    flight of, 444
Seven(s), 224–25, 236–37, 404–5, 452–53, 570
Seventh Day Adventists, 406–7
Seventy weeks, 445. *See also* Eschatology
    and Jeremiah's seventy years, 451
    divisions of, 468–76
    interpretation of, 60
    meaning of, 452–65
    purpose of, 465–68
Seventy years, 435, 451, 459, 469–70
Shadrach, Meshach, and Abednego
    accusation of, 179–80, 182–84
    and Daniel, 299
    and fiery furnace, 192
    and First Commandment, 31
    and idolatry, 164
    as possible eunuchs, 90–91
    deliverance of, 165–66, 193, 195–97
    diet of, 93, 96–97, 99–100
    faith of, 30–31, 181, 197–98
    faithfulness of, 93–94, 99–100, 161–65, 176, 185–87
    gifts of, 29
    God of, 190
    in Babylonian captivity, 106
    names of, 89, 92–93
    Nebuchadnezzar's treatment of, 118
    nobility of, 91
    prayer of, 124–26
    promotion of, 143, 199–200
    threatening of, 184–85
    training of, 91–92, 94
    wisdom of, 97–98, 100–101
Shame, 432, 438
Shea, William, on Belteshazzar, 88
Shekel, 281, 285–87
Shinar (land of), 80, 271
Ships from Kittim, 27, 516–17, 528–29
Sign, 212
Silver
    gods of, 223–24, 273
    in dream of statue, 132
    significance of, 134, 136, 150
    vessels of, 267
Simon bar Kozibah, 475
Simony, 553
Sin
    and law, 31, 34–36
    completion of, 445–46, 465
    confession of, 33–34, 36, 104–5, 425–26, 432–33, 436–39
    end of, 475
    forgiveness of, 206, 329
    of Israel, 437–39
    of Nebuchadnezzar, 241–42, 245
    victory over, 481
Sisera, 409
Slander, 179–80
Sleep
    as death, 561
    of Daniel, 409, 413, 491–92
Solomon
    crown of, 490
    prayer of, 437
Son, 261–62
Son of God. *See also* Divine man; Jesus Christ; Son of gods; Son of Man
    and Michael, 495
    as divine man, 498–501
    in Qumran tradition, 73
    versus kings of Persia, 492
Son of God Text (Qumran), 73
Son of gods. *See also* Jesus Christ; Messiah
    in fiery furnace, 189–90, 193–95, 197
    Messiah as, 26
Son of Man. *See also* Jesus Christ; Messiah
    advent of, 38
    and holy ones, 367, 369
    and kingdom of God, 366, 382–84
    and Marduk, 333
    as divine man, 498
    before Ancient of Days, 351–52
    dominion of, 340, 372
    enthronement of, 384
    identity of, 355–59
    Jesus as, 43–45
    Messiah as, 26–27, 328–29
    throne of, 350–51
    title of, 339–40
Son of man, Daniel as, 413
Song of the Three Young Men, 69–70, 220
    and fiery furnace narrative, 192
    and textual tradition, 64

Index of Subjects

Sons of Israel, 86, 91. *See also* Israel; Jews; Judeans

Sons of men, 493

Soothsayers. *See also* Chaldeans; Diviners; Magicians; Occult; Wise men
  and interpretation of dream of tree, 232
  in Babylonian court, 98–99

Sorcerers, 114–15. *See also* Chaldeans; Diviners; Magicians; Occult; Soothsayers; Wise men

Source criticism, 134–35, 147. *See also* Higher criticism

South, king/kingdom of, 520–32, 544–45. *See also* Ptolemaic king/kingdom; Ptolemy I–VII

Sovereignty of God, 18–19, 28–29, 77, 109. *See also* Authority; Dominion
  and Babylonian captivity, 105
  and Daniel's prayer, 125
  and dominion, 331
  and dream of tree, 244–45
  and Gospel, 206
  and history, 328, 480
  and human authorities, 185
  and human kingdoms, 149
  and Nebuchadnezzar, 84–85, 142–43, 203–4, 251–52
  and persecution of Jews, 531–32
  and salvation, 181

Sphinx, 175

Spirit
  in Daniel (*See* Holy Spirit, working in Daniel)
  of antichrist, 420
  of gods, 270

Spiritual warfare, 492–93, 502–4. *See also* Angel; Divine man; Gabriel; Michael; Warfare
  and divine man, 480–82, 505–7

Stars, 402, 557

Statue
  as idol, 170–71, 174–76
  description of, 134–36

Statute, 308–9

Stone
  gods of, 223–24
  in dream of statue, 46, 130–31, 135–36, 138–41, 147–48

Strength, 511

Structure of Daniel, 1, 20–25, 331–32, 427–29

Suffering, 101–2

Susa, 399

Susanna, 67–68, 220
  and textual tradition, 64

Tale of Ahikar, 38–39

Tammuz, 537

Tarshish, 490

Teaching, 433

Tekel. *See* Shekel

Temple. *See also* Jerusalem; Most Holy Place; Sacrifice; Second temple; Vessels of temple
  and worship, 475
  anointing of, 466
  Antichrist in, 552
  daily sacrifice in, 151–52
  dedication of, 437
  defilement of, 416–17
  desecration of, 378–79, 463–64, 530, 540
  desolation of, 549–50
  destruction of, 396–97, 447–48, 469
  function of, 272
  Jesus as, 467–68
  reconstruction of, 398, 403
  rededication of, 405, 467
  sacking of, 528
  worship at, 450

Temple fortress, 517

Ten Commandments. *See* Commandment(s); Law of God

Ten horns of fourth beast, 347–48
  dispensationalism on, 380–81
  explanation of, 373
  higher criticism on, 378

Ten plagues, 212

Text of Daniel, 62–73

Theodoret, on dream of statue, 140

Theodotion (person), 63–67

Theodotion version of Daniel, 63–67

Threat
  of dismemberment, 118
  of fiery furnace, 177–78, 184–85
  of Nebuchadnezzar's advisors, 116

Thrones, in heavenly court, 339, 350–51, 353
Tiamat, 333, 342
Tiglath-pileser III, 544
Tigris, 489, 568
Time, times, and half a time, 152, 363, 375–76, 565, 569–70. *See also* End, time of; Eschatology; Last days
    dispensationalism on, 381
    significance of, 574–76
Titus, 448
Topaz, 490
Torah. *See also* Commandment(s); Law of God
    Daniel on, 437
    fulfillment of, 433, 438–39
Transgression. *See also* Sin
    desolation of, 397–98, 567
    end of, 410, 445, 465
    of Antiochus IV Epiphanes, 403–4
Transgressors, end of, 410, 415
Treasurers in Babylonian Empire, 171
Treasury
    and vessels of the temple, 84
    of temples, 80
Treaty, 515
Tree
    description of, 231, 233–34
    interpretation of, 242–43
Tribulation, 60. *See also* Antichrist; Dispensationalism; Eschatology; Last days; Millennium
Truth, 362, 488, 495, 506, 510
Typology
    and desolation, 476
    and seventy weeks, 455–57

Ulai Canal, 393, 399, 412
Understanding. *See also* Insight; Knowledge; Wisdom
    and Gabriel's ministry, 450–51
    command to acquire, 489
    mystery of, 410–11
    of vision, 394
    seeking of, 412
Unity
    critical theories on, 5–6
Uphaz
    land of, 490

Versification, 208–9
    and vision of divine man, 507
    of Daniel in lions' den, 304

Vessels of temple, 29, 32, 77, 84, 267
    and Belshazzar's feast, 271–72
    Menelaus' theft of, 526
    use of, 257, 272–73
Vision, 393–94
    sealing of, 417, 446, 466
Vision of divine man, 479. *See also* Divine man
    content of, 497–501
    Daniel's reaction to, 501, 504–5
    date of, 482–83, 496–97
    higher criticism of, 483–84
    structure of, 484–86
Vision of four beasts, 57, 341–49. *See also* Babylon, in vision of four beasts; Beasts; Greece, in vision of four beasts; Persia, in vision of four beasts; Rome, in vision of four beasts
    and dream of statue, 327–28
    and eschatology, 349–50
    and kingdom of God, 327–30
    and myth, 332–35
    and structure of Daniel, 331–32
    Daniel's reaction to, 364, 385–86
    explanation of, 364–70
    Son of Man in, 355–59
Vision of heavenly court, and messianic psalms, 359–60
Vision of ram and goat. *See also* Greece, in vision of ram and goat; Persia, in vision of ram and goat
    and dream of statue, 150
    and last days, 409
    Daniel's reaction to, 417
    description of, 398–403
    dispensationalism on, 418–21
    explanation of, 412–17
    historical setting of, 390–91
Vision of ten horns, and dream of statue, 138
Vision of the netherworld, and vision of four beasts, 333
Visions, 129
    and First Commandment, 32
    and narratives, 106–7
    and structure of Daniel, 21
    and unity of Daniel, 5–6
    as *ex eventu*, 28
    as predictive prophecy, 3–4, 12, 18–19
    chronology of, 2
    in prophetic ministry, 41
    interpretations of, 101

Warfare, 511–12. *See also* Spiritual warfare
    between angels and demons, 502–4
    between Seleucids and Ptolemies, 520–32
    in vision of divine man, 488–89
    of evil king, 544–45
    of little horn of Daniel 7, 371–76
    of papacy against saints, 553
Warrior
    God as, 413
    Jesus Christ as, 500, 502–7
    Michael as, 503–4
Watchers. *See also* Angel
    and God, 237–38
    angels as, 231
    in dream of tree, 234
    interpretation of, 244–45
Weeks. *See* Eschatology; Seven(s); Seventy weeks
White, 352–53
Wind
    in dream of statue, 135–36
    of heaven, 150–51, 341
Wine, 39, 267
Wings of leopard, 150–51
Wisdom, 42–43. *See also* Insight; Knowledge; Understanding
    and Daniel's prayer, 439
    and discernment, 87
    and revelation, 125–26, 130
    as gift of God, 109
    of Daniel, 270
    of Judean youths, 97–98, 100–101
Wise men, 115. *See also* Chaldeans; Diviners; Magicians
    and Daniel, 110–11, 133, 287–88
    and dream of tree, 232, 238
    and handwriting on wall, 274–76, 282
    and Nebuchadnezzar, 117–20
    execution of, 116, 123
    of Belshazzar, 269
Wonderful things. *See* Means of grace
Wood
    gods of, 223–24

Word of God. *See also* Gospel; Law and Gospel; Law of God
    and Antichrist, 371–74
    and Moses, 438–39
    and revelation, 488
    as means of grace, 543
    Daniel's study of, 426, 428, 434–35, 451, 497
    power of, 494, 505
    sound of, 491, 504
    study of, 563
Worship
    altering of, 549, 551–52
    and Antichrist, 374
    and Daniel in lions' den, 299–300
    and diet, 99–100
    and idolatry, 162–63, 199
    and temple, 475
    and Third Commandment, 33–34
    call to, 172
    Law of Moses on, 308
    of demons, 502
    of false gods, 174–75
    of God, 125, 321–22, 450
    of idols, 132, 173, 176–78
    of Son of Man, 358
Wrath of God, 414, 434, 437, 440–41. *See also* Judgment

Xerxes, 149, 518–19

Yahweh, 427–28, 432, 435. *See also* God
Yamauchi, Edwin, 11
Young, Ian, 7–8

Zedekiah, 2
    idolatry of, 163
    Nebuchadnezzar's treatment of, 118
    reign of, 167–69
Zerubbabel, 92, 463
Zeus. *See also* Idolatry
    and Antiochus IV Epiphanes, 536
    idol of, 403, 530
Zoroastrianism, 134–35

Index of Passages

Old Testament
Genesis
  1, 236, 404, 453
  1–2, 375, 570
  1:1–2, 342
  1:2, 333
  1:6–8, 557
  1:14–17, 557
  1:28–3:6, 52
  2:14, 489
  2:17, 288
  2:21, 114, 409
  3:1, 415
  3:15, 142, 197
  3:19, 561
  4:1–8:14, 52
  5–11, 71
  6:13, 409
  7:11, 333
  8:2, 333
  8:15–11:32, 52
  9:6, 21
  10:2, 516
  10:4, 516
  10:8–10, 80
  10:10, 80
  11:1–9, 84
  11:2, 80
  11:4, 234
  12:1–3, 53
  12:1–Exodus 18:27, 52
  12:3, 123
  12:7, 53
  12:8, 32
  13:14–17, 53
  14:1, 80
  14:9, 80
  14:20, 190
  15:1, 501
  15:5, 402, 562
  15:6, 31, 197, 206, 562
  15:12, 114, 409
  15:13, 406
  15:18, 489
  16:7–10, 197
  16:11, 197
  17:1–8, 53
  17:12, 236
  18–19, 197, 500, 568
  18:1, 197, 568
  18:2, 197
  18:10–14, 197
  18:13, 568
  18:22–33, 197
  19, 234
  19:1, 568
  19:24, 353
  19:27, 317
  21:22, 396
  21:32, 396
  22:8, 497
  22:17, 402
  22:18, 123
  24:3, 122, 565
  24:7, 122
  24:16, 90
  24:27, 403
  24:50, 469
  24:63, 317
  26:2–5, 53
  26:4, 562
  26:5, 433
  26:7, 90
  26:15, 417
  26:18, 417
  26:24, 501
  27:11, 410
  27:15, 445
  27:23, 410
  28:10–17, 114
  28:11, 317
  28:13–15, 53
  29:27–28, 431, 445
  30:12, 38
  31:51, 339
  32:11 (ET 32:10), 403
  32:24–30 (MT 32:25–31), 194
  32:25 (ET 32:24), 503
  35:9–12, 53
  37:3, 268
  37:5–8, 238
  37:5–11, 101
  37:8, 101
  37:9–10, 238
  37:10, 101
  37:12–36, 37
  37:22, 535
  37:23, 268
  37:31, 394
  37:32, 268
  37:36, 38, 90
  39, 37
  39:1, 38, 90
  39:9, 439
  40, 239
  40:2, 38
  40:5, 38
  40:6, 38, 96
  40:7, 38
  40:8, 38
  40:16, 38
  40:18, 38
  40:22, 38
  40–41, 38
  41, 233, 236, 239
  41:1, 489
  41:1–3, 568
  41:1–7, 114
  41:1–38, 37
  41:2, 97
  41:4, 97
  41:4–5, 114
  41:8, 37–38, 98, 114
  41:11, 38
  41:12–13, 38
  41:15, 38
  41:16, 38
  41:18, 97
  41:24, 37, 98
  41:25, 38
  41:28, 38
  41:38, 38, 233
  41:39–45, 37
  41:45, 92
  41:46, 37
  43:16, 121
  43:23, 505
  43:34, 98
  49:1, 129, 504
  49:10, 335
  49:24, 139
  49:25, 333
  50:20, 38

Exodus
  1:22, 568
  2:3, 568
  2:5, 568
  3:2, 197, 353
  3:4–6, 197
  3:5, 403
  3:13, 541
  3:15–16, 541
  3:19, 440
  4:5, 541
  4:12, 426
  4:15, 426
  6:1, 440
  6:6, 191
  6:7, 542
  7:3, 212
  7:4, 402
  7:11, 37, 98, 115
  7:11–12, 98, 232
  7:22, 37, 98, 232

599

8:3 (ET 8:7), 37, 98, 232
8:14–15 (ET 8:18–19), 37, 98, 232
9:11, 37, 98
12:1–6, 497
12:5, 497
12:23, 234
12:40–41, 406
12:41, 402
13:9, 440
13:20–21, 195
13:21–22, 353, 481
14:7, 269
14:13–14, 426
14:19, 195
14:19–31, 481
14:24, 195
15:5, 333
15:8, 333
15:11, 411, 541
15:19, 116
15:26, 438
16:28, 433
18:10, 191
18:16, 433
18:20, 433
19:3–Acts 1:26, 52
19:5, 438
19:6, 369, 566
19:18, 353
20:2, 299
20:3, 299
20:3–6, 31
20:4–5, 163
20:6, 437
20:7, 32
20:8–11, 33, 299, 375, 570
20:12, 34
20:18, 490–91
22:2 (ET 22:3), 447
22:7 (ET 22:8), 535
22:10 (ET 22:11), 535
22:17 (ET 22:18), 115
23:10–12, 570
23:11, 245
23:11–12, 375
23:14–17, 497
23:23, 481
23:26, 431
25:18–20, 444
26:33–34, 466
28:42, 489
29:7, 473
29:20, 490
29:37, 466
29:38–42, 396
29:45–46, 119

29:46, 542
30:7–8, 317
30:10, 466
30:23–32, 467
30:29, 466
30:30, 473
30:36, 466
31:2–5, 207
32:11, 433, 440
32:13, 562
32:32, 37
32:32–33, 350, 559
32:34, 481, 503
33:2, 503
33:9–10, 195
34:6, 403
34:6–7, 436
34:22, 445
34:24, 497
35:31, 101
36:20 (ET 39:13), 490
39:13, 490
39:28, 489
40:10, 466–67
40:13, 473
40:15, 473
40:35, 119

Leviticus
2:3, 466
2:10, 466
4:23, 394
6:3 (ET 6:10), 489, 501
6:10 (ET 6:17), 466
6:18 (ET 6:25), 466
6:22 (ET 6:29), 466
7:1, 466
7:6, 466
7:36, 473
8:12, 473
9:5, 176
10:2, 353
10:12, 466
10:17, 466
11, 99
11:45, 366
12:3, 236
12:5, 445
14:13, 466
15:3, 446
16:4, 489
16:23, 489
16:29, 502
16:31, 502
16:32, 473, 489, 501
19:12, 565
19:26, 221
20:8, 366
21:8, 366
21:22, 466

21:23, 366
22:9, 366
22:16, 366
22:32, 366
23:27, 502
23:32, 502
24:9, 466
25:3–4, 375, 570
25:8, 459
26, 439, 459
26:14–39, 439
26:27–35, 459
26:31, 431
26:33, 431, 438
26:34–35, 459
26:40–45, 439
26:46, 433
27:28, 466

Numbers
3:3, 473
4:4, 466
4:19, 466
6:24–26, 441
6:25, 436, 441
6:27, 92, 441
7:10–11, 171
7:16, 394
11:25–29, 207
12:1–15, 433
12:5, 195
12:6, 41
12:8, 411
12:11, 433
14:14, 195
14:34, 407
16:27–33, 323
18:9, 466
18:9–10, 466
22:23–31, 321
23:3–8, 396
23:19, 192, 356
24, 529
24:4, 41
24:14, 26, 129, 376, 504, 570
24:16, 41
24:17, 27, 475, 529
24:23, 529
24:24, 27, 516, 529
27:18, 207
28:10, 397
28:26, 445
34:6–7, 341
35:25, 473

Deuteronomy
1:7, 489
1:10, 562
1:11, 541
1:21, 541

Index of Passages

1:43, 280
3:11, 171
4:1, 541
4:28, 284
4:30, 129, 438
4:34, 212, 440
4:35, 542
4:39, 542
5:6, 299
5:7, 299
5:7–10, 31
5:8–9, 163
5:11, 32
5:12–15, 33, 299
5:15, 440
5:16, 34
5:26, 320
6:3, 541
6:13, 32
6:21, 440
6:22, 212
7:6, 370
7:8, 440
7:9, 542
7:9–12, 436
7:19, 440
8:7, 333
9:5, 433
9:26, 440
10:17, 132, 533
10:20, 32
12:1, 541
12:2, 230
12:5, 93
12:21, 93
13:2–4 (ET 13:1–3), 212
14:2, 370
14:21, 370
14:24, 93
15:11, 245
16:9, 445
16:10, 445
16:16, 445, 497
17:6, 568
18:10, 115
18:10–14, 221
18:20, 280
18:20–22, 18, 137, 147
18:21–22, 41, 452
19:15, 568
19:16–21, 322
21:13, 489
24:16, 322
26:7, 541
26:8, 440
26:19, 370
27:3, 541
27–28, 439

28:9, 370
28:15–68, 410, 439
28:36–37, 438
28:50, 410
28:63, 542
29:24 (ET 29:25), 541
30:1, 438
30:1–5, 426
30:1–10, 439
30:11, 411
31:6, 505
31:7, 494, 505
31:10, 14
31:16–29, 439
31:23, 494
31:29, 129, 504
31:32, 505
32:4, 139
32:7, 362
32:15, 139
32:15–35, 439
32:18, 139
32:30–31, 139
32:36, 186, 439
32:40, 569
32:40–43, 569
33:3, 368
33:11, 268
33:13, 333
33:17, 348, 394
34:5, 438

Joshua
1:1, 438
1:4, 341, 489
1:6–7, 494, 505
1:9, 494, 505
1:13, 438
1:15, 438
1:18, 494, 505
2:11, 95
3:10, 320
4:22, 116
5:13–15, 195, 481
5:14, 503
5:14–15, 402
6:10, 469
6:19, 80
6:24, 80
7:21, 80
7:24–25, 323
8:31, 438–39
8:33, 438
9:1, 341
9:4–5, 363
10:25, 505
11:12, 438
12:6, 438
13:8, 438
13:22, 221

14:7, 96, 438
14–21, 568
15:1, 568
16:1, 568
17:1, 568
18:3, 541
18:7, 438
22:2, 438
22:4–5, 438
22:22, 533
23:4, 341

Judges
2:1, 197
2:12, 541
3:10, 207
3:19, 115
4:2, 396
4:7, 396, 491
4:21, 409
5:12, 494
5:18–20, 503
6:11–12, 197, 505
6:14, 197
6:21–22, 505
6:23, 494, 501, 505
6:34, 207
7, 114
8:15, 444
8:31, 93
9:8, 473
9:15, 473
10:14, 559
11:29, 207
13:3, 197
13:6, 409
13:13–21, 197
13:22, 197
14:12–19, 411
14:14, 271
16:3, 114

Ruth
1:8, 436
2:20, 436
3:8–13, 114
3:10, 436

1 Samuel
2:2, 139
2:7, 280
2:9, 238
3:15, 41
4:4, 353
4:14, 491
4:19, 493
6:9, 439
9:2, 171
9:16, 473
9:20, 542
10:1, 473

10:12, 261
12:19, 397
12:24, 394
13:13, 46
13:14, 473
15:1, 473
15:17, 473
15:29, 192
16:3, 473
16:12–13, 473
17:26, 320
17:34–35, 335
17:34–37, 343
17:36, 320
17:55, 115
22:18, 489, 501
24:7 (ET 24:6), 535
24:11 (ET 24:10), 535
25:26, 242
25:30, 473
25:37, 288
26:9, 535
26:11, 535
26:12, 114, 409
26:23, 535
27:8, 362
28:8–25, 114

2 Samuel
2:4, 473
2:7, 473
3:39, 473
5:2, 473
5:3, 473
5:17, 473
6:2, 353
6:21, 473
7:3, 96
7:8, 473
7:12–16, 335
7:13, 46
7:16, 46
7:17, 41
7:29, 335
11:2, 90
12:7, 473
12:16, 317
12:20, 497
13:16, 439
13:18–19, 268
13:23, 489
14:2, 497
14:28, 489
15:25, 119
16:2, 444
16:7, 494
18:32, 242
19:11 (ET 19:10), 473
19:44 (ET 19:43), 98
20:16, 494

22:3, 139
22:12, 328–29, 358
22:29, 239
22:32, 139
22:33, 543
22:47, 139
23:3, 139
24:16, 234

1 Kings
1:34, 473
1:35, 473
1:39, 473
1:45, 473
2:3, 439
3:3–15, 126
3:5, 114
3:25–26, 130
5:15 (ET 5:1), 473
6:16, 466
6:23–28, 444
7:50, 466
8:6, 466
8:10–13, 119
8:15, 431
8:17, 96
8:23, 436
8:24, 431
8:27, 119
8:27–53, 316
8:28, 441
8:28–29, 15
8:30, 442
8:34, 442
8:36, 426, 442
8:39, 119, 397, 442
8:43, 119, 397
8:47, 437
8:49, 119, 397
8:54, 317
9:3, 93, 316, 437
9:5, 46
9:22, 269
10:11, 411
11:36, 93
12:10, 268
13:6, 433
14:7, 473
14:21, 93
14:23, 230
16:2, 473
18:21, 162
18:22, 503
19:5–7, 321
19:10, 503
19:14, 503
19:15, 473
19:16, 473
20:13, 491
20:28, 491

20:35, 261
20:43, 96
21:4, 96
21:8, 446
21:17–29, 41
22, 118
22:11, 348
22:19, 350, 353
22:19–22, 350
22:19–23, 237

2 Kings
1:10–14, 353
2:3, 261
2:5, 261
2:7, 261
2:12, 261
2:15, 261
3:19, 417
3:25, 417
4:1, 261
4:38, 261
5:1, 396
5:16, 176
5:22, 261
6:1, 261
6:14–17, 481
6:15–17, 501
7:2, 269
7:17, 269
7:19, 269
9:1, 261
9:3, 473
9:6, 473
9:12, 473
9:25, 269
10:1–17, 261
10:25, 269
11:12, 473
13:4, 433
13:23, 438
14:6, 322, 439
14:9–10, 233
15:13, 489
15:25, 269
17:1–23, 104
17:12, 104
17:17, 221
17:18–20, 104
17:34, 93
18:12, 438
18:17, 90
18:26, 115
19:4, 320
19:15, 353
19:16, 320, 441
20:5, 473
21:4, 93
21:7, 93
21:22, 541

23:21, 439
23:30, 473
24:1, 83–84
24:1–6, 84
24:10–12, 84
24:11, 79
24:15–16, 85
24:17, 84
25:7, 118
25:8, 121
25:10–12, 121
25:11, 85
25:15, 121
25:18, 121
25:20, 121
25:22, 79
25:27–30, 259

1 Chronicles
1:7, 516
3:1, 88
5:25, 541–42
5:26, 293
6:1 (ET 6:16), 72
6:34 (ET 6:49), 438, 466
9:11, 473
9:20, 473
11:2, 473
11:3, 473
11:10, 495
12:18 (ET 12:17), 541–42
12:28 (ET 12:27), 473
14:8, 473
16:12, 541
17:7, 473
17:14, 46
17:15, 41
21:27, 362
22:10, 46
22:13, 494
23:13, 466–67
23:25, 119
28:4, 473
28:7, 46
28:20, 494
29:11, 125, 131
29:20, 541
29:22, 473
36:17–20, 436

2 Chronicles
1:3, 438
1:10–12, 100
3:8, 466
3:10, 466
4:22, 466
5:7, 466
6:4, 431
6:5, 473
6:13, 317
6:14, 436
6:15, 431
6:19–20, 15
6:20, 93
6:30, 119
6:33, 119
6:39, 119
7:12, 316
7:15, 316
7:22, 541
8:9, 269
8:13, 445
9:1, 411
9:29, 41
11:16, 541
11:22, 473
12:13, 93
13:5, 46
13:12, 541
14:3 (ET 14:4), 541
15:12, 541
16:9, 495, 563
16:10, 96
19:4, 541
19:11, 474
20:6, 541
20:17, 512
20:25, 445
20:33, 541–42
21:10, 541
22:7, 473
23:11, 473
23:18, 439
24:6, 438
24:9, 438
24:18, 541
24:24, 541
25:4, 439
26:19, 96
28:6, 54`1
28:9, 96, 541
28:25, 541
29:5, 541
29:21, 394
30:5, 439
30:7, 541
30:9, 438
30:18, 439
30:19, 541
30:22, 541
31:3, 439
31:12, 474
31:13, 473
31:14, 466
32:3–4, 417
32:18, 535
32:21, 432
32:30, 417
32:32, 41
33:6, 115
33:7, 93
33:11–13, 84
33:12, 433, 541
34:32–33, 541
35:12, 439
35:21, 535
35:26, 439
36:2, 431, 435
36:5–7, 436
36:5–8, 84
36:6, 83
36:6–7, 79, 84
36:9, 84
36:9–10, 436
36:10, 79, 84, 542
36:13, 79
36:15, 119, 541
36:15–16, 436
36:15–21, 435
36:17, 436
36:18–21, 459
36:20, 85
36:21, 436
36:22–23, 277, 289–90, 295, 300, 460, 469, 483
36:23, 122

Ezra, 7, 210, 467
1–3, 295
1–6, 504
1–7, 461–62, 470
1:1–2, 290, 483
1:1–4, 460, 469
1:1–5, 470
1:1–11, 277, 289, 295, 300
1:2, 122
1:7–8, 290
1:7–11, 277
1:8, 483
2:62, 96
2:63, 466
3:2, 439
3:4, 439
3:7, 290, 483
3:8, 3, 482
3:8–6:15, 300
4:3, 290, 483
4:4, 535
4:5, 290, 483
4:7, 115
4:12, 461
4:12–13, 181
4:15, 362
4:19, 362
4:22, 191, 307
4:24, 3

5:8, 181
5:11–12, 122
5:13–14, 290
5:14–15, 267
5:17, 290
6:1–5, 469–70
6:3, 290
6:4, 269
6:5, 267
6:6–12, 470
6:9, 191, 307
6:9–10, 122
6:10, 309
6:14, 290
6:17, 394
7:11–26, 462
7:12, 122
7:12–26, 470
7:15, 119
7:17, 182
7:19, 267
7:21, 122
7:23, 122
7:27, 541
8:2, 88
8:21, 502
8:27, 445
8:28, 541
8:35, 394
9:5, 317
9:7, 432
10:11, 541

Nehemiah, 7, 210
1:3, 439, 461
1:4–5, 122
1:5, 436–37
1:5–11, 429
1:6, 15–16
2:1–9, 470
2:3, 461
2:4, 122
2:4–6, 460
2:8, 461
2:10, 439
2:13, 461
2:15, 461
2:17, 461
2:20, 122
4:1 (ET 4:7), 417
6:19, 469
7:64, 96
7:65, 466
7:69 (ET 7:70), 79
8:6, 317
8:15, 439
9, 437
9:7, 93
9:10, 280
9:13, 433

9:16, 280
9:26–37, 70
9:27, 559
9:29, 280
9:32, 436–37
10:1–2 (ET 9:38–10:1), 446
10:7 (ET 10:6), 88
10:30 (ET 10:29), 438
10:35 (ET 10:34), 439
10:37 (ET 10:36), 439
11:11, 473
13:21, 535
13:27, 439

Esther, 7
1, 39
1:1, 313
1:3, 86, 149
1:11, 90
1:14, 149
1:17, 469
1:18–19, 149
1:19, 39, 149, 316, 469
1:20, 181
2:2–3, 90
2:6, 79
2:7, 90
2:9, 535
2:19, 39, 132
2:21, 39, 132, 535
3, 39
3:2–3, 39
3:6, 535
3:12, 446
3:15, 469
4:2, 39
4:3, 436
4:6, 39
4:14, 40
5:9, 39
5:9–7:10, 39
5:13, 39
6:2, 535
6:7–11, 39
6:9, 86
6:10, 39
6:12, 39
7:8, 469
7:10, 322
8:7, 535
8:8, 316, 446
8:9, 313
8:10, 446
9:2, 535
9:22, 245
9:29, 308
9:30, 313
10:2, 149

Job
1–2, 237
1:6, 237, 350
1:6–2:7, 481
1:6–12, 350
1:7, 563
1:21, 123
2:1, 350
2:1–6, 350
2:2, 563
4:13, 114, 409
5:1, 367
6:2, 412
6:19, 218
7:1, 488
7:21, 561
11:19, 433
12:18, 42
13:25, 135
14:7, 235, 238
14:12, 561
14:14, 488
14:17, 446
15:15, 367
16:21, 356
21:18, 135
21:26, 561
22:10, 535
22:14, 329, 358
22:15, 362
24:16, 446
25:6, 356
28:14, 333
28:16, 490
31:7, 87
33:15, 114, 409
34:15, 561
35:8, 356
36:30, 491
36:32, 491
37:5, 411
37:7, 446
38:6, 339
38:7, 503
38:8, 337
38:16, 333
38:25, 448
38:30, 333
39:2, 431
40:16, 268
40:23, 337
41:24 (ET 41:32), 333
42:3, 411

Psalms
1:3, 233
1:4, 135
2, 335, 359
2:1–3, 360
2:4–9, 360

2:5, 535
2:7, 139
2:10–12, 360
2:12, 360
4:3 (ET 4:2), 340
7:2 (ET 7:1), 432
7:4 (ET 7:3), 432
7:15–17 (ET 7:14–16), 322
8:5 (ET 8:4), 340, 356–57
9:8 (ET 9:7), 353
9:12 (ET 9:11), 353
11:4, 353
12:5 (ET 12:4), 448
13:4 (ET 13:3), 432, 556, 561
14:1–3, 438
16:3, 368
17:15, 556
18:3 (ET 18:2), 139, 348
18:9 (ET 18:8), 353
18:12 (ET 18:11), 329, 358
18:13–14 (ET 18:12–13), 353
18:29 (ET 18:28), 239
18:32 (ET 18:31), 139
18:47 (ET 18:46), 139
19:2 (ET 19:1), 557
19:15 (ET 19:14), 139
20:5–6 (ET 20:4–5), 431
21:4 (ET 21:3), 561
21:10 (ET 21:9), 353
22:2 (ET 22:1), 503
22:7 (ET 22:6), 441
22:16 (ET 22:15), 561
22:17 (ET 22:16), 130, 446
25:3, 273
25:6, 438
25:10, 436
26:1, 186
27:1, 543
27:11, 426
28:1, 139
28:2, 317
28:8, 543
28:9, 561
30:1 (ET superscription), 172
30:3 (ET 30:2), 432
30:13 (ET 30:12), 432
31:3 (ET 31:2), 139, 543
31:5 (ET 31:4), 543
31:17 (ET 31:16), 441

33:7, 333
33:20, 576
34:10 (ET 34:9), 368
35:5, 135
35:13, 502
35:26, 394
36:5 (ET 36:4), 114
36:7 (ET 36:6), 333
37:18, 561
37:27–28, 561
37:35–36, 233
37:39, 543, 559
38:16 (ET 38:15), 431
40:6 (ET 40:5), 540
40:18 (ET 40:17), 531
41:2 (ET 41:1), 245
41:13 (ET 41:12), 561
42:8 (ET 42:7), 333
43:1, 186
43:2, 543
44:16 (ET 44:15), 432
45, 550
45:8 (ET 45:7), 497
45:7 (ET 45:6), 46
45:10 (ET 45:9), 490
46:2 (ET 46:1), 531
49:3 (ET 49:2), 340
49:5 (ET 49:4), 411
50:1, 132, 533
50:3, 353
50:15, 247
51:8 (ET 51:6), 417
52:10 (ET 52:8), 230, 233
53:2–4 (ET 53:1–3), 438
55:13 (ET 55:12), 394
55:18 (ET 55:17), 316
55:21 (ET 55:20), 535
56:9 (ET 56:8), 350
62:3 (ET 62:2), 139
62:7–8 (ET 62:6–7), 139
62:10 (ET 62:9), 340
63:5 (ET 63:4), 317
63:7 (ET 63:6), 114
66:20, 190
67:2 (ET 67:1), 441
68:17 (ET 68:16), 119
68:19 (ET 68:18), 119
68:36 (ET 68:35), 190
69:7 (ET 69:8), 441
69:24 (ET 69:23), 268
69:29 (ET 69:28), 350, 559
70:6 (ET 70:5), 531
71:3, 139
71:20, 333
72:14, 501

72:18, 540
75:8 (ET 75:7), 280
75:11 (ET 75:10), 348
76:3 (ET 76:2), 119
76:6 (ET 76:5), 561
76:13 (ET 76:12), 473
77:5 (ET 77:4), 114
77:7 (ET 77:6), 114
77:17 (ET 77:16), 333
78:2, 411
78:15, 333
78:21, 353
78:35, 139
78:43, 212
79:9, 441
80:2 (ET 80:1), 353
80:4 (ET 80:3), 441
80:8 (ET 80:7), 441
80:18 (ET 80:17), 340, 356–57
80:20 (ET 80:19), 441
82:1, 237
83:14 (ET 83:13), 135
83:16 (ET 83:15), 535
84:2 (ET 84:1), 119
86:10, 540
86:11, 426
86:12, 431
89:6 (ET 89:5), 367
89:8 (ET 89:7), 367
89:27 (ET 89:26), 139
89:29 (ET 89:28), 436
89:47 (ET 89:46), 353
90:5, 561
90:17, 431
92:13–16 (ET 92:12–15), 233
92:15 (ET 92:14), 230
92:16 (ET 92:15), 139
94:22, 139
95:1, 139
97:2, 328, 358
97:3, 353
98:1, 540
98:8, 54
99:1, 353
103, 70
103:19, 353
104:3, 328, 358
104:6, 333
104:29, 561
105:45, 433
106:9, 333
106:45, 436
107:26, 333
110, 335, 351, 359, 474
110:1, 350–51
110:1–3, 360
110:4, 360

110:5–6, 360
112:4, 239
113:2, 123
115:1, 441
115:4–7, 284
116:15, 501
118:22, 139–40, 571
118:22–23, 46
118:26, 474
119:22, 441
119:33, 426
119:35, 441
119:55, 114
119:58, 433
119:62, 114
119:102, 426
119:148, 114
119:164, 316
121:1–2, 531
122:7, 411
126:2–3, 394
131:1, 411
132:7, 119
132:13, 119
132:17, 348
133:13, 561
134:2, 317
135:6, 333
135:15–17, 284
136:2, 132, 533
136:4, 540
137, 104–5
137:7, 494
139:14, 411
139:16, 350
141:2, 317
144:1, 139
144:6, 491
145:11–12, 131
145:13, 46, 213–14
146:5, 531
148, 70
148:7, 333
150:1, 557

Proverbs
1:1–7, 101
1:6, 411
2:2, 95
2:5, 101
3:20, 333
4:4, 426
4:11, 426
4:19, 238
6:1–19, 484
6:16–19, 519
8:6, 474
8:24, 333
8:27 28, 333
9:2, 121

9:10, 368
10:25, 561
10:29, 543
10:30, 561
11:3–11, 484
14:21, 245
14:35, 42
16:12–15, 42
19:3, 96
19:5, 322
19:6, 433
19:9, 322
19:11, 101, 562
19:12, 42, 96
19:15, 114
19:17, 245
20:2, 42
20:28, 42
21:1, 42
21:28, 322
22:11, 42
22:28, 362
22:29, 42
23:5, 444
23:10, 362
24:16, 192
26:16, 192
28:15, 335, 343
30, 519
30:3, 368
30:15, 494, 519
30:15–16, 519
30:18, 519
30:18–19, 519
30:21, 519
30:21–23, 519
30:29, 519
30:29–31, 519

Ecclesiastes
2:1, 156
2:11, 156
2:15, 156
2:17, 156
2:19, 156
2:20, 95
2:21, 156
2:23, 156
2:26, 156
5:1, 469, 535
7:9, 535
7:12, 101
8:1, 38
8:1–4, 42
9:8, 497
10:20, 100

Song of Songs, 550
3:1–5, 114
4:12, 446
5:2–8, 114

5:11, 490
5:14, 490
5:14–15, 491
7:1 (ET 6:13), 494

Isaiah
1:1, 41, 129, 446
1:18, 352
2:2, 26, 129, 376, 504, 570
2:2–3, 560
2:2–5, 142
2:3, 426, 469
2:12–13, 243
4:2, 514
4:3, 559
6, 350, 365
6:1–7, 350
6:2, 444
6:5, 413
6:6–7, 505
6:7, 414
6:8, 505
6:13, 235, 238
7:12, 41
8:8, 475
8:11, 17, 505
8:11–15, 139
8:14, 46
8:14–15, 139–40
8:16, 446
8:17, 576
8:18, 212
9:5 (ET 9:6), 411
9:5–6 (ET 9:6–7), 335, 403
9:6 (ET 9:7), 46
10:23, 448, 534
10:33–34, 243
11, 48, 330
11:1, 235, 238
11:10, 495
11:11, 80
11:11–16, 426
12:4, 32
13:4, 491
13:12, 490
13:17, 291, 295
17:10, 139, 543
17:12, 342
17:13, 135
19:1, 328, 358
20:3, 212
21:2, 41, 291, 295
21:14, 218
22:1, 41
22:5, 41
23:1, 516
23:12, 516
24:5, 433

24:7, 95
24:21, 503
25:4–5, 543
26:4, 139
26:19, 556, 561
28:16, 46, 139–40
28:16–17, 139
28:22, 448, 534
29:5, 135, 491
29:10, 114
29:11, 446
30:3, 96
30:25, 393
30:29, 139
33:2, 559
33:3, 491
33:21, 516
36:11, 115
37:4, 320
37:17, 320, 441
37:19, 273
38:16, 226
39:7, 85, 91
40:1, 494
40:2, 397, 488
40:18–20, 273
40:19–20, 187
40:24, 135
40:28, 444
40:29, 444
40:31–32, 444
41:2, 135
41:15–16, 135
42:6, 53, 495
44:4, 393
44:8, 139
44:8–20, 187
44:9–20, 273
44:12, 444
44:15, 173
44:17, 173
44:19, 173
44:24–28, 471
44:24–45:8, 288
44:26, 431
44:28, 289–90, 295, 425, 469
45:1, 290, 295, 495
45:1–6, 289
45:4, 289
45:13, 469
46:6, 173
49:6, 53
49:8, 448
49:19, 448
50:4, 444
50:10, 239
51:1–2, 138
51:9, 362, 494

51:10, 333
51:12, 356
51:17, 494
52:1, 494
52:9, 431
52:11, 494
52:13–53:12, 449, 560
52:14, 449, 491
52:14–15, 560
52:15, 449, 556, 560
53, 53
53:1, 440
53:3, 473, 571
53:7, 497
53:8, 130, 446
53:11, 449, 558, 562
53:11–12, 556, 560
53:12, 449
54:10, 436
55:1–3, 206
55:3, 436
55:10–11, 494, 505
55:11, 469
55:12, 54
56:2, 356
56:4–5, 91
57:14, 494
57:19, 494
57:20, 342
58:5, 436
58:12, 362
59:3, 96
60:2–3, 239
61:1, 501
61:3, 497
61:4, 362, 448
61:10, 352
62:10, 494
62:12, 566
63:3, 96
63:9, 362
63:11, 362
63:13, 333
64:3 (ET 64:4), 576
65:17–25, 48, 330
65:20, 431
66:1, 353
66:6, 491
66:19, 410
66:24, 557, 561

Jeremiah
1, 365
1:4–10, 505
1:9, 414, 505
1:11–19, 41
1:12, 440
1:18, 437
2:10, 516
2:24, 444

3:1–4:31, 104
4:4, 438
4:7, 335, 342
4:11–12, 135
4:13, 335, 342
5:1, 563
5:6, 440
5:24, 445
6:5, 114
6:16, 362
6:23, 342
7:10, 176
7:19, 432, 438
7:25, 437
9:2, 104
10:9, 490
10:10, 320
11:2, 438
11:9, 438
13:24, 135
14:7, 441
14:8, 559
14:14, 41, 221
14:21, 441
15:11, 559
15:19, 247
16:10, 439
16:14–15, 426
16:15, 438
16:19, 543
17:8, 393
17:25, 438
18:11, 438
18:15, 362
20:1, 473
21:2, 79
23:3, 438
23:6, 562
23:8, 438
23:9–32, 137
23:16, 41
23:20, 129, 504
23:36, 320
23:40, 440
24, 163
24:1–10, 41
24:9, 440
*25:1, 4, 12, 80, 435
25:3–4, 438
25:4, 437
25:11–12, 257, 288, 295, 406, 426, 435, 469–70, 570
25:12, 435
25:13, 469
25:19–26, 435
25:23, 218
26:4–5, 438
26:5, 437

26:19, 433, 439
27, 168–69
27:1–22, 168
27:6, 79
27:8, 79
27:20, 79
28, 168–69
28:1, 168
28:1–17, 41
28:3, 79, 489
28:8, 362
28:11, 489
28:17, 169
29:1, 79, 469
29:1–2, 435
29:3, 79
29:8, 226
29:10, 257, 288, 406, 426, 435, 469–70, 570
29:14, 469
29:18, 440
29:19, 437–38
29:22, 118, 178
30:1–31:40, 469
30:3, 469
30:7, 559
30:18, 463
30:24, 129, 504
30–31, 463, 469
31:28, 440
31:31–34, 474
31:34, 475
31:38–39, 463
32:10–11, 446
32:14, 446
32:20–21, 212, 440
32:23, 433, 438
32:32, 438
32:37, 438
32:42, 439
32:44, 446
33:16, 562
35:13, 438
35:15, 437–38
35:17, 439
36:7, 442
36:9–26, 84
36:31, 439
37:20, 442
38:26, 442
39:3, 90, 259
39:9–11, 121
39:13, 90, 121, 259
40:1–2, 121
40:5, 121
41:10, 121
42:2, 442
42:9, 442

43:6, 121
44:4, 437
44:4–5, 438
44:7, 439
44:17, 438, 469
44:21, 437
44:27, 440
48:26, 394
48:40, 335, 342, 475
48:47, 26, 129, 376, 504, 570
49:18, 356
49:19, 335, 342
49:20, 218
49:22, 335, 342, 475
49:33, 356
49:36, 335, 341
49:39, 26, 129, 376, 504, 570
50:8, 400
50:17, 335, 342
50:29, 280
50:40, 356
50:44, 335, 342
51:2, 135
51:11, 5, 257, 291, 295
51:28, 5, 257, 291, 295
51:39, 561
51:43, 356
51:51, 440
51:57, 561
51:58, 444
51:59–64, 84, 163, 167, 169
51:64, 444
52:12, 121
52:14–16, 121
52:19, 121
52:24, 121
52:26, 121
52:29, 167
52:30, 121

Lamentations
1:4, 448
2:1–22, 104
2:19, 317
3:10, 343
3:33, 340
3:40, 104
3:41, 317
4:14, 96
4:15, 494
4:18, 409
4:19, 335, 342–43
5:18, 448

Ezekiel
1, 498–99
1:1, 41, 114
1:4, 328, 358, 499

1:4–28, 499
1:13, 499
1:13–14, 491
1:15–21, 353
1:16, 490
1:22–23, 557
1:24, 491, 499
1–24, 104, 272
1:25–26, 557
1:26, 340
1:26–27, 499
1:26–28, 339
1:27, 499, 557
1:28, 364, 413
2:1, 340
2:1–2, 505
2:1–3, 414
2:3, 340
2:6, 340
2:8, 340
3:1, 494
3:1–3, 505
3:14–15, 364
3:18–19, 288
3:23, 413
3:25–26, 364
4:6, 407
6:53–63, 105
7:2–3, 409
7:6, 409
7:13, 41
7:20, 514
7:26, 41
8:2, 557
8:3, 41, 114
8:4, 41
8:14, 537
9–10, 564
9:1–8, 234
9:2–3, 489, 497
9:11, 489, 497
10:1, 557
10:2, 489, 497
10:5, 491
10:6–7, 489, 497
10:7, 499
10:9, 490
11:16, 301, 467
11:24, 41
12:22, 41
12:23, 41
12:24, 41, 221
12:27, 41, 412
13:6–7, 221
13:7, 41
13:16, 41
13:23, 221
14:14, 88, 104
14:20, 88, 104

14:22–23, 105
17, 238, 491
17:1–4, 233
17:2, 411
17:3, 335, 342, 475
17:7, 475
18, 322
18:21, 246
18:22, 246
20:6, 401, 514
20:15, 401, 514
21:15 (ET 21:10), 121
21:26 (ET 21:21), 119
21:30 (ET 21:25), 409
21:34 (ET 21:29), 409
23:15, 269
23:23, 269
25–32, 272
26:7, 79
26:19, 333
27:6, 516
28:2, 315, 473
28:3, 88, 104, 417
28:9, 315
28:13, 490
30:9, 516
31, 234–35, 238, 243
31:1, 234
31:4, 333
31:15, 333
33:11, 494
33:28, 448
33:30, 469
33:48, 272
34:11–16, 288
34:21, 394
34:23–24, 272
35:5, 409
35:12, 448
36:4, 448
37:1–14, 41
37:9, 335, 341
37:23, 17
37:24–25, 272
38:6, 376
38:8, 26, 376
38:16, 26, 129, 376, 570
38–39, 573–74
39:9, 574
39:9–16, 573
39:12, 574
39:14, 574
39:21–24, 105
40–48, 330, 365, 573–74
40:1–48:35, 41
40:2, 41
40:3, 365, 409
40:5, 171
41:4, 466
42:13, 466
43:4, 41
43:11, 433
43:12, 466
44:3, 272
44:4, 413
44:5, 433
44:13, 466
44:15, 17
44:24, 433
45:3, 466
45:7, 272
45:16, 272
45:21, 445
47:10, 341
47:15, 341
47:19–20, 341
48:12, 466
48:28, 341

Daniel
1, 3, 28, 32, 34, 64, 77, 80, 109–12, 161–62, 165, 183, 203, 220, 233, 272, 300, 331–32
1–2, 183, 314
1–3, 162
1–4, 253
1–5, 300–301, 331
1–6, 1, 5–6, 20, 37, 58, 105–6, 227, 319, 324, 331–32
1–7, 24
1:1, 20–21, 79–84, 237, 288
1:1–2, 4, 12, 28, 77, 79–86, 112, 185–86, 257, 277, 283, 300, 436
1:1–2:4, 5, 21, 63, 331, 390
1:1–3, 349
1:1–6:29 (ET 1:1–6:28), 21
1:1–7, 37
1:1–7:28, 23
1:1–21, 22–23
1:2, 18, 23, 29, 79–80, 83–85, 101, 105, 125, 136, 227, 262, 267, 271–72, 295
1:2–3, 85, 163
1:2–4, 410
1:2–7, 77, 282
1:3, 38, 65, 85–87, 89–91, 112, 339, 341
1:3–4, 93
1:3–7, 38, 86–94, 112
1:4, 23, 30, 37, 87, 90–91, 97, 100–101, 106, 439, 517, 531, 562, 567
1:4–5, 100
1:5, 79, 87–88, 111–12, 237, 288
1:6, 88, 91
1:6–7, 88, 164
1:7, 88–89, 92–93, 129, 164, 166, 183, 269, 293, 410, 496
1:7–11, 38, 86, 89, 492
1:8, 87, 93, 95–96
1:8–14, 99–100
1:8–15, 30
1:8–17, 112
1:8–21, 95–103
1:9, 28, 96, 101, 105, 227
1:10, 38, 96
1:10–17, 62
1:11, 88, 96, 100, 164
1:12, 96–97
1:13, 87, 96–97
1:14, 96
1:15, 79, 87, 97, 105
1:15–16, 96
1:15–17, 100–102
1:16, 87, 96–97
1:16–20, 62
1:17, 28, 30, 37, 41, 97, 100–101, 105, 129, 227, 439, 446, 450, 562, 566–67, 577
1:18, 38, 79, 86, 89, 110–11, 492
1:18–19, 111–12
1:18–21, 102–3
1:19, 87–88, 97–98, 110, 164
1:19–20, 482
1:19–21, 106
1:20, 30, 37, 57–58, 98–99, 102, 106, 110–11, 114, 192, 227, 347, 373, 382, 450, 577
1:21, 3, 103, 237, 288, 290, 295, 488, 496
1:22, 473
2, 12, 23, 26, 28–30, 32, 34, 36–37, 40–41, 55–57, 60, 77, 80, 99, 101, 106, 109, 112, 134–35, 137–38, 143–44,

146–48, 150, 153, 155–56, 161–62, 165, 174, 183, 203, 206–7, 211, 213, 224–25, 230–33, 243, 251–52, 258, 270, 272, 276, 287, 289, 327–29, 331, 355, 371, 376, 381–83, 389, 391, 400–401, 414, 418, 435, 458, 476, 480, 502, 506
2–3, 498
2–5, 225, 228
2–6, 77, 222, 331
2–7, 331–32
2:1, 20–21, 38, 80, 111, 113–14, 117, 231, 237, 288
2:1–3, 117, 124
2:1–7:28, 23
2:1–11, 110, 257
2:1–13, 113–20, 123
2:1–49, 22–23
2:2, 37, 87, 98, 110, 114–15, 182, 541
2:2–6, 62
2:3, 38, 114, 117, 231
2:3–11, 133
2:4, 63, 87, 115, 117, 129, 182, 213, 268–69
2:4–6, 117–18
2:4–6:29 (ET 2:4–6:28), 331
2:4–7, 115
2:4–7:28, 5, 21, 63
2:5, 87, 116, 118, 182, 191, 199
2:5–6, 109
2:6, 116, 118
2:6–7, 115, 271
2:7, 118–19
2:7–8, 116
2:7–9, 118–19
2:8, 116, 118
2:8–9, 109, 118, 236, 339
2:9, 115, 118–19, 308
2:9–11, 62
2:10, 9, 87, 98, 116, 182, 185, 269
2:10–11, 123, 251
2:10–13, 119–20
2:11, 30, 109, 116, 119, 133, 143, 190, 227, 268, 492

2:12, 116, 182, 184, 191, 242
2:12–14, 110–11
2:13, 116, 120, 308
2:14, 121, 123, 267
2:14–16, 123–24
2:14–23, 121–26
2:15, 116, 122–23, 308
2:16, 115, 122, 128, 132, 309, 339
2:17, 88, 122, 164
2:17–18, 124
2:18, 110–11, 122, 124, 309
2:18–19, 32, 122, 124, 402
2:18–23, 227
2:19, 41, 109, 122–23, 129, 337
2:19–23, 124–26
2:19–33, 62
2:20, 115–16, 122–23, 125–26
2:20–23, 25, 106, 109, 122, 132, 492
2:21, 34, 37, 98, 110, 122, 125, 131, 236, 270, 295, 316, 339–40, 415
2:21–22, 18
2:22, 122, 270
2:22–23, 125
2:23, 122, 125–26, 309, 341
2:24, 110, 115, 128, 182, 268
2:24–25, 122
2:24–26, 132–33
2:24–49, 125, 127–43
2:25, 91, 128–29, 222, 498
2:26, 93, 116, 123, 129, 186
2:27, 9, 98, 110–11, 116, 129, 133, 185, 221, 230, 268
2:27–28, 41, 106, 125, 142
2:27–30, 43, 122, 133–34
2:28, 26, 38, 79, 122, 129–30, 133, 227, 337, 339, 341, 376, 504, 559, 570
2:29, 109, 129, 133, 143
2:29–30, 133
2:30, 19, 129–30, 133, 143, 343

2:31, 130, 268
2:31–35, 134–37
2:32–33, 56
2:33, 130–31, 224
2:33–34, 347
2:33–35, 347
2:33–46, 62
2:34, 26, 130–31, 135, 138–40, 147, 170, 224, 258, 446
2:34–35, 125, 312, 321, 327, 330, 382, 389, 458, 492, 574
2:35, 135–36, 139–41, 224, 273, 355
2:36, 131
2:36–38, 136, 327
2:36–43, 136–38
2:37, 32, 122, 131, 295, 402, 412
2:37–40, 134
2:38, 131, 136–37, 141, 148, 365
2:39, 131, 136, 149
2:39–40, 365
2:40, 137, 347
2:40–43, 137
2:40–45, 347
2:41, 131, 138, 224
2:41–42, 56, 130–31, 347
2:41–43, 155
2:42, 131, 224, 347
2:43, 131–32, 138, 155, 224
2:44, 24, 32, 45, 115, 117, 122, 126, 132, 138, 141, 147–48, 224, 323, 340, 355, 402
2:44–45, 46, 125, 130, 138–42, 213–14, 227, 239, 252, 258, 273, 289, 312, 321, 327, 330, 354, 358, 382, 389, 458, 492, 574
2:45, 26, 130, 132, 138, 170, 224, 258, 362, 446
2:46, 132, 173
2:46–47, 142–43
2:46–49, 482
2:47, 9, 30, 32, 47, 69, 79, 106, 109, 122, 129, 132, 185, 227, 252, 533
2:47–3:2, 62

610

2:48, 37, 110, 126, 131, 171, 184, 276, 327
2:48–49, 37, 106, 111–12, 143
2:49, 39, 93, 132, 143, 162, 176, 183–84, 196, 309
3, 11–12, 28–29, 31, 33, 39, 63–64, 70, 77, 93, 109, 134, 143, 161, 183, 203–4, 209, 211, 220, 223, 225, 227, 233, 253, 272–73, 299–300, 304, 314, 358, 383, 399
3–4, 85
3:1, 20–21, 162–63, 167, 170–71, 175–76
3:1–3, 174–76
3:1–7, 170–78
3:1–30, 22
3:2, 166, 170–72, 175–76, 339, 341
3:2–3, 163–64, 166, 168, 171, 176, 184, 199, 406
3:3, 170, 175–76
3:4, 47, 163, 166, 172, 176, 358
3:4–6, 198
3:4–7, 176–78
3:5, 10, 132, 163–65, 170, 172–74, 177–78, 339
3:5–7, 173
3:6, 163, 174, 177, 249, 267
3:7, 10, 163–66, 170, 172–74, 178, 182, 358
3:7–8, 339
3:8, 24, 87, 179, 182, 199, 223, 299, 498
3:8–10, 62
3:8–12, 176, 182–84
3:8–18, 179–87
3:9, 115–17, 179
3:10, 10, 163–65, 172–74, 180, 267
3:10–11, 183
3:10–12, 173
3:11, 163, 174
3:12, 142, 162–63, 168, 170, 174, 176, 180, 182–84, 190, 193, 222–23, 267, 310, 312

3:12–13, 498
3:12–14, 93, 163, 166
3:13, 180, 188, 191
3:13–15, 184–85
3:14, 142, 162–63, 170, 174, 180, 184, 186, 193
3:14–15, 173, 183
3:14–18, 106
3:15, 10, 105, 163–66, 170, 172, 174, 180–81, 185, 190, 197, 249, 251, 267, 273, 310, 315, 339
3:16, 93, 116, 163, 166, 181, 185
3:16–18, 185–87
3:17, 65, 174, 180–81, 185–87
3:17–18, 19, 31, 165
3:18, 142, 162, 170, 173–74, 181–82, 186–87, 190, 193, 200
3:19, 57–58, 188–89, 191–92, 225, 236, 382, 491
3:19–20, 93, 163, 166
3:19–22, 242
3:19–23, 163, 191–92
3:19–30, 188–200
3:20, 174
3:20–21, 118
3:21, 174, 189, 339
3:22, 122, 182, 189
3:22–23, 93, 163, 166
3:22–30, 62
3:23, 64, 70, 174, 192
3:23–25, 47, 62
3:23–28, 105
3:23–33 (ET 4:2–3), 106
3:24, 128, 189, 192–93, 269
3:24–25, 189
3:24–25 (OG/θ´), 192
3:24–27, 185, 192–96
3:24–45 (OG/θ´), 64, 70, 192
3:25, 26, 30, 142, 165–66, 174, 189–90, 193–94, 196, 268, 271, 321, 340, 458, 498
3:26, 20, 32, 93, 166, 174, 190, 196–97, 212, 251, 253, 435

3:27, 37, 166, 171, 189–90, 193, 196, 312
3:28, 162, 173–74, 180, 185, 190, 196–98, 252, 321
3:28–29, 69–70, 106
3:28–30, 93, 166, 196–200
3:29, 116, 118, 142, 166, 180, 185, 190, 198–99, 246, 253, 267, 269, 289, 307, 312, 323–24, 358, 492
3:29–30, 198–200, 204, 299
3:30, 37, 106, 176, 184, 199, 313, 482
3:31 (ET 4:1), 20–21, 209, 323, 358
3:31–4:34 (ET 4:1–37), 22, 323
3:31–33 (ET 4:1–3), 1, 20, 63, 208–9, 212–14
3:32 (ET 4:2), 32, 190, 196, 212–13, 220, 251, 253, 312, 435
3:32–33 (ET 4:2–3), 204, 206, 212–13, 324
3:33, 212–13
3:33 (ET 4:3), 19, 36, 117, 249, 312, 323, 331, 338
3:33 (ET 4:30), 45
3:46 (OG), 192
3:46–50 (OG/θ´), 64, 70, 192
3:50 (OG/θ´), 193
3:51 (OG/θ´), 192
3:51–90 (OG/θ´), 64, 70, 192
3:91–92 (θ´; MT/ET 3:24–25), 194
3:91–97 (OG/θ´; MT/ET 3:24–30), 64, 192
3:92 (θ´; MT/ET 3:25), 194
4, 2, 16, 23–24, 28–30, 32, 35, 37, 40–41, 63, 71, 101, 110, 201, 213, 215–28, 236–37, 243, 246, 251, 257–59, 270, 272, 276–77, 283,

611

287, 304, 343, 375–76, 399, 435
4–5, 314
4–6, 64, 122
4:1 (ET 4:4), 207–8, 230, 250
4:1–5 (ET 4:3–8), 231–33
4:1–15 (ET 4:4–18), 229–39
4:1–34 (ET 4:4–37), 208–9
4:2, 362
4:2 (ET 4:5), 122, 129, 231, 234, 337
4:3 (ET 4:6), 110, 180, 232, 267
4:3 (ET 4:7), 230
4:4, 87
4:4 (ET 4:7), 98, 221, 230, 232, 238–39, 257, 268
4:4–5 (ET 4:7–8), 110, 221, 239
4:5 (ET 4: 8), 217
4:5 (ET 4:8), 88, 232–33, 253, 259, 270
4:5–6 (ET 4:8–9), 31, 38, 93, 106, 142, 190, 204, 207, 210, 245, 253, 257–58, 262, 276–77, 282, 314, 367
4:5–9 (ET 4:8–12), 62
4:5–24 (ET 4:8–27), 217
4:6 (ET 4:9), 98, 122, 221, 230–32, 270, 282
4:6–7 (ET 4:9–10), 122, 129, 231
4:6–9 (ET 4:9–12), 233–34
4:7 (ET 4:10), 129–30, 231, 234, 337
4:7–9 (ET 4:10–12), 242
4:7–14 (ET 4:10–17), 238
4:8 (ET 4:11), 231, 234, 241, 280
4:8–9 (ET 4:11–12), 238
4:9 (ET 4:12), 47, 206, 231, 234, 242–43
4:10 (ET 4:13), 122, 129–30, 210, 231, 234, 238, 243–44, 337, 339, 341, 367, 404
4:10–14 (ET 4:13–17), 234–38, 244–45
4:11 (ET 4:14), 244
4:11–12 (ET 4:14–15), 234–35
4:12 (ET 4:15), 231, 235, 245
4:12–13 (ET 4:15–16), 216, 241, 248, 251
4:12–16 (ET 4:15–19), 62
4:13 (ET 4:16), 207–8, 224–25, 235–36, 238, 244, 251, 288, 339, 343, 375, 405
4:13 (ET 4:17), 233
4:14 (ET 4:17), 32, 131, 205, 207, 210, 220, 231–32, 234–35, 237–38, 244, 246, 251, 253, 258, 262, 295, 367
4:14 (ET 4:17), 196
4:14–15 (ET 4:17–18), 210
4:15 (ET 4:18), 31, 38, 110, 142, 185, 190, 207, 232, 238–39, 245, 253, 257–58, 262, 270, 277, 282, 314, 367
4:15–16 (ET 4:18–19), 93, 230
4:16 (ET 4:19), 217, 232, 241–42, 268, 274, 283, 364
4:16–24 (ET 4:19–27), 209, 240–47
4:16–30 (ET 4:19–33), 210
4:17 (ET 4:20), 231, 241–42, 280
4:17–19 (ET 4:20–22), 242–43
4:17–23 (ET 4:20–26), 210, 250
4:17–24 (ET 4:29–27), 210
4:18 (ET 4:21), 47, 206, 231, 242–43
4:19 (ET 4:22), 241, 243, 280, 331, 338
4:20 (ET 4:23), 208, 210, 216, 224–25, 231, 241, 244, 248, 251, 288, 339–40, 367, 375, 404–5
4:20–23 (ET 4:23–26), 243
4:21 (ET 4:24), 220, 230, 238, 244
4:21–22 (ET 4:24–25), 32, 232, 251, 253
4:21–22 (ET 24–25), 196
4:21–23 (ET 4:24–27), 244–45
4:21–24 (ET 4:24–27), 262
4:21–34 (ET 4:24–37), 105
4:22 (ET 4:25), 131, 208, 216–17, 224–25, 231, 236, 241, 244–45, 248, 251, 267, 288, 295, 339, 405
4:22–23 (ET 4:25–26), 205, 244, 251
4:23 (ET 4:26), 236, 245, 251, 252
4:24 (ET 4:27), 13–14, 30, 35, 41, 198, 203, 205, 210, 217, 241–47, 250, 252, 411
4:25–30 (ET 4:28–33), 209–10, 217, 226, 250–51
4:25–34 (ET 4:28–37), 248–53
4:26 (ET 4:29), 250, 402
4:26–29 (ET 4:29–32), 207, 217
4:27 (ET 4:30), 203–4, 250–51, 257
4:27 (MT 4:24), 247
4:28 (ET 4:31), 289, 316, 340
4:28–29 (ET 4:31–32), 251
4:29 (ET 4:32), 32, 131, 196, 208, 216–17, 224–25, 232, 236, 248–49, 251, 253, 258, 267, 288, 295, 339, 375, 405
4:29–30 (ET 4:31–32), 62
4:29–30 (ET 4:32–33), 217, 231, 248
4:30 (ET 4:33), 174, 236, 249, 251, 267

4:31 (ET 4:34), 19, 32, 35–36, 45, 117, 196, 209, 212–14, 232, 237, 246, 249, 251, 253, 257, 270, 323, 331, 338, 343
4:31–32 (ET 4:34–35), 25, 69, 106, 204, 251, 253
4:31–33 (ET 4:34–36), 205
4:31–34 (ET 4:34–37), 206, 209, 213, 262, 277, 289
4:32 (ET 4:35), 18, 246, 249, 251–53, 295, 313, 402, 415
4:33 (ET 4:36), 189, 209, 223, 249–50, 252, 268, 270, 283, 339, 343
4:33–34 (ET 4:36–37), 246, 252–53
4:34 (ET 4:37), 36, 106, 185, 204, 246, 250, 252–53, 257, 402, 492
5, 2, 4, 12, 21, 23, 28–30, 32, 35, 39–41, 77, 101, 105, 110, 167, 220, 223–25, 227, 243, 257, 260, 263, 271, 284, 286, 304, 337, 376, 390, 399
5–6, 498
5:1, 4, 20–21, 266–67, 269
5:1–3, 260, 263, 265
5:1–4, 271–73
5:1–6:1 (ET 5:1–31), 22
5:1–12, 266–77
5:1–30, 88
5:2, 4, 260–62, 265, 267, 271–72
5:2–3, 262, 267, 276
5:2–4, 277
5:3, 267, 272
5:4, 190, 223, 273, 284, 321
5:5, 174, 249, 267–68, 280
5:5–6, 273–74
5:5–7, 62
5:6, 268–69, 271, 274, 364, 491

5:7, 87, 98, 110, 115, 221, 230, 268–69, 271, 282, 330
5:7–8, 282, 495
5:8, 110, 257, 268–69, 271, 275
5:8–9, 274–76
5:8–12, 110
5:9, 269, 276, 364, 491
5:9–10, 268
5:10, 115, 117, 268–70, 282, 364
5:10–12, 62, 276–77
5:11, 4, 38, 87, 98, 106, 190, 207, 221, 227, 230, 232, 257–58, 260, 262, 265, 268, 270, 272, 282, 314, 367
5:11–12, 30, 37, 439, 562
5:12, 38, 93, 115, 227, 268, 270–71, 314
5:12–14, 62
5:13, 4, 91, 129, 222, 260, 262, 265, 272
5:13–6:1 (ET 5:13–31), 278–89
5:13–16, 281–82
5:14, 30, 37–38, 190, 207, 257–58, 262, 270, 282, 314, 439, 562
5:14–16, 62
5:15, 98, 110, 115, 257, 279, 282
5:15–17, 268, 271, 495
5:16, 38, 185, 268–69, 271, 279, 282, 330, 482
5:16–19, 62
5:17, 34, 116, 279, 283, 288, 341
5:17–21, 282–84
5:18, 4, 32, 190, 196, 220, 223, 260, 262, 265, 272, 279, 283–84, 435
5:18–21, 24, 221–22, 277, 279, 283
5:18–22, 262
5:18–23, 41
5:19, 279–80, 283, 312, 358
5:19–22, 62
5:20, 243, 280, 316, 340–41
5:20–21, 257, 284, 343

5:21, 32, 190, 196, 220, 231, 267, 280, 283, 295, 435
5:21–23, 492
5:22, 4, 260, 262, 265, 279, 284
5:22–24, 284–85
5:22–28, 221
5:23, 79, 190, 223, 262, 267, 273, 280, 283–84, 307, 321, 402
5:24, 280
5:24–25, 309, 494–95
5:25, 275, 280–81, 285, 288
5:25–28, 274–75, 285–88
5:26, 268, 280, 286
5:26–28, 285
5:27, 285, 287
5:28, 150, 258, 281, 285, 287, 295
5:29, 37, 39, 269, 283, 330, 482
5:29–6:1 (ET 5:29–31), 288–89
5:30, 87, 106, 258, 268, 277, 281, 288
5:30–6:1 (ET 5:30–31), 271
5:31, 149
6, 2, 12, 28–30, 33, 37, 39, 63, 69, 105, 109, 162, 164, 167, 211, 225, 290–92, 294, 299, 314, 319, 324, 331, 358, 383, 390, 434
6:1 (ET 5:31), 1, 5, 11, 20, 63, 150, 237, 258, 277, 282, 288–90, 292, 294–95, 301, 304, 375, 498, 506
6:2 (ET 6:1), 5, 20–21, 149, 290, 292, 294–95, 301, 306
6:2–3 (ET 6:1–2), 37, 292, 302–3
6:2–4 (ET 6:1–3), 106, 313–14
6:2–5 (ET 6:1–4), 314
6:2–6 (ET 6:1–5), 106
6:2–29 (ET 6:1–28), 22, 305–24
6:3 (ET 6:2), 269, 302, 307

613

Index of Passages

6:4 (ET 6:3), 269, 292, 303, 307, 313, 318–20, 322, 324
6:4–5 (ET 6:3–4), 307
6:5 (ET 6:4), 185, 191, 307, 311, 341
6:5–6 (ET 6:4–5), 106, 314, 322
6:5–29 (ET 6:4–28), 304
6:6 (ET 6:5), 301, 307–8, 314, 363
6:7 (ET 6:6), 5, 115, 117, 149, 290, 295, 308, 310, 315
6:7–8 (ET 6:6–7), 307
6:7–10 (ET 6:6–9), 315–16
6:7–11 (ET 6:6–10), 30
6:8 (ET 6:7), 171, 189, 292–94, 303, 308–9, 315
6:8–11 (ET 6:7–10), 106
6:8–22 (ET 6:7–21), 62
6:9 (ET 6:8), 39, 149, 295, 308–9, 314, 316
6:9–11 (ET 6:8–10), 309, 495
6:10 (ET 6:9), 5, 149, 182, 290, 295, 309
6:11 (ET 6:10), 301, 309–10, 317–18, 339
6:11–12 (ET 6:10–11), 308, 316–17
6:12 (ET 6:11), 308, 310, 315, 317
6:12–14 (ET 6:11–13), 301, 309
6:13 (ET 6:12), 39, 149, 292–95, 303, 308, 310, 314, 316, 318, 362
6:13–14 (ET 6:12–13), 309, 318, 495
6:14 (ET 6:13), 91, 129, 180, 222, 267, 301, 309–10, 312, 318, 339
6:15 (ET 6:14), 180, 300, 307, 310, 319, 322
6:15–16 (ET 6:14–15), 318–19
6:15–17 (ET 6:14–16), 301
6:16 (ET 6:15), 39, 149, 295, 308, 310–11, 315
6:17 (ET 6:16), 180, 300, 310–11, 319–20
6:17–19 (ET 6:16–18), 319–20
6:18 (ET 6:17), 301, 320, 446, 558
6:19 (ET 6:18), 114, 311
6:19–21 (ET 6:18–20), 307
6:20 (ET 6:19), 128, 185, 301
6:20–24 (ET 6:19–23), 320–22
6:21 (ET 6:20), 180, 185, 300–301, 310–12, 320
6:22 (ET 6:21), 34, 115, 117, 311, 321
6:23 (ET 6:22), 26, 301, 311–12, 321–22, 338, 362, 458, 492, 498
6:24 (ET 6:23), 189, 300–301, 311, 317, 322, 340
6:24–25 (ET 6:23–24), 303
6:25 (ET 6:24), 24, 106, 179, 299, 311–12, 319, 322–23, 338
6:26 (ET 6:25), 5, 149, 290, 295, 323, 358
6:26–28 (ET 6:25–27), 69–70, 227, 293–94, 299, 323–24
6:27 (ET 6:26), 45, 106, 117, 180, 267, 279, 301, 310, 312, 320–21, 323, 331, 338, 340, 358, 363
6:27–7:4 (ET 6:26–7:4), 62
6:27–28 (ET 6:26–27), 106, 323, 492
6:28 (ET 6:27), 180, 212, 310, 312–13
6:29 (ET 6:28), 5, 149, 290, 293, 295, 301–2, 313, 324, 339, 341, 482
7, 1–2, 4, 21, 23–26, 32, 34, 36, 41, 46, 54–59, 80, 106, 138, 144, 146, 150–56, 252, 327–35, 337–38, 341–42, 346, 348, 351, 355–59, 363, 370–71, 373, 376–77, 379–80, 382–84, 389–91, 399–401, 414, 418–19, 435, 443–44, 450, 455–56, 458, 476, 480, 486, 496, 502, 506, 539, 547–48, 571
7–9, 1, 496
7–12, 3, 5–6, 21, 25, 28, 32, 57, 65, 77, 106, 299, 319, 324, 332, 346, 365, 389, 425, 444
7:1, 21, 41, 80, 88, 129, 237, 263, 288, 304, 330, 337, 339–41, 375, 390, 414, 507
7:1–2, 122, 129
7:1–8, 329, 355, 360
7:1–12:13, 21, 23
7:1–14, 336–60
7:1–28, 22–23
7:2, 41, 47, 54, 150, 333, 337, 341–42, 345–46, 380, 382
7:2–3, 341–42, 346
7:2–8, 365
7:3, 337–38, 342, 365–66
7:4, 338, 342–43, 345, 347
7:4–6, 358
7:4–7, 354
7:5, 338, 343–45, 347, 354, 400
7:5–6, 62
7:5–7, 62
7:6, 150–51, 331, 338, 345–47, 400, 520
7:7, 41, 47, 122, 129, 137, 155, 337–39, 341, 347–48, 362, 370–71, 373, 385
7:7–8, 337, 385, 570
7:7–14, 370–71
7:8, 130, 151, 154–55, 339, 348–49, 354, 362, 370–71, 373, 377, 395, 401, 421, 547–48, 553
7:8–10, 360

614

7:9, 47, 328, 339, 350–53, 531
7:9–10, 47, 349–50, 352–53, 355, 372, 384, 574
7:9–14, 329, 349, 365–66, 389, 480, 496, 559
7:9–27, 329
7:10, 47, 339, 349–51, 353, 364, 505
7:10–11, 354
7:11, 47, 62, 154, 334, 337, 342, 349, 353–54, 356, 362, 374, 377, 500, 533, 547–48, 570
7:11–12, 354–55, 360, 372, 384, 574
7:11–13, 148
7:11–14, 385
7:12, 224, 236, 316, 331, 338–41, 354–55, 375
7:13, 26, 29, 32, 38, 41, 47, 122, 129, 145, 148, 194, 252, 258, 328, 337, 339–40, 344, 347, 350–52, 356–58, 408, 450, 474, 493, 498–99, 504
7:13–14, 24, 26, 31, 36, 43–44, 46, 48, 73, 239, 321, 328, 340, 349, 352, 355–60, 366–67, 372, 383–84, 458, 492, 498, 500, 504, 574
7:14, 19, 24, 26, 37, 45, 252, 316, 323, 329, 331, 338, 340, 347, 349, 351, 356, 358–59, 364, 384
7:15, 1, 41, 122, 129, 361–62, 364, 417
7:15–16, 364–65
7:15–23, 62
7:15–28, 329, 361–86
7:16, 309, 362, 364, 366, 412, 444, 450
7:17, 337, 342, 360, 365–66, 373
7:17–18, 364–70
7:18, 33, 274, 323, 327–29, 347, 351, 360, 362, 365–66, 368, 383, 571

7:19, 155, 267, 347, 362, 370–71, 373, 385
7:19–20, 364
7:19–21, 360
7:19–22, 364, 370–72
7:19–27, 500
7:20, 47, 137, 154–55, 337, 362, 370–71, 373, 377, 385
7:20–21, 371–72, 385, 421, 547–48
7:20–22, 339
7:20–27, 574
7:21, 47, 151, 154, 330, 339, 355, 362, 371, 533
7:21–22, 327, 356, 364, 367–68, 370
7:21–26, 570
7:22, 33, 328–29, 339, 351–52, 356, 360, 362–64, 366–70, 372, 383, 385, 547, 571
7:23, 365, 385
7:23–25, 360, 373–84
7:23–27, 364
7:24, 47, 57–58, 137, 151, 154, 373, 385
7:24–25, 385, 548
7:25, 33, 47, 57, 151–52, 154, 156, 196, 224, 308, 327, 330, 339, 355, 362–63, 366–70, 373–85, 389, 405, 421, 455, 457, 533, 540, 547, 565, 569–70, 573–74
7:25–8:5, 62
7:26, 154, 312, 316, 331, 338, 340, 355–56, 360, 363, 547
7:26–27, 331, 384–85
7:26–28, 62
7:27, 24, 33, 37, 45, 117, 141, 154, 252, 323, 327–29, 331, 338, 347, 356, 358, 360, 362, 364, 366–70, 384, 571
7:28, 1, 29, 268, 327, 362–64, 385–86, 417, 491, 562
8, 2, 4, 16, 21, 29, 32, 34, 41, 55, 58–59, 61, 80, 144, 146,

150–54, 156, 331, 346, 349, 365, 371, 389–91, 394, 401, 404, 407, 410, 413, 418–21, 450, 456, 486, 496, 500, 536, 539
8:1, 1, 21, 41, 63, 80, 88, 237, 263, 288, 390, 393, 398, 444, 450, 507
8:1–2, 129, 446
8:1–8, 62
8:1–12:13, 5, 21, 23, 63
8:1–14, 392–407
8:1–27, 22
8:2, 25, 41, 393, 399
8:2–3, 393
8:2–4, 399
8:3, 25, 150–51, 344, 393–94, 400
8:4, 394, 396, 399–401, 520, 535, 540
8:5, 151, 346, 394–95, 400, 409–10, 444
8:5–7, 399–400
8:6, 393, 395
8:6–7, 150
8:7, 395, 398, 400, 444
8:8, 341, 345–46, 394–96, 400–401, 404, 409–10, 520
8:8–10, 395
8:9, 151, 154–55, 394–95, 401–2, 514, 545
8:9–12, 401–3
8:9–14, 520, 540
8:10, 47, 249, 394–96, 402
8:10–12, 404
8:11, 27, 321, 394, 396–97, 401–3, 412, 481, 492, 498, 500, 567
8:11–12, 398
8:11–13, 396, 405
8:11–14, 152, 154, 389
8:12, 151, 397–98, 403, 411, 495
8–12, 16, 331
8:12–13, 410, 445
8:13, 41, 47, 129, 357, 367, 393, 397–98, 404, 473, 517, 530, 567
8:13–14, 404–7, 568
8:13–16, 62

615

Index of Passages

8:14, 151–53, 398,
    404–7, 412–14, 530,
    572–73
8:15, 1, 41, 98, 129,
    394, 408–10,
    412–13, 498
8:15–18, 412–14
8:15–27, 408–17, 481
8:16, 41, 46, 365,
    412–13, 431, 450,
    481, 498, 567–68
8:16–17, 62
8:16–18, 501
8:16–26, 568
8:17, 41, 129, 340, 409,
    413–14, 418, 420,
    493, 539, 544, 567
8:17–18, 498
8:18, 114, 409–10, 444,
    450, 492, 498, 501
8:19, 13–14, 25, 58,
    409, 413–14, 420,
    536, 540
8:19–22, 414
8:20, 365, 396, 399,
    409
8:20–21, 62, 150
8:20–22, 59, 418, 421
8:21, 346, 365, 394,
    400, 409–10, 418
8:21–22, 345, 414
8:22, 346, 415, 520
8:22–23, 410, 510
8:23, 154, 271, 410–11,
    415, 418
8:23–25, 414, 540
8:23–26, 59, 415–21
8:24, 151, 367–68, 397,
    402, 411, 415–16,
    536, 540, 565–66
8:24–25, 540
8:25, 25, 101, 154,
    394, 396, 398, 402,
    411–12, 415–16,
    439, 492, 498, 500,
    515, 540, 562
8:26, 41, 47, 129,
    404–5, 412–14, 417,
    450, 495, 566
8:27, 1, 29, 41, 241,
    364, 385, 398, 410,
    412, 417, 571
9, 2, 16, 21, 26–27,
    33, 36, 55, 60, 70,
    80, 91, 104, 106,
    292, 331, 390, 425,
    427–29, 433, 437,
    445, 450, 455–56,
    459, 470, 480, 496

9–12, 331, 390
9:1, 5, 21, 80, 87, 149,
    288, 290, 292,
    294–95, 429, 498,
    507
9:1–2, 237, 288, 431,
    434–35, 488
9:1–4, 425
9:1–19, 430–42
9:1–27, 22
9:2, 1, 79, 224, 237,
    426–28, 431,
    434–35, 444, 451,
    453, 456, 459,
    468–69, 471, 489,
    497, 570
9:2–20, 36
9:3, 425, 431–32, 436,
    441, 444, 496
9:3–4, 79, 433
9:3–6, 436–37
9:4, 79, 104, 425, 427,
    432, 436–37
9:4–6, 425
9:4–9, 427
9:4–11, 104
9:4–19, 70, 104, 425,
    496
9:5, 432, 436–37
9:5–6, 425, 436, 438
9:6, 104, 437, 492
9:6–10, 427
9:7, 91, 432–33, 438,
    456
9:7–11, 437–39
9:7–14, 425
9:8, 79, 427, 432, 438,
    492
9:9, 79, 104, 124,
    431–32, 438
9:9–10, 432
9:10, 79, 104, 427,
    432–33, 438
9:10–11, 426, 433, 438
9:11, 91, 104, 427–28,
    432–33, 438–39,
    449
9:12, 433, 439, 456
9:12–14, 62, 439–40
9:13, 101, 425, 427–28,
    432–33, 439, 495,
    517, 562
9:13–14, 79, 427
9:13–15, 432
9:14, 432–33, 438, 440
9:15, 431, 433, 440
9:15–16, 426, 433,
    440–41
9:15–17, 62, 79, 432

9:16, 398, 432–34, 438,
    440, 456
9:17, 13, 15–16, 432,
    434, 441
9:17–18, 425, 436, 441
9:17–19, 105, 426,
    432–34, 441–42
9:18, 398, 428, 433–34,
    438, 441–43, 448
9:18–19, 441
9:19, 79, 425, 432, 434,
    441–42
9:20, 79, 91, 398,
    427, 432, 441–43,
    450–51
9:20–23, 450–57
9:20–27, 425, 443–76,
    481
9:21, 41, 46, 129, 365,
    413, 443–44, 450,
    481, 498
9:21–22, 501
9:22, 30, 37, 98, 101,
    428, 431, 439,
    444–45, 450, 517,
    562, 566–67, 577
9:23, 41, 425, 445,
    451, 458, 468, 470,
    488–89, 534, 543,
    567
9:24, 27, 36, 41, 129,
    224, 398, 410, 427,
    445–46, 451–68,
    471, 474–76, 489,
    558, 562
9:24–26, 445
9:24–27, 60, 407, 427,
    445, 451–76, 480,
    488–89, 496, 498,
    570
9:25, 27, 101, 224,
    398, 425–28, 439,
    446, 448, 452–53,
    455–56, 458,
    460–64, 468–74,
    480, 482, 517, 530,
    562
9:25–26, 27, 29, 34,
    38, 44, 48, 321,
    448, 451, 453, 458,
    465–67, 472–74,
    489
9:25–27, 34, 36, 470
9:26, 27, 36, 224, 398,
    409, 446–48, 456,
    458, 461, 463–65,
    467, 471–75, 516,
    534
9:26–27, 258, 473, 550

616

9:27, 27, 31, 47, 225,
  398, 428, 445,
  448–50, 452–53,
  455–57, 463–65,
  473–76, 517, 530,
  534, 556, 575
10, 489, 498–500
10–12, 1–2, 21, 26, 32,
  34, 80, 144, 146,
  150–51, 176, 331,
  346, 365, 390, 450,
  479–80, 482–83,
  488, 492, 496, 506,
  510, 524, 529,
  535–36, 539, 559,
  564–65, 568, 575,
  577
10:1, 21, 41, 80, 93,
  98, 103, 176, 237,
  288, 290, 302, 324,
  431, 444, 482–83,
  488–89, 495–96,
  506–7, 510, 518
10:1–11:1, 477, 479,
  484, 487–507
10:1–12:13, 22
10:2, 1
10:2–3, 224, 445, 489,
  496–97
10:3, 99, 398, 445, 489,
  520, 534
10:4, 25, 103, 176, 482,
  489, 497, 568
10:4–6, 357, 497–501,
  564, 568
10:4–21, 27, 321, 458,
  481, 484
10:5, 25, 47, 489–90,
  498–99
10:5–6, 493, 498–99,
  562, 568
10:5–9, 62, 500
10:6, 47, 398, 408, 482,
  490–91, 499, 504
10:7, 1, 41, 491
10:7–9, 501
10:8, 41, 488, 491, 511
10:8–16, 62
10:9, 114, 409, 413,
  491–92, 498, 504
10:10, 413, 444, 450,
  498, 504
10:10–11, 364, 385,
  501
10:10–12, 504
10:11, 445, 489, 492,
  501, 534, 543
10:11–16, 62
10:12, 492, 497, 501–2

10:12–14, 501–4
10:13, 402, 481, 489,
  492–95, 498, 500,
  502–4, 556, 559
10:14, 26, 41, 129, 376,
  431, 493, 504, 559,
  570
10:15, 504
10:15–17, 488
10:15–18, 364, 385
10:15–19, 504–5
10:16, 41, 340, 444,
  450, 493, 498–99,
  504, 511
10:16–17, 504–5
10:16–20, 62
10:18, 340, 409, 444,
  450, 493–94,
  498–99, 505
10:18–19, 495, 501
10:19, 445, 489, 492,
  494, 505, 534, 543
10:20, 410, 484, 492,
  494–95, 503, 505
10:20–11:1, 482, 498,
  505–7
10:20–21, 492
10:21, 62, 72, 369,
  402, 481, 484, 492,
  494–95, 500, 505–6,
  510, 556, 559
11, 16–18, 29, 72, 153,
  155–56, 295, 411,
  480, 489, 512, 520,
  529, 539, 545, 548,
  550
11:1, 5, 149, 237, 288,
  290, 293, 295–96,
  494–95, 498, 506–7,
  511, 518
11:1–2, 62
11:2, 146, 296, 346,
  410, 483–86, 495,
  506, 510, 518–20
11:2–3, 539
11:2–4, 510
11:2–12:4, 479, 484–85
11:2–31, 510
11:2–35, 477, 482,
  508–32
11:3, 486, 524, 540
11:3–4, 151, 346,
  484–85, 520
11:3–35, 146
11:3–45, 146
11:4, 341, 401, 484–85,
  520
11:4–6, 539
11:4–40, 483

11:5, 492, 510, 520–22
11:5–6, 486, 539
11:5–35, 145, 365,
  484–85, 520
11:6, 131, 155, 237,
  409, 510–11,
  513–14, 516,
  521–22
11:6–8, 539
11:7, 510–11, 522
11:7–9, 521–22
11:8, 237, 510–12, 522
11:9, 522
11:10, 473, 511–12,
  516, 521, 523, 535
11:10–13, 491
11:10–19, 521
11:11, 395, 513, 523,
  539
11:11–12, 513, 521,
  523, 538
11:11–13, 512
11:12, 280, 511, 513,
  523
11:13, 237, 409, 510,
  512–13, 539
11:13–16, 62, 513
11:13–17, 62
11:13–19, 521, 523–25
11:14, 41, 129, 510,
  514, 524, 539
11:15, 512, 514, 539
11:16, 401, 510, 514,
  524, 540, 545
11:17, 131, 155,
  514–15, 521, 524
11:17–18, 512, 538
11:18, 514–15, 524–25
11:19, 511–12, 514–15,
  525
11:20, 225, 515, 521,
  525
11:20–21, 510–11
11:21, 411–12, 515–16,
  525, 538
11:21–24, 525–27, 545
11:21–30, 544
11:21 35, 153, 483,
  486, 521, 536, 538,
  540, 544–45, 547
11:21–45, 153
11:22, 446, 448, 514,
  516, 521, 525–26
11:22–23, 526
11:22–24, 525
11:23, 511, 516, 526
11:23–24, 526
11:24, 411–12, 515,
  527

617

11:25, 512, 539
11:25–26, 525, 527
11:25–27, 521
11:25–28, 527–28, 545
11:25–29, 62
11:26, 87, 473, 516
11:27, 13–14, 25, 409, 414, 510, 516, 528, 539
11:28, 398, 526, 528
11:29, 414, 516
11:29–30, 528–29
11:29–35, 545
11:30, 27, 156, 398, 512, 516–17, 526, 528–29, 536, 540, 544
11:30–32, 529–31, 544
11:31, 47, 396, 398, 449, 463, 473, 476, 510–11, 514, 517, 523, 530, 540, 550, 567, 575
11:32, 17, 40, 62, 511, 516–17, 526, 530, 542
11:33, 30, 37, 43, 87, 101, 225, 431, 439, 484–85, 517, 531, 562, 567
11:33–35, 101, 514, 531–32, 562
11:33–36, 62
11:34, 515, 517, 531
11:35, 13–15, 25, 29–30, 37, 43, 87, 101, 352, 409, 414, 439, 484–85, 510, 516, 518, 538–39, 544, 562, 567, 572
11:35–45, 547
11:36, 25, 47, 132, 284, 411, 448, 486, 533–36, 539–41, 547, 553, 565–66, 571
11:36–12:4, 483–85
11:36–37, 541, 552
11:36–38, 536
11:36–39, 420, 536, 540–45, 548, 552
11:36–45, 144, 146, 153, 411, 477, 483, 486, 533–46, 548, 559, 562, 565, 570–71, 574
11:37, 517, 534, 541–42, 547–48, 550

11:37–39, 534
11:38, 62, 445, 489, 511, 534, 542–43, 547–48, 551–52
11:38–39, 511
11:39, 533–34, 542–43, 547
11:40, 409, 473, 484–85, 516, 535, 539, 544–45, 547
11:40–45, 3, 145, 153, 536, 538, 544–46
11:41, 401, 514, 535, 540, 544–45, 547
11:42, 535, 544
11:42–43, 545
11:43, 445, 489, 534–35, 543–44, 548
11:44, 535
11:44–45, 546
11:45, 398, 401, 409, 514, 533, 535, 540, 545–47
12, 18, 55, 60, 64, 68, 144
12:1, 37, 47, 72, 295, 350, 369, 402, 410, 481, 492, 495, 505–6, 510, 556, 559
12:1–2, 49
12:1–3, 19, 544, 559–62, 572
12:1–4, 146, 477, 483, 556–63
12:2, 27, 37, 47, 72, 323, 556–57, 560–61, 568, 577
12:2–3, 27, 30, 48, 141, 156, 161, 187, 198, 200, 207, 311, 321–22, 329–30, 482, 496, 504, 531, 533, 559
12:3, 27, 30, 37, 42–43, 47, 87, 101, 402, 439, 482, 484, 517, 557–58, 561–62, 567, 577
12:4, 42–43, 72, 100, 386, 409, 414, 417, 446, 484–85, 495, 539, 544, 557–58, 562–63, 566, 571
12:5, 1, 568
12:5–6, 500
12:5–7, 568–71

12:5–13, 477, 479, 484, 564–77
12:6, 409, 564–66, 568, 571
12:6–7, 489, 497, 499, 564, 568
12:6–11, 500
12:7, 357, 363, 370, 398, 405, 414, 457, 500, 564–66, 568–74, 576–77
12:7–8, 575
12:8, 496, 545, 571–72, 574–76
12:8–10, 571–72
12:9, 409, 417, 446, 539, 544, 558, 562, 564, 566, 571, 577
12:10, 17, 30, 37, 40, 47, 62, 87, 101, 352, 417, 439, 517, 562–63, 566–67, 571–72
12:11, 47, 396, 398, 449, 463, 473, 476, 517, 550, 567, 572–76
12:11–12, 60, 224, 404, 571–77
12:12, 444, 500, 572–76
12:13, 409, 479, 567–68, 575, 577

Hosea
3:5, 26, 129, 376, 504, 570
7:16, 414
12:1 (ET 11:12), 368
12:11 (ET 12:10), 41
13:3, 135
13:6, 513
13:7–8, 335
13:8, 343
14:9 (ET 14:8), 230

Joel
2:14, 246
2:20, 394
3:1 (ET 2:28), 41
3:5 (ET 2:32), 32
4:16 (ET 3:16), 543
4:18 (ET 3:18), 54

Amos
1:3, 519
1:6, 519
1:9, 519
1:11, 519
1:13, 519
2:1, 519

2:4, 519
2:6, 519
5:15, 246
5:19, 335, 343
6:6, 497
7:4, 333
7:7–9, 41
7–8, 365
7:15, 505
8:1–3, 41
8:2, 409
8:4–6, 245
8:12, 563
9:13, 54

Obadiah
1, 41, 129, 446
9, 218

Jonah
1:5–6, 409
1:9, 116, 122
1:12, 341
1:13, 116
1:15, 96
1:16, 409
2:6 (ET 2:5), 333
2:11 (ET 2:10), 116
3, 204
3:4, 40, 204
3:7–9, 199, 204
4:1, 439
4:2, 436

Micah
2:1–2, 114
3:6, 41
4:1, 26, 129, 376, 504, 570
4:1–5, 142
4:2, 469
5:1 (ET 5:2), 26, 139, 193, 352
7:9, 96
7:14, 362

Nahum
1:1, 41, 129, 446
1:7, 543
2:9 (ET 2:8), 494

Habakkuk
1–2, 40
1:8, 335, 342
1:12, 139
2:2, 41
2:3, 14, 41
2:6, 411
2:13, 444
3, 40
3:10, 333

Zephaniah
2:2, 135
2:10, 394
3:1, 96
3:8, 576

Haggai, 7, 291
1:1–15, 470
1:4, 461–62, 470
1:14, 461–62, 470
2:7, 542
2:10, 497
2:18, 497

Zechariah, 7, 71, 291
1–6, 365
1:1, 436
1:1–17, 470
1:3, 247
1:7, 436, 497
1:7–6:8, 41
1:12, 435–36
2:6, 341
3:1–2, 481
3:9, 139
4:7, 139
4:10, 563
5:11, 80
6:5, 341
7:2, 433
7:10, 245
8:21–22, 433
9:10, 494
10:3, 400
11:16, 97
12:10, 130, 446
13:1–6, 466
13:4, 41
13:9, 353
14:3, 49
14:5, 367

Malachi, 7
1:7, 96
1:9, 433
1:12, 96
3:2, 518
3:2–3, 353
3:4, 362
3:5, 115
3:6, 192

New Testament

Matthew
1:1, 261
1:18–25, 53, 110, 193
1:21, 94
2:13, 321
2:19–20, 321
3:2, 26, 366
3:8, 247

3:9, 53
3:11, 357
3:17, 412
4:1–10, 503
4:1–11, 481, 505
4:6–10, 301
4:11, 500, 503
4:17, 26, 366
5–7, 206
5:3, 366
5:10, 366
5:11–12, 441
6:8, 451
6:9–13, 316
6:10, 252, 366
6:13, 131
6:17, 497
7:15, 456
8:11, 571
8:28–32, 481
8:29, 357
9:24, 561
10:1, 370
10:7, 26
10:8, 232
10:14–25, 200
10:32–33, 33, 300
10:40, 501
11:2–3, 45
11:3, 357
11:27, 359
12:6, 142, 467
12:28, 26, 55, 137, 144, 232, 360
12:41, 204
12:41–42, 560
12:45, 370
13:10–17, 417
13:24–43, 355
13:31–32, 234
13:32, 47
13:39–43, 49
13:41, 500
13:43, 37, 47, 562
13:49, 49
14:25–26, 564
14:25–29, 412
14:27, 502
14:33, 564
15:1–9, 315
16:16, 320
16:18, 46, 117, 457
16:21, 53
16:27, 49, 500
17:2, 491
17:7, 502
18:16, 568
19:21, 245
19:28, 47, 351

20:19, 27
20:28, 449
21:42, 571
21:42–44, 36, 140
21:44, 46
22:15–21, 34
22:15–46, 301
22:21, 162
22:42–44, 351
23:37, 571
24:1–31, 455
24:5, 456
24:6–31, 330, 344
24:11, 456
24:15, 40, 47, 398, 449, 455, 463, 473, 475, 517, 530, 567
24:15–23, 473
24:21, 559
24:22, 207, 414, 457, 565
24:22–24, 559
24:27, 48, 491
24:29–30, 559
24:30, 43, 48, 145, 148, 351, 356–58, 360, 474
24:30–31, 49, 384
24:31, 341, 500
24:36, 49
24:42, 49
24:44, 49
25:1–13, 114
25:9–10, 114
25:13, 49
25:14–30, 49
25:21, 164
25:23, 164
25:31, 44, 49, 351, 356–58, 360, 474
25:31–46, 49, 560–61
25:34, 55, 360, 559, 571
25:46, 47, 561
26:24, 357
26:28, 449, 474
26:32, 27
26:47–50, 301
26:54, 53
26:62–63, 185
26:63, 301, 320
26:64, 36, 44, 145, 148, 351, 356–60, 474
27:1–2, 301
27:11–14, 301
27:12–14, 185
27:18–26, 301
27:19, 320
27:31, 447
27:35, 447
27:37, 307

27:43, 185, 301, 311
27:45–50, 450
27:46, 447–48, 503
27:66, 301, 320
28:1, 236, 301, 320
28:1–20, 185
28:2–3, 503
28:10, 502
28:18, 207, 328, 359
28:19, 352, 441

Mark
1:14–15, 504
1:15, 26, 360
1:24, 467
4:32, 47
5:1–20, 98
5:39, 561
7:5–13, 315
7:6, 439
9:1, 26, 55, 144, 360, 504
9:37, 501
9:47, 55, 148
10:30, 572
12:18–27, 321
12:33, 198
13:1–26, 455
13:14, 47, 398, 449, 455, 463, 473, 475, 517, 530, 567
13:14–20, 473
13:19, 559
13:24–26, 48
13:24–27, 559
13:25, 481
13:26, 44, 145, 148, 356–58, 360, 474
13:27, 341
13:32, 576
14:21, 357
14:24, 474
14:40–43, 114
14:58, 131, 447
14:62, 44, 48, 145, 148, 356–60, 474
15:43, 532
16:2, 236
16:5, 412, 503
16:17, 232

Luke
1:8–10, 317
1:11–19, 413
1:13, 501
1:19, 46, 446, 450, 462
1:26, 46, 446, 450, 462
1:26–33, 413
1:26–56, 193
1:30, 501
1:31–33, 328

1:32–33, 73
1:33, 46
1:35, 73
1:52, 206
1:69, 348
1:77, 101
2:1, 144
2:1–7, 106, 137, 144
2:1–20, 193
2:8–15, 500
2:9, 446, 462
2:11, 446, 462
2:14, 313
2:25–38, 532
2:40, 102
2:46–47, 102
3:1–23, 137, 144
3:4, 439
3:8, 53
3:15, 532
4:18, 467, 501
4:43, 328
5:10, 502
5:16, 301
6:20, 328
6:22, 441
7:18–20, 45
7:21, 370
8:52, 561
9:22, 571
9:27, 26, 55, 144, 360
9:30–31, 557
9:31, 233
9:48, 501
9:51, 514
9:51–19:28, 514
10:9, 26, 55, 144, 360
10:11, 26, 360
10:16, 501
10:16–20, 142
10:18, 370, 481
10:20, 559
11:2, 328
11:2–4, 316
11:5, 114
11:20, 26, 55, 137, 144, 360
11:31–32, 560
11:32, 204
12:8–9, 33, 300
12:32, 502
13:19, 47
13:34, 571
14:13, 245
17:10, 442
17:20–21, 55, 137, 144
17:21, 26, 61, 360
17:22–24, 48
17:25, 571

18:1–8, 502
18:7, 414
18:18–23, 253
19:8, 245
19:9, 261
19:11, 55
19:11–27, 148
20:17–18, 140
20:18, 46
21:5–28, 455
21:12, 572
21:20, 475, 530
21:20–24, 473
21:24, 475, 531
21:25–27, 559
21:27, 44, 48, 145, 148, 356–58, 360, 474
21:31, 26, 360
21:35, 48
22:18, 55, 148
22:20, 474
22:22, 357
22:30, 351, 384
22:41, 317
22:43, 500
22:69, 360
23:11, 441
23:42, 328
23:50–51, 532
24:1, 236
24:4, 412, 503
24:5, 301, 321
24:25–26, 53
24:27, 54
24:36, 494
24:44–53, 53
24:45, 572

John
1:1, 26, 139, 193, 312, 352
1:3, 359
1:10, 359
1:11, 473, 571
1:14, 106, 110, 119, 139, 142, 316, 403, 467–68, 506
1:17, 403, 506
1:18, 139
1:29, 53, 497
1:30, 357
1:36, 497
1:51, 500
2:18–22, 316, 403, 467–68
2:19, 447
2:19–21, 142
3:31, 359
3:35, 359
4:10, 29

4:20–26, 34
4:23–24, 353
4:25, 357
4:34, 501
5:21, 359
5:22–23, 384
5:23–24, 501
5:25, 37
5:27, 49, 359
5:27–29, 49
5:28–29, 560–61
5:29, 47
5:30, 501
5:36–38, 501
6:14, 532
6:29, 501
6:38–39, 501
6:39, 359, 376
6:39–40, 49
6:40, 359, 376
6:44, 49, 376, 501
6:54, 49, 376
6:57, 501
6:63, 276
6:69, 467
7:16, 501
7:28–29, 501
7:33, 501
8:12, 239, 491
8:16, 501
8:26, 501
8:29, 501
8:31–32, 320
8:32, 506
8:39–44, 53
8:40, 506
8:42, 501
8:56–58, 197
9:4, 501
10:16, 52
10:22–39, 406
10:36, 501
11, 382
11:11–13, 561
11:24, 382
11:24–25, 376
11:25, 37, 382
11:42, 501
11:43–44, 382
11:49–52, 195
12:44–45, 501
12:46, 239
12:49, 501
13:3, 359
13:20, 501
13:27, 505
14:6, 403, 506
14:13–14, 316
14:24, 426, 501

15:4–6, 320
15:5, 247
15:16, 316
15:18–19, 301
15:20, 572
15:21, 501
16:5, 501
16:23, 442
16:23–27, 316
16:32, 447
16:33, 328
17, 55
17:1–5, 54
17:3, 501
17:8, 501
17:18, 501
17:21, 501
17:23, 501
17:25, 501
18:1–19:15, 301
18:37, 506
19:8–16, 301, 319
19:11, 205, 416
19:15–16, 301
20:1, 236
20:19, 494
20:21, 494, 501
20:26, 494

Acts
1:3, 36
1:7, 49
1:8, 426
1:11, 48
2, 123
2:1–Revelation 19, 52
2:17, 26, 129, 376, 504, 570
2:17–18, 207
2:23, 572
2:27, 467
2:33, 360
2:38, 441
2:38–39, 207, 497
2:38–40, 206
4:12, 53, 162, 200
4:18–20, 162
4:23–31, 124
4:27, 467
4:29–30, 440
5:5, 288
5:10, 288
5:19, 321
5:29, 34, 162, 317
5:31, 360
6:10, 232
7:44–50, 468
7:55–56, 359–60
7:56, 36
7:60, 317

621

8:12, 36, 141
8:23, 497
8:26, 321
9:3–7, 491
9:7, 501
9:40, 317
10:22, 321
10:38, 467
10:42, 49
10:48, 441
11:21, 440
12:6–7, 193
12:7–11, 321
12:21–23, 205, 251
12:23, 288
13:35, 467
14:11–13, 142
14:15, 320
14:22, 200
16:11–40, 114
16:16–18, 98
16:25–26, 193
16:31, 206
17:31, 49
18:9, 502
19:8, 36
21:5, 317
22:9, 501
22:9–11, 491
24:15, 47
24:22–26, 253
25:10–12, 34
26:28, 441
26:28–31, 253
27:24, 501
28:23, 36, 141
28:31, 36, 141

Romans
1:5, 441
1:7, 323, 367
1:16, 505
1:16–17, 566, 571
1:17, 427
1:24–28, 550
1:26, 534
1:27, 534
1:32, 288
2:16, 49
3:10–18, 438
3:20, 35
3:21–26, 427
3:22–24, 272
4, 31
4–5, 53, 455
4:3–6, 427
4:15, 35
4:16, 53
5, 197
5:1, 323

5:3–5, 566
5:5, 207
5:6–8, 384
5:9–10, 384
5:15, 449
5:17, 61, 329, 427
5:20, 164
5:21, 61
6:1–4, 380
6:1–11, 61
6:23, 29, 288
7:6, 207
7:7, 35
8:2, 207
8:7, 51, 439
8:14–16, 207
8:27, 367
8:28, 29, 328
8:30, 329
8:31–39, 321
8:34, 36, 360
8:35–39, 328
9:4–5, 447
9:5, 197
9:6–7, 53
9:6–8, 53
9:6–23, 53
9:26, 320
9:30–31, 425
9:32–33, 36
10:8–17, 494
10:9–11, 300
10:12, 52
11:1–6, 571
11:7, 571
11:7–10, 571
11:25, 571
11:25–27, 571
11:25–32, 531
11:26, 571
11:33, 125
12:1, 198
12:4–5, 140
12:5, 468
12:11, 314
12:13, 367
13:1, 78, 416
13:1–7, 162, 205, 347
13:1–10, 34, 320
13:6, 125
13:12–14, 49
14:17, 36, 61
15:4, 26
15:9, 441
15:26, 245
16:20, 142, 232, 421, 505

1 Corinthians
1:2, 34, 441

1:3, 323
1:7, 49
1:9, 30
1:18–30, 43
1:18–31, 374
1:19, 232
1:25, 288
1:30, 232, 562
2:7, 37
2:7–16, 258, 276
2:14, 35, 51, 439
3:11–15, 353
3:16–17, 142, 468
5:7, 497
6:9–10, 55, 148, 360, 504
6:9–11, 550
6:11, 441
6:15–20, 198
8–10, 99
8:4, 284
10:1–4, 426
10:16–22, 272
10:20, 187
10:20–21, 284, 502
10:21, 114
11:25, 474
11:27–31, 272
11:31, 247
12, 207
12:3, 51, 439
12:12–27, 140
12:27, 468
13:3, 198
13:8, 320, 466
13:13, 320
14:7, 172
15, 53
15:12–27, 49
15:20, 27
15:24, 504
15:25, 360
15:26, 49
15:27, 359
15:40–57, 27
15:41, 557
15:43, 557
15:47–57, 482
15:50, 55, 148, 360
15:50–52, 571
15:51, 561
15:52, 561
15:54–57, 49
15:56–57, 197

2 Corinthians
1:20, 427
1:21, 467–68
1:22, 441, 497
2:14, 43

3:3, 320
3:6, 474
3:7–16, 572
3:14–18, 258
4:4, 55, 238
4:6, 37, 43, 55, 239
4:7, 451, 501
5:1, 131
5:4, 352
5:10, 49
5:17, 53, 236
5:21, 427, 448, 562
6:16, 320
8:9, 447
11:14, 456
13:1, 568
13:4, 500

Galatians
1:6, 374
2:10, 245
3, 53, 123, 197, 455
3–5, 197
3:7–9, 53
3:13–14, 53
3:22–29, 566
3:26–29, 53, 562, 571
3:27, 352
3:28, 52
3:29, 441
4:4, 29, 119, 193, 289
4:4–5, 77
4:22–28, 53
4:26, 455, 545
5:19–21, 55, 360

Ephesians
1:4, 559
1:7, 289, 316
1:7–9, 258
1:8, 37, 100
1:10, 29
1:13, 207, 441, 497
1:17, 37, 100, 126
1:20–23, 207, 360
1:22, 359
2:1, 439
2:6, 61
2:8, 29
2:8–9, 51, 439
2:17, 494
2:19–21, 540
2:19–22, 142, 468
3:4–6, 258
3:14, 317
4:4–5, 52, 207
4:12, 468
4:13, 100
4:30, 207, 497
4:32, 441
5:8, 239

5:14, 561
5:21–33, 550
6:1–9, 314
6:5–8, 40
6:10–18, 481
6:12, 503
6:17, 371
5:21, 148
6:15–16, 53

Philippians
1:20, 198
2:5–9, 207
2:5–11, 54
2:6–8, 500
2:6–11, 187
2:10–11, 384
2:15, 37, 47, 562
3:9, 427
3:20–21, 482
3:21, 27
4:3, 37, 350
4:18, 198
4:22, 40

Colossians
1:3, 352
1:9, 232
1:9–10, 43, 100
1:12, 577
1:13, 504
1:13–14, 239
1:14, 289
1:15–19, 119
1:15–20, 140
1:17, 352
1:19–20, 142, 468
1:23, 141
1:25–27, 143
1:26–27, 258
1:28, 232
2:2, 258
2:2–3, 43
2:3, 37, 100, 232
2:9, 119, 140
2:9–15, 481
2:10, 360
2:11, 131
2:11–13, 380
2:11–14, 61
2:19, 140
2:23, 551
3:1, 36, 360
3:4, 557
3:10, 43
3:11, 52
3:16–24, 314
3:22–25, 40

1 Thessalonians
1:9, 320

1:10, 576
2, 547
2:18, 505
4:13–17, 49
4:13–18, 577
4:16–18, 384
4:17, 381
5, 49
5:2, 49
5:5, 239
5:16–17, 317
5:16–18, 316
5:17, 320, 502
5:24, 30

2 Thessalonians
1:6–10, 49
1:7, 49
1:11–12, 316
2, 421, 571
2:1–10, 371
2:1–12, 456, 476
2:3, 156, 571
2:3–4, 374, 541
2:3–8, 385
2:3–12, 538, 543, 548
2:4, 47, 542, 552
2:6, 385
2:6–7, 376, 385, 455
2:6–8, 533, 562, 571
2:7, 376, 562, 571
2:7–8, 385
2:8, 49, 156, 376, 385, 421, 456, 533–34, 546, 571
2:8–10, 541
2:9–12, 456

1 Timothy
2:4, 345
2:8, 34, 317
3:9, 258
3:15, 320
3:16, 258
4:1–3, 550
4:10, 320, 441
5:14, 550
5:19, 568
6:14, 49
6:15, 412, 533

2 Timothy
1:10, 55
1:12, 273
2:8, 55
2:10, 559
2:11–13, 30, 300
2:12, 384
2:19, 441, 559
3:1, 26, 129, 376, 504, 570

3:12, 572
3:15, 451
3:16, 147, 276
4:1, 49, 141, 504
4:8, 49
4:18, 504

Titus
2:11–13, 49
2:13, 49, 205, 532, 576–77

Philemon, 40
3, 323

Hebrews
1, 139
1:2, 26, 129, 376, 504, 570
1:3, 207
1:3–14, 500
1:7, 237, 321, 353
1:8, 46, 351, 353
1:9, 467
1:13–14, 353
1:14, 237, 321, 481
2:6–8, 357
2:8, 359
2:14, 110, 232, 503
3:12, 320
4:12, 371
4:14, 501
4:16, 351
5:7, 187
7:22, 474
7:27, 466
8:1, 351
8:1–9:28, 468
8:8, 474
8:13, 474
9, 416
9:3, 466
9:12, 466
9:14, 320
9:15, 474
9:28, 49, 576
10:11–14, 466
10:13, 441
10:23, 30
10:28, 568
10:31, 320
11, 164, 481
11:13–16, 53
11:32–35, 187
11:33, 301, 321
11:33–34, 164
11:34, 47, 187, 200
12:2, 351
12:22, 320, 455, 545
12:24, 474
13:4, 550
13:8, 192
13:13, 441
13:16, 198
13:20, 474

James
1:2–4, 566
1:5, 126
1:17, 192
5:3, 26, 129, 376, 504, 570
5:14–15, 316

1 John
1:5, 239
2:18, 26, 129, 376, 383, 419, 548, 562, 570
2:18–22, 456
2:19, 542
2:20, 100, 467–68
2:22, 562
2:22–24, 419
2:24, 320
2:27, 467–68
3:2, 49
3:2–3, 49
3:6–10, 426
3:8, 232, 503
3:13, 301
4:1, 137
4:2, 110
4:3, 419–20, 562
4:9–10, 501
4:9–14, 196
4:14, 501
5:21, 284

2 John
7, 456, 562

1 Peter
1:4–5, 49
1:5, 376
1:7, 49, 451, 501
1:10–11, 276, 385
1:10–12, 546
1:11, 31, 147
1:13–15, 49
1:19, 451, 497
1:20, 376
2:4, 451
2:4–5, 140
2:4–6, 540
2:4–9, 142, 468
2:6, 451
2:9, 239, 566
2:12–25, 322
2:13–14, 125
3:4, 451, 501
3:18–22, 481
3:19–20, 370
4:13, 49

4:14, 441
4:16, 441
4:17, 272
5:4, 49
5:8, 505

2 Peter
1:1, 427
1:3, 101
1:11, 46, 117
1:19–21, 276
1:21, 31
2:1, 541
2:18, 541
3, 49
3:1–10, 414
3:3, 26, 129, 376, 504, 570
3:4–13, 563
3:9, 49
3:10–13, 49
3:11–12, 49

Jude
4, 541
9, 481, 492, 500, 504
14, 49
14–15, 49
16, 541
18, 26, 129, 376
20–21, 316
21, 532
24, 49

Revelation
1, 498–99
1:1, 328, 365
1:4, 45
1:4–5, 45
1:5, 360
1:7, 44, 47–48, 145, 148, 357, 360, 384
1:8, 45
1:9, 328
1:13, 44, 47, 357, 490, 499
1:13–16, 499
1:13–18, 357
1:14, 47, 353, 491, 499, 531
1:15, 491, 499
1:16, 491, 499
1:17, 501
1:17–18, 501
1:18, 357
1:19, 47
1:20, 503
2:5, 45
2:10, 187
2:16, 45
2:17, 353

2:18, 47, 353, 491
3:4–5, 353, 532
3:5, 47, 350, 559
3:7, 467
3:11, 45
3:12, 142, 455, 468
3:18, 353, 532
4, 340
4–5, 329, 349
4:4, 351, 353, 481, 532
4:5, 353, 491
4:8, 45
4:10, 441, 481
5, 417
5:1–8:1, 446, 563, 570
5:5, 349, 498
5:5–14, 481
5:6, 497
5:8, 172, 317
5:9, 366
5:9–10, 329
5:10, 366
5:11, 47, 353
5:12, 125, 497
5:13, 351
6:1–8, 234, 342, 345
6:7–8, 338
6:11, 353, 532, 567
6:12–7:17, 350
7:1, 47, 341
7:1–8, 481
7:2, 320, 345
7:3–8, 497
7:9, 353, 531, 567
7:9–17, 481
7:10–17, 381
7:12, 125
7:13, 567
7:13–14, 353, 531
7:13–17, 360
7:14, 47, 381, 567
7:17, 351
8:2–11:19, 570
8:3–4, 317
8:5, 353
8:7–8, 353
8:7–9:21, 234
9:13–11:14, 350
9:14, 489
9:17–18, 353
9:20, 284, 345
10, 491, 498
10:1, 353, 491
10:4, 47
10:5–7, 569
10:5–11, 365
10:11, 47
11:2, 457, 573, 575
11:2–3, 457, 461

11:3, 457, 568, 573, 575
11:5, 353
11:7, 47
11:7–8, 200
11:7–12, 273
11:13, 122
11:15, 46, 117, 329, 360
11:16, 351
12, 232
12:3, 47
12:4, 47, 370, 402, 503
12:6, 457, 461, 573, 575
12:6–17, 572
12:7, 504
12:7–8, 559
12:7–11, 492–93, 503
12:7–12, 481
12:10, 131
12–13, 68, 354
12:13–13:18, 505
12:13–17, 481
12:13–18, 354
12:14, 47, 457, 461, 569
12:18–13:10 (ET 12:17–13:10), 342, 348, 372
13, 354, 366, 372, 456
13:1, 47, 366
13:1–2, 57, 381–82
13:1–10, 372
13:4, 456
13:5, 47, 457, 461, 573, 575
13:6–7, 47
13:7, 47
13:8, 37, 47, 350, 559
13:11, 348, 366, 372
13:11–18, 342, 348, 354, 372, 383, 421, 456, 476, 543
13:12–18, 456
14:1–5, 481
14:2, 172
14:10, 353
14:11, 567
14:13, 567
14:14, 44, 47, 353, 357
14:15, 345
14:15–16:21, 234
14:18, 345, 353
15:1–16:21, 570
15:2, 172, 353
15:7, 320
16:1, 345
16:8, 353

16:9, 345
16:11, 122, 345
16:12, 489
16:12–16, 350
16:13, 68, 348, 354, 372, 421
16:15, 45
17, 354
17:1, 348, 372
17:1–18, 365
17:3, 57, 381–82
17:7, 57, 381–82
17:8, 350, 559
17:9, 47
17:12, 47
17:12–13, 382
17:12–18, 57, 381
17:14, 47, 412, 500, 533
17:15–16, 348, 372
17:16, 353
18:8, 353
19:1, 47
19:1–10, 349, 353
19:2, 348, 372
19:3, 349
19:11, 353
19:11–14, 49
19:11–16, 349
19:11–21, 372, 456, 476
19:12, 47, 353, 491
19:14, 532
19:15, 372
19:16, 412, 500, 533
19:17–18, 345
19:17–21, 354
19:19–20, 349
19:20, 47, 342, 348, 353–54, 372, 421, 456, 476
19–20, 329, 349
20, 51–52, 54, 380
20:1–6, 54, 61, 350, 380
20:1–7, 51, 54, 574
20:1–10, 574
20:2, 68
20:3, 455
20:4, 47, 351
20:7–9, 565, 571
20:7–10, 372, 544
20:7–15, 350
20:9–10, 349, 353
20:10, 49, 342, 348, 354, 372, 421, 476
20:11, 47, 353
20:11–15, 49, 372, 544

20:12, 37, 47, 339, 349–50, 559
20:12–15, 560–61
20:14, 49
20:14–15, 353
20:15, 350, 559
21, 455, 468
21:1–8, 360
21:8, 353
21:9–22:6, 365
21:22, 142, 468
21–22, 34, 330, 574
21:27, 350, 559
22:1, 351
22:3, 351
22:3–5, 329
22:6, 30
22:7, 45
22:10, 385, 563
22:11, 47
22:12, 45
22:12–13, 45
22:17, 206
22:20, 45

Apocrypha, Old Testament Pseudepigrapha, and Other Jewish Literature

1 Esdras
4:58, 316

Tobit, 210
1:21–22, 39
2:10, 39
3:11, 316
11:18, 39
12:15, 368
14:10, 39

Judith
10:3, 497
11:17, 114
12:5–6, 114

Wisdom of Solomon
10:10, 368
18:14–19, 114

Ben Sira
3:30, 13–14, 16, 242
36:1–11, 15
36:10, 13–16
36:22, 13, 15–16
42:17, 368

Baruch
1:11, 4, 260

Prayer of Azariah, 64, 69–70, 192–93, 220

Song of the Three Young Men, 64, 69–70, 192–93, 220

Susanna, 64, 67–68, 220

Bel and the Serpent, 64, 68–69
1, 293
41, 69

1 Maccabees, 371, 467
1:11, 416
1:11–15, 416
1:15, 416
1:16–19, 401
1:20–24, 377, 402, 405, 416, 528
1:20–62, 401
1:21–22, 416
1:24, 371
1:29, 405, 416
1:29–35, 529
1:29–40, 377
1:30, 412, 416
1:31, 465
1:33, 517
1:38, 465
1:41–51, 402–3, 405, 530
1:41–53, 406
1:44–46, 403
1:46, 368
1:47, 403, 530
1:54, 378, 403, 405–6, 416, 463, 530
1:56–57, 403, 530
1:59, 403, 530
1:62–63, 530
3:30, 527
3:31, 401
4:52–53, 378, 405
6:1, 401
6:1–16, 416
6:1–17, 527
6:5, 401
6:56, 401

2 Maccabees, 371, 467
1:11–17, 527
3, 525
4:7–10, 526
4:23–26, 526
4:32–33, 526
4:34, 526
5–6, 401
6:1, 403
6:1–2, 403, 416, 530
6:1–11, 402
6:4, 403, 530

6:6, 403
6:7, 537
7, 177
9:1–2, 401
9:1–28, 416
9:1–29, 527
13:4–8, 177

1 Enoch, 71
1–36, 231
10–16, 231
10:11–12, 453
12:2, 368
14:23, 368
39:12–13, 231
46:1–5, 357
48:3–7, 357
48:10, 357
52:4, 357
71:7, 231
91:12–19, 453
93:1–10, 453
93:6, 368

Sibylline Oracles, 135

4 Ezra
5:13, 497
9:24–25, 497
12:10–12, 144
13, 357

2 Baruch
9:2–10:1, 497
12:5–13:1, 497
20:5–22:1, 497
39:5–6, 144
47:2–48:1, 497
48:25–28, 497

Testament of Reuben
5:6–7, 231

Testament of Levi
3:3, 368
18:11, 368
18:14, 368

Testament of Issachar
5:4, 368

Testament of Naphtali
3:5, 231

Jubilees
4:15, 231
4:22, 231
7:21, 231
10:5, 231
17:11, 368

Qumran
1QapGen 2:1, 368
1QDan^a, 62–63, 87, 115
1QDan^b, 62–63

1QH 3:21–22, 369
1QM 3:4–5, 368
1QM 10:10, 368
1QM 12:8, 369
1QM 15:14, 368
4QDan^a, 62–63, 98–99, 123, 268, 271, 393–94
4QDan^b, 62–63, 310, 312, 337, 393
4QDan^c, 17, 62, 506, 515
4QDan^d, 62–63
4QDan^e, 62
4QDaniel Suzanna? ar, 70
4QFlorilegium, 17, 40, 62
4QFour Kingdoms^{a-b} ar, 70
4QpapApocalypse ar, 70
6QDan^a, 62
Genesis Apocryphon, 231
Pesher on the Periods, 453
Prayer of Nabonidus (4QPrNab ar), 70–71, 215, 218–27
Pseudo-Daniel (4Qps-Dan^{a-c} ar), 71–73
Son of God Text (4QApocalypse ar), 73

Josephus
Antiquities, 4.212, 317
Antiquities, 10.86, 83
Antiquities, 10.186, 90
Antiquities, 10.190, 65
Antiquities, 10.192–93, 65
Antiquities, 10.195, 117
Antiquities, 10.210, 40
Antiquities, 10.217, 224, 236
Antiquities, 10.220–22, 83
Antiquities, 10.231, 4, 260
Antiquities, 10.237, 276
Antiquities, 10.266, 40
Antiquities, 10.266–81, 40
Antiquities, 10.276, 144
Antiquities, 11.1–18, 469
Antiquities, 11.337, 40
Antiquities, 12.322, 40

Against Apion, 1.135–37, 83
Against Apion, 1.149–53, 219
Against Apion, 1.153, 259

Babylonian Talmud
Berakoth, Mishnah 4:1, 317
Berakoth, Mishnah 5:1, 317
Berakoth, 26b, 317
Berakoth, 31a, 317
Ḥagigah, 14a, 350
Sanhedrin, 22a, 274
Sanhedrin, 38b, 350
Sanhedrin, 93b, 91
Sanhedrin, 98a, 357
Taʿanith, 21b, 286

Midrash Rabbah Numbers
13:14, 357

'Aggadat Berešit
14:3, 357
23:1, 357

New Testament Pseudepigrapha
Apocalypse of Thomas, 453

Literature of the Early Christian Era
Andrew of Caesarea
Commentary on the Apocalypse, 352

Chrysostom
Discourses against Judaizing Christians, 538
On the Incomprehensible Nature of God, 11, 351

Cyril of Alexandria
Commentary on Daniel, 352

Cyril of Jerusalem
Catechetical Lectures, 15, 351

Didache
8, 317
8:2, 131

Ephraim of Syria, 405

Epistle of Barnabas
4:1–5, 144

Eusebius
Demonstration of the Gospel, 144
Ecclesiastical Theology, 3.17, 351

Hippolytus
Commentary on Daniel, 144, 343, 345, 405, 467, 538
"Scholia on Daniel," 194, 351

Irenaeus
Against Heresies, 21.7, 140

Jerome
Commentary on Daniel, 3, 140, 144–45, 194, 224, 236, 343, 345, 351, 404, 468, 479, 518, 538

John of Damascus
On the Divine Images, 352

Justin Martyr
Dialogue with Trypho, 76, 140

Porphyry
Against the Christians, 3, 144–45, 479

Pseudo-Dionysius
The Divine Names, 352

Tertullian
Against the Jews, 467–68

Theodoret of Cyrus
Commentary on Daniel, 140, 352, 404, 467, 538

Ecumenical Creeds
Apostles' Creed, 144, 352
Nicene Creed, 94, 139, 141, 144, 352, 555
Athanasian Creed, 139, 352, 384

Lutheran Confessions
Augsburg Confession
IV, 31
V, 439
VI, 31, 242
VI 1, 198
VII 1, 457
XIII 1–2, 551
XVIII 1, 199, 204, 322

XVIII 1–3, 35
XX, 31

Apology of the Augsburg Confession
IV, 31
IV 24–25, 246
IV 33–35, 199, 204, 322
IV 38, 35
IV 69, 197
IV 79, 198
IV 122–82, 242
IV 142, 199, 204, 322
IV 250, 439
IV 261, 198
IV 261–68, 204, 246, 252
IV 262, 242
IV 328–38, 442
VII/VIII, 548
VII/VIII 4, 548, 552
VII/VIII 9, 457
VII/VIII 23–24, 549, 552
VII/VIII 24, 548
VII/VIII 48, 548
XV, 548
XV 18, 548
XV 18–19, 548, 551
XV 18–21, 549
XV 19, 548
XV 21, 548
XV 21–22, 551
XVIII 4, 35
XVIII 4–10, 199, 204, 322
XXI 4–6, 164
XXIII, 548
XXIII 25, 548, 550
XXIV, 548
XXIV 44–47, 476
XXIV 44–48, 549
XXIV 51, 548–49, 552
XXIV 98, 549

Smalcald Articles
II III 25, 549
II IV, 548
II IV 4, 549
II IV 10–13, 552
III II 1–5, 31
III III 25, 548
III XI 1–3, 550

Treatise on the Power and Primacy of the Pope, 548
39, 548
39–40, 548
39–59, 548

Small Catechism
I 1–2, 299
II 6, 439

Large Catechism
I 2, 543
I 4, 162
I 48, 34
I 89, 33
III 65–67, 61
Preface, 11, 505

Formula of Concord Epitome
IV, 242
VI, 31, 199, 242
VI 1, 31, 34
XI, 28, 560
XI 3, 133

Formula of Concord Solid Declaration
IV, 242
V 17, 35
VI, 31, 199, 242
VIII 54–55, 359
XI, 28, 134, 560
XI 6, 134
XI 8, 134

Works of Martin Luther

American Edition
31:25, 425
31:40, 61
35:295, 144
35:296, 131, 139
35:298–99, 322
35:299, 338
35:300, 373, 548
35:302, 404–5
35:303, 459
35:303–4, 460, 470
35:303–5, 453
35:305, 455
35:305–6, 502–3
35:306, 518
35:313, 538, 542
54:476, 245

Weimarer Ausgabe
39/1:342–58, 35

Weimarer Ausgabe Deutsche Bibel
11/2.144–45, 209
11/2.154–55, 304

Lutheran Hymnals

Lutheran Service Book
319, 139, 352
320, 384
321, 299
670, 231
930, 67
931, 67

Lutheran Worship
9, 67

Ancient Near Eastern Literature

Babylonian Chronicle, 81–84, 167–68, 208

Dynastic Prophecy, 135

Enuma Elish, 332–34

Harran Inscriptions of Nabonidus, 218

Nabonidus Chronicle, 215, 218, 292, 302, 483

Persian Verse Account of Nabonidus, 218, 264

Tale of Ahikar, 38–39

Vision of the Netherworld, 333

Classical Literature

Arrian
Anabasis Alexandri, 4.11, 294

Herodotus
Histories, 1.74.3, 219
Histories, 1.86, 177
Histories, 1.112, 294
Histories, 1.113–14, 294
Histories, 1.188, 263
Histories, 1.191, 271
Histories, 8.105.1, 90

Hesiod
Works and Days, 109–201, 134–35

Ovid
Metamorphoses, 1.89–162, 134

Pliny
Natural History, 34.18, 175

Polybius
Histories, 5.79, 523
Histories, 5.107, 523
Histories, 14.12, 523
Histories, 16.39, 524
Histories, 26.1, 416, 527
Histories, 28.18, 415
Histories, 29.27, 528–29
Histories, 30.25, 537
Histories, 31.11, 416, 527

Xenophon
Cyropaedia, 7.5.15, 271
Cyropaedia, 7.5.21, 271
Cyropaedia, 7.5.25, 271
Cyropaedia, 7.5.29–32, 288–89
Cyropaedia, 8.5.19, 294